AF380651

SIGNS FOR PEACE

AN IMPOSSIBLE VISUAL ENCYCLOPEDIA

EDITED BY DESIGN2CONTEXT RUEDI BAUR AND VERA BAUR KOCKOT

LARS MÜLLER PUBLISHERS

CONTENTS

LE CHANT DE LA PAIX (THE SONG OF PEACE*)

Choeur alsacien (arabe)

A izza i ana sacranou
A izza i ana sacranou
Askaratni kaasoun kaasoun khalidah   Chers amis

Ana mal' anou bihoubbinn raasikhinn   Je suis ivre, ivre d'une coupe éternelle
Lan yatroukani abada   Rempli d'un amour solide
Ana mal' anou bihoubbinn raasikhinn   Qui ne m'abandonnera jamais
Lan yatroukani abada

Katica Illényi (yiddish)

Kim shoyn lied   Viens chanson
Kim shoyn lied
Hayss men zol trinken   Donne l'ordre de boire
Zikh oupshikeren   Pour devenir ivre
Fil yeder bekher   Remplis chaque coupe
yaaaa...
Vouss trinkt zikh oyss   Chaque coupe qui se vide

Choeur alsacien (arabe)

Hatta tamtali'aal arnahou houbba   Pour que les âmes se remplissent d'amour
Hatta tamtali'aal arnahou houbba

Hayet Ayad (arabe)

Hatta tahriqa jaloudana   Pour que le feu de l'amour
Naarou, naarou l houbbi   Nous brûle la peau
Hatta tahriqa jaloudana
Naarou, naarou l houbbi
Ida ma faraghna min anfousina   Pour que vides de nous-mêmes
Namtali a houbba   On se remplisse d'amour

* Dear Friends/I am drunk, drunk from an eternal chalice/Filled with an everlasting love/
That will never abandon me/Come song/Tell people to drink/And get drunk/Refill each
chalice/Each chalice that is empty/So the souls may be filled with love/So the love's
fire/May burn our skin/So that, emptied of ourselves, we may be filled with love

Choeur alsacien (arabe)

A izza i ana sacranou

A izza i ana sacranou

Askaratni kaasoun kaasoun khalidah

Ana mal' anou bihoubbinn raasikhinn

Lan yatroukani abada

Ana mal' anou bihoubbinn raasikhinn

Lan yatroukani abada

Ana mal' anou bihoubbinn raasikhinn

Lan yatroukani abada

Ana mal' anou bihoubbinn raasikhinn

Lan yatroukani abada

Chers amis

Je suis ivre, ivre d'une coupe éternelle

Rempli d'un amour solide

Qui ne m'abandonnera jamais

Rempli d'un amour solide

Qui ne m'abandonnera jamais

Mitzu (romani)

Av de gilija

Vorba pijasz te avasz

Car le coeur de celui

Qui n'a pas brûlé à l'amour

Choeur alsacien (arabe)

Li anna qalba mann

Lam yahtariqa houbbann

Car le coeur de celui

Qui n'a pas brûlé à l'amour

Mitzu (romani)

Av de gilija

Vorba pijasz te avasz

Birevurja

Te amende

Car le coeur de celui

Qui n'a pas brûlé à l'amour

Celui qui n'a pas été

Esclave de l'amour

Choeur alsacien (arabe)

Lann yarifa lann yarifa

Asraara l houbbi

Lann yarifa lann yarifa

Asraara l houbbi

Ne connaîtra jamais

Les secrets de l'au-delà

Dear friends/I am drunk, drunk from an eternal chalice/Filled with an everlasting love/ That
will never abandon me/Filled with an everlasting love/That will never abandon me/ For he
whose heart/Has not burned with love/For he whose heart/Has not burned with love/ For
he whose heart/Has not burned with love/He who has not been/The slave of love/Will never
know/The secrets of the hereafter

Mitzu [romani]

Te perguvas kamipe   Ne connaîtra jamais les secrets
                                            de l'au-delà

Katica Illényi [yiddish]

In vert kaynmoul nisht vissn   Et ne connaîtra jamais
Di aynskayt fin ayns tse zahn   L'unicité d'être un

Hayet Ayad [arabe]

Walann yarifa abadann   Et ne connaîtra jamais
Wihdata l waahidi   L'unicité d'être un

Choeur alsacien [arabe]

Walann yarifa abadann   Et ne connaîtra jamais
Wihdata l waahidi   L'unicité d'être un
Walann yarifa abadann
Wihdata l waahidi
Walann yarifa abadann
Wihdata l waahidi

Tony Gatlif, "Le Chant de la paix,"
from his film *Swing,* France, 2002.

Will never know, The secrets of the hereafter/And will never know/The uniqueness of being
one/And will never know/The uniqueness of being one/And will never know/The uniqueness of
being one

ON ENCYCLOPEDIC IMPOSSIBILITY

THE PROJECT'S ORIGINS 1

Let's go back to that moment when the decision was taken to put together a collection. Not every book allows one to tell the story of its beginnings so clearly. Of course some need can always be cited, but aren't there quite a number of themes that are well worth the energy one might devote to them? In our case, we can point to a project taking a wrong turn or rather being turned toward another. For a publisher or a director of a research institution, there is never a lack of appeals coming from artists with more or less relevant projects in tow. Freshly graduated from architecture or design programs that are too narrowly tailored to a miserable job market, or boasting longer work experience, certain artists who find themselves at odds with what their profession holds out for them try to put their know-how to uses that both make sense and go beyond the monetary dimension. In our case, we were facing that unappealing subject that involves bringing a brand and visual identity to an organization generally concerned with making a profit; in other words, corporate identity, these days often called branding. It was the former term and not the latter that our visitor employed.[1] He wanted to develop "a corporate identity for peace," and was asking for our advice and support. Besides the fact that peace is hardly a matter for the limited liability company, as far as we know, and that lots of signs of that type already exist, the very intention of unifying the various expressions of peace under one and the same representation seemed to us to be a part of that post-colonial cultural genocide that Johan Galtung has described so well.[2] In the ensuing discussion, we argued our refusal with the friendly young designer. During the exchange, however, we eventually arrived at a completely different project, which involved bringing together and trying to understand a group of signs that express peace in a great variety of ways. And so this inevitably incomplete visual collection debuted in 2005.

THE PROJECT'S ORIGINS 2

This project emerged from a challenge. A research focus of the institute has been the investigation of images at the levels of both production and reception. We were contracted to produce an issue of the magazine *Abstract* on the topic "The Future." Increasingly evident after extensive research was the astonishing absence of visions that went beyond the coming thirty years. The images we found either sketched out a future based on the aesthetics of 1970s science fiction à la "Starship Enterprise," or else anticipated an apocalypse. Everything which extended more than thirty years into the future took written form — a more abstract and innocuous medium. This absence of alternatives to the excess of images reproduced by the mainstream horrified us. The question now posed itself: How might pictures of a sought-after future appear? How would we visualize peace? During this period, young researchers committed to investigating the impact of images came to the institute with related questions. Maru Martinez, for example, explored the use of images in the context of NGOs and aid organizations. She examined the deployment of images in a range of contexts and in relation to the respective target groups. She devoted special attention to the central question of how dignity and protection could be represented visually, and at the same time how veracity in relation to the depicted situation could be insured, and hence how a targeted transla-tion could succeed in the context of the specific utilization. This issue also consistently accompanied research for the encyclopedia. Manifesting itself was the power of images that, in Marie José Mondzain's felicitous characterization, is expressed in an iconophobia when faced with the simultaneous flood of the perpetually identical. We were repeatedly confronted with this anxiety in the face of images and their impact, among other things when we sought support for our research. Our application was rejected by numerous international organizations acting on behalf of a consortium of nations because our project plan made no allowance for the exclusion of images that might offend a given member state. Later, we were invited to present our already extensive collection at an exhibition in Paris. More than 50 percent of the images were refused. Here, we encountered a central problem of current research that extends into the realm of political communication: Has such research become toothless in order to protect various sensibilities? This has become a key question for us. Are we unable to find certain images because they have no fora, or because access to them is encrypted? Might one consequence of this be that critical or problematical images no longer surface, or are simply no longer produced? Might a kind of premature self-censorship come into play because the market or stage for controversial images is absent? For us, this also raises the question: Is it possible to engender a culture of constructive debate around images and the subjects they depict, one that sustains — or better yet harnesses — our attention?

CONTEMPORARY EVENTS, CONTEXT

The Second Gulf War launched by the Bush family and American conservatives was in full swing. Conservative American forces were wrapping the most abject events of war in an arrogance that has rarely been equaled, placing the Western world as a whole in an uncomfortable position vis-à-vis the role of exemplary democracy to which it laid claim. Even the Geneva Conventions on the rights of prisoners of war were shamelessly flouted. The CIA was transporting prisoners to countries where torture could be performed outside of the pressure normally exerted by the media. The staged prisoner photos coming out of Abu Ghraib prison shocked the entire world. After an initial moment of silence corresponding to the alarm at the monstrosity of the events and the power of war propaganda, the community of artists creating images of resistance gradually set to work. An output of visuals that has rarely been surpassed in number swept through international electronic networks. As both actors and sponsors (001),[3] we were then able to analyze, doubtless with a certain lack of objectivity on our part, this immense corpus of images calling for an end to the bellicose attitude. Several irrefutable truths came to the fore. First, nearly all of these images were produced outside of the immediate theater of conflict and generally by persons who were not directly involved in it. Only a few rare calls for desertion, for example, were formulated. These were only rarely expressed visually. The most powerful icons sprang illegally from Abu Ghraib. They were very quickly appropriated by those who opposed the war in order to symbolize the barbarism, inconceivable in the twenty-first century [002]. In this regard, we can state that the greater part of the visual expressions involved a rejection of war rather than something in favor of peace. Apart from the contextual icons, most of the other symbols employed to talk about this particular war could have applied to any other; they corresponded to a kind of decontextualized global language. In these images there exists a kind of cool distancing that is due to those graphic treatments produced by the usual programs for working digitally with images. Thus, a shoe thrown during a press conference may remain the symbol of this incomparable difference in power between the advanced technology of some and the limited means of others [003]. That spontaneous visual expression has its place in this book, as does the more carefully wrought expression from the world of images. Against war in general, against that war in particular, against the invader or against the enemy, the limit is sometimes very subtle and the instances of reappropriation and possible conflation are many. It is, moreover, what pacifists are accused of. This war, like so many others, was fought in the name of a so-called peace [004]. We had to take a stand, then, in the selection of images and themes.

THE ESSENTIAL ONES

The collection came out. The eye grew sharper. The signs seemed to grow in number: "Peace Hotel," "Peace Street and Square," candles, and above all doves en masse; flags boasting rainbows, and especially the circular "peace-and-love" sign, which

001

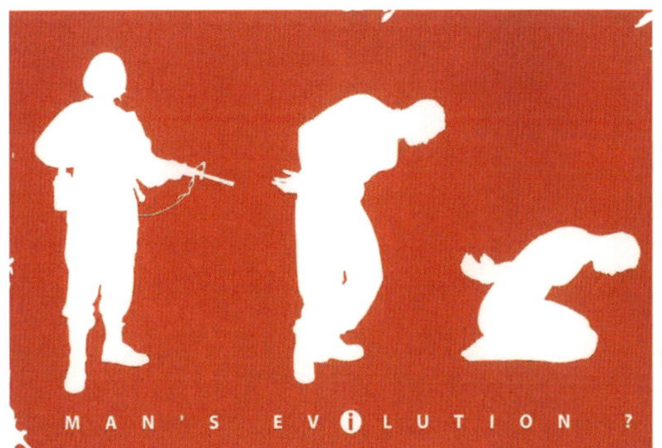

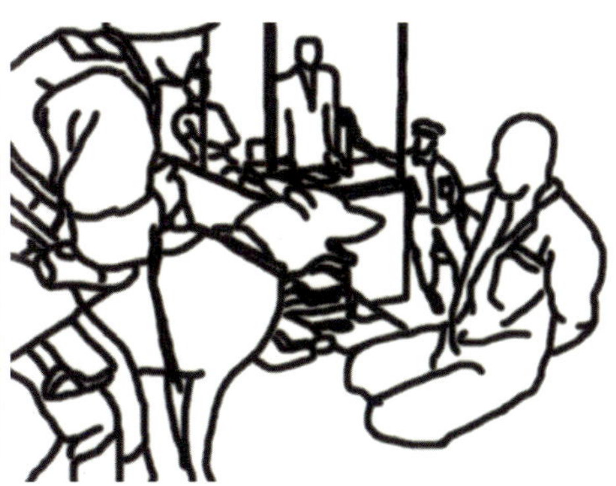

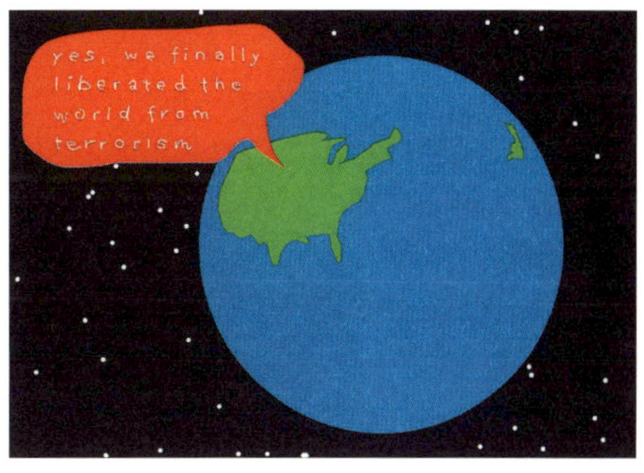

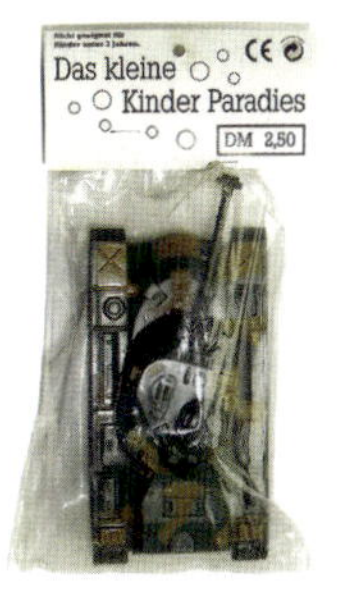

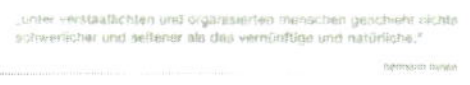

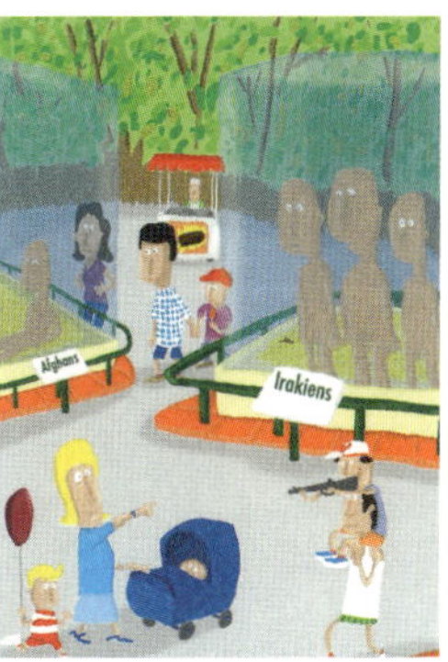

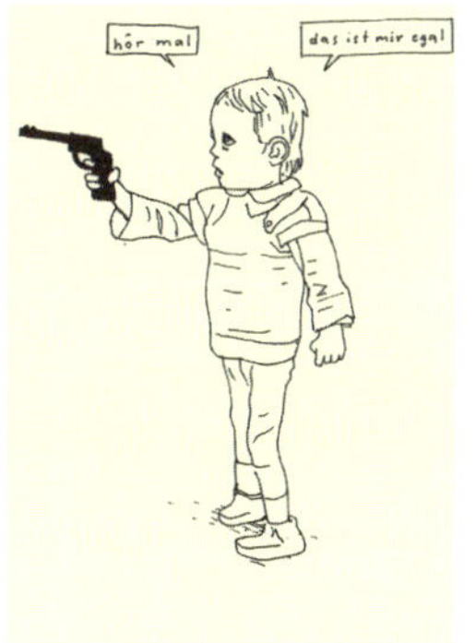

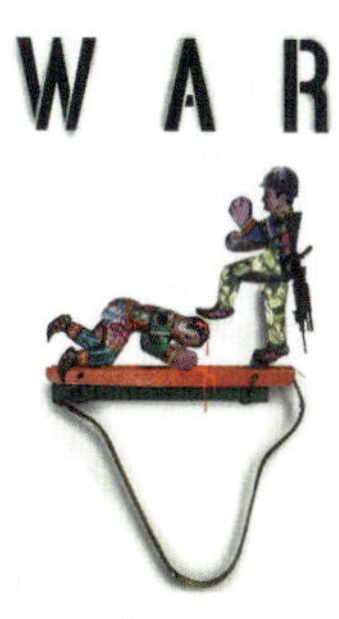

demoilcracy

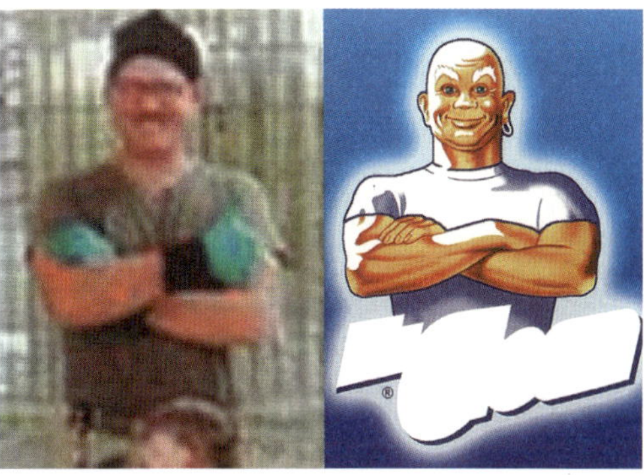

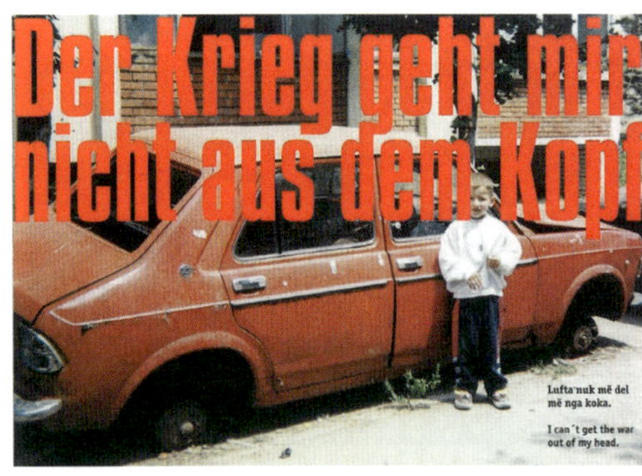
Der Krieg geht mir nicht aus dem Kopf
Lufta nuk më del më nga koka.
I can´t get the war out of my head.

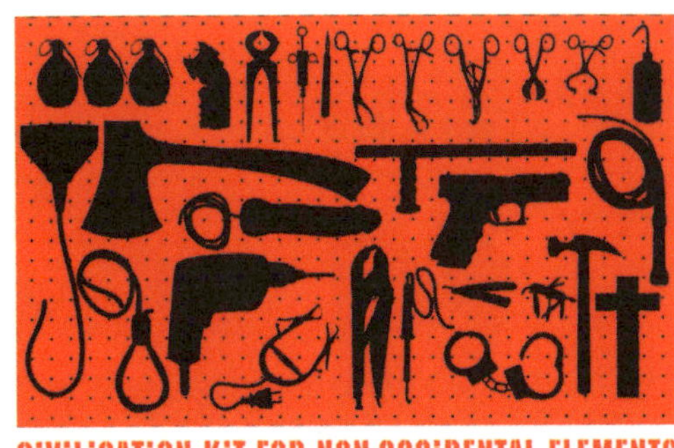
CIVILISATION KIT FOR NON-OCCIDENTAL ELEMENTS

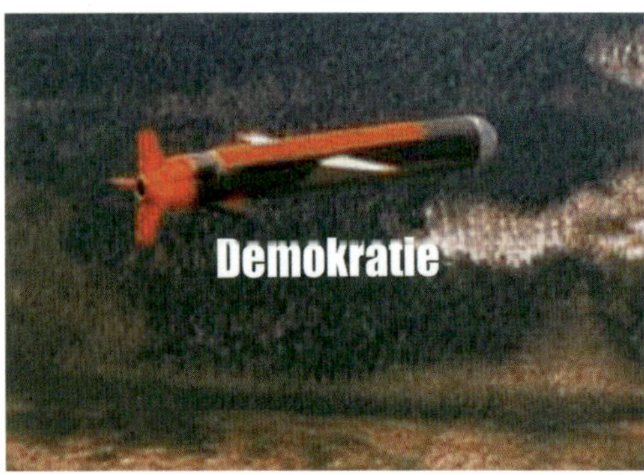
Demokratie

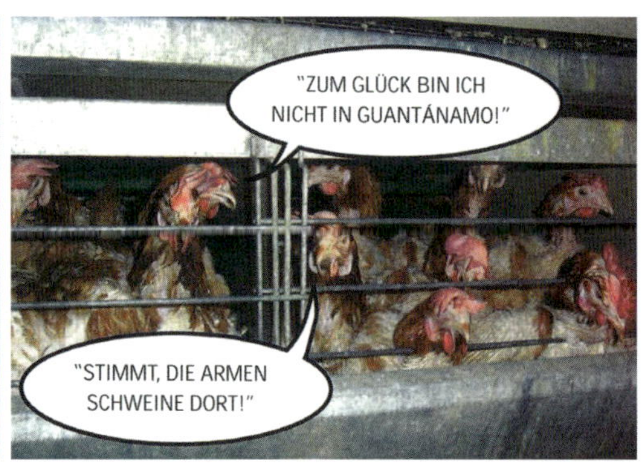
"ZUM GLÜCK BIN ICH NICHT IN GUANTÁNAMO!"
"STIMMT, DIE ARMEN SCHWEINE DORT!"

002
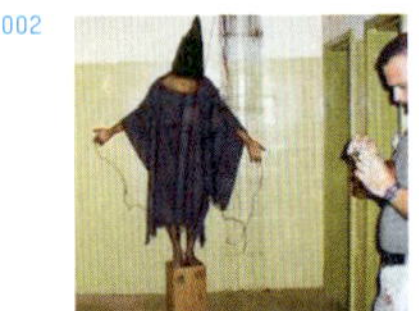
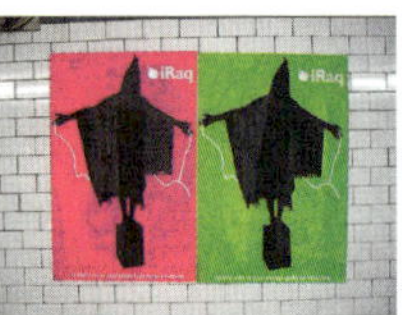
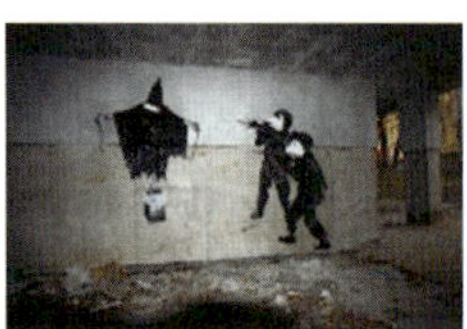
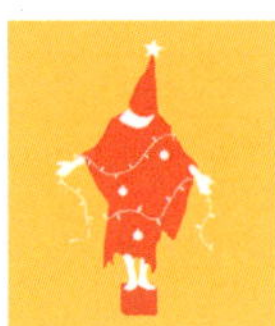
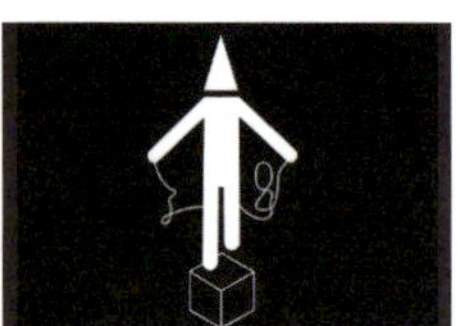

003
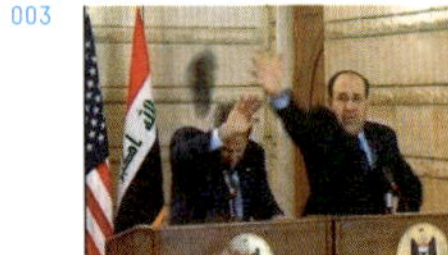
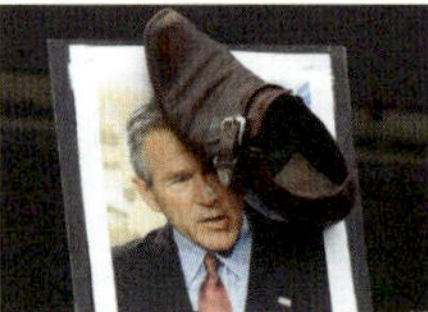
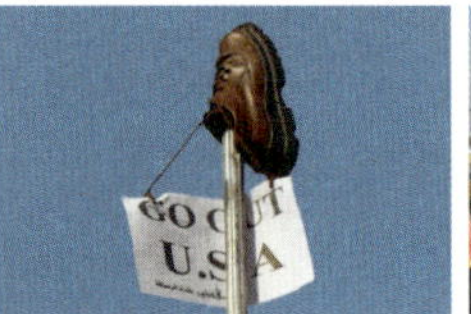
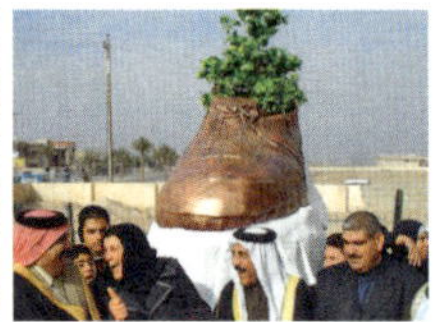

004
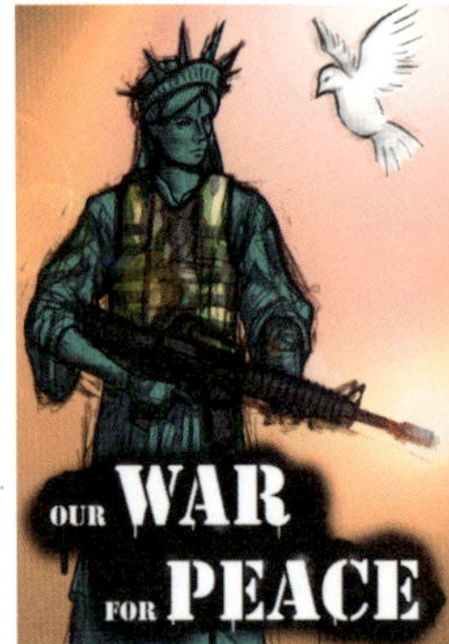
OUR WAR FOR PEACE
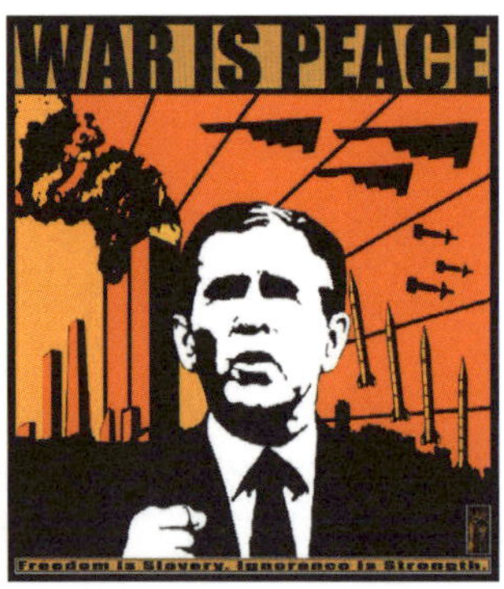
WAR IS PEACE
Freedom is Slavery. Ignorance is Strength.

proved impossible to avoid. You need only enter one of these terms into Google to see an undifferentiated avalanche of each of the signs come spilling out (005, 006, and 007). Do we have here interchangeable symbols springing from a global visual language? Fashion, advertising campaigns, and marketing are not mistaken. They make abundant use of these symbols, but to their own ends. Unfortunately, we know all too well that if public opinion started trending toward other values, toward more patriotic or even bellicose ones, the same strategists would exchange these peace symbols in a flash for others expressing, for instance, triumphant nationalism, xenophobia, even a call for war. There is no lack of examples, unfortunately, including in countries said to be above all suspicion. It is interesting to recall, in this regard, the atmosphere of peace that developed in certain periods and contexts, an atmosphere that has often been built around a single symbol. Thus, we tend to associate Pablo Picasso's doves with peace movements from the time of the Cold War and calls for disarmament. Their appearance on dinner plates remains engraved in our memory (008). Personal experiences at times, but also lasting symbols of an age, as we see, for instance, in that fantastic movement against the Vietnam War. The peace-and-love sign of the Woodstock festival or Volkswagen camper vans came to summarize the movement (009). We also recall that impressive wave of *pace* rainbow flags that were hung in the windows of our apartment blocks after the morose G8 summit in Genoa. The movement had begun in Italy and spread like wildfire throughout Europe. An atmosphere for peace at a particular moment (010). We might likewise mention the Carnation Revolution in the spring of 1974 during which the Portuguese dictatorship was ousted. It involved planting this flower in the barrel of rifles to move beyond violence (011). There is likewise the olive branch and of course the entire olive tree. Symbols dating back to Ancient Greece, today they are identified with the conflict in the Middle East stretching back over several generations. These symbols remain anchored in our memory. They correspond to a specific atmosphere, context, and time, and lose their pertinence and their power once they are used in a more general, indistinct way. Only very rarely can they be recycled or transferred to another context. In this regard, then, the signs that we call global lose their pertinence when applied to a specific cause; they do not signify international solidarity.

005

006

007
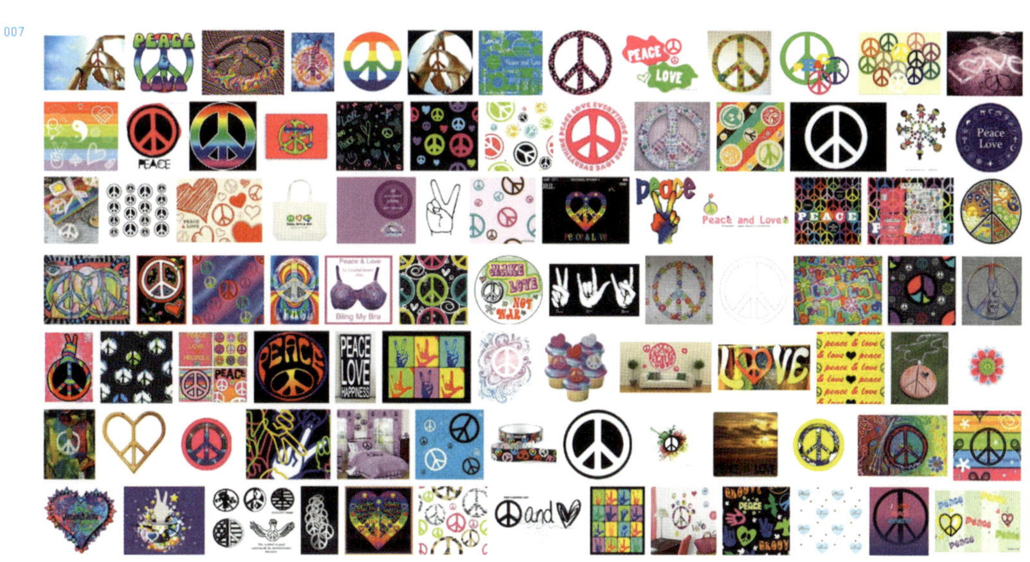

008
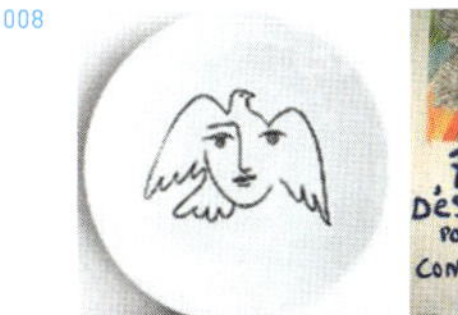
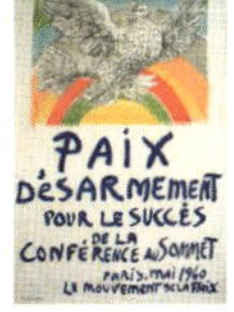

009
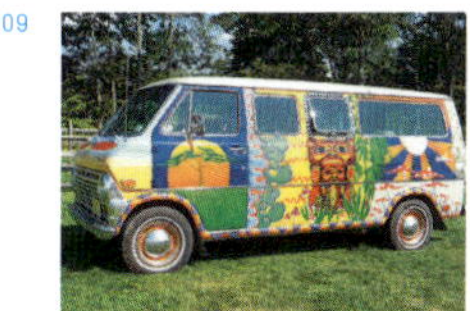
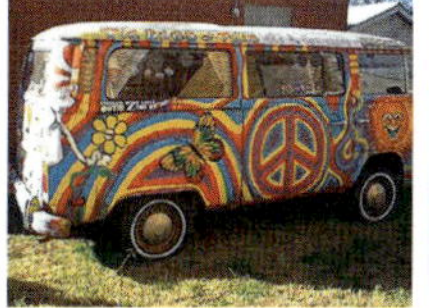
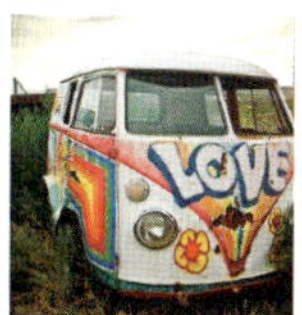
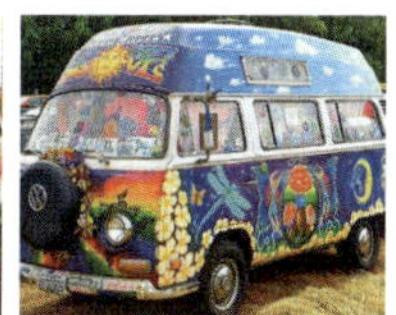

010
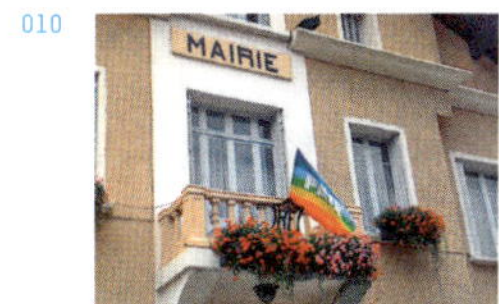

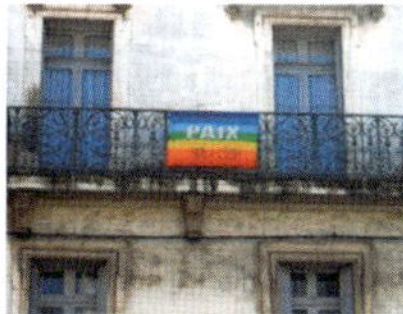

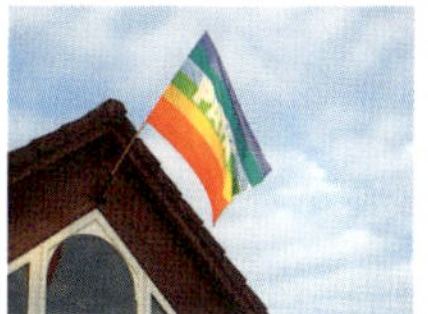

011
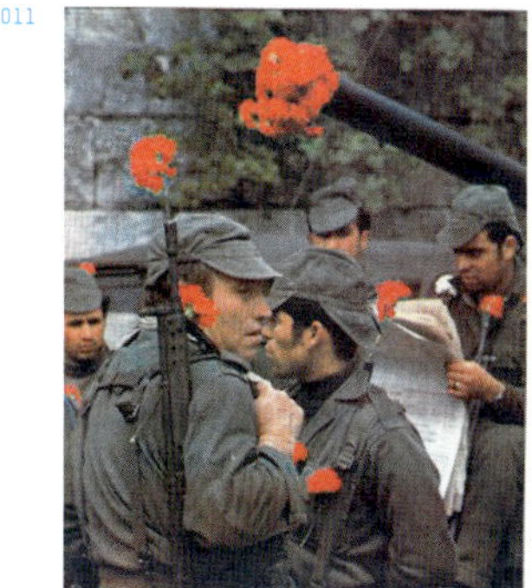

FRIEDENSSTULLE

The "peace slice of bread and butter," the Berlin expression referring to an especially thick slice of buttered bread, indirectly conjures up the famine that haunted the city during and just after the war. In search of such symbols that are especially bound up with a particular context, culture, period, or occasionally a corporation, community, or family, the Design2context Institute organized a number of workshops in places that had recently witnessed conflicts. The idea was to create visuals, but avoid starting off from generalities. Participants were invited to point out to us the places, objects, shapes, or situations that represented peace for them in these times of conflict. The responses were fairly unexpected in some cases. Coming back to us from Central America there was the beauty salon, a place one could return to once the situation calmed down; conversely, Beirut's nightclubs allowed one to forget the absurdity of the conflict. A more ambivalent image is the Kalashnikov, which some were happy to possess in case of an attack. In her research into the iconography of the Second Gulf War, Megan Hall, who is also responsible for the present book's layout, found an incredible video that shows two young Iraqis swimming in the private pool of a sumptuous abandoned house [012]. Not all of these images made their way directly into this encyclopedia, yet they much more clearly symbolize peace for those who manage to decode them—above all for those who lived through the events—than the ones presented here. This provides us with an initial version of the impossibility that figures in the title of the book.

THE PEACE BEACH

During another workshop we put together with Jordi Cano in Barcelona at the Elisava School, one student's response struck us in particular. We had decided to tackle our theme by starting with questions of public space. This involved distinguishing public areas that give rise to aggression and fear from those that spread peace and solidarity. Arena Vent began to talk

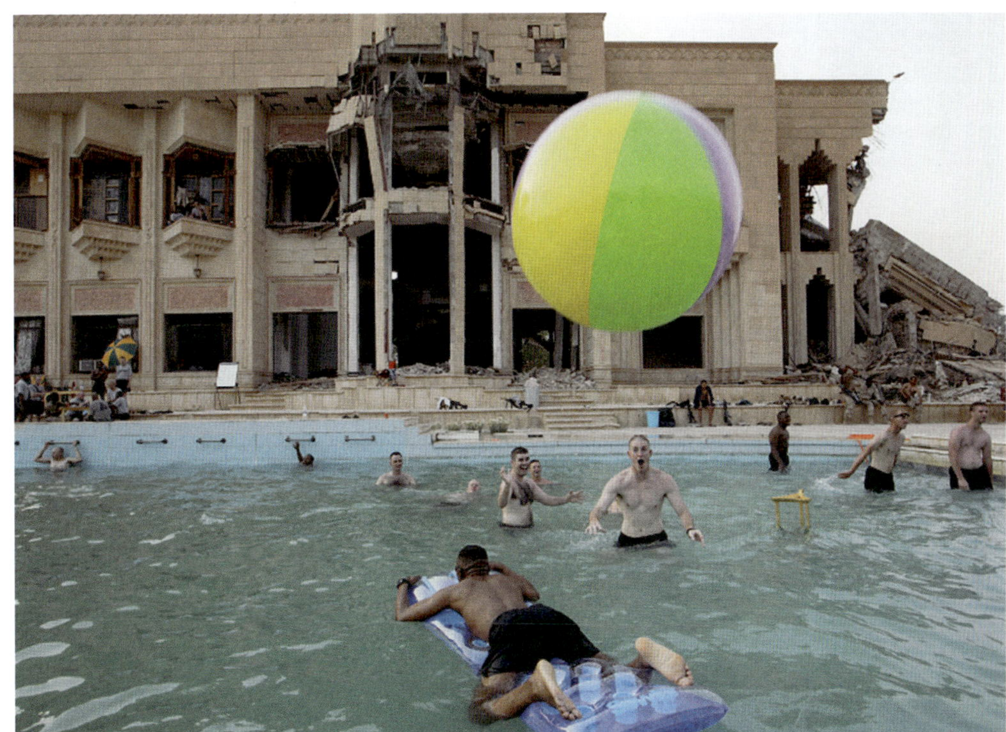

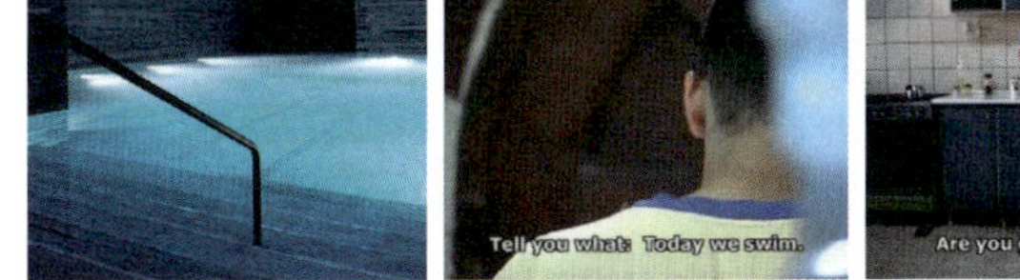

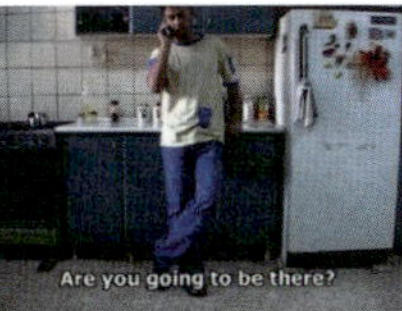

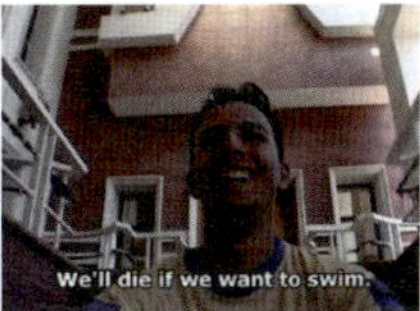

about the beach in her city, where she likes to slip away to because of the area's peace and quiet. Yet the measures that have been gradually put in place to ensure that calm and protect vacationers from a few possible petty thefts have done much more to destroy the potential for a peaceful setting. An artificial peace, a protected peace, a peace where the security is staged does not express well-being, harmony, and serenity. It is not at all pleasant to take a swim on a beach surrounded by barbed wire or policemen [013]. In just a few images she showed us all of the subject's ambivalence,

PEACE ZONE

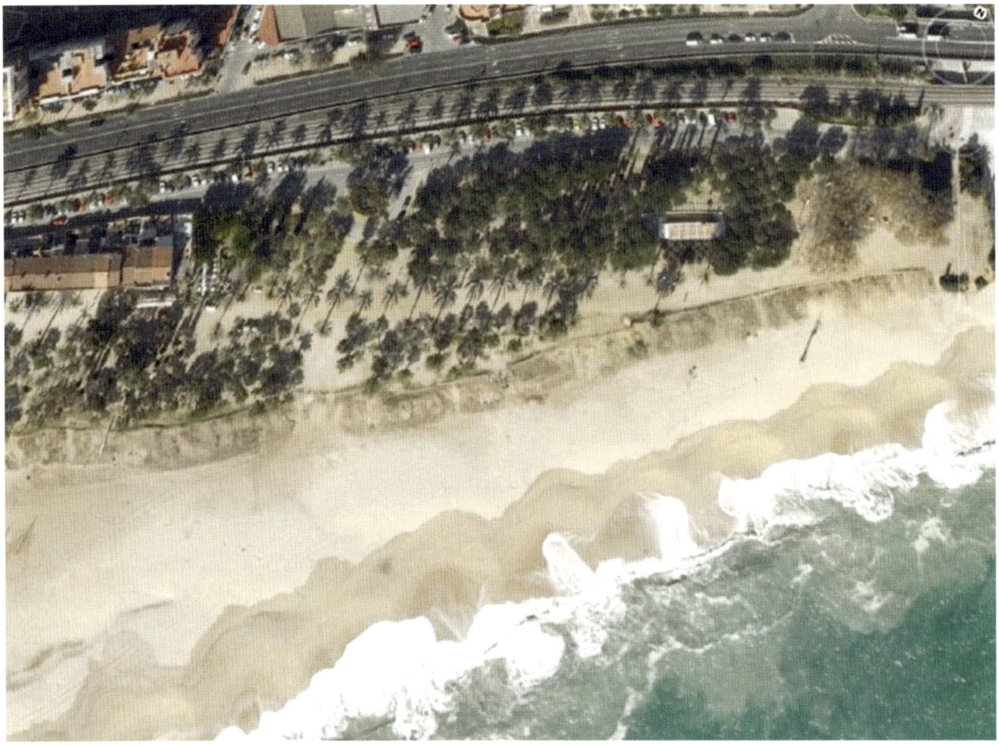

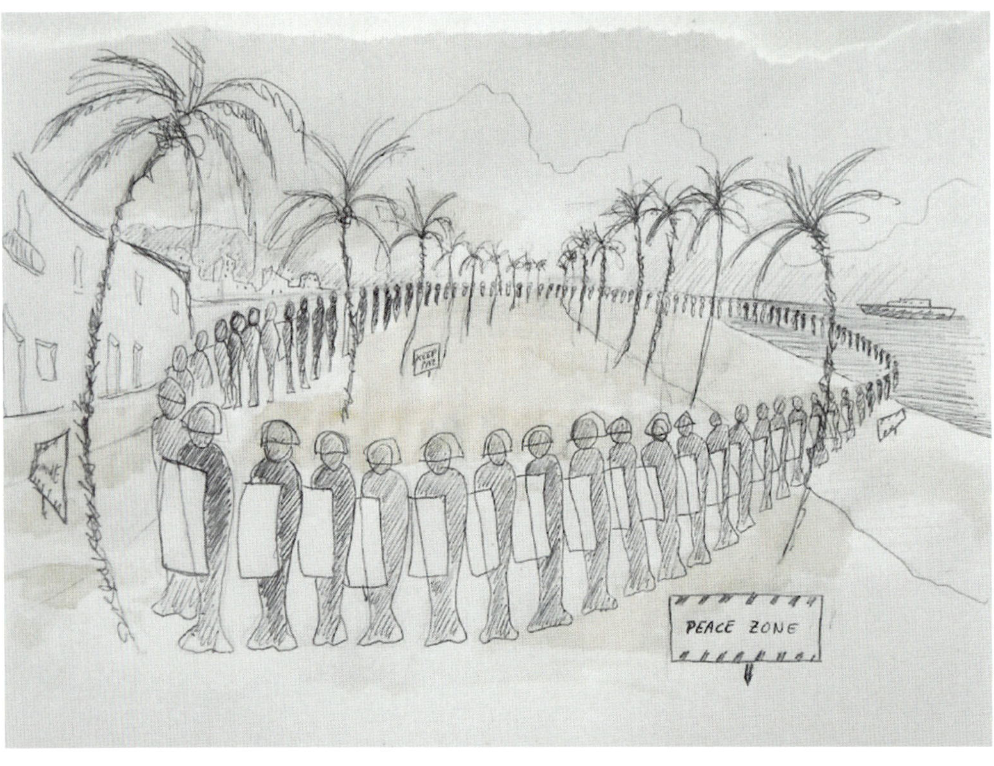

indirectly bringing to mind those countries, neighborhoods, businesses, and properties that have to isolate themselves from the rest of the world in order to preserve their privileges. Peace behind walls, fences, and other forms of excessive protection is sometimes much more aggressive, bellicose, or uncivil than the mild chaos of a public beach. Yet how does one represent that difference between harmony, public peace, and a place that is well protected vis-à-vis a typically imagined enemy? In search of that kind of depiction, and seeing that the capitalist West, waging permanent economic war, manages at best to represent non-war, not real peace, we realized we had to examine other visual cultures.

THAT UNKNOWN ANIMAL

We were told the story of a mystical animal well after our arrival in China. A kind of unicorn only appeared when peace and harmony reigned throughout the land. The *qilin* is the very incarnation of harmony: its voice is melodious, its gait steady. It never takes a step without having looked beforehand where it is going to tread and tramples nothing beneath its hoof, not even blades of grass. It only crosses good areas and lies down on flat terrain. A plant eater, it is called the "benevolent animal." The call of the female *qilin* presages the return of peace. Gentle and friendly, with the body of a deer and the tail of an ox, it sports a single horn wrapped in flesh, unlike the horn of the rhinoceros. The horn is a symbol of wisdom and not a weapon; it allows the *qilin* to separate the righteous from those who have something weighing on their conscience. Looking for contemporary visualizations of these pacifist animal symbols, and once again as part of a workshop, in this case in Dailin, we were made aware of the incredible diminishment in the symbolic diversity of our planet. Of course the students knew the symbol. In the end it constitutes, along with several other figures, the foundation of their mythological culture. They brought us, moreover, several interesting

014

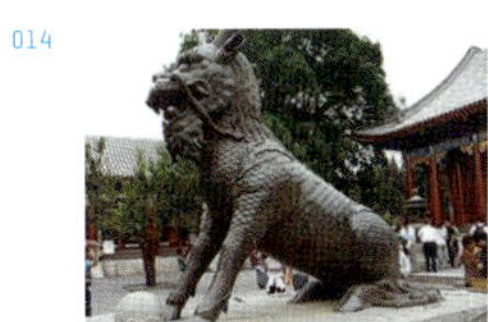
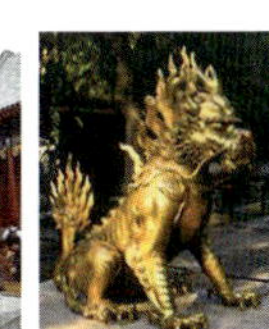
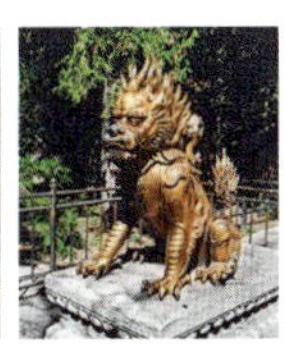

historical depictions (014). But it was almost impossible to get them to work on more contemporary interpretations of this myth. For them it smacked of an outdated past or popular art. Graphic design could not tell us whether that culture nurtured them or not. The rest of the workshop clearly showed this mimeticism with respect to the global graphic output, which is strongly influenced by the West. The referents spring from both graphic style and symbols that have been worked in some way. We can almost say that creativity remains in a kind of pre-established straitjacket, a fine international genre outside of which graphic designers fear they will limit their credibility and understandability. Even the yin and yang symbol, which has managed to pass the hurdle of truly international under-standability, is often accompanied by the peace-and-love sign at the risk of redundancy, as if it weren't sufficient unto itself (015). And since each of them addresses all of the others as a whole in our world, it is simpler to forget particular codes than to make them comprehensible to others. In other words, in terms of images there exists the same dangerous dialectic that applies to languages: on the one hand, modern, contemporary "globish," accessible to everyone and intended for one and all; and on the other, the coded, which remains specific to the community and is kept half-alive almost in secret through nostalgia. If our encyclopedia has come to be filled out, it is indeed through the confrontation and revitalization of that multitude of local symbols directly expressing peace, justice, and harmony. It is the work of an ethnologist that without question remains to be perfected.

015

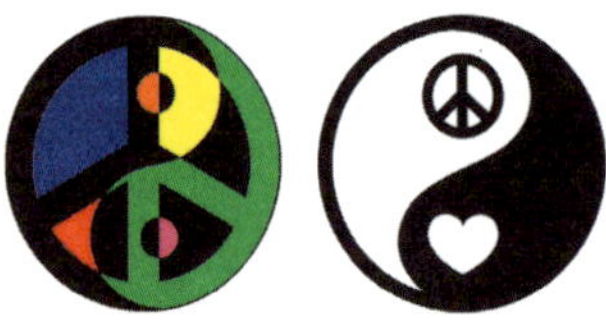

AROUSING IMAGES
The workshops played a sensitive role. While our task as seekers of images in China and Barcelona consisted of going

behind the globally sanctioned mainstream in order to endow
with credibility and update visualizations of the special,
the personal, that which had been relegated to the obsolete,
the kitschy, the workshops held in crisis contexts acquired a
further dimension. In Beirut, San Salvador, and Delhi, we were
initially confronted with the images the participants assumed
that we—as designers and researchers—expected of them. Only
after several days did personal, tender, hard, emotionally
charged images emerge. Including those one would have preferred
not to view because the pain seemed unendurable. These inner
pictures elicited more than visual impressions. They are
accompanied by a range of meanings, and their effects are
inescapable for those who seek to collect and transmit them.
We realized that our search involved a completely different
level of responsibility than simply an obligation to truth and
sensitivity. We who arrive from outside and reawaken emotions
that are perhaps submerged in a restorative sleep leave the
scene again after just a few days. We hope that this opening
up of wounds contributes to the healing process, and does not
simply aggravate suffering. It is clear that exceptional
significance must be attributed to these very different types
of images; they have much to show and to communicate of great
importance to us all.

THE FORCE OR WEAKNESS OF THE IMAGE

What can an image do against someone who has decided to take up
arms, to impose his position by force? It is rather symptomatic
that the two motifs most reproduced by Picasso, the ones
the artist made accessible to a broad audience, were the dove
of peace and reproductions of Don Quixote (016). In a way these
series of images mirrored each other. To fight against the
impossible, to depict windmills and pursue the struggle for
peace and the well-being of humans, and do so with pen or
paintbrush—the fragile bird of freedom, in a word, battles the
impossible, made up of windmills, steamrollers, closed systems,
and the tanks of today, piloted from afar. What does it matter,

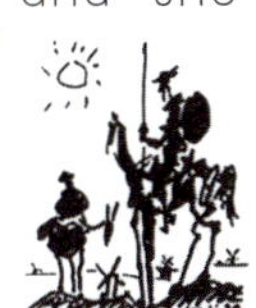

this impossible struggle against the vastly more powerful?
It is really about engaging in the fight like a dove, with just
wings, symbols, words, and images. Through the use of "soft"
means, in a way. It is about taking on the fight in the face
of the very worst dangers, or more comfortably in a country
at peace. Even in this it is about going beyond the comfort
of indifference and silence, making an effort to leave behind
inaction and anonymity, announcing one's position, even an
unpopular one, bearing witness, crying out, manifesting one's
outrage, trying to convince others and awaken their conscience,
making another, different position heard, contradicting the
propaganda or the prevailing thought, breaking the silence;
in short, resisting, fighting, not throwing in the towel, not
giving in. In this respect, then, the act of creating an image
corresponds to that of putting pen to paper. It is about
finding a way to proclaim something while avoiding the banality
of a message that is too direct, showy, simplistic. This
intention, however, guarantees neither the quality of the image
nor how it will be received by the intended audience. Most
end up in the wastepaper basket before even being sent out into
the world. Some will make it into print, and only a few will
remain fixed in our memory.

Thus, many images in the present book were designed to be
printed as posters. They were pasted up legally or illegally,
sometimes very locally, rarely on a wide scale, outside of
conflict zones or within. The digital media have erased the
boundaries between creation, production, and diffusion. They
are also breaking down geographic borders. On their computers
graphic designers create their images, which are immediately
sent out over the networks, cross borders, and are passed on.
The image created is added to the heap of others out there. If
noticed, it generally has an impact on a very brief moment in
time, then finds itself just as quickly forgotten. The right
image, the high-quality one that comes at the right time, spreads
like word of mouth, from computer to computer. It moves people,

offers food for thought, is eventually reused, and becomes
a symbol, almost an icon. It brings people together and
occasionally even manages, however slightly, to transform
a conflict situation.

CLASSIFICATION

With images pouring in from everywhere, our collection was
gradually growing; we needed to define a way for classifying
them. The long work session with Sébastien Thierry is still
fresh in our memory. We had a small conference room at the
institute at our disposal and it was very quickly covered with
photographs and their corresponding titles. Of course the
exercise itself was not as easy as all that. A great number of
images belonged to a range of categories simultaneously, and
unlike an Internet site, where such multifaceted indexing could
have been done, in a book one has to make choices. Moreover,
the creation of one category automatically imposed other
corresponding ones, categories for which we often did not as
yet have images. Generally, introducing a title forced us
to begin our search once again for images while focusing on
the theme in question. But before beginning that search, we had
to finalize the selection of entries. While some were obvious
choices, for others the discussion was more heated. What to
do, for example, with everything related to famous people? Whom
should we select and whom should we leave aside? Did we have
to reproduce the sometimes surprising Nobel Peace Prize winners,
choose other criteria, and if so, which? In the end we decided
to remain in the narrow category of depictions of peace.
We eliminated the living symbols by limiting ourselves to
symbols that had gone through a real visual production process.
And what to do with certain religions, which for some, in
their imperial conquest, lie at the heart of so many wars and
conflicts? While the image of that likable figure of the
Buddha seemed to be a given, Christian peace was, for example,
more emblematic, yet at the same time it was impossible to
eliminate Christian actions taken in the struggle for peace.

What to do with the Muslim faith, even contemporary Islam, stigmatized as a source of aggression? Didn't it have the right to sit at the table of contents, just like Christianity in its pacifist iteration? The search for common ground among faiths certainly contributes to peace [017]. Then again, non-belief also had to be respected. The discussion around religious diversity led us to talk about the different relationships to peace. Despite our efforts to avoid the clichés in order to get beyond the Eurocentric ambient, as well as our wish not to limit ourselves to a single point of view on the conflicts and broaden the choice of viewpoints, we had no interest in finding ourselves in a kind of pseudo-neutrality in which taking any stand would no longer be possible. Here again we had to transcend the notion of a Voltairian encyclopedia in that the present book aims to be neither objective nor neutral; it is rather the work of several authors acting side by side, with their own way of seeing the project, and a range of levels of tolerance and intensity of research.

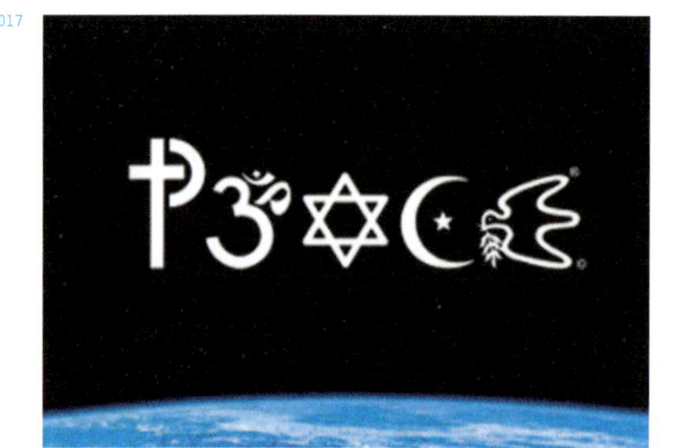
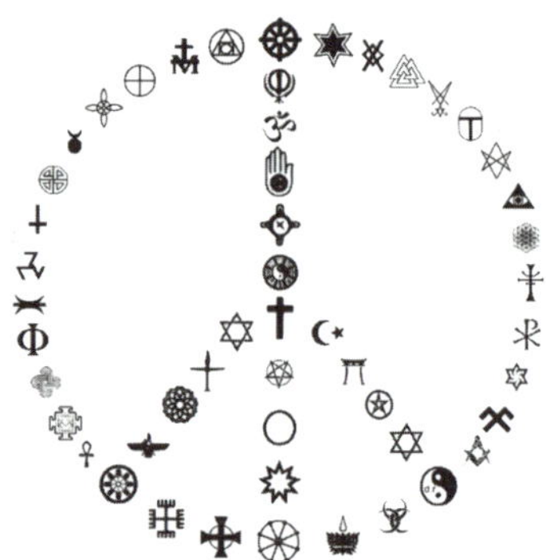

LAMBS AND SHEPHERDESSES

To return to the difficulty of depicting peace in the West juxtaposed with the abundance of images of non-war: for example, the positive iconography unabashedly expressed in China like a vital purpose is projected by Western religions into either a distant past forever lost to us, that of Adam and Eve before the story of the apple, or a hypothetical future, that of a heavenly paradise. Its transposition to Earth puts it within hailing distance of utopia. On the other hand, the Church builds its image by taking care of those in the worst circumstances. Mother Theresa, Abbé Pierre, and many others thus become symbols of that nearly impossible struggle for happiness on earth. This iconographic construct is laid over the dominant ideology of marketing, which is based on erasing the negative, wrinkles, ugliness, tears, death, and war, and leads to that generalized "happyness" that is found in the American Declaration of Independence. It is seemingly guaranteed, if only through consumption, at least by political power. It is the construction of an immediate happiness, which one might set against both the paradise of religion and the struggle for that far-off happiness known as communism. Not to mention the deliberately simplistic iconographies of the Far Right and religious sects, which contrast the hell of today with an iconography made up of golden hair and smiles, a safe world in which nothing negative could ever occur (018). Thus, depictions of family harmony, a carefree existence, children's games, joy, fraternity, the simple pleasures of life, mutual aid, and so on have been co-opted by worlds that we keep a wary eye on nowadays. They read as either nostalgia, utopian future, illusory paradise, or simply advertising, populism, and dangerous propaganda.

018
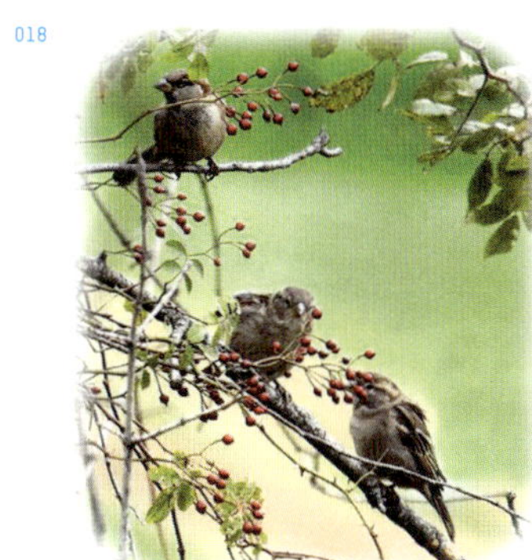
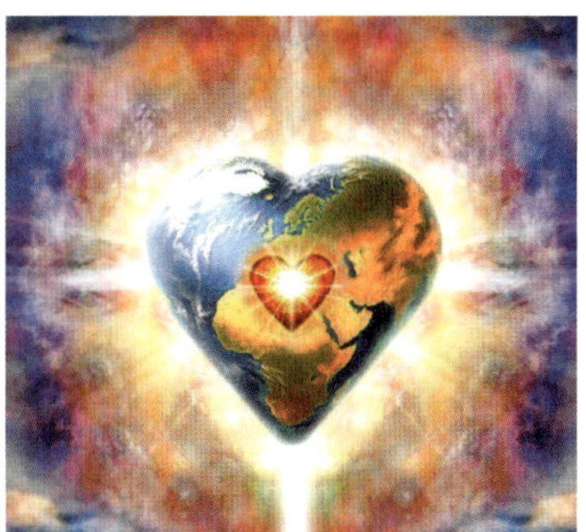

WE'VE LOST EVERYTHING

Life's little coincidences: Philippe Madec gave us his latest book called *Architecture et paix* (Architecture and Peace).[4] From the first pages, he tackles the theme of the difficulty of positively depicting peace. "Basically I knew that the subject of architecture is peace, and that the possibility of repose that it authorizes is its most fundamental expression. But how does one grasp the banal? How does one make present just how much the wall, roof, floor, right there within reach, and devoid of any obvious quality even, are in fact indispensable to our lives, even essential as an organization of our survival?… Standing among all of the members of her family, shivering from everything but the cold, the mother says they have lost everything. And that phrase, always the same, all of us would say it in the same circumstances if faced with what amounts to absolute material tragedy." For us this text conjures up photographers and creators of documentaries. We cannot include them in the present encyclopedia, but they do remarkable work and manage, perhaps better than graphic artists, to depict those moments of real peace, that unconsciousness, those walls and roofs and floors that reassure us. They show us that indispensable thing, the peace that is sometimes present, including in places facing the greatest difficulty and conflict zones. Through the parallels drawn between war and peace, they reveal the invisible and show other aspects of reality without distancing us from the worst. Unfortunately, their work is generally reduced in the press to merely spectacular clichés.

BANNED IMAGES

We remember Christine Breton returning from a trip to Bethlehem with a series of photographs. "These images are in danger; they represent a world of peace that is unbearable to religious extremists," she confided to us. The photos show a town where Christians, Jews, and Muslims live peacefully side by side. Nothing more than normal life, but which, in the current situation, points up all the absurdities of mutual aggression. They show that the stigmatized enemy could be our dear neighbor of yesterday. How many of these images were destroyed in Israel and elsewhere in the world? Images of Constantinople with Greek shops, Yugoslavia, and a unified Korea. We shall always lack those of nineteenth-century Europe before the rise of nationalisms, of pre-colonial Africa… Why have so many libraries been bombarded in the last few decades? They contain evidence that is impossible to bear for those who attack peaceful societies.

IMAGE FOR PEACE

The result of this collection, then, has more to do with images for peace than images of peace, as we had initially anticipated. Each of these posters, tracts, protest marches, installations, and signs of various types says in its own way "No" to the fatality of the logic of violence, public safety at all costs, armaments, bombardments, war, and, beyond that, armies. Each was created either during conflicts as forthright cries against the absurdity of the situation, or as a commemorative act and remembrance of horrors that should never be repeated, or, in a more abstract way, against the very concept of these bellicose mindsets. This category includes images that unfortunately never really lose their contemporary look. We are thinking of an image, so simple and so fitting, by the Japanese graphic designer Shigeo Fukuda (019). As is often the case, it is the link between text and image that creates the tension. Here the term "victory," generally employed for a military victory, is turned around, like a bomb going back into the barrel of its cannon.

We would like to mention the project's online archive,[5] which contains more images, and which moreover remains open-ended and invites future contributions. And although the focus of this encyclopedia has shifted, it remains committed to the challenge of developing visions of peace. In connection with our work,

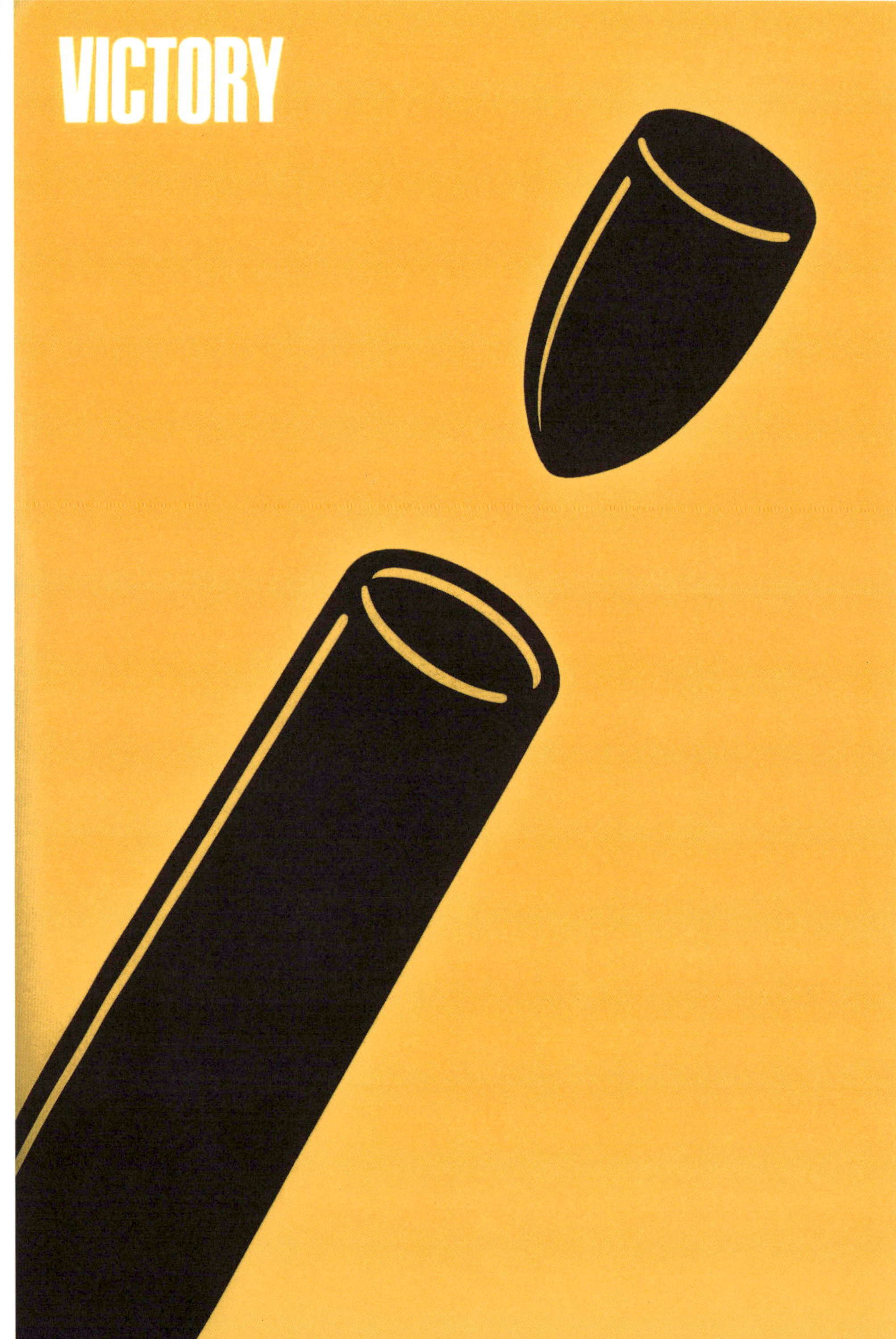
019
VICTORY

the peace researcher Johann Galtung has spoken of a *causa materialis,* one that recognizes in visual presence a step toward the engendering of a new reality. Altered in a similar fashion was the perspective of Carolin Emcke, a renowned philosopher and foreign correspondent from crisis regions who directed two workshops at the institute in the course of the project. At the start, she regarded the central task on the path toward peace to be the depiction of its infringement. But over the past year, she has emphasized the necessity for bringing visions of potential futures to individuals and communities whose realities and whose image worlds have been impacted by violence. To cite the philosopher Ernst Bloch, "It is a question of learning to hope,"[6] or as Christa Wolf wrote, "If we cease to hope, then that which we fear will surely come."[7]

IMPOSSIBILITY

The book now goes to the printer. We would like to thank the many individuals who have had a hand in it, as well as all of those who will understand that it is impossible for us, in such a situation, to compensate each of the creators of these images. The cause, we hope, surpasses monetary interests. Given the quantity of images involved, it is impossible to respect the laws concerning the reproduction of works of art.

NECESSARILY INCOMPLETE

One need only open the newspaper to understand that the need for images continues to make itself felt daily. Each day brings its new needs for explanations, persuasion, and reminders. We harbor the modest hope that this collection will be a factor in inspiring future struggles.

At the same time, we are aware of a fear of images that leads to total control, as in the case of "embedded journalism," or even to censorship. This fear is also expressed in a profound distrust of images. In response to a question concerning the forms of credible documentation, students in the visual design course at the Zurich University of the Arts informed us that they believed such documentation should be in black and white and devoid of images. When those who have chosen the image as their métier are seized by such despair, then one can only confront them with another vision, with different images, in order to make them aware of the important role they have to play. The question remains whether—in this age of the flood of images—we really find ourselves in the middle of an iconic or pictorial turn, or whether we are dealing with a mass of uniform image worlds, ones that call for new visual positions. Who if not young designers will feel themselves called upon to make inspired and responsible contributions to this effort? The objective of research into images can only be to exit a state of resigned indifference, one that is often the result of visual illiteracy, and to generate an impetus leading toward the more aware treatment of images. It is a question of a critical school of the gaze for the sake of a reflexive relationship with images and an investigative image praxis. With the present volume, it is our intention to contribute to this effort, if only to the extent that dissatisfaction with the collection would lead toward its further development, or even to an entirely new collection and production. Which is why we now cite Marie-José Mondzain, whose marvelous essay "Can Images Kill?,"[8] which invokes the alternative of iconophobia or phobocracy, concludes with the appeal: "Make images!"

RUEDI BAUR AND VERA BAUR KOCKOT

1 The visitor was Chris Steurer. The graphic artist remained by our side throughout the first phase of the project, between 2005 and 2008, along with Karin Prätorius, Clemens Bellut, Sébastien Thierry, Maru Martinez, and Maria Fahringer. The second phase, between 2008 and 2010, mainly involved Megan Hall, Monya Pletsch, Meriem Bouhara, Clemens Bellut, and us. Several workshops and shows were put together at the time in various countries around the world and at UNESCO in Paris. The project was taken over by the publisher Lars Müller at the closing of the Design2context Institute in late 2010, and finalized over the summer of 2012 by a smaller team, namely Megan Hall, Sophie Loschert, Lars Müller, and ourselves.

2 See "Kulturozid" in Johan Galtung, *Eurotopia. Die Zukunft eines Kontinents,* Vienna 1993, p. 11.

3 In May 2004, the Design2context Institute launched an appeal for images entitled "Unworthy of democracy: be human in wartime as well!" Two thousand invitations and emails were sent out; 300 contributions against abuses of the Geneva Conventions came back to us from seven countries. The images were published as a small booklet by Scalo Editions, Zurich, in July of 2004.

4 Philippe Madec, *L'architecture et la paix, éventuellement une consolation,* Paris 2012.

5 See *Imagine Peace!—A Visual Encyclopedia,* at http://peace.civic-city.org.

6 From the foreword of Ernst Bloch, *The Principle of Hope,* trans. Neville Plaice, Stephen Plaice, and Paul Knight, Cambridge, Mass. 1986, p. 3; originally published in German as *Das Prinzip Hoffnung* in 1959.

7 Christa Wolf, *No Place on Earth,* trans. Jan Van Heurck, New York 1982, p. 117; originally published in German as *Kein Ort. Nirgends* in 1979.

8 Marie-José Mondzain, "Can Images Kill?," *Critical Inquiry* 36, no. 1 (2009); originally published in French as *L'Image peut-elle tuer?* in 2002.

001 BE HUMANE IN WARTIME AS WELL!
Contribution protesting
violations of the Geneva
Convention
CREATOR Romain Benichou, Paris
SOURCE Institut Design2Context
DATE 2004

001 BE HUMANE IN WARTIME AS WELL!
Contribution protesting
violations of the Geneva
Convention
CREATOR Ruth Blesi, Zurich
SOURCE Institut Design2Context
DATE 2004

001 BE HUMANE IN WARTIME AS WELL!
Contribution protesting
violations of the Geneva
Convention
CREATOR Jean-Christophe
Bollache, Lyon
SOURCE Institut Design2Context
DATE 2004

001 BE HUMANE IN WARTIME AS WELL!
Contribution protesting
violations of the Geneva
Convention
CREATOR Stefan Nowak, Düsseldorf
SOURCE Institut Design2Context
DATE 2004

001 BE HUMANE IN WARTIME AS WELL!
Contribution protesting
violations of the Geneva
Convention
CREATOR Yessica Younes, Düsseldorf
SOURCE Institut Design2Context
DATE 2004

001 BE HUMANE IN WARTIME AS WELL!
Contribution protesting
violations of the Geneva
Convention
CREATOR Franck Fortuna, Saumur
SOURCE Institut Design2Context
DATE 2004

001 BE HUMANE IN WARTIME AS WELL!
Contribution protesting
violations of the Geneva
Convention
CREATOR Niklaus Rüegg, Zurich
SOURCE Institut Design2Context
DATE 2004

001 BE HUMANE IN WARTIME AS WELL!
Contribution protesting
violations of the Geneva
Convention
CREATOR Ghislain Bailly, Lille
SOURCE Institut Design2Context
DATE 2004

001 BE HUMANE IN WARTIME AS WELL!
Contribution protesting
violations of the Geneva
Convention

CREATOR Ruth Blesi, Zurich
SOURCE Institut Design2Context
DATE 2004

001 BE HUMANE IN WARTIME AS WELL!
Contribution protesting
violations of the Geneva
Convention
CREATOR Ali Zitouni, Paris
SOURCE Institut Design2Context
DATE 2004

001 BE HUMANE IN WARTIME AS WELL!
Contribution protesting
violations of the Geneva
Convention
CREATOR Anna Berkenbusch and
Linda Wölfel, Berlin
SOURCE Institut Design2Context
DATE 2004

001 BE HUMANE IN WARTIME AS WELL!
Contribution protesting
violations of the Geneva
Convention
CREATOR Félix Müller and Thomas
Decker, Paris
SOURCE Institut Design2Context
DATE 2004

001 BE HUMANE IN WARTIME AS WELL!
Contribution protesting
violations of the Geneva
Convention
CREATOR Seraina Bucher-Feuerstein,
Zurich
SOURCE Institut Design2Context
DATE 2004

001 BE HUMANE IN WARTIME AS WELL!
Contribution protesting
violations of the Geneva
Convention
CREATOR Birgit Kölz and Christine
Hebrank, Cologne
SOURCE Institut Design2Context
DATE 2004

002 ABU GHRAIB
The abuse of detainees at
Abu Ghraib
SOURCE marvinlindsay.typepad.com/
DATE 2004

002 ABU GHRAIB
The abuse of detainees at
Abu Ghraib
SOURCE www.flickr.com/photos/
amerigo/388831667/
DATE 2004

002 ABU GHRAIB
The abuse of detainees at
Abu Ghraib
SOURCE arabadvertising.blogspot.ch
DATE 2004

002 ABU GHRAIB
The abuse of detainees at Abu Ghraib

SOURCE design961.blogspot.ch
DATE 2004

002 BE HUMANE IN WARTIME AS WELL!
Contribution protesting violations
of the Geneva Convention
CREATOR Fons Hickmann, Berlin
SOURCE Institut Design2Context

003 MAN THROWS SHOES AT BUSH
SOURCE news.bbc.co.uk/
DATE 2008

003 MAN THROWS SHOES AT BUSH
SOURCE www.gala.fr/
DATE 2008

003 MAN THROWS SHOES AT BUSH
SOURCE naim.over-blog.org/
DATE 2008

003 A BRONZE SHOE MONUMENT
CREATOR Mahmud Saleh
SOURCE www.guardian.co.uk/
DATE 2008

004 WAR IS PEACE
SOURCE www.fanpop.com/

004 WAR IS PEACE
SOURCE mancelovici.wordpress.com/

005 PEACE
Google Image Research
SOURCE Google

006 FREEDOM DOVE
Google Image Research
SOURCE Google

006 PEACE AND LOVE
Google Image Research
SOURCE Google

008 FREEDOM FACE
CREATOR Pablo Picasso
SOURCE www.mvtpaix.org/

008 FREEDOM FACE
CREATOR Pablo Picasso
SOURCE en.amorosart.com/

009 PSYCHEDELIC BUS 1960S
Woodstock Festival
SOURCE www.flickr.com/
DATE 1969

009 PSYCHEDELIC BUS 1960S
Woodstock Festival
SOURCE number-a.com/
DATE 1969

009 PSYCHEDELIC BUS 1960S
Woodstock Festival
SOURCE blog.hippiecouture.com/

009 PSYCHEDELIC BUS 1960S
Woodstock Festival
SOURCE web420.com/

010 PEACE FLAG
SOURCE www.21septembre.org/

010 PEACE FLAG
SOURCE archives-lepost.
huffingtonpost.fr/

010 PEACE FLAG
SOURCE www.21septembre.org/

011 THE CARNATION REVOLUTION
SOURCE avengers-in-time.blogspot.ch
DATE 1974

012 Soliers from the first armored
division celebrate American
Independence Day at a palace
that belonged to Saddam Hussein's
son Uday.
CREATOR Yuri Kozyrev
SOURCE timbuktu.dk/archives/tag/
dispatches
DATE 4 July 2003

012 THERMAL VALS SPA, SWITZERLAND
SOURCE travelwithfrankgehry.
blogspot.com/2009/04/therme-
vals-spa-by-peter-zumthor.html

012 SCREENSHOT SEQUENCE FROM THE
SHORT FILM *LAST RESORT*
Hometown Baghdad is an online
web series that tells the
stories of three young Iraqis
struggling to survive during
the war.
CREATOR chattheplanet.com
DATE 2007

013 THE PEACE BEACH, BARCELONA
CREATOR Arena Vent

013 THE PEACE BEACH, BARCELONA
CREATOR Arena Vent

014 QILIN STATUE
SOURCE en.wikipedia.org/
DATE 2009

014 QILIN STATUE
SOURCE living-vegan.blogspot.ch/

014 QILIN STATUE
SOURCE fr.wikipedia.org/

015 PEACE, YIN AND YANG
SOURCE subtlehippie.com

015 PEACE, YIN AND YANG
SOURCE subtlehippie.com

016 DON QUIXOTE
SOURCE multimedia.uqam.ca

017 PEACE AND RELIGION
SOURCE mountzion144.ning.com

017 PEACE AND RELIGION
SOURCE media.photobucket.com/

018 RELIGIOUS SECTS
SOURCE peacelovelove.blogspot.ch/

018 RELIGIOUS SECTS
SOURCE zeblog.majest.net/

019 VICTORY
CREATOR Shigeo Fukuda
SOURCE Alain Le Quernec,
Fukuda. C'est fou (Quimper:
Le Quartier, 1991).

001
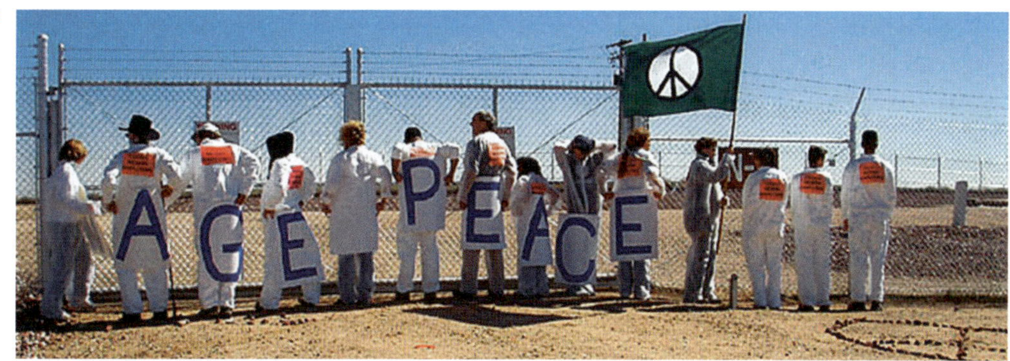

002
003
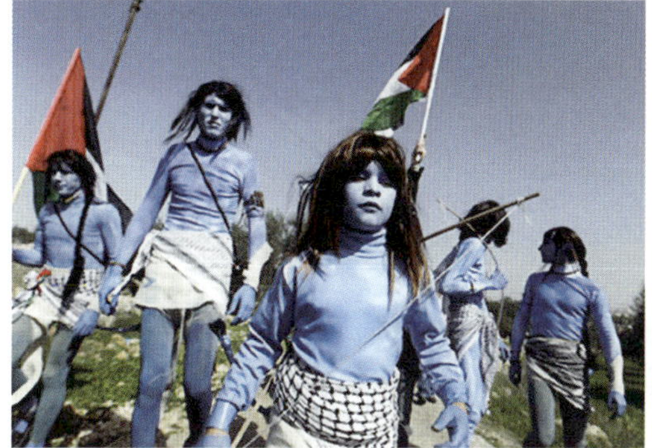
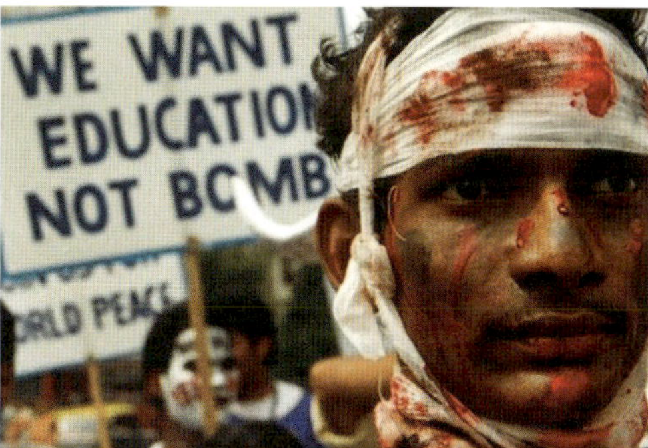

004
005
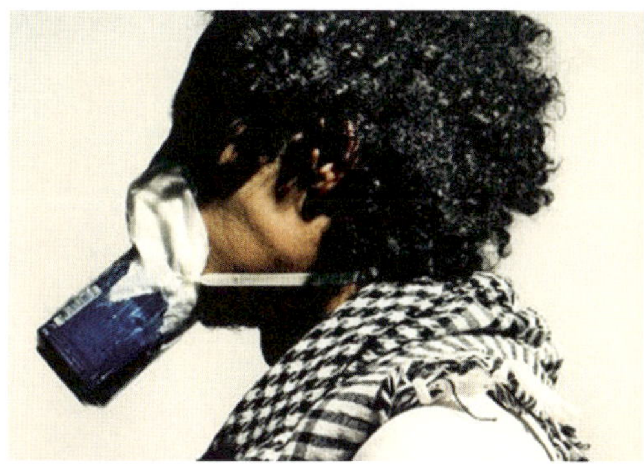
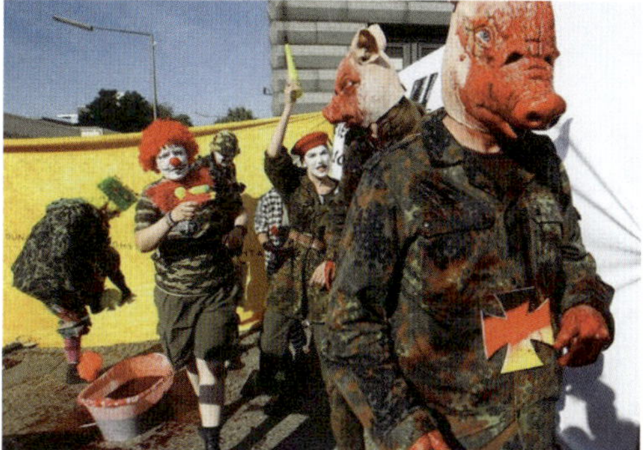

006
007
NEXT
008
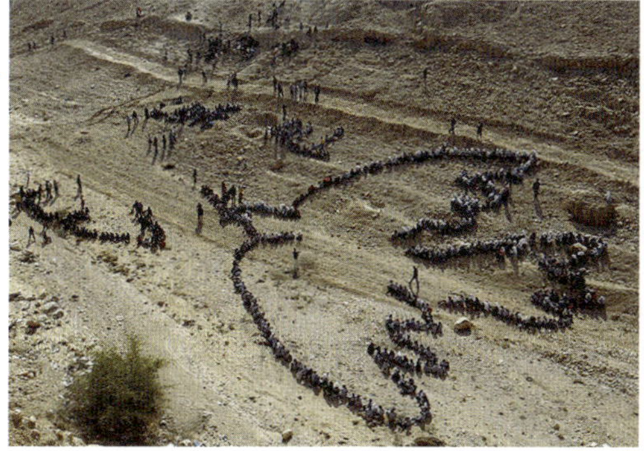
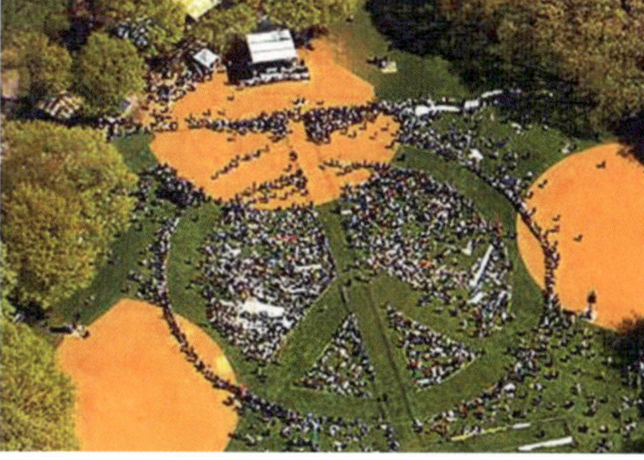

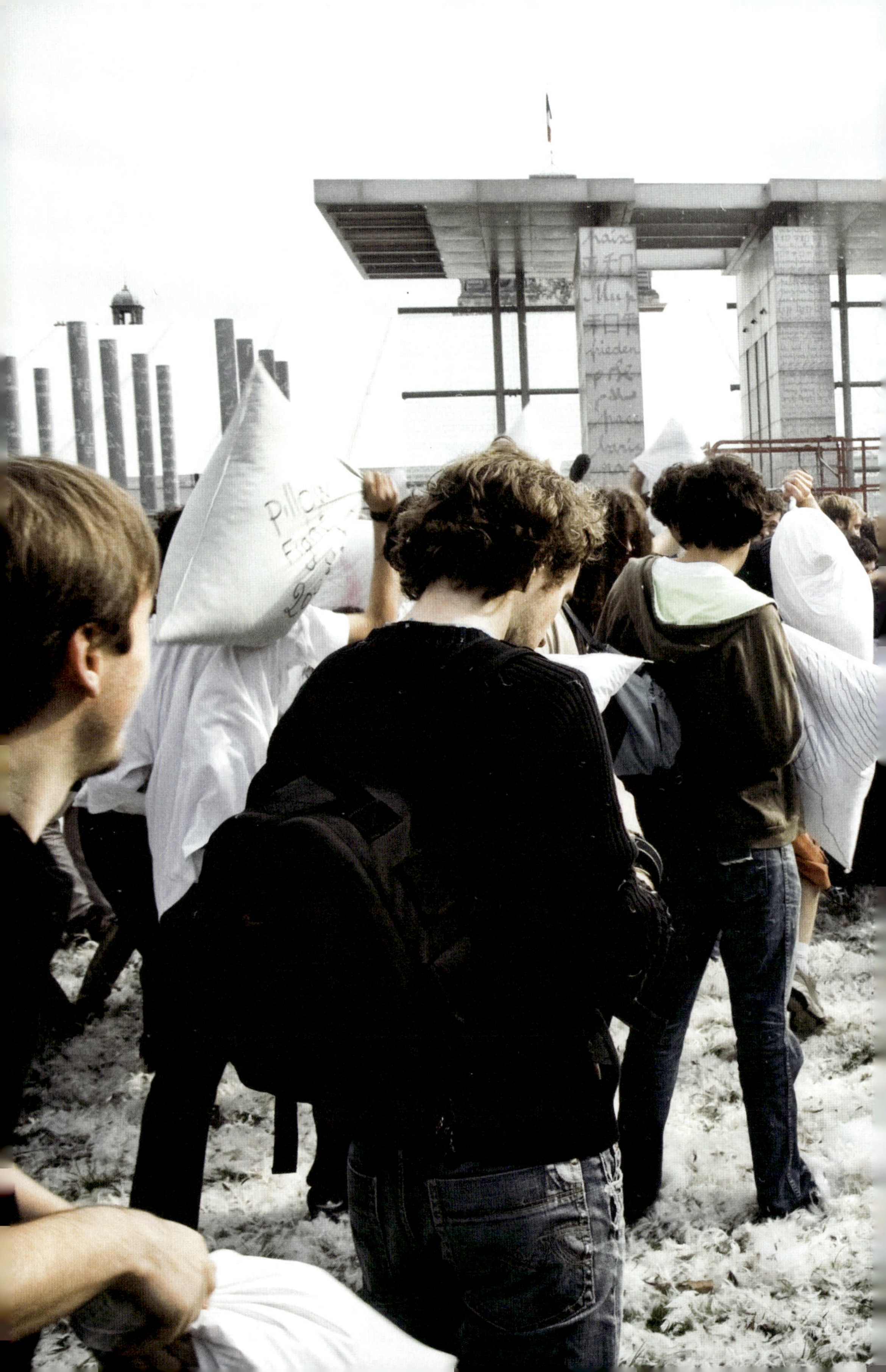

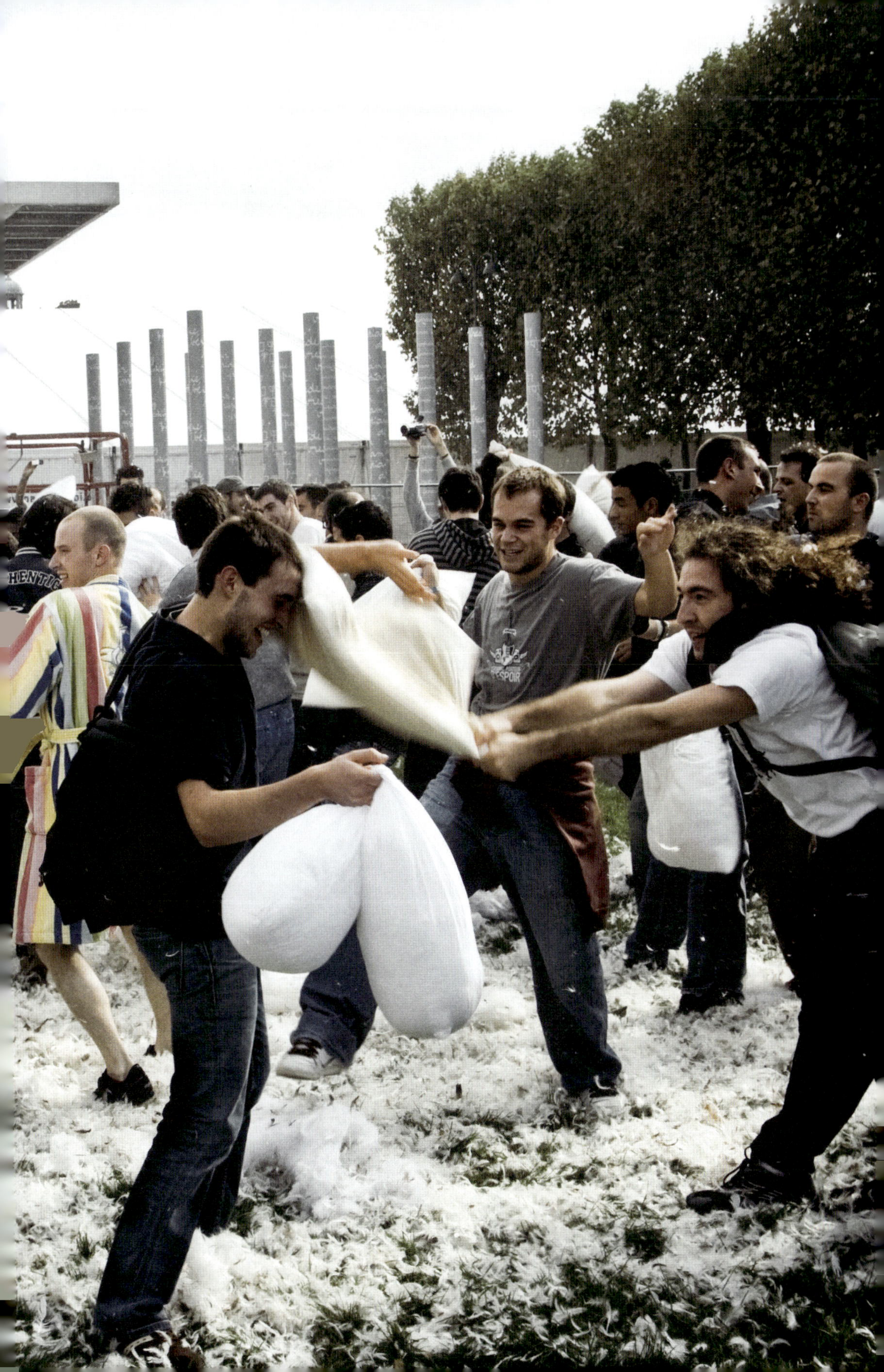

009
010
011

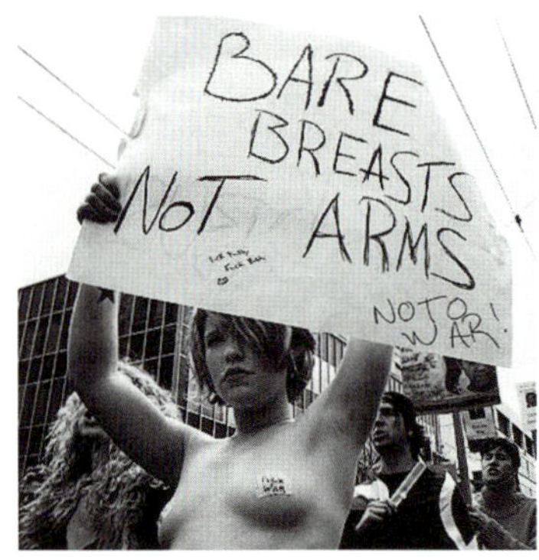

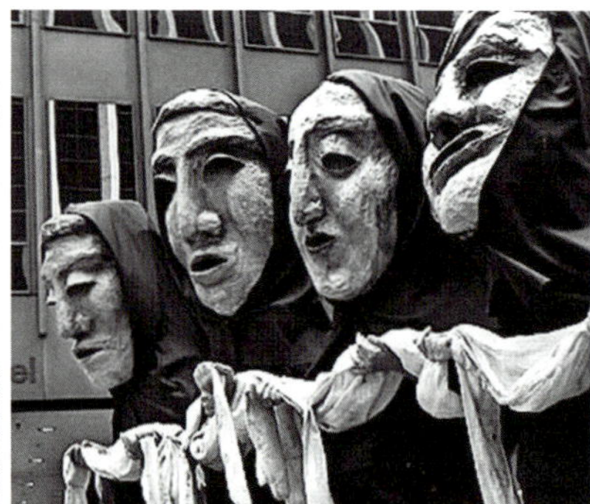
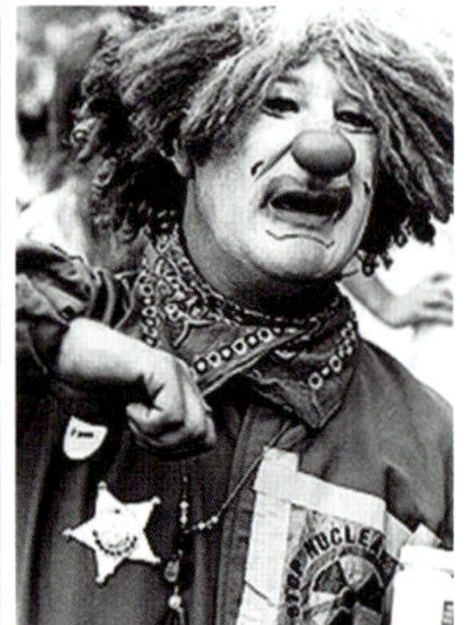

012
013
014
015

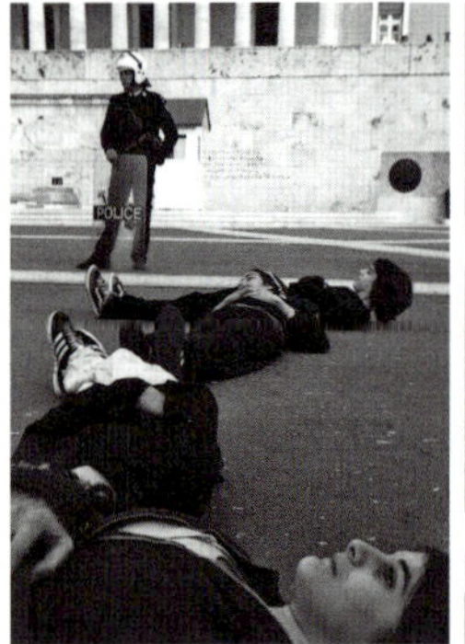
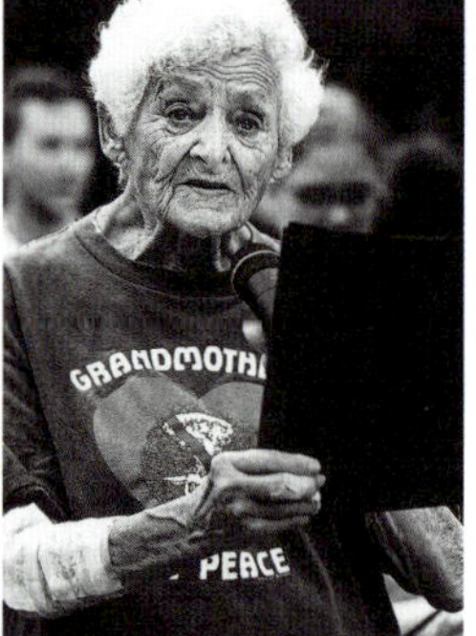

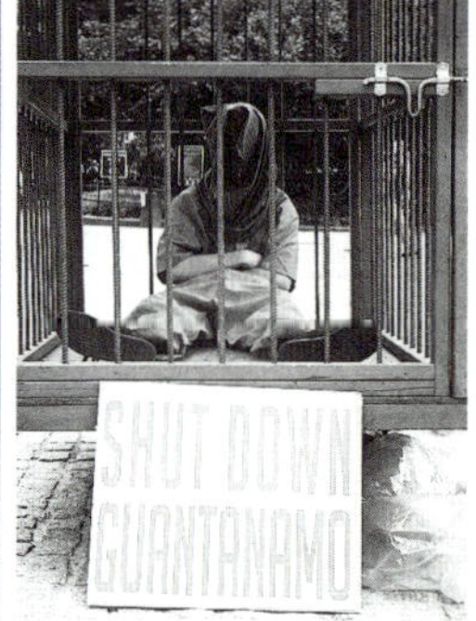

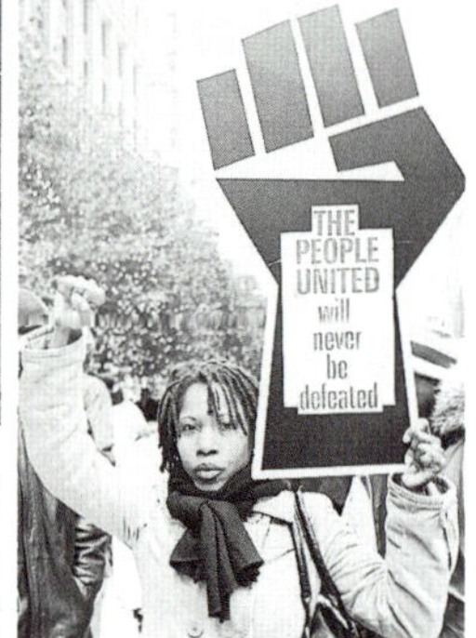

016
017

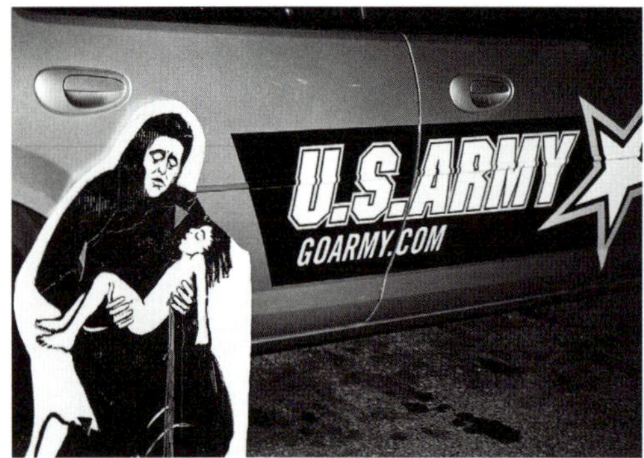

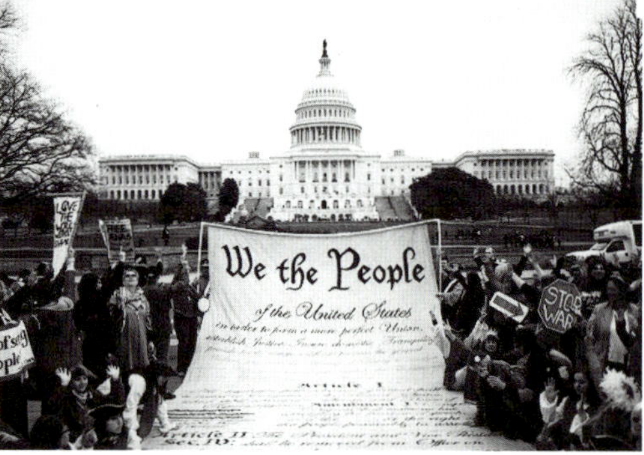

018
019
020

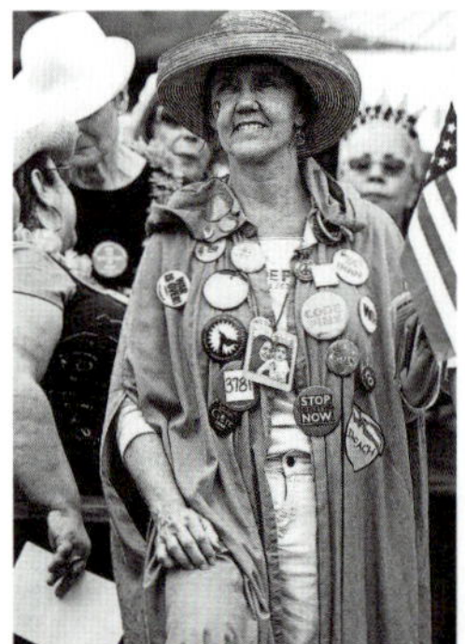

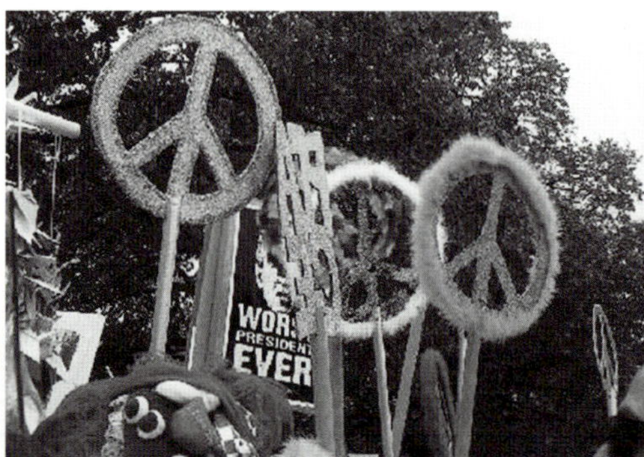

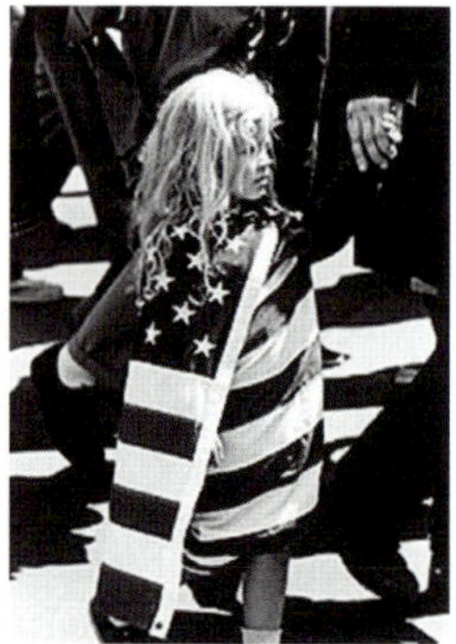

021
022
023

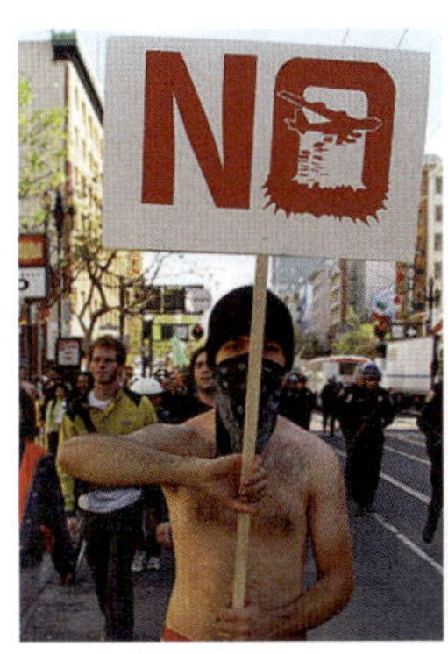

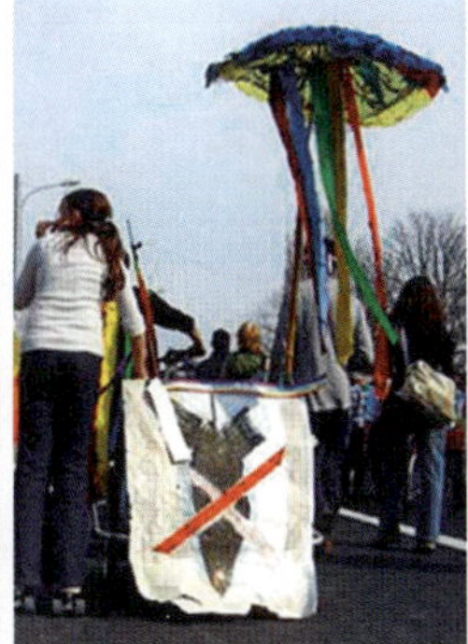

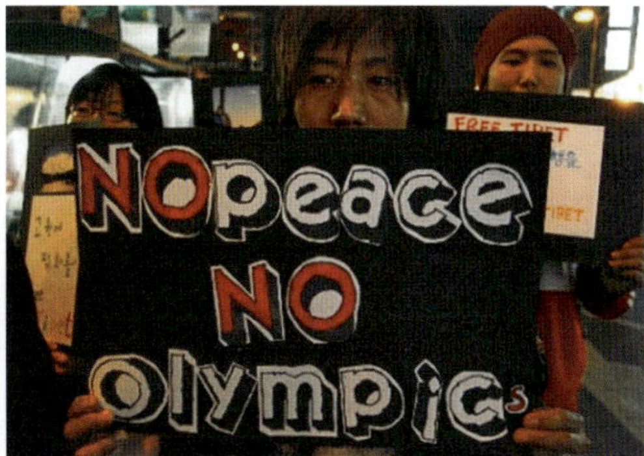

024
025

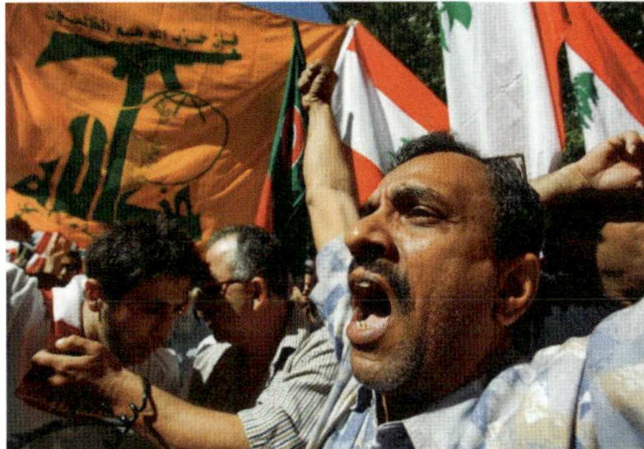

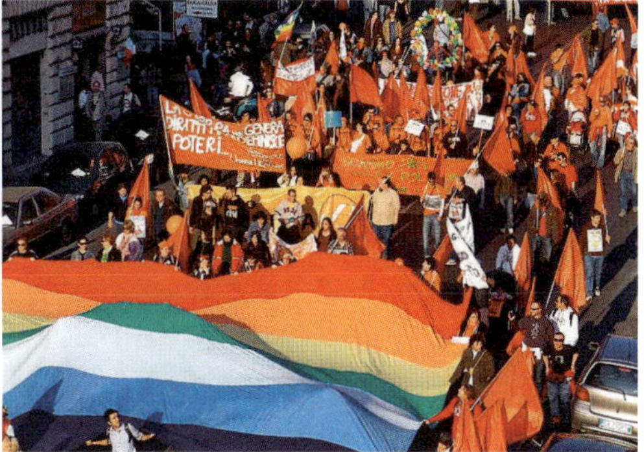

026
027
028

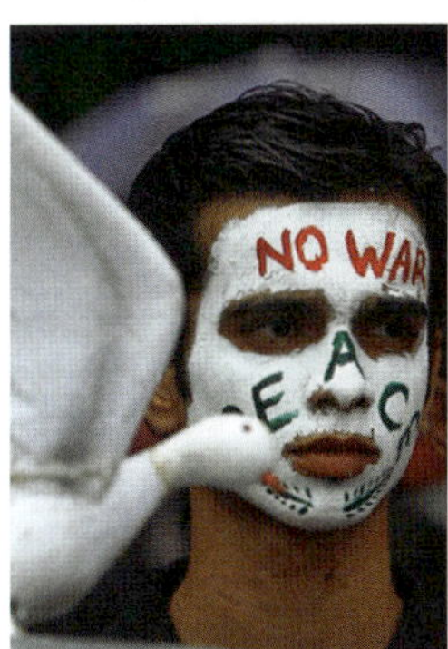

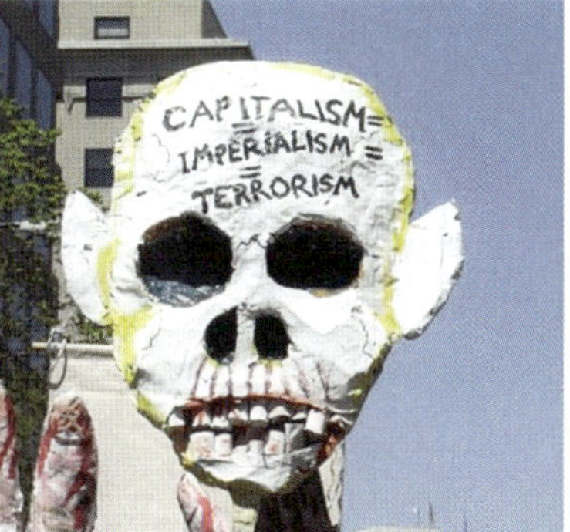

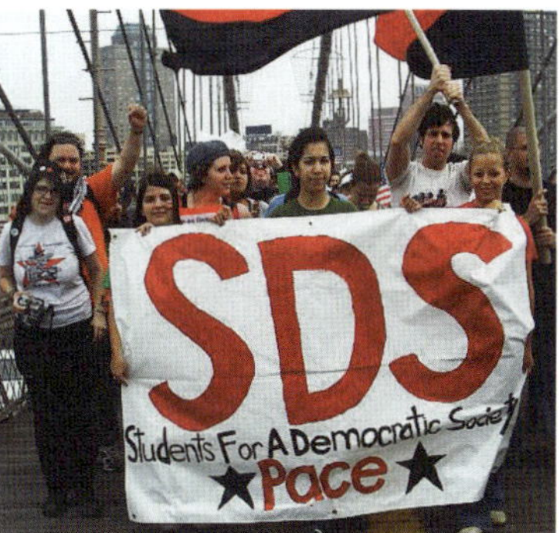

029
030

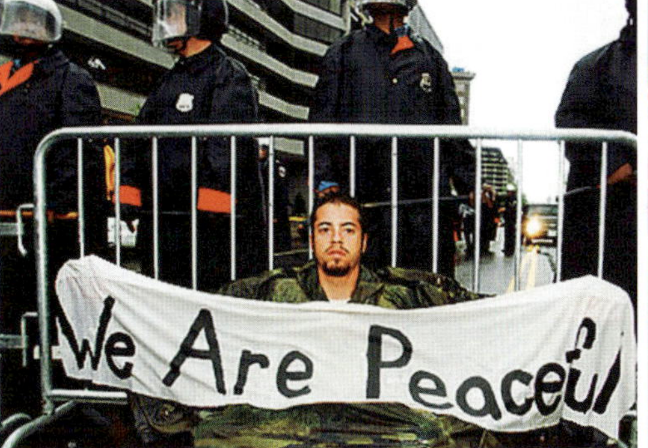

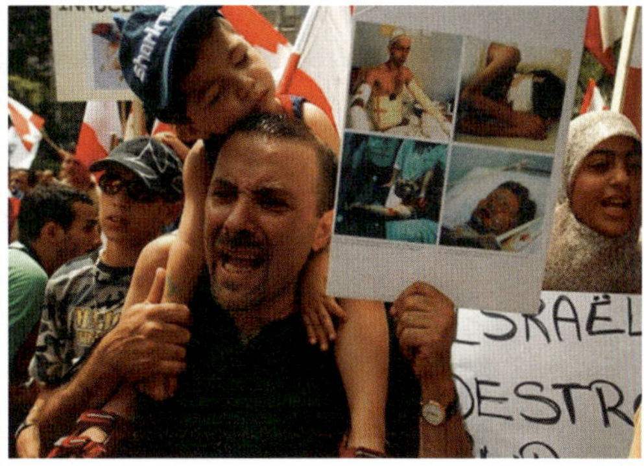

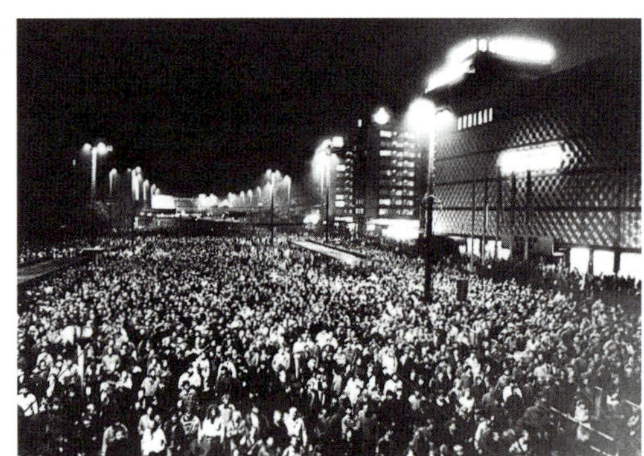
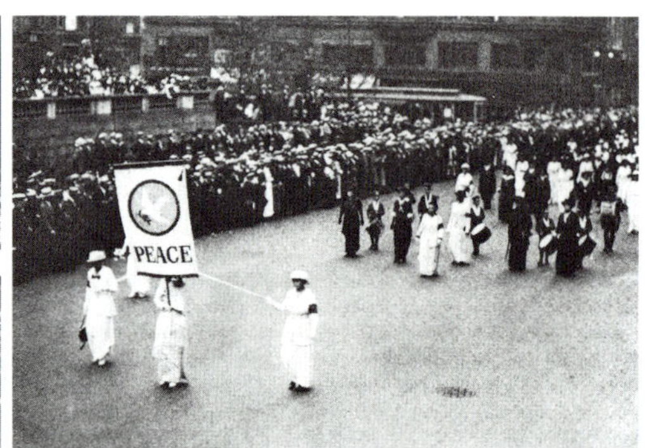
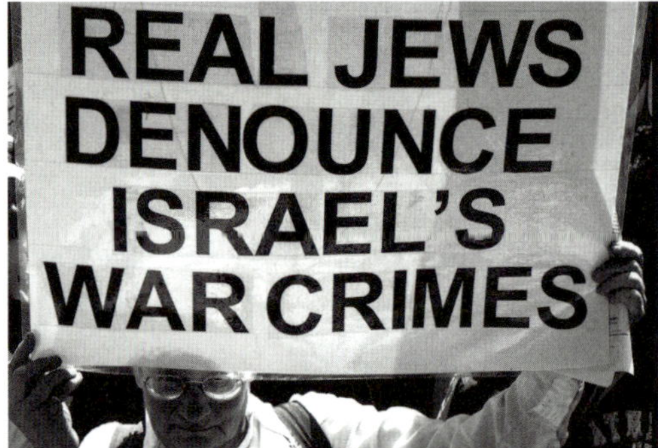

REAL JEWS
DENOUNCE
ISRAEL'S
WAR CRIMES

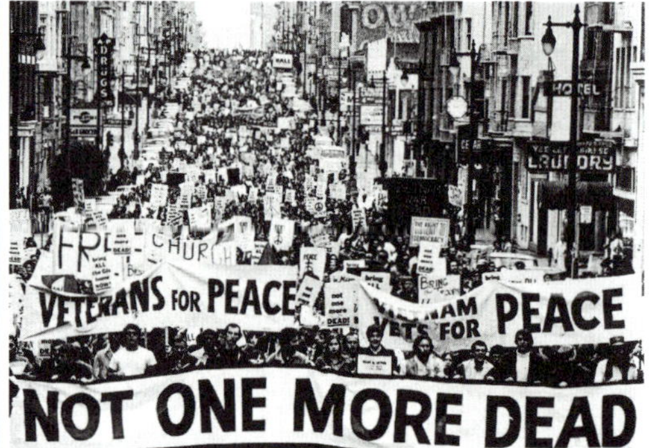

VETERANS FOR PEACE
VETS FOR PEACE
NOT ONE MORE DEAD

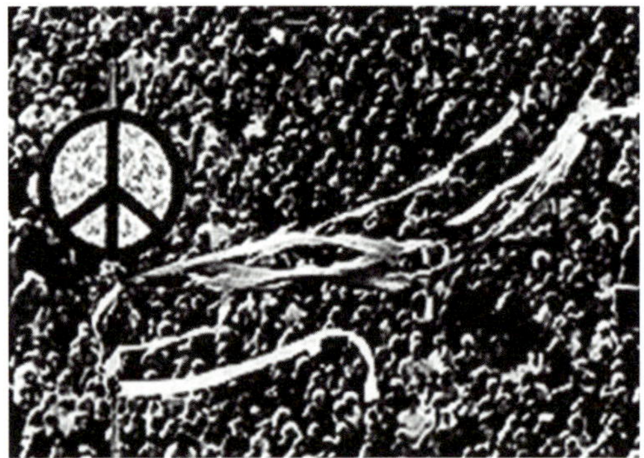
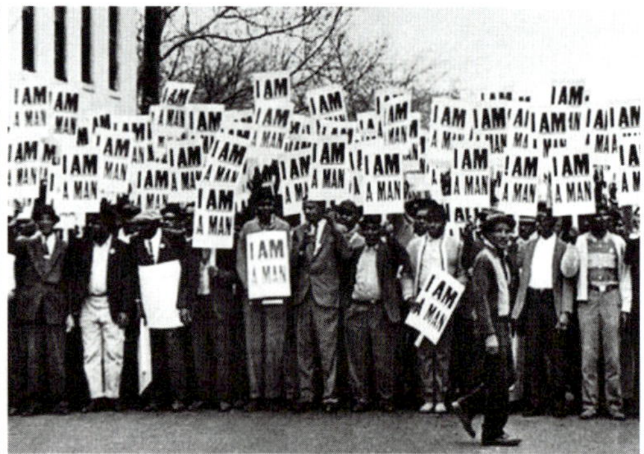

I AM A MAN

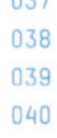
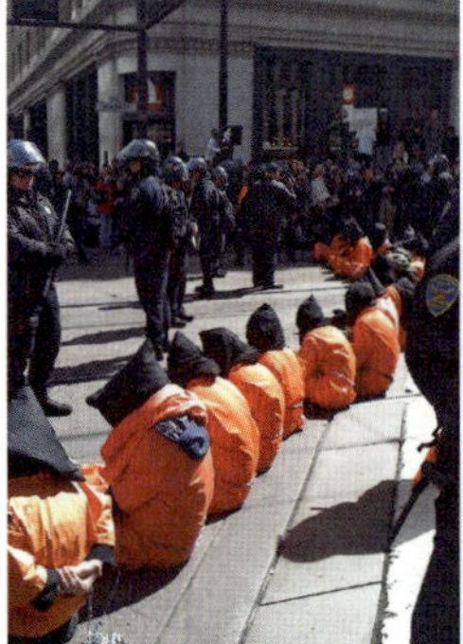
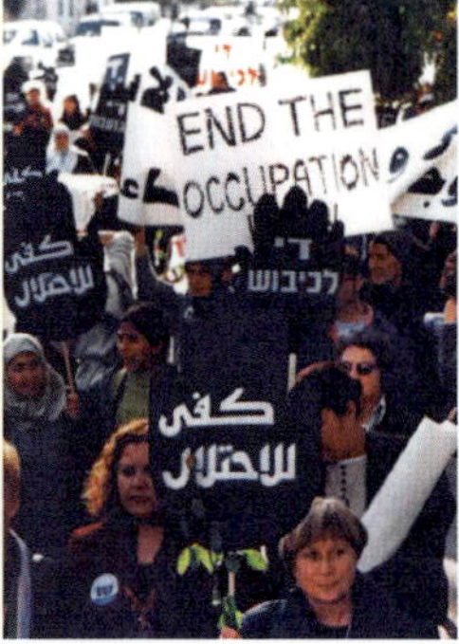

END THE
OCCUPATION

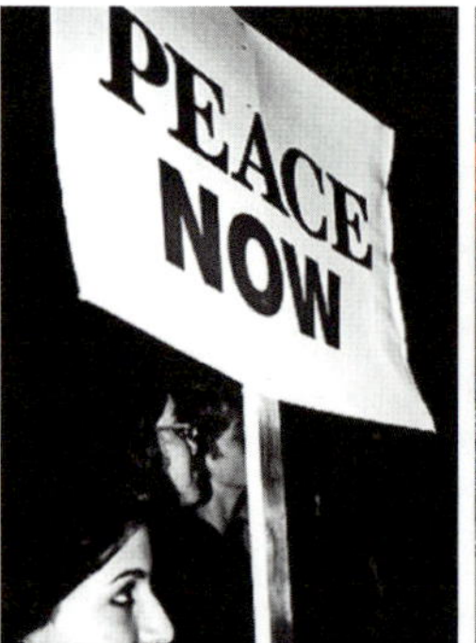

PEACE
NOW

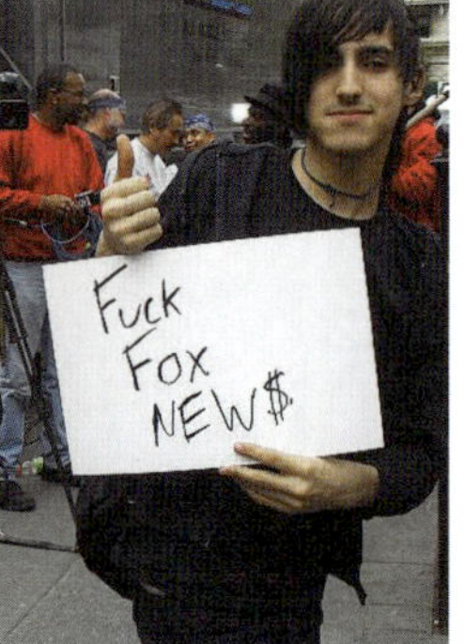

Fuck
Fox
NEW$

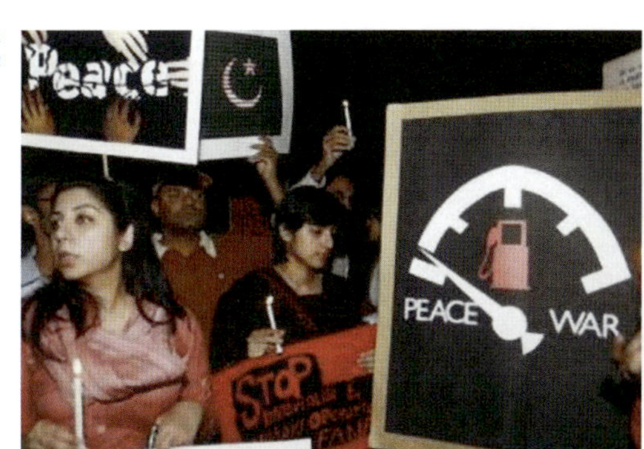
PEACE
WAR
STOP

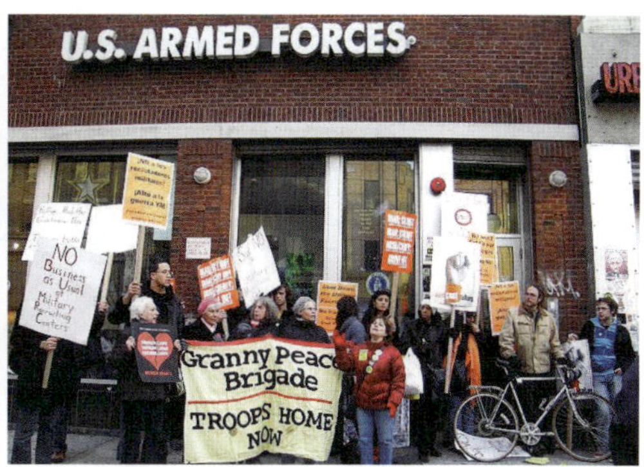
U.S. ARMED FORCES
NO
Business
as Usual
Military
Recruiting
Centers
Granny Peace
Brigade
TROOPS
HOME
NOW

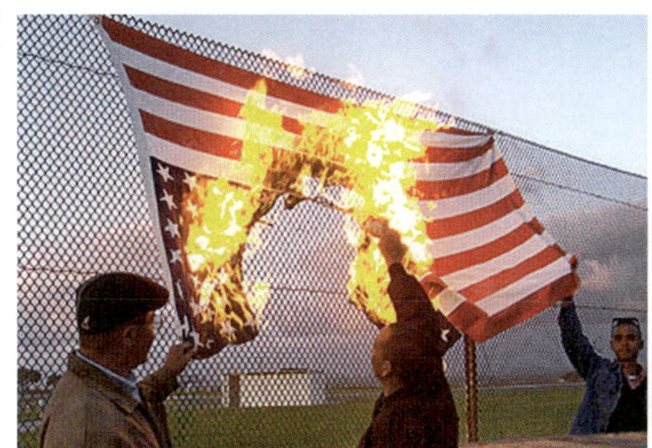

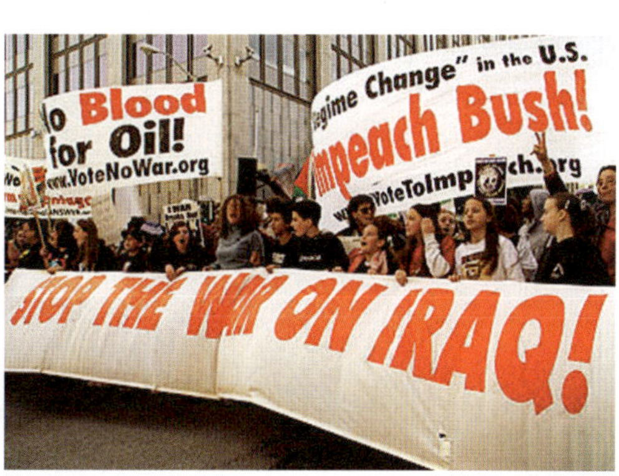
No Blood
for Oil!
www.VoteNoWar.org
Regime Change" in the U.S.
Impeach Bush!
www.VoteToImpeach.org
STOP THE WAR ON IRAQ!

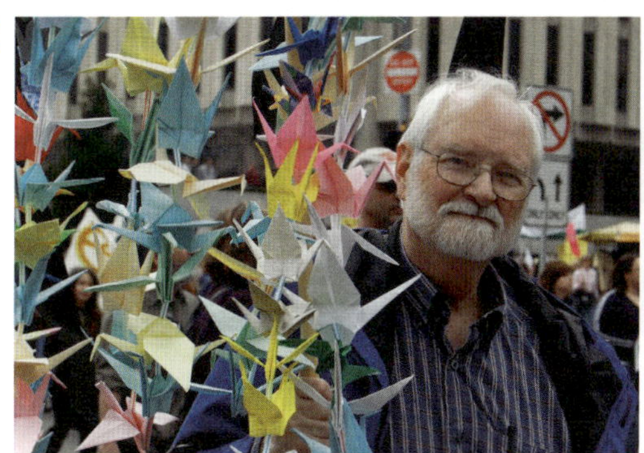

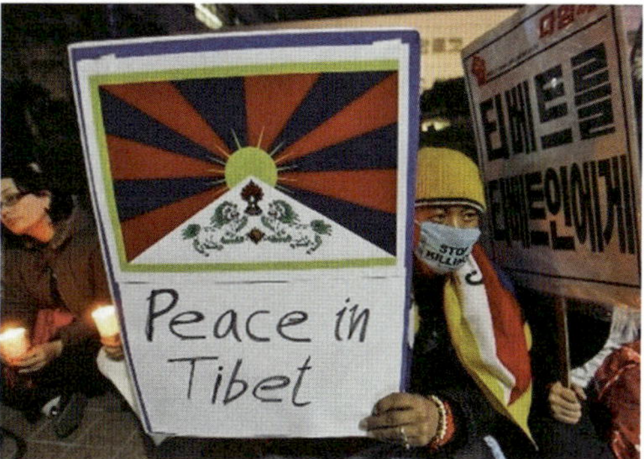
Peace in
Tibet

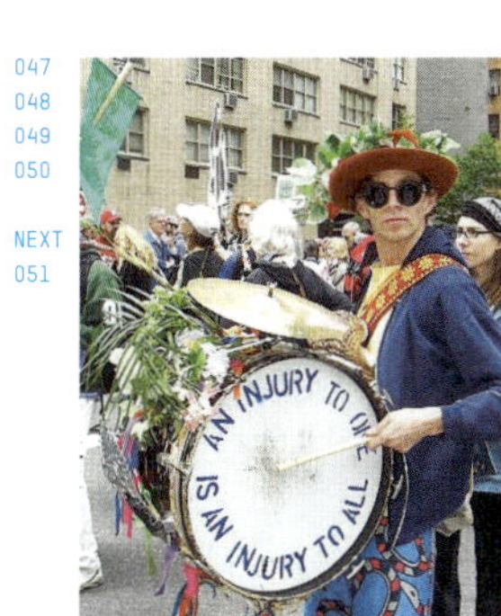
AN INJURY TO ONE
IS AN INJURY TO ALL

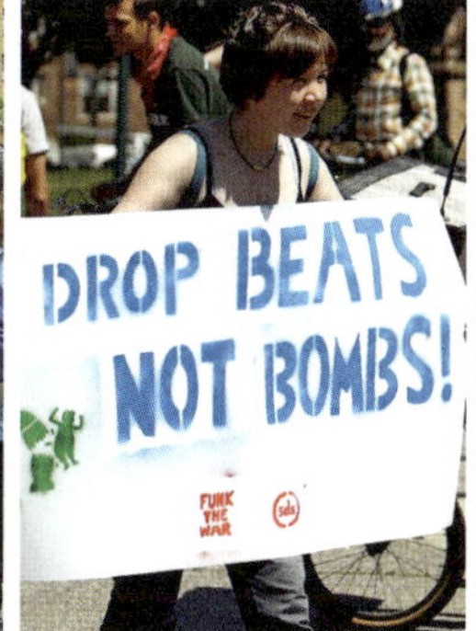
DROP BEATS
NOT BOMBS!
FUNK
THE
WAR

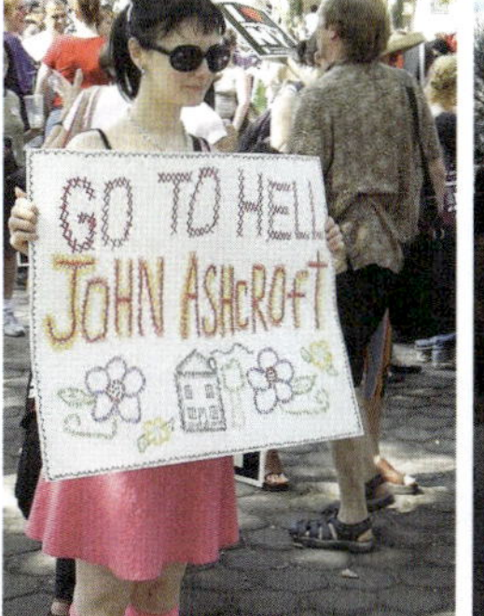
GO TO HELL
JOHN ASHCROFT

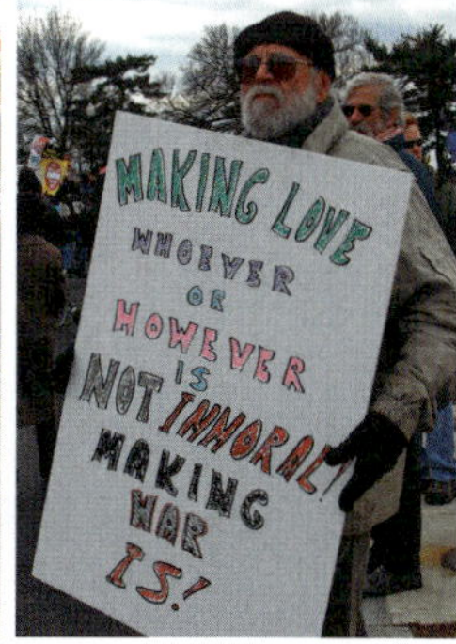
MAKING LOVE
WHOEVER
OR
HOWEVER
IS
NOT IMMORAL
MAKING
WAR
IS!

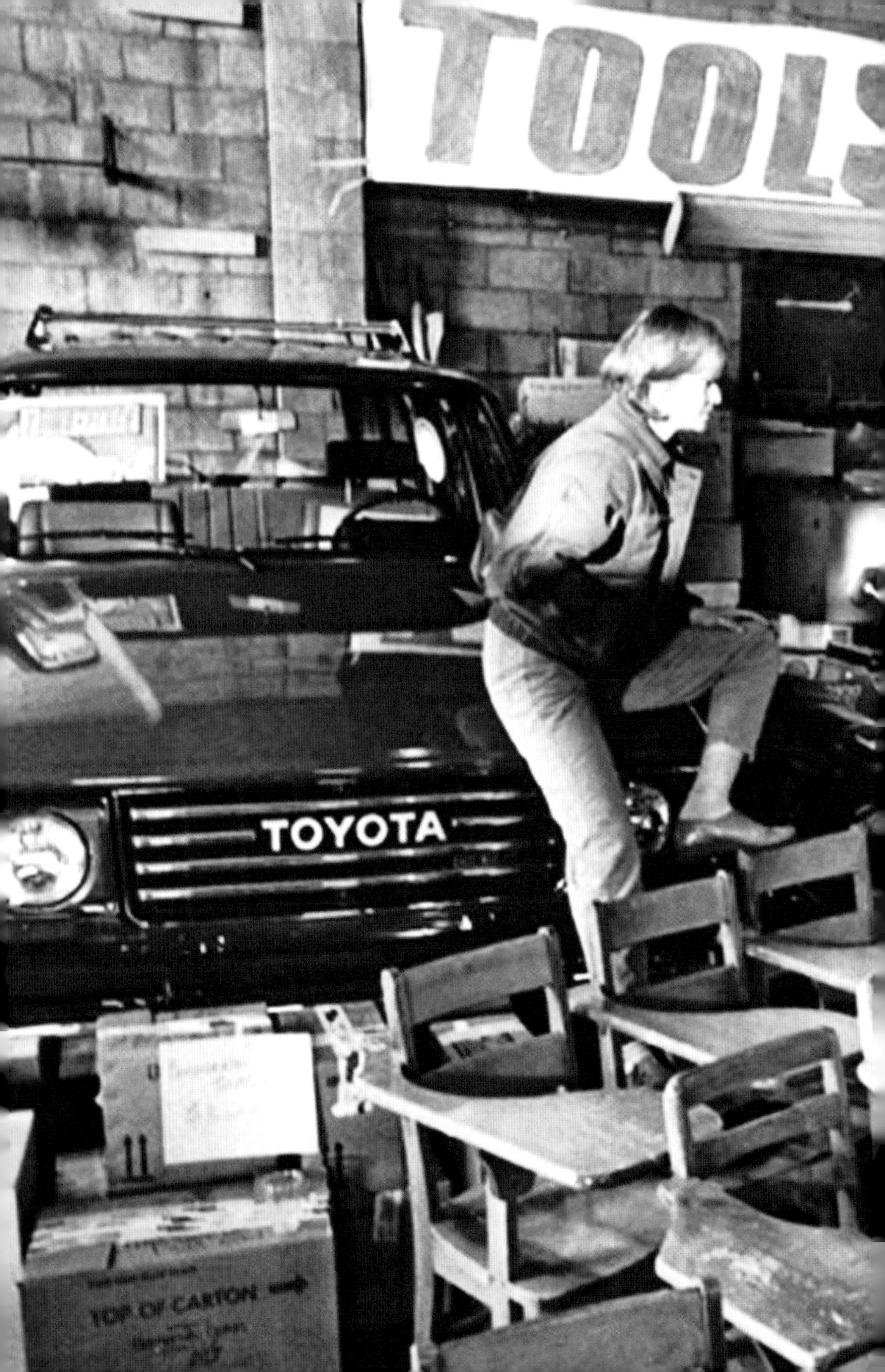

TOOLS
TOYOTA
TOP OF CARTON

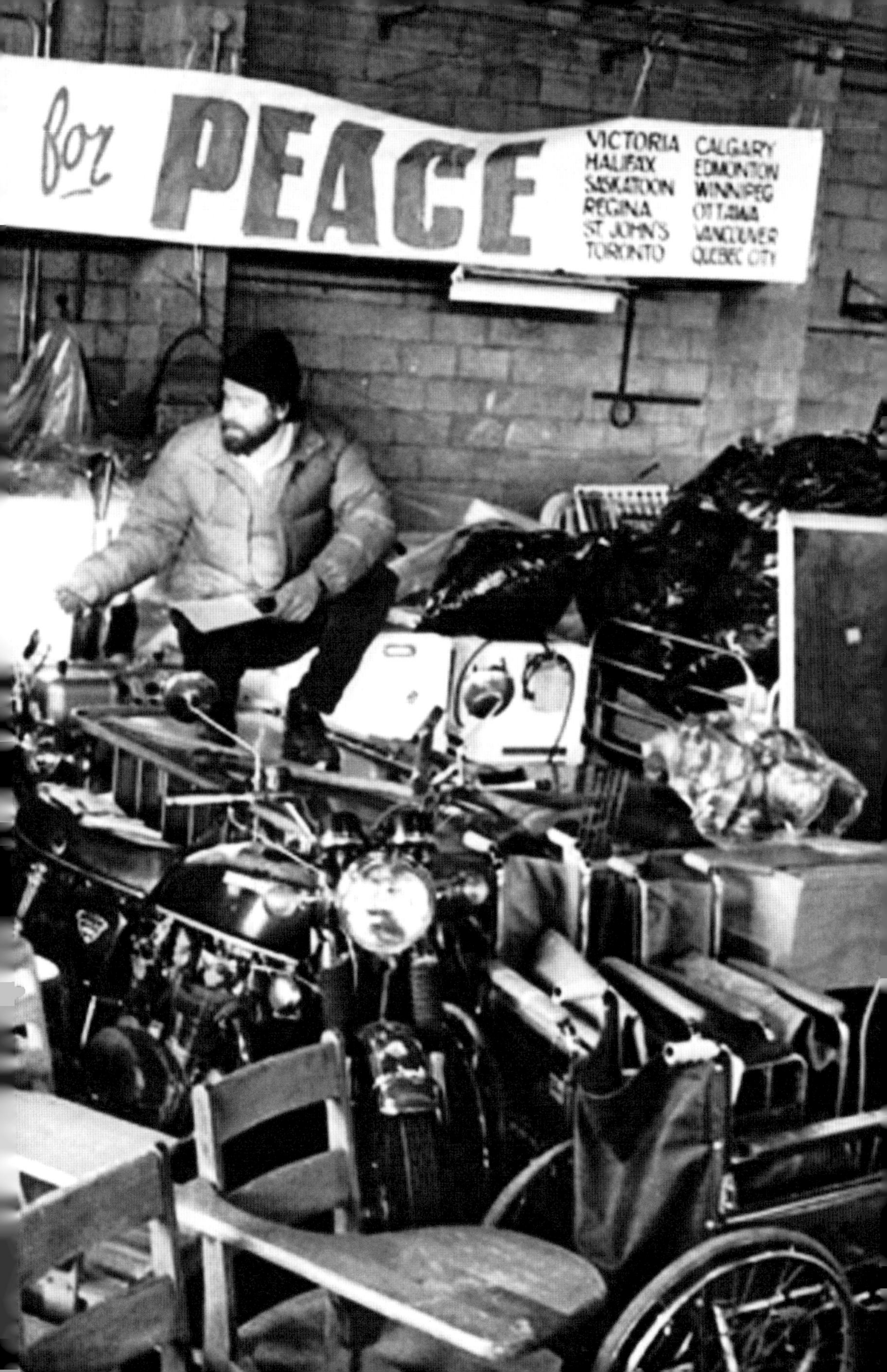
for PEACE
VICTORIA CALGARY
HALIFAX EDMONTON
SASKATOON WINNIPEG
REGINA OTTAWA
ST. JOHN'S VANCOUVER
TORONTO QUEBEC CITY

001 WAGE PEACE 2
Activism at a Colorado missile
silo with the Rocky Mountain
Peace and Justice Center.
CREATOR Provided by Bee-Butt
SOURCE www.flickr.com/photos/
mercedeson
DATE 2007

002 AVATAR PROTEST [WEST BANK BARRIER]
Protesters painted themselves
blue and donned long hair and
loincloths to draw a parallel
between their struggle and that
of the film's alien characters.
CREATOR Darren Whiteside
SOURCE Reuters
DATE 12 February 2010

003 INDIA HIROSHIMA DAY
Students in Mumbai, India,
participate in a peace rally
to commemorate the dropping
of the first atomic bomb on
the Japanese city of Hiroshima,
Monday, August 6, 2007.
CREATOR Gautam Singh
SOURCE AP
DATE 6 August 2007

004 THE PROTESTER
El Teneen, a prominent Egyptian
graffiti artist, wears a homemade
gas mask.
CREATOR Peter Hapak for TIME
SOURCE lightbox.time.com

005 THE DEAD OF OUR ARMED FORCES
FOR PEACE, JUSTICE, AND FREEDOM
Demonstration outside of the
inauguration of the memorial
to the Bundeswehr located at
the Bendlerblock in Berlin.
SOURCE probe.20minutes-blogs.fr/
tag/bundeswehr
DATE 2009

006 A DOVE OF PEACE FROM JERICHO
Nearly 1,000 children from UN
schools in Jericho gathered
together to form the outline
of Pablo Picasso's *Dove of
Peace* at the base of the Mount
of Temptation located outside
the West Bank city of Jericho.
The project was conceived by
British artist John Quigley
and the United Nations Relief
Works Agency to send a message
of peace to the world.
CREATOR Ahmad Gharabli
SOURCE hungeree.com/culture/
a-dove-of-peace-from-jericho/
DATE 25 November 2011

007 PEACE ACTIVISM
SOURCE www.peacenowar.net/newpeace/
index.php?option=com_content&task=
blogcategory&id=25&Itemid=38

008 PILLOW FIGHT, PARIS, FRANCE
CREATOR Philippe Leroyer
SOURCE www.flickr.com/photos/
philippeleroyer
DATE 13 October 2007

009 BOOBS NOT BOMBS, SAN FRANCISCO
With creativity and humor, Boobs
Not Bombs advocates peaceful
resolutions to US policies
towards Iraq, Afghanistan, and
the Middle East.
CREATOR David Hanks
SOURCE www.davidhanks.org
DATE 22 March 2003

010 MOURNING MOTHERS, SAN FRANCISCO
Associated with Direct Action to
Stop the War, the Mourning Mothers
dress in black veils and robes to
represent the grieving mothers
whose children have died. They
carry cloth dolls, which symbolize
Iraqi children killed by coalition
troops and years of UN sanctions.
CREATOR David Hanks
SOURCE www.davidhanks.org
DATE 5 June 2003

011 WAVY GRAVY, TRUE TO HIS SCHOOL
"The only hippie that I know
who is true to his school is
Wavy Gravy [Hugh Romney]. Every
day of his life he works with
kids, every day since the 1960s.
Through his Hog Farm, camps,
summer camps and hospital visits,
etc. Wavy is a great example of
unconditional love."
CREATOR Larry Keenan
SOURCE www.emptymirrorbooks.com

012 WE COME IN PEACE
CREATOR murplejane
SOURCE www.flickr.com/photos/
murplejane/

013 GRANDMOTHERS FOR PEACE
United for Peace and Justice
Antiwar National Mobilization.
CREATOR Danny Hammontree
SOURCE www.flickr.com/photos/
digitalgrace

014 SHUT DOWN GUANTANAMO
CREATOR Thomas Good
SOURCE www.antiauthoritarian.net
DATE 2006

015 DAY OF OUTRAGE DEMONSTRATION
CREATOR Thomas Good
SOURCE www.antiauthoritarian.net
DATE 2006

016 4000 UNITED STATES MILITARY
PERSONNEL DEAD
CREATOR Thomas Good
SOURCE www.antiauthoritarian.net
DATE CREATED 2008

017 PROTESTING THE BUSH
ADMINISTRATION ON CAPITOL HILL
Antiwar activists from Code Pink
and affiliated organizations
protest, outside the US Capitol
in Washington, DC. The protest,
an "Action Day to Take Back the
Constitution," took place one day
before the fifth anniversary of
the start of the war in Iraq.
CREATOR Thomas Good
SOURCE www.antiauthoritarian.net
DATE CREATED 18 March 2008

018 LYDIA VICKERS
Lydia Vickers participates in
the United for Peace and Justice
Antiwar National Mobilization.
CREATOR Danny Hammontree
SOURCE www.flickr.com/photos/
digitalgrace
DATE 27 October 2007

019 GIVE PEACE A CHANCE
March on Washington to end the
War in Iraq on 24 September 2005.
The march was sponsored by United
for Peace and Justice.
CREATOR Kelly Dowd
SOURCE www.tcnjsignal.net
DATE 24 September 2005

020 DAUGHTER OF THE NEW AMERICAN
REVOLUTION, SPRING MOBILIZATION
CREATOR Larry Keenan
SOURCE www.emptymirrorbooks.com
DATE 1967

021 SAN FRANCISCO, 19 MARCH 2004
CREATOR David Hanks
SOURCE www.davidhanks.org
DATE 19 March 2004

022 ANTIWAR MARCH
SOURCE www.wri-irg.org

023 DEMONSTRATION FOR TIBET
SOURCE photos.cyberpresse.ca

024 DEMONSTRATION FOR LEBANON
Demonstrators in front of the
Israeli consulate in Montreal wave
flags of Lebanon and Hezbollah.
libanais et du Hezbollah.
CREATOR David Boily
SOURCE photos.cyberpresse.ca

025 PEACE MARCH
SOURCE www.giorgioschultze.eu/

026 STUDENT AT ANTINUCLEAR
DEMONSTRATION, MUMBAI
SOURCE photos.cyberpresse.ca
DATE 6 August 2008

027 SIGN OF THE TIMES
CREATOR Thomas Good
SOURCE www.antiauthoritarian.net
DATE 2005

028 STUDENTS FOR A DEMOCRATIC
SOCIETY [SDS]
Pace University Students for
a Democratic Society demonstrate
for immigrant rights on the
Brooklyn Bridge in New York City.
CREATOR Donyal Svilar
SOURCE www.antiauthoritarian.net/
DATE 2007

029 WE ARE PEACEFUL
CREATOR Dang Ngo
SOURCE www.dangngo.com

030 DEMONSTRATION FOR LEBANON
A man protests his opposition
to Israel during a Lebanese
demonstration in Montreal.
CREATOR David Boily
SOURCE photos.cyberpresse.ca
DATE 16 July 2006

031 AMASSING PROTEST
About 700,000 people gathered
in central Leipzig during one
of the so-called Monday Marches
against East Germany's Communist
regime. The Monday Marches forced
communist dictator Erich Honecker
from power and led to the fall of
the Berlin Wall.
SOURCE www.globalpost.com
DATE 9 October 1989

032 WOMEN MARCHING FOR PEACE
SOURCE University of California,
San Diego
DATE 1915

033 REAL JEWS
Protest denouncing the US-
supported Israeli bombings and
invasion of Lebanon.
CREATOR Danny Hammontree
SOURCE www.flickr.com/photos/
digitalgrace
DATE 12 August 2006

034 PEACE MARCH SAN FRANCISCO
CREATOR Dang Ngo
SOURCE University of California,
San Diego
DATE 1969

035 PEACE RALLY, KEZAR STADIUM,
SAN FRANCISCO
"There were over 67,000 people
protesting the Vietnam war. They
all ended up at Kezar after the
march [Spring Mobilization] to
hear speakers, songs, etc."
CREATOR Larry Keenan
SOURCE www.emptymirrorbooks.com
DATE 1967

036 I AM A MAN
More than 5,000 men lined up prior
to the 28 March 1968 march led
by Martin Luther King during the
sanitation workers' strike.
CREATOR Ernest C. Withers
SOURCE johnedwinmason.typepad.com/
john_edwin_mason_photogra/2010/09/
index.html

037 DEMONSTRATION AGAINST GUANTANAMO,
SAN FRANCISCO
SOURCE www.peacenowar.net

038 MARCHING THROUGH JERUSALEM
Coalition Peace March on
the Pentagon against the
war in Iraq.
CREATOR Gina Benevento
SOURCE www.gilasvirsky.com
DATE 29 December 2000

039 DEMONSTRATION FOR PEACE, PLACE
DE FRANCE - "NOW"
CREATOR Sandra Renard
SOURCE sandrarenard.blog.lemonde.fr/
DATE November 2005

040 FUCK FOX NEWS
CREATOR Thomas Good
SOURCE www.antiauthoritarian.net
DATE 2007

041 ANTIBOMBING DEMONSTRATION,
PAKISTAN
Students and peace activists
carry posters for peace during
a protest against US military
strikes in Pakistan's tribal areas
along the Afghanistan border.
CREATOR Mohsin Raza
SOURCE Reuters
DATE 5 November 2008

042 HARLEM COUNTER-RECRUITMENT ACTION
CREATOR Thomas Good
SOURCE www.antiauthoritarian.net
DATE 2008

043 TIJUANA / SAN DIEGO BORDER
CREATOR David Hanks
SOURCE www.davidhanks.org
DATE 21 April 2001

044 ANTIWAR DEMONSTRATION,
SAN FRANCISCO
CREATOR David Hanks
SOURCE www.davidhanks.org
DATE 20 March 2003

045 PEACE MARCH, PITTSBURGH
CREATOR mknobil
SOURCE www.flickr.com/photos/
knobil

046 PRO-TIBET DEMONSTRATION, SEOUL
SOURCE photos.cyberpresse.ca

047 KENNY WOLLESEN,
EXTRAORDINARY DRUMMER
CREATOR Thomas Good
SOURCE www.antiauthoritarian.net
DATE 2005

048 DROP BEATS NOT BOMBS
A student protests during an
antiwar rally.
CREATOR Jason Gareau
SOURCE media.www.commonwealth
times.com
DATE 2008

049 PRICELESS!
CREATOR Thomas Good
SOURCE www.antiauthoritarian.net
DATE 2004

050 ANSWER COALITION PEACE MARCH
ON THE PENTAGON
CREATOR jcolman
SOURCE www.flickr.com/photos/
jcolman
DATE 17 March 2007

051 TOOLS FOR PEACE
CREATOR Tools for Peace Branch
Office [Hamilton, Ont.]
SOURCE pw20c.mcmaster.ca

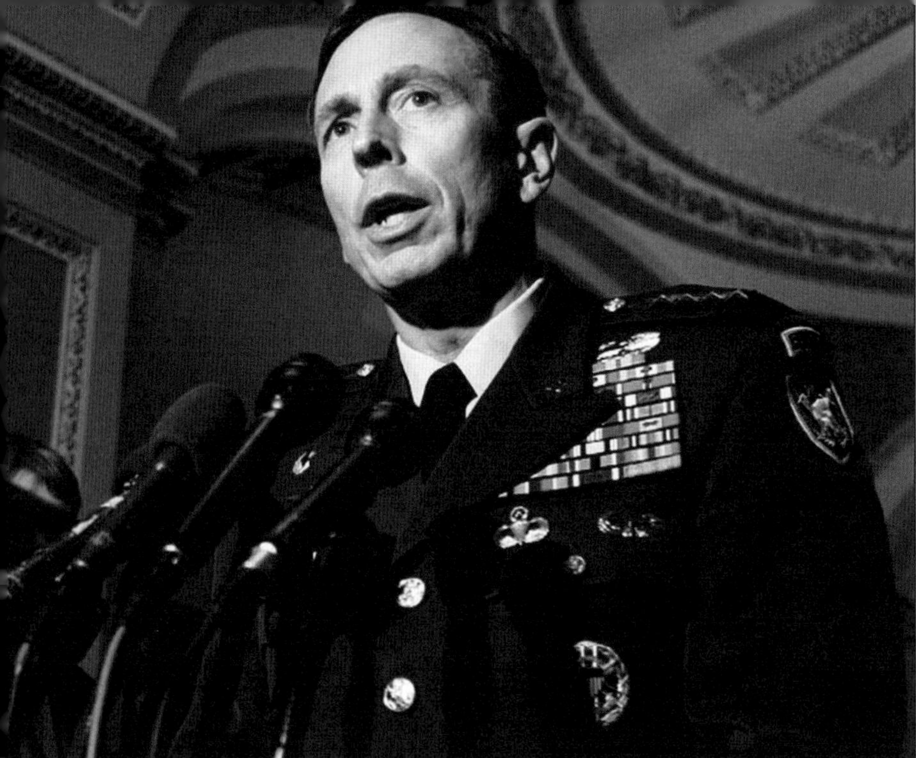

GENERAL PETRAEUS OR GENERAL BETRAY US?

Cooking the Books for the White House

General Petraeus is a military man constantly at war with the facts. In 2004, just before the election, he said there was "tangible progress" in Iraq and that "Iraqi leaders are stepping forward." And last week Petraeus, the architect of the escalation of troops in Iraq, said, "We say we have achieved progress, and we are obviously going to do everything we can to build on that progress."

Every independent report on the ground situation in Iraq shows that the surge strategy has failed. Yet the General claims a reduction in violence. That's because, according to the *New York Times*, the Pentagon has adopted a bizarre formula for keeping tabs on violence. For example, deaths by car bombs don't count. The *Washington Post* reported that assassinations only count if you're shot in the back of the head — not the front. According to the Associated Press, there have been more civilian deaths and more American soldier deaths in the past three months than in any other summer we've been there. We'll hear of neighborhoods where violence has decreased. But we won't hear that those neighborhoods have been ethnically cleansed.

Most importantly, General Petraeus will not admit what everyone knows: Iraq is mired in an unwinnable religious civil war. We may hear of a plan to withdraw a few thousand American troops. But we won't hear what Americans are desperate to hear: a timetable for withdrawing all our troops. General Petraeus has actually said American troops will need to stay in Iraq for as long as ten years.

Today, before Congress and before the American people, General Petraeus is likely to become General Betray Us.

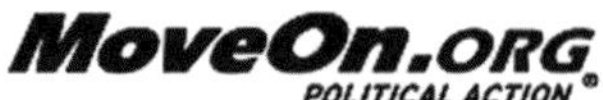

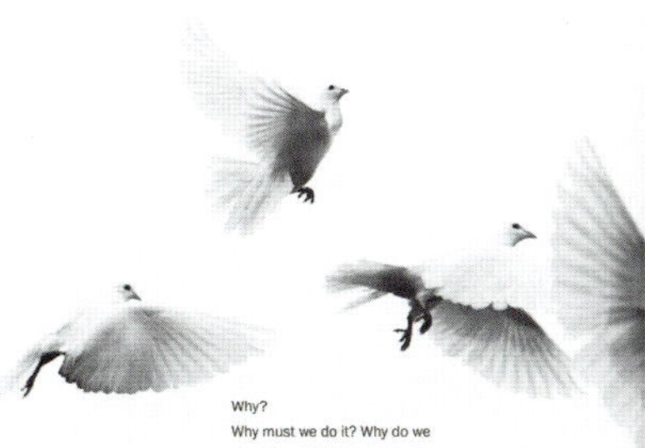

THE TIMES OF INDIA

PRICE RS 4.50 ALONG WITH MUMBAI MIRROR OR THE ECONOMIC TIMES OR MAHARASHTRA TIMES

LOVE PAKISTAN

Feels odd to see those two words side by side doesn't it?

Terror, hatred and fanaticism somehow sit more comfortably in our minds when we think of the other side of the border.

Words that we've been fed in daily doses over the last six decades. And in greater doses over the last one year.

Shutting our minds to the undeniable truth that people across the border are, above all, people. Like us.

So here's the question. Is there any chance at all, that we could still raise a hand, not in anger but in greeting?

Depends on who raises his hand first, some of us would say. Also how, whisper a few others. But mostly, it all boils down to one simple question.

Why?

Why must we do it? Why do we need them? Why don't they first say sorry for what they've done? And the answer is simple.

It's easier to say Hi than to say Sorry. It's shorter too. Besides, there is no rule that says a book has to be closed before a new one is opened. Not even if it's a history book.

So on the first day of this new year, we're going to make a start. Again.

With Aman Ki Asha. A brave, new people-to-people initiative by The Times of India and Pakistan's Jang Group to bring the people of two fine nations closer together. Culturally, emotionally and peacefully.

Starting with a series of cross-border cultural interactions, business seminars, music & literary festivals and citizens meets that will give the bonds of humanity a chance to survive outside the battlefields of politics, terrorism and fundamentalism.

In the hope that one day, words like Pakistan, India and Love will not seem impossible in the same sentence.

aman ki asha
AN INDO-PAK PEACE PROJECT
THE FIRST STEP

The right-hand advertisement is a reproduction of a MoveOn.org political ad:

THE BUSH LEGACY: WAGING WAR FOR POLITICAL GAIN.

In 2002, an election year, Karl Rove and George Bush began the march to war with Iraq. The American people were told that Iraq was tied to the attacks on 9/11 and that it posed a threat to the United States. Bush said Iraq already had weapons of mass destruction and was developing nuclear weapons. We now know his reasons for going to war were false. And George Bush must have known some were untrue even as he repeated them.

HERE COMES WORLD WAR III.

Now, with a Presidential election likely to turn on the disaster in Iraq, George Bush has been threatening war with Iran, arguing falsely that the country is on the verge of developing nuclear weapons. *The Washington Post* reported that National Security Advisor Stephen Hadley "said Bush first learned in August or September about intelligence indicating Iran had halted its weapons program..." Yet on October 17, Bush continued to paint a picture of a nuclear Iran and invoked the specter of World War III. On December 4, Bush lied about when he found out Iran had no nuclear weapons program, saying: "I was made aware of the NIE [National Intelligence Estimate] last week." His rhetoric against Iran goes on unabated.

GEORGE BUSH MUST BE STOPPED.

A resolution is being introduced in the House of Representatives by Neil Abercrombie of Hawaii. It explicitly states that George Bush has been given no authority to go to war with Iran. It is a sad commentary on the Bush presidency that the resolution is vital and must be passed. Otherwise, there's no telling what George Bush might do.

MoveOn.ORG
POLITICAL ACTION

OUR NAME IS NEW. THE NEED IS NOT.

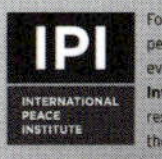

Terrorism. Failed states. Weapons proliferation. Private armies. Transnational criminal syndicates. Mass atrocities. Energy, food, and water scarcity.
The world remains a dangerous place.

IPI
INTERNATIONAL PEACE INSTITUTE

For nearly four decades, the International Peace Academy trained peacekeepers and promoted conflict resolution. But as our agenda evolved to address changing threats, so did our name. Now the International Peace Institute is at the forefront of independent policy research, analysis, and dialogue on emerging security challenges. With the new Trygve Lie Center for Peace, Security & Development, IPI is poised to redouble its efforts to facilitate international cooperation and renovate international institutions to meet the next generation of complex threats and opportunities.

777 United Nations Plaza, New York, NY 10017 USA
www.ipinst.org

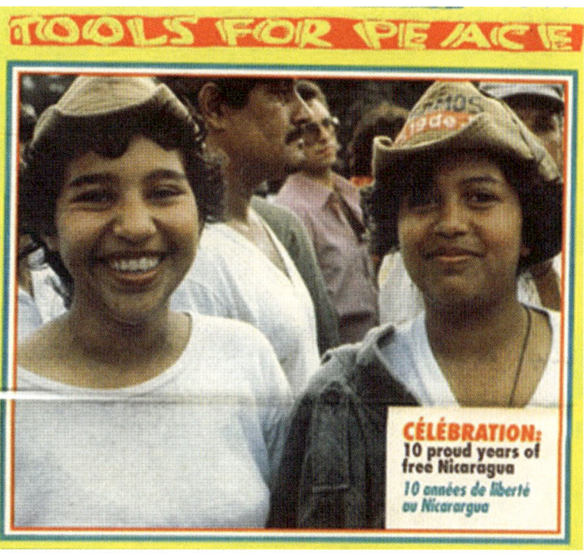

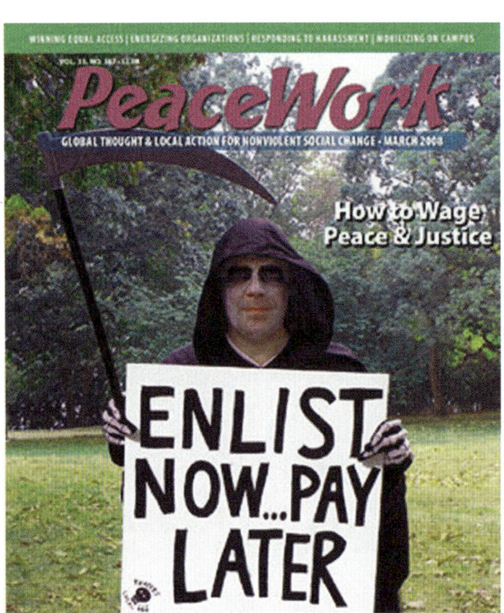
WINNING EQUAL ACCESS | ENERGIZING ORGANIZATIONS | RESPONDING TO HARASSMENT | MOBILIZING ON CAMPUS
VOL. 38, NO 387 - $3.50
PeaceWork
GLOBAL THOUGHT & LOCAL ACTION FOR NONVIOLENT SOCIAL CHANGE · MARCH 2008
How to Wage
Peace & Justice
ENLIST NOW...PAY LATER

006

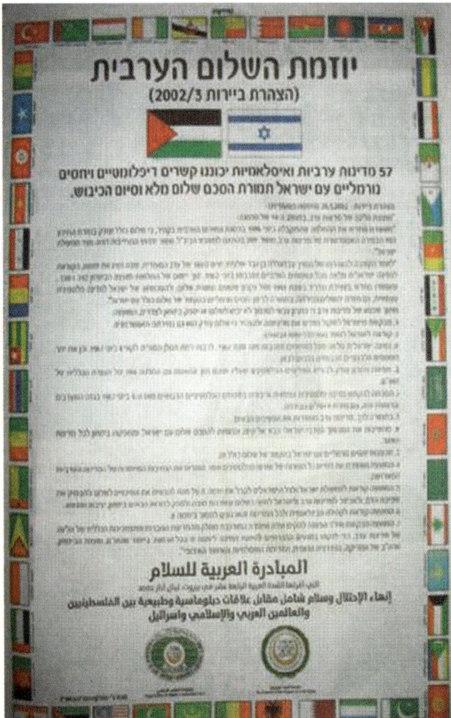
יוזמת השלום הערבית
(הצהרת ביירות 2002/3)
57 מדינות ערביות ואיסלאמיות יכוננו קשרים דיפלומטיים ויחסים
נורמליים עם ישראל תמורת הסכם שלום מלא וסיום הכיבוש.
המבادرة العربية للسلام
إنهاء الإحتلال وسلام شامل مقابل علاقات دبلوماسية وطبيعية بين الفلسطينيين
والعالمين العربي والإسلامي وإسرائيل

007

001 GENERAL PETRAEUS OR GENERAL
     BETRAY US?
     CREATOR Moveon.org
     SOURCE pol.moveon.org
     DATE 2007

002 AMAN KI ASHA. INDO-PAK
     PEACE PROJECT.
     On the first of January 2010,
     readers of *The Times of India*
     woke up to this front-page ad.
     CREATOR Taproot India
     SOURCE www.campaignindia.in/
     DATE 1 January 2010

003 THE WASHINGTON FOLLIES
     CREATOR Moveon.org
     SOURCE pol.moveon.org/bushroveira-
     nad.html
     DATE 2008

004 OUR NAME IS NEW. THE NEED IS NOT.
     CREATOR Matt Ipcar
     SOURCE osocio.org
     DATE 2008

005 TOOLS FOR PEACE
     SOURCE pw20c.mcmaster.ca
     DATE 1989

006 PEACEWORK MAGAZINE: NLN EDITOR
     THOMAS GOOD ON THE COVER
     CREATOR Nathaniel Good
     SOURCE www.antiauthoritarian.net
     DATE 2008

007 PALESTINIAN AUTHORITY REACHES OUT
     TO ISRAELIS IN HEBREW
     Palestinian Authority newspaper
     ad in Hebrew urging Israeli
     support for the Arab League Peace
     Initiative. The ad explains the
     details of a peace plan originally
     proposed by Saudi King Abdullah
     in 2002 and later adopted by
     the Arab League. The subtitle
     reads "57 Arab and Islamic States
     will establish normal diplomatic
     relations with Israel in exchange
     for full peace and an end to
     the occupation." The P.A. placed
     full-page newspaper ads in Israel's
     four largest Hebrew dailies.
     CREATOR The Palestinian Authority
     SOURCE peacenow.org/entries/archive
     5579#.UAVtonBnSas
     DATE 20 November 2008

001

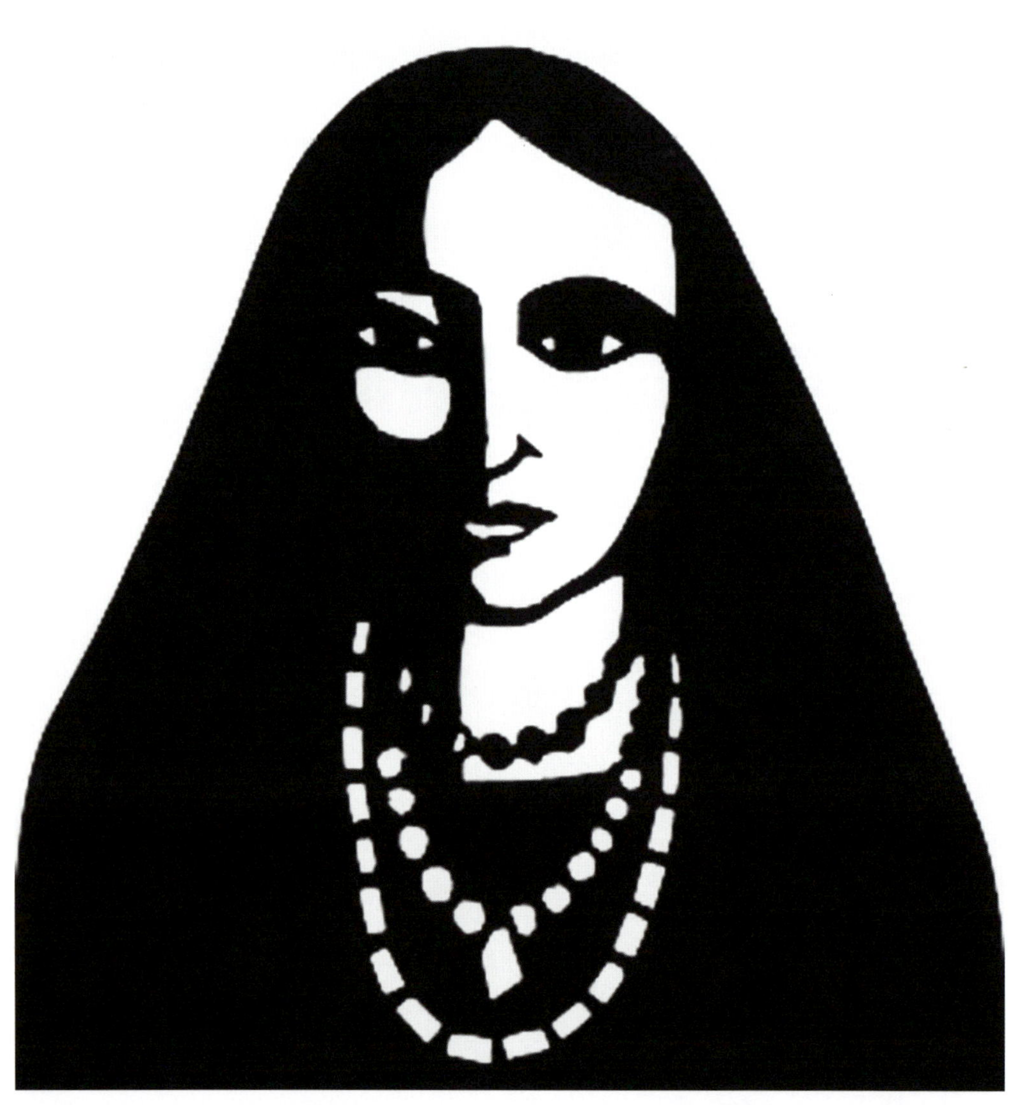

002
003
004
005

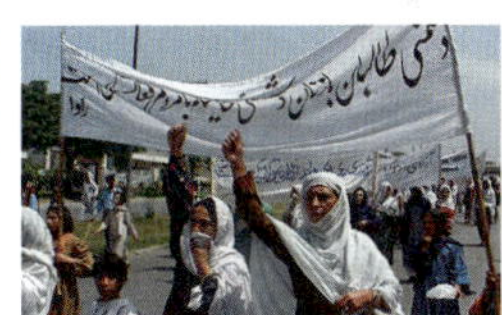

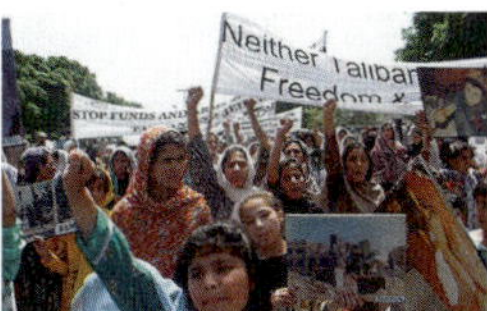

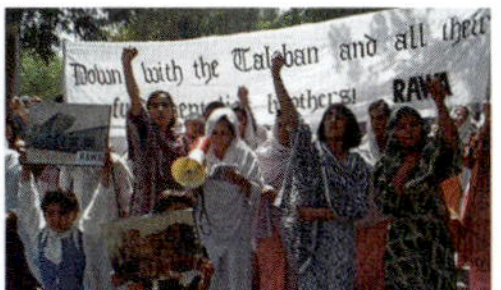

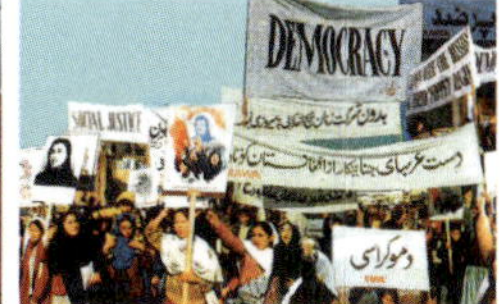

006
007

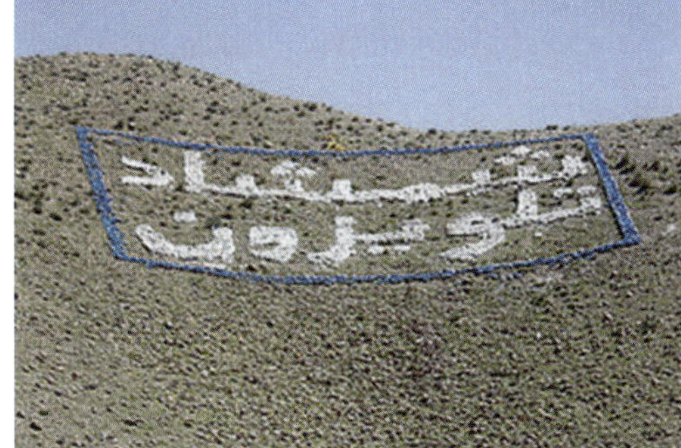
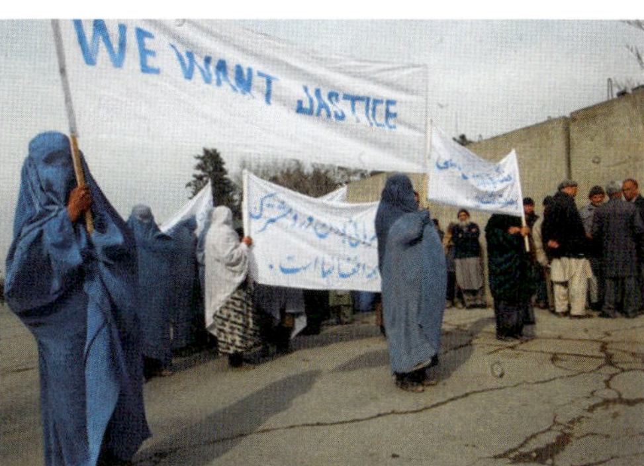

008

NEXT
009

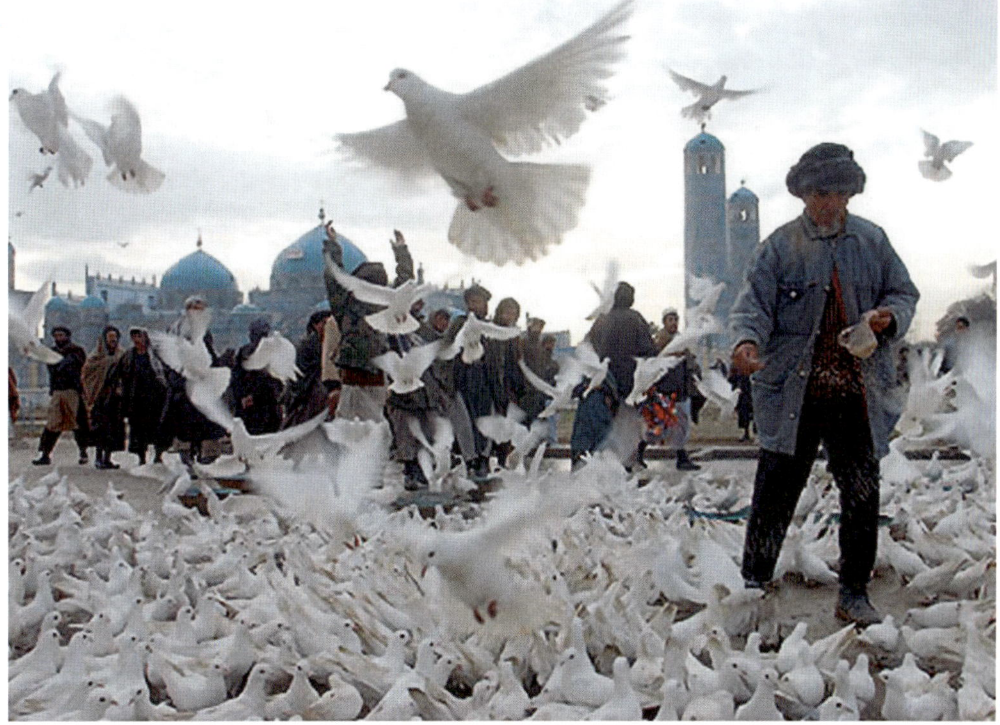

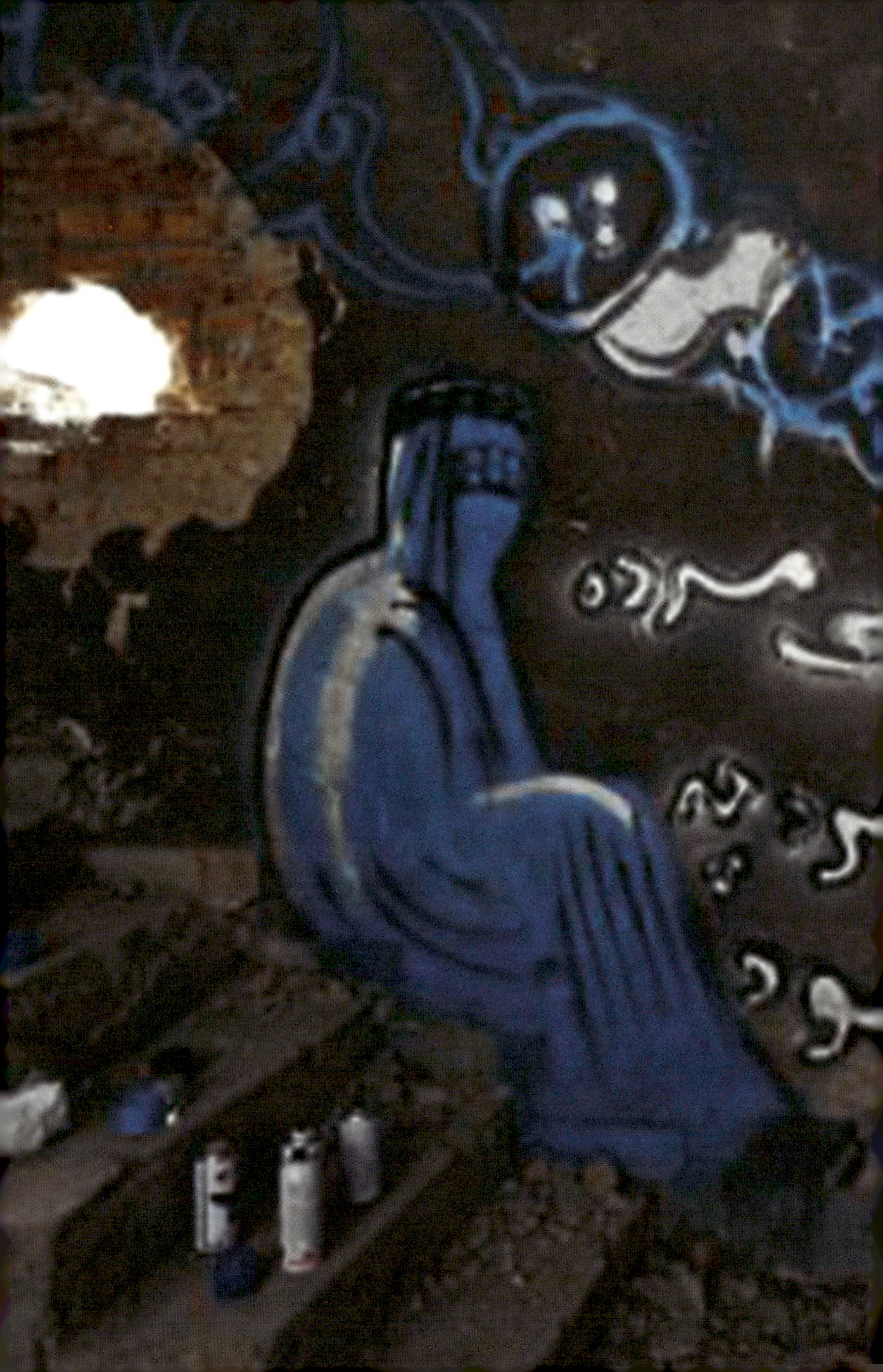

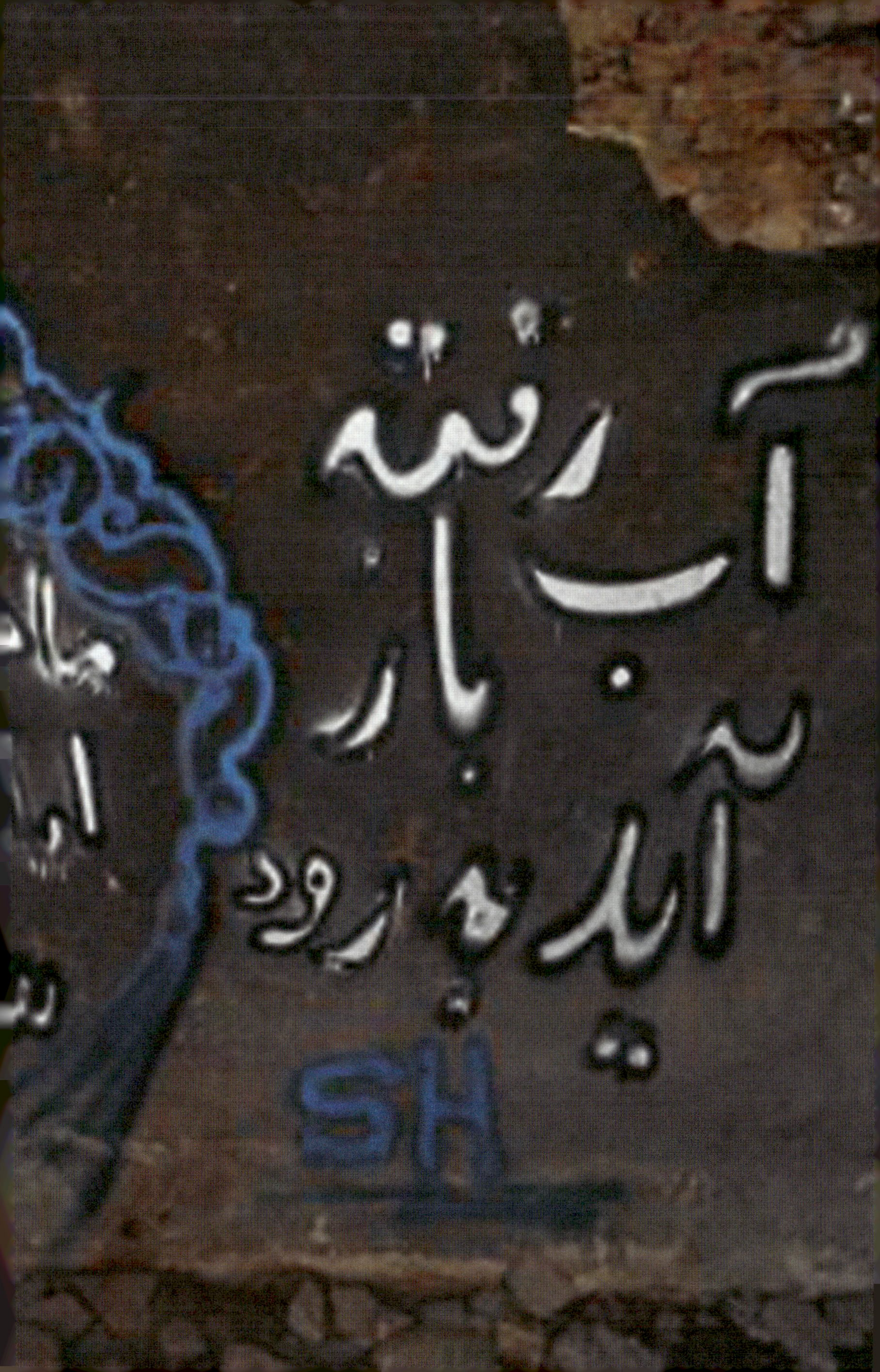
آب بازه
آینده رود
SH

010
011

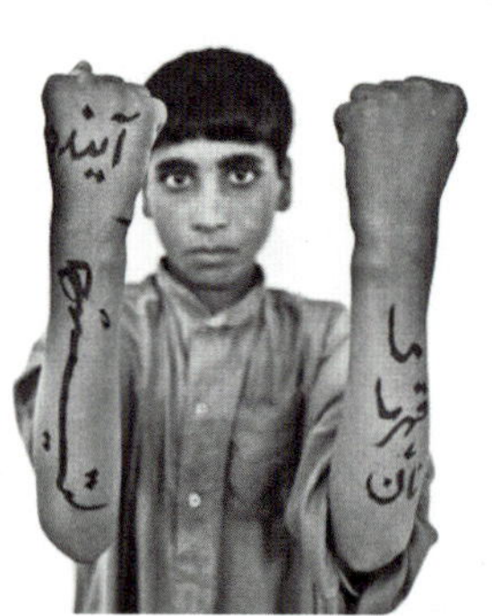
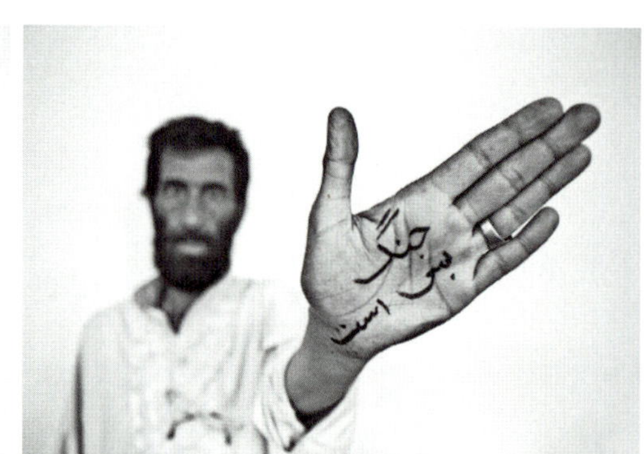

012
013

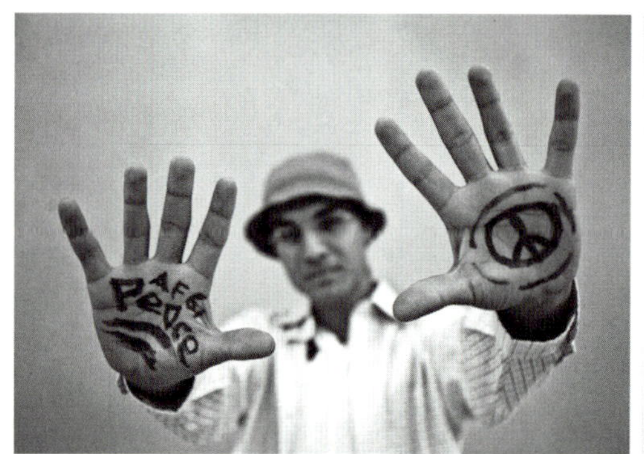

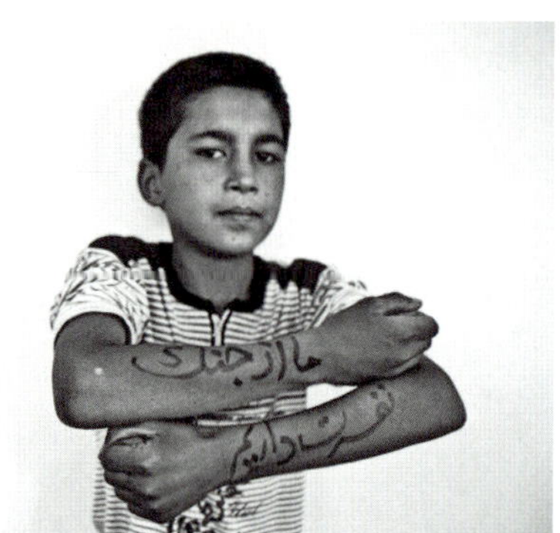

014

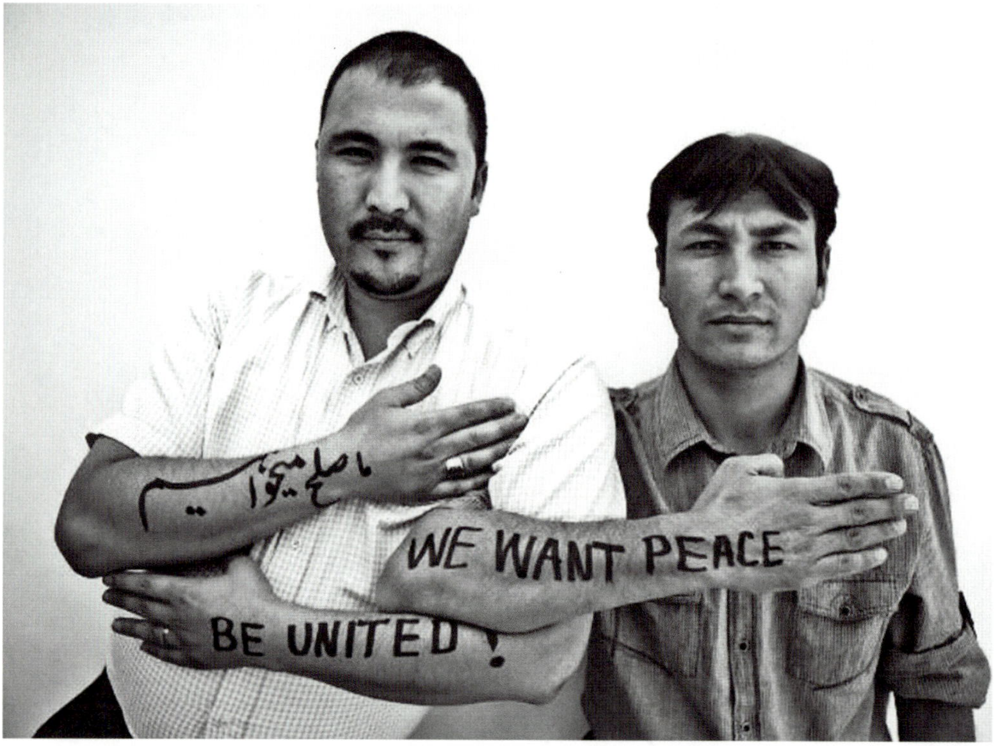

015
016

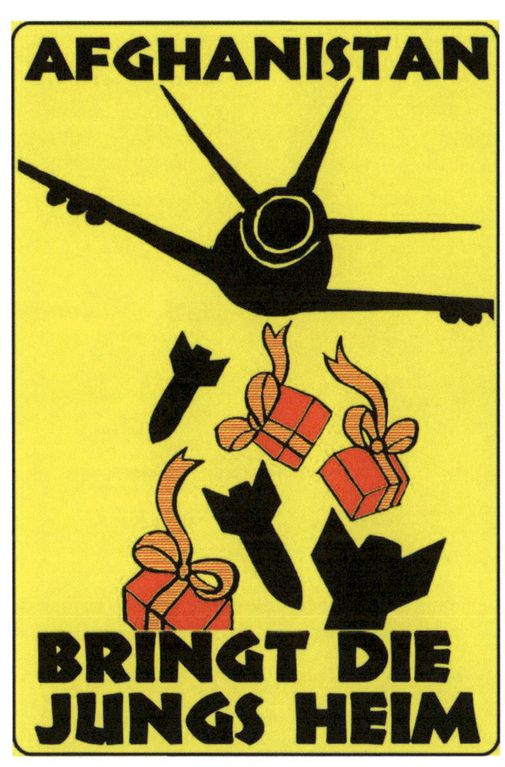
AFGHANISTAN
BRINGT DIE
JUNGS HEIM

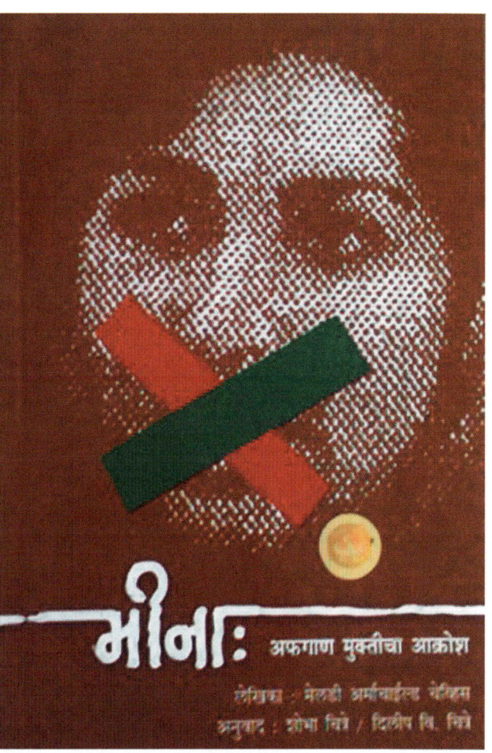
मीना:
अफगाण मुक्तीचा आक्रोश
लेखिका - मेलडी आर्मोचाइल्ड चेविस्हम
अनुवाद : शोभा चिते / दिलीप वि. चिते

017

KEIN SOLDAT
MEHR NACH
AFGHANISTAN

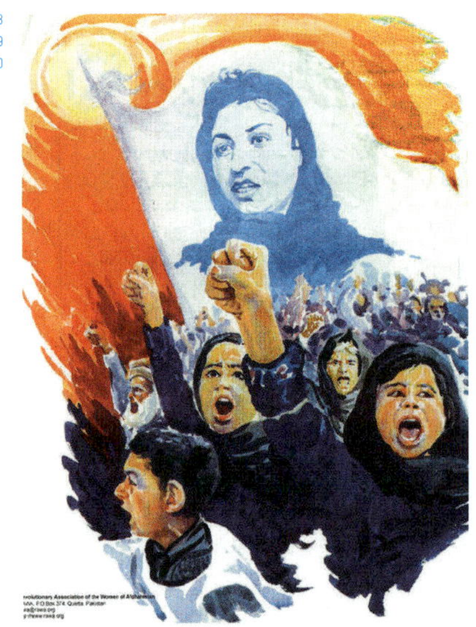

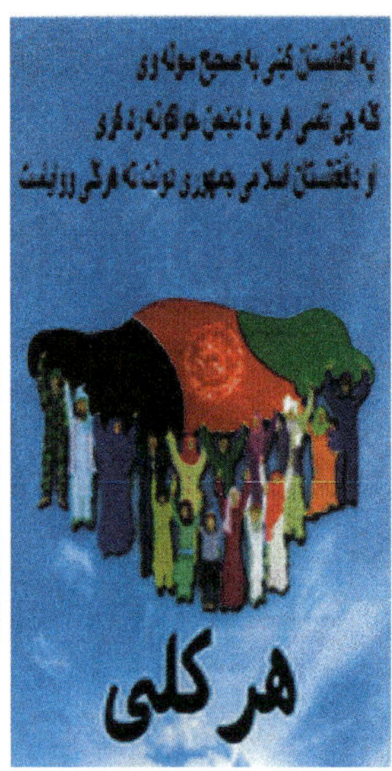
هر کلی

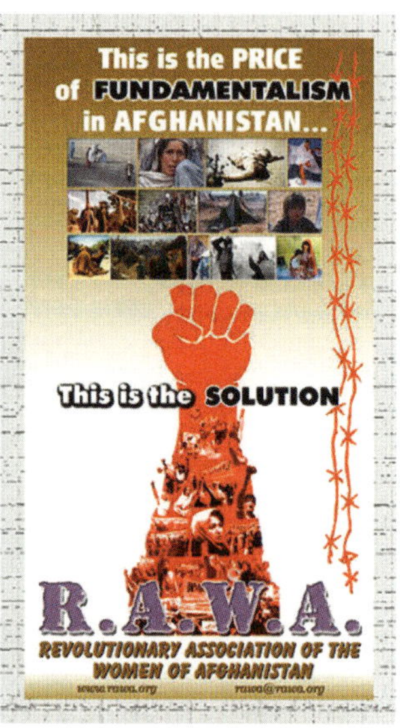
This is the PRICE
of FUNDAMENTALISM
in AFGHANISTAN...
This is the SOLUTION
R.A.W.A.
REVOLUTIONARY ASSOCIATION OF THE
WOMEN OF AFGHANISTAN
www.rawa.org   rawa@rawa.org

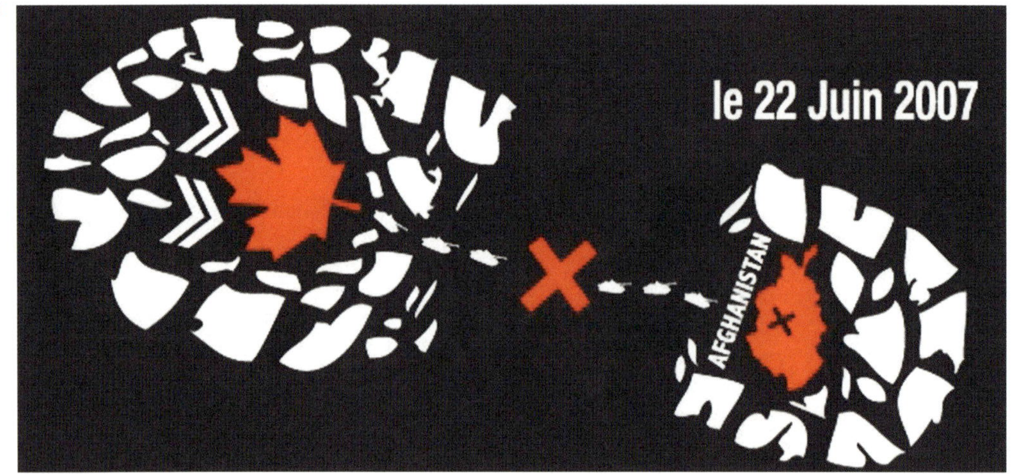
le 22 Juin 2007
AFGHANISTAN

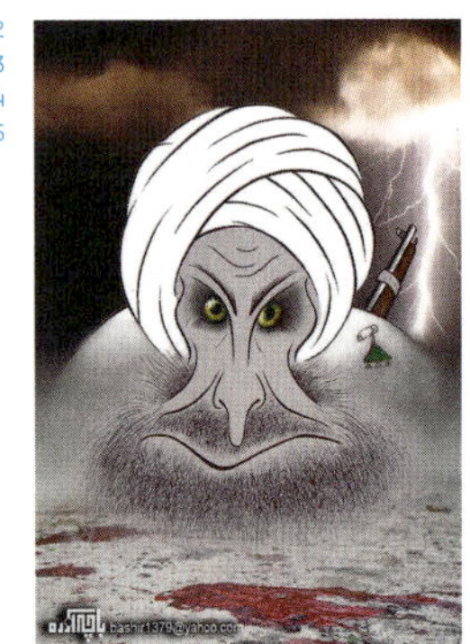

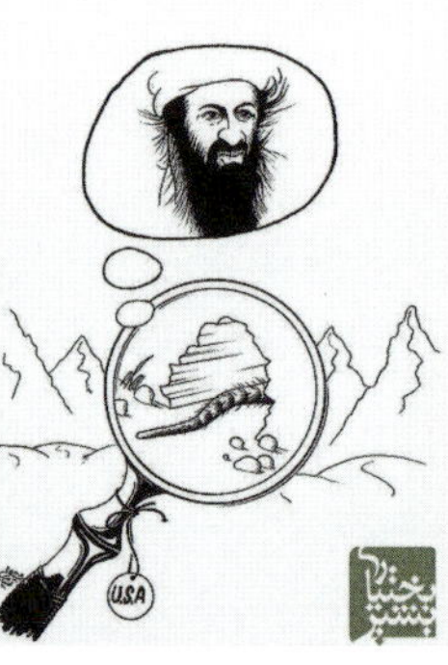
USA

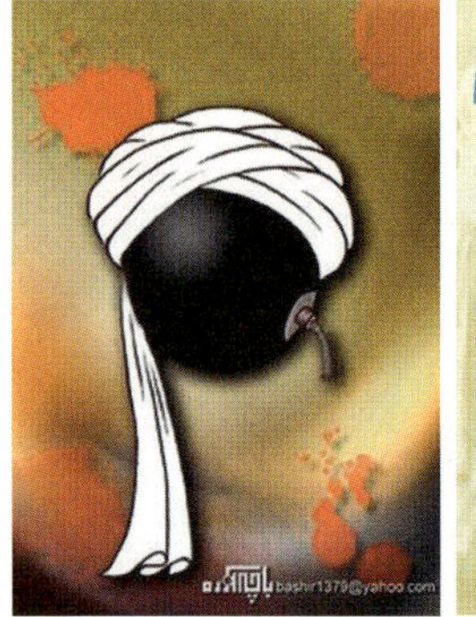

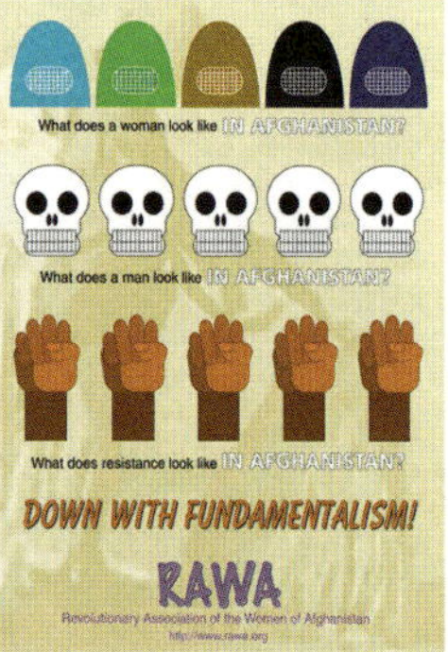
What does a woman look like IN AFGHANISTAN?
What does a man look like IN AFGHANISTAN?
What does resistance look like IN AFGHANISTAN?
DOWN WITH FUNDAMENTALISM!
RAWA
Revolutionary Association of the Women of Afghanistan
http://www.rawa.org

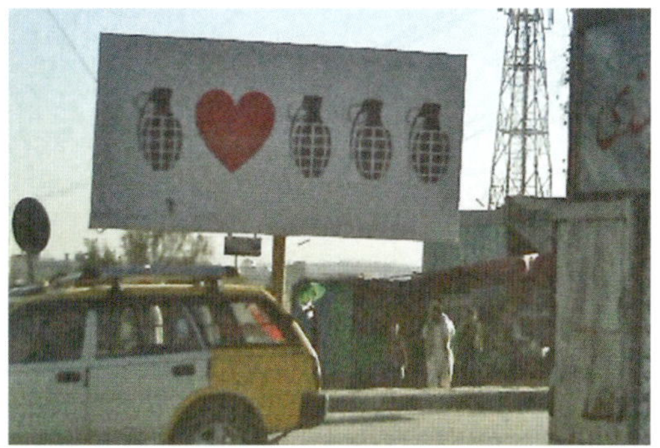

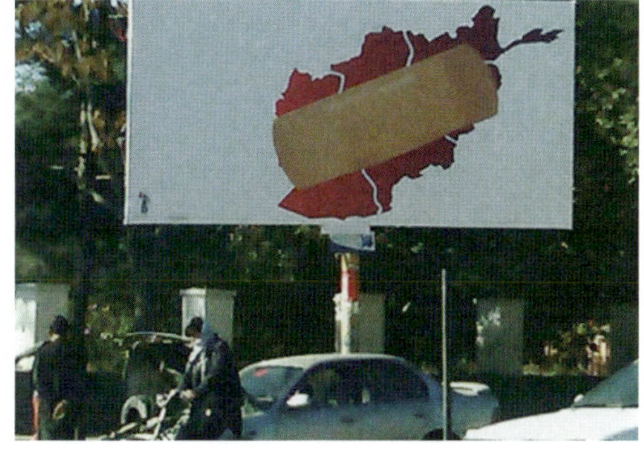

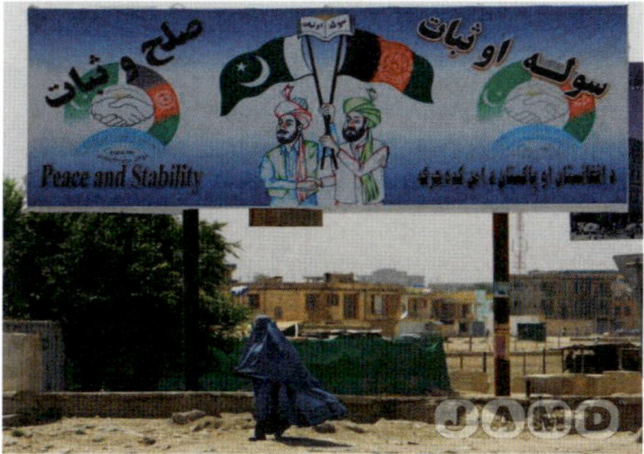

صلح و ثبات
سوله او ثبات
Peace and Stability

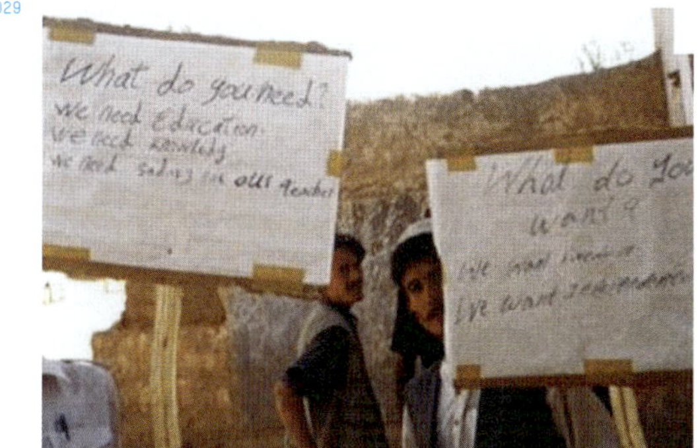

What do you need?
We need education.
We need knowledge
We need salary for our teacher

What do you
want?

001   DON'T BOMB AFGHANISTAN
      SOURCE www.voices.netuxo.co.uk/
      stopbombingafghanistan.htm

002   REVOLUTIONARY ASSOCIATION OF
      THE WOMEN OF AFGHANISTAN [RAWA]
      DEMONSTRATION, ISLAMABAD
      Hundreds of women and girls
      participate in this demonstration
      condemning the seizure of Kabul
      by fundamentalists.
      CREATOR Revolutionary Association
      of the Women of Afghanistan [RAWA]
      SOURCE www.rawa.org
      DATE 28 April 2000

003   REVOLUTIONARY ASSOCIATION OF
      THE WOMEN OF AFGHANISTAN [RAWA]
      SOURCE www.rawa.org

004   REVOLUTIONARY ASSOCIATION OF
      THE WOMEN OF AFGHANISTAN [RAWA]
      SOURCE www.rawa.org

005   A PROTEST RALLY OF RAWA AGAINST
      THE CRIMES OF THE FUNDAMENTALISTS
      IN AFGHANISTAN
      CREATOR Revolutionary Association
      of the Women of Afghanistan [RAWA]
      SOURCE www.rawa.org

006   PEACE
      Rocks proclaiming peace on the
      road from Kabul to Jalalabad.
      CREATOR Todd Huffman
      SOURCE www.flickr.com/photos/
      oddwick/4461400109/

007   AFGHAN WOMEN
      Almost seven years after the fall
      of the Taliban, newspapers report
      that the situation for women has
      become worse.
      CREATOR Nasim Fekrat
      SOURCE www.afghanlord.org/

008   DOVES AT THE AZRAT ALI SHRINE
      According to the mullah of the
      shrine, when doves return they
      bring peace with them. And if
      they leave, it is war again.
      CREATOR James Hill
      SOURCE www.iwpr.net

009   THE WATER CAN COME BACK TO
      A DRIED-UP RIVER, BUT WHAT
      ABOUT THE FISH THAT DIED?
      This piece is painted on a wall
      in the ruins of a cultural center
      in Kabul, and the script
      is a poem [the title of the piece].
      CREATOR Shamsia Hassani
      SOURCE peacenews.info

010   WE ARE THE HEROES OF THE FUTURE
      CREATOR Grace Chung
      SOURCE www.facebook.com/media/
      set/?set=a.2073504693191
      81.63852.159338960786999

011   STOP FIGHTING
      CREATOR Grace Chung
      SOURCE www.facebook.com/media/
      set/?set=a.2073504693191
      81.63852.159338960786999

012   AFGHANISTAN, PEACE
      CREATOR Grace Chung
      SOURCE www.facebook.com/media/
      set/?set=a.2073504693191
      81.63852.159338960786999

013   WE HATE FIGHTING
      CREATOR Grace Chung
      SOURCE www.facebook.com/media/
      set/?set=a.2073504693191
      81.63852.159338960786999

014   DEAR WORLD, AFGHANISTAN
      An online project to unite
      people through pictures.
      CREATOR Grace Chung
      SOURCE www.facebook.com/media/
      set/?set=a.2073504693191
      81.63852.159338960786999

015   AFGHANISTAN BRINGT DIE JUNGS HEIM
      [AFGHANISTAN / BRING THE BOYS HOME]
      CREATOR www.mitwelt.org
      SOURCE mitwelt.org/afghanistan-
      krieg-tornados.html

016   MEENA - HEROINE OF AFGHANISTAN
      CREATOR Revolutionary Association
      of the Women of Afghanistan [RAWA]
      SOURCE www.rawa.org

017   KEIN SOLDAT MEHR NACH AFGHANISTAN
      [NO MORE SOLDIERS TO AFGHANISTAN]
      CREATOR Revolutionary Association
      of the Women of Afghanistan [RAWA]
      SOURCE www.rawa.org

018   RAWA POSTER FOR MARTYRED MEENA
      Meena's blood inspires all
      freedom-loving women!
      CREATOR Revolutionary Association
      of the Women of Afghanistan [RAWA]
      SOURCE www.rawa.org

019   C-130J TAILOR-MADE FOR MISSION
      OVER AFGHANISTAN
      A C-130J performed a leaflet
      drop over Afghanistan. The
      leaflet translates, "There will
      be true peace in Afghanistan
      when everyone rejects the
      enemy forces and embraces the
      government of the Islamic
      Republic of Afghanistan."
      CREATOR United States Air Force
      SOURCE www.379aew.afcent.af.mil

020   THIS IS THE PRICE OF FUNDAMENTALISM
      IN AFGHANISTAN
      CREATOR Revolutionary
      Association of the Women of
      Afghanistan [RAWA]
      SOURCE www.rawa.org

021   POSTER FOR MARCH IN OPPOSITION TO
      CANADIAN INVOLVEMENT IN AFGHANISTAN
      CREATOR Coalition de Quebec pour
      la Paix
      SOURCE www.quebecsolidaire.net
      DATE 22 June 2007

022   MULLAH TROJAN, THE STRONGEST
      VIRUS AGAINST PEACE, SECURITY,
      AND JUSTICE IN AFGHANISTAN
      CREATOR Bashir Bakhtiari
      SOURCE 1.bp.blogspot.com

023   IS THERE ANY IDEA, WHEN OSAMA
      BIN LADEN WILL BE CAUGHT BY THE
      US FORCES?
      CREATOR Bashir Bakhtiari
      SOURCE farm4.static.flickr.
      com/3193/2904888655_ac8f1393a0.jpg

024   TALIBAN IDEOLOGY
      CREATOR Bashir Bakhtiari
      SOURCE 1.bp.blogspot.com

025   IN AFGHANISTAN
      CREATOR Revolutionary Association
      of the Women of Afghanistan [RAWA]
      SOURCE www.rawa.org

026   AFGHANISTAN: PROSPECTS FOR
      THE FUTURE
      In July 2011 Afghanistan launched
      the process for a complete tran-
      sition of security responsibili-
      ties from NATO to Afghan security
      forces by 2014.
      CREATOR Revolutionary Association
      of the Women of Afghanistan [RAWA]
      SOURCE www.insightonconflict.org/
      2011/12/afghanistan-10-years-on/

027   AFGHANISTAN: PROSPECTS FOR
      THE FUTURE
      SOURCE www.insightonconflict.org/
      2011/12/afghanistan-10-years-on/

028   AFGHANISTAN AND PAKISTAN PEACE
      JIRGA BEGINS IN KABUL
      An Afghan woman walks by a sign
      advertising the Peace jirga in
      Kabul to discuss combating the
      Taliban and Al Qaeda and the
      ongoing violence in the tribal
      region along the border of the
      two countries.
      CREATOR Paula Bronstein
      SOURCE www.jamd.org
      DATE 9 August 2007

029   OVER 3000 TEACHERS AND STUDENTS
      PROTEST AGAINST WARLORDS IN
      TAKHAR PROVINCE
      CREATOR Revolutionary Association
      of the Women of Afghanistan [RAWA]
      SOURCE www.rawa.org

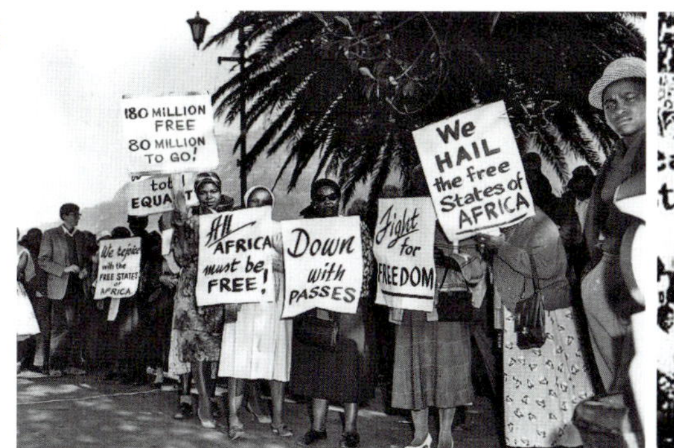
180 MILLION FREE
80 MILLION TO GO!
tot EQUAT
We rejoice with the FREE STATES of AFRICA
All AFRICA must be FREE!
Down with PASSES
Fight for FREEDOM
We HAIL the free States of AFRICA

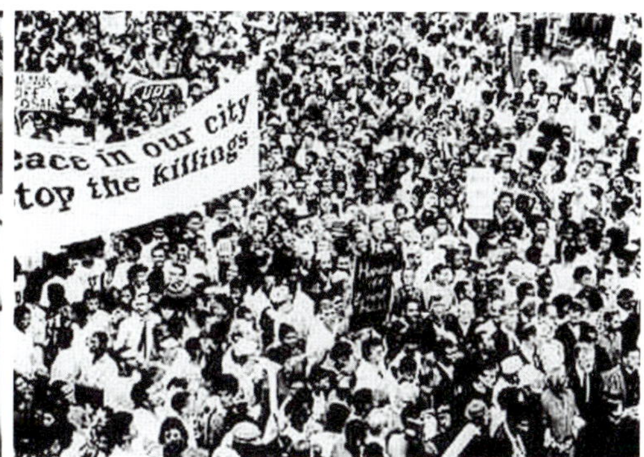
UDF
eace in our city
top the killings

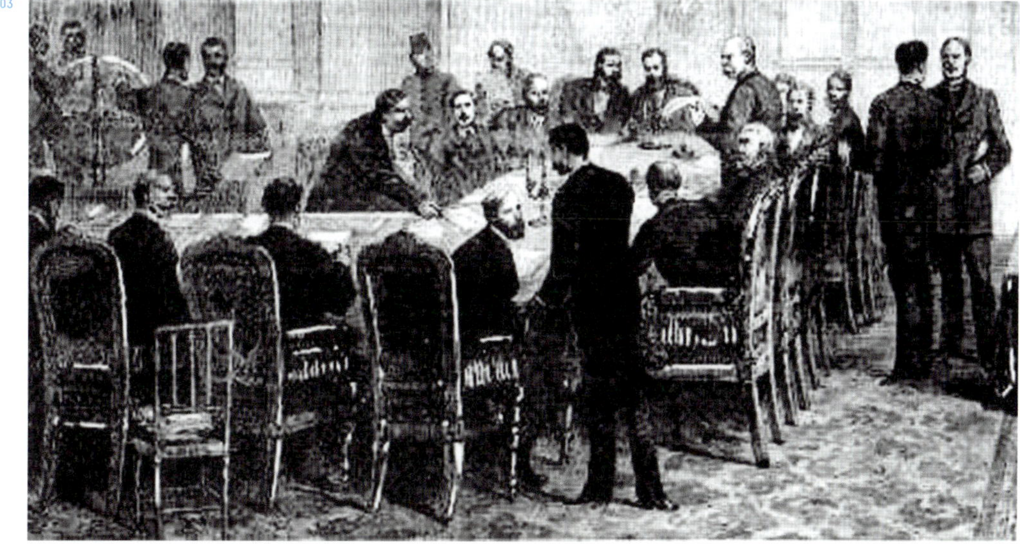

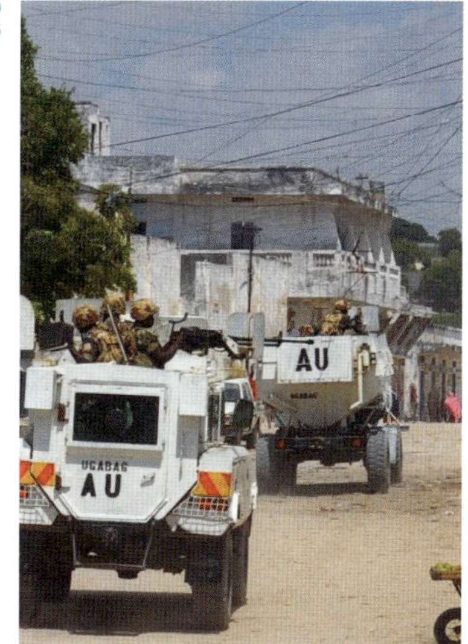
AU
UGABAG
AU

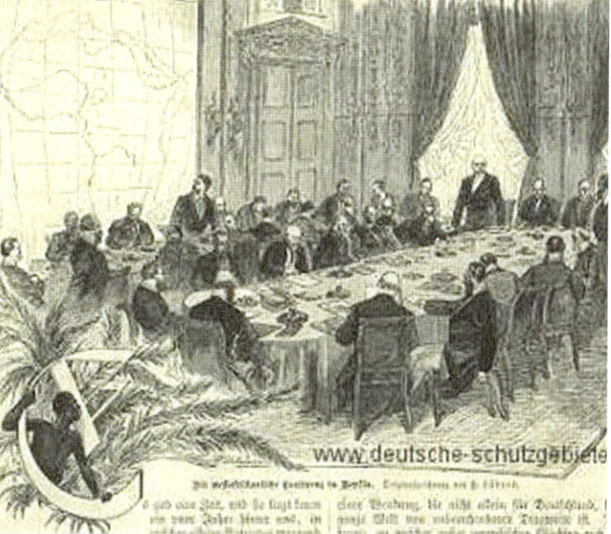
www.deutsche-schutzgebiete

006
007

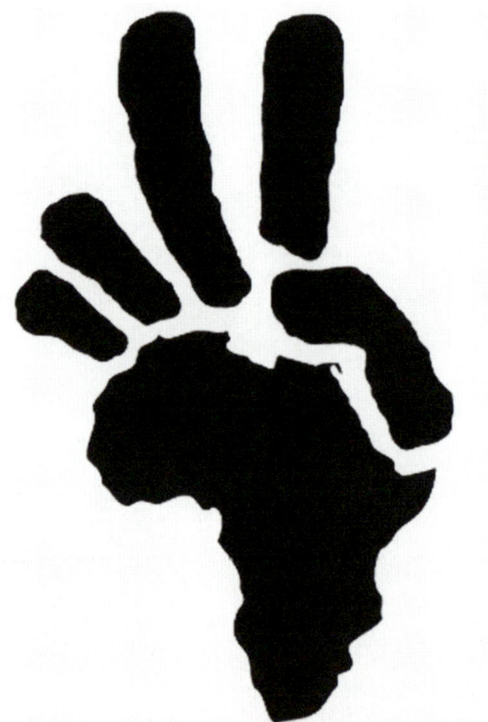

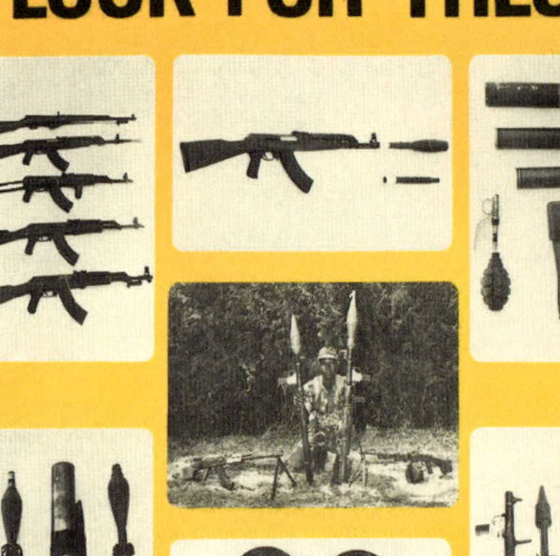

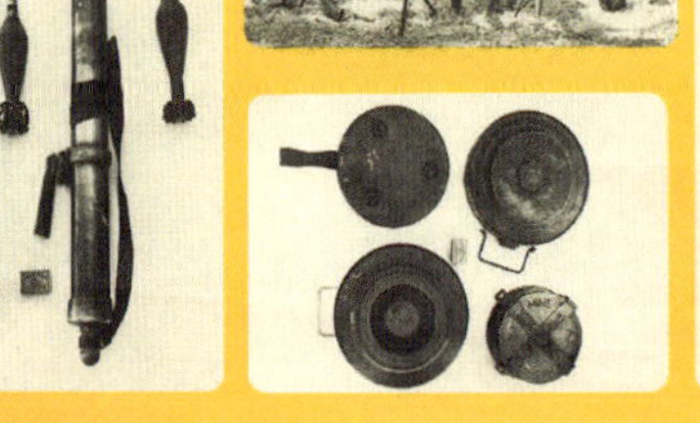

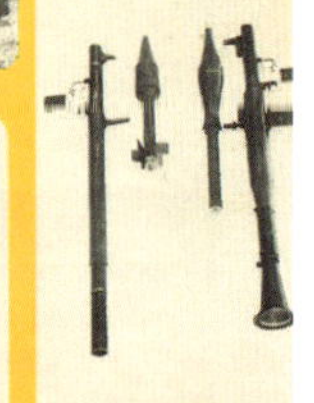

008
009

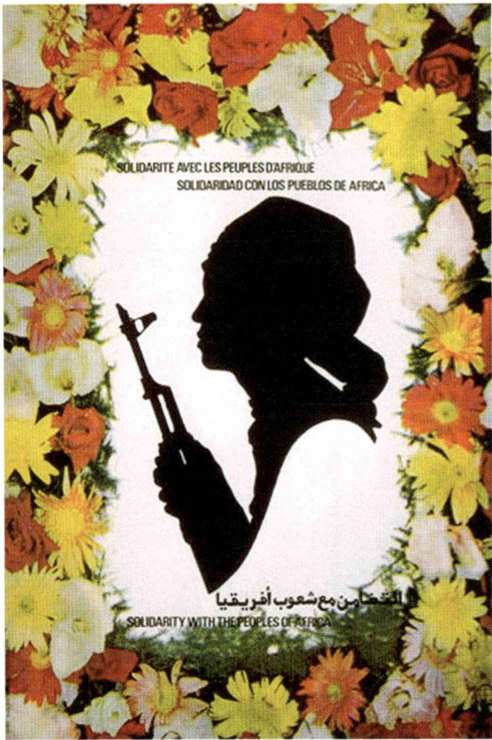

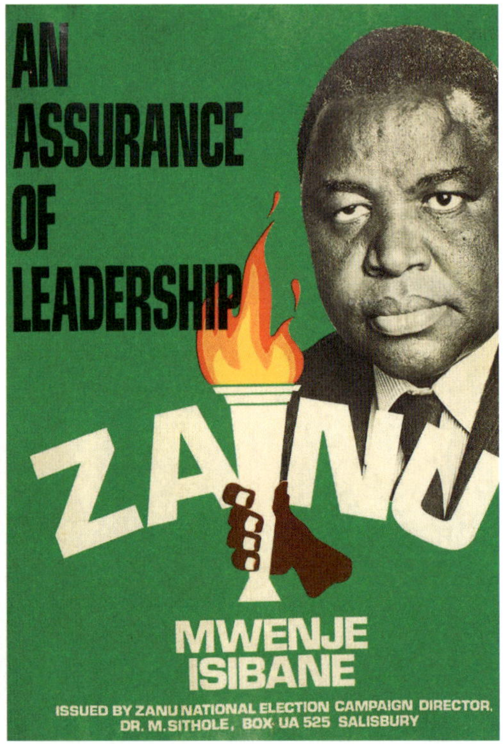

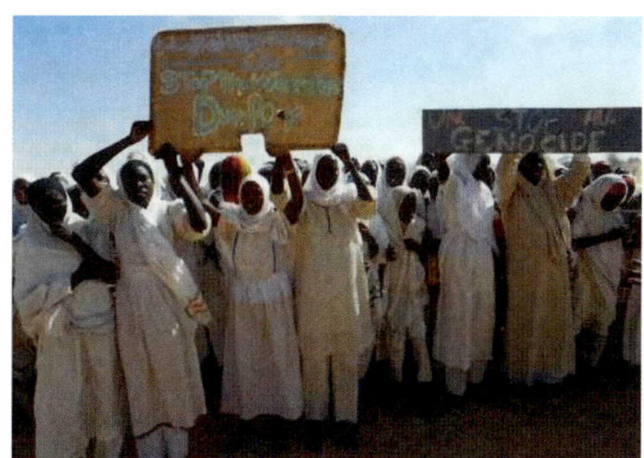

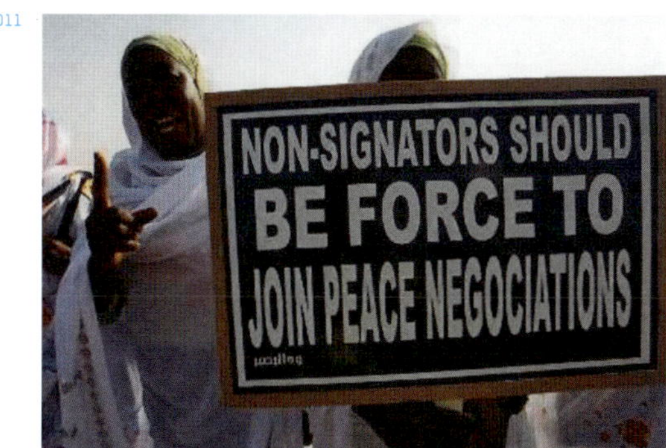

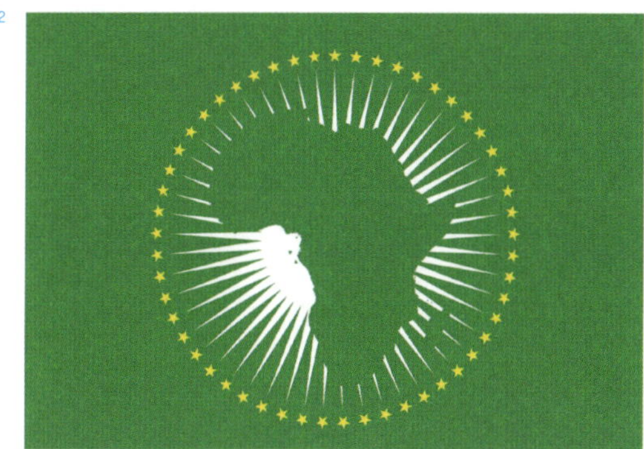

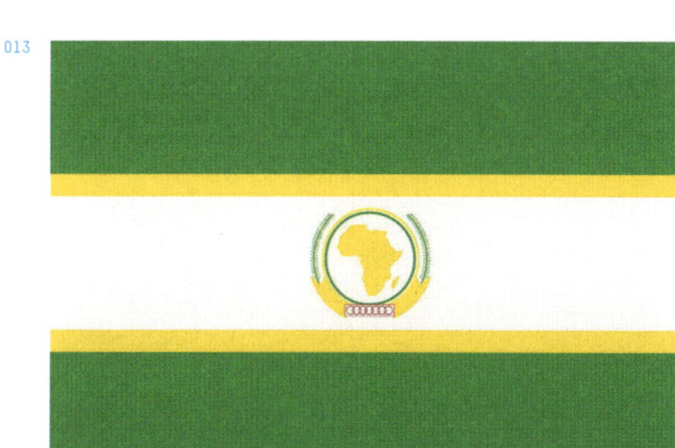

001 AFRICA DAY PROTEST IN CAPE TOWN
     SOURCE my.ilstu.edu
     DATE 16 April 1962

002 CAPE TOWN PEACE MARCH
     On 13 September 1989 Archbishop
     Tutu, Mayor Gordon Oliver, and
     others led a march for peace in
     defiance of apartheid laws and
     the ban on political protests.
     Five months later, President de
     Klerk would reverse the ban on
     the ANC and free Nelson Mandela.
     SOURCE www-cs-students.stanford.edu
     DATE 13 September 1989

003 BERLIN WEST AFRICA CONFERENCE
     SOURCE Photos from African
     Unification Front on Facebook

004 AFRICAN PEACEKEEPERS PATROL
     STREETS IN SOMALIA
     SOURCE Photos from African
     Unification Front on Facebook

005 BERLIN WEST AFRICA CONFERENCE
     SOURCE Photos from African
     Unification Front on Facebook

006 AFRICAN UNION
     CREATOR Provided by comoananse
     SOURCE www.flickr.com/photos/comoa-
     nanse/2556643564/

007 MAKE MONEY: LOOK FOR THESE
     SOURCE legionantiques.com

008 SOLIDARITY WITH THE PEOPLES
     OF AFRICA
     CREATOR Rafael Morante
     SOURCE www.docspopuli.org

009 AN ASSURANCE OF LEADERSHIP / ZANU
     CREATOR Rafael Morante
     SOURCE commonwealth.sas.ac.uk
     DATE 1980

010 DARFUR PROTEST, BERADIK
     School girls hold placards before
     a meeting between Special envoy to
     Darfur Jan Eliasson and the SLM
     Unity in Beradik town.
     CREATOR Mohamed Abdalla
     SOURCE Reuters
     DATE 6 December 2007

011 DARFUR PROTEST, BERADIK
     SOURCE Reuters

012 FLAG OF THE AFRICAN UNION
     SOURCE nv.wikipedia.org
     DATE 2010

013 FLAG OF THE AFRICAN UNION
     SOURCE www.icnl.org
     DATE 2010

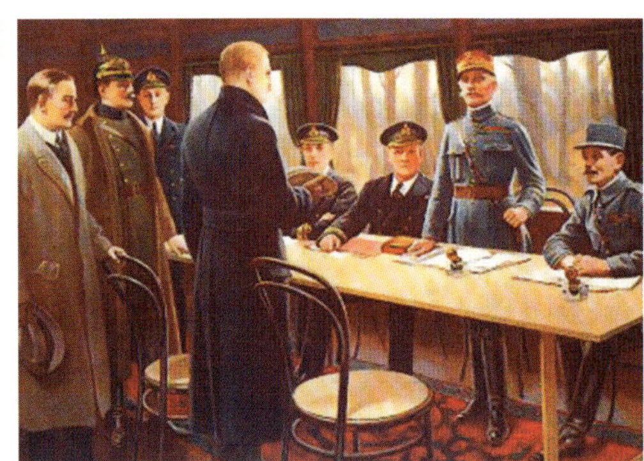
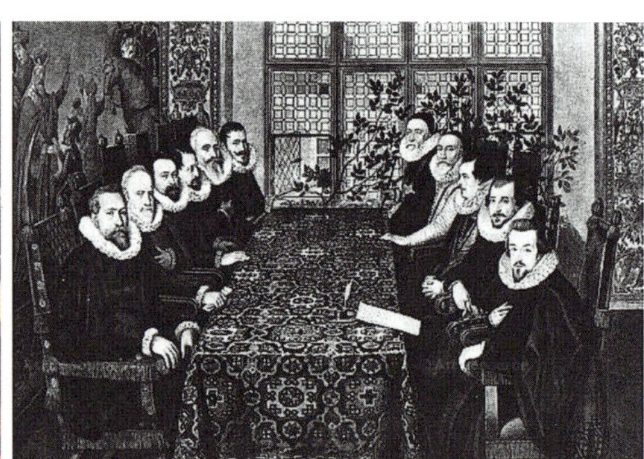
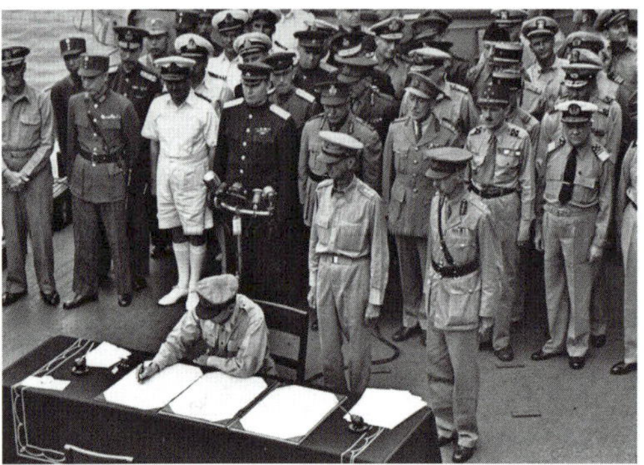
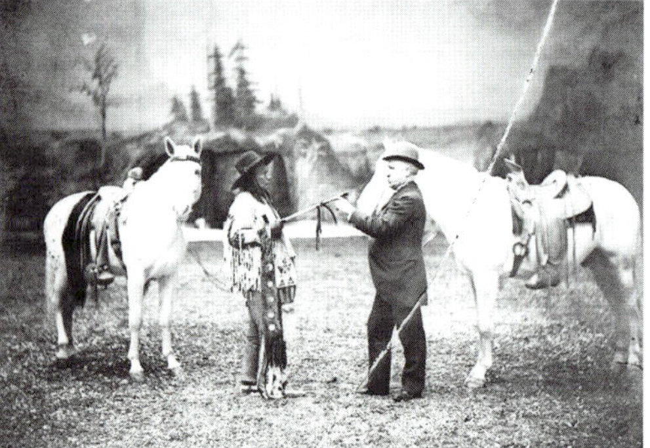
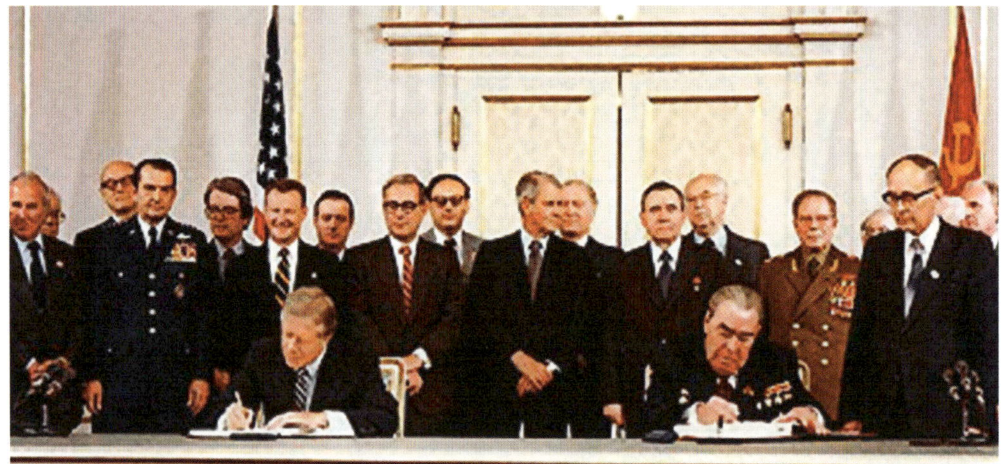
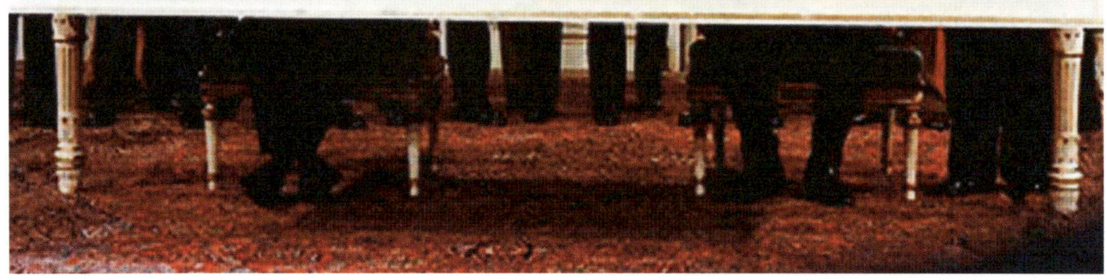

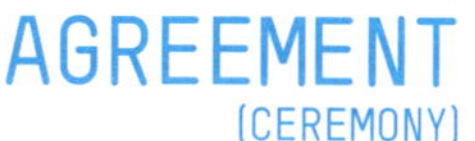
A
AGREEMENT
(CEREMONY)

006
007
008

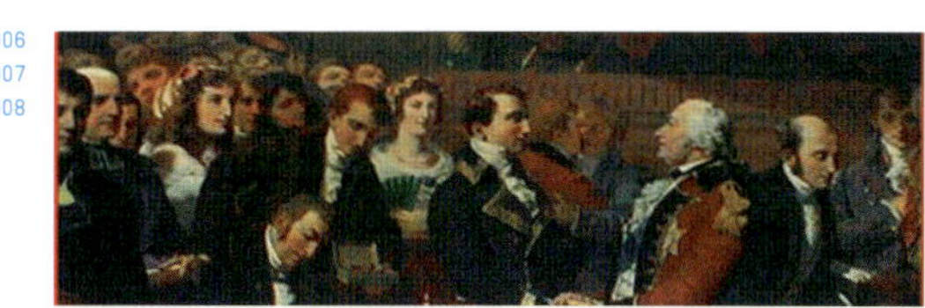

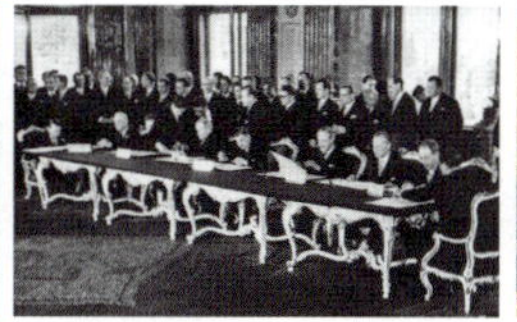

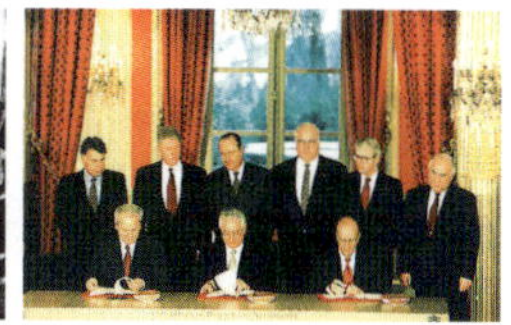

009
010
011
012

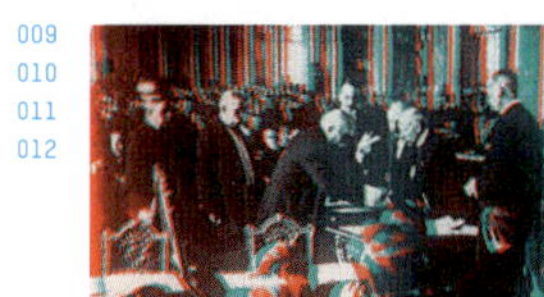

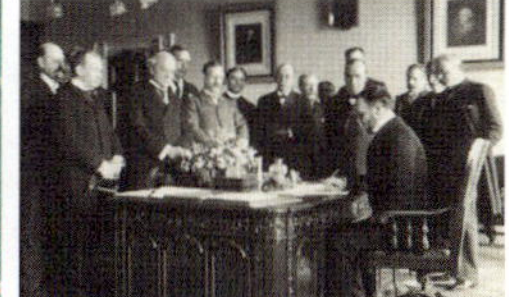

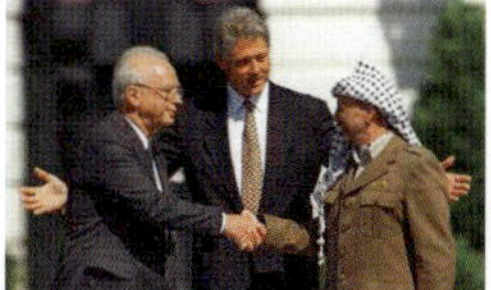

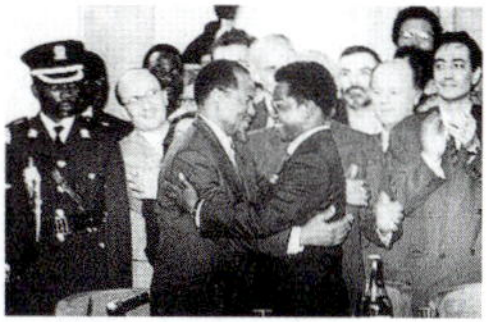

013

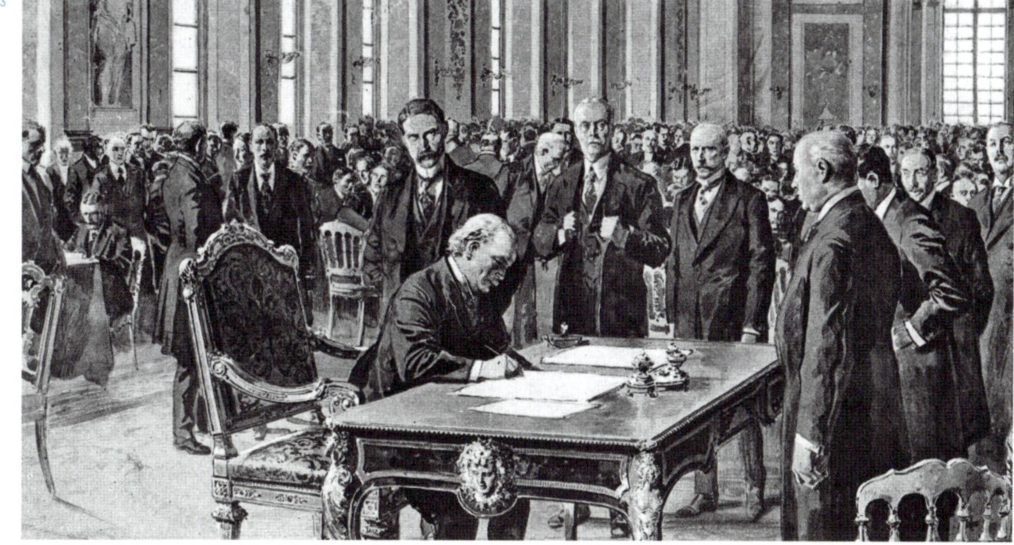

014
015
016
017

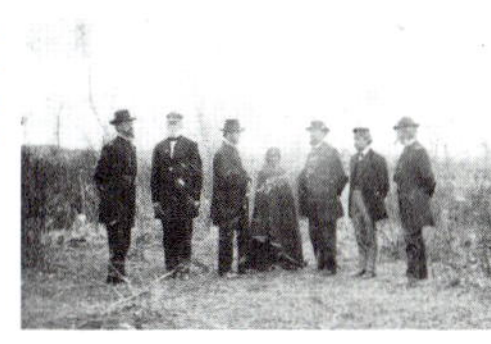

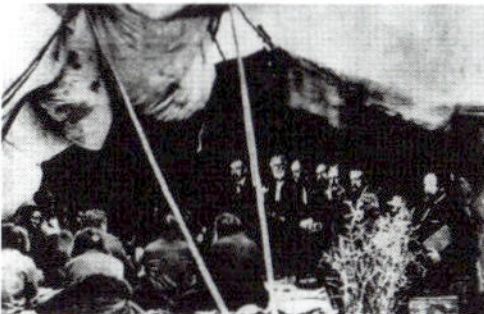

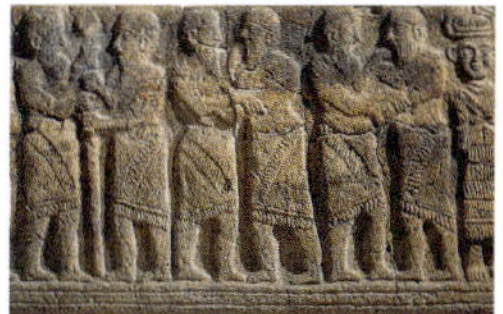

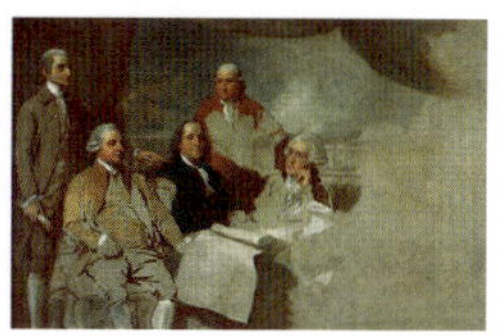

018
019

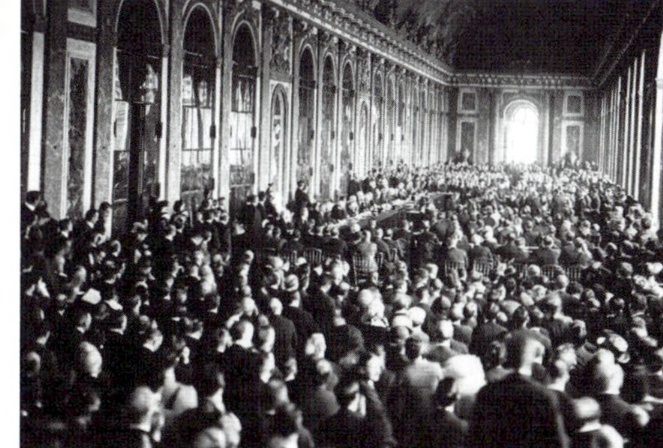

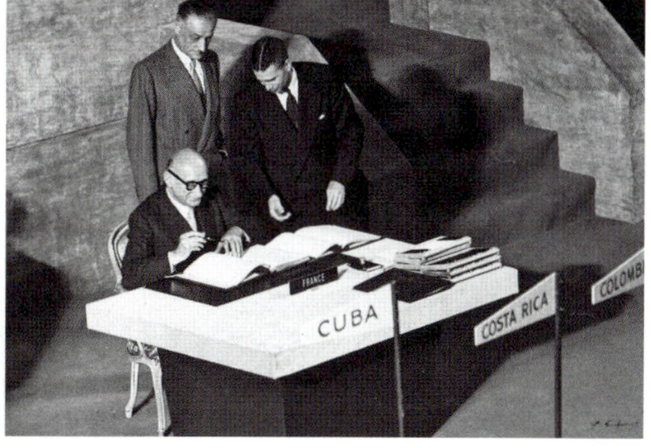

020

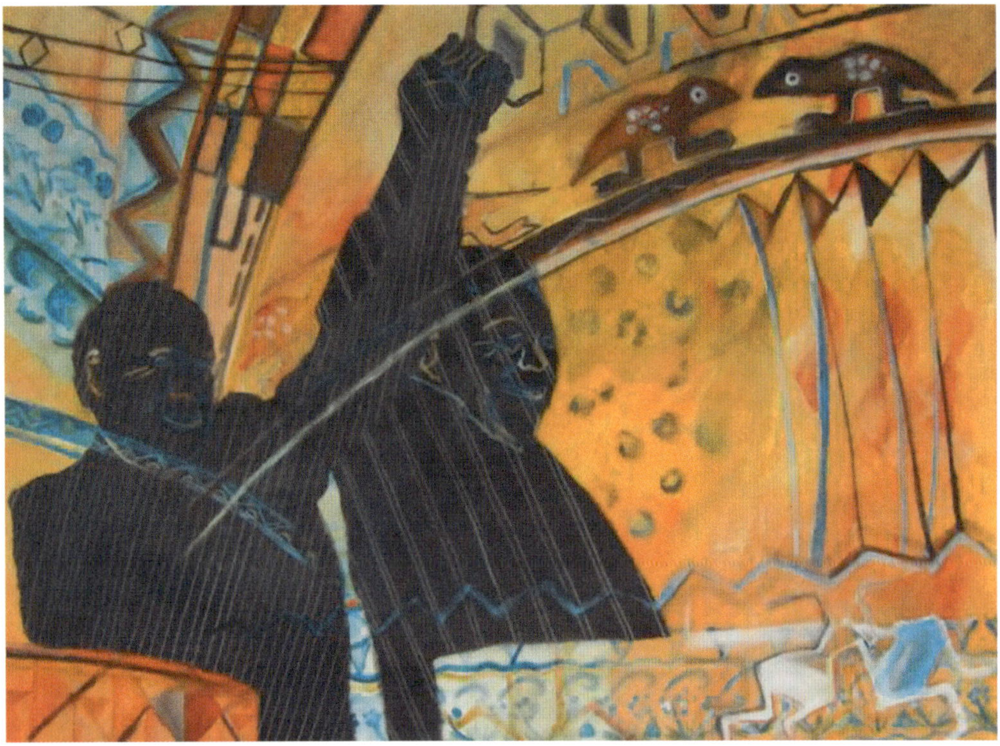

021

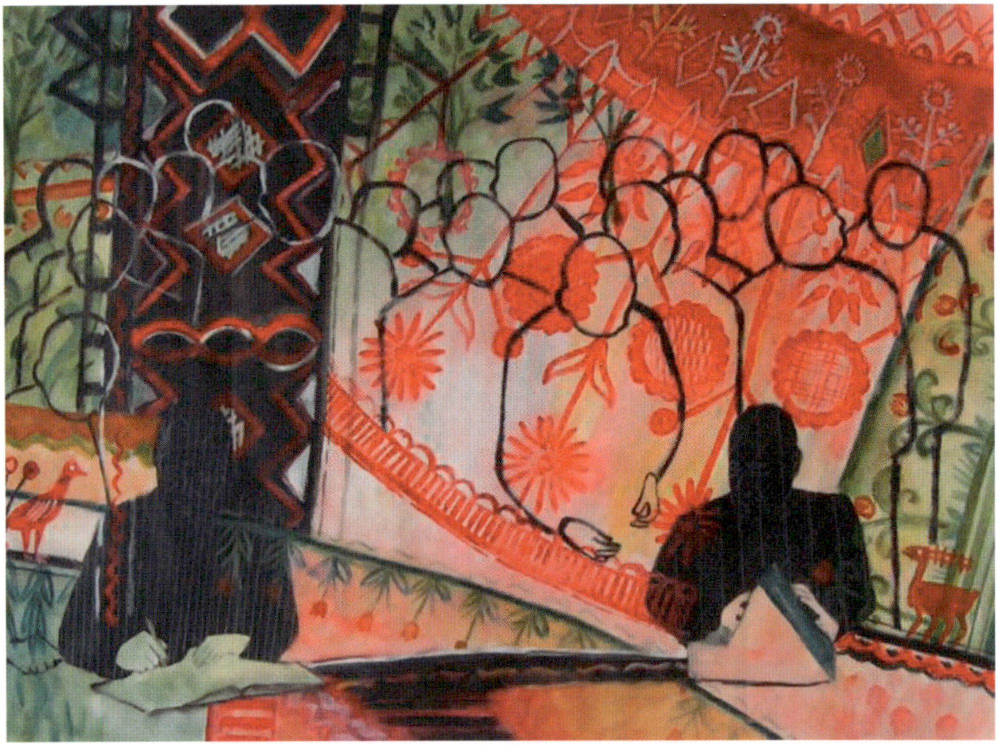

022

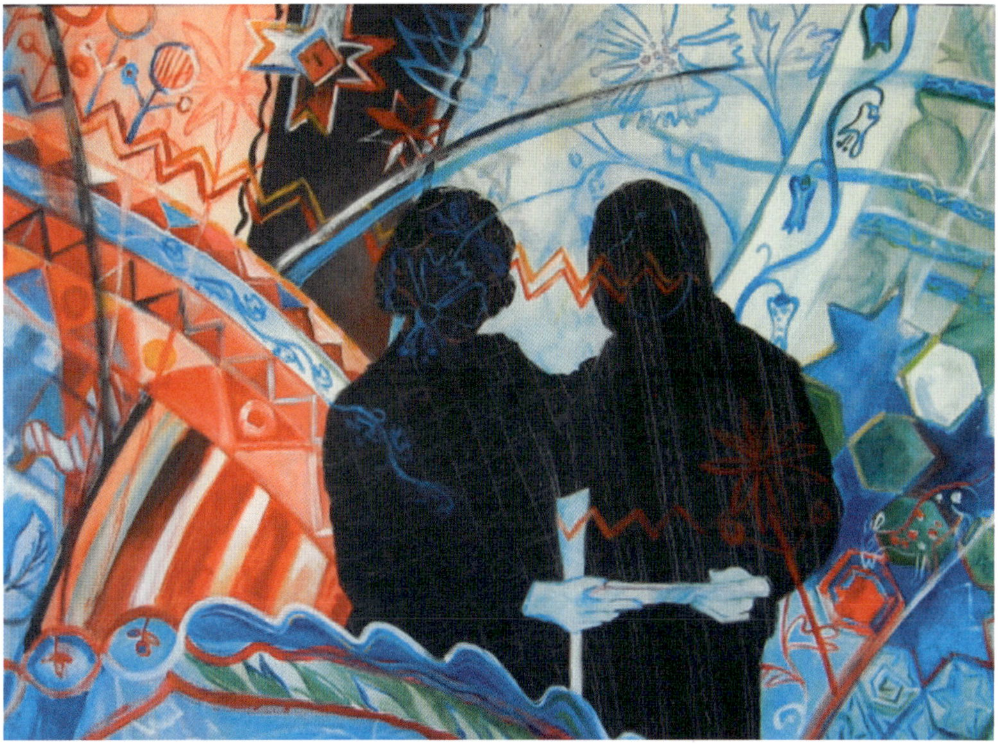

023

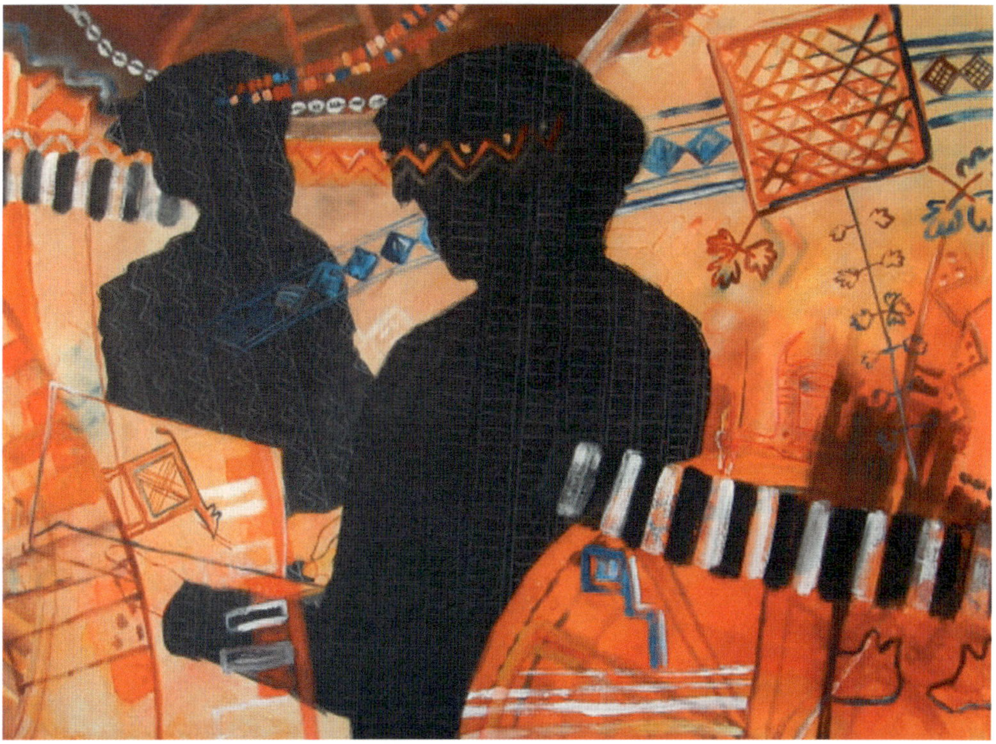

001 TREATY OF RETHONDES
     SOURCE bravepatrie.com
     DATE 11 November 1918

002 THE SOMERSET HOUSE CONFERENCE
     The Somerset House Conference:
     Spanish-Flemish [left] and the
     English [right] delegations
     negotiating a peace treaty
     to end the nineteen-year-long
     Anglo-Spanish War.
     SOURCE www.artres.com
     DATE 19 August 1604

003 JAPANESE SURRENDER-MISSOURI
     Gen. Douglas MacArthur signing
     official surrender of Japan,
     as Gen. Jonathan Wainwright &
     British Gen. Arthur E. Percival
     look on aboard the US battleship
     USS Missouri in Tokyo Bay.
     CREATOR J. R. Eyerman
     SOURCE www.life.com

004 CHIEF JOSEPH AND CAPTAIN JEROME
     WITH BUFFALO BILL'S HORSES
     Chief Joseph, Nez Perce, and
     Captain Jerome with Buffalo Bill's
     saddled horses, photographed at
     Madison Square Garden, full-
     length with painted backdrop in
     background; Chief Joseph passes
     a peace pipe to Captain Jerome.
     CREATOR Barry, David Frances
     SOURCE memory.loc.gov

005 SALT II ACCORDS
     President Jimmy Carter and Soviet
     General Secretary Leonid Brezhnev
     sign the Strategic Arms Limitation
     Talks [SALT II] treaty, 16 June
     1979, in Washington DC.
     CREATOR Bill Fitz-Patrick
     SOURCE en.wikipedia.org
     DATE 16 June 1979

006 ACCORDS DE PAIX D'AMIENS
     [TREATY OF AMIENS]
     This treaty temporarily ended
     hostilities between France
     and England during the French
     Revolutionary Wars.
     CREATOR Jules Ziegler
     SOURCE www.histoire-image.org
     DATE 27 March 1802

007 WORLD LEADERS SIGN AUSTRIAN
     STATE TREATY
     CREATOR Ralph Crane
     SOURCE www.life..com
     DATE May 1955

008 ACCORDS DE DAYTON À PARIS
     [SIGNING OF THE DAYTON ACCORDS
     IN PARIS]
     Slobodan Milosevic, President
     of Serbia, Franjo Tudjman,
     President of Croatia and Alija
     Izetbegovic, President of Bosnia

and Herzegovina, signed the Gene-
ral Framework Agreement for Peace
in Bosnia and Herzegovina, in the
presence of Felipe Gonzalez, Bill
Clinton, Jacques Chirac, Helmut
Kohl, John Major and Viktor
Chernomyrdin.
SOURCE www.ladocumentationfran-
caise.fr
DATE 14 December 1995

009 CLÉMENCEAU SIGNS THE PEACE TREATY
     AT VERSAILLES
     SOURCE etienne.jacqueau.free.fr
     DATE 28 June 1919

010 RATIFICATION OF THE PEACE TREATY
     BETWEEN SPAIN AND THE UNITED STATES
     Secretary of State John Hay signs
     the ratification of the treaty
     ending the Spanish-American War
     on behalf of the United States at
     the White House.
     SOURCE www.doc.diplomatie.gouv.fr
     DATE 1899

011 PEACE TREATY
     Prime Minister Yitzhak Rabin
     shakes hands with PLO leader
     Yasser Arafat, watched over by
     President Bill Clinton. This
     marked the signing of the
     Declaration of Principles,
     which would lead to the first
     withdrawals from occupied
     territories by Israel.
     CREATOR Gary Hershorn
     SOURCE Reuters
     DATE 13 September 1993

012 PEACE AGREEMENT IN MOZAMBIQUE
     [LUSAKA ACCORD]
     On 7 September 1974 Portugal and
     Mozambique signed the Lusaka
     Accord, which formally recognized
     Mozambique's right to independence.
     SOURCE ccfmoz.com
     DATE 7 September 1974

013 BRITISH PRIME MINISTER
     LLOYD GEORGE
     Signs the Treaty of Versailles,
     formally ending World War I.
     SOURCE www.life.com
     DATE 28 June 1919

014 INDIAN PEACE COMMISSION
     A Native American [Modoc or Dakota]
     woman stands outdoors in the center
     of a group of six white men, three
     in military uniforms, three in suits
     and coats; she wears a blanket
     wrapped around her shoulders.
     SOURCE memory.loc.gov

015 TREATY SIGNING BY WILLIAM T.
     SHERMAN AND THE SIOUX AT FORT
     LARAMIE, WYOMING
     CREATOR Alexander Gardner

SOURCE University of California,
San Diego
DATE 1868

016 THREE PAIRS OF WARRIORS EMBRACING
     TO SEAL PEACE TREATY.
     Detail of the long side of basalt
     sacrificial basin. Temple N, Tel
     Mardikh, Ebla, Syria.
     CREATOR Photograph by Erich
     Lessing / Art Resource, NY
     SOURCE www.artres.com

017 AMERICAN COMMISSIONERS OF THE
     PRELIMINARY PEACE NEGOTIATIONS
     WITH GREAT BRITAIN
     CREATOR Benjamin West
     SOURCE Winterthur Museum

018 TREATY OF VERSAILLES
     Crowd of diplomats gathered
     in the Hall of Mirrors for the
     signing of the treaty ending
     World War I.
     SOURCE www.life.com
     DATE 28 June 1919

019 ROBERT SCHUMAN, OF FRANCE, SIGNING
     JAPANESE PEACE TREATY.
     The Japanese Peace Treaty was
     signed in the War Memorial
     Opera House in San Francisco,
     California, on 8 September 1951.
     CREATOR J. R. Eyerman
     SOURCE www.life.com

020 NELSON MANDELA REPLACES FREDERIK
     WILLEM DE KLERK AS PRESIDENT, 1994
     CREATOR Violetta Vollrath
     SOURCE www.violetta.de/fried.htm
     DATE 2006

021 JÓZEF CYRANKIEWICZ AND WILLY
     BRANDT, TREATY OF WARSAW 1970
     CREATOR Violetta Vollrath
     SOURCE www.violetta.de/fried.htm
     DATE 2006

022 MADAME PRESIDENT OF THE USA
     AND MADAME PRESIDENT OF IRAN,
     PEACE TREATY
     CREATOR Violetta Vollrath
     SOURCE www.violetta.de/fried.htm
     DATE 2008

023 LEADER OF THE NATIONAL CONGRESS
     DARFUR AND MADAME PRESIDENT OF
     SUDAN, INTERGOVERNMENTAL AGREEMENT
     CREATOR Violetta Vollrath
     SOURCE www.violetta.de/fried.htm
     DATE 2008

001
002
003

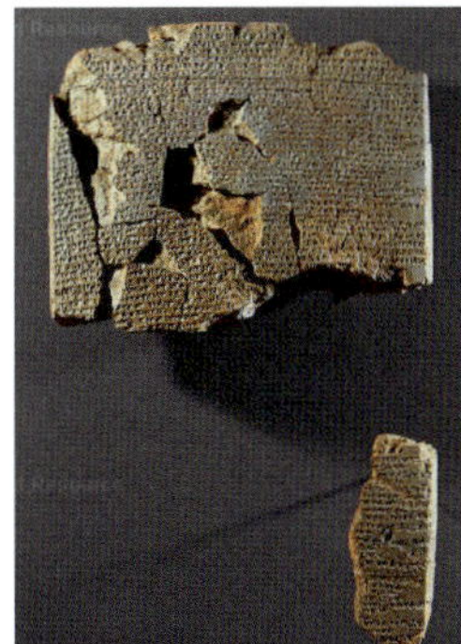
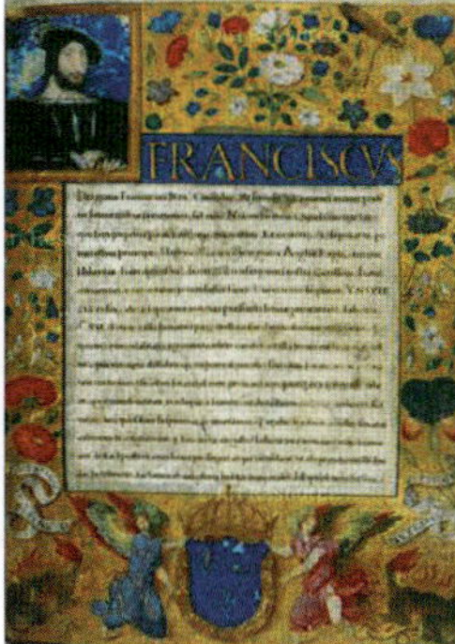
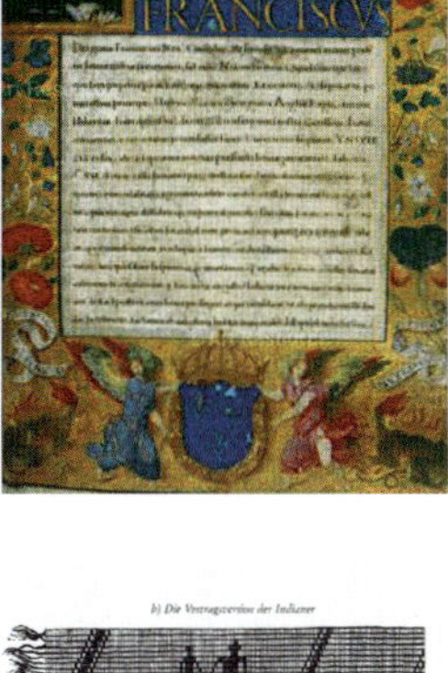
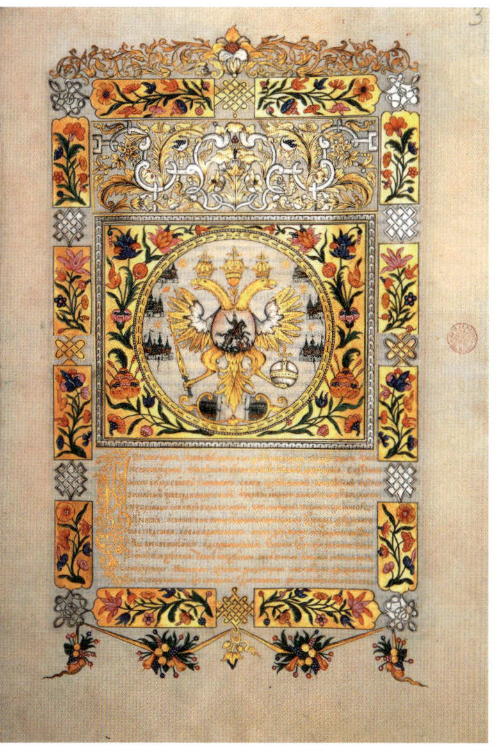

004
005

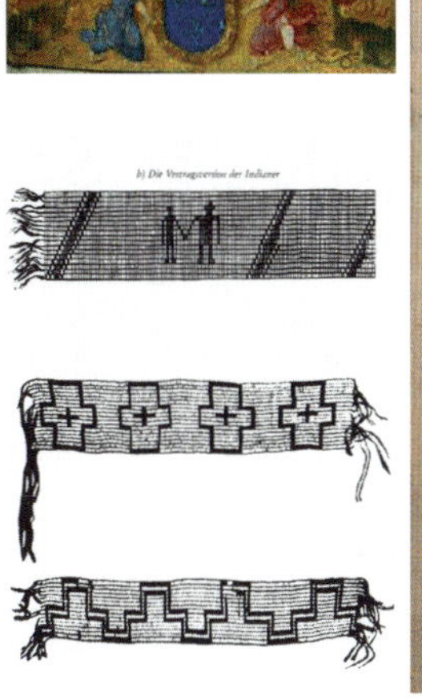

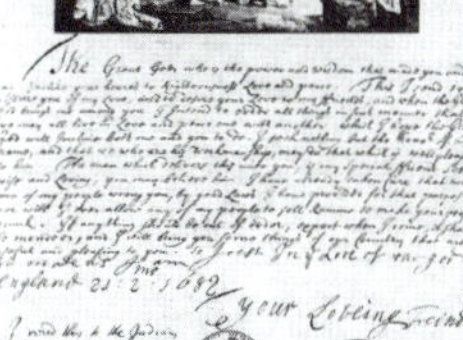

006

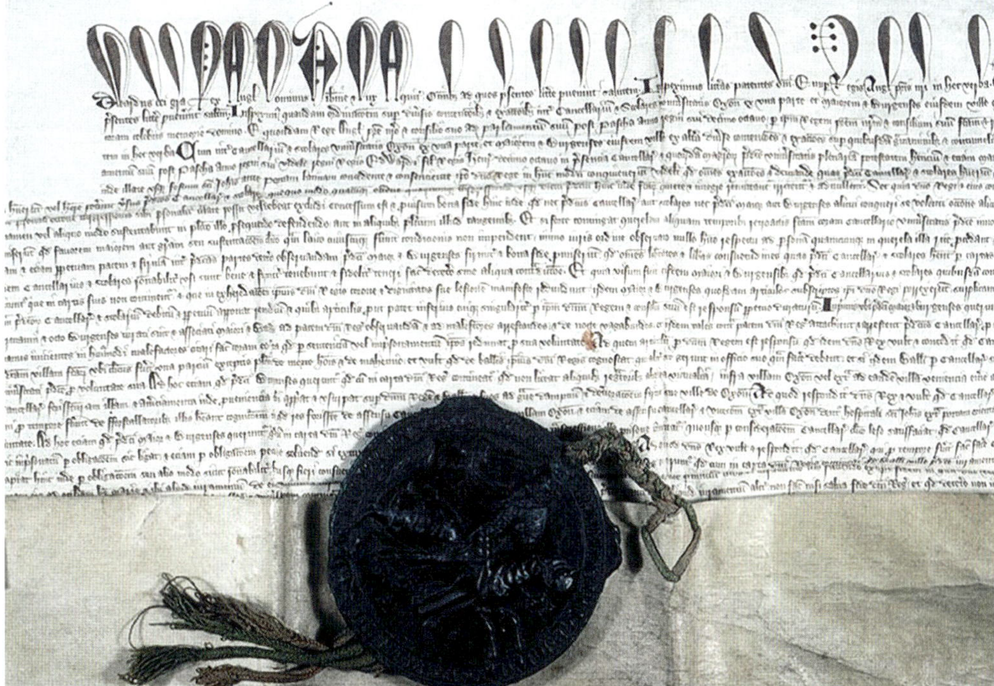

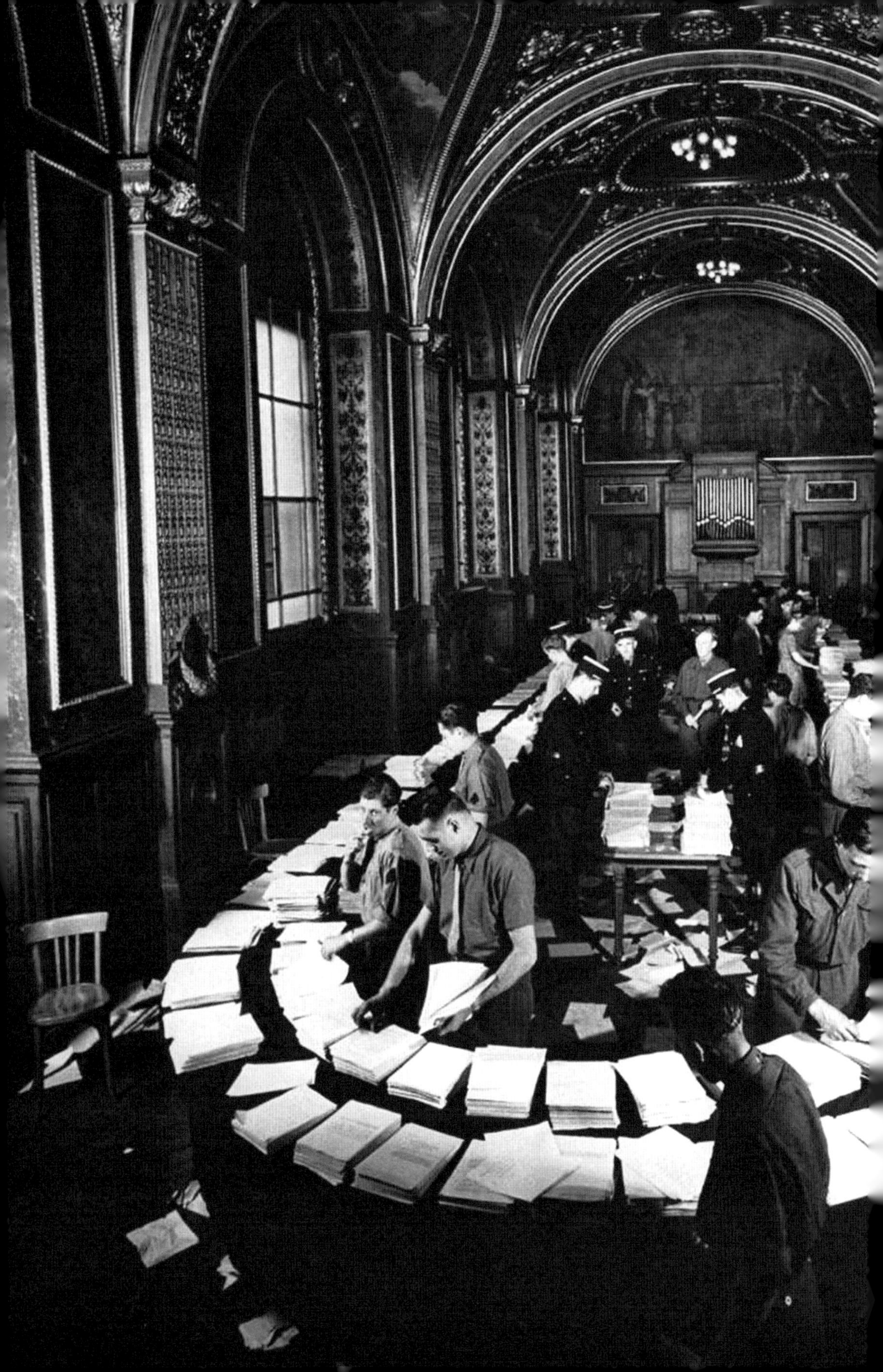

LEFT
007

008
009
010
011

012
013
014

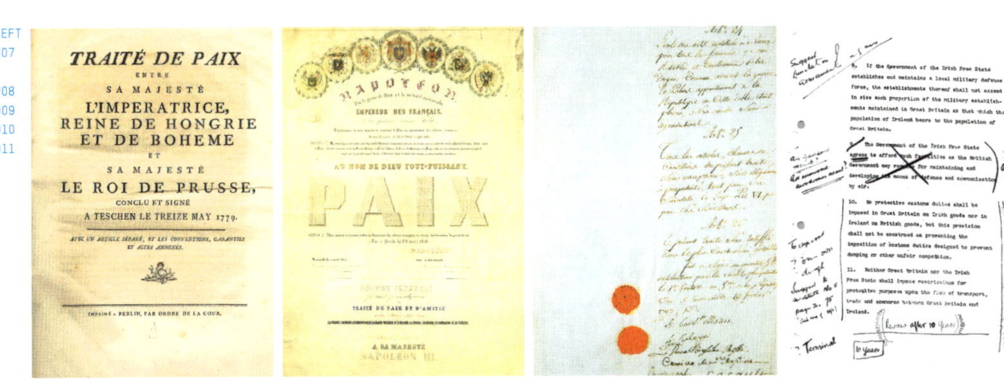

015
016
017

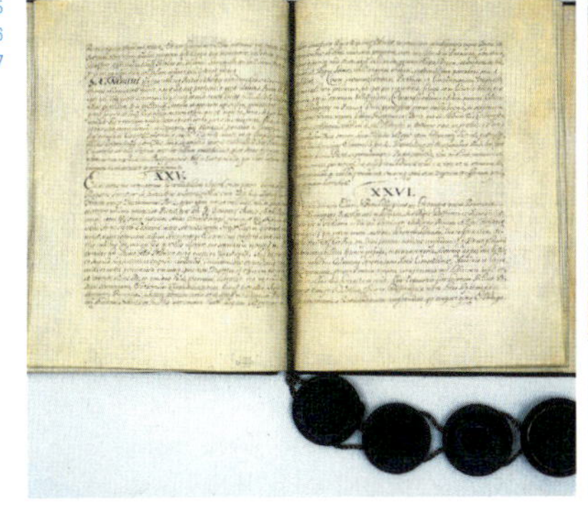

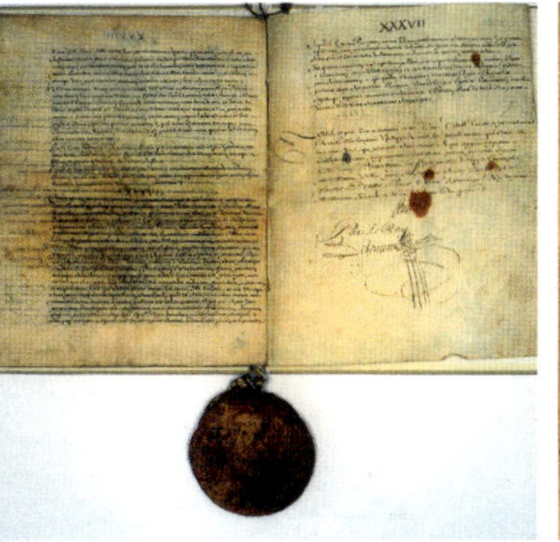

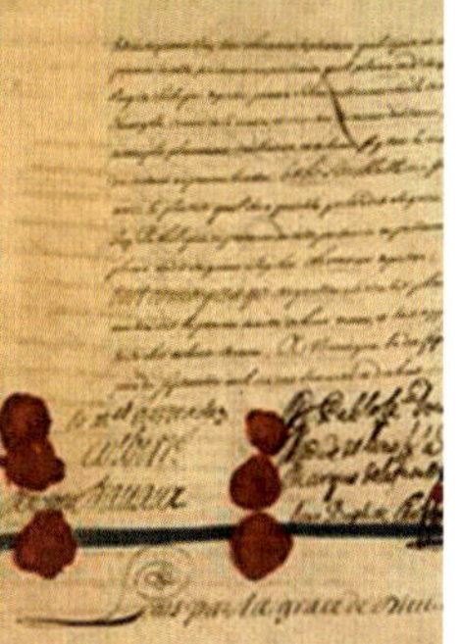

018
019

NEXT
020

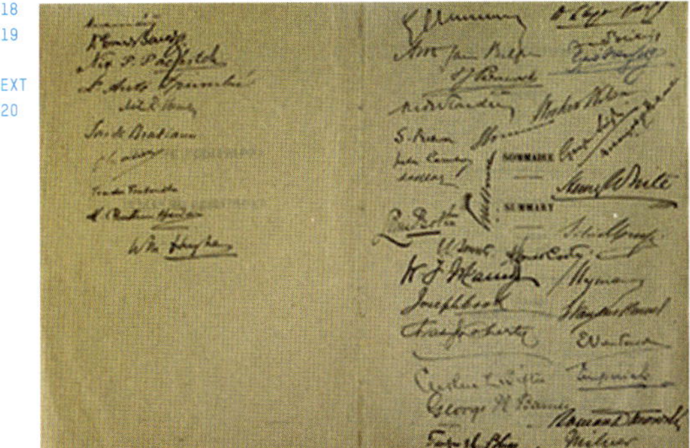

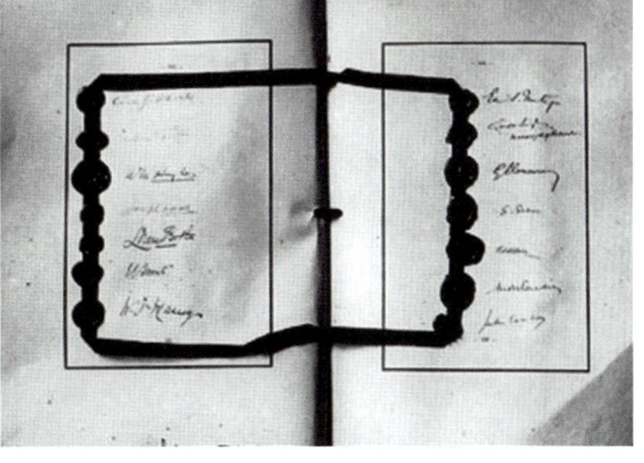

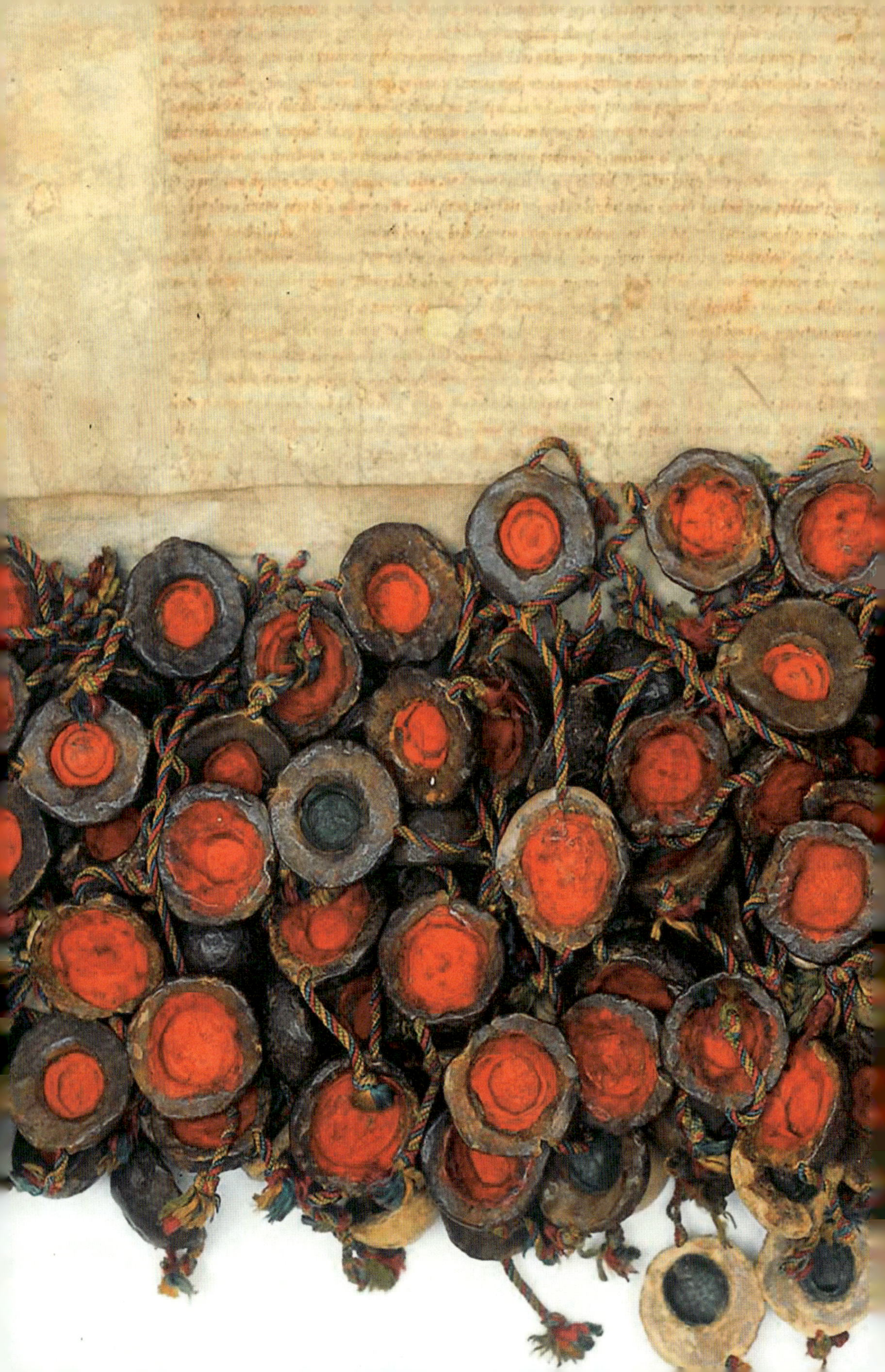

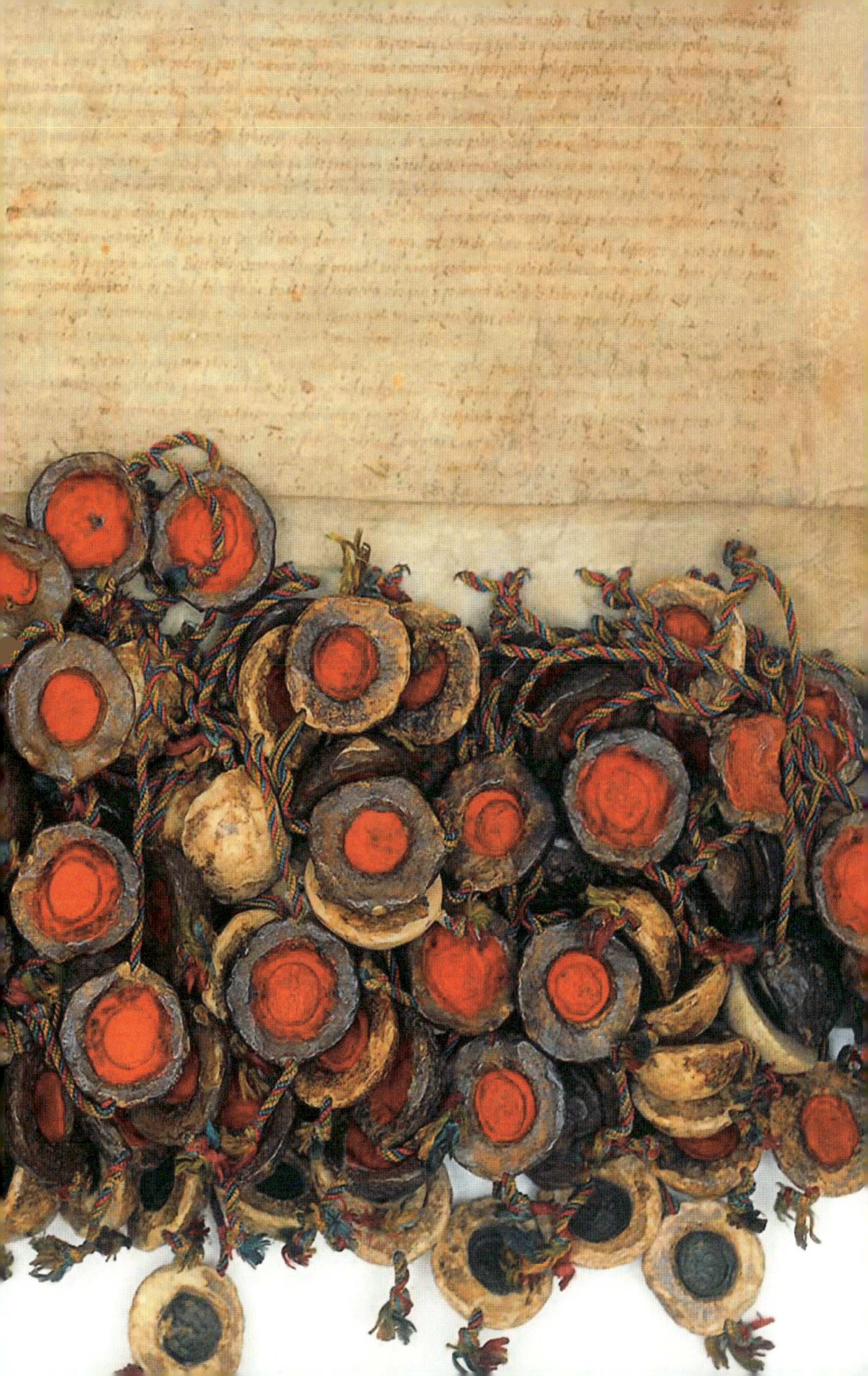

001   TREATY CONCLUDED AFTER THE
      BATTLE OF KADESH BETWEEN PHARAOH
      RAMSES II AND THE HITTITE KING
      MUVATALLISH
      Fragment of a terracotta tablet in
      Akkadian language, the diplomatic
      language of the 13th century BC.
      CREATOR Photograph by Erich
      Lessing / Art Resource, NY
      SOURCE www.artres.com
      DATE 1272 BC

002   ILLUMINATED TITLE PAGE FROM THE
      TREATY OF PEACE BETWEEN HENRY VII
      AND FRANCIS I
      CREATOR Photograph by HIP / Art
      Resource, NY
      SOURCE www.artres.com
      DATE c. 1500

003   POLISH RUSSIAN PEACE AGREEMENT
      [GRZYMULTOWSKI TREATY]
      SOURCE de.wikipedia.org
      DATE 1686

004   WILLIAM PENN'S TREATY
      This broadside combines a
      lithograph commemorating Penn's
      1682 treaty with the Delaware
      Indians and a reproduction of
      a letter Penn sent to the Lenape
      Indians before his arrival in the
      New World.
      SOURCE Unknown
      DATE C. 1840-1850

005   WAMPUM BELTS RELATED TO
      PENN'S TREATY
      SOURCE Unknown
      DATE 1682

006   LETTERS PATENT
      Letters patent confirming terms of
      peace, between town and University
      of Oxford, drawn up in 1290 by
      Edward I. Dated at Waltham.
      SOURCE Bodleian Library
      DATE 1290

007   PEACE CONFERENCE
      Workers collating documents
      in the Salle de Brosse of the
      Luxembourg Palace during the
      Paris Peace Conference.
      CREATOR Gjon Mili
      SOURCE www.life.com
      DATE October 1946

008   PEACE TREATY OF TESCHEN
      The Peace Treaty of Teschen ended
      the War of the Bavarian Succession,
      fought between the Hapsburgs and
      a Saxon-Prussian alliance.
      SOURCE Unknown
      DATE 13 May 1779

009   ANNOUNCEMENT OF THE PROMULGATION
      OF THE TREATY OF PARIS
      "It is a peace, as Lord Clarendon
      said to Parliament, that is
      honorable for all and humiliating
      to no one."
      SOURCE Ministère des Affaires
      étrangères et européennes
      DATE 28 April 1856

010   TREATY OF PEACE OF TOLENTINO
      BETWEEN THE HOLY SEE AND FRANCE
      During the French Revolutionary
      Wars, the Vatican was forced
      to cede Avignon and the Comtat
      Venaissin to France, ending 500
      years of papal rule.
      SOURCE asv.vatican.va/
      DATE 1797

011   ANGLO-IRISH TREATY
      Annotated draft from the
      Anglo-Irish Treaty that
      established the Irish Free
      State and independence for
      26 out of 32 Irish counties.
      SOURCE National Archives
      of Ireland
      DATE 1921

012   PEACE AGREEMENT BETWEEN THE
      GOVERNMENT OF THE REPUBLIC
      OF RWANDA AND THE RWANDESE
      PATRIOTIC FRONT
      SOURCE www.docstoc.com/docs/2944643/
      peace-agreement-between-the-
      government-of-the-republic-
      of-rwanda
      DATE 1 October 1990

013   TEXT OF SHARI'A-FOR-PEACE DEAL
      BETWEEN TALIBAN AND PAKISTAN
      SOURCE Roznama Express
      DATE 16 February 2009

014   PEACE TREATY WITH THE EMPIRE
      This treaty between France
      and the Holy Roman Empire was
      one of several treaties
      concluding the Franco-Dutch
      War of 1672-78.
      SOURCE www.diplomatie.gouv.fr
      DATE 1679

015   PEACE TREATY OF OLIWA — VERSION
      ISSUED BY THE SWEDISH SIDE
      The Swedish commissioners conclude
      peace with Jan Kazimierz, King of
      Poland, the emperor Leopold, and
      Friedrich Wilhelm, margrave of
      Brandenburg.
      SOURCE www.poland.pl
      DATE 3 May 1660

016   RATIFICATION OF THE PEACE TREATY
      OF OLIWA BY LOUIS XIV, KING OF
      FRANCE, AS GUARANTOR
      SOURCE www.poland.pl
      DATE 22 September 1660

017   PEACE TREATY BETWEEN FRANCE
      AND SPAIN
      This treaty is one of several
      that concluded the Franco-Dutch
      War of 1672-78.
      SOURCE www.diplomatie.gouv.fr/
      DATE 17 September 1678

018   TREATY OF VERSAILLES
      SOURCE pastel.diplomatie.gouv.fr
      DATE 28 June 1919

019   SIGNATURE PAGE OF THE TREATY
      OF VERSAILLES
      SOURCE pastel.diplomatie.gouv.fr
      DATE 28 June 1919

020   ACT OF THE WARSAW GENERAL
      CONFEDERATION
      A general seym of nobles, meeting
      in Warsaw after the death of King
      Zygmunt August of Poland, adopts
      articles intended to preserve the
      peace and domestic order prior to
      the election of a new monarch.
      SOURCE www.poland.pl
      DATE 28 January 1573

001

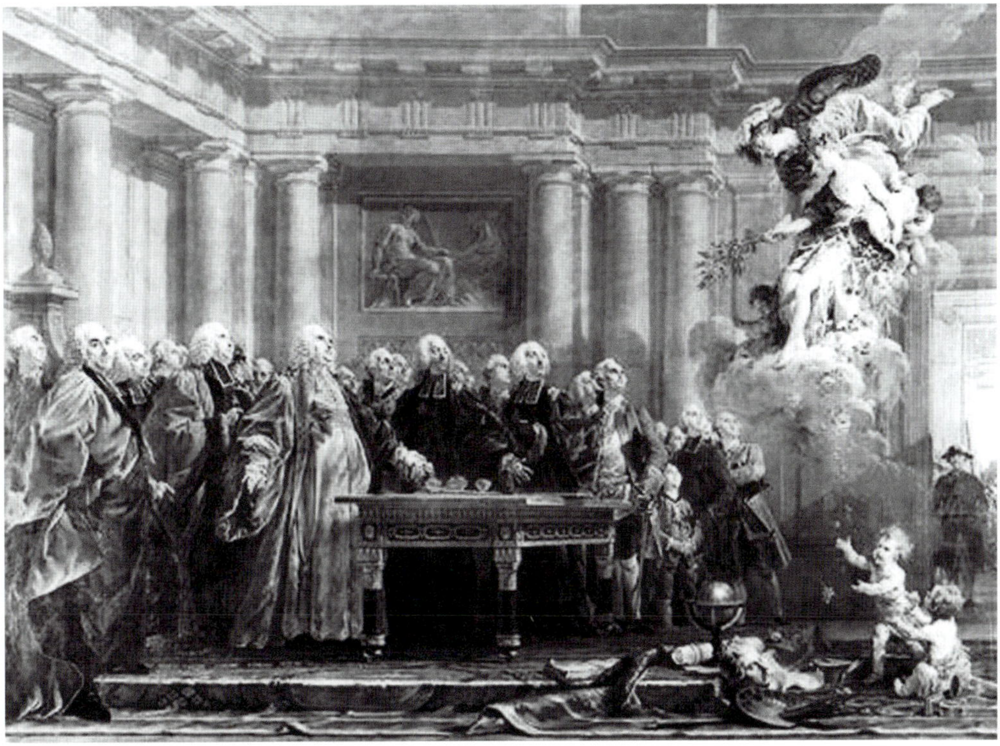

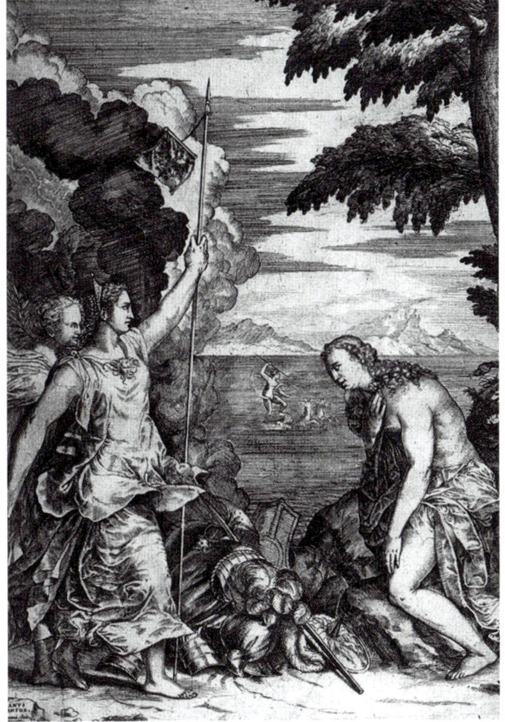

002
003

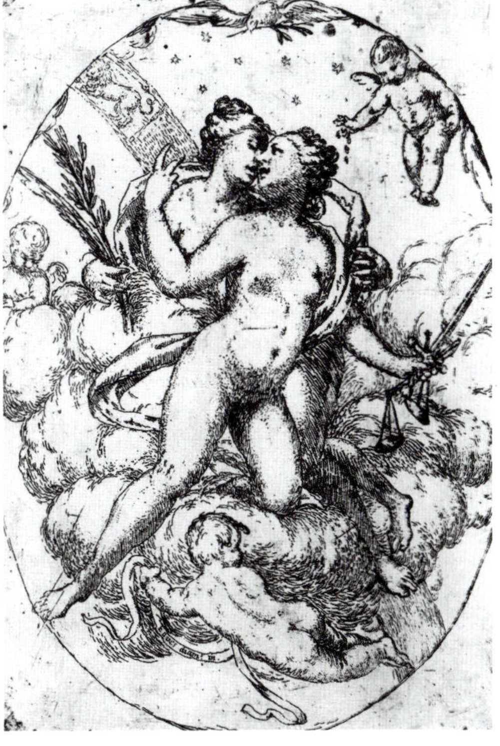

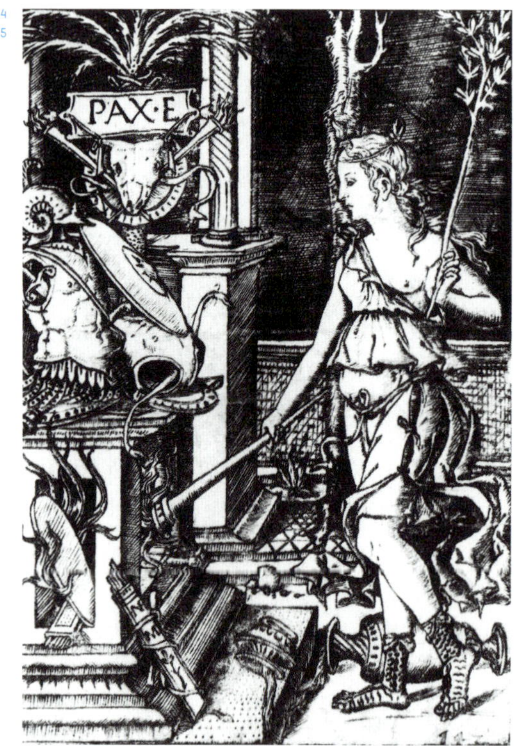

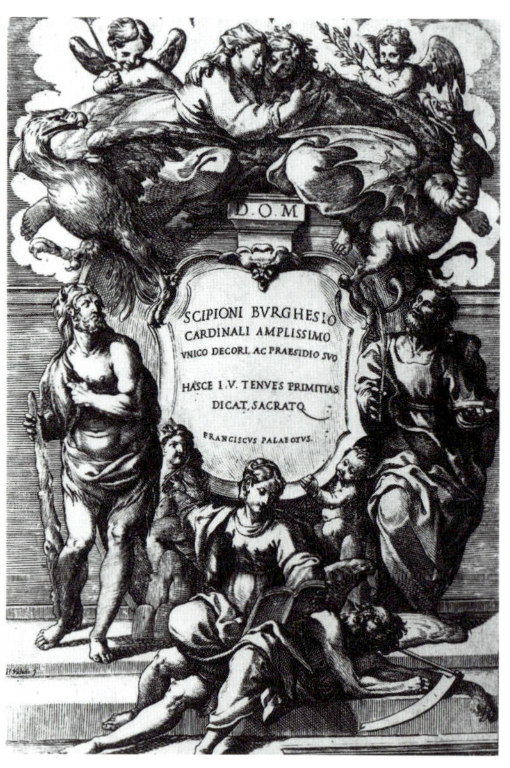

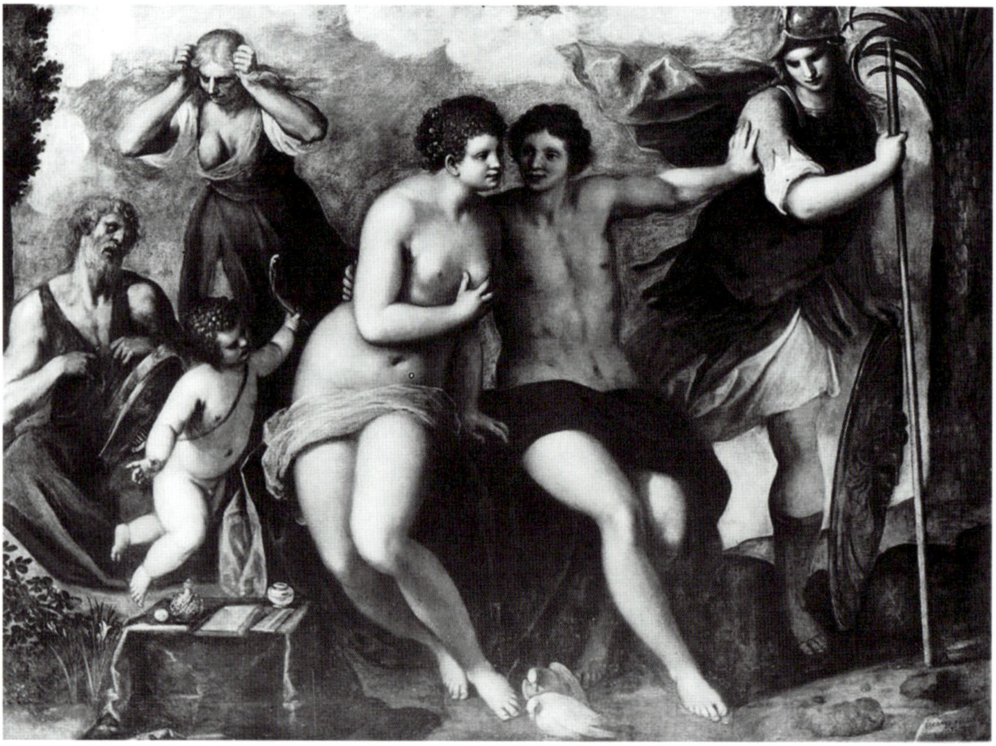

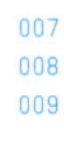
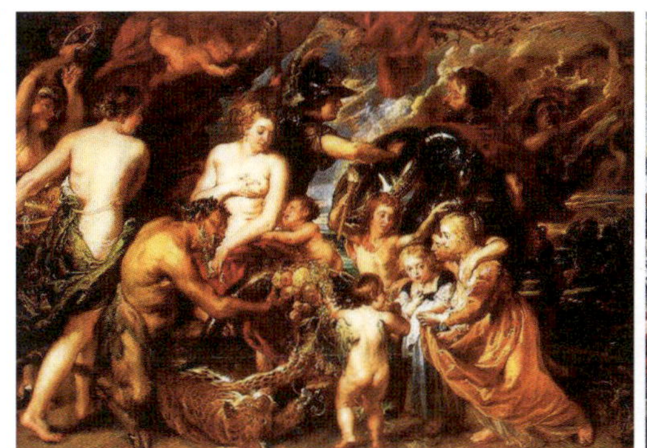
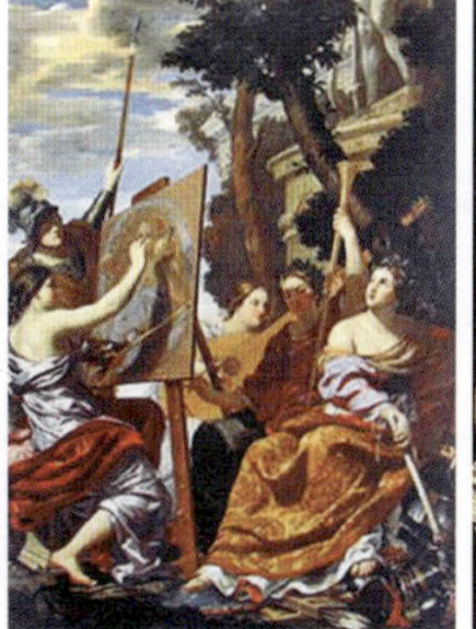
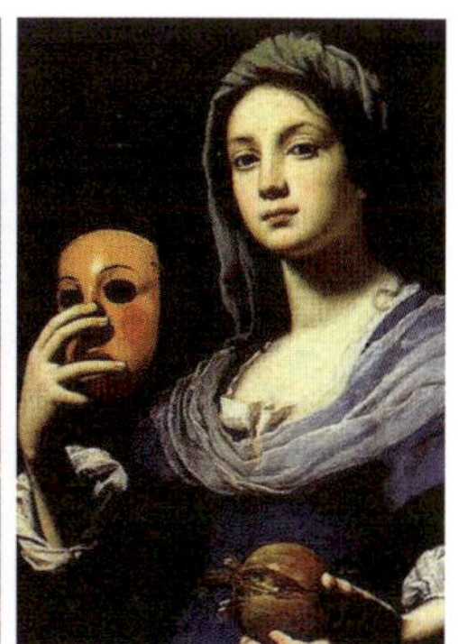
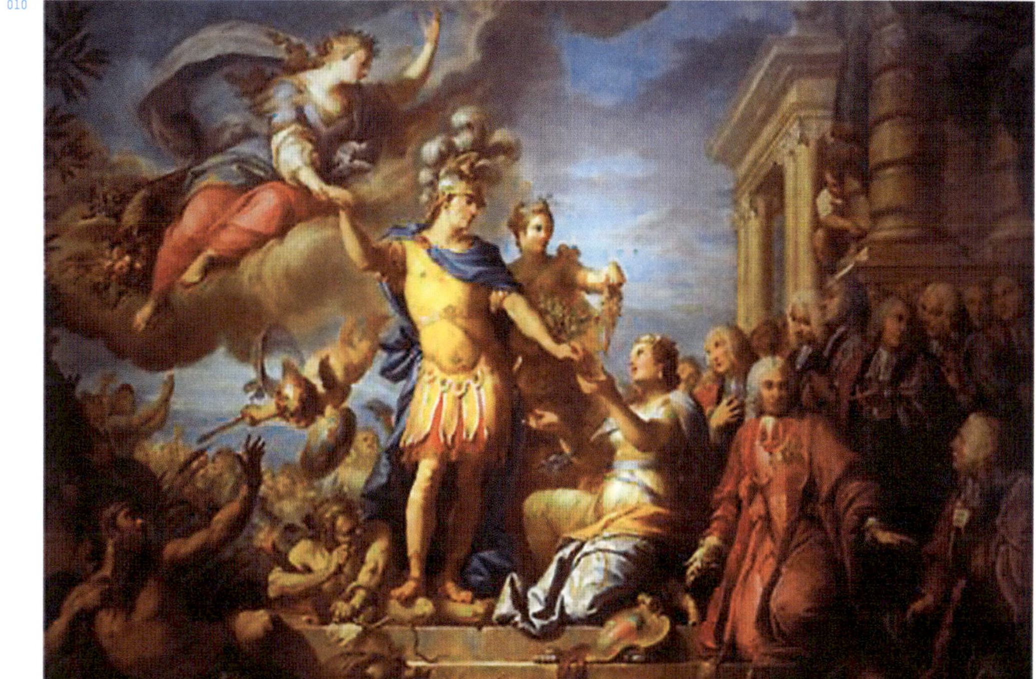
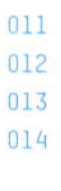
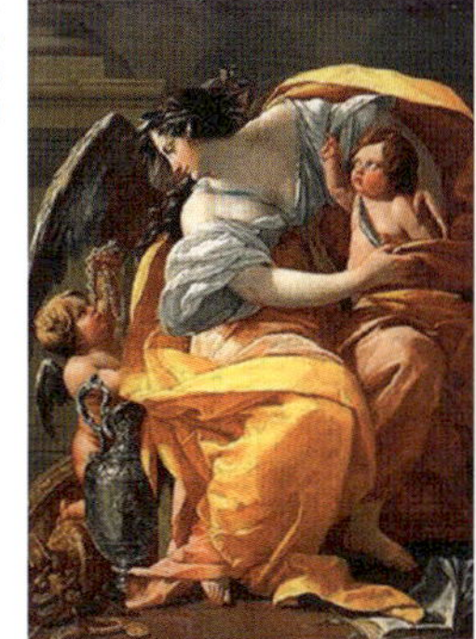
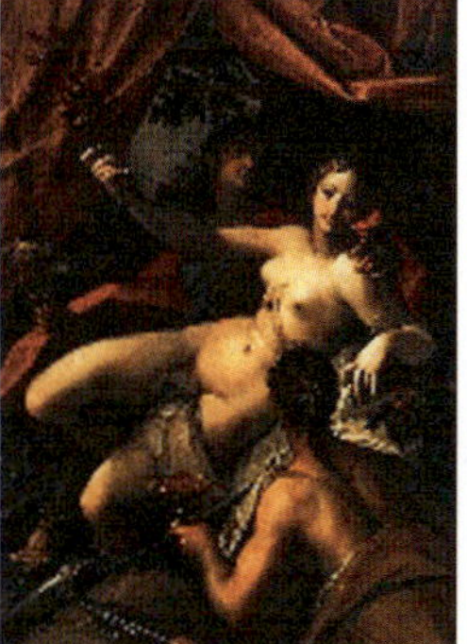
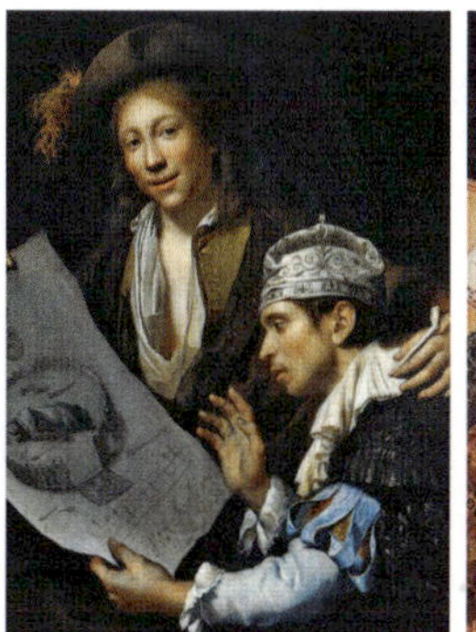
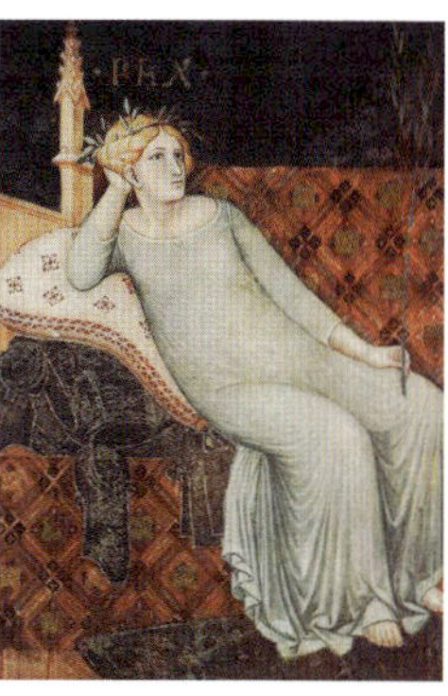

001 ALLEGORY OF PEACE OF 1763
CREATOR Noël Hallè
SOURCE www.univ-montp3.fr
DATE 1763

002 CAESARIS INVICTI PIA
RELLIGIONIS IMAGO [AN ALLEGORY ON
PEACE AND RELIGION]
CREATOR Giulio Fontana
SOURCE Fine Arts Museums of San
Francisco

003 ALLEGORY OF JUSTICE AND PEACE
CREATOR Giuseppe Diamantini
SOURCE *The Illustrated Bartsch.
Vol. 47, Italian Masters of the
Seventeenth Century.*
DATE 1682

004 ALLEGORY OF PEACE
CREATOR Nicoletto da Modena
SOURCE *The Illustrated Bartsch.
Vol. 25, Early Italian Masters.*

005 ALLEGORY OF JUSTICE AND PEACE
CREATOR Giovanni Luigi Valesio
SOURCE *The Illustrated Bartsch.
Vol. 40, Italian Masters of
the Sixteenth and Seventeenth
Centuries.*

006 ALLEGORY OF WAR AND PEACE
CREATOR Palma il Giovane, Jacopo
SOURCE Frick Art Reference
Library

007 ALLEGORY ON THE BLESSINGS
OF PEACE
CREATOR Peter Paul Rubens
SOURCE National Gallery, London
DATE 1629-30

008 PEACE AND THE ARTS
CREATOR Charles Mellin
SOURCE National Gallery, London
DATE 1627

009 DECEPTIVE MAUVE
CREATOR Lorenzo Lippi
SOURCE Musée des Beaux-Arts,
Angers
DATE 1779

010 ALLEGORY OF THE PEACE OF
AIX-LA-CHAPELLE
CREATOR Jacques Dumont
SOURCE Musée Carnavalet, Paris
DATE 1761

011 ALLEGORY OF WEALTH
CREATOR Jan van Wijckersloot
SOURCE Louvre
DATE c. 1640

012 ALLEGORY OF PEACE, ART,
AND ABUNDANCE
CREATOR Hans van Aachen
SOURCE Hermitage
DATE 1602

013 ALLEGORY OF THE DISASTER
CREATOR Jan van Wijckersloot
SOURCE www.rijksmuseum.nl
DATE 1672

014 ALLEGORY OF PEACE [FROM THE
ALLEGORY OF GOOD GOVERNMENT]
CREATOR Ambrogio Lorenzetti
SOURCE Palazzo Pubblico, Siena
DATE 1338-39

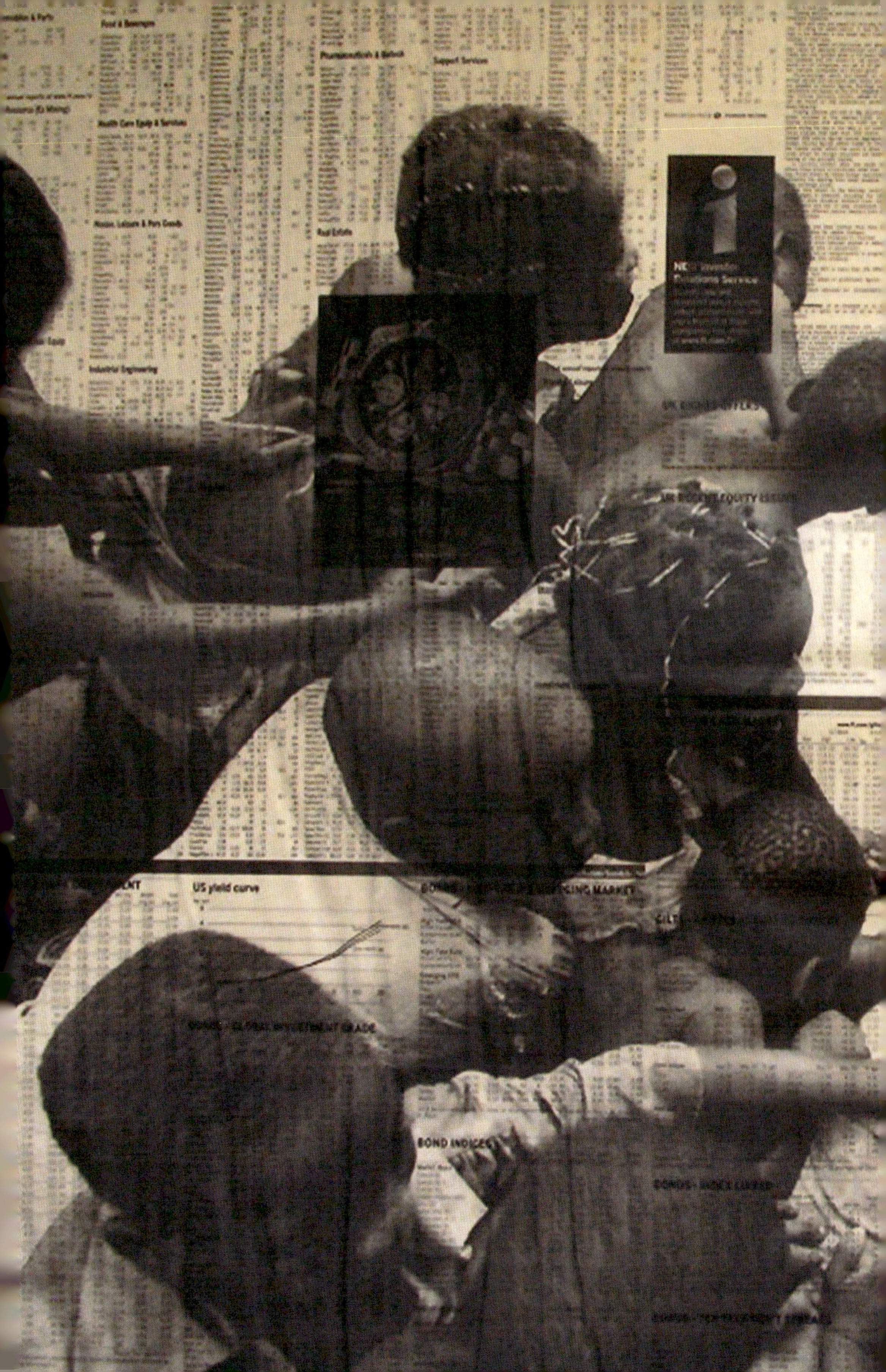

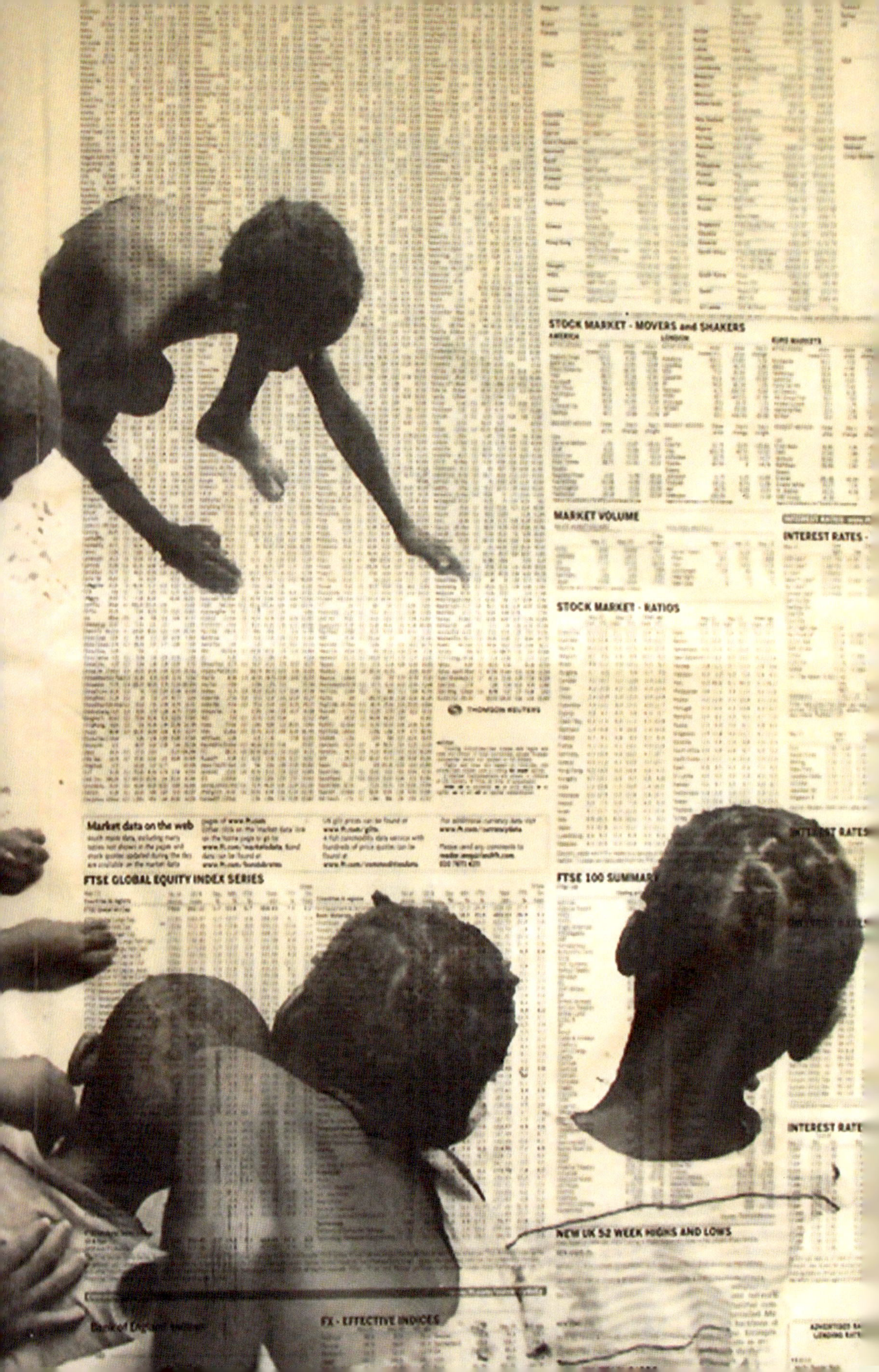

001 CAFE OF EQUIVALENT$
"Playing around with the the
concoction, fabrication of value
in the global capitalist financial
system, we engaged city workers
with some simple truth derivatives
during their lunchbreak, equating
their salaried/bonus income with
the cost of lunch for a worker
in the producing countries, that
is, Mozambique, Brazil, Indonesia,
Bangladesh."
CREATOR Peter Kennard and Cat
Picton Phillips
SOURCE www.kennardphillipps.com
DATE 2008

Mandela, held in South African prison for 27 years

Apartheid

Boy

SHELL OUT OF
NAMIBIA
AND
SOUTH AFRICA

NO FUEL FOR
APARTHEID

ANTI APARTHEID MOVEMENT 13 Mandela St·London NW1· 01·387 7966

LOOK BEFORE YOU BUY • BOYCOTT THE PRODUCTS OF
BOYCOTT
APARTHEID

ANTI APARTHEID MOVEMENT 13 Mandela St·London NW1· 01·387 7966

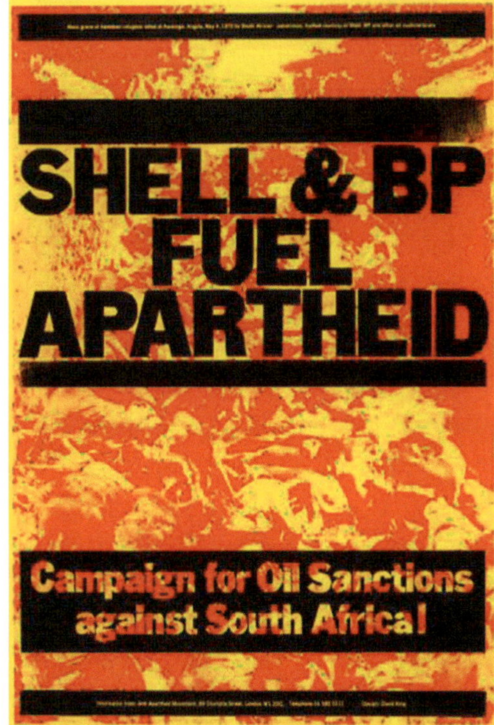
SHELL & BP
FUEL
APARTHEID

Campaign for Oil Sanctions
against South Africa!

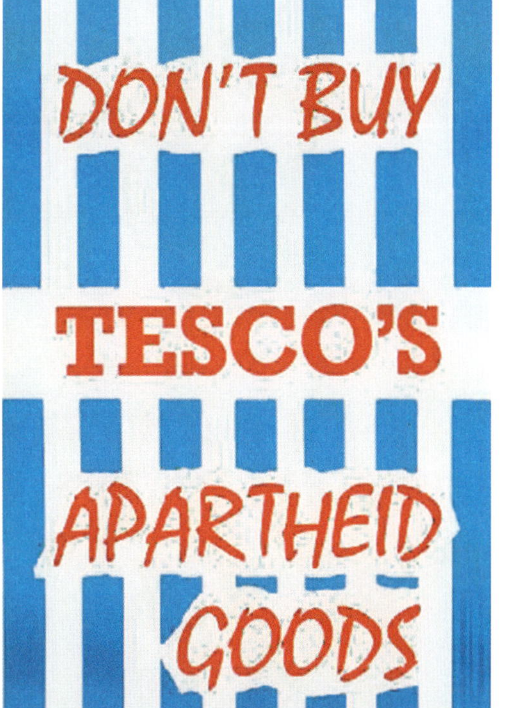
DON'T BUY
TESCO'S
APARTHEID
GOODS

006

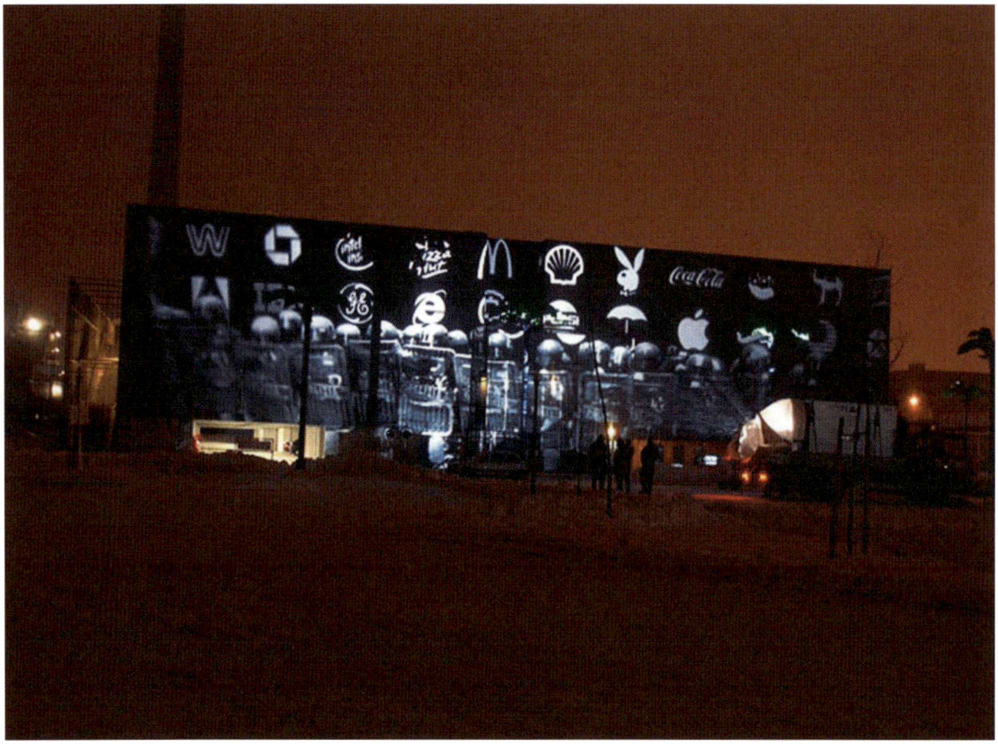

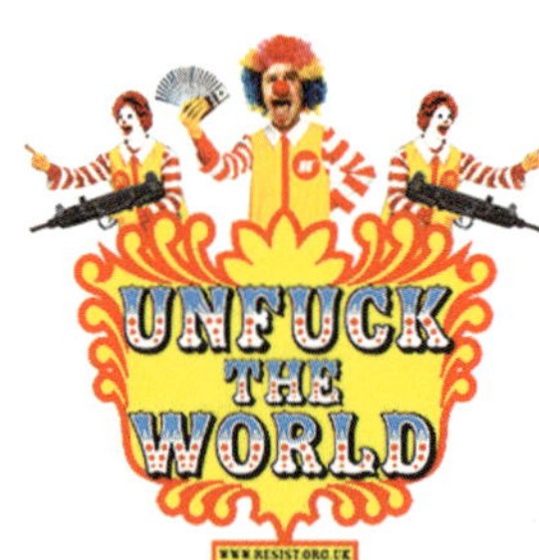

007
008

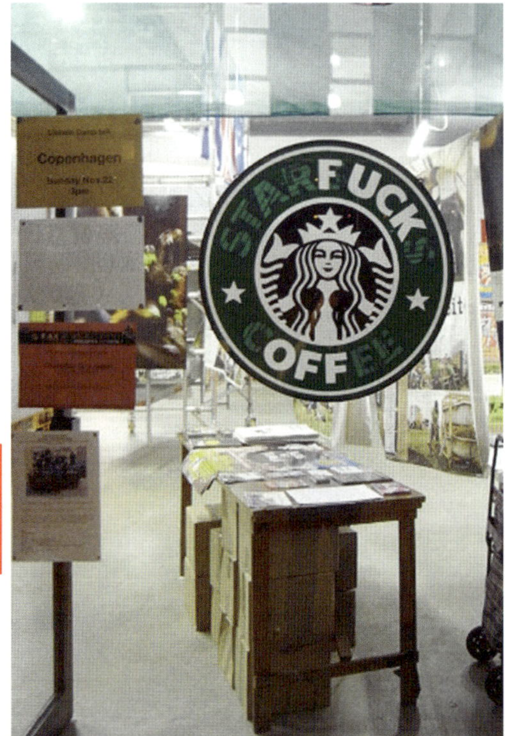

009

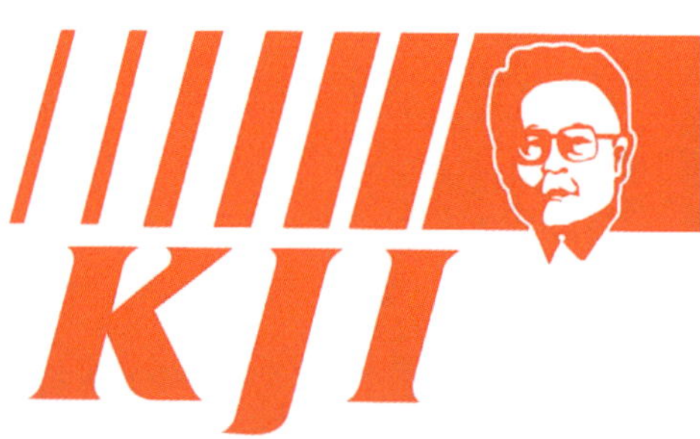

001 NELSON MANDELA HELD IN SOUTH
AFRICAN PRISON FOR 27 YEARS
CREATOR Grapus
SOURCE Steven Heller and Carol
Wells, eds., *The Graphic Impera-
tive: International Posters for
Peace, Social Justice, and the
Environment,* 1965-2005 [Boston:
Massachusetts College of Arts,
2005], p. 28.

002 SHELL OUT OF NAMIBIA AND SOUTH
AFRICA: NO FUEL FOR APARTHEID
SOURCE www.library.northwestern.edu

003 SANCTIONS YEAR AGAINST APARTHEID
SOURCE www.library.northwestern.edu

004 SHELL & BP FUEL APARTHEID:
CAMPAIGN FOR OIL SANCTIONS
AGAINST SOUTH AFRICA!
"Mass grave of Namibian refugees
killed at Kassinga, Angola, May 4,
1978, by South African paratroops,
fueled courtesy of Shell, BP
and other oil multinationals."
Information from Anti Apartheid
Movement.
SOURCE www.library.northwestern.edu

005 DON'T BUY TESCO'S APARTHEID GOODS
SOURCE www.library.northwestern.edu

006 HUMO PROJECTIONS, "COMPLEX CONTROL"
PROJECTION ONTO A CINEPLEX
A week-long series of HUge and
MObile projections using Europe's
largest slide projector on the
back of a truck.
CREATOR Movement of the
Imagination
SOURCE www.movementoftheimaginati-
on.org/humo5.html

007 WHOSE WORLD? OUR WORLD
CREATOR Noel Douglas
SOURCE www.taipeibiennial.org/2008/
DATE 2008

008 FUCK OFF
CREATOR Noel Douglas
SOURCE www.flickr.comphotos/
48714801@N00sets/72157623716667011
DATE 2009

009 KJI 2004
Inspired by "an omnipresent fast-
food character" Kim Jong-il, the
North Korean dictator watches
over the exhibition space. "The
first reaction to this piece
of work from most people is to
laugh," says Barnbrook. "I kind of
like that. Making a valid political point by entertaining rather
than ranting is always a better
way to go."
CREATOR Jonathan Barnbrook
SOURCE Wallpaper.com

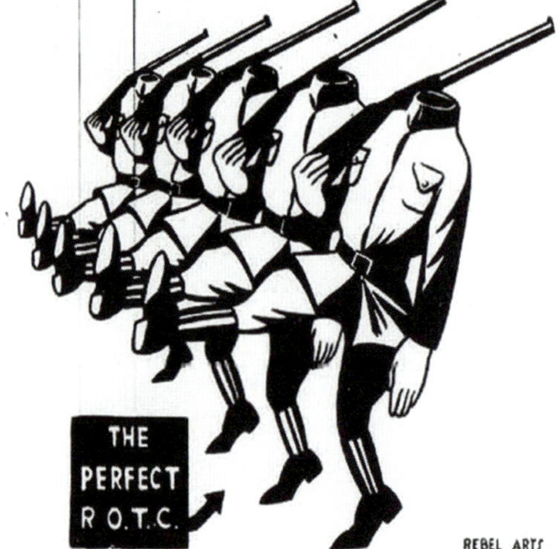
ABOLISH!
the R.O.T.C.!
THE PERFECT R.O.T.C.
REBEL ARTS

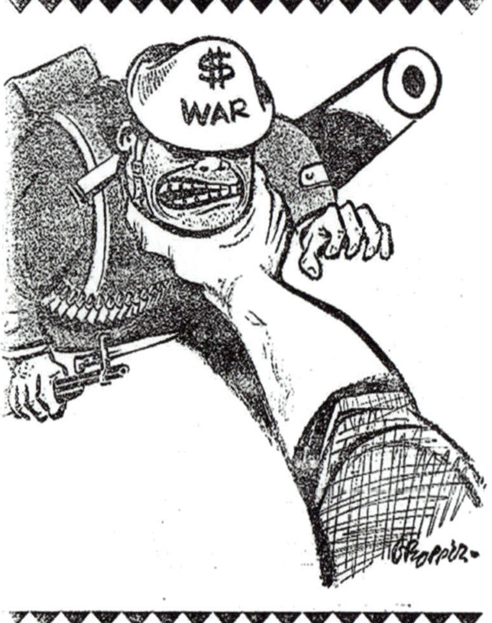
FIGHT WAR!
$ WAR
National Committee for the Student Congress Against War

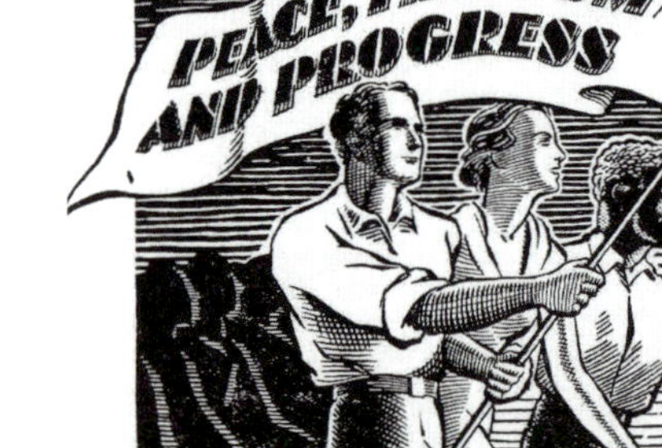
PEACE, FREEDOM AND PROGRESS

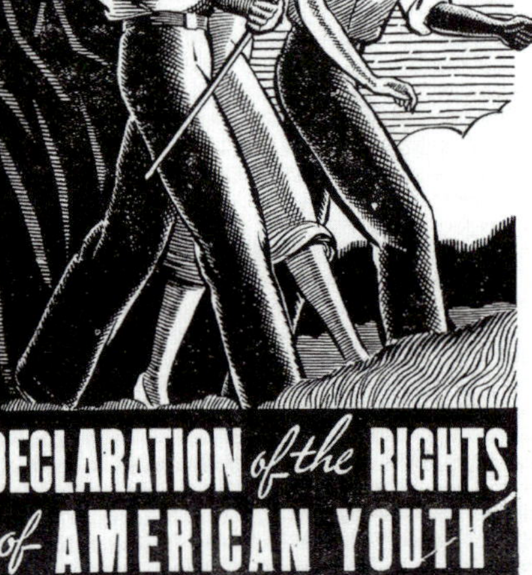
DECLARATION of the RIGHTS of AMERICAN YOUTH

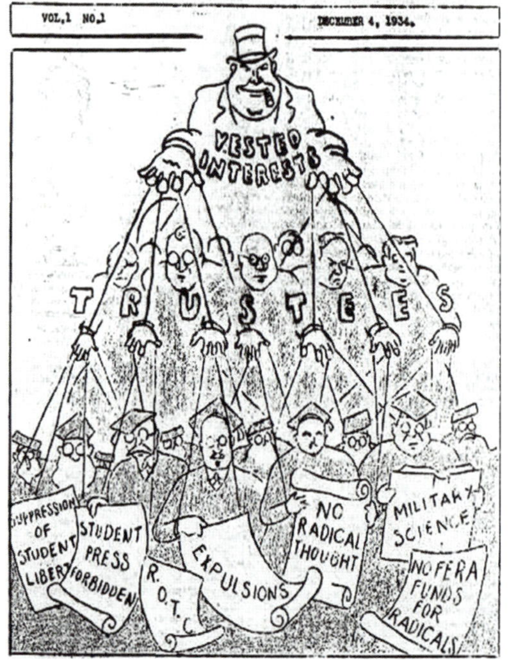
THE STUDENT CALL
VOL.1 NO.1
DECEMBER 4, 1934.
VESTED INTERESTS
TRUSTEES
SUPPRESSION OF STUDENT LIBERTY
STUDENT PRESS FORBIDDEN
R.O.T.C.
EXPULSIONS
NO RADICAL THOUGHT
MILITARY SCIENCE
NO FERA FUNDS FOR RADICALS

005

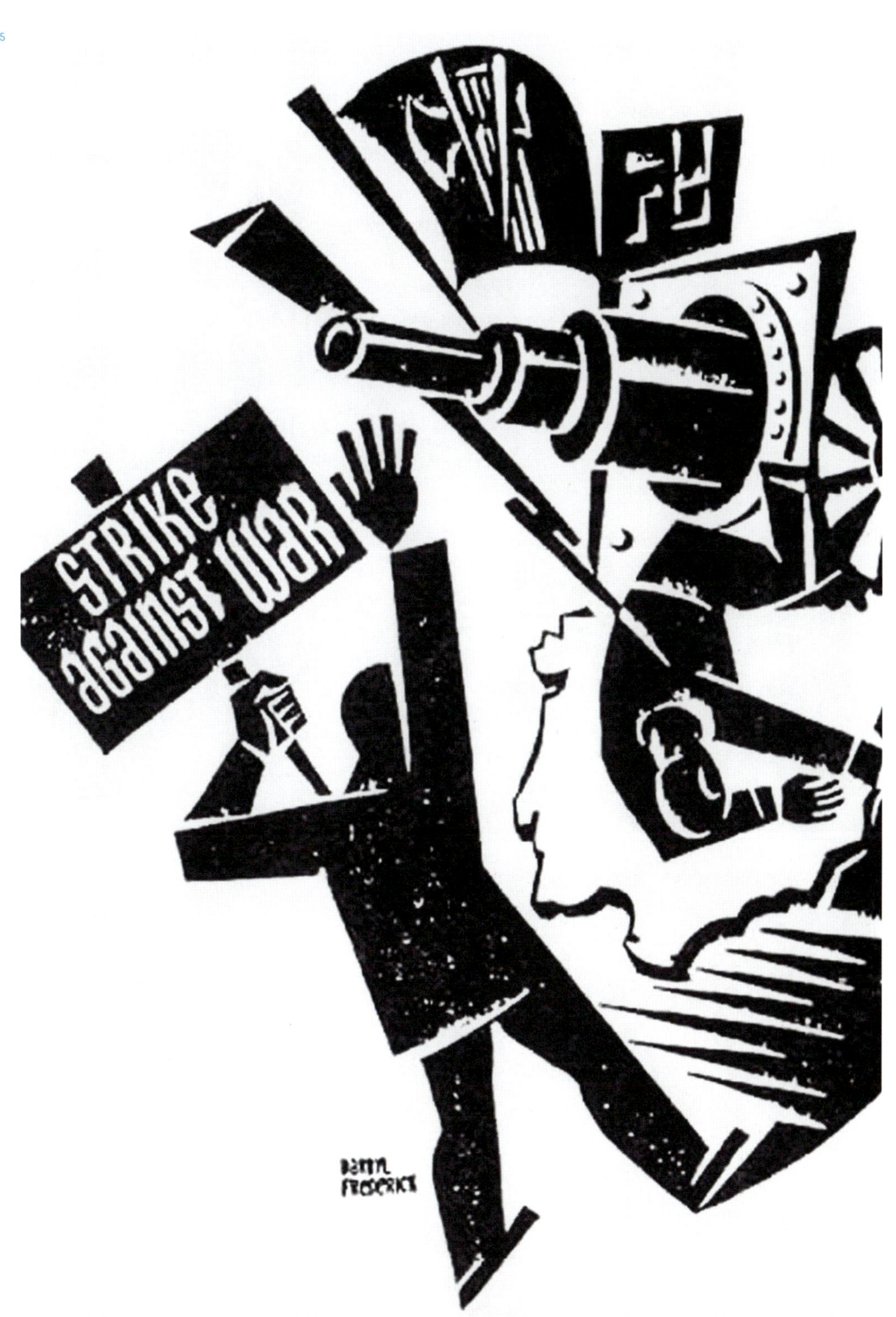

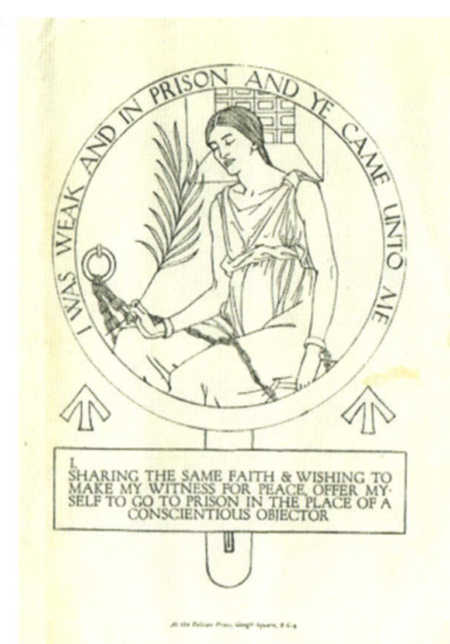
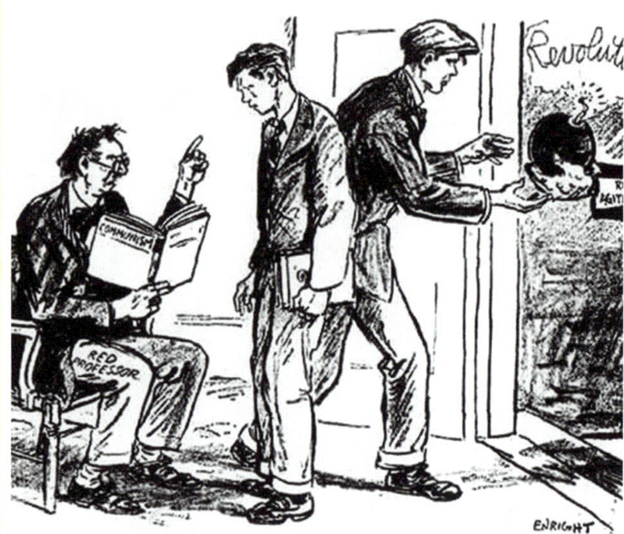

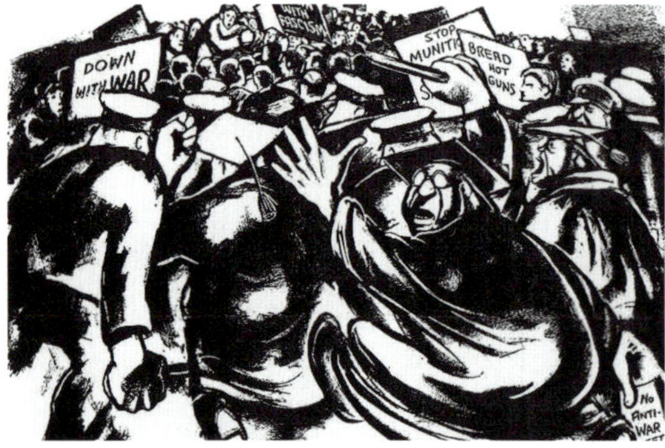
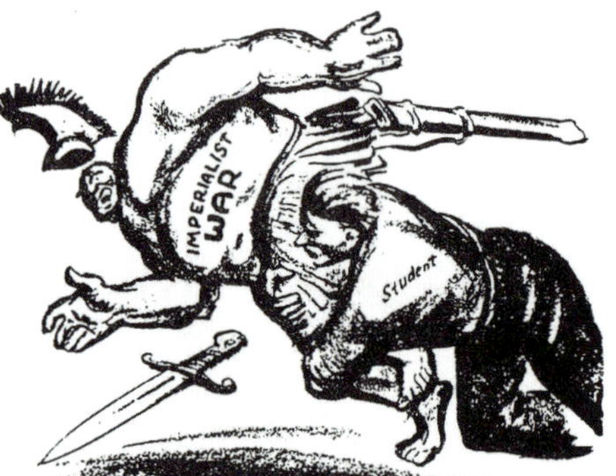

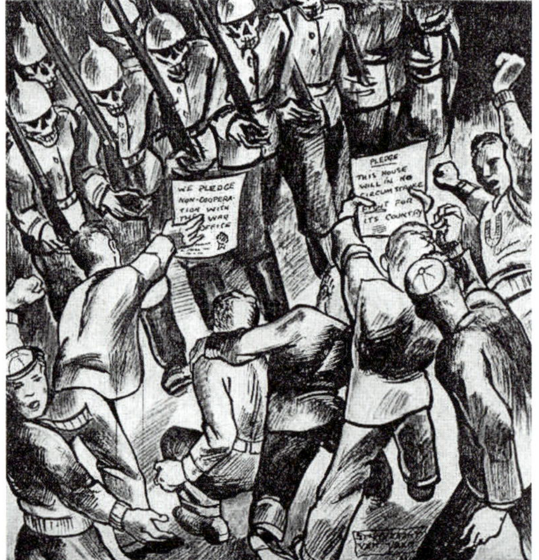
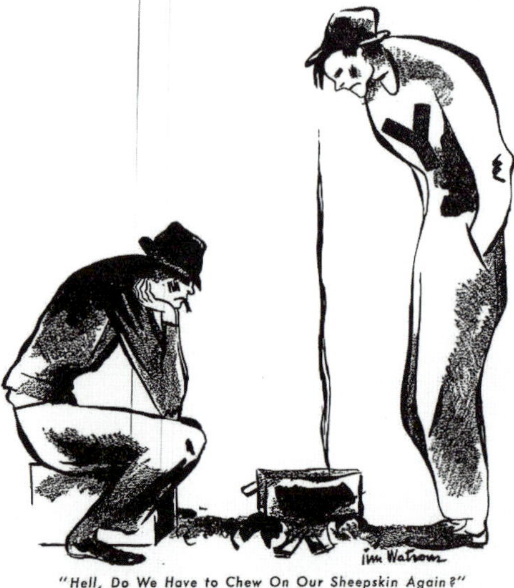

"Hell, Do We Have to Chew On Our Sheepskin Again?"

012
013

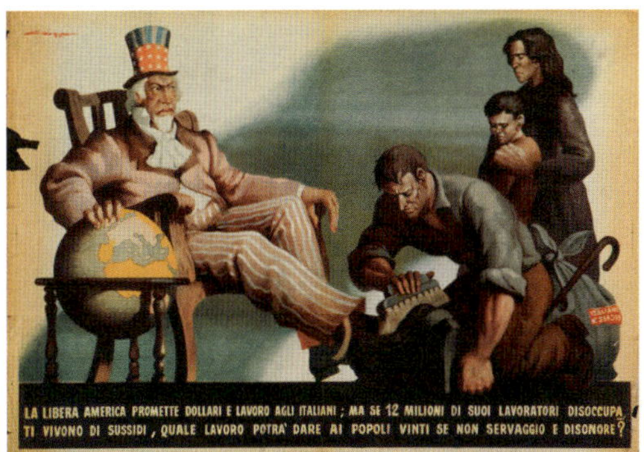

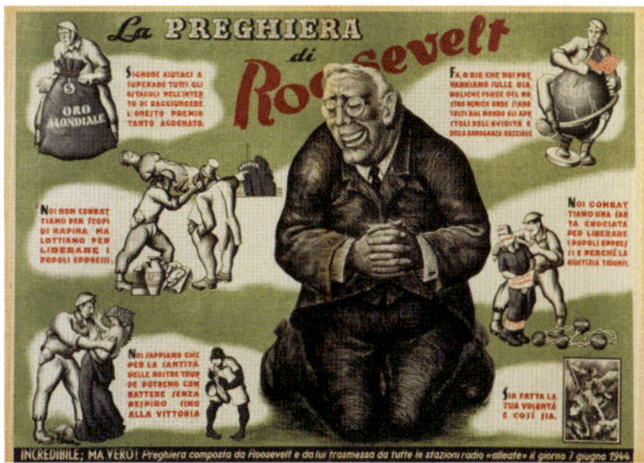

014
015
016

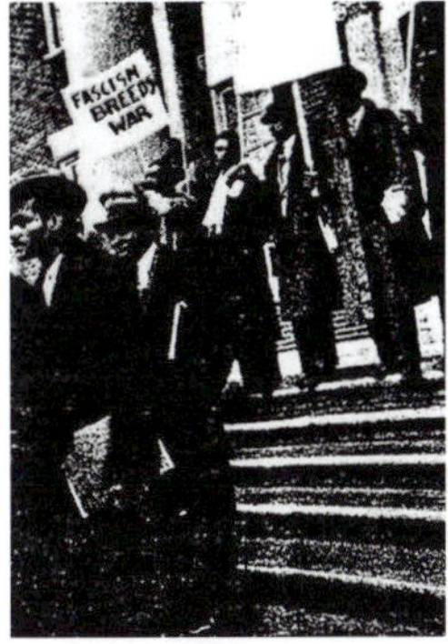

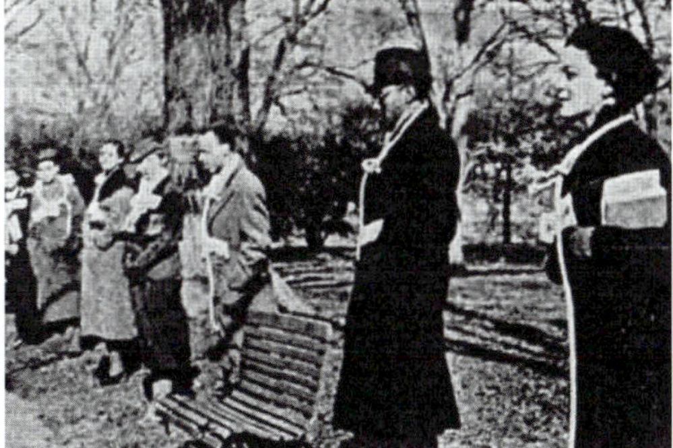

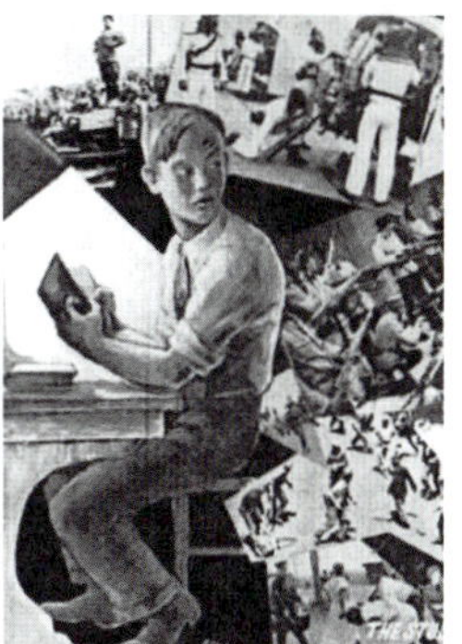

017
018

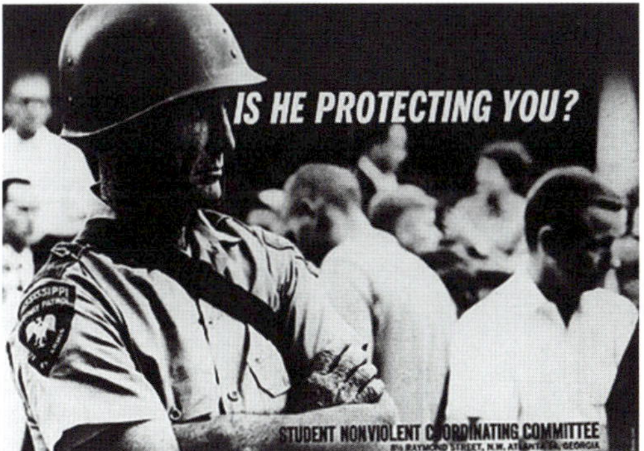

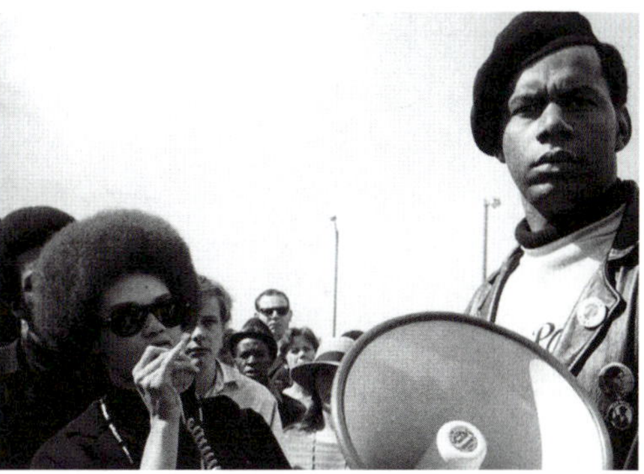

019
020
021

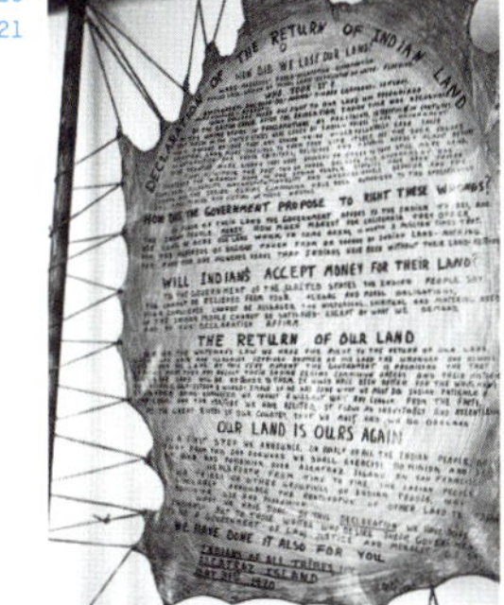

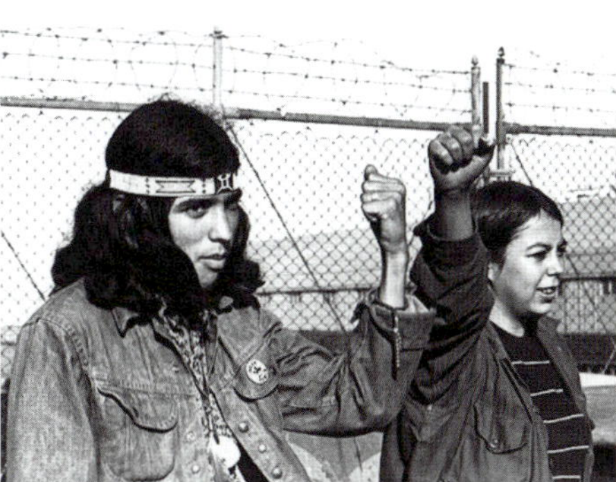

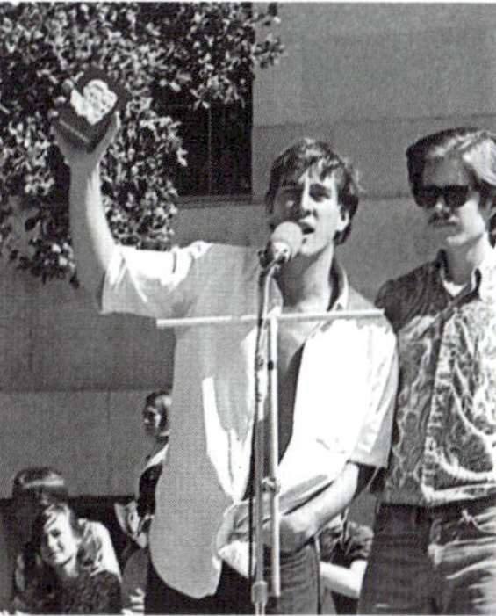

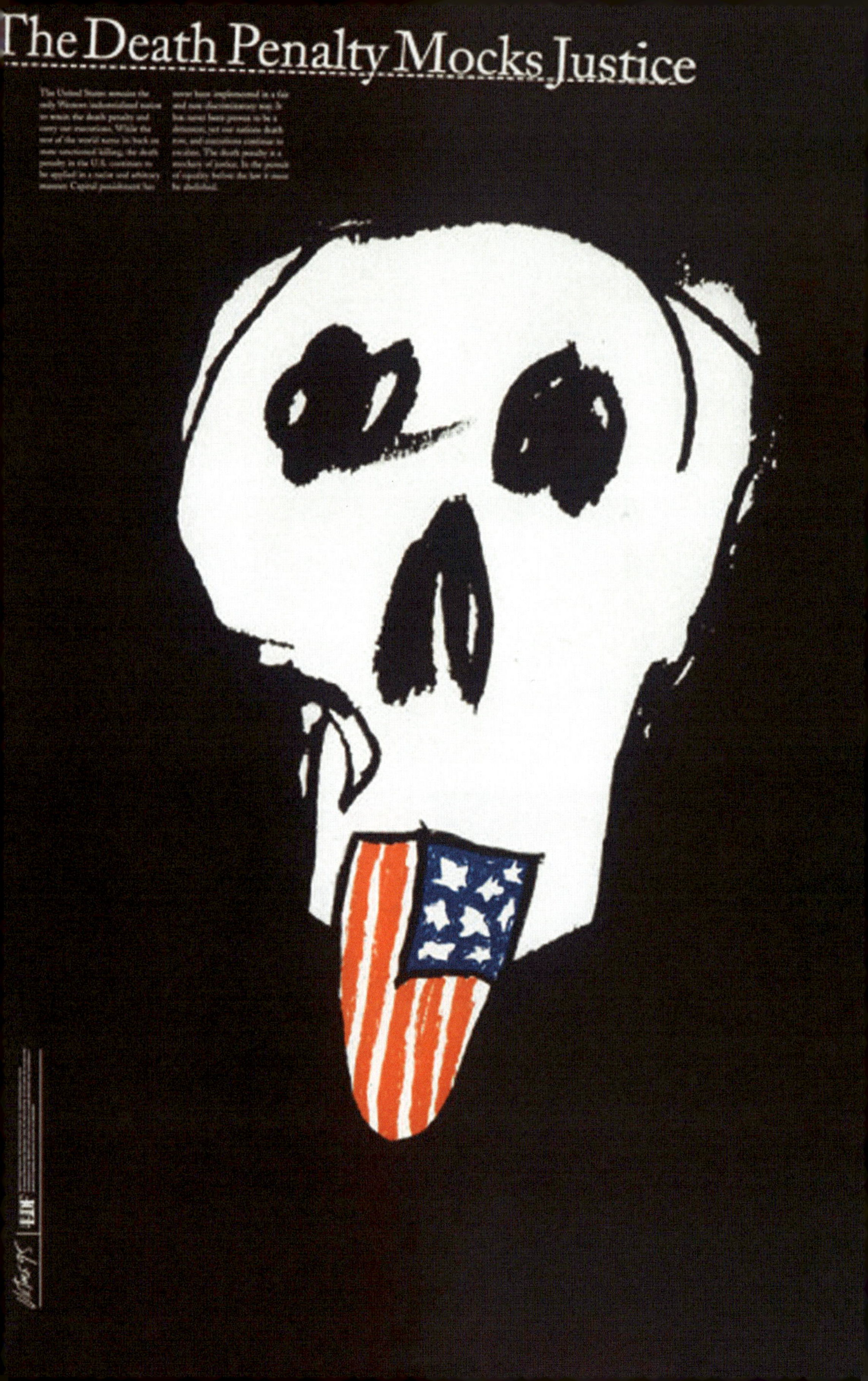

The Death Penalty Mocks Justice

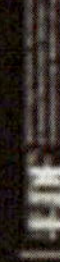

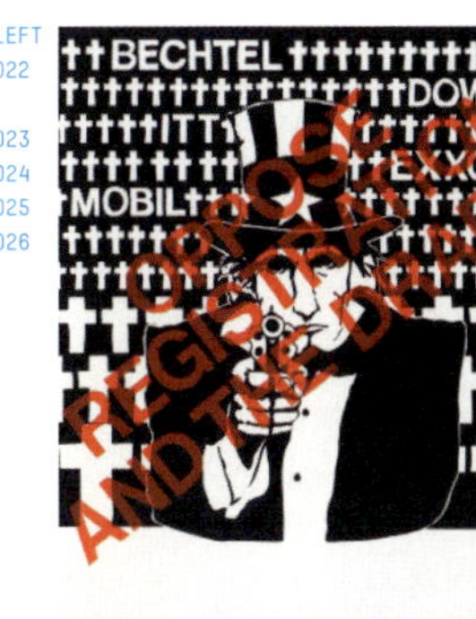

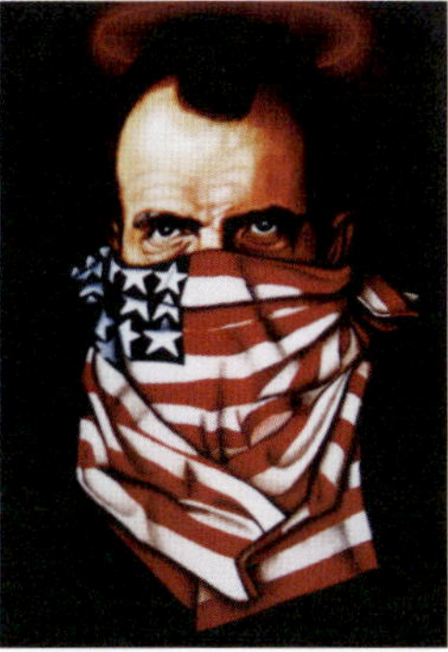

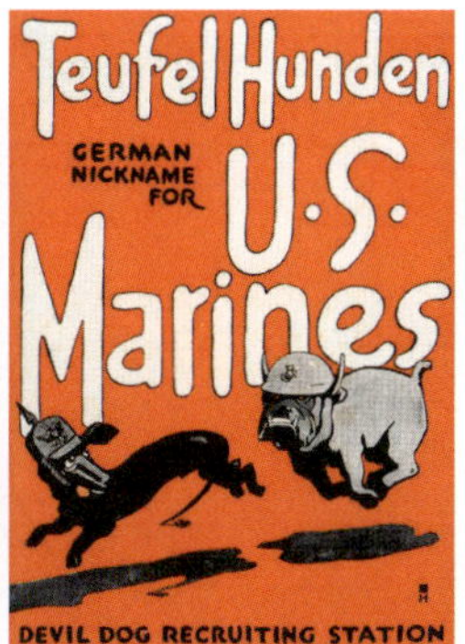

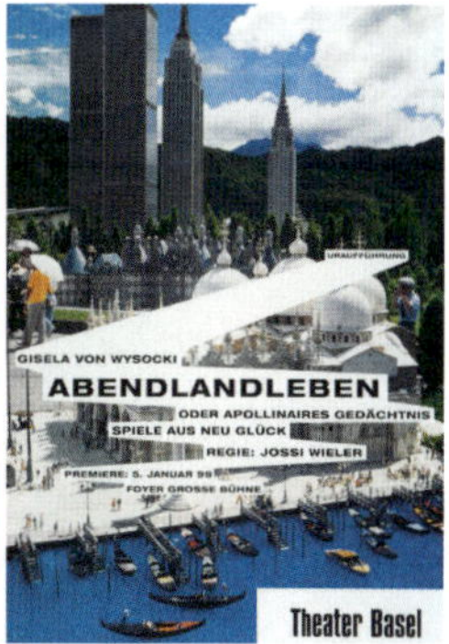

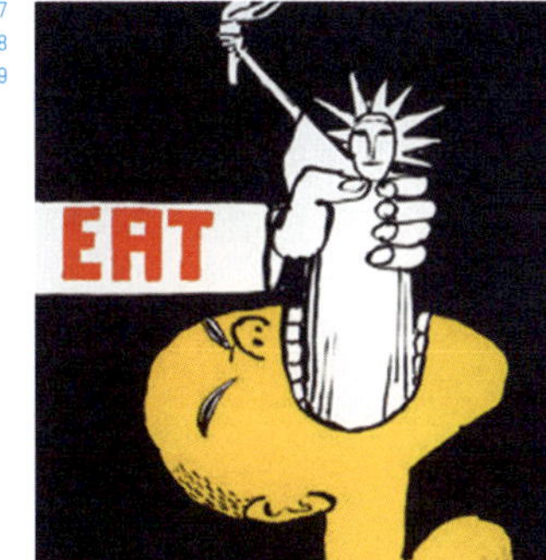

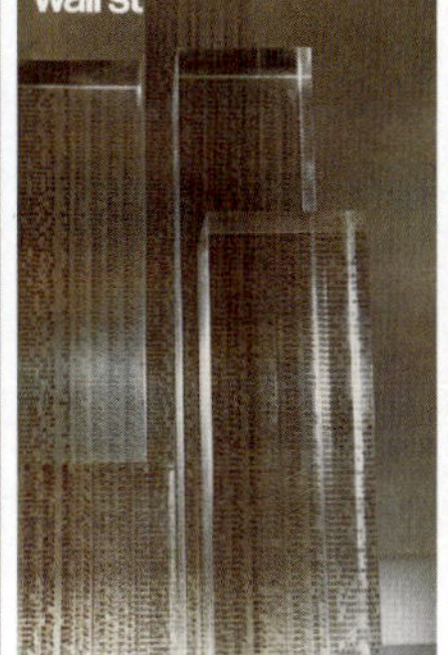

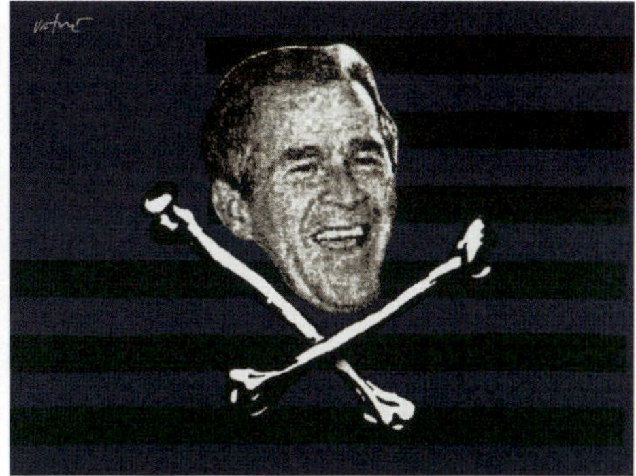

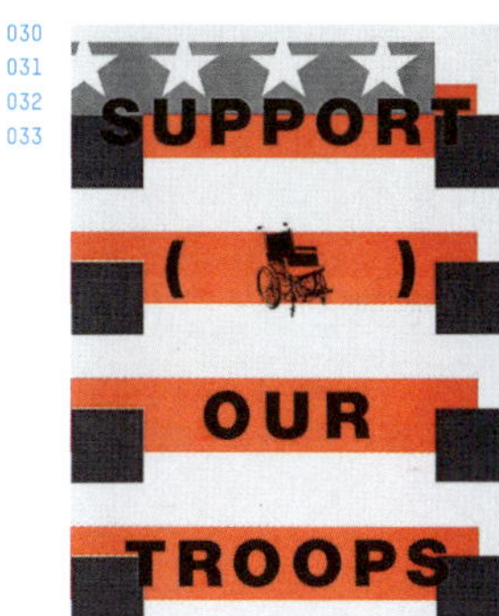

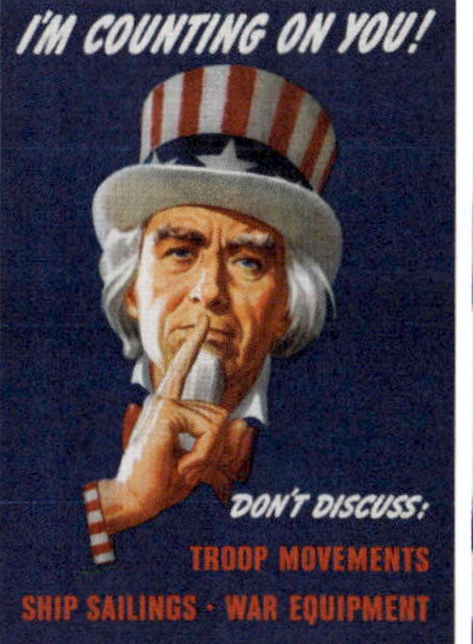

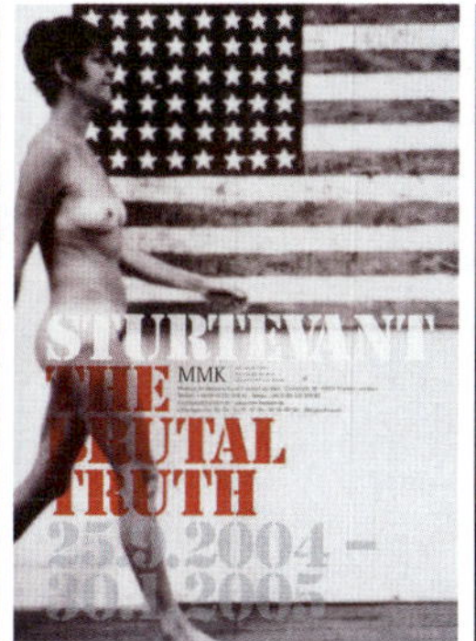

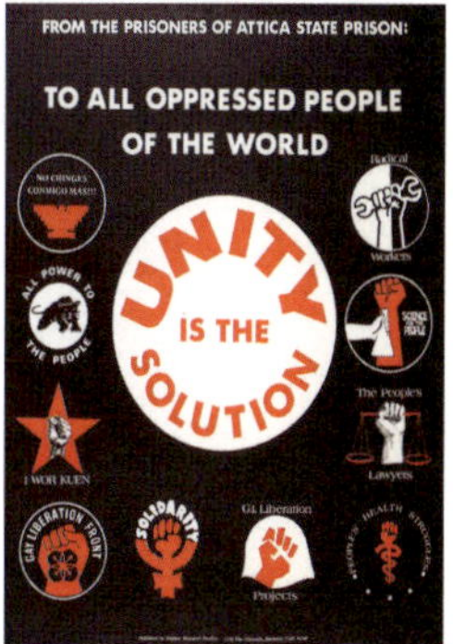

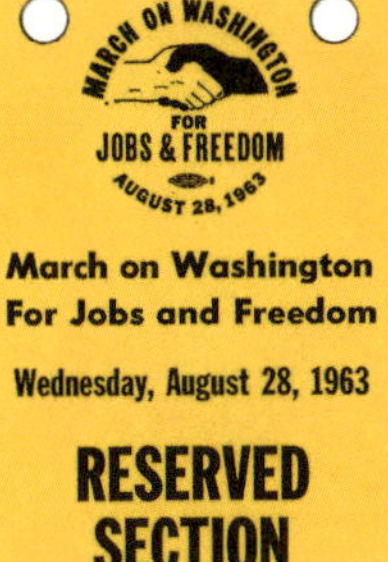
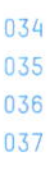

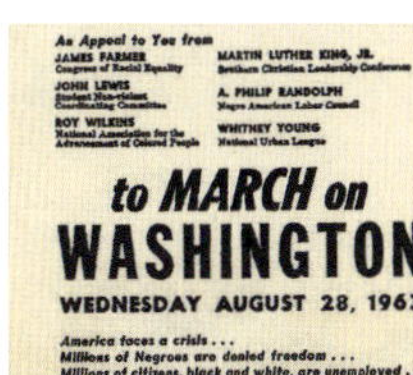
An Appeal to You from
JAMES FARMER
Congress of Racial Equality
MARTIN LUTHER KING, JR.
Southern Christian Leadership Conference
JOHN LEWIS
Student Nonviolent
Coordinating Committee
A. PHILIP RANDOLPH
Negro American Labor Council
ROY WILKINS
National Association for the
Advancement of Colored People
WHITNEY YOUNG
National Urban League

to MARCH on WASHINGTON

WEDNESDAY AUGUST 28, 1963

America faces a crisis...
Millions of Negroes are denied freedom...
Millions of citizens, black and white, are unemployed...

We demand: — Meaningful Civil Rights Laws
— Massive Federal Works Program
— Full and Fair Employment
— Decent Housing
— The Right to Vote
— Adequate Integrated Education

In our community, groups and individuals are mobilizing for
the August 28th demonstration. For information regarding
your participation, call the local Coordinating Committee
for the

MARCH ON WASHINGTON
FOR JOBS AND FREEDOM

1417 You Street, N.W.
ADams 2-2320

CO-CHAIRMEN
Rev. Walter E. Fauntroy, Coordinator
Joseph A. Beavers
E. Charles Brown
Edward A. Hailes
Julius W. Hobson
Sterling Tucker

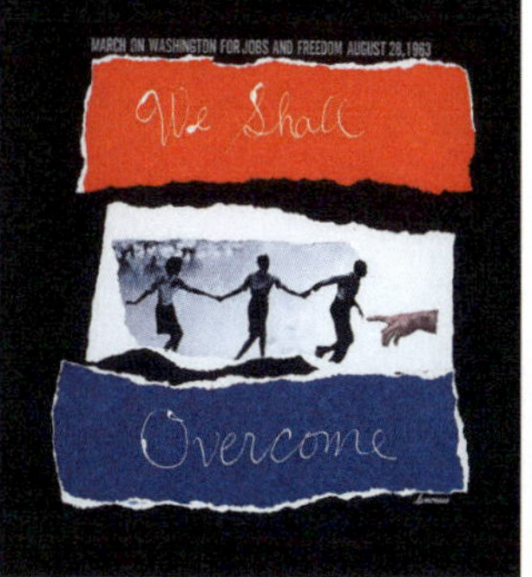

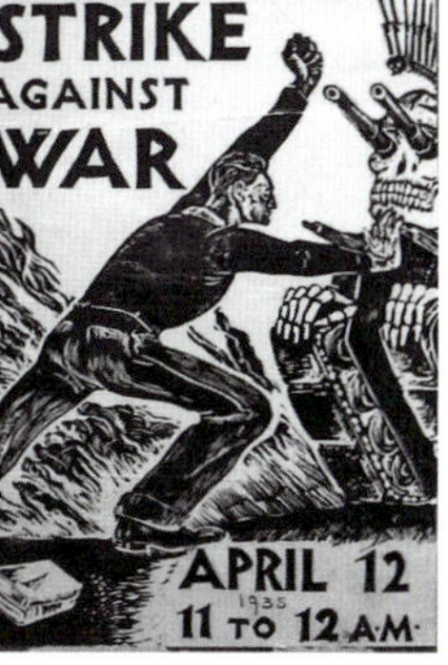

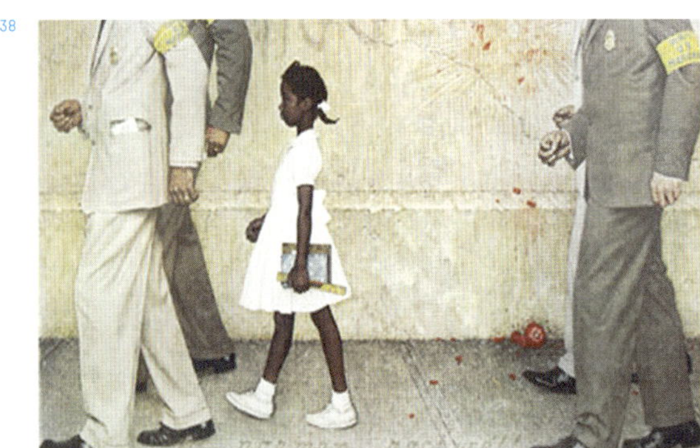

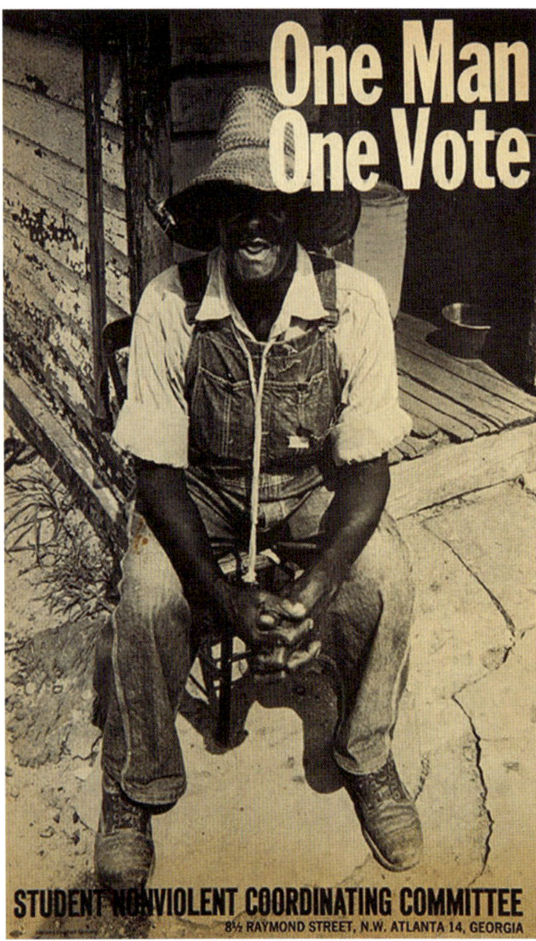

038

039

001 ABOLISH THE R.O.T.C.!
Graphic from *The Student Outlook*
3, nos. 3-4.
CREATOR Rebel Arts / *The Student Outlook*
SOURCE newdeal.feri.org
DATE 1934

002 FIGHT WAR
Cover illustration for pamphlet
of the National Committee for the
Student Congress Against War.
CREATOR William Gropper
SOURCE Chicago Historical Society
DATE 27 December 1932

003 DECLARATION OF THE RIGHTS OF
AMERICAN YOUTH
CREATOR American Youth Congress
SOURCE newdeal.feri.org

004 VESTED INTERESTS
Cover to *The Student Call* 1, no. 1.
CREATOR *The Student Call*
SOURCE newdeal.feri.org
DATE 4 December 1934

005 STRIKE AGAINST WAR
Cover art from *The Student Advocate*,
the American Student Union magazine.
CREATOR Darryl Frederick
SOURCE www.docspopuli.org
DATE 12 April 1935

006 I WAS WEAK AND IN PRISON AND YE
CAME UNTO ME
Leaflet from the No-Conscription
Fellowship.
CREATOR No-Conscription Fellowship
SOURCE pw20c.mcmaster.ca
DATE 1916

007 THEORY AND PRACTICE
Editorial cartoon from the *New
York American*.
CREATOR *New York American*
SOURCE newdeal.feri.org

008 WE NEVER TAUGHT 'EM THAT
Refers to the attempt of antira-
dical vigilantes and repressive
college administrators to disrupt
the first national student strike
against war.
SOURCE newdeal.feri.org
DATE 24 April 1934

009 JINGOISM
CREATOR *The Daily Worker*
SOURCE newdeal.feri.org

010 WE PLEDGE NON-COOPERATION
CREATOR *The Student Outlook*
SOURCE newdeal.feri.org
DATE December 1933

011 HELL, DO WE HAVE TO CHEW ON OUR
SHEEPSKINS AGAIN?
CREATOR SLID magazine *Revolt*

SOURCE newdeal.feri.org
DATE December 1932

012 LA LIBERA AMERICA...
[FREE AMERICA PROMISES DOLLARS
AND WORK TO ITALIANS]
CREATOR Dante Coscia
SOURCE Plakatsammlung Museum
für Gestaltung Zürich
DATE 1944

013 LA PREGHIERA DI ROOSEVELT
[ROOSEVELT'S PRAYER]
SOURCE Plakatsammlung Museum
für Gestaltung Zürich
DATE 1944

014 STUDENTS IN DEMONSTRATION,
HOWARD UNIVERSITY
CREATOR NAACP's *Crisis Magazine*
SOURCE newdeal.feri.org

015 HOWARD UNIVERSITY ANTILYNCHING
PROTEST
CREATOR *The Student Outlook*
SOURCE newdeal.feri.org
DATE February 1935

016 THE STUDENTS RETURN
CREATOR *The Student Outlook*
SOURCE newdeal.feri.org
DATE October 1934

017 IS HE PROTECTING YOU?
CREATOR Student Nonviolent
Coordinating Committee
SOURCE americanhistory.si.edu
DATE 1963

018 KATHLEEN CLEAVER SPEAKING AT
BLACK PANTHER RALLY
CREATOR Roz Payne
SOURCE www.newsreel.us
DATE 1969

019 THE PROCLAMATION
CREATOR Ilka Hartmann
SOURCE www.ilkahartmann.com

020 WE WILL NOT GIVE UP
Indian occupiers moments after
the removal from Alcatraz Island.
CREATOR Ilka Hartmann
SOURCE www.ilkahartmann.com
DATE 11 June 1971

021 BURN DRAFT CARDS, UC BERKELEY
CREATOR Ilka Hartmann
SOURCE www.ilkahartmann.com
DATE c. 1967-68

022 DEATH PENALTY MOCKS JUSTICE
CREATOR James Victore
SOURCE Plakatsammlung Museum
für Gestaltung Zürich
DATE 1995

023 OPPOSE REGISTRATION AND THE DRAFT
CREATOR Students for Peace

SOURCE newdeal.feri.org
DATE 1980

024 NIXON
CREATOR Bengt Nystrom
SOURCE Plakatsammlung Museum
für Gestaltung Zürich

025 TEUFEL HUNDEN
[DEVIL DOGS]
CREATOR US Marine Corps
SOURCE Library of Congress
DATE 1918

026 ABENDLANDLEBEN
[OCCIDENTAL LIFE, OR APPOLINAIRE'S
MEMORY: PLAYS FROM NEW LUCK]
CREATOR Emanuel Tschumi
SOURCE www.emanuel-tschumi.ch

027 EAT
CREATOR Tomi Ungerer
SOURCE Plakatsammlung Museum
für Gestaltung Zürich

028 WALL STREET
CREATOR Tomoko Miho
SOURCE Plakatsammlung Museum
für Gestaltung Zürich

029 BUSH PIRATE
CREATOR James Victore
SOURCE Plakatsammlung Museum
für Gestaltung Zürich

030 SUPPORT OUR TROOPS
CREATOR David Hutchins
SOURCE Plakatsammlung Museum
für Gestaltung Zürich

031 I'M COUNTING ON YOU!
CREATOR Leon Helguera
SOURCE Plakatsammlung Museum
für Gestaltung Zürich

032 STURTEVANT — THE BRUTAL TRUTH
CREATOR Gesellschaft für
Gestaltung, Frankfurt am Main
SOURCE MMK Museum für moderne Kunst
DATE 2004

033 UNITY IS THE SOLUTION
CREATOR Student Research Facility
SOURCE www.docspopuli.org
DATE mid 1970s

034 PLATFORM PASS
From the March on Washington,
where Martin Luther King
proclaimed, "I have a dream."
SOURCE americanhistory.si.edu
DATE 28 August 1963

035 HANDBILL, MARCH ON WASHINGTON
SOURCE americanhistory.si.edu
DATE 28 August 1963

036 WE SHALL OVERCOME
This souvenir portfolio was

produced by the National Urban
League for participants in the
March on Washington.
CREATOR Louis Lo Monaco
SOURCE americanhistory.si.edu
DATE 28 August 1963

037 STRIKE AGAINST WAR
SOURCE www.docspopuli.org
DATE 12 April 1935

038 THE PROBLEM WE ALL LIVE WITH
CREATOR Norman Rockwell
SOURCE en.wikipedia.org

039 ONE MAN, ONE VOTE
SOURCE americanhistory.si.edu

001

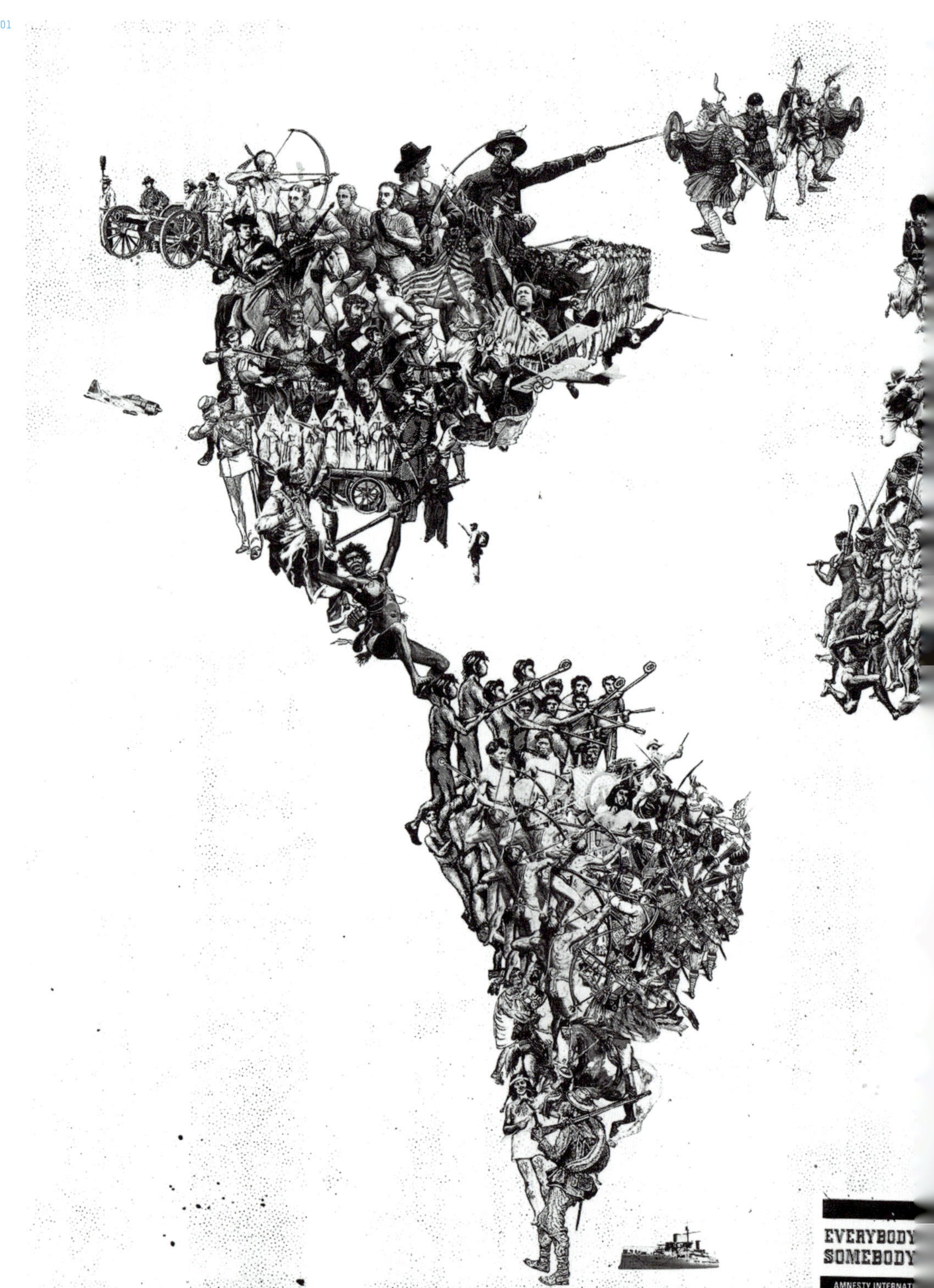

AMNESTY INTERNATIONAL

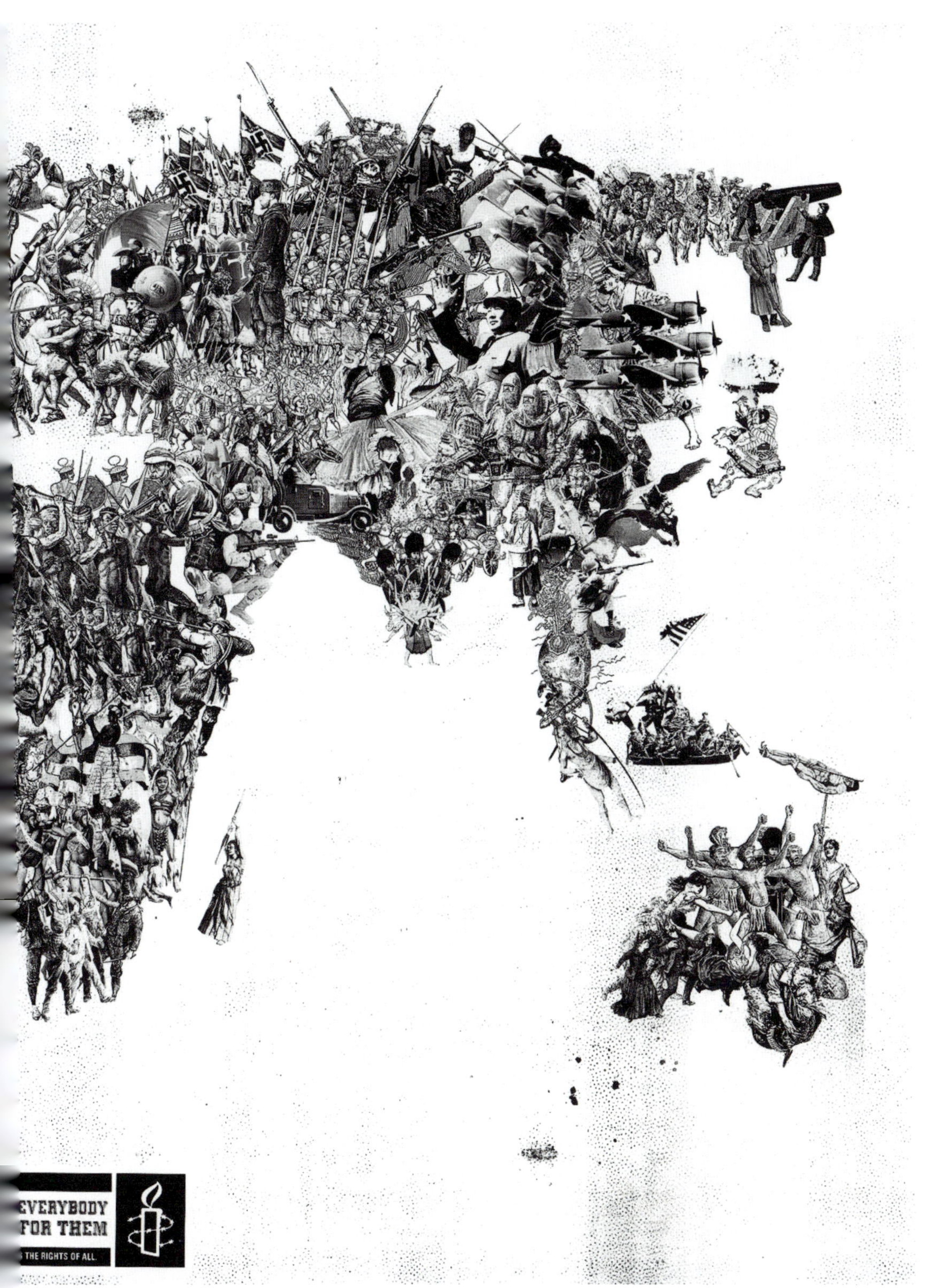
EVERYBODY
FOR THEM
THE RIGHTS OF ALL.

002

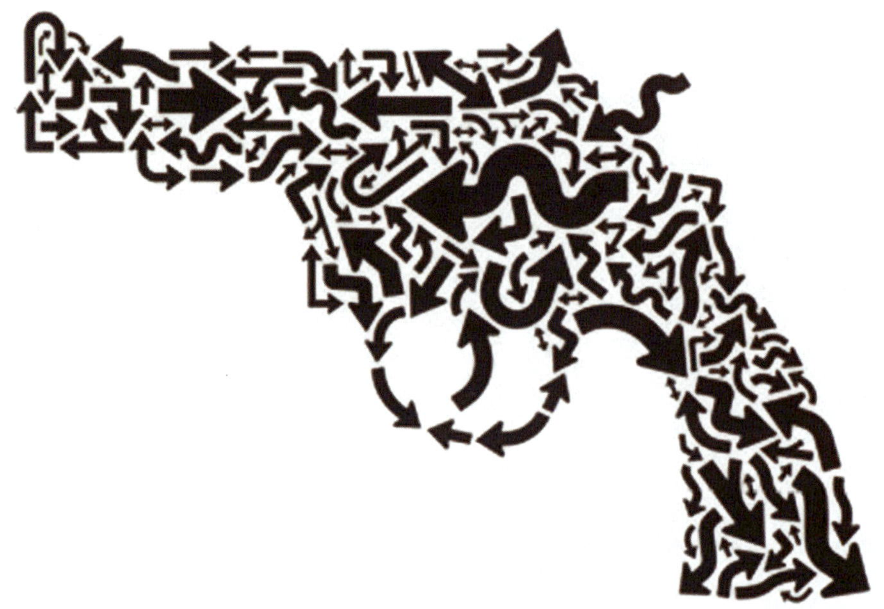

003

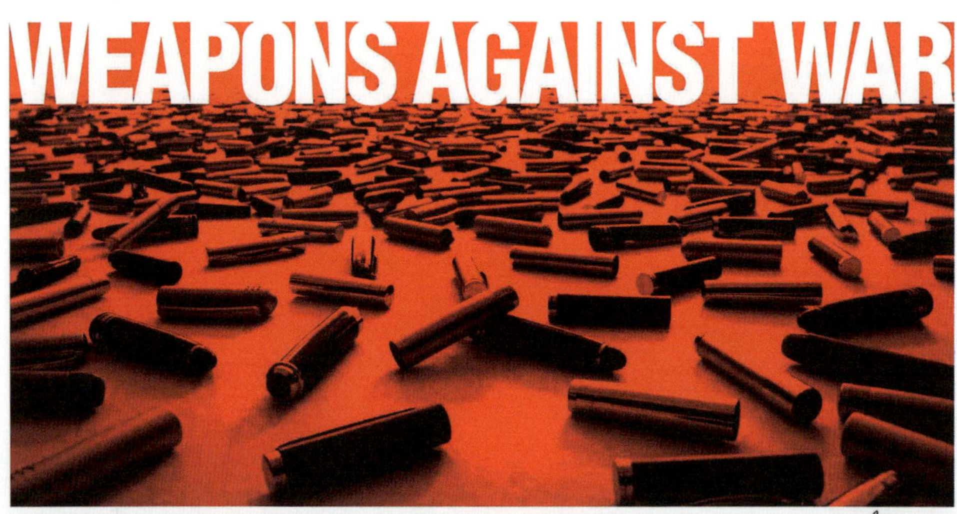

WEAPONS AGAINST WAR
By putting pen to paper, you can help end armed conflict in Darfur and Eastern Chad. Join thousands of others around the world in writing to Sudanese MPS and asking them (pleading with them if we must) to put an end to the atrocities being committed in these countries. To find out how you can make a difference, visit http://www.amnesty.org/en/armed-conflict
amnesty international

004
005

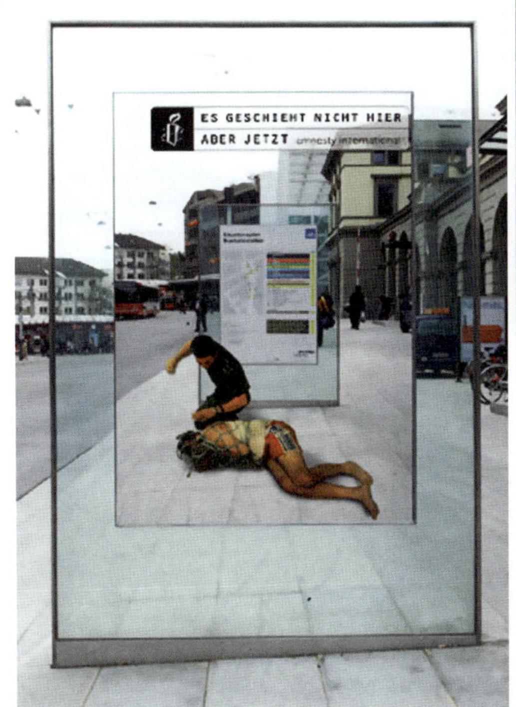

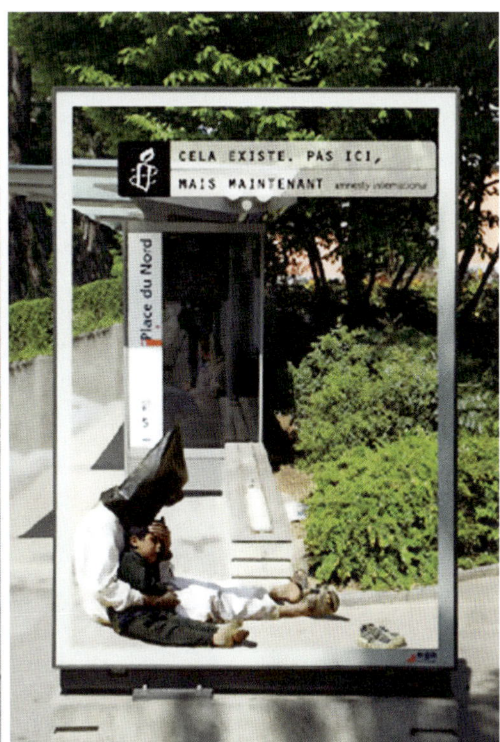

006
007

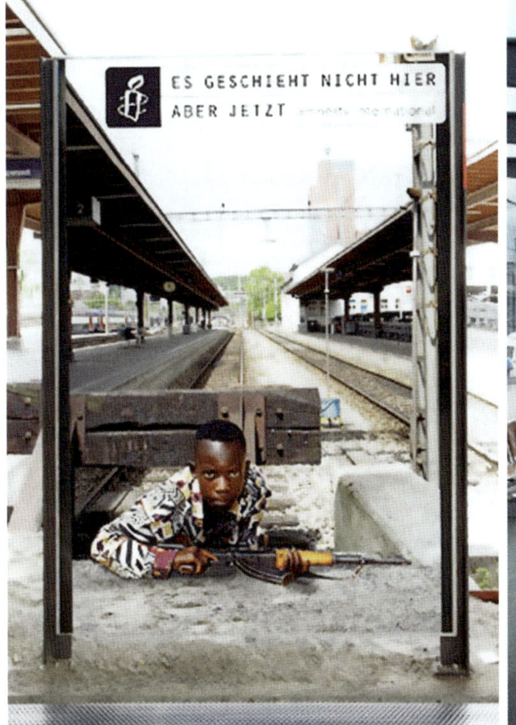

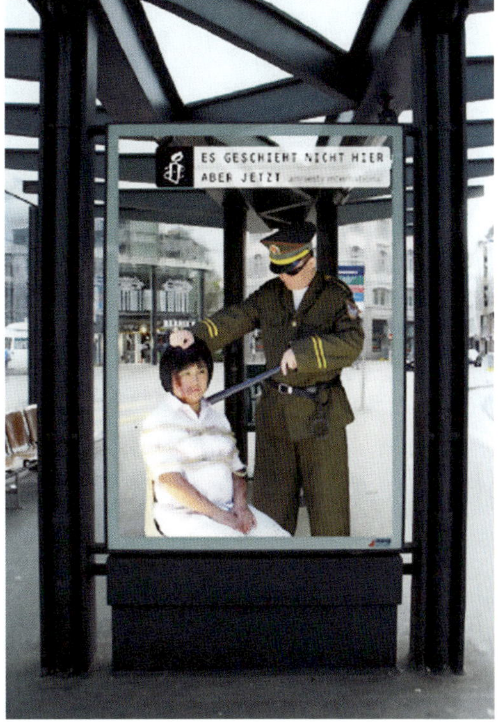

008
009
010
011

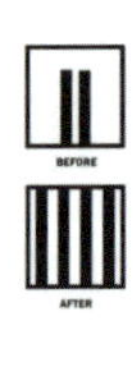

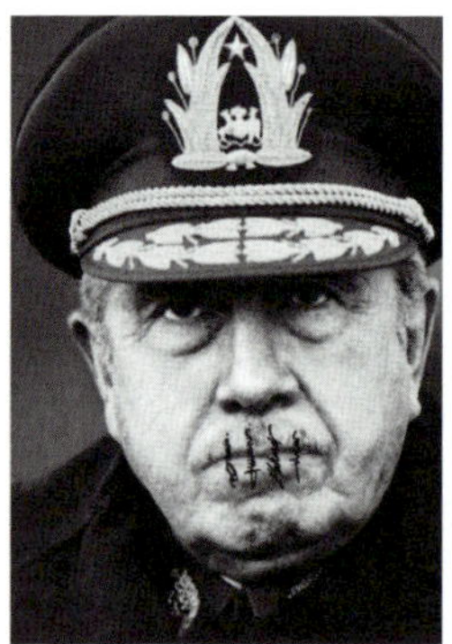

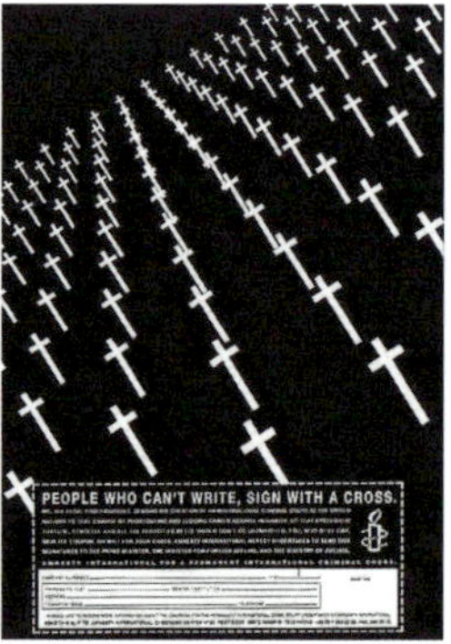

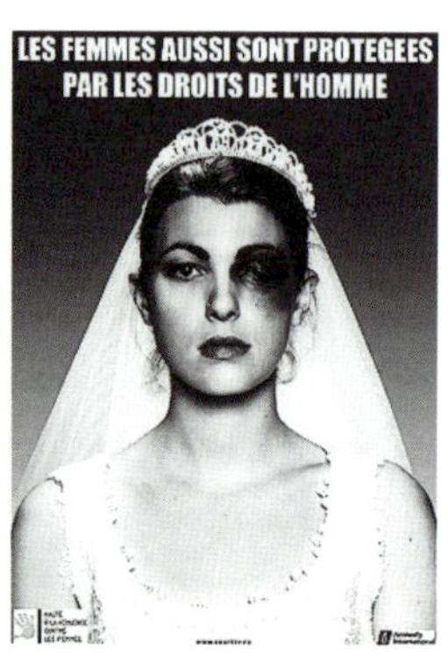

012
013
014
015

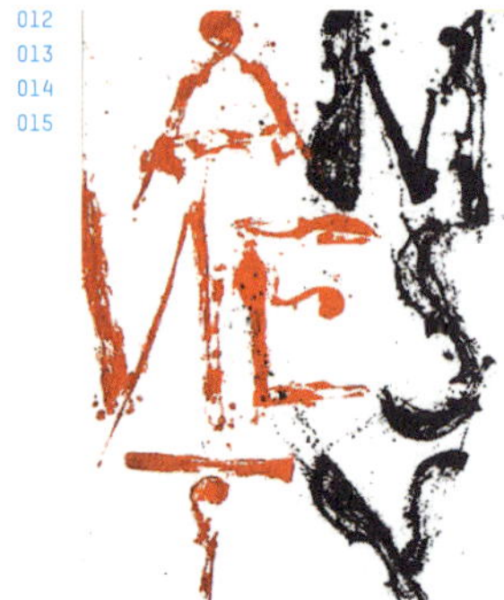

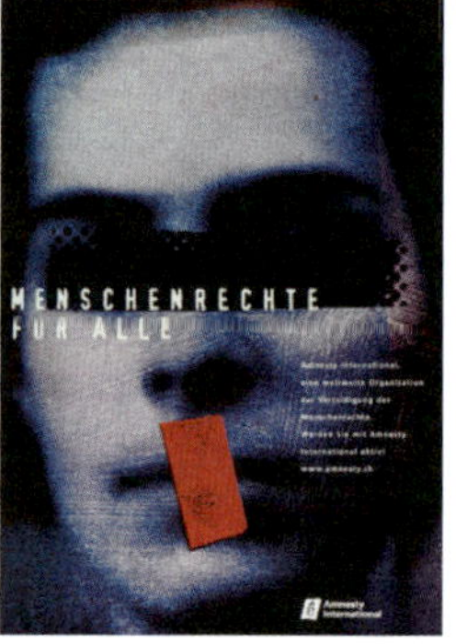

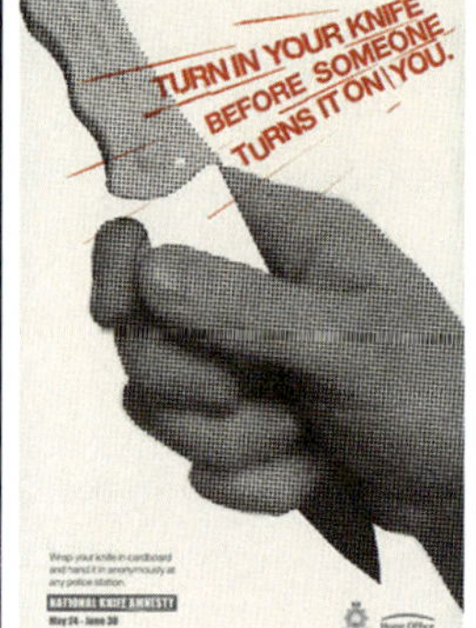

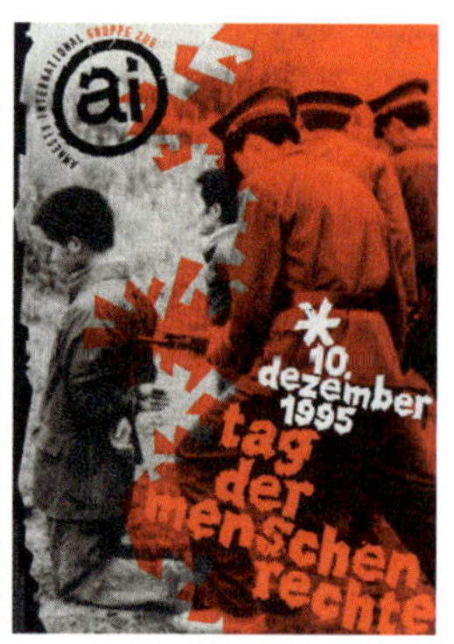

016
017
018
019

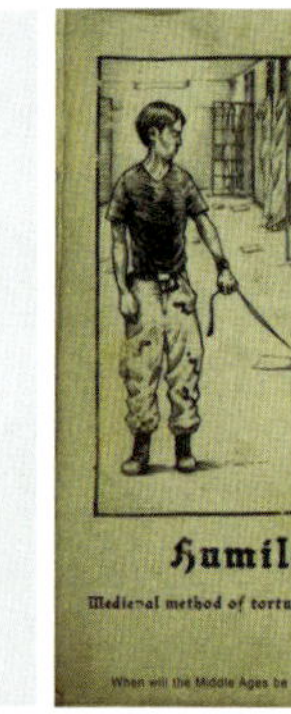

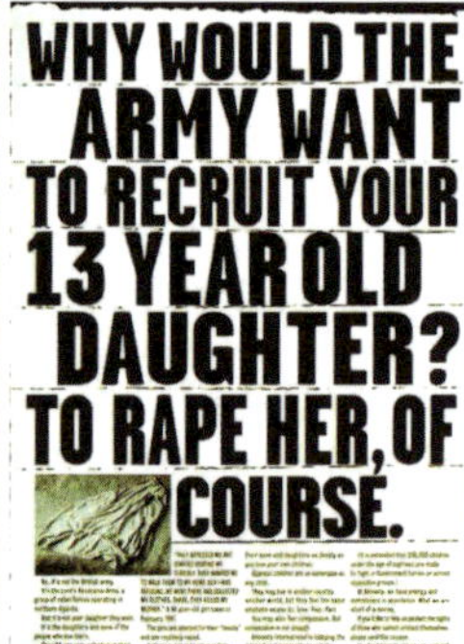

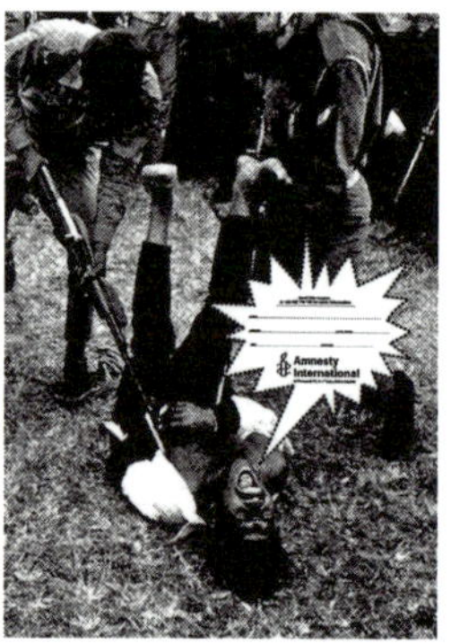

020
021

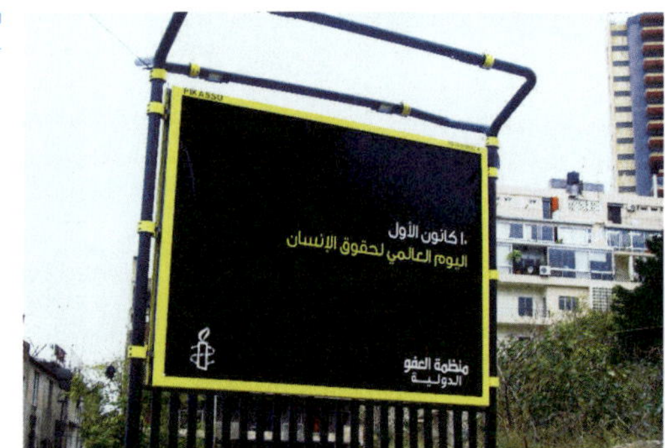

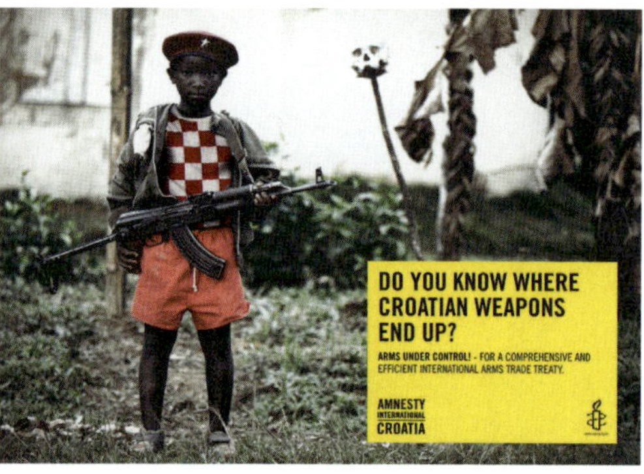

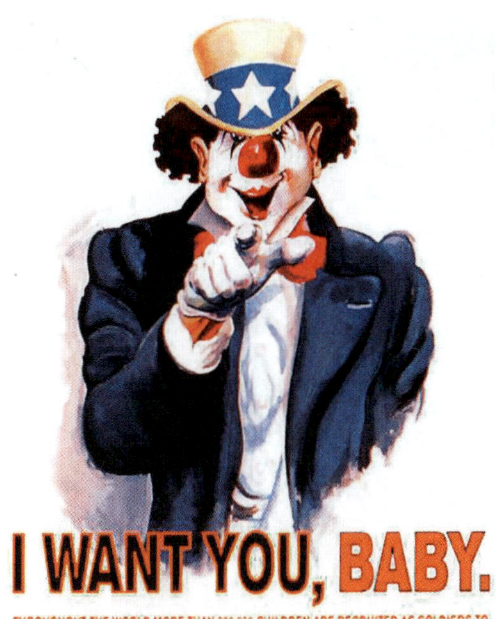

I WANT YOU, BABY.
THROUGHOUT THE WORLD MORE THAN 300.000 CHILDREN ARE RECRUITED AS SOLDIERS TO
PARTICIPATE IN WARS. WE WANT YOU TO HELP US STOP THE WORST ABUSES OF CHILD LABOUR.

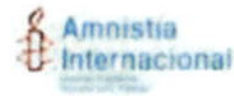

Amnistía
Internacional

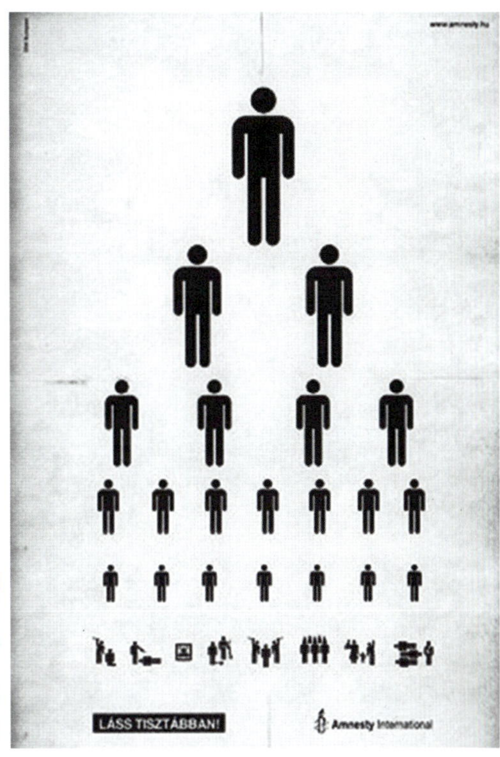

www.amnesty.hu
AMNESTY
LÁSS TISZTÁBBAN!
Amnesty International

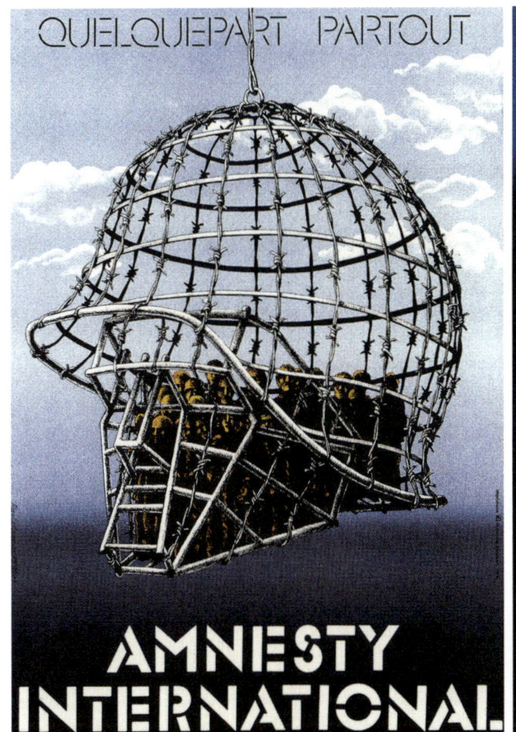

QUELQUEPART PARTOUT
AMNESTY
INTERNATIONAL.

夢をみる
鳥になる夢を
鳥になりどこかに
翔び去る夢を
狂ったように……
詩・著行　金芝河
AMNESTY

026

OGGI
231
232
MAKE SOME NOISE FOR THOSE WHO CAN'T BE HEARD
FREEDOM WEEK 30 JULY - 5 AUGUST
AMNESTY
INTERNATIONAL

027

WE WILL NEVER LET MONEY
HIDE REALITY FROM US.
WE REFUSE MONEY FROM MULTINATIONAL CORPORATIONS
AND GOVERNMENTS. OUR ACTION IS SUPPORTED BY YOUR
DONATIONS ONLY. WWW.AMNESTY.FR
AMNESTY
INTERNATIONAL

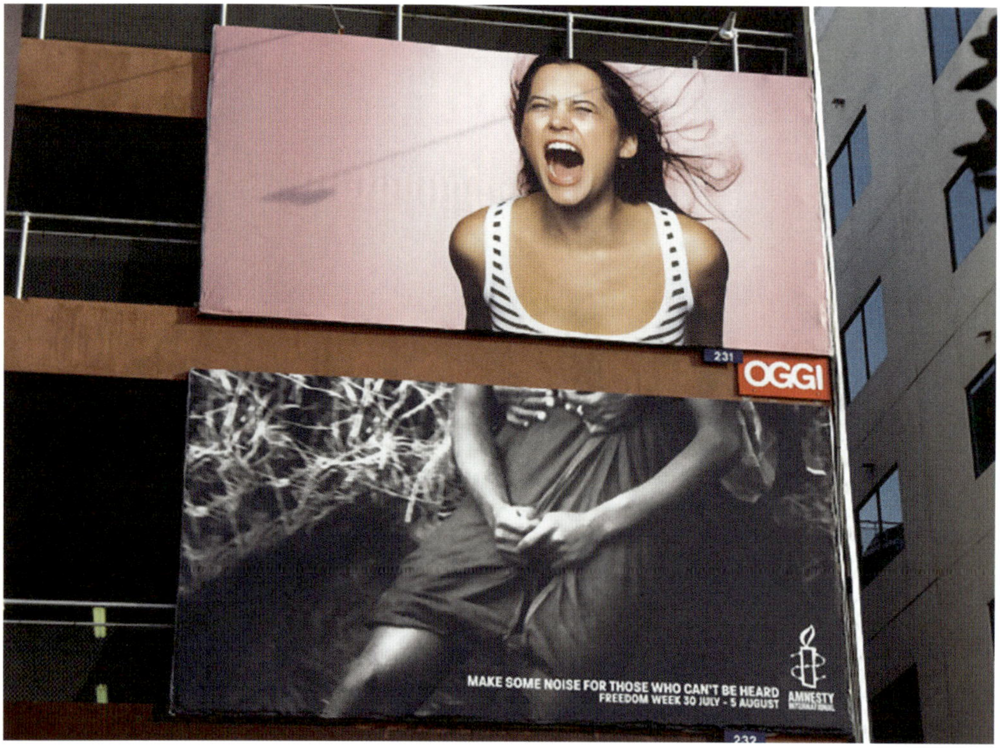

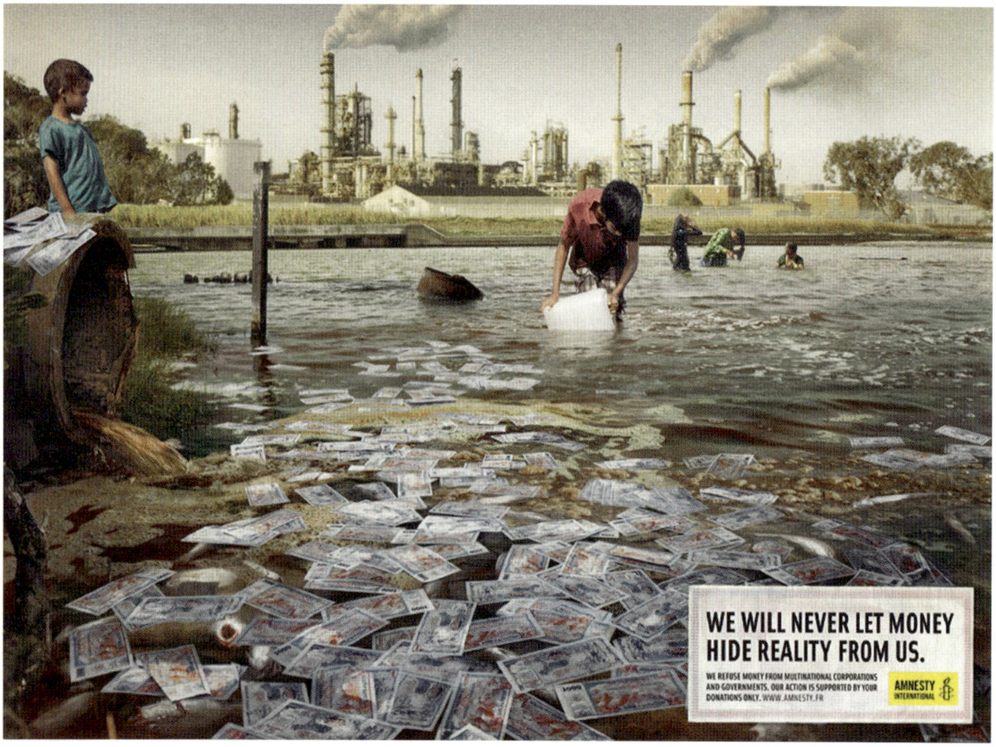

028
029

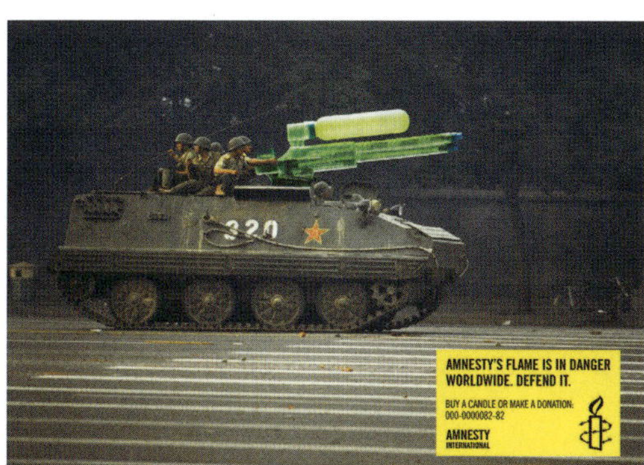

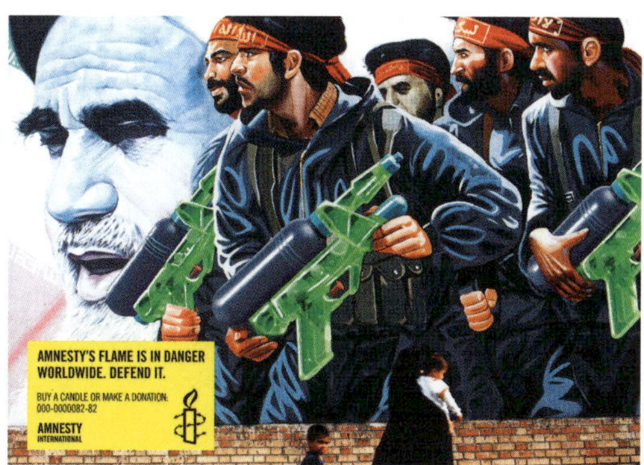

030
031

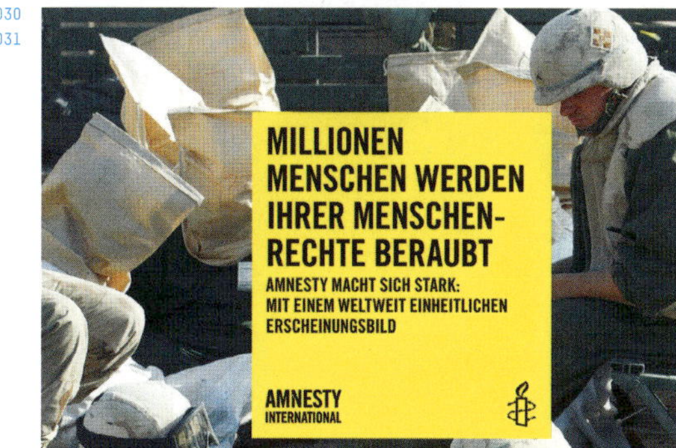

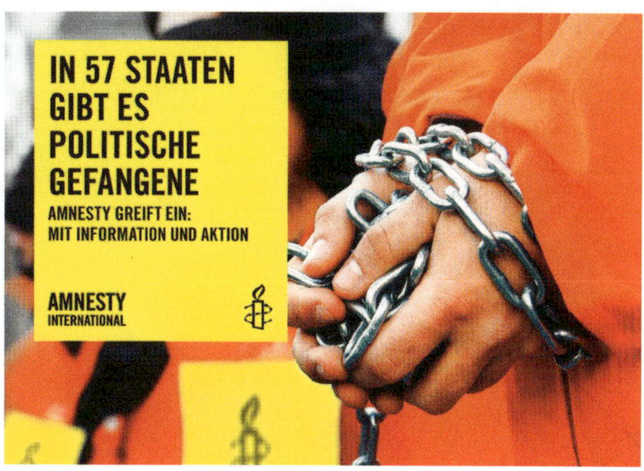

032

033

AMNESTY
INTERNATIONAL

034

INDIFFERENCE TURNS REALITY INTO
CONTRADICTION
(((DEMAND DIGNITY)))   AMNISTÍA
INTERNACIONAL
LA PAZ
CALLE 11

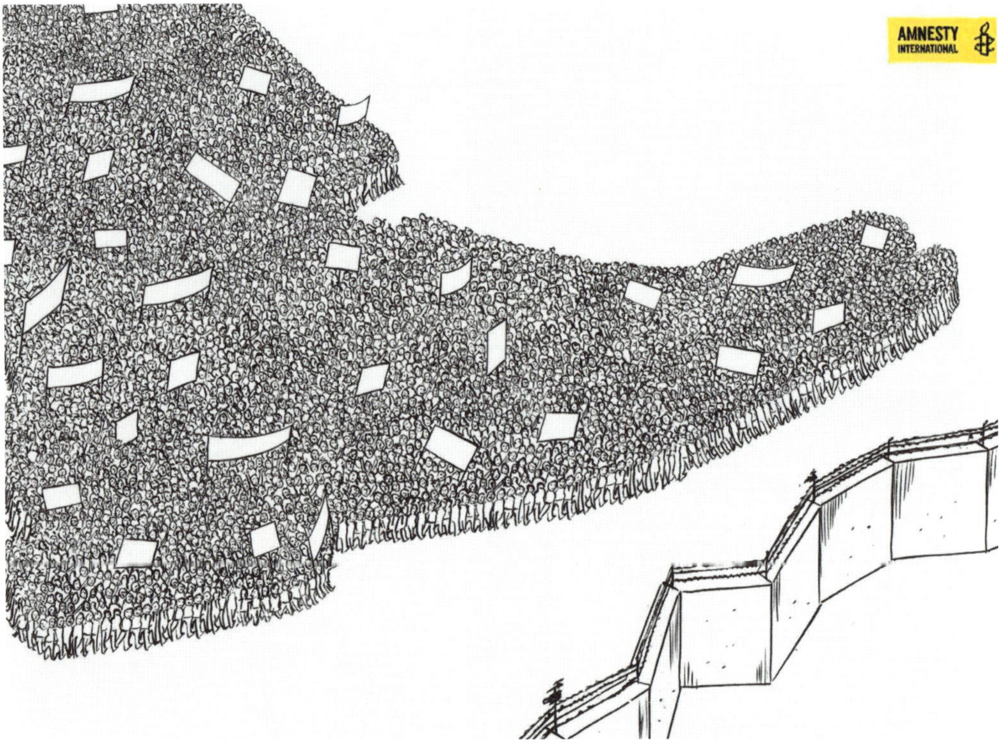

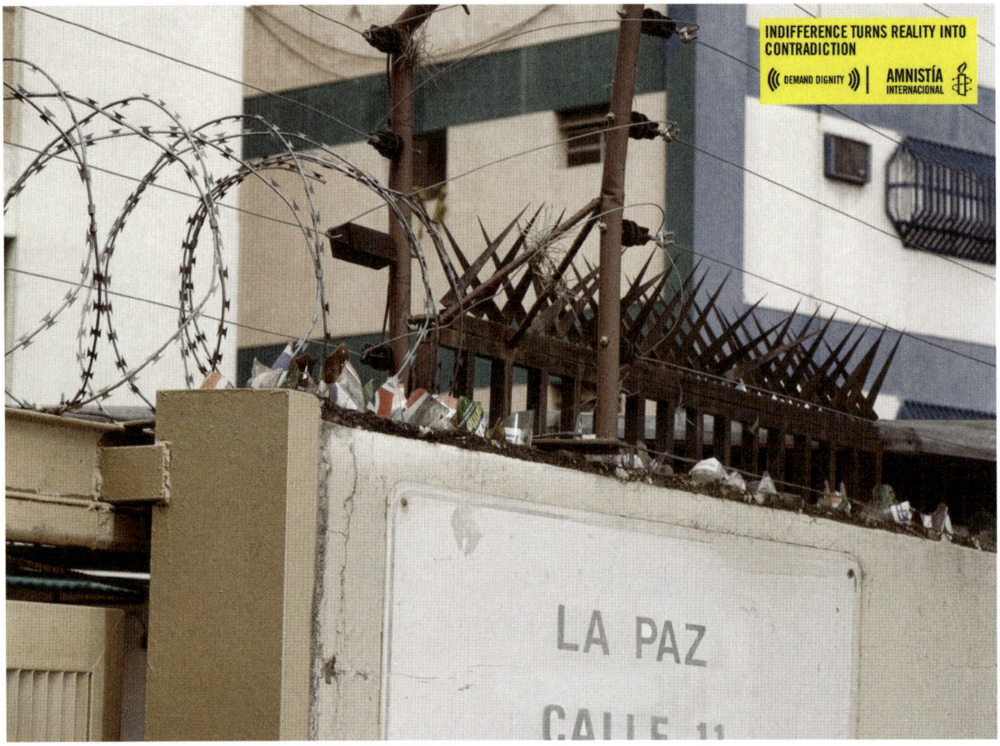

001 EVERYBODY IS AGAINST EVERYBODY.
    SOMEBODY HAS TO BE FOR THEM.
    CREATOR Leo Burnett Lisbon for
    Amnesty International
    SOURCE osocio.org

002 STOP GUN TRAFFICKING
    CREATOR Amnesty International
    SOURCE www.icollector.com

003 WEAPONS AGAINST WAR
    CREATOR Saatchi + Saatchi
    for Amnesty International
    SOURCE osocio.org

004 ES GESCHIEHT NICHT HIER, ABER JETZT
    [IT EXISTS. NOT HERE, BUT NOW]
    CREATOR Amnesty International
    SOURCE www.flickr.com/photos/
    pomgod/188675364/

005 CELA EXISTE. PAS ICI,
    MAIS MAINTENANT
    [IT EXISTS. NOT HERE, BUT NOW]
    CREATOR Amnesty International
    SOURCE www.flickr.com/photos/
    pomgod/188675365/

006 ES GESCHIEHT NICHT HIER, ABER JETZT
    [IT EXISTS. NOT HERE, BUT NOW]
    CREATOR Amnesty International
    SOURCE www.flickr.com/photos/
    pomgod/188675345/

007 ES GESCHIEHT NICHT HIER, ABER JETZT
    [IT EXISTS. NOT HERE, BUT NOW]
    CREATOR Amnesty International
    SOURCE www.flickr.com/photos/
    pomgod/188675310/

008 AMNESTY INTERNATIONAL:
    SEPTEMBER 11TH
    CREATOR Bates Paris for Amnesty
    International
    SOURCE www.coloribus.com
    DATE 2003

009 HUMAN RIGHTS AWARENESS: PINOCHET
    CREATOR TBWA / Paris for Amnesty
    International
    SOURCE www.coloribus.com

010 AMNESTY INTERNATIONAL: CROSS
    CREATOR Ammirati Puris Lintas for
    Amnesty International
    SOURCE www.coloribus.com
    DATE 1998

011 LES FEMMES AUSSI SONT PROTEGEES
    PAR LES DROITS DE L'HOMME
    [WOMEN ARE ALSO PROTECTED BY
    THE RIGHTS OF MAN]
    CREATOR Amnesty International
    SOURCE www.coloribus.com
    DATE 2005

012 AMNESTY
    CREATOR Arman
    SOURCE artistsposters.com

013 MENSCHENRECHTE FÜR ALLE
    [HUMAN RIGHTS FOR ALL]
    CREATOR Urs Grünig for Amnesty
    International
    SOURCE Plakatsammlung Museum
    für Gestaltung Zürich

014 TURN IN YOUR KNIFE BEFORE
    SOMEONE TURNS IT ON YOU
    CREATOR Amnesty International
    SOURCE www.north-wales.police.uk

015 TAG DER MENSCHENRECHTE
    [HUMAN RIGHTS DAY]
    CREATOR Ueli Kleeb for Amnesty
    International
    SOURCE Plakatsammlung Museum
    für Gestaltung Zürich
    DATE 1995

016 AMNESTY INTERNATIONAL: PETE
    CREATOR Publicis Mojo, New Zealand
    for Amnesty International
    SOURCE www.coloribus.com
    DATE 2007

017 HUMAN RIGHTS ORGANIZATION:
    HUMILIATION
    CREATOR Ogilvy Frankfurt
    for Amnesty International
    SOURCE www.coloribus.com
    DATE 2006

018 AMNESTY INTERNATIONAL: RAPE
    CREATOR Abbott Mead Vickers
    for Amnesty International
    SOURCE www.coloribus.com
    DATE 1999

019 CAMPAIGN AGAINST TORTURE:
    SCREAM
    CREATOR Contrapunto for
    Amnesty International
    SOURCE www.coloribus.com
    DATE 2001

020 DECEMBER 10TH / INTERNATIONAL
    DAY FOR HUMAN RIGHTS
    CREATOR Lowe Pimo, Beirut
    for Amnesty International
    SOURCE osocio.org

021 DO YOU KNOW WHERE CROATIAN
    WEAPONS END UP?
    CREATOR Croatia, Digitel&
    for Amnesty International
    SOURCE osocio.org

022 I WANT YOU, BABY
    CREATOR SAATCHI & SAATCHI
    for Amnesty International
    SOURCE www.coloribus.com
    DATE 2000

023 EYE CHART
    CREATOR DDB Budapest for
    Amnesty International
    SOURCE www.pop-ology.com
    DATE 2006

024 QUELQUEPART PARTOUT
    [ANYWHERE, EVERYWHERE]
    CREATOR Alain Le Quernec
    for Amnesty International
    SOURCE JAGDA Peace Posters
    International Exhibition
    DATE 1978

025 AMNESTY
    CREATOR Yusaku Kamerkura
    for Amnesty International
    SOURCE JAGDA Peace Posters
    International Exhibition

026 SCREAM — MAKE SOME NOISE FOR
    THOSE WHO CAN'T BE HEARD
    CREATOR Publicis Mojo Auckland,
    New Zealand for Amnesty
    International
    SOURCE adlandtv.com

027 WE WILL NEVER LET MONEY HIDE
    REALITY FROM US
    CREATOR TWBA / Paris for Amnesty
    International
    SOURCE www.ibelieveinadv.com

028 AMNESTY'S FLAME IS IN DANGER
    WORLDWIDE. DEFEND IT. BUY A CANDLE
    OR MAKE A DONATION.
    CREATOR Air Brussels Belgium
    for Amnesty International
    SOURCE osocio.org

029 AMNESTY'S FLAME IS IN DANGER
    WORLDWIDE. DEFEND IT. BUY A CANDLE
    OR MAKE A DONATION
    CREATOR Air Brussels Belgium
    for Amnesty International
    SOURCE osocio.org

030 MILLIONEN MENSCHEN WERDEN IHRER
    MENSCHENRECHTE BERAUBT.
    [MILLIONS ARE DEPRIVED OF THEIR
    HUMAN RIGHTS]
    CREATOR Amnesty International
    SOURCE www.marketing-blog.biz

031 IN 57 STAATEN GIBT ES
    POLITISCHE GEFANGENE
    [IN 57 COUNTRIES THERE ARE
    POLITICAL PRISONERS]
    CREATOR Amnesty International
    SOURCE www.marketing-blog.biz

032 AMNESTY INTERNATIONAL CANDLE
    CREATOR Amnesty International
    SOURCE www.thebigidea.co.nz

033 HAMMER, HAND, FOOT
    CREATOR Amnesty International
    SOURCE www.ibelieveinadv.com

034 INDIFFERENCE TURNS REALITY
    INTO CONTRADICTION
    CREATOR Amnesty International
    SOURCE theinspirationroom.com/
    daily/2012/amnesty-international-
    irony/

001

„Vor der Gewalt
kapitulieren ist ein
Zeichen von Unmännlichkeit."
Mahatma Gandhi

002

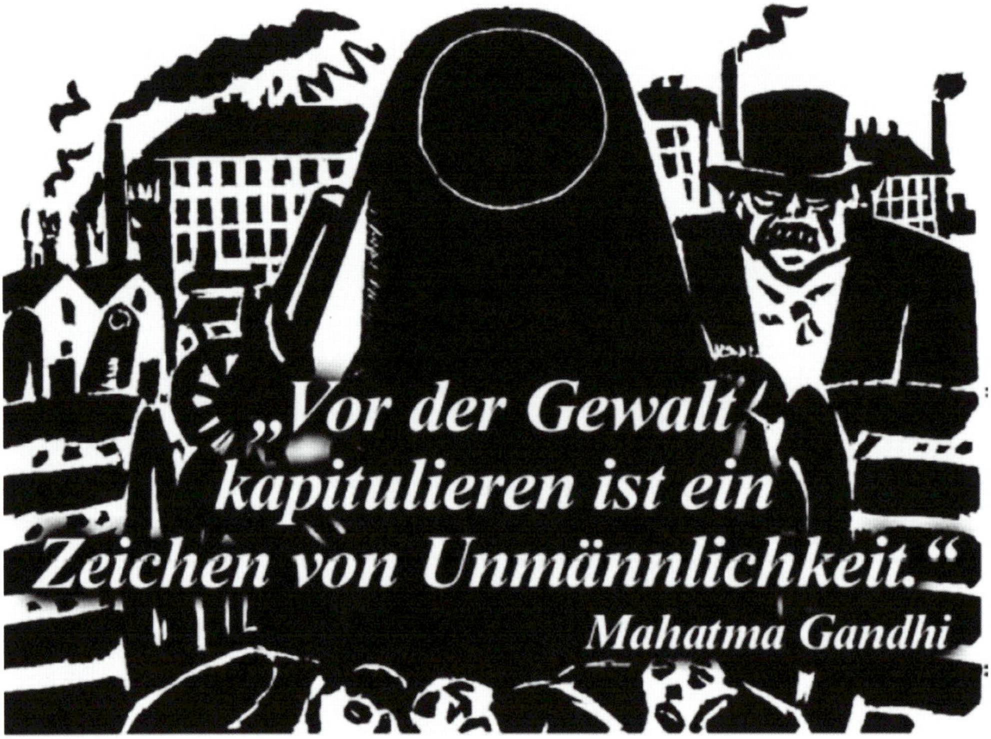

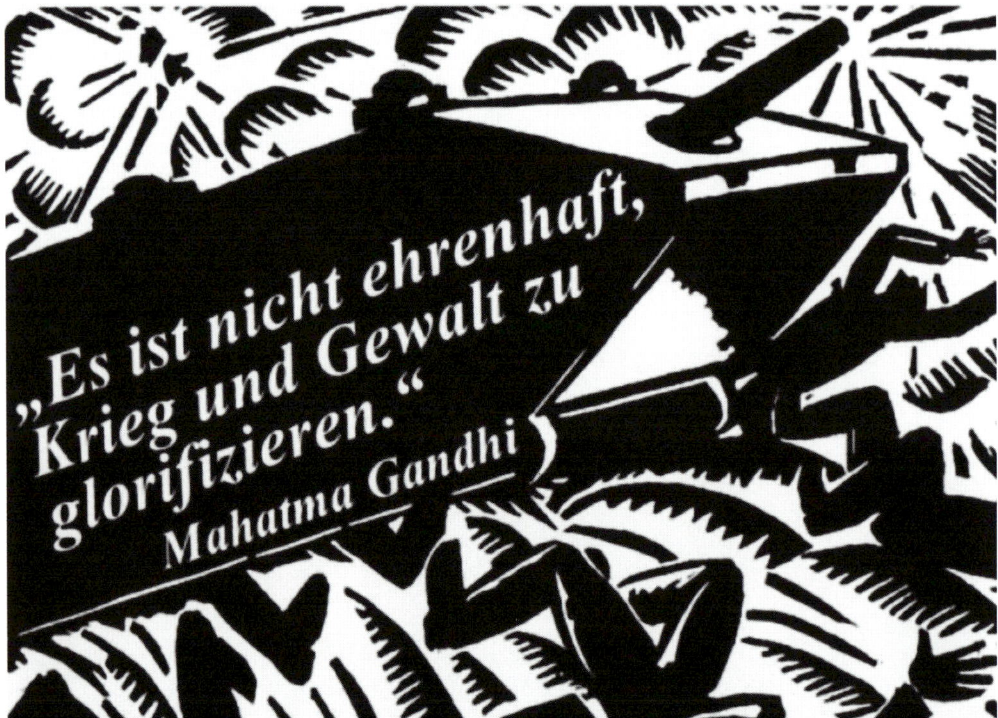

„Es ist nicht ehrenhaft,
Krieg und Gewalt zu
glorifizieren."
Mahatma Gandhi

003

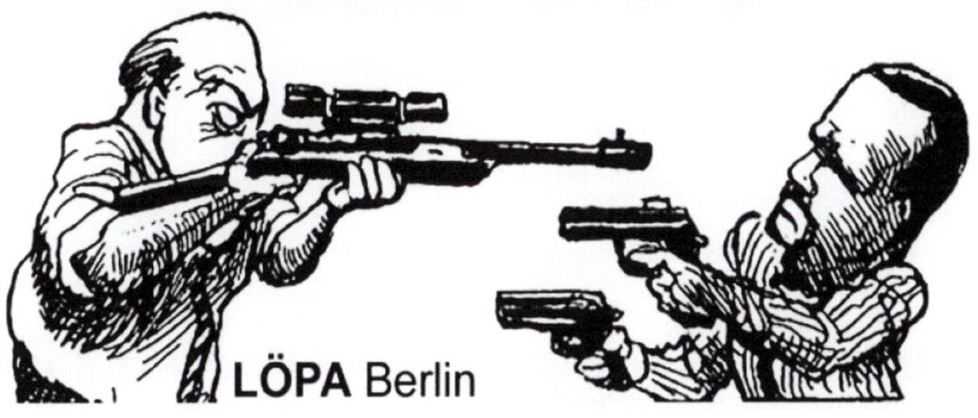
Kein Kriegsspielzeug
für Generäle und
andere Kinder!
LÖPA Berlin

004

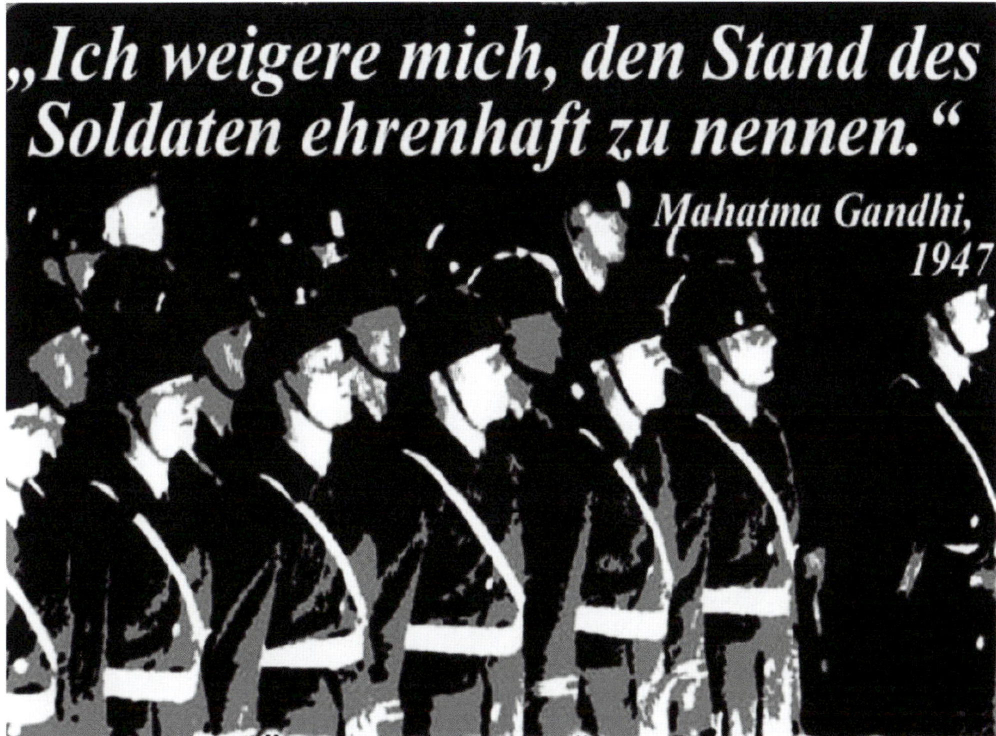
„Ich weigere mich, den Stand des
Soldaten ehrenhaft zu nennen."
Mahatma Gandhi,
1947

005
006

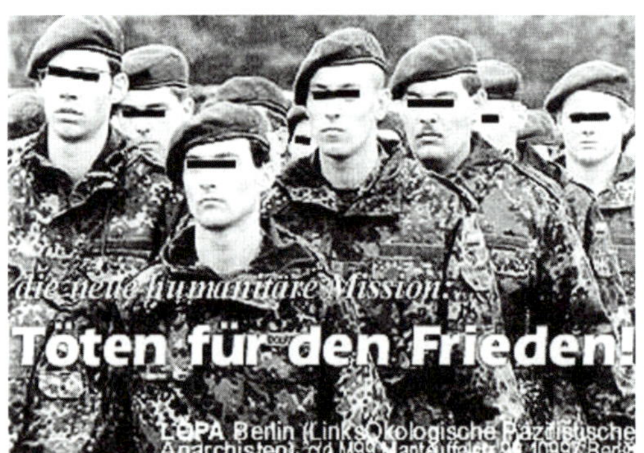

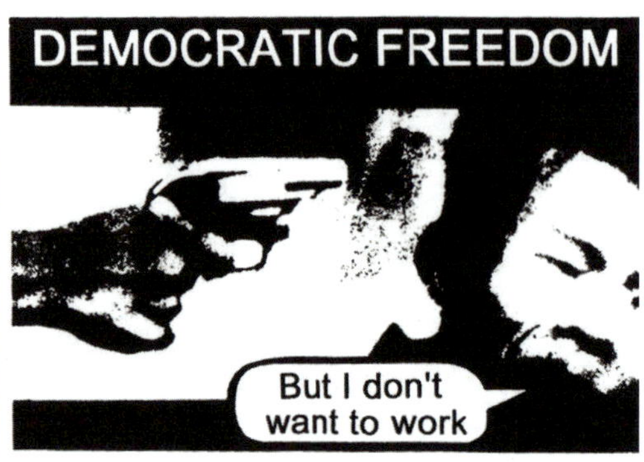

007
008

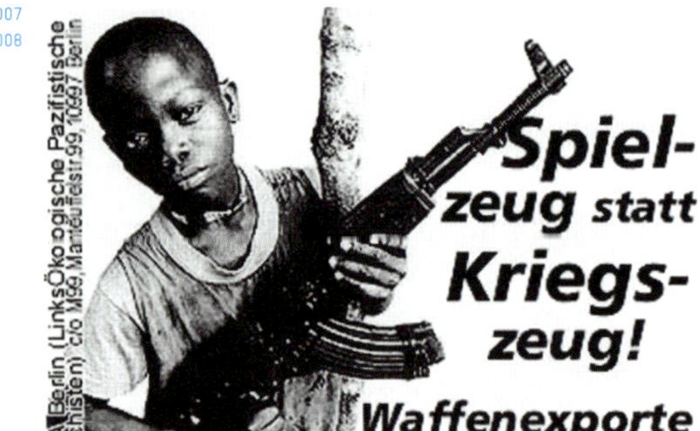

009
010

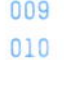

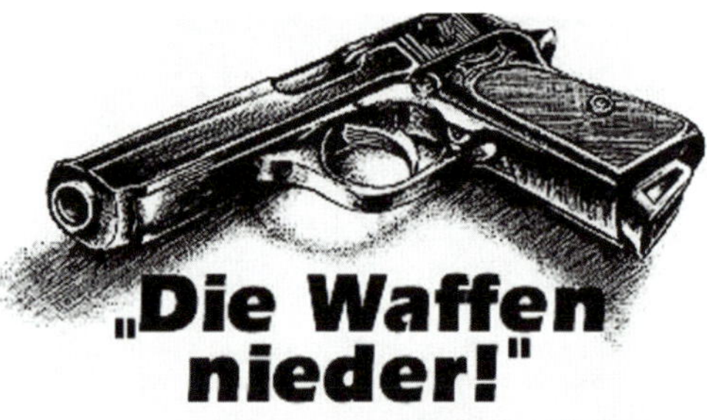

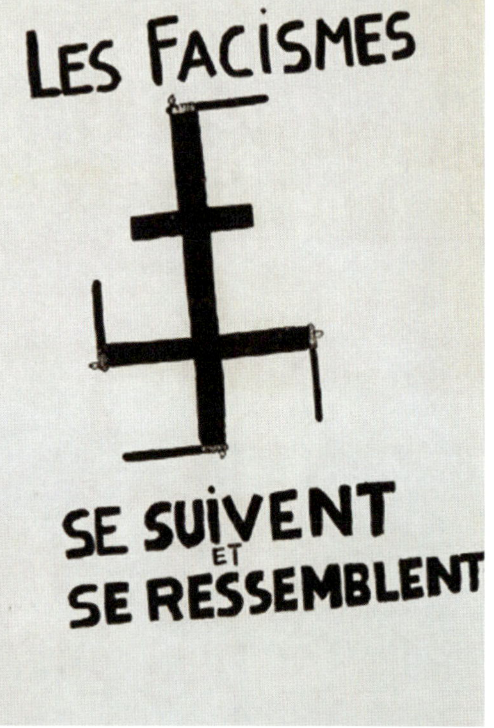

011

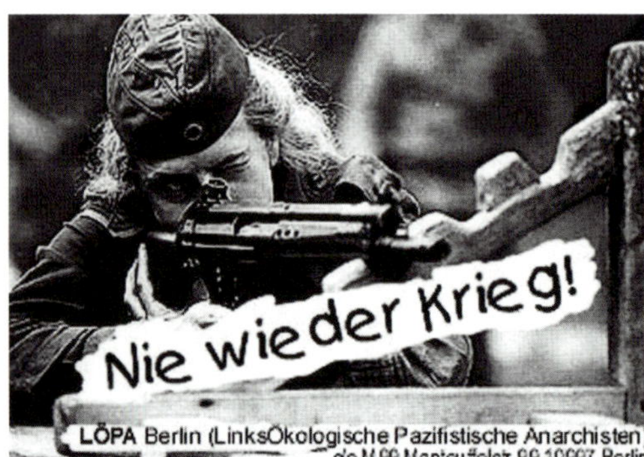

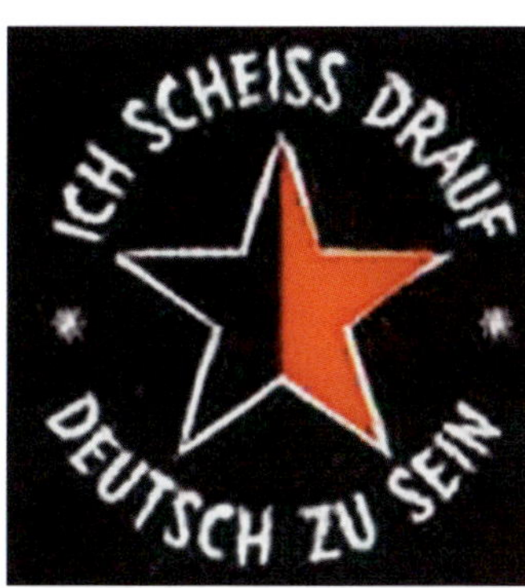

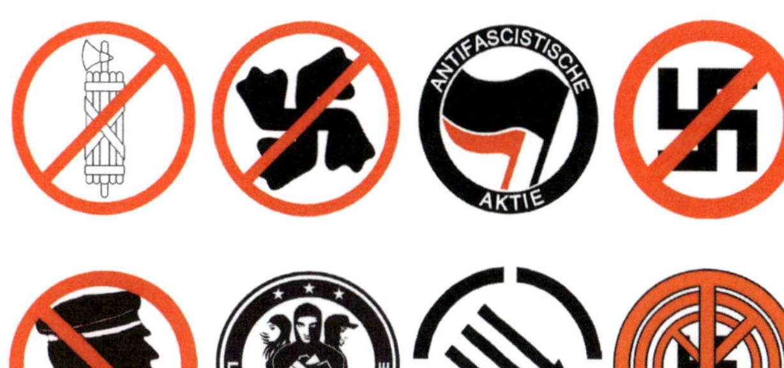

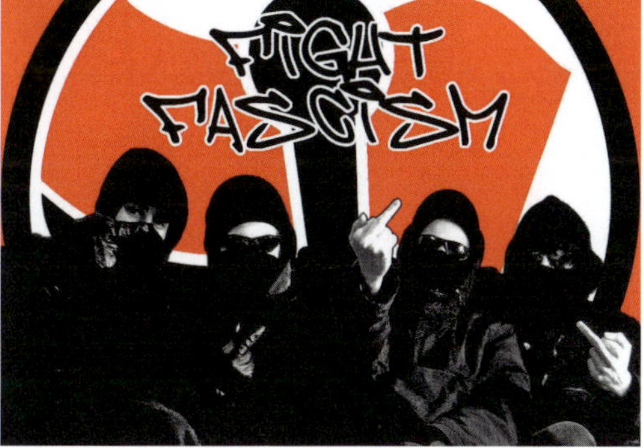

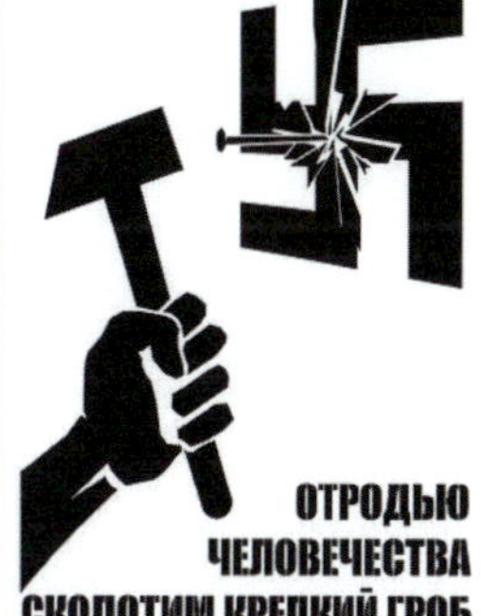

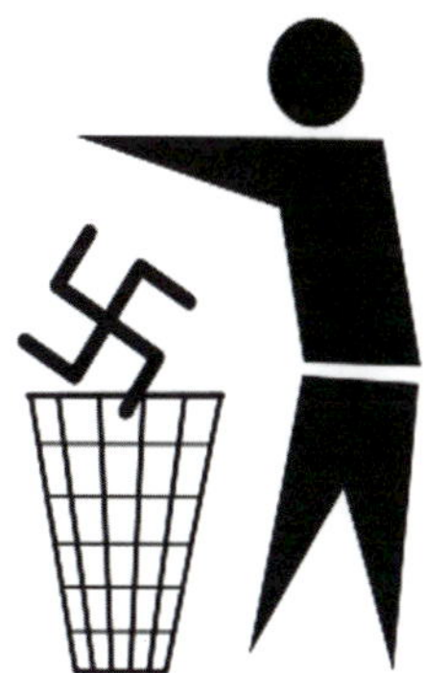

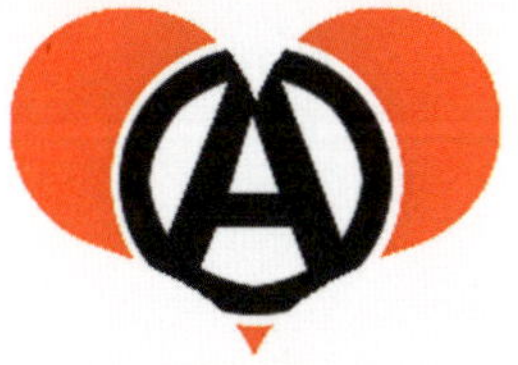

free love? as if love is anything but free! man has bought brains, but all the millions in the world have failed to buy love. man has subdued bodies, but all the power on earth has been unable to subdue love. man has conquered whole nations, but all his armies could not conquer love. man has chained and fettered the spirit, but he has been utterly helpless before love. high on a throne, with all the splendor and pomp his gold can command, man is yet poor and desolate, if love passes him by. and if it stays, the poorest hovel is radiant with warmth, with life and color. thus love has the magic power to make of a beggar a king. yes, love is free; it can dwell in no other atmosphere. - emma goldman

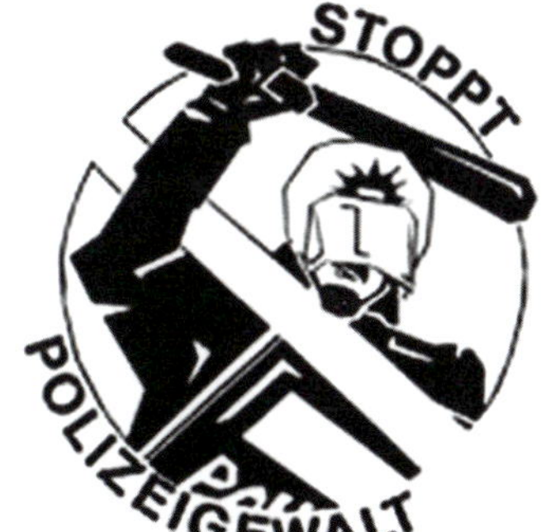

001 VOR DER GEWALT KAPITULIEREN IST
EIN ZEICHEN VON UNMÄNNLICHKEIT
[CAPITULATING TO VIOLENCE IS
A SIGN OF UNMANLINESS]
CREATOR Löpa Berlin
SOURCE www.oocities.org

002 ES IST NICHT EHRENHAFT, KRIEG UND
GEWALT ZU GLORIFIZIEREN
[IT IS NOT HONORABLE TO GLORIFY
WAR AND VIOLENCE]
CREATOR Löpa Berlin
SOURCE www.oocities.org

003 KEIN KRIEGSSPIELZEUG FÜR GENERALE
UND ANDERE KINDER!
[NO WAR TOYS FOR GENERALS AND
OTHER CHILDREN!]
CREATOR Löpa Berlin
SOURCE www.oocities.org

004 ICH WEIGERE MICH, DEN STAND DES
SOLDATEN EHRENHAFT ZU NENNEN
[I REFUSE TO CALL THE PROFESSION
OF THE SEPOY HONORABLE]
CREATOR Löpa Berlin
SOURCE www.oocities.org

005 DIE NEUE HUMANITÄRE MISSION:
TÖTEN FÜR DEN FRIEDEN!
[THE NEW HUMANITARIAN MISSION:
DIE FOR PEACE]
CREATOR Löpa Berlin
SOURCE www.oocities.org

006 DEMOCRATIC FREEDOM
SOURCE www.anarchosyndicalism.net

007 SPIELZEUG STATT KRIEGSZEUG!
WAFFENEXPORTE STOPPEN!
[TOYS INSTEAD OF ARMS!
STOP ARMS EXPORTS!]
CREATOR Löpa Berlin
SOURCE www.oocities.org

008 NO BORDERS AND WALLS AND
FORCED DEPORTATIONS
SOURCE anarchyagogo.tumblr.com

009 DIE WAFFEN NIEDER!
[LAY DOWN YOUR ARMS!]
CREATOR Löpa Berlin
SOURCE www.oocities.org

010 LES FACISMES — SE SUIVENT ET
SE RESSEMBLENT
[FASCISMS FOLLOW AND RESEMBLE
ONE ANOTHER]
CREATOR Atelier Populaire, Paris
SOURCE Plakatsammlung Museum
für Gestaltung Zürich

011 NIE WIEDER KRIEG!
[NO MORE WAR]
CREATOR Löpa Berlin
SOURCE www.oocities.org

012 ICH SCHEISS DRAUF DEUTSCH
ZU SEIN
[BEING GERMAN? I SAY SHIT ON IT]
SOURCE deutschelobby.com

013 ANTI-FASCIST SYMBOL
Anti-Fascist/Anti-Nazi symbol
without using a swastika, which
is forbidden in Germany.
CREATOR Piast
SOURCE commons.wikimedia.org

014 AGAINST KACZYZM
"Kaczyzm," a contemptuous term
for the ideology of of Lech and
Jaroslaw Kaczynski, is derived
from the Polish word kaczka [duck].
CREATOR Piast
SOURCE commons.wikimedia.org

015 ANTIFACISTISCHE AKTIE
Logo for the Anti-Facist Action
in the Netherlands.
CREATOR Eilexe
SOURCE commons.wikimedia.org

016 ANTI-NAZI SYMBOL
CREATOR Zeimusu
SOURCE commons.wikimedia.org

017 UNTITLED
SOURCE projektwerkstatt.de

018 LET'S FIGHT WHITE PRIDE
SOURCE freiraumtanz.noblogs.org

019 SOURCE streetart.antispe.org

020 ANTI-NAZI SYMBOL
SOURCE dagegen-bleiben.de

021 FIGHT FASCISM
CREATOR antifaschistische Aktion
Rochlitz Geringswalde Burgstädt
SOURCE aargb.blogsport.de

022 ANTIFA STENCIL 1
SOURCE Unknown

023 ANTIFA
CREATOR PavelD
SOURCE commons.wikimedia.org

024 TO LOVE AND RESPECT
CREATOR PavelD
SOURCE www.anarchosyndicalism.net

025 REDEEMING THE STREET
SOURCE plainputzsky.blogspot.ch

026 STOPPT POLIZEIGEWALT
[STOP POLICE VIOLENCE!]
SOURCE www.futurelife.de

027 GLOBAL SOLIDARITY
SOURCE heisseluft.wordpress.com

001
002
003

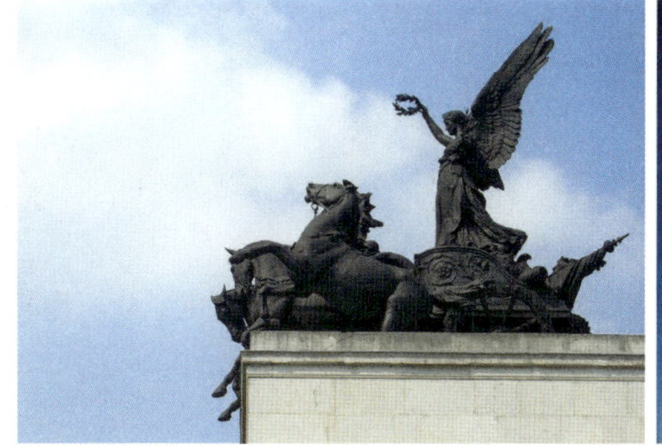 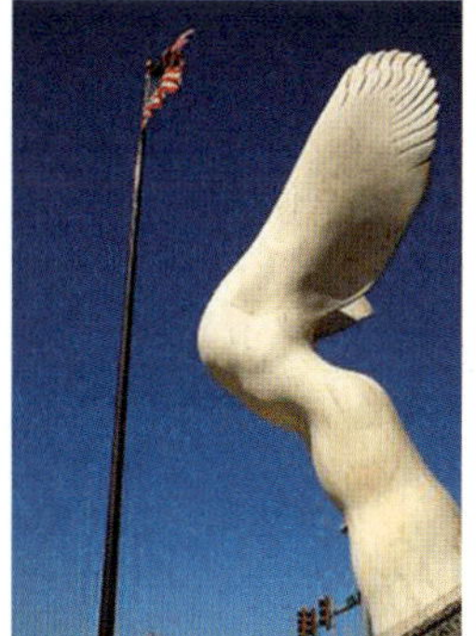 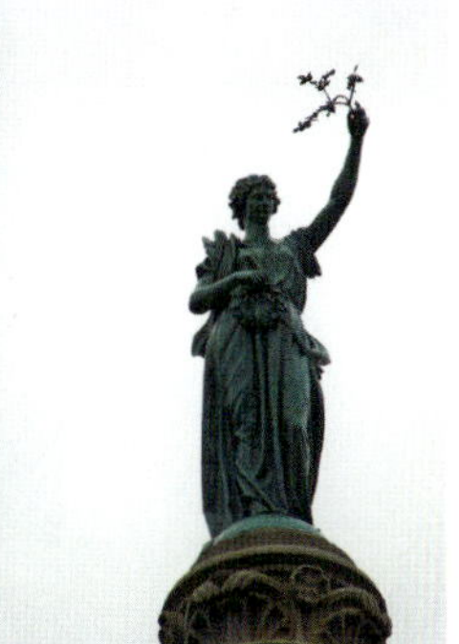

004
005
006

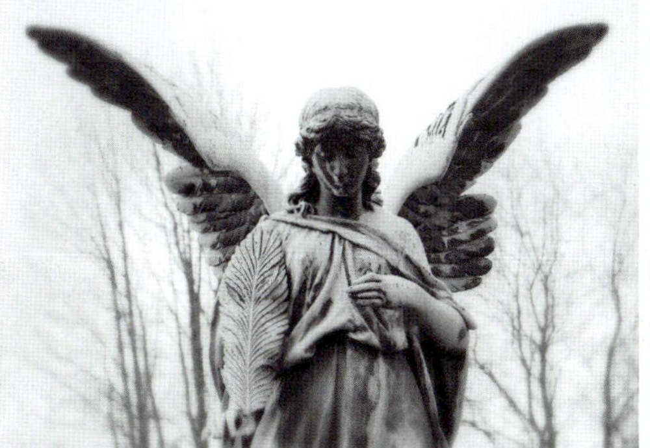 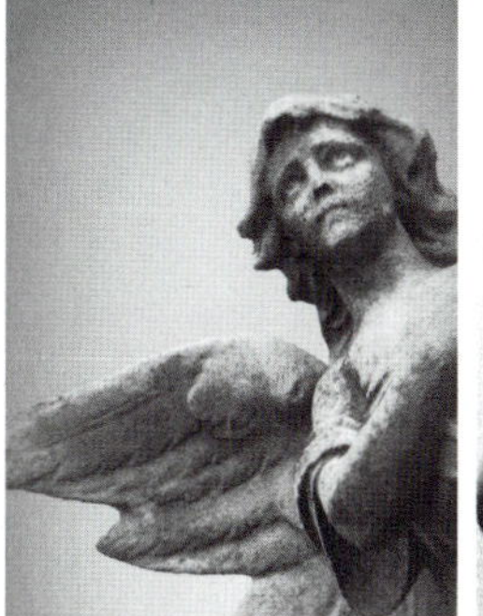 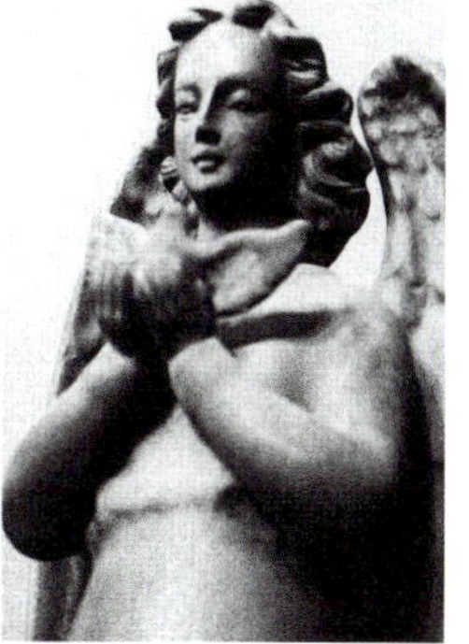

007
008
009

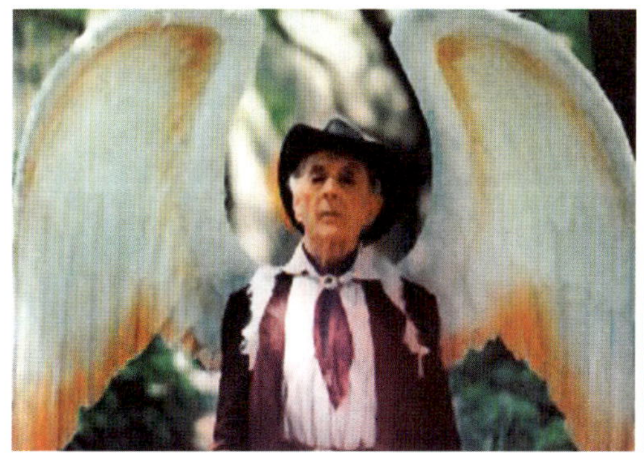 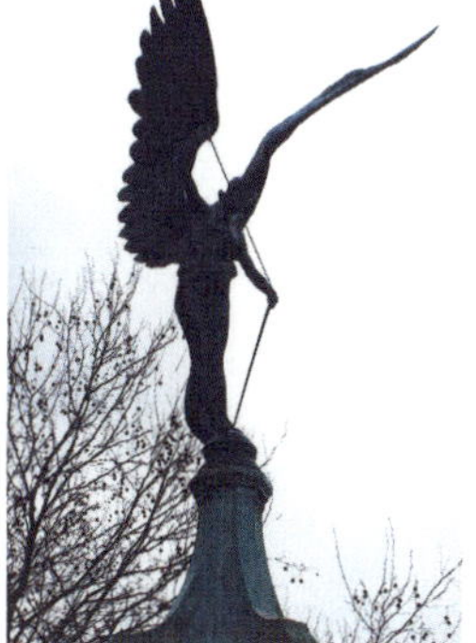 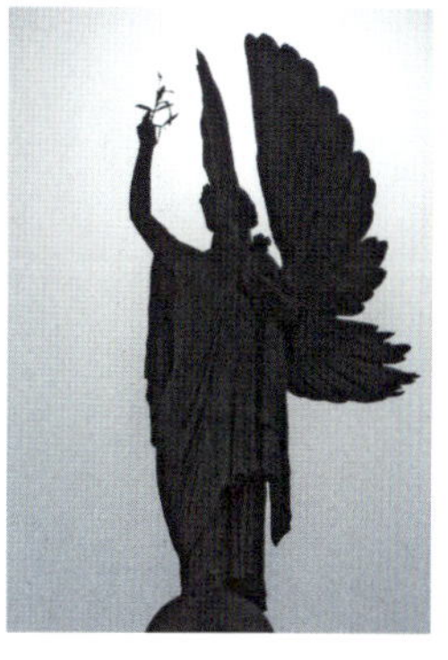

010
011
012

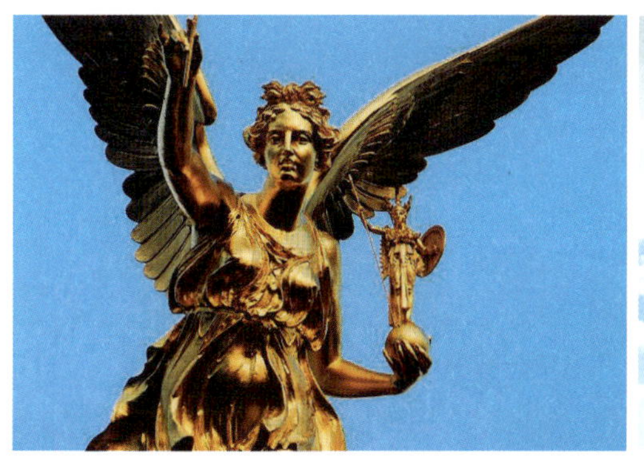 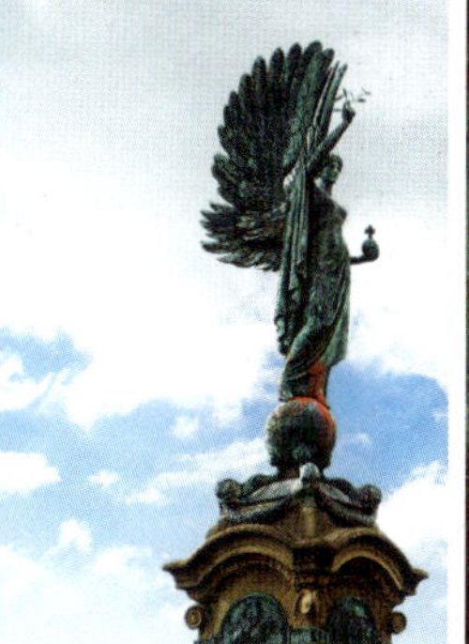 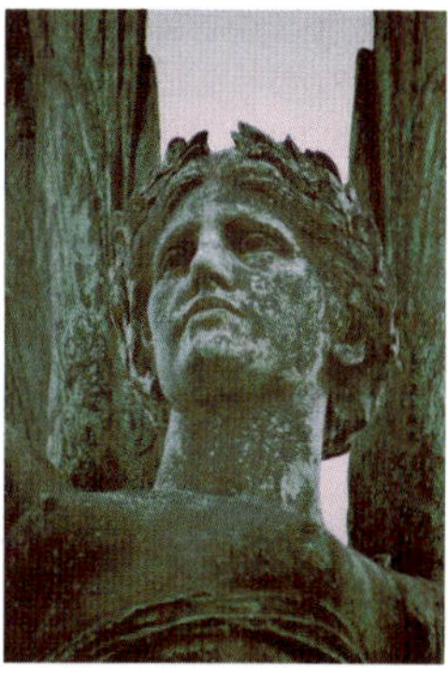

013
014

015
016
017
018

019
020
021
022

023
024

RIGHT
025

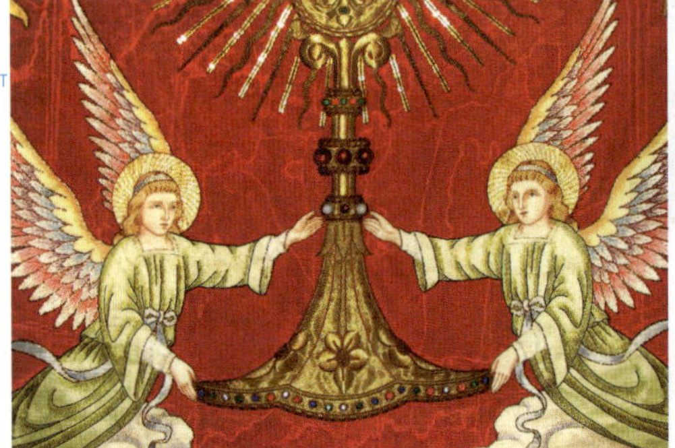

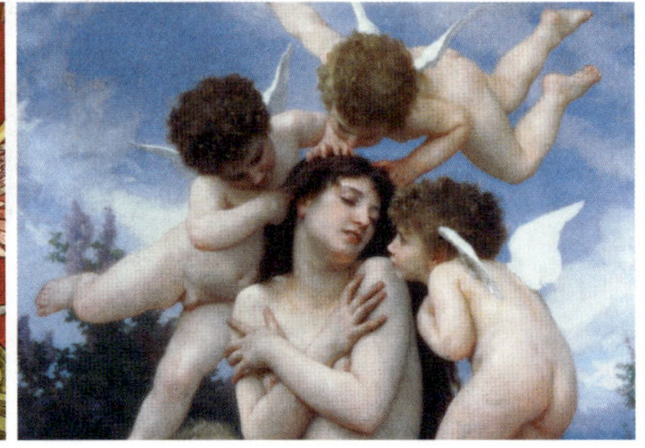

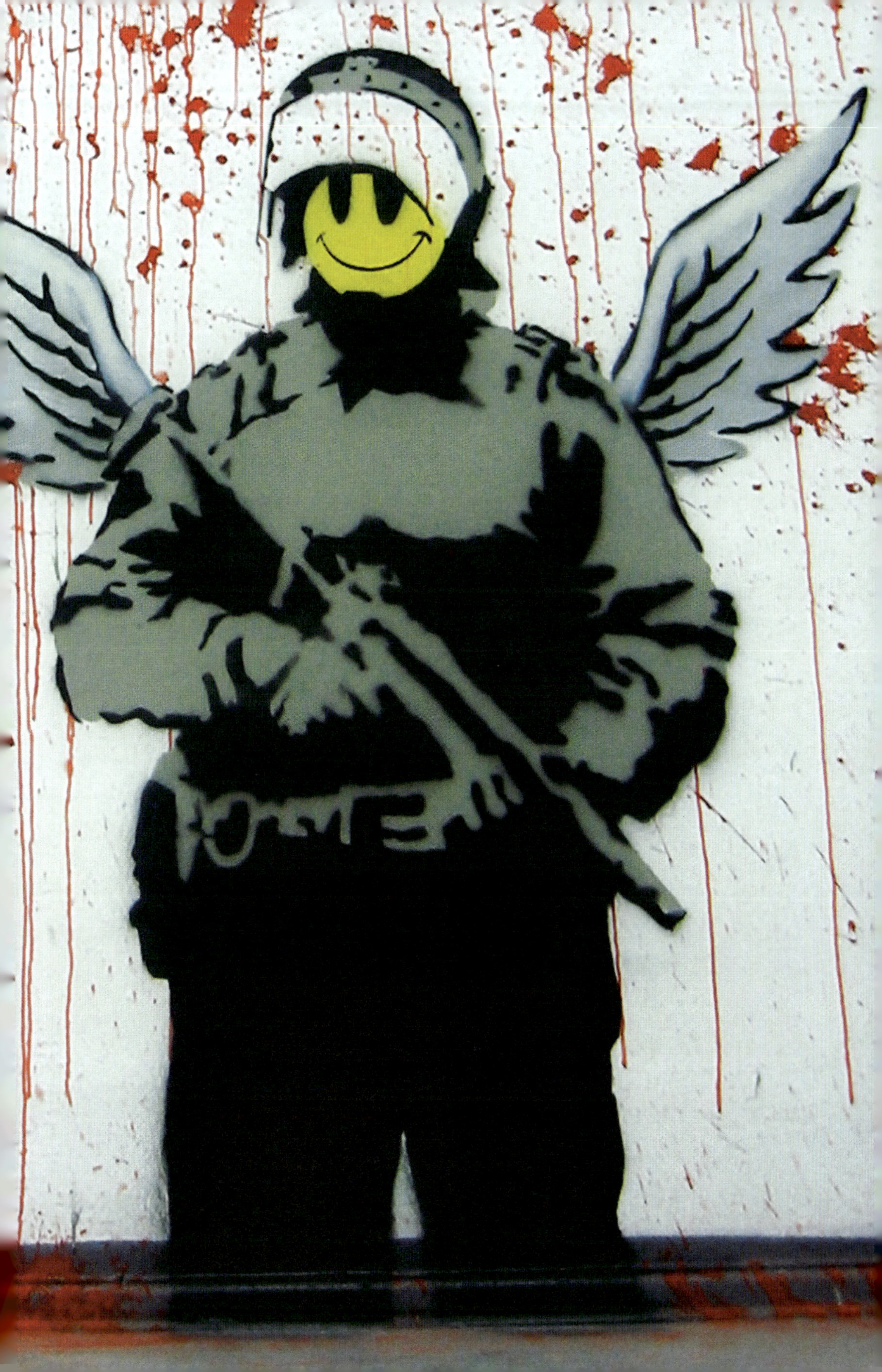

026
027

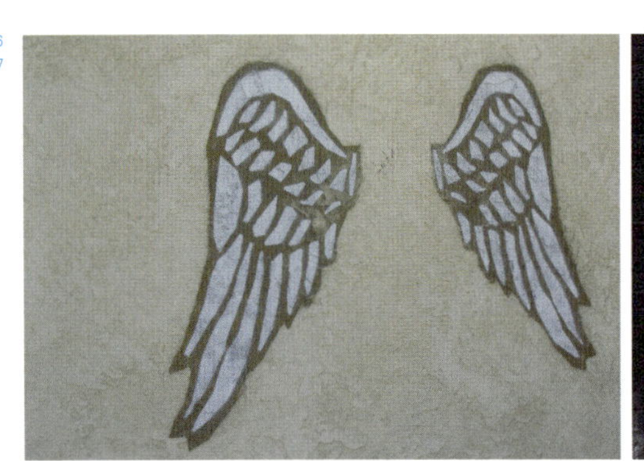
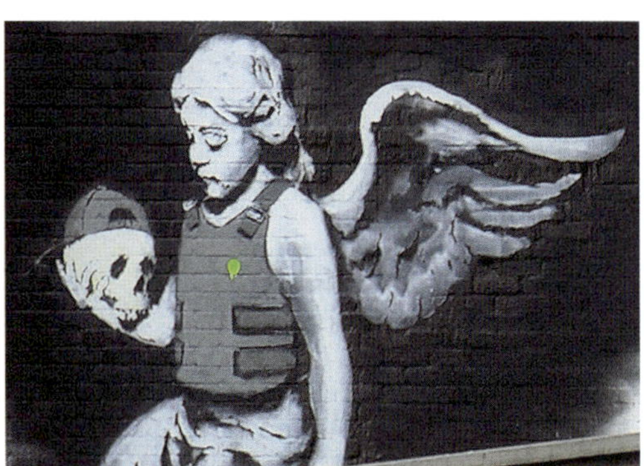

028
029

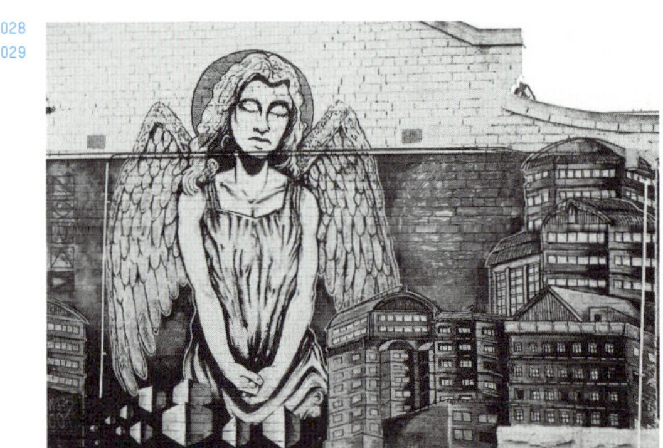
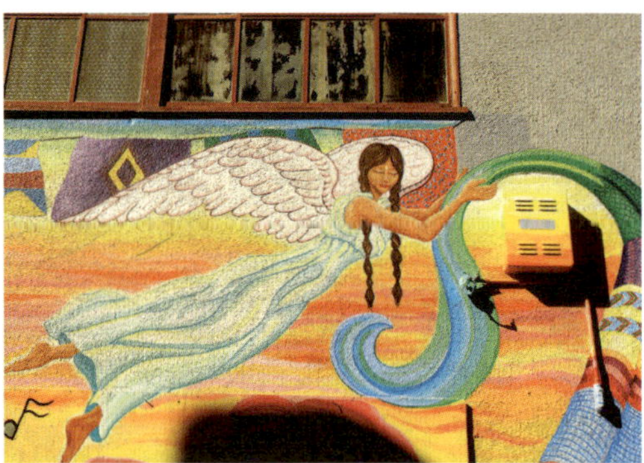

030
031
032
033

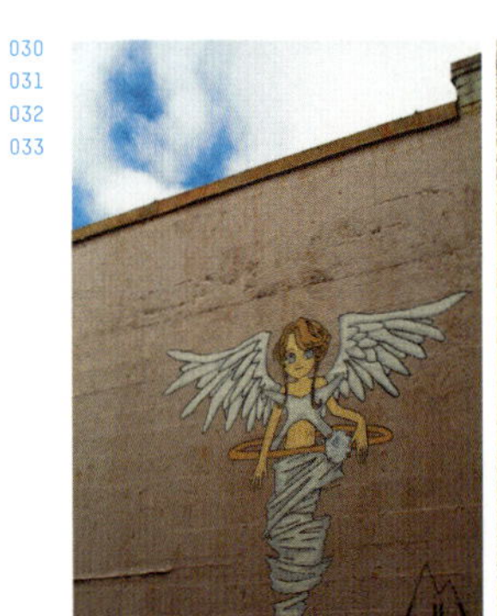
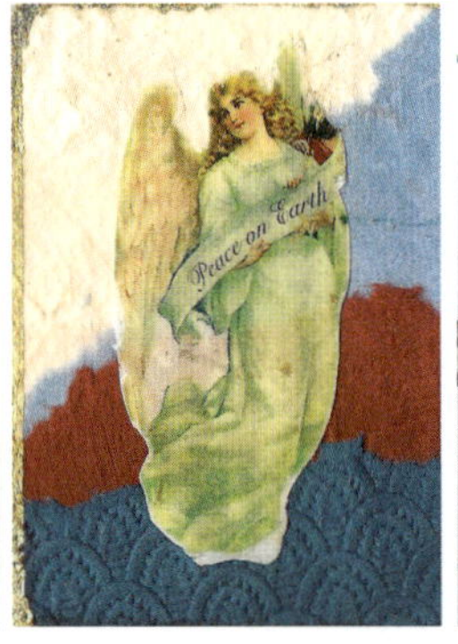

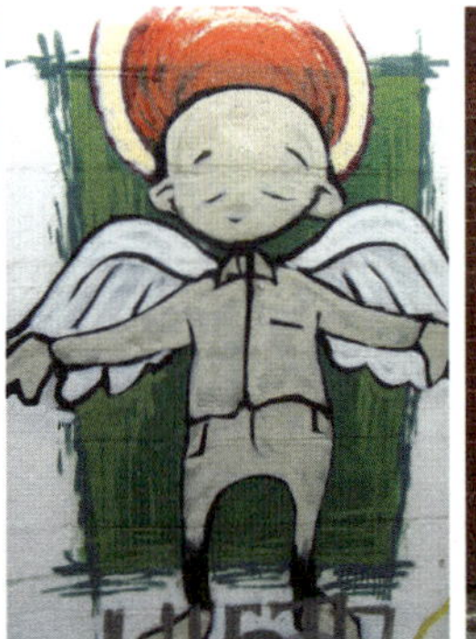
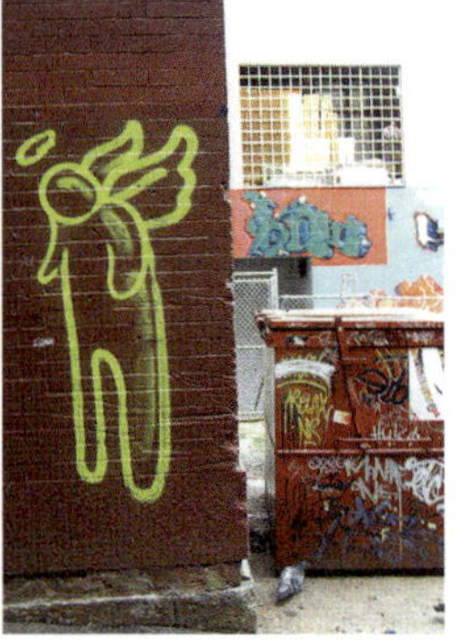

034
035

RIGHT
036

NEXT
037

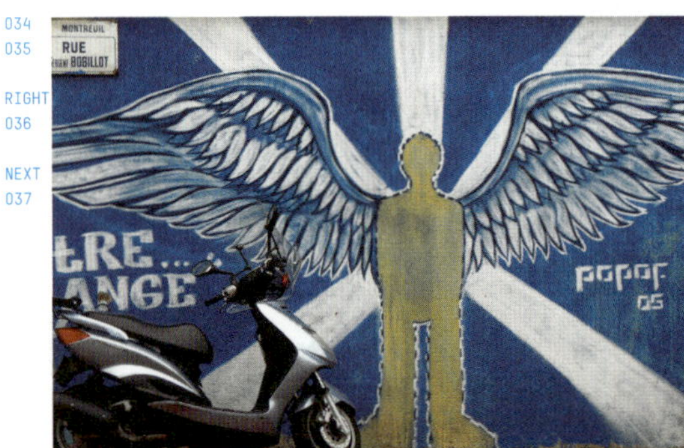

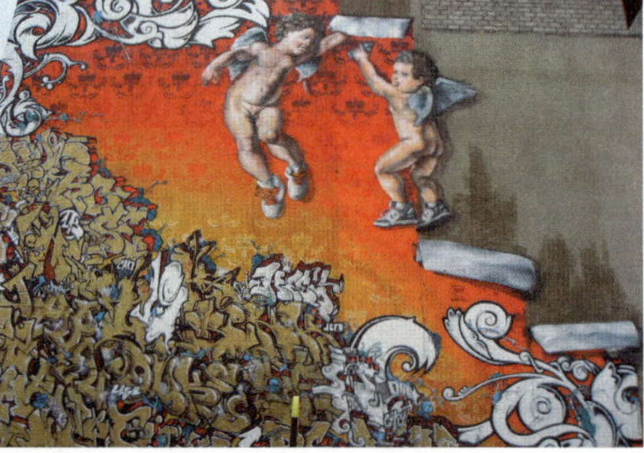

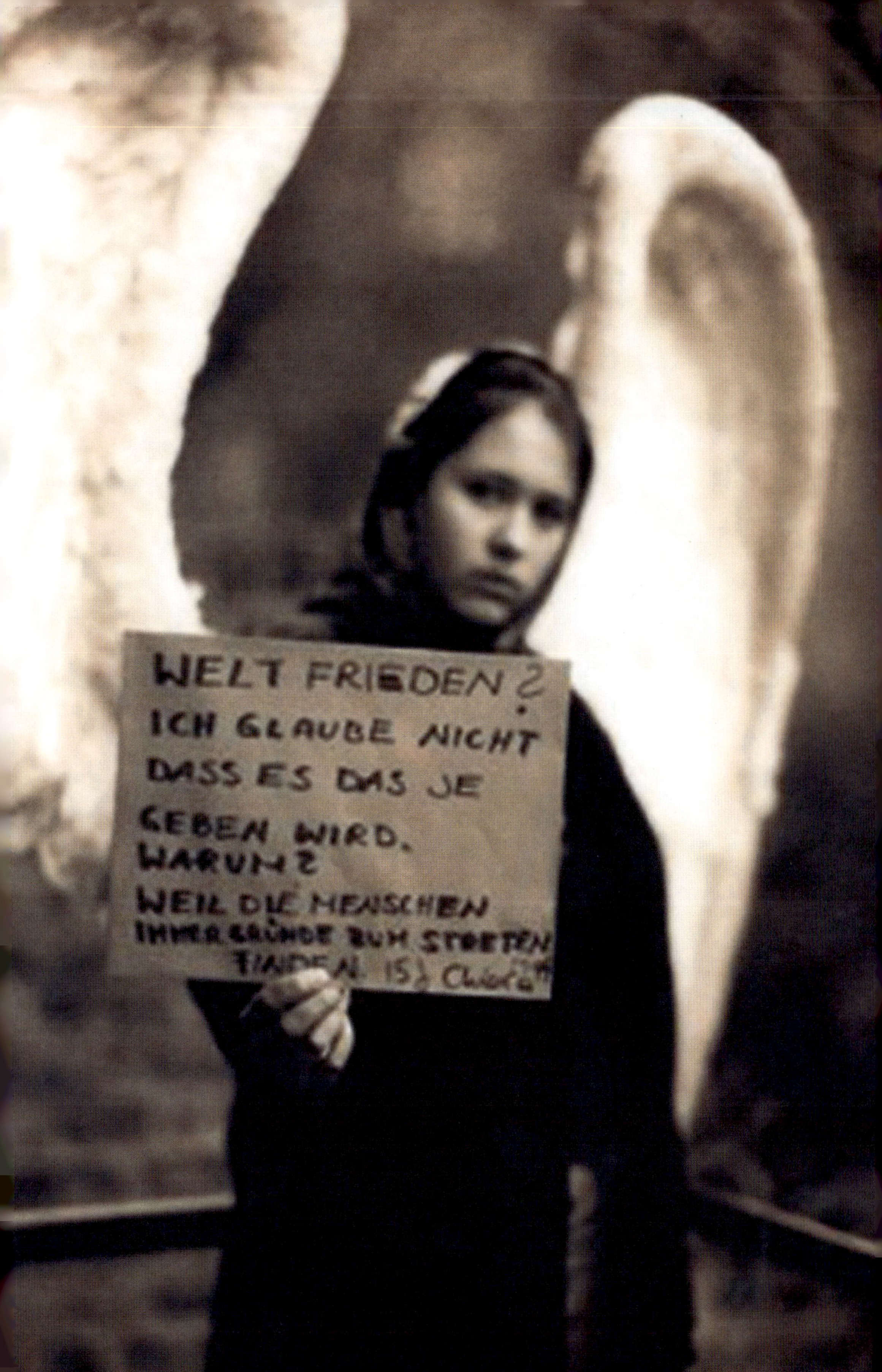
WELT FRIEDEN?
ICH GLAUBE NICHT
DASS ES DAS JE
GEBEN WIRD.
WARUM?
WEIL DIE MENSCHEN
IMMER GRÜNDE ZUM STREITEN
FINDEN. 15j.

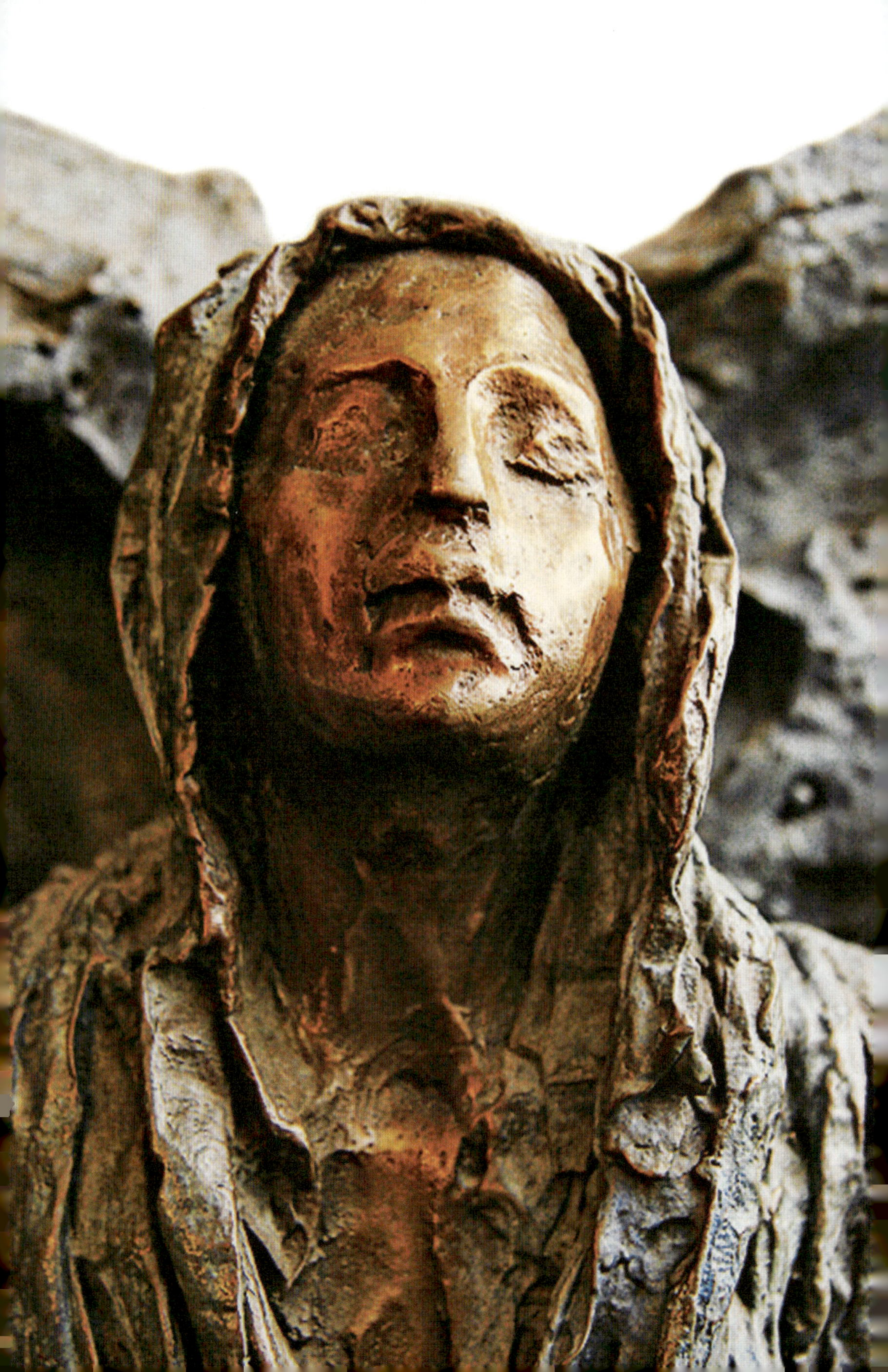

001 PEACE HOLDS THE REIGNS OF WAR
Adrian Jones's depiction of the
Angel of Peace descending on the
Chariot of War over Wellington
Arch in Hyde Park, London.
CREATOR Provided by penguin_strut
SOURCE www.flickr.com/photos/
95666471@N00/632498793/

002 WINGS OF PEACE AND FREEDOM
MONUMENT, DIXON, IL, USA
CREATOR Wayne Wilkinson
SOURCE saukvalleyphotography.
blogspot.com

003 ANGEL OF PEACE
New Haven's 119-year-old Angel
of Peace statue, which sits atop
East Rock.
CREATOR Provided by nkhorst
SOURCE www.flickr.com/photos/
11187056@N07/2490419957/

004 LONELY ANGEL
CREATOR Provided by bogenfreund
SOURCE www.flickr.com/photos/
bogenfreund/356014489/

005 ANGEL OF PEACE
CREATOR Provided by floralgal
SOURCE www.flickr.com

006 LADY OF PEACE
CREATOR Provided by oclark53
SOURCE www.flickr.com/photos/
oliverclark/2490443165/

007 WINGS OF PEACE
CREATOR Panja Jürgens
SOURCE theangelsarewithyoucatas.
blogspirit.com

008 ANGEL OF PEACE
CREATOR Provided by tan-tanl
SOURCE www.flickr.com/photos/
22635884@N08/2173705556/

009 PEACE STATUE – BRIGHTON & HOVE
CREATOR Provided by Mark Wordy
SOURCE www.flickr.com/photos/
61798879@N00/466327076/

010 FRIEDENSENGEL, MÜNCHEN
[ANGEL OF PEACE, MUNICH]
CREATOR Provided by DizzyFlores
SOURCE picasaweb.google.com

011 ANGEL OF PEACE
CREATOR Provided by powerpig
SOURCE www.flickr.com/photos/
powerpig/2378331305/

012 ANGEL OF PEACE
CREATOR Provided by Mike
SOURCE www.flickr.com

013 GOD GETTING BUSTED
CREATOR Banksy
SOURCE www.banksy.co.uk

014 ANGEL
CREATOR Provided by Paul Green
SOURCE www.flickr.com/photos/
paulgreen/2677894850/

015 ANGEL
CREATOR Banksy
SOURCE s85.photobucket.com

016 PEACE
CREATOR Provided by disneyfarm
SOURCE www.flickr.com/photos/
disneyfarm/366510602/

017 ANGEL OF PEACE
CREATOR Provided by
Toronto_photographer
SOURCE www.flickr.com/photos/
20666617@N00/202168076/

018 ANGEL, THE SIGN OF PEACE
CREATOR Provided by afkatws
SOURCE www.flickr.com/photos/
drewbuddie/113901015/

019 ANGEL OF PEACE
CREATOR Panja Jürgens
SOURCE theangelsarewithyoucatas.
blogspirit.com

020 ROMAN CATHOLIC CATHEDRAL OF
ST. JOHN THE BAPTIST, NORWICH,
NORFOLK, UK
CREATOR Provided by Elly
SOURCE www.flickr.com/photos/
ecr/1391476515/

021 ANGEL OF PEACE
Depicted holding an orb and an
olive branch, it is a memorial to
Edward VII, The Peacemaker.
CREATOR Provided by Saint.Tobias
SOURCE www.flickr.com/photos/
sainttobias/262274158/

022 MADONNA AND CHILD WITH SAINT
JOHN THE BAPTIST [ALLEGORY OF
THE PEACE OF WESTPHALIA]
CREATOR Joachim von Sandrart
SOURCE www.lwl.org
DATE 1648

023 EMBROIDERED ANGELS
From a banner in the Holy Cross
parish, Leicester.
CREATOR Provided by Lawrence OP
SOURCE www.flickr.com/photos/
paullew/1471330145/

024 RETURN OF SPRING
CREATOR William-Adolphe Bouguereau
SOURCE commons.wikimedia.org

025 EVERY PICTURE TELLS A LIE
CREATOR Banksy
SOURCE www.kreativ-reaktor.com

026 WALL ART, MISSION BEACH,
SAN DIEGO, CA, USA
CREATOR Provided by wmpe2000
SOURCE www.flickr.com/photos/
28372328@N00/1601989507/

027 BULLETPROOF ANGEL IN GREAT
EASTERN STREET LONDON
CREATOR Provided by Howard.Gees
SOURCE www.flickr.com/photos/
cyberslayer/1885895500/

028 ANGEL WALL, OFF EASY STREET
CREATOR Provided by
Felix Kirsch
SOURCE www.flickr.com/pho-
tos/9696110@N07/2056904140/

029 WALL ART, MISSION BEACH,
SAN DIEGO, CA, USA
CREATOR Provided by jablife
SOURCE www.flickr.com/photos/
belchshots/1806753321/

030 ANGEL
CREATOR Provided by smohundro
SOURCE www.flickr.com/photos/
belchshots/1806753321/

031 ANGEL OF PEACE
CREATOR Provided by nayski
SOURCE www.flickr.com/photos/
nayski/2478665712/

032 WALL ANGEL OFF BENEVOLENT STREET
IN PROVIDENCE, RI, USA
CREATOR Provided by Mr. Ducke
SOURCE www.flickr.com/photos/
dippy_duck/2490037957/

033 URBAN ANGEL MAKES AN APPEARANCE
CREATOR Provided by
victoria potter
SOURCE www.flickr.com/photos/
blindphotography/393570641/

034 ANGEL
CREATOR Provided by Tiffereth
SOURCE www.flickr.com/photos/
tiffereth/2564163638/

035 URBAN ANGELS
CREATOR Provided by Maxi Maxi
SOURCE www.flickr.com/photos/
maxiccs/2300444325/

036 WELTFRIEDEN?
[WORLD PEACE? I DON'T THINK IT
WILL EVER HAPPEN. WHY? BECAUSE
PEOPLE WILL ALWAYS FIND SOMETHING
TO FIGHT ABOUT]
CREATOR Panja Jürgens
SOURCE theangelsarewithyoucatas.
blogspirit.com

037 RENAISSANCE PEACE ANGEL
CREATOR Lin Evola-Smidt
SOURCE sierraclub.typepad.com/
greenlife/2009/06/the-recycled-art-
of-war.html

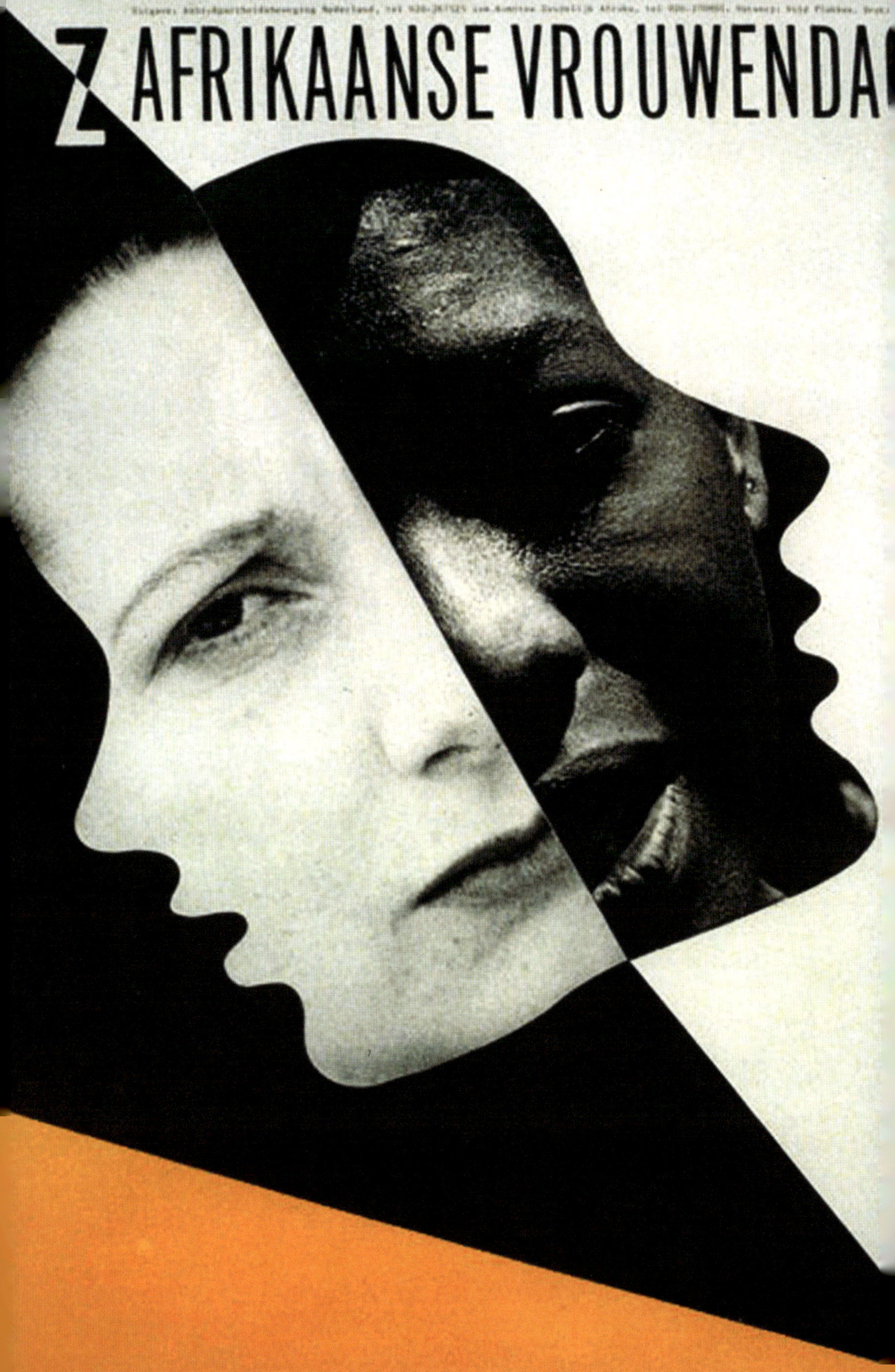

Z AFRIKAANSE VROUWENDAG

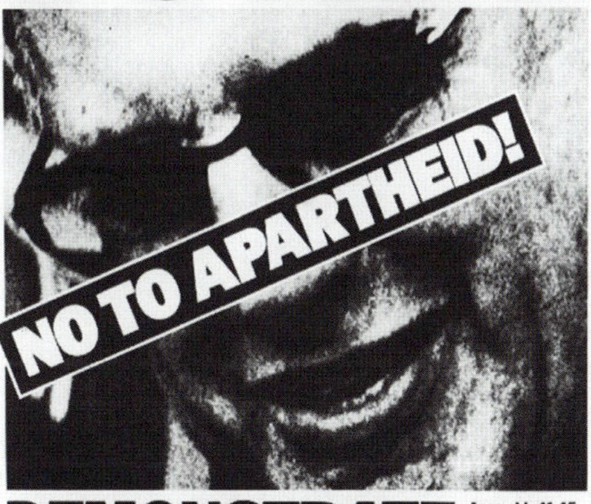
NO TO
BOTHA!
NO TO APARTHEID!
DEMONSTRATE
SATURDAY JUNE 2ND
Assemble 11.45
Speaker's Corner
Hyde Park

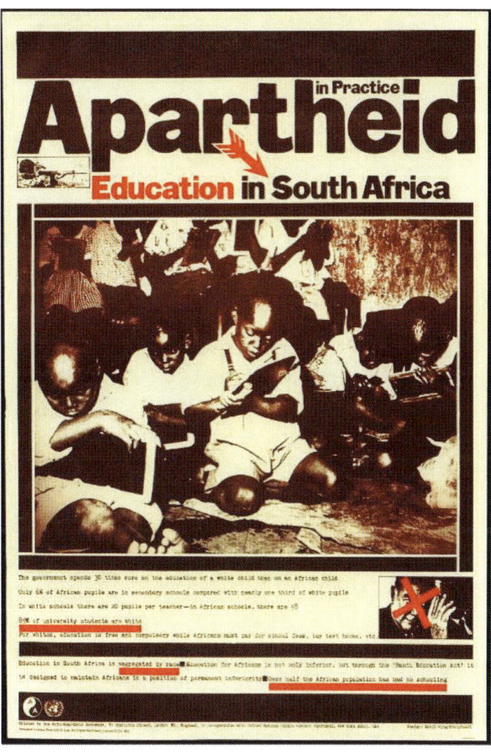
in Practice
Apartheid
Education in South Africa
ANTI-APARTHEID-BEWEGUNG

Apartheid is enough
to turn any civilized
human being into
a political prisoner.

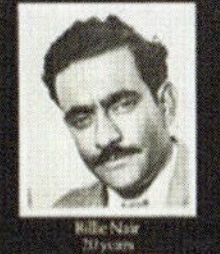
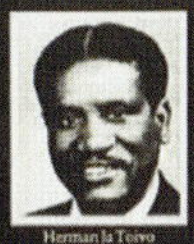
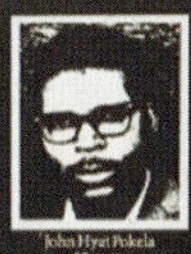
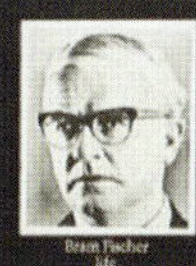
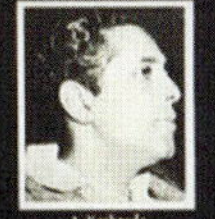
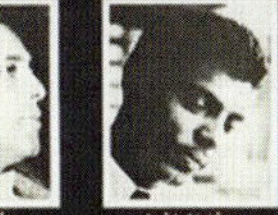
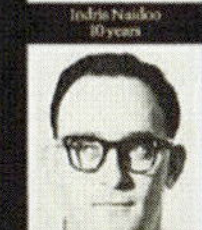
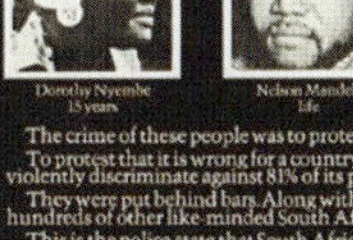

Billie Nair
20 years
Herman Ja Toivo
20 years
John Hyat Pokela
13 years
Bram Fischer
life
A. Kathrada
life
Indris Naidoo
10 years
Dorothy Nyembe
15 years
Nelson Mandela
life
Walter Sisulu
life
Denis Goldberg
life
The crime of these people was to protest.
To protest that it is wrong for a country to
violently discriminate against 81% of its people.
They were put behind bars. Along with
hundreds of other like-minded South Africans.
This is the police state that South Africa has
become.
A state without justice.
Yet, how could it be otherwise, in a state
without equality!
If you wish to protest, you can do so without fear. You only have to join the Anti-Apartheid
Movement, 89 Charlotte Street, London, W.1. Telephone 01-580 5311.

APARTHEID –
NEIN
DANKE!
1982
UNO-Jahr der
Mobilisierung
für Sanktionen
gegen Südafrika
ANTI-APARTHEID-BEWEGUNG (AAB) · Blücherstr. 14, D-5300 Bonn 1

006
007

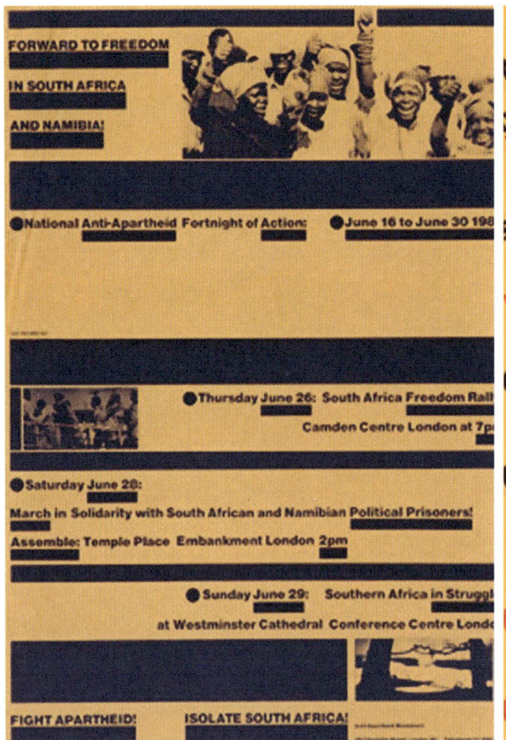

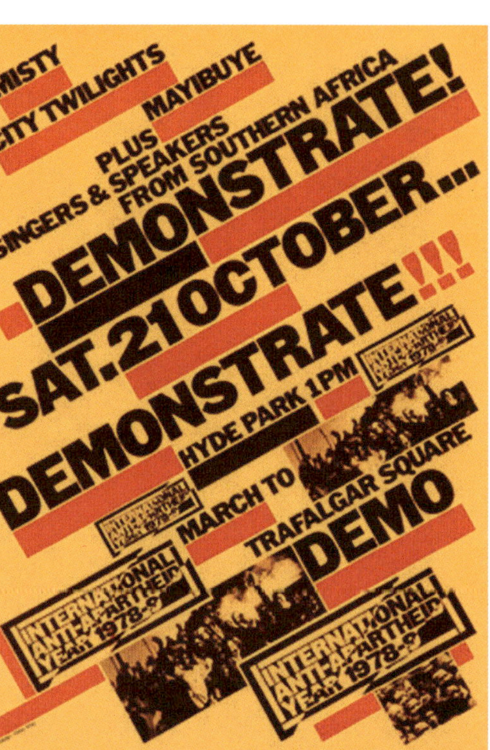

008
009

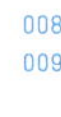

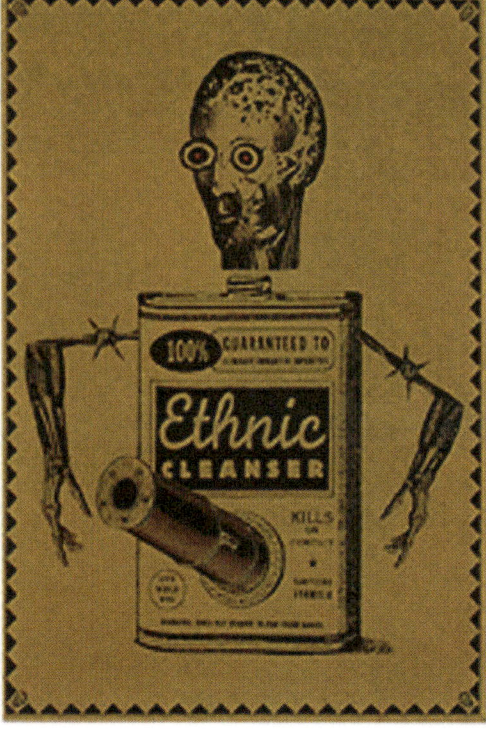

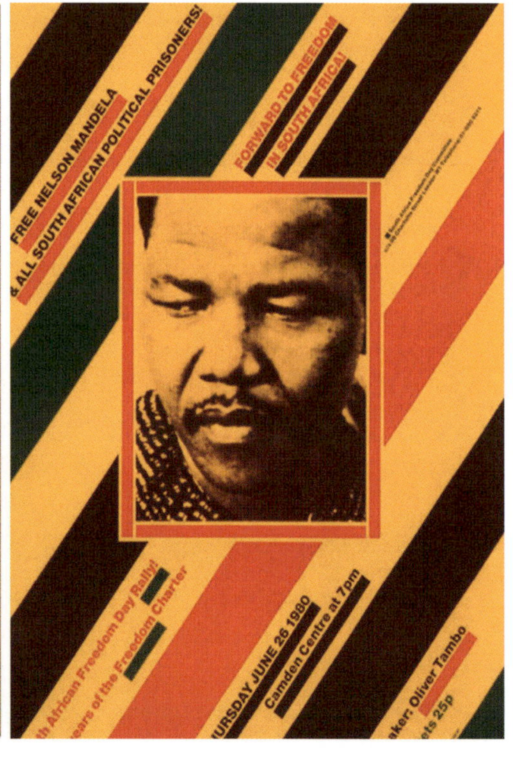

010
011

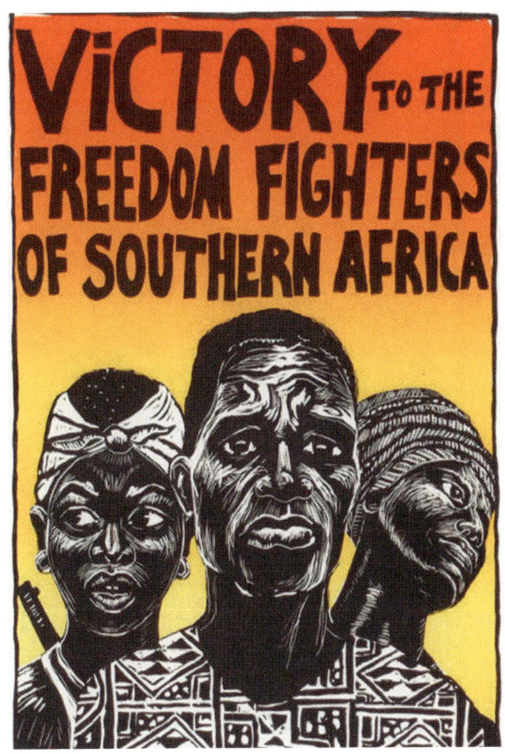

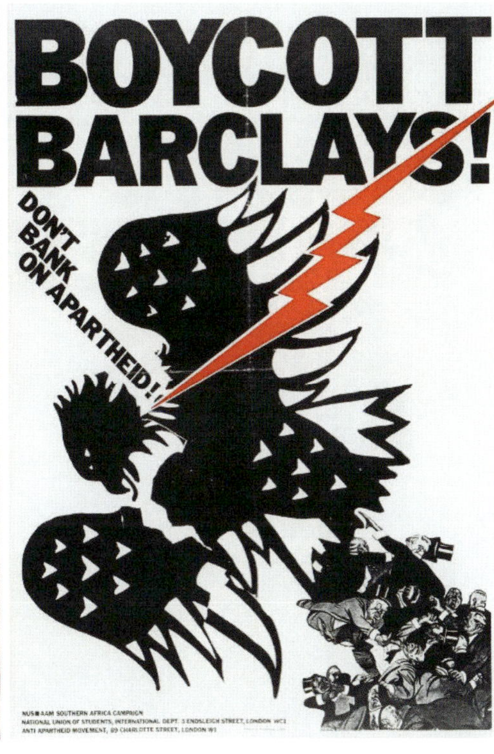

012
013

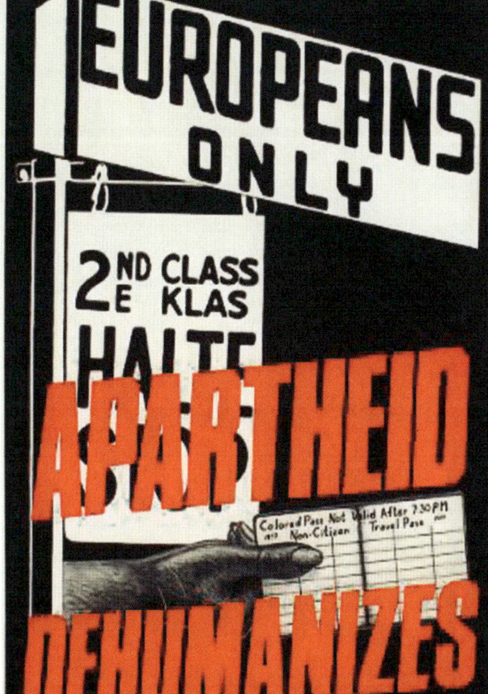

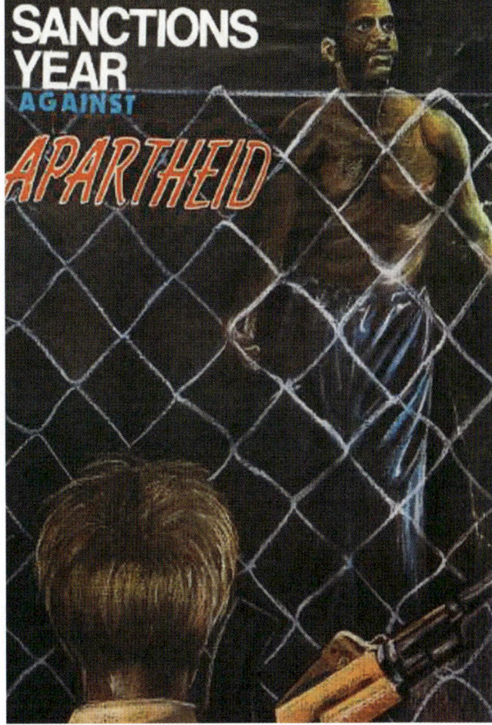

014
015

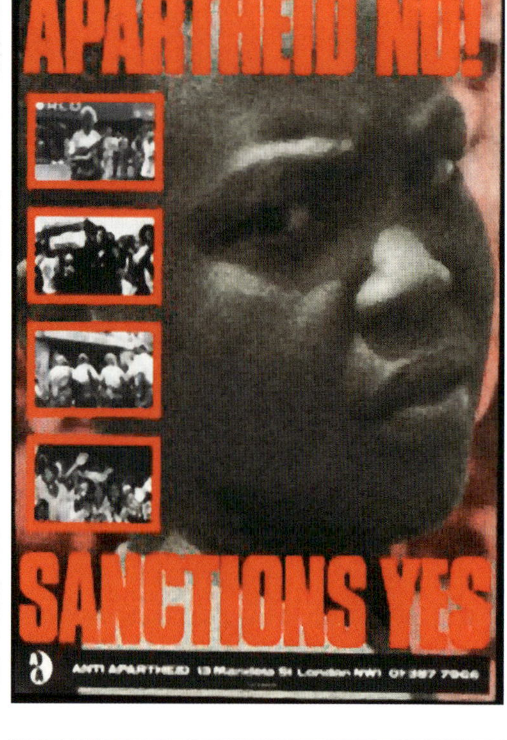

016
017

RIGHT
018

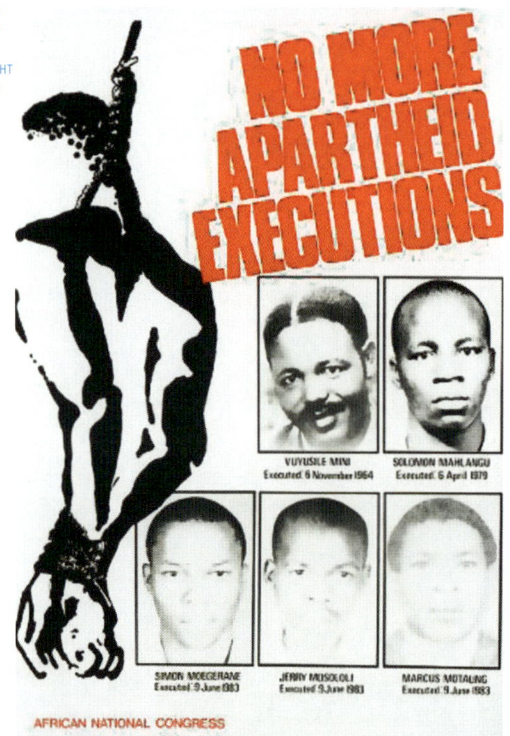

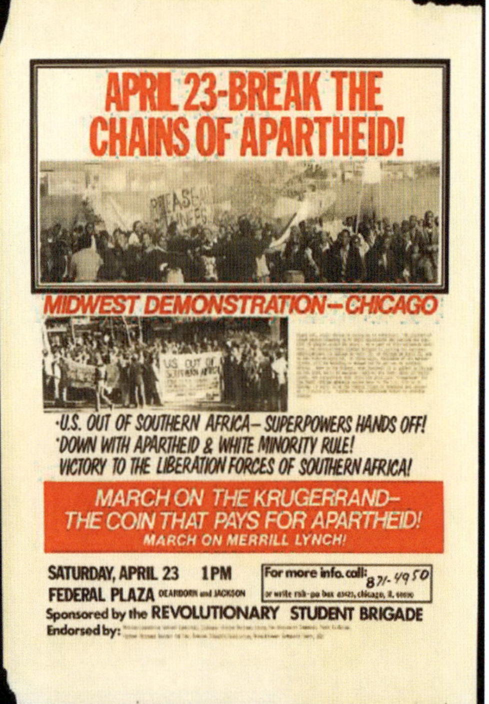

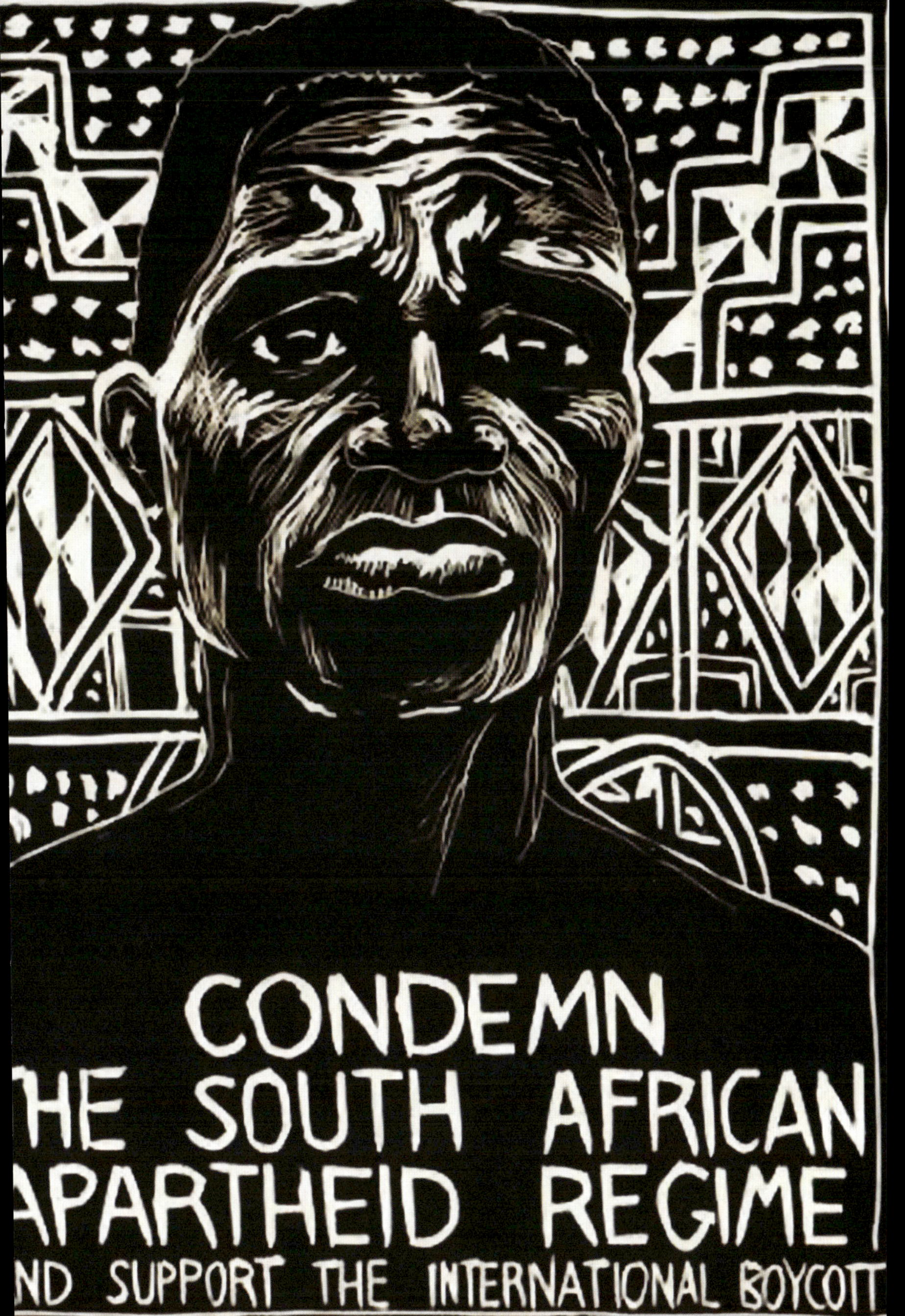
CONDEMN
THE SOUTH AFRICAN
APARTHEID REGIME
AND SUPPORT THE INTERNATIONAL BOYCOTT

019
020

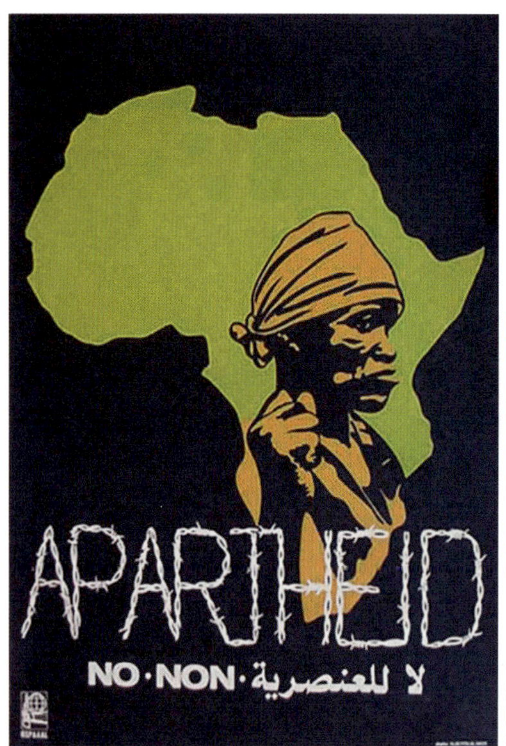

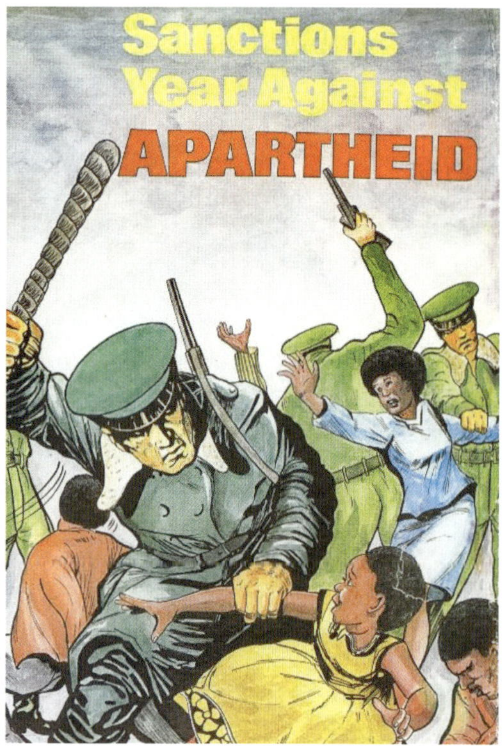

021
022

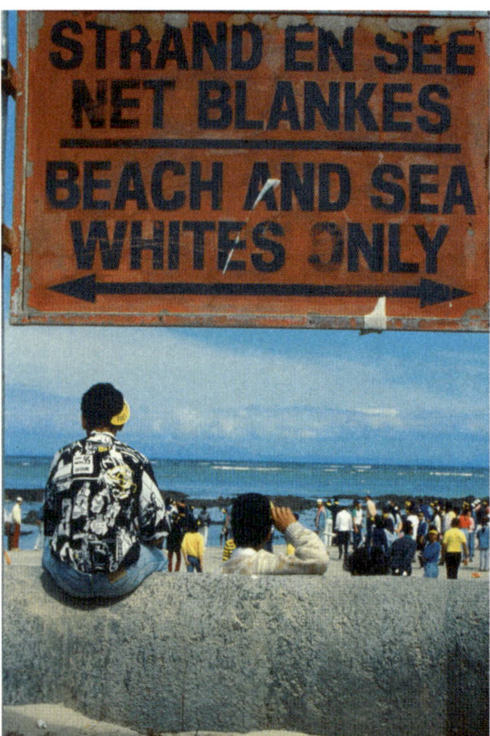

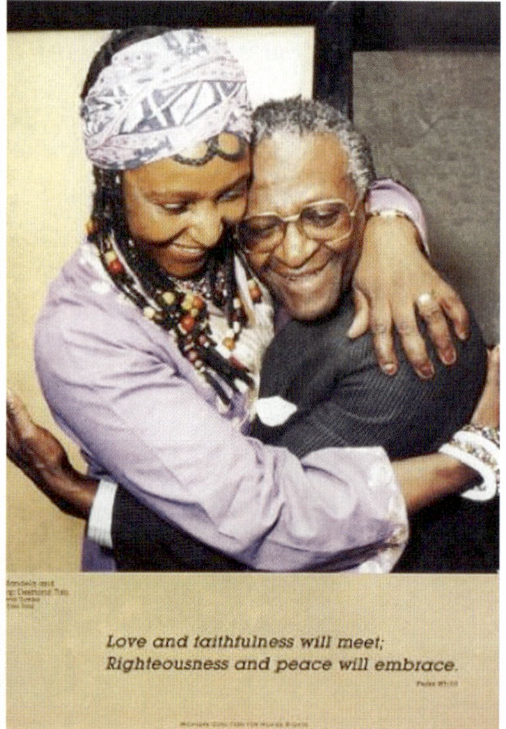

023
024

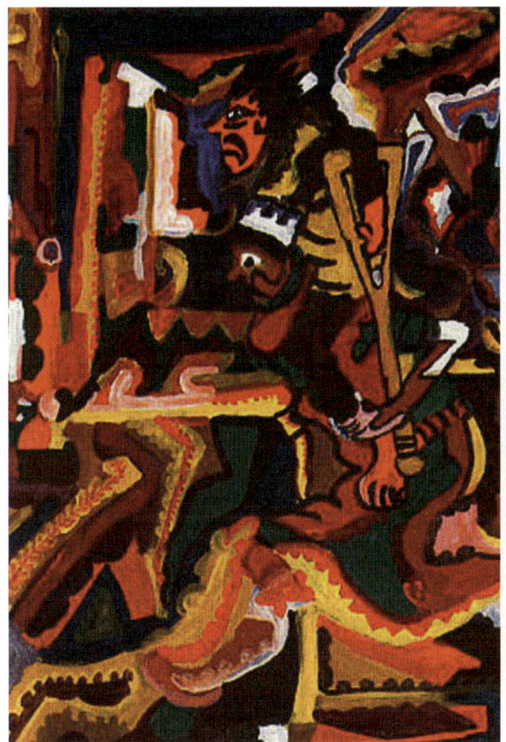

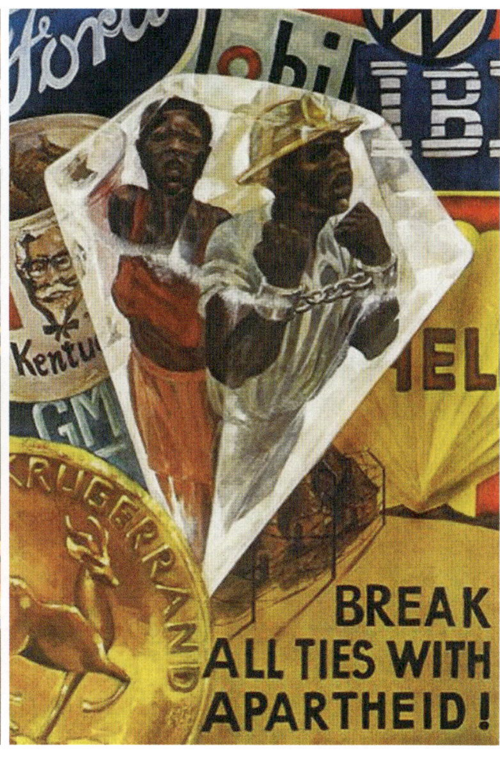

025
026

NEXT
027

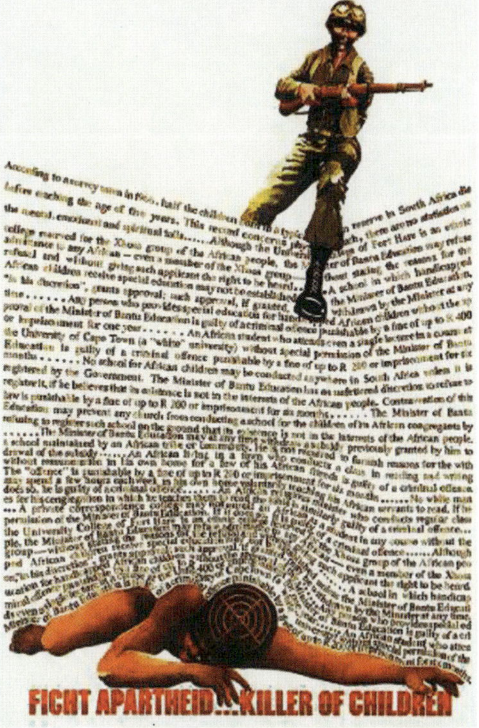

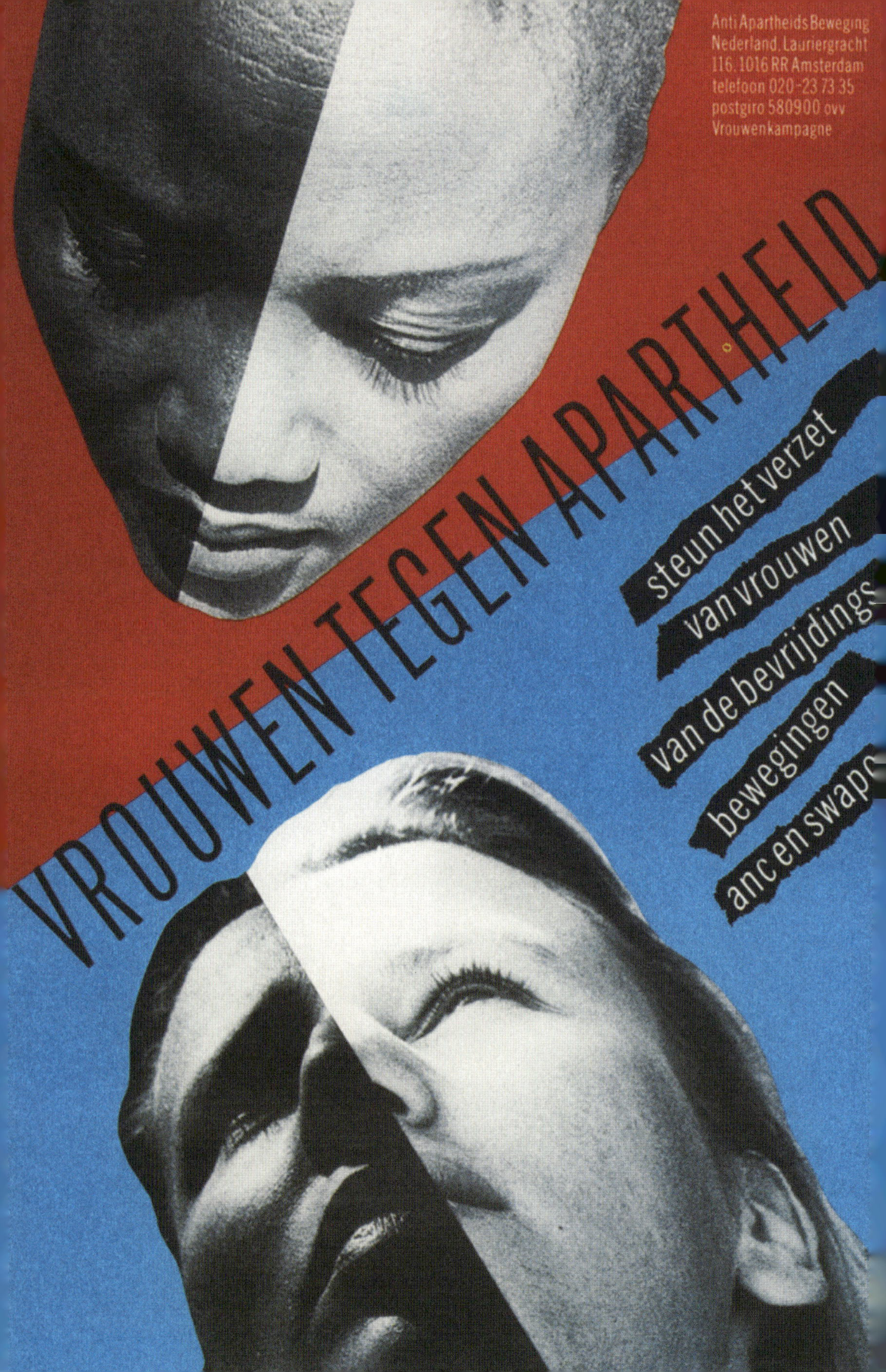
Anti Apartheids Beweging
Nederland, Lauriergracht
116, 1016 RR Amsterdam
telefoon 020-23 73 35
postgiro 580900 ovv
Vrouwenkampagne
VROUWEN TEGEN APARTHEID
steun het verzet
van vrouwen
van de bevrijdings
bewegingen
anc en swapo

001 SOUTH AFRICAN WOMEN
CREATOR Wild Plakken
SOURCE www.geheugenvannederland.nl
DATE 1998

002 NO TO BOTHA! NO TO APARTHEID!
SOURCE www.library.northwestern.edu

003 APARTHEID IN PRACTICE:
EDUCATION IN SOUTH AFRICA!
SOURCE www.library.northwestern.edu

004 APARTHEID IS ENOUGH TO TURN ANY
CIVILIZED HUMAN BEING INTO A
POLITICAL PRISONER
SOURCE www.library.northwestern.edu

005 APARTHEID — NEIN, DANKE!
[APARTHEID — NO THANKS! 1982 —
UN YEAR OF MOBILIZATION FOR
SANCTIONS AGAINST SOUTH AFRICA]
SOURCE www.library.northwestern.edu
DATE 1892

006 FORWARD TO FREEDOM IN SOUTH
AFRICA AND NAMIBIA!
Anti-Apartheid Movement, London
CREATOR David King
SOURCE Plakatsammlung Museum
für Gestaltung Zürich
DATE 1980

007 DEMONSTRATE!
Anti-Apartheid Movement, London
CREATOR David King
SOURCE Plakatsammlung Museum
für Gestaltung Zürich
DATE 1978

008 ETHNIC CLEANSER
CREATOR Joe Scorsone, Alice Drueding
SOURCE "L'engagement politique et
social," Le festival d'affiches,
Chaumont, 19 May - 16 July 2000

009 FREE NELSON MANDELA AND ALL SOUTH
AFRICAN POLITICAL PRISONERS!
Anti-Apartheid Movement, London
CREATOR David King
SOURCE Plakatsammlung Museum
für Gestaltung Zürich
DATE 1978

010 VICTORY TO THE FREEDOM FIGHTERS
OF SOUTHERN AFRICA
CREATOR San Francisco Poster
Brigade
SOURCE Plakatsammlung Museum
für Gestaltung Zürich

011 BOYCOTT BARCLAYS!
SOURCE www.library.northwestern.edu

012 EUROPEANS ONLY
SOURCE www.library.northwestern.edu

013 SANCTIONS YEAR AGAINST APARTHEID
Nigerian National Committee against
Apartheid marks International

Year of Mobilization for
Sanctions against South Africa.
SOURCE www.library.northwestern.edu

014 ANTI-APARTHEID MOVEMENT SAYS
ISOLATE APARTHEID SOUTH AFRICA
SOURCE www.library.northwestern.edu

015 APARTHEID NO!: SANCTIONS YES
SOURCE www.library.northwestern.edu

016 NO MORE APARTHEID EXECUTIONS
SOURCE www.library.northwestern.edu

017 BREAK THE CHAINS OF APARTHEID!
Midwest demonstration in Chicago.
SOURCE www.library.northwestern.edu

018 CONDEMN THE SOUTH AFRICAN
APARTHEID REGIME AND SUPPORT THE
INTERNATIONAL BOYCOTT
SOURCE www.library.northwestern.edu

019 APARTHEID
SOURCE www.odg.cat

020 SANCTIONS YEAR AGAINST APARTHEID
SOURCE www.library.northwestern.edu

021 BEACH AND SEA WHITES ONLY
SOURCE media-2.web.britannica.com

022 LOVE AND FAITHFULNESS WILL MEET,
RIGHTEOUSNESS AND PEACE WILL
EMBRACE — PSALM 85:10
Winnie Mandela, wearing
traditional African clothing,
and Archbishop Desmond Tutu in
a business suit happily embrace.
SOURCE media-2.web.britannica.com
DATE 1987

023 UNTITLED
SOURCE Julius Njau, Permanent
Collection, Museum für Volkerkunde
DATE 1988

024 BREAK ALL TIES WITH APARTHEID!
CREATOR Mary H. Nash
SOURCE www.library.northwestern.edu

025 SOUTH AFRICA
CREATOR Rafael Enriquez
SOURCE Steven Heller and Carol
Wells, eds., *The Graphic
Imperative: International Posters
for Peace, Social Justice, and the
Environment, 1965-2005* [Boston:
Massachusetts College of Arts,
2005], p. 28.

026 FIGHT APARTHEID, KILLER OF CHILDREN
CREATOR Pat Cummings
SOURCE www.library.northwestern.edu

027 VROUWEN TEGEN APARTHEID
[WOMEN AGAINST APARTHEID]
CREATOR Wild Plakken
SOURCE www.geheugenvannederland.nl

001
002

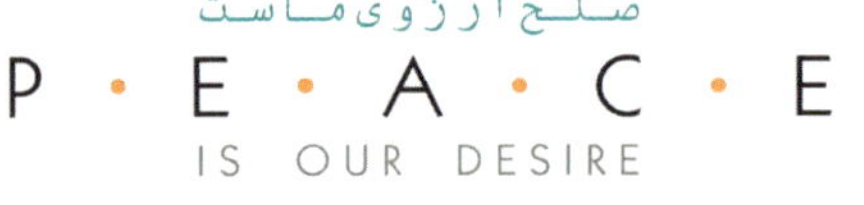

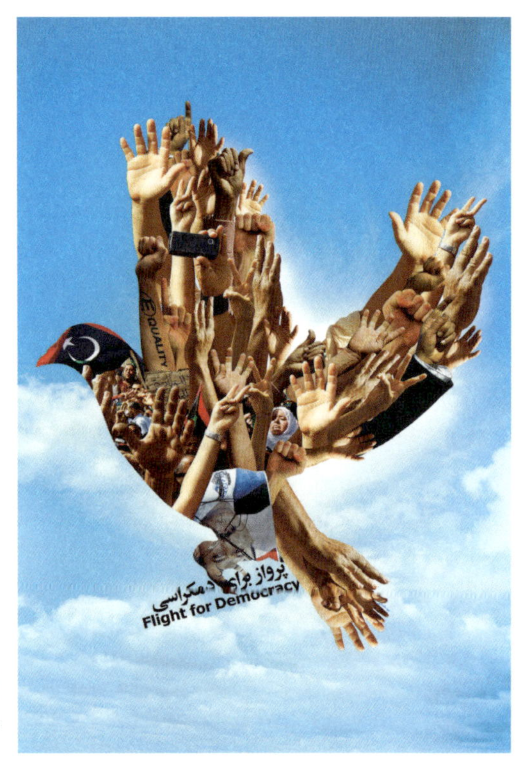

003
004

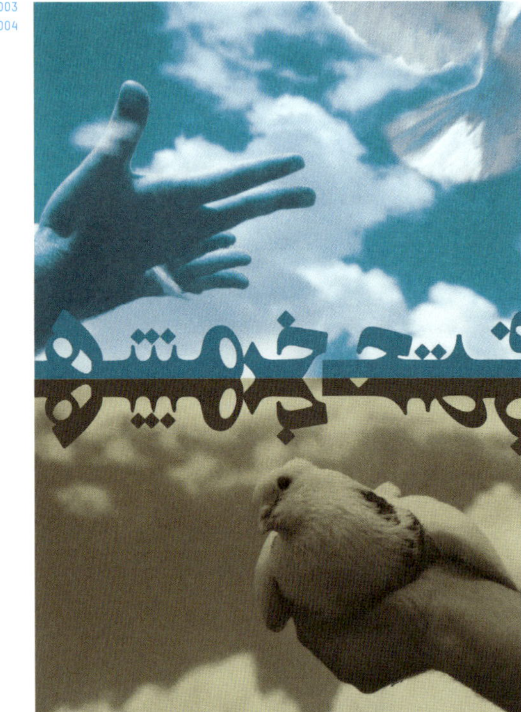

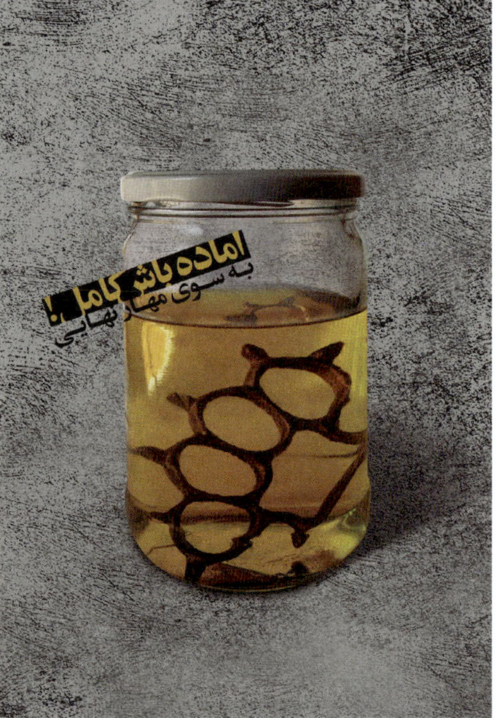

005
006

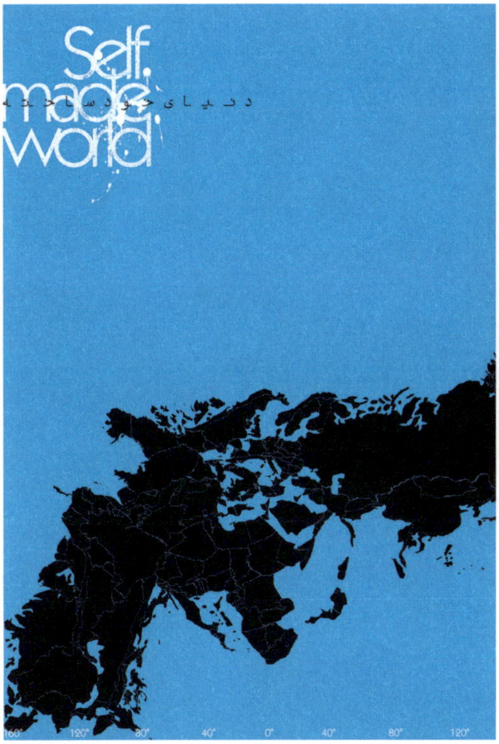

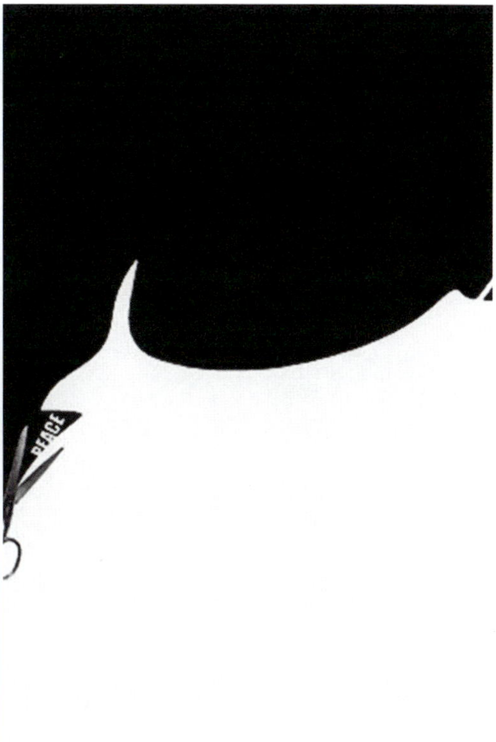

007
008

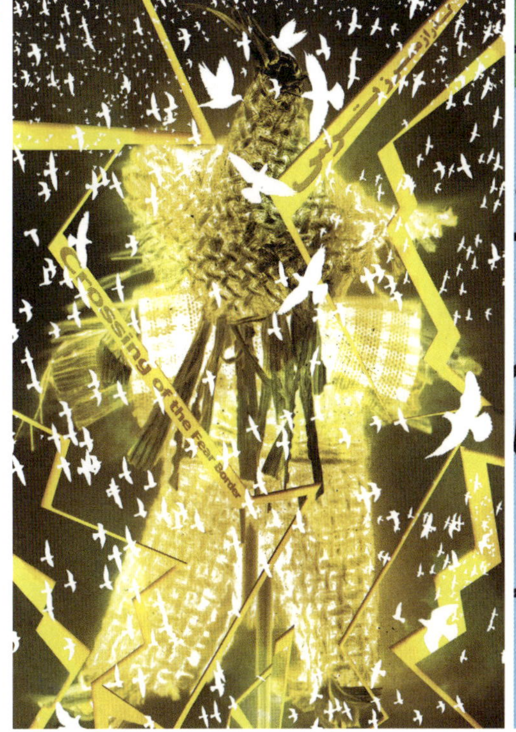

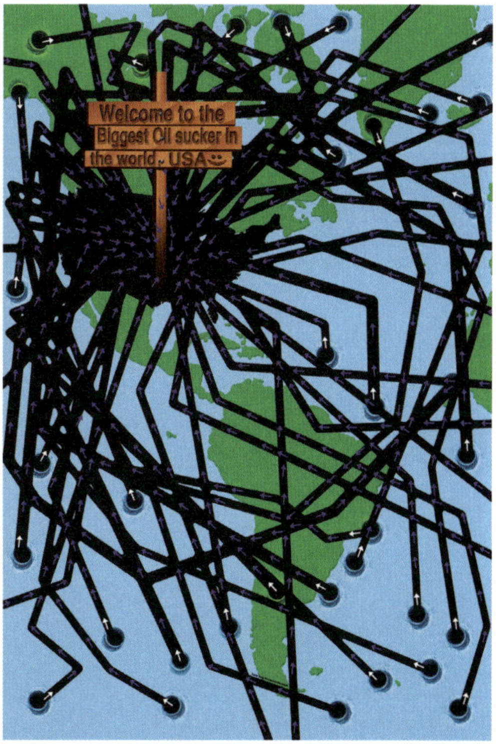

009
010

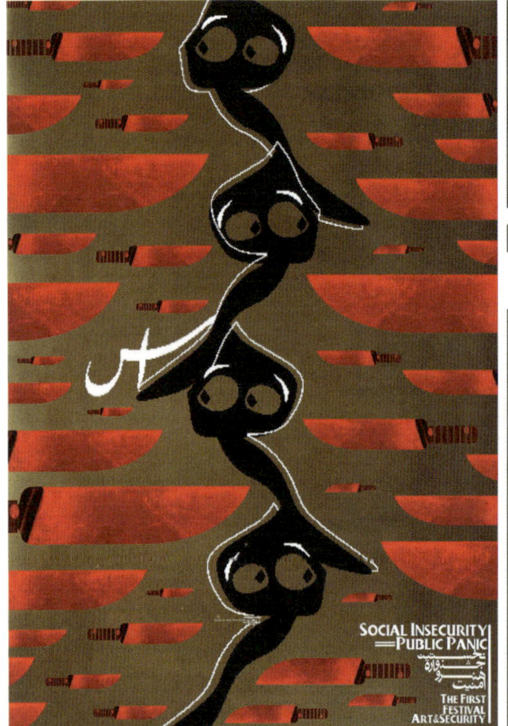

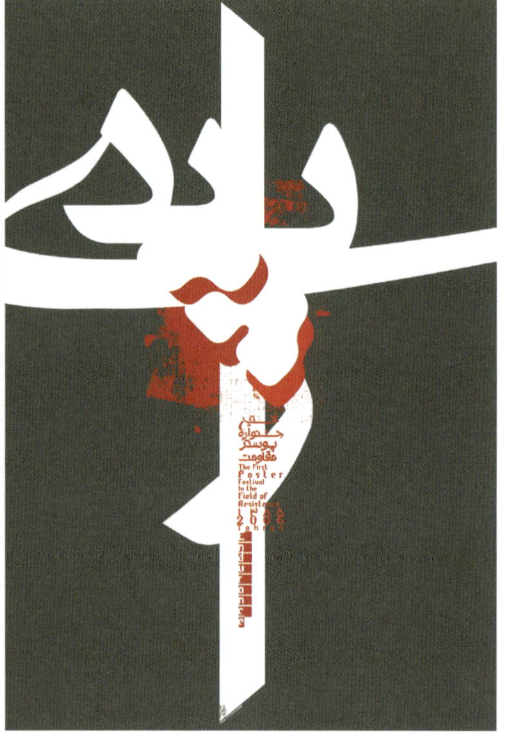

011
012

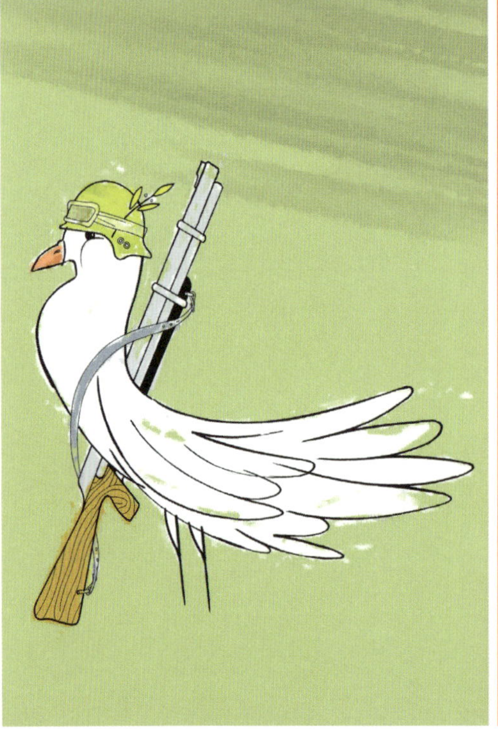

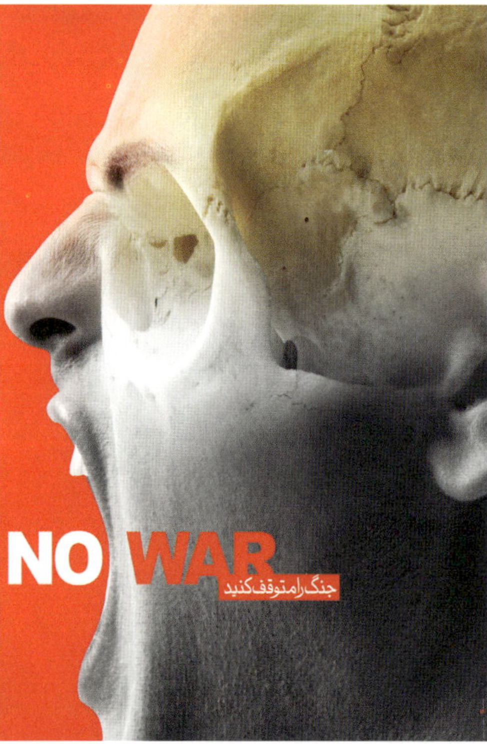

013
014

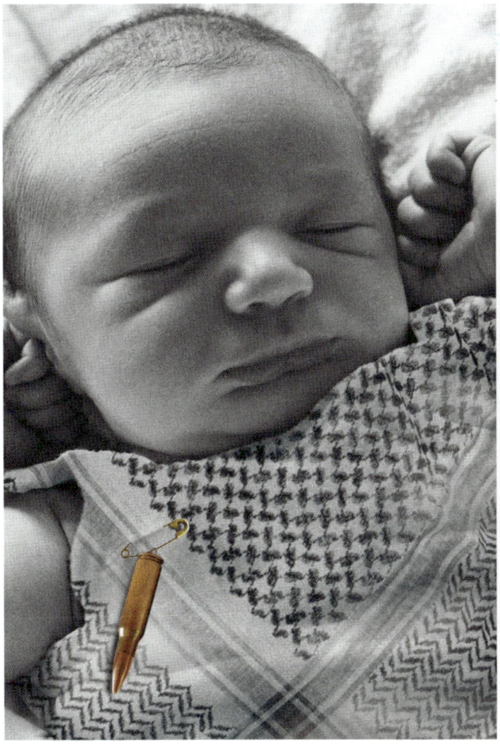

015
016

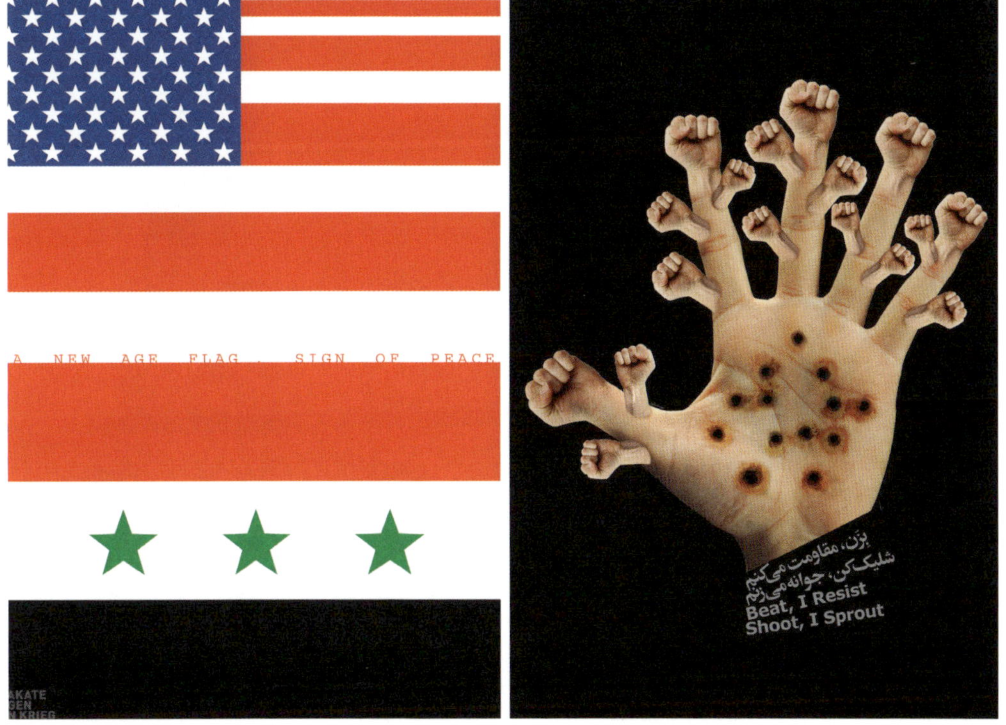

017
018

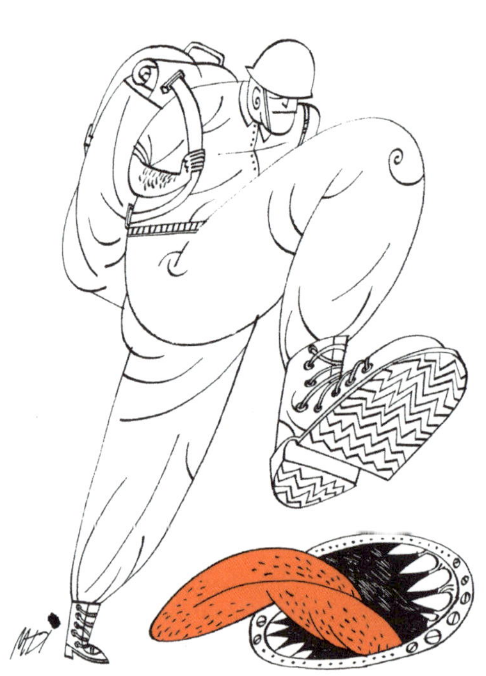

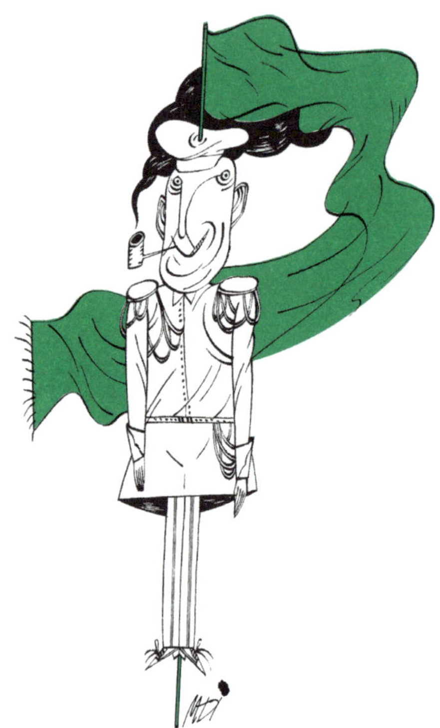

019
020

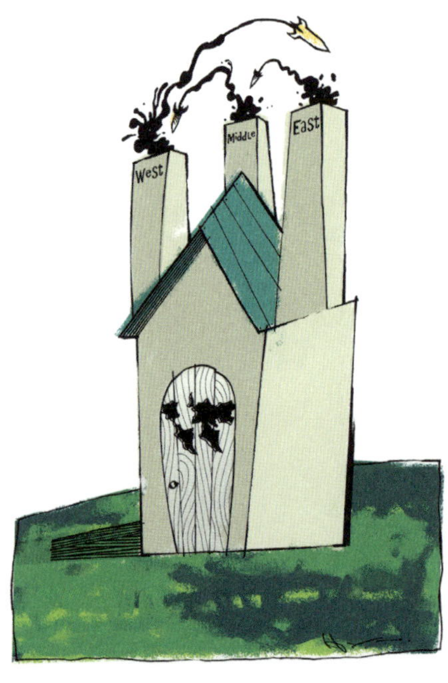

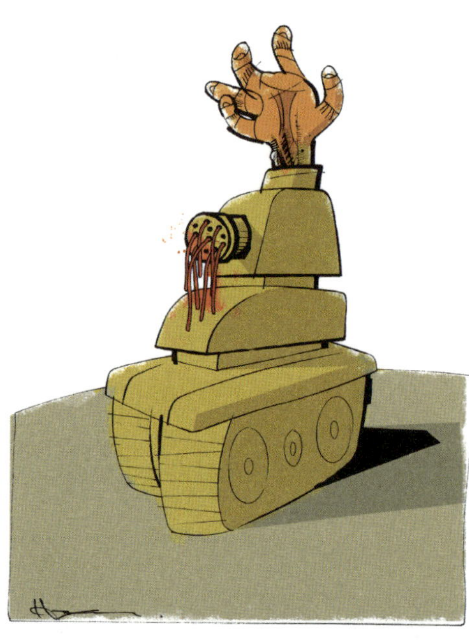

001 PEACE IS OUR DESIRE
CREATOR Hassan Karimyadeh
DATE 2007

002 FLIGHT FOR DEMOCRACY
CREATOR Parisa Tashakori
DATE 2012

003 FREEDOM OF KHORAMSHAR
CREATOR Parisa Tashakori
DATE 2007

004 SECURITY
CREATOR Parisa Tashakori
DATE 2007

005 SELF-MADE WORLD
CREATOR Hassan Karimyadeh
DATE 2012

006 PEACE
CREATOR Mehdi Saeedi

007 CROSSING THE FEAR BORDER
CREATOR Amirhossein Ghoochibeik
DATE 2012

008 WELCOME TO THE BIGGEST OIL SUCKER
IN THE WORLD "USA"
CREATOR Amirhossein Ghoochibeik
DATE 2012

009 SOCIAL INSECURITY = PUBLIC PANIC
CREATOR Amirhossein Ghoochibeik
DATE 2007

010 ENDURANCE
CREATOR Amirhossein Ghoochibeik
DATE 2006

011 PEACEMAKER
CREATOR Hassan Karimyadeh
DATE 2005

012 NO WAR
CREATOR Sohrab Marzban

013 UNTITLED
CREATOR Parisa Tashakori

014 PEACE
CREATOR Parisa Tashakori
DATE 2009

015 AGAINST WAR IN IRAQ
CREATOR Parisa Tashakori
DATE 2002

016 BEAT I RESIST, SHOOT I SPROUT
CREATOR Parisa Tashakori
DATE 2012

017 THE MINE'S LUST
CREATOR Mahdi Karimzadeh

018 THE VANGUARD OF PEACE
CREATOR Mahdi Karimzadeh

019 UNITED NATIONS
CREATOR Hassan Karimyadeh
DATE 2007

020 WAR CAR
CREATOR Hassan Karimyadeh
DATE 2008

001

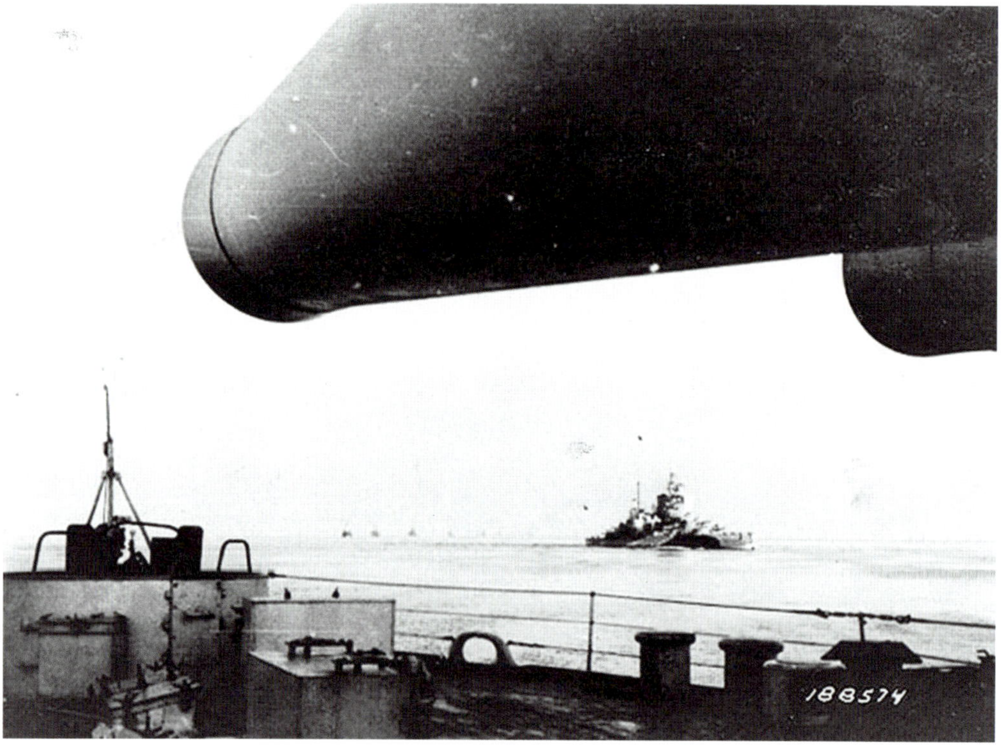

002
003

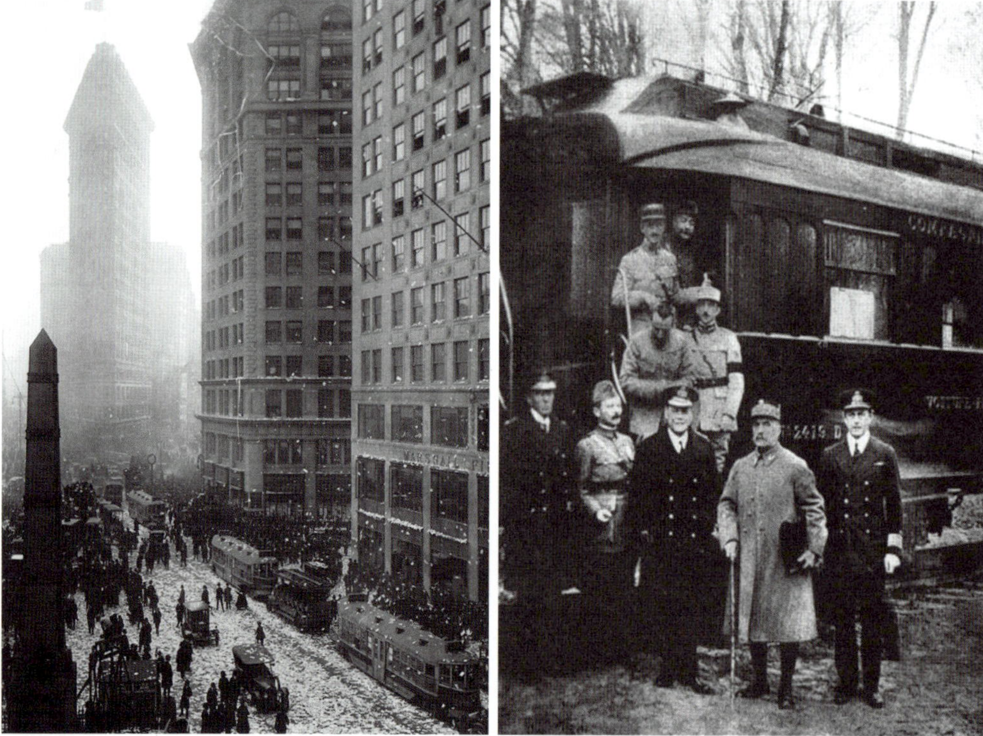

004
005

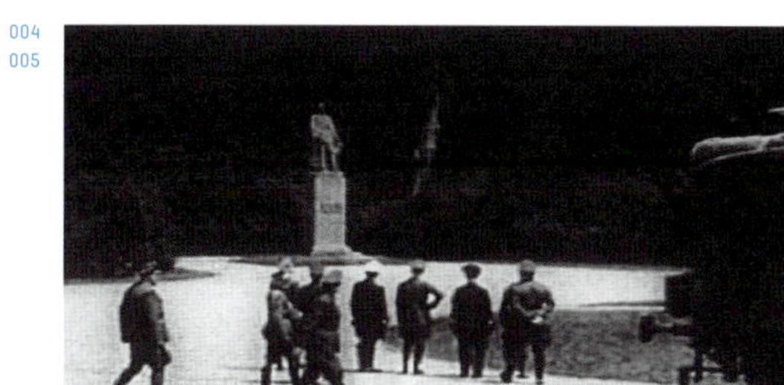

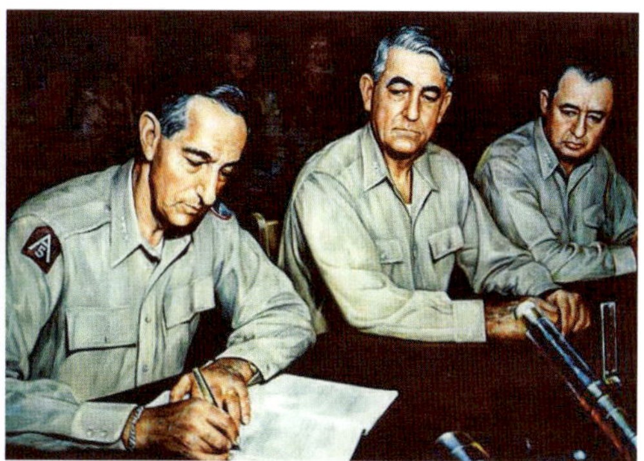

006
007

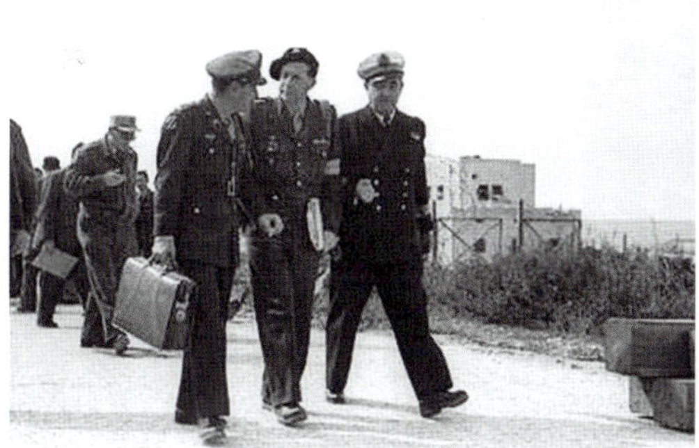

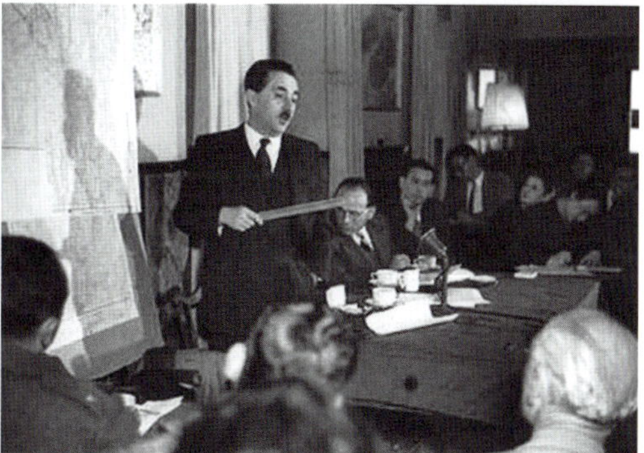

008
009

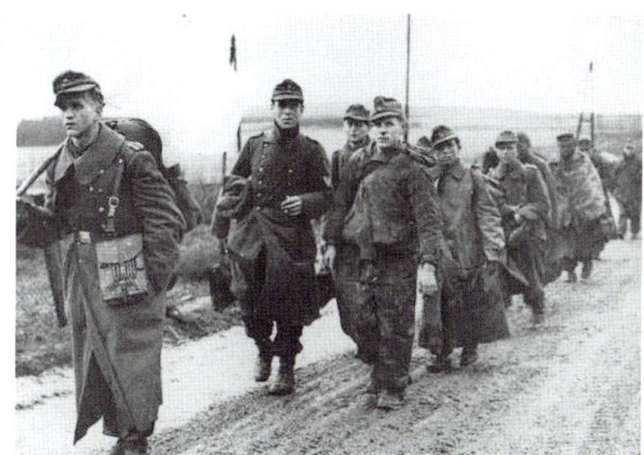

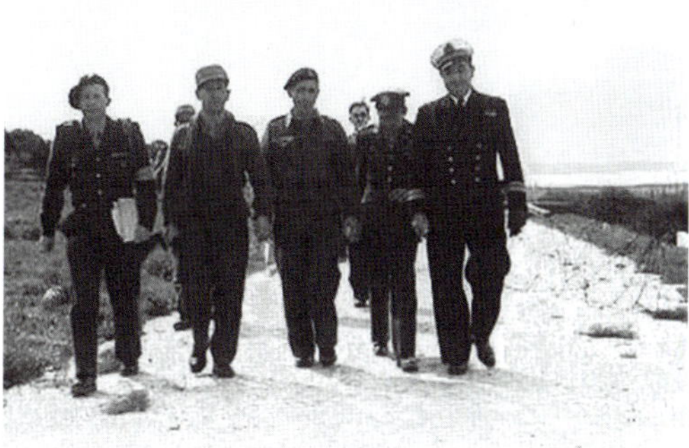

010
011

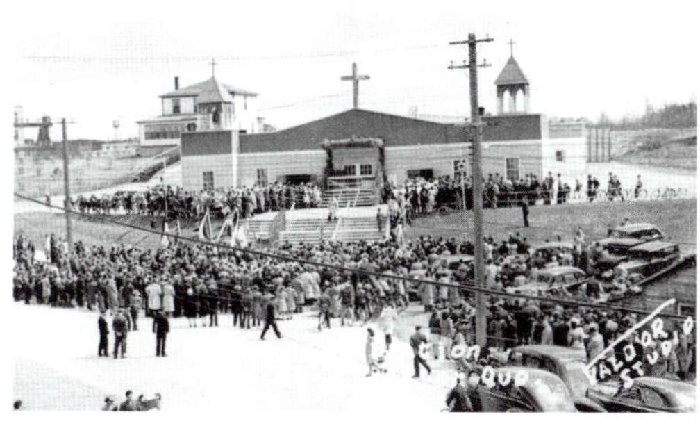

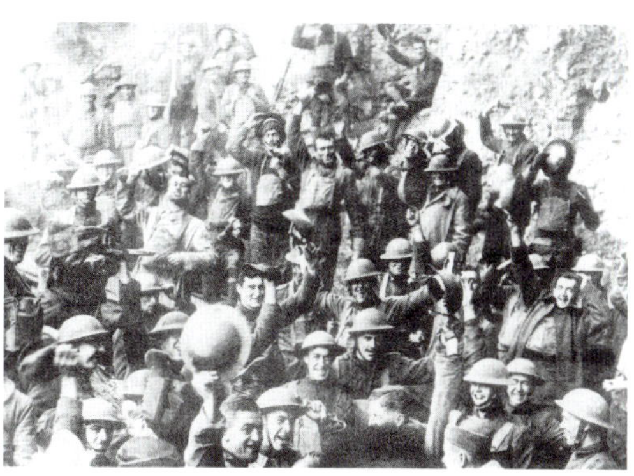

012
013

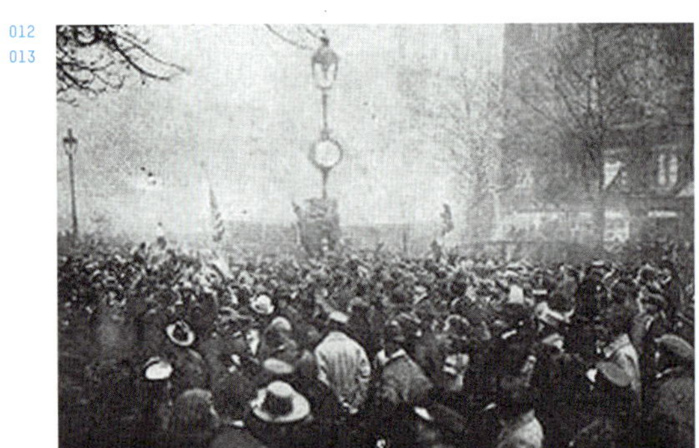
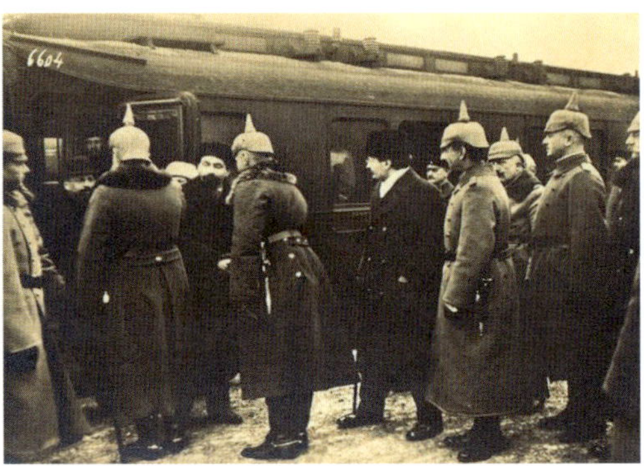

014
015

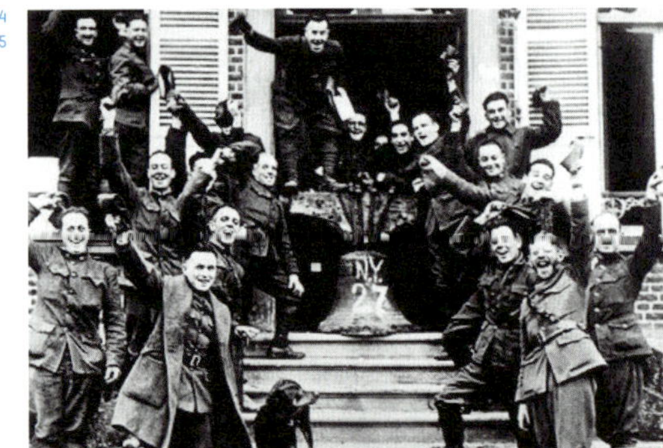
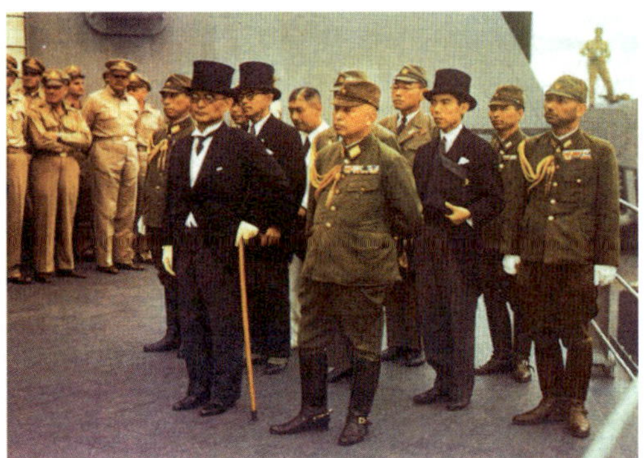

016
017

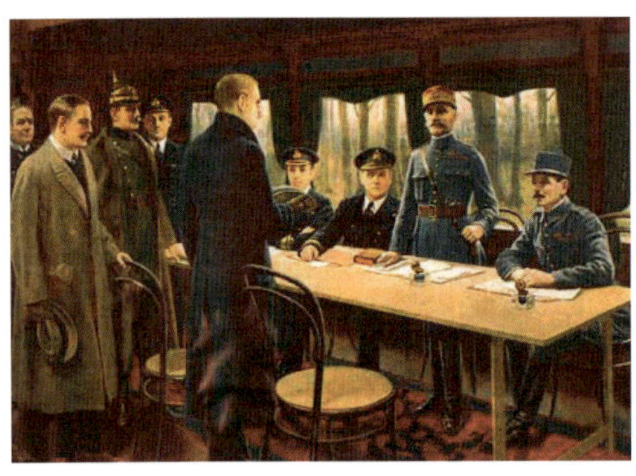
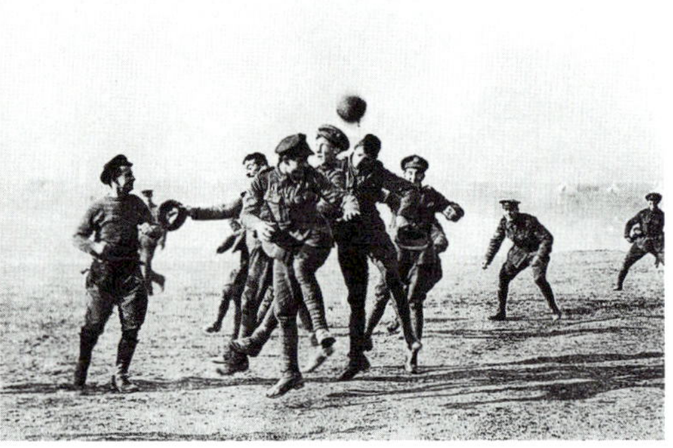

018
019

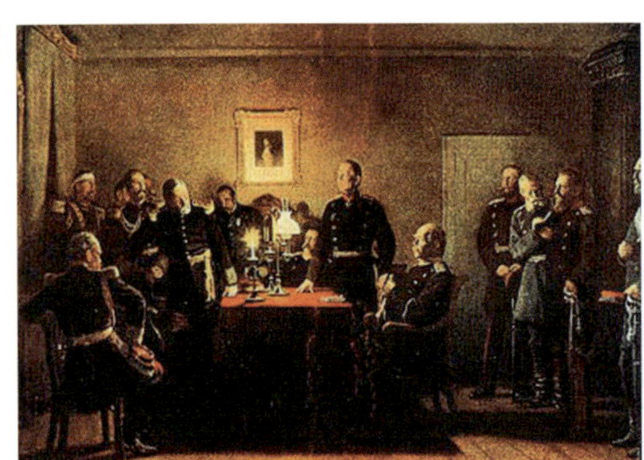
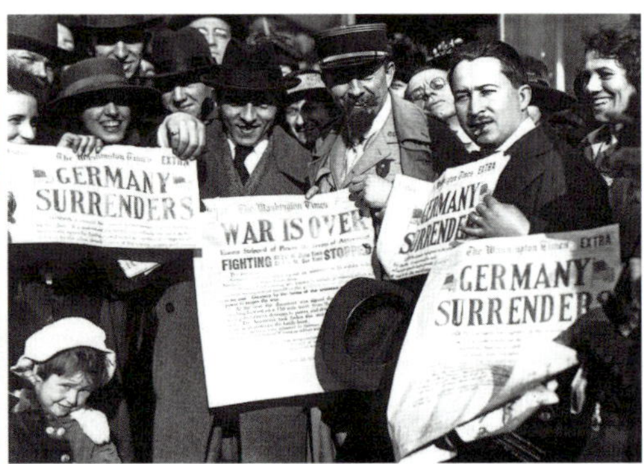

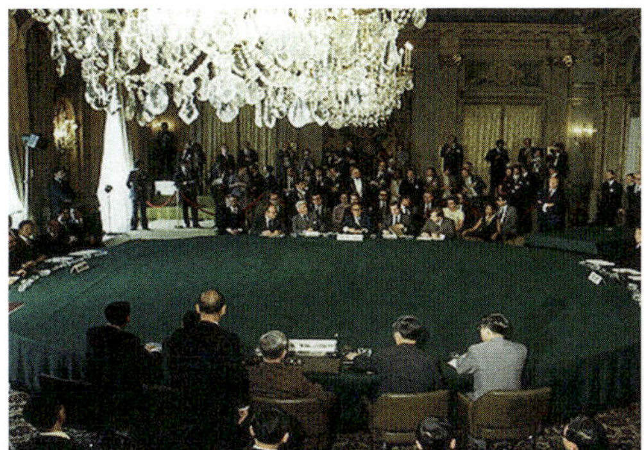
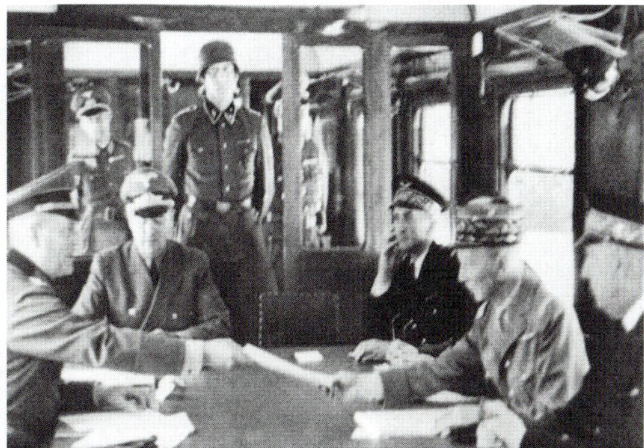
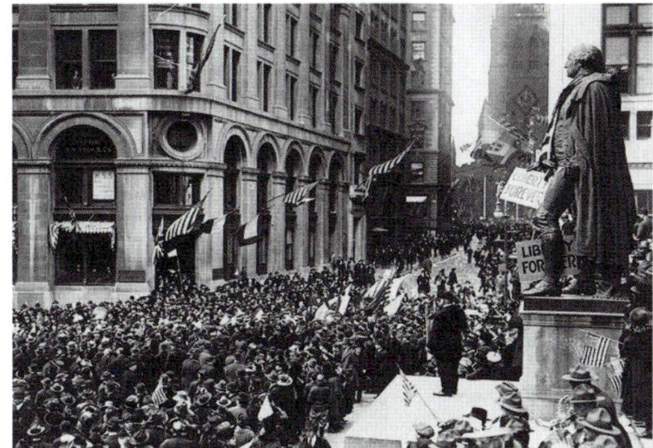
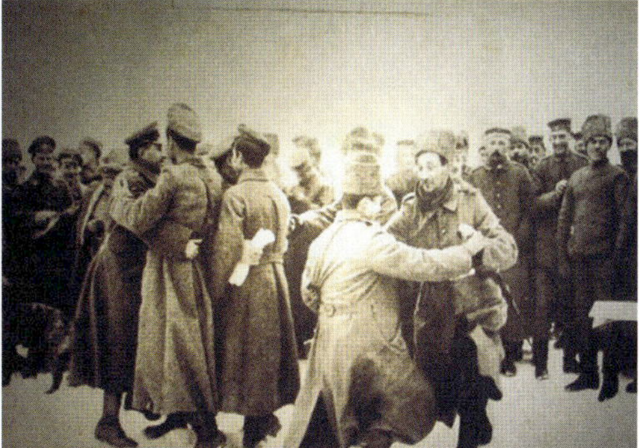
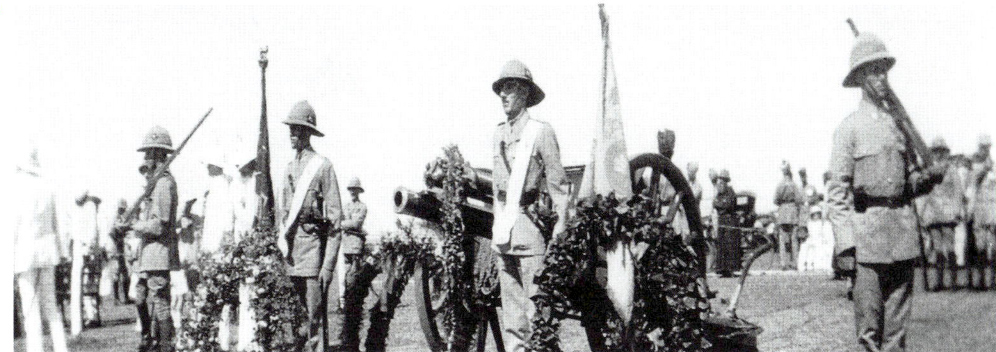
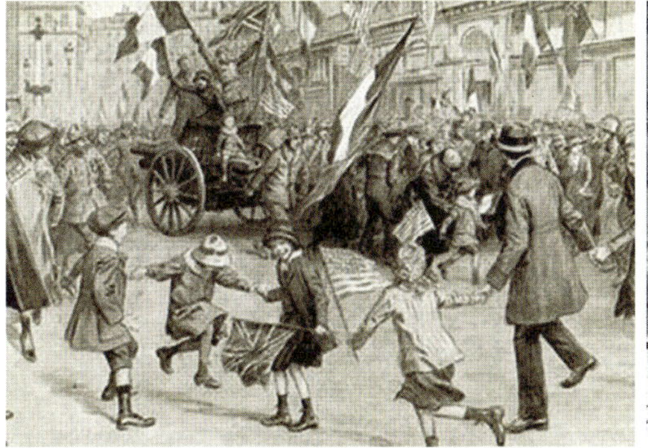
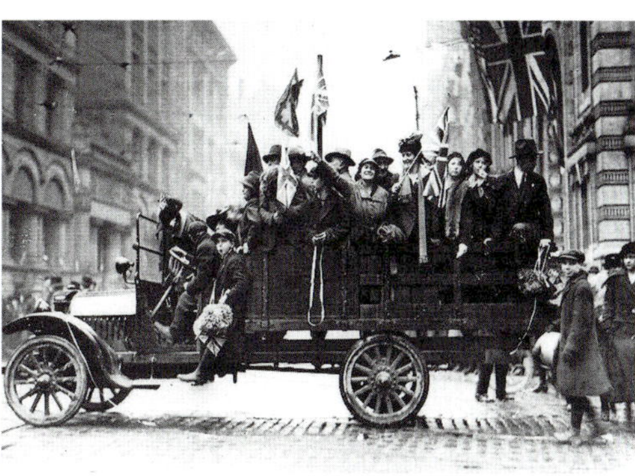

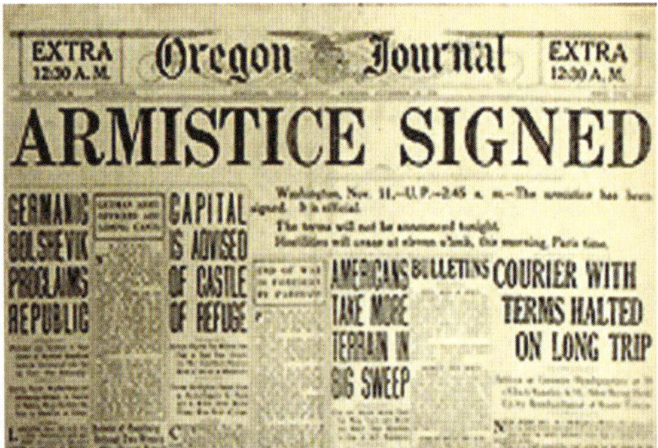
EXTRA
12:30 A.M.
Oregon Journal
EXTRA
12:30 A.M.
ARMISTICE SIGNED

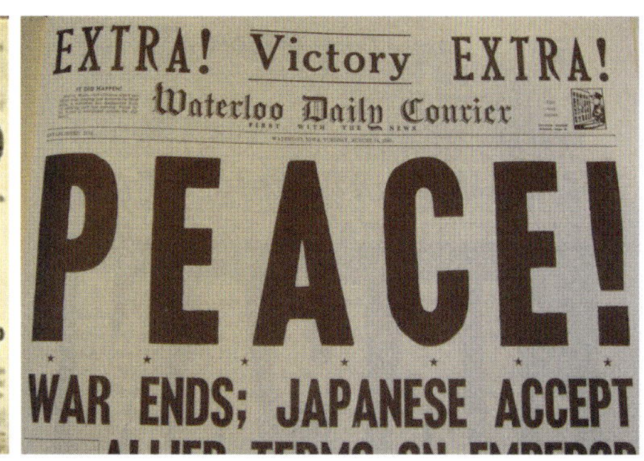
EXTRA! Victory EXTRA!
Waterloo Daily Courier
PEACE!
WAR ENDS; JAPANESE ACCEPT

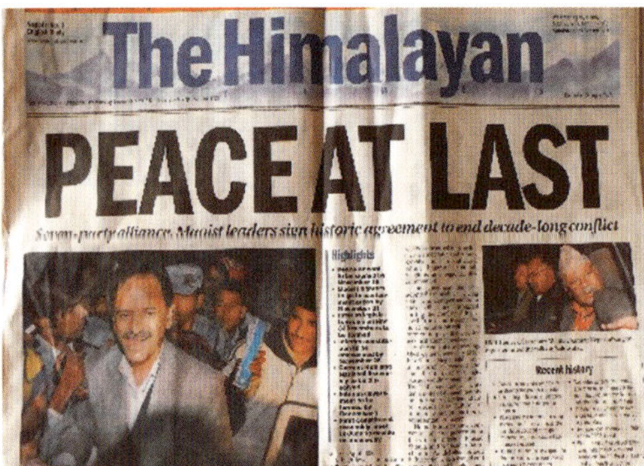
The Himalayan
PEACE AT LAST

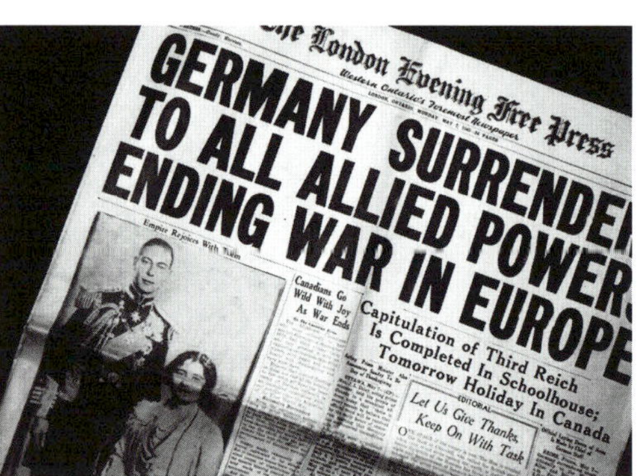
London Evening Free Press
GERMANY SURRENDERS
TO ALL ALLIED POWERS
ENDING WAR IN EUROPE

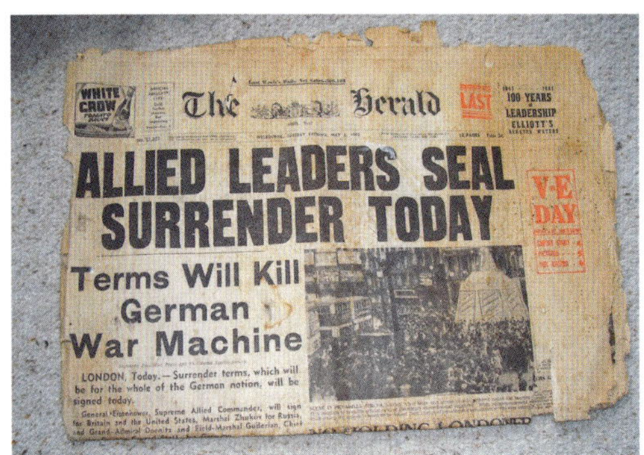
The Herald
ALLIED LEADERS SEAL
SURRENDER TODAY
Terms Will Kill
German
War Machine
V-E
DAY

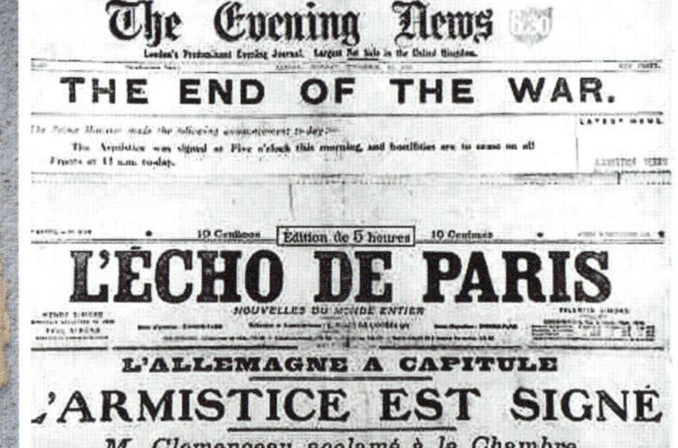
The Evening News
THE END OF THE WAR.
L'ÉCHO DE PARIS
L'ALLEMAGNE A CAPITULE
L'ARMISTICE EST SIGNÉ
M. Clemenceau acclamé à la Chambre

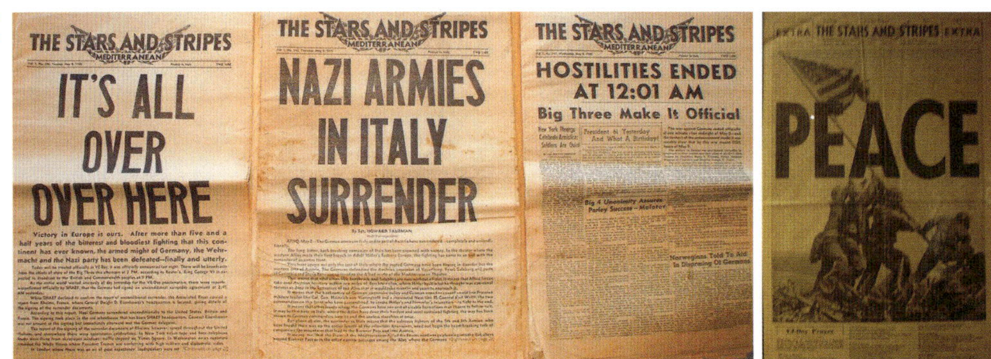
THE STARS AND STRIPES
IT'S ALL
OVER
OVER HERE
THE STARS AND STRIPES
NAZI ARMIES
IN ITALY
SURRENDER
THE STARS AND STRIPES
HOSTILITIES ENDED
AT 12:01 AM
Big Three Make It Official
EXTRA THE STARS AND STRIPES EXTRA
PEACE

035
036

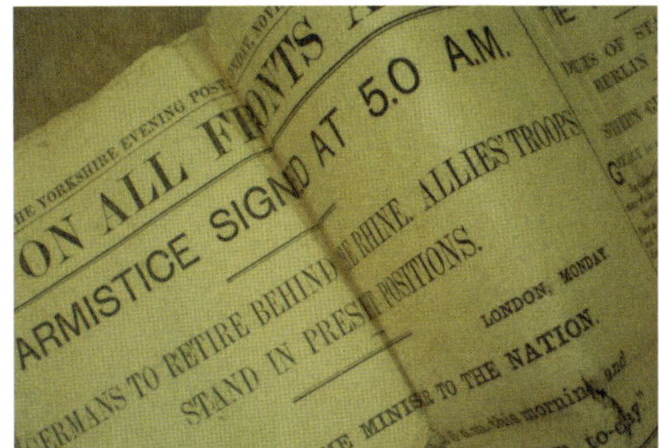

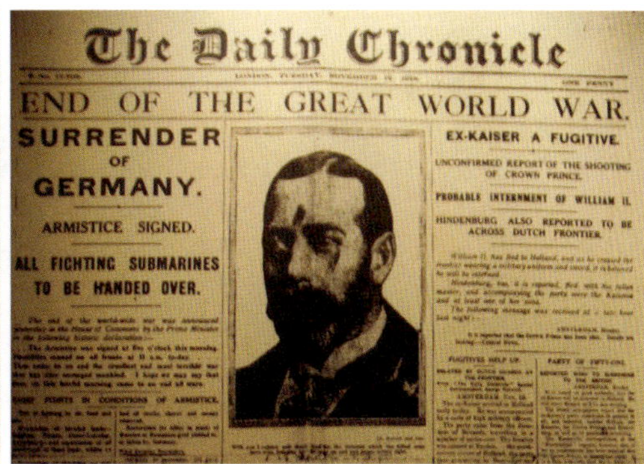

037
038
039
040

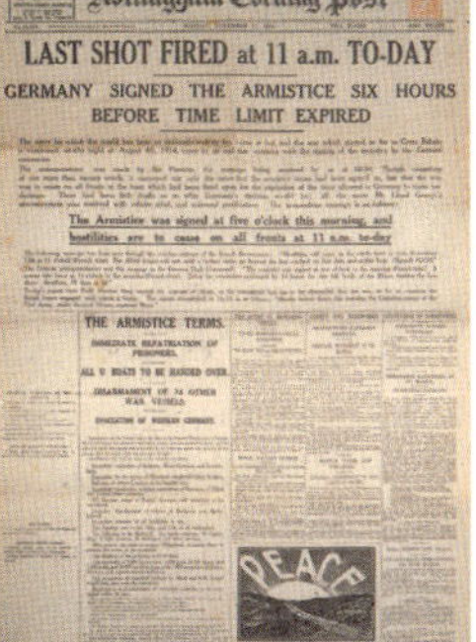

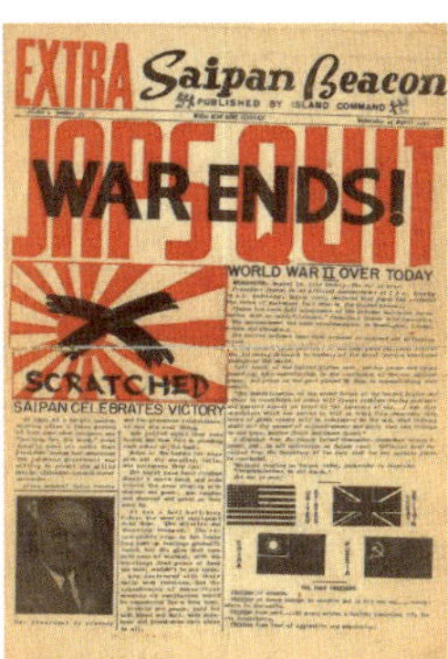

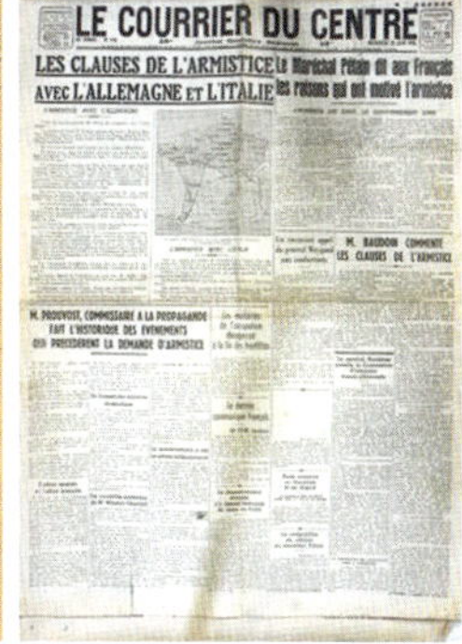

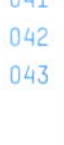

LE COURRIER DU CENTRE
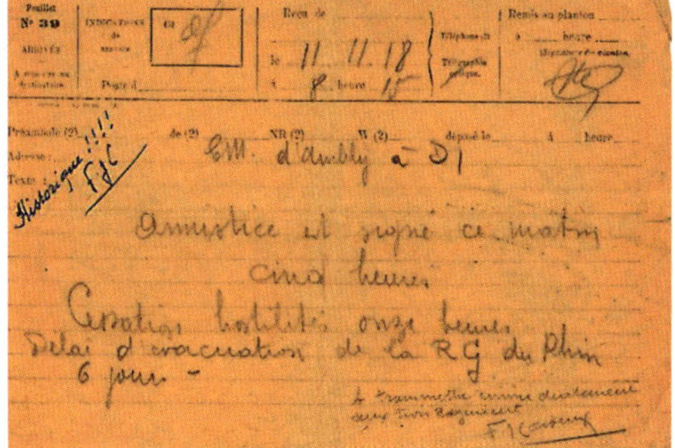

041
042
043

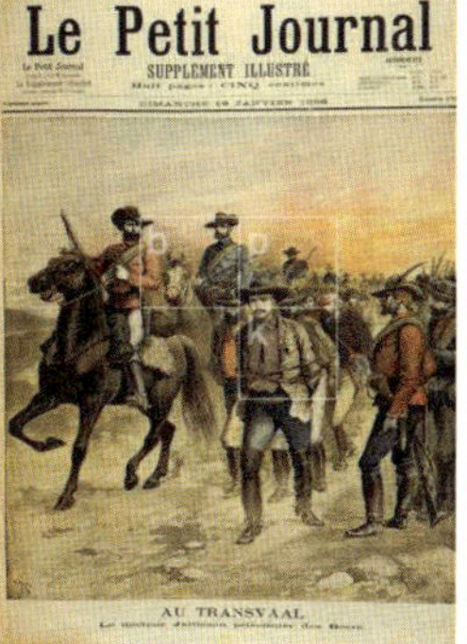

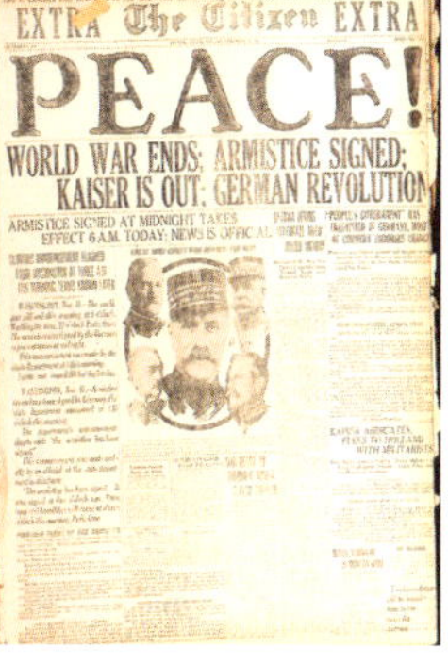

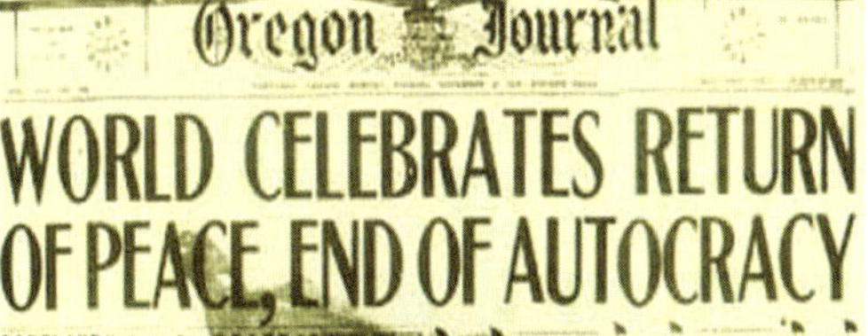

044
045

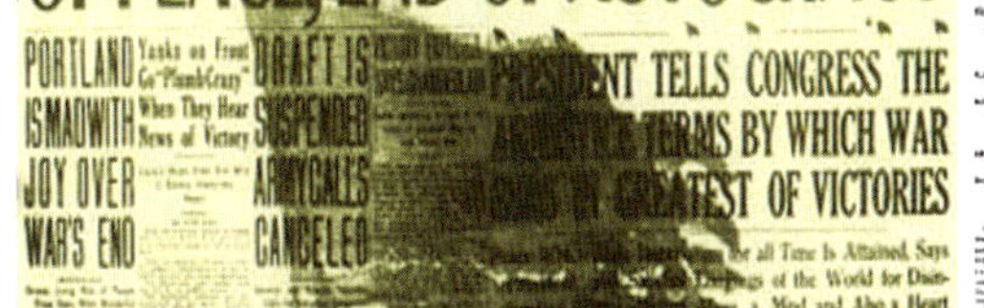

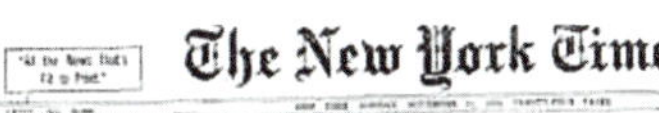

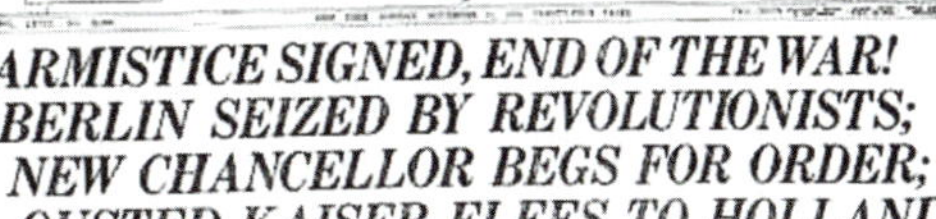

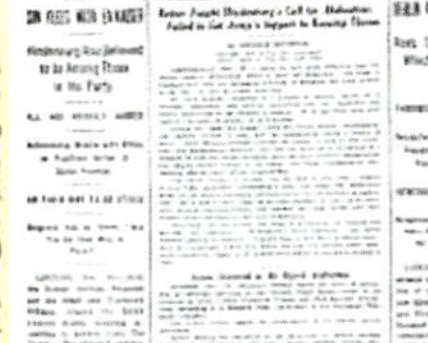

001 HMS VALIANT
HMS Valiant leads the line as the Italian fleet steams into Malta, under the terms of the Italian Armistice.
SOURCE commons.wikimedia.org
DATE 10 September 1943

002 ARMISTICE DAY, FLATIRON BUILDING
CREATOR The Press Illustrating Service
SOURCE commons.wikimedia.org

003 The allied representatives at the signing of the armistice. Ferdinand Foch, second from right, seen outside his railway carriage in the forest of Compiègne.
CREATOR The Press Illustrating Service
SOURCE en.wikipedia.org/wiki/
DATE 11 November 1918

004 HITLER AND GERMAN-NAZI OFFICERS STARING AT FRENCH MARSHAL FOCH STATUE
Hitler [hand on his waist] and German Military officers staring at French marshal Ferdinand Foch's memorial statue before entering the railway carriage where will be signed the 1940 armistice, at Compiègne, France.
SOURCE commons.wikimedia.org
DATE 25 June 1940

005 CLARK SIGNING ARMISTICE
General Mark Clark signs the Military Armistice Agreement ending the Korean War on behalf of the UN Command, believing himself to be the first US commander to agree to an Armistice without victory. Clark stated afterward, "I cannot find it in me to exalt at this hour."
SOURCE commons.wikimedia.org
DATE 27 July 1953

006 UN OFFICERS ON THEIR WAY TO LEBANESE ARMISTICE TALKS, ENDING THE 1948 ARAB-ISRAELI WAR
SOURCE 147.237.72.31/scripts/topsrch/topapi.dll
DATE 1949

007 FOREIGN MINISTER MOSHE SHARETT AT PIO PRESS CONFERENCE, IN TEL AVIV AFTER THE SIGNING OF ARMISTICE WITH EGYPT.
CREATOR Amirhossein Ghoochibeik
SOURCE 147.237.72.31/scripts/topsrch/topapi.dll
DATE 1949

008 GERMAN ARMY SURRENDER
SOURCE en.wikipedia.org

009 LEBANESE ARMISTICE TALKS
SOURCE 147.237.72.31/scripts/topsrch/topapi.dll
DATE 1949

010 VICTORY CELEBRATION, VAL D'OR
CREATOR William Gallaway
SOURCE commons.wikimedia.org
DATE 2006

011 MEN OF US 64TH REGIMENT, 7TH INFANTRY DIVISION, CELEBRATE THE NEWS OF THE ARMISTICE.
SOURCE US National Archive
DATE 11 November 1918

012 PEACE TREATY, BREST-LITOVSK
SOURCE www.greatwardifferent.com
DATE 1918

013 ARMISTICE NEGOTIATIONS, BREST-LITOVSK
The Brest-Litovsk treaty marked Russia's exit from World War I. Here, the Russian delegation, including Leon Trotsky, is greeted by the staff of Germany's Field Marshal von Hindenburg.
SOURCE www.nexusboard.net
DATE 1917

014 NEW YORK TROOPS ON THE CAMBRIA FRONT RIG UP A LIBERTY BELL TO CELEBRATE THE SIGNING OF THE ARMISTICE
SOURCE www.n24.de
DATE 11 November 1918

015 THE END OF THE WAR IN THE PACIFIC
The Japanese delegation aboard the USS Missouri BB-63.
SOURCE www.maritimequest.com
DATE 2 September 1945

016 SIGNING OF THE ARMISTICE ON 11 NOVEMBER 1918 IN RAILWAY DINING CAR NO. 2419 D
SOURCE de.academic.ru

017 FOOTBALL MATCH, 11 NOVEMBER 1918
This Armistice Day football match at Dale Barracks between German soldiers and Royal Welsh fusiliers commemorates the famous Christmas Day truce between Germany and Britain.
SOURCE www.sodahead.com

018 NEGOTIATIONS FOR SURRENDER IN DONCHERY THE NIGHT OF 1-2 SEPTEMBER 1870
CREATOR Lutz Braun
SOURCE bpkgate.picturemaxx.com
DATE 1870

019 JUBILANT AMERICANS
Residents of Washington DC show newspaper headlines announcing the surrender of Germany, ending

World War I.
SOURCE Unknown
DATE 8 November 1918

020 PARIS PEACE ACCORDS
[L] South Vietnam Deputy Prime Minister Nguyen Luu Vien; [R] Vietcong representatives led by Gen. Ng V Hieu; Front row: North Vietnam, le Duc Tho; in the center at the back is Secretary of State Henry Kissinger.
SOURCE banmeonline.org
DATE 13 June 1973

021 ARMISTICE OF COMPIÈGNE, NEGOTIATORS
SOURCE de.wikipedia.org
DATE 1940

022 ARMISTICE DAY, WALL STREET.
Thousands gather at the Subtreasury Building on Wall Street during Armistice Day.
SOURCE commons.wikimedia.org
DATE 1918

023 ARMISTICE
Russian and German soldiers fraternize after the armistice.
SOURCE www.cassiodor.com
DATE 1918

024 ARMISTICE DAY OF 1928: OBSERVED IN INDIA
CREATOR Provided by Lenton Sands
SOURCE www.flickr.com/photos/lenton_sands/1592502449/

025 ARMISTICE
The citizens of Paris celebrated in the streets, while watching a parade of captured cannons.
SOURCE skyvington.blogspot.com
DATE 1918

026 ARMISTICE DAY, TORONTO
SOURCE commons.wikimedia.org
DATE 1918

027 OREGON JOURNAL: ARMISTICE SIGNED
CREATOR Provided by CommandZed
SOURCE www.flickr.com/photos/zara/120169387
DATE 10 November 1918

028 WATERLOO DAILY COURIER: PEACE!
CREATOR Provided by CommandZed
SOURCE www.flickr.com/photos/zara/120169387
DATE 14 August 1945

029 THE HIMALAYAN TIMES: PEACE AT LAST
CREATOR The Himalayan Times
SOURCE www.zeblog.com
DATE 7 November 2006

030 THE LONDON EVENING FREE PRESS: GERMANY SURRENDERS TO ALL ALLIED

POWERS ENDING WAR IN EUROPE
CREATOR Provided by peterkelly
SOURCE www.flickr.com/photos/
peterkelly1/2390324670/
DATE 8 May 1945

031 THE HERALD: ALLIED LEADERS SEAL
SURRENDER TODAY
CREATOR Provided by Pete Morgan
SOURCE www.flickr.com/photos/
petermorgan/129239951/
DATE 8 May 1945

032 THE EVENING NEWS: THE END OF
THE WAR / L'ECHO DE PARIS:
L'ARMISTICE EST SIGNÉ
SOURCE rostock57.over-blog.com
DATE 11 November 1918

033 THE STARS AND STRIPES: IT'S ALL
OVER OVER HERE / NAZI ARMIES IN
ITALY SURRENDER / HOSTILITIES
ENDED AT 12:01 AM
CREATOR Provided by Kendall
Sterling
SOURCE www.flickr.com/photos/
21403390@N08/2075301630/
DATE 8 May 1945, 3 May 1945, 9
May 1945

034 THE STARS AND STRIPES: PEACE!
CREATOR Provided by Piedmont
Fossil
SOURCE www.flickr.com/photos/
piedmont_fossil/205028054/sizes/o/
DATE 15 August 1945

035 THE YORKSHIRE EVENING POST:
ARMISTICE SIGNED AT 5.0 A.M
CREATOR Provided by Mig_R
SOURCE www.flickr.com/photos/
fawbs/500889294/
DATE 11 November 1918

036 THE DAILY CHRONICLE: END OF THE
GREAT WORLD WAR
CREATOR Provided by Marcin Wichary
SOURCE www.flickr.com/photos/
mwichary/2254924345/
DATE 12 November 1918

037 POSTER ANNOUNCING THE ARMISTICE
OF 11 NOVEMBER 1918
CREATOR Republique Francaise
SOURCE www.parisenimages.fr/fr/
popup-photo.html?photo=850-7

038 NOTTINGHAM EVENING POST:
LAST SHOT FIRED AT 11 A.M. TO-DAY
CREATOR Provided by Marcin Wichary
SOURCE www.flickr.com/photos/
mwichary/2254924345/
DATE 11 November 1918

039 SAIPAN BEACON: JAPS QUIT / WAR ENDS!
CREATOR Provided by maryannec
SOURCE www.flickr.com/photos/
7584734@N08/456001923/
DATE 15 August 1945

040 LE COURRIER DU CENTRE: LES
CLAUSES DE L'ARMISTICE AVEC
L'ALLEMAGNE ET L'ITALIE
[THE TERMS OF THE ARMISTICE
WITH GERMANY AND ITALY]
CREATOR Le Courrier Du Centre
SOURCE journaux-anciens.chapitre.com
DATE 26 June 1940

041 A SENT TELEGRAM
Armistice was signed this morning
at 5:00. Cessation of hostilities
at 11:00. Delay of evacuation
of the right bank of the Rhine
six days.
CREATOR Le Courrier Du Centre
SOURCE alecole.educ.cg86.fr
DATE 11 November 1918

042 LE PETIT JOURNAL — AU TRANSVAAL:
LE DOCTEUR JAMESON PRISONNIER
DES BOERS
[LE PETIT JOURNAL — IN THE
TRANSVAAL: DR. JAMESON, PRISONER
OF THE BOERS]
SOURCE Unknown
DATE 19 January 1896

043 THE CITIZEN: PEACE!
CREATOR Library and Archives Canada
SOURCE www65.statcan.gc.ca
DATE 11 November 1918

044 OREGON JOURNAL: WORLD CELEBRATES
RETURN OF PEACE, END OF AUTOCRACY
CREATOR Oregon Journal
SOURCE Oregon State Archives
DATE 11 November 1918

045 NEW YORK TIMES: ARMISTICE SIGNED,
END OF THE WAR!
CREATOR Library and Archives
Canada
SOURCE www.solarnavigator.net
DATE 11 November 1918

001

002

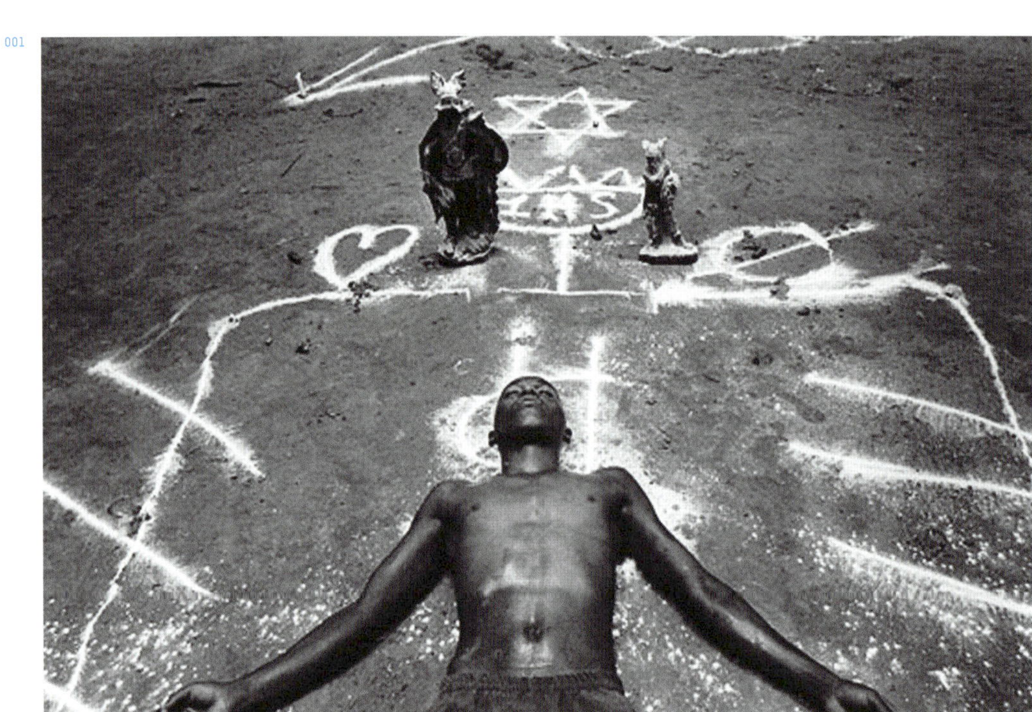

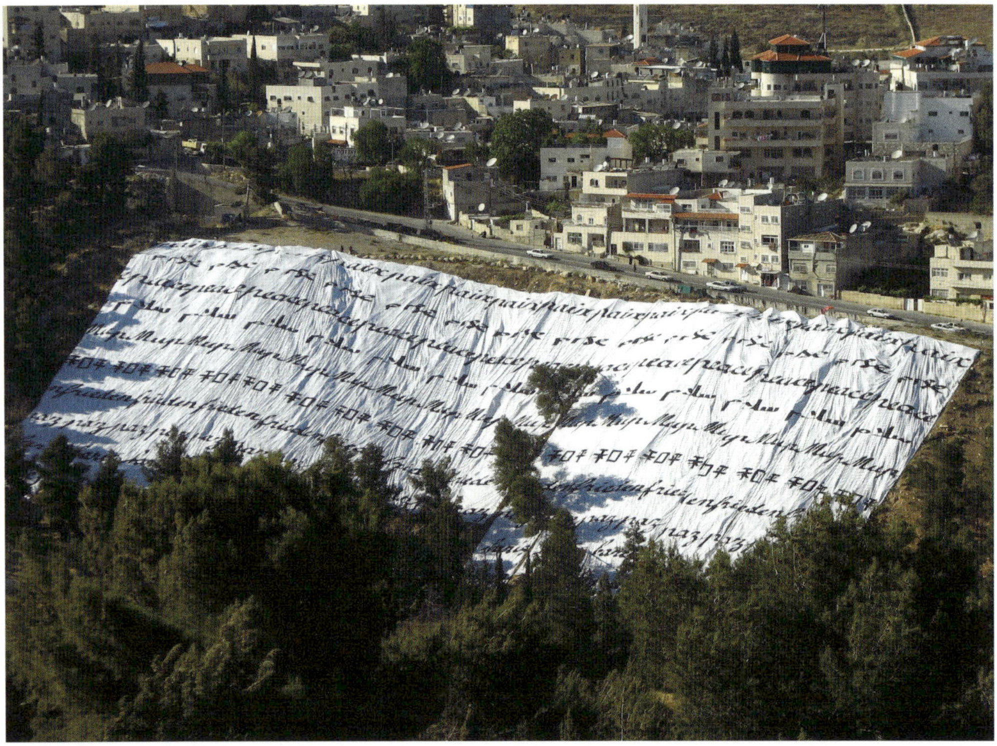

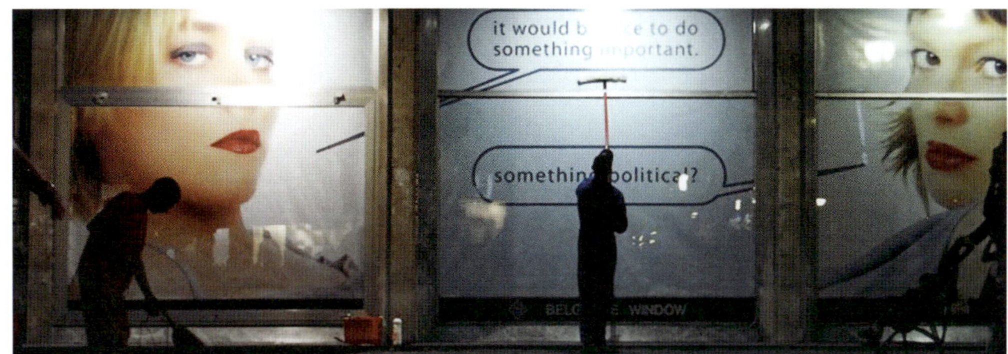
it would b   e to do
something   mportant.
something political?
BELO   WINDOW

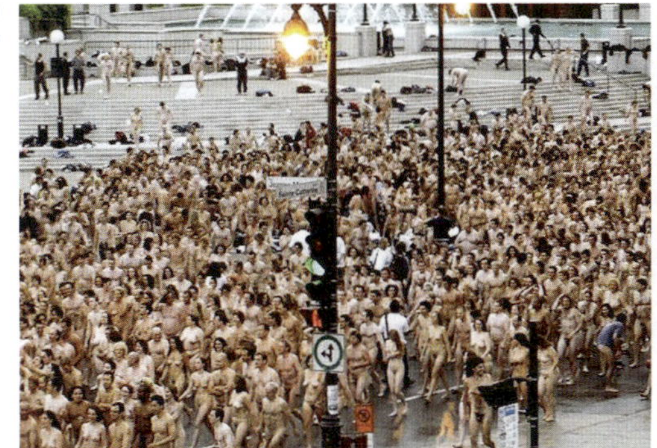

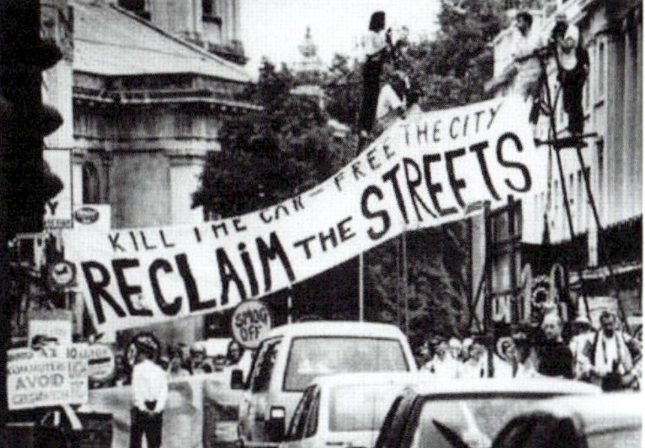
KILL THE CAR — FREE THE CITY
RECLAIM THE STREETS

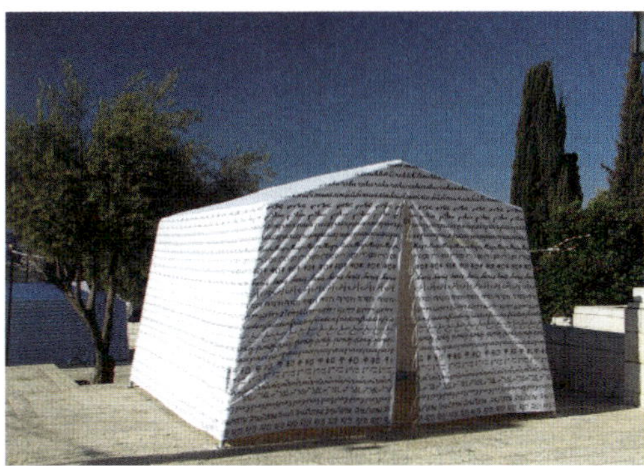

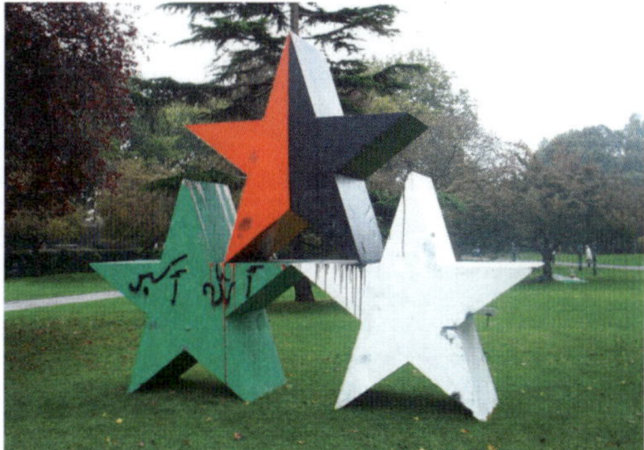

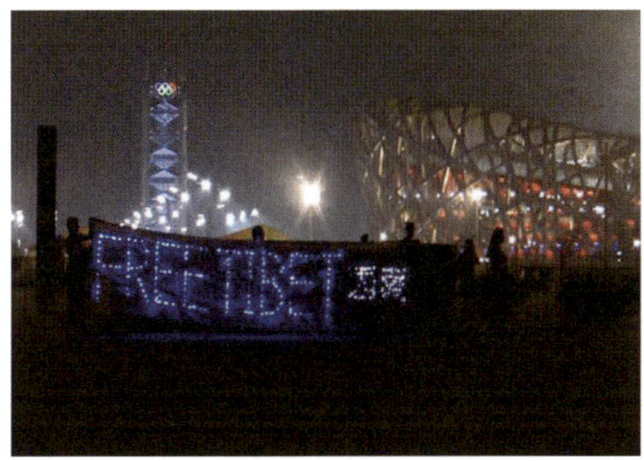
FREE TIBET

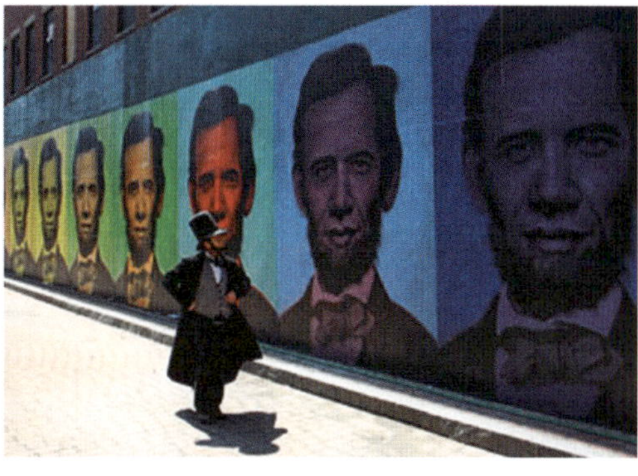

010

PEACE ON EAR
GOODWILL TO
STOP
KILLING
KIDS
MAKE
PEACE
NOT WAR
LET IRAQ
FACE
OF THE
ENEMY
IN KABUL
This The Kids
USA) 6,000 Under 5's
2,000 Over 5's We
PROTECT
THE
HUMAN
FATHER FORGIVE THEM
FOR THEY KNOW NOT WHAT THEY DO
SCOS AD
CHILDREN FORGIVE US FOR NOW WE DO
THE MURDERED
CHILDREN
AS YOU DO TO THE LEAST
IT IS OURS HUMANE BEINGS
YOU
DO
TO
ME

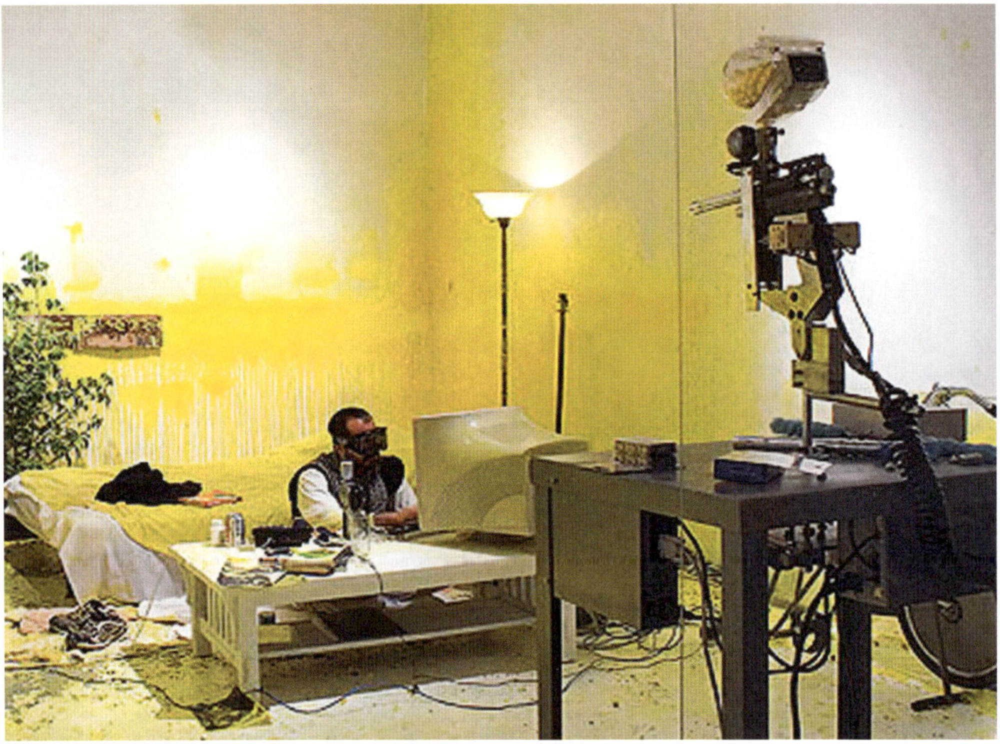

011

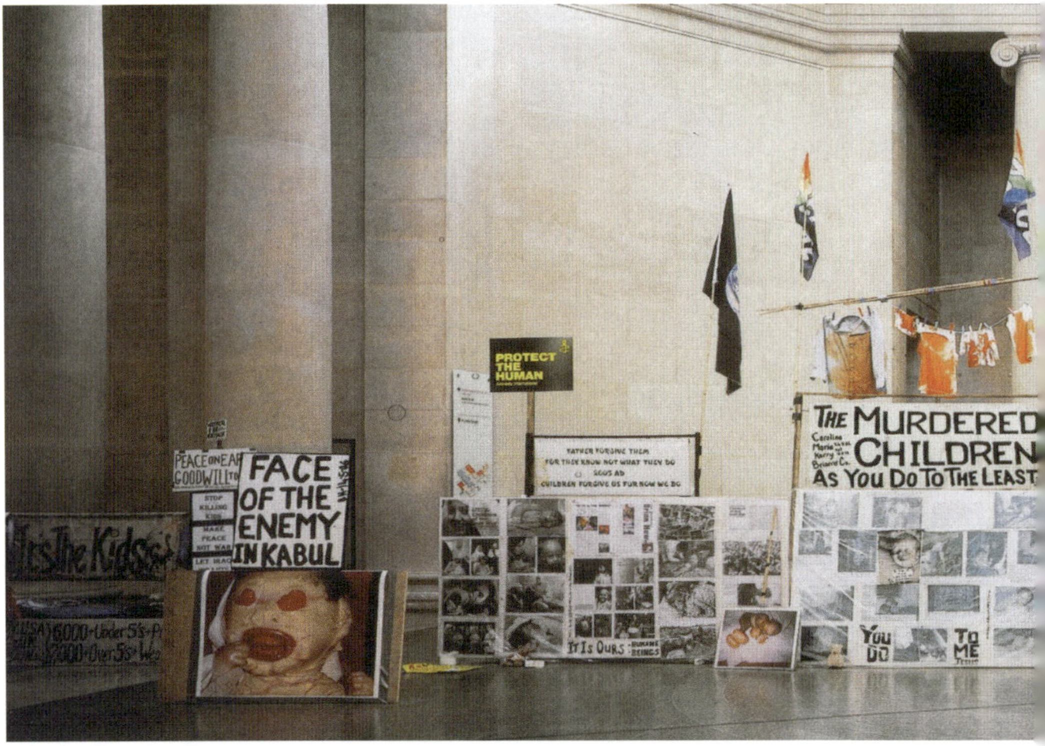

012

GLOBAL WOMEN'S STRIKE
Community Anti-War Picket & Open Mic
every Wednesday 5.30–7pm
www.globalwomenstrike.net   tel 020 7482 2496
Community picket Wednesdays
5.30–7pm

SUPPORT
BRIAN
PAX-USA/UK SHAME
ALL GODS CHILDREN
ALL THE SAME
BLAIR BLIAR
NO MORE WAR
Australians say NO to war on IRAQ
STOP killing our kids
SUPPORT OUR TROOPS
BRING H
BLAIR LIED
ALL GODS CHILDREN
PRAYING FOR PEACE
UK TROOPS OUT OF IRAQ
Peace Salam Shalom
THE PROUD PARENTS

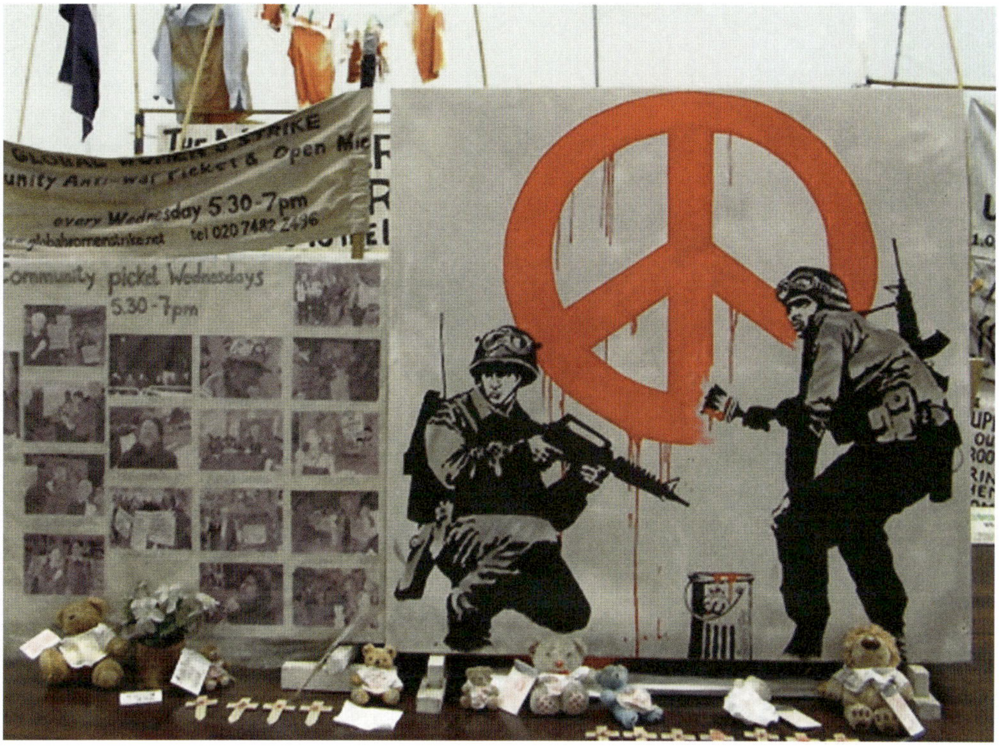

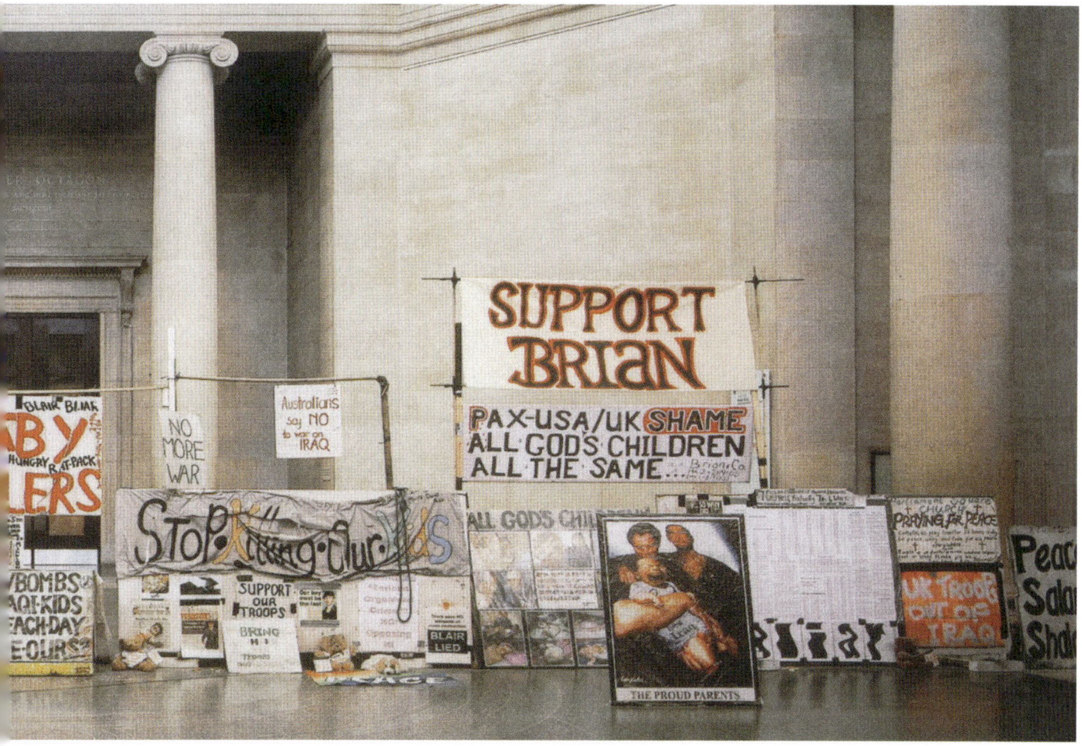

013

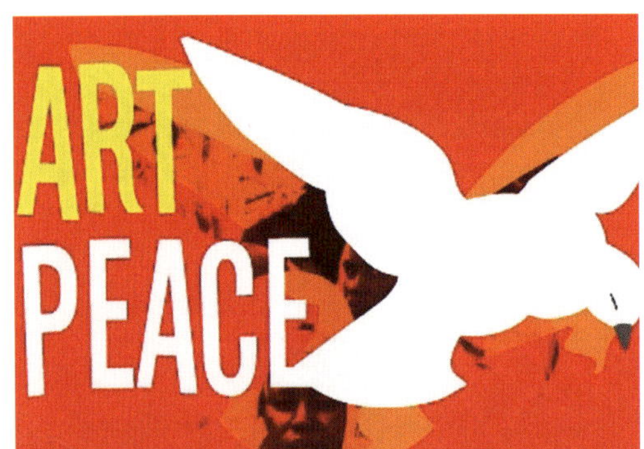

014

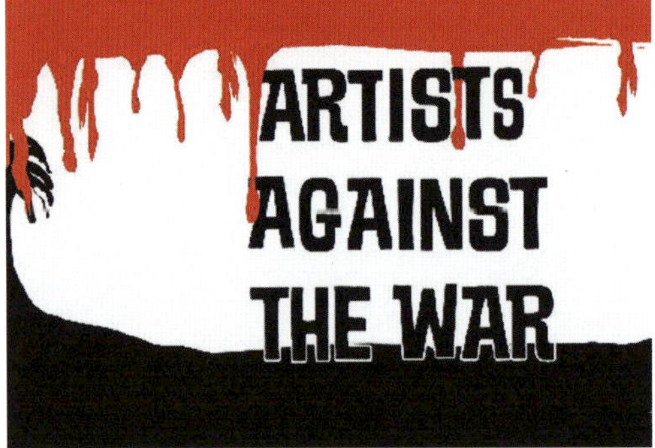

015

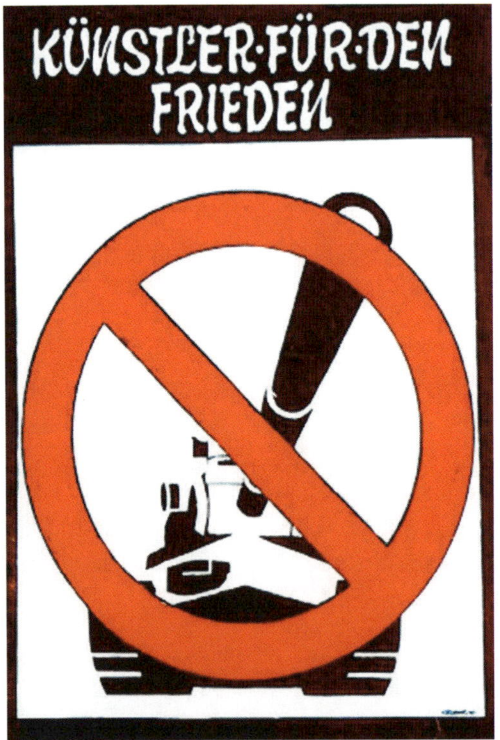

001 UNTITLED
Venezuela. Yaracuy state. Sorte
mountain. Maria Lionza cult.
Prayers for love, fortune, and
peace under the Viking Court.
CREATOR Cristina Garcia Rodero
SOURCE www.magnumphotos.com
DATE 2005

002 LES TENTES DE LA PAIX
[PEACE TENTS]
CREATOR Clara Halter
SOURCE www.flickr.com/photos/me-
kron/147745916/in/photostream/
DATE 2006

003 IT WOULD BE NICE TO DO
SOMETHING POLITICAL
CREATOR Toril Goksøyr & Camilla
Martens
SOURCE www.g-m.as
DATE 2007 [Venice Biennale]

004 SPENCER TUNICK PHOTO SHOOT AT
MUSÉE D'ART CONTEMPORAIN DE
MONTRÉAL, 2001
SOURCE Unknown

005 RECLAIM THE STREETS
SOURCE www.eco-action.org

006 LES TENTES DE LA PAIX
[PEACE TENTS]
CREATOR Clara Halter
SOURCE www.flickr.com/photos/
mekron/147745916/in/photostream/
DATE 2006

007 INSTALLATION
SOURCE Unknown

008 FREE TIBET, 2008 BEIJING OLYMPICS
CREATOR James Powderly
SOURCE antiadvertisingagency.com

009 OBAMA-LINCOLNS
CREATOR Mural by Ron English.
Photograph taken by Will Kerr.
SOURCE www.adbusters.org
DATE 2008

010 DOMESTIC TENSION
Wafaa Bilal, an Iraqi-born
artist, dodges paintballs in
this interactive performance
piece. The paintballs, fired by a
remote-control gun controlled by
visitors to his website, reproduce
the conditions of bombardment
felt by citizens of his homeland.
Bilal calls the piece "an open
narrative written by everybody
who participated" and is pleased
that "through a merging of art
and technology I could speak of
a political issue in real time."
CREATOR Artist, Wafaa Bilal. Photo
taken for the *Chicago Tribune* by
Chris Walker.

SOURCE www.bobedwardsradio.com
DATE 2007

011 STATE BRITAIN
Tate Britain, London. This
installation re-creates an
antiwar display set up by
Brian Haw outside Parliament,
which was confiscated by police.
CREATOR Mark Wallinger
SOURCE www.titien.net
DATE 2007

012 STATE BRITAIN
Tate Britain, London
CREATOR Mark Wallinger
SOURCE www.titien.net
DATE 2007

013 ART PEACE
SOURCE www.phantomgalleries.com

014 ARTISTS AGAINST THE WAR
SOURCE www.reverbnation.com

015 ARTISTS FOR PEACE
CREATOR Mark Wallinger
SOURCE schmoll-et-copains.typepad.
com

001

PEACE
IS
HERE.
IF YOU WANT IT
War is over – if you want it
Rochdale—Peace Centre
Toronto—The Peace City
Canada – The Peace Maker
We live in
Peace Community
All we are saying is give peace a chance
Toronto Rochdale Peace Centre
Rochdale College,
Room 1411, 341 Bloor St. West,
Toronto 181, Ontario   928-3188

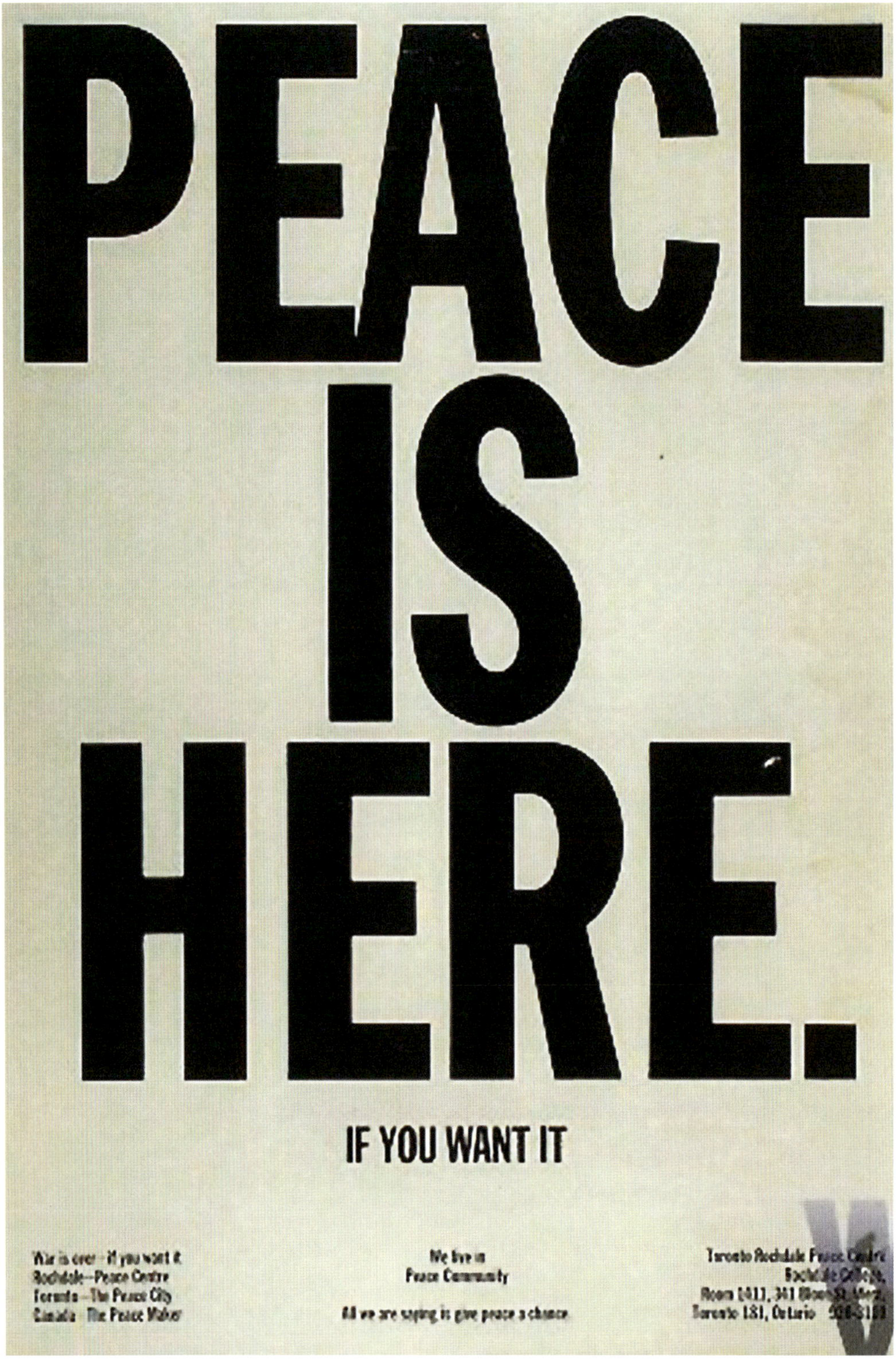

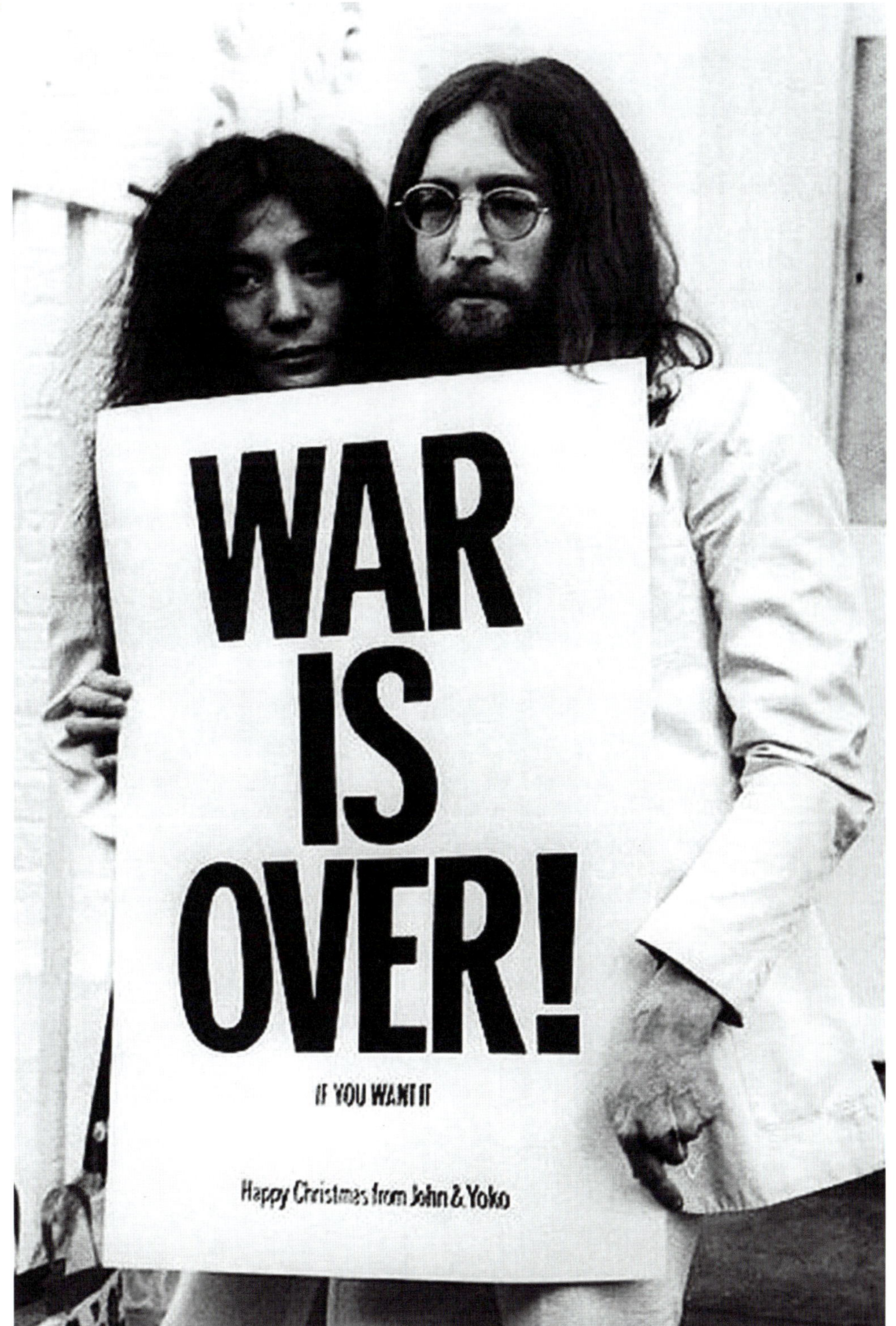
WAR
IS
OVER!
IF YOU WANT IT
Happy Christmas from John & Yoko

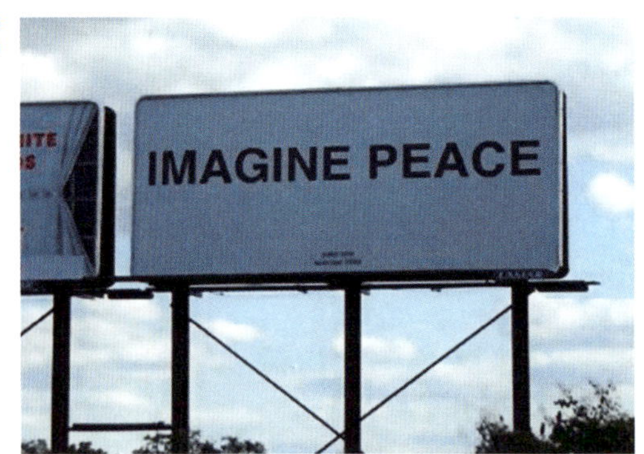

Everybody's talking 'bout

Bagism   Ministers   revolution   John & Yoko
Shagism   Sinisters   evolution   Timmy Leary
Dragism   Banisters   masturbation   Tommy Smothers
Madism   Canisters   flagellation   Bobby Dylan
Ragism   Bishop &   regulations   Tommy Cooper
Tagism   Fishop's   integrations   Derek Taylor
This-ism   Rabbi &   meditations   Norman Mailer
That-ism   Pop eyes   United Nations   Alen Ginsberg
                Bye byes.   Congratulations Hare Krishna
                                                  Hare Krishna

All we are saying is give peace a chance.

John Lennon

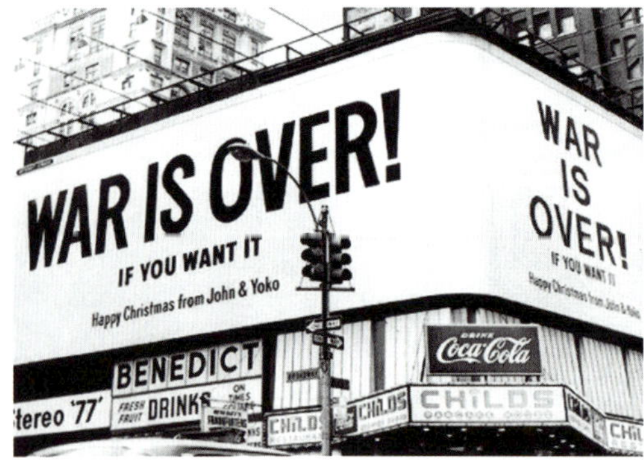

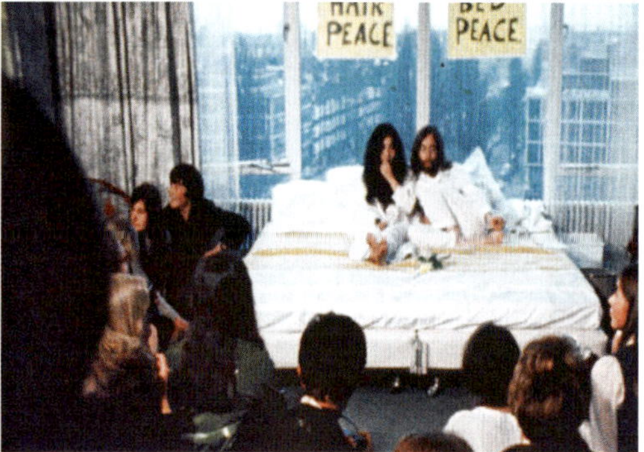

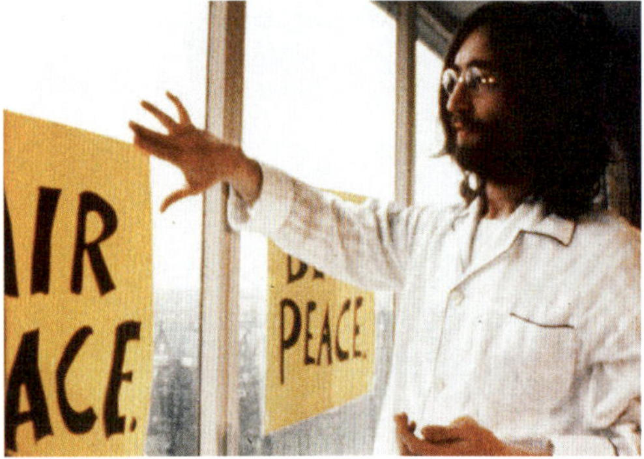

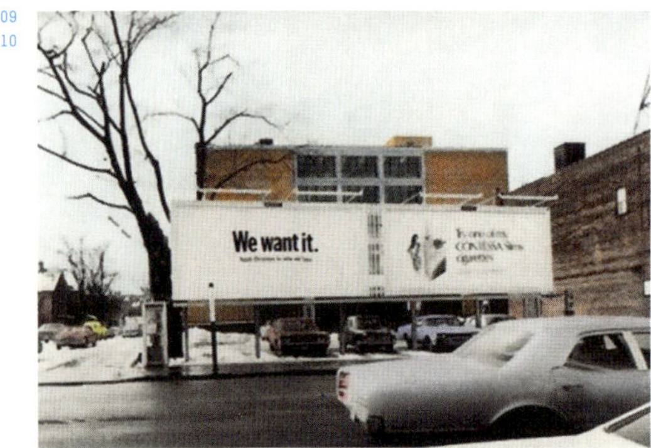

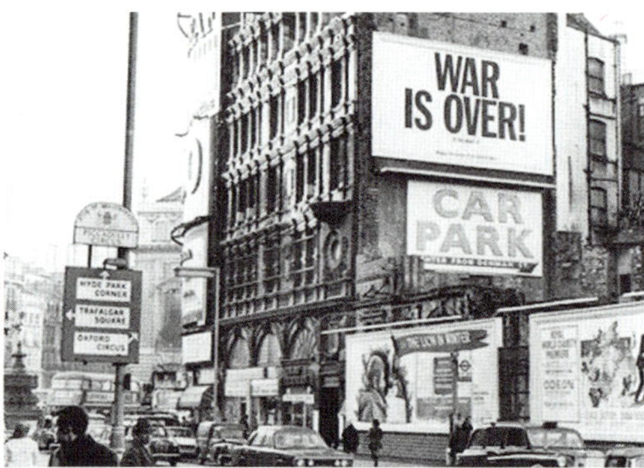

001 PEACE IS HERE. (IF YOU WANT IT)
     CREATOR John Lennon / Yoko Ono
     SOURCE imaginepeace.com

002 WAR IS OVER! (IF YOU WANT IT)
     CREATOR John Lennon / Yoko Ono
     SOURCE imaginepeace.com

003 IMAGINE PEACE
     CREATORJohn Lennon / Yoko Ono
     SOURCE imaginepeace.com

004 EVERYBODIES TALKING BOUT
     CREATOR John Lennon / Yoko Ono
     SOURCE imaginepeace.com

005 WAR IS OVER! (IF YOU WANT IT)
     CREATOR John Lennon / Yoko Ono
     SOURCE imaginepeace.com

006 BED-IN
     CREATOR John Lennon / Yoko Ono
     SOURCE imaginepeace.com

007 BED-IN
     CREATOR John Lennon / Yoko Ono
     SOURCE imaginepeace.com

008 DER KRIEG IST AUS
     (WAR IS OVER!)
     CREATOR John Lennon / Yoko Ono
     SOURCE imaginepeace.com

009 WE WANT IT.
     CREATOR John Lennon / Yoko Ono
     SOURCE imaginepeace.com

010 WAR IS OVER! (IF YOU WANT IT)
     CREATOR John Lennon / Yoko Ono
     SOURCE imaginepeace.com

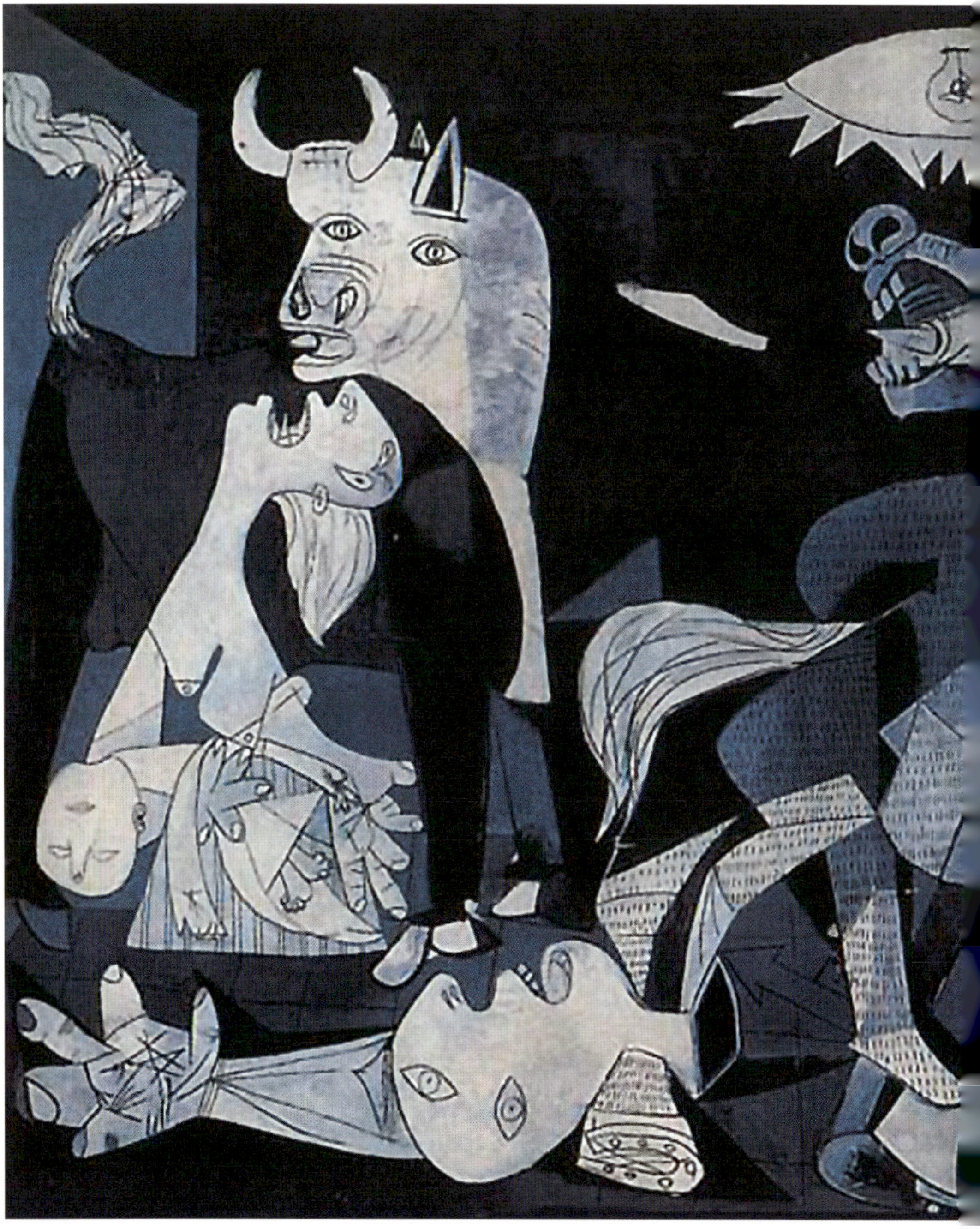

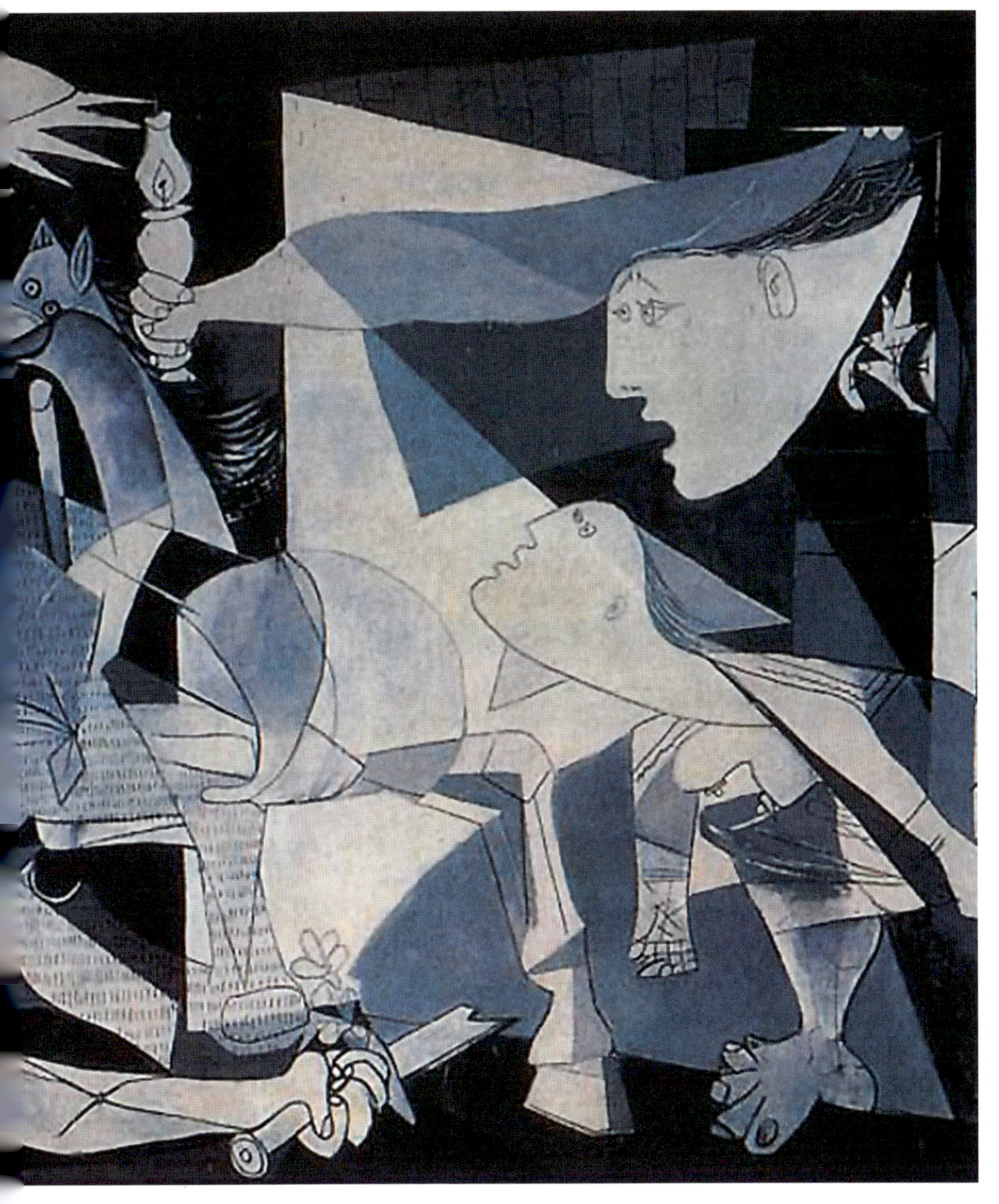

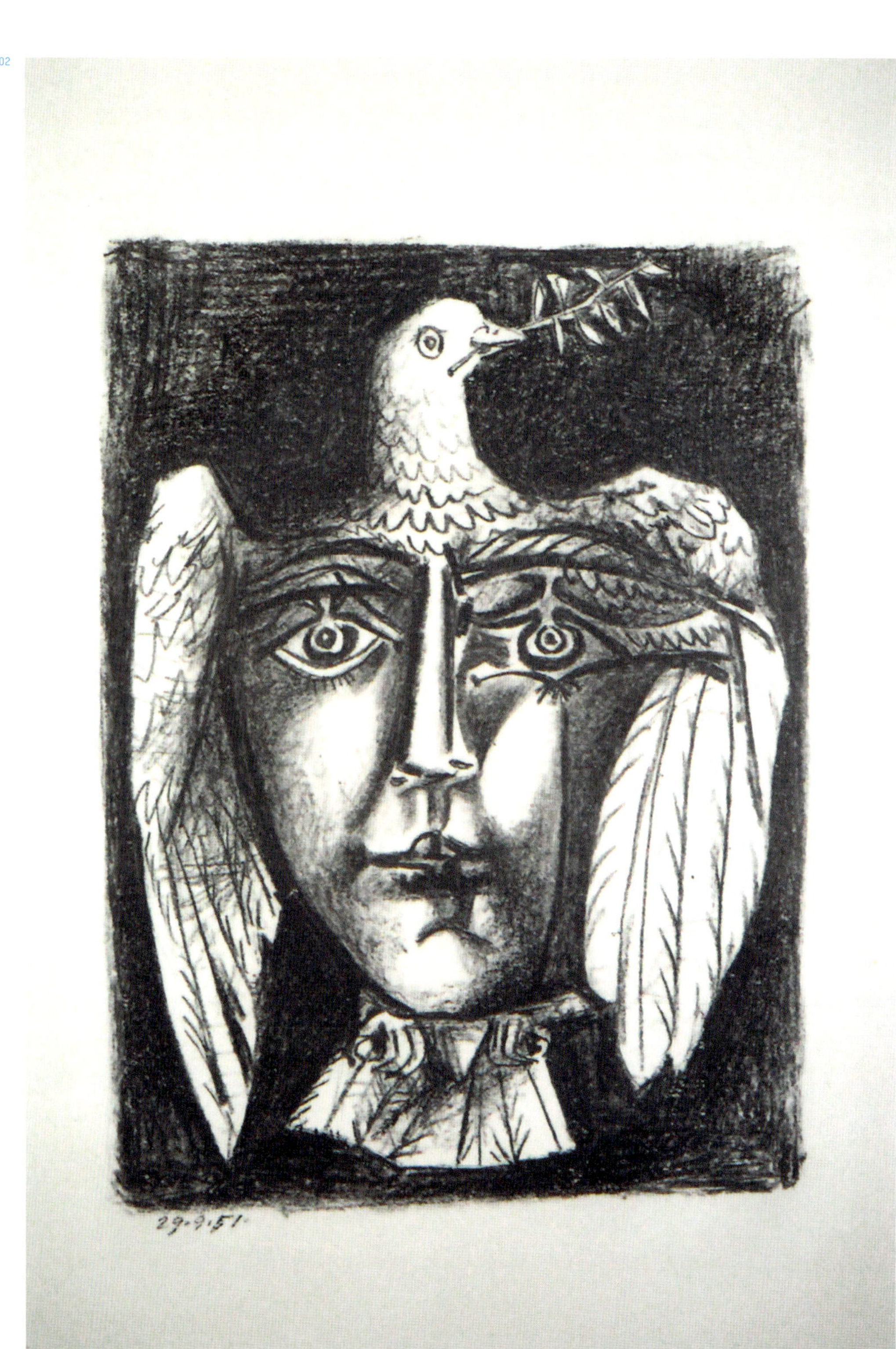
29.9.51.

003
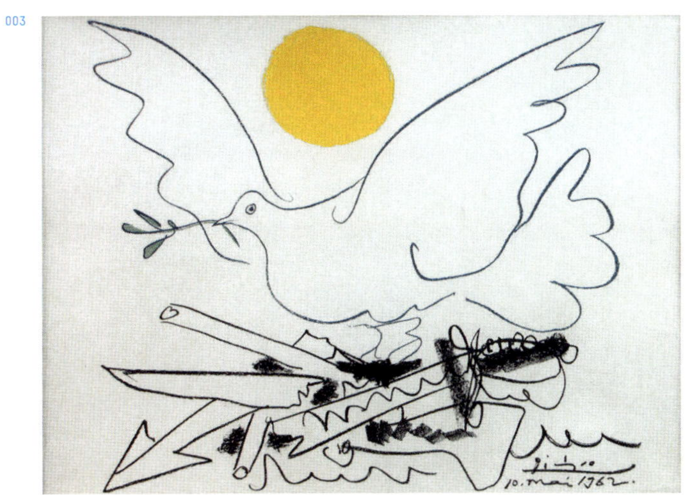

004
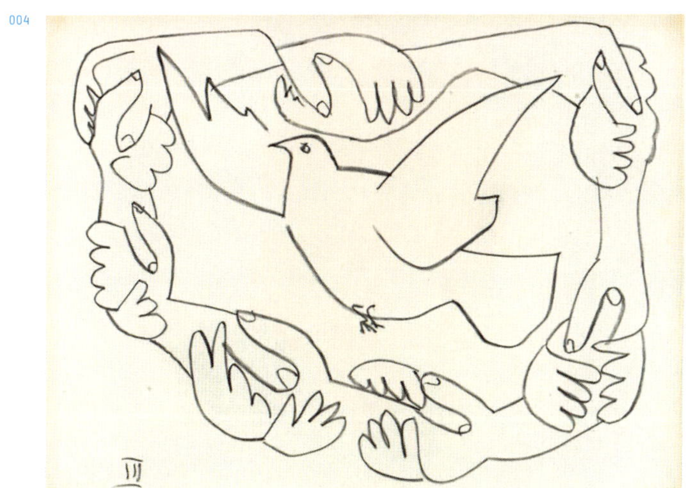

005
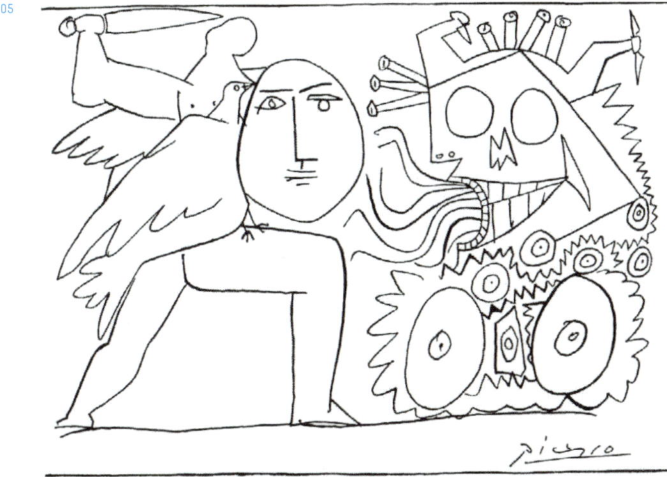

001 GUERNICA
     CREATOR Pablo Picasso
     SOURCE www.metasurface.net/
     DATE 1937

002 THE FACE OF PEACE
     CREATOR Pablo Picasso
     SOURCE denisbloch.com
     DATE 1951

003 PEACE POSTER
     CREATOR Pablo Picasso
     SOURCE voiceseducation.org
     DATE 1962

004 HANDS ENTRWINED III
     CREATOR Pablo Picasso
     SOURCE voiceseducation.org

005 WAR AND PEACE
     CREATOR Pablo Picasso
     SOURCE voiceseducation.org
     DATE 1951

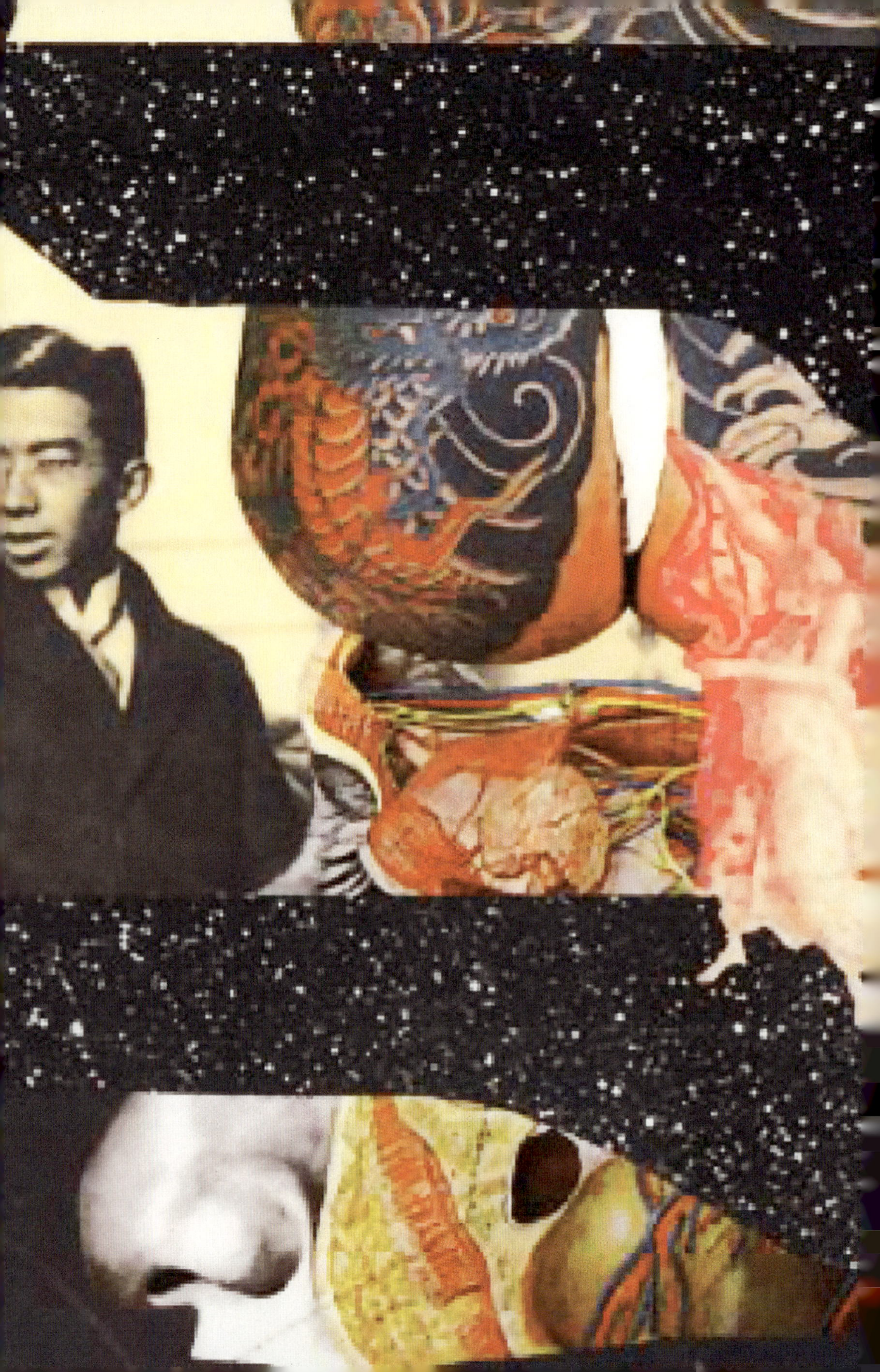

LEFT
001

002
003

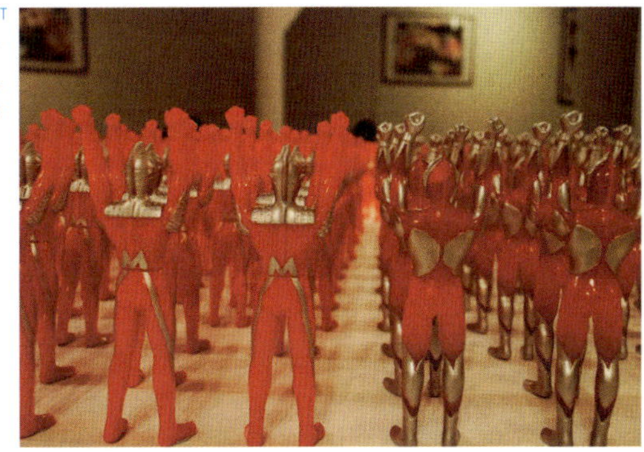
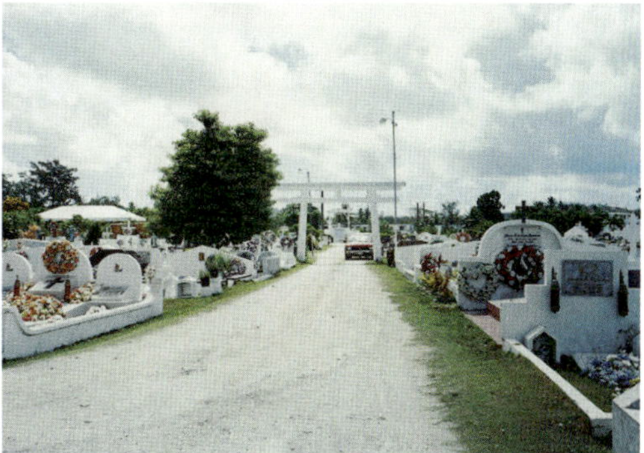

004
005

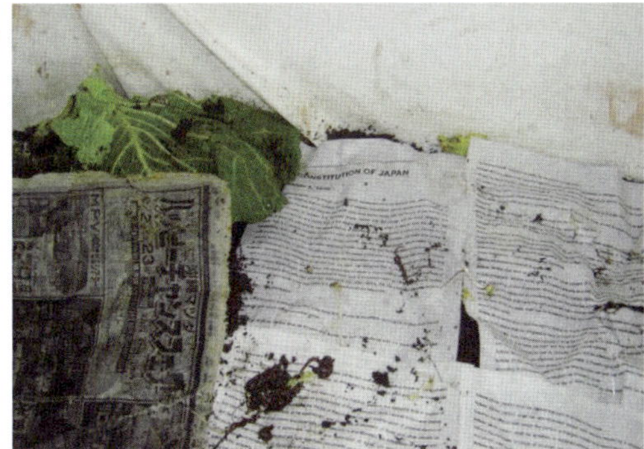
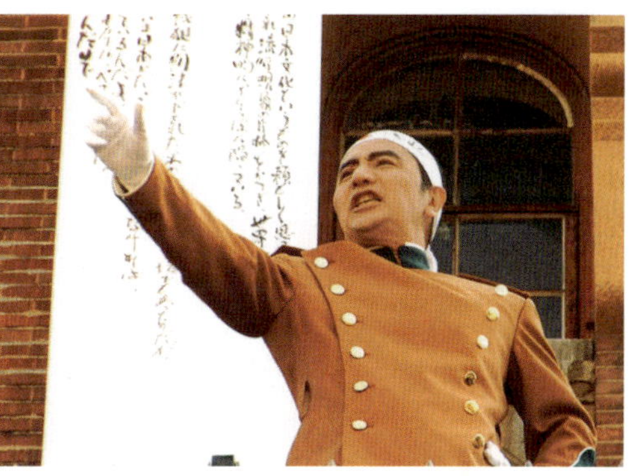

006
007

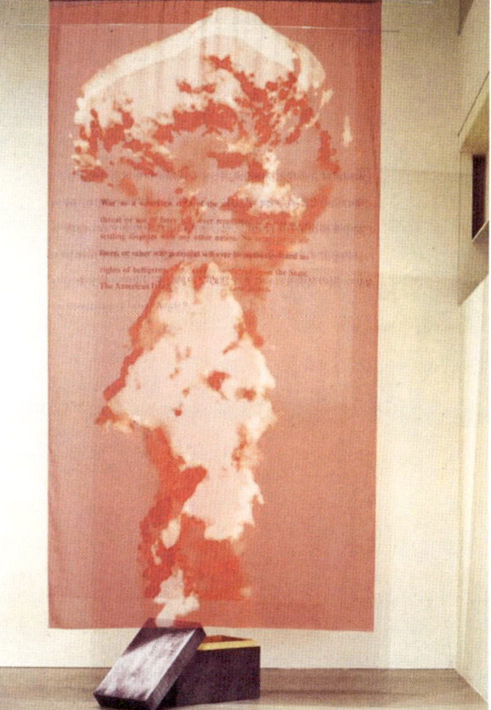
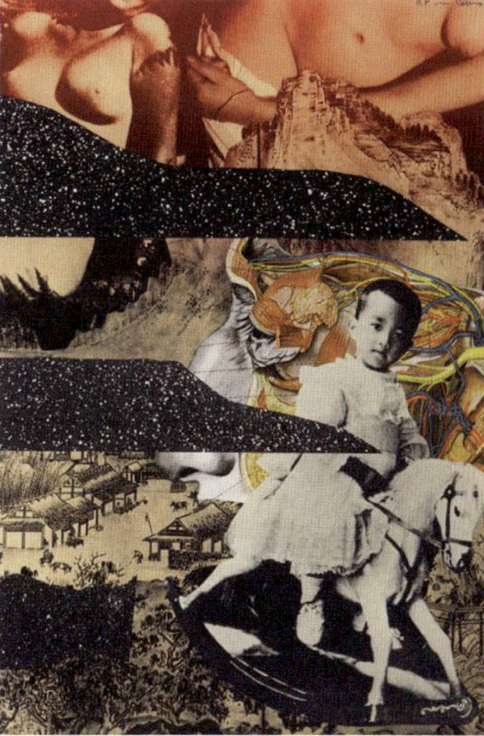

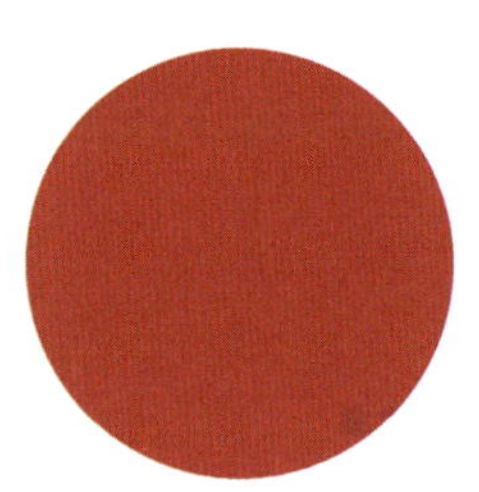

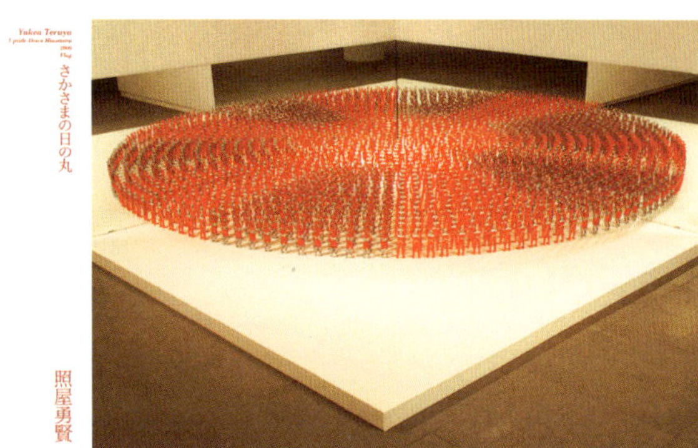

Article 9

1) Aspiring sincerely to an international peace based on justice and order, the Japanese people forever renounce war as a sovereign right of the nation and the threat or use of force as a means of settling international disputes.

2) In order to accomplish the aim of the preceding paragraph, land, sea, and air forces, as well as other war potential, will never be maintained. The right of belligerency of the state will not be recognized.

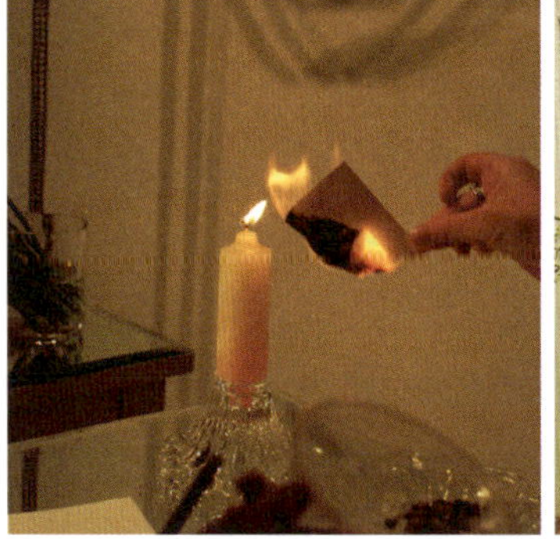

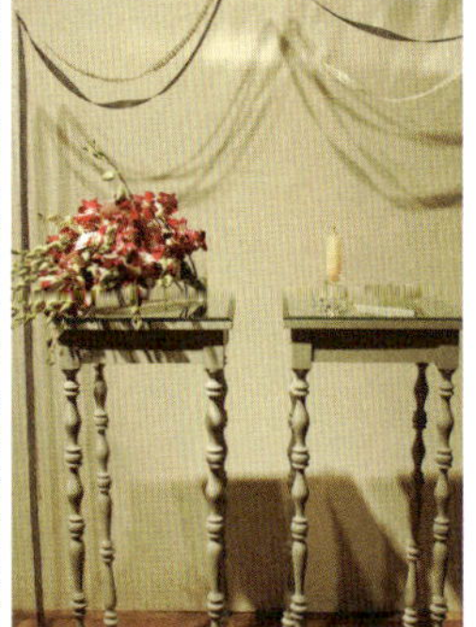

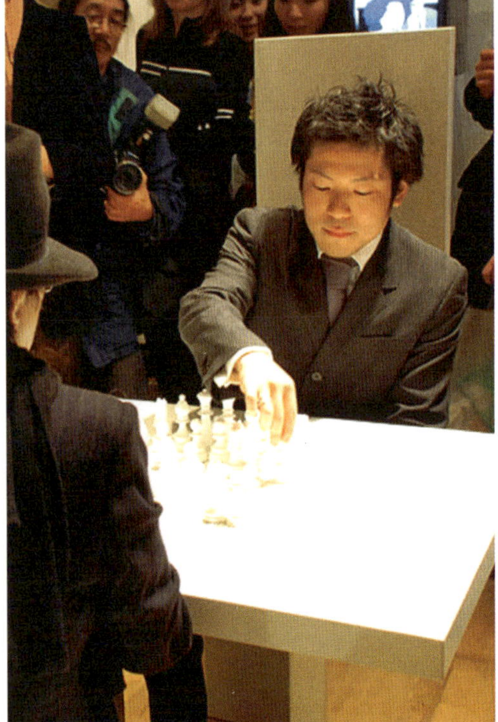

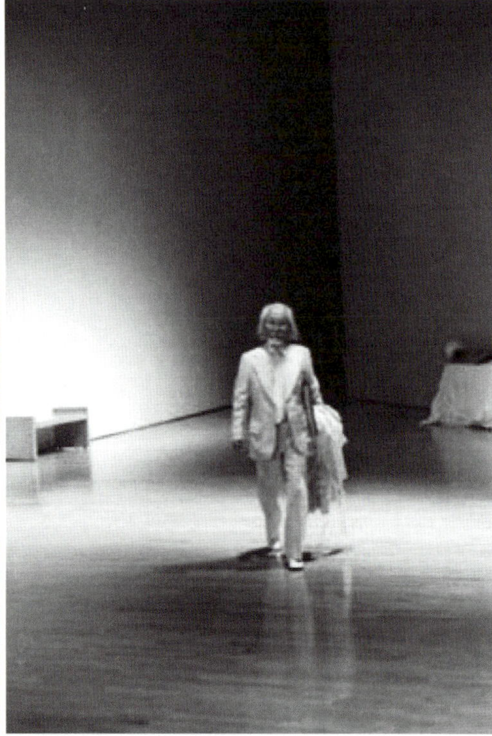

001 WORK I FROM HOLDING PERSPECTIVE
CREATOR Oura Nobuyuki
SOURCE www.shift.jp.org/en/archives/
2008/02/into_the_atomic_sunshine_
exhibition.html

002 BANZAI CORNER
CREATOR Yukinori Yanagi
SOURCE www.spoon-tamago.
com/2012/08/14/yukinori-yanagi-ban
zai-corner/

003 UNTITLED [TORII]
CREATOR Motoyuki Shitamichi
SOURCE www.tokyoartbeat.com/tablog/
entries.en/2008/08/into-the-atomic-
sunshine.html
DATE 2007

004 JAPANESE CONSTITUTION WORM
AUTODAFÉ
CREATOR Eric van Hove
SOURCE www.shift.jp.org/en/archives/
2008/07/eric_van_hove.html
DATE 2005

005 SEASON OF PASSION — A REQUIEM:
MISHIMA 1970.11.25 — 2006.4.6
CREATOR Yasumasa Morimurae
SOURCE www.artabase.net/exhibition/
374-yasumasa-morimura-seasons-of-
passion

006 THE FORBIDDEN BOX
CREATOR Yukinori Yanagi
SOURCE www.yanagistudio.net/works/
projectarticle902_view.html
DATE 1995

007 FIGURE 1
CREATOR Oura Nobuyuki
SOURCE Unknown

008 FIGURE UPSIDE-DOWN HINOMARU [FLAG]
CREATOR Yuken Teruya
SOURCE www.japantimes.co.jp/text/
fa20080807a1.html
DATE 2006

009 BANZAI CORNER
CREATOR Yukinori Yanagi
SOURCE www.tokyoartbeat.com/tablog/
entries.en/2008/08/into-the-atomic-
sunshine.html
DATE 2006

010 ARTICLE 9
CREATOR Provided by the Article 9
Association
SOURCE www.9-jo.jp/en/index_en.html

011 UNTITLED
CREATOR Photograph by Yuka
Takamatsu
SOURCE Unknown

012 YOUR FEARS, MY HOPES
CREATOR Vanessa Albury
SOURCE www.shift.jp.org/en/archives/
2008/02/into_the_atomic_sunshi-
ne_exhibition.html
DATE 2007

013 WHITE CHESS
CREATOR Yuka Takamatsu
SOURCE japanfocus.org/-Shinya-
Watanabe/2700

014 VANISHING ACT
CREATOR Matsuzawa Yutaka
SOURCE Unknown

Albert Einstein
Old Grove Rd.
Nassau Point
Peconic, Long Island

August 2nd, 1939

F.D. Roosevelt,
President of the United States,
White House
Washington, D.C.

Sir:

Some recent work by E.Fermi and L. Szilard, which has been communicated to me in manuscript, leads me to expect that the element uranium may be turned into a new and important source of energy in the immediate future. Certain aspects of the situation which has arisen seem to call for watchfulness and, if necessary, quick action on the part of the Administration. I believe therefore that it is my duty to bring to your attention the following facts and recommendations:

In the course of the last four months it has been made probable - through the work of Joliot in France as well as Fermi and Szilard in America - that it may become possible to set up a nuclear chain reaction in a large mass of uranium,by which vast amounts of power and large quantities of new radium-like elements would be generated. Now it appears almost certain that this could be achieved in the immediate future.

This new phenomenon would also lead to the construction of bombs, and it is conceivable - though much less certain - that extremely powerful bombs of a new type may thus be constructed. A single bomb of this type, carried by boat and exploded in a port, might very well destroy the whole port together with some of the surrounding territory. However, such bombs might very well prove to be too heavy for transportation by air.

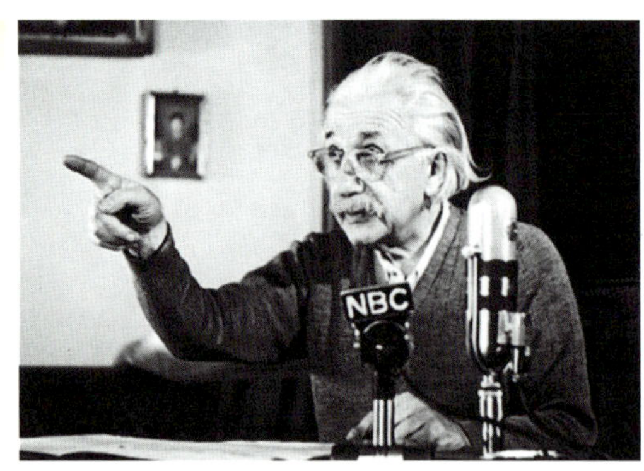

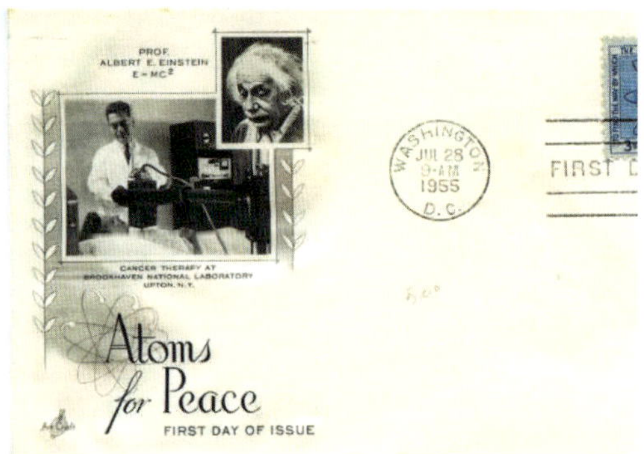

EMERGENCY COMMITTEE *of* ATOMIC SCIENTISTS
INCORPORATED
ROOM 28, 90 NASSAU STREET
PRINCETON, NEW JERSEY

Trustees
ALBERT EINSTEIN
Chairman
HAROLD C. UREY
Vice-Chairman
HANS A. BETHE
T. R. HOGNESS
PHILIP M. MORSE
LINUS PAULING
LEO SZILARD
V.F. WEISSKOPF

October 9, 1947

Dr. Donald Kundiger
1030 Steiner Street
San Francisco 15, Calif.

Dear Dr. Kundiger:

I have received with pleasure your generous answer to my letter enclosing the recent Statement of the Emergency Committee of Atomic Scientists with it urgent appeal for the necessity of effective international control of atomic energy. Thank you for your continued help in our campaign to arouse the American people to an understanding of the present very serious situation.

An article by Cord Meyer in a recent issue of the _Atlantic Monthly_ develops further some of the topics touched upon in our Statement. If you have not seen Mr. Meyer's article, I think you will be interested in the enclosed reprint.

Thank you for your long and thoughtful letter, with its pertinent comments and suggestions. I have referred it to one of my colleagues for his consideration as well.

It was thoughtful of you to send us the names of your friends. We are contacting them as you suggested.

With cordial greetings,

Sincerely yours,

A. Einstein

AE:mr

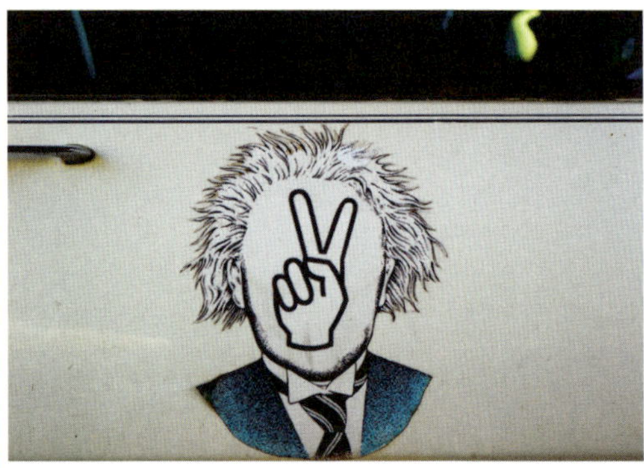

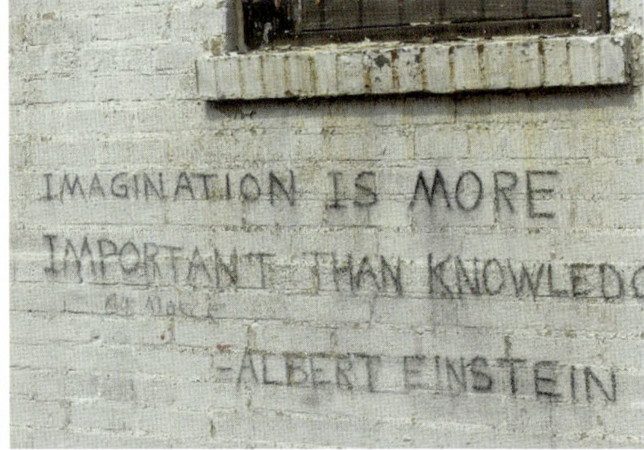

007
008

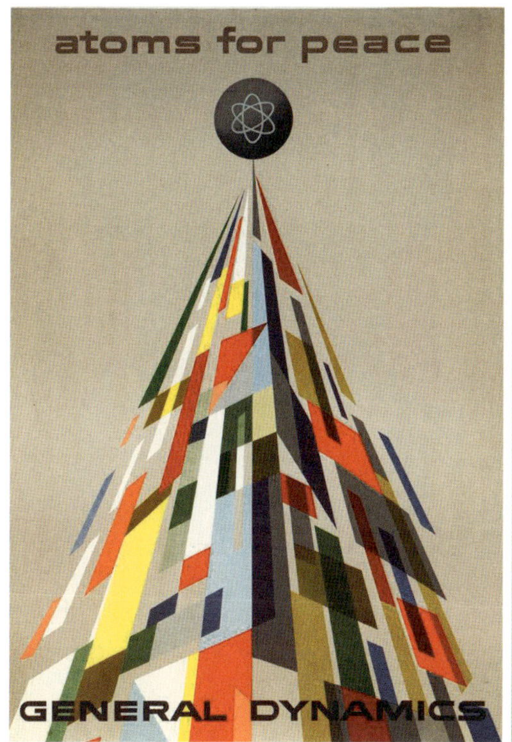

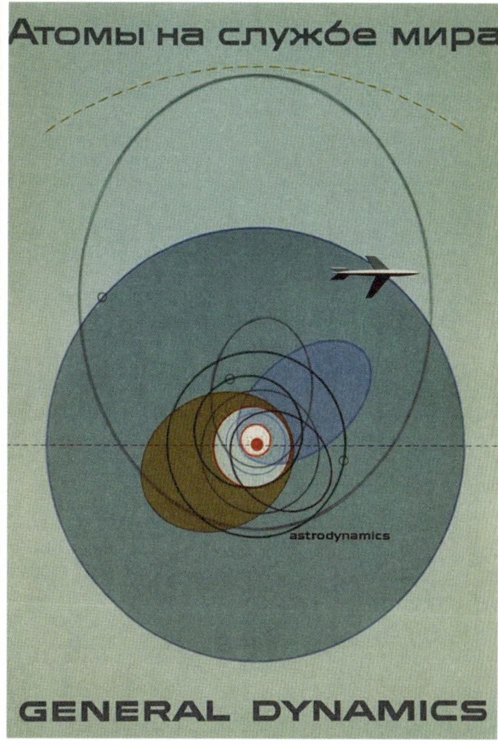

009
010

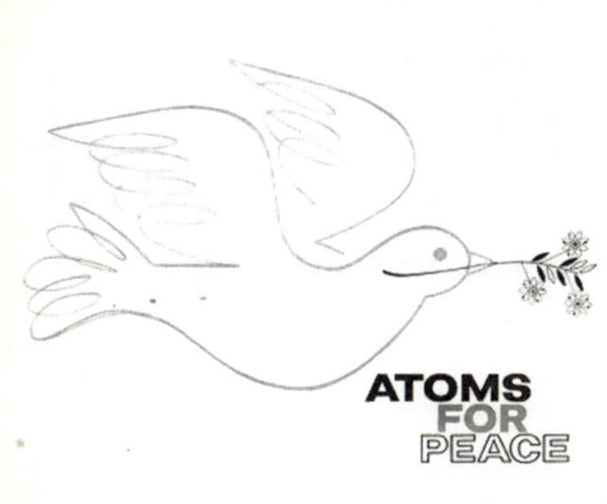

Lockheed, always in the forefront of aeronautic and scientific achievement, now extends its leadership into a significant new field—Nuclear Energy for the World's Work.

For eight years, Lockheed's nuclear scientists, physicists and engineers have been working on the development of a nuclear-powered airplane. Now, these scientists are also ready to put the atom to work for industry—with research and process heat reactors, food irradiation facilities and the applications of radioisotopes.

At Dawsonville, Georgia, Lockheed will begin operating the Georgia Nuclear Laboratories later this year. This new installation will provide the largest radiation effects research capability in the United States.

LOCKHEED MEANS LEADERSHIP

LOCKHEED NUCLEAR PRODUCTS

MARIETTA, GEORGIA

*Operated by the Georgia Division
Lockheed Aircraft Corporation*

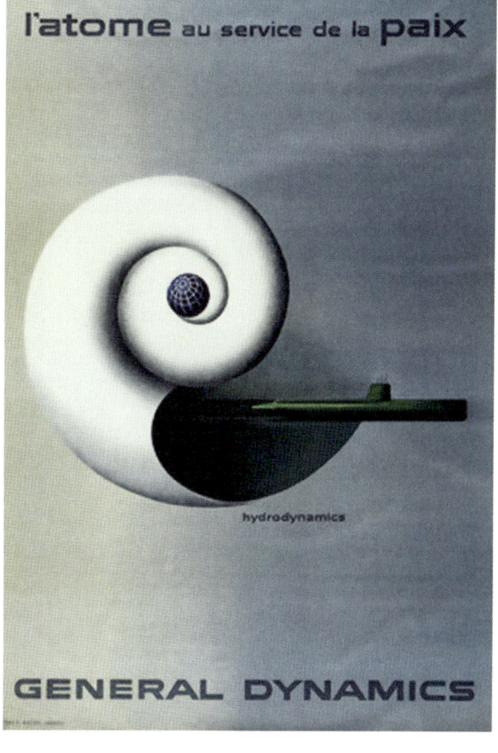

001 LETTER TO PRESIDENT FRANKLIN
D. ROOSEVELT
CREATOR Albert Einstein
SOURCE www.teslasociety.com

002 EINSTEIN NBC
Never comfortable with the
title "father of atomic energy,"
Einstein was haunted by the fear
that the atomic bomb would be
used again. In 1950, with the
development of the hydrogen
bomb, Einstein televised via NBC
his idea for peace in a nuclear
world: a single world government
drawn up by the US, the USSR,
and Great Britain, that would
control knowledge of atomic bomb
construction.
CREATOR Provided by thirdwise
SOURCE www.flickr.com/photos/
10912019@N05/2428315500/
DATE 1939

003 ATOMS FOR PEACE — FIRST DAY COVER
CREATOR United States of America
SOURCE people.maths.ox.ac.uk
DATE 1955

004 EMERGENCY COMMITTEE OF ATOMIC
SCIENTISTS
CREATOR Albert Einstein
SOURCE www.einsteinsworld.com

005 E=MCPEACED
CREATOR Artwork by Troy Torgerson,
Photograph by Squid Vicious
SOURCE www.flickr.com/photos/
fat_hobo/2173022232/sizes/o/

006 IMAGINATION
CREATOR Provided by oppositeofsuper
SOURCE www.flickr.com/photos/
oppositeofsuper/154820924/sizes/o/

007 ATOMS FOR PEACE
Produced for the Atomic Energy
Conference, Geneva, 1955.
CREATOR Erik Nitsche
SOURCE The Museum of Modern Art
DATE 1955

008 THE ATOM IN THE SERVICE OF PEACE
Produced for the Atomic Energy
Conference, Geneva, 1955.
CREATOR Erik Nitsche
SOURCE The Museum of Modern Art
DATE 1955

009 ATOMS FOR PEACE
CREATOR Lockheed
SOURCE blog.modernmechanix.com
DATE 1958

010 THE ATOM IN THE SERVICE OF PEACE
CREATOR Erik Nitsche
SOURCE The Museum of Modern Art
DATE 1955

001

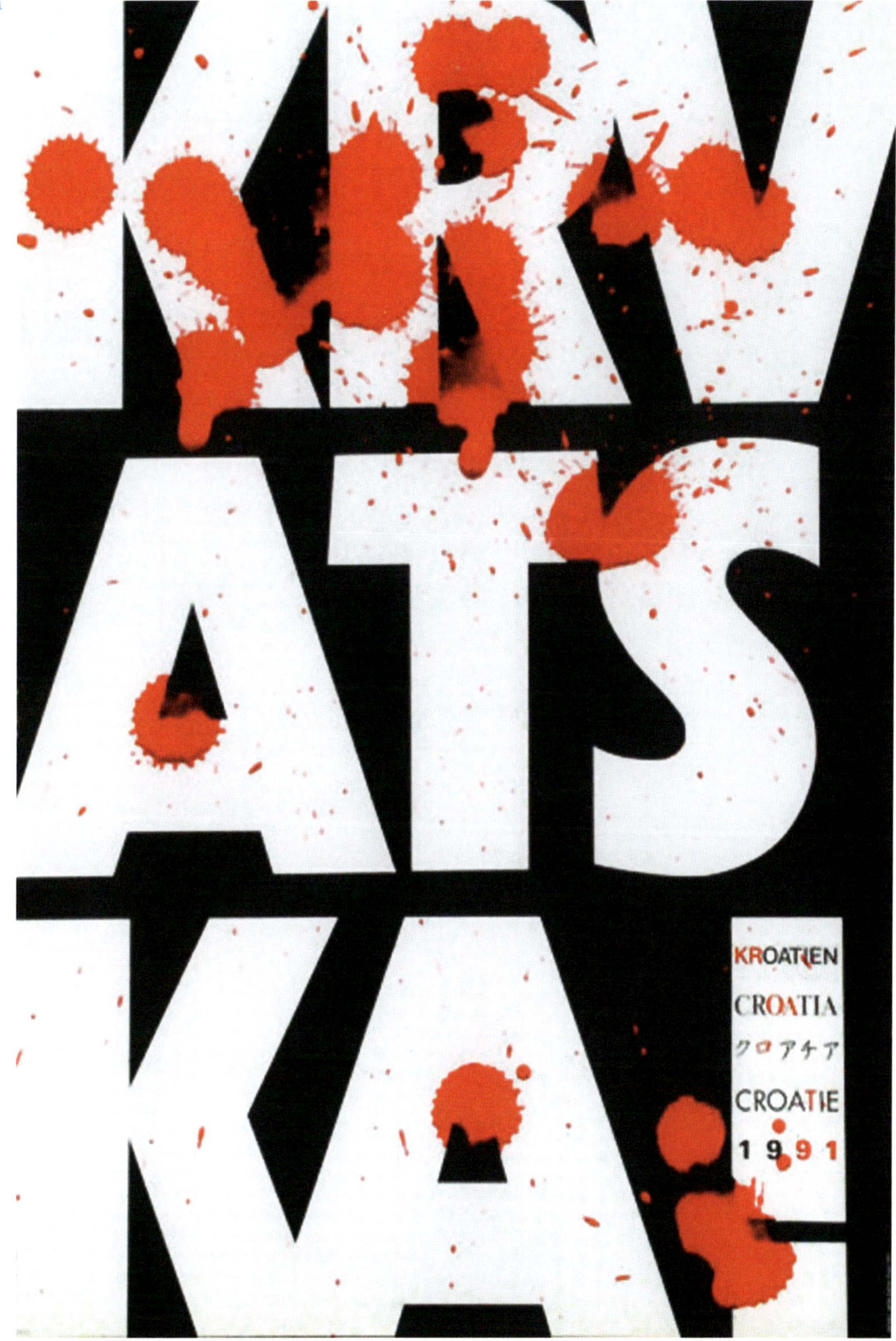

002

Vukovar is a thousand years old Croatian city on the Danube, and majority of its citizens are Croatian.
– Read
between
the lines
Vukovar was razed and occupied on 18 November 1991 by the forces of Greater Serbia in their aggression on the Republic of Croatia. Before the very eyes of the whole world more than 700 of its defenders and 1600 civilians were killed, and 3600 of its inhabitants disappeared without trace.
Vukovar was deprived of its homes, churches, factories and museums, even of its trees and birds, and life itself came to a standstill.
Croatia will be free only when Vukovar is liberated and when the banished Vukovarians return to their homes. On the third anniversary of the occupation of Vukovar, 18 November 1994, Council of the City of Vukovar in Exile, Zagreb, Croatia.

003
004

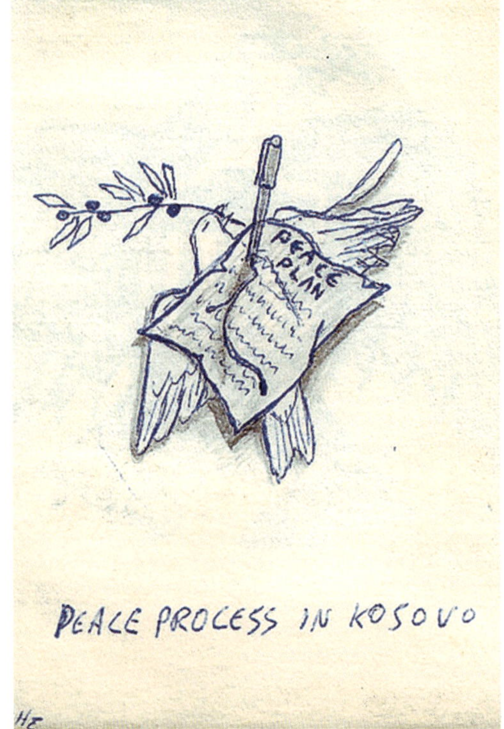
PEACE
PLAN
PEACE PROCESS IN KOSOVO
HE

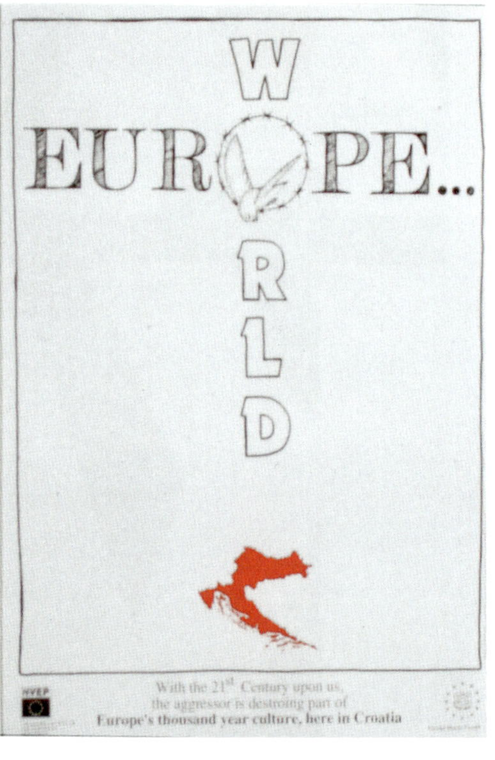
W
EUR PE...
O
R
L
D
HVEP
With the 21st Century upon us,
the aggressor is destroying part of
Europe's thousand year culture, here in Croatia

005

PSYHOANALYSIS
LINGUISTICS
ANTHROPOLOGY
PHILOSOPHY
AESTHETICS
ETHICS
KORREAN
LEAR
MACBETH
TIMON
FALSTAFF
RICHARD III
CALIBAN
HENRY V
TIMON
HAMLET
OTHELLO

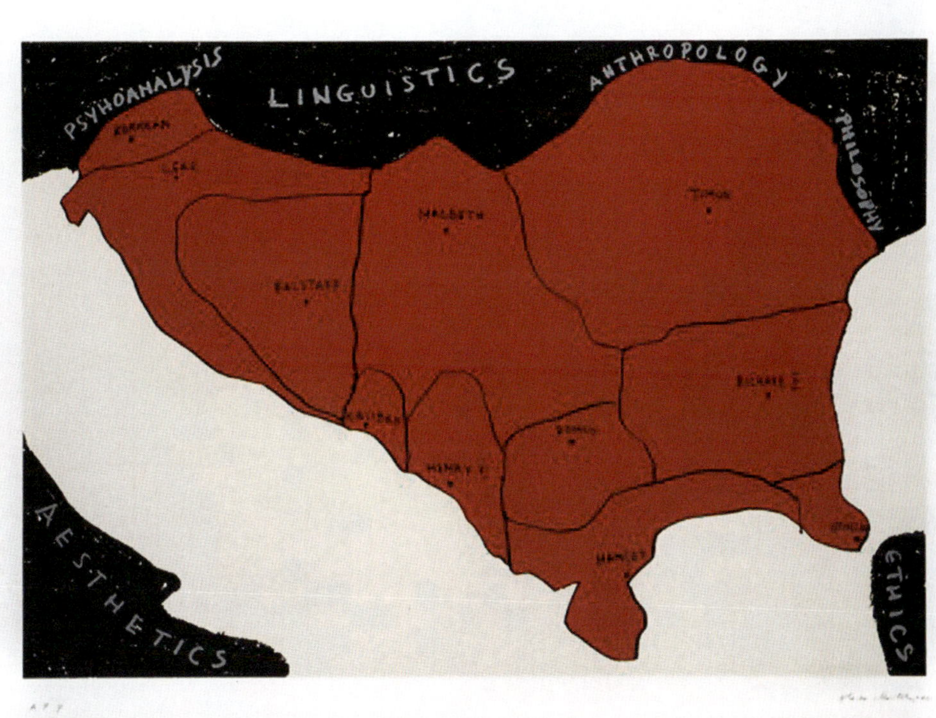

006

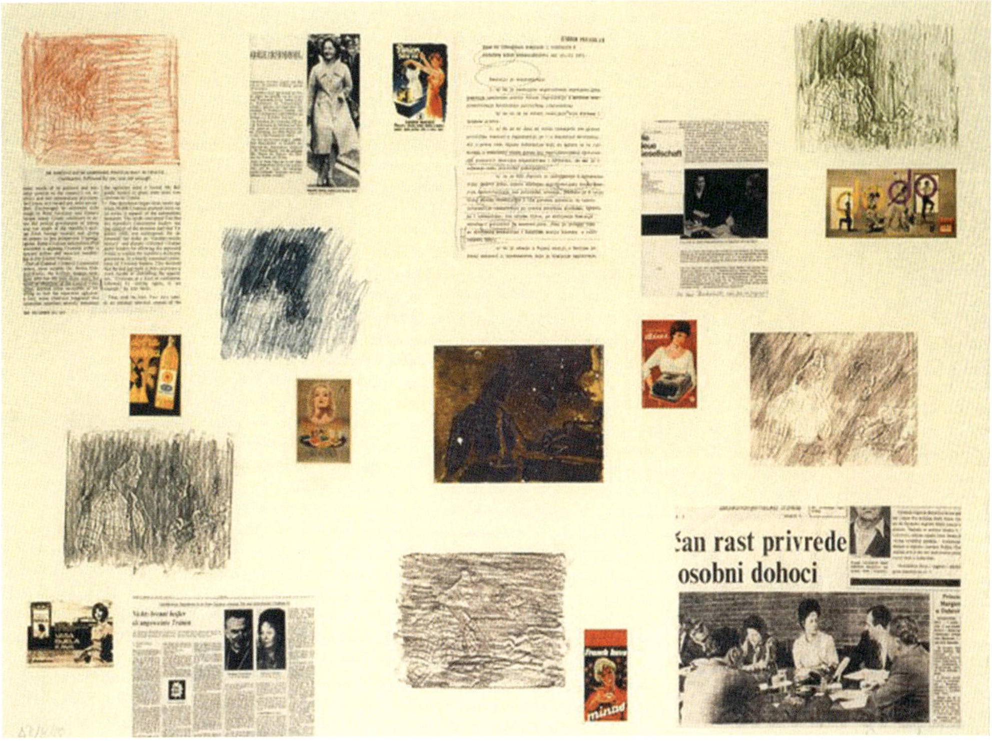

007
008

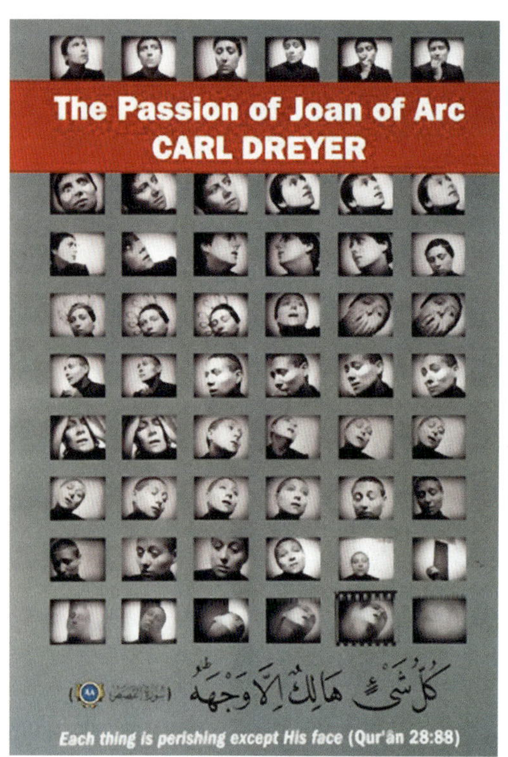

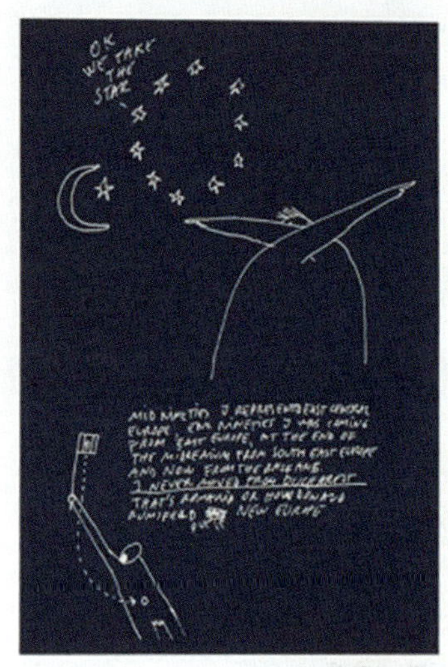

009
010

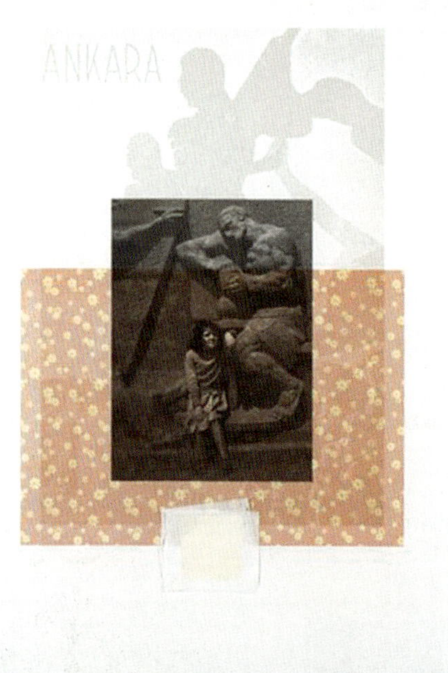

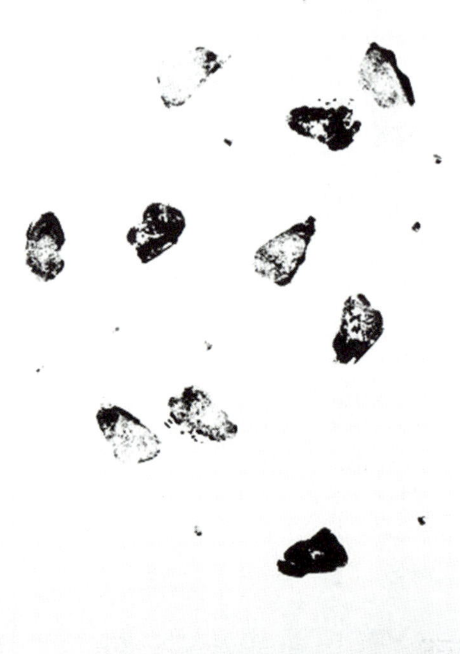

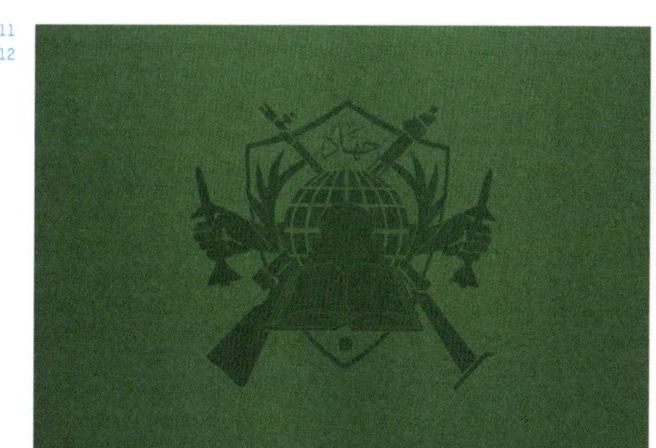
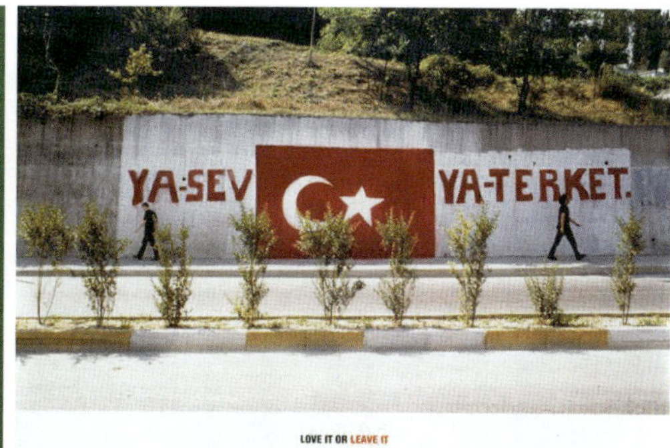
YA·SEV
www.eastartmap.org
YA·TERKET.
LOVE IT OR LEAVE IT

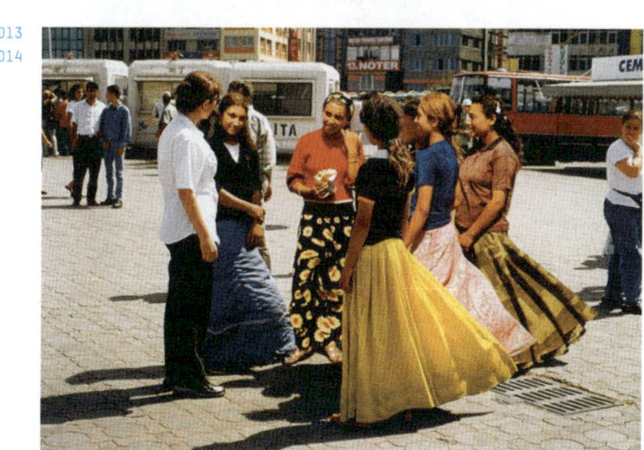
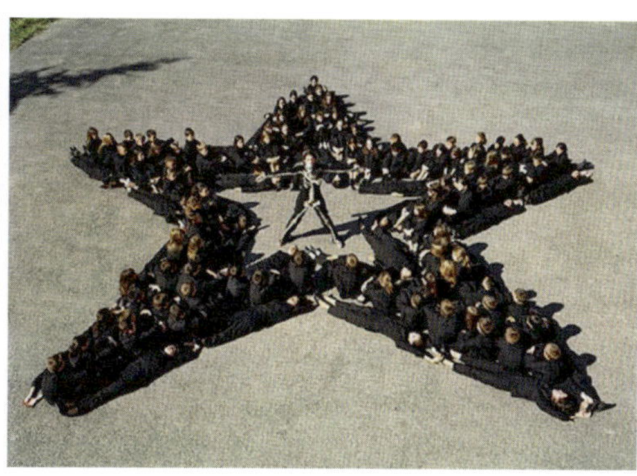

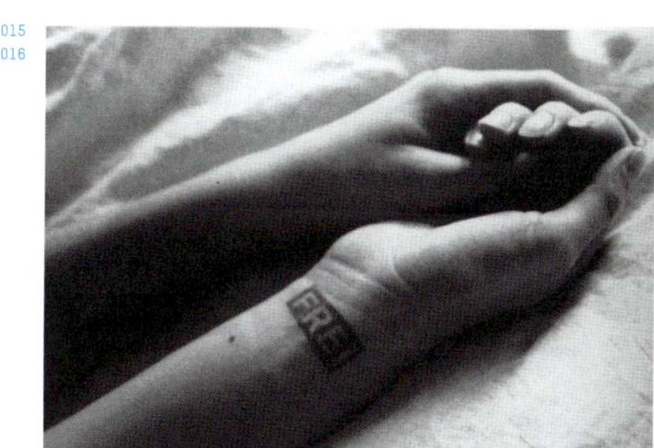
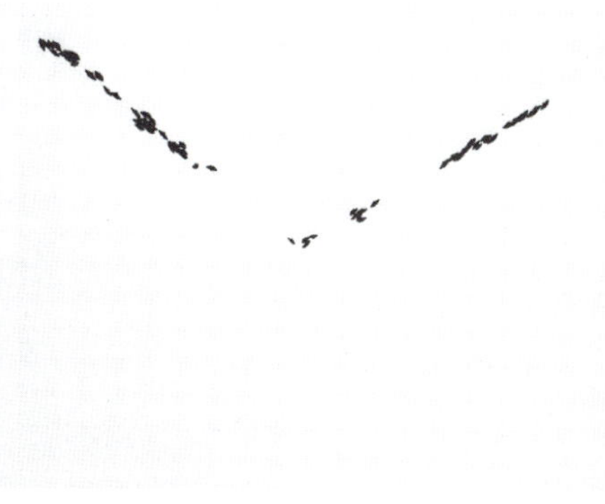

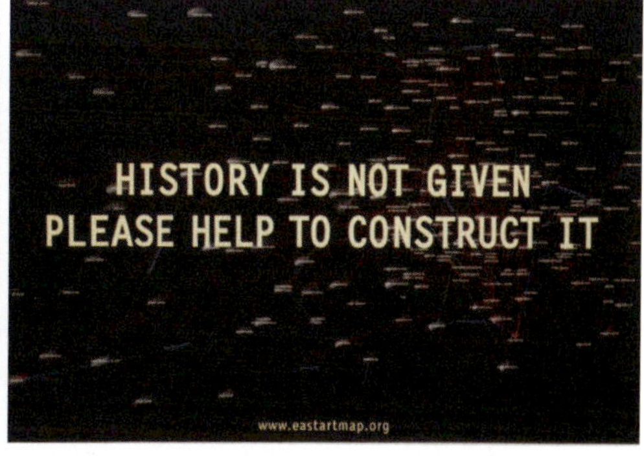
I believe more in horoscope
than in nationalities.
HISTORY IS NOT GIVEN
PLEASE HELP TO CONSTRUCT IT
www.eastartmap.org

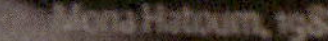

OVER
MY
DEAD
BODY
Mona Hatoum, 1988

LEFT
019

020
021

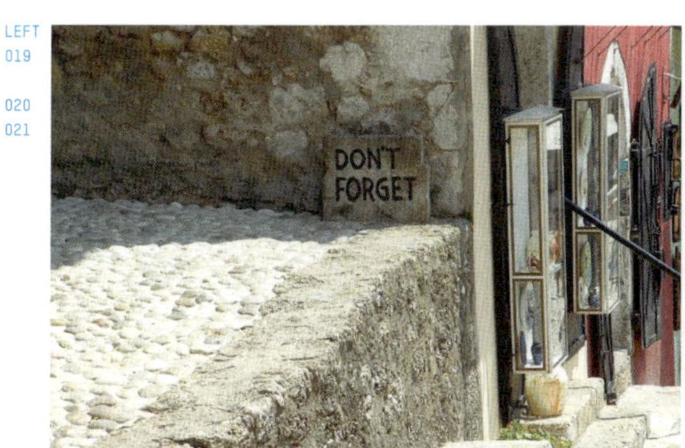

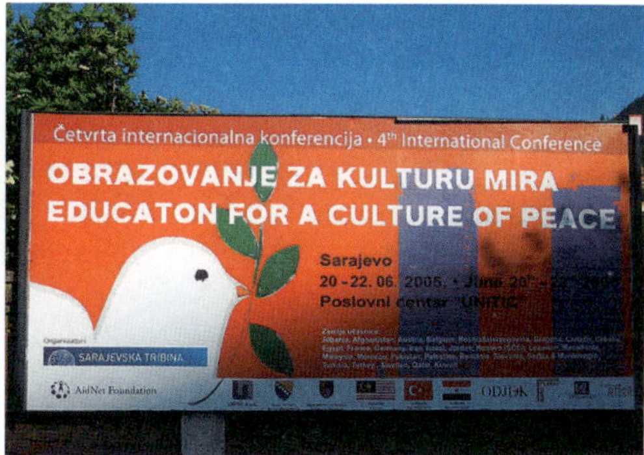

022
023

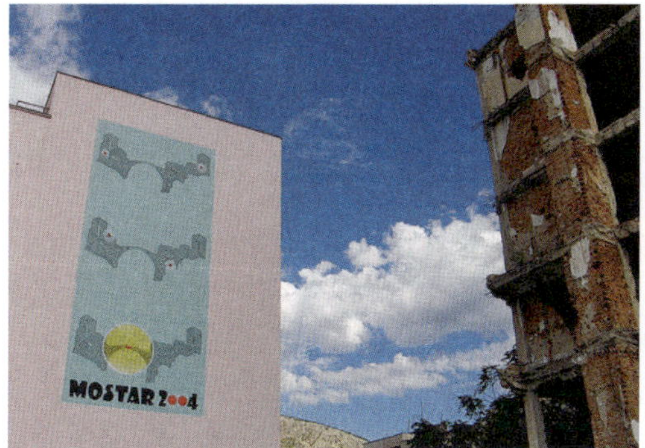

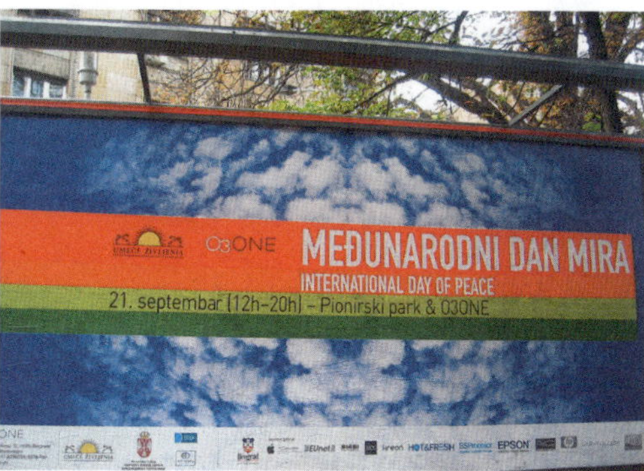

024
025

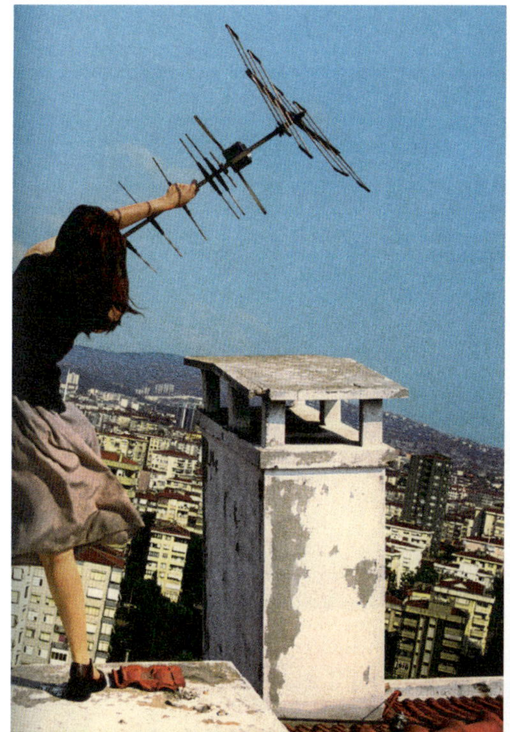

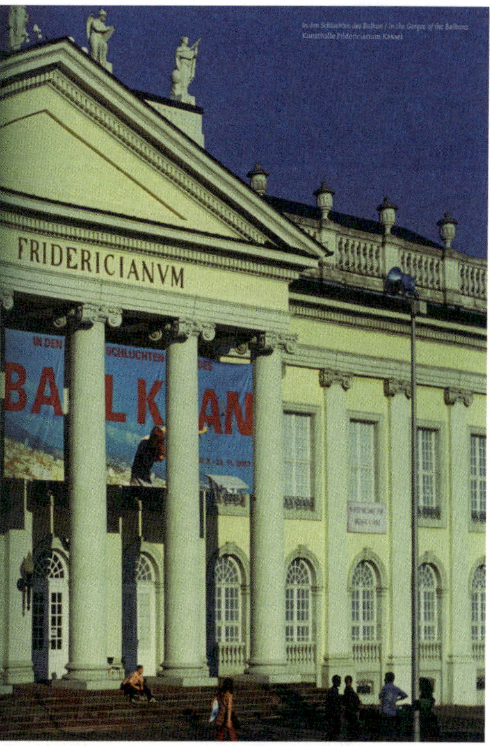

026

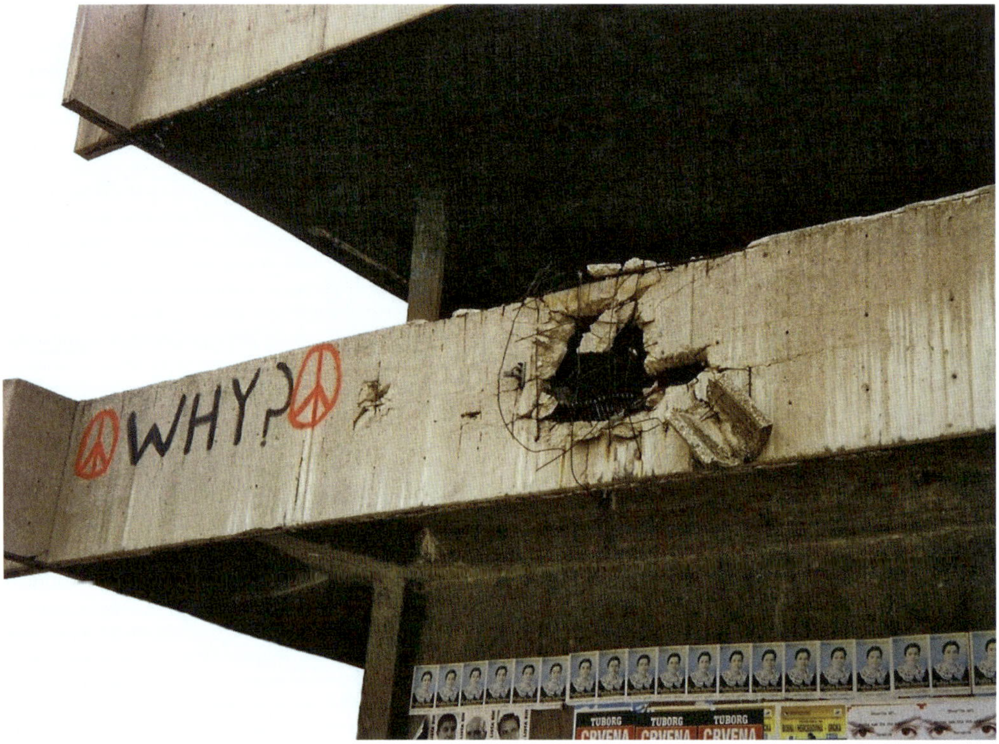

027

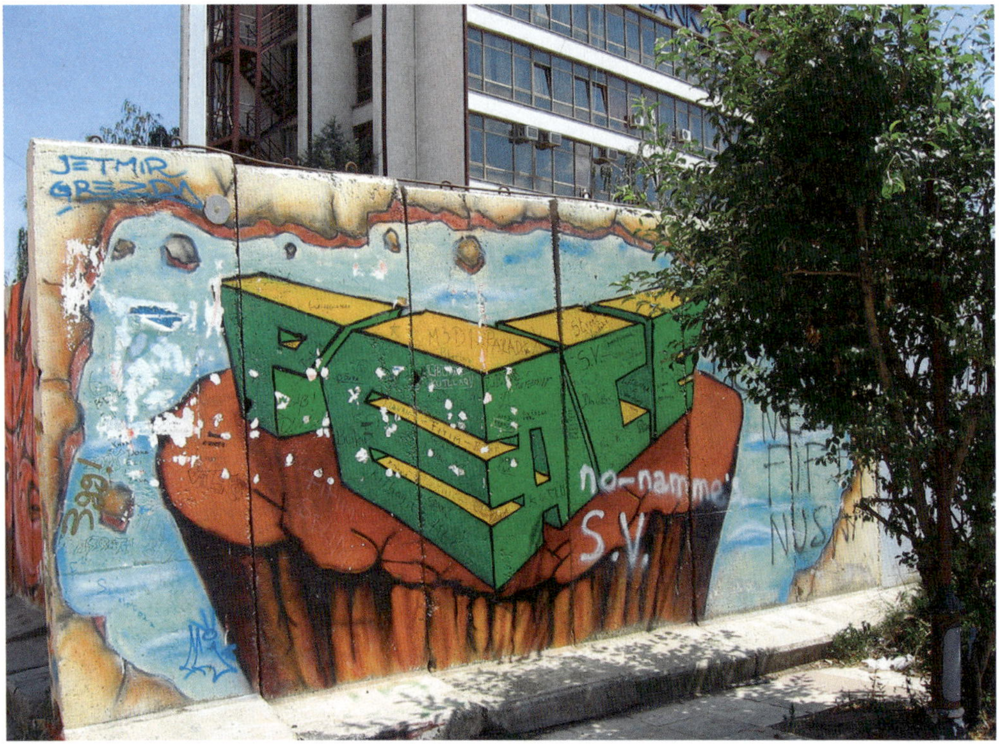

001 KRUATSKA!
SOURCE Plakatsammlung Museum
für Gestaltung Zürich

002 READ BETWEEN THE LINES
CREATOR Boris Ljubicic
SOURCE Plakatsammlung Museum
für Gestaltung Zürich
DATE 1996

003 PEACE PROCESS IN KOSOVO, PEACE PLAN
CREATOR Provided by view-askew
SOURCE www.flickr.com/photos/
nicalibre

004 WORLD EUROPE …
With the 21st Century upon us, the
aggressor is destroing [sic] part
of Europe's thousand-year culture,
here in Croatia.
SOURCE HVEP

005 SHAKESPEARE WITH US
CREATOR Vlado Martek
SOURCE www.editionblockberlin.de
DATE 2005

006 SARKA D. K
CREATOR Sanja Ivekovic
SOURCE www.editionblockberlin.de
DATE 2005

007 THE PASSION OF JOAN OF ARC
CREATOR Jalal Toufic
SOURCE www.editionblockberlin.de
DATE 2005

008 UNTITLED
CREATOR Dan Perjovschi
SOURCE www.editionblockberlin.de
DATE 2005

009 IN THE SHADE
CREATOR Karamustafa
SOURCE www.editionblockberlin.de
DATE 2005

010 ONE-MINUTE DANCE
CREATOR Nevin Aladag
SOURCE www.editionblockberlin.de
DATE 2005

011 THE FLAG
CREATOR Oliver Musovik
SOURCE www.editionblockberlin.de
DATE 2005

012 LOVE IT OR LEAVE IT
CREATOR Halil Altindere
SOURCE www.editionblockberlin.de
DATE 2005

013 PILOT, 2001 — 2003
CREATOR Aydan Murtezaoglu
SOURCE www.editionblockberlin.de
DATE 2005

014 COUNT ON US
CREATOR Marina Abramovic

SOURCE www.editionblockberlin.de
DATE 2005

015 FREI
CREATOR Sejla Kameric
SOURCE René Block and Marius
Babias, eds, *The Balkan Trilogy*
[Munich: Silke Schreiber, 2007].

016 UNTITLED
CREATOR Anri Sala
SOURCE www.editionblockberlin.de
DATE 2005

017 I BELIEVE MORE IN HOROSCOPE THAN
IN NATIONALITIES
CREATOR Maja Bajevic
SOURCE www.editionblockberlin.de
DATE 2005

018 HISTORY IS NOT GIVEN PLEASE HELP
TO CONSTRUCT IT
CREATOR Edi Hila
SOURCE René Block and Marius
Babias, eds, *The Balkan Trilogy*
[Munich: Silke Schreiber, 2007].

019 OVER MY DEAD BODY
CREATOR Mona Hatoum
SOURCE René Block and Marius
Babias, eds, *The Balkan Trilogy*
[Munich: Silke Schreiber, 2007].

020 DON'T FORGET
CREATOR Provided by gianita
SOURCE www.flickr.com/photos/
gianita/211236894/

021 SARAJEVO: EDUCATION FOR
A CULTURE OF PEACE
CREATOR Provided by Wes Burns
SOURCE www.flickr.com/photos/
jetsetwes/84231340/

022 MOSTAR 2004
This mural in Mostar depicts two
balls rolling through mazes and
meeting in the middle of the
newly repaired Old Bridge, which
had been destroyed during the
Balkan Wars.
SOURCE Unknown

023 PEACE DAY 2006: SERBIA –
ANTITRAFFICKING CENTER [ATC]
CREATOR Provided by Wes Burns
SOURCE www.flickr.com/photos/
9221746@N08/580812855/

024 UNTITLED
CREATOR Aydan Murtezaoglu
SOURCE René Block and Marius
Babias, eds, *The Balkan Trilogy*
(Munich: Silke Schreiber, 2007).

025 UNTITLED
SOURCE René Block and Marius
Babias, eds, *The Balkan Trilogy*
[Munich: Silke Schreiber, 2007].

026 PEACE
SOURCE www.flickr.com/photos/
nicalibre/79845317/

027 PEACE
SOURCE www.flickr.com/photos/
nicalibre

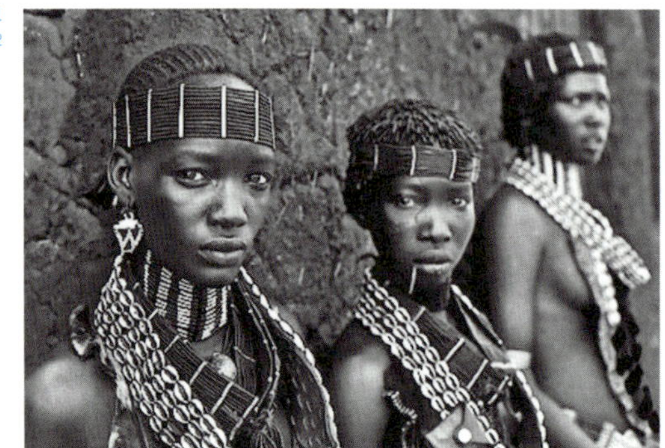
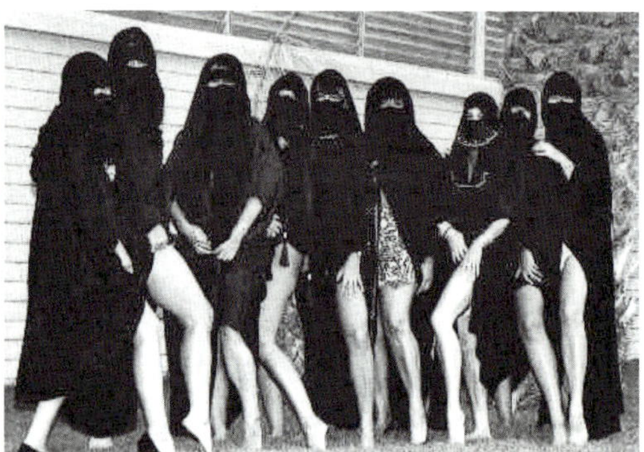

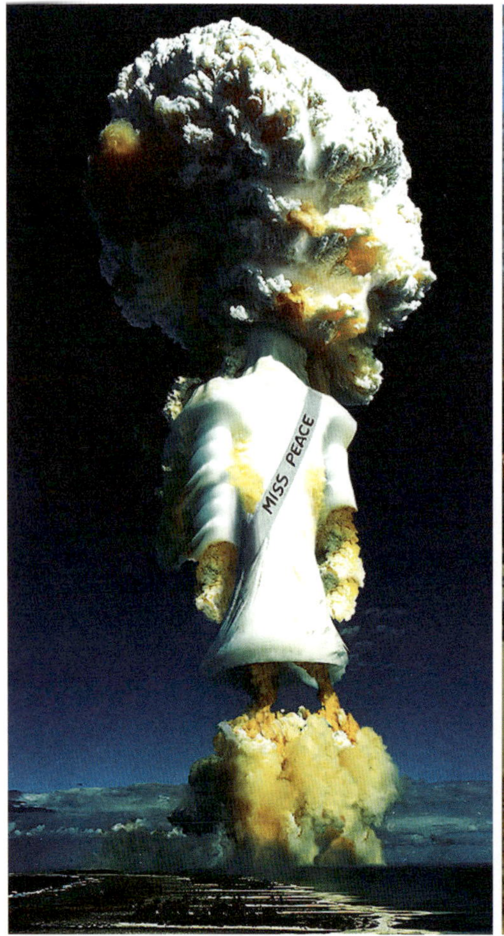
MISS PEACE

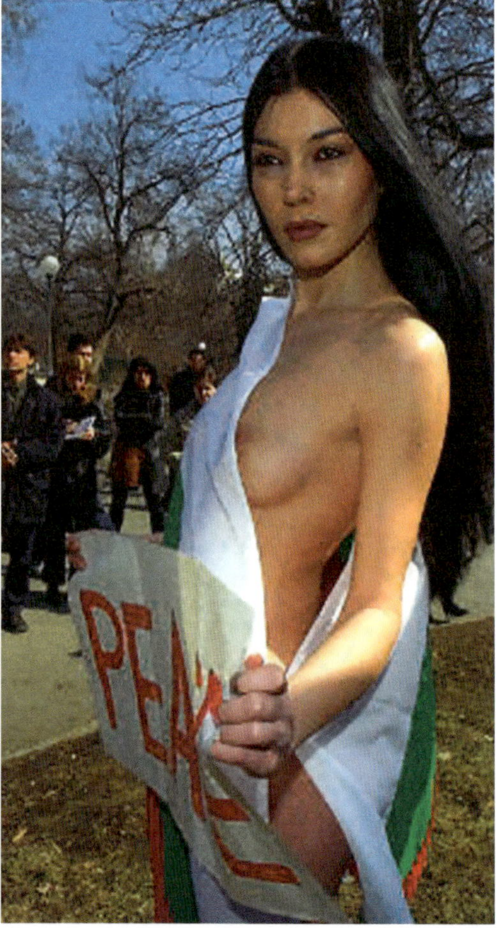
PEA

005

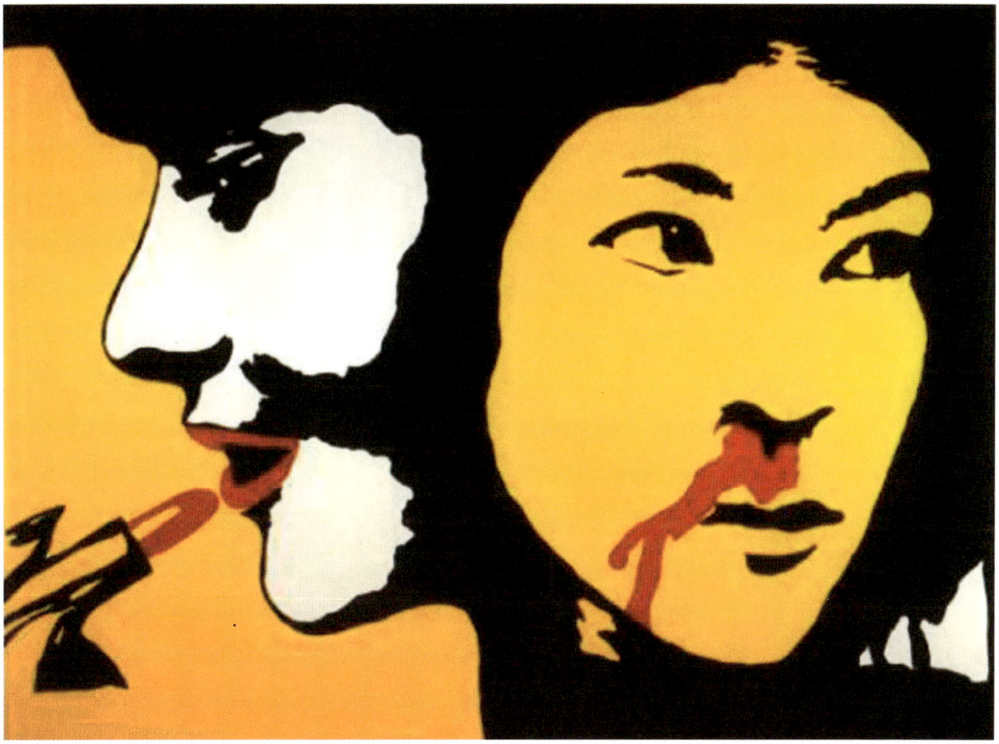

006

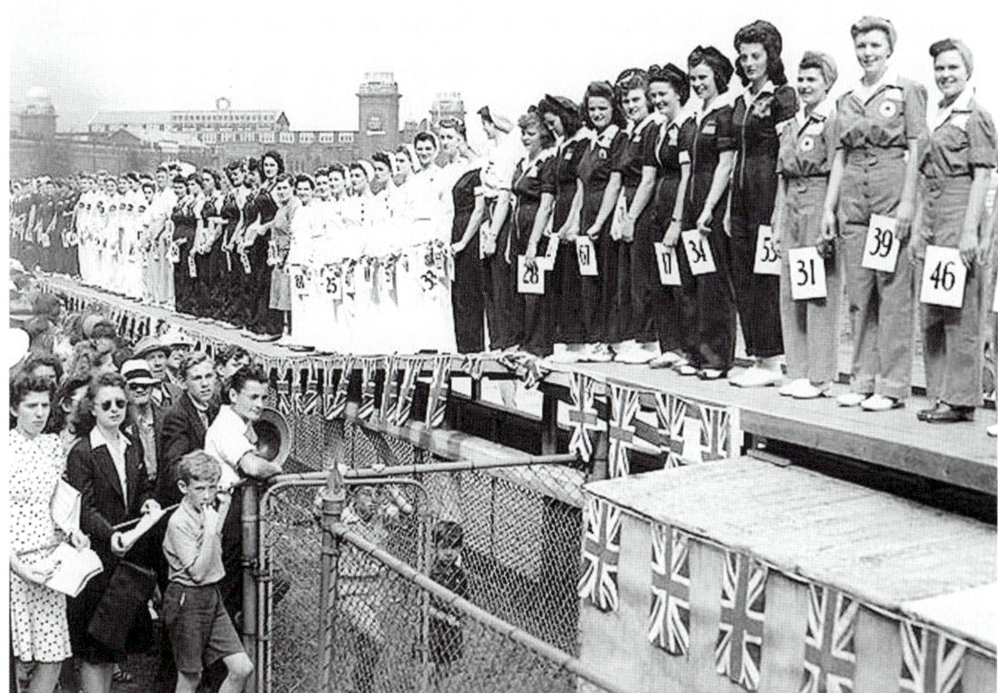

007

Մաքրում եմ լռության
իմ դիմակը
Լռության օր
Day of Silence

008

MISTO
LE RESTAURANT MISTO S'ASSOCIE À L'ANEB
POUR COMBATTRE L'ANOREXIE-NERVEUSE-BOULIMIE

ANEB
ASSOCIATION QUÉBÉCOISE D'AIDE AUX PERSONNES
SOUFFRANT D'ANOREXIE-NERVEUSE ET DE BOULIMIE

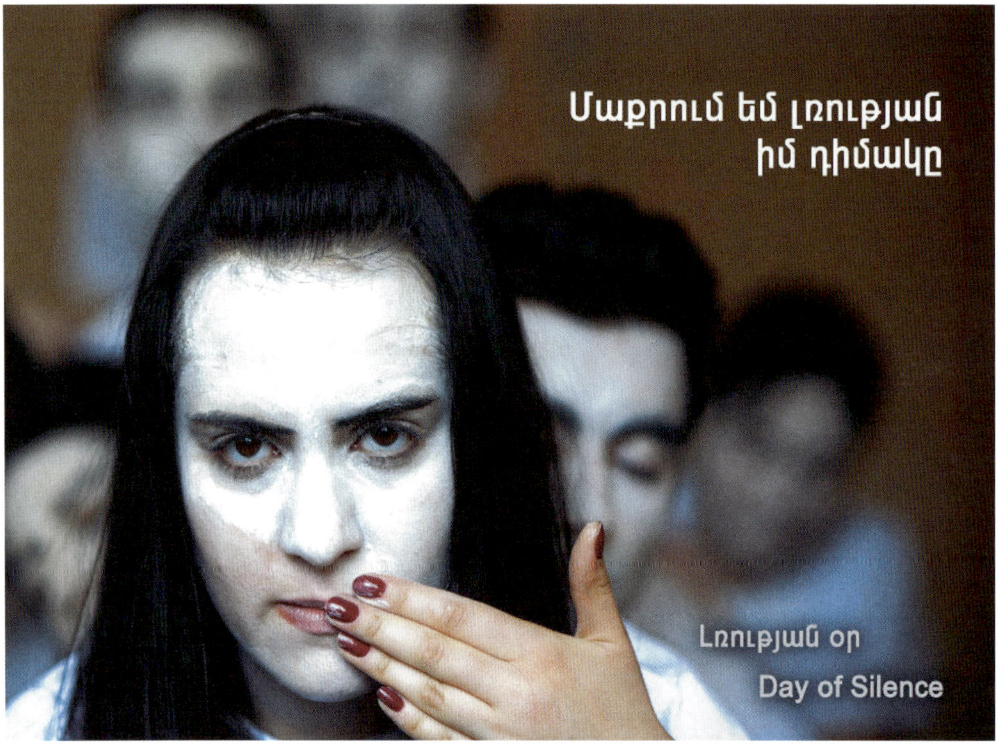

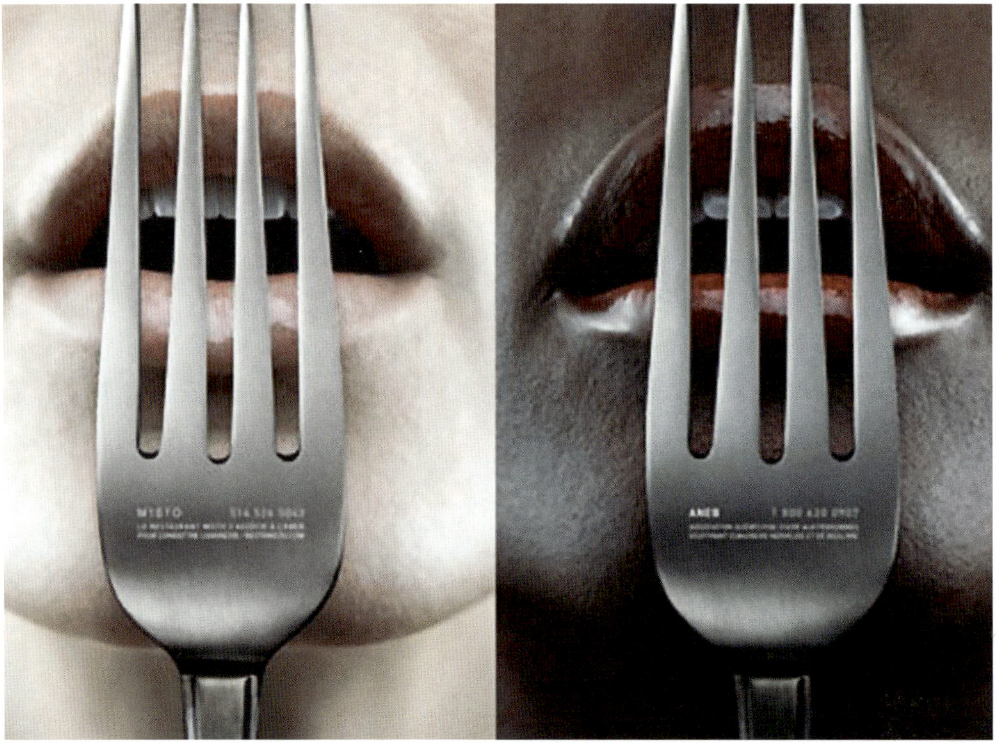

009
010

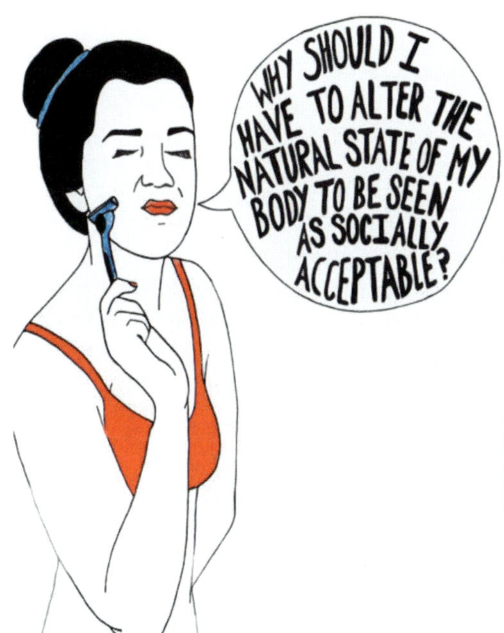

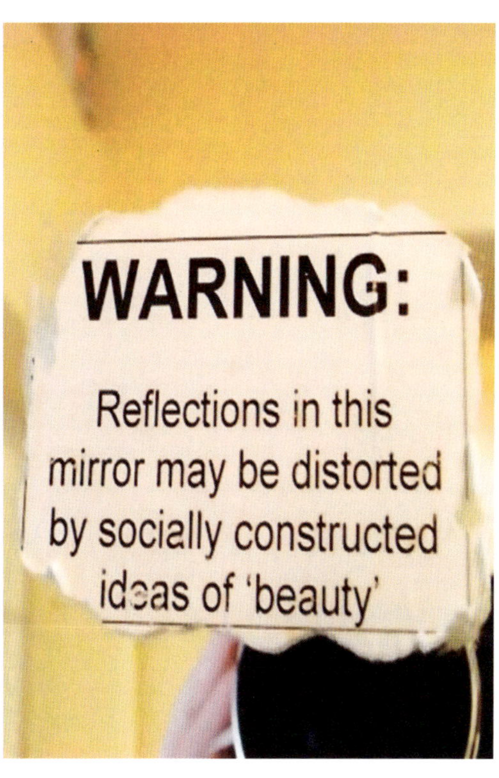

011
012

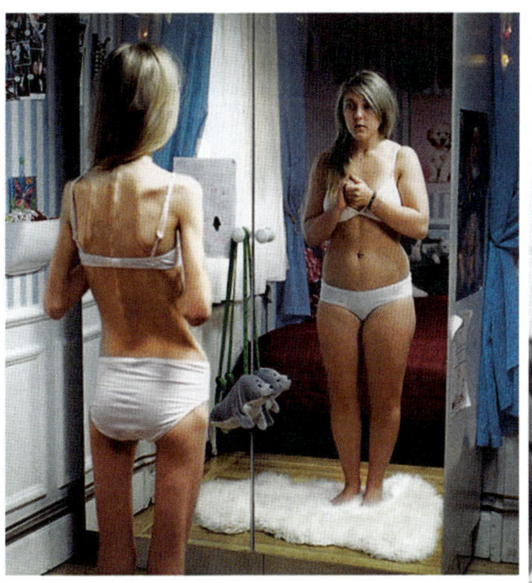

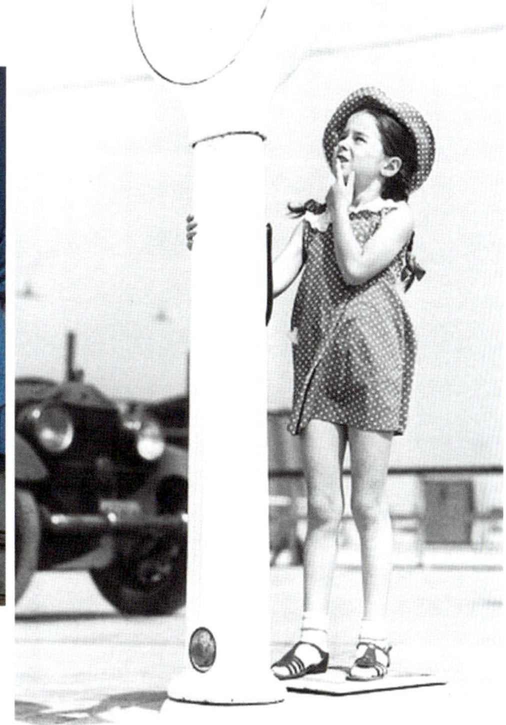

001 BEAUTY BEYOND EGO
     Artist's statement: "With this
     exhibition I would like to pay a
     special and self-standing tribute
     to rural African women. The value
     of this collection is not only in
     its photographic value, but mainly
     in the subjects portrayed. There
     is a beauty in rural African
     women that goes beyond what we
     normally think beauty is, beyond
     the egocentric concept of looks,
     appearance and even beyond the
     concept of inner beauty."
     CREATOR Giulio d'Ercole
     SOURCE www.africancolours.com
     DATE 2011

002 UNTITLED
     SOURCE atlasshrugs2000.typepad.com

003 MISS PEACE
     SOURCE designyoutrust.com

004 TANYA KARABELOVA OUTSIDE THE US
     EMBASSY IN SOFIA
     The former Miss Bulgaria protested
     against military intervention
     in Iraq.
     SOURCE yves.a.free.fr

005 LA MODELO Y LA VIETNAMITA
     [THE MODEL AND THE
     VIETNAMESE WOMAN]
     CREATOR José Gómez Fresquet
     SOURCE whatcalicodidnext.word-
     press.com
     DATE c. 1970

006 MISS WAR WORKER BEAUTY CONTEST
     SOURCE commons.wikimedia.org
     DATE 1942

007 I AM ERASING MY MASK OF SILENCE
     The Day of Silence [April 20]
     focuses attention on the spread
     of hate crimes against the
     LGBT community, from homophobia,
     bullying, discrimination, and
     intolerance to psychological
     and physical abuse.
     CREATOR Women's Rights Center
     [a Yerevan-based NGO]
     SOURCE human-rights-for-all.
     tumblr.com/

008 ANEB QUEBEC
     Association for people suffering
     from anorexia and bulimia.
     CREATOR Amen-Expoxy
     SOURCE osocio.org

009 WHY SHOULD I HAVE TO ALTER THE
     NATURAL STATE OF MY BEING TO BE
     SEEN AS SOCIALLY ACCEPTABLE?
     SOURCE fuckyougenderbinary.
     tumblr.com/

010 WARNING
     SOURCE weheartit.com

011 LITTLE SNOW WHITE AND THE
     MIRROR ISSUE
     CREATOR Anorexi Bulimi Kontakt,
     Grey Stockholm
     SOURCE osocio.org

012 LITTLE GIRL LOOKING CONFUSED
     BY A SCALE
     SOURCE www.picturesfromourpast.com/
     detail/41990.html

001
002

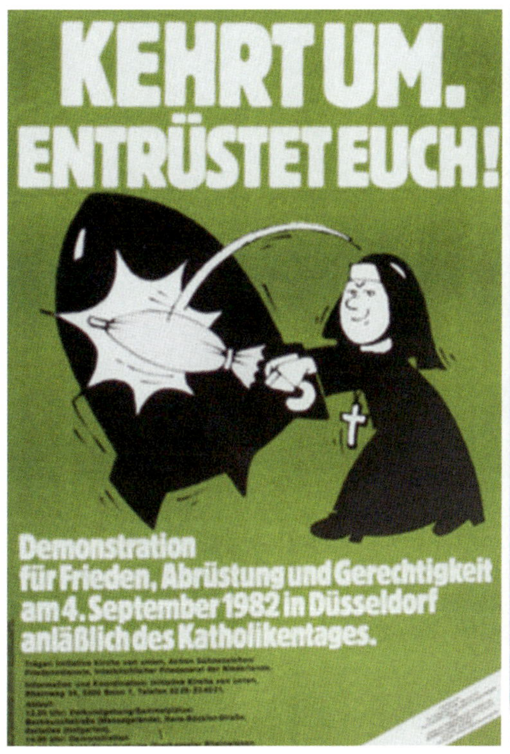

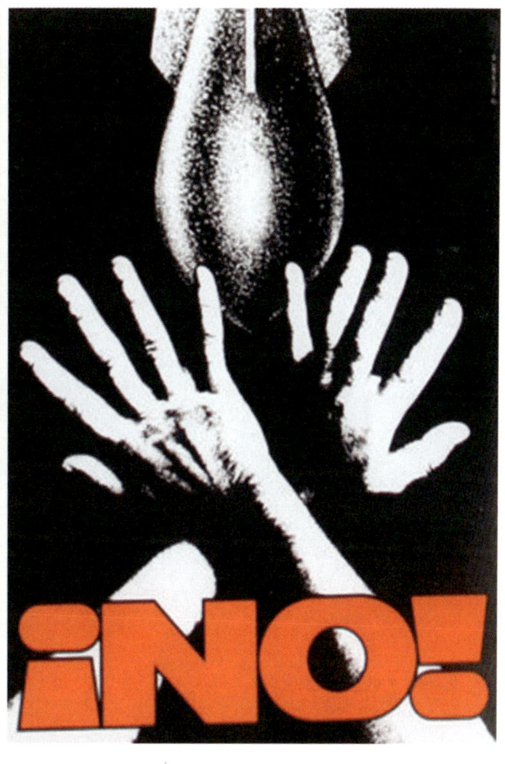

003
004

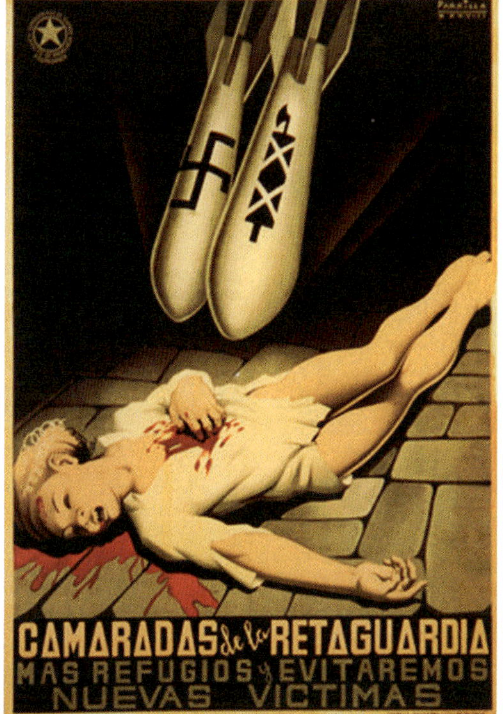

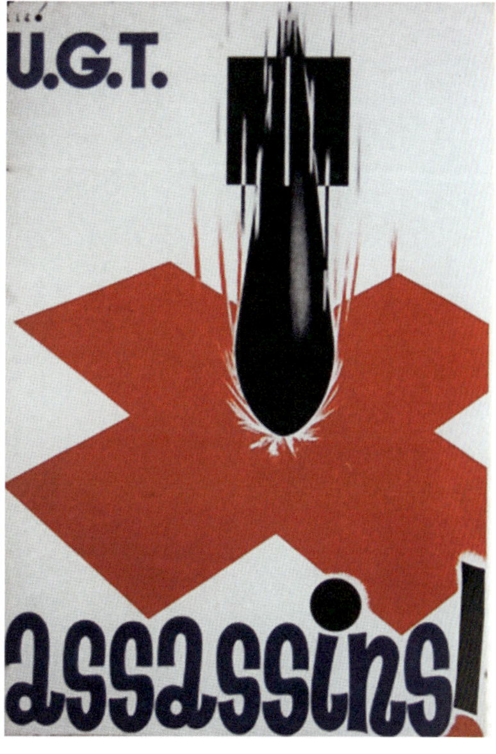

005
006

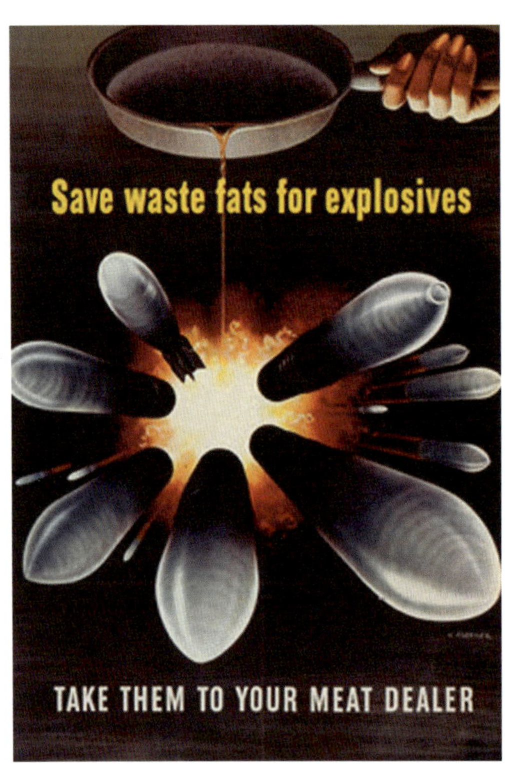
Save waste fats for explosives
TAKE THEM TO YOUR MEAT DEALER

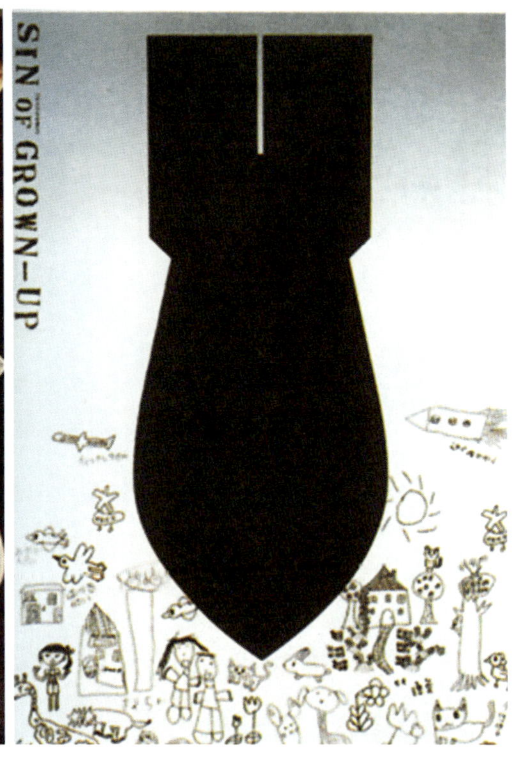
SIN OF GROWN-UP

007
008

RIGHT
009

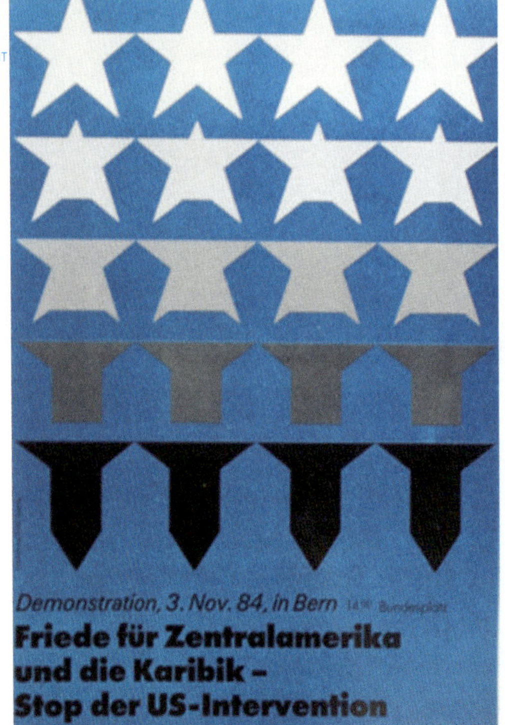
Demonstration, 3. Nov. 84, in Bern
Friede für Zentralamerika
und die Karibik –
Stop der US-Intervention

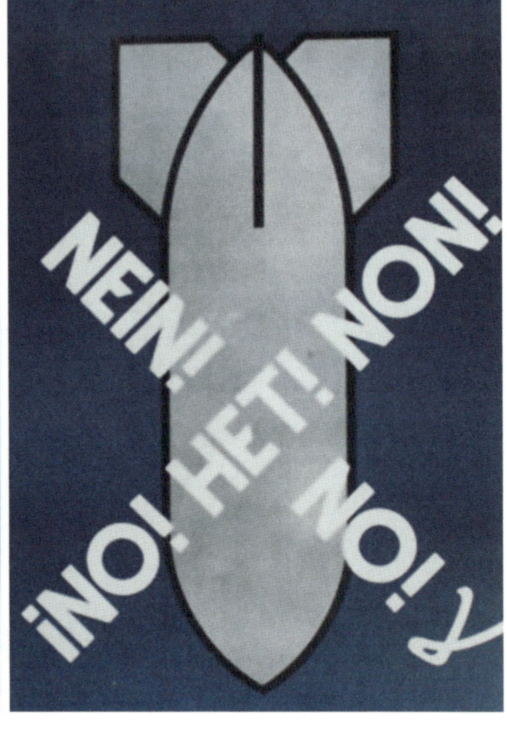
NEIN! HET! NON!
¡NO!

PEACE
IS IN OUR
HANDS
PEACE

010
011

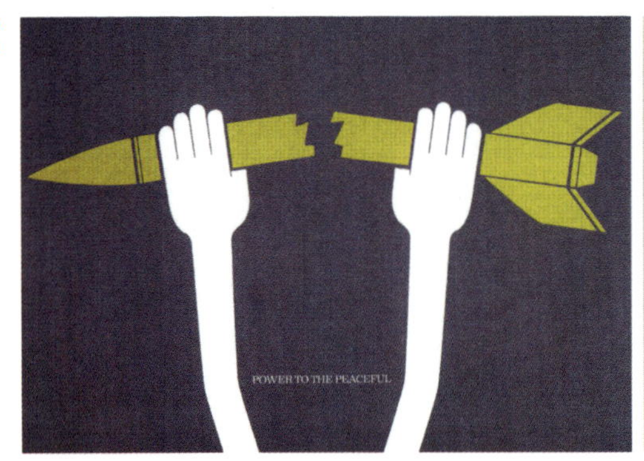

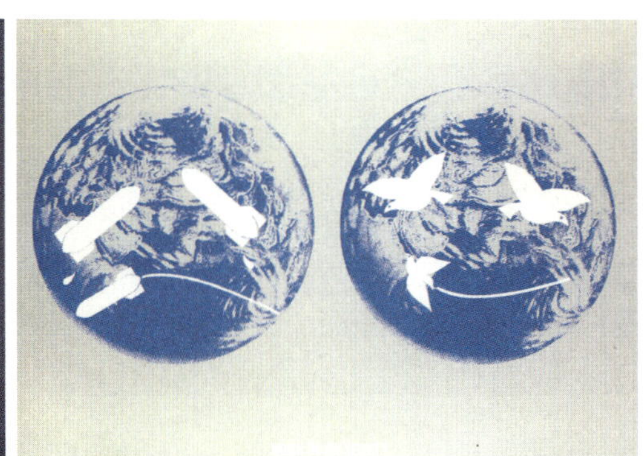

012
013

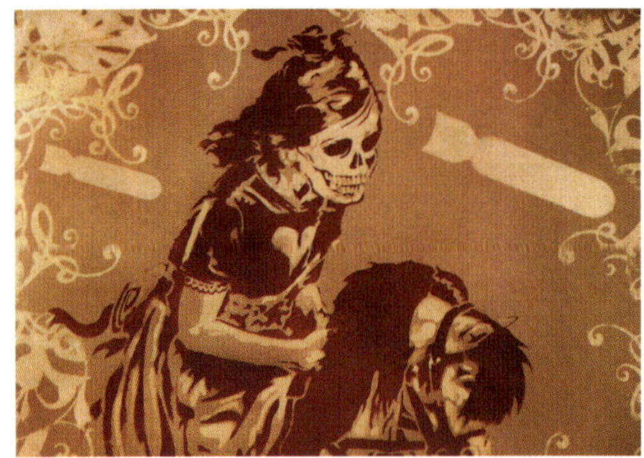

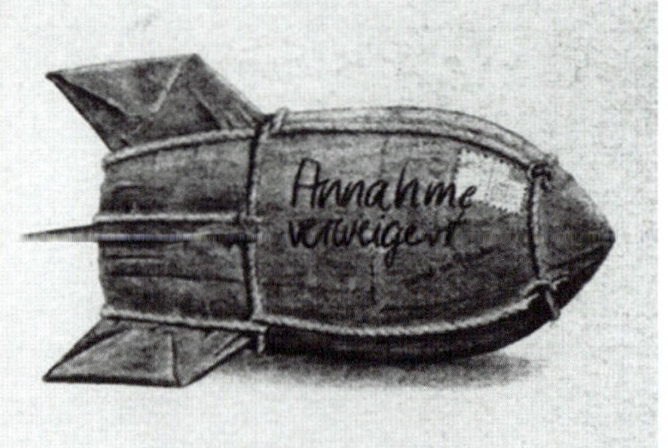

014
015

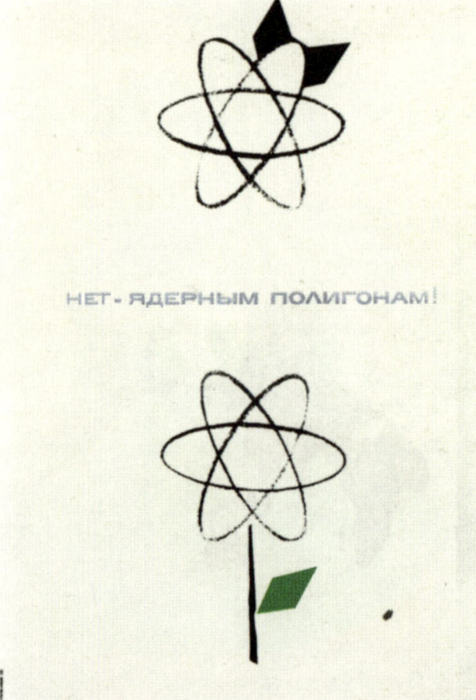

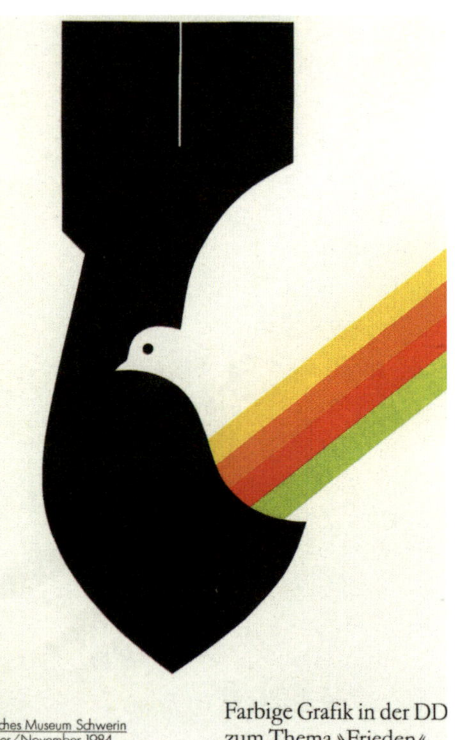

016
017

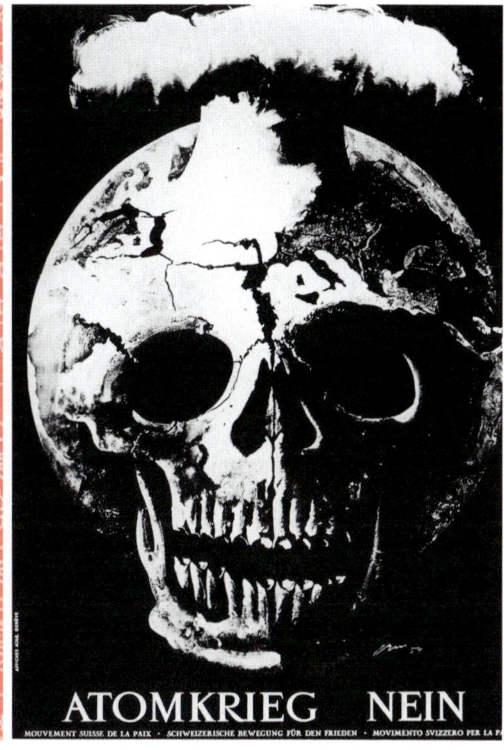

018
019

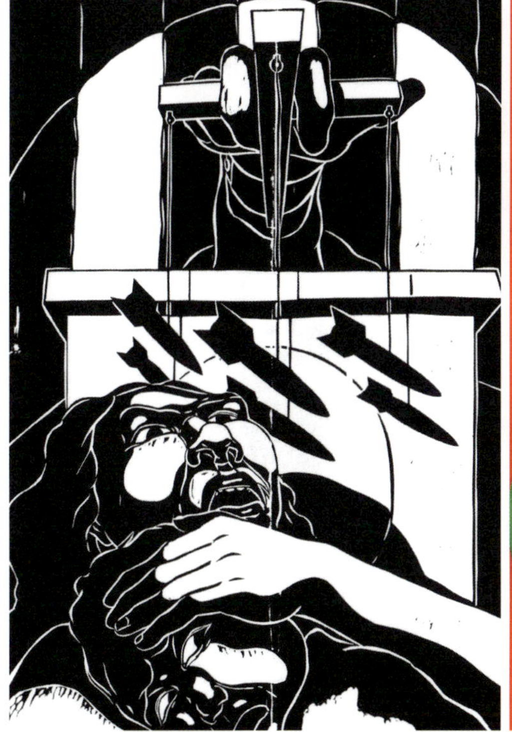

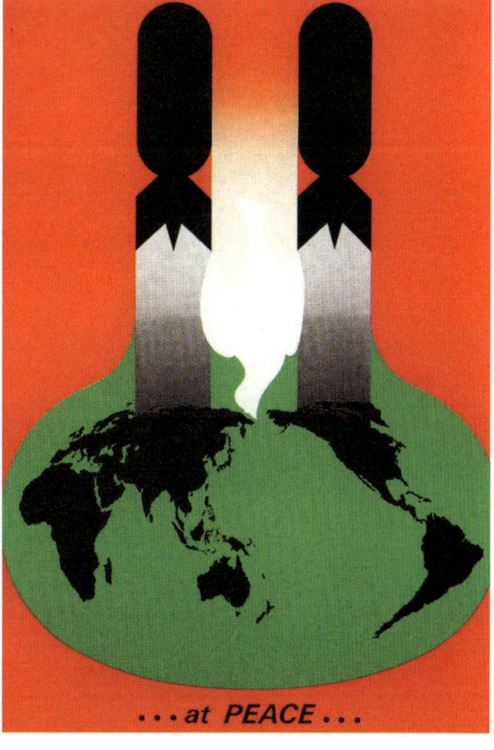

020
021

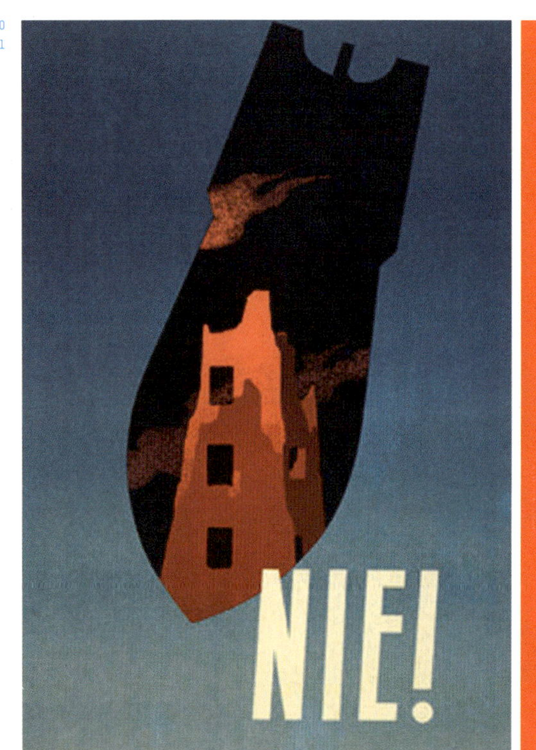

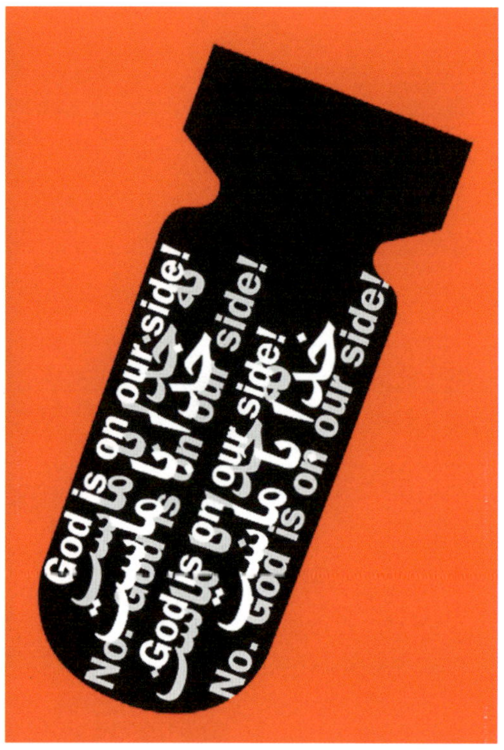

022
023

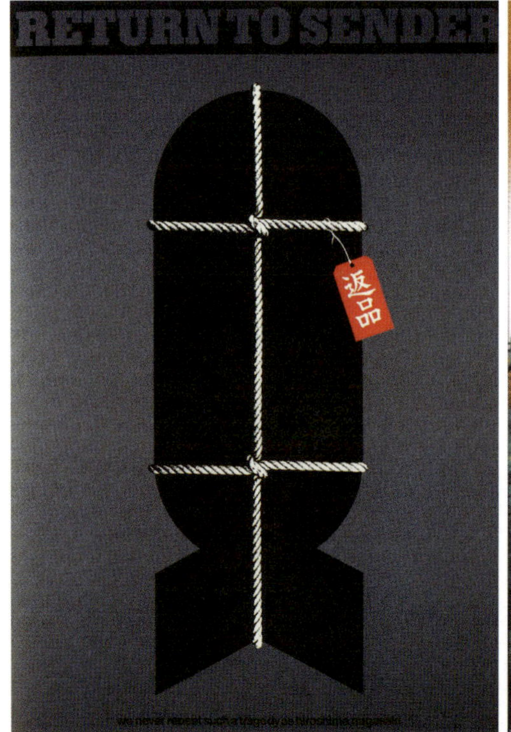

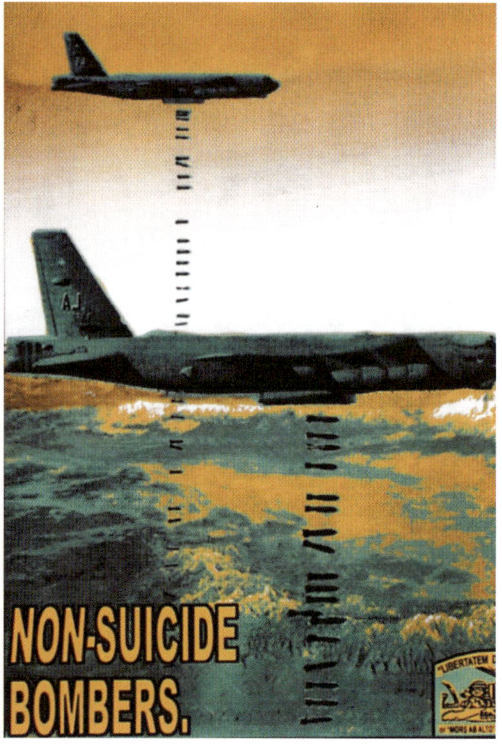

024
025

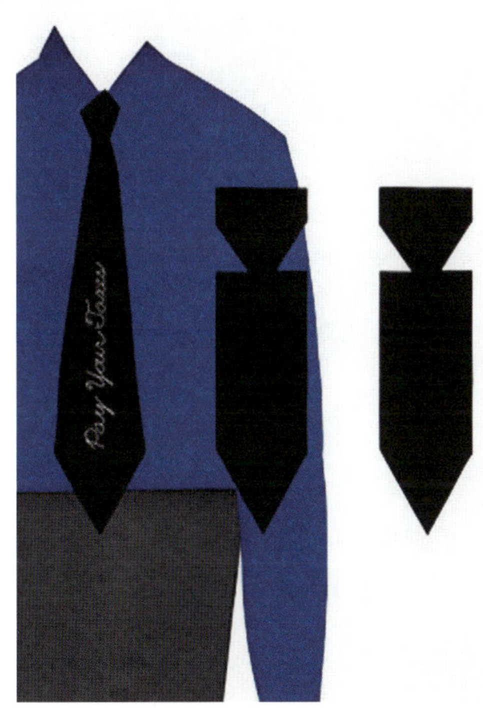

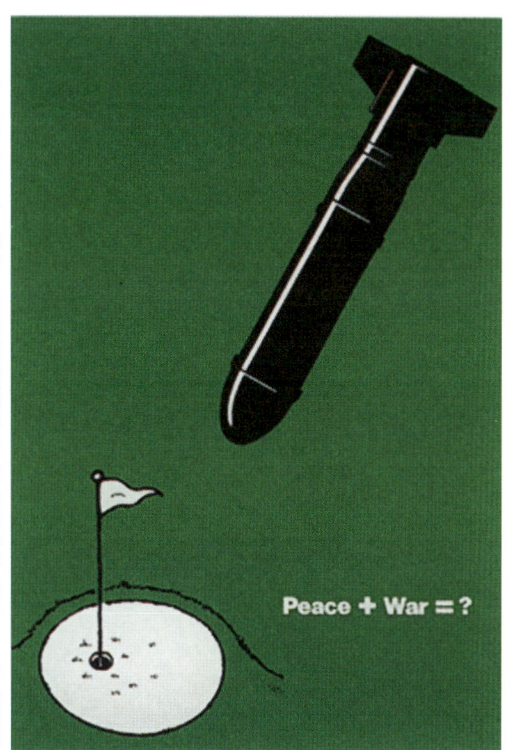

026
027

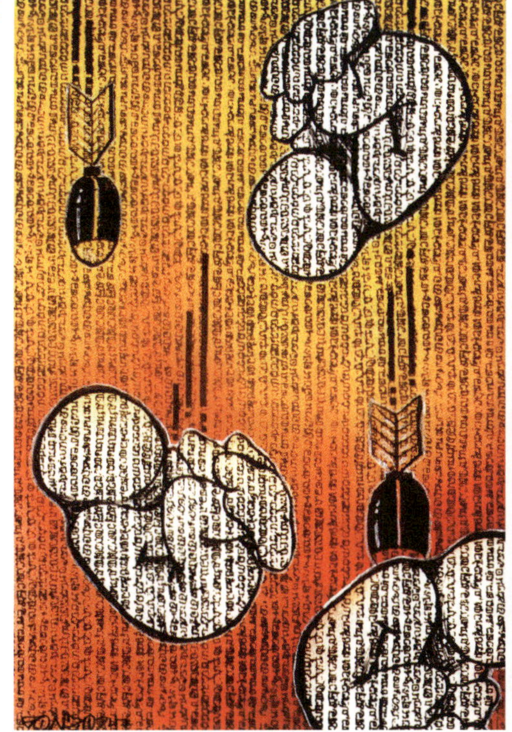

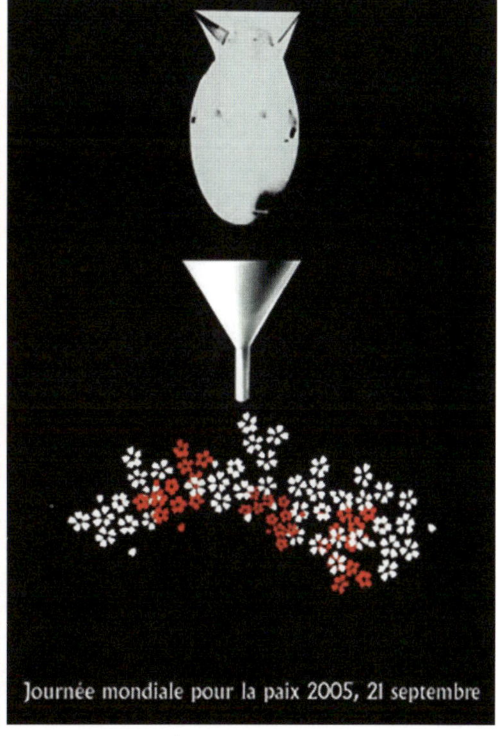

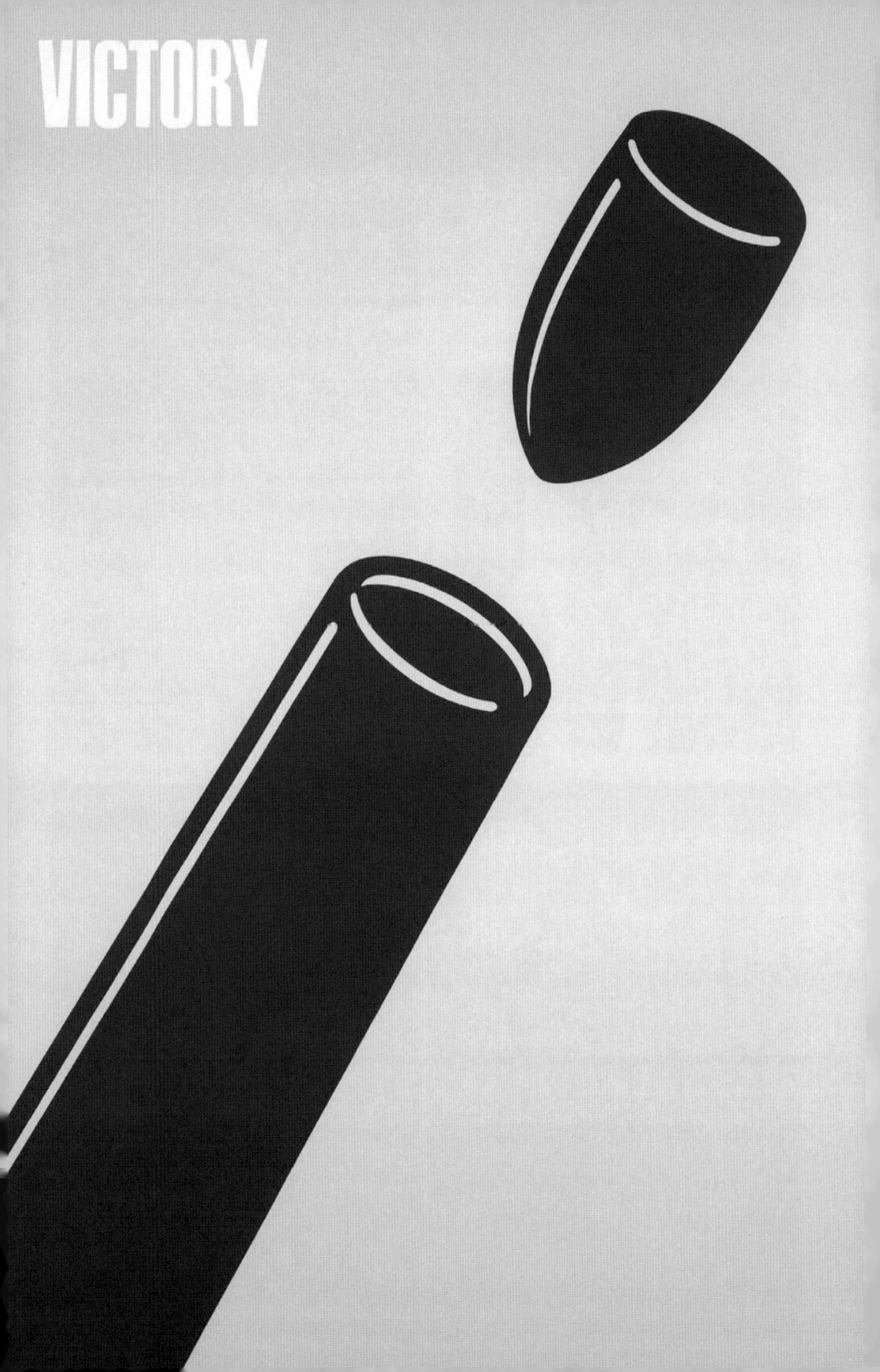

VICTORY

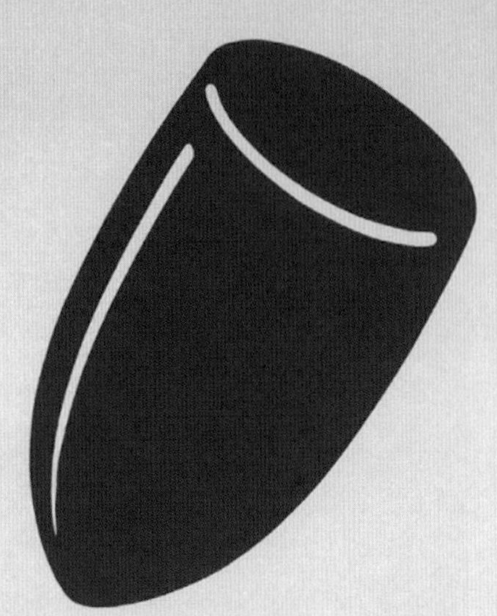

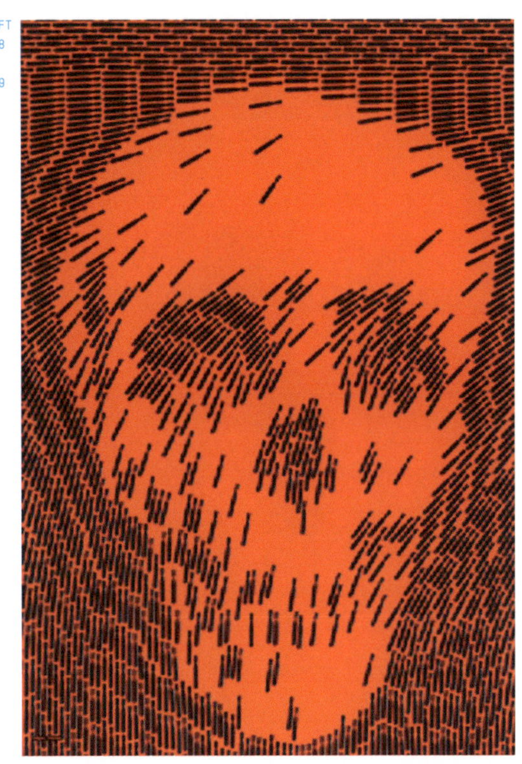

030

001 KEHRT UM. ENTRÜSTET EUCH
[REPENT. DISARM]
CREATOR Serviceteam Werbung
& Grafik
SOURCE Plakatsammlung Museum
für Gestaltung Zürich

002 NO!
CREATOR Chovanec
SOURCE Plakatsammlung Museum
für Gestaltung Zürich

003 CAMARADAS DE LA RETAGUARDIA
MAS REFUGIOS Y EVITAREMOS
NUEVAS VICTIMAS
[COMRADES - MORE HOUSING AND
FEWER VICTIMS]
CREATOR Parilla
SOURCE Plakatsammlung Museum
für Gestaltung Zürich

004 U.G.T. ASSASINS!
This poster from the Spanish Civil
War was produced by the fascist
Nationalists. It labels the Union
General de Trabajadores [UGT],
a Socialist trade organization,
as assassins.
CREATOR L. Leo
SOURCE Plakatsammlung Museum
für Gestaltung Zürich

005 SAVE WASTE FATS FOR
EXPLOSIVES
CREATOR Henry Koerner
SOURCE Plakatsammlung Museum
für Gestaltung Zürich

006 SIN OF GROWN-UP
CREATOR Hiroshi Sato
SOURCE Plakatsammlung Museum
für Gestaltung Zürich

007 FRIEDE FÜR ZENTRALAMERIKA UND DIE
KARIBIK — STOP DER US-INTERVENTION
[PEACE TO CENTRAL AMERICA AND THE
CARIBBEAN - STOP US INTERVENTION]
CREATOR Edith Spettig
SOURCE Plakatsammlung Museum
für Gestaltung Zürich

008 NEIN! NO! iNO! HET! NON!
SOURCE Plakatsammlung Museum
für Gestaltung Zürich

009 PEACE IS IN OUR HANDS
CREATOR David Gillhespy
SOURCE www.davidgillhespy.com

010 POWER TO THE PEACEFUL
CREATOR Christopher Ryan
SOURCE Change to: John Carr, ed.,
Yo! What Happened to Peace?
[Rome: Federico Zesi, 2007], p. 46.

011 WHICH DO YOU SELECT?
CREATOR Yuji Baba
SOURCE Poster from JAGDA Peace
Posters International Exhibition

012 TIL DEATH BROKE HER HEART
CREATOR John Pundt
SOURCE John Carr, ed., Yo! What
Happened to Peace? [Rome: Federico
Zesi, 2007], p. 46.

013 ANNAHME VERWEIGERT — ZURÜCK
AN ABSENDER
[DELIVERY REFUSED — RETURN
TO SENDER]
SOURCE Plakatsammlung Museum
für Gestaltung Zürich

014 NOT ATOMIC BOMB
CREATOR Stanislaw Wieczorek
SOURCE Poster from JAGDA Peace
Posters International Exhibition

015 COLOR GRAPHICS IN THE GERMAN
DEMOCRATIC REPUBLIC ON THE THEME
OF PEACE
CREATOR Rolf Felix Müller
SOURCE Poster from JAGDA Peace
Posters International Exhibition
DATE 1984

016 JOURNEÉ MONDIALE POUR LA PAIX
[WORLD PEACE DAY 2005]
CREATOR Courot
SOURCE www.mairie-vitry94.fr

017 ATOMKRIEG NEIN [ATOMIC WAR - NO]
CREATOR Hans Erni
SOURCE Poster from JAGDA Peace
Posters International Exhibition

018 WE HAVE NOTHING TO FEAR, BUT
FEAR ITSELF!
CREATOR Glenn Brooks
SOURCE Change to: John Carr, ed.,
Yo! What Happened to Peace?
[Rome: Federico Zesi, 2007], p. 19.

019 AT PEACE
CREATOR Noboru Matsuura
SOURCE Poster from JAGDA Peace
Posters International Exhibition

020 NIE! [NEVER!]
CREATOR Tadeusz Trepkowski
SOURCE Plakatsammlung Museum
für Gestaltung Zürich

021 GOD IS ON OUR SIDE!
CREATOR David Lancashire
SOURCE Beiträge macht Bilder

022 RETURN TO SENDER
CREATOR Masahide Abe
SOURCE Poster from JAGDA Peace
Posters International Exhibition

023 NON-SUICIDE BOMBERS
SOURCE Poster from JAGDA Peace
Posters International Exhibition

024 PAY YOUR TAXES
CREATOR Quinn Mahoney
SOURCE acg.media.mit.edu

025 PEACE + WAR = ?
CREATOR Takashi Sekiguchi
SOURCE "L'engagement politique et
social," Le festival d'affiches,
Chaumont, 19 May - 16 July 2000

026 UNTITLED
SOURCE John Carr, ed., Yo!
What Happened to Peace?
[Rome: Federico Zesi, 2007].

027 JOURNEE MONDIALE POUR LA PAIX
2005, 21 SEPTEMBRE
CREATOR Desfonaine
SOURCE www.mairie-vitry94.fr

028 VICTORY
CREATOR Shigeo Fukuda
SOURCE img.listen.no
DATE 1975

029 NO MORE
CREATOR Shigeo Fukuda
SOURCE www.moma.org
DATE 1968

030 NOT WHAT I HAD IN MIND
CREATOR Tsunehisa Kimura
SOURCE pichaus.com
DATE 1968

001
002

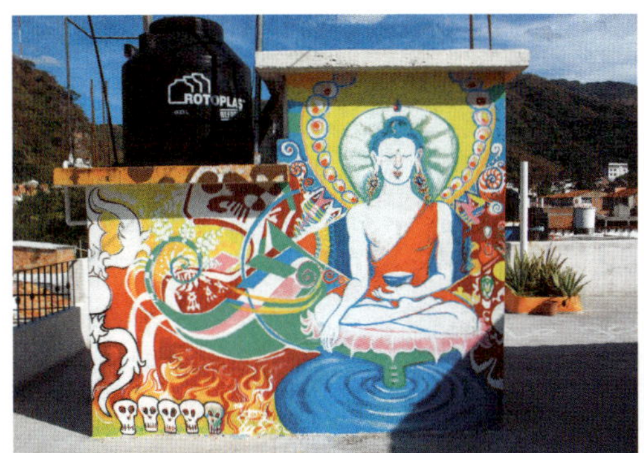
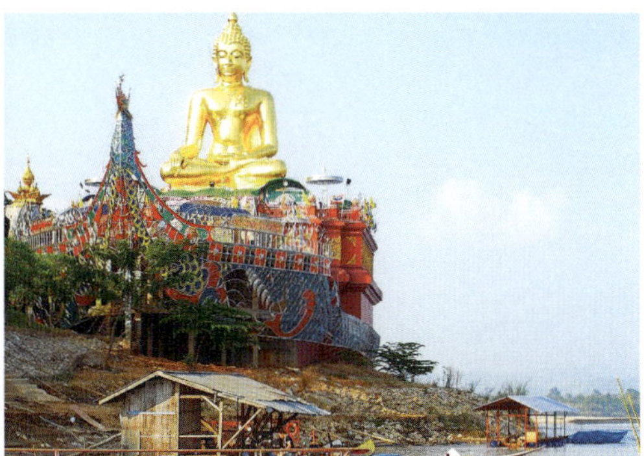

003
004

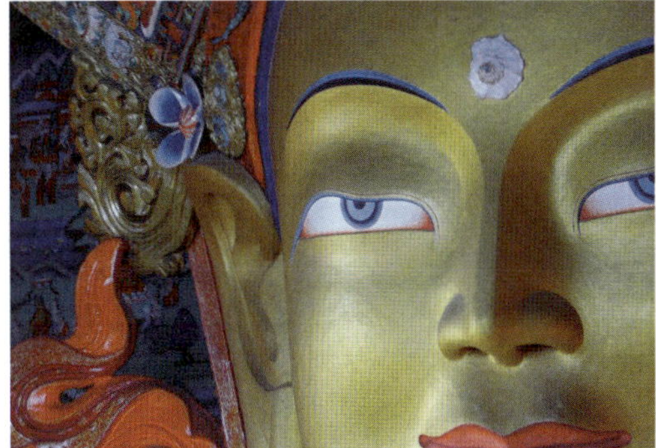
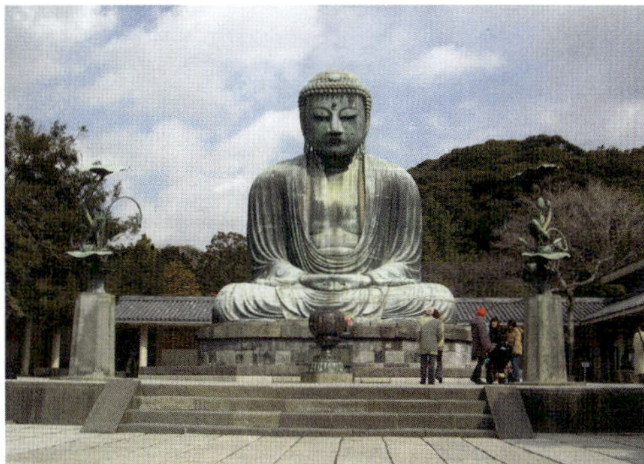

005
006

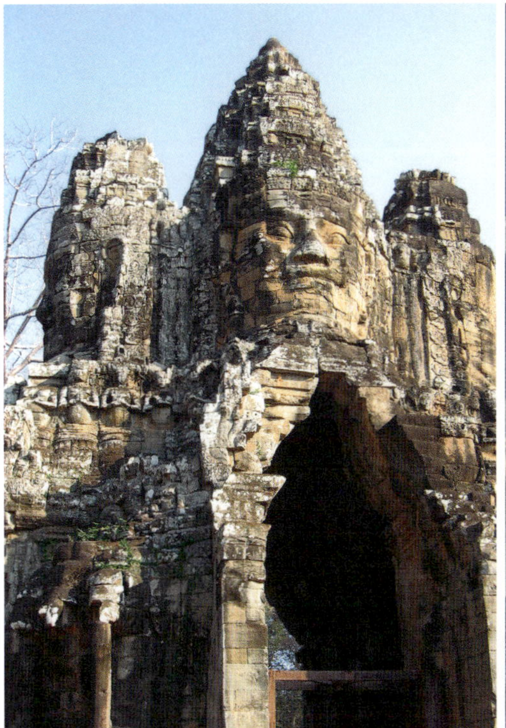
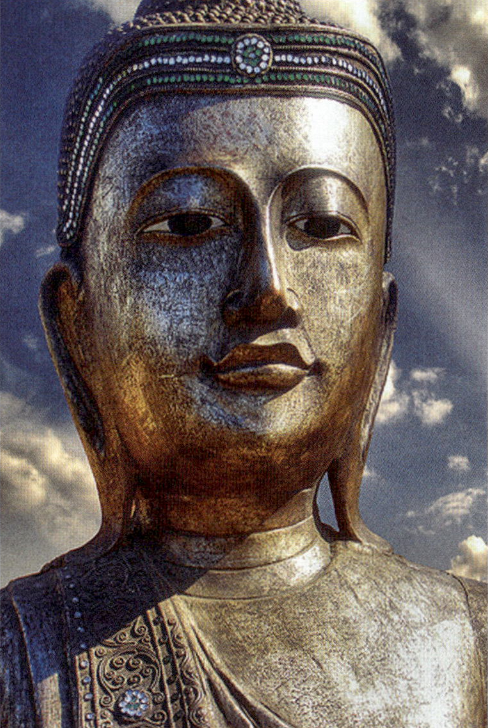

007
008

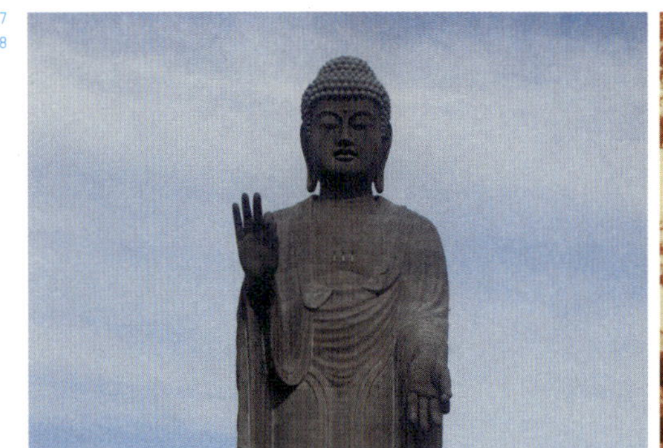
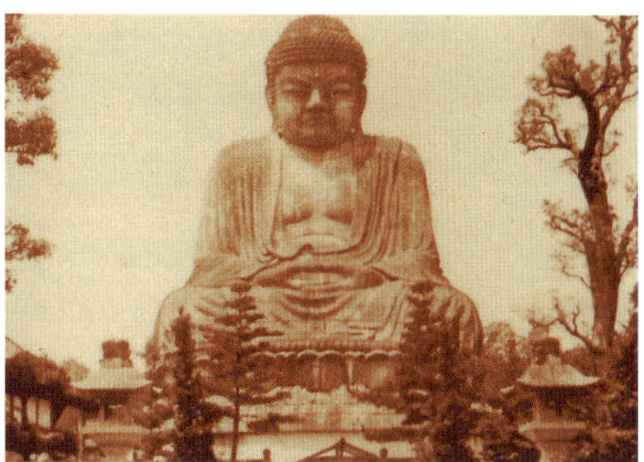

009
010

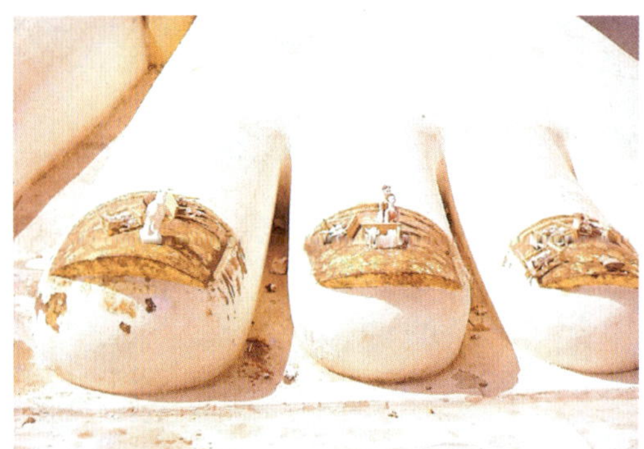
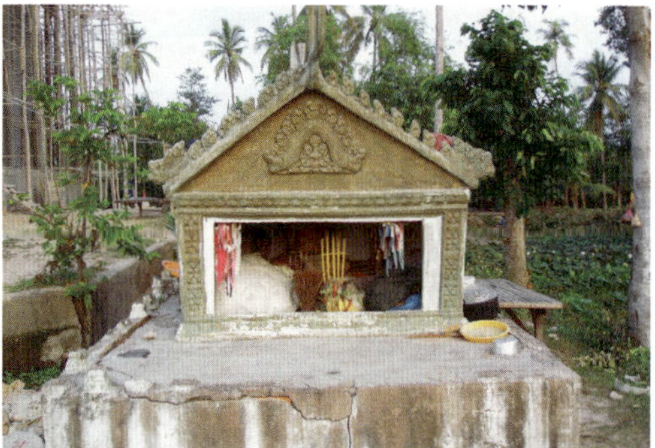

011
012

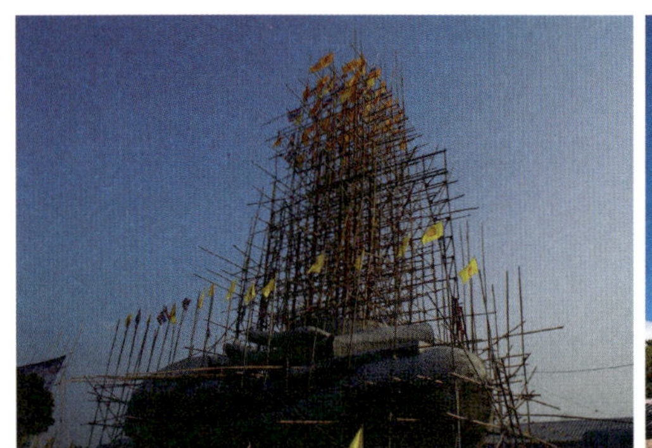
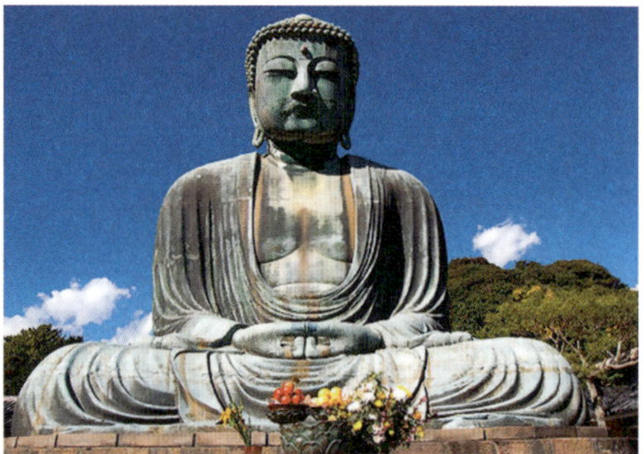

013
014

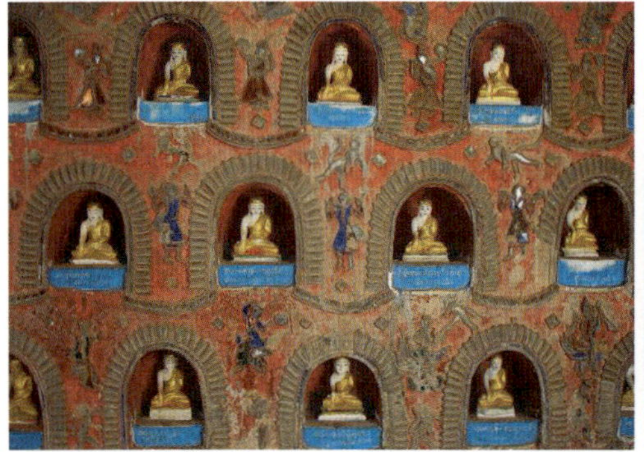
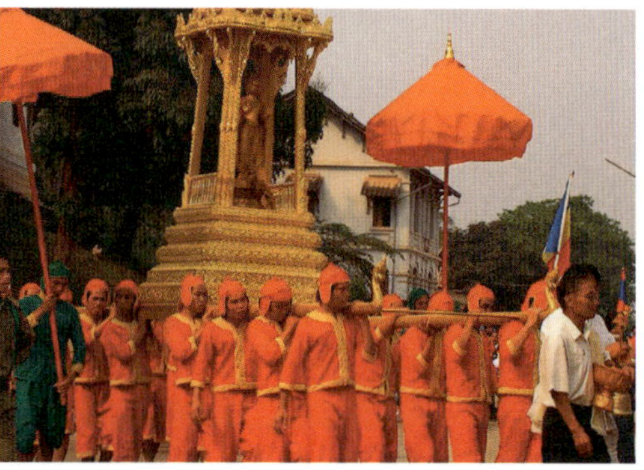

015
016

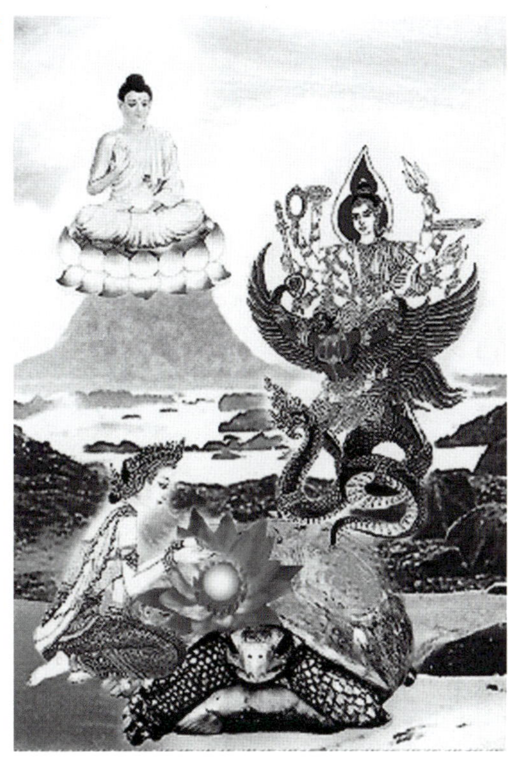

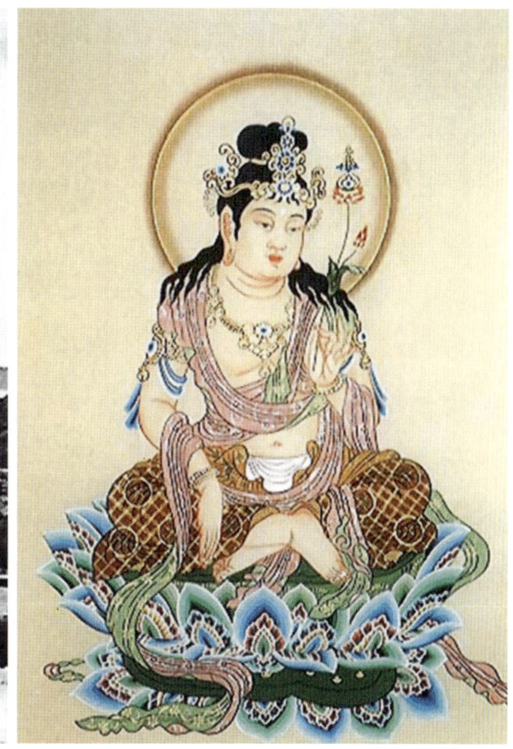

017
018

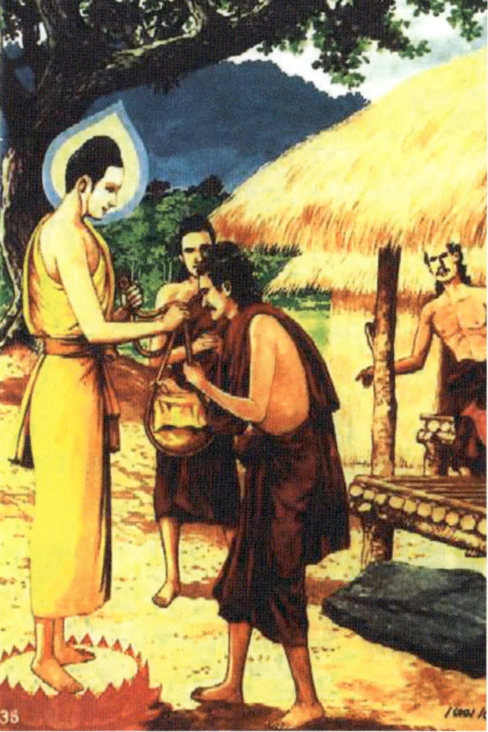

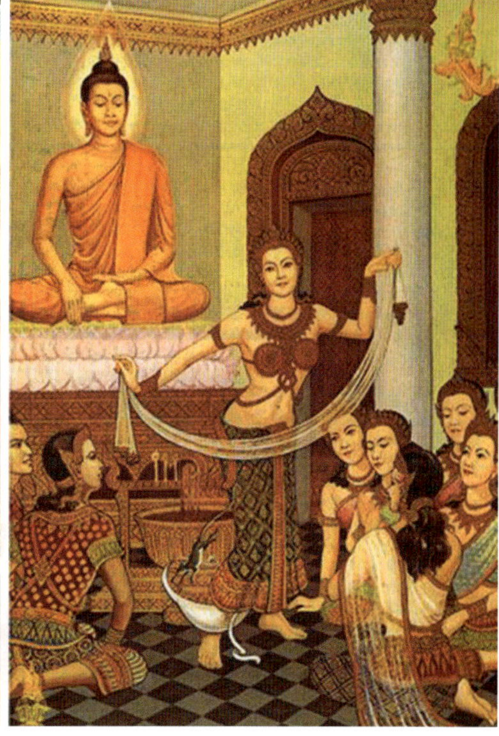

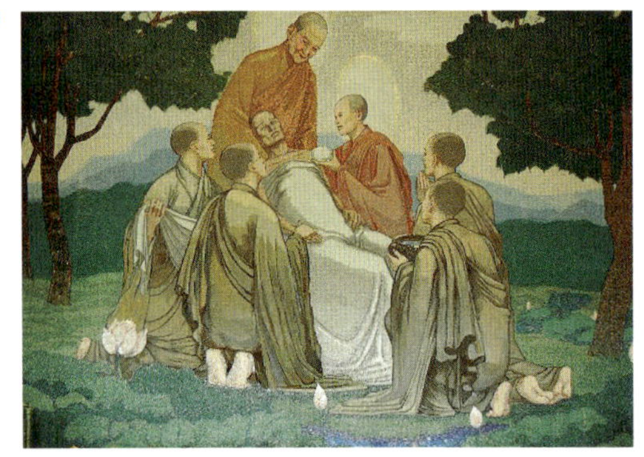

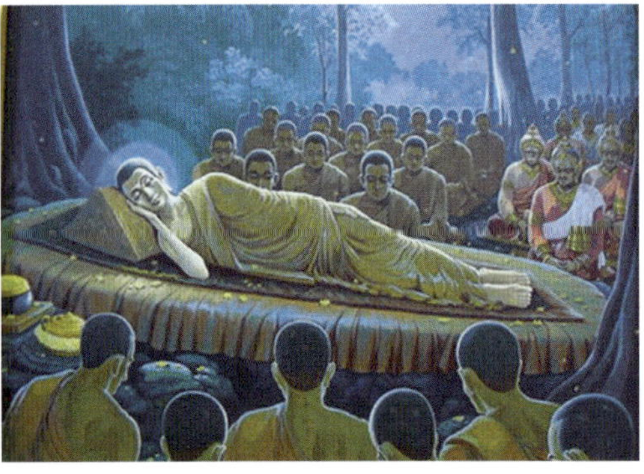

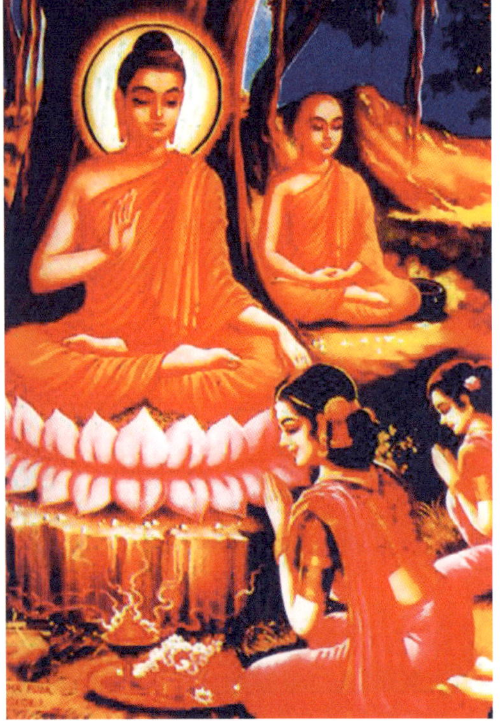

001 VAJRASATTVA, A MEXICAN TIBETAN
BUDDHA
CREATOR Provided by Wonderlane
SOURCE www.flickr.com/photos/
wonderlane/351494912/

002 BUDDHA ON THE MEKONG
CREATOR Provided by pninaN
SOURCE www.flickr.com/photos/
49206401@N00/2162458670/

003 BUDDHA IN LADAKH
CREATOR Provided by crazyegg95
SOURCE www.flickr.com/photos/
crazyegg95/97122091/

004 KAMAKURA'S GREAT BUDDHA
Located in Kamakura near Tokyo.
[Kamakura, Central Honshu, Japan].
CREATOR Provided by freakland
SOURCE www.flickr.com/photos/
freakland/117177628/

005 BUDDHA
Buddha heads at the southern gate,
Siem Reap, Siem Reap Province, KH.
CREATOR Provided by Grandmaster
Chang
SOURCE www.flickr.com/photos/
grandmasterchang/707867200

006 BUDDHA
CREATOR Provided by Kris Kros
SOURCE www.flickr.com/photos/
kros/103378534/

007 THE LARGEST BUDDHA STATUE IN
THE WORLD
The Ushiku Amida Buddha is
located in Ibaraki Prefecture,
east of Tokyo. It is 120m in
height and is found in the
Guinness Book of World Records
as the tallest Buddha statue in
the world. By comparison, it is
three times taller than the
Statue of Liberty.
CREATOR Provided by Nicolas
Welzel
SOURCE www.flickr.com/photos/
welzlnxq/2230255419/

008 JAPAN — BUDDHA AT BEPPU
Second-largest Buddha statue
in Japan.
CREATOR Provided by Rebecca
Ocarina
SOURCE www.flickr.com/photos/
rebeccaholder/161965312/

009 OFFERINGS ON BUDDHA'S TOES
People placed small statues
and other offerings on the
toes of the standing Buddha
statue. The toenails were
covered in gold leaf. This
photo was taken in Siam [now
Thailand] in 1956.
CREATOR Provided by Terry McTigue

SOURCE www.flickr.com/photos/
terrymct/153938063/

010 CEREMONY IN KOMPONG SPEU
On March 31, 2006, This temple
held a ceremony called "Bun Bark
Netr Preah Puttharup" — the
ceremony of opening the eye of
the Buddha image. During the
central moment of the ceremony,
the pupils of the Buddha are
painted into the central Buddha
image, thereby completing and
"enlivening" it.
CREATOR Provided by Erik Davis
SOURCE www.flickr.com/photos/
erikwdavis/2446288217/

011 BEGINNINGS OF A GIANT BUDDHA
CREATOR Provided by Adam Howarth
SOURCE www.flickr.com/photos/
puppydogbites/2161251976/

012 BUDDHA
CREATOR Provided by dpalac
SOURCE www.flickr.com/pho-
tos/9795581@N03/791020738/

013 BUDDHA WALL STATUE
CREATOR R. Lichius / Chromorange
SOURCE picture-alliance/
chromorange

014 GOLDEN BUDDHA PROCESSION
CREATOR Provided by Tony Yang
SOURCE www.flickr.com/photos/
iamtonyang/22375081/

015 BUDDHA
SOURCE www.cungduongphap.com

016 BUDDHA
SOURCE www.cungduongphap.com

017 BUDDHA
SOURCE ecurriculum.mv.ac.th

018 BUDDHA
SOURCE www.banphra.com

019 BUDDHA
SOURCE photo.tokyo.idv.tw

020 BUDDHA
SOURCE www.agalico.com

021 BUDDHA
SOURCE www.chinawts.com

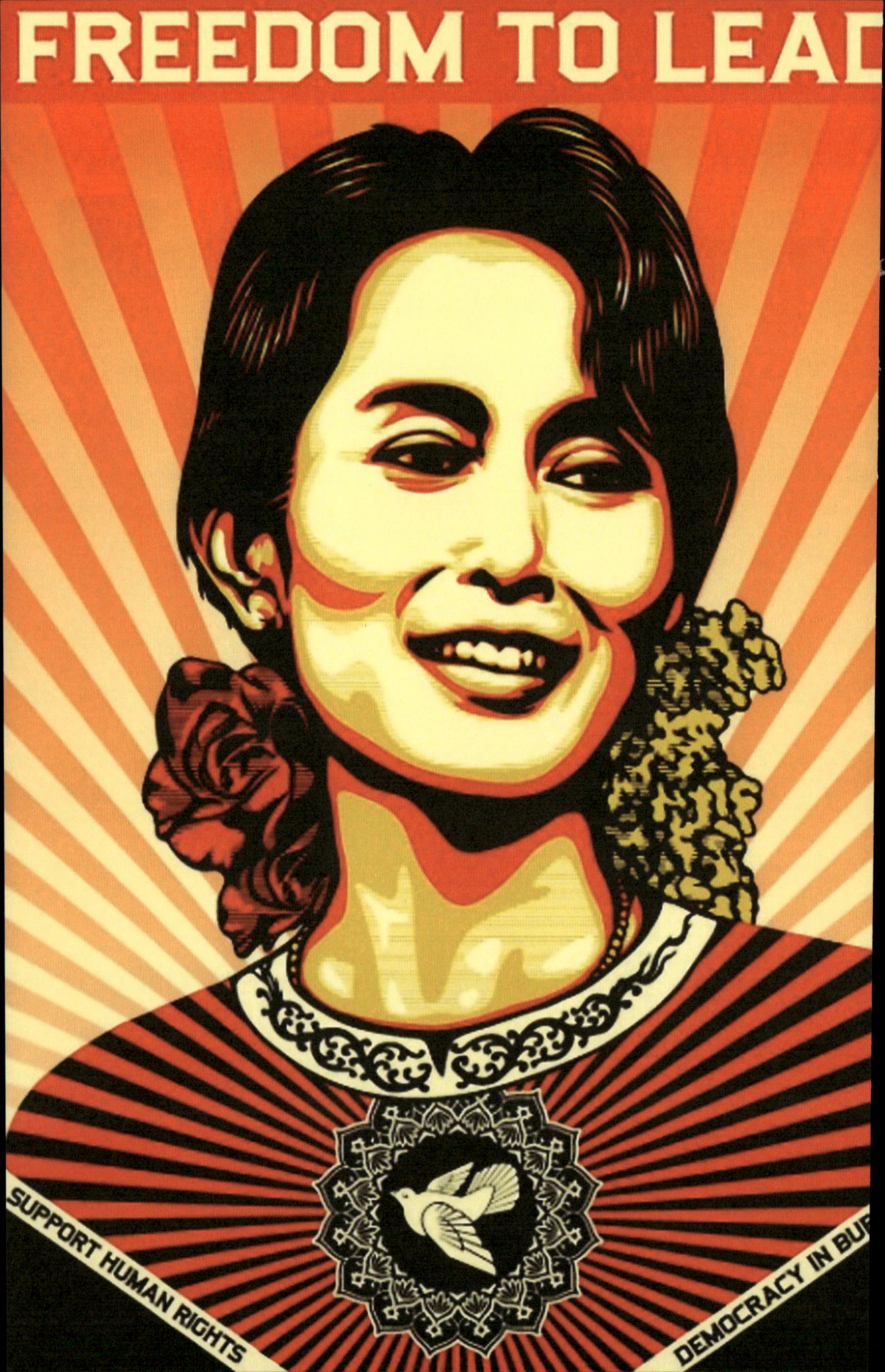

FREEDOM TO LEAD
SUPPORT HUMAN RIGHTS
DEMOCRACY IN BUR

LEFT
001
002
003

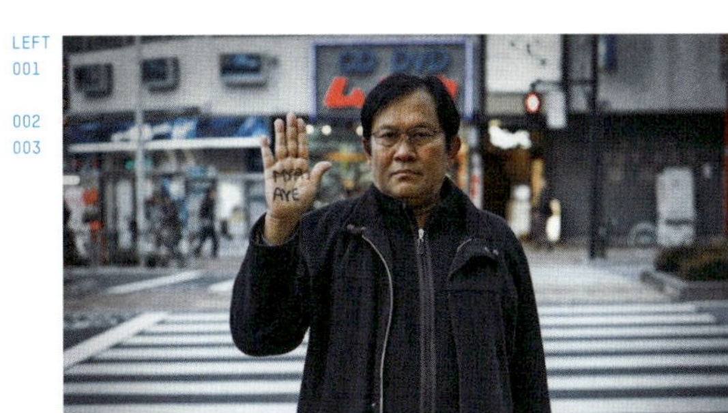

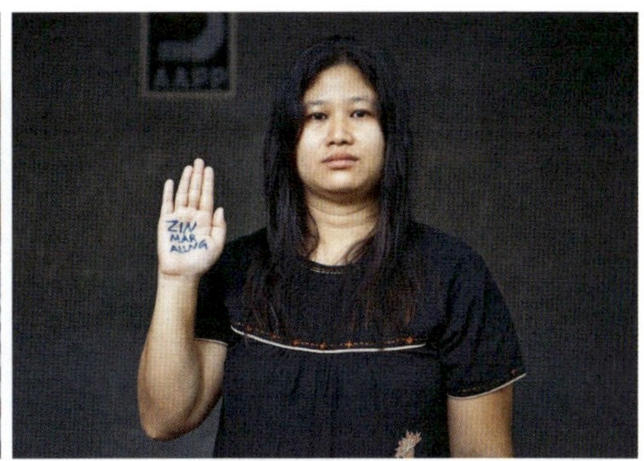

004
005

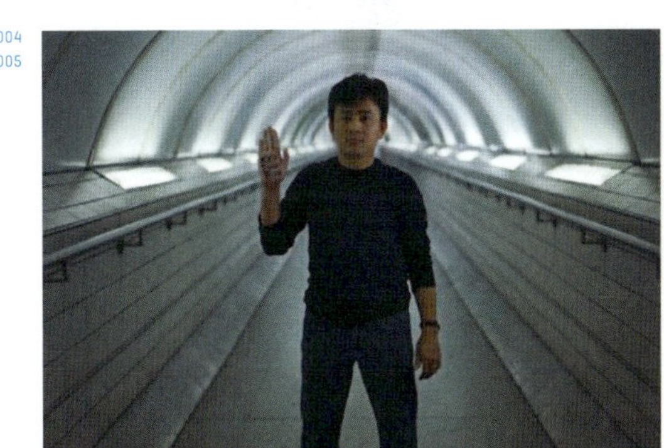

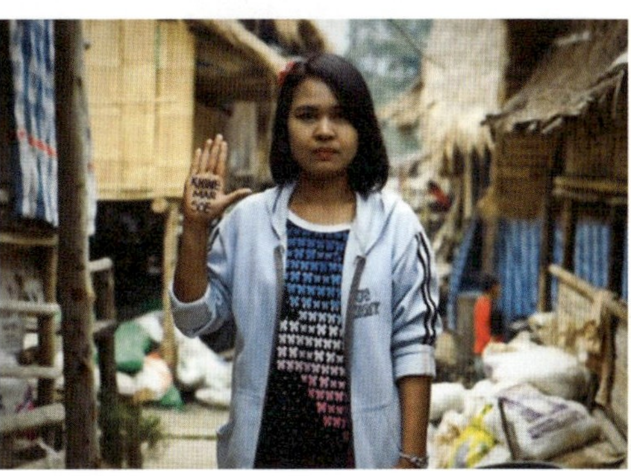

006

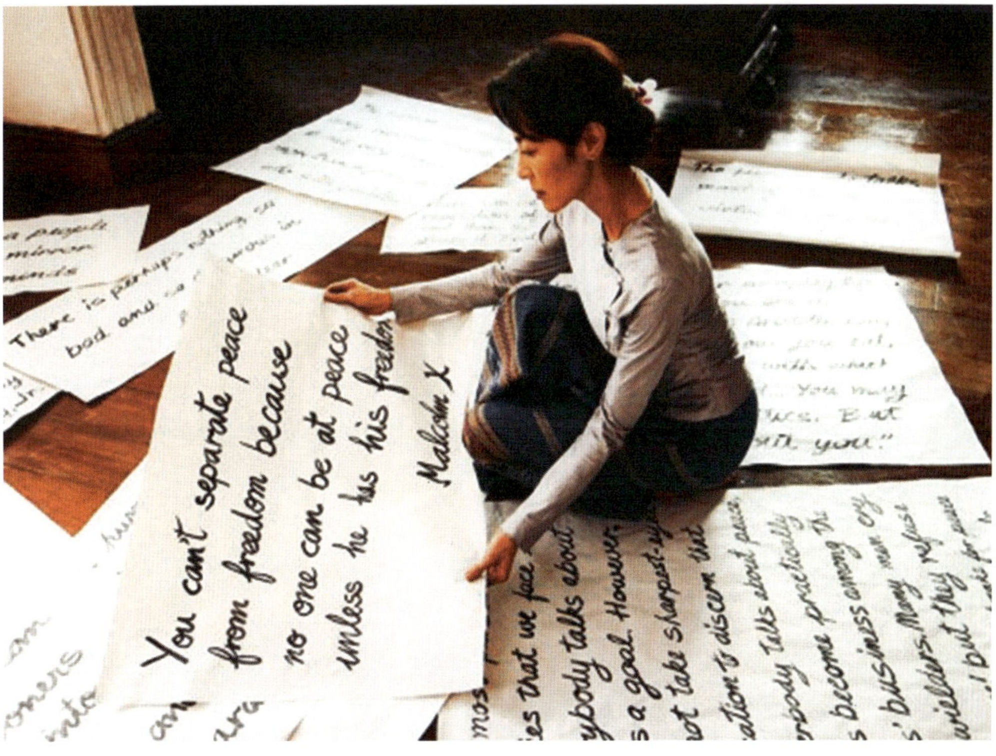

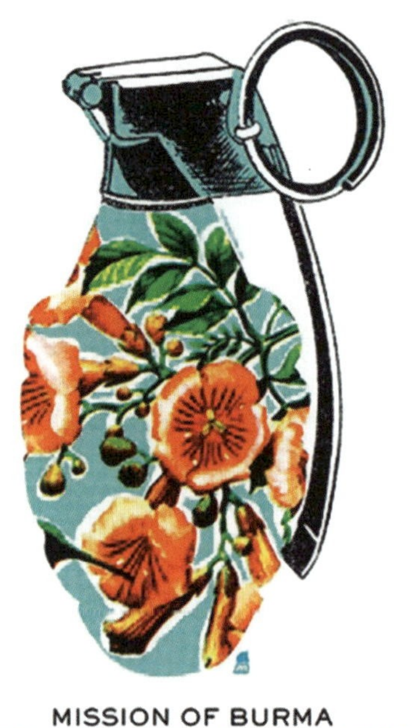
MISSION OF BURMA
SOME SOVIET STATION · REUNION SHOW! JAN. 13, 2007 THE EARL

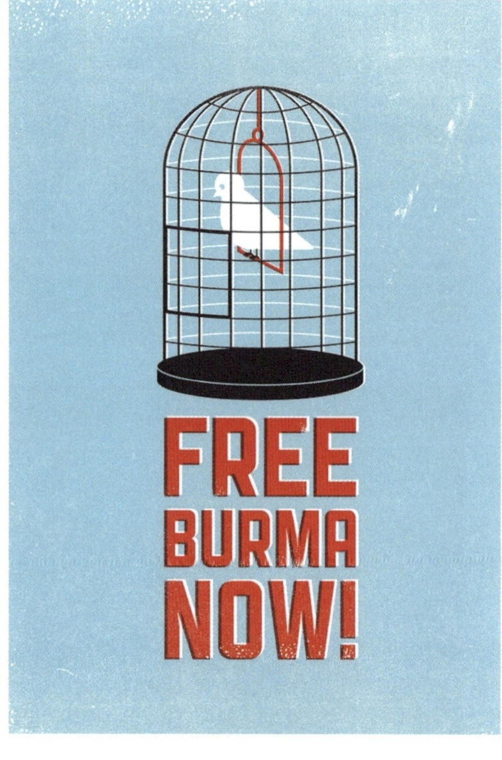
FREE
BURMA
NOW!

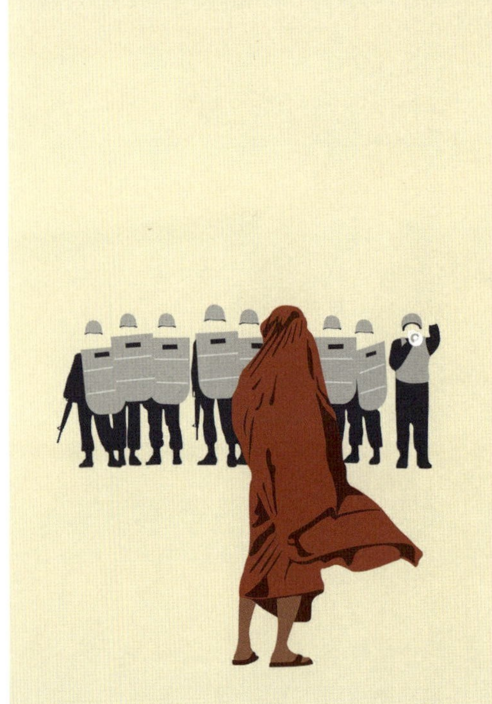

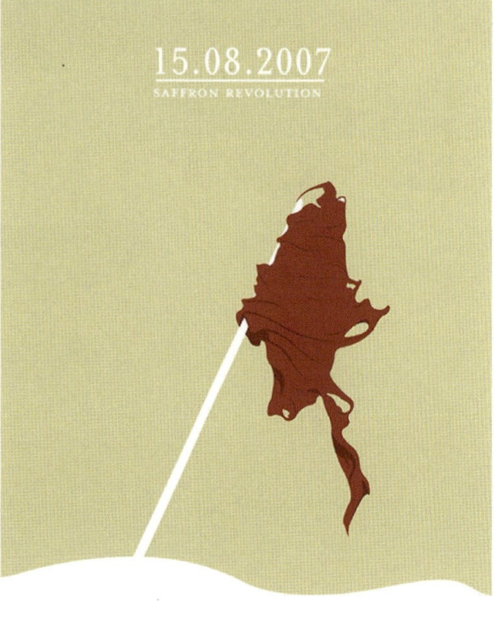
15.08.2007
SAFFRON REVOLUTION

011

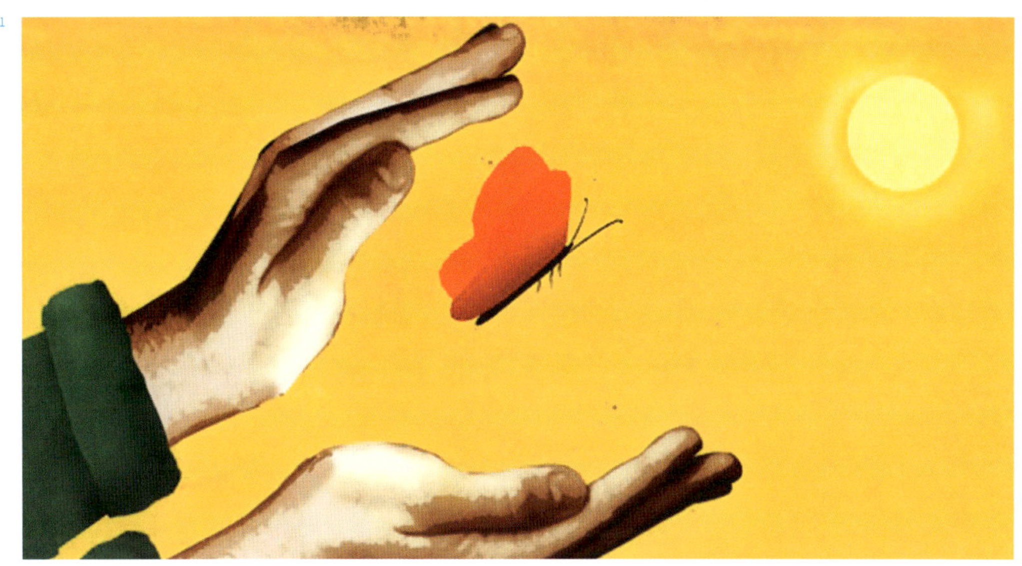

012

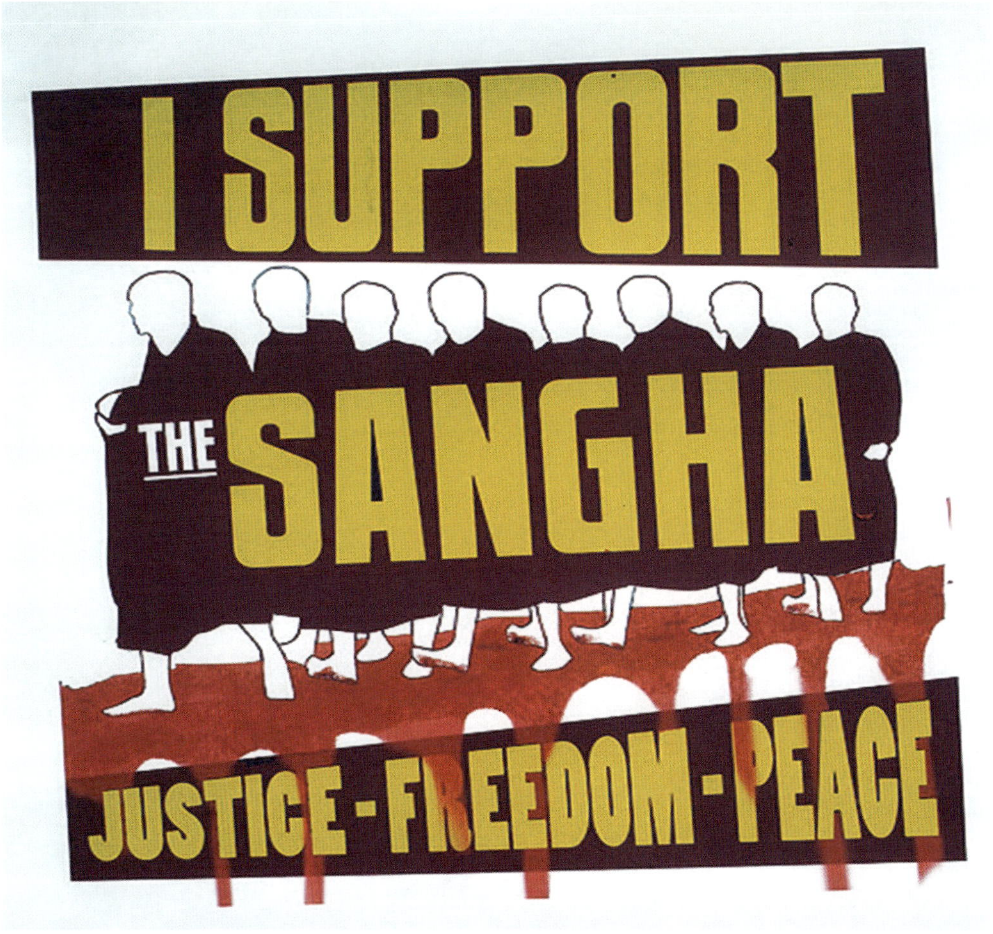

001 AUNG SAN SUU KYI
     Shepard Fairey created this
     portrait of Aung San Suu Kyi to
     raise awareness of her ongoing
     house arrest and the oppressive
     nature of the military regime
     ruling Burma.
     CREATOR Shepard Fairey
     SOURCE osocio.org.

002 EVEN THOUGH I'M FREE I AM NOT
     A global documentary photography
     project about Burma's political
     prisoners. Traveling across the
     world to Southeast Asia, Australia,
     Japan, Europe, USA, and Canada as
     well as into Burma itself, hun-
     dreds of Burma's former political
     prisoners who have fled the
     country and are now forced to
     live in exile often as stateless
     people, have been photographed,
     coming together to raise awareness
     of the tragic plight of their
     colleagues still detained in jail.
     SOURCE osocio.org

003 EVEN THOUGH I'M FREE I AM NOT
     SOURCE osocio.org

004 EVEN THOUGH I'M FREE I AM NOT
     SOURCE osocio.org

005 EVEN THOUGH I'M FREE I AM NOT
     SOURCE osocio.org

006 MISSION OF BURMA: THE LADY
     CREATOR EuropaCorp
     SOURCE www.vogue.com

007 MISSION OF BURMA
     SOURCE postercabaret.com/

008 FREE BURMA NOW
     CREATOR Brian Hurst
     SOURCE www.flickr.com/photos/
     51073266@N08/5172823849
     DATE 2010

009 SAFFRON REVOLUTION
     CREATOR Scott Broadley
     SOURCE www.flickr.com/photos/
     40280667@N08/5080025604
     DATE 2010

010 SAFFRON REVOLUTION
     CREATOR Scott Broadley
     SOURCE www.flickr.com/photos/
     40280667@N08/5079641593
     DATE 2010

011 CREATOR Michael Morganstern
     SOURCE postonpolitics.blogspot.ch

012 I SUPPORT THE SANGHA [MONKS]
     POSTER: JUSTICE, FREEDOM, PEACE
     CREATOR Provided by Alan Chan
     SOURCE www.flickr.com/photos/
     alanchan/1456875842

001

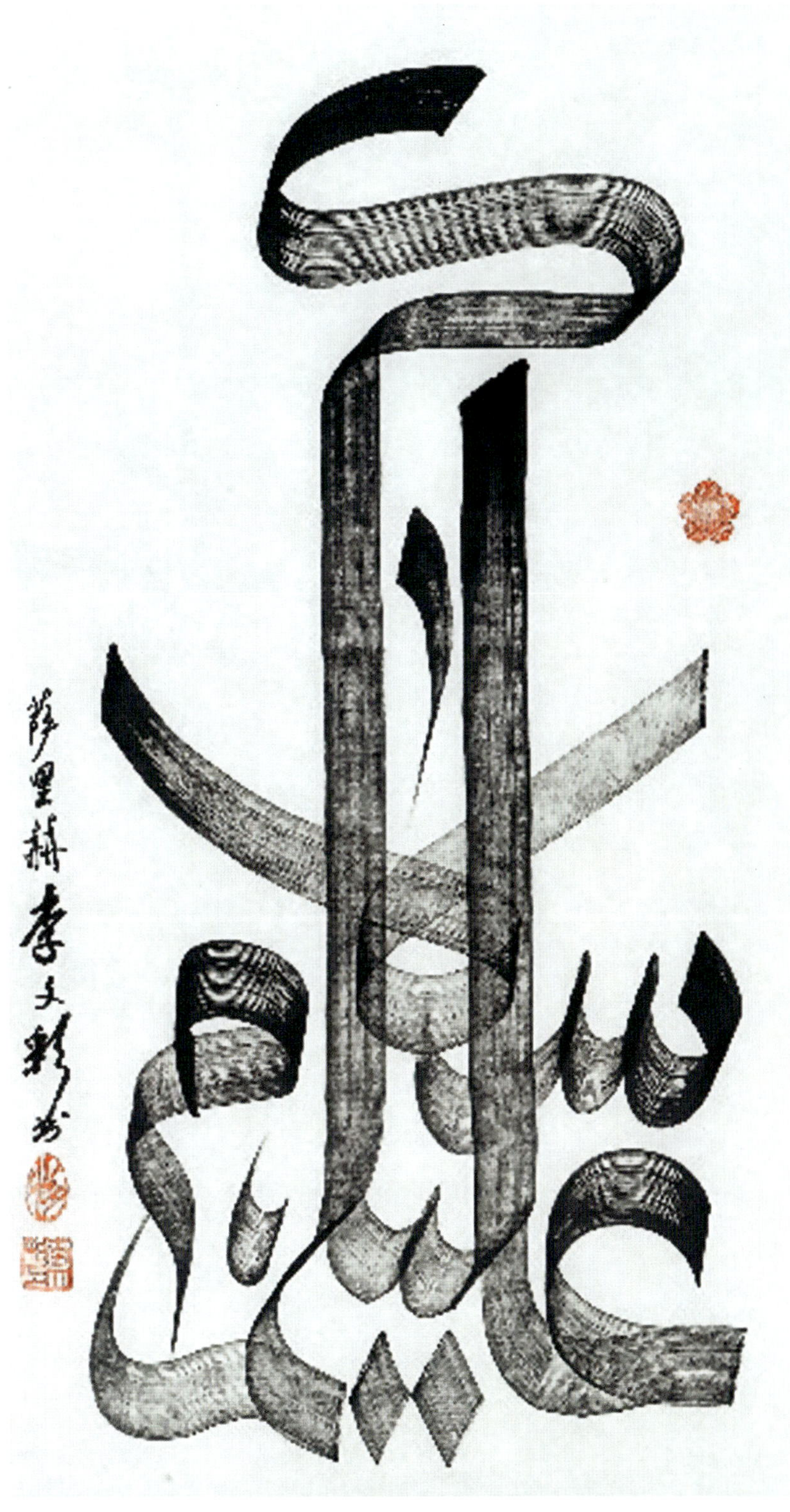

002

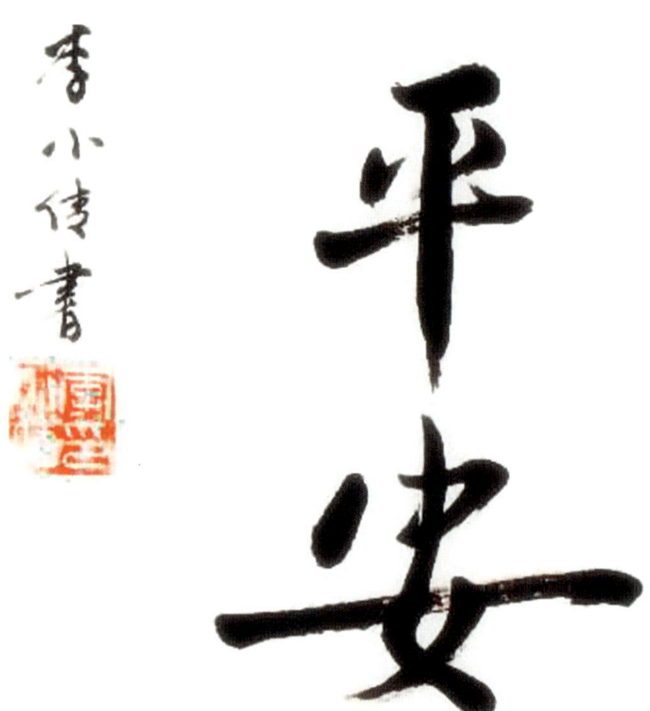

003
004

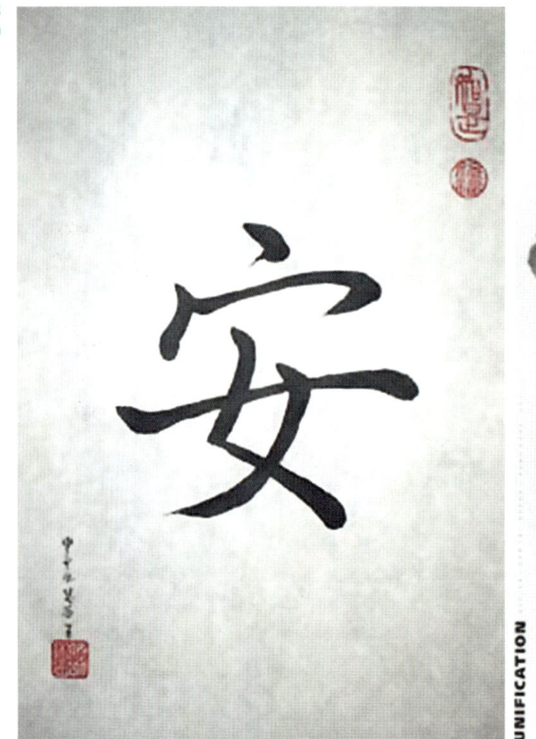

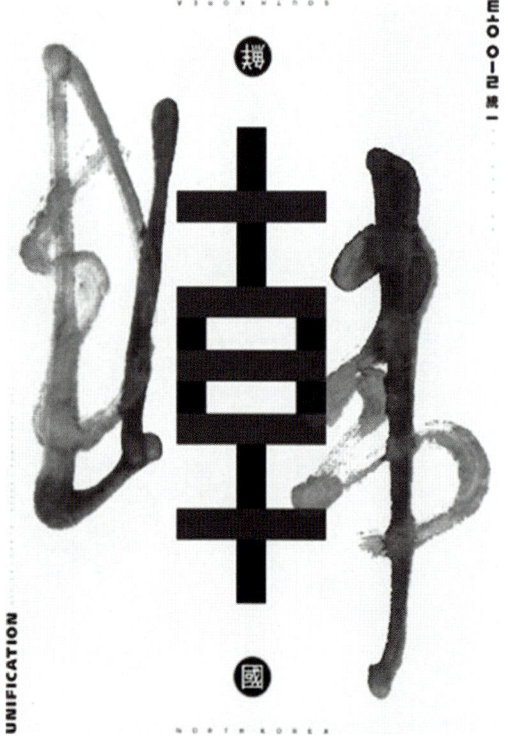

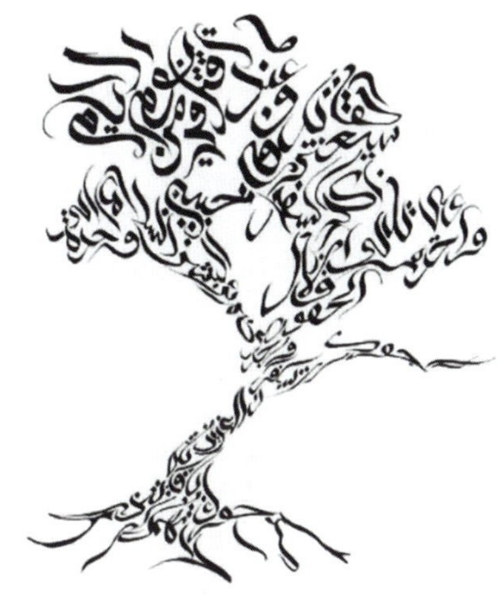

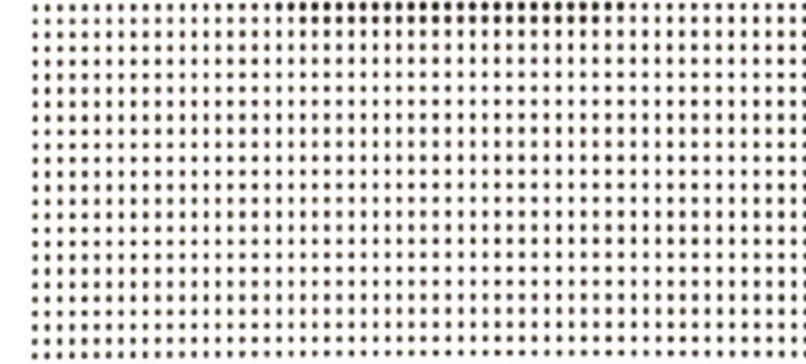

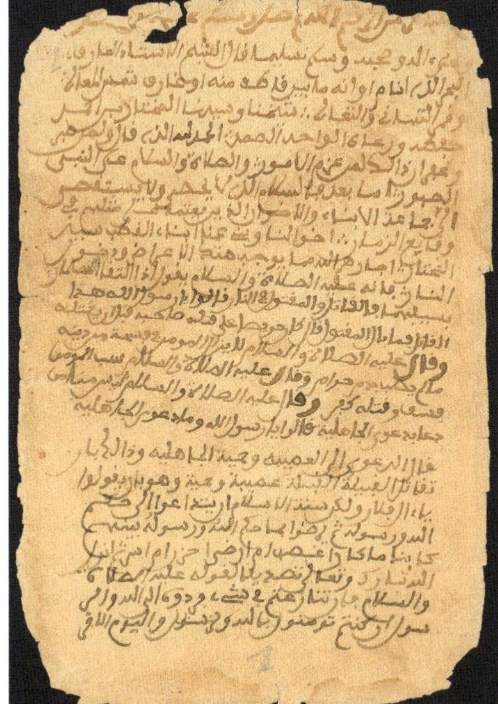

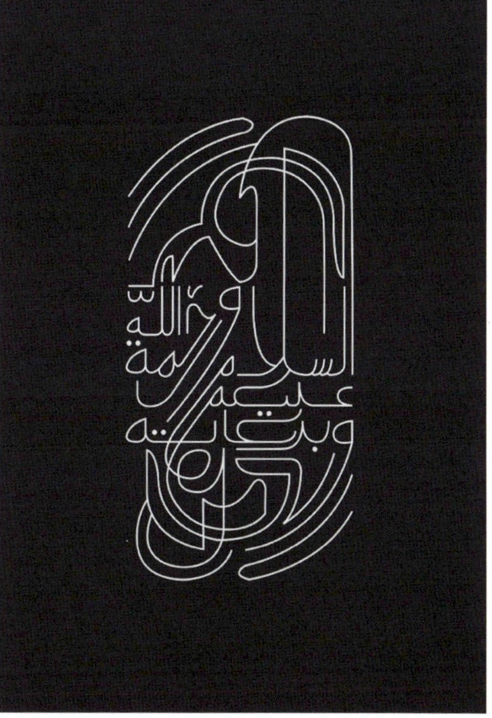

009

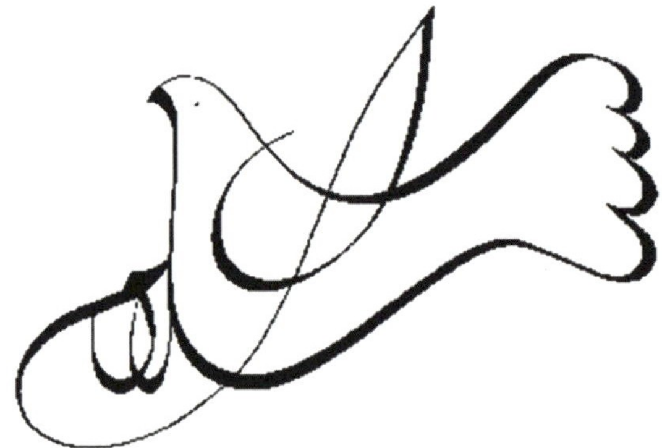

010

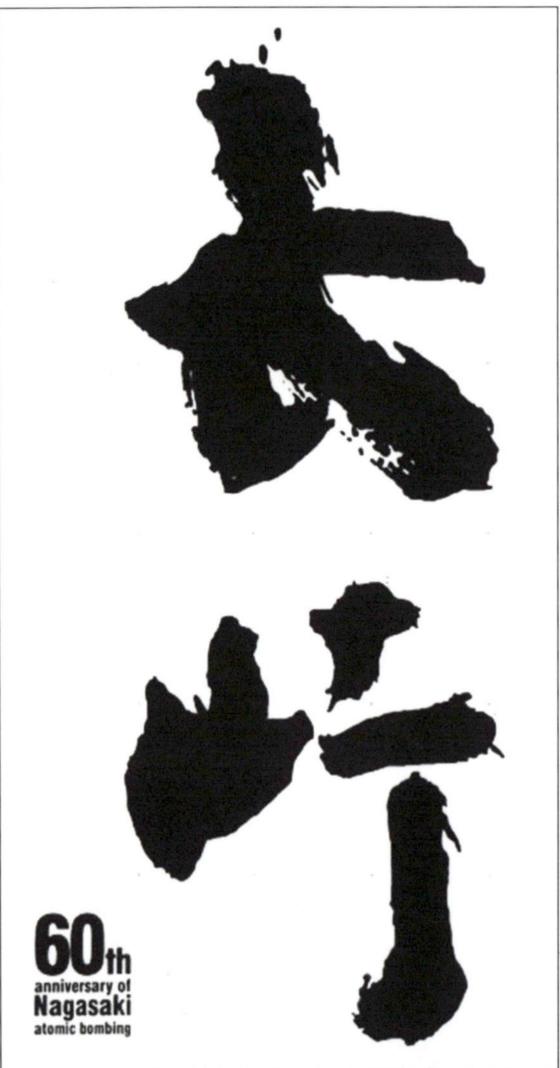

001 A SINO-ARABIC CALLIGRAPHY
Alaykum Salam [May Peace be
upon you]
CREATOR Salihe Li Wencai
SOURCE Koller Auktionen Zurich

002 PEACE IN CHINESE CALLIGRAPHY
CREATOR Xiaoqian Li-Columeau
SOURCE peinturechinoisexiaoqian.
wifeo.com

003 PEACEFUL
SOURCE massarts.stumbleupon.com

004 UNIFICATION — NORTH KOREA AND
SOUTH KOREA
CREATOR Tai-Keung Kan
SOURCE Plakatsammlung Museum
für Gestaltung Zürich

005 PEACE OF MIND
CREATOR Hung Lam
SOURCE Plakatsammlung Museum
für Gestaltung Zürich

006 TRAVEL TICKETS
The day I'm killed, my killer,
rifling through my pockets, will
find travel tickets: One to peace,
one to the fields and the rain,
and one to the conscience of
humankind. Dear killer of mine,
I beg you: Do not stay and waste
them. Take them, use them. I beg
you to travel. [Samih al-Qasim,
Palestinian poet]
CREATOR Josh Berer
SOURCE joshberer.wordpress.com/
page/4/

007 LETTER TO THE WARRING TRIBES
In this work, the author, a
scholar and religious leader,
urges warring factions to make
peace and live in peace. He
supports his argument with
quotations from the Koran and
allusions to the practice of
Muhammad and his companions,
which require the faithful to
avoid discord, to reconcile, and
to live in peace and tolerance.
CREATOR al-Mukhtar ibn Ahmad ibn
Abi Bakr al-Kunti al-Kabir, Sayyid
SOURCE www.wdl.org/en/item/199/
DATE c. 1300–1499

008 SALAAM [PEACE]
Peace be upon you with the mercy
of Allah and his blessings.
CREATOR Provided by Ibraheem
Youssef
SOURCE www.flickr.com/photos/
heemaz/4537314011/

009 SALAAM [PEACE]
CREATOR Hasan Mas'soudy
SOURCE iraqifamilyrelief.
blogspot.com

010 60TH ANNIVERSARY OF NAGASAKI
ATOMIC BOMBING
CREATOR Xu Wang
SOURCE Plakatsammlung Museum
für Gestaltung Zürich

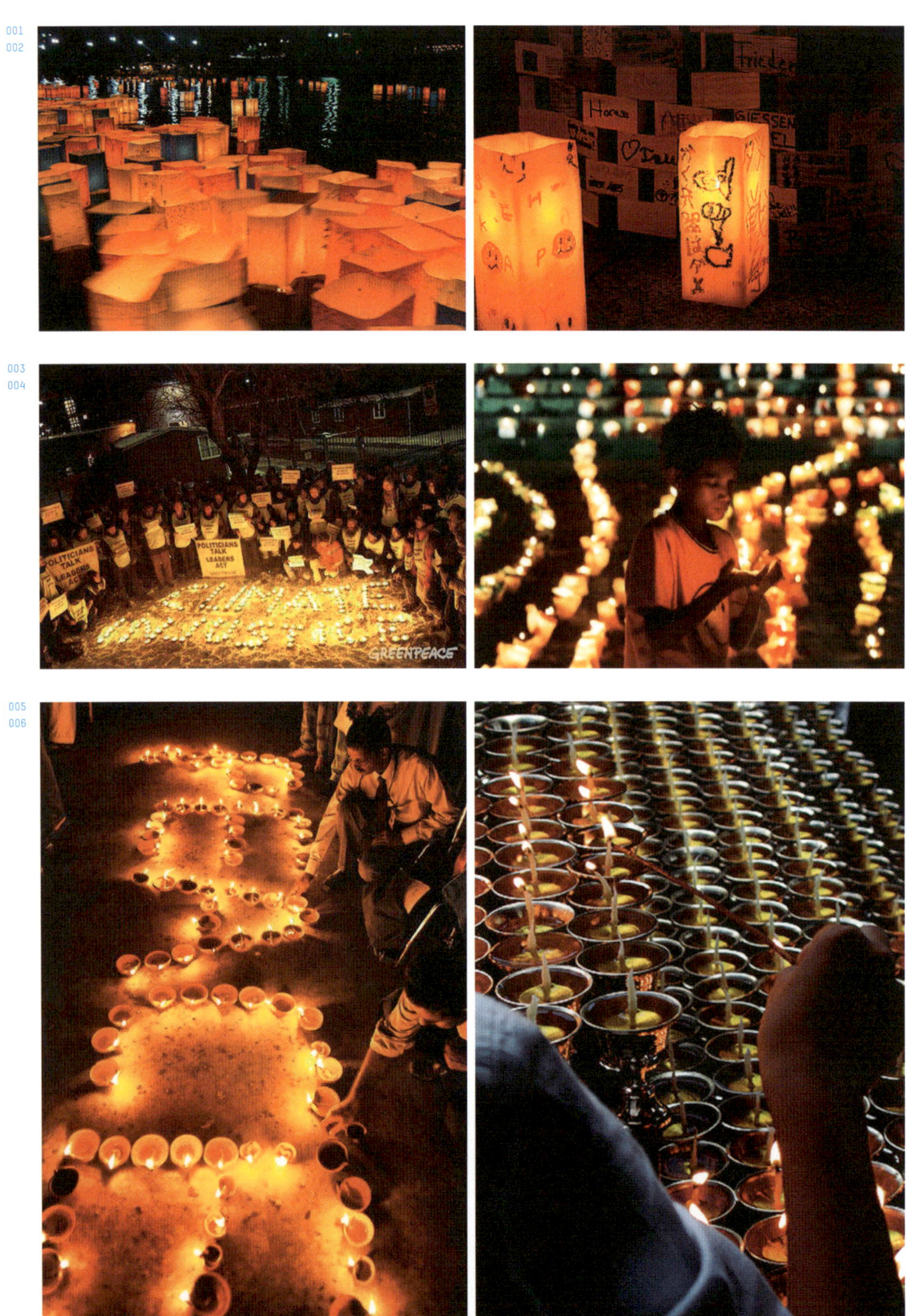
POLITICIANS
TALK
LEADERS
ACT
POLITICIANS
TALK
LEADERS
ACT
GREENPEACE

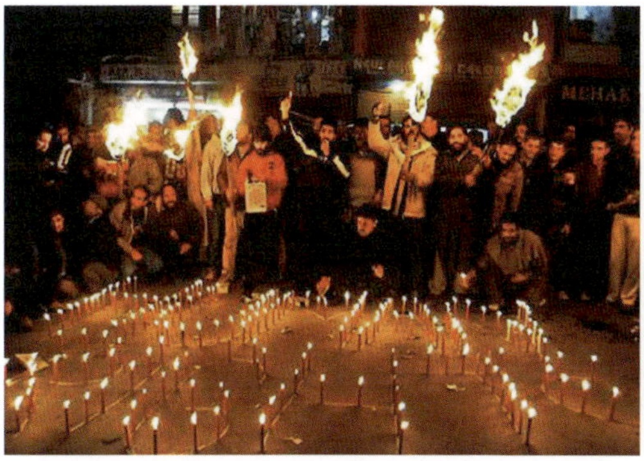

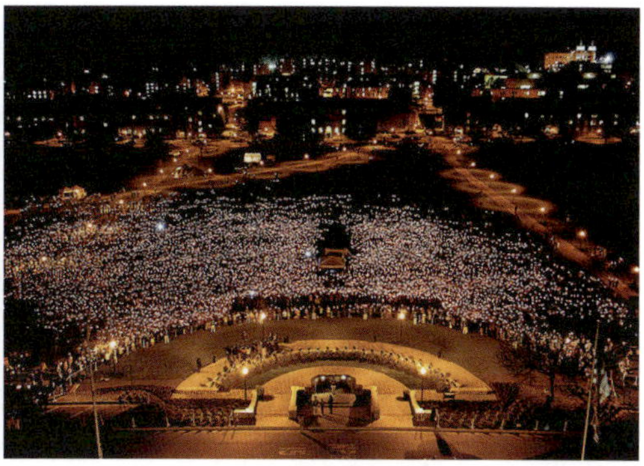

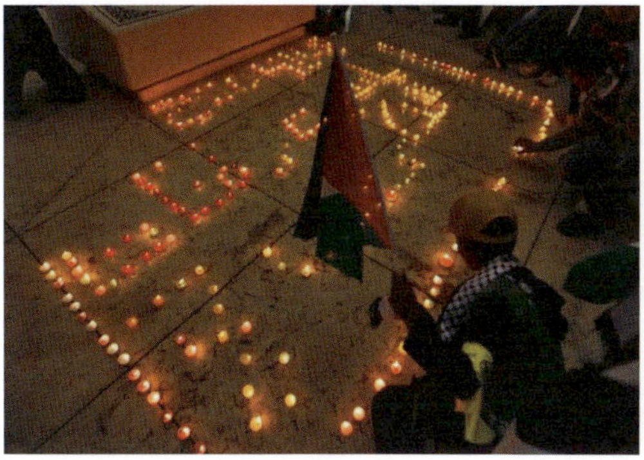

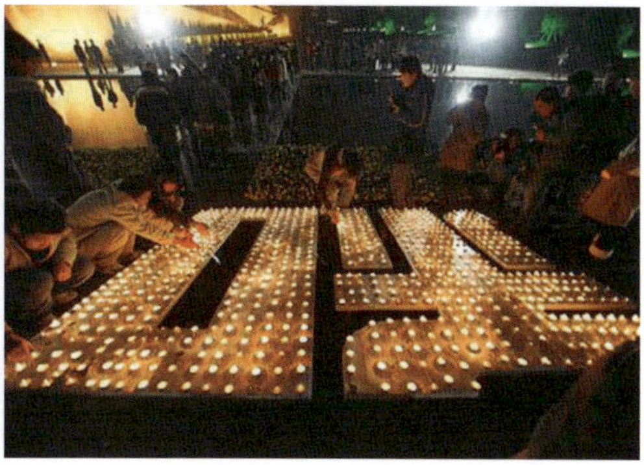

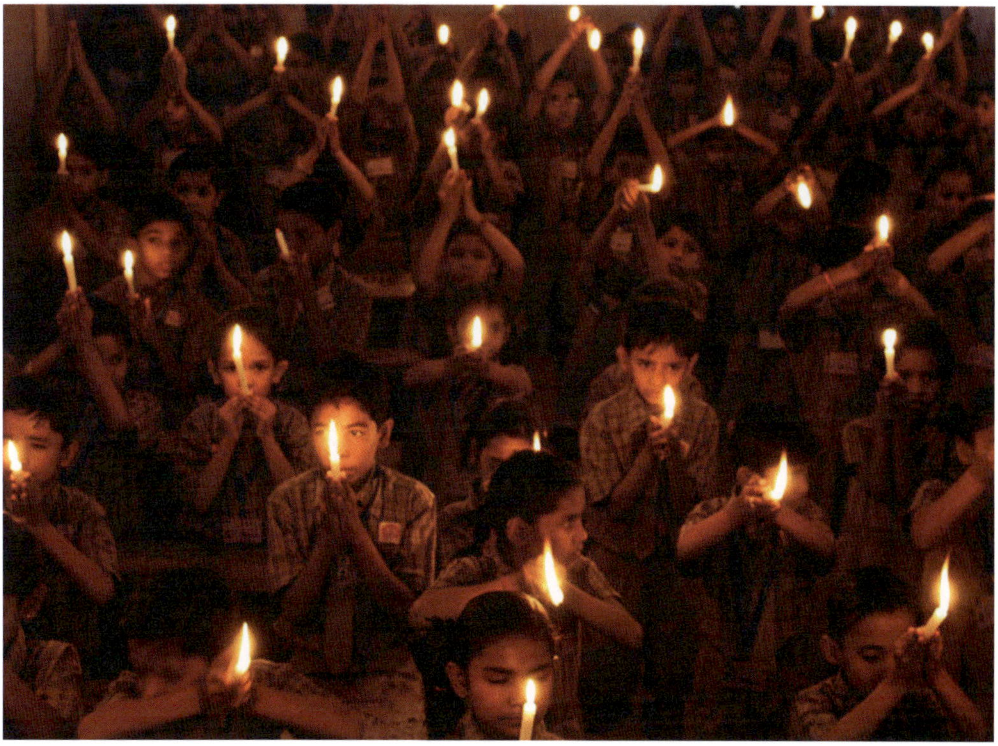

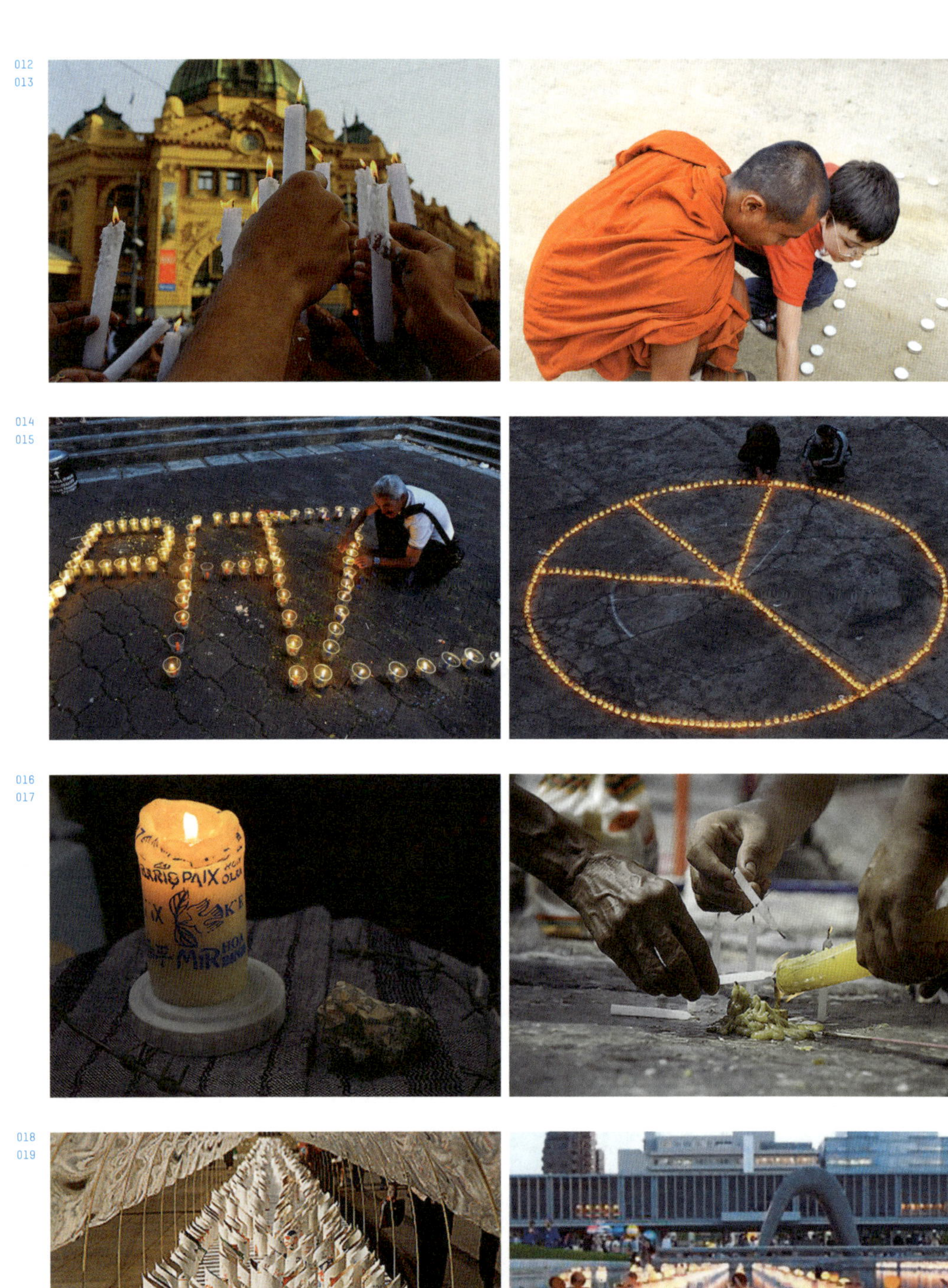

001 PEACE FOR EVERYONE
CREATOR Provided by HAPPYCHAN
SOURCE www.flickr.com/photos/
happygolucky/210613502/

002 WISH FOR THE ABOLITION OF
NUCLEAR WEAPONS
60th memorial service for
Hiroshima. A Buddhist ceremony
in which paper lanterns float
in the water.
CREATOR Provided by Giyu [Velvia]
SOURCE www.flickr.com/photos/
giyu/31871686/

003 CLIMATE INJUSTICE
More than 100 Greenpeace
supporters held a candlelit
vigil outside the Vestre Faengsel
prison, where four Greenpeace
activists were being held. They
spent Christmas in jail.
SOURCE www.greenpeace.org

004 CLIMATE INJUSTICE
CREATOR Provided by Daily Life
SOURCE www.greenpeace.org

005 PAKISTANIS LIGHT CANDLES FOR
PEACE — BUT PEACE WITH OR WITHOUT
ISLAMIC SUPREMACY
Pakistani human rights activists
light earthenware lamps during a
peace rally in Karachi. A massive
car bomb, killing 118 people on
October 28 in Peshawar, oversha-
dowed talks and underscored the
gravity of the Islamist threat,
considered a backlash against the
government's alliance with the US.
SOURCE islamizationwatch.
blogspot.ch
DATE 31 October 2009

006 JOKHANG PALACE, YAK BUTTER
CANDLES, LHASA, TIBET
CREATOR Provided by James Marzano
SOURCE www.flickr.com/photos/jam-
marz/2402747874/

007 CANDLELIGHT PROTESTS
Jammu Kashmir Liberation Front
[JKLF] activists stage a candle-
light protest against alleged
human rights violations in Jammu
and Kashmir.
CREATOR Habib Naqash
SOURCE www.greaterkashmir.com

008 CANDLELIGHT VIGIL FROM THE ROOF
OF BURRUS HALL [VIRGINIA TECH]
CREATOR Provided by Mark [mumansky]
SOURCE www.flickr.com/photos/
7295018@N03/3449572547
DATE 2009

009 CLIMATE INJUSTICE
A Palestinian boy places a candle
near the grave of late Palestinian
leader Yasser Arafat in the West
Bank city of Ramallah, during a
vigil to mark the anniversary of
Arafat's death.
CREATOR Mohamad Torokman
SOURCE occupiedpalestine.
wordpress.com
DATE 10 November 2011

010 NANJING NEVER HAPPENED
Visitors place candles to create
the Chinese character "peace"
in the new section of the Nanjing
Massacre museum, as part of a
ceremony marking the seventieth
anniversary of the Nanjing
massacre.
CREATOR Nir Elia
SOURCE uk.reuters.com
DATE 13 December 2007

011 MUMBAI TERRORIST ATTACKS
Schoolchildren hold candles
during a vigil held in memory
of the victims of shootings in
Mumbai, in the western Indian city
of Ahmedabad.
CREATOR Amit Dave
SOURCE www.boston.com
DATE 27 November 2008

012 CANDLES FOR PEACE
Indian students hold up candles,
protesting against what they say
is targeted violence against the
Indian community.
CREATOR Will Ockenden
SOURCE www.flickr.com/photos/
scissorhands33/3580256149/
DATE 2009

013 CANDLES FOR PEACE, BURMA
SOURCE www.thebestfriend.org

014 PAZ [PEACE]
Colombia
SOURCE www.pearltrees.com
DATE 6 January 2012

015 CZECH-US RADAR DEMONSTRATION
In Breznice, peace activists light
candles to form a peace sign as
some two hundred people protested
the war in Iraq and the antimissile
radar base the US proposed to
construct in the Czech Republic.
CREATOR Michal Cizek
SOURCE www.daylife.com
DATE 20 October 2007

016 PEACE CANDLE
In the CPT Hebron delegation
apartment. A rock and a piece of
barbed wire.
CREATOR Photograph by Jill
Granberg. Provided by delayed
gratification.
SOURCE www.flickr.com/photos/
joshhough/315552780/

017 PEACE
CREATOR Provided by **luisa**
SOURCE www.flickr.com/photos/
luisapuccini/2138060150/

018 PEACE CANDLES
CREATOR My Lai Peace Park Project
SOURCE www.mylaipeacepark.org

019 CREATOR Provided by aguszka
SOURCE www.flickr.com/photos/
8536096@N05/524772123/

001

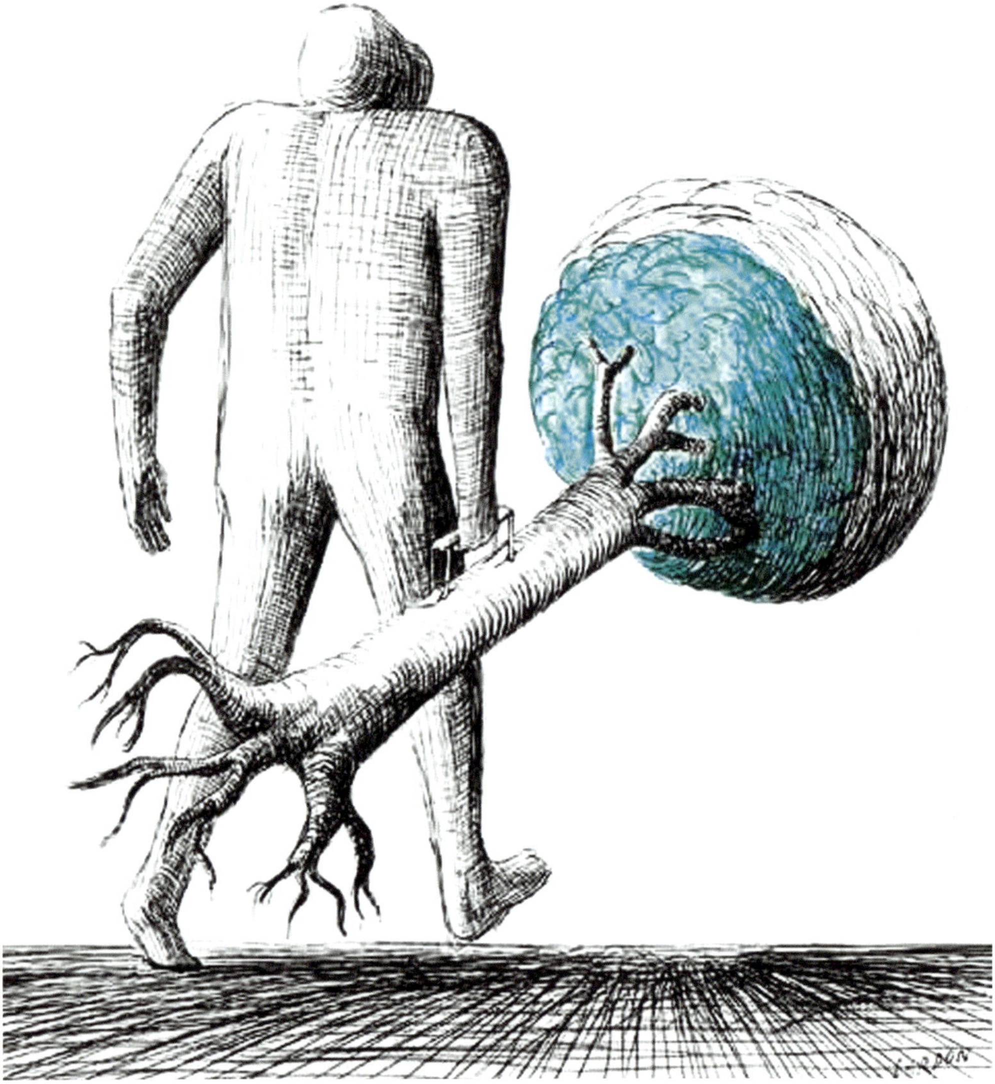

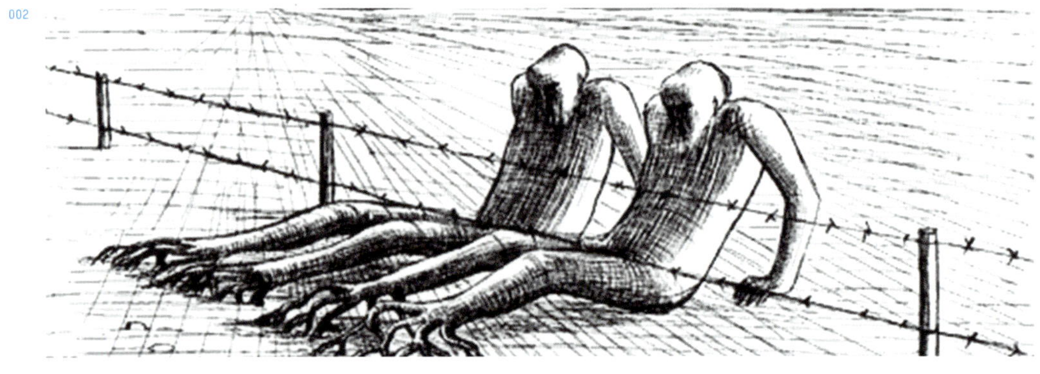

002

003

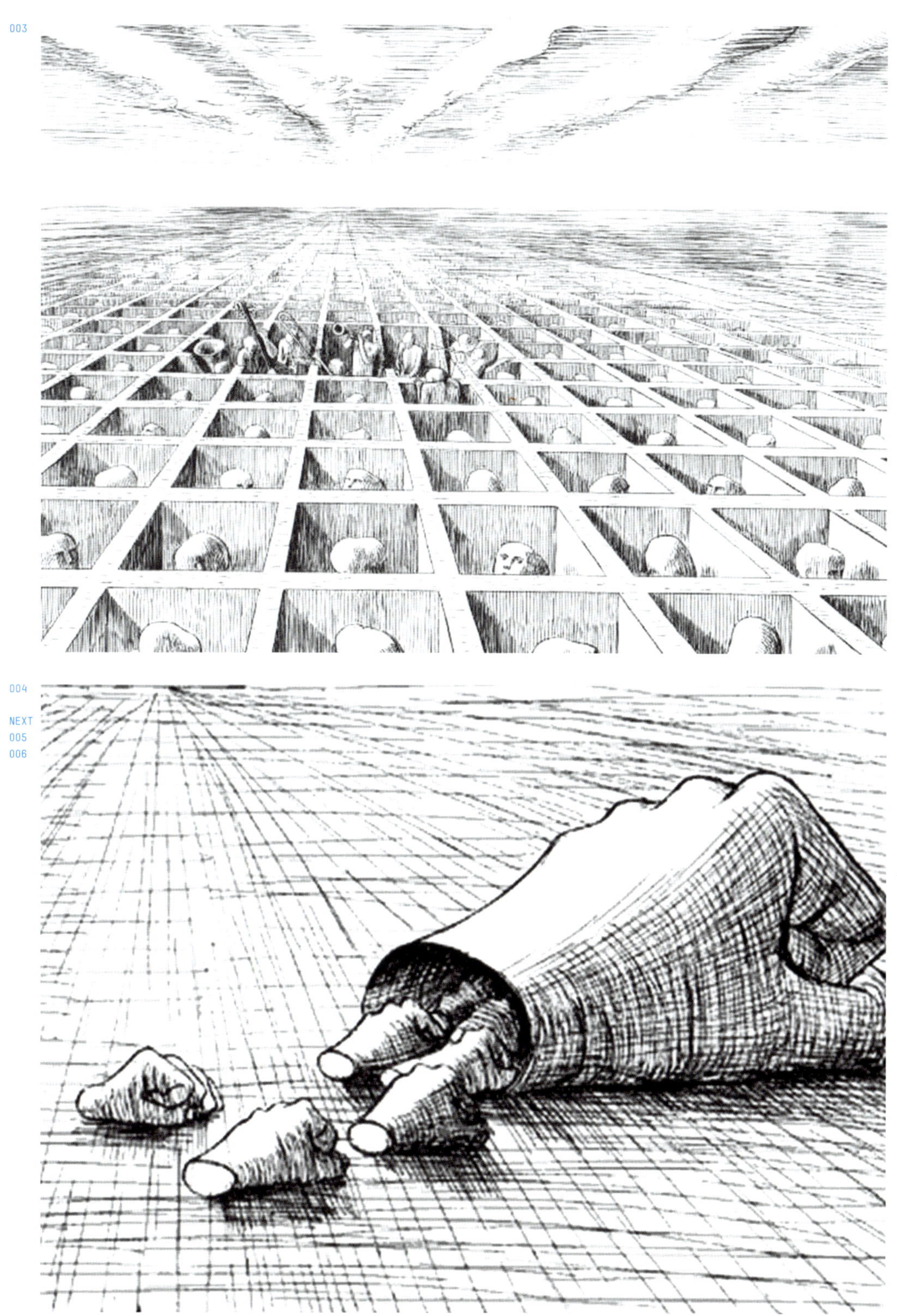

004
NEXT
005
006

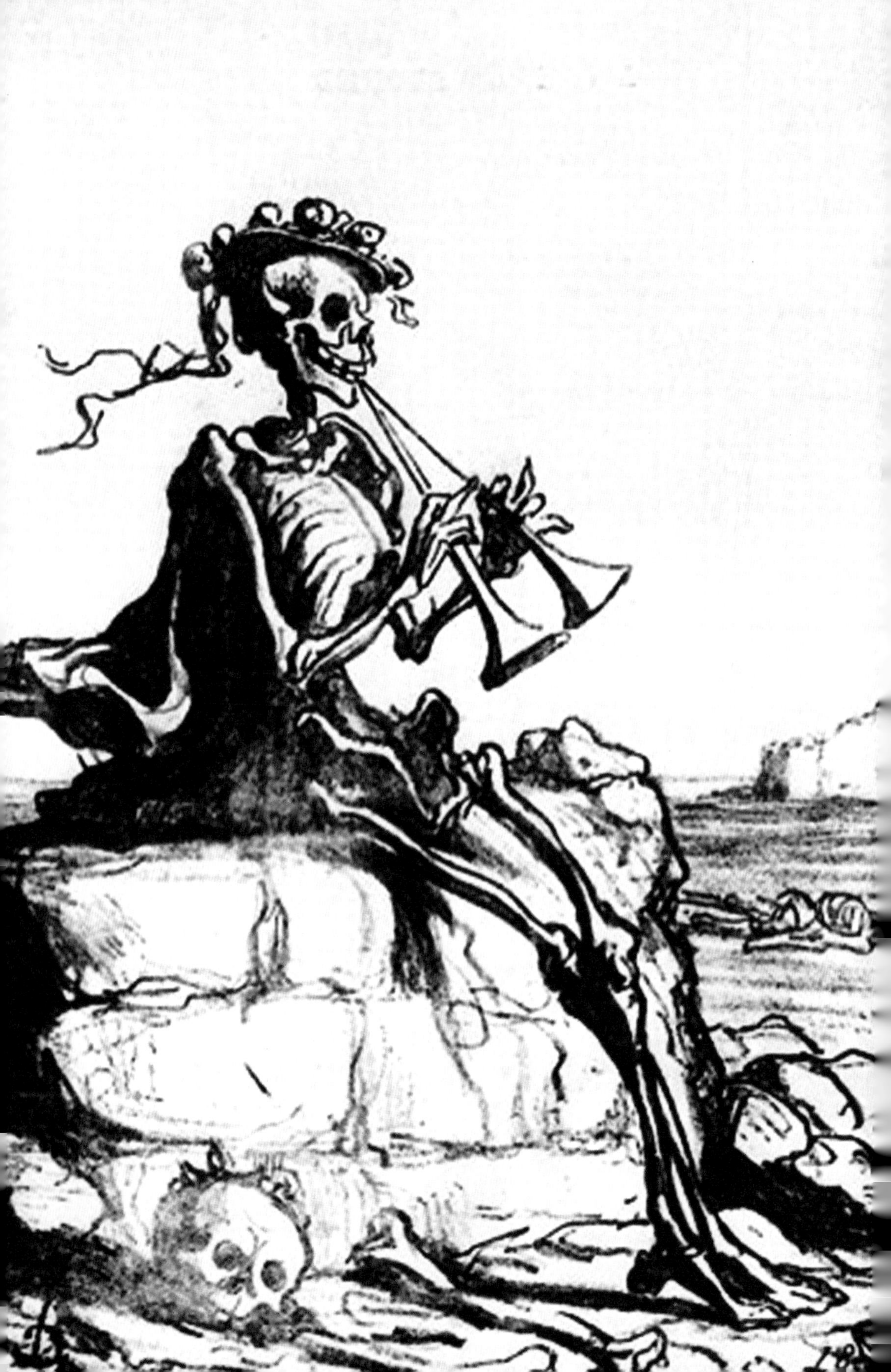

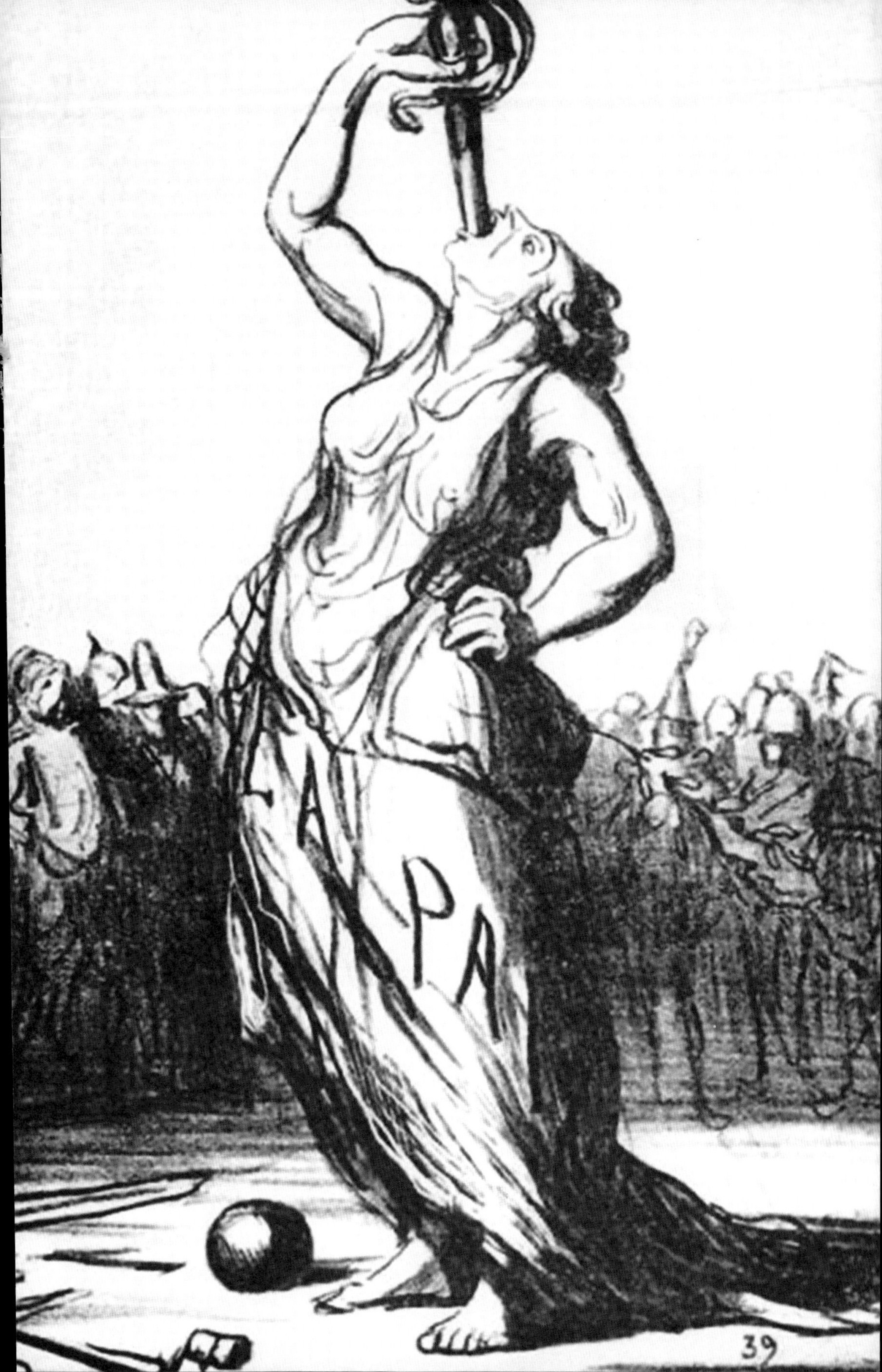

LA
PA
39

007

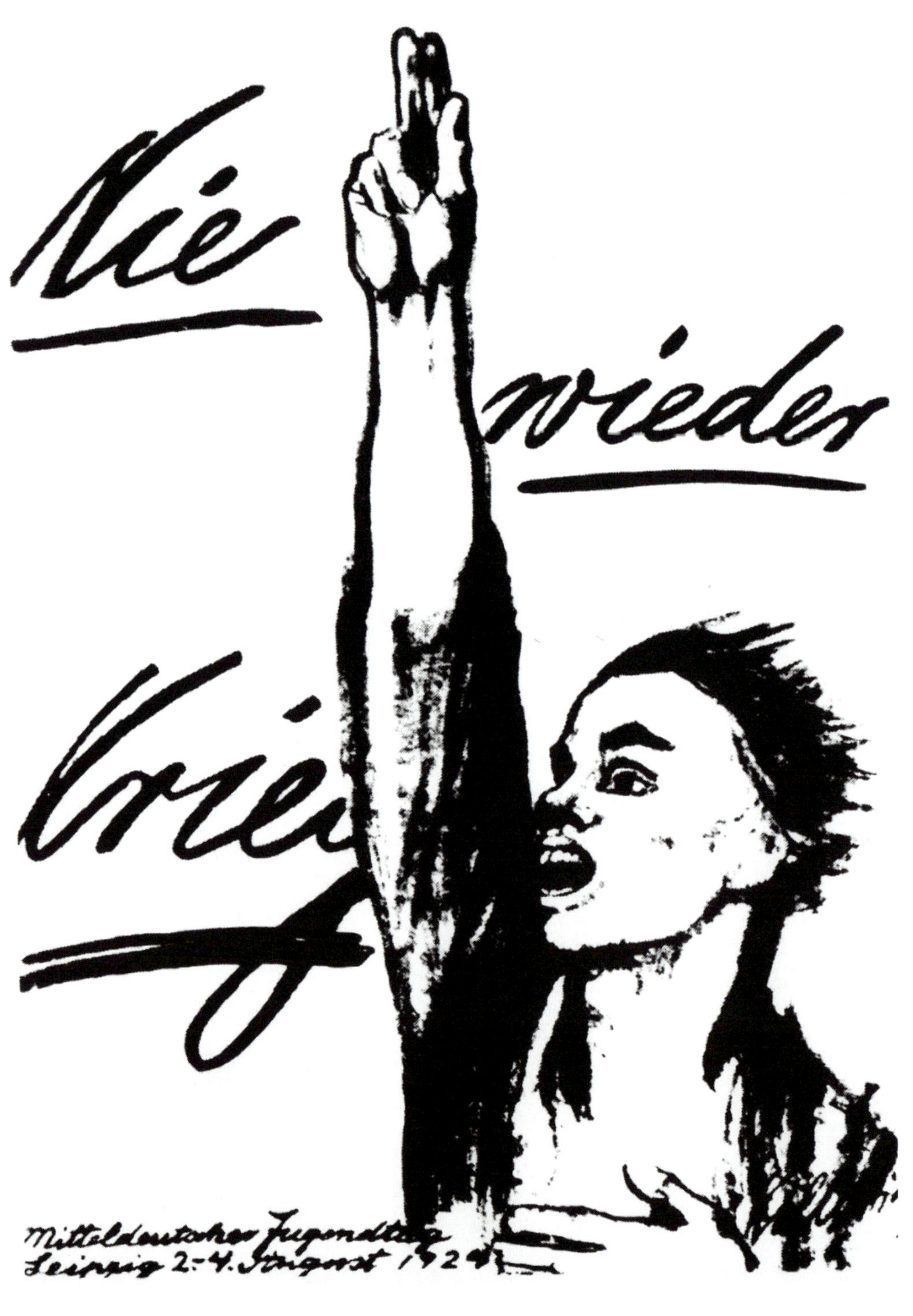
Nie
wieder
Krieg
Mitteldeutscher Jugendtag
Leipzig 2-4. August 1924

008
009

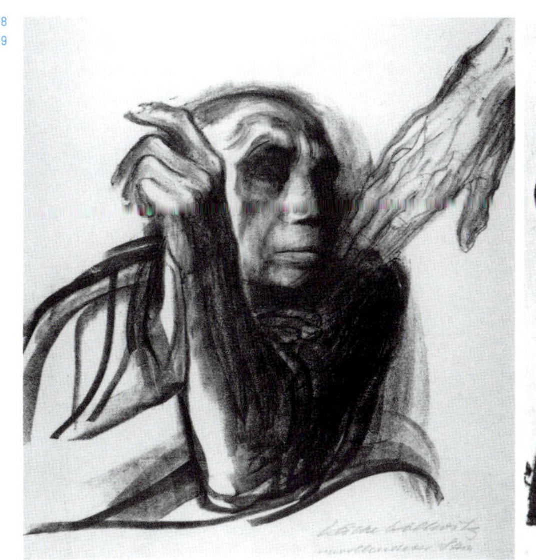
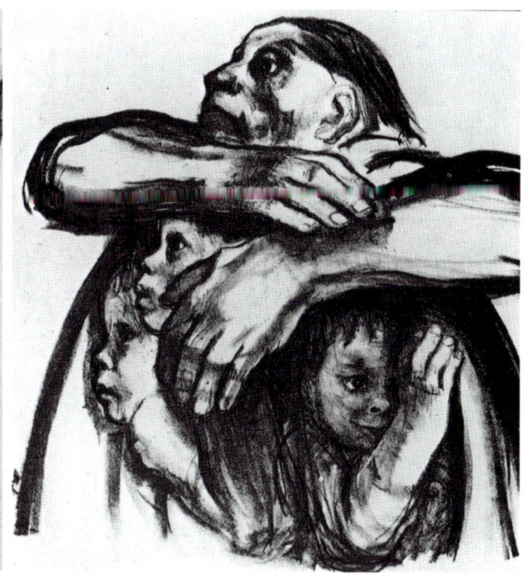

010
011

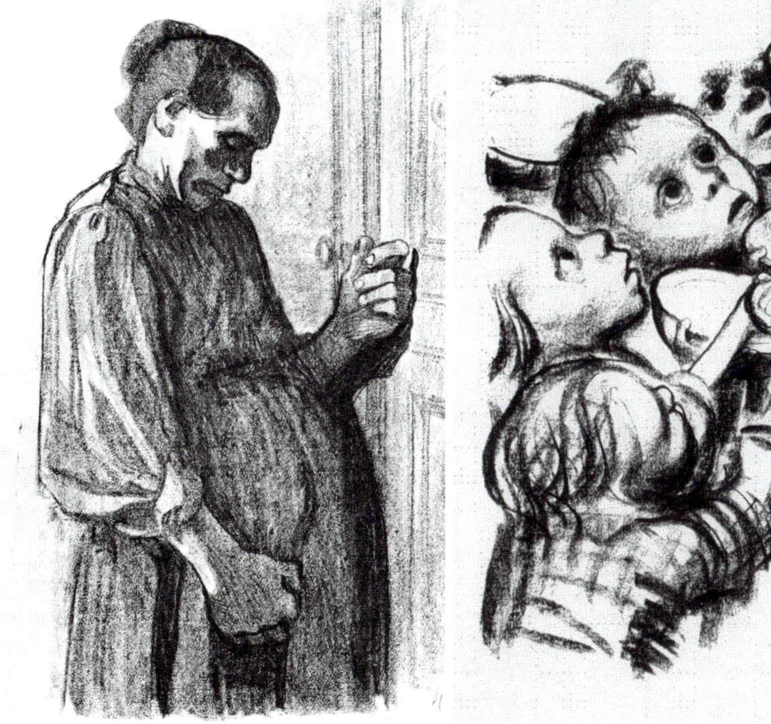

012
013

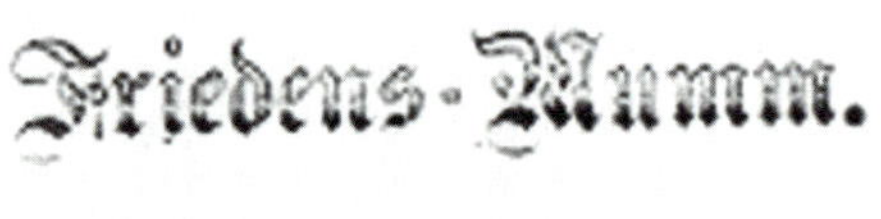

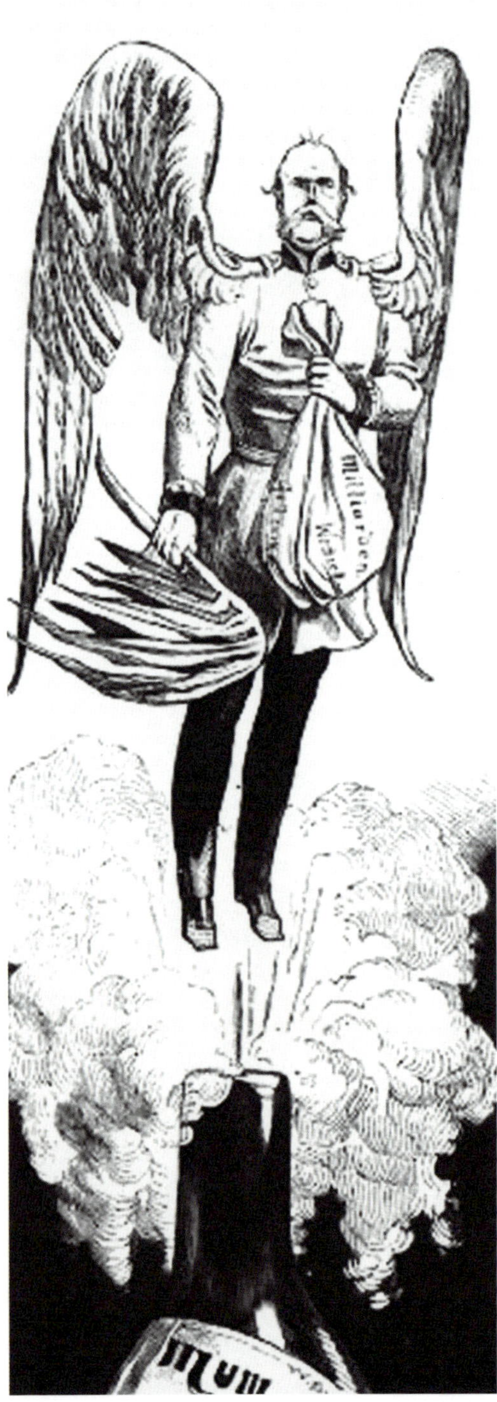

014

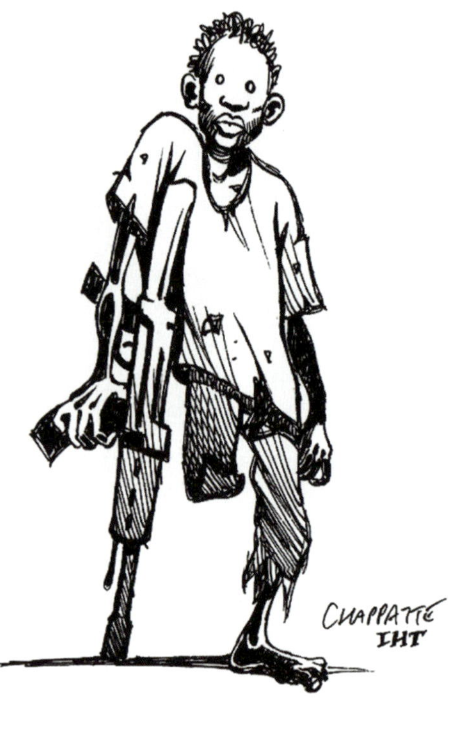

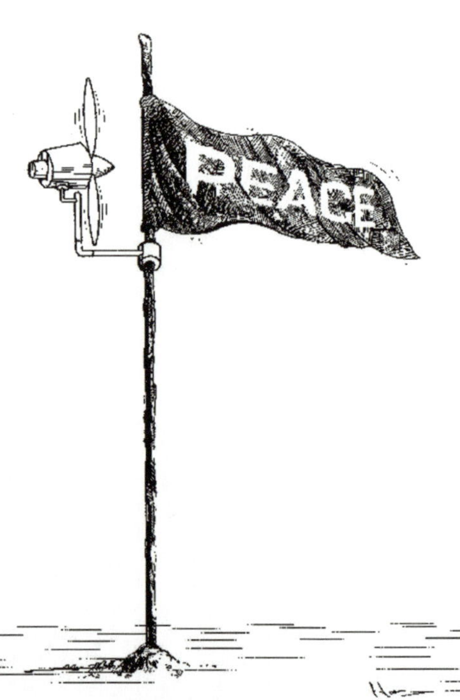

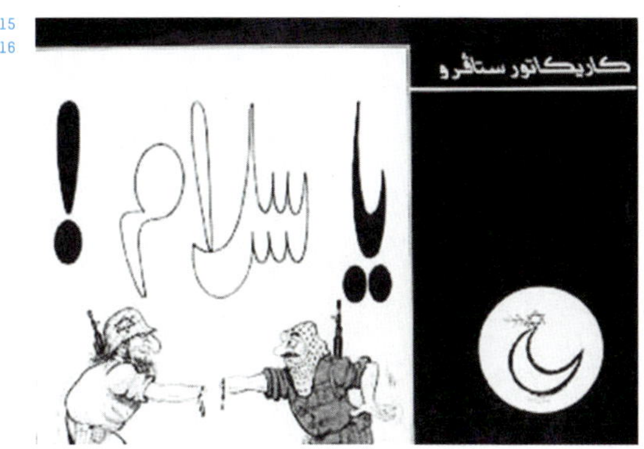
كاريكاتور ستاڤرو
يا سلام !
!

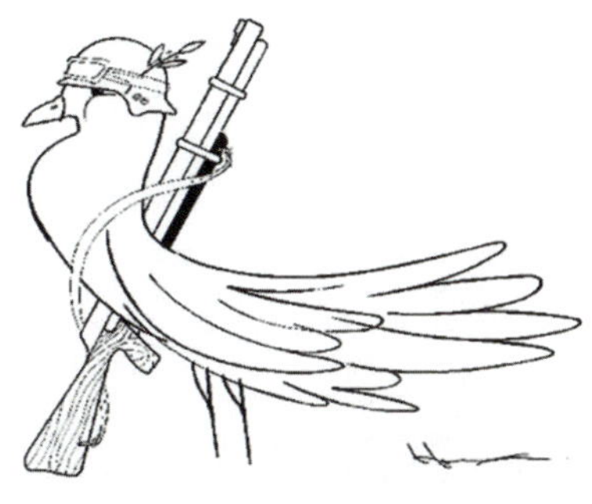

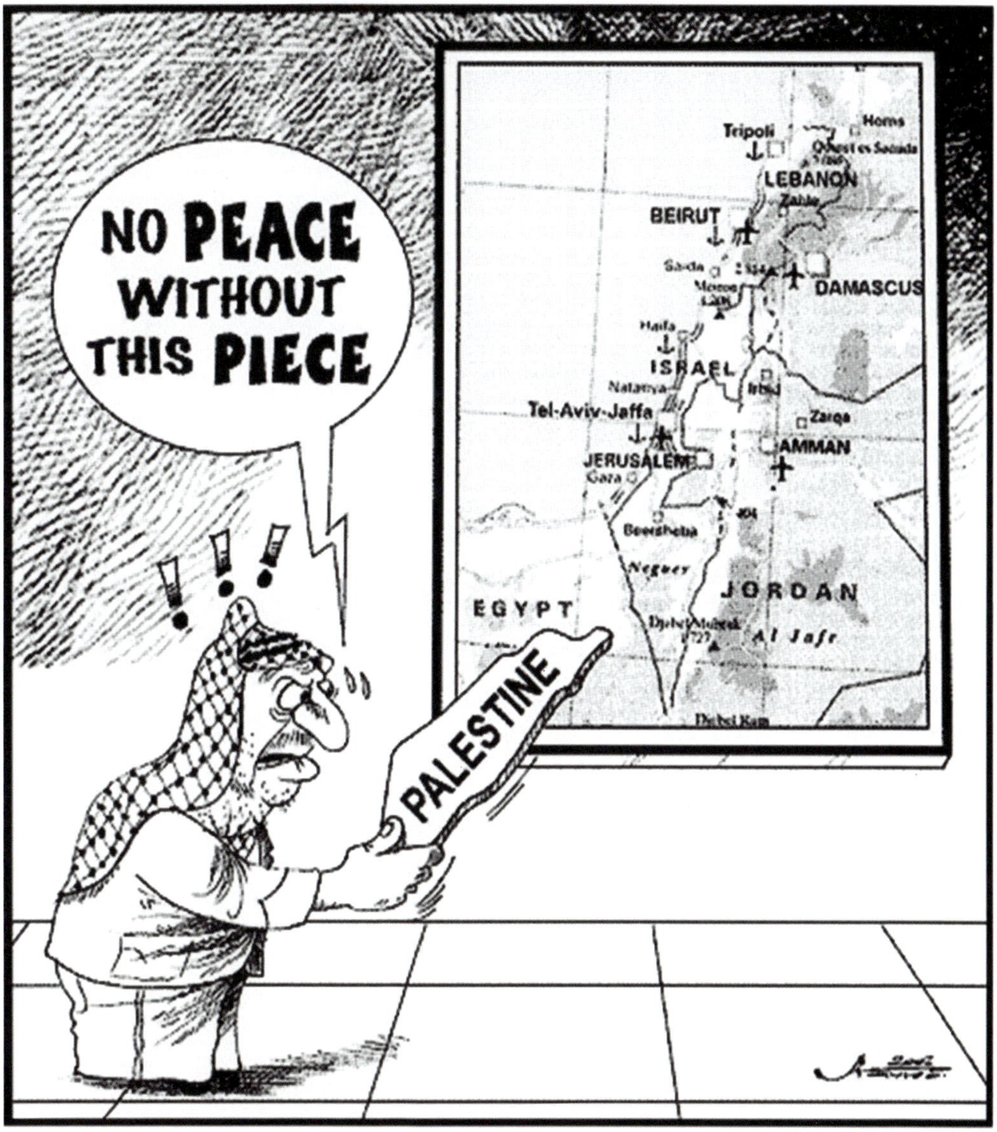

NO PEACE
WITHOUT
THIS PIECE

PALESTINE

Tripoli
Homs
LEBANON
BEIRUT
Saïda
DAMASCUS
Haifa
ISRAEL
Natanya
Tel-Aviv-Jaffa
JERUSALEM
Gaza
Zarqa
AMMAN
Beersheba
Neguev
JORDAN
EGYPT
Al Jafr

018

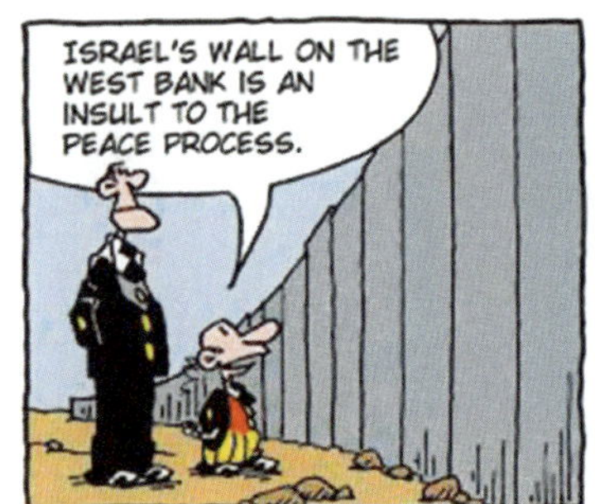
ISRAEL'S WALL ON THE WEST BANK IS AN INSULT TO THE PEACE PROCESS.

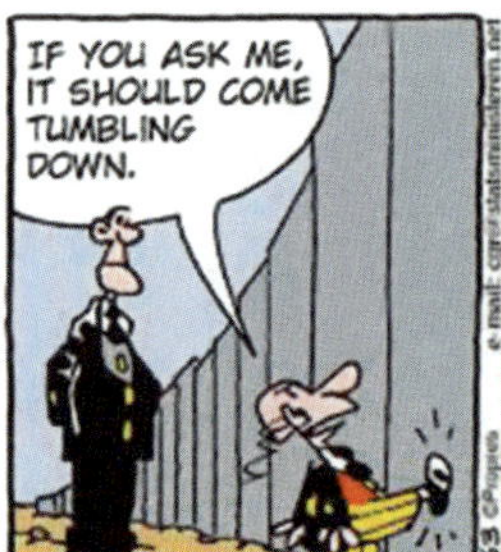
IF YOU ASK ME, IT SHOULD COME TUMBLING DOWN.

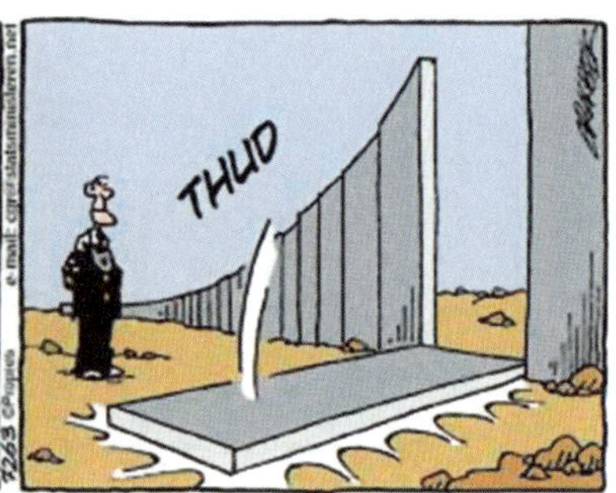
THUD

019

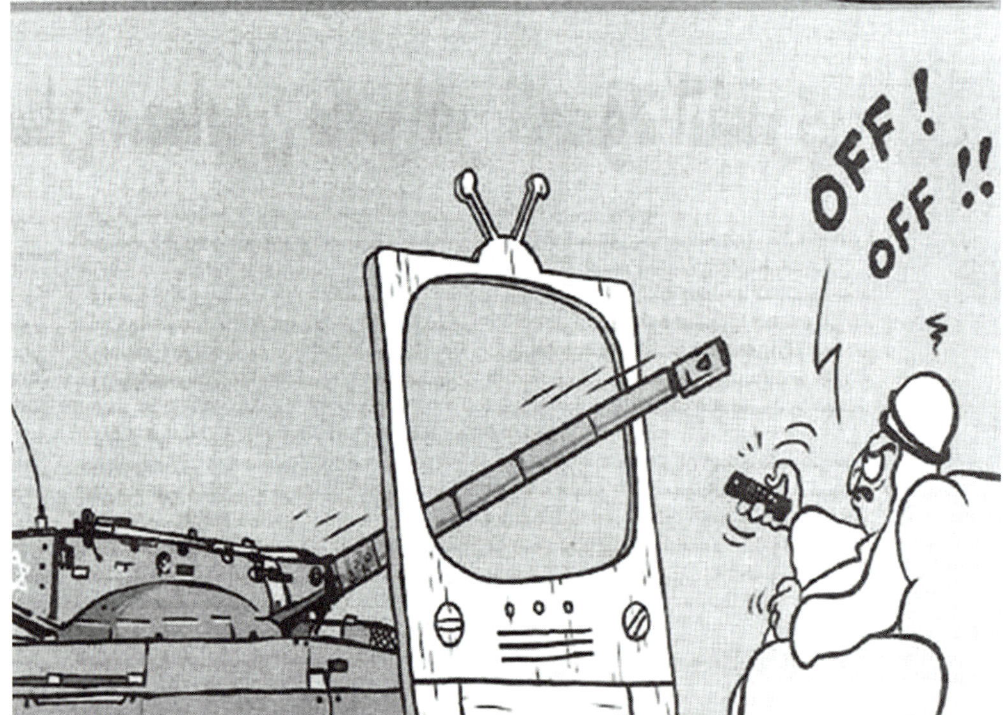
29/06/2006
القدس
OFF !
OFF !!

020
021

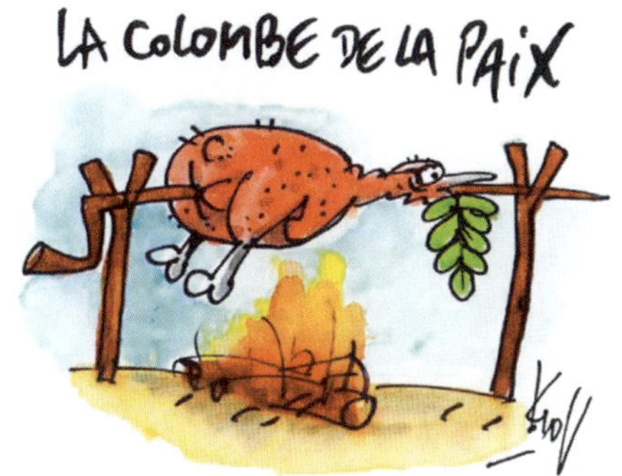

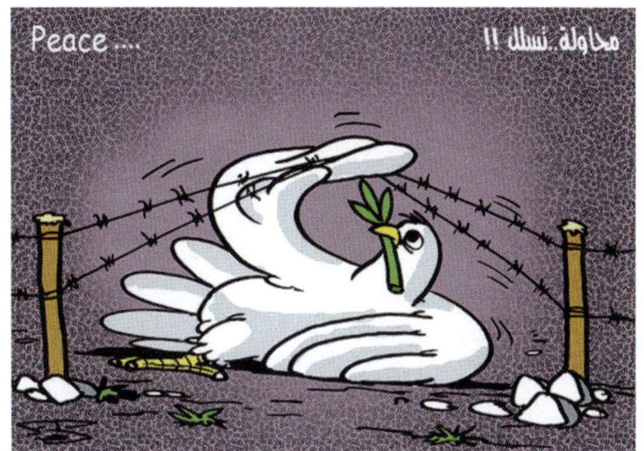

022
023

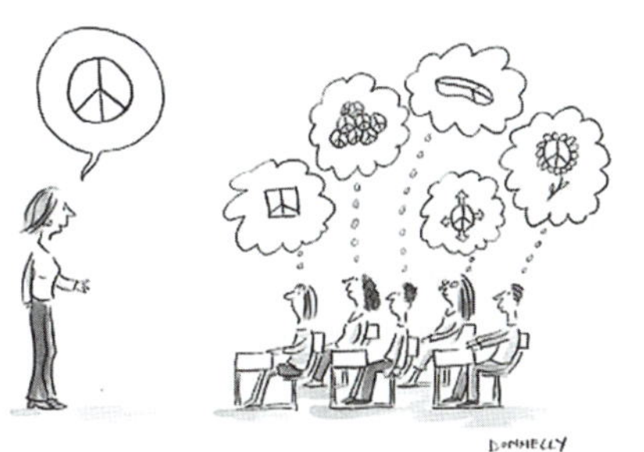

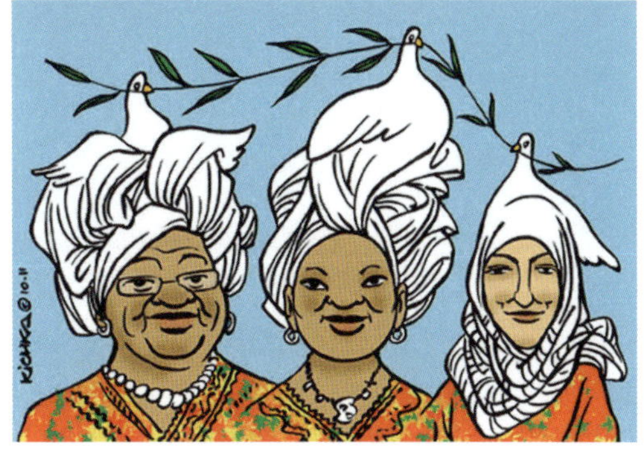

024
025

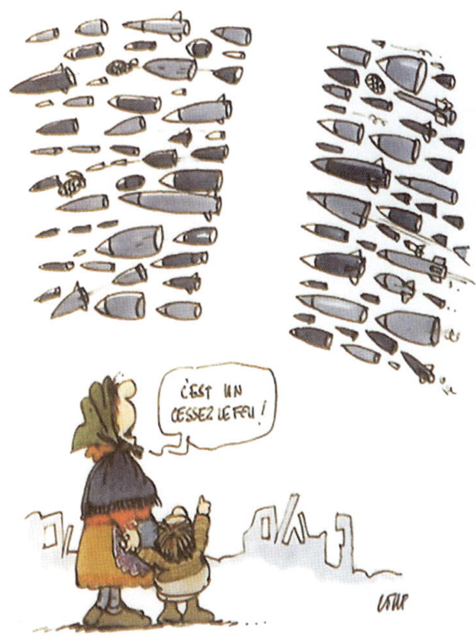

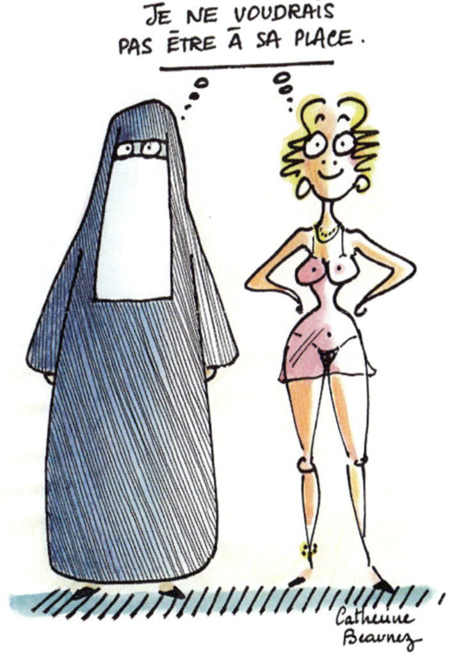

001 UNTITLED
CREATOR Jacques-Armand Cardon
SOURCE www.irancartoon.com

002 UNTITLED
CREATOR Jacques-Armand Cardon
SOURCE www.irancartoon.com

003 UNTITLED
CREATOR Jacques-Armand Cardon
SOURCE www.irancartoon.com

004 UNTITLED
CREATOR Jacques-Armand Cardon
SOURCE www.irancartoon.com

005 UMA PAZ IDÍLICA [AN IDYLLIC PEACE]
CREATOR Honorè Daumier
SOURCE gitacao.wordpress.com
DATE 1871

006 LA PAIX ARMEE [PEACE ARMY]
CREATOR Dessins Daumier
SOURCE coloriages.dessins.free.fr

007 NIE WIEDER KRIEG!
[NO MORE WAR!]
CREATOR Kaethe Kollwitz
SOURCE www.of.shuttle.de
DATE 1922

008 RUF DES TODES [CALL OF DEATH]
CREATOR Kaethe Kollwitz
SOURCE my.hamilton.edu
DATE 1937

009 SAATFRÜCHTE SOLLEN NICHT
VERMAHLEN WERDEN
[SEEDS FOR SOWING SHOULD NOT
BE MILLED]
CREATOR Kaethe Kollwitz
SOURCE D. J. R. Bruckner, Seymour
Chwast, and Steven Heller, eds.,
Kunst Gegen den Krieg [Basel:
Birkhäuser, 1984], p. 68.
DATE 1941

010 BEIM ARTZ [AT THE DOCTOR'S]
CREATOR Kaethe Kollwitz
SOURCE www.uni-leipzig.de
DATE 1908/09

011 HUNGERNDE KINDER [GERMANY'S
CHILDREN ARE STARVING!]
CREATOR Kaethe Kollwitz
SOURCE www.badische-zeitung.de
DATE 1924

012 FRIEDENS-MUMM
[PEACE MUMM]
Otto von Bismarck returns from
Frankfurt with the signed treaty
ending the Franco-Prussian War.
CREATOR Wilhelm Scholz
SOURCE photomaniak.com

013 CREATOR Patrick Chappatte, IHT
SOURCE www.cartooningforpeace.org/

014 UNTITLED
SOURCE www.cartooningforpeace.org/

015 LA PAIX ISRAELO-PALESTINIENNE.
YA SALAAM
[THE ISRAELI-PALESTINIAN PEACE]
SOURCE www.stavrotoons.com

016 SOURCE www.cartooningforpeace.org

017 NO PEACE WITHOUT THIS PIECE
CREATOR Stavro Ad-Dabbour
SOURCE www.planetenonviolence.org

018 THE KINGDOM
CREATOR Carsten Graabaek

019 SOURCE www.elmandjra.org
DATE 2006

020 LA COLOMBE DE LA PAIX
[THE DOVE OF PEACE]
CREATOR Kroll
SOURCE www.cartooningforpeace.org
DATE 2001

021 PEACE...
CREATOR Boukhari
SOURCE www.cartooningforpeace.org

022 THINKING PEACE
CREATOR Liza Donnelly
SOURCE www.cartooningforpeace.org

023 CREATOR Michel Kichka
SOURCE www.cartooningforpeace.org
DATE 2001

024 C'EST UN CESSEZ LE FEU!
[IT'S A CEASE-FIRE!]
CREATOR Loup [France]
SOURCE www.cartooningforpeace.org

025 JE NE VOUDRAIS PAS ETRE A SA PLACE
[I WOULDN'T WANT TO BE IN HER PLACE]
CREATOR Catherine Beaunez
SOURCE www.cartooningforpeace.org

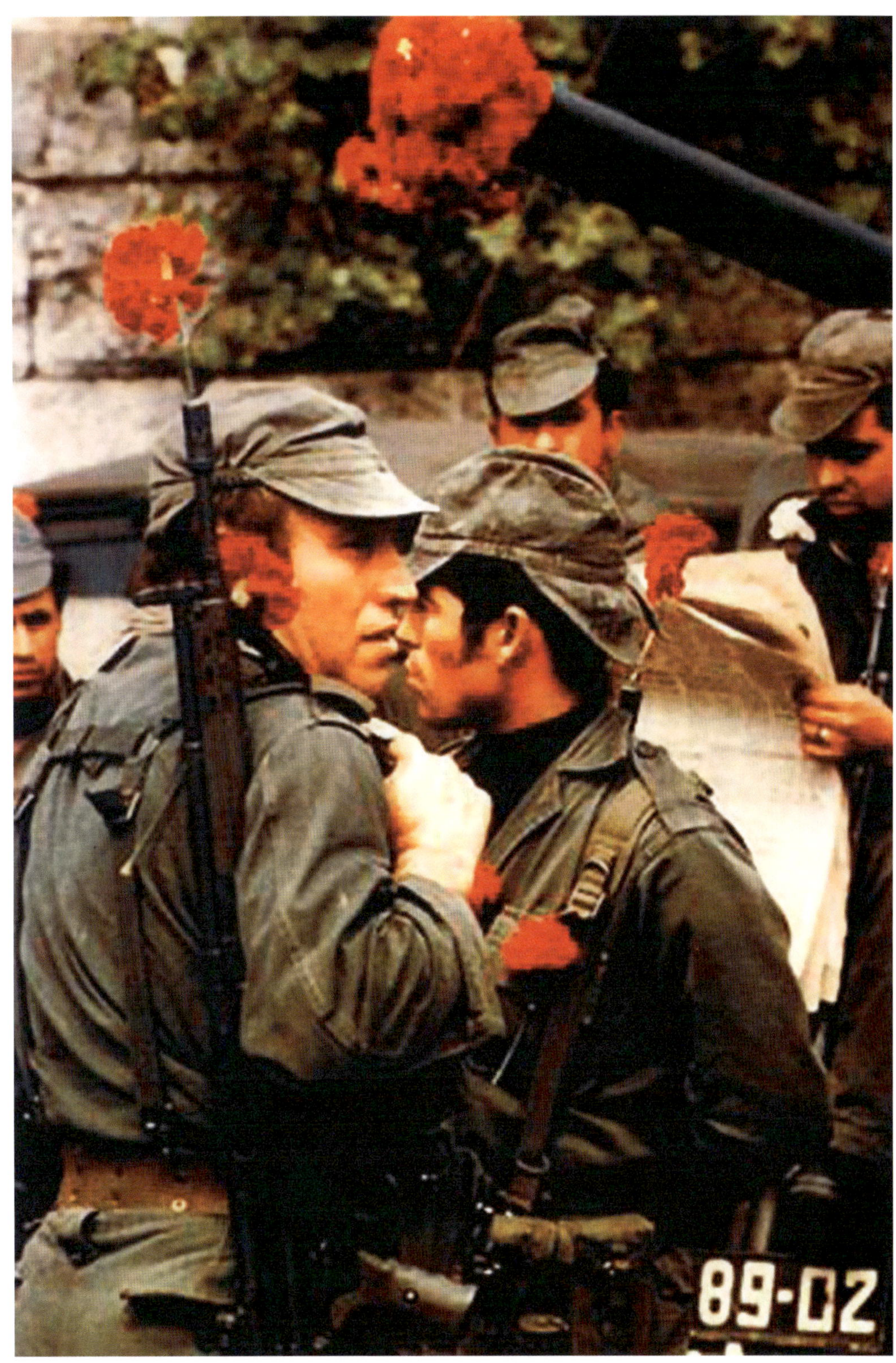

89-02

002
003
004

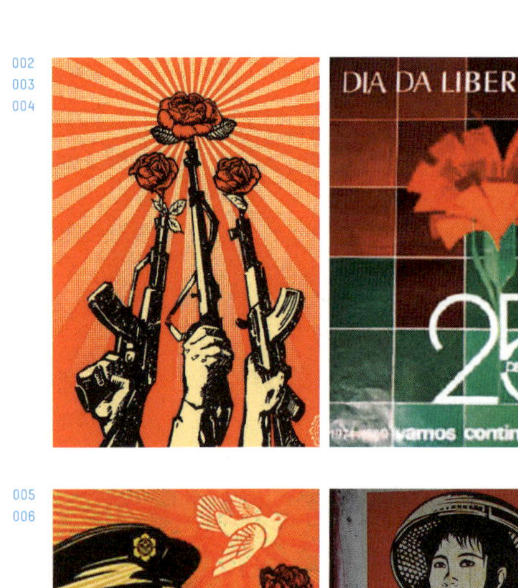

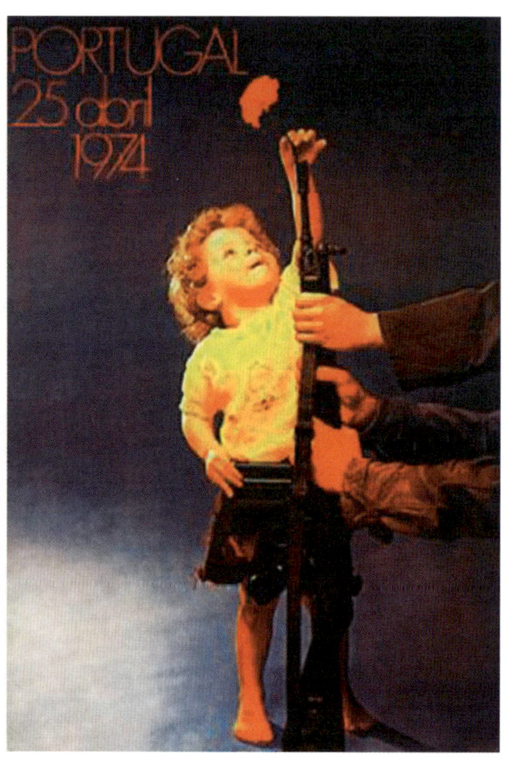

005
006

007
008

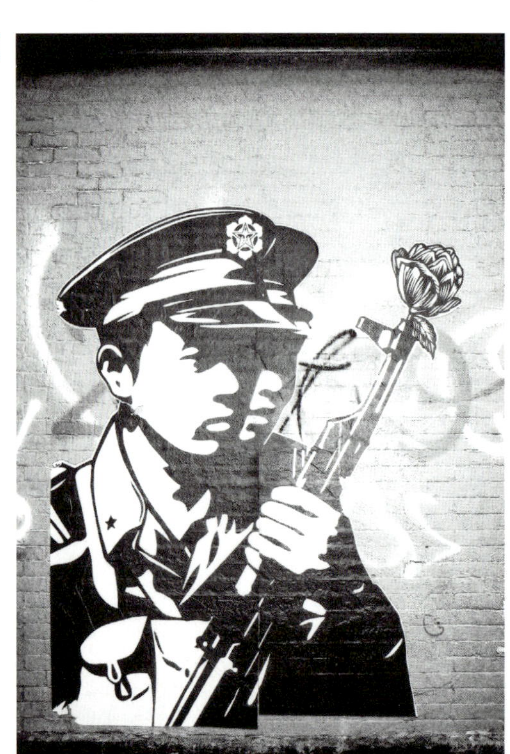

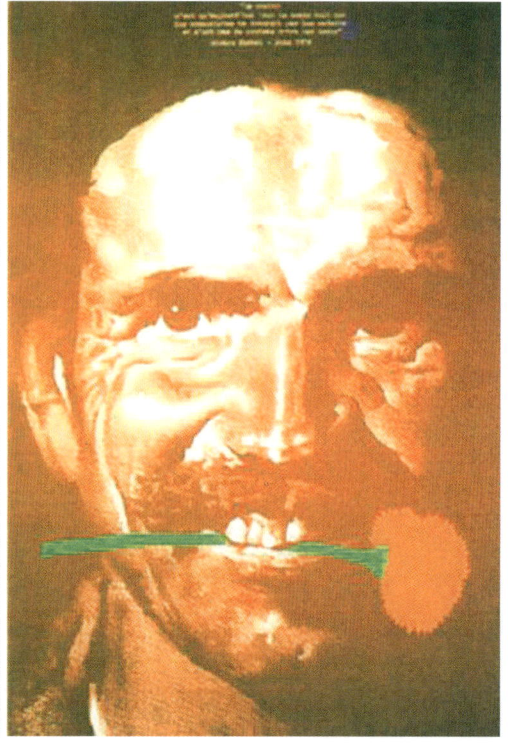

009
010

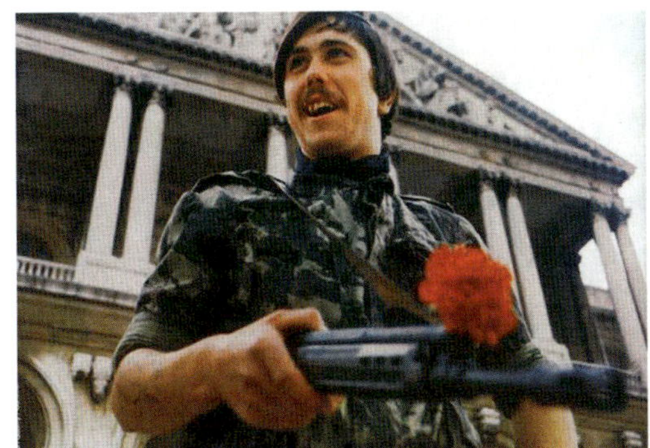

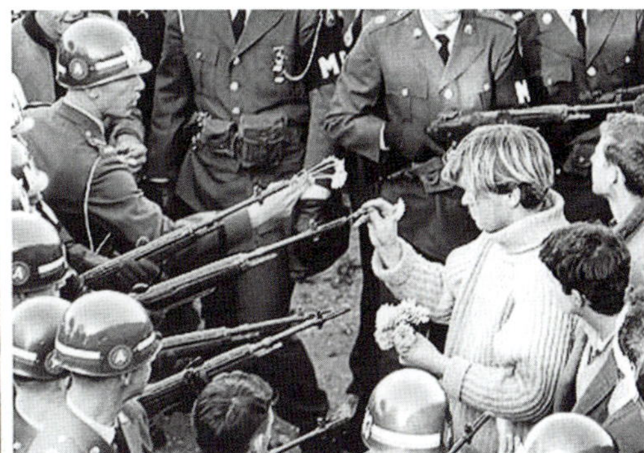

011
012

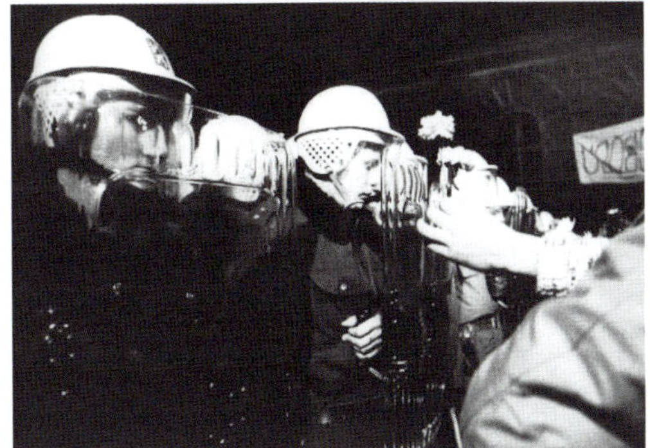

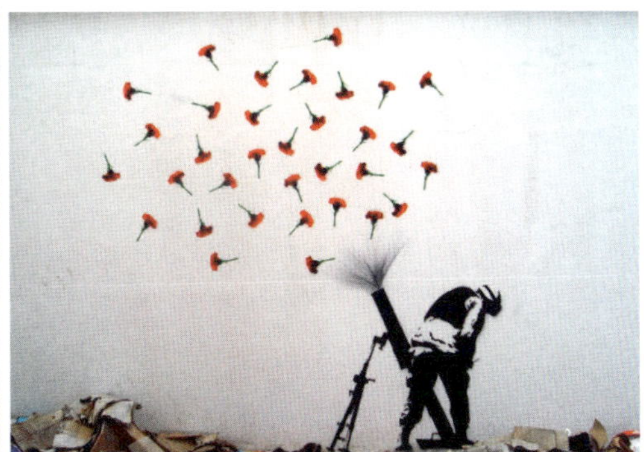

013
014

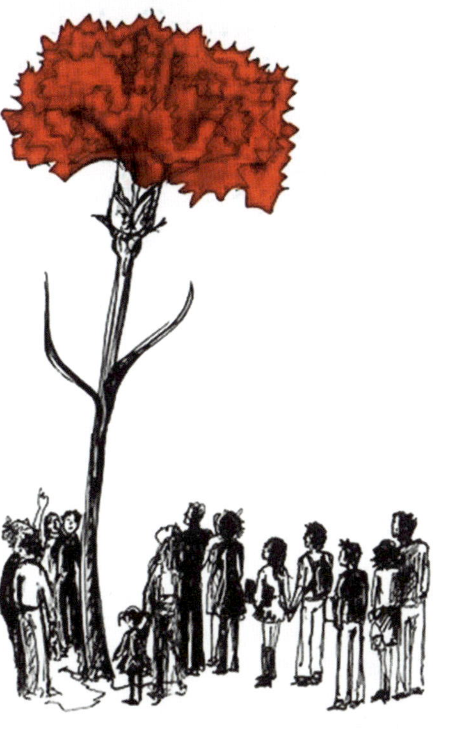

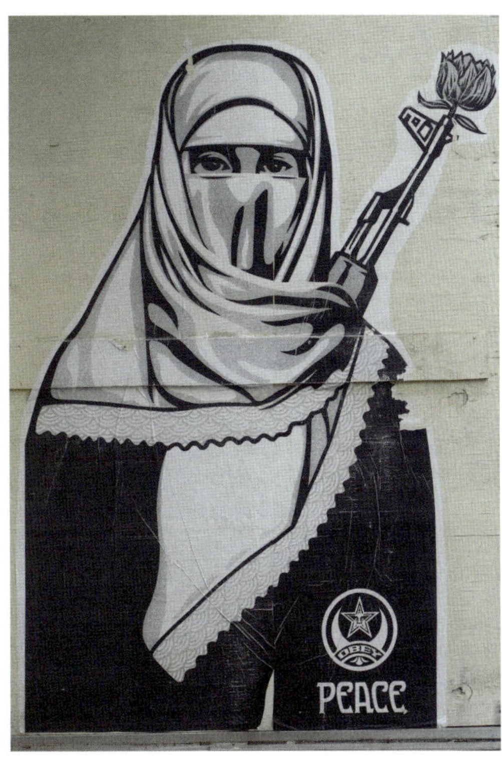

015

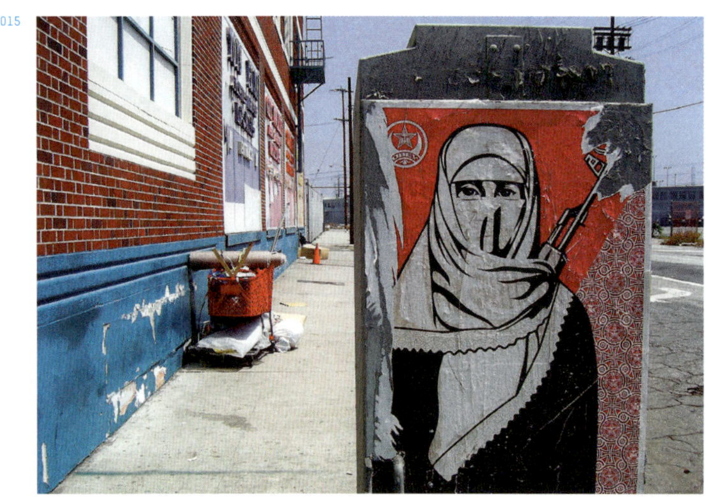

016

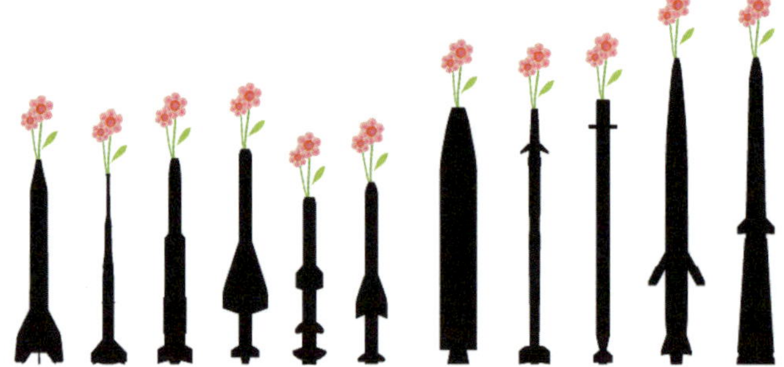

017

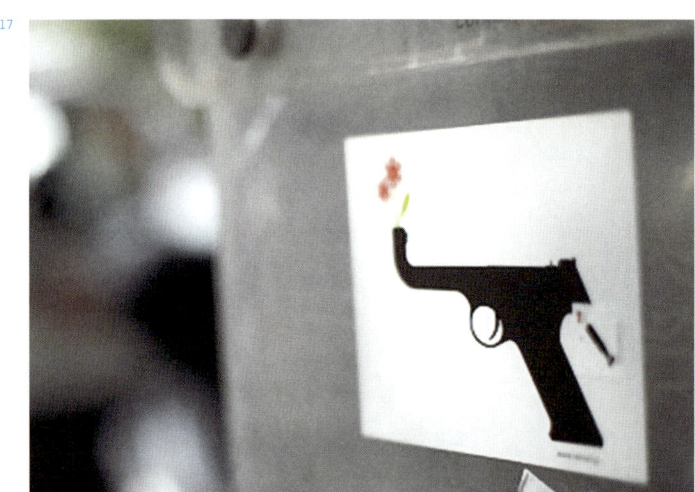

001 The Carnation Revolution, Portugal
     SOURCE www.profesorenlinea.cl
     DATE 25 April 1974

002 GUNS AND ROSES
     CREATOR Shepard Fairey
     SOURCE obeygiant.com

003 DIA DA LIBERDADE
     [FREEDOM DAY]
     SOURCE www.dhnet.org.br

004 PORTUGAL, 25 ABRIL 1974
     CREATOR José Afonso
     SOURCE info-graf.fr

005 PEACE = RED ROSE IN A BARREL?
     CREATOR Poster by Obey, Provided
     by ZenzenOK
     SOURCE www.flickr.com/photos/
     zenzenok/76194182/

006 CHINESE SOLDIERS
     CREATOR Shepard Fairey
     SOURCE obeygiant.com

007 GUNS & ROSES, WILLIAMSBURG,
     BROOKLYN
     CREATOR Poster by Obey, Provided
     by Todd W. Shaffer
     SOURCE www.flickr.com/photos/
     toddwshaffer/910558865/

008 UM TRACTOR
     SOURCE apor.blogspot.com

009 CARNATION REVOLUTION, PORTUGAL
     SOURCE media.photobucket.com
     DATE 25 April 1974

010 BYE BYE "MR FLOWER"
     1960s photograph of a Vietnam
     War protester placing flowers in
     soldiers' gun barrels.
     CREATOR Provided by Bernie Boston
     SOURCE www.flickr.com/photos/
     silipo/2215691957/

011 VELVET REVOLUTION, CZECHOSLOVAKIA
     Nonviolent protesters face
     armored policemen.
     SOURCE www.mzv.cz
     DATE 1989

012 UNTITLED
     CREATOR Provided by
     steventannock209
     SOURCE media.photobucket.com

013 UNTITLED
     CREATOR Provided by kimixcore
     SOURCE media.photobucket.com

014 MUSLIM GRAFFITI, HOUSTON
     CREATOR Poster by Obey, Provided
     by EDgAr H.
     SOURCE www.flickr.com/photos/
     dptlc/116803253/

015 OBEY POSTER
     CREATOR Poster by Shepard Fairey,
     Provided by El Photo
     SOURCE www.flickr.com/photos/
     46818804@N00/161356595/

016 RETIRED WEAPONS WEBSITE
     CREATOR Yuji Tokuda, Junya
     Ishikawa
     SOURCE retired.jp/

017 MILAN, DESIGNWEEK 07
     CREATOR Bart Claeys
     SOURCE www.flickr.com/photos/
     bartclaeys/486362015/

TCHETCHENIE
KOSMOR
TCHEKOV

001 KOSOVO — TIMOR — TCHETCHENIE
CREATOR Nous Travaillons Ensemble
SOURCE Plakatsammlung Museum für
Gestaltung Zürich

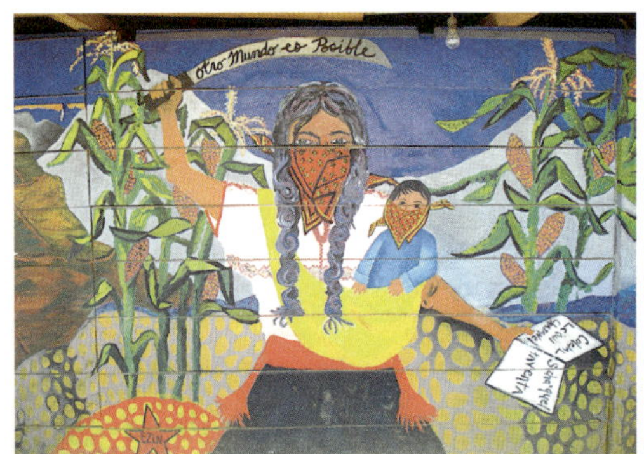
Otro Mundo es Posible

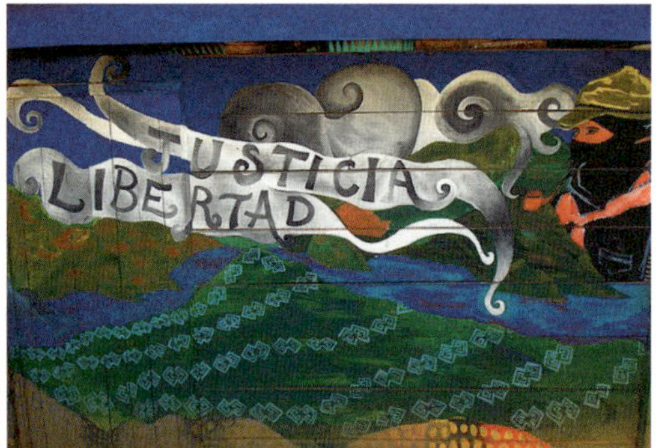
JUSTICIA
LIBERTAD

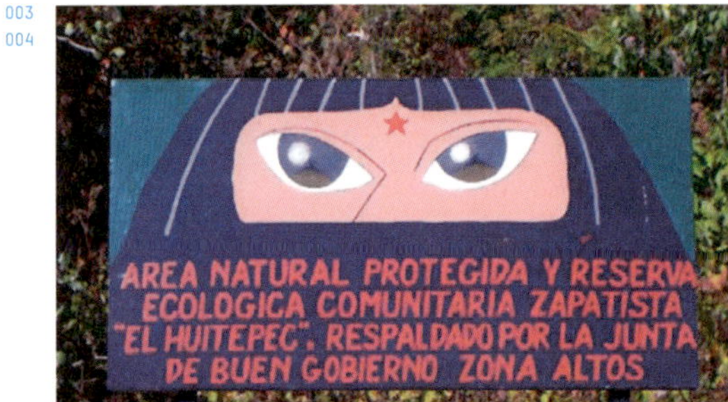
AREA NATURAL PROTEGIDA Y RESERVA
ECOLOGICA COMUNITARIA ZAPATISTA
"EL HUITEPEC". RESPALDADO POR LA JUNTA
DE BUEN GOBIERNO ZONA ALTOS

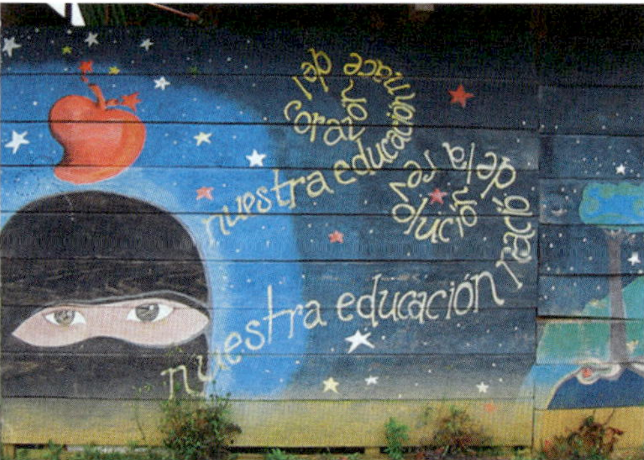
nuestra educación
nuestra educación nació

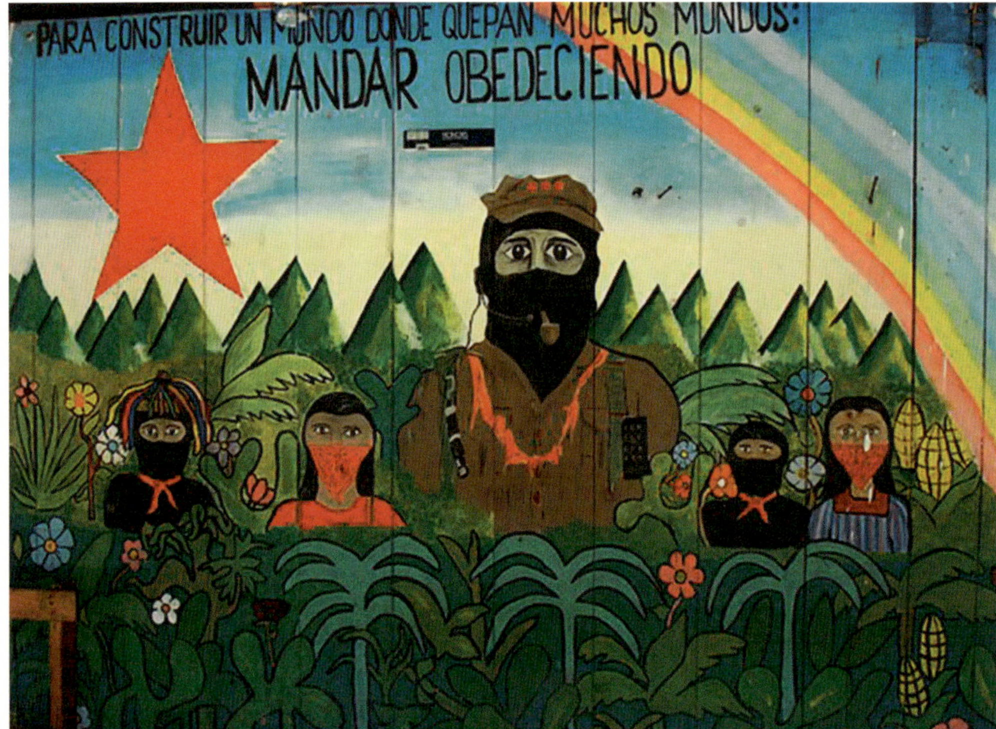
PARA CONSTRUIR UN MUNDO DONDE QUEPAN MUCHOS MUNDOS:
MANDAR OBEDECIENDO

006
007

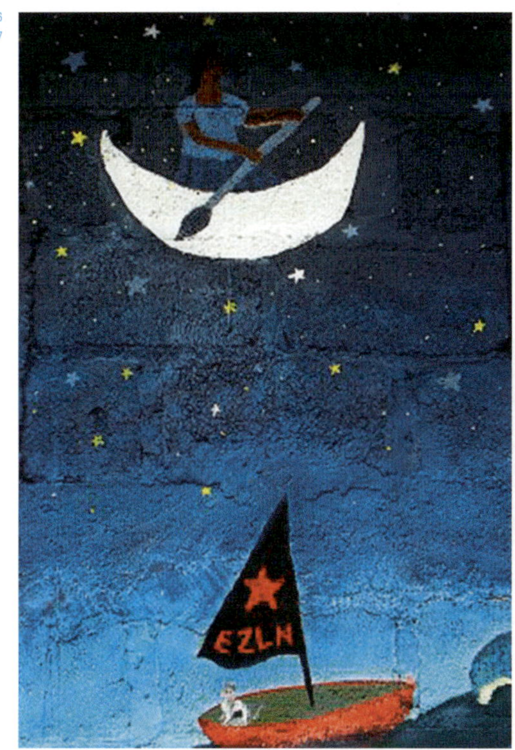

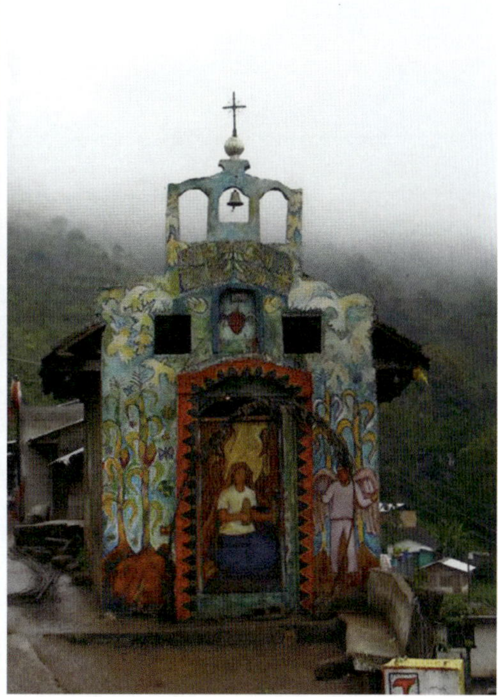

008

NEXT
009

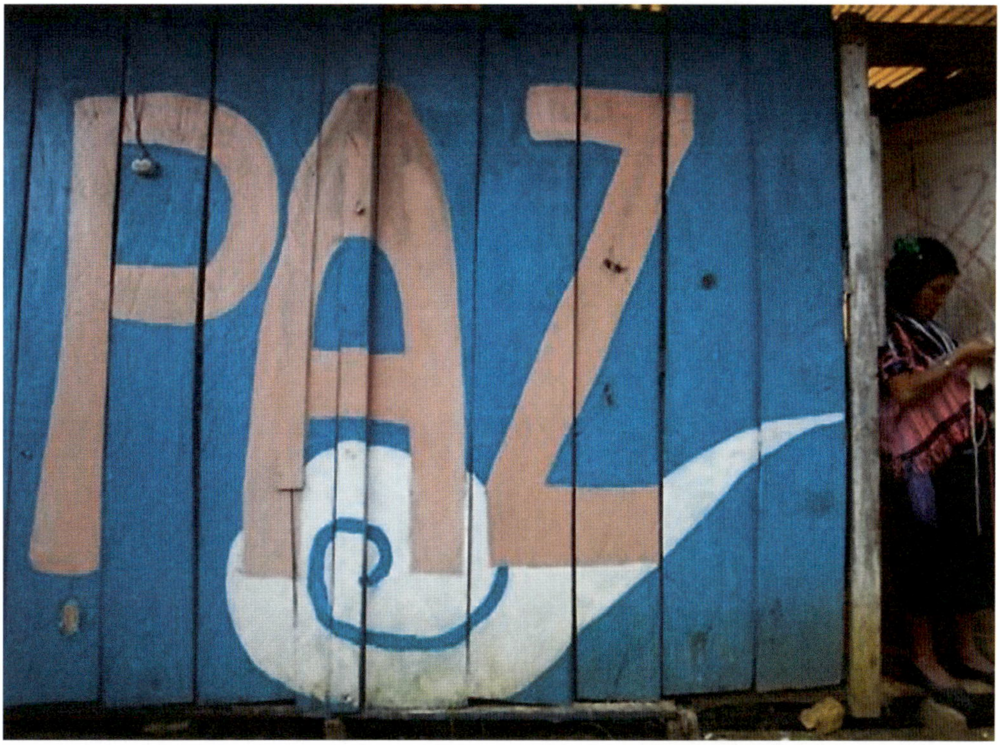

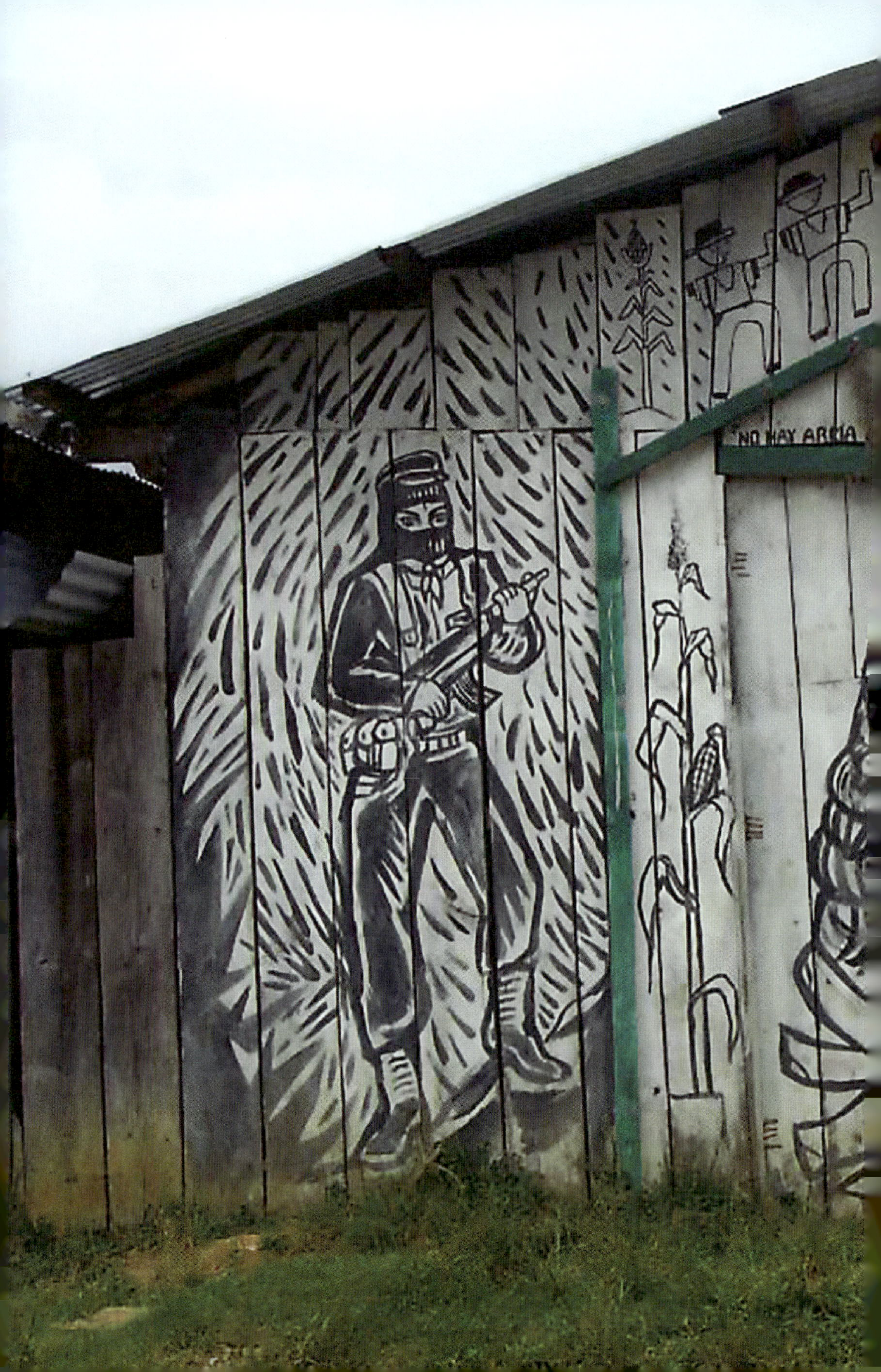
NO HAY AREA

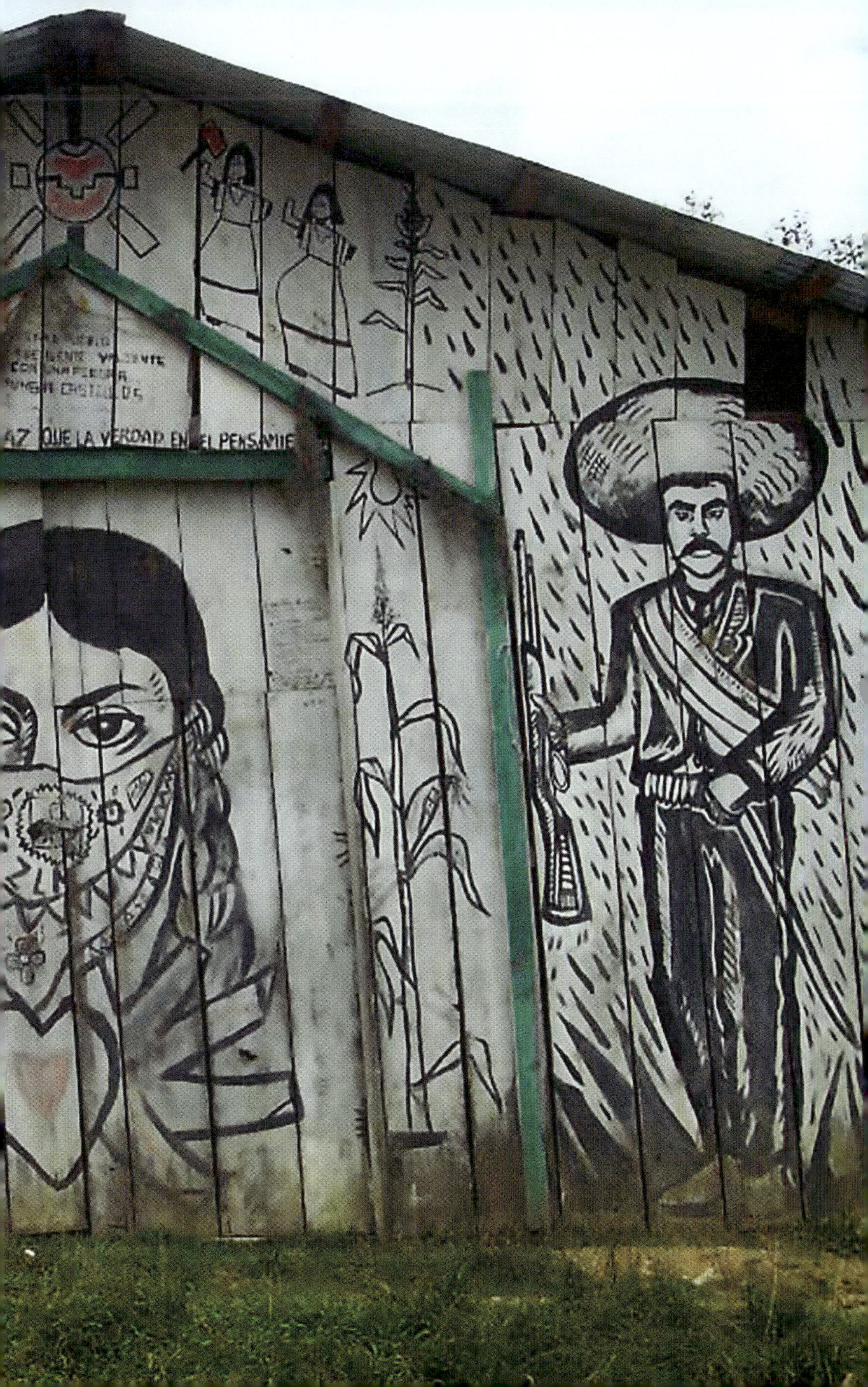

...PRE PUEBLO
...IENTE VALIENTE
CON SU RIQUEZA
...EN CASTILLOS
...AZ QUE LA VERDAD EN EL PENSAMIE...

010
011

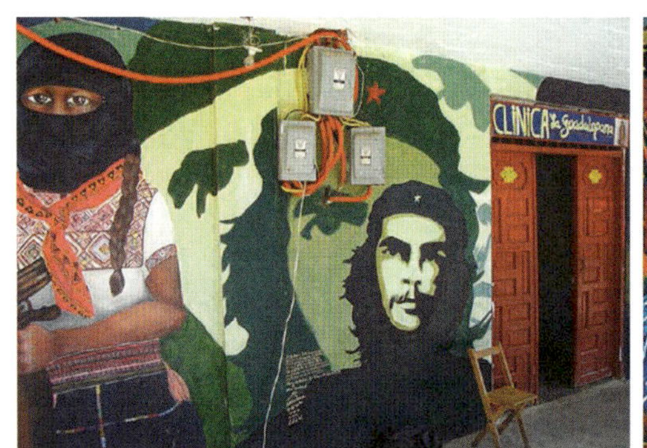

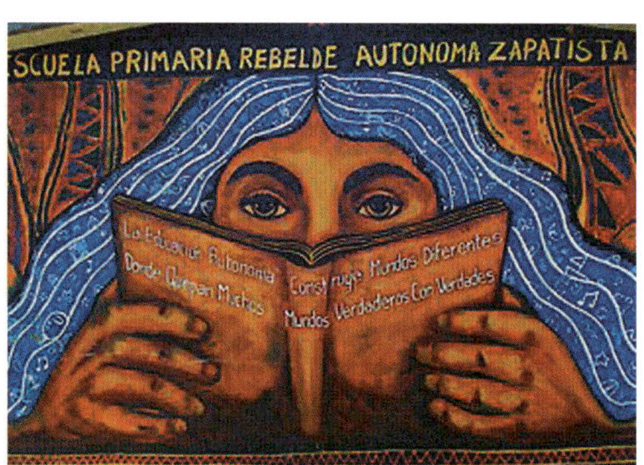

012
013

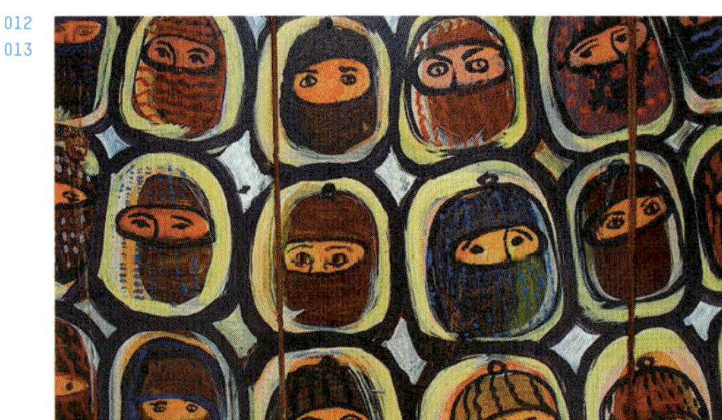

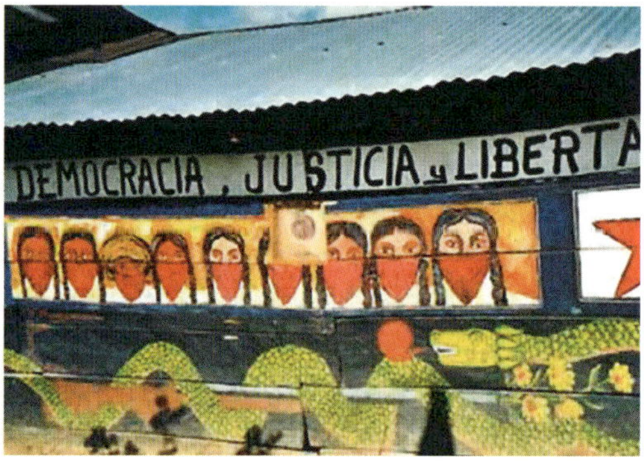

014

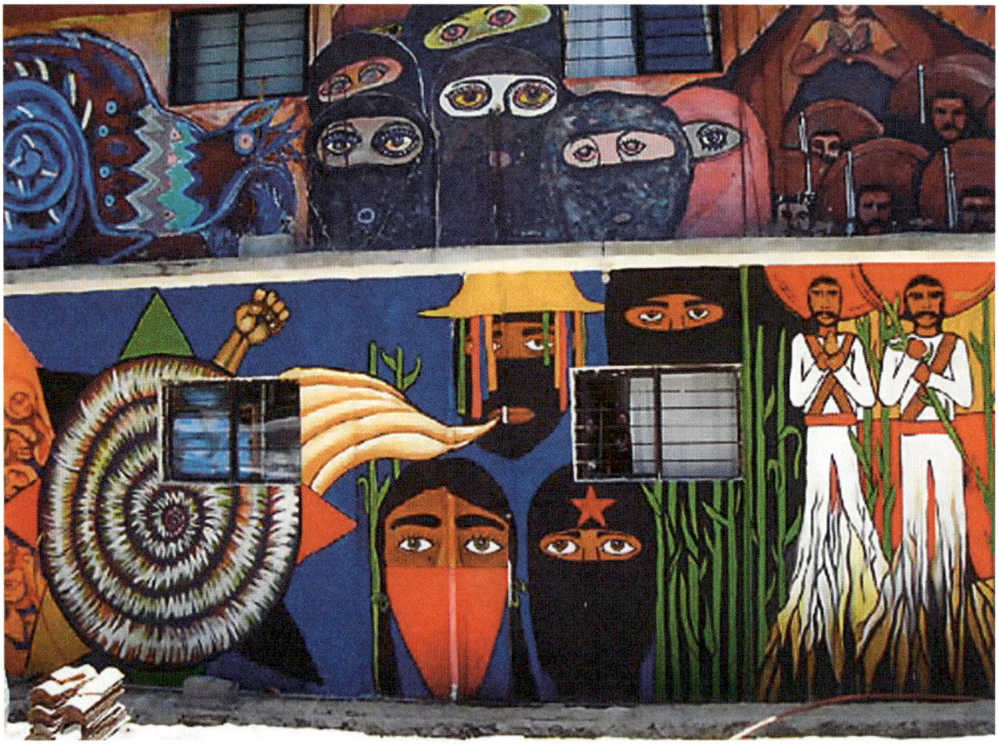

015
016

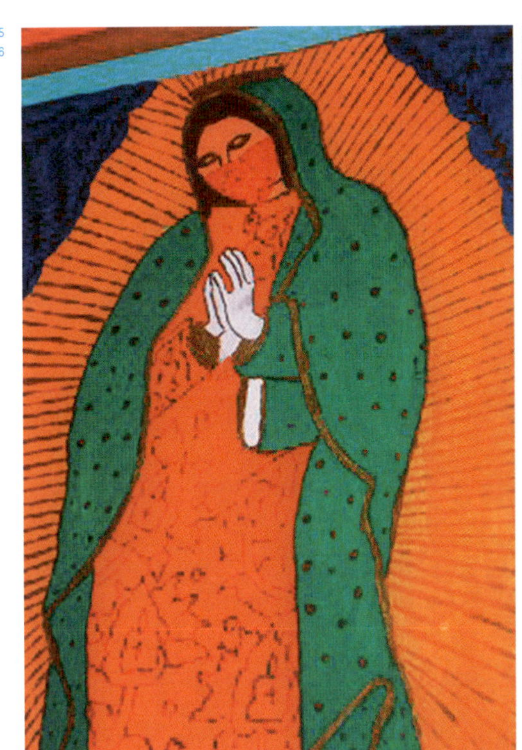

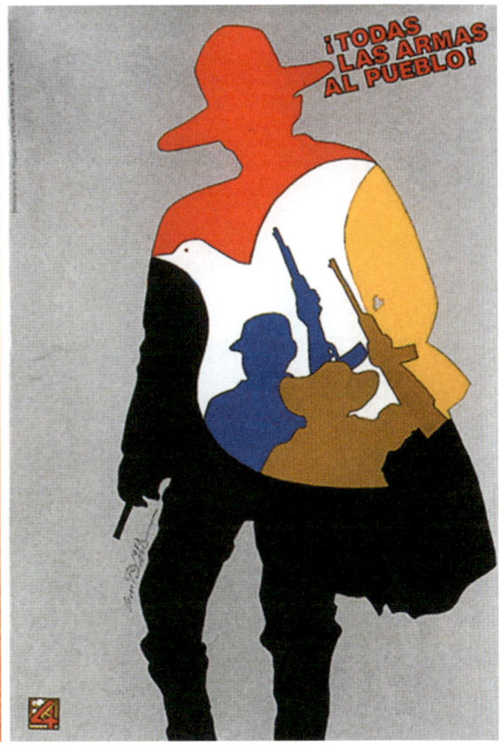

017

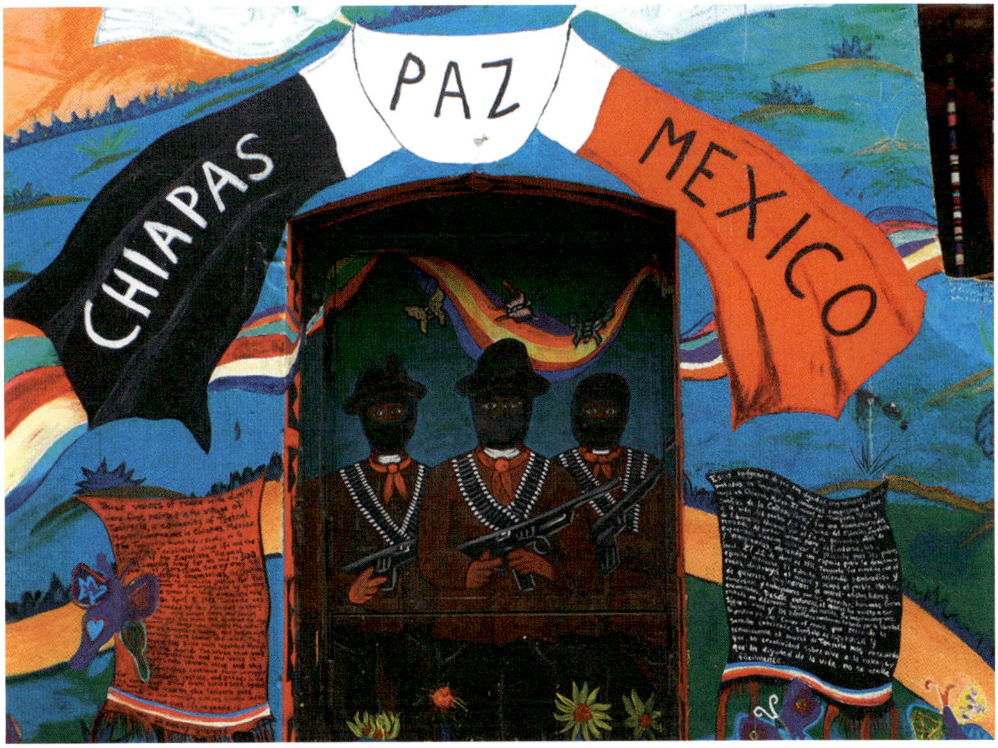

001 OTRO MUNDO ES POSIBLE
[ANOTHER WORLD IS POSSIBLE]
With naive images, the murals
of Chiapas depict the active
role of women in the fight
for education, and use slogans
such as: "Education through
revolution and with all our
hearts," and "In the independent
Zapatista schools, a collective
spirit of the world is conveyed
to the children. Our philosophy is
that humankind is a part
of nature."
CREATOR Maria de Cossio

002 JUSTICIA / LIBERTAD
[JUSTICE / FREEDOM]
CREATOR Maria de Cossio

003 AREA NATURAL PROTEGIDA
Y RESERVA ECOLOGICA
[PROTECTED AREA AND
ECOLOGICAL RESERVE]
CREATOR Maria de Cossio

004 NUESTRA EDUCACION NACE
DEL CORAZON
[OUR EDUCATION COMES FROM
THE HEART]
CREATOR Maria de Cossio

005 PARA CONSTRUIR UN MUNDO
[TO BUILD A WORLD]
CREATOR Maria de Cossio

006 EZLN
CREATOR Maria de Cossio

007 JOURNEY TO CHIAPAS, MEXICO
CREATOR Just Journey
SOURCE www.uusc.org

008 MEXICO INDIAN MASSACRE
CREATOR Eduardo Verdugo

009 NO HAY ARMA MAS EFICAZ QUE
LA VERDAD
[NO WEAPON MORE EFFECTIVE
THAN TRUTH]
CREATOR Maria de Cossio

010 CLINIC WITH PORTRAIT OF
CHE GUEVARA
CREATOR Maria de Cossio

011 ESCUELA PRIMARIA REBELDE
[REBEL PRIMARY SCHOOL]
CREATOR Maria de Cossio

012 MURAL OF WOMEN'S FACES
CREATOR Maria de Cossio

013 DEMOCRACIA, JUSTICIA Y LIBERTAD
[DEMOCRACY, JUSTICE, AND FREEDOM]
CREATOR Maria de Cossio

014 UNTITLED
CREATOR Maria de Cossio

016 UNTITLED
CREATOR Maria de Cossio

016 TODAS LAS ARMAS AL PUEBLO! — ALLE
WAFFEN DEM VOLK
[ALL WEAPONS TO THE PEOPLE!]
CREATOR Cim P. Davic
SOURCE Bruno Margadant and
Hans-Rudolf Lutz, *Hoffnung und
Widerstand: das 20 Jahrhundert
im Plakat der internationalen
Arbeiter- und Friedensbewegung*
(Zurich: Lutz, 1998).

017 ZAPATISTA MURAL
CREATOR Provided by donkeycart
SOURCE www.flickr.com/photos/
donkeycart/2602506443/

001

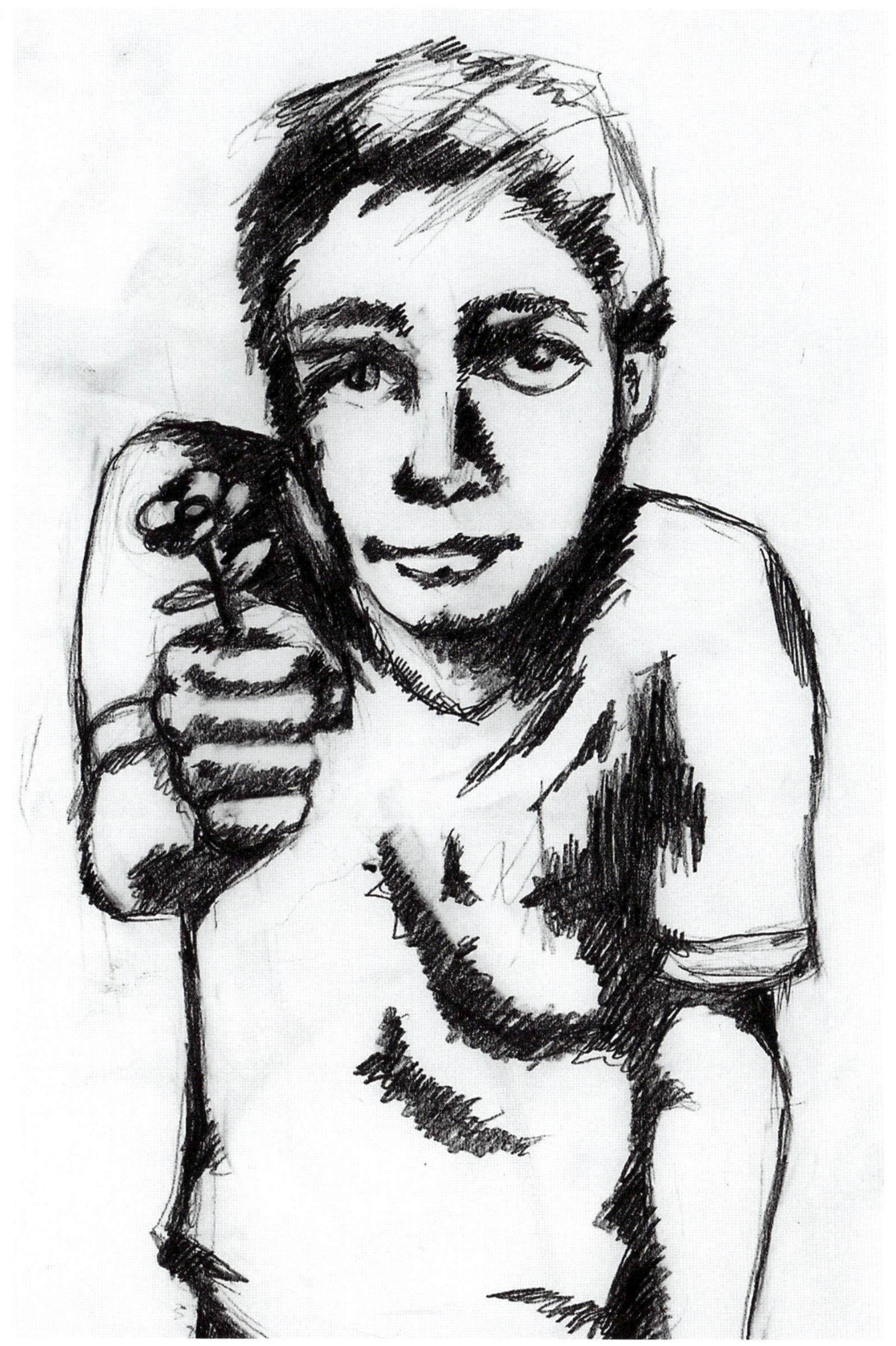

002
003

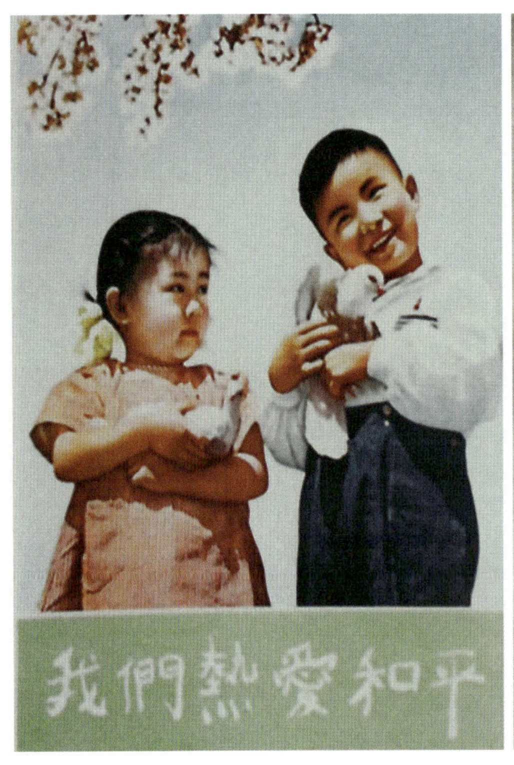

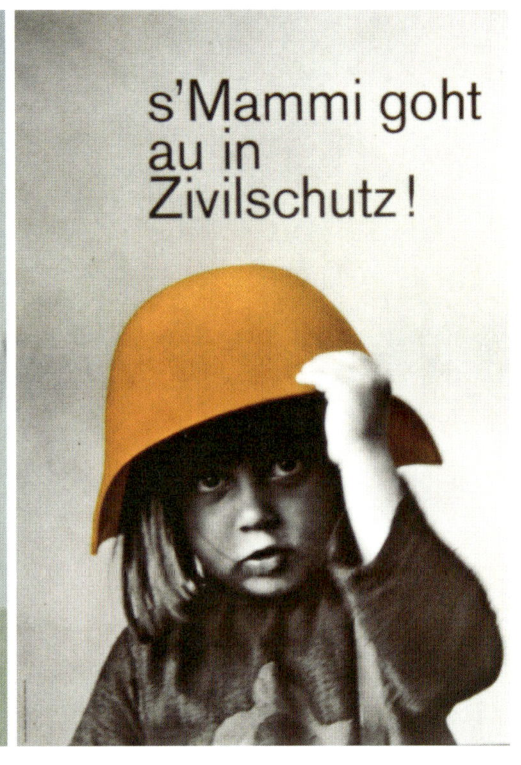

004
005

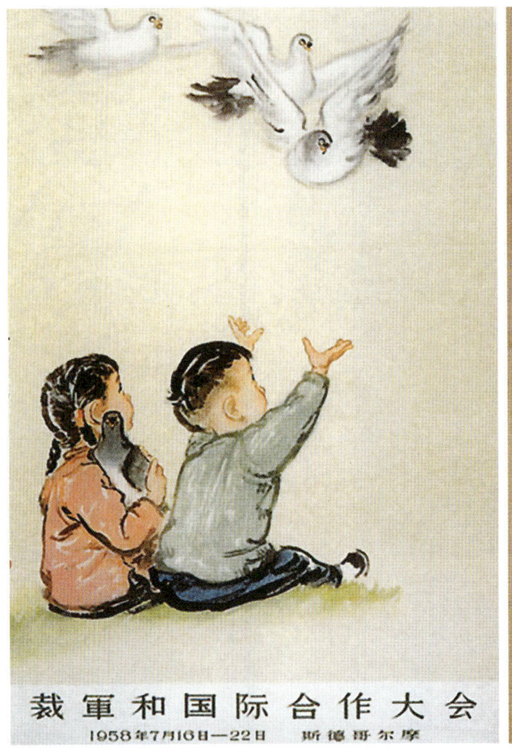

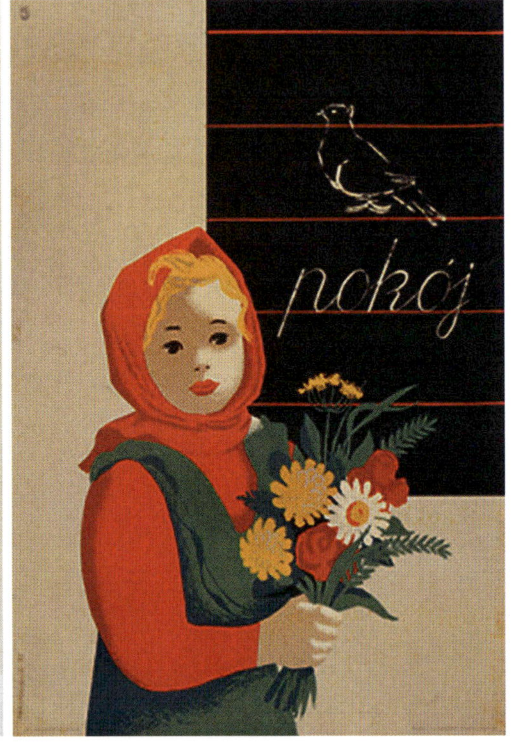

Why?

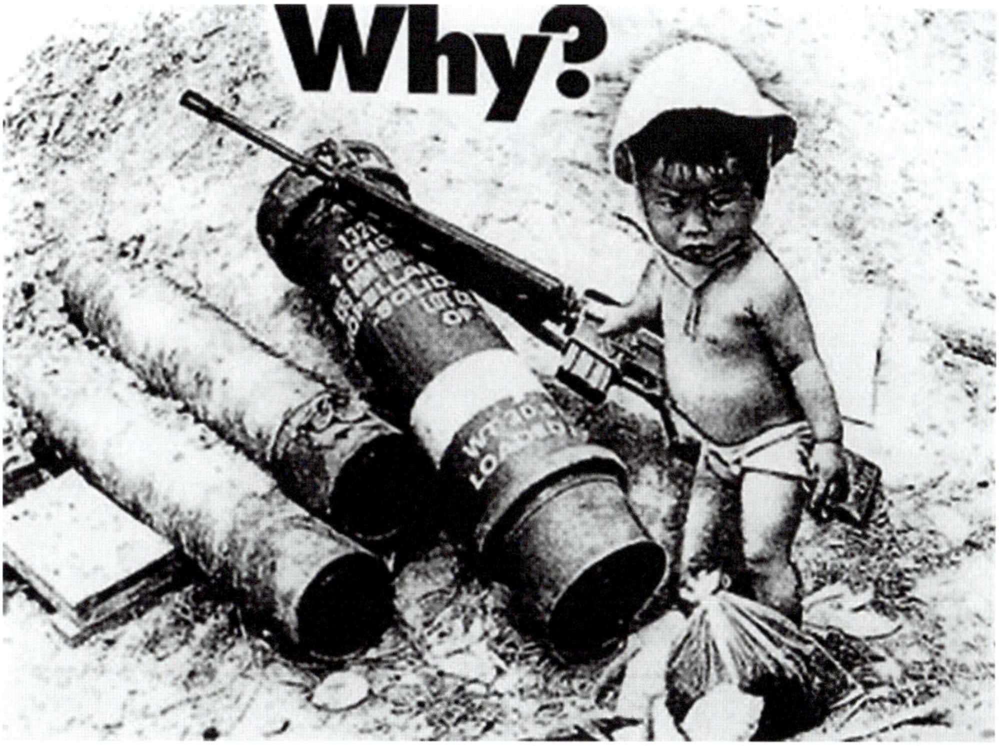

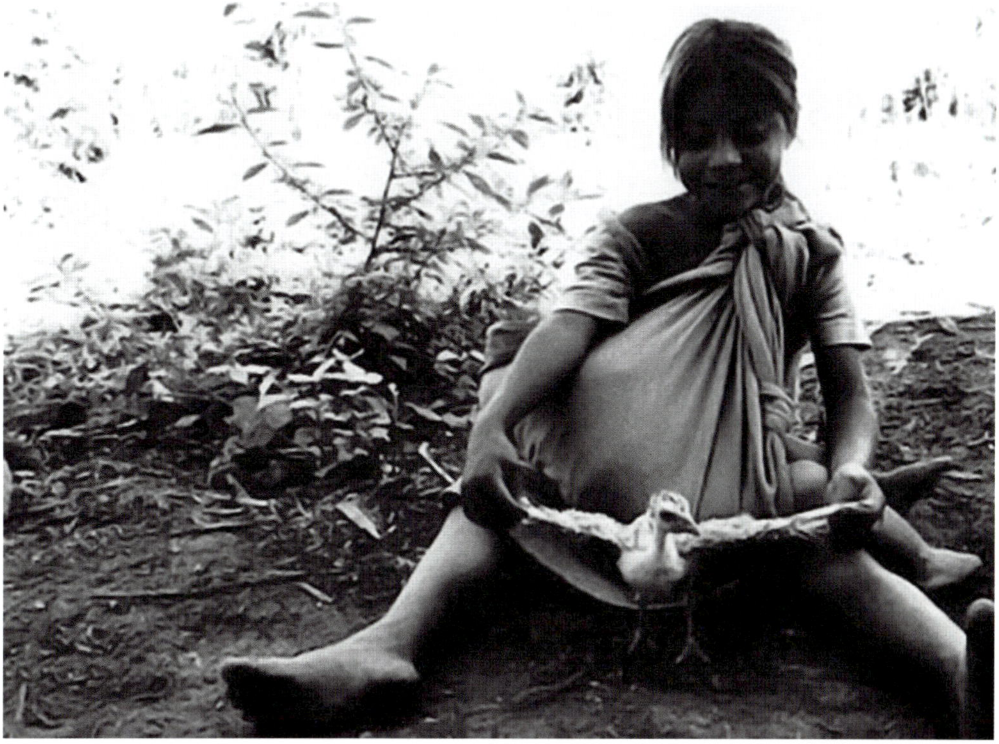

008

fête pour la paix
Appel des 100/19 juin 1983/Paris

009

Q. And babies?
A. And babies.

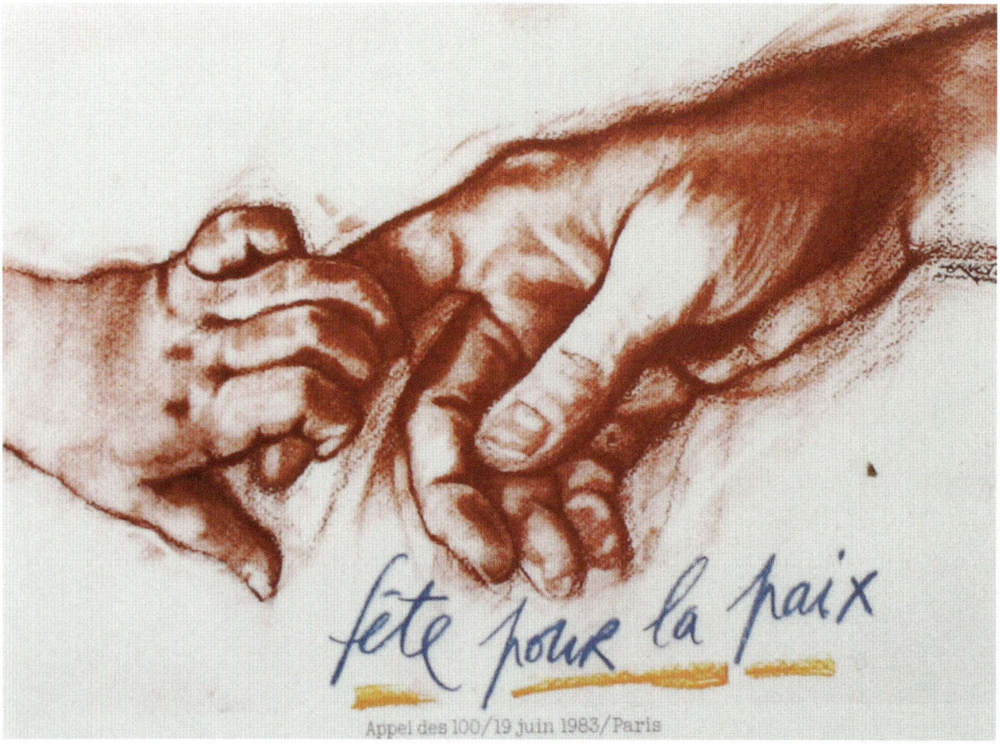

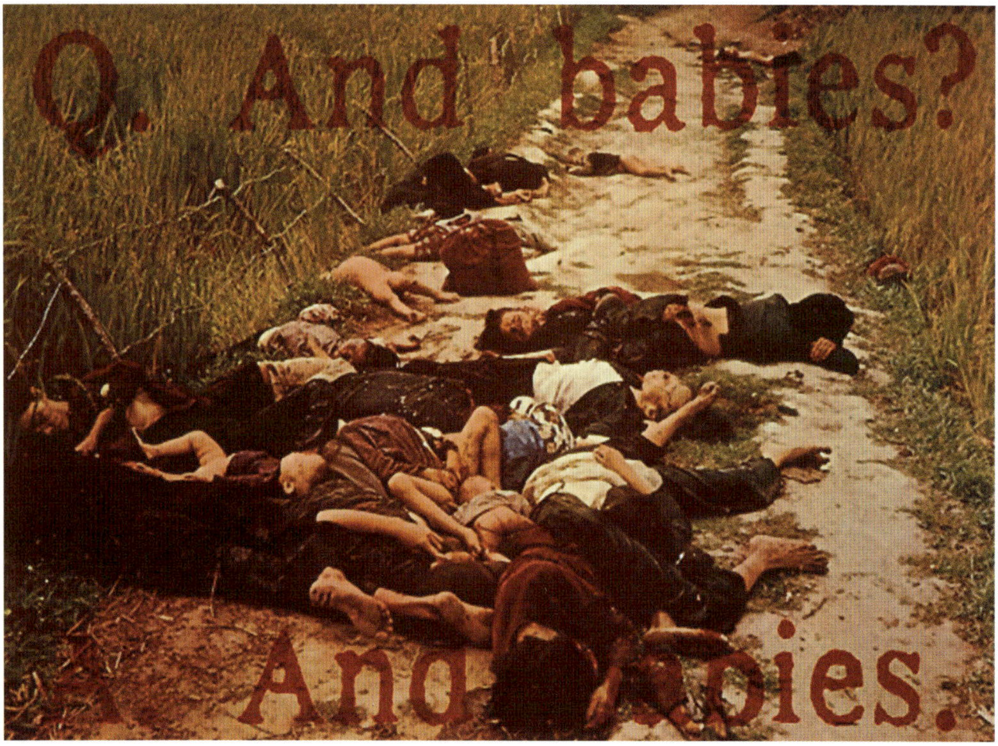

001   CREATOR Gerrit Wigger
      SOURCE Beiträge macht Bilder

002   WE LOVE PEACE ARDENTLY
      SOURCE Plakatsammlung Museum
      für Gestaltung Zürich

003   S'MAMMI GOHT AU IN ZIVILSCHUTZ
      [MY MOMMY IS ALSO IN THE CIVIL
      PROTECTION SERVICE]
      CREATOR Gerrit Wigger
      SOURCE Plakatsammlung Museum
      für Gestaltung Zürich

004   UNTITLED
      CREATOR Jiang Zhache
      SOURCE Bruno Margadant and
      Hans-Rudolf Lutz, *Hoffnung und
      Widerstand: das 20 Jahrhundert
      im Plakat der internationalen
      Arbeiter- und Friedensbewegung*
      [Zurich: Lutz, 1998].

005   POKOJ
      [PEACE]
      CREATOR Jozef Mroszczak
      SOURCE Plakatsammlung Museum
      für Gestaltung Zürich
      DATE 1951

006   WHY?
      CREATOR DPA
      SOURCE Plakatsammlung Museum
      für Gestaltung Zürich

007   UNTITLED
      CREATOR Samantha Dietmar
      SOURCE Beiträge macht Bilder

008   FÉTE POUR LA PAIX
      [PARTY FOR PEACE]
      CREATOR Ernest Ernest-Pignon
      SOURCE Plakatsammlung Museum
      für Gestaltung Zürich

009   Q. AND BABIES? — A. AND BABIES.
      CREATOR Peter Brandt
      SOURCE Plakatsammlung Museum
      für Gestaltung Zürich

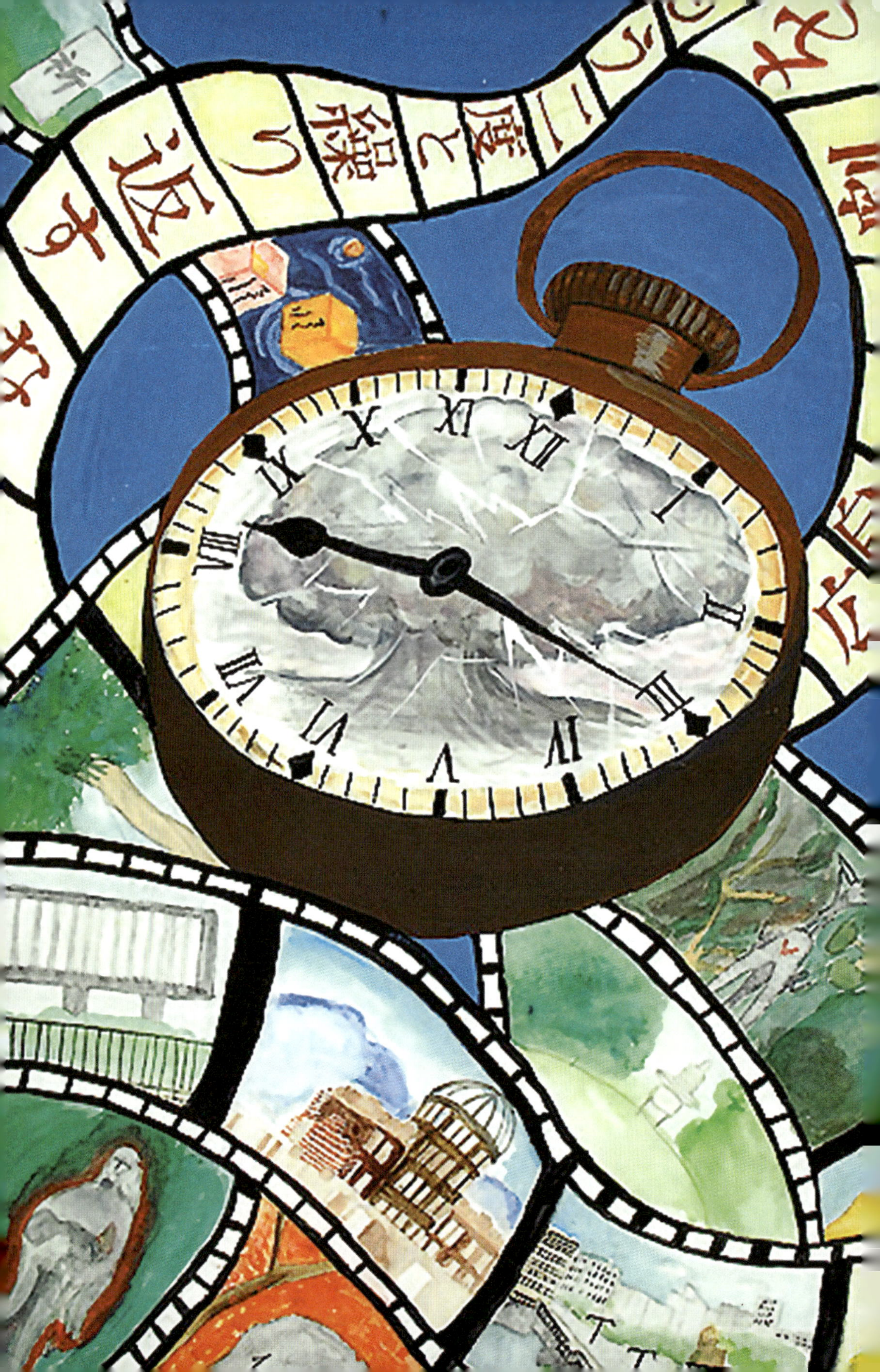

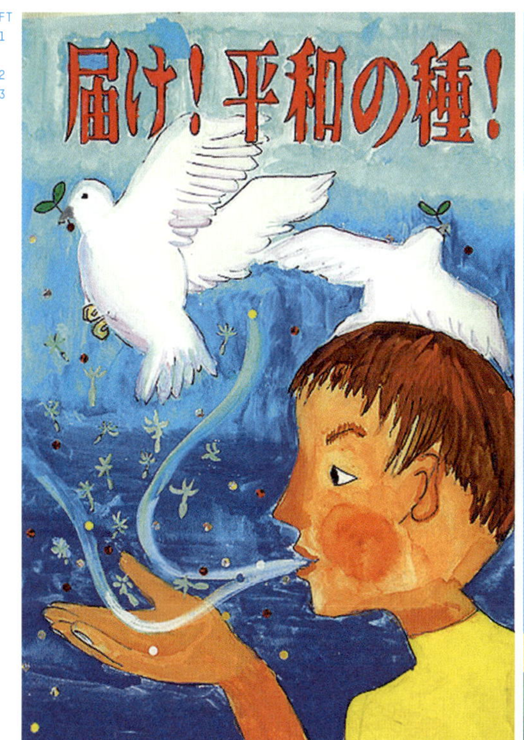
届け！平和の種！

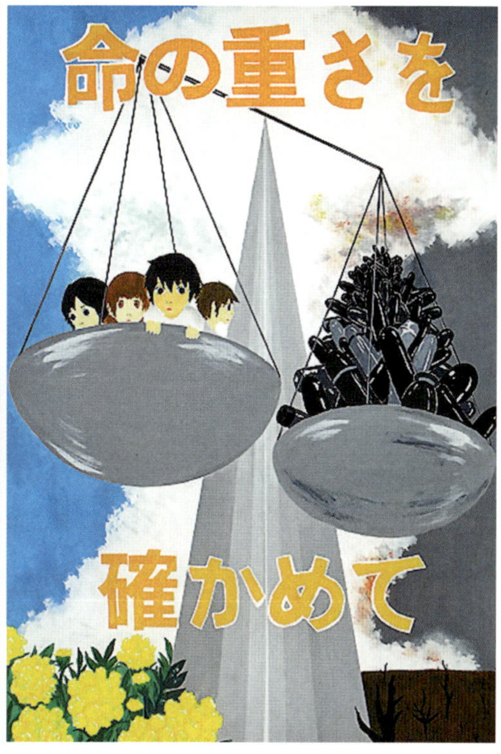
命の重さを
確かめて

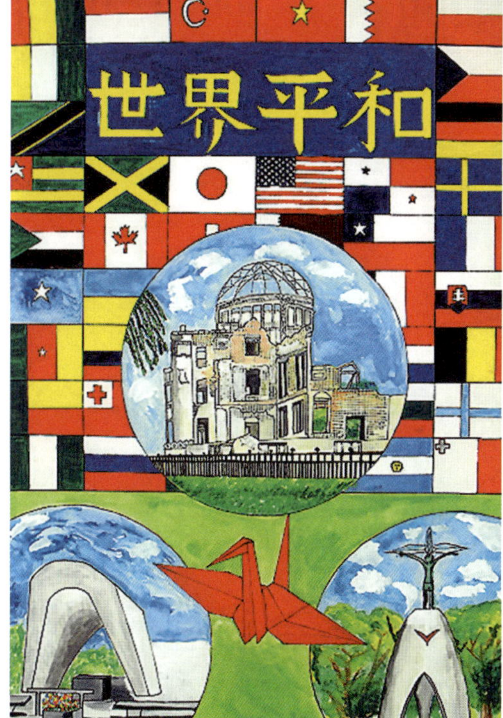
世界平和

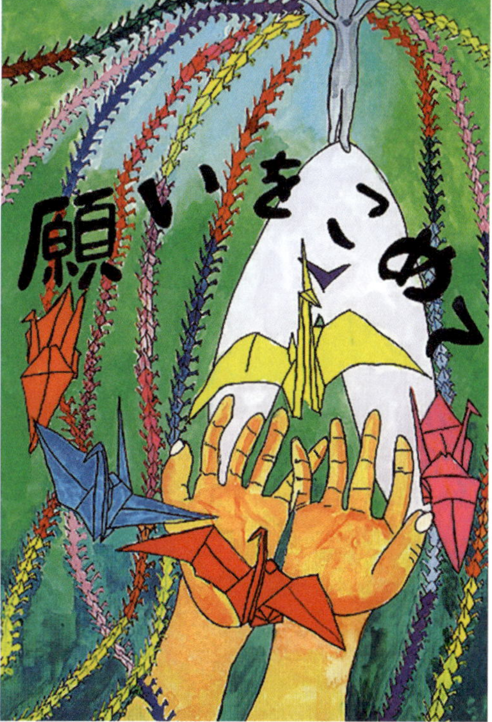
願いをこめて

006

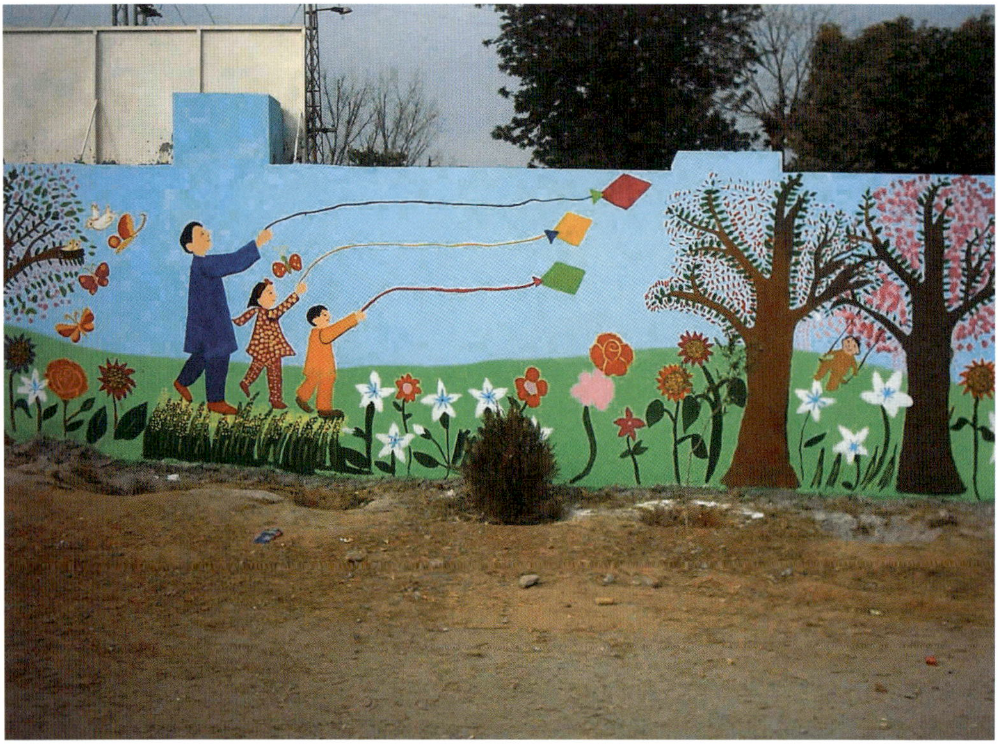

007

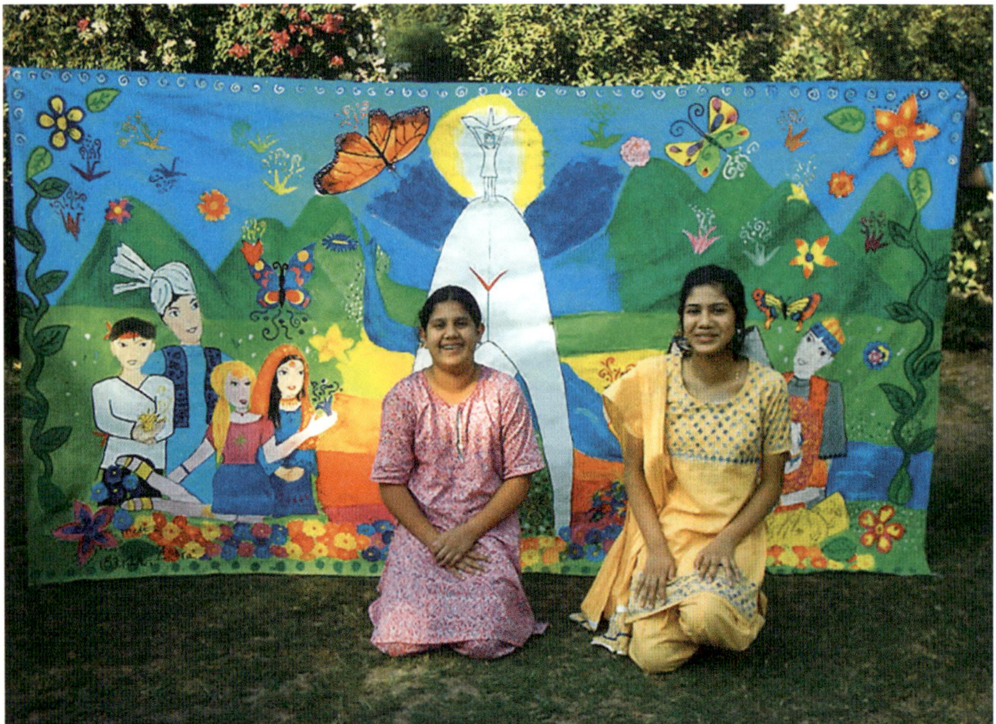

008
009

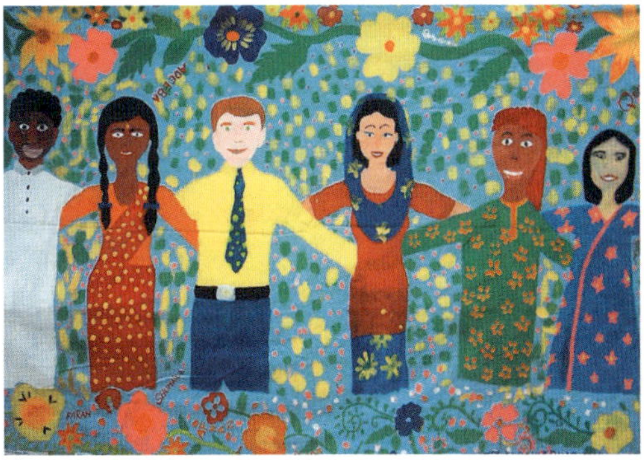

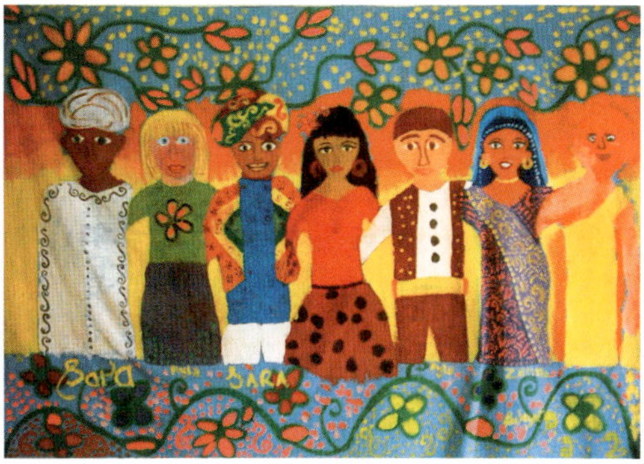

010
011

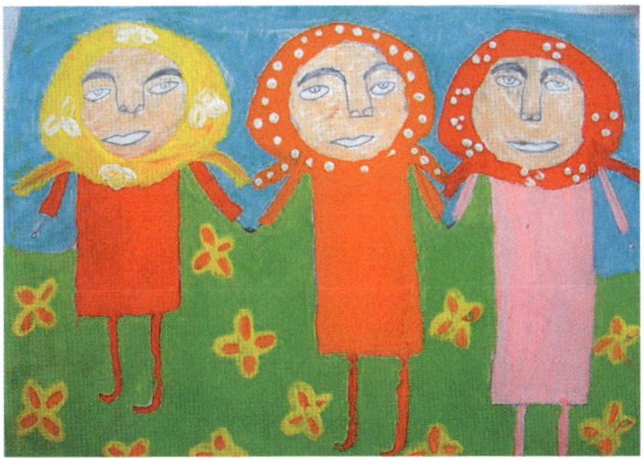

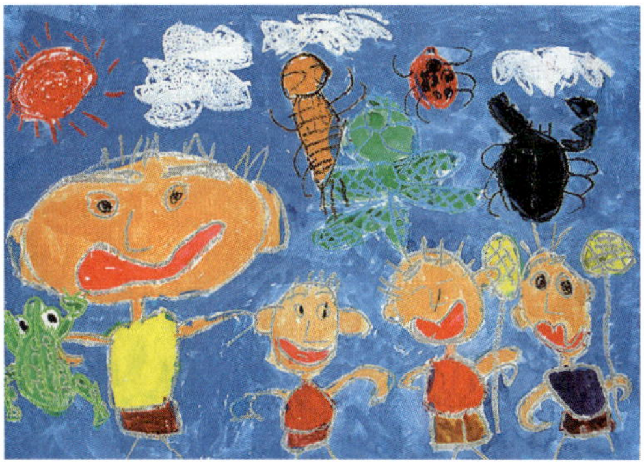

012
013

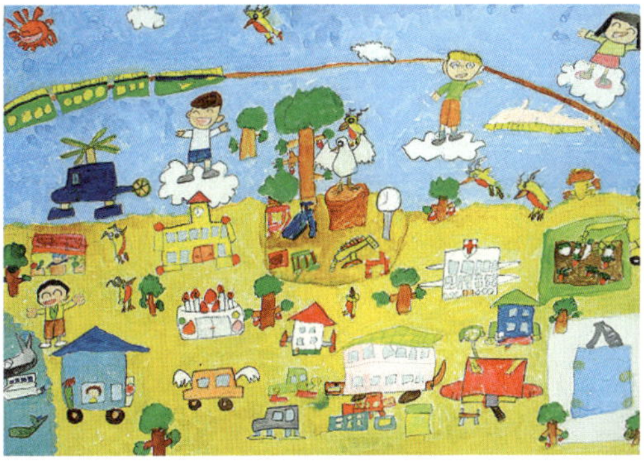

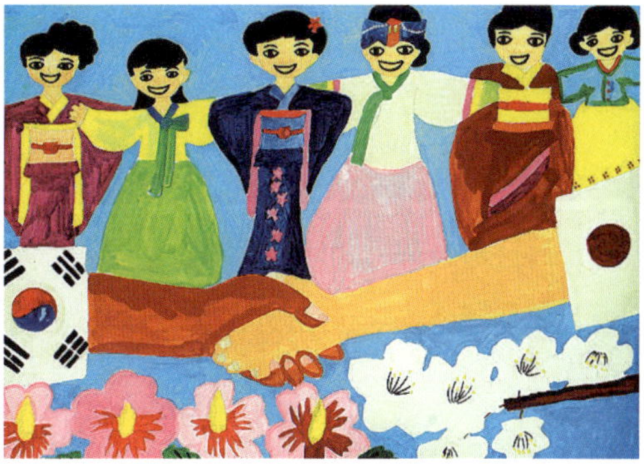

014
015

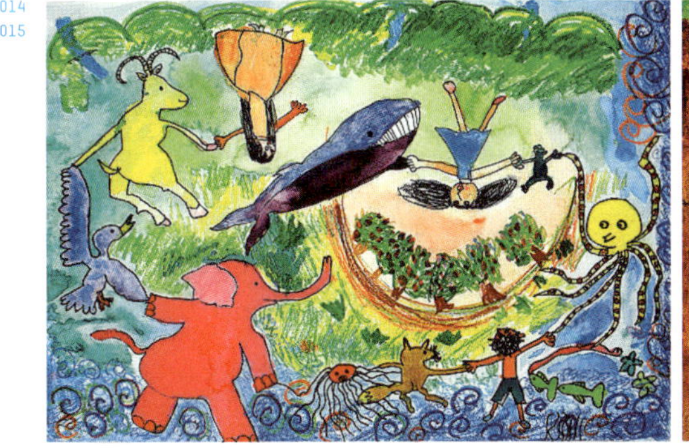

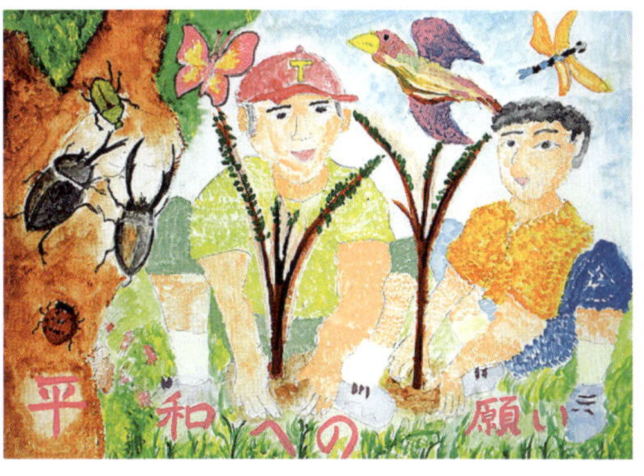

001 UNTITLED
Children's Peace Drawings Competition. This competition started
in 1986 as a commemoration of the
United Nations' International Year
of Peace. Every year we solicit
drawings on the theme of peace
from elementary and junior high
school students in Hiroshima City
as well as overseas.
CREATOR Komi Terada
SOURCE www.pcf.city.hiroshima.jp

002 UNTITLED
CREATOR Taiga Fukushima
SOURCE www.pcf.city.hiroshima.jp

003 UNTITLED
CREATOR Tsuaki Sato
SOURCE www.pcf.city.hiroshima.jp

004 UNTITLED
CREATOR Hiroe Taura
SOURCE www.pcf.city.hiroshima.jp

005 UNTITLED
CREATOR Sakura Yamamoto
SOURCE www.pcf.city.hiroshima.jp

000 SEASONS
Two-hundred-foot-long mural
painted on the walls of the
school by students.
SOURCE www.funkorchildart.com

007 PEACE
Sara Khan [11] and Zehra Khan [13].
CREATOR Hiroe Taura
SOURCE www.pcf.city.hiroshima.jp

008 MULTICULTURAL HARMONY
Shalamar School for Hearing
Impaired, Lahore.
SOURCE www.funkorchildart.com

009 MULTICULTURAL HARMONY
Sara [10], Zehra [12], Ayla [11].
SOURCE www.funkorchildart.com

010 UNTITLED
CREATOR Sumaira Bibi
SOURCE www.funkorchildart.com

011 UNTITLED
CREATOR Naoki Murata
SOURCE www.pcf.city.hiroshima.jp

012 UNTITLED
CREATOR Ryohei Kaneshina
SOURCE www.pcf.city.hiroshima.jp

013 UNTITLED
CREATOR Park Ji Eun
SOURCE www.pcf.city.hiroshima.jp

014 UNTITLED
CREATOR Mio Takinami
SOURCE www.pcf.city.hiroshima.jp

015 UNTITLED
CREATOR Keisuke Tomotaki
SOURCE www.pcf.city.hiroshima.jp

001
002

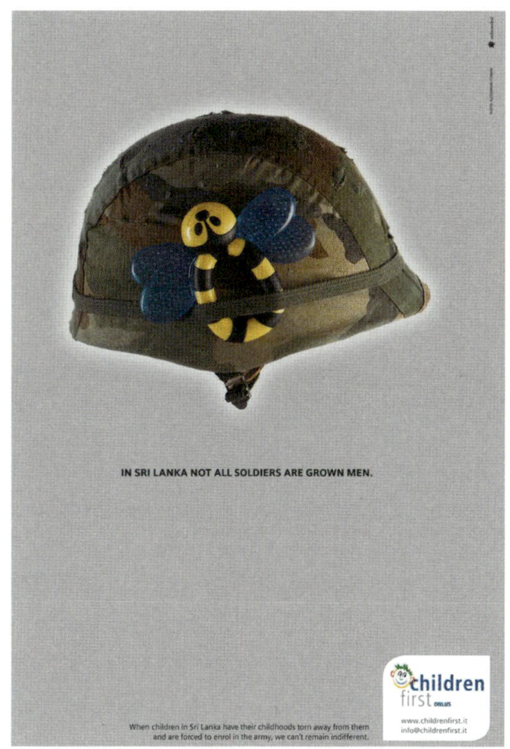

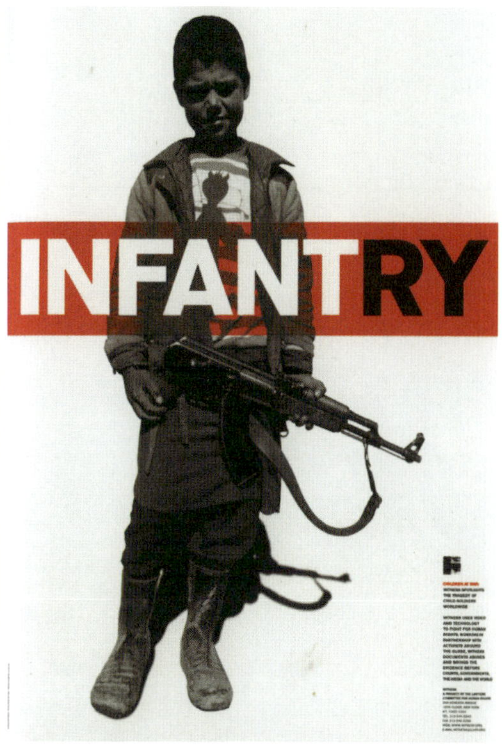

003
004

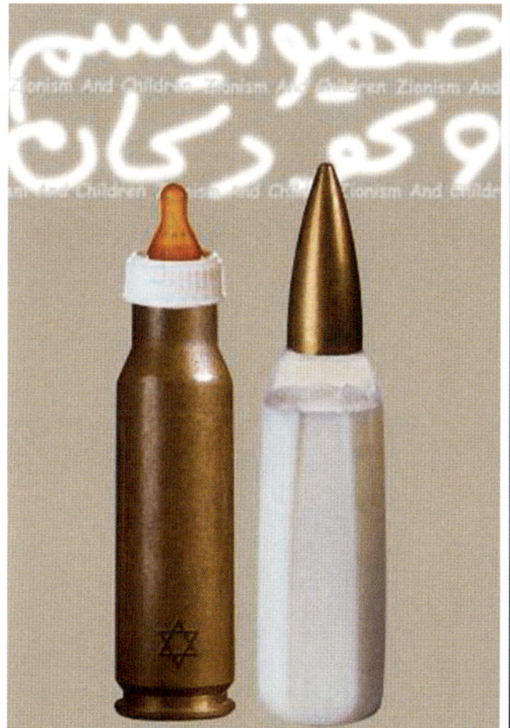

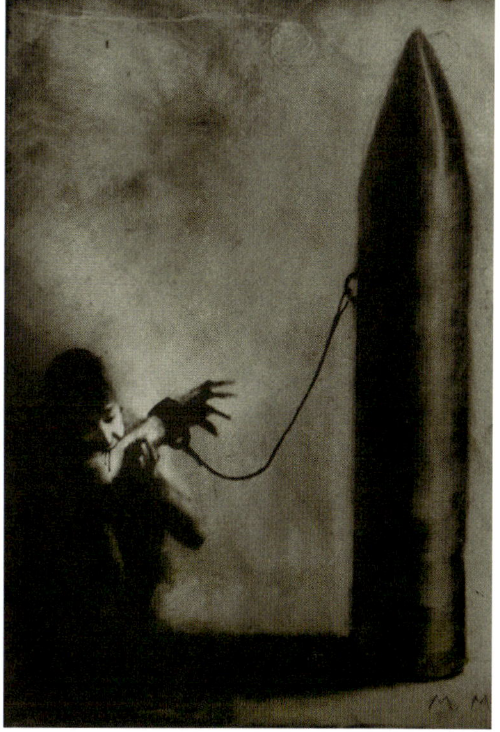

005
006

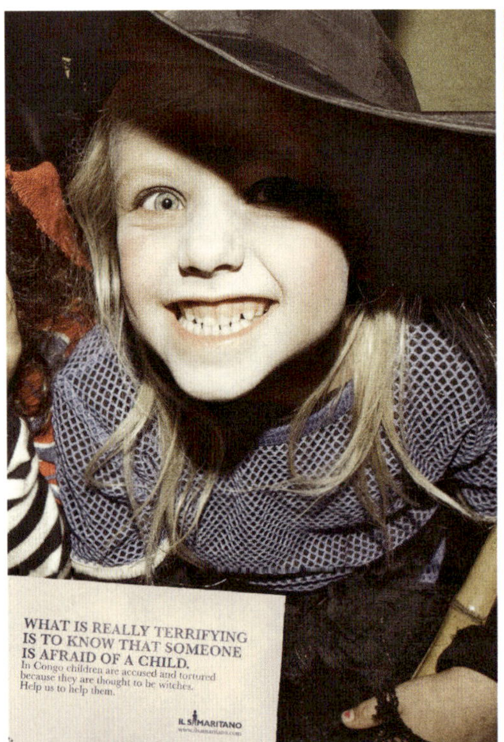

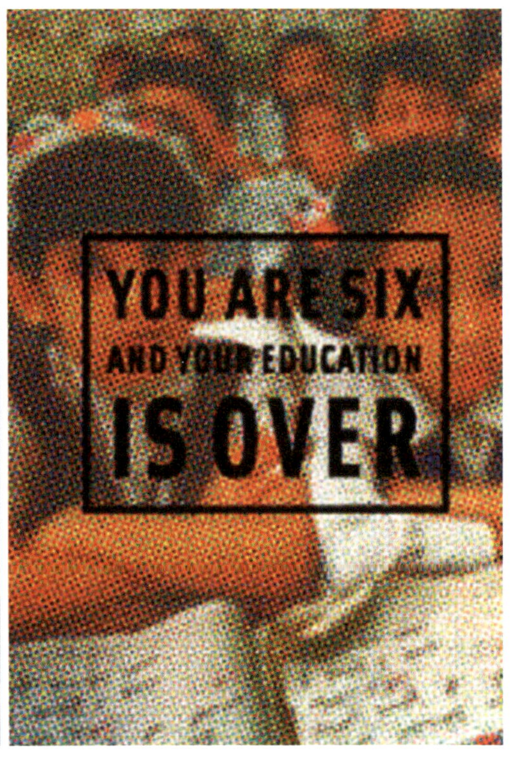

007
008

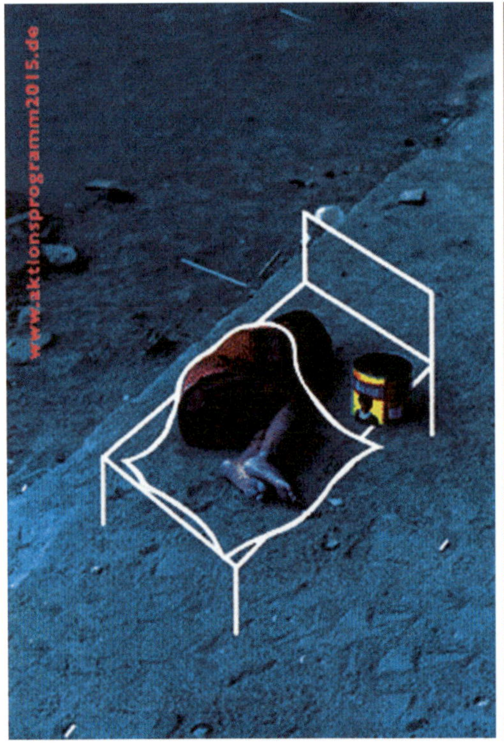

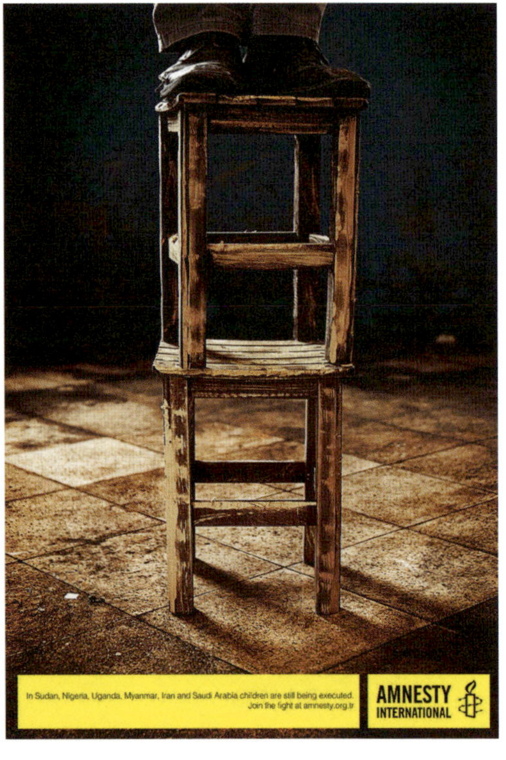

009
010

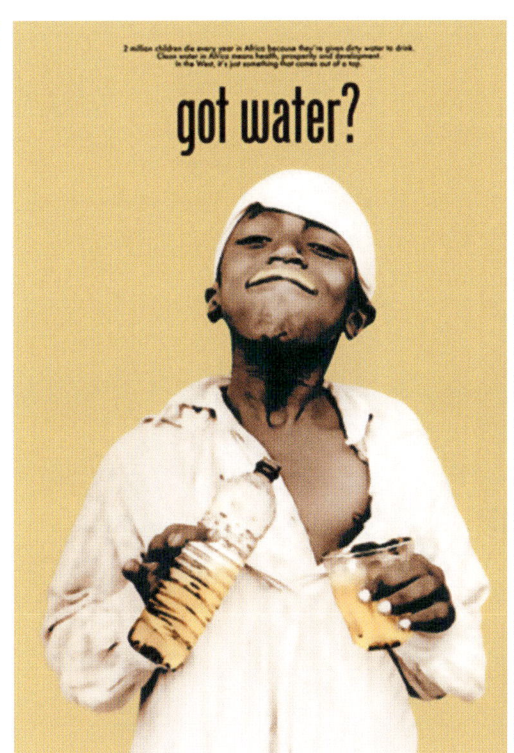

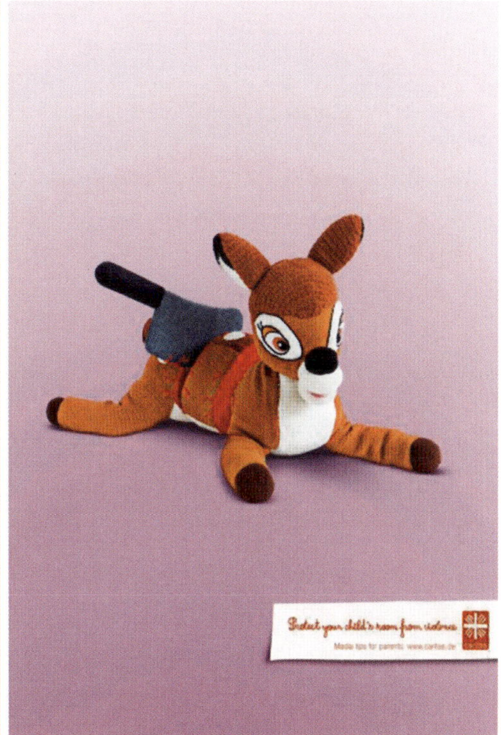

011

NEXT
012

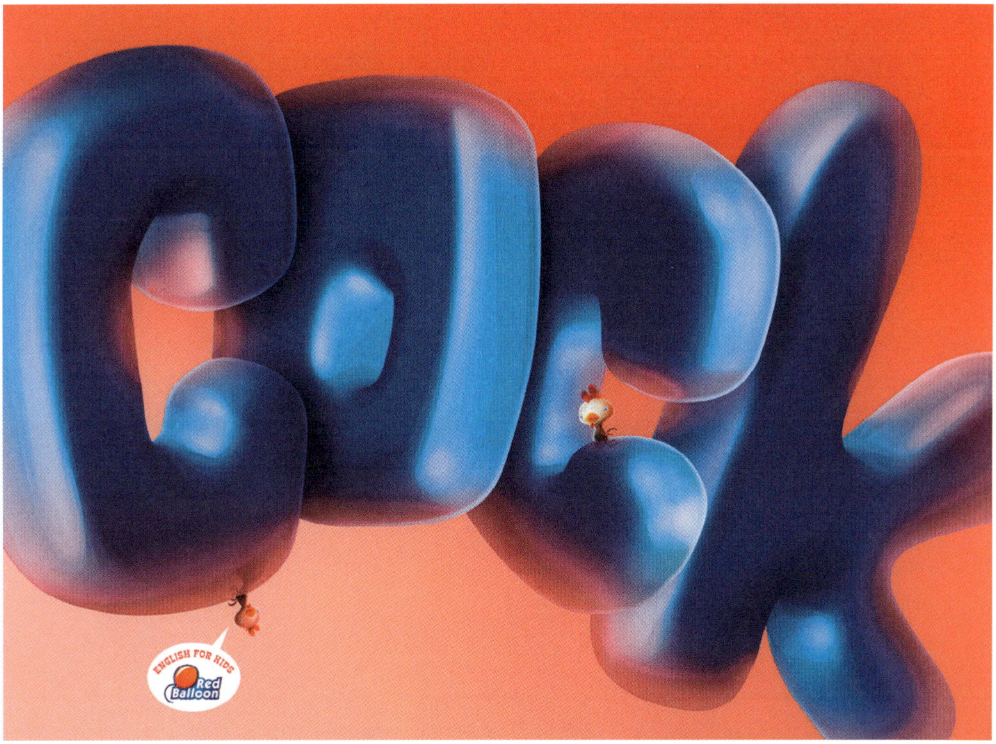

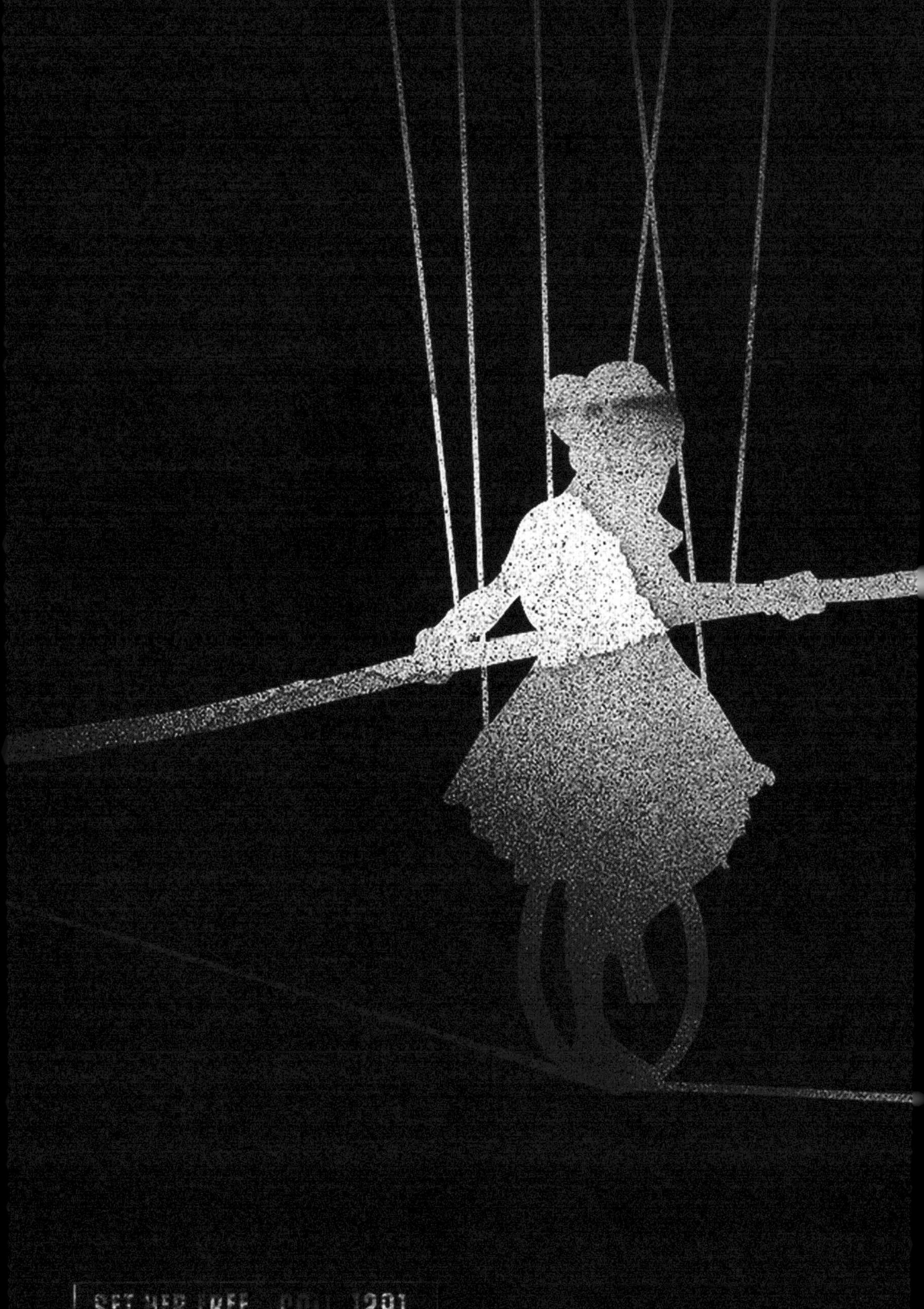

SET HER FREE - CALL 1291
A DELHI POLICE INITIATIVE TO ABOLISH CHILD ABUSE

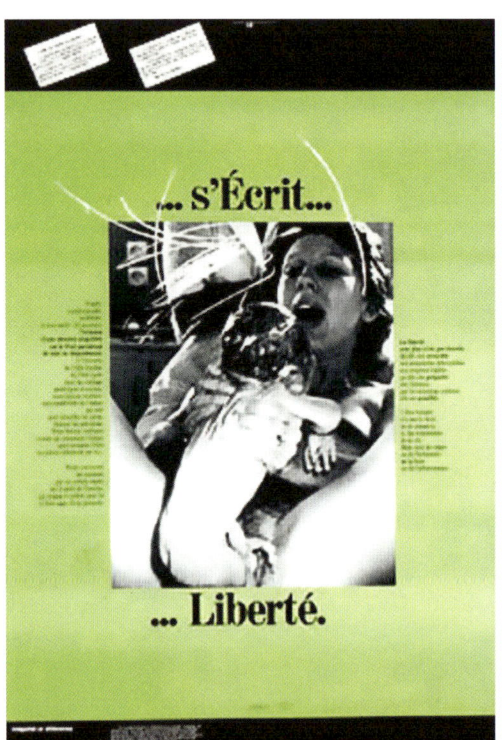
... s'Écrit...
... Liberté.

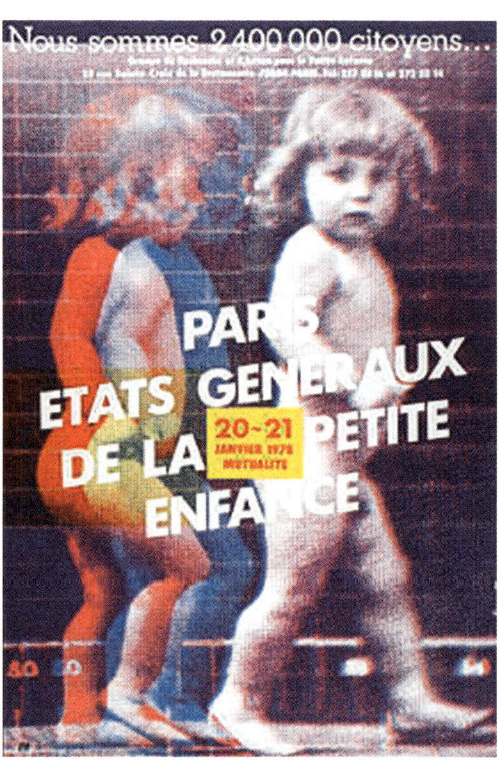
Nous sommes 2 400 000 citoyens...
PARIS
ETATS GENERAUX
DE LA PETITE
ENFANCE
20~21
JANVIER 1978
MUTUALITE

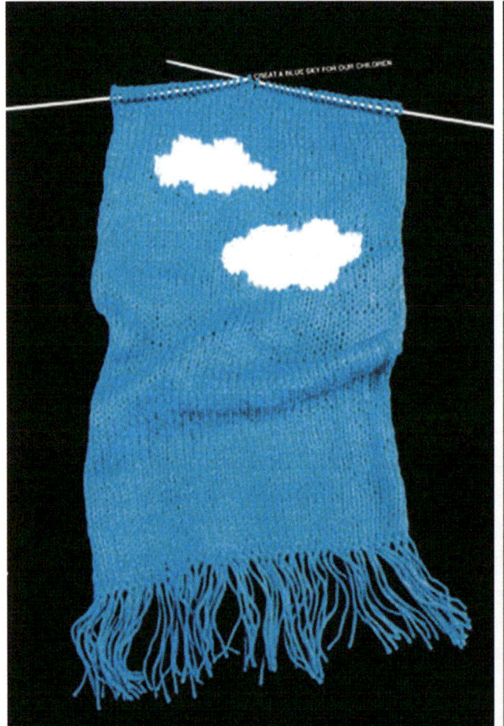
CREAT A BLUE SKY FOR OUR CHILDREN

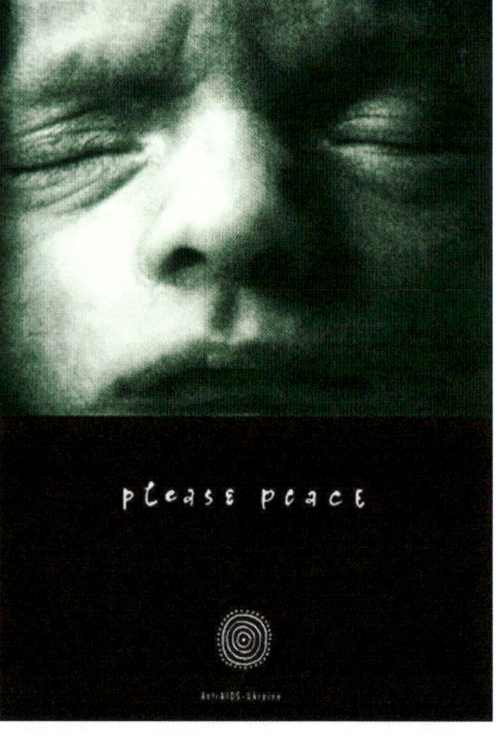
please peace

017
018

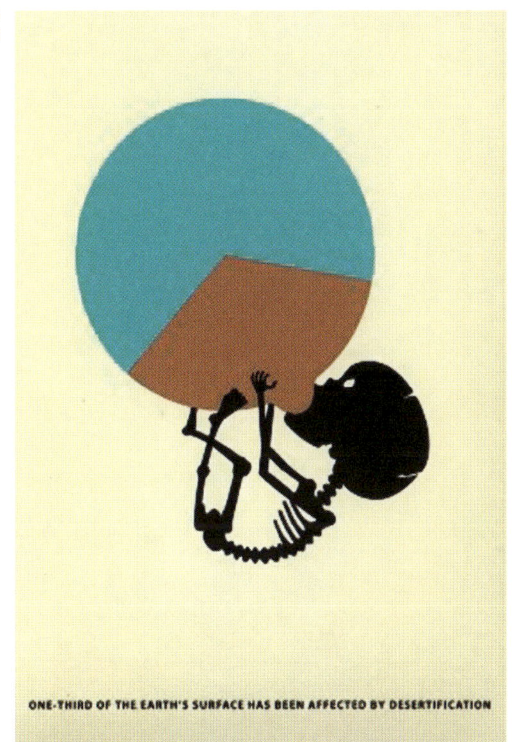

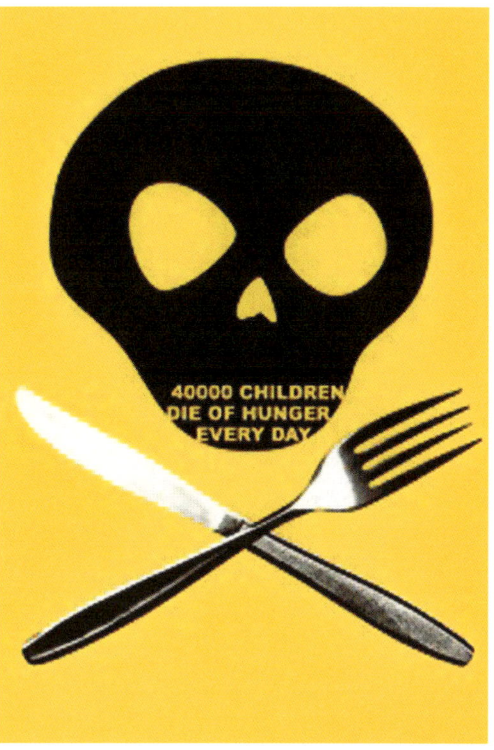

019
020

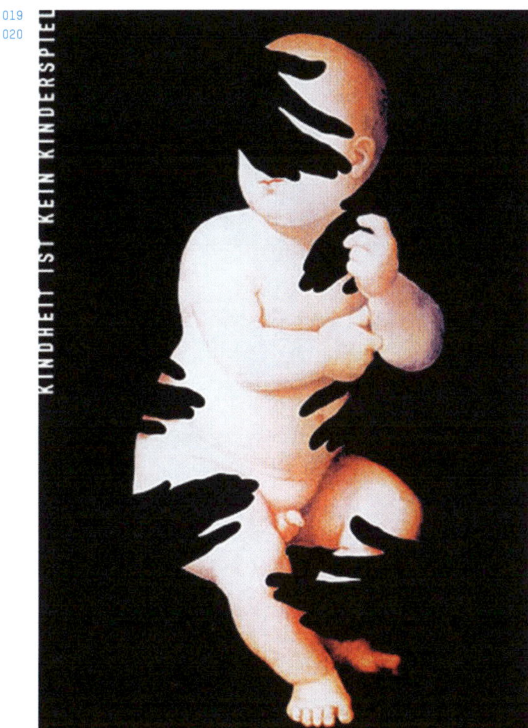

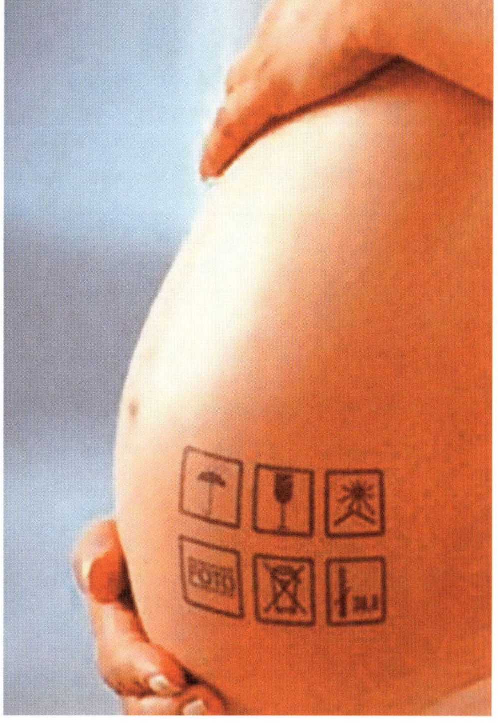

021
022

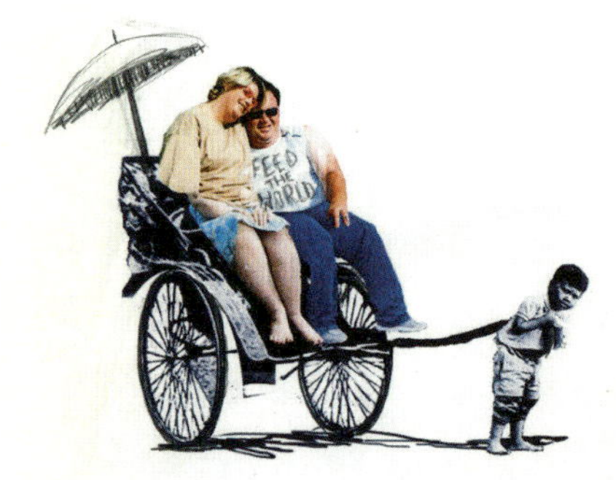

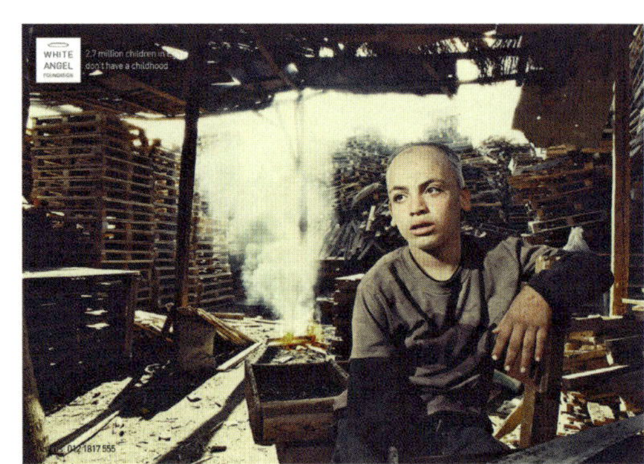

023
024

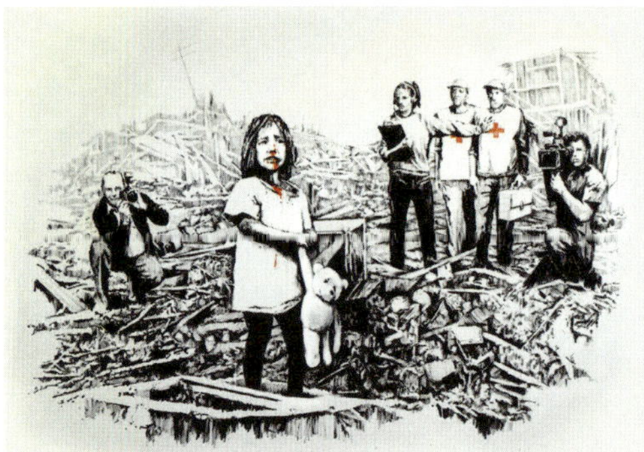

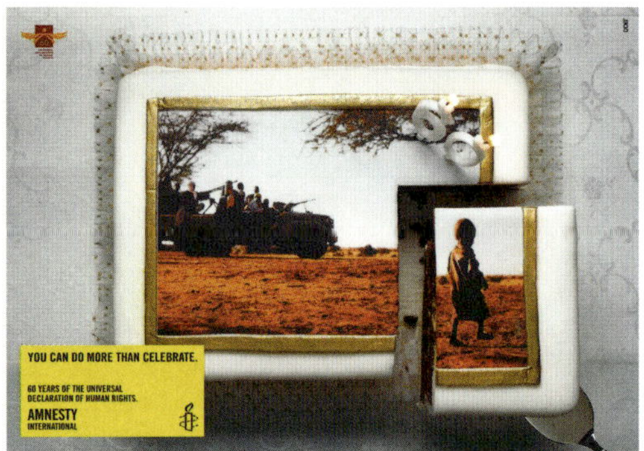

025

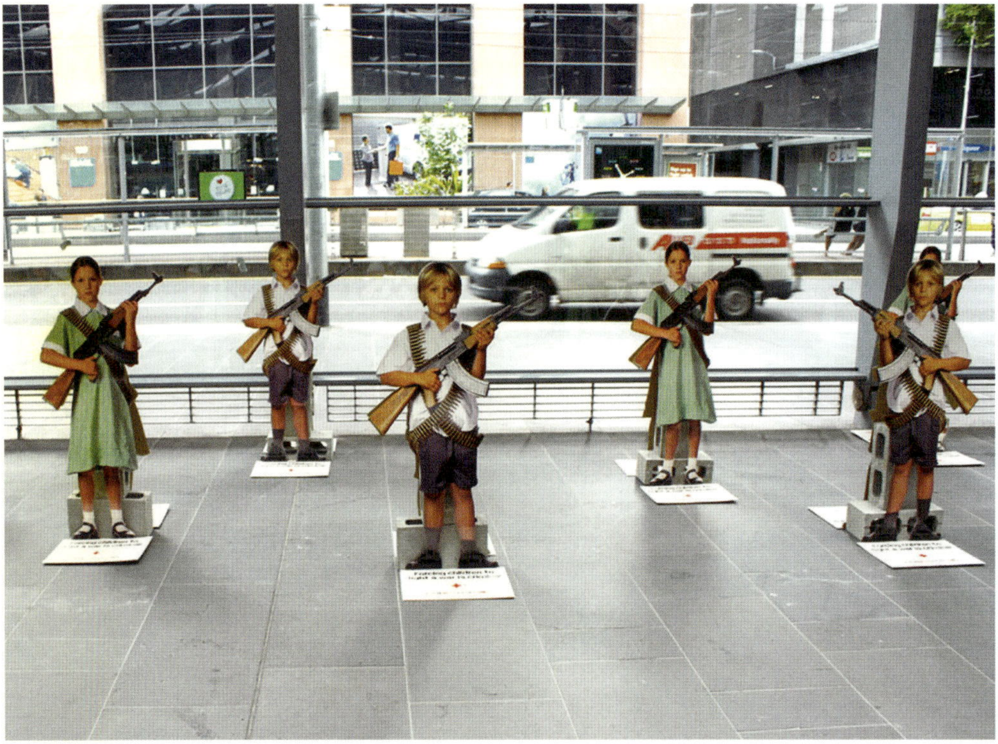

001 IN SRI LANKA NOT ALL SOLDIERS
ARE GROWN MEN
CREATOR Childrenfirst.it
SOURCE Unknown

002 INFANTRY
CREATOR Andy Mosley, Harry Pearce,
Lippa Pearce
SOURCE Steven Heller and Carol
Wells, eds., *The Graphic Imperative:
International Posters for Peace,
Social Justice, and the Environment,
1965-2005* [Boston: Massachusetts
College of Arts, 2005], p. 33.

003 ZIONISM AND CHILDREN
CREATOR Maysam-khazaei
SOURCE good50x70.org

004 FEAR OF NUCLEAR WAR
CREATOR Matt Mahurin
SOURCE 11oz.com

005 CHILD WITCHES
What is really terrifying is to
know that someone is afraid of a
child. In the Congo children are
accused and tortured because they
are thought to be witches. Help
us to help them.
CREATOR Il Samaritano, Italy
SOURCE www.coloribus.com

006 CHILDREN'S RIGHTS CAMPAIGN
The Convention of the Rights of
the Child [CRC], an international
treaty to protect the rights of
children throughout the world, was
adopted by the UN General Assembly
in 1989. Within ten years, 191
countries had ratified this treaty,
making it the most widely ratified
human rights instrument in history.
CREATOR Grapus
SOURCE earthaction.org
DATE 2001-2003

007 UNTITLED
CREATOR Markus Gröpl
SOURCE www.aktionsprogramm2015.de

008 IN SUDAN, NIGERIA, UGANDA, MYANMAR,
IRAN AND SAUDI ARABIA CHILDREN
ARE STILL BEING EXECUTED
CREATOR TBWA / Istanbul, Turkey
SOURCE www.ibelieveinadv.com

009 GOT WATER?
CREATOR Andrea Lo Vetere
SOURCE ww.logorevue.sk

010 PROTECT YOUR CHILD'S ROOM
FROM VIOLENCE
CREATOR BBDO, Düsseldorf
SOURCE www.ibelieveinadv.com

011 ENGLISH FOR KIDS
CREATOR Ogilvy, Sao Paulo
SOURCE www.ibelieveinadv.com

012 SET HIM/HER FREE. CALL 1291.
A DELHI POLICE INITIATIVE TO
ABOLISH CHILD LABOUR
CREATOR Rediffusion Y&R,
Gurgaon, India
SOURCE www.ibelieveinadv.com
DATE 2009

013 S'ÉCRIT ... LIBERTÉ
[SPELL ... FREEDOM]
CREATOR Grapus
SOURCE www.aubervilliers.fr

014 NOUS SOMMES 2,400,000 CITOYENS...
[WE ARE 2.4 MILLION CITIZENS]
CREATOR Grapus
SOURCE www.aubervilliers.fr

015 LET'S CREATE A BLUE SKY FOR
OUR CHILDREN
The 100th anniversary of Sadeq
Hedayat's birthday.
CREATOR Firouz Shafei
SOURCE www.tehran-poster-biennial.
com

016 PLEASE PEACE
CREATOR Marita Herold
SOURCE www.logorevue.sk

017 ONE THIRD OF THE EARTH'S
SURFACE HAS BEEN AFFECTED
BY DESERTIFICATION
CREATOR Lourdes Zolezzi
SOURCE www.posterpage.ch
DATE 2000

018 400,000 CHILDREN DIE OF HUNGER
CREATOR Lourdes Zolezzi
SOURCE www.posterpage.ch
DATE 2000

019 CHILDHOOD IS NOT CHILD'S PLAY
The Essen Poster Museum in Germany
organized an international competition advocating for the protection
of children in general, and against
pedophilia in particular.
CREATOR Alain Le Quernec
SOURCE good50x70
DATE 1998

020 UNTITLED
CREATOR Yvgeny Šilin
SOURCE www.logorevue.sk

021 FEED THE WORLD 2
CREATOR Banksy
SOURCE www.banksy.co.uk

022 2.7 MILLION CHILDREN IN EGYPT
DON'T HAVE A CHILDHOOD
CREATOR White Angel Foundation,
TBWA / Egypt
SOURCE www.coloribus.com

023 MEDIA
CREATOR Banksy
SOURCE www.banksy.co.uk

024 YOU CAN DO MORE THAN CELEBRATE
CREATOR DDB, Budapest, Hungary
SOURCE www.ibelieveinadv.com

025 FORCING CHILDREN TO FIGHT IN WAR
IS CRIMINAL
Red Cross Australia recently
hit the news with a series of
ambient installations designed
to raise public awareness of the
international laws relating to
torture, landmines, and child
soldiers. The Geneva Conventions
aim to limit suffering and
protect the vulnerable during
times of armed conflict. While
they are not always followed,
these laws of war continue to
save lives: of civilians including children, humanitarian
workers and journalists, as well
as the captured and wounded.
CREATOR Red Cross Australia,
The Fuel Agency
SOURCE theinspirationroom.com

001
002
003
004
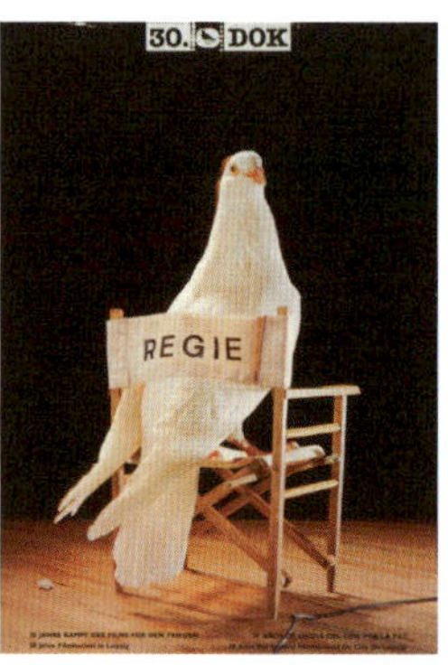
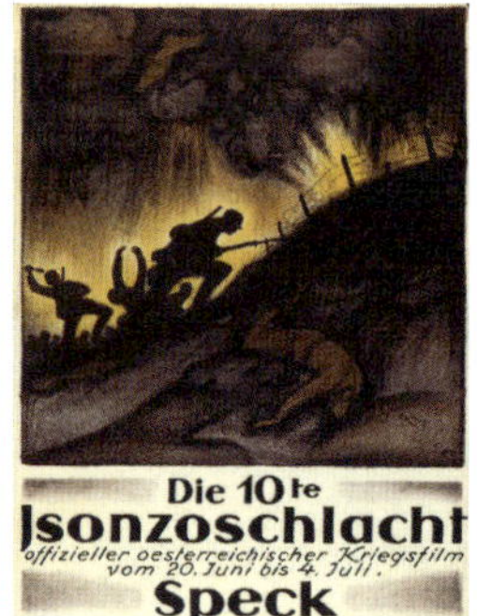
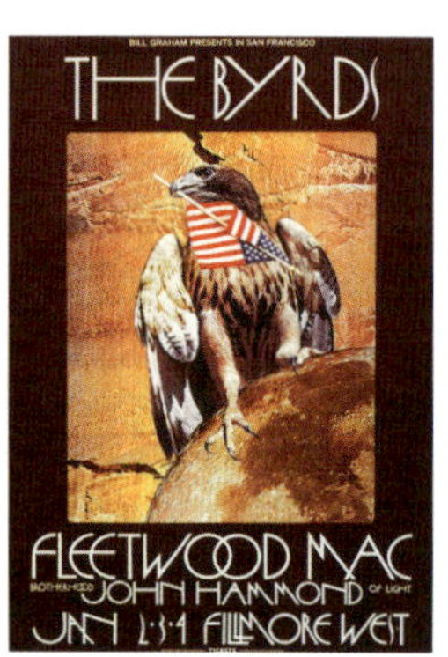

005
006
007
008
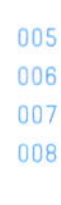
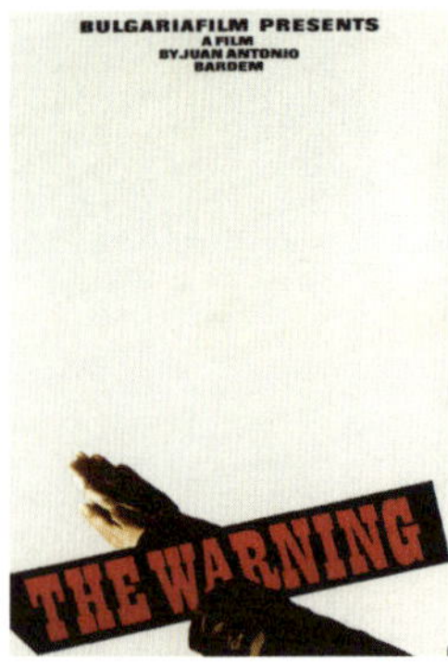
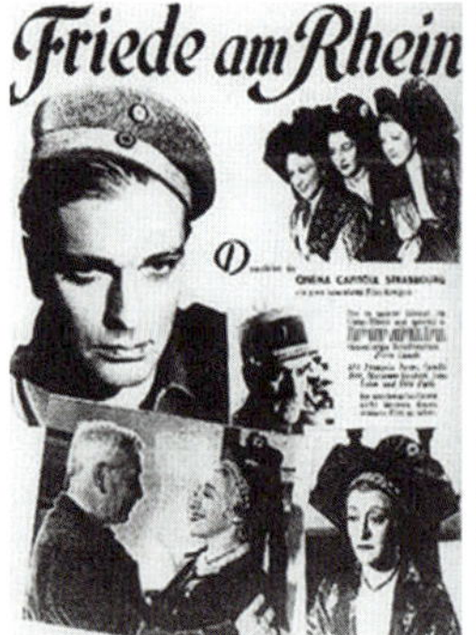
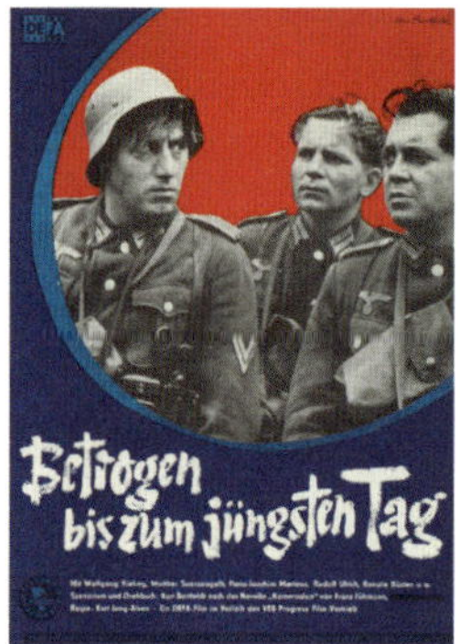
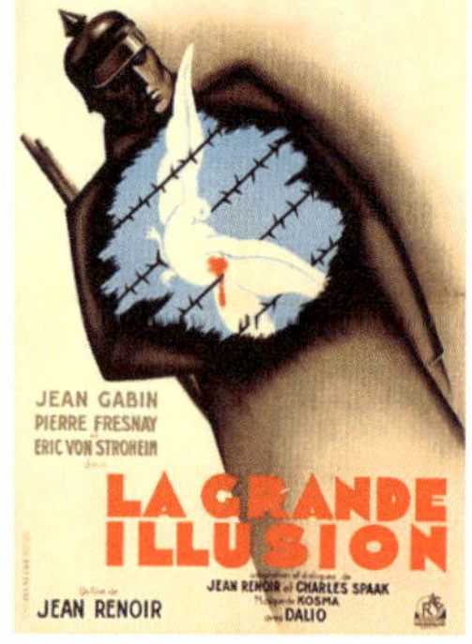

009
010
011
012
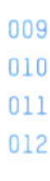
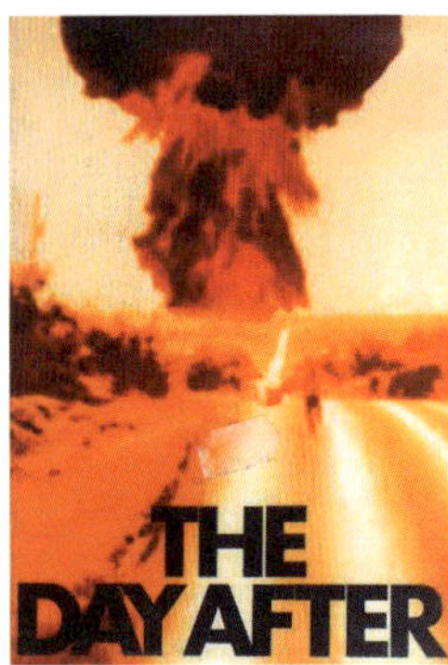
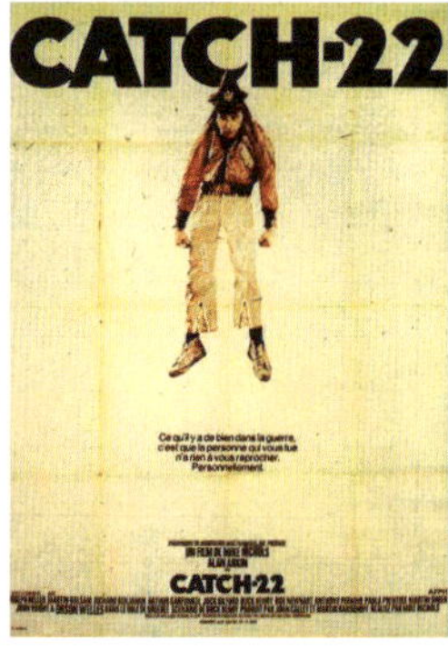
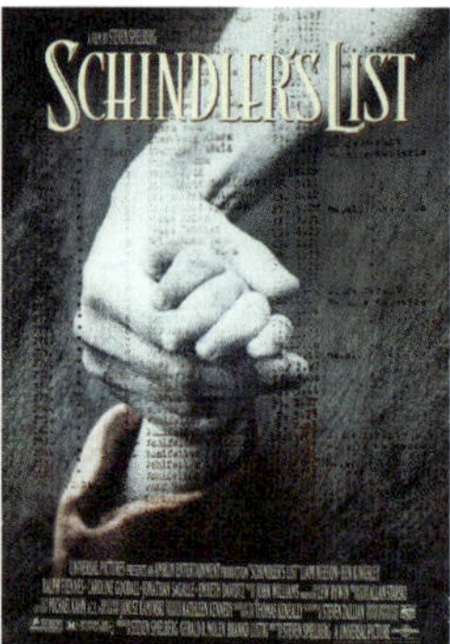
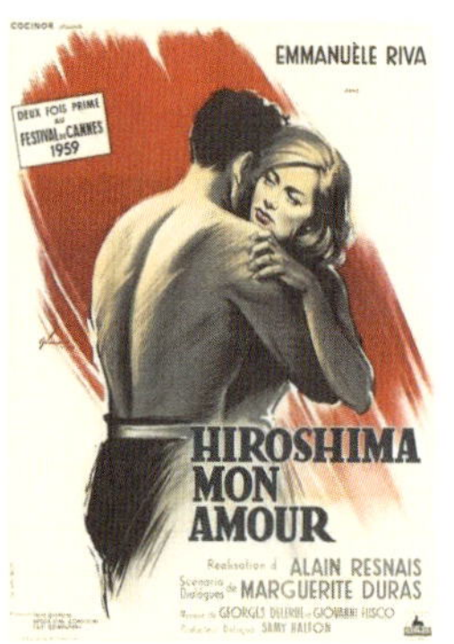

013
014
015
016
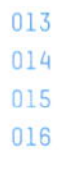
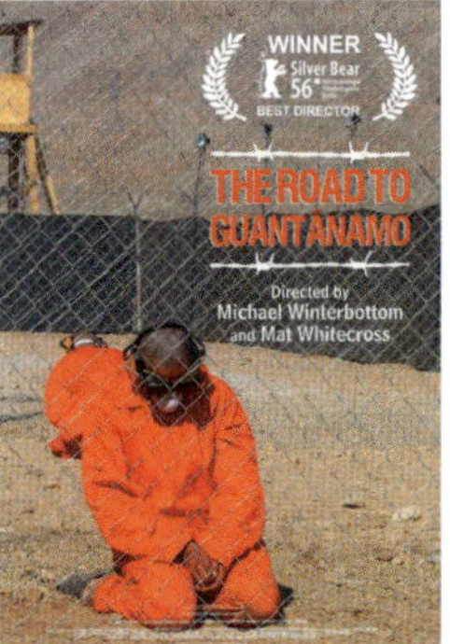
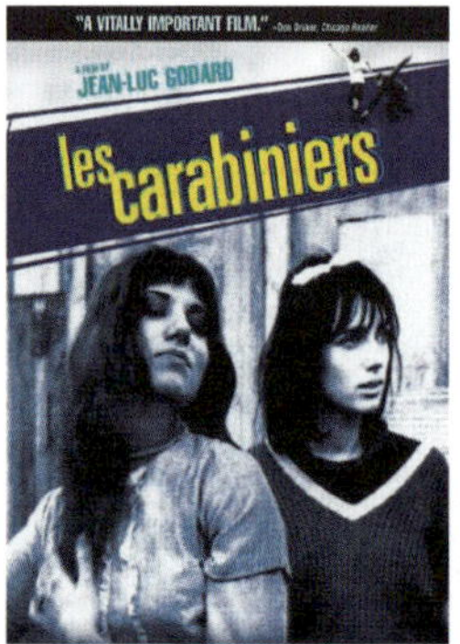
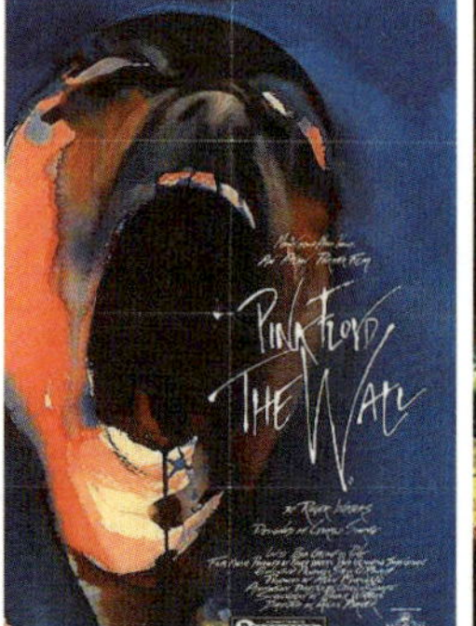
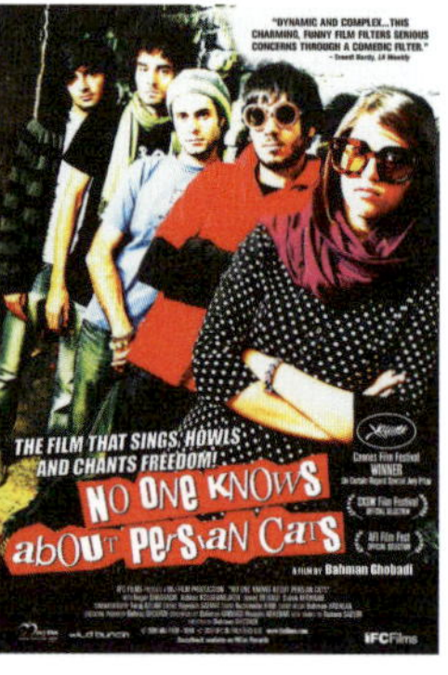

017
018
019

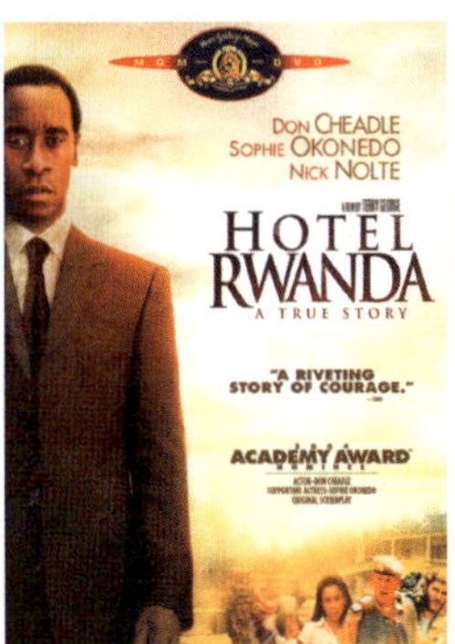
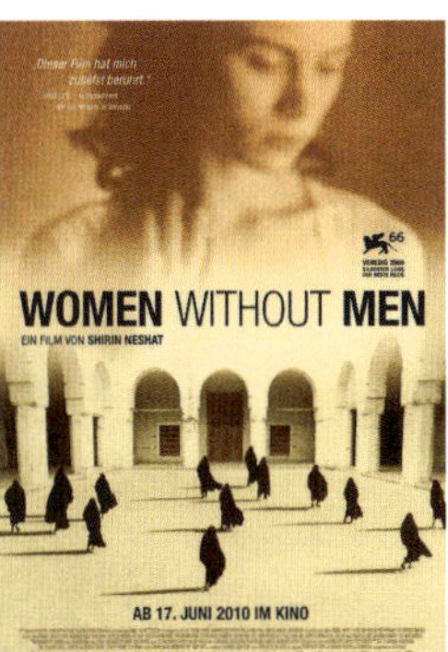
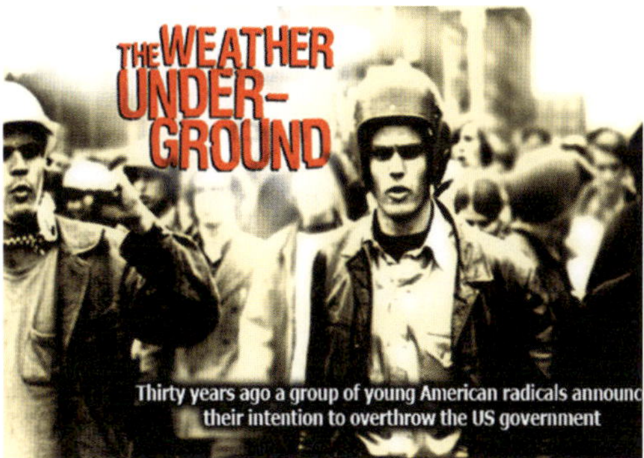

020
021
022

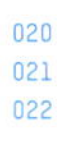
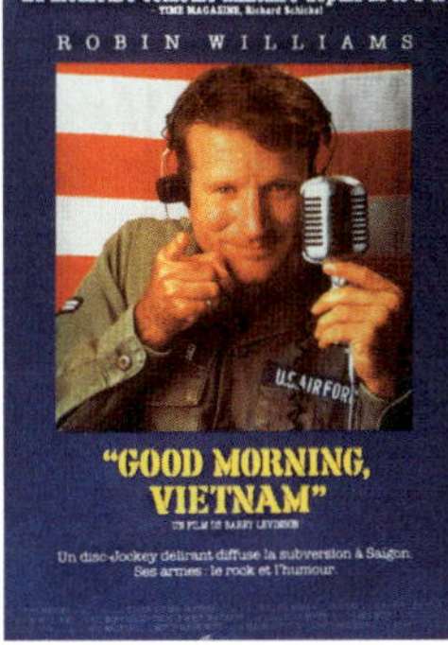
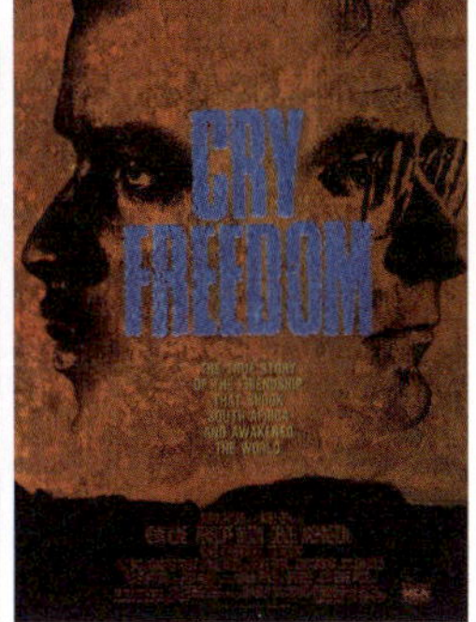
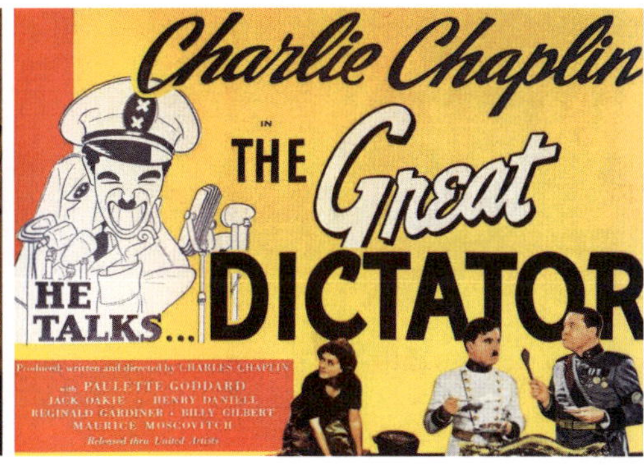

023
024
025

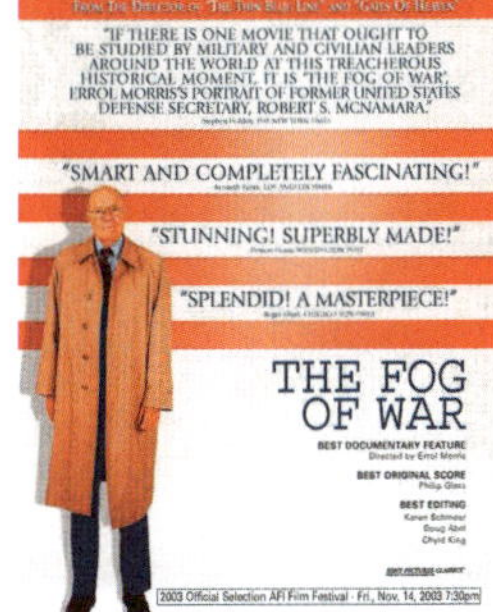
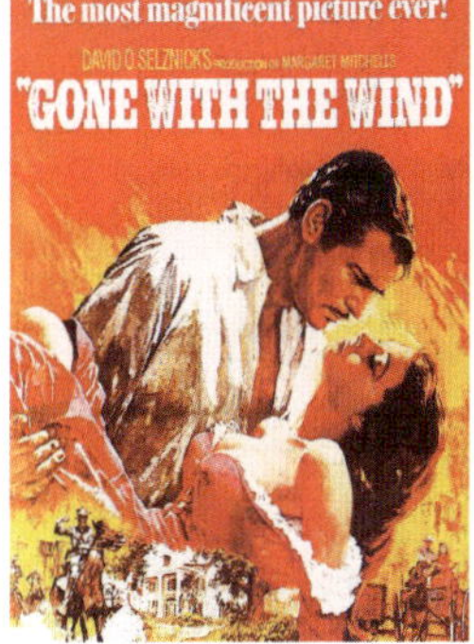
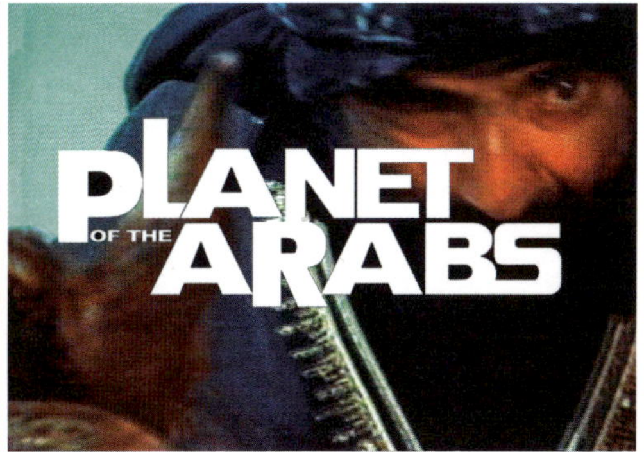

026
027
028

NEXT
029

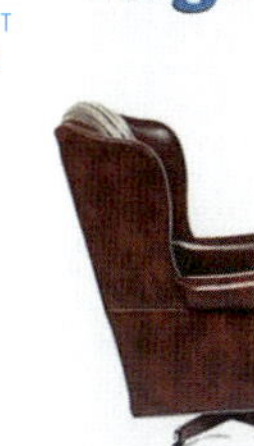
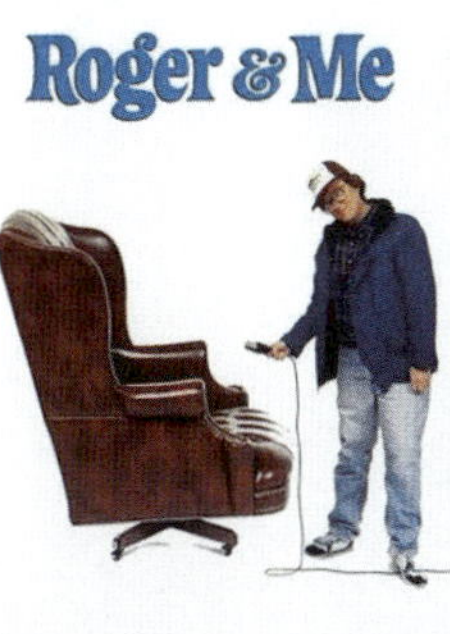
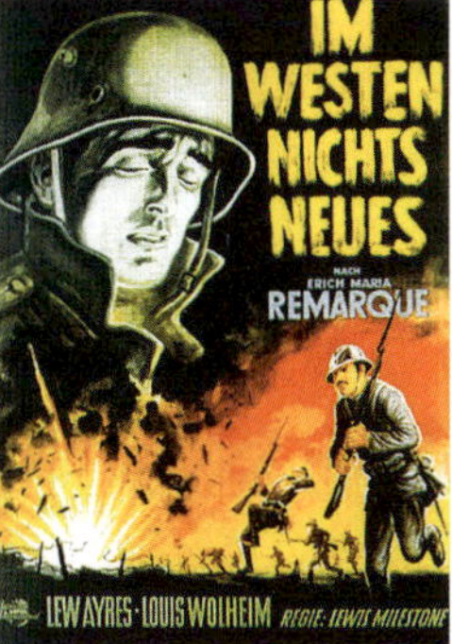
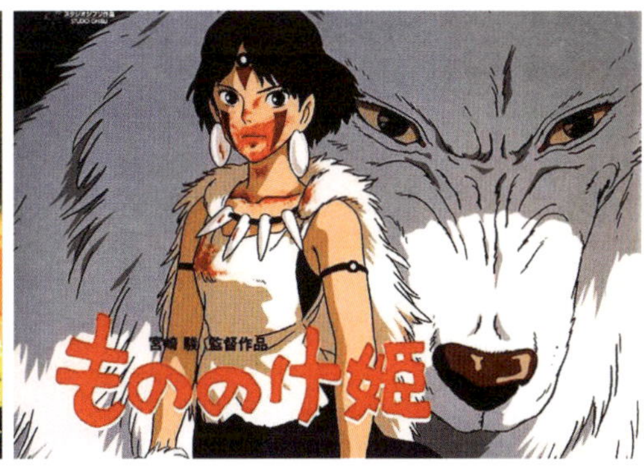

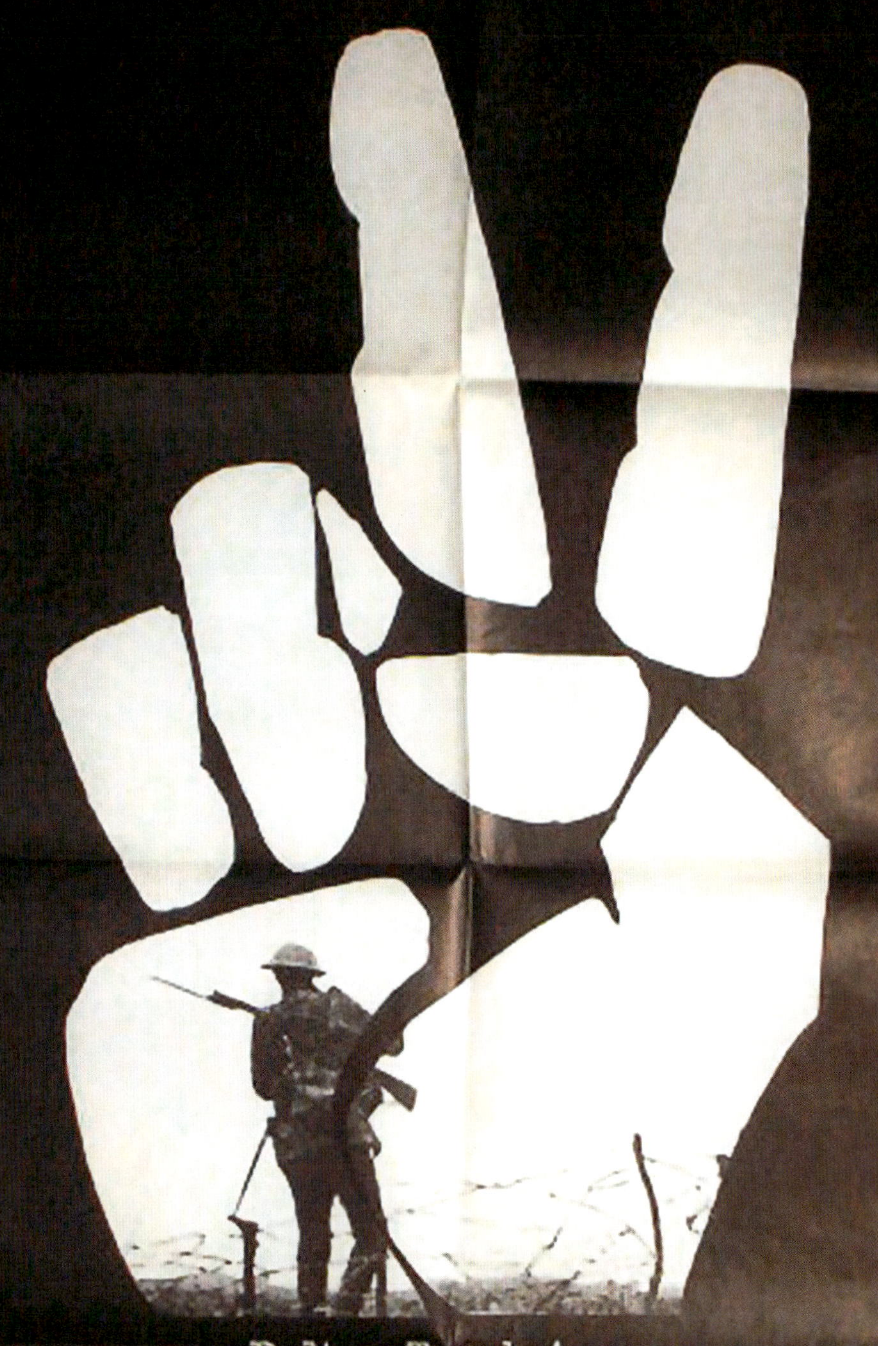

Dalton Trumbo's
johnny got his gun
A Bruce Campbell Production   Jerry Gross Presents A Cinemation Industries Rel

001 LA GUERRE EST FINIE
[THE WAR IS OVER]
CREATOR Hans Hillmann
SOURCE Plakatsammlung Museum
für Gestaltung Zürich

002 30 YEARS OF FIGHTING FOR FILMS OF
PEACE - DOCUMENTARY AND SHORT
FILMS FOR CINEMA AND TELEVISION
SOURCE Plakatsammlung Museum
für Gestaltung Zürich

003 DIE 10. ISONZOSCHLACHT
[THE 10TH BATTLE OF ISONZO]
CREATOR Carl Moos
SOURCE Plakatsammlung Museum
für Gestaltung Zürich

004 THE BYRDS
CREATOR David Singer
SOURCE Plakatsammlung Museum
für Gestaltung Zürich

005 THE WARNING
CREATOR Stefan Borisov
SOURCE Posters from JAGDA Peace
Posters International Exhibition
DATE 1983

006 FRIEDE AM RHEIN
[PEACE ON THE RHINE]
SOURCE judaisme.sdv.fr
DATE 1939

007 BETROGEN BIS ZUM JÜNGSTEN TAG
[DUPED RIGHT UP TO DOOMSDAY]
CREATOR John Heartfield
SOURCE Plakatsammlung Museum
für Gestaltung Zürich

008 LA GRANDE ILLUSION
[THE GRAND ILLUSION]
CREATOR John Heartfield
SOURCE imagecache2.allposters.com

009 THE DAY AFTER
The film postulates a fictional
war between NATO forces and the
Warsaw Pact that rapidly esca-
lates into a full-scale nuclear
exchange between the United
States and the Soviet Union.
CREATOR John Heartfield
SOURCE www.video-zentrale.de
DATE 1983

010 CATCH 22
SOURCE movieposters.2038.net
DATE 1970

011 SCHINDLER'S LIST
A film about Oskar Schindler,
a German businessman who saved
the lives of more than a thousand
mostly Polish-Jewish refugees
during the Holocaust by employing
them in his factories.
SOURCE en.wikipedia.org
DATE 1993

012 HIROSHIMA MON AMOUR
[HIROSHIMA, MY LOVE]
It is the documentation of an
intensely personal conversation
between a French-Japanese couple
about memory and forgetfulness.
It was a major catalyst for the
Nouvelle Vague [French New Wave],
making highly innovative use of
flashbacks to create a uniquely
nonlinear storyline.
SOURCE en.wikipedia.org
DATE 1959

013 THE ROAD TO GUANTANAMO
SOURCE www.impawards.com
DATE 2006

014 LES CARABINIERS
[THE CARABINEERS]
SOURCE voiceseducation.org
DATE 1963

015 PINK FLYOD: THE WALL
SOURCE www.moviepostershop.com
DATE 1982

016 NO ONE KNOWS ABOUT PERSIAN CATS
SOURCE www.ifcfilms.com

017 HOTEL RWANDA
A true story based on the 1994
Rwandan genocide.
SOURCE www.ifcfilms.com
DATE 2004

018 WOMEN WITHOUT MEN
The story chronicles the inter-
twinined lives of four Iranian
women during the summer of 1953;
a cataclysmic moment in Iranian
history when an American-led,
British-backed coup d'ètat brought
down the democratically elected
prime minister, Mohammad Mossadegh,
and reinstalled the Shah to power.
SOURCE bt.eutorrents.com
DATE 2009

019 THE WEATHER UNDERGROUND
DATE 2002
SOURCE Unknown

020 GOOD MORNING VIETNAM
SOURCE www.thecelebritycity.com
DATE 1987

021 CRY FREEDOM
A romantic look at the short life
of South African activist Steven
Biko, and his friendship with
white news editor, Donald Woods.
SOURCE www.geschichte.uni-konstanz.de

022 THE GREAT DICTATOR
Chaplin's film advanced a stirring,
controversial condemnation of Adolf
Hitler, Benito Mussolini's fascism,
antisemitism, and the Nazis.
SOURCE www.stellasmagazine.com
DATE 1949

023 THE FOG OF WAR
An American documentary film
about the life and times of
former US Secretary of Defense
Robert S. McNamara.
SOURCE en.wikipedia.org
DATE 2003

024 GONE WITH THE WIND
SOURCE garethrussellpopular.
blogspot.com
DATE 1939

025 PLANET OF THE ARABS
Out of 1000 films that have Arab
and Muslim characters, from years
1896 to 2000, 12 were postive
depictions.
SOURCE www.jsalloum.org/films.html
DATE 2006

026 ROGER AND ME
SOURCE roswellpoliticaltheory.
blogspot.ch
DATE 1989

027 IM WESTEN NICHTS NEUES
[ALL QUIET ON THE WESTERN FRONT]
SOURCE www.geschichte.uni-konstanz.
de
DATE 1930

028 PRINCESS MONONOKE
SOURCE movie.zing.vn
DATE 1997

029 JOHNNY GOT HIS GUN
SOURCE www.tower.com

001
002

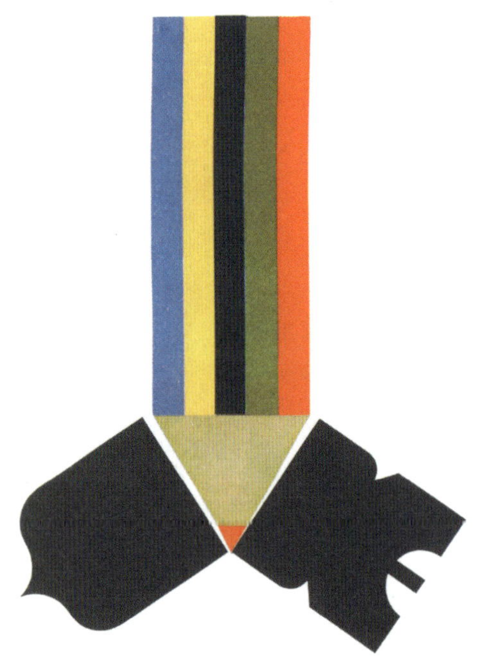

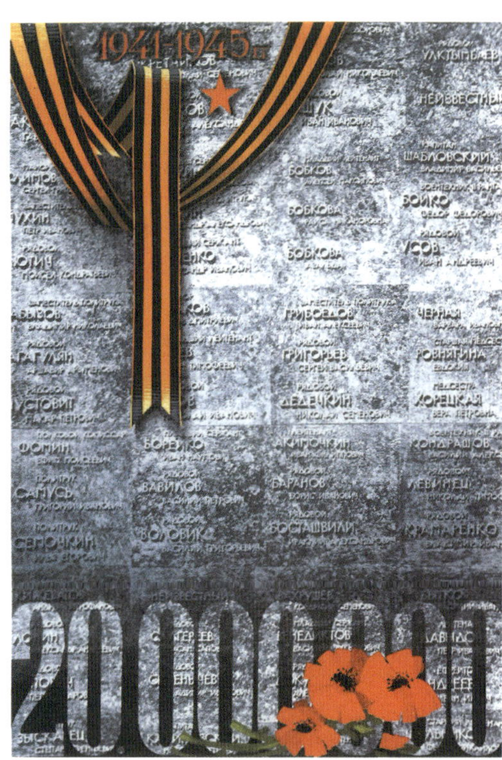

003
004

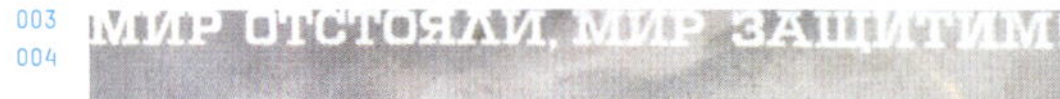

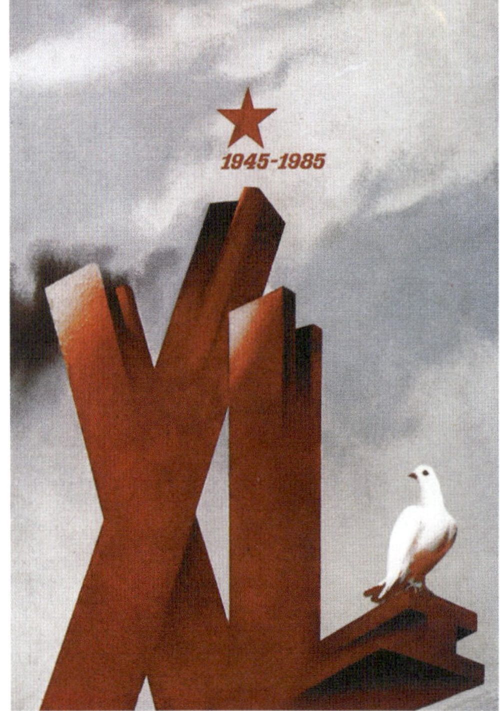

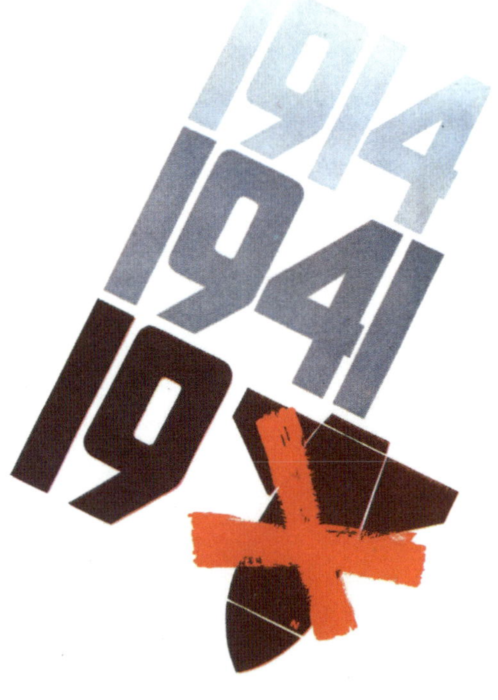

005
006

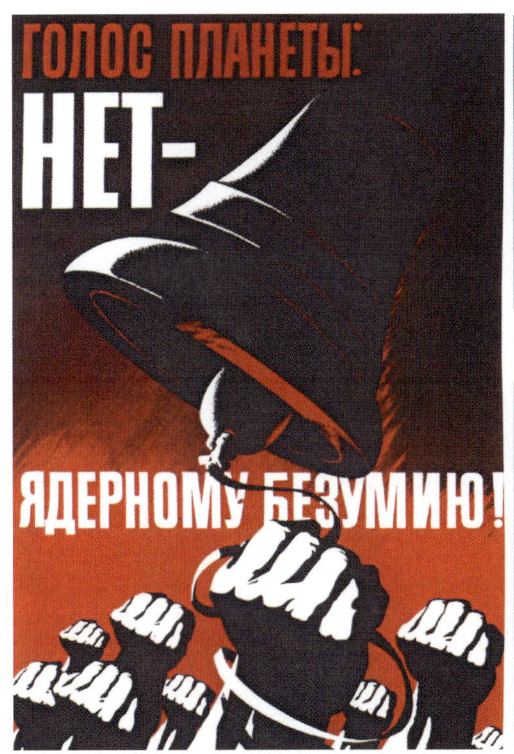

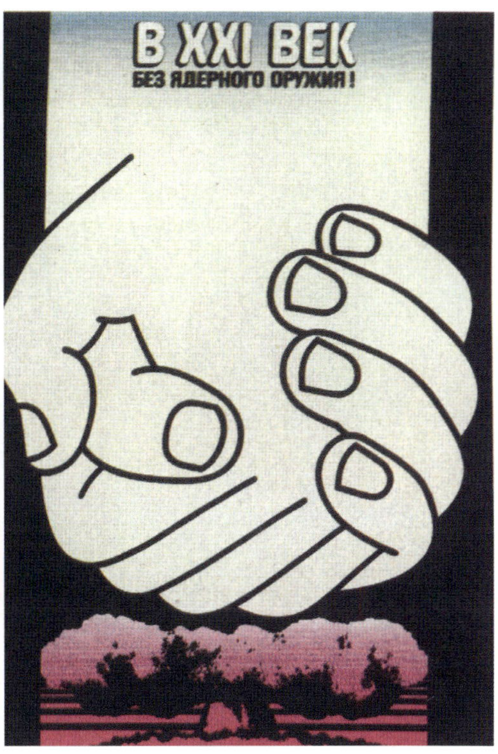

007
008

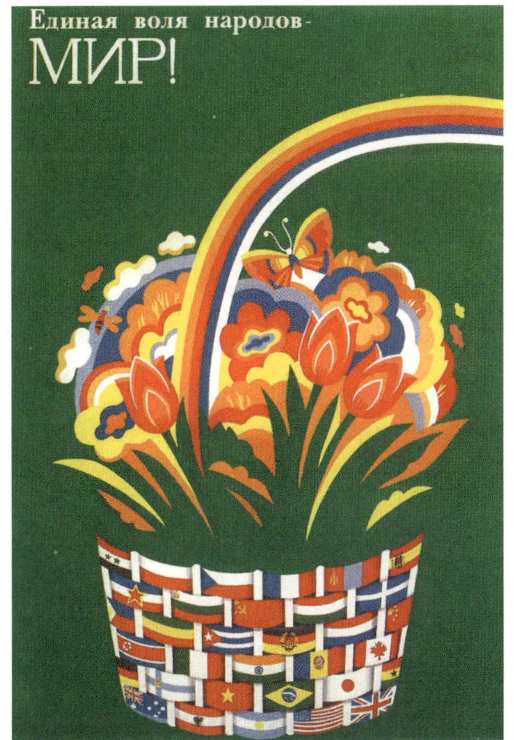

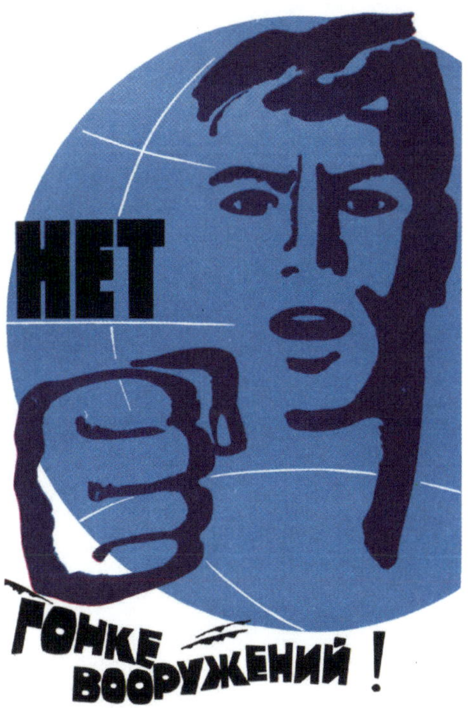

009
010

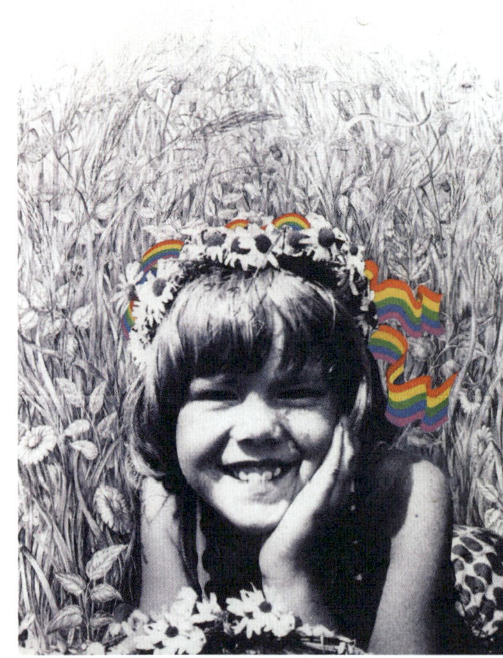
Моя планета голубая, я люблю тебя и обнимаю!

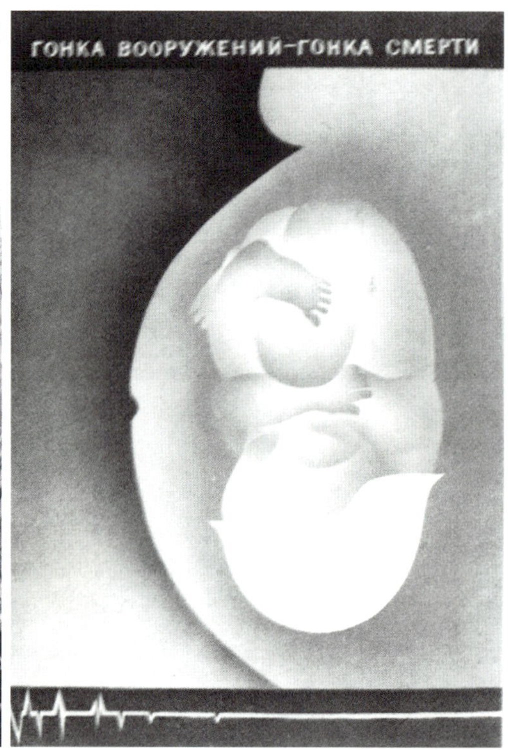
ГОНКА ВООРУЖЕНИЙ–ГОНКА СМЕРТИ

011
012

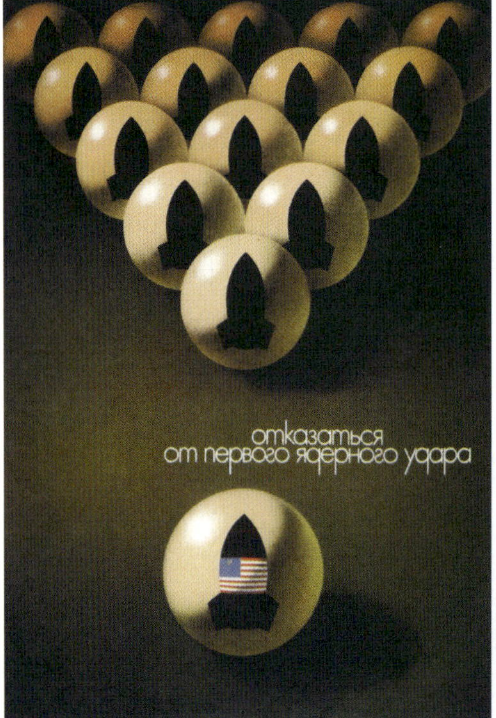
отказаться
от первого ядерного удара

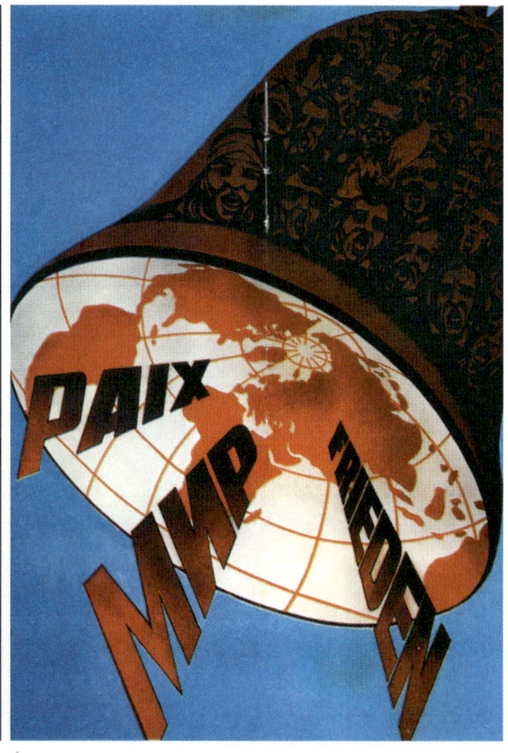
PAIX
МИР
FREEDOM

013
014

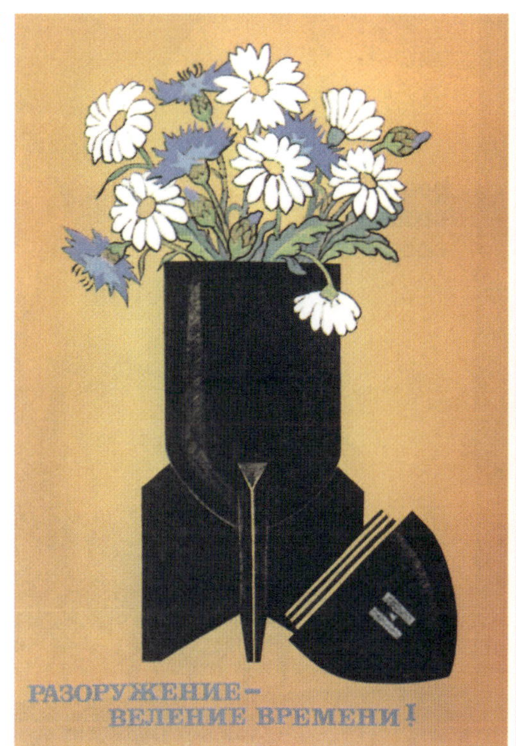

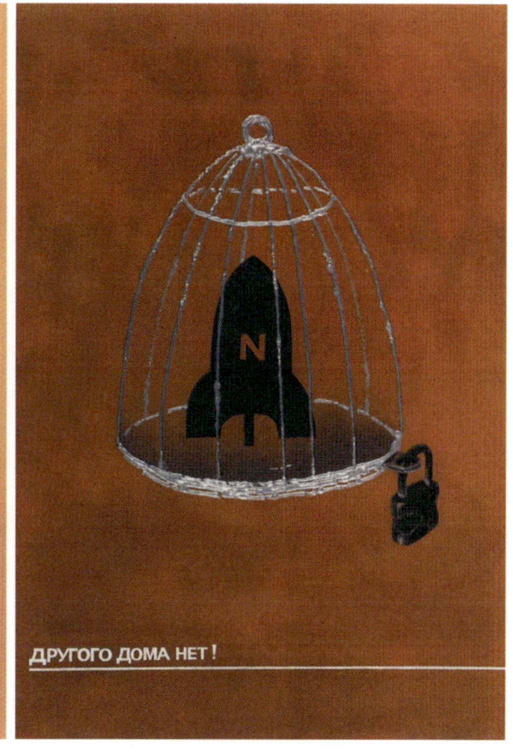

015
016

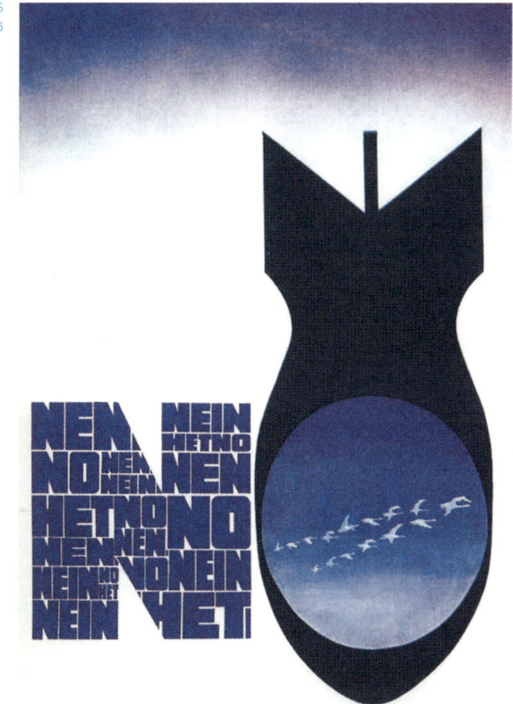

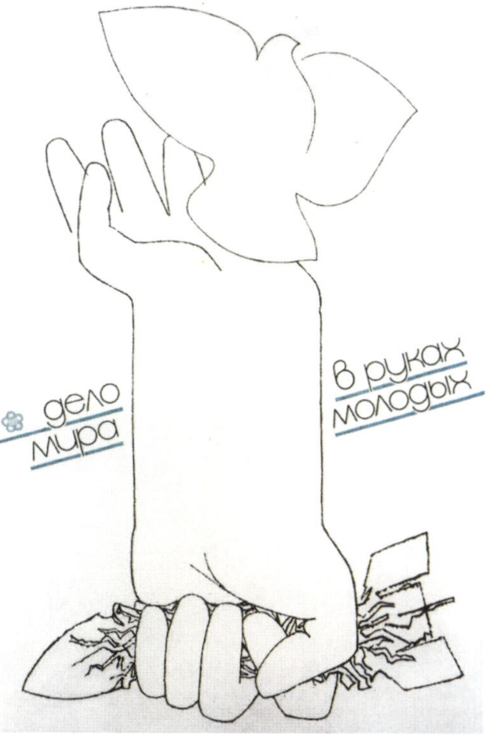

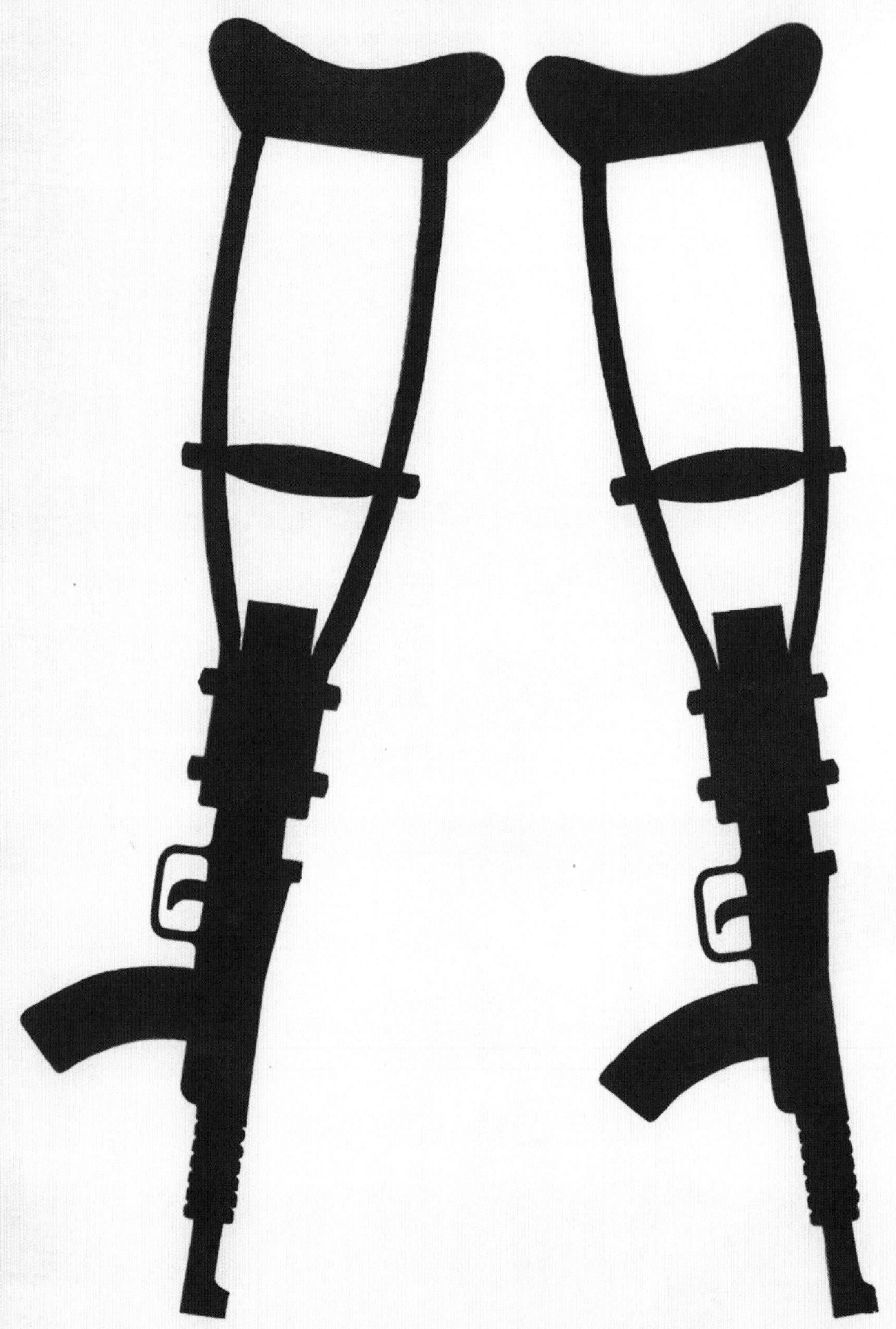
НЕОТДЕЛИМОЕ

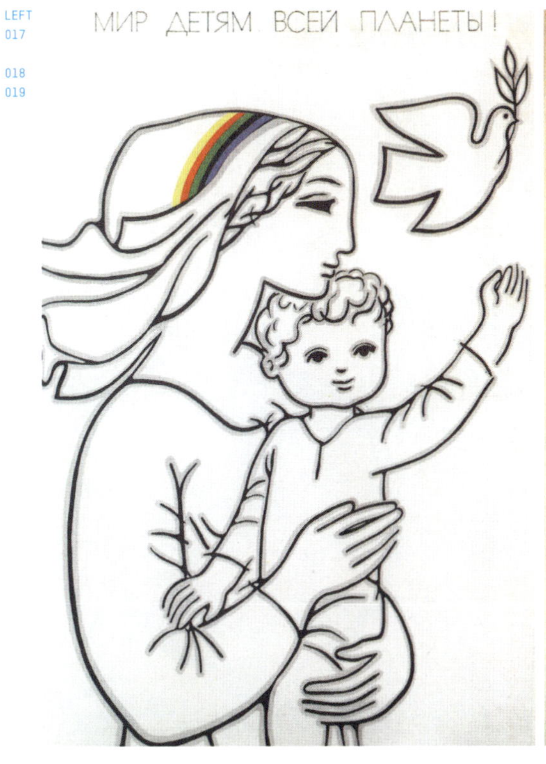
МИР ДЕТЯМ ВСЕЙ ПЛАНЕТЫ!

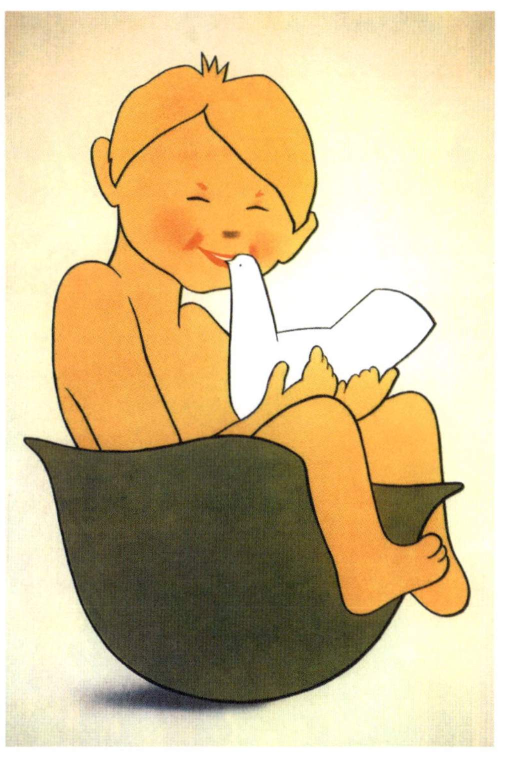

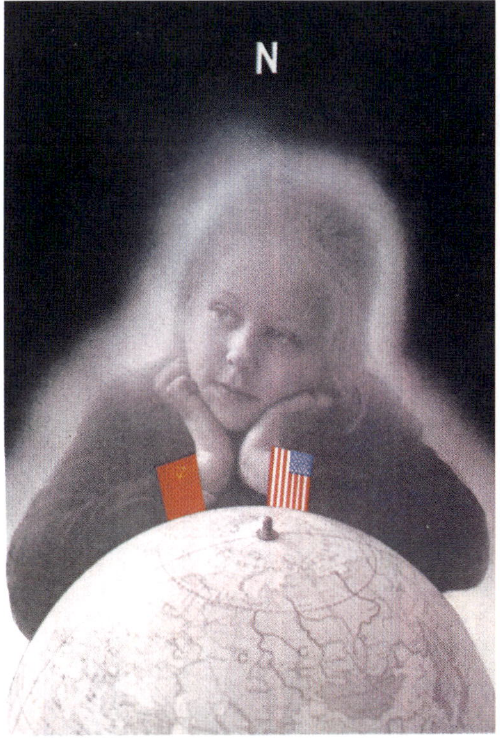
N

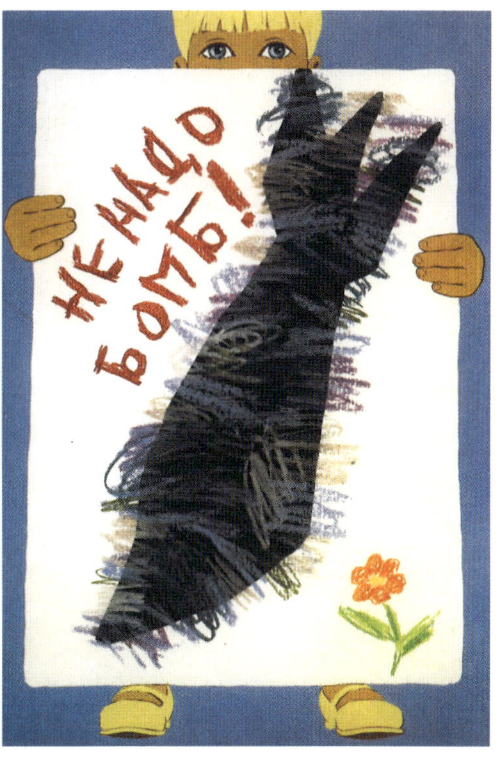
НЕ НАДО
БОМБ!

022
023

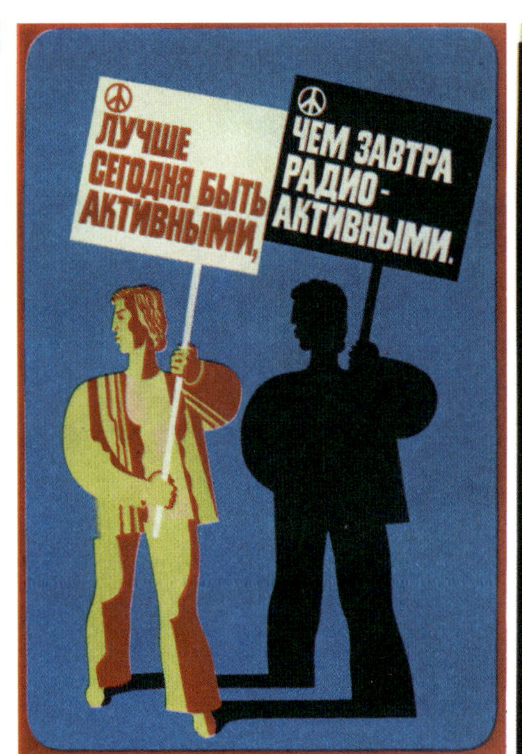

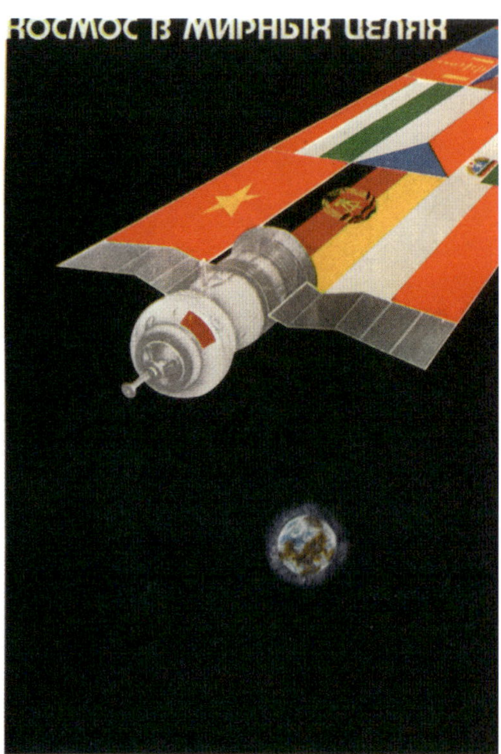

024
025

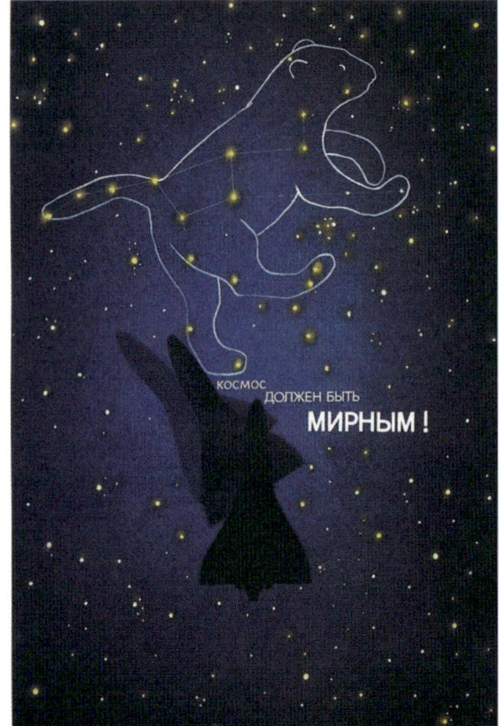

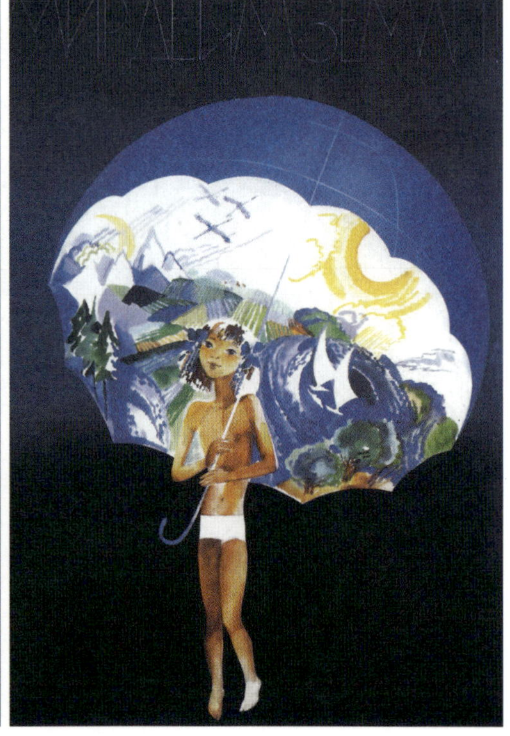

026
027

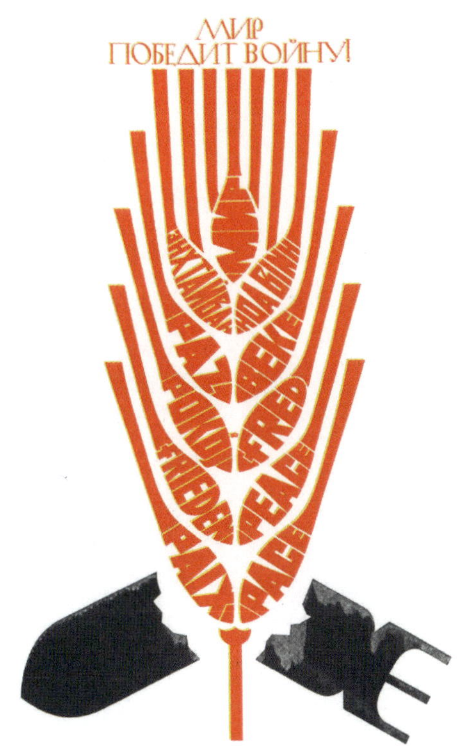

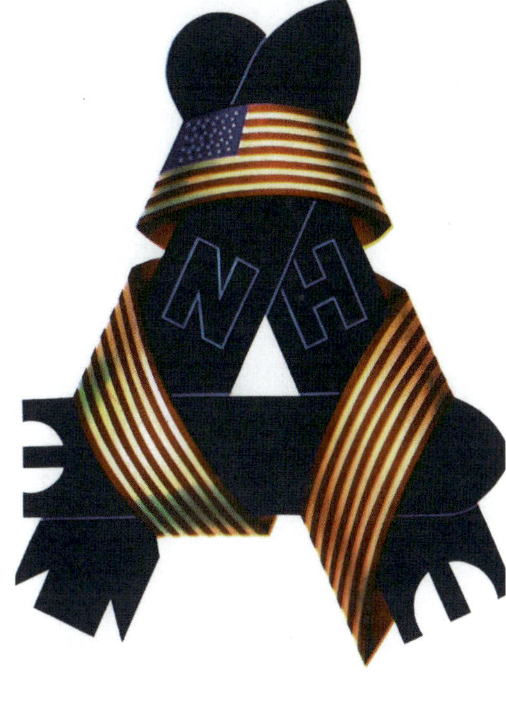

028
029

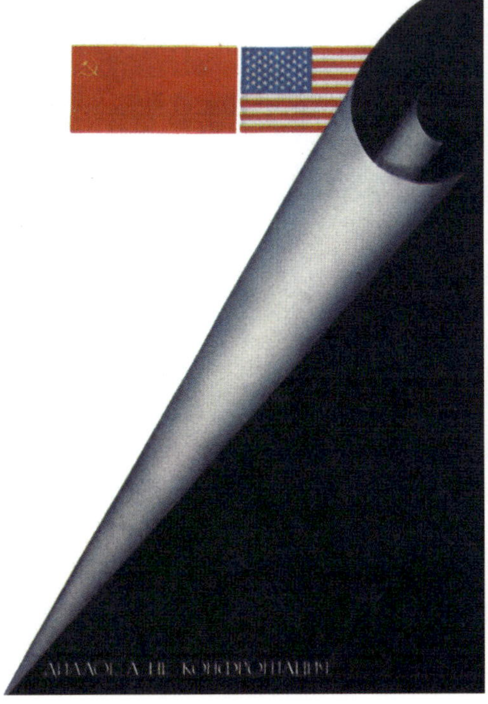

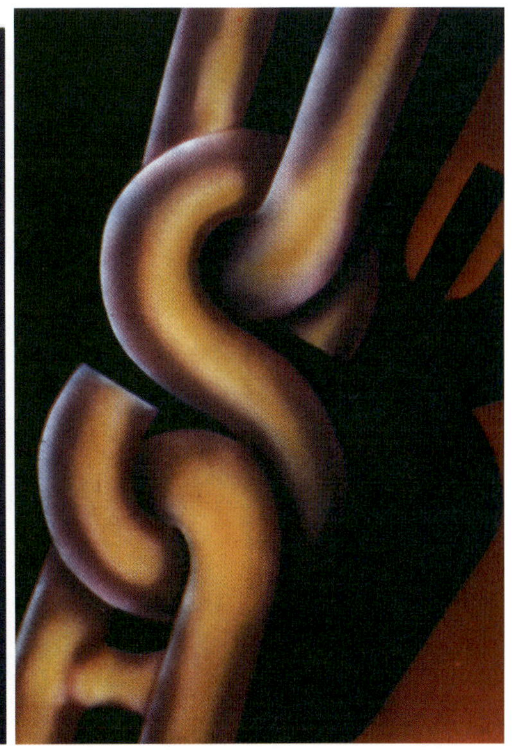

030
031

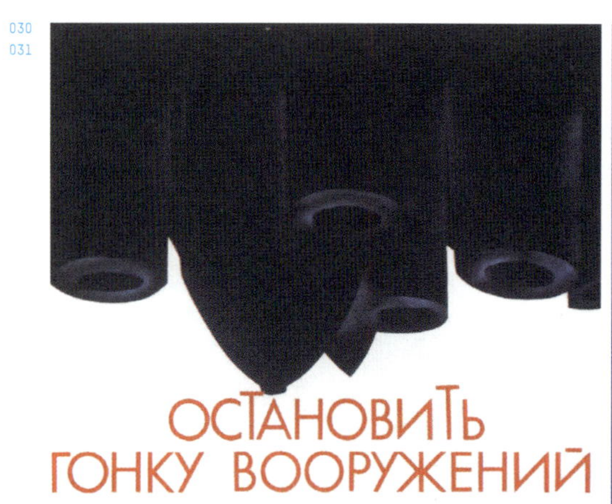

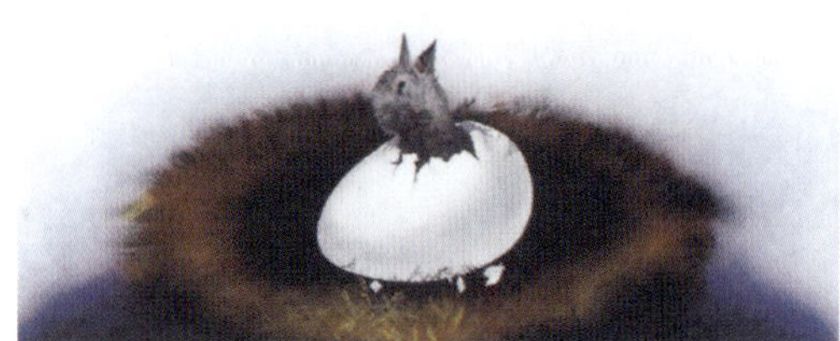

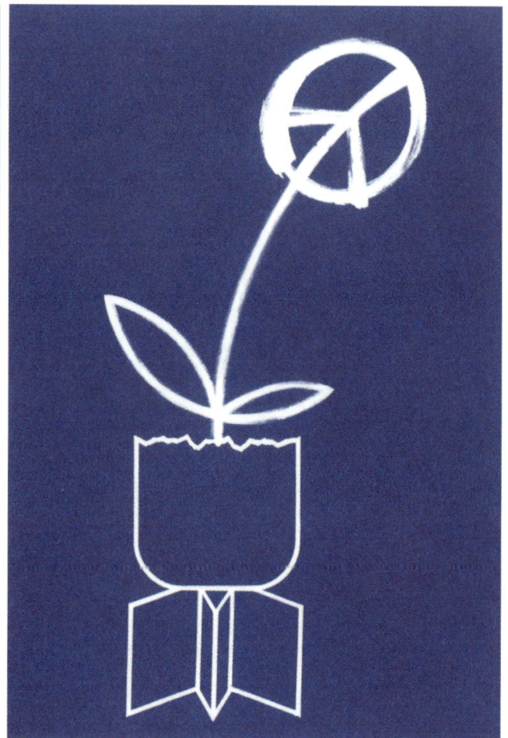

032
033

RIGHT
034

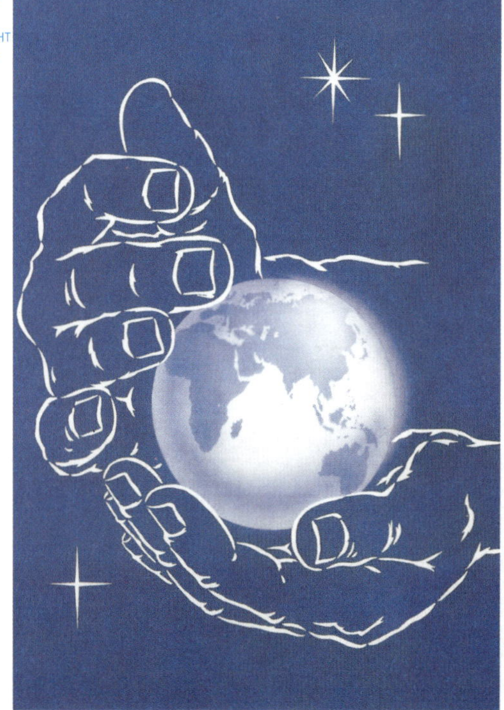

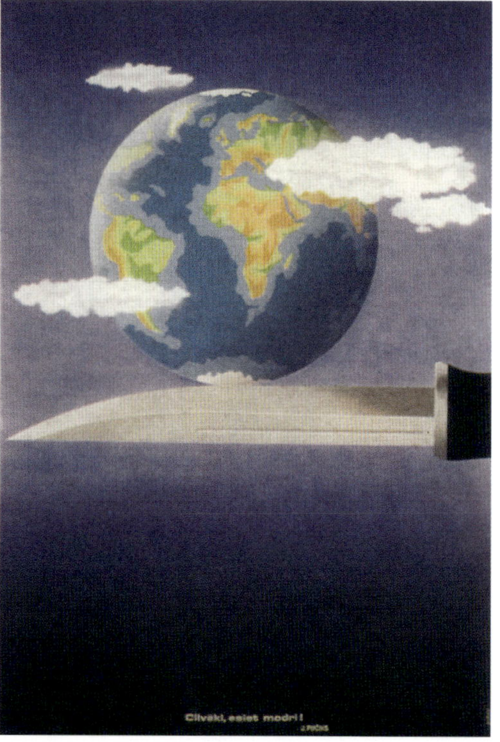

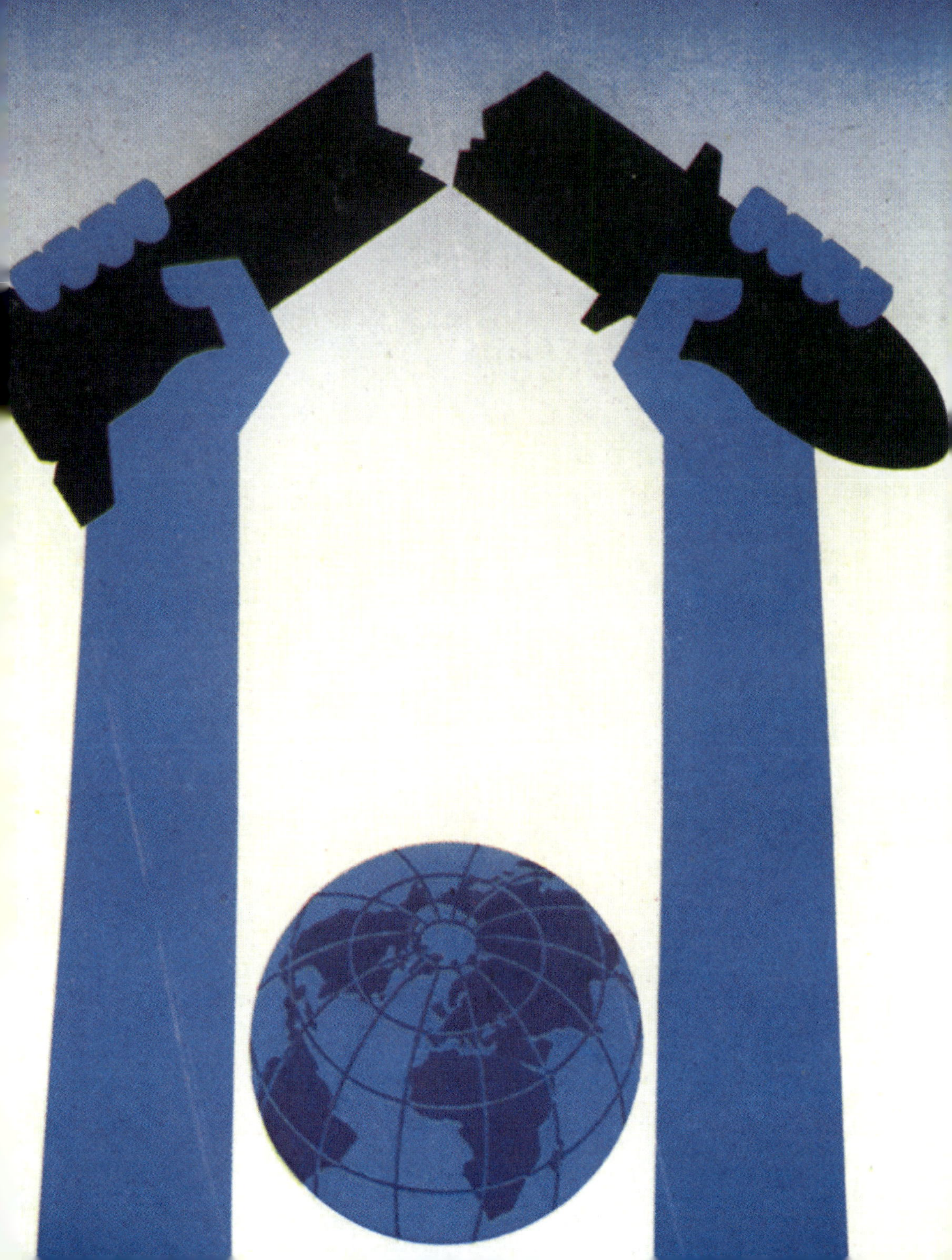
МИР ПОБЕДИТ!

035
036

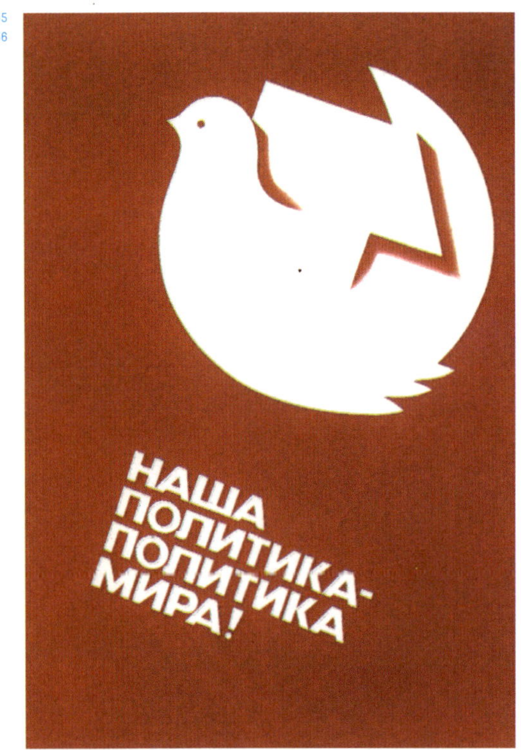

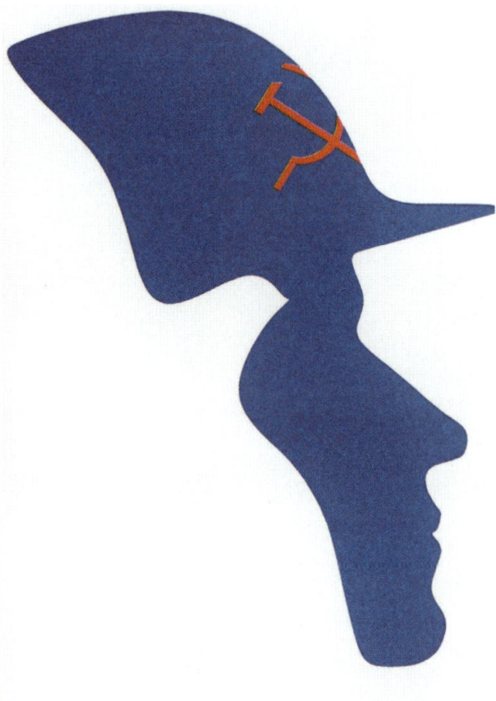

037
038

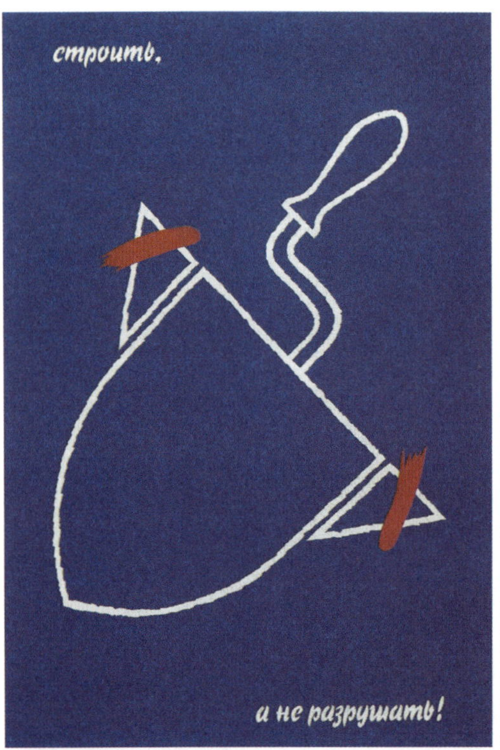

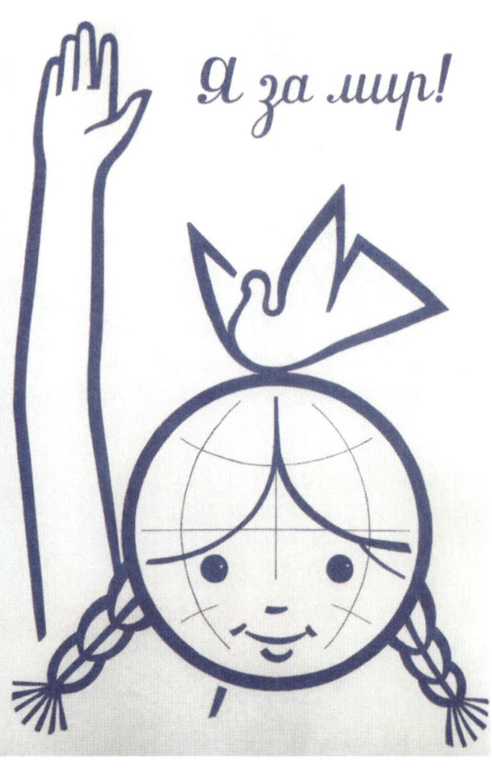

039
040

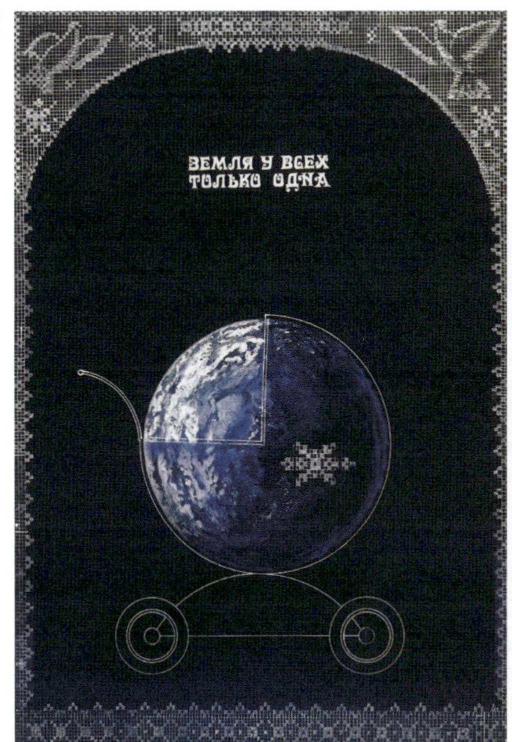

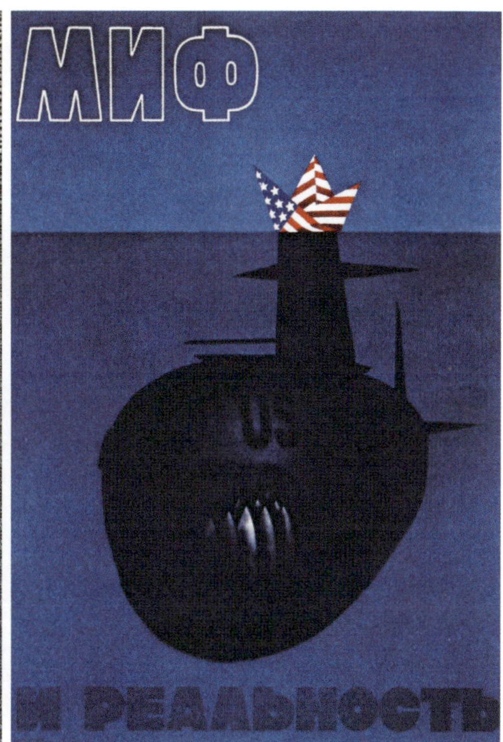

041
042

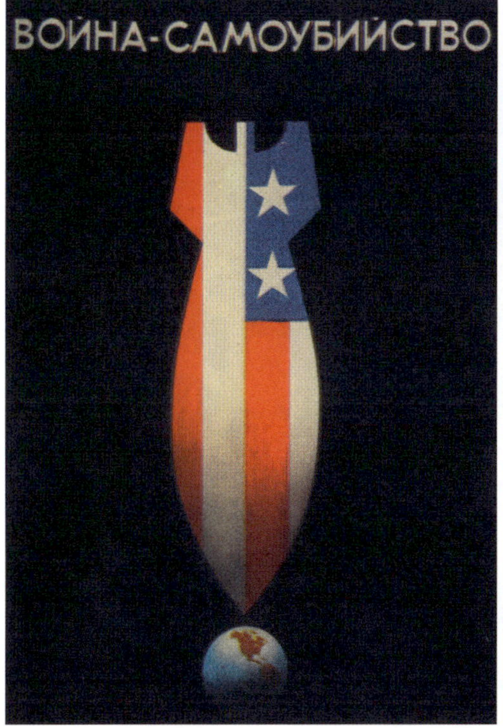

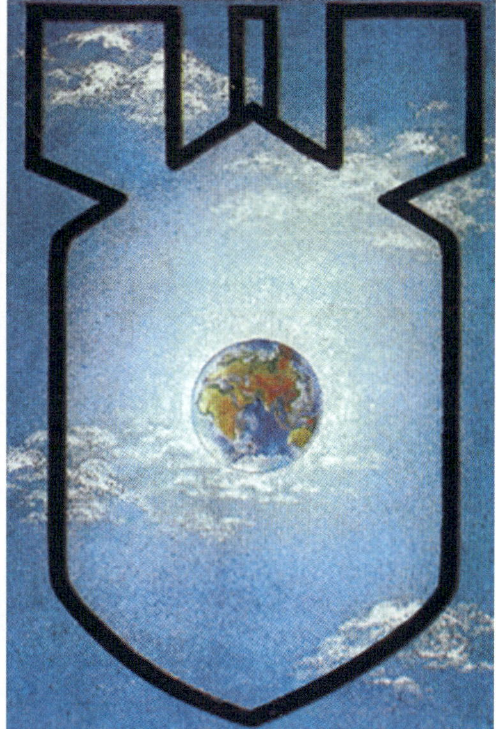

043
044

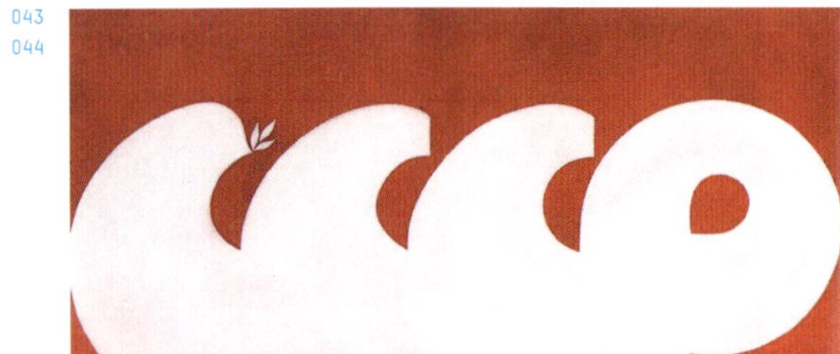

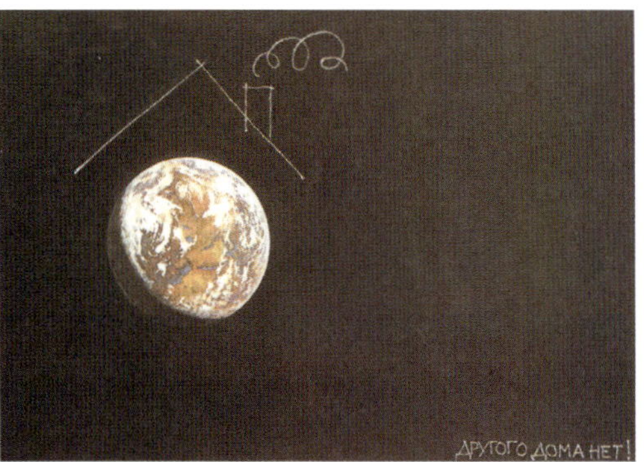

045

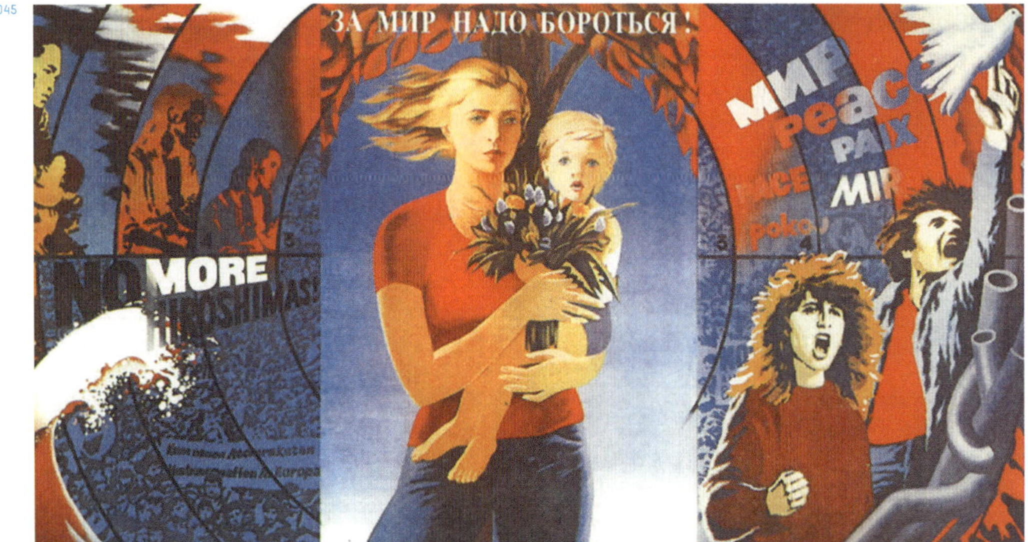

046

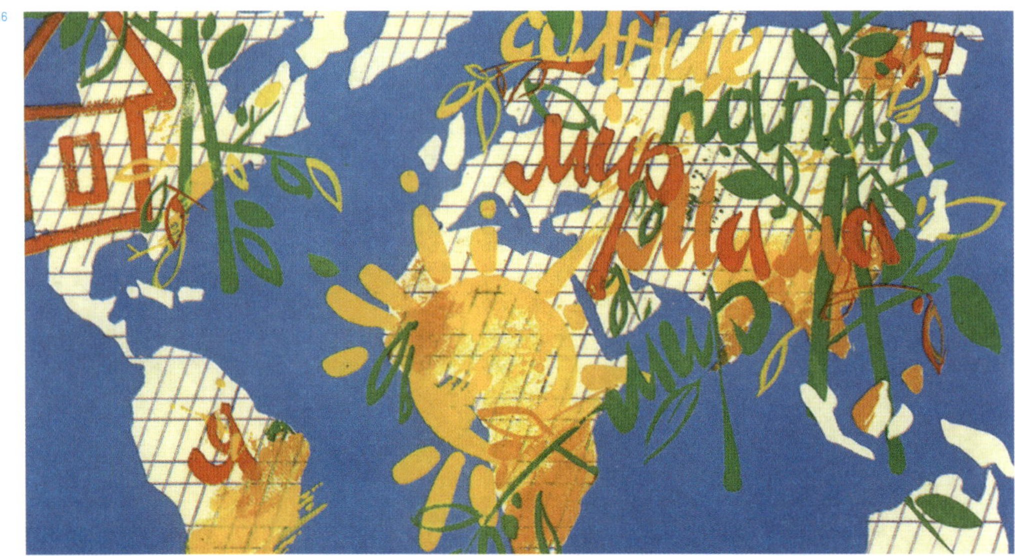

047
048
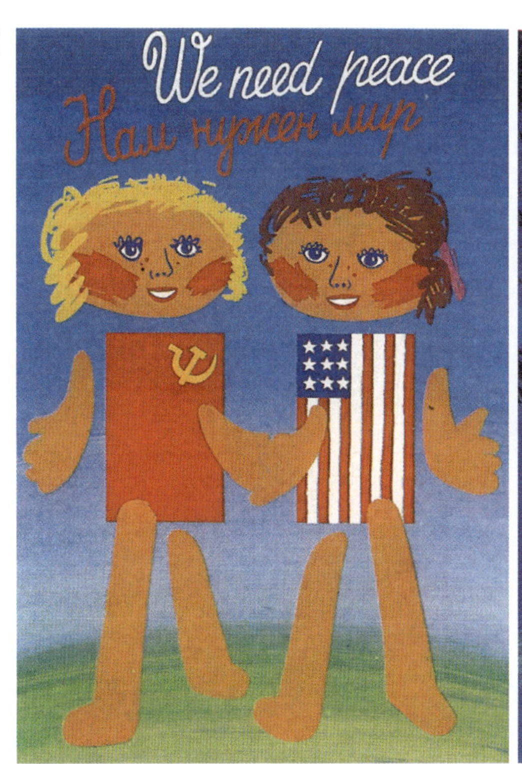

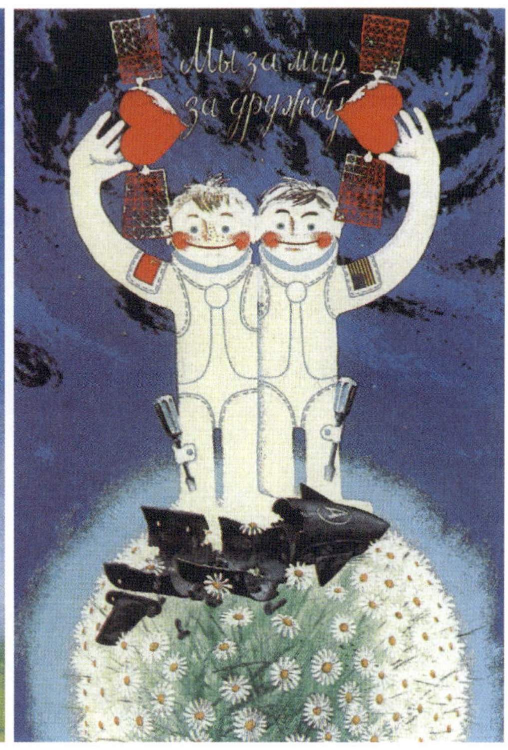

049
050
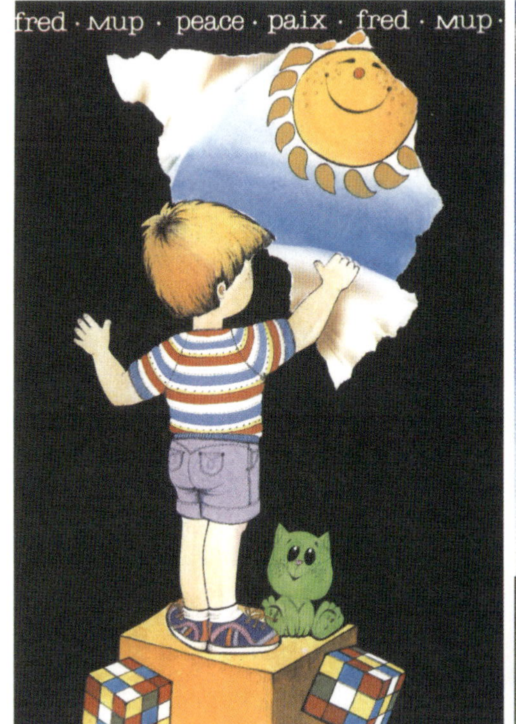

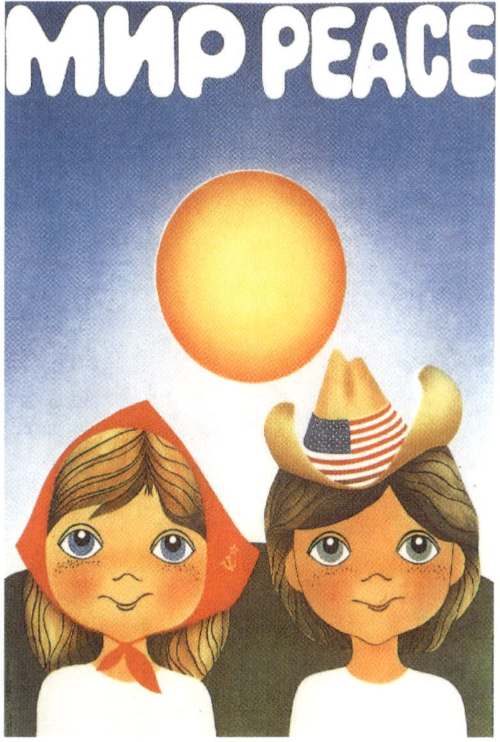

051
052

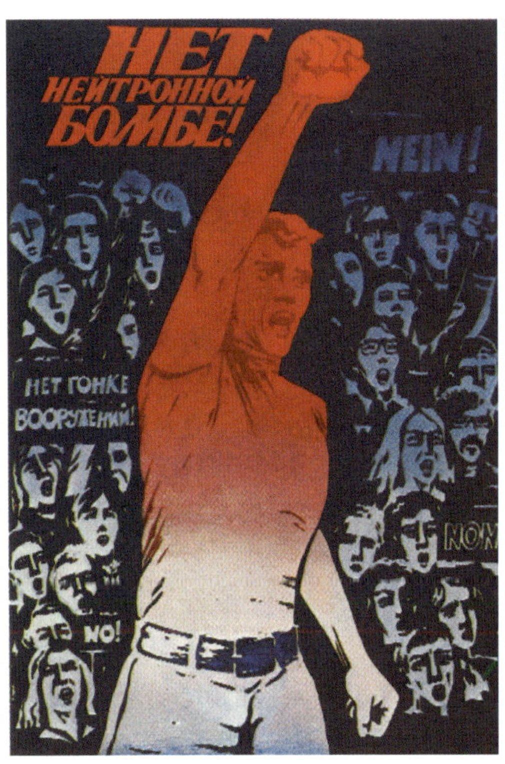

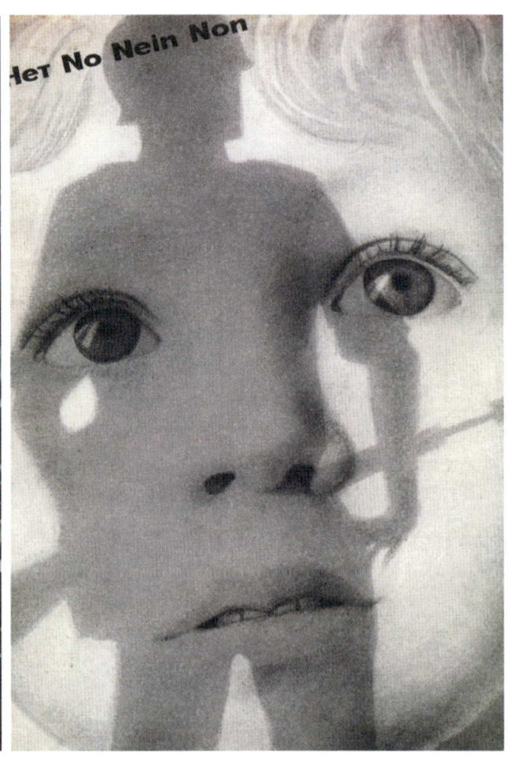

053
054

RIGHT
055

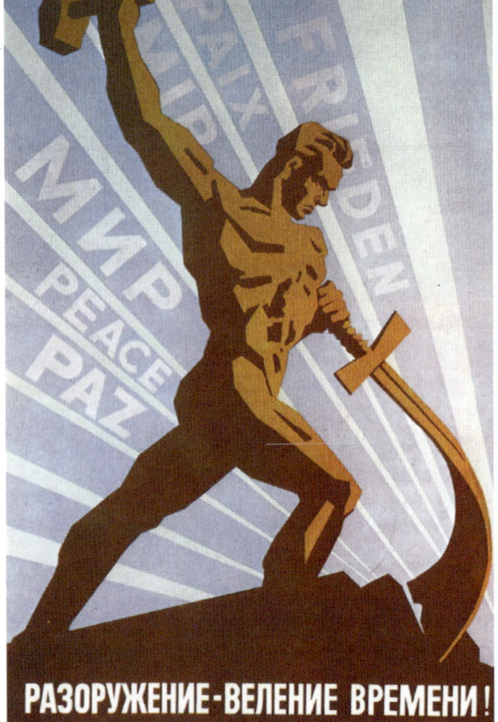

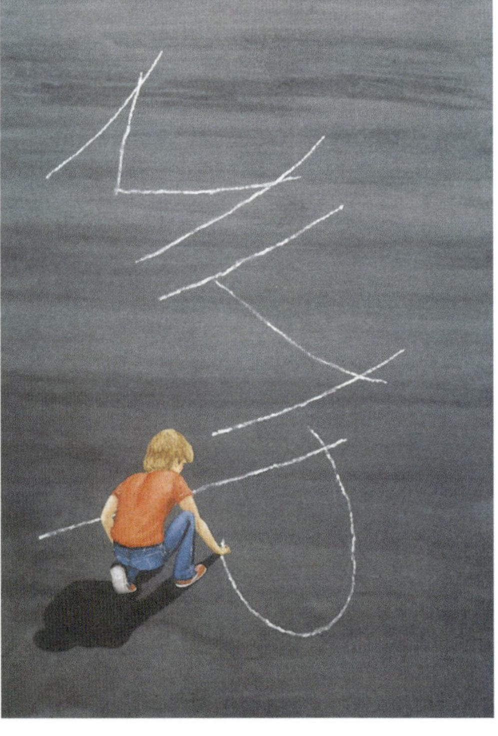

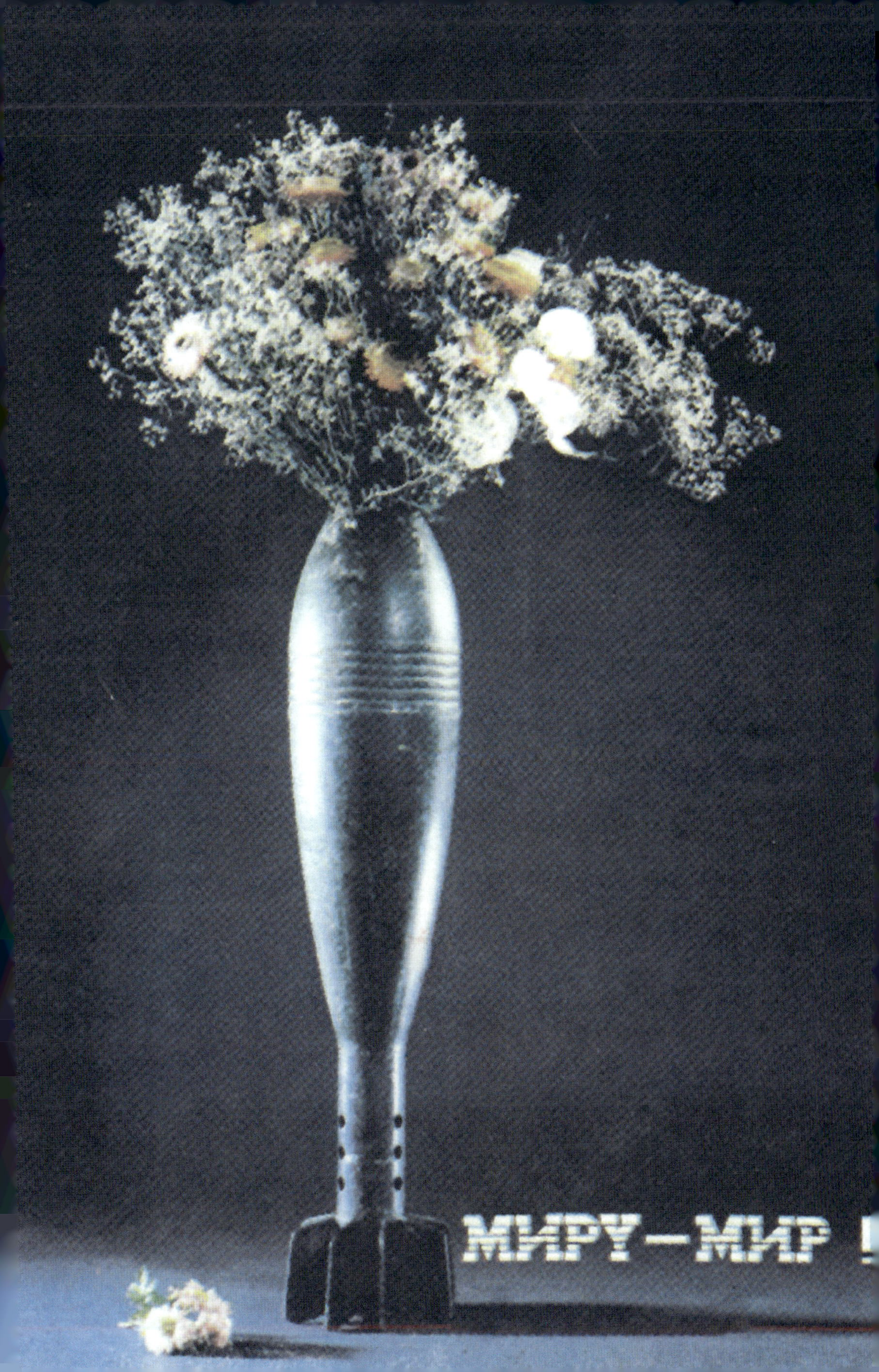

МИРУ — МИР !

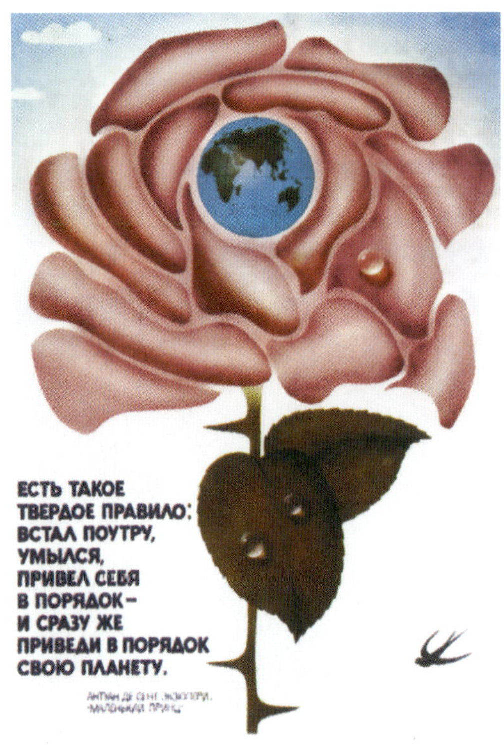

056
ЕСТЬ ТАКОЕ
ТВЕРДОЕ ПРАВИЛО:
ВСТАЛ ПОУТРУ,
УМЫЛСЯ,
ПРИВЕЛ СЕБЯ
В ПОРЯДОК —
И СРАЗУ ЖЕ
ПРИВЕДИ В ПОРЯДОК
СВОЮ ПЛАНЕТУ.
АНТУАН ДЕ СЕНТ-ЭКЗЮПЕРИ,
«МАЛЕНЬКИЙ ПРИНЦ»

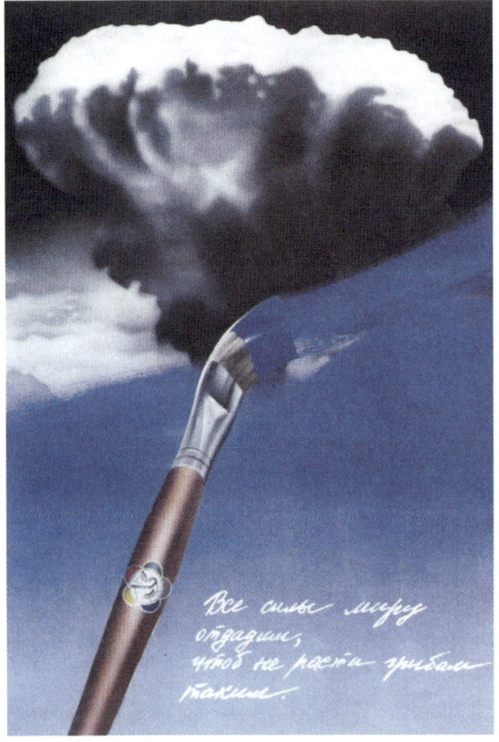

057
Все силы миру
отдадим,
чтоб не расти грибам
таким.

001 A PENCIL CUTS A BOMB
SOURCE www.sovietposters.com

002 20,000,000, 1941–1945
SOURCE www.sovietposters.com

003 WE DEFENDED THE PEACE, WE WILL
PROTECT THE WORLD!
SOURCE www.sovietposters.com

004 1914 1941 19X
SOURCE www.sovietposters.com

005 THE VOICE OF THE PLANET: NO TO
NUCLEAR MADNESS!
SOURCE www.sovietposters.com

006 ENTER THE 21ST CENTURY WITHOUT
NUCLEAR WEAPONS!
SOURCE www.sovietposters.com

007 PEACE!
SOURCE www.sovietposters.com

008 NO TO THE [NUCLEAR] ARMS RACE!
SOURCE www.sovietposters.com

009 MY BLUE PLANET, I LOVE YOU
AND HUG [YOU].
SOURCE www.sovietposters.com

010 ARMS RACE – IS A RACE OF DEATH!
SOURCE www.sovietposters.com

011 TO REFUSE [TO DO] THE FIRST
NUCLEAR STRIKE
SOURCE www.sovietposters.com

012 PAIX, MIR, FRIEDEN [PEACE]
SOURCE www.sovietposters.com

013 DISARMAMENT – IS A DICTATE
OF THE TIME!
SOURCE www.sovietposters.com

014 THERE IS NO OTHER HOME!
SOURCE www.sovietposters.com

015 NET NO NEIN
SOURCE www.sovietposters.com

016 THE CAUSE OF PEACE IS IN THE
HANDS OF YOUNG [PEOPLE]!
SOURCE www.sovietposters.com

017 INSEPARABLE
SOURCE www.sovietposters.com

018 PEACE TO THE CHILDREN OF
ALL THE PLANET
SOURCE www.sovietposters.com

019 A CHILD IS INSIDE A SOLDIERS'
HELMET – KASKA
SOURCE www.sovietposters.com

020 PEACE BETWEEN THE USA AND
THE SOVIET UNION
SOURCE www.sovietposters.com

021 NO NEED FOR BOMBS!
SOURCE www.sovietposters.com

022 IT IS BETTER TODAY TO BE PROACTIVE,
THAN TO BE RADIOACTIVE TOMORROW
SOURCE www.sovietposters.com

023 PEACEFUL COSMOS
SOURCE www.sovietposters.com

024 COSMOS MUST BE PEACEFUL!
SOURCE www.sovietposters.com

025 PEACE TO THE CHILDREN OF
THE EARTH!
SOURCE www.sovietposters.com

026 PEACE WILL WIN OVER WAR
SOURCE www.sovietposters.com

027 NUCLEAR AND HYDROGEN BOMBS
WRAPPED INTO AN AMERICAN FLAG
SOURCE www.sovietposters.com

028 DIALOGUE, NOT CONFRONTATION
SOURCE www.sovietposters.com

030 STOP ARMS RACE
SOURCE www.sovietposters.com

031 PEACE SYMBOL FLOWER IS GROWING
OUT OF THE BROKEN BOMB
SOURCE www.sovietposters.com

032 PALMS HOLDING THE EARTH
SOURCE www.sovietposters.com

033 CILVEKI, ESIET MODRI!
[PEOPLE, BE VIGILANT!]
CREATOR Juliuss Fuciks
SOURCE www.sovietposters.com

034 PEACE WILL BE VICTORIOUS!
SOURCE www.sovietposters.com

035 OUR POLITICS – IS THE
POLITICS OF PEACE!
SOURCE www.sovietposters.com

036 WE [ARE] A PEACEFUL PEOPLE
SOURCE www.sovietposters.com

037 TO BUILD, NOT TO DESTROY!
SOURCE www.sovietposters.com

038 I [VOTE] FOR PEACE!!
SOURCE www.sovietposters.com

039 WE ALL HAVE ONLY ONE EARTH
SOURCE www.sovietposters.com

040 MYTH AND REALITY
SOURCE www.sovietposters.com

041 WAR IS SUICIDE
SOURCE www.sovietposters.com

042 NUCLEAR BOMB
SOURCE www.sovietposters.com

043 THE MAIN TARGET OF OUR FOREIGN
POLICY IS PEACE!
SOURCE www.sovietposters.com

044 THERE IS NO OTHER HOME!
SOURCE www.sovietposters.com

045 WE HAVE TO FIGHT FOR PEACE!
SOURCE www.sovietposters.com

046 PEACE TO THE CHILDREN OF
THE WHOLE PLANET
SOURCE www.sovietposters.com

047 WE NEED PEACE
SOURCE www.sovietposters.com

048 WE [VOTE] FOR PEACE, FOR FRIENDSHIP
SOURCE www.sovietposters.com

049 FRIED MIR PEACE PAIX
SOURCE www.sovietposters.com

050 MIR [PEACE]
SOURCE www.sovietposters.com

051 NO TO THE NEUTRON BOMB!
SOURCE www.sovietposters.com

052 NET NO NEIN NON
SOURCE www.sovietposters.com

053 DISARMAMENT IS A DICTATE
OF THE TIME!
SOURCE www.sovietposters.com

054 MIR [PEACE]
SOURCE www.sovietposters.com

055 PEACE TO THE WORLD!
SOURCE www.sovietposters.com

056 CLEAN UP THE PLANET
SOURCE www.sovietposters.com

057 WE WILL USE FOR PEACE ALL OUR
STRENGTH, NOT TO HAVE MUSHROOMS
LIKE THIS RAISED
SOURCE www.sovietposters.com

001
002
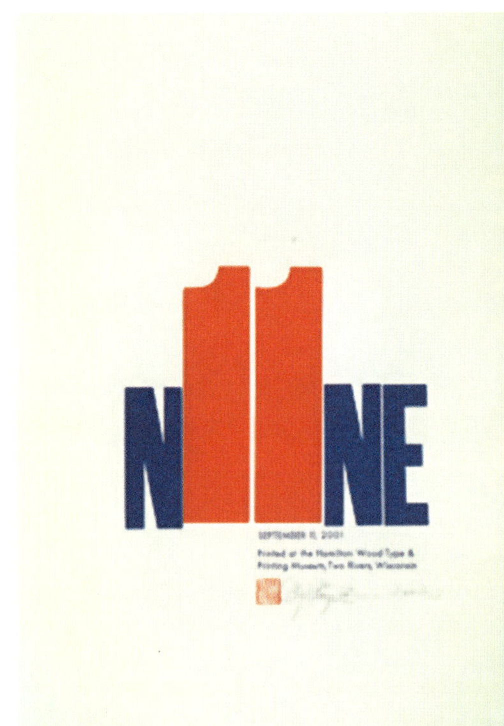
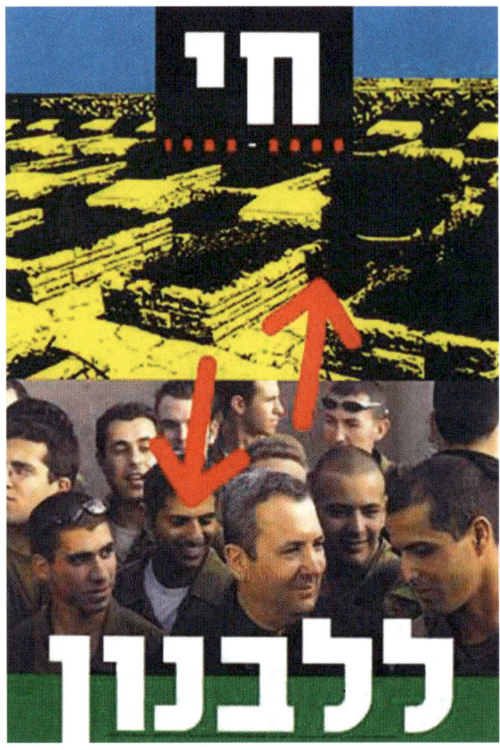

003
004
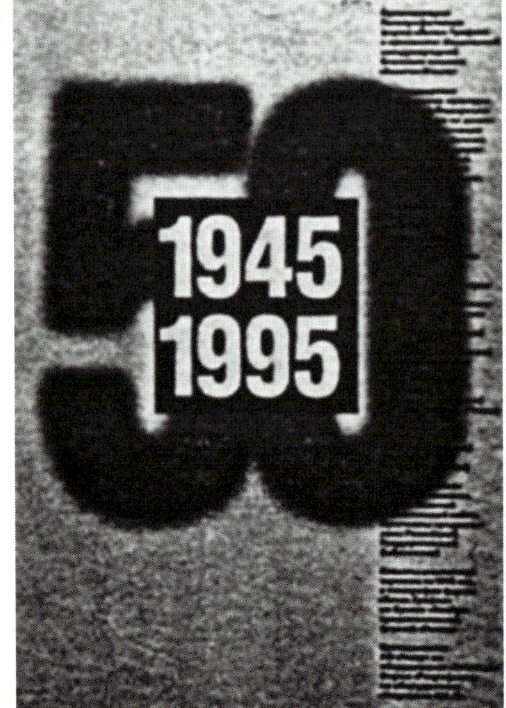

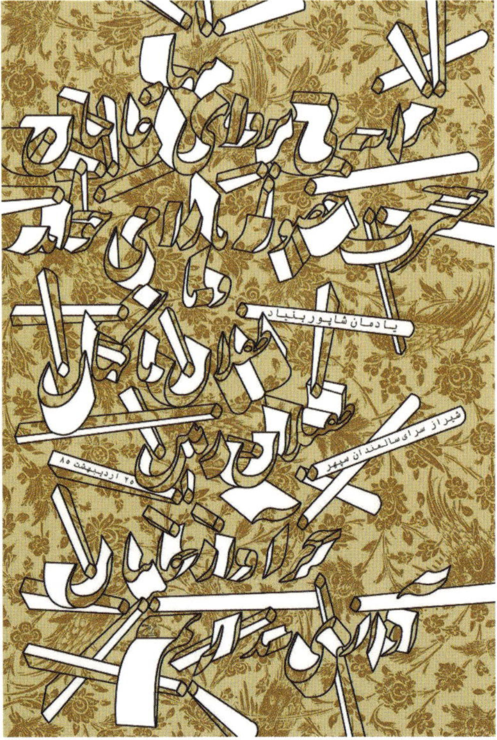

005
006

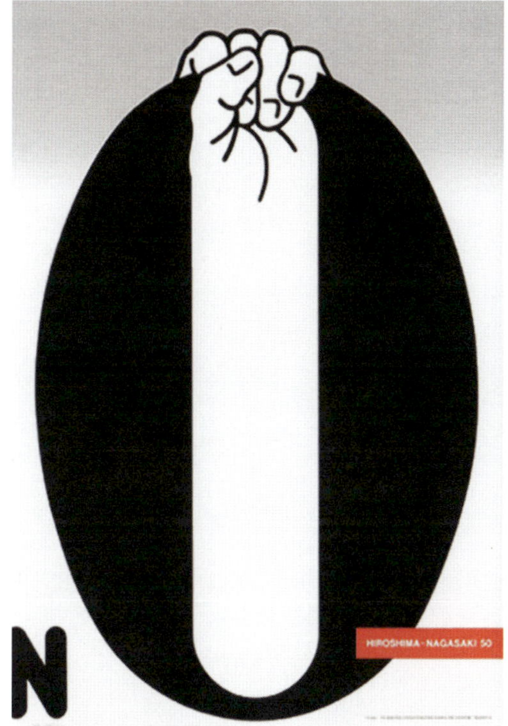

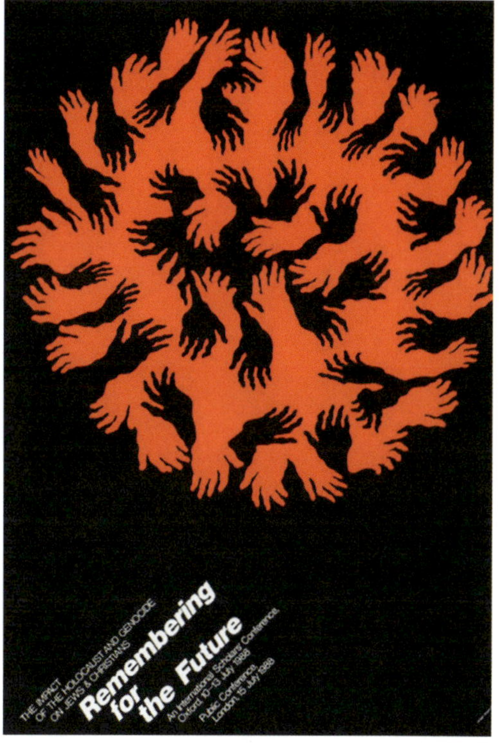

007
008

NEXT
009

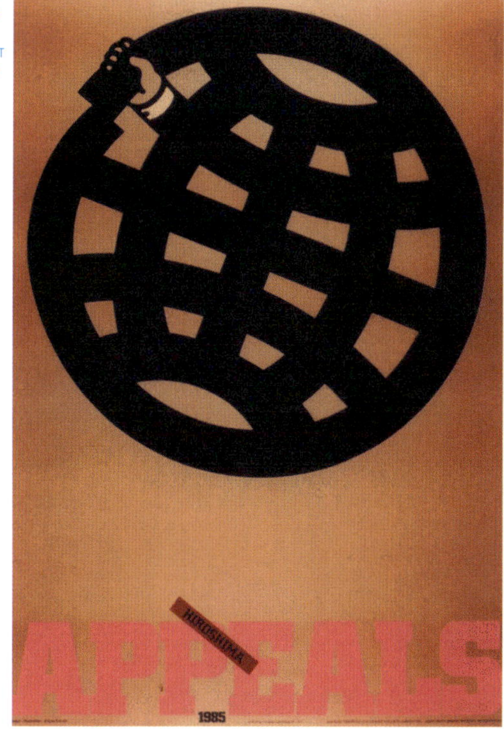

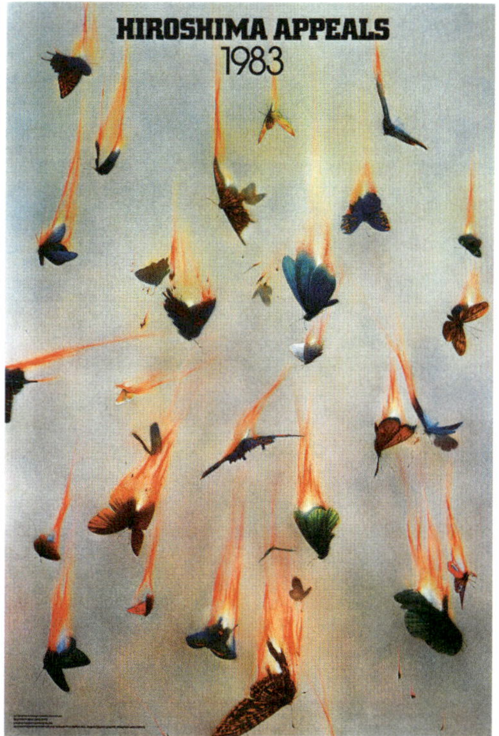

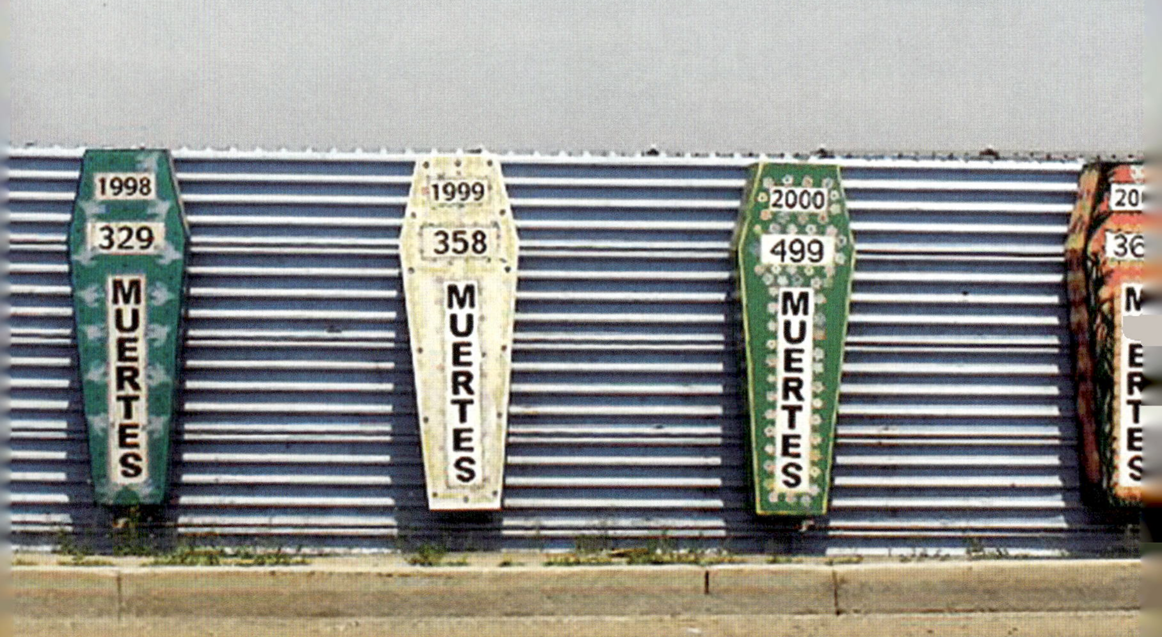

1998
329
MUERTES
1999
358
MUERTES
2000
499
MUERTES
200
36
MUERTES

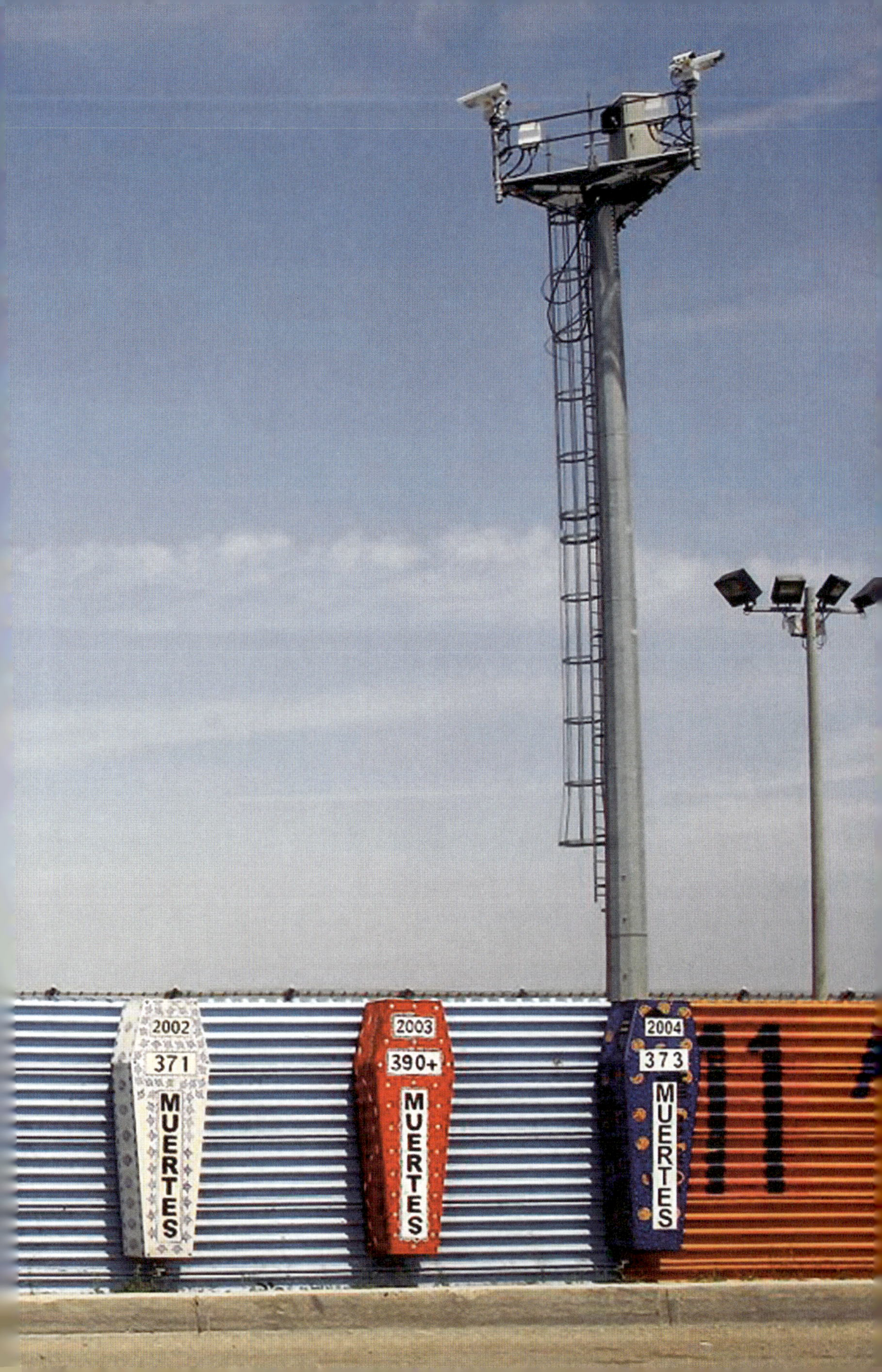

2002
371
MUERTES
2003
390+
MUERTES
2004
373
MUERTES

010
011

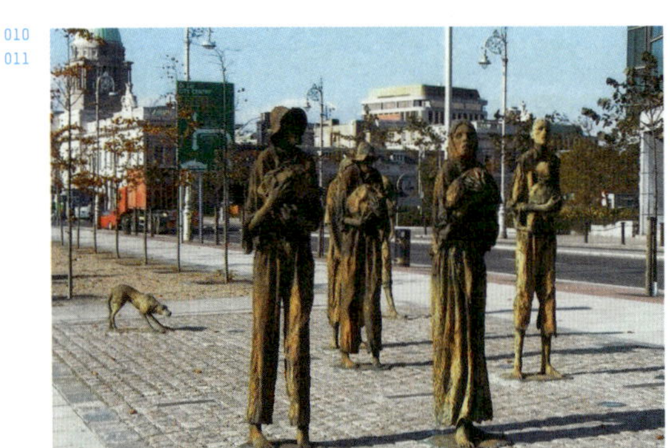
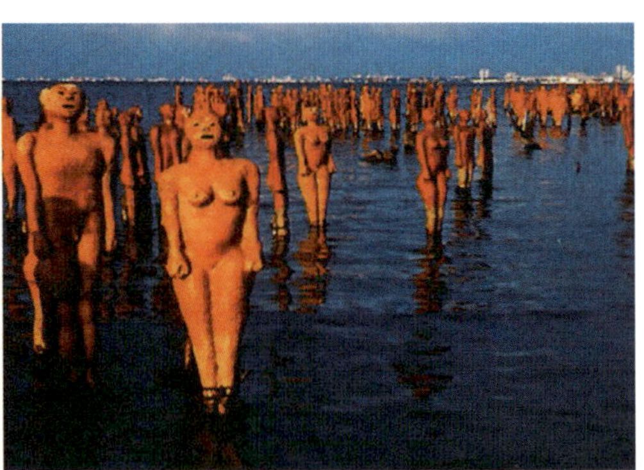

012
013

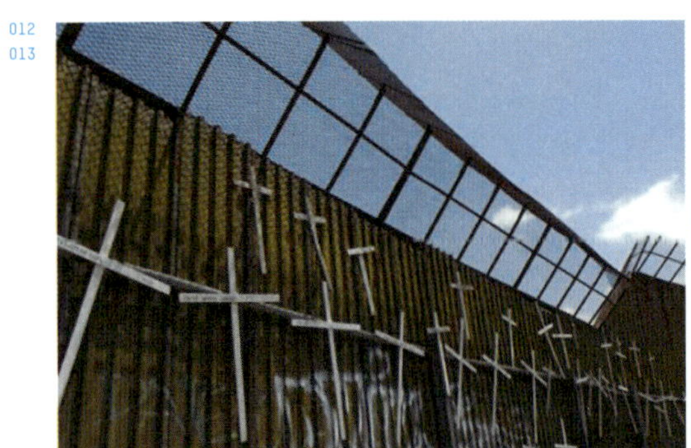
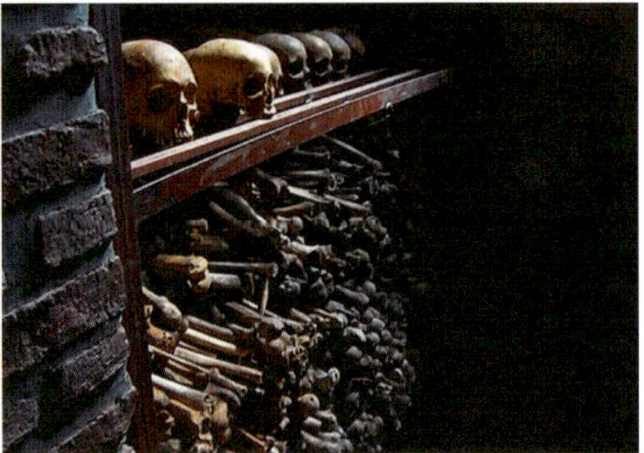

014

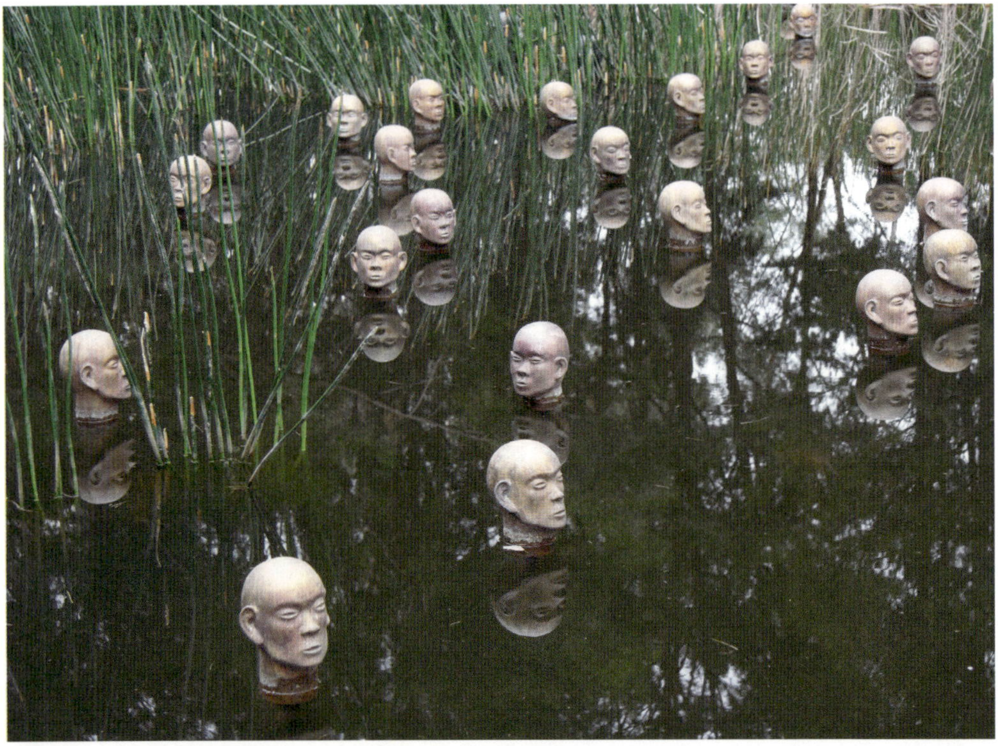

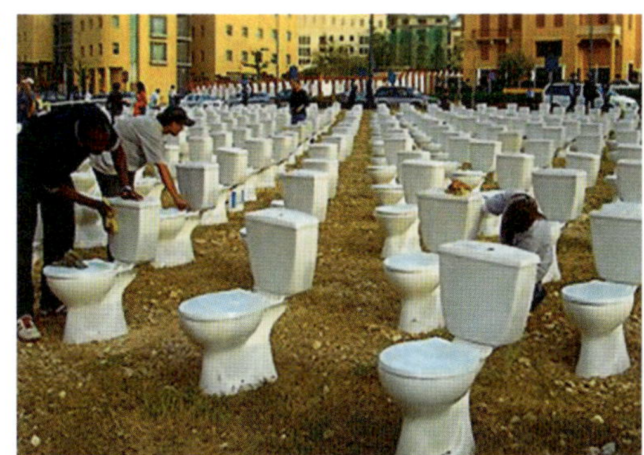
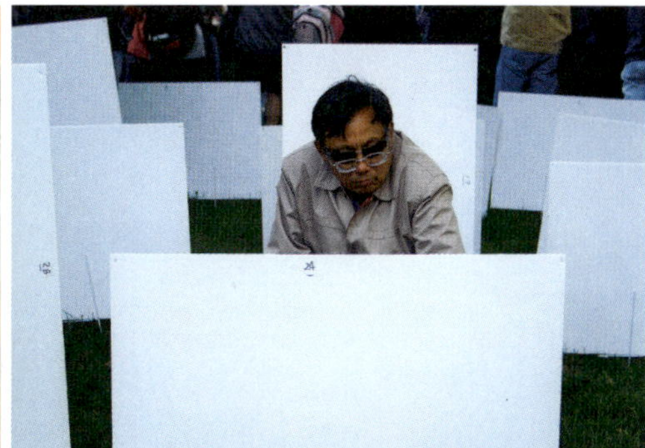
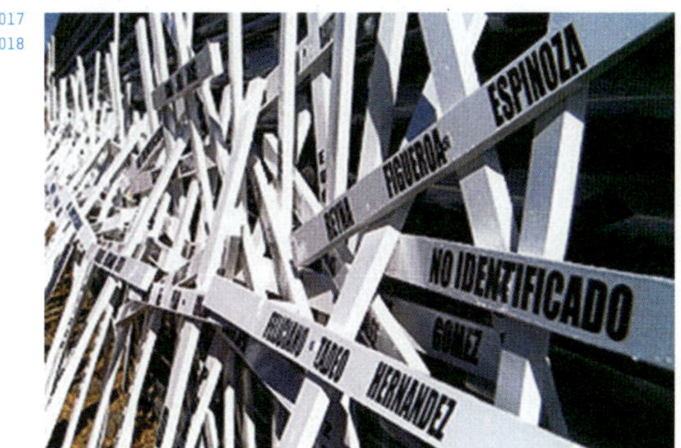

ESPINOZA
FIGUEROA
NO IDENTIFICADO
GOMEZ
HERNANDEZ

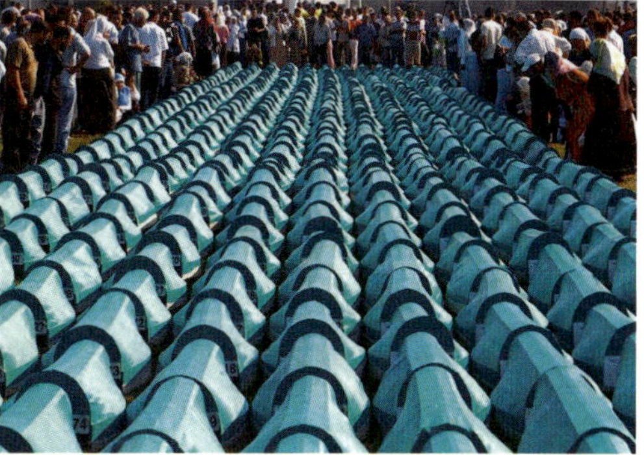

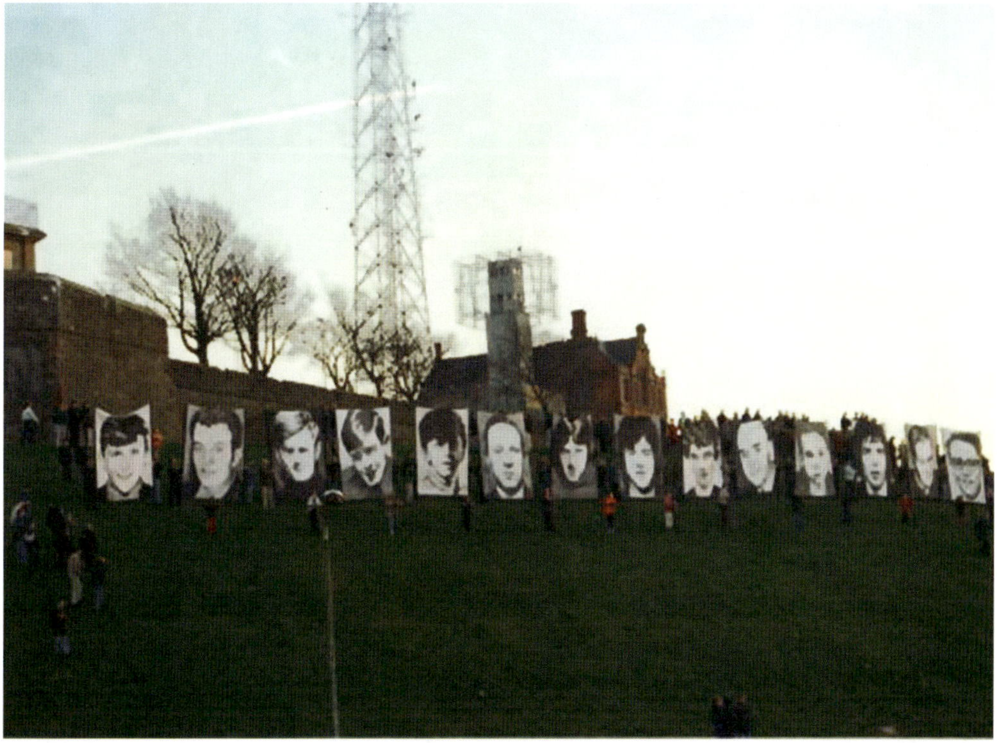

020

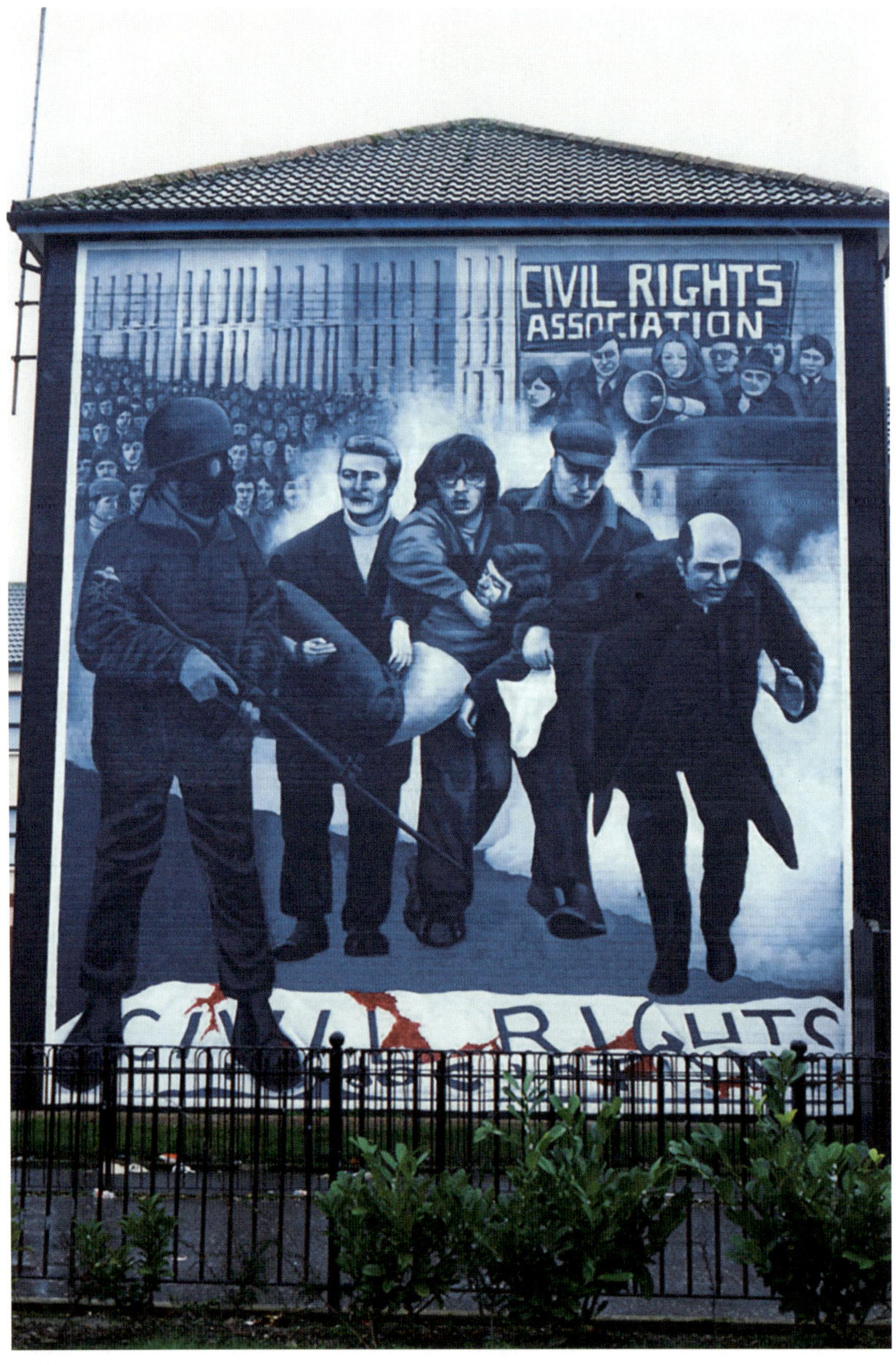

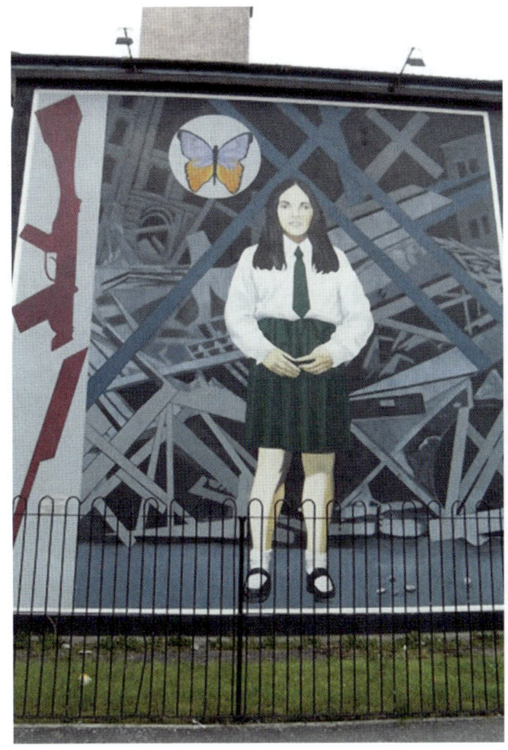

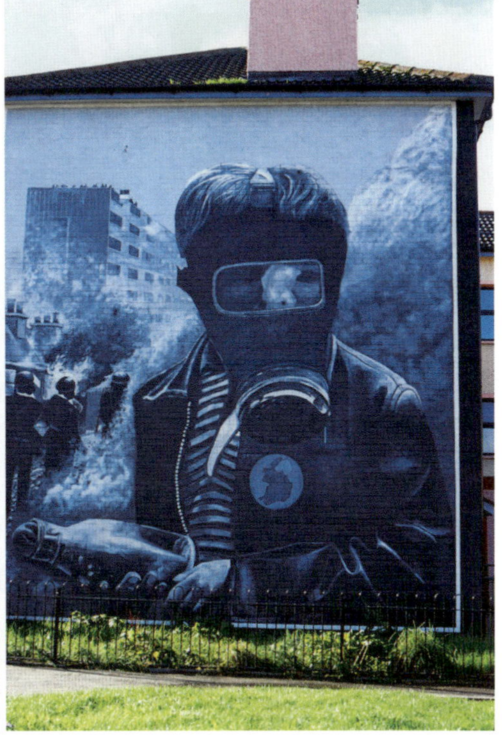

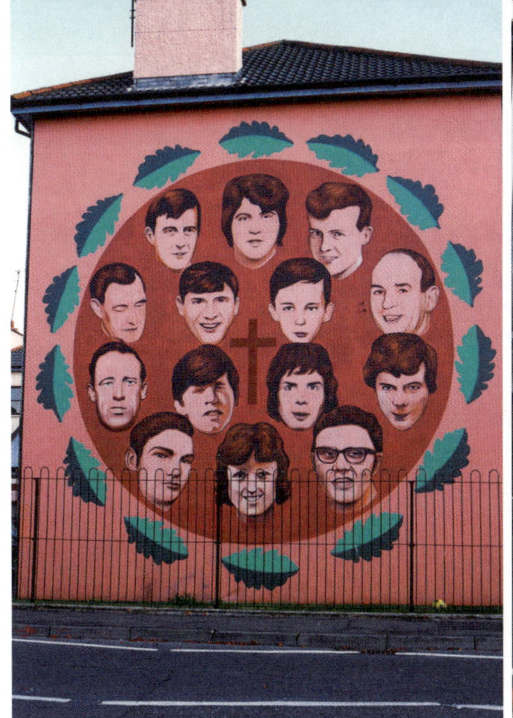

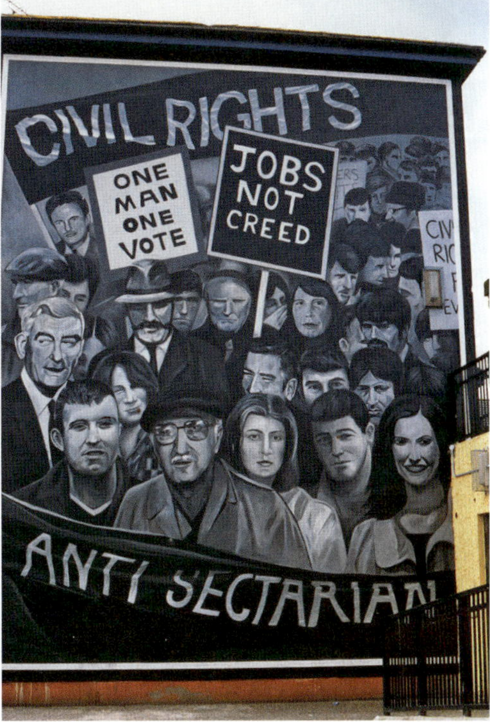
CIVIL RIGHTS
ONE MAN ONE VOTE
JOBS NOT CREED
CIVIL RI...
ANTI SECTARIAN

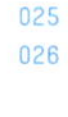

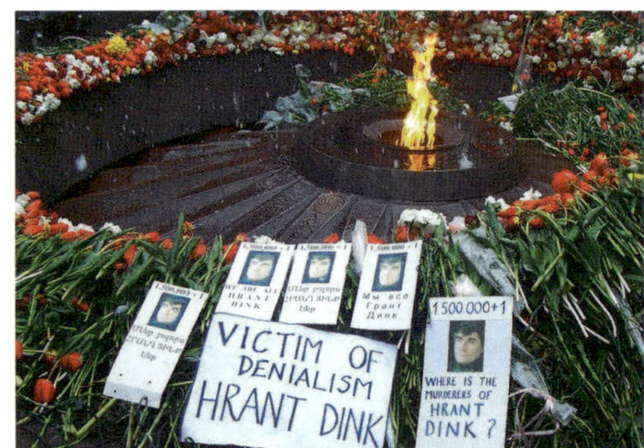
VICTIM OF
DENIALISM
HRANT DINK
1 500.000+1
WHERE IS THE
MURDERERS OF
HRANT
DINK ?

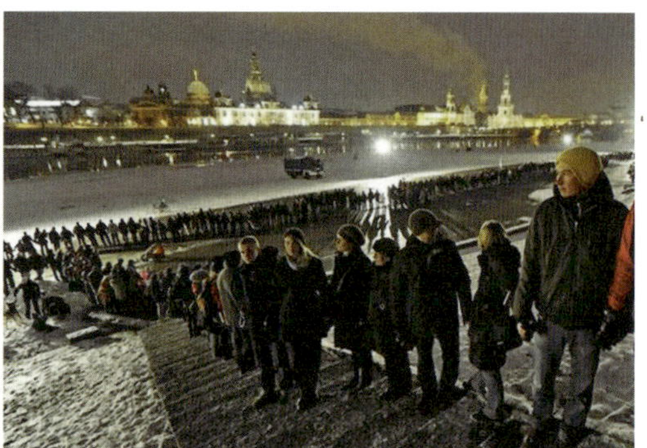

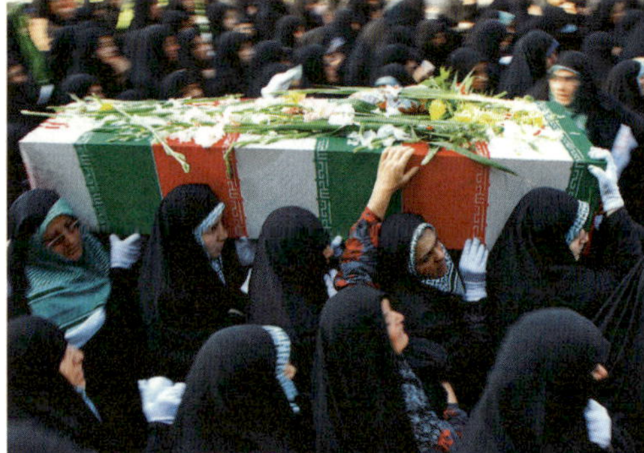

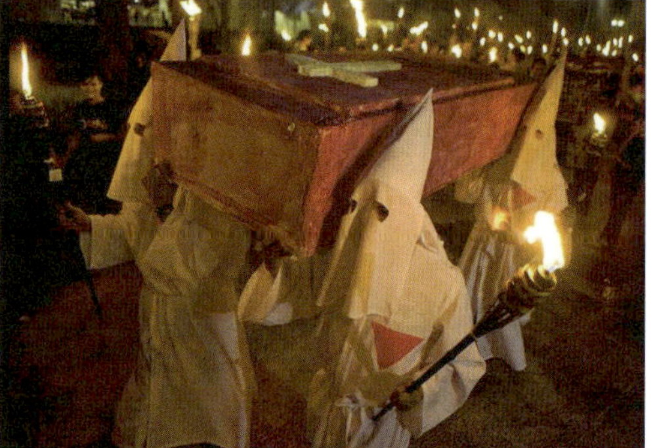

Ashnag

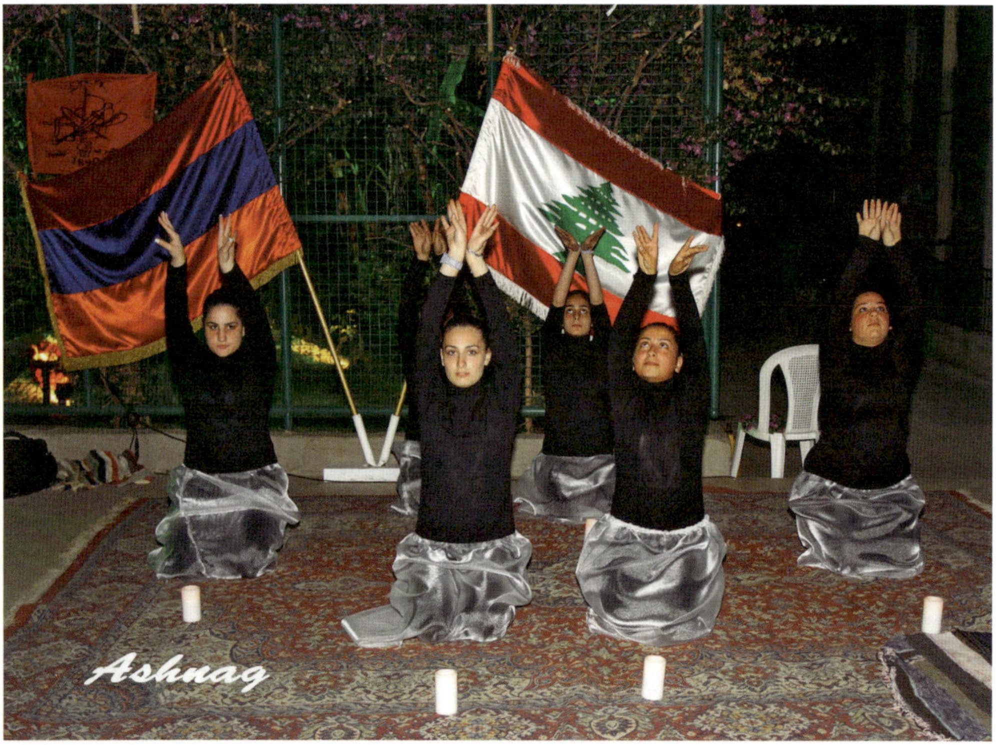

030
031

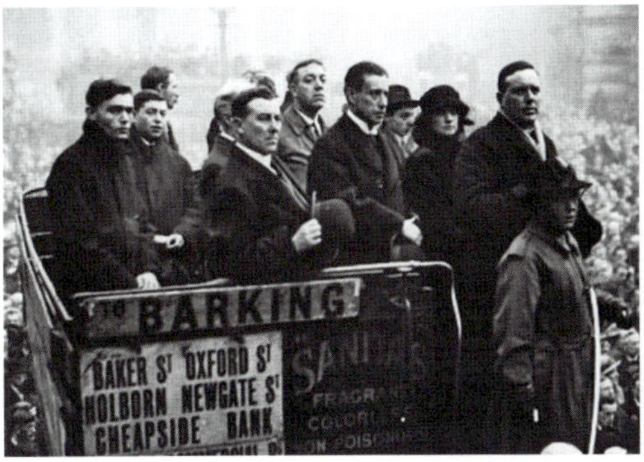
TO BARKING
BAKER ST OXFORD ST
HOLBORN NEWGATE ST
CHEAPSIDE BANK

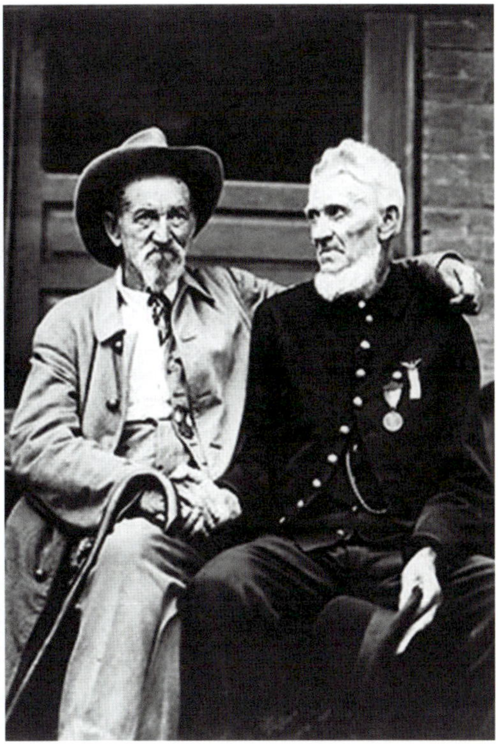

032

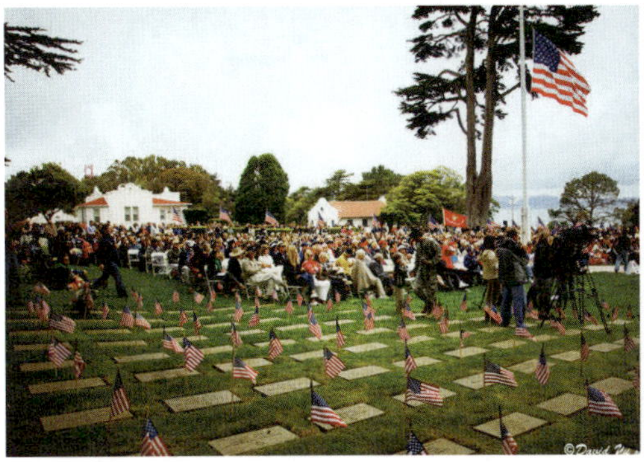

033

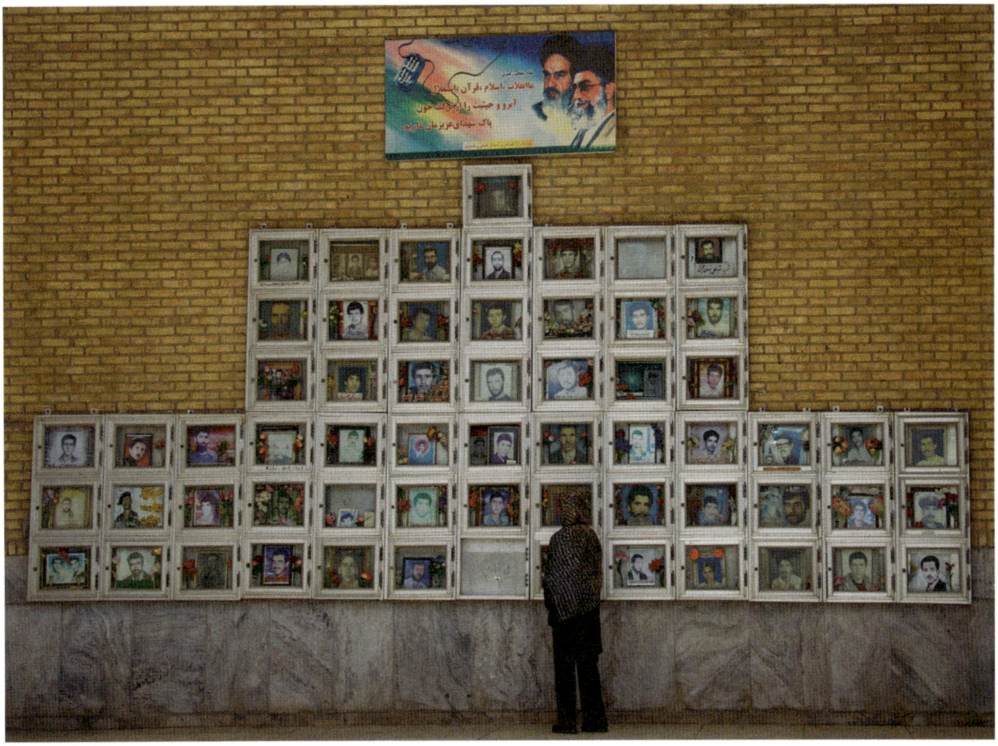

001 NINE/11
CREATOR Dennis Y. Ichiyama
SOURCE Plakatsammlung Museum
für Gestaltung Zürich

002 LIFE TO LEBANON
Poster commemorating the
eighteenth anniversary of
the Lebanon War and the I.D.F.
withdrawal.
CREATOR David Tartakover.
SOURCE www.oocities.org
DATE 2000

003 1945-1995
CREATOR Vladimir Cajka
SOURCE Plakatsammlung Museum
für Gestaltung Zürich

004 COMMEMORATION OF SHAHPOUR BONYAD
CREATOR Morteza Mahallati
SOURCE www.odatv.com
DATE 2006

005 THINKING FOR A LIVING
CREATOR Shigeo Fukuda
SOURCE ffffound.com

006 REMEMBERING FOR THE FUTURE
CREATOR Shigeo Fukuda
SOURCE thenoisyneighbor.tumblr.com
DATE 1989

007 HIROSHIMA APPEALS
CREATOR Shigeo Fukuda
SOURCE proyectofukuda.blogspot.ch
DATE 1985

008 HIROSHIMA APPEALS
CREATOR Yusaku Kamekura
SOURCE workthatmatters.blogspot.ch
DATE 1983

009 UNTITLED
In 2003 artists bolted coffins
to the Mexican side of the border
wall. Each was decorated and inscribed with a year and the number
of crossers who died that year.
For 1995 the number of confirmed
dead was 61; in 2000 there were
499. They are both a warning to
crossers and a reproach to the
United States. Three years after
their installation, and two weeks
before the US midterm elections,
Congress passed the Secure Fence
Act of 2006, calling for more than
700 miles of border wall modeled
on the barrier from which the
coffins hang.
CREATOR Artists in Tijuana, Mexico
SOURCE notexasborderwall.blogspot.
com
DATE 2003

010 A COMMEMORATION OF THE STARVING
PEASANTS OF DUBLIN [ON THE BANK
OF THE LIFFEY]

CREATOR Eve Andersson
SOURCE www.eveandersson.com

011 1001 EARTH HUMANS
[JAKARTA, INDONESIA]
CREATOR Dadang Christanto
SOURCE www.anu.edu.au
DATE 1996

012 A JOURNEY ALONG THE MIGRANT TRAIL
Crosses hang on the Mexican side
of the border wall in Nogales,
Mexico, commemorating the 4,000
people who have lost their lives
attempting to cross the desert
in search of a better life in the
United States.
CREATOR Tim Hoover
SOURCE mcc.org

013 THE FIFTEENTH COMMEMORATION OF
THE 1994 TUTSI GENOCIDE IN RWANDA
CREATOR Provided by hoteldephil
SOURCE csis.org

014 HEADS FROM THE NORTH, NATIONAL
GALLERY, CANBERRA
CREATOR Art by Dadang Christanto.
Provided by Ian Stehbens.
SOURCE commondatastorage.google-
apis.com

015 LEBANON: COMMEMORATING THE
CIVIL WAR
SOURCE globalvoicesonline.org

016 TIANANMEN VIGIL
CREATOR Provided by John Packman
SOURCE www.flickr.com/photos/
johnpackman/3710142381

017 CROSSES COMMEMORATE VICTIMS OF
VIOLENCE, SOME LEFT UNIDENTIFIED,
IN MEXICO
CREATOR Pies Cansados
SOURCE worldfocus.org

018 SREBRENICA MASSACRE COMMEMORATED
SOURCE www.rferl.org

019 BLOODY SUNDAY PROTEST STREET ART
On "Bloody Sunday" [30 January
1972] the British Army opened fire
on a civil rights demonstration
and killed 14 people. As part of
the commemoration, the Bogside
Artists produced fourteen large
black and white portraits of
those killed. The paintings are
shown displayed on the hillside
overlooking the route taken by
the march on 30 January 1972.
CREATOR Martin Melaugh
SOURCE cain.ulst.ac.uk

020 BLOODY SUNDAY 30 JANUARY 1972
The Bogside Artists are best
known for the wall murals that
they painted in the Bogside area

of Derry, Northern Ireland. This
collection of murals has become
known as The People's Gallery.
CREATOR Martin Melaugh
SOURCE cain.ulst.ac.uk

021 DEATH OF INNOCENCE
CREATOR Martin Melaugh
SOURCE cain.ulst.ac.uk

022 PETROL BOMBER BATTLE OF
THE BOGSIDE
CREATOR Martin Melaugh
SOURCE cain.ulst.ac.uk

023 BLOODY SUNDAY VICTIMS
CREATOR Martin Melaugh
SOURCE cain.ulst.ac.uk

024 CIVIL RIGHTS, THE BEGINNING
CREATOR Martin Melaugh
SOURCE cain.ulst.ac.uk

025 HRANT DINK
CREATOR Provided by nersess
SOURCE www.flickr.com/photos/
nersess/2078182343/sizes/l/in/
photostream/

026 DRESDEN COMMEMORATES WORLD WAR II
BOMBING ANNIVERSARY
SOURCE www.dw.de

027 IRANIAN MUSLIM WOMEN COMMEMORATE
THOSE WHO WERE KILLED DURING THE
IRAN-IRAQ WAR [1980-88], TEHRAN
CREATOR Ali Mohammadi
SOURCE www.lightstalkers.org
DATE 29 November 2009

028 DAY IN PHOTOS
Members of the gay rights
community take part in a rally
to commemorate International Day
Against Homophobia in Monterrey,
Mexico. The participants' costumes
represent intolerance and the
coffin symbolizes those who have
died of HIV/AIDS as well as those
who have suffered from persecution.
CREATOR Tomas Bravo
SOURCE www.washingtonpost.com

029 COMMEMORATING 95TH ANNIVERSARY
OF ARMENIAN GENOCIDE
CREATOR Provided by Ashnag
SOURCE www.flickr.com/photos/
studioashnag/4540973635

030 SILENCE TO COMMEMORATE THE
ANNIVERSARY OF THE OFFICIAL END
OF WORLD WAR I IS OBSERVED NEAR
BANK, LONDON.
SOURCE www.dailymail.co.uk

031 HOW WE HAVE COMMEMORATED
THE CIVIL WAR
An unidentified Confederate and
Union soldier shake hands on the

fiftieth anniversary reunion at
Gettysburg.
CREATOR Associated Press
SOURCE www.smithsonianmag.com/

032 MEMORIAL DAY COMMEMORATION
CREATOR Provided by David Yu
SOURCE www.flickr.com/photos/
davidyuweb/2525280573/
DATE 2008

033 WAR MEMORIAL
The men in the photographs on the
wall are soldiers who perished in
the Iran-Iraq war of the 1980s.
Above them is a poster with a
dog tag in the upper left corner
and the visages of Iran's past
and present Supreme Leaders, the
late Ayatollah Khomeini and the
Ayatollah Sayyed Ali Khamenei.
In the precincts of the Mausoleum
of Khawje Rabie, Mashhad, Iran,
CREATOR Provided by A Davey
SOURCE www.flickr.com/photos/
adavey/4823633803/

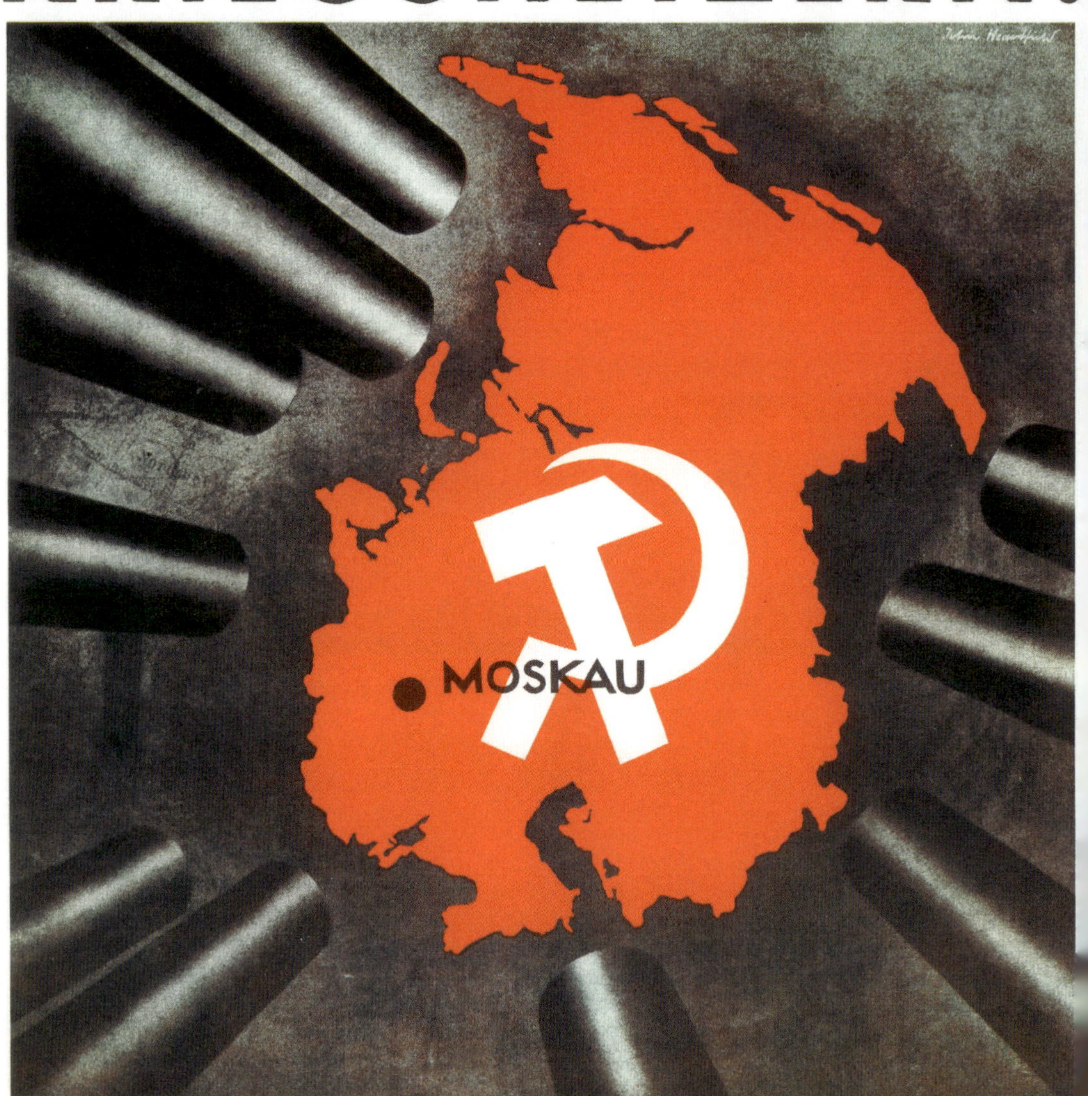

NIEDER MIT DEN KRIEGSHETZERN!
MOSKAU
KÄMPFT FÜR DIE SOWJETUNION!
HERAUS ZUM KAMPFMAI 1932
Herausgeber und für den Inhalt verantwortlich: Ernst Schneller, MdR., Berlin. — Druck: Westdeutsche Buchdruck-Werkstätten AG., Düsseldorf, Kölner Straße 44.

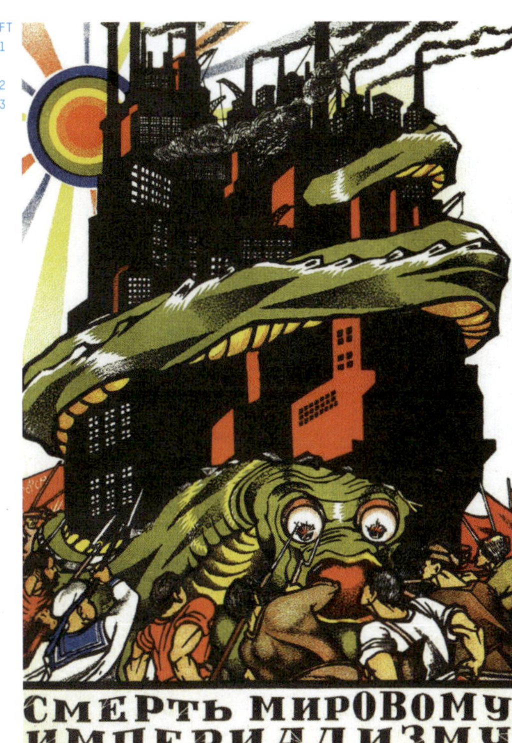
СМЕРТЬ МИРОВОМУ
ИМПЕРИАЛИЗМУ

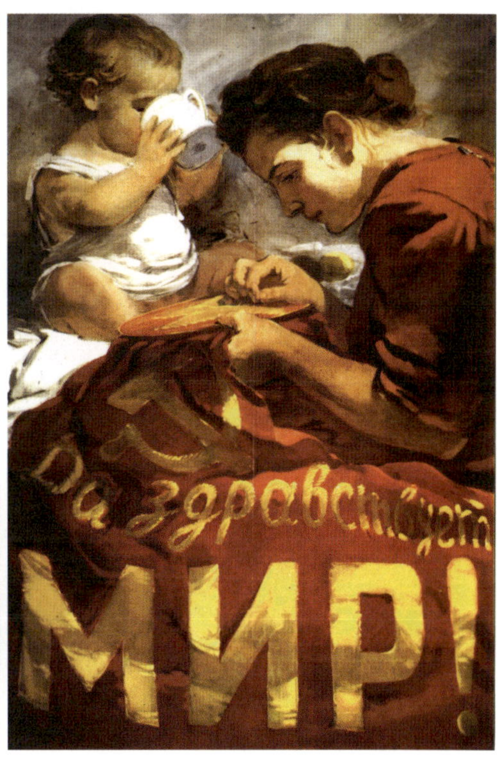
Да здравствует
МИР!

· Р · С · Ф · С · Р ·
ПРОЛЕТАРИИ ВСЕХ СТРАН, СОЕДИНЯЙТЕСЬ!
ДА
ЗДРАВСТВУЕТ
СОЛНЦЕ!

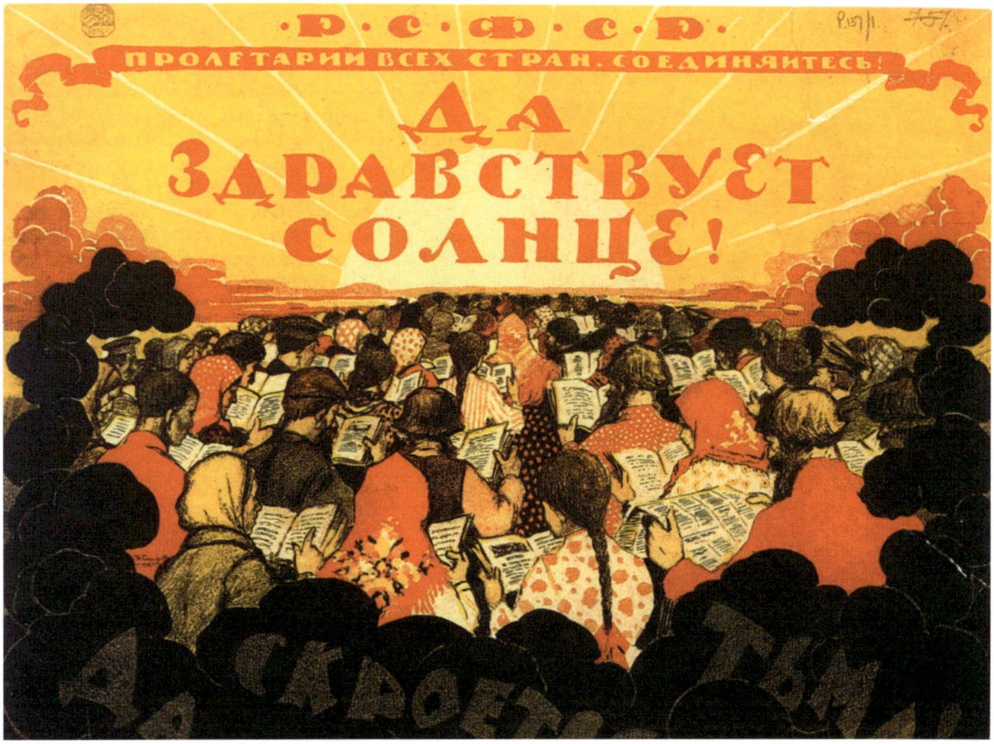

005
006

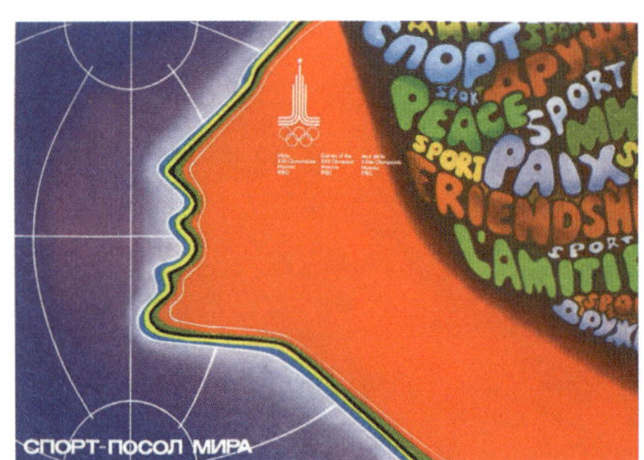

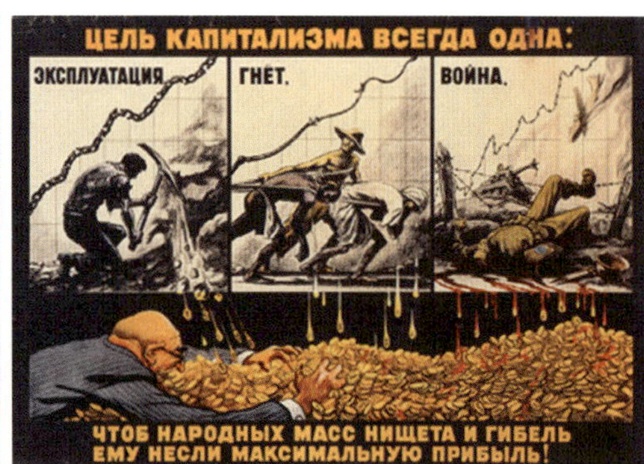

007
008

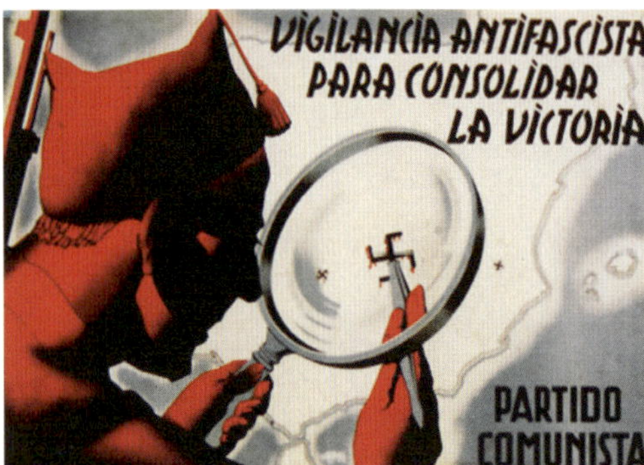

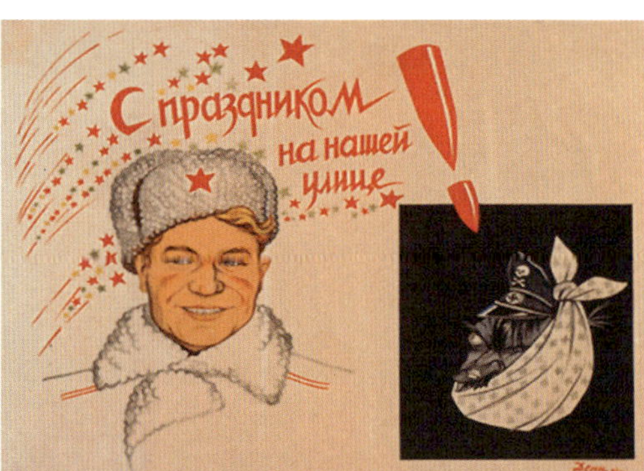

009
010

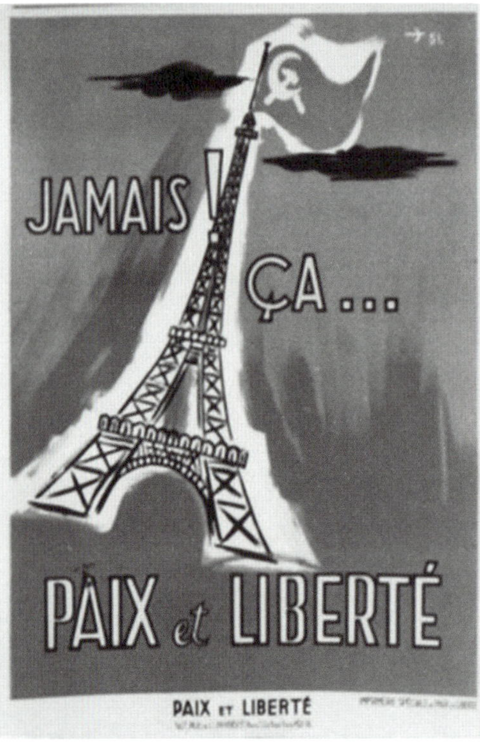

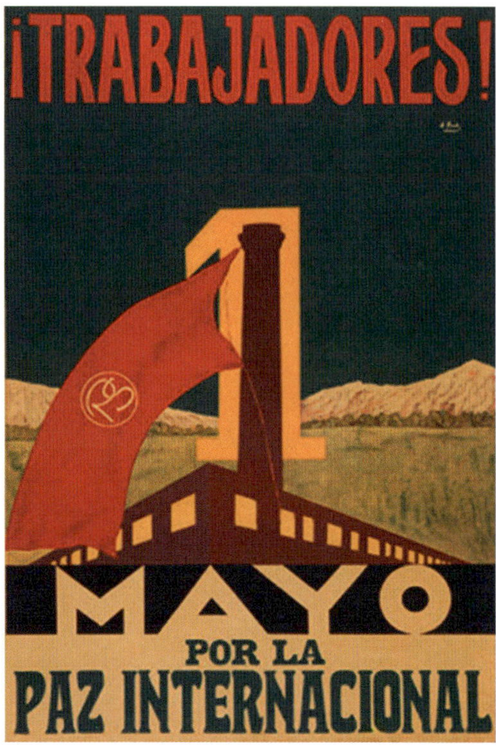

001 NIEDER MIT DEN KRIEGSHETZERN!
[DOWN WITH WARMONGERS!]
CREATOR John Heartfiled

002 DEATH TO WORLDS' IMPERIALISM
SOURCE www.sovietposters.com

003 LONG LIVE PEACE!
SOURCE www.sovietposters.com

004 LONG LIVE THE SUN, LET THE
DARKNESS DISAPPEAR
SOURCE www.sovietposters.com

005 SPORTS ARE AN AMBASSADOR OF PEACE
CREATOR David Yu
SOURCE www.sovietposters.com

006 CEL' KAPITALIZMA VSEGDA ODNA:
EKSPLUATICIJA, GNET,...
[THE GOAL OF CAPITALISM IS ALWAYS
THE SAME]
CREATOR I. Semenov
SOURCE Plakatsammlung Museum
für Gestaltung Zürich

007 VIGILANCIA ANTIFASCISTA
PARA CONSOLIDAR LA VICTORIA
PARTIDO COMUNISTA
[KEEP THE FASCISTS UNDER
SURVEILLANCE IN ORDER TO ATTAIN
VICTORY FOR THE COMMUNIST PARTY]
CREATOR Seccion Artes Plasticas
A.I.D.C.
SOURCE Plakatsammlung Museum
für Gestaltung Zürich

008 S PRAZDNIKOM NA NASEJ ULICE!
[A JOYFUL CELEBRATION ON
OUR STREET]
CREATOR Viktor Nikolaevic Deni
SOURCE Plakatsammlung Museum
für Gestaltung Zürich

009 JAMAIS ÇA ... PAIX ET LIBERTÉ
[NEVER THIS ... PEACE AND LIBERTY]
CREATOR Bernhard Bloom
SOURCE Plakatsammlung Museum
für Gestaltung Zürich

010 TRABAJADORES!
[WORKERS!]
CREATOR J. Foch
SOURCE Plakatsammlung Museum
für Gestaltung Zürich

001

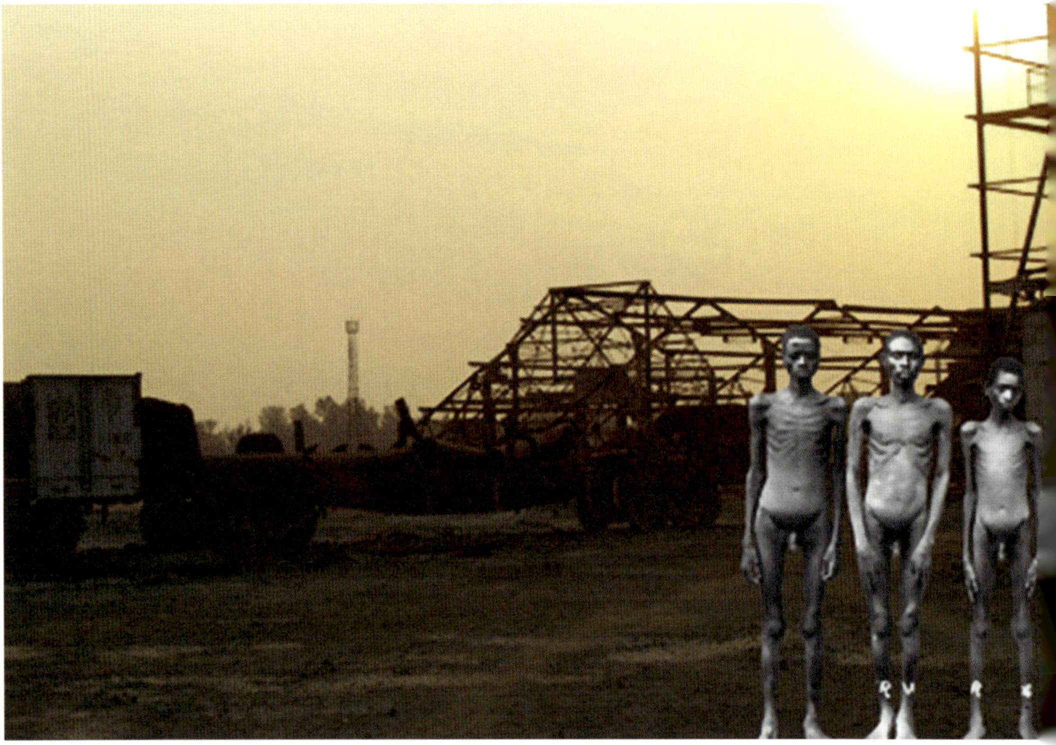

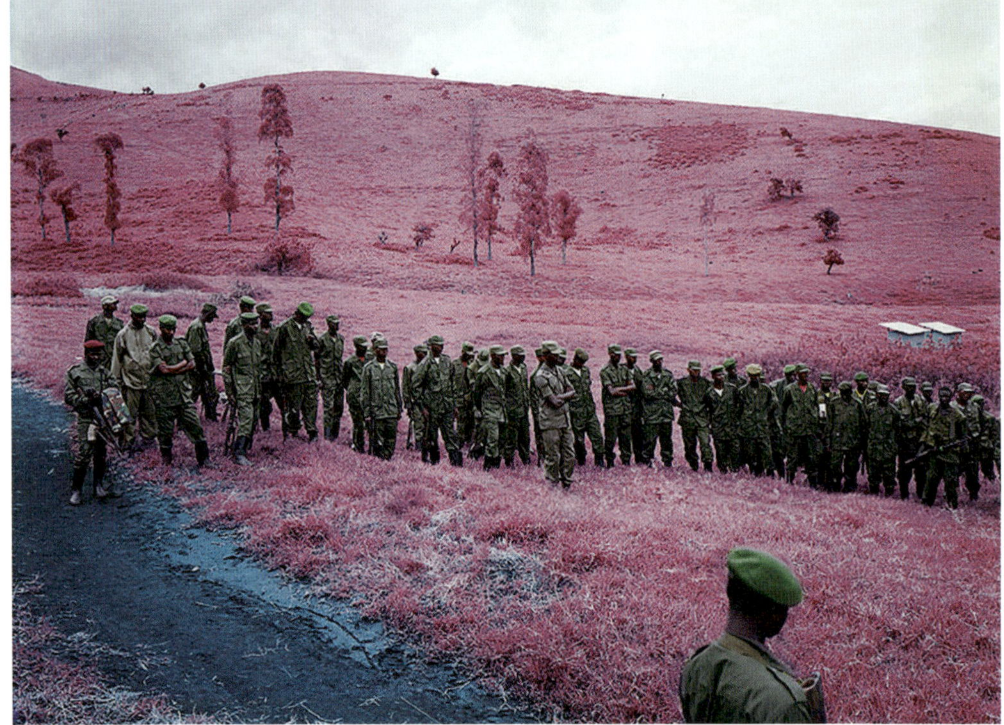

002

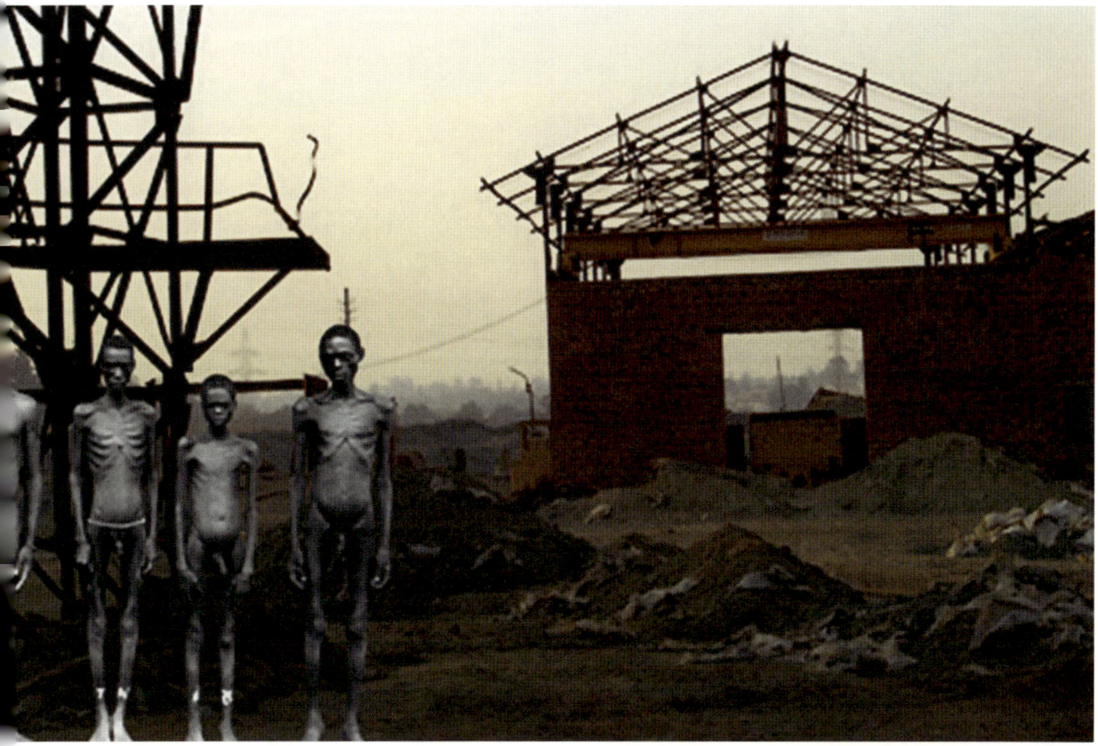

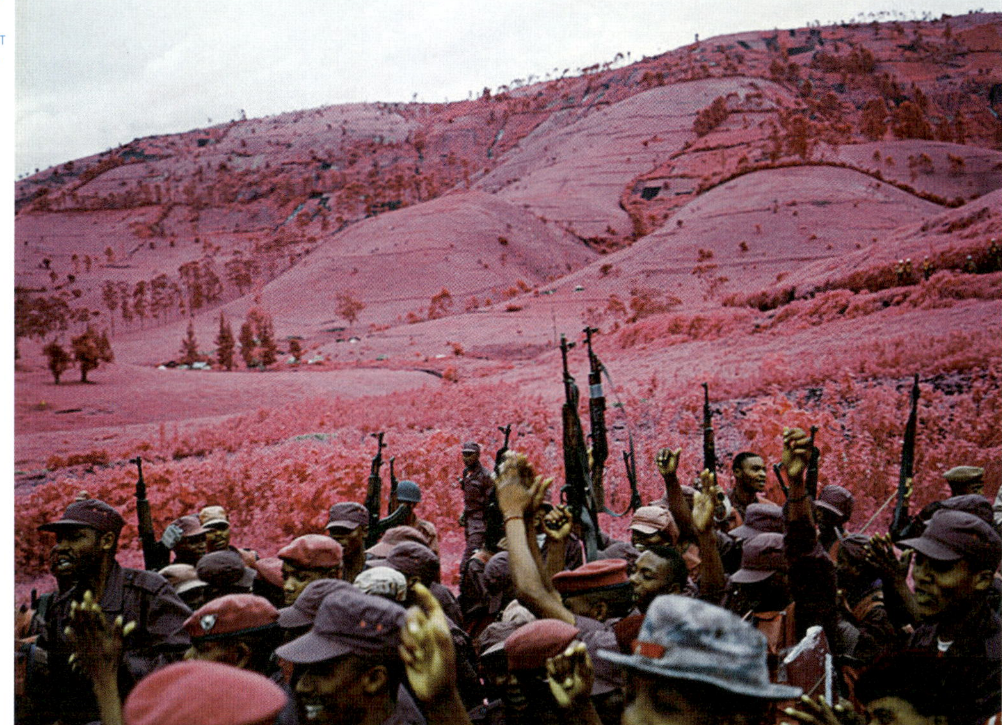

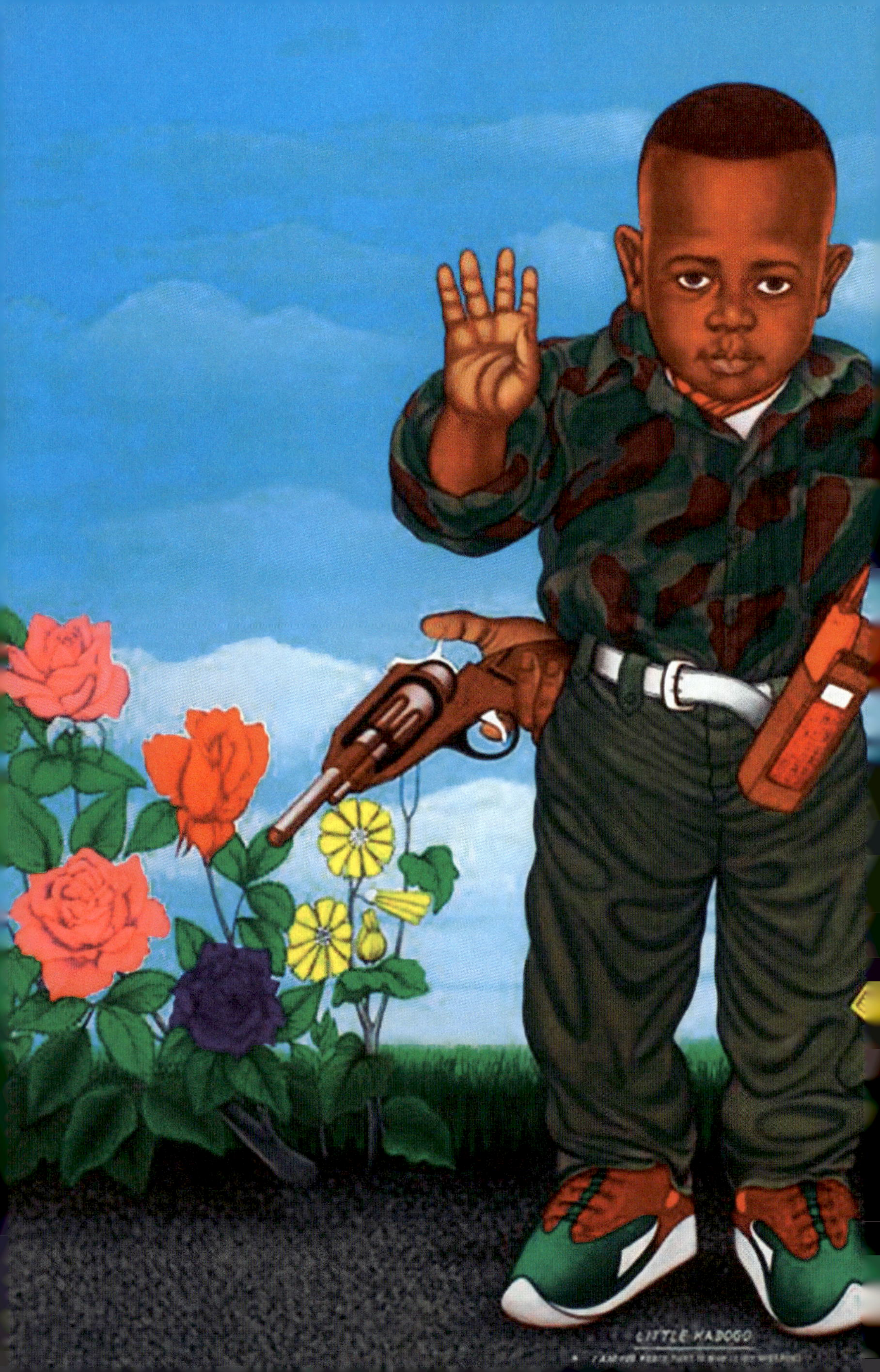
LITTLE KADOGO

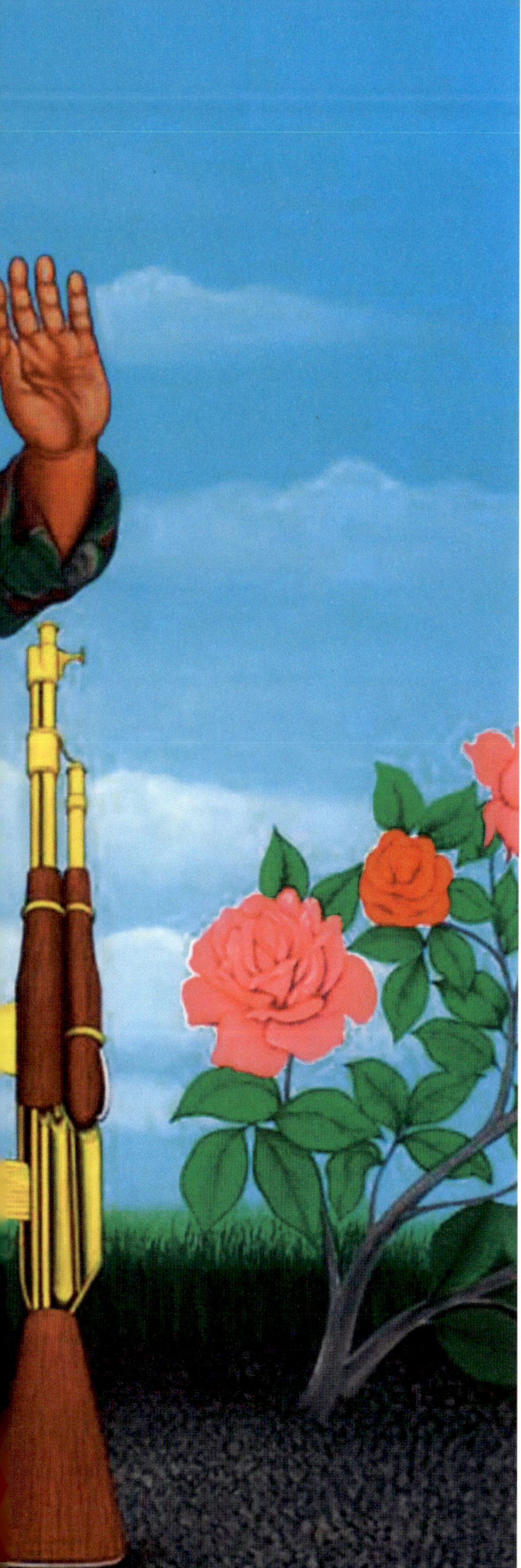

001 MEMORY
     Katanga, Congo [DRC]. He says
     "To superimpose past onto present
     reveals the will to denounce past
     and present abuses."
     CREATOR John Heartfiled
     DATE 2006

002 COLONEL SOLEIL'S BOYS, NORTH KIVU,
     EASTERN CONGO
     CREATOR Richard Mosse
     SOURCE www.richardmosse.com
     DATE 2010

003 LA VIE EN ROSE, NORTH KIVU,
     EASTERN CONGO
     CREATOR Richard Mosse
     SOURCE www.richardmosse.com
     DATE 2010

004 TIME FOR REBELS
     CREATOR Chèri Cherin
     SOURCE alexandrepomar.typepad.com
     DATE 2008

001
002

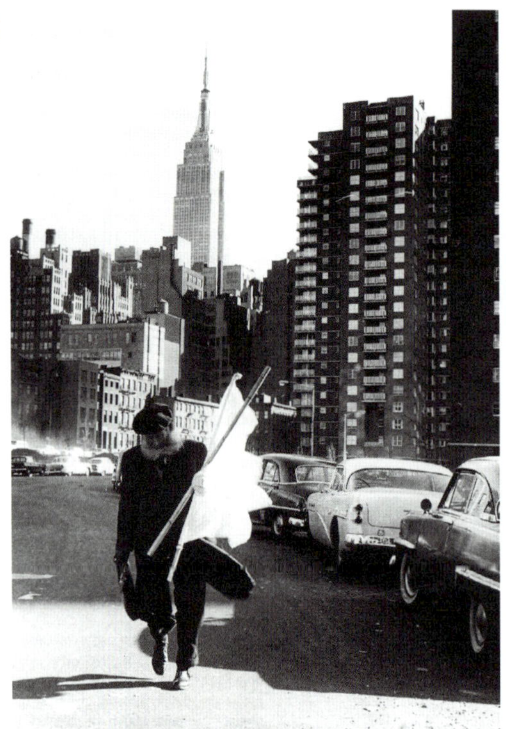

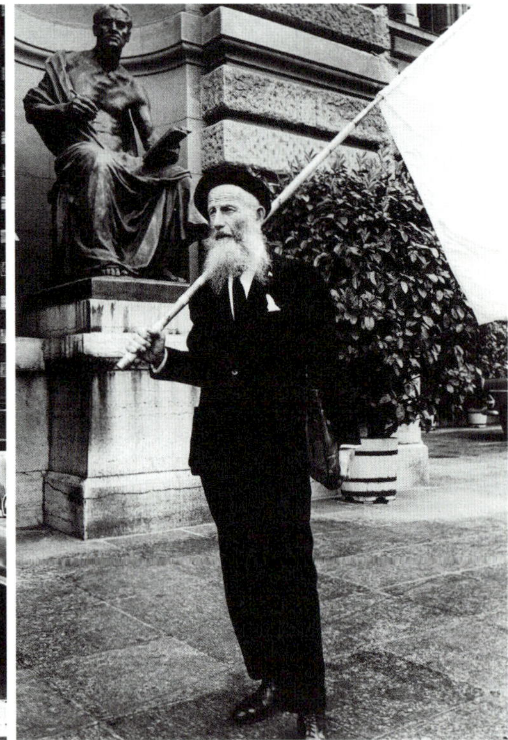

003

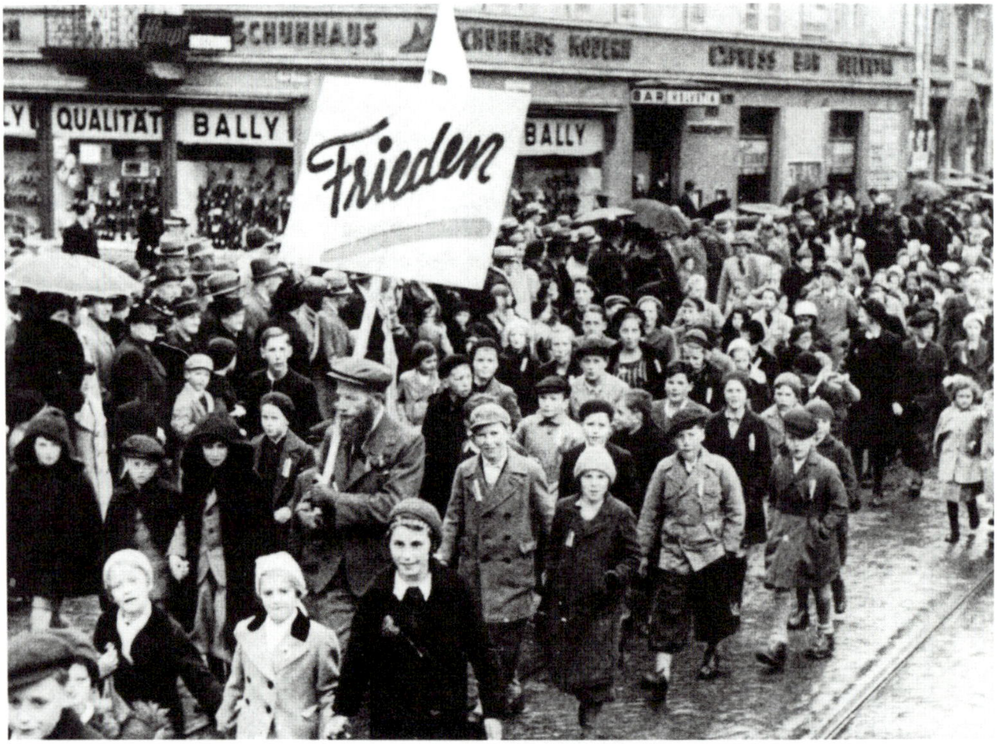

004
005

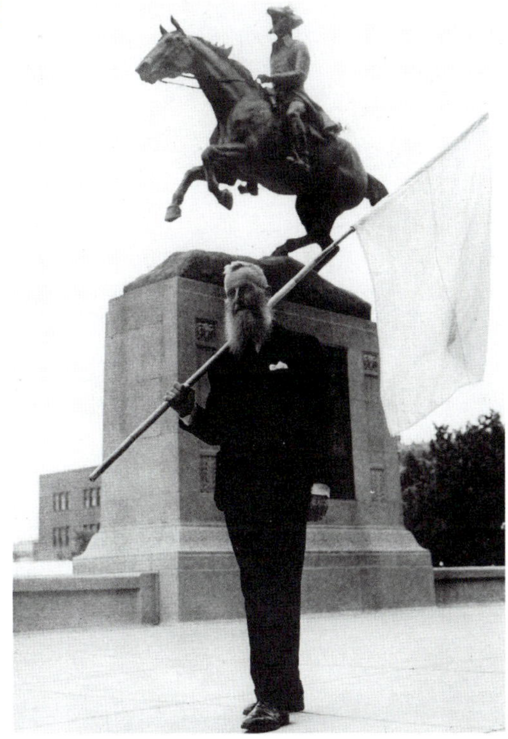

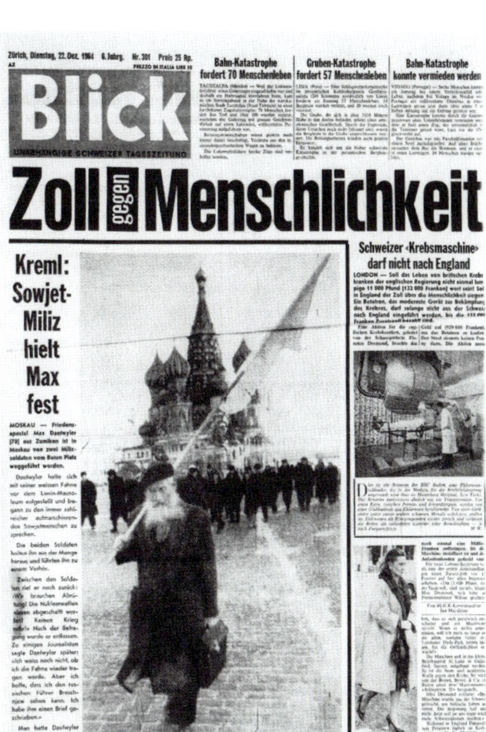

006
007

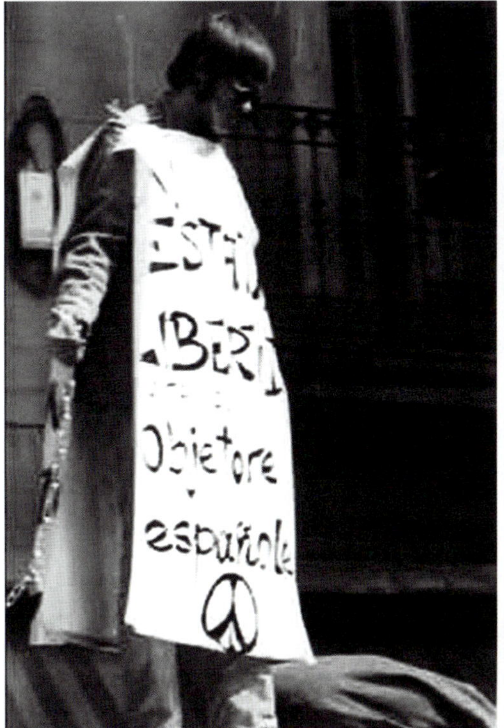

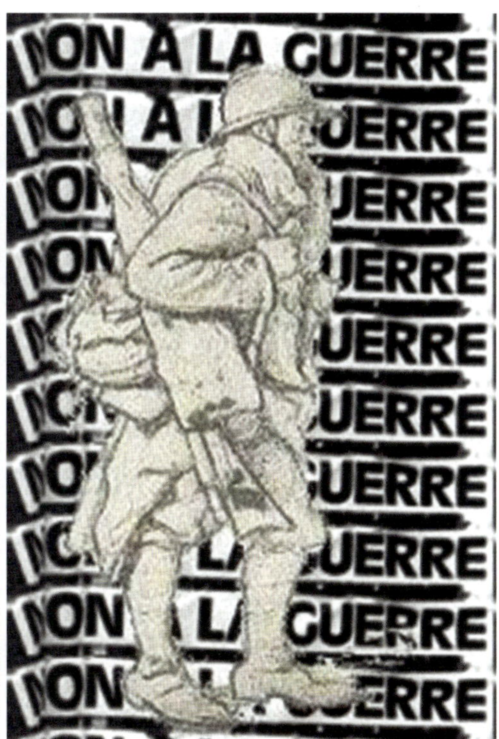

008

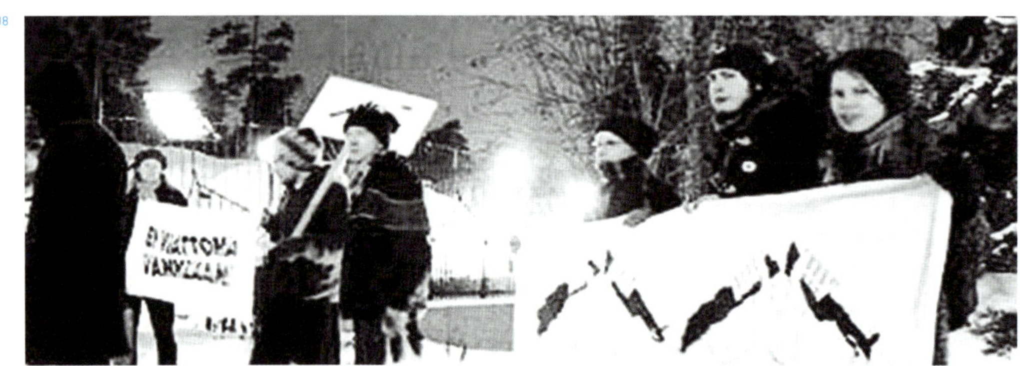

009

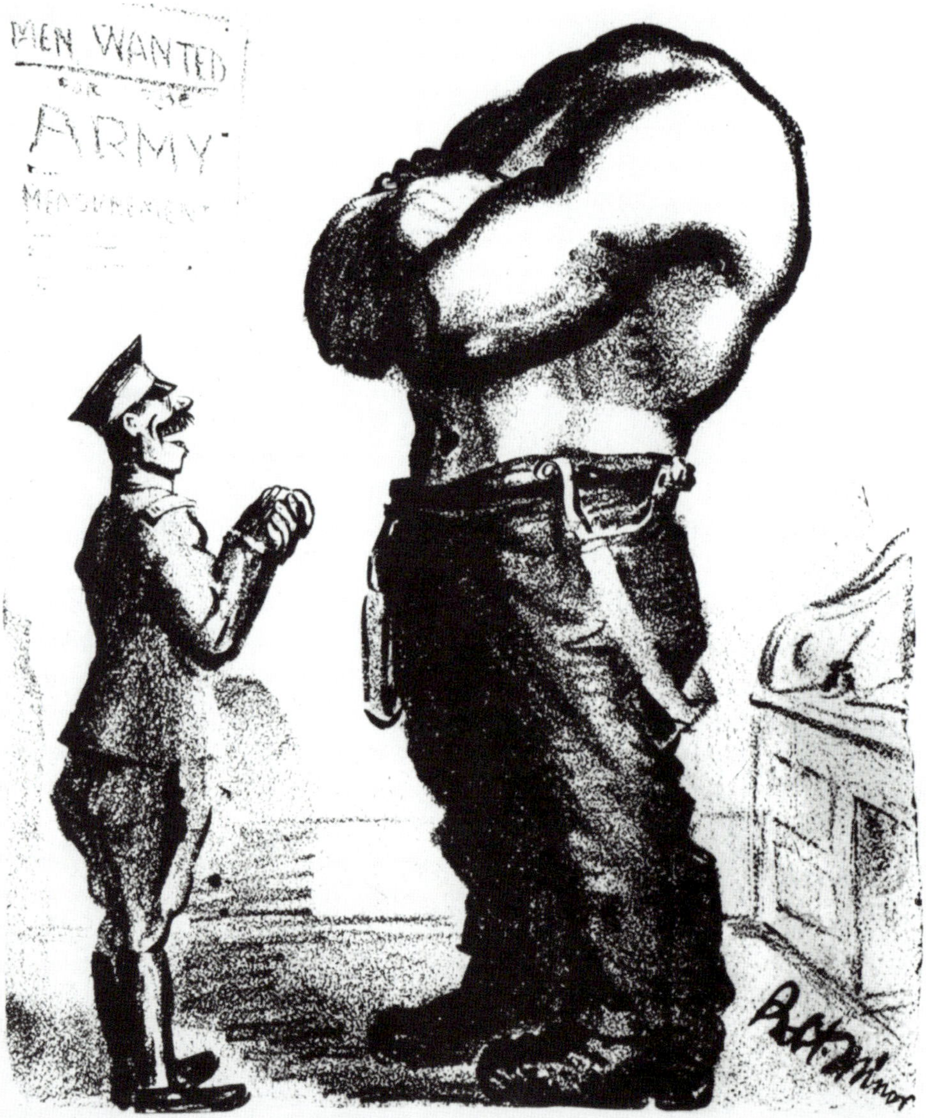

010

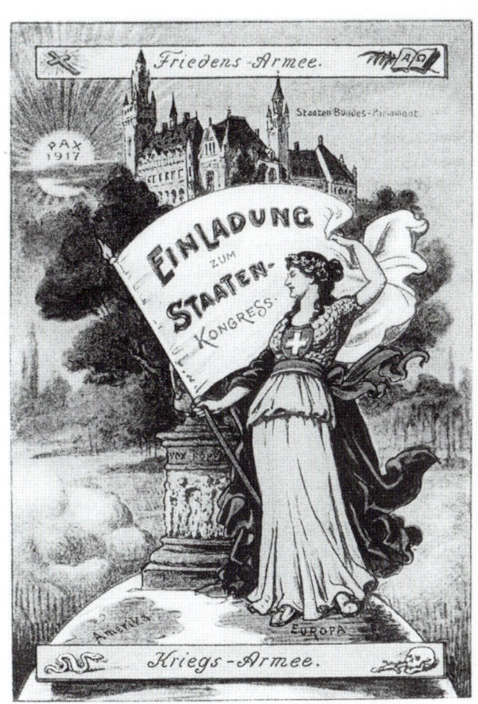

011

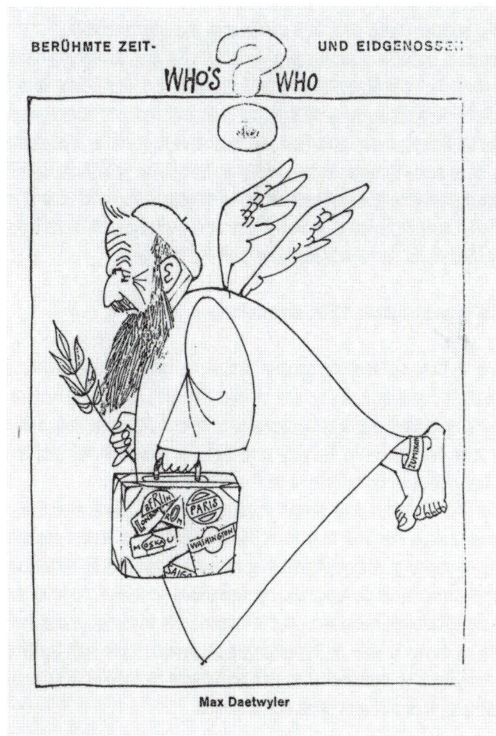

Max Daetwyler

001 MAX DAETWYLER
SOURCE Hans von Rütte, *Max Daetwyler: Friedensapostel, apotre de la pax, 1886-1976*, p. 43.

002 MAX DAETWYLER
SOURCE Hans von Rütte, *Max Daetwyler: Friedensapostel, apotre de la pax, 1886-1976*, p. 22.

003 PEACE MARCH
SOURCE Hans von Rütte, *Max Daetwyler: Friedensapostel, apotre de la pax, 1886-1976*, p. 37.

004 MAX DAETWYLER
SOURCE Hans von Rütte, *Max Daetwyler: Friedensapostel, apotre de la pax, 1886-1976*, p. 21.

005 MAX DAETWYLER
SOURCE Hans von Rütte, *Max Daetwyler: Friedensapostel, apotre de la pax, 1886-1976*, p. 101.

006 UNTITLED
CREATOR anarchism et non violence
SOURCE anarchismenonviolence2.org

007 NON A LA GUERRE
[NO TO WAR]
CREATOR planete non violence
SOURCE www.planetenonviolence.org

008 UNTITLED
CREATOR War Resisters'
SOURCE www.wri-irg.org

009 AT LAST, A PERFECT SOLDIER
SOURCE Hans von Rütte, *Max Daetwyler: Friedensapostel, apotre de la pax, 1886-1976*, p. 48.

010 EINLADUNG ZUM STAATEN-KONGRESS
[INVITATION TO THE STATES CONGRESS]
SOURCE Hans von Rütte, *Max Daetwyler: Friedensapostel, apotre de la pax, 1886-1976*, p. 60.

011 MAX DAETWYLER
SOURCE Hans von Rütte, *Max Daetwyler: Friedensapostel, apotre de la pax, 1886-1976*, p. 60.

001
002

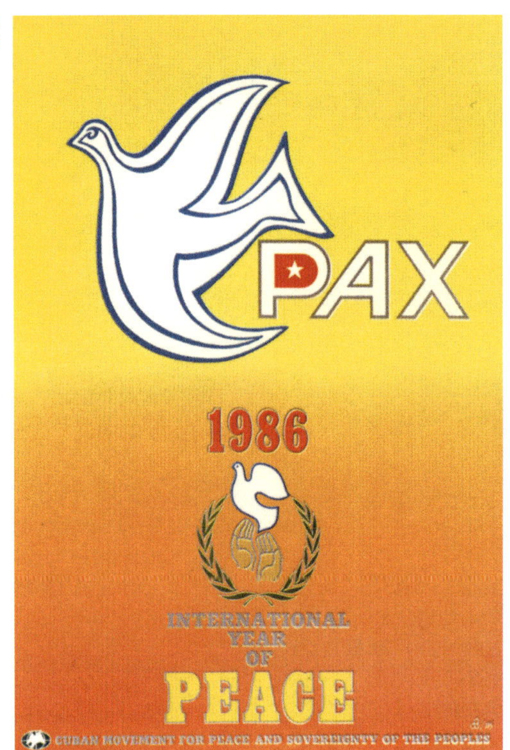

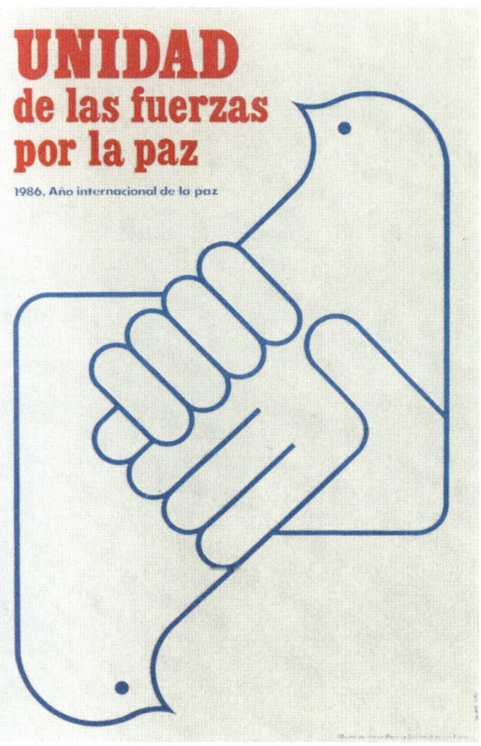

003
004

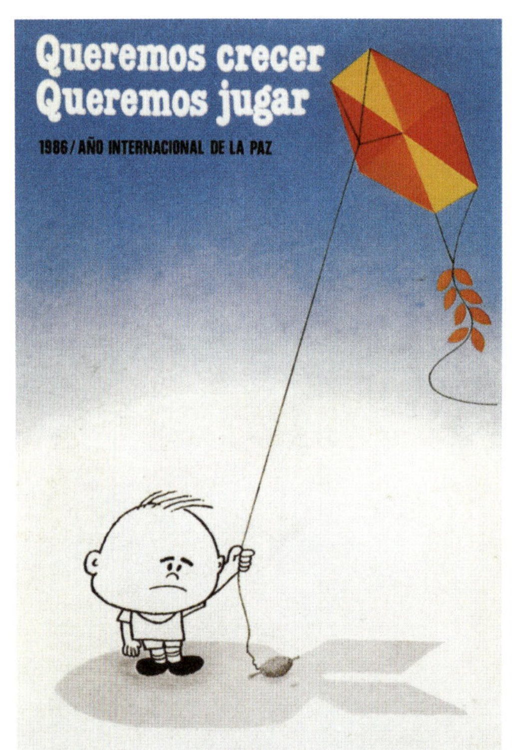

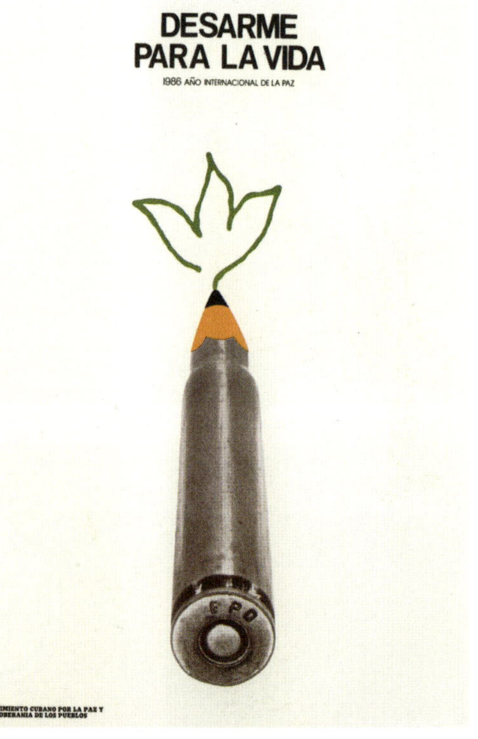

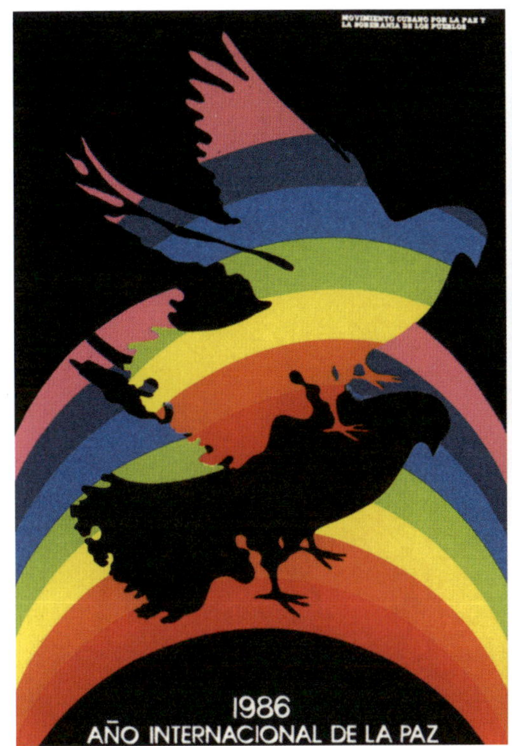
MOVIMIENTO CUBANO POR LA PAZ Y
LA SOBERANIA DE LOS PUEBLOS
1986
AÑO INTERNACIONAL DE LA PAZ

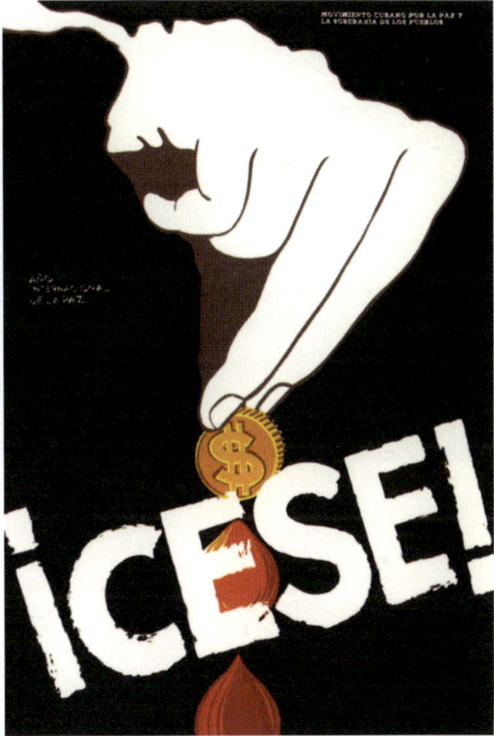
MOVIMIENTO CUBANO POR LA PAZ Y
LA SOBERANIA DE LOS PUEBLOS
AÑO
INTERNACIONAL
DE LA PAZ
¡CESE!

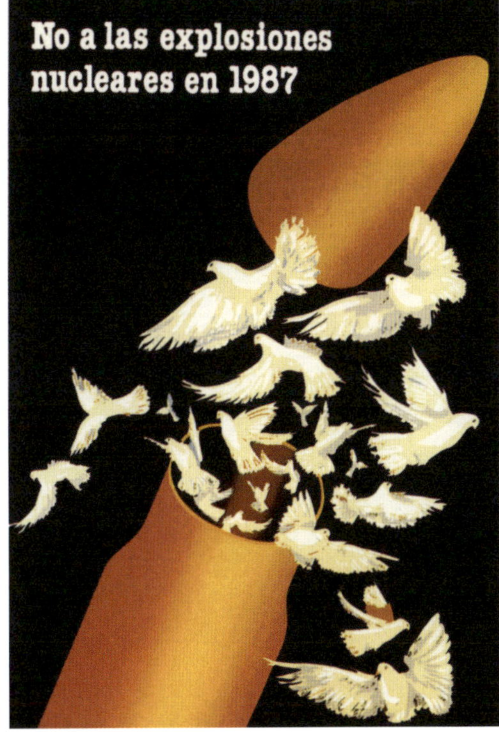
No a las explosiones
nucleares en 1987

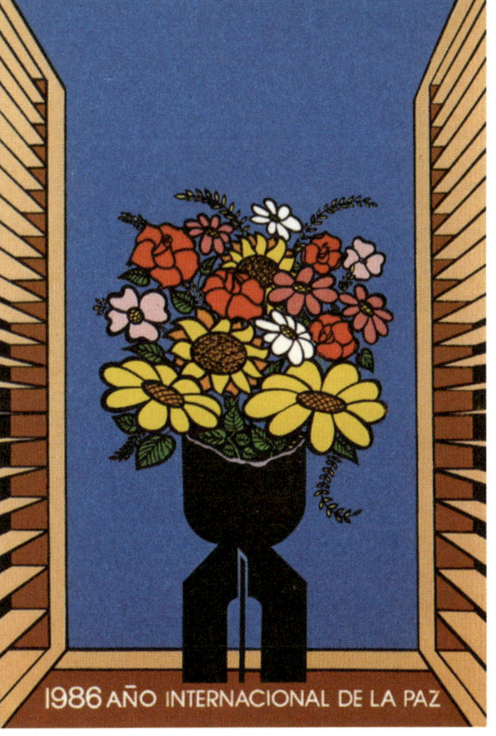
1986 AÑO INTERNACIONAL DE LA PAZ

001 PAX 1986
[PEACE 1986]
CREATOR Cuban Committee of
the Movement for Peace and
Sovereignty
SOURCE Posters from JAGDA Peace
Posters International Exhibition

002 UNITY OF ALL PEACE FORCES
CREATOR Cuban Committee of
the Movement for Peace and
Sovereignty
SOURCE Posters from JAGDA Peace
Posters International Exhibition

003 QUEREMOS CRECER / QUEREMOS JUGAR
[WE WANT TO GROW UP / WE WANT TO
PLAY GAMES]
CREATOR Cuban Committee of
the Movement for Peace and
Sovereignty
SOURCE Posters from JAGDA Peace
Posters International Exhibition

004 DESARME PARA LA VIDA
[DISARMAMENT FOR LIFE]
CREATOR Cuban Committee of
the Movement for Peace and
Sovereignty
SOURCE Posters from JAGDA Peace
Posters International Exhibition

005 1986 AÑO INTERNACIONAL DE LA PAZ
[1986, INTERNATIONAL YEAR OF PEACE]
CREATOR Cuban Committee of
the Movement for Peace and
Sovereignty
SOURCE Posters from JAGDA Peace
Posters International Exhibition

006 ¡CESE! [STOP]
CREATOR Cuban Committee of
the Movement for Peace and
Sovereignty
SOURCE Posters from JAGDA Peace
Posters International Exhibition

007 NO A LAS EXPLOSIONES NUCLEARES
EN 1987
[NO TO 1987 NUCLEAR EXPLOSIONS]
CREATOR Cuban Committee of
the Movement for Peace and
Sovereignty
SOURCE Posters from JAGDA Peace
Posters International Exhibition

008 1986 AÑO INTERNACIONAL DE LA PAZ
[1986, INTERNATIONAL YEAR OF PEACE]
CREATOR Cuban Committee of
the Movement for Peace and
Sovereignty
SOURCE Posters from JAGDA Peace
Posters International Exhibition

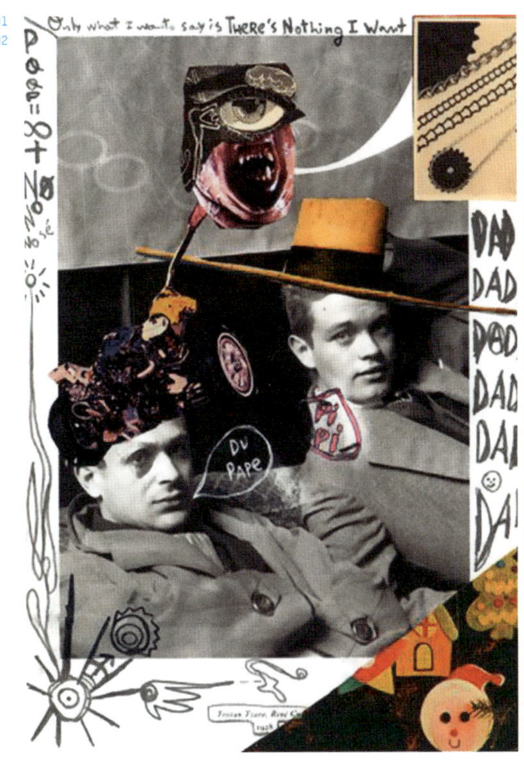
Only what I want to say is THERE's Nothing I Want
DAD
DAD
DAD
DAD
DAD
DA
Du Pape
PiPi

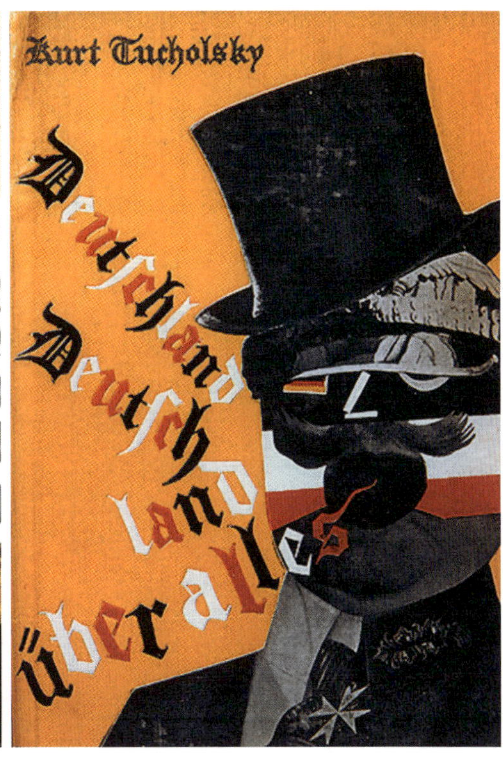
Kurt Tucholsky
Deutschland Deutschland über alles

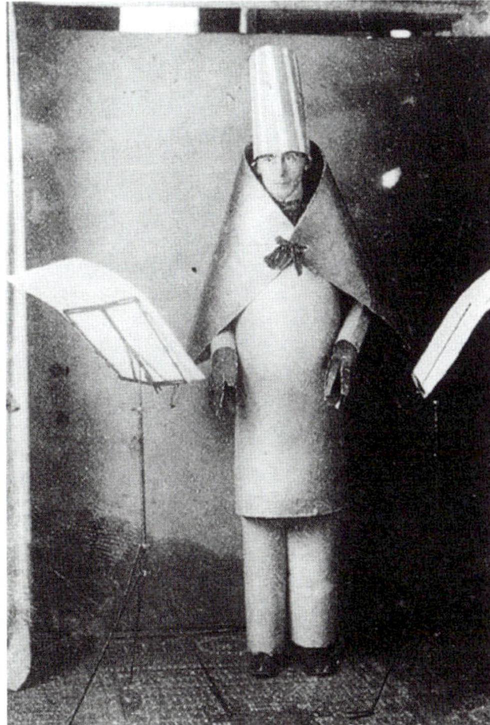

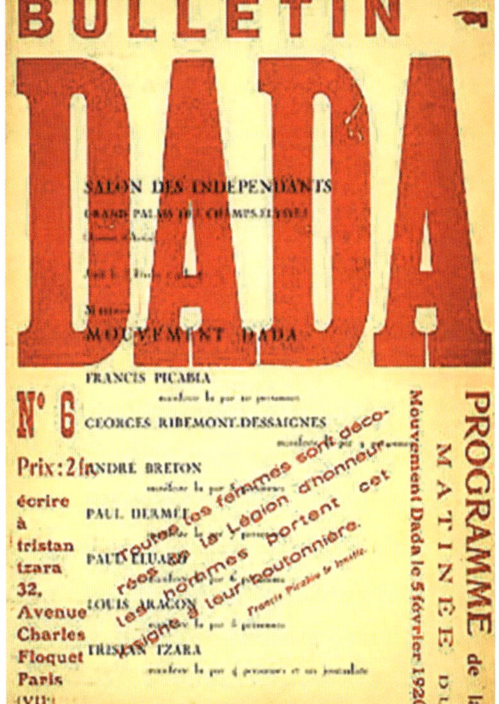
BULLETIN
DADA
SALON DES INDÉPENDANTS
MOUVEMENT DADA
FRANCIS PICABIA
N° 6
GEORGES RIBEMONT-DESSAIGNES
Prix : 2 f ANDRÉ BRETON
écrire
à
tristan
tzara
PAUL DERMÉE
PAUL ÉLUARD
32,
Avenue
LOUIS ARAGON
Charles
Floquet
TRISTAN TZARA
Paris
(VII)
PROGRAMME de la MATINÉE
Mouvement Dada le 5 février 1920

005
006

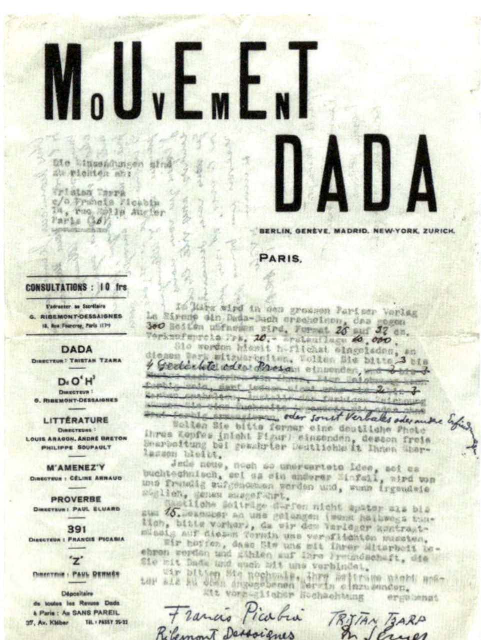

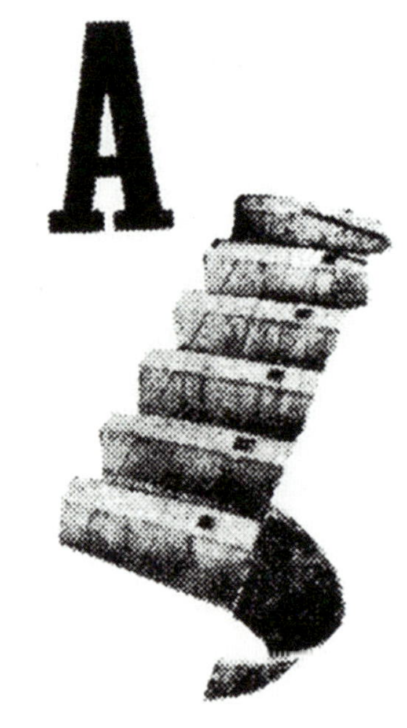

007
008

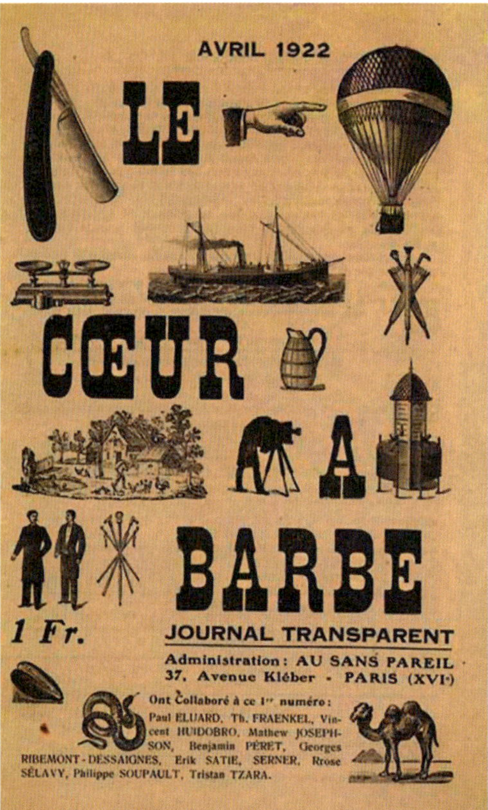

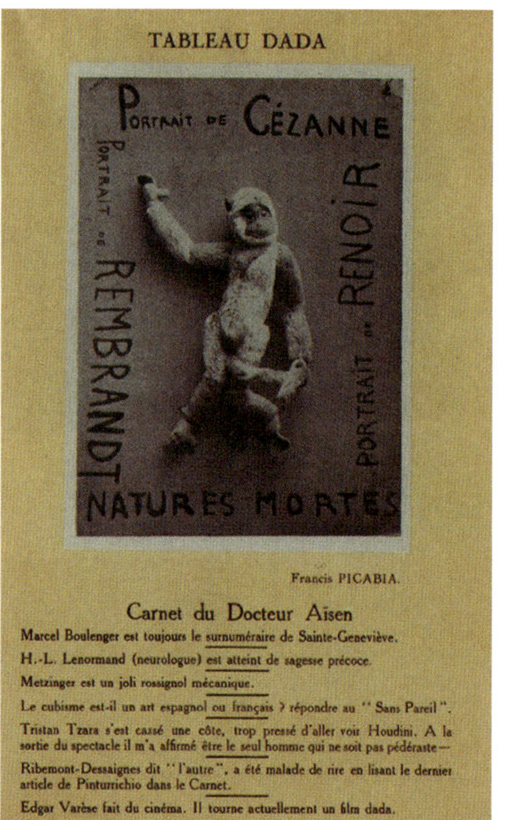

Carnet du Docteur Aïsen

Marcel Boulenger est toujours le surnuméraire de Sainte-Geneviève.

H.-L. Lenormand (neurologue) est atteint de sagesse précoce.

Metzinger est un joli rossignol mécanique.

Le cubisme est-il un art espagnol ou français ? répondre au " Sans Pareil ".

Tristan Tzara s'est cassé une côte, trop pressé d'aller voir Houdini. A la sortie du spectacle il m'a affirmé être le seul homme qui ne soit pas pédéraste —

Ribemont-Dessaignes dit " l'autre ", a été malade de rire en lisant le dernier article de Pinturrichio dans le Carnet.

Edgar Varèse fait du cinéma. Il tourne actuellement un film dada.

009
010

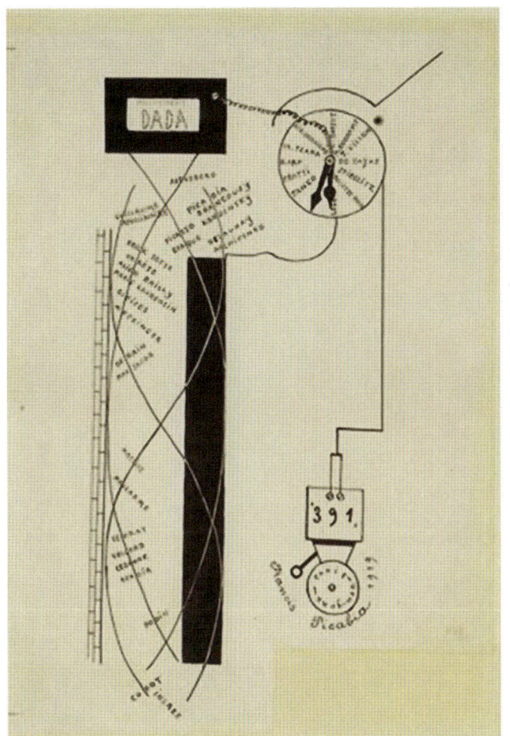

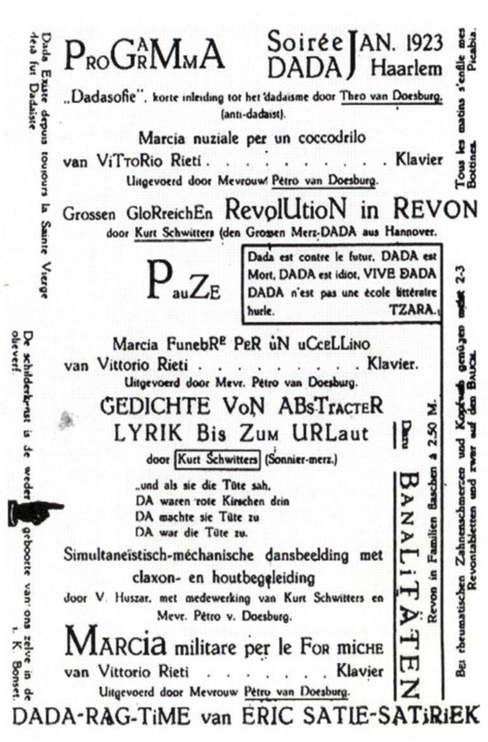

PRoGrAMMA — Soirée DADA — JAN. 1923 Haarlem

„Dadasofie", korte inleiding tot het dadaisme door Theo van Doesburg. (anti-dadaist).

Marcia nuziale per un coccodrilo van ViTtoRio Rieti . . . . Klavier. Uitgevoerd door Mevrouw Pètro van Doesburg.

Grossen GloRreichEn RevolUtioN in REVON door Kurt Schwitters (den Grossen Merz-DADA aus Hannover.

PauZe

Dada est contre le futur, DADA est Mort, DADA est idiot, VIVE ĐADA DADA n'est pas une école littéraire hurle. TZARA.

Marcia FunebRe PeR üN uCceLLino van Vittorio Rieti . . . . Klavier. Uitgevoerd door Mevr. Pètro van Doesburg.

GEDICHTE VoN ABsTracteR LYRIK Bis Zum URLaut door Kurt Schwitters (Sonnier-merz.)

...und als sie die Tüte sah,
DA waren rote Kirschen drin
DA machte sie Tüte zu
DA war die Tüte zu.

Simultaneïstisch-méchanische dansbeelding met claxon- en houtbegeleiding door V. Huszar. met medewerking van Kurt Schwitters en Mevr. Pètro v. Doesburg.

Marcia militare per le For miche van Vittorio Rieti . . . . Klavier. Uitgevoerd door Mevrouw Pètro van Doesburg.

DADA-RAG-TiME van ERIC SATIE-SATiRIEK

011
012

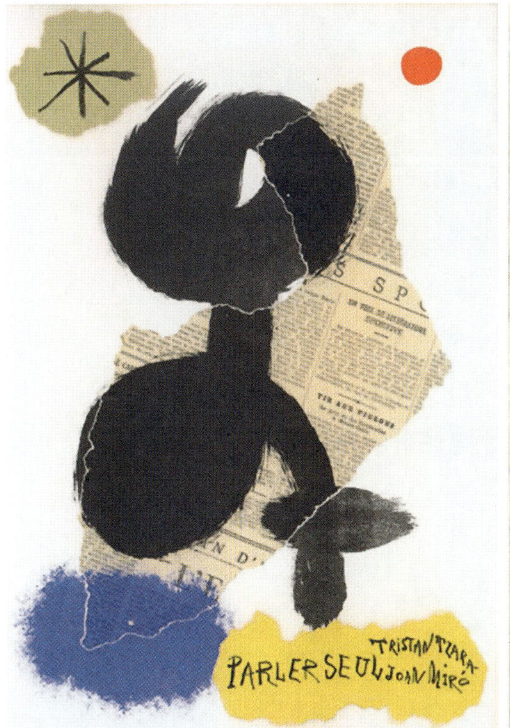

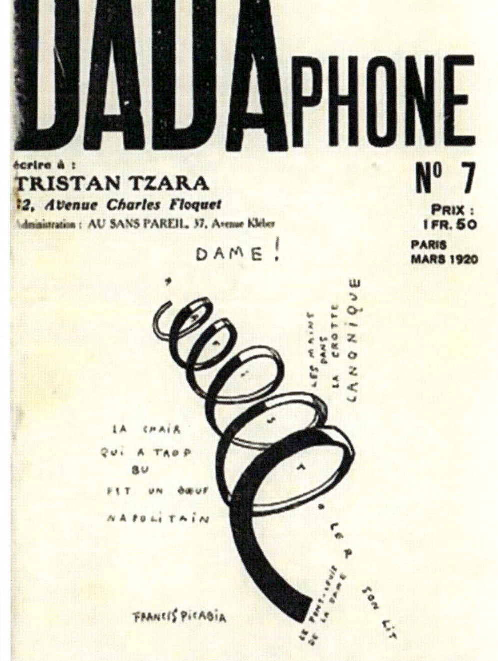

013

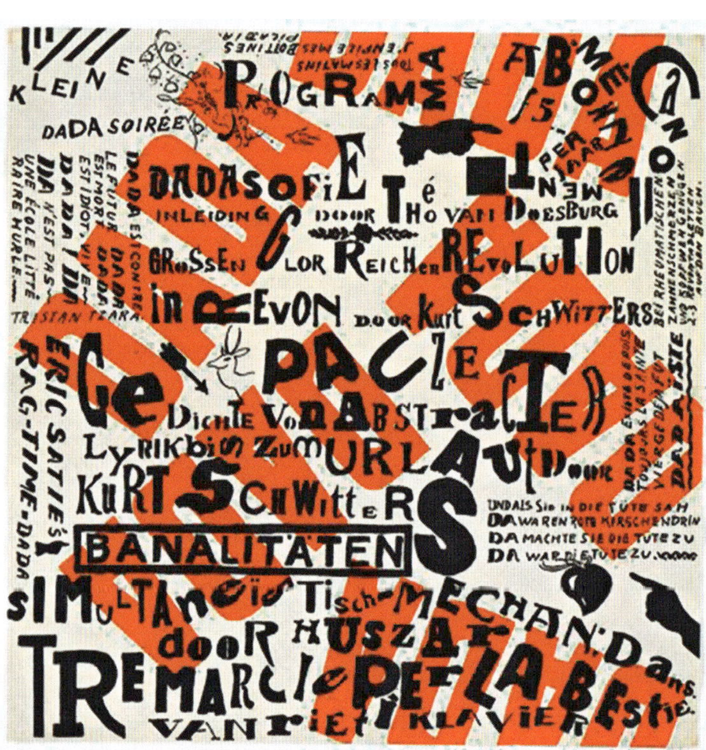

014

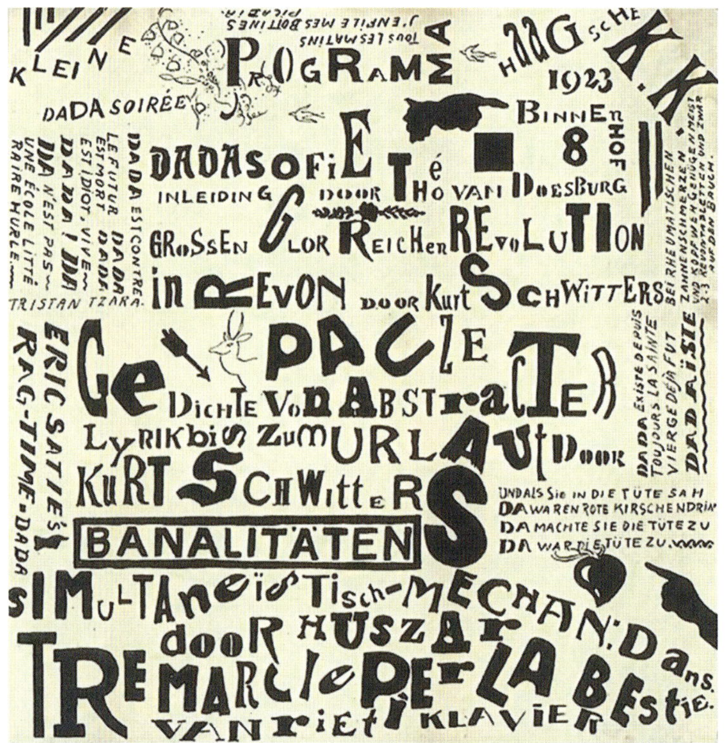

001 UNTITLED
SOURCE i153.photobucket.com

002 DEUTSCHLAND, DEUTSCHLAND, ÜBER ALLES
[GERMANY, GERMANY ABOVE ALL!]
CREATOR John Heartfield
SOURCE www.ozanne-rarebooks.com

003 HUGO BALL, CABARET VOLTAIRE, ZURICH
SOURCE barriochino.files.word
press.com
DATE 1916

004 BULLETIN DADA
SOURCE www.artic.edu

005 MOUVEMENT DADA [DADA MOVEMENT]
CREATOR Tristan Tzara
SOURCE www.arslibri.com

006 BONSET CONSTRUCTION 1
CREATOR Theo van Doesburg
SOURCE commons.wikimedia.org
DATE c. 1921

007 LE COEUR À BARBE
[THE BEARDED HEART]
CREATOR Francis Picabia
SOURCE www.personal.kent.edu
DATE 1922

008 TABLEAU DADA
[DADA PAINTING: PORTRAIT OF
CEZANNE, PORTRAIT OF REMBRANDT, ...]
CREATOR Francis Picabia
SOURCE www.personal.kent.edu
DATE 1920

009 MOVIMENTO DADA [DADA MOVEMENT]
CREATOR Francis Picabia
SOURCE www.moma.org
DATE 1919

010 PROGRAMME DADA-SOIREE HAARLEM
[DADA PROGRAM-HAARLEM SOIREE]
CREATOR Theo van Doesburg
SOURCE commons.wikimedia.org
DATE 1923

011 POÈME [POEM]
CREATOR Tristan Tzara / Joan Miro
SOURCE sarahwilson.files.
wordpress.com

012 DADA PHONE
CREATOR Tristan Tzara
SOURCE sarahwilson.files.
wordpress.com

013 KLEINE DADA SOIRÉE
[SMALL DADA EVENING]
CREATOR Theo van Doesburg
SOURCE commons.wikimedia.org
DATE 1922

014 KLEINE DADA SOIRÉE
[SMALL DADA EVENING]
CREATOR Theo van Doesburg
SOURCE commons.wikimedia.org

001

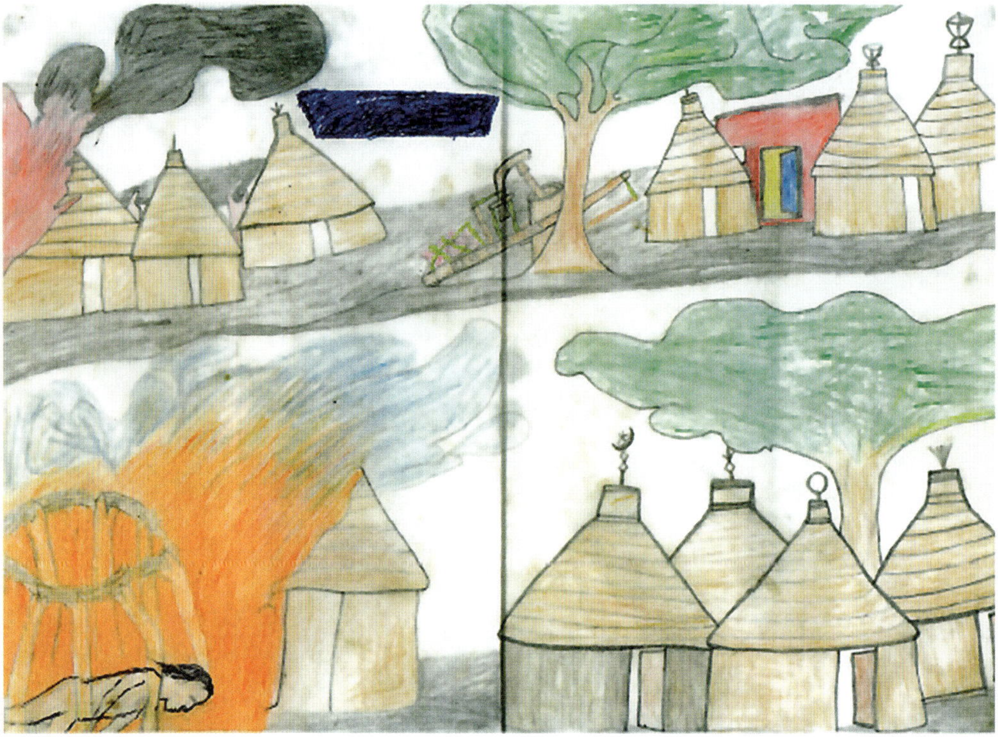

002

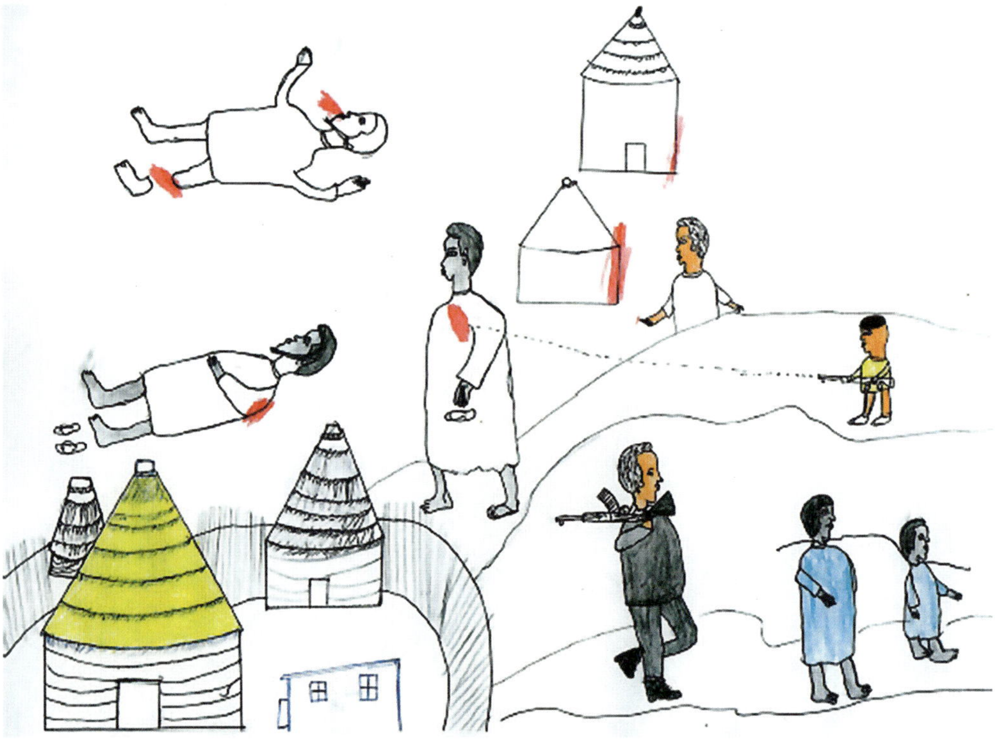

003

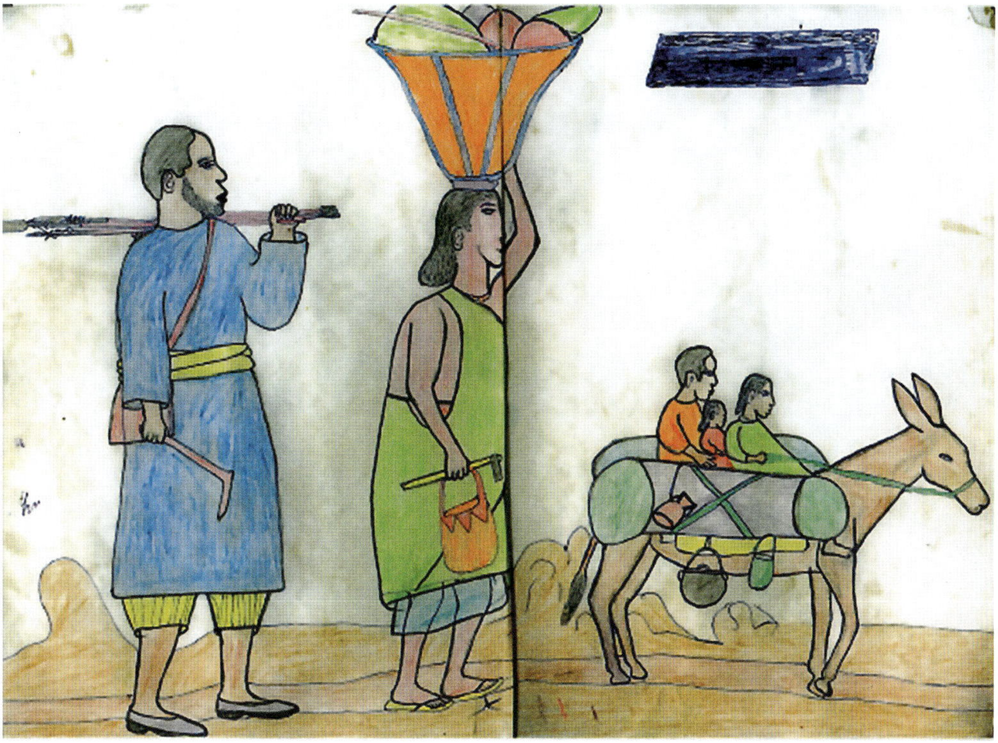

004
NEXT
005

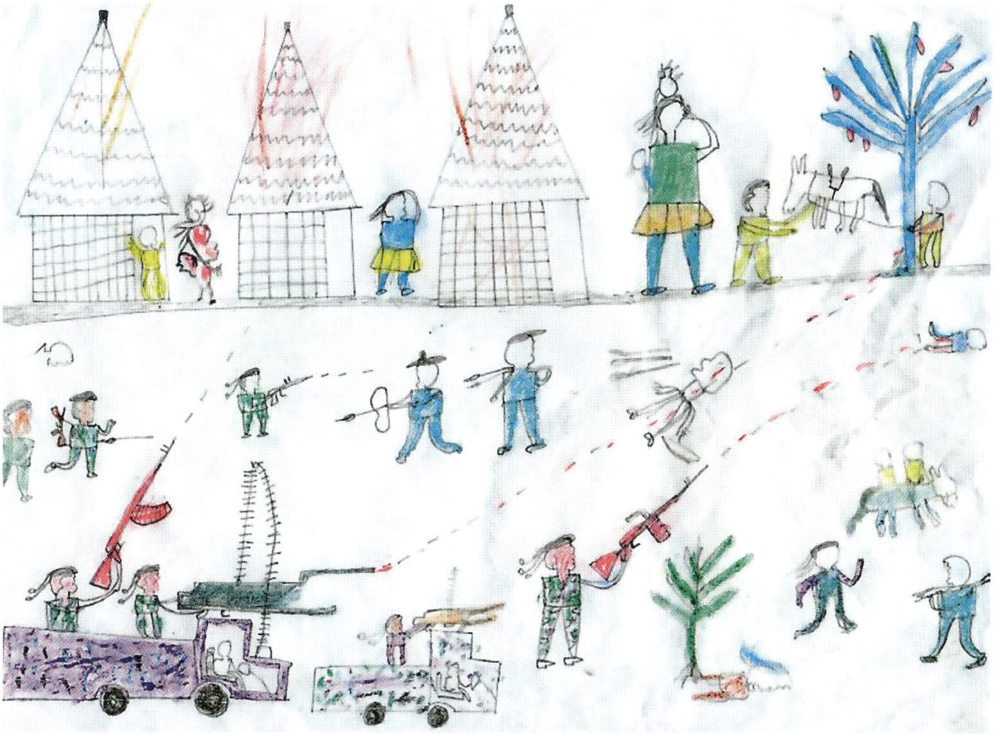

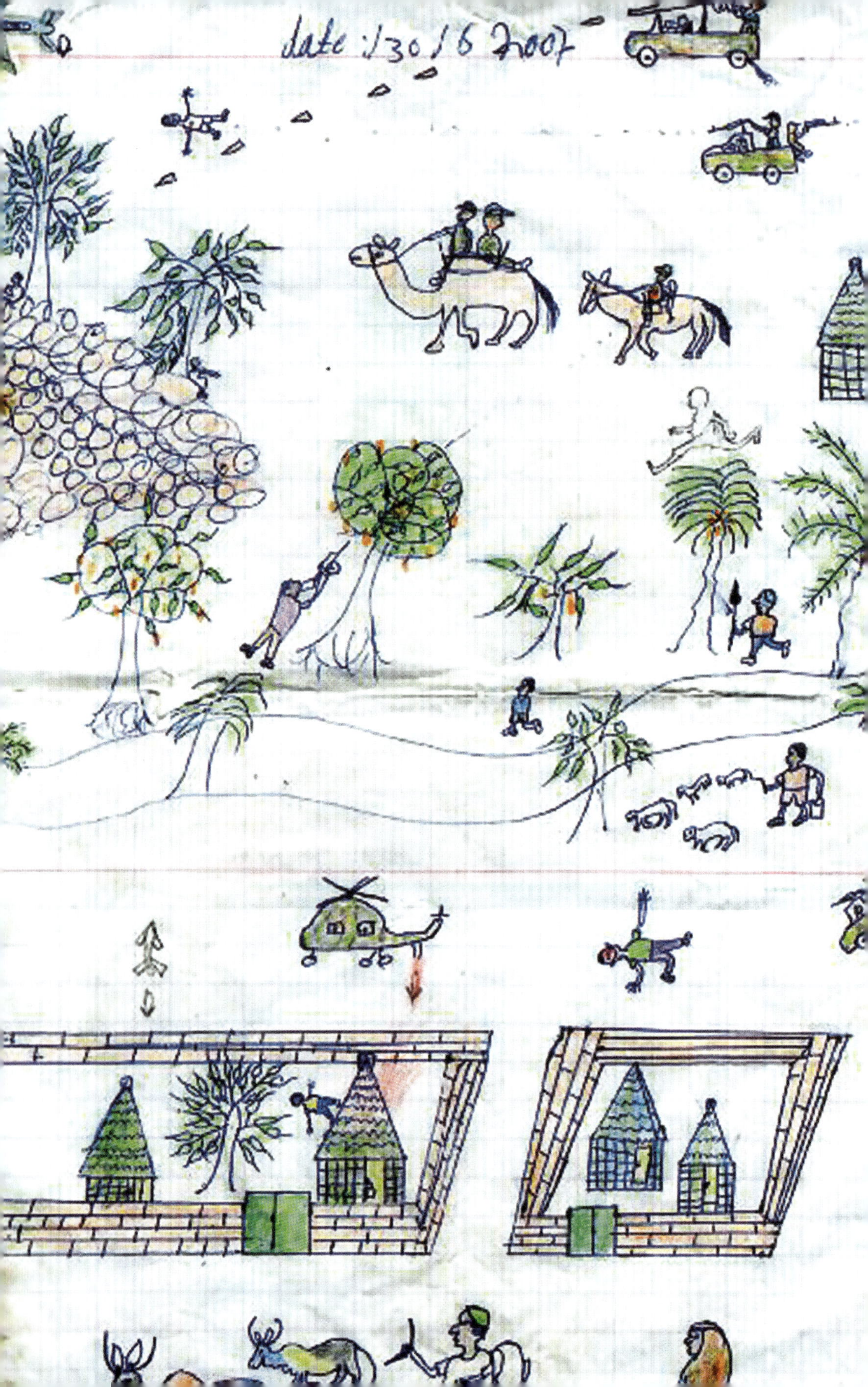
date : 30 / 6 2007

001   DRAWINGS OF GENOCIDE
      CREATOR Darfuri children
      SOURCE www.wagingpeace.info

002   DRAWINGS OF GENOCIDE
      This boy was nine when his
      village in the area of Aishbarra,
      Darfur, was attacked in 2003 by
      the Sudanese government forces
      and Janjaweed militia. The drawing
      shows houses burning, villagers
      being shot and even amputated.
      The villagers who are attacked
      are colored in black, while the
      attackers have lighter [orange]
      skin - showing the ethnic
      character of the attacks. In the
      bottom right of the drawing are
      two young men, attached by the
      neck, led away by a Janjaweed
      fighter. These boys could be taken
      into slavery, or may become child
      soldiers.
      CREATOR Darfuri children
      SOURCE www.wagingpeace.info

003   DRAWINGS OF GENOCIDE
      CREATOR Darfuri children
      SOURCE www.wagingpeace.info

004   DRAWINGS OF GENOCIDE
      This drawing describes an attack
      by Sudanese government forces
      on the village in Eastern Chad.
      Sudanese armed forces, identi-
      fiable by their berets and
      uniforms, arrive in the village
      on machine gun-mounted pickup
      trucks and by foot. They shoot
      at the fleeing population that
      only has arrows to protect itself,
      while the houses are set alight.
      CREATOR Darfuri children
      SOURCE www.wagingpeace.info

005   DRAWINGS OF GENOCIDE
      In this drawing, a young girl
      from Darfur shows the peaceful
      life in her village being
      disrupted by a violent attack
      by Sudanese government forces
      and the Janjaweed militia. Some
      villagers are seen herding cattle
      and sheep or sitting under
      trees. But this sense of calm is
      contrasted by Sudanese airplanes
      and helicopters bombing the
      village and setting fire to the
      houses. Government forces in
      pickup trucks and Janjaweed on
      horse- and camelback are shooting
      at civilians.
      CREATOR Darfuri children
      SOURCE www.wagingpeace.info

001
002

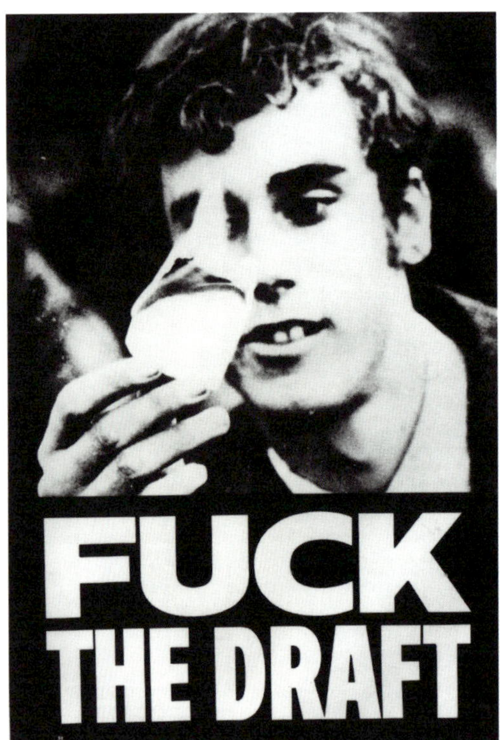

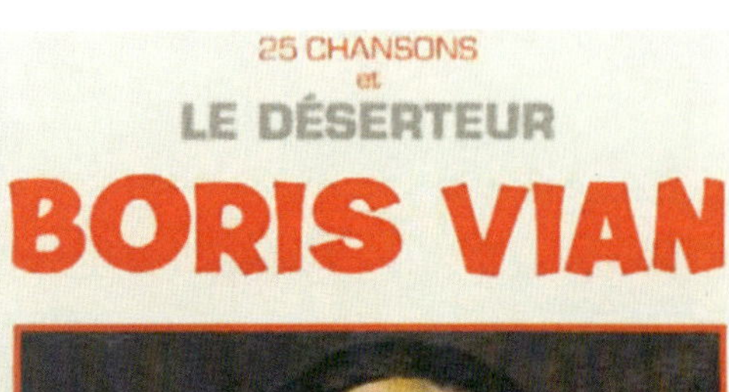

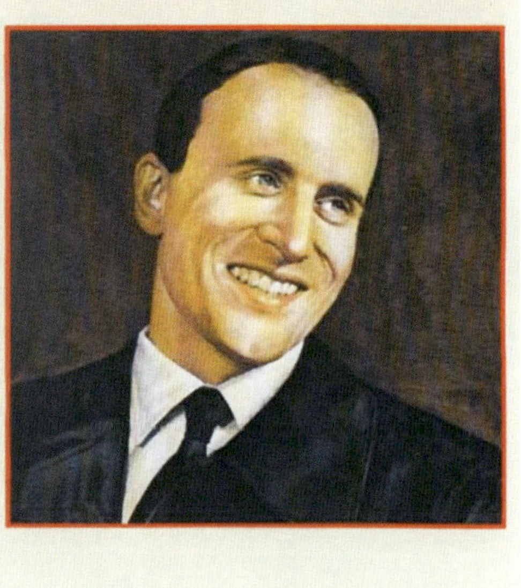

003
004

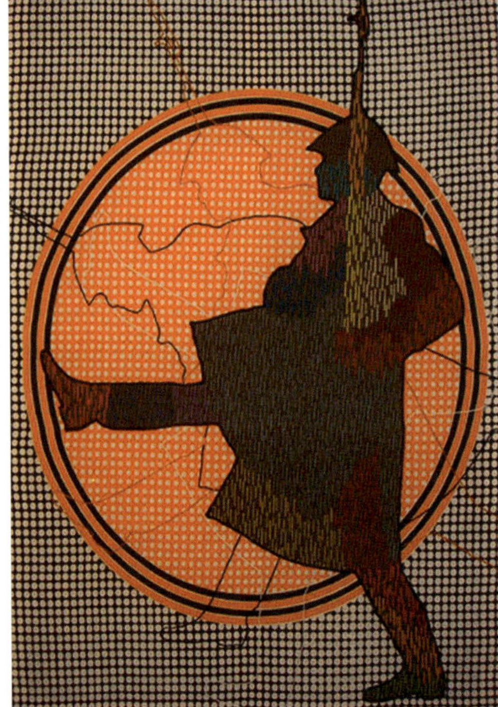

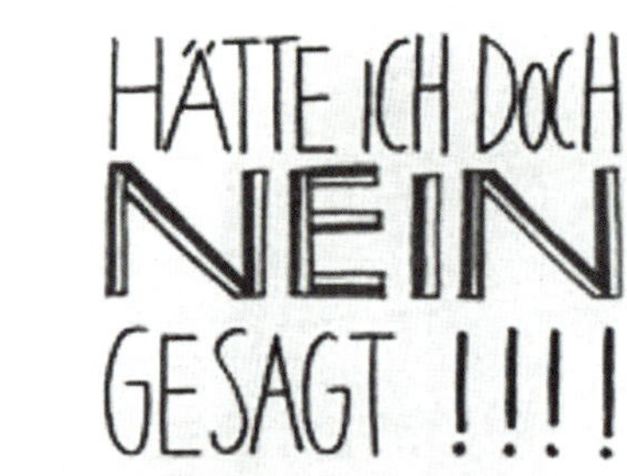

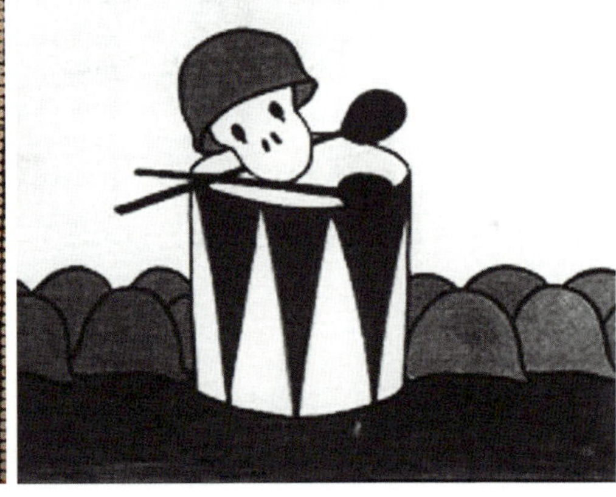

005
006

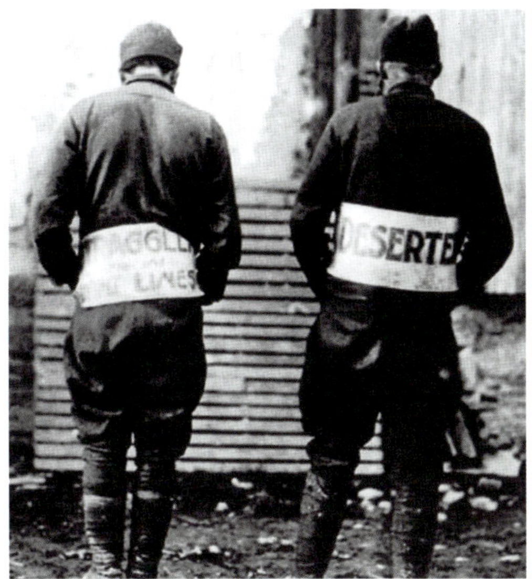

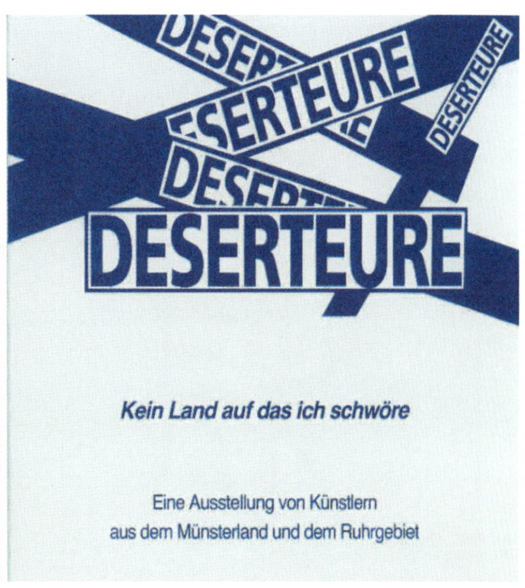

007
008

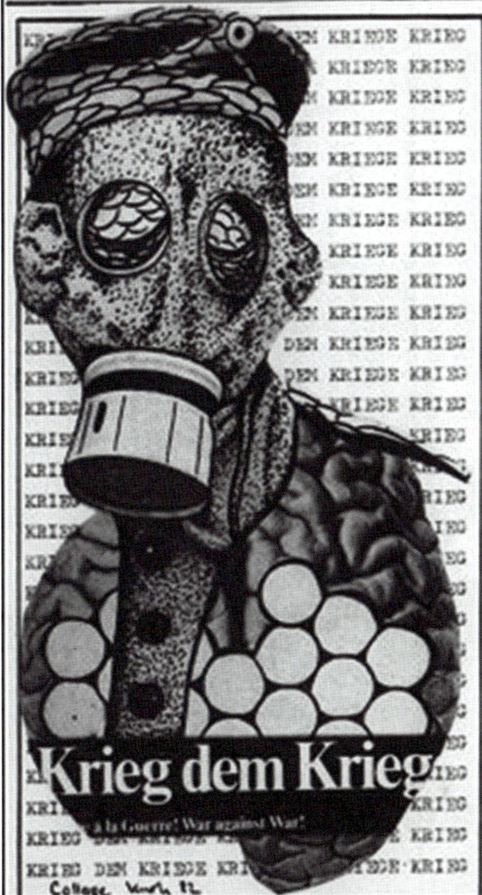

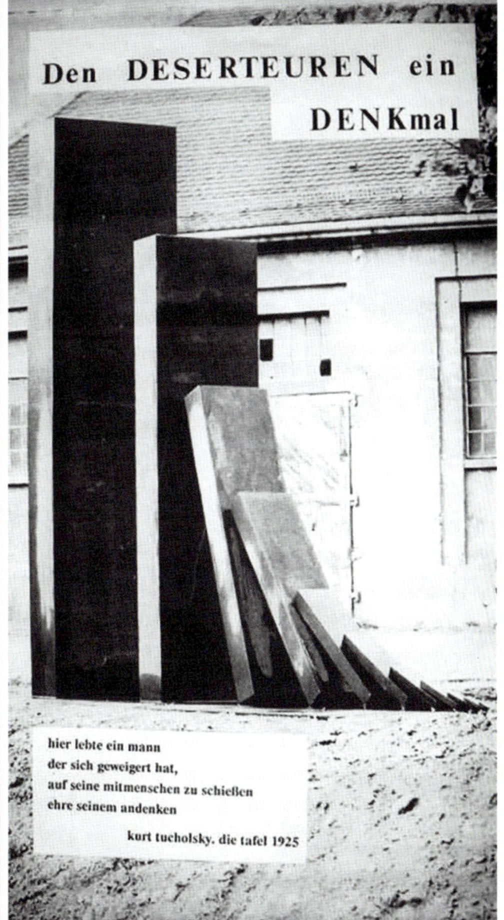

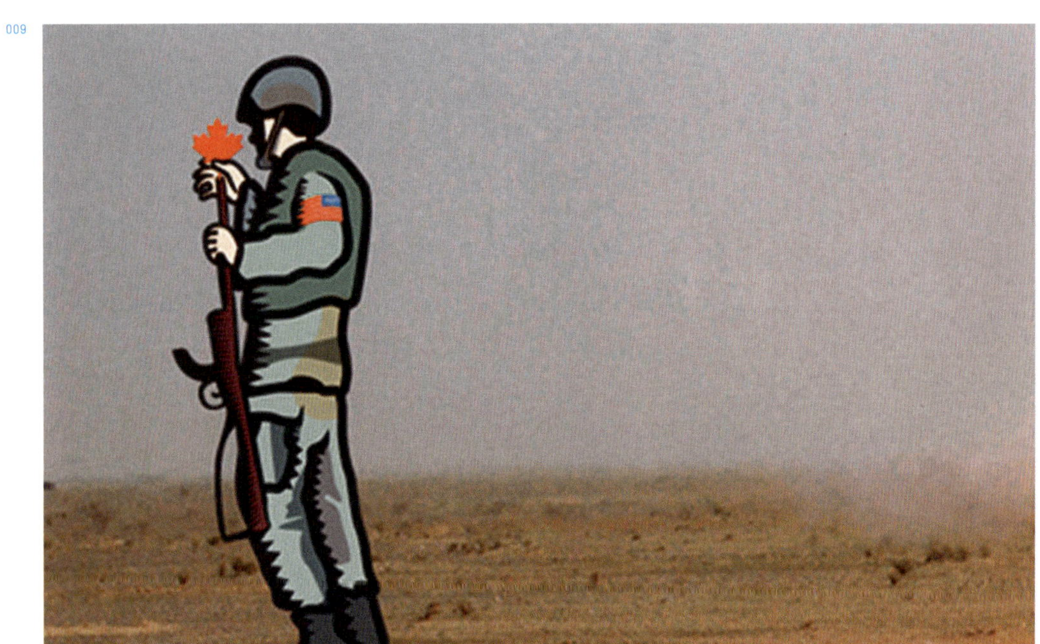

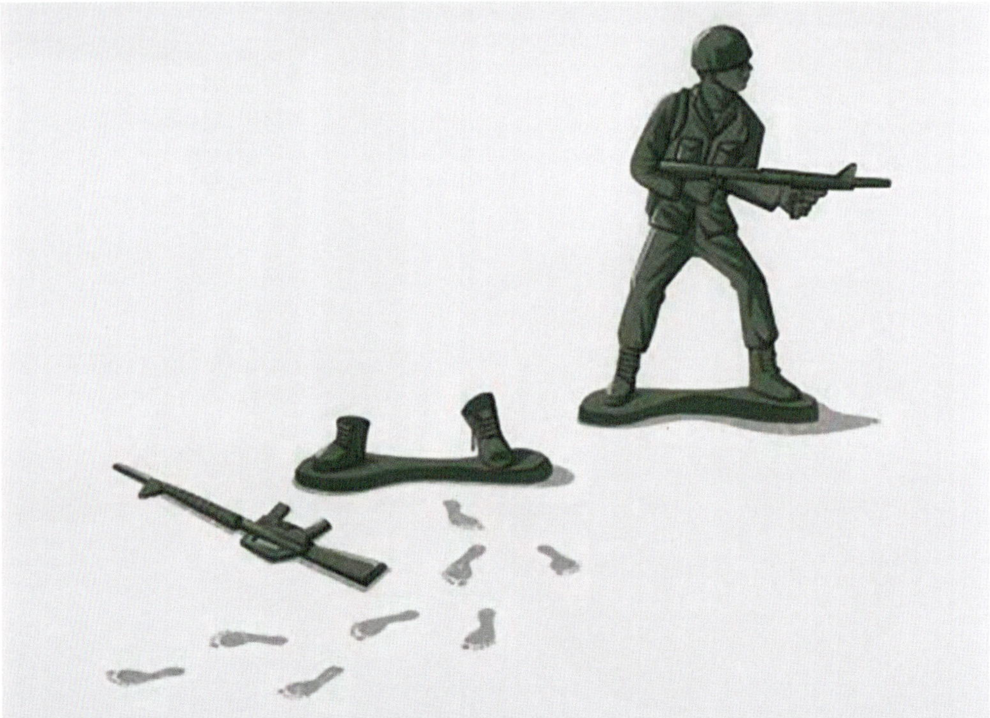

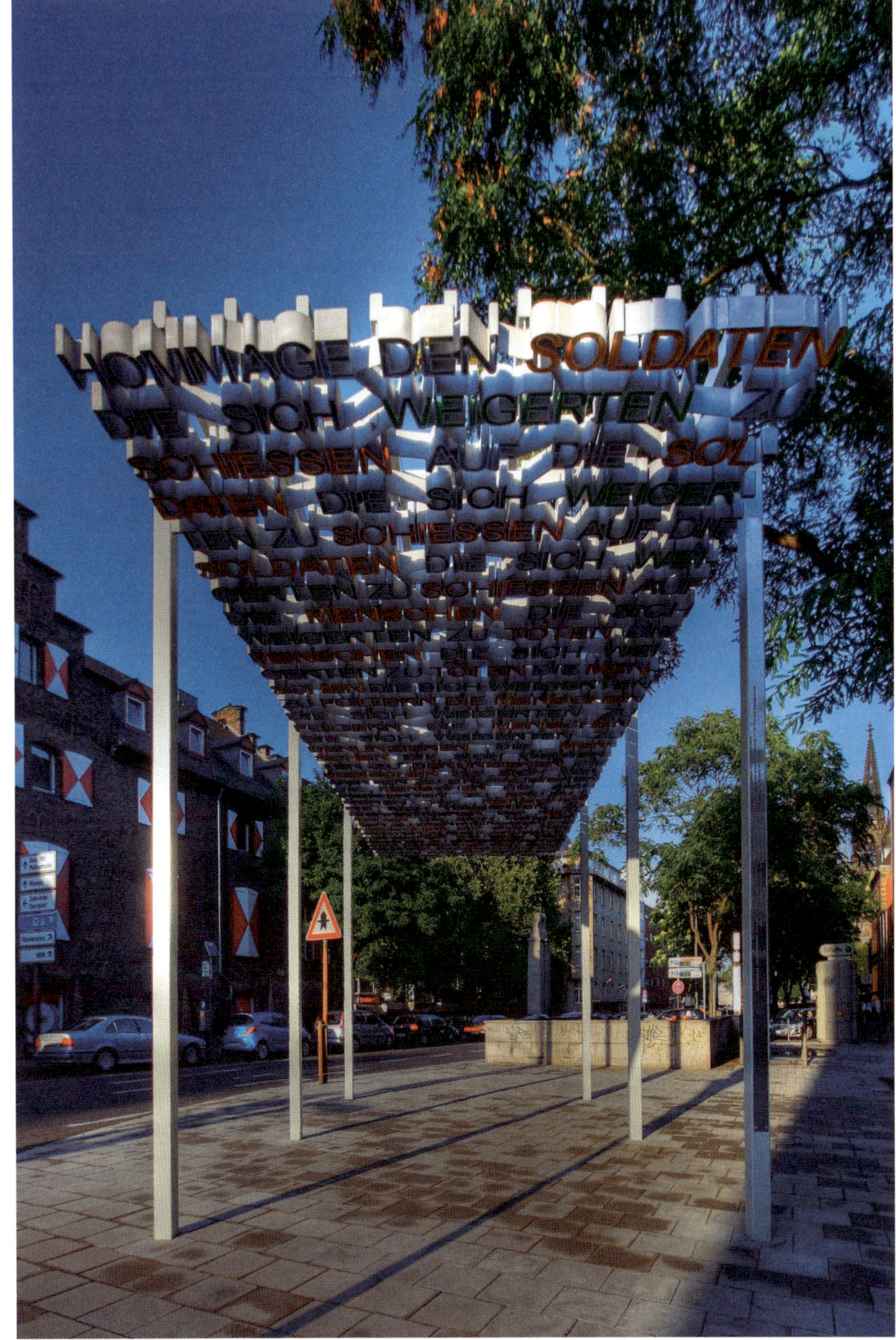
HOMMAGE DEN SOLDATEN
DIE SICH WEIGERTEN ZU
SCHIESSEN AUF DIE SOL-
DATEN DIE SICH WEIGER-
TEN ZU SCHIESSEN AUF DIE
SOLDATEN DIE SICH WEI-
GERTEN ZU SCHIESSEN AUF
DIE MENSCHEN DIE SICH
WEIGERTEN ZU TÖTEN

001 FUCK THE DRAFT
SOURCE Carol Wells, David Kunzle,
and Nguyen Ngoc Dung, *Decade of
Protest: Political Posters from
the United States, Vietnam, and
Cuba, 1965–1975* [Santa Monica:
Smart Art Press, 1996], p. 41.

002 25 CHANSONS ET LE DÉSERTEUR
BORIS VIAN
[25 SONGS AND THE DESERTER
BORIS VIAN]
SOURCE www.di-arezzo.del

003 DESERTION
CREATOR Jan Bejaiovec
SOURCE www.testbildlabor.de

004 HÄTTE ICH DOCH NEIN GESAGT
[BUT I HAD SAID NO]
CREATOR Renate Grünewald
SOURCE www.fi-nottuln.de

005 HUMILIATION
American straggler and a deserter
publicly humiliated at Florient,
France.
CREATOR Provided by Chow Hon Lam
SOURCE www.greatwar.nl
DATE 5 November 1010

006 COVER FOR AN EXHIBITION CATALOG
SOURCE www.fi-nottuln.de

007 KRIEG DEM KRIEG
[WAR AGAINST WAR]
SOURCE www.medeasy.de

008 DESERTEURDENKMAL IN ULM
[MEMORIAL TO DESERTERS IN ULM]
SOURCE www.friedensfahnen.de

009 CLÉMENT DE GAULEJAC
CREATOR Corey Glass
SOURCE www.rue89.com

010 DESERTER
CREATOR Provided by Chow Hon Lam
SOURCE www.flickr.com/photos/
65414366@N00/6104723903/

011 DENKMAL FÜR DIE DESERTEURE
DER WEHRMACHT
[MONUMENT TO DESERTERS FROM
THE WEHRMACHT]
CREATOR Design by Ruedi Baur
SOURCE upload.wikimedia.org

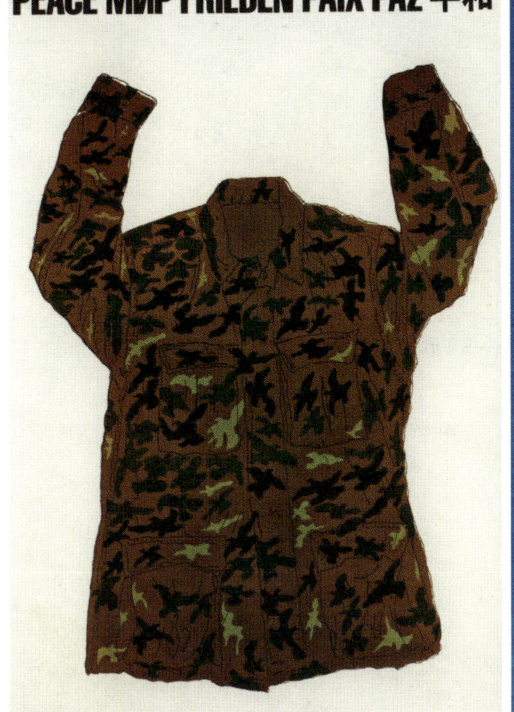
PEACE МИР FRIEDEN PAIX PAZ 平和

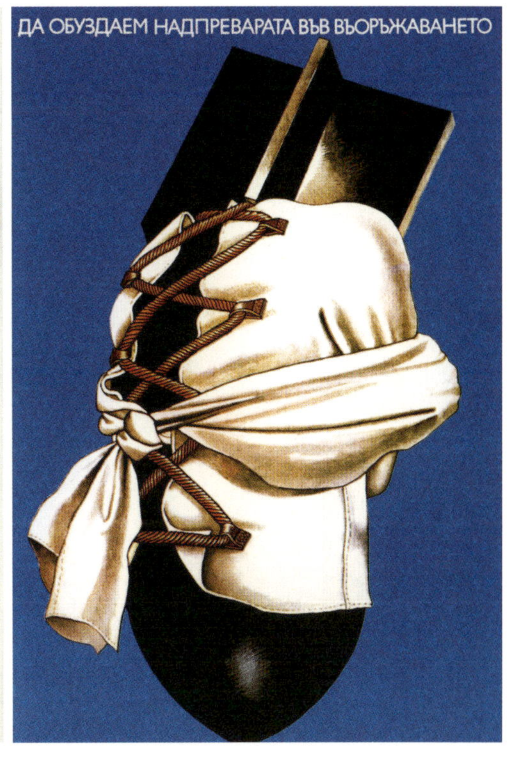
ДА ОБУЗДАЕМ НАДПРЕВАРАТА ВЪВ ВЪОРЪЖАВАНЕТО

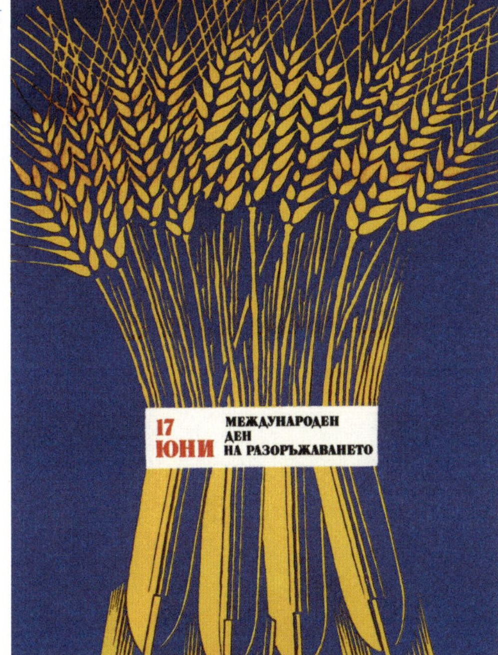
17
ЮНИ
МЕЖДУНАРОДЕН
ДЕН
НА РАЗОРЪЖАВАНЕТО

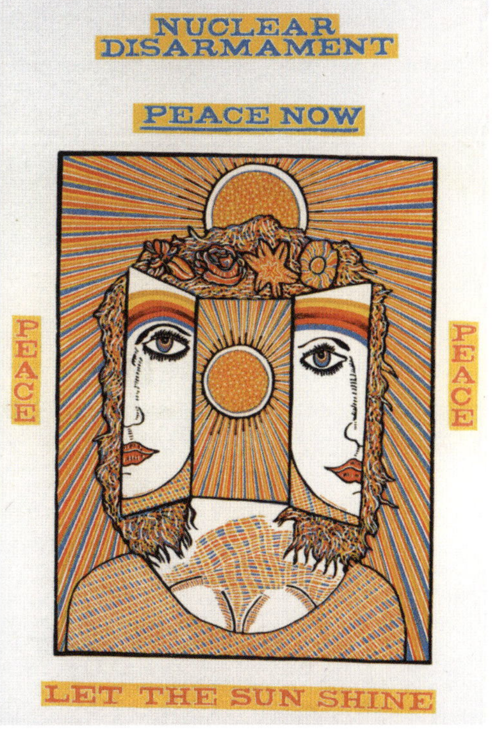
NUCLEAR
DISARMAMENT
PEACE NOW
PEACE
PEACE
LET THE SUN SHINE

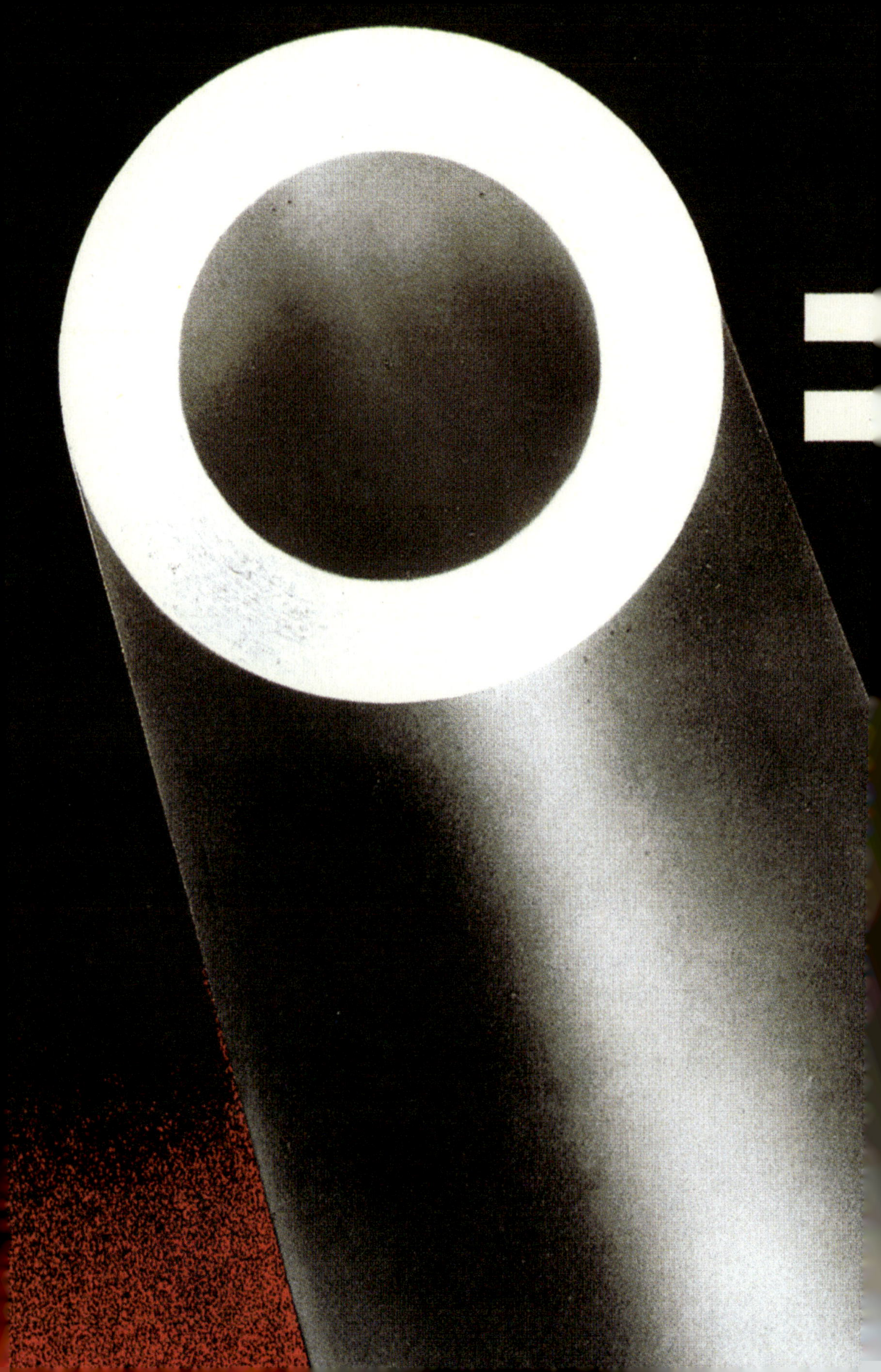

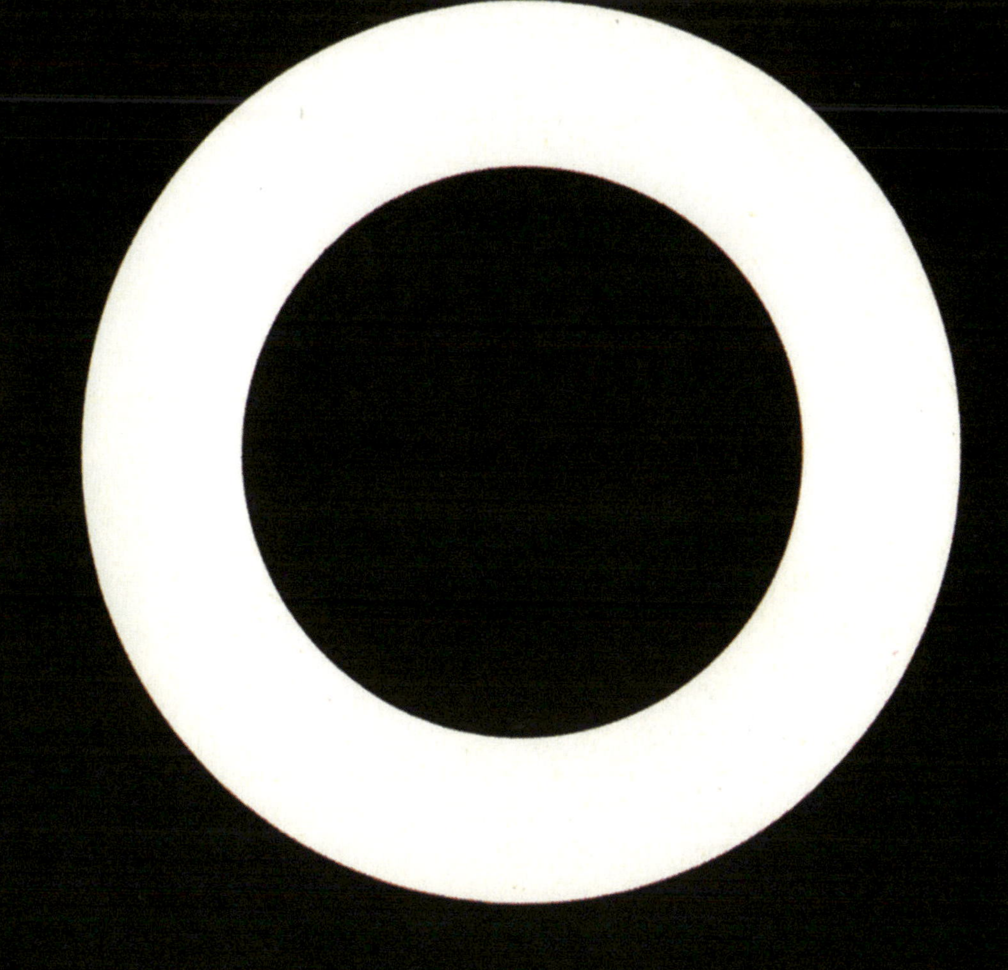

ЗА ПЪЛНО
РАЗОРЪЖАВАНЕ!

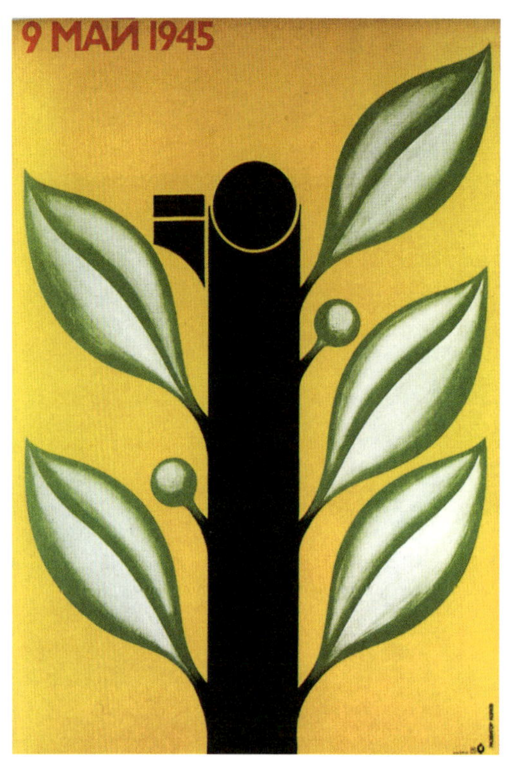
9 МАЙ 1945

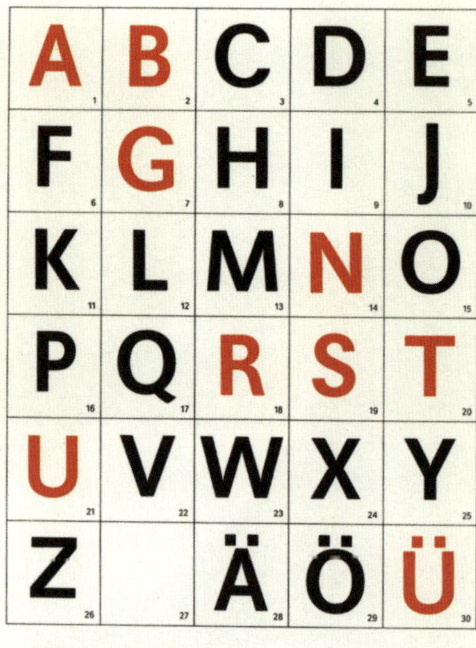
A B C D E
F G H I J
K L M N O
P Q R S T
U V W X Y
Z Ä Ö Ü
1, 2, 18, 30, 19, 20, 21, 14, 7 –
einzige Chance zur Erhaltung des Lebens
auf der Erde

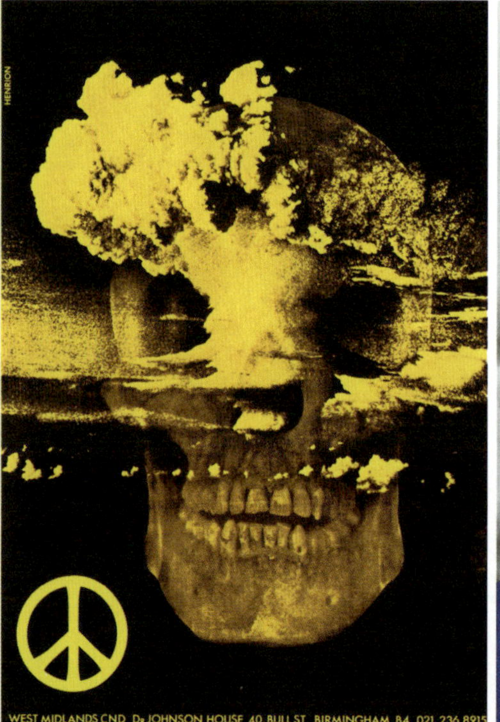
HENRION
WEST MIDLANDS CND D₂ JOHNSON HOUSE 40, BULL ST BIRMINGHAM B4 021 236 8915

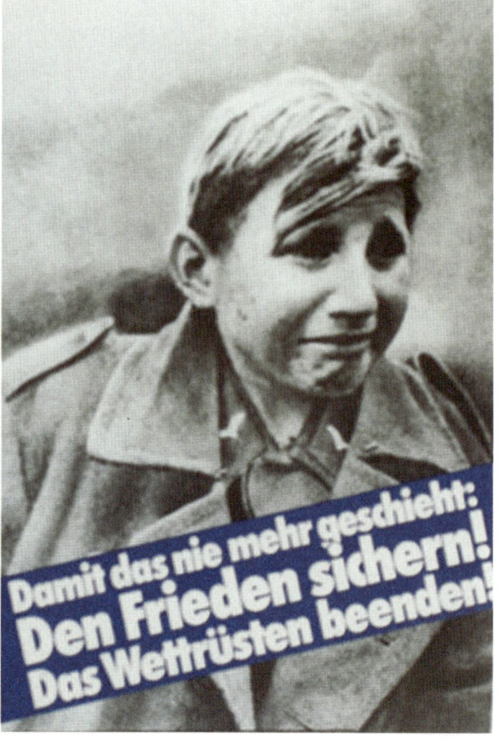
Damit das nie mehr geschieht:
Den Frieden sichern!
Das Wettrüsten beenden!

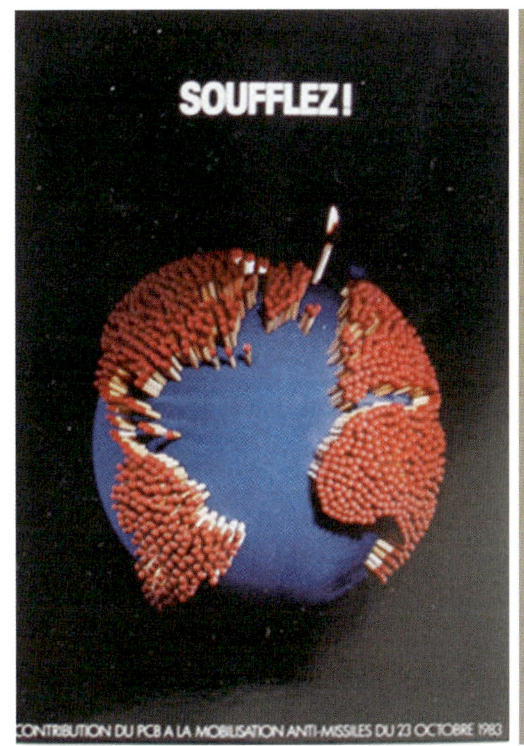
SOUFFLEZ!
CONTRIBUTION DU PCB A LA MOBILISATION ANTI-MISSILES DU 23 OCTOBRE 1983

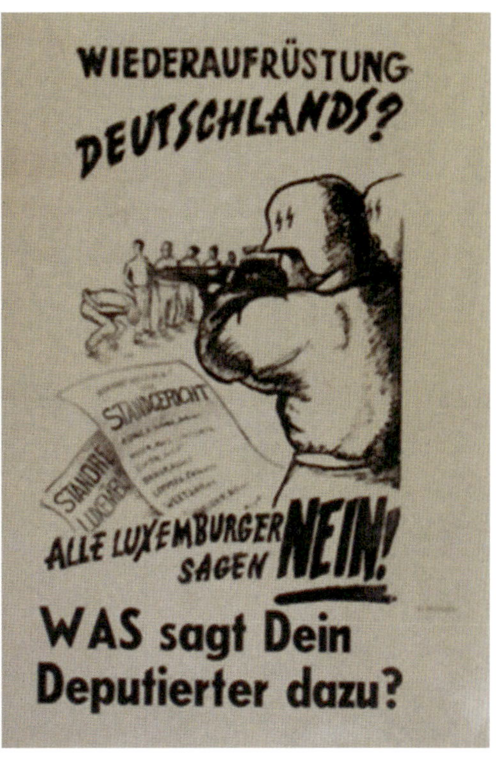
WIEDERAUFRÜSTUNG
DEUTSCHLANDS?
STANDGERICHT
ALLE LUXEMBURGER SAGEN NEIN!
WAS sagt Dein
Deputierter dazu?

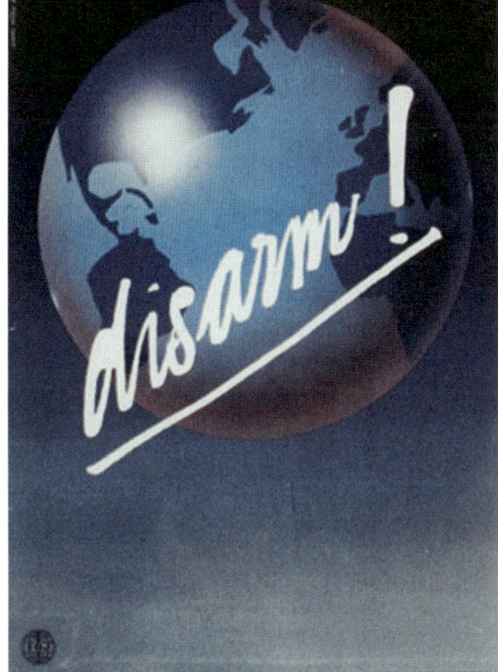
disarm!
THE INTERNATIONAL ORGANIZATION OF JOURNALISTS

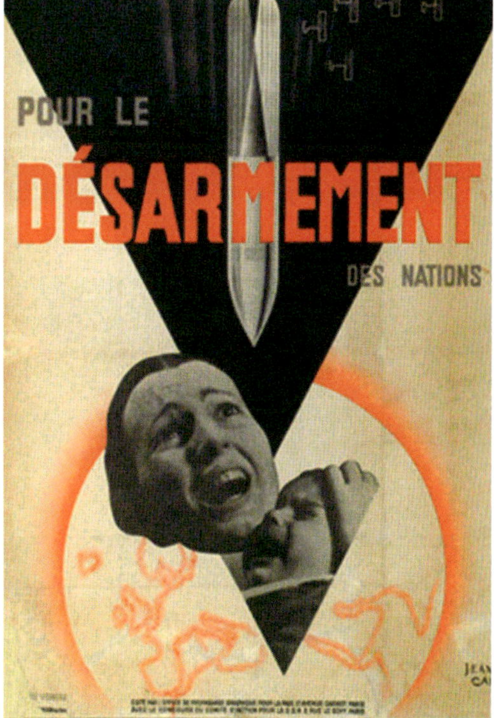
POUR LE
DÉSARMEMENT
DES NATIONS

014

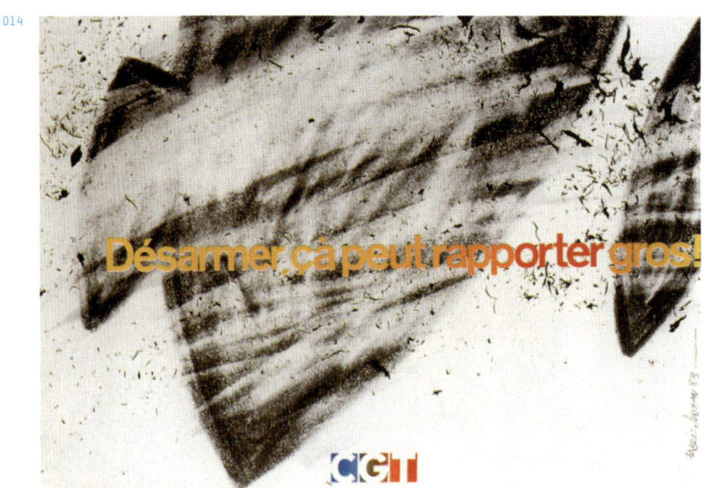
Désarmer, çà peut rapporter gros!
CGT

015

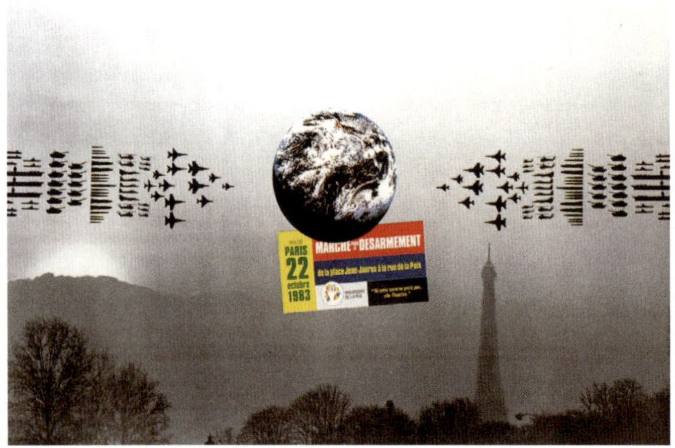
PARIS
22
octobre
1983
MARCHE POUR LE DÉSARMEMENT
de la place Jean-Jaurès à la rue de la Paix

016

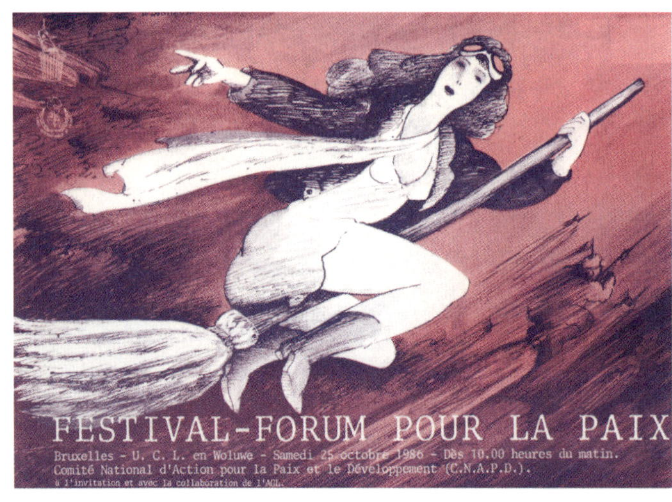
FESTIVAL-FORUM POUR LA PAIX
Bruxelles - U. C. L. en Woluwe - Samedi 25 octobre 1986 - Dès 10.00 heures du matin.
Comité National d'Action pour la Paix et le Développement (C.N.A.P.D.).
à l'invitation et avec la collaboration de l'AGL.

001 PEACE
CREATOR Masuteru Aoba
SOURCE Poster from JAGDA Peace
Posters International Exhibition

002 STOP THE COURSE OF ARMAMENT
CREATOR Simeon Krastev
SOURCE Poster from JAGDA Peace
Posters International Exhibition

003 INTERNATIONAL DAY OF DISARMAMENT
CREATOR Petar Petrov
SOURCE Poster from JAGDA Peace
Posters International Exhibition
DATE 1985

004 NUCLEAR DISARMAMENT, LET THE
SUN SHINE
CREATOR Jim Cave
SOURCE Poster from JAGDA Peace
Posters International Exhibition
DATE 1987

005 FOR DISARMAMENT
CREATOR Kiril Karapanov
SOURCE Poster from JAGDA Peace
Posters International Exhibition

006 9TH OF MAY 1945
CREATOR Razvigor Kolev
SOURCE Poster from JAGDA Peace
Posters International Exhibition

007 DISARMAMENT
CREATOR Gert Wunderlich
SOURCE Poster from JAGDA Peace
Posters International Exhibition
DATE 1987

008 NUCLEAR DISARMAMENT
CREATOR FHK Henrion
SOURCE Poster from JAGDA Peace
Posters International Exhibition

009 DAMIT DAS NIE WIEDER GESCHIEHT...
[SO THIS NEVER HAPPENS AGAIN...]
SOURCE Poster from JAGDA Peace
Posters International Exhibition

010 SOUFFLEZ!
[BLOW!]
CREATOR Philippe Deltour
SOURCE Poster from JAGDA Peace
Posters International Exhibition

011 WIEDERAUFRÜSTUNG DEUTSCHLANDS?
[GERMAN REARMAMENT?]
CREATOR Lu
SOURCE Poster from JAGDA Peace
Posters International Exhibition

012 DISARM
CREATOR Karel Misek
SOURCE Poster from JAGDA Peace
Posters International Exhibition

013 POUR LE DÉSARMEMENT DES NATIONS
[FOR THE DISARMAMENT OF NATIONS]
CREATOR Jean Carlu

SOURCE Poster from JAGDA Peace
Posters International Exhibition

014 THE GREAT FRUITS OF DISARMAMENT
CREATOR Loyau Martine
SOURCE Poster from JAGDA Peace
Posters International Exhibition

015 MARCH FOR DISARMAMENT - BOMBS
CREATOR Grapus
SOURCE Poster from JAGDA Peace
Posters International Exhibition

016 FESTIVAL - FORUM FOR PEACE
CREATOR Grapus
SOURCE Poster from JAGDA Peace
Posters International Exhibition

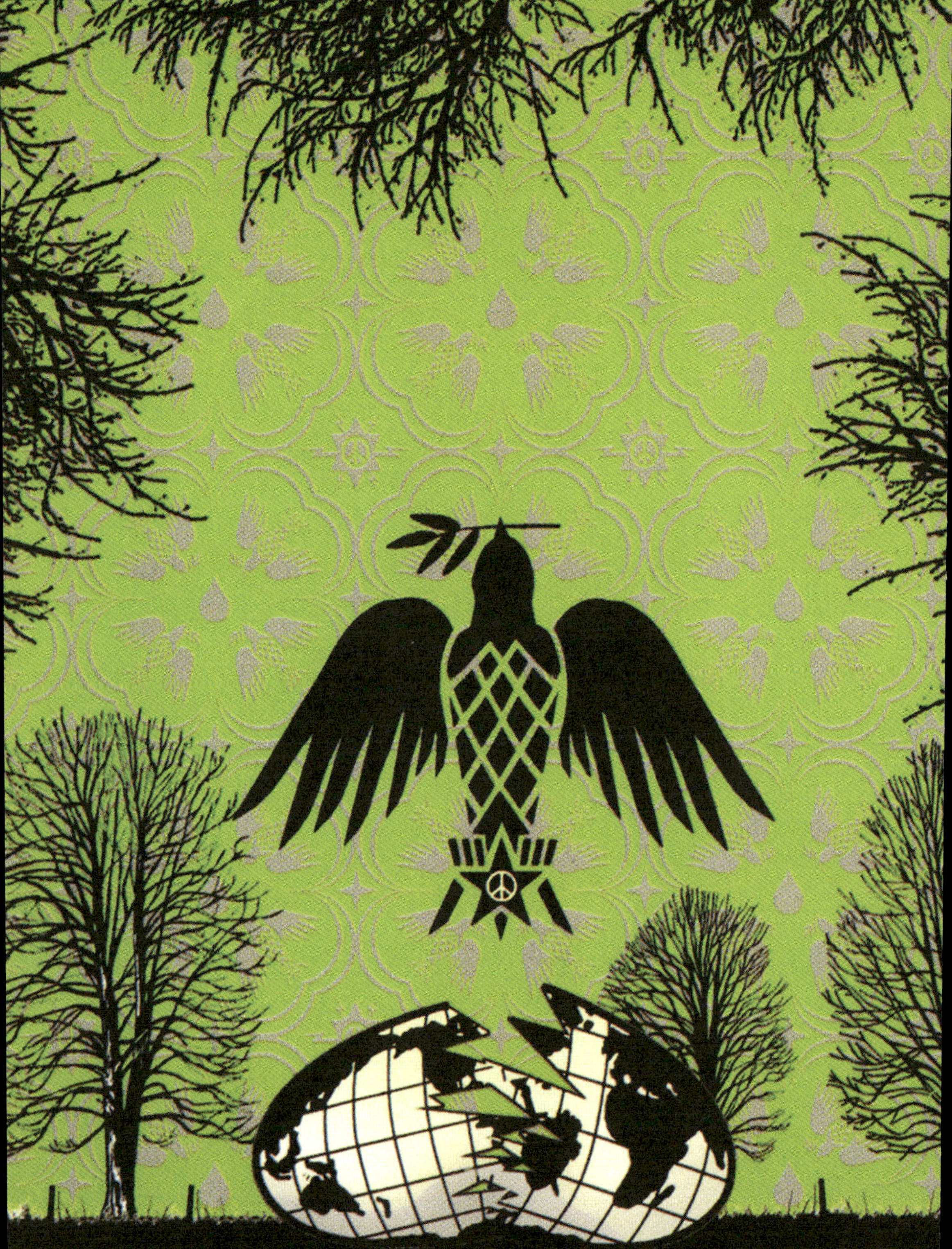

LEFT
001
002
003

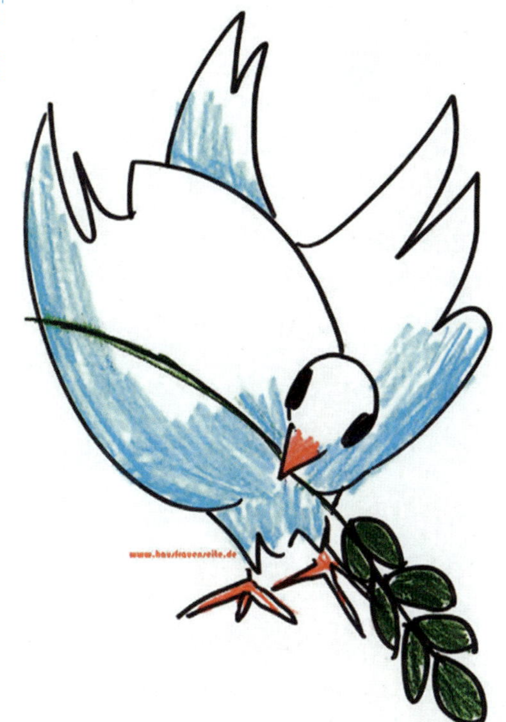

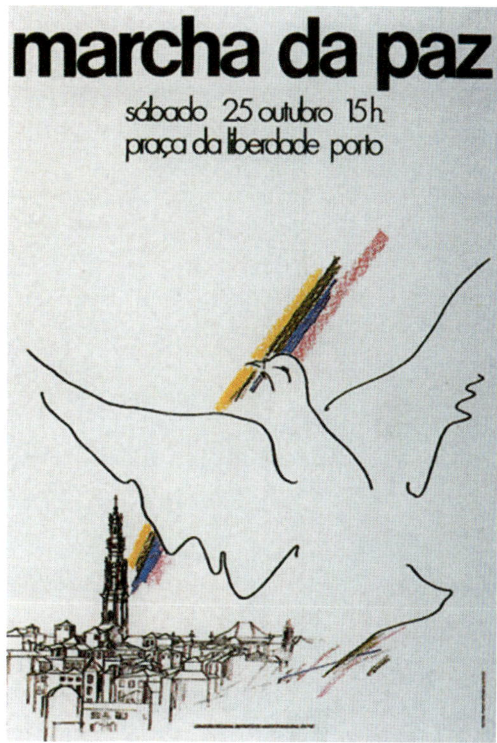

004
005

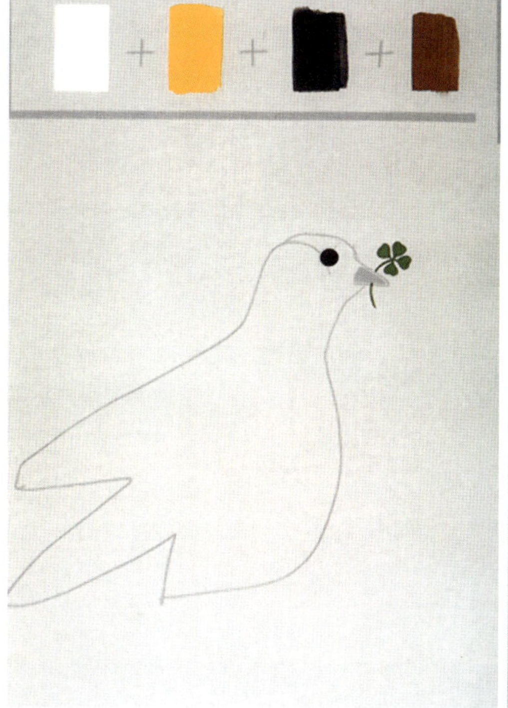

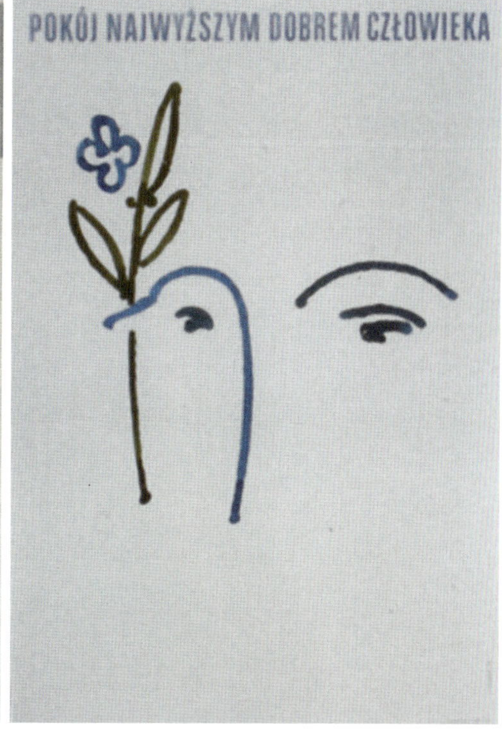

006
007

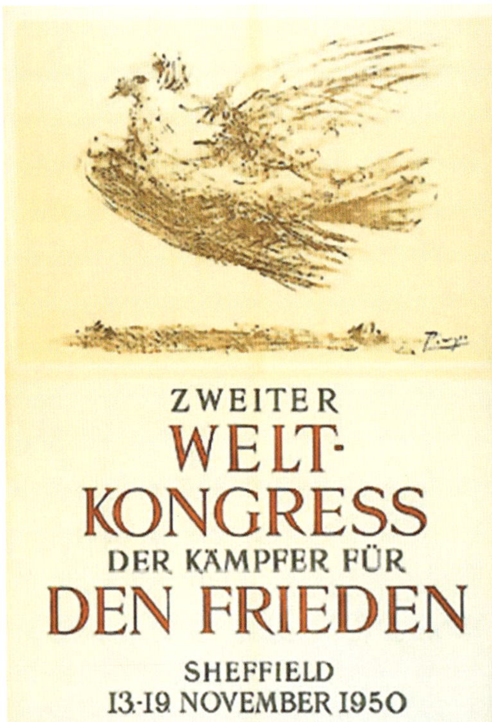

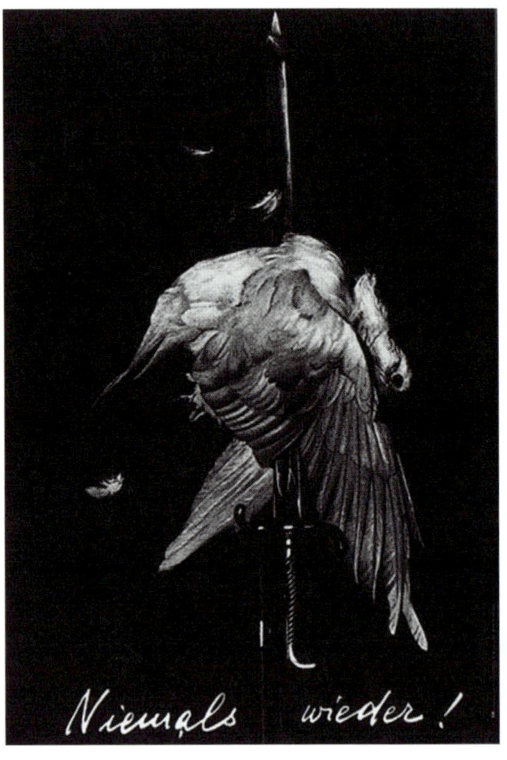

008
009

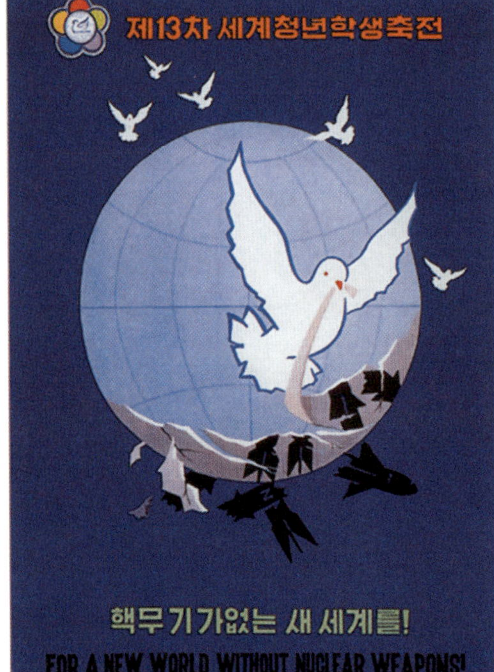

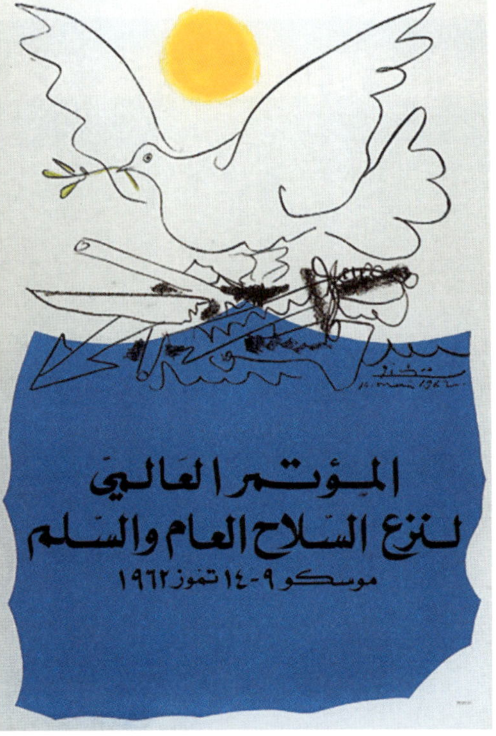

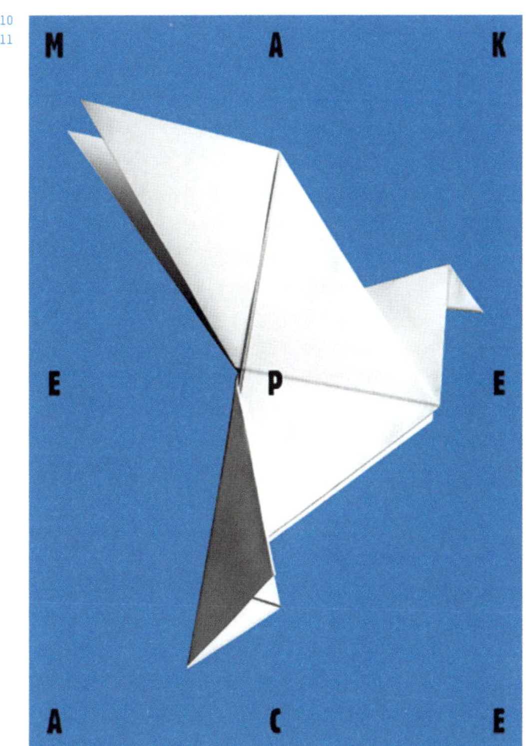
M
A
K
E
P
E
A
C
E

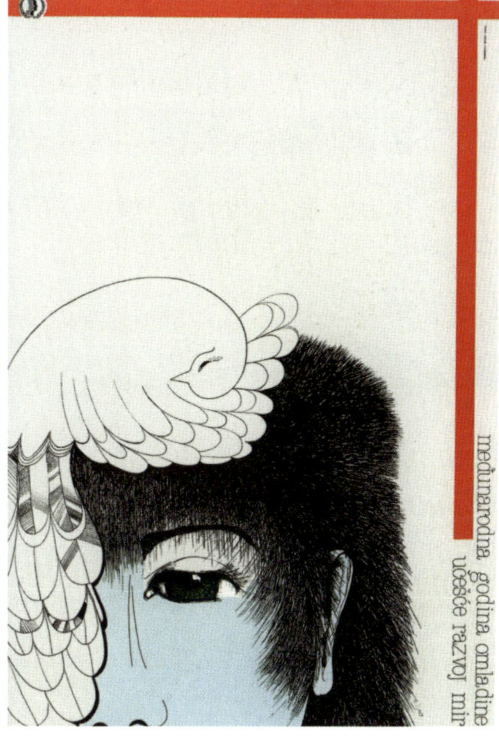
medunarodna godina omladine
učešće razvoj mir

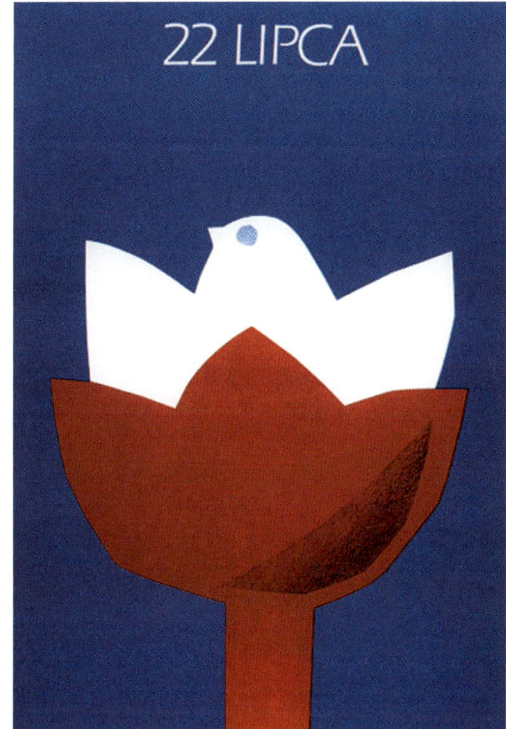
22 LIPCA

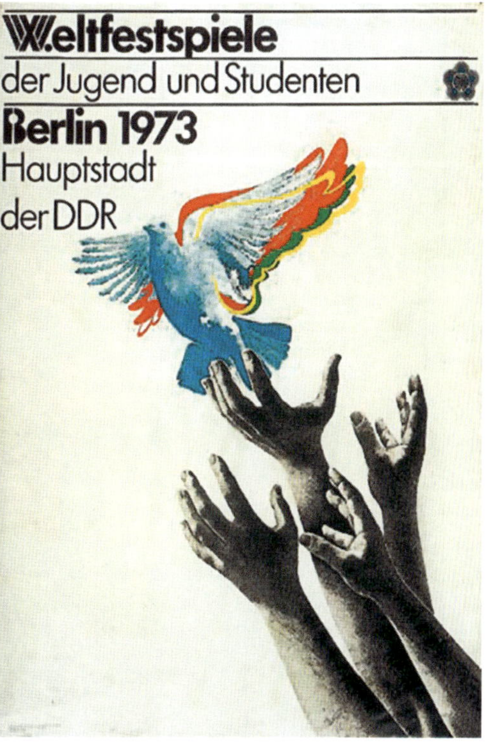
Weltfestspiele
der Jugend und Studenten
Berlin 1973
Hauptstadt
der DDR

014
015

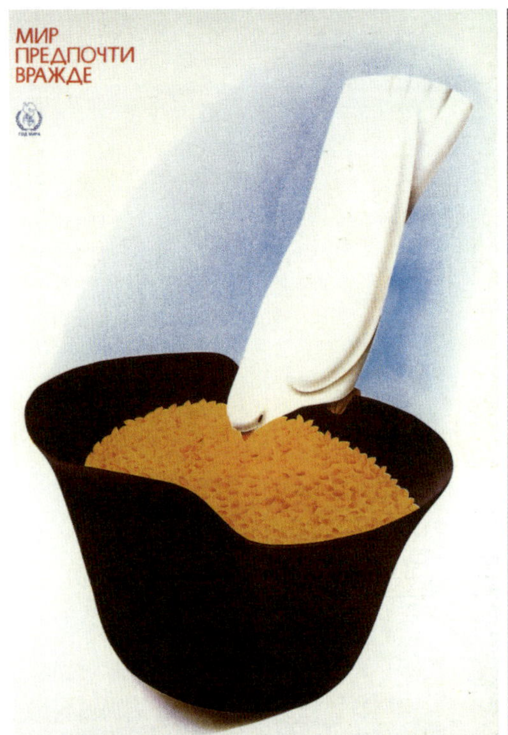

МИР
ПРЕДПОЧТИ
ВРАЖДЕ

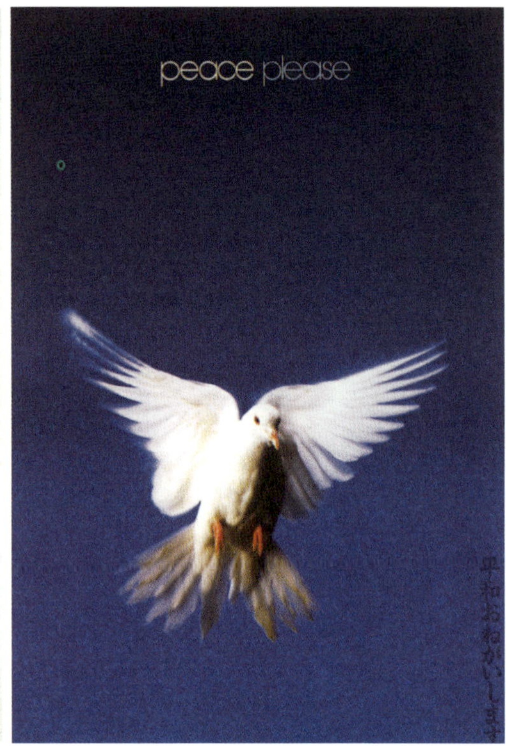

peace please

016
017

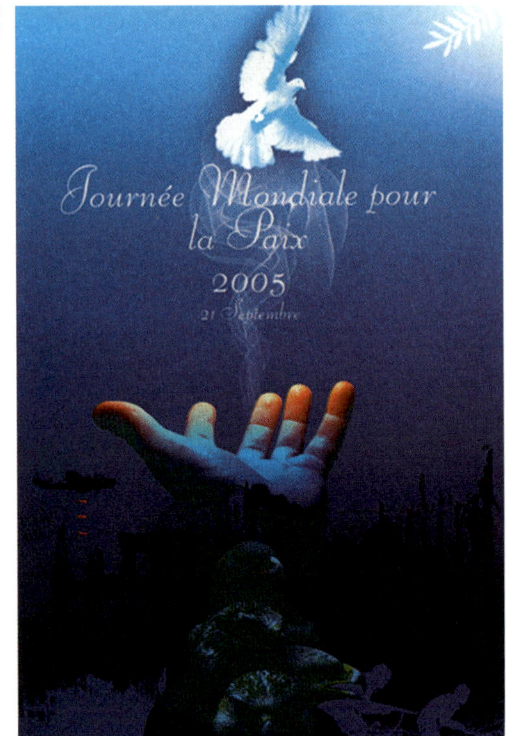

Journée Mondiale pour
la Paix
2005
21 Septembre

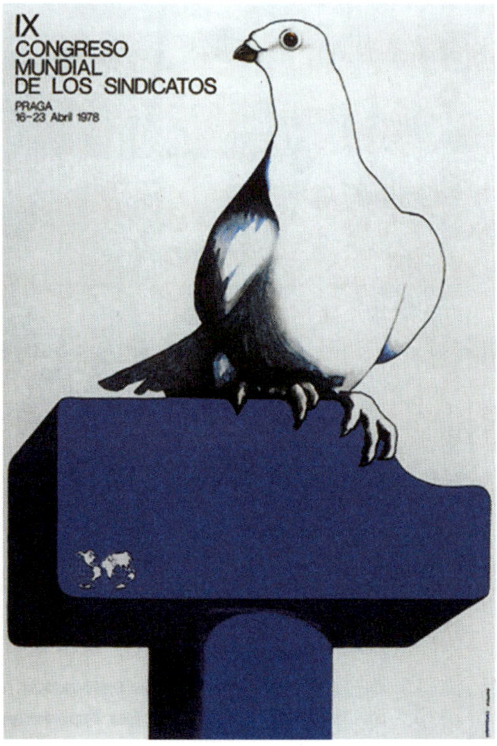

IX
CONGRESO
MUNDIAL
DE LOS SINDICATOS
PRAGA
16-23 Abril 1978

018
019

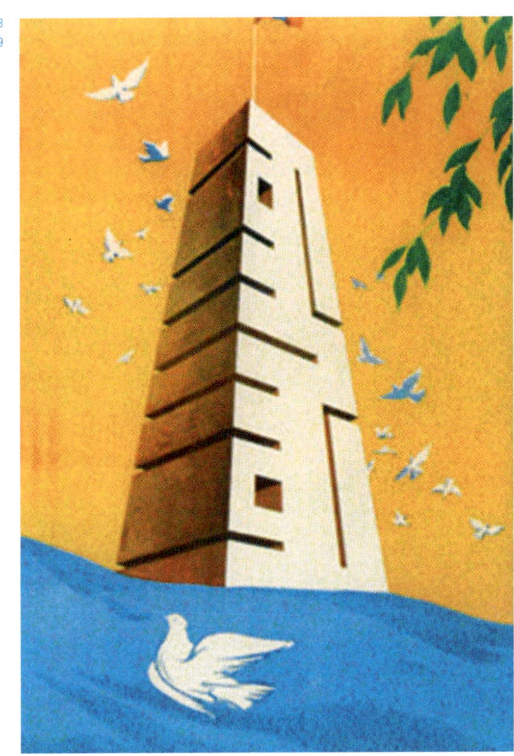

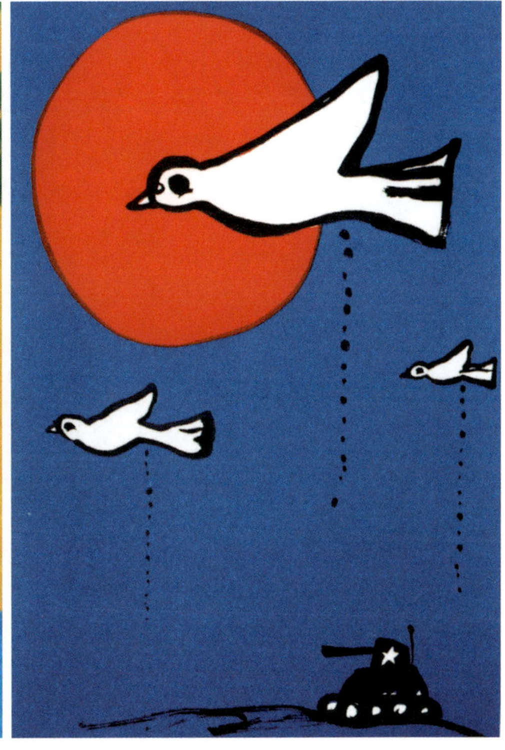

020
021

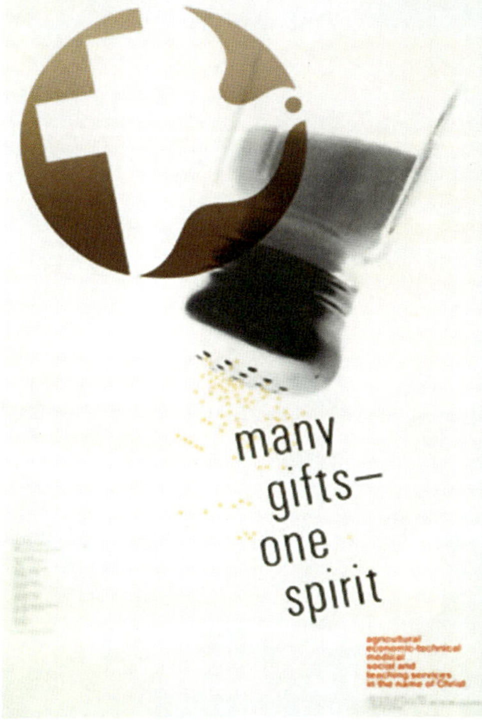

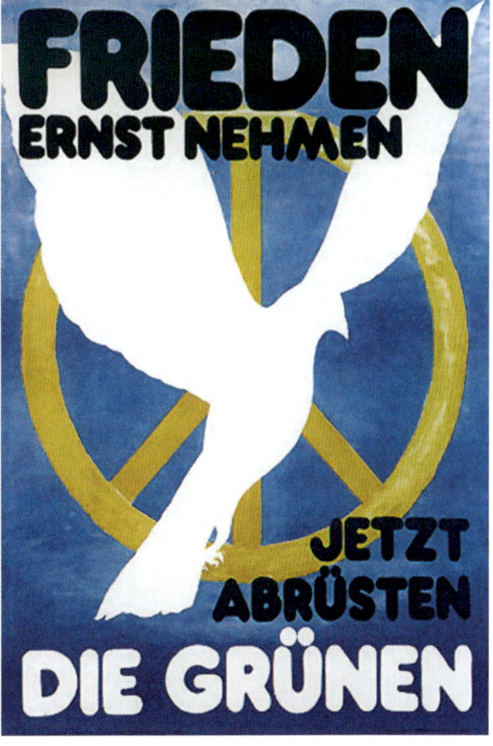

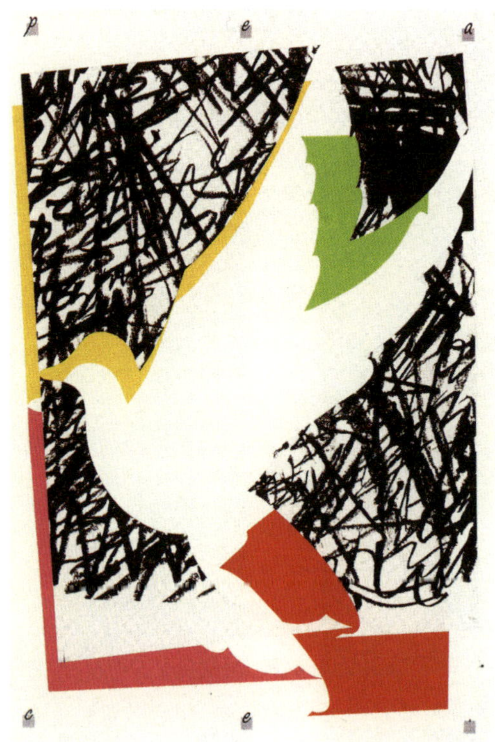

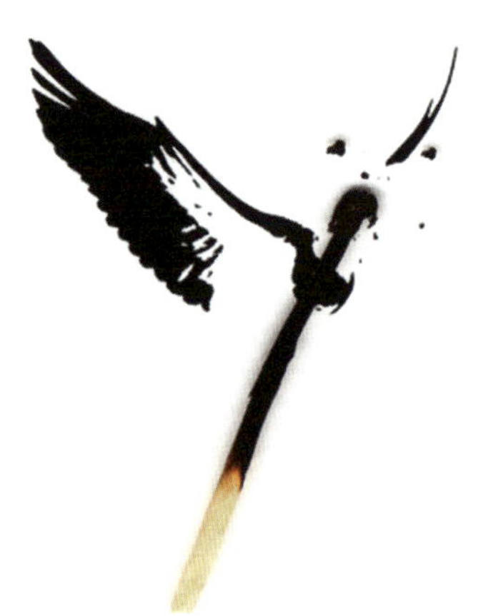

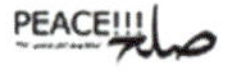
PEACE!!!

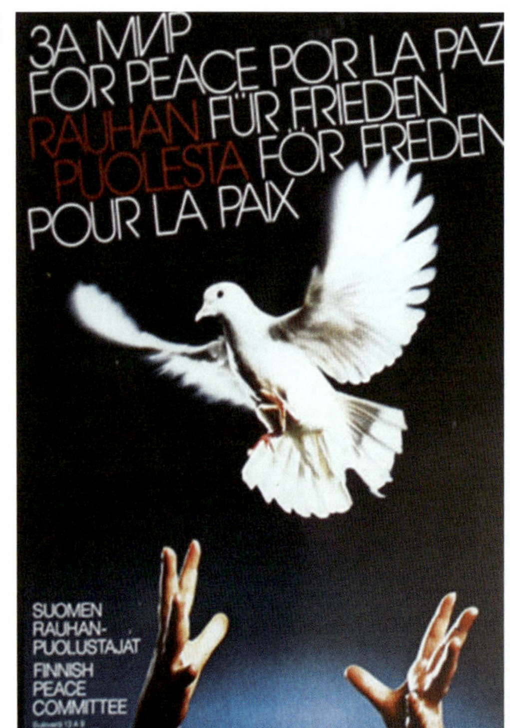
ЗА МИР
FOR PEACE POR LA PAZ
RAUHAN FÜR FRIEDEN
PUOLESTA FÖR FREDEN
POUR LA PAIX
SUOMEN
RAUHAN-
PUOLUSTAJAT
FINNISH
PEACE
COMMITTEE

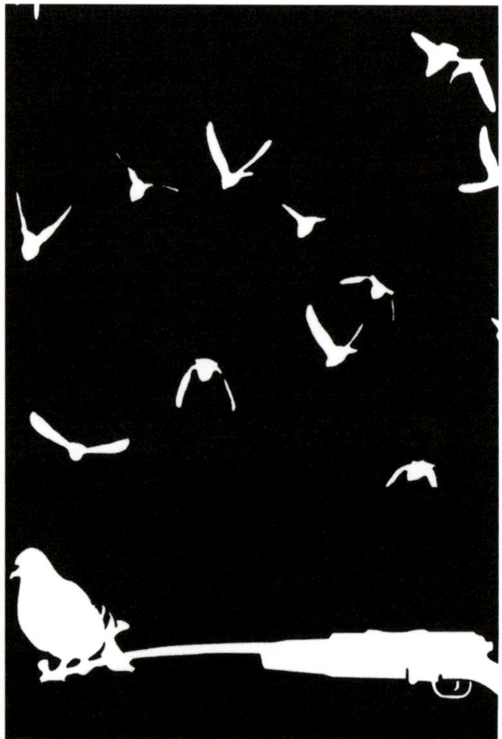

026
027

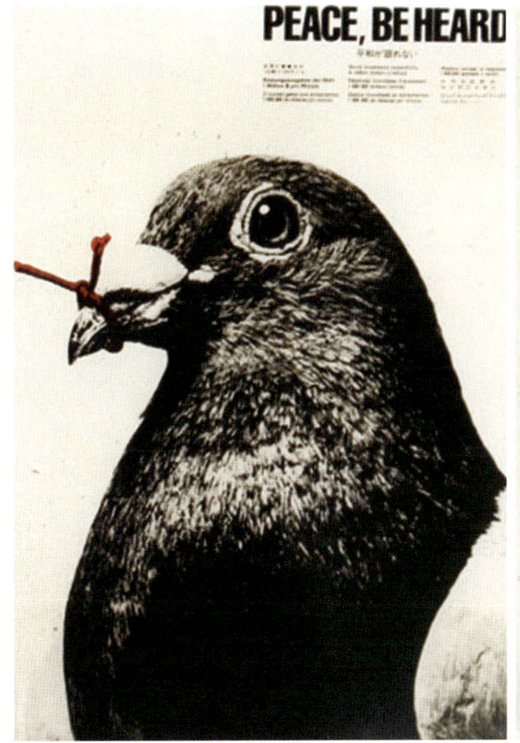

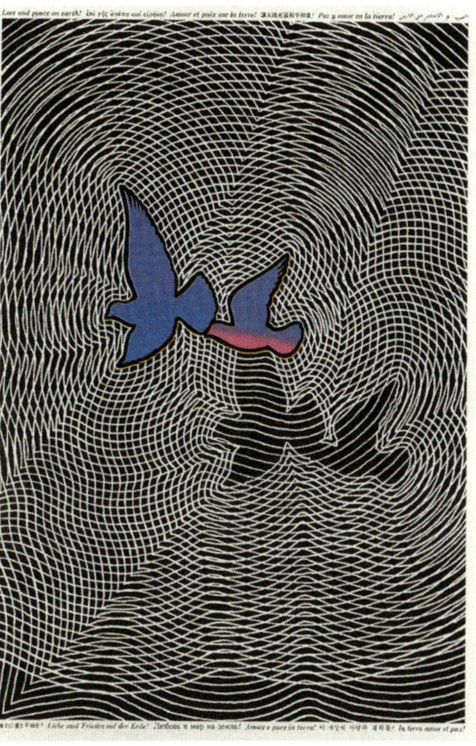

028
029

NEXT
030

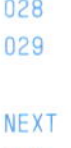

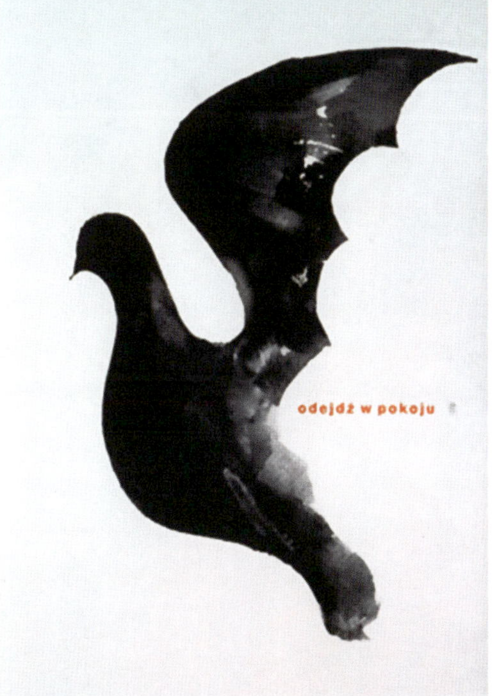

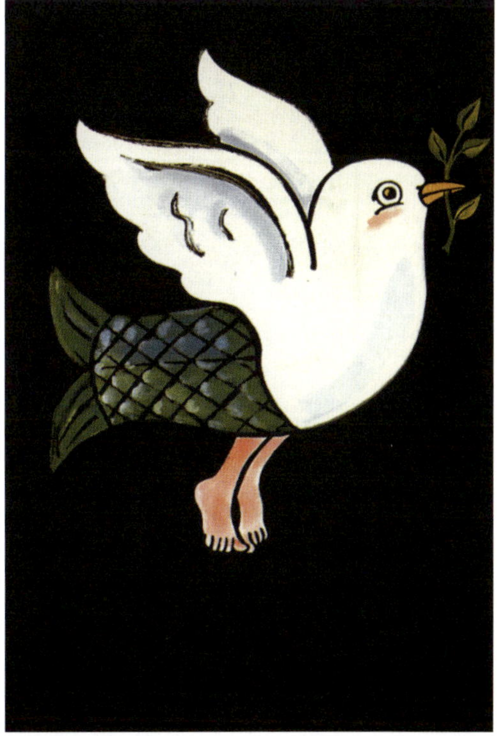

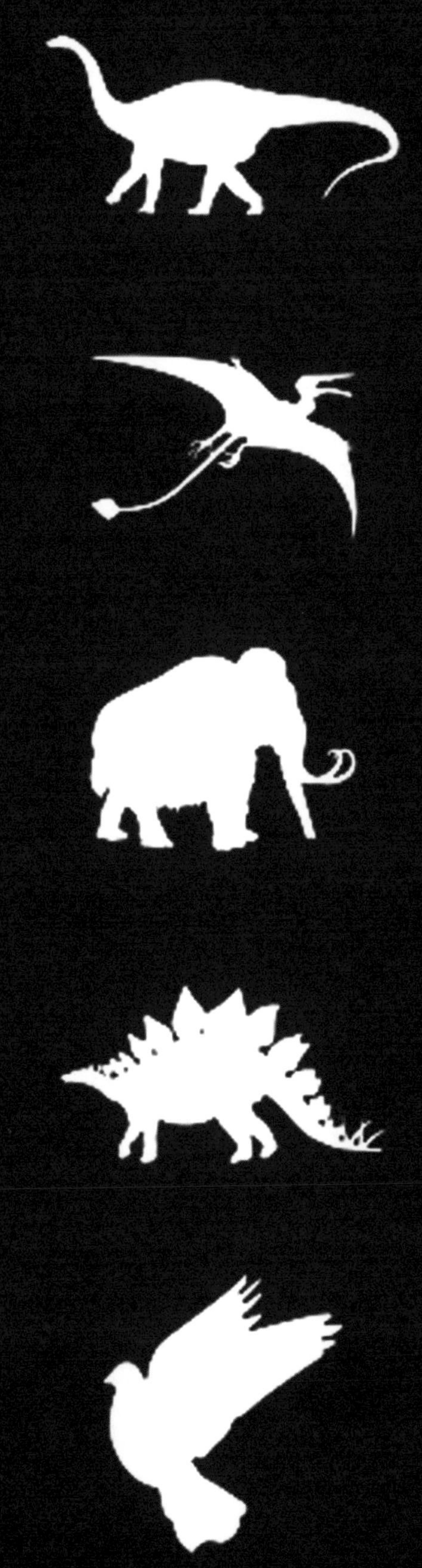

001 PEACE
CREATOR Delanorock
SOURCE John Carr, ed., *Yo! What Happened to Peace?* [Rome: Federico Zesi, 2007], p. 84.

002 FRIEDENSTAUBE
[DOVE OF PEACE]
CREATOR Ludwig Szmtag
SOURCE Beiträge macht Bilder

003 MARCHA DA PAZ
[PEACE MARCH]
CREATOR Paulo Hernani
SOURCE Bruno Margadant, *Hoffnung and Wiederstand* [Zurich: Verlag Hans-Rudolf Lutz, 1998]

004 PEACE DOVE
CREATOR Henryk Tomaszewski
SOURCE Bruno Margadant, *Hoffnung and Wiederstand* [Zurich: Verlag Hans-Rudolf Lutz, 1998]

005 POKOJ NAJWYZSZYM DOBREM CZLOWIEKA
[PEACE IS THE GREATEST GOOD OF PEOPLE]
CREATOR Karol Sliwka
SOURCE Plakatsammlung Museum für Gestaltung Zürich

006 ZWEITER WELT-KONGRESS DER KÄMPEN FÜR DEN FRIEDEN
[SECOND WORLD CONGRESS OF THE SUPPORTERS OF PEACE]
SOURCE www.dhm.de

007 NIEMALS WIEDER!
[NEVER AGAIN!]
CREATOR John Heartfield
SOURCE Bruno Margadant, *Hoffnung and Wiederstand* [Zurich: Verlag Hans-Rudolf Lutz, 1998]

008 FOR A NEW WORLD WITHOUT NUCLEAR WEAPONS
SOURCE Bruno Margadant, *Hoffnung and Wiederstand* [Zurich: Verlag Hans-Rudolf Lutz, 1998]

009 CREATOR Pablo Picasso
SOURCE Bruno Margadant, *Hoffnung and Wiederstand* [Zurich: Verlag Hans-Rudolf Lutz, 1998]

010 MAKE PEACE
SOURCE Beiträge macht Bilder

011 INTERNATIONAL YOUTH YEAR
CREATOR Aleksandra Boman Visic
SOURCE Poster from JAGDA Peace Posters International Exhibition

012 22 LIPCA
[22 JULY]
CREATOR Andrzei Przygodzk
SOURCE Bruno Margadant, *Hoffnung and Wiederstand* [Zurich: Verlag Hans-Rudolf Lutz, 1998]

013 PLAKAT ZU DEN X. WELTFESTSPIELEN DER JUGEND UND STUDENTEN
[10TH FESTIVAL OF YOUTH AND STUDENTS]
SOURCE www.dhm.de
DATE 1973

014 PREFER PEACE TO HOSTILITY
CREATOR The Poster Publishing House
SOURCE Poster from JAGDA Peace Posters International Exhibition

015 PEACE, PLEASE
CREATOR Charles Michael Helmken
SOURCE Poster from JAGDA Peace Posters International Exhibition

016 JOURNÉE MONDIALE POUR LA PAIX, 21 SEPTEMBRE 2005
[WORLD DAY FOR PEACE, 21 SEPTEMBER 2005]
CREATOR Charlie Le Nouail
SOURCE www.mairie-vitry94.fr

017 CREATOR Wlodzimierz Terechowicz
SOURCE Bruno Margadant, *Hoffnung and Wiederstand* [Zurich: Verlag Hans-Rudolf Lutz, 1998]

018 MOGOLEI [MONGOLIA]
SOURCE Plakatsammlung Museum für Gestaltung Zürich

019 PEACE OF SHIT
CREATOR Yuri Shimojo
SOURCE John Carr, ed., *Yo! What Happened to Peace?* [Rome: Federico Zesi, 2007], p. 17.

020 MANY GIFTS - ONE SPIRIT
CREATOR Kenneth Hiebert
SOURCE Plakatsammlung Museum für Gestaltung Zürich

021 WAHLPLAKAT ZUR BUNDESTAGSWAHL
[POSTER FOR THE PARLIAMENTARY ELECTION]
SOURCE home.arcor.de
DATE 1983

022 FOREVER
CREATOR Marco Fogliatti
SOURCE Poster from JAGDA Peace Posters International Exhibition

023 PEACE
CREATOR Harby Pedram
SOURCE Beiträge macht Bilder

024 FÜR FRIEDEN [FOR PEACE]
CREATOR Mika Launis, Aulis Nyqvist
SOURCE Plakatsammlung Museum für Gestaltung Zürich

025 SOURCE John Carr, ed., *Yo! What Happened to Peace?* [Rome: Federico Zesi, 2007].

026 PEACE, BE HEARD
CREATOR Masuteru Aoba, Kenny-Lui Kam Yuen, Hiroshi Koiwai
SOURCE Plakatsammlung Museum für Gestaltung Zürich

027 LOVE AND PEACE ON EARTH!
CREATOR Hirokatsu Hijikata
SOURCE Poster from JAGDA Peace Posters International Exhibition

028 ODEJDZ W POKOJU [GO IN PEACE]
CREATOR Stefan Lechwar
SOURCE Plakatsammlung Museum für Gestaltung Zürich

029 WORLD PEACE
CREATOR Thomas Schleusing
SOURCE Poster from JAGDA Peace Posters International Exhibition

030 EXTINCTION
CREATOR Tahamtan Aminian
SOURCE Beiträge macht Bilder
DATE 2006

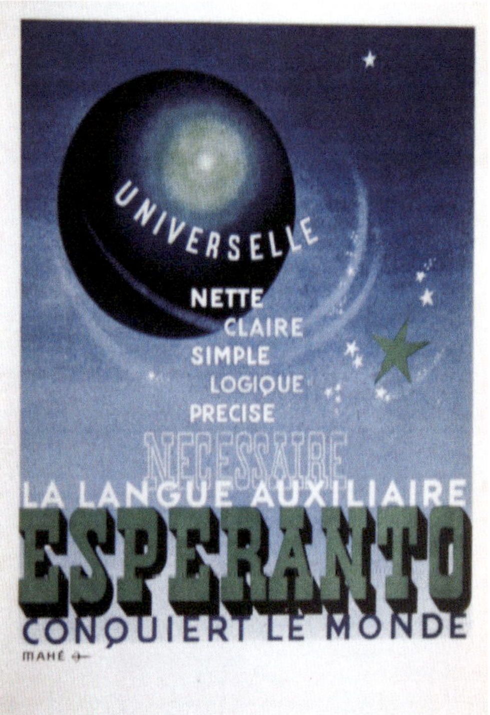
UNIVERSELLE
NETTE
CLAIRE
SIMPLE
LOGIQUE
PRECISE
NECESSAIRE
LA LANGUE AUXILIAIRE
ESPERANTO
CONQUIERT LE MONDE
MAHÉ

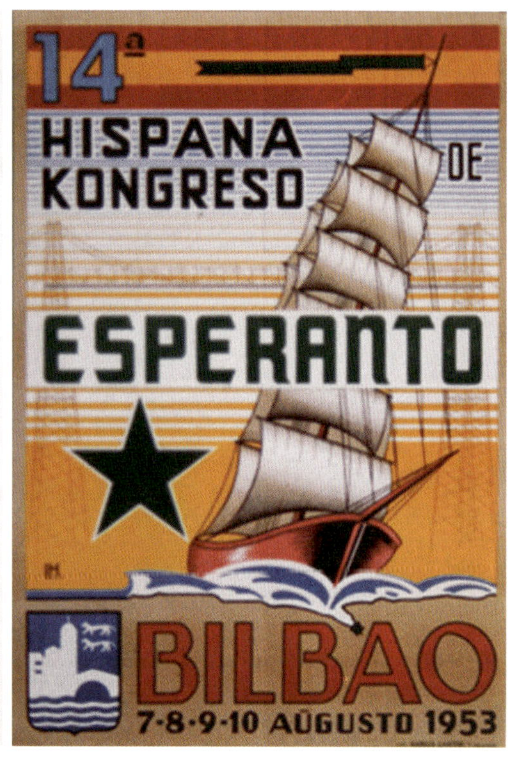
14ª
HISPANA
KONGRESO
DE
ESPERANTO
BILBAO
7·8·9·10 AÚGUSTO 1953

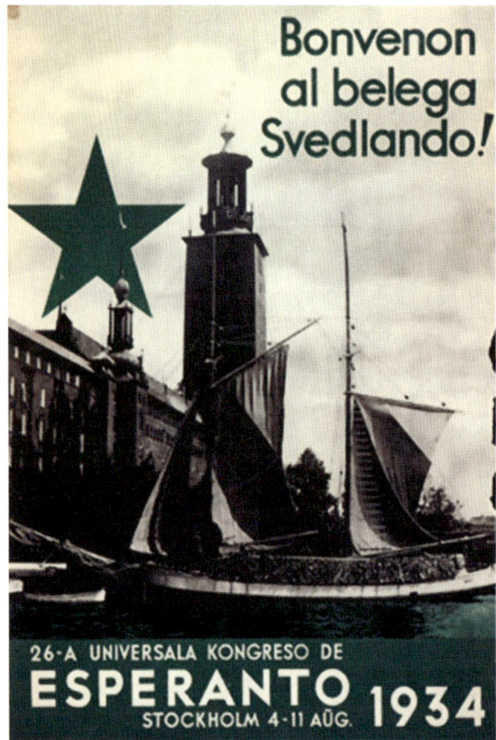
Bonvenon
al belega
Svedlando!
26-A UNIVERSALA KONGRESO DE
ESPERANTO 1934
STOCKHOLM 4-11 AÜG.

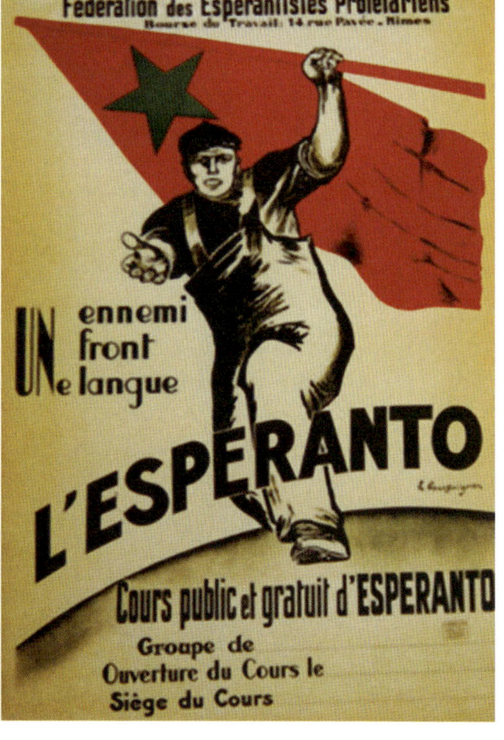
Fédération des Espérantistes Prolétariens
Bourse du Travail: 14 rue Pavée - Nimes
UN ennemi
front
UNe langue
L'ESPERANTO
Cours public et gratuit d'ESPERANTO
Groupe de
Ouverture du Cours le
Siège du Cours

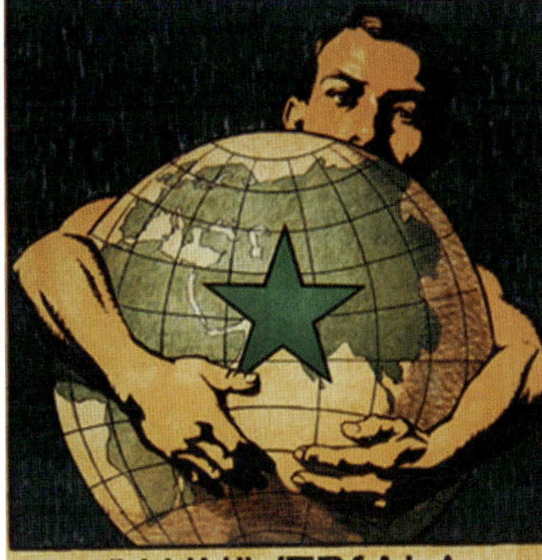

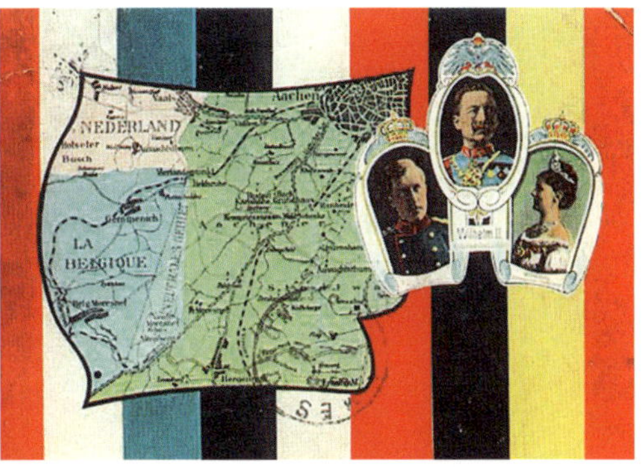

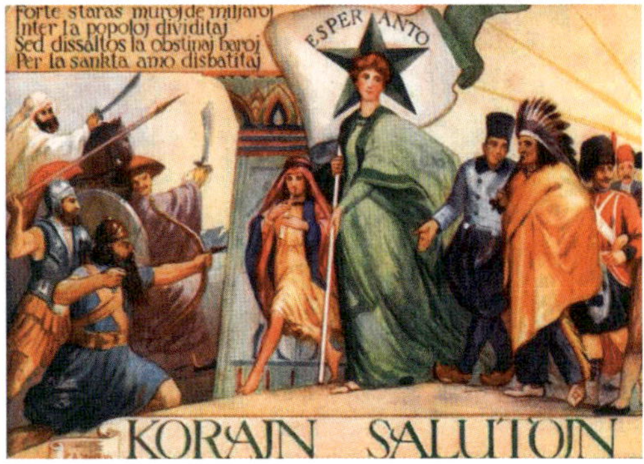

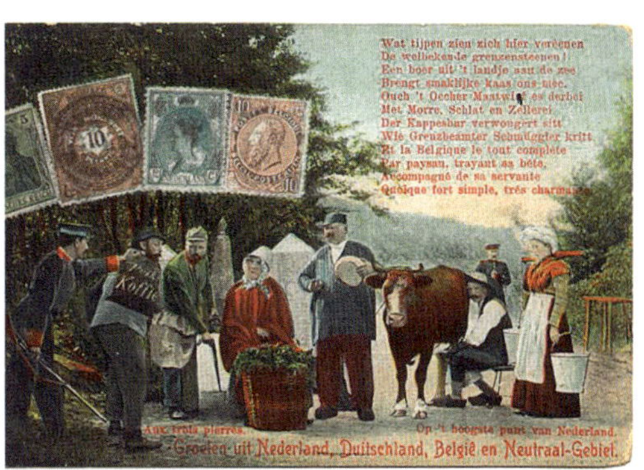

Einwohner von Neutral-Moresnet!

Ziert die Häuser!   Steckt Fahnen auf!

Böllerschießen hat Euch soeben verkündet daß der

Friede

gezeichnet ist.

Hiermit ist zugleich das Geschick d. Neutralen Gebietes besiegelt!
Neutral-Moresnet ist von der Landkarte verschwunden!
Belgien, dass uns in schwerer Zeit vor Hunger schützte, soll
unser Vaterland sein! Was vor 25 Jahren angestrebt wurde,
hat heute seine Verwirklichung gefunden.   Drum

Flaggen heraus!

und zum Zeichen der Freude, beteiligt Euch an der

Volks=Versammlung

die heute Abend 8 Uhr am Schützenlokale stattfinden wird,
stimmt dabei ein in die Hymne an Belgien und nehmet Teil an
dem daurauffolgenden

Fackelzug.

Die Gemeinde-Verwaltung von Neutral-Moresnet.

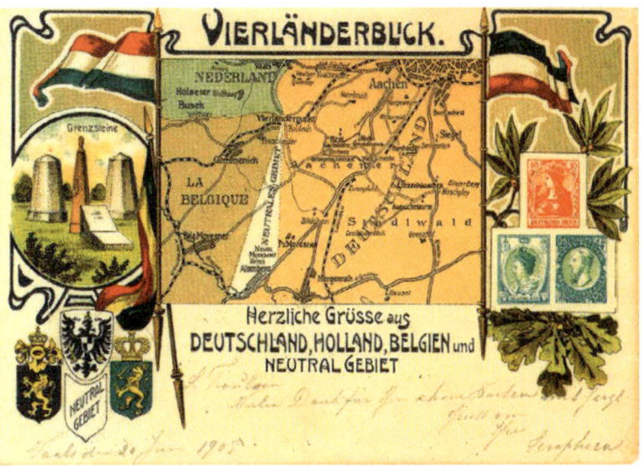

001 ESPERANTO CONQUIERT LE MONDE
[ESPERANTO CONQUERS THE WORLD]
SOURCE Plakatsammlung Museum
für Gestaltung Zürich
DATE 1930/1940

002 14A HISPANA KONGRESO DE
ESPERANTO - BILBAO
[14TH CONGRESS OF
ESPERANTO - BILBAO]
CREATOR LH
SOURCE Plakatsammlung Museum
für Gestaltung Zürich

003 BONVENON AL BELEGA: SVEDLANDO!
[WELCOME TO BEAUTIFUL SWEDEN!]
CREATOR LH
SOURCE Plakatsammlung Museum
für Gestaltung Zürich
DATE 1934

004 UNE ENNEMI, UNE FRONT, UNE
LANGUE - L'ESPERANTO
[ONE ENEMY, ONE FRONT, ONE
LANGUAGE - ESPERANTO]
CREATOR H. Bourgignon
SOURCE Plakatsammlung Museum
für Gestaltung Zürich
DATE 1934

005 IX UNIVERSALA KONGRĚSŎ
DE ESPERANTO
[NINTH UNIVERSAL CONGRESS
OF ESPERANTO]
SOURCE Plakatsammlung Museum
für Gestaltung Zürich
DATE 1913

006 POSTCARD OF NEUTRAL MORESNET
In 1908, there was a proposal
to make Neutral Moresnet the
first Esperanto-speaking state.
After World War I, the region
became part of Belgium.
CREATOR Gemeindeverwaltung
Neutral-Moresnet
SOURCE www.moresnet.nl

007 KORAJN SALUTOJN
[WARM GREETINGS]
Postcard with lyrics from "La
Espero," the anthem of Esperanto:
The walls of a thousand years
stand firm / Between the divided
peoples / But the stubborn barri-
ers will crumble / Knocked down
with sacred love
SOURCE www.metropostcard.com

008 POSTER ANNOUNCING PEACE AND
DISSOLUTION OF NEUTRAL MORESNET
IN FAVOR OF BELGIUM
CREATOR Gemeindeverwaltung
Neutral-Moresnet
SOURCE www.moresnet.nl

009 GROETEN UIT NEDERLAND,
DUITSCHLAND, BELGIË EN
NEUTRAAL-GEBIET
[GREETINGS FROM THE NETHERLANDS,
GERMANY, BELGIUM AND NEUTRAL
MORESNET]
CREATOR Gemeindeverwaltung
Neutral-Moresnet
SOURCE www.moresnet.nl

010 VIERLÄNDERBLICK - HERZLICHE
GRÜSSE AUS DEUTSCHLAND, HOLLAND,
BELGIEN UND NEUTRAL GEBIET
[VIEW OF FOUR COUNTRIES - CORDIAL
GREETINGS FROM GERMANY, HOLLAND,
BELGIUM, AND NEUTRAL MORESNET]
CREATOR Gemeindeverwaltung
Neutral-Moresnet
SOURCE www.moresnet.nl

001
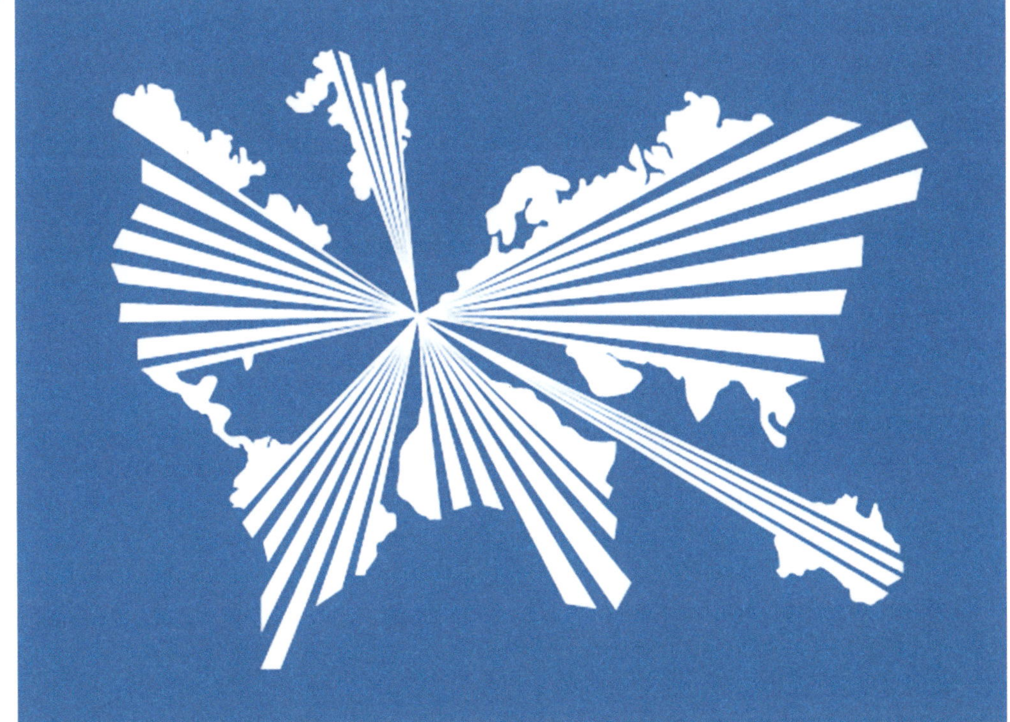

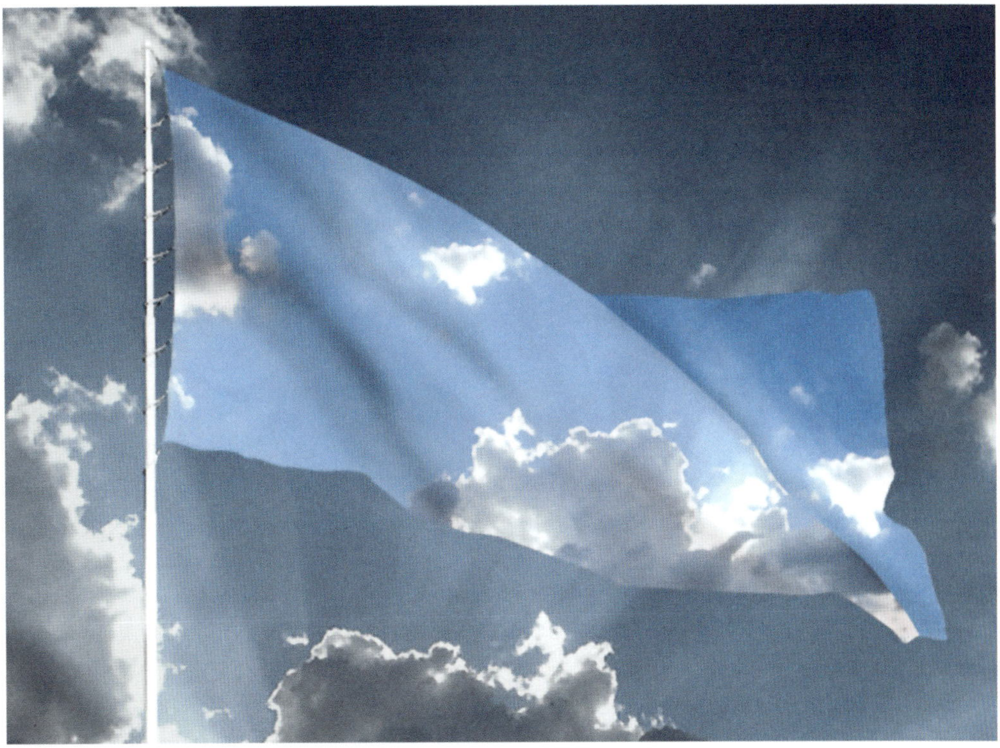

002

003

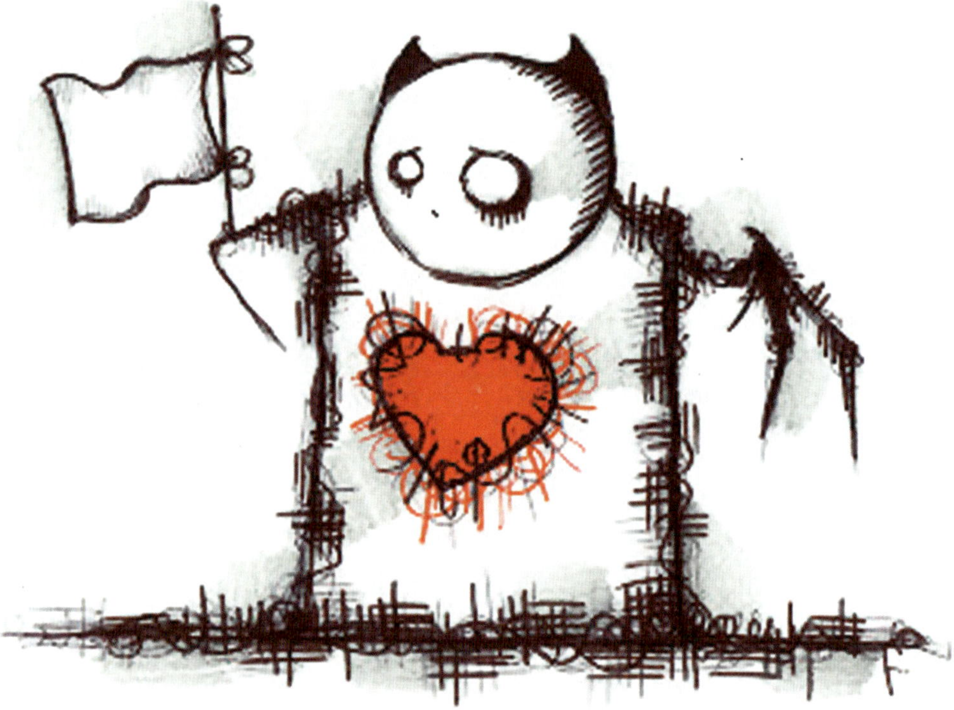

004

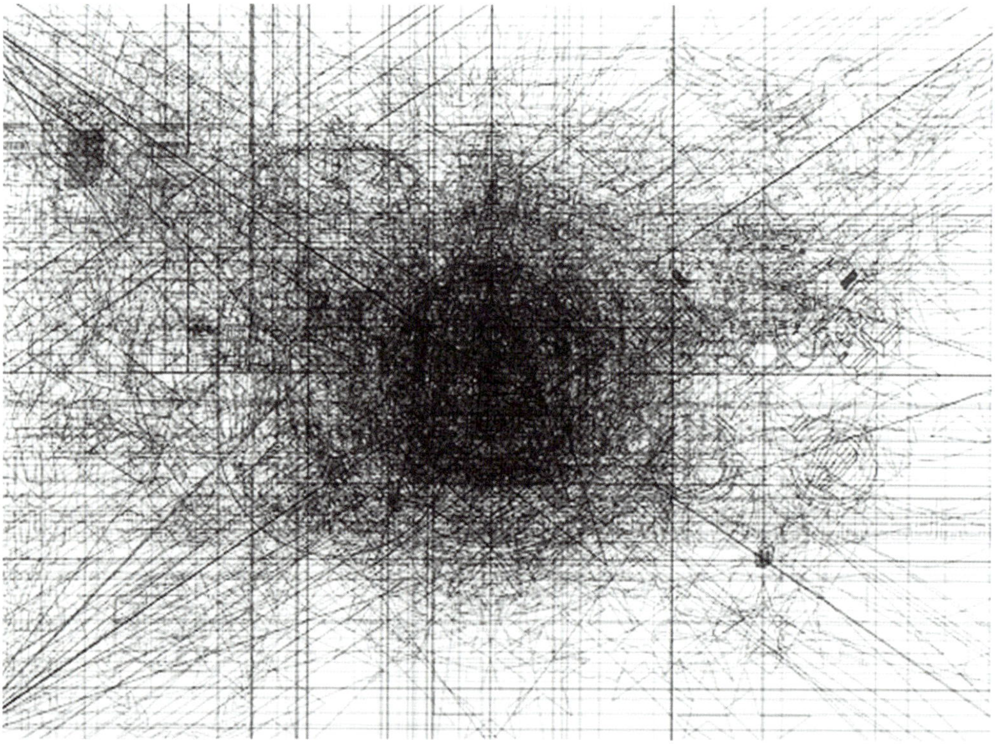

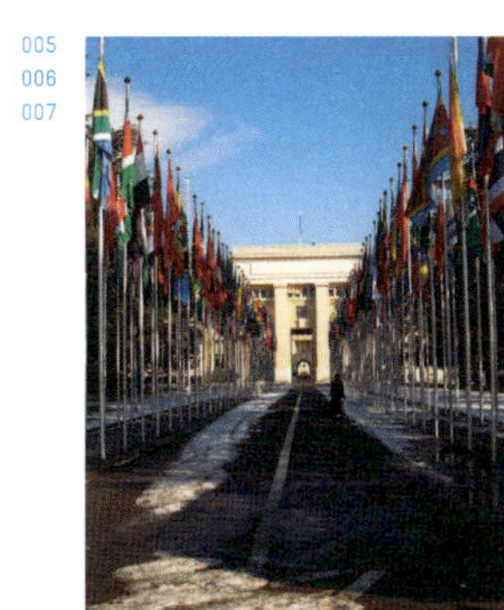
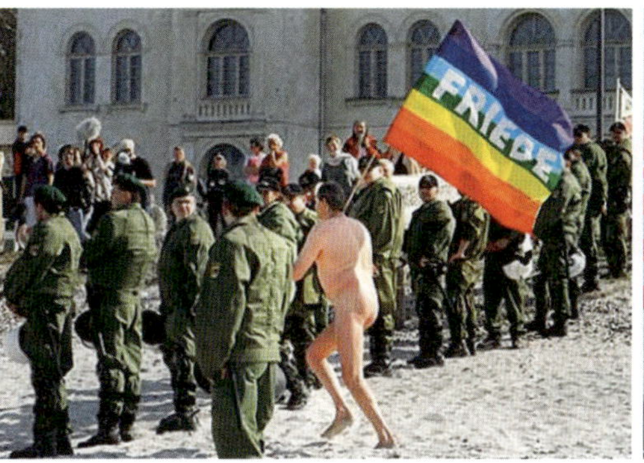
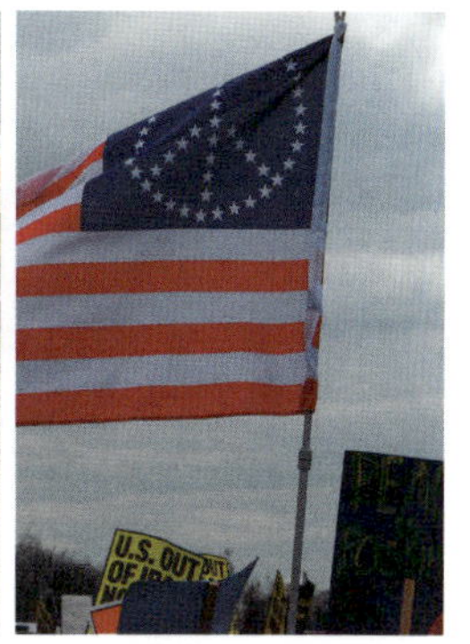
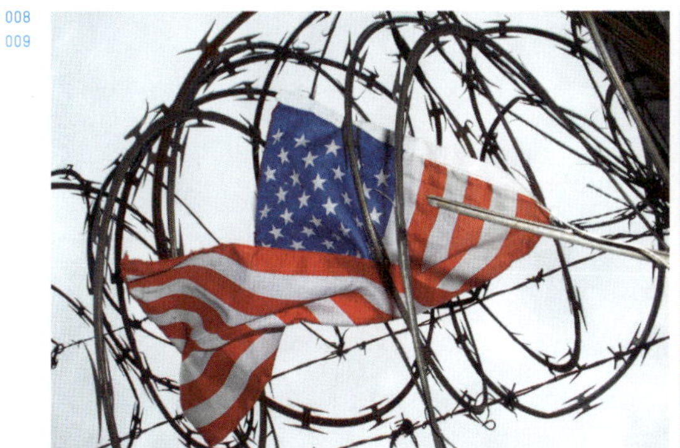
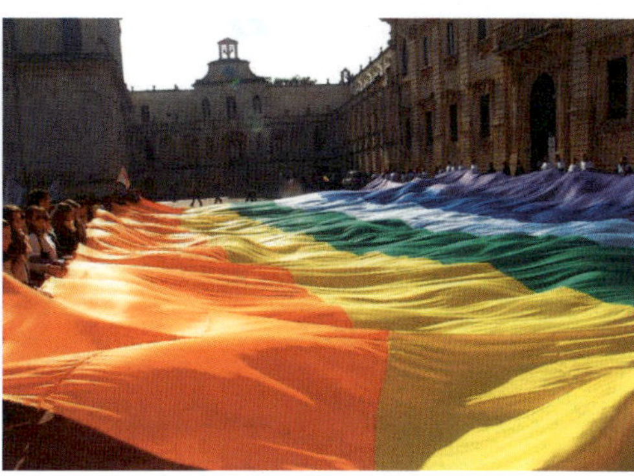
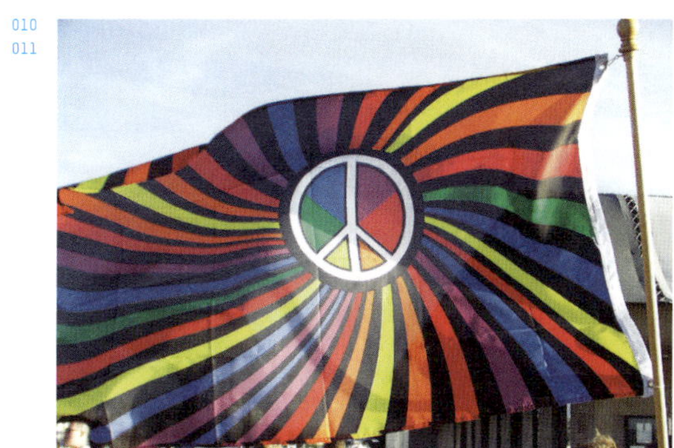
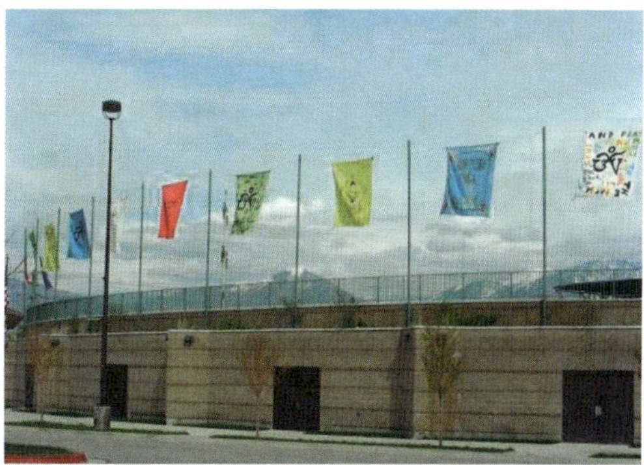
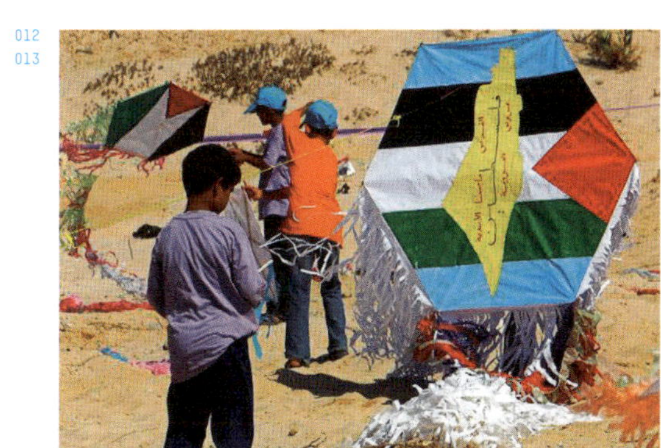
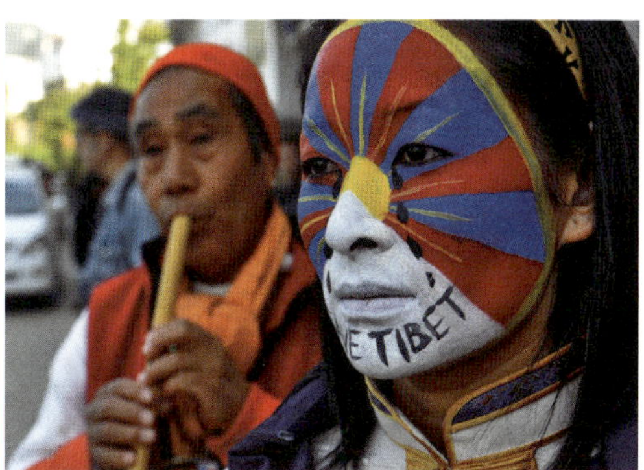

014
015

016

017
018

019

020
021

022

023
024

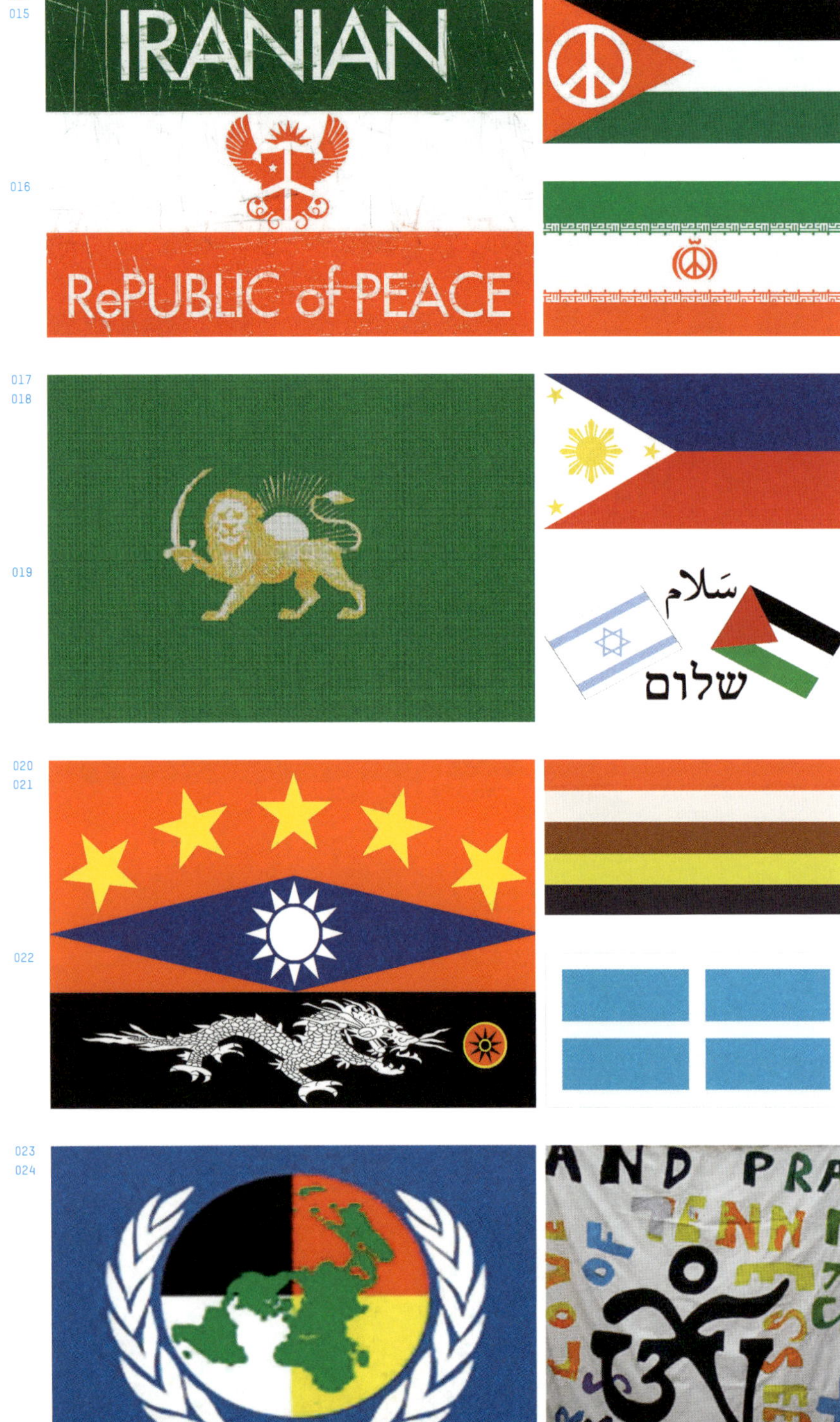

025
026

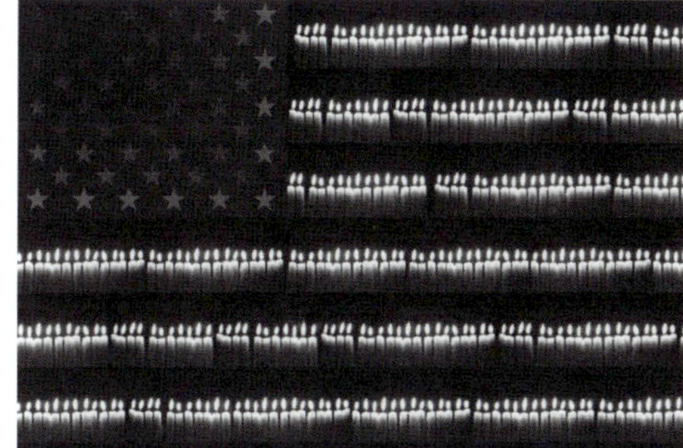

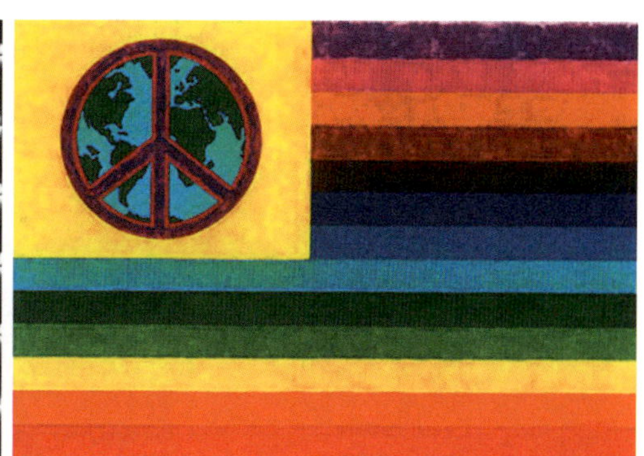

027
028
029

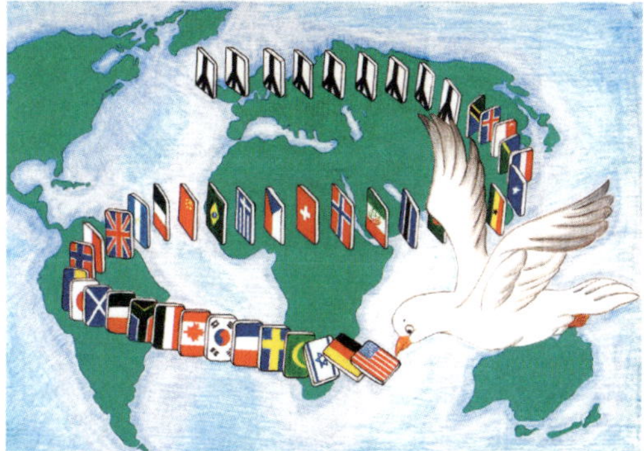

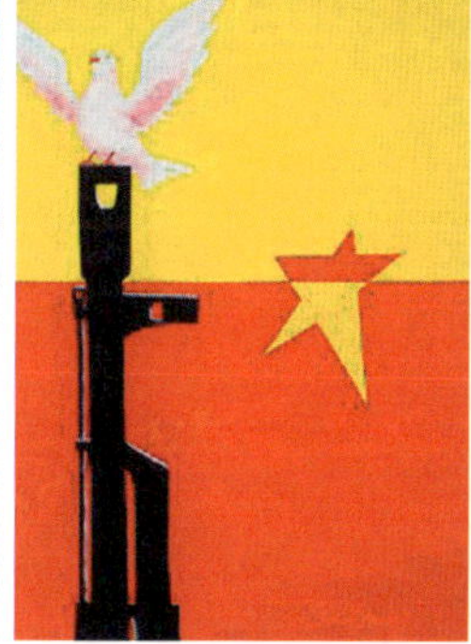

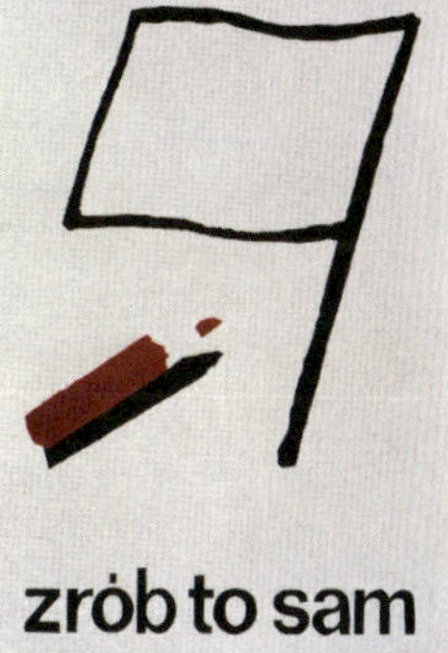

030

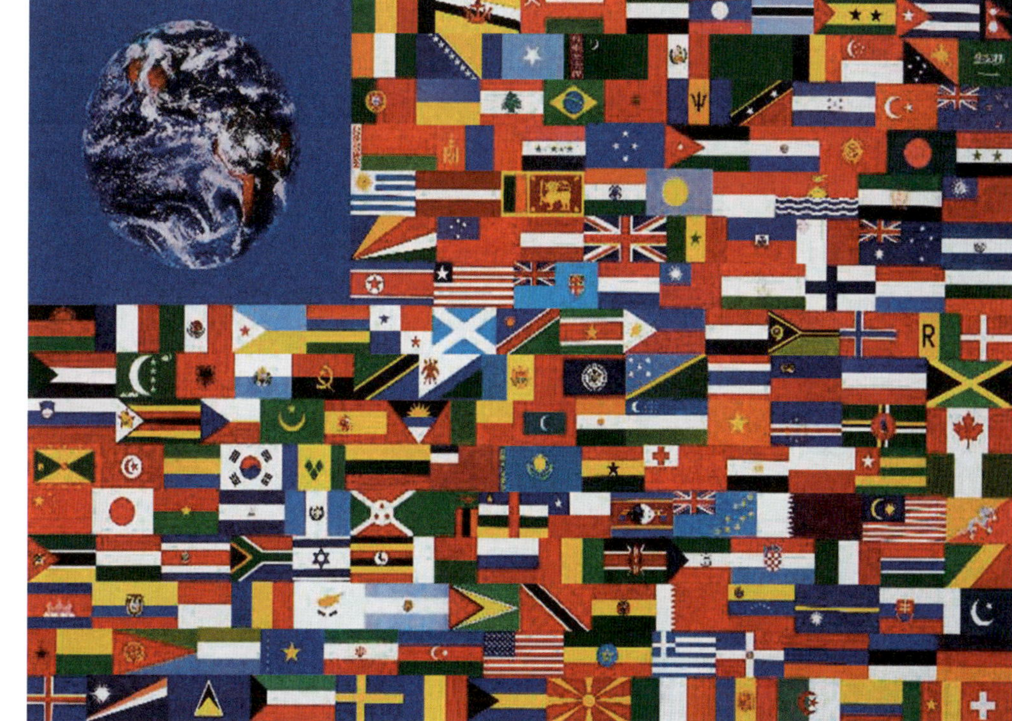

001 MARC'S FLAG
     Image created for One Flag
     competition held by Adbusters.
     CREATOR Marc Arroyo Ortiga
     SOURCE www.adbusters.org

002 THE FLAG OF UNION
     Image created for One Flag
     competition held by Adbusters.
     CREATOR Luba Mikhnovsky
     SOURCE www.adbusters.org

003 UNTITLED
     SOURCE hintermschein.blogspot.ch

004 210 = 1
     "My flag takes the 210 flags
     from the countries in the world
     as outlines layered on top of
     one another to create a global
     flag. The flag contains 295 stars,
     13 moons, 19 suns, 16 birds and 4
     dragons." Image created for One
     Flag competition held by Adbusters.
     CREATOR Rory Brady
     SOURCE www.adbusters.org

005 UNITED NATIONS HEADQUARTERS, GENEVA
     SOURCE www.lawcf.org

006 A NAKED MAN WITH A PEACE FLAG
     CROSSING A POLICE CHAIN
     CREATOR Matthias Marburg
     SOURCE bloeser.blogspot.com

007 ANSWER COALITION PEACE MARCH
     ON THE PENTAGON
     CREATOR Provided by jcolman
     SOURCE www.flickr.com/photos/
     jcolman/424492465/

008 CONCENTRATION CAMPS IN THE US
     SOURCE earthhopenetwork.net

009 RICUCIAMO LA PACE, THE LARGEST
     PEACE FLAG IN THE WORLD
     CREATOR Provided by GPACE
     SOURCE www.gpace.net

010 PEACE FLAG, SAN DIEGO
     CREATOR Provided by cleopatra69
     SOURCE www.flickr.com/photos/
     cleopatra69/4013263844/

011 THE PEACE FLAG PROJECT
     CREATOR Barton Moody
     SOURCE www.bartonmoody.com

012 CHILDREN IN GAZA ATTEMPT TO
     SET GUINNESS WORLD RECORD FOR
     KITE FLYING
     SOURCE www.telegraph.co.uk

013 EXPRESSING IT
     CREATOR Jatin Gandhi
     SOURCE www.theothergandhi.com

014 IRANIAN REPUBLIC
     OF PEACE

     CREATOR Ofunne Obiamiwe
     SOURCE www.republicofpeace.com

015 SUDAN DARFUR PEACE FLAG
     CREATOR PeaceSymbol.org
     SOURCE www.peacesymbol.org

016 IRAN PEACE FLAG
     CREATOR Nik Bear Brown
     SOURCE www.peacesymbol.org

017 IRAN PEACE FLAG
     SOURCE arteshe-iran.blogspot.com

018 PHILIPPINES PEACE FLAG
     SOURCE www.loeser.us

019 ISRAEL AND PALESTINE PEACE
     CREATOR Ogre
     SOURCE commons.wikimedia.org

020 CHINA PEACE FLAG
     CREATOR Henry Churchyard
     SOURCE www.crossmyt.com

021 WORLD PEACE ASSOCIATION:
     BROTHERHOOD FLAG
     CREATOR Rob Davis
     SOURCE flagspot.net

022 MERCHANT'S ENSIGN
     This flag was used by peaceful
     merchant ships [i.e., not warships]
     sailing for Mexico along the
     coasts of the Gulf between Mexico
     and North America.
     SOURCE www.loeser.us

023 ALL NATIONS PEACE
     CREATOR All Nations Peace
     SOURCE www.allnationspeace.com

024 UNITARIAN CHURCH PEACE FLAG
     CREATOR Unitarian Church
     SOURCE www.bartonmoody.com

025 SEPTEMBER 11
     CREATOR Cedomir Kosovic
     SOURCE Steven Heller and
     Carol Wells, eds., *The Graphic
     Imperative: International Posters
     for Peace, Social Justice, and the
     Environment, 1965-2005* [Boston:
     Massachusetts College of Arts, 2005].

026 WORLD PEACE FLAG
     CREATOR Sally Marr / Peter Dudar
     SOURCE www.coalitionforworldpeace.
     org

027 UNTITLED
     SOURCE multivu.prnewswire.com

028 GUNS AND PEACE
     CREATOR Sun Mu
     SOURCE www.crestock.com

029 CAN YOU SMILE WHEN YOU ARE OLD
     CREATOR Keizo Matsui

     SOURCE Plakatsammlung Museum
     für Gestaltung Zürich

030 WORLD PEACE FLAG
     SOURCE www.globaleye2000.com

001

EVERY TARGET IS A HOME!
PEACE
Geg
eden
GEGEN JEDEN
KRIEG
WIEDERENTWAFFNUNG
jetzt
HEUTE IST NICHT
ALLE TAGE...

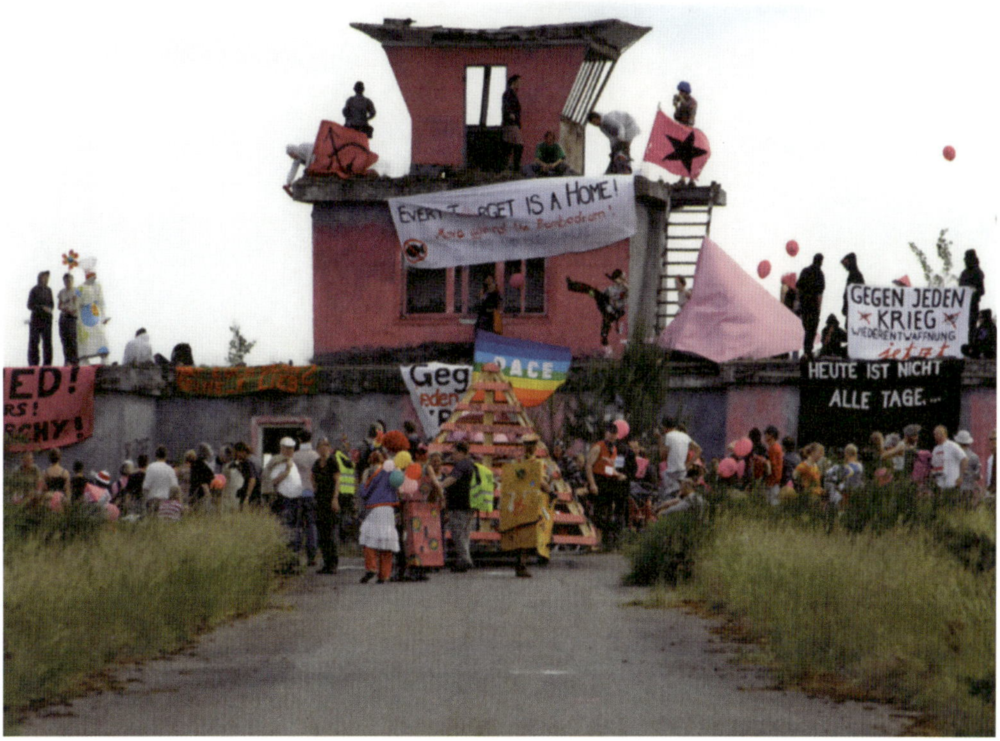

002

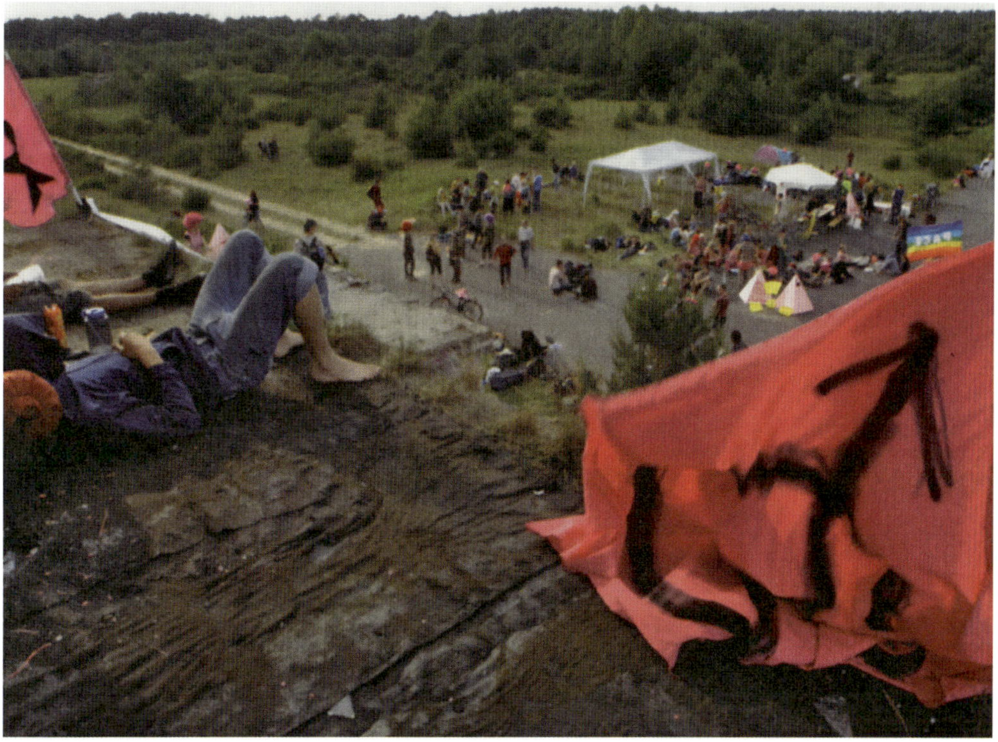

003
004
005
006
007
008
009
010

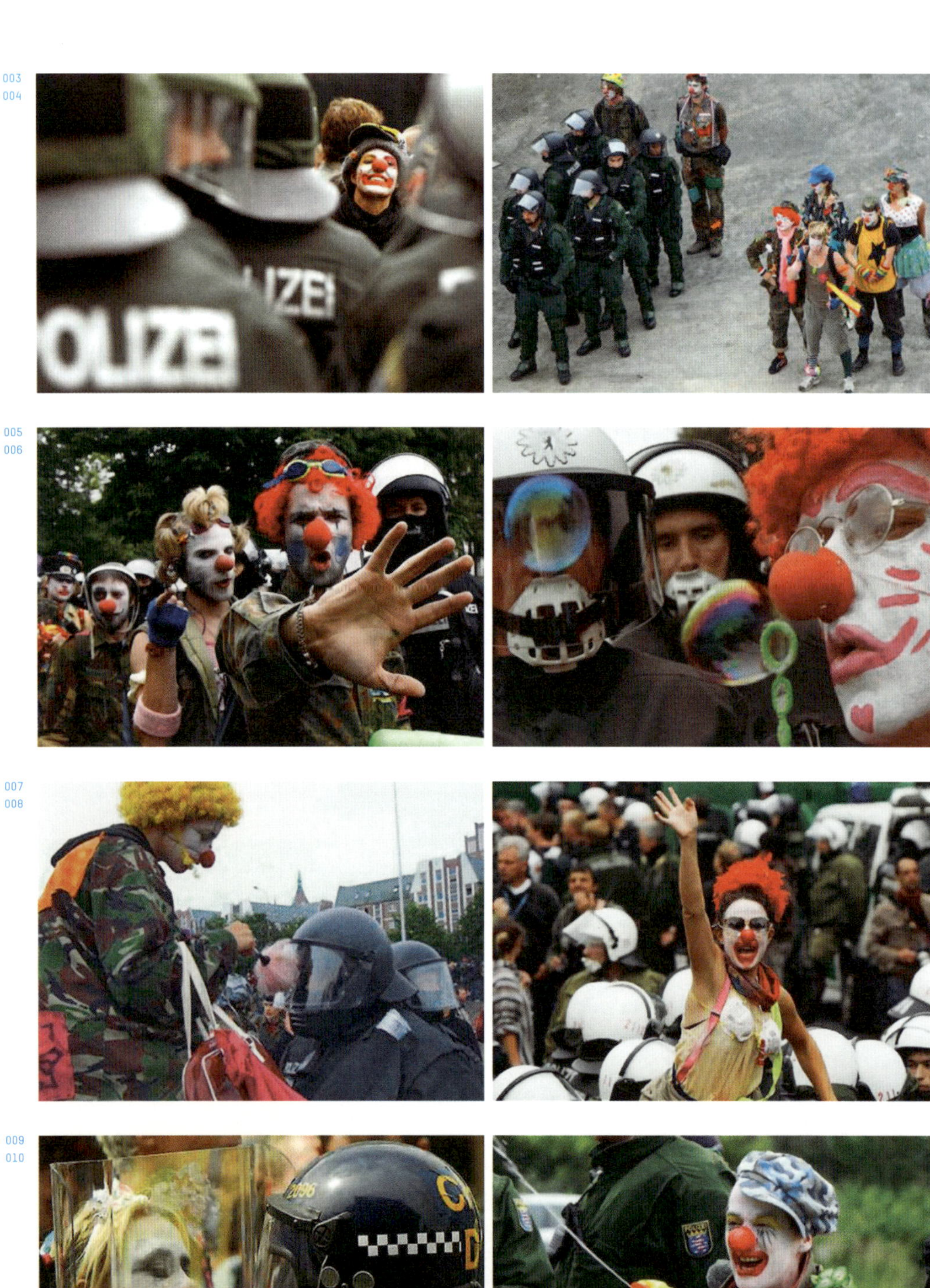

011
012

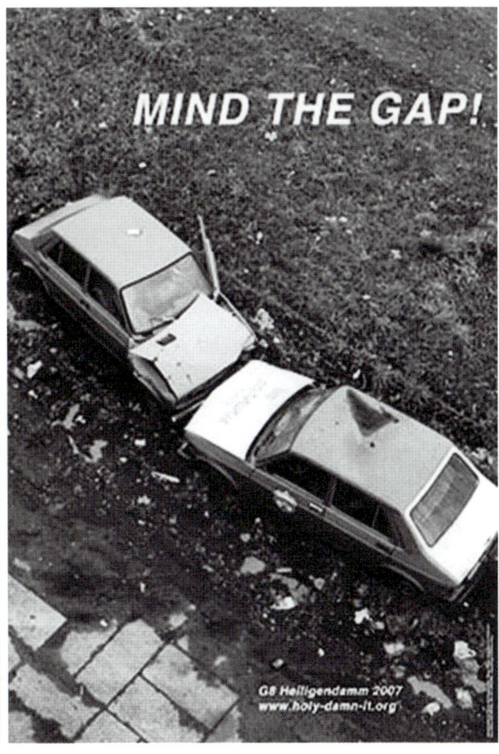

013

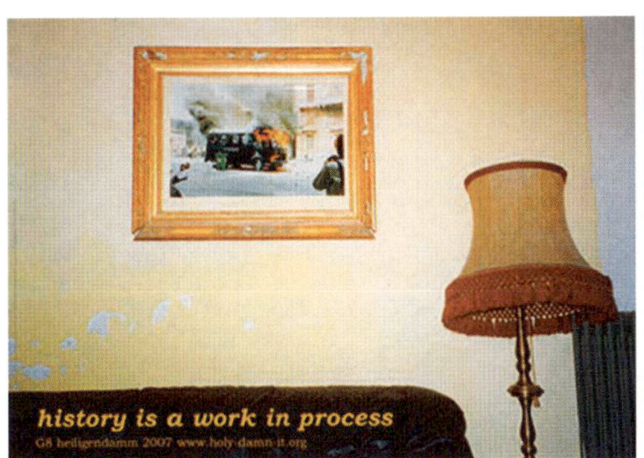

014
NEXT
015

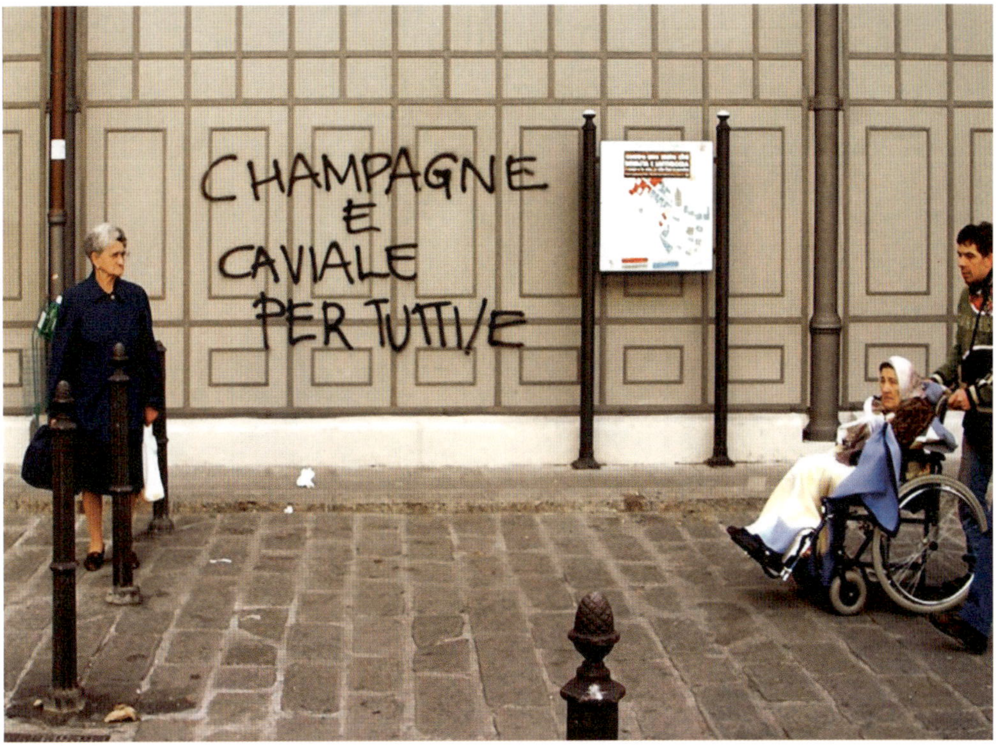

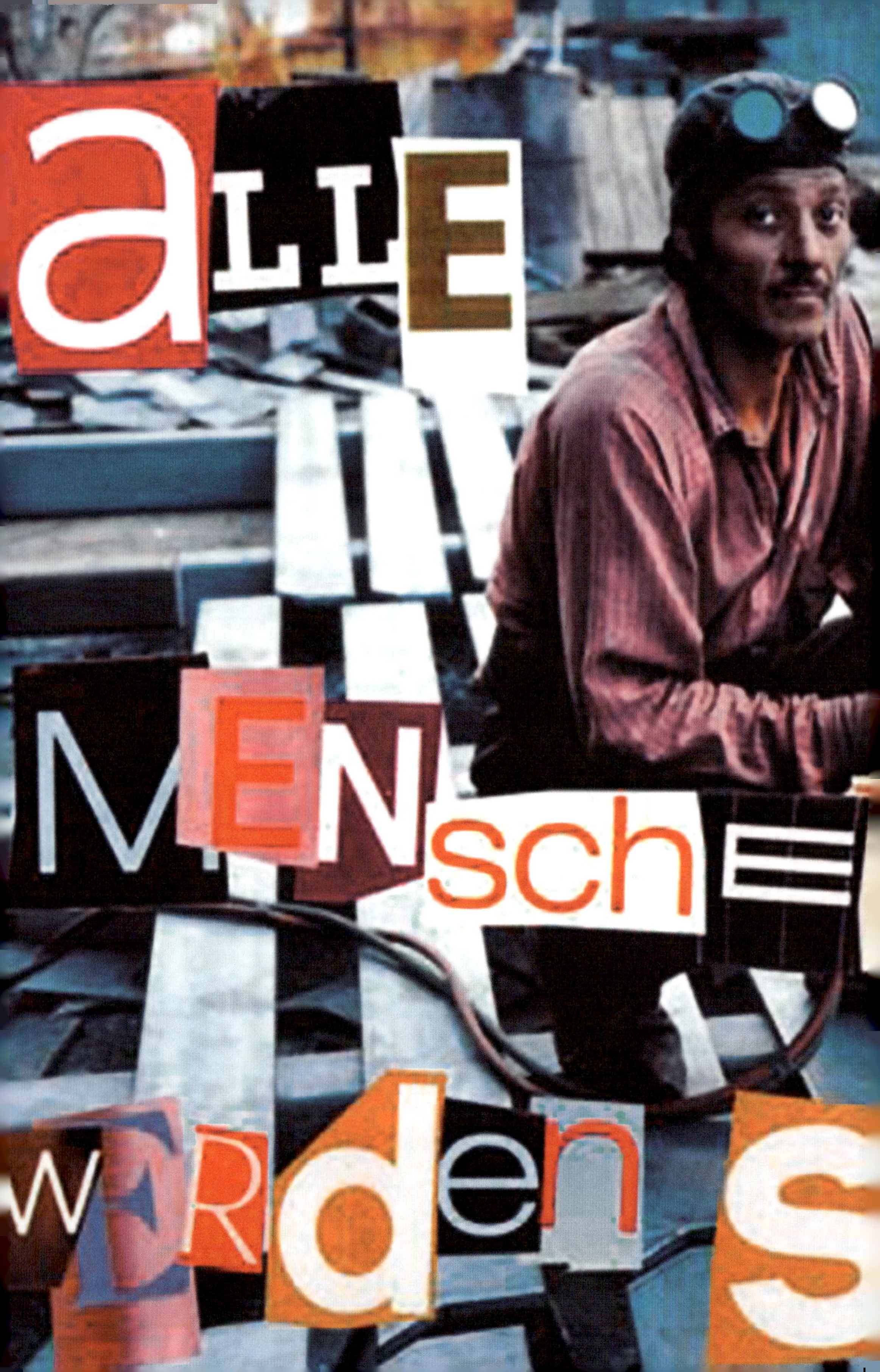

alle
Menschen
werden's

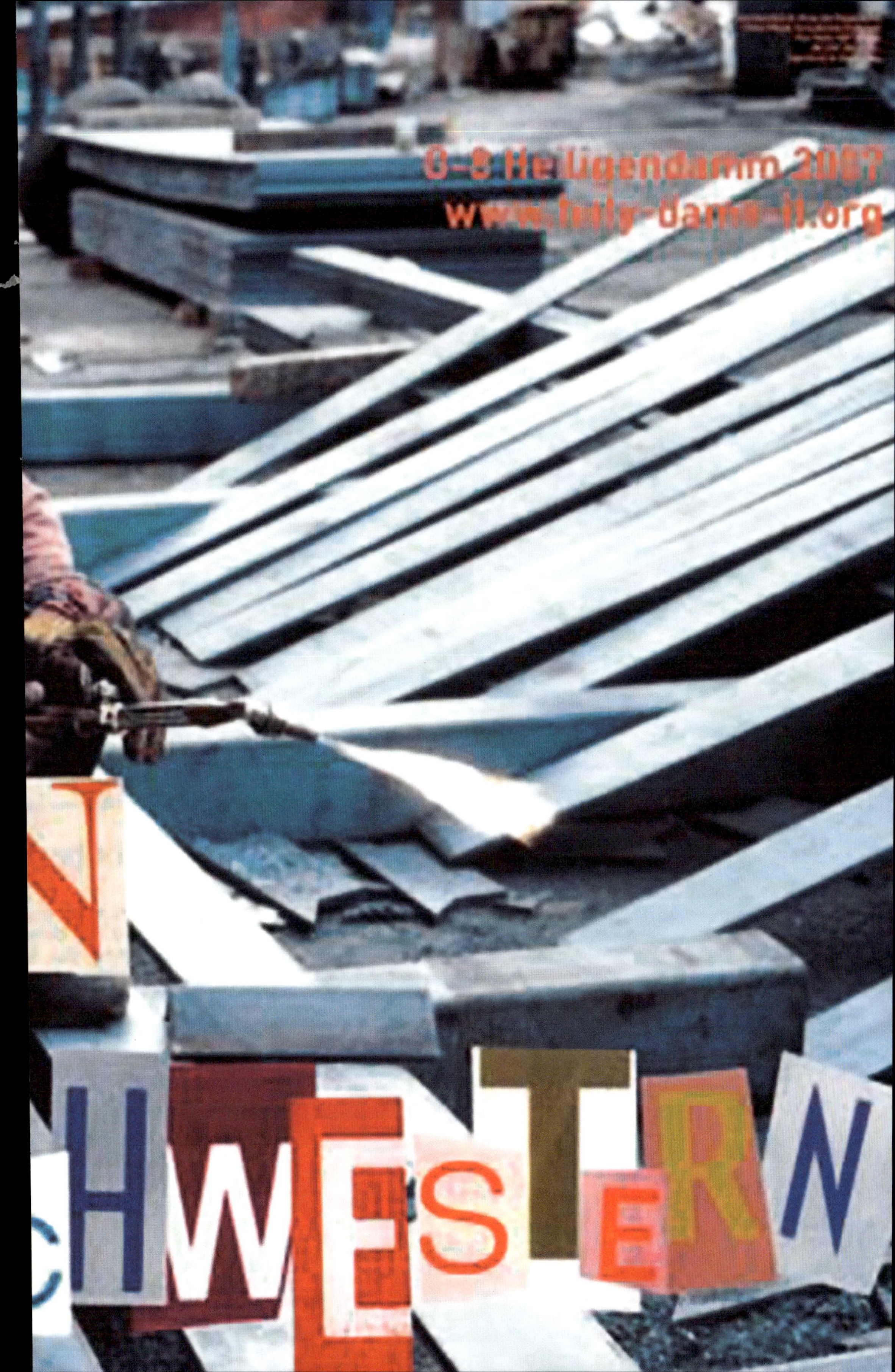
G-8 Heiligendamm 2007
www.heily-dame-it.org
SCHWESTERN

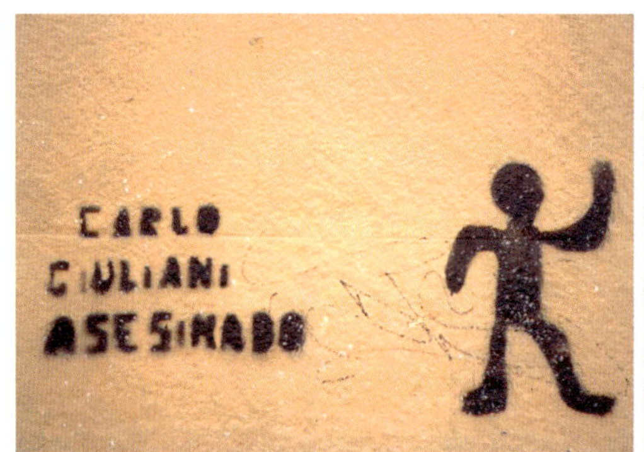
CARLO
GIULIANI
ASESINADO

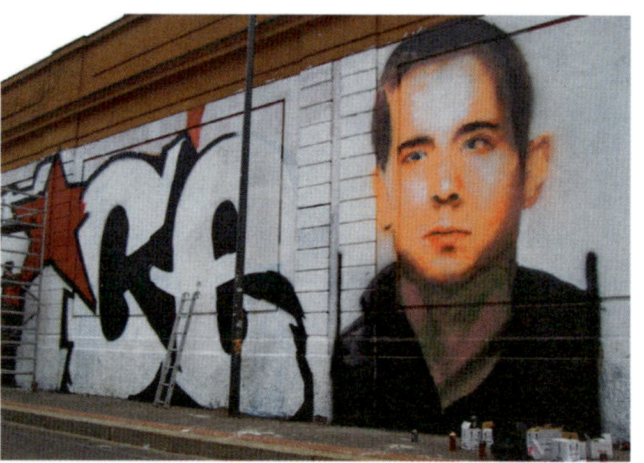

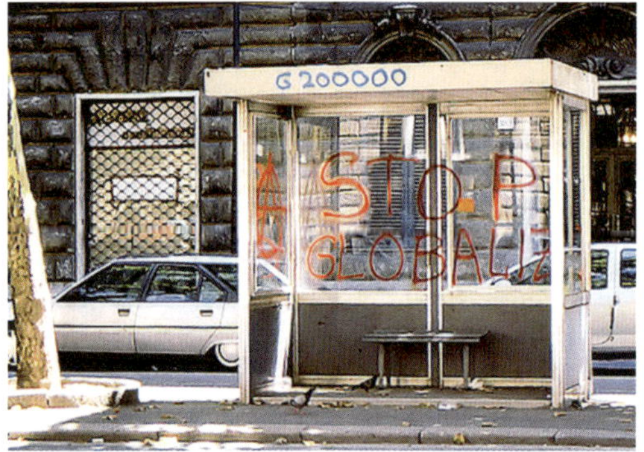
G 200000
STOP
GLOBALIZ

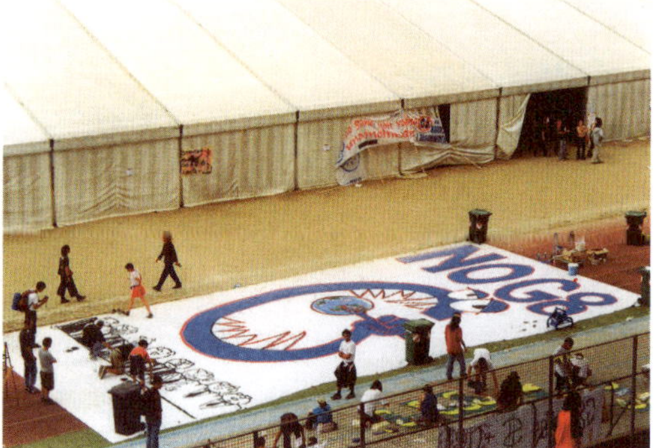
NO G8

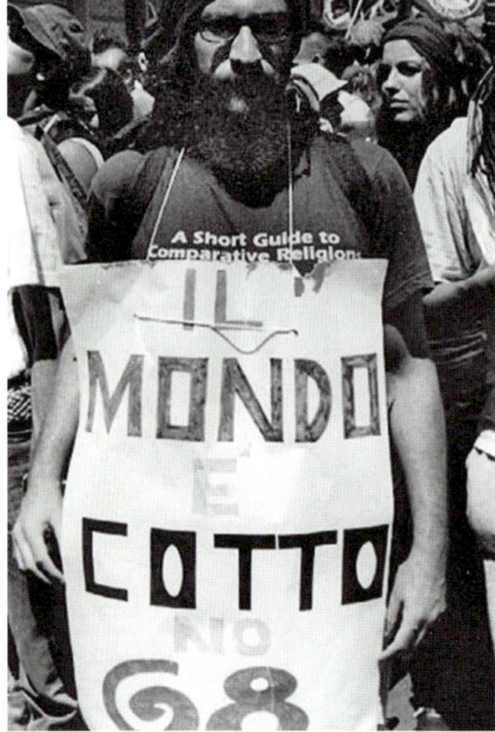
A Short Guide to
Comparative Religion
IL
MONDO
È
COTTO
NO
G8

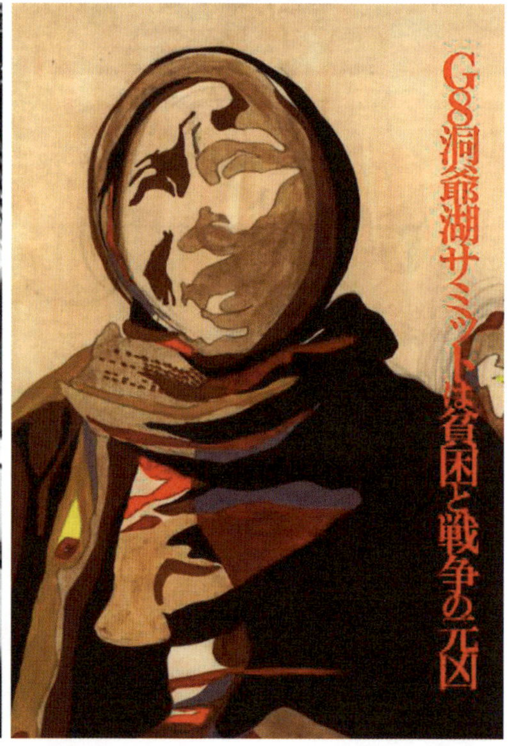
G8洞爺湖サミットは貧困と戦争の元凶

001 UNTITLED
Ofog is a Swedish peace network
working against increased
militarization in the EU.
CREATOR Ofog
SOURCE Karin Kasböck, *Theater
of Peace: Peace and Visibility
in an Asymmetrical World* [Berlin:
Argobooks, 2010], p. 21.

002 UNTITLED
CREATOR Ofog
SOURCE Karin Kasböck, *Theater
of Peace: Peace and Visibility
in an Asymmetrical World* [Berlin:
Argobooks, 2010], p. 21.

003 CLOWN PARADE IN ROSTOCK, GERMANY
CREATOR Associated Press
SOURCE www.welt.de

004 CLOWN PARADE IN ROSTOCK, GERMANY
CREATOR Associated Press
SOURCE www.welt.de

005 CLOWN PARADE IN ROSTOCK, GERMANY
CREATOR Associated Press
SOURCE www.welt.de

006 CLOWN PARADE IN ROSTOCK, GERMANY
CREATOR Associated Press
SOURCE www.welt.de

007 CLOWNS PROTESTING G8
CREATOR Projektwerkstatt
SOURCE www.heise.de

008 CLOWN PARADE IN ROSTOCK, GERMANY
CREATOR Associated Press
SOURCE www.welt.de

009 KISS
CREATOR Provided by yaritoyota
SOURCE www.flickr.com/photos/
12190970@N06/2345384727/

010 CLOWN PARADE IN ROSTOCK, GERMANY
CREATOR Associated Press
SOURCE www.welt.de

011 SOURCE socialforumtuebingen.
wordpress.com

012 G8 SUMMIT IN HEILIGENDAMM,
GERMANY
CREATOR Walter Seidl
SOURCE www.holy-damn-it.org

013 G8 SUMMIT IN HEILIGENDAMM,
GERMANY
CREATOR Petra Gerschner
SOURCE www.holy-damn-it.org

014 CHAMPAGNE E CAVIALE PER TUTTI/E
[CHAMPAGNE AND CAVIAR FOR ALL]
CREATOR Provided by Morgan Fuse
SOURCE www.flickr.com/photos/
morganfuse83/2065720698/

015 G8 SUMMIT IN HEILIGENDAMM, GERMANY
CREATOR Allan Sekular
SOURCE www.holy-damn-it.org

016 CARLO
This graffito, photographed in
Madrid, pays tribute to Carlo
Giuliani, who was killed by
Italian police during a protest
against the July 2001 G8 Economic
Forum meeting in Genoa.
CREATOR Provided by zokete
SOURCE www.flickr.com/photos/
madbastard/533387428/

017 MILAN, GRAFFITO ON THE
VIA BRAMANTE
CREATOR Provided by agitazioni
SOURCE www.flickr.com/photos/
agitazioni/968225517/
DATE 21 July 2007

018 G8, GENEVA
CREATOR Provided by .ste.
SOURCE www.flickr.com/photos/
gocciolina77/527807526/
DATE 2001

019 G8, GENEVA
CREATOR Provided by milafafa
SOURCE www.flickr.com/photos/
milafafa/2048695774/
DATE 2001

020 TIZIANO FECIT
CREATOR Provided by milafafa.
SOURCE www.flickr.com/photos/
milafafa

021 G8 IS THE RINGLEADER OF WAR
AND POVERTY
CREATOR Provided by irregular
SOURCE linux7.sanpal.co.jp

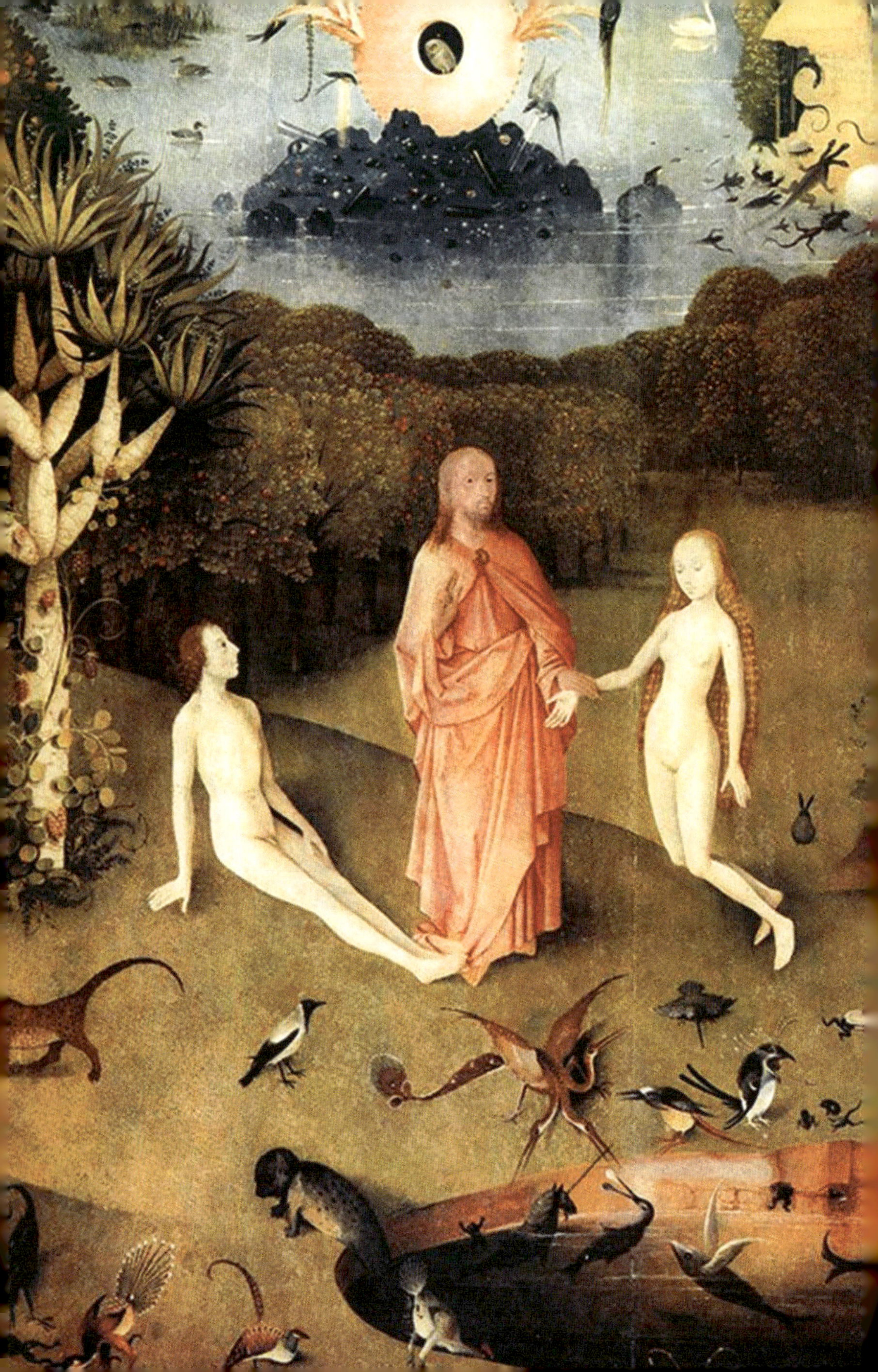

LEFT
001
002
003

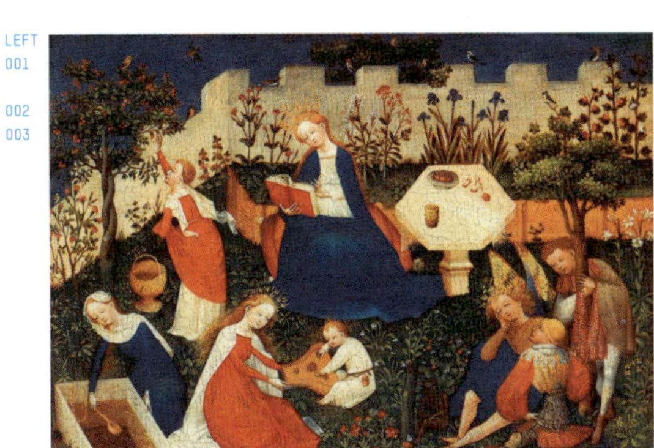
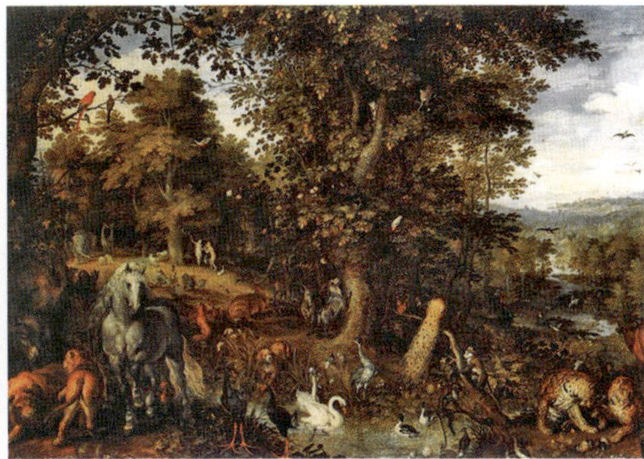

004
005

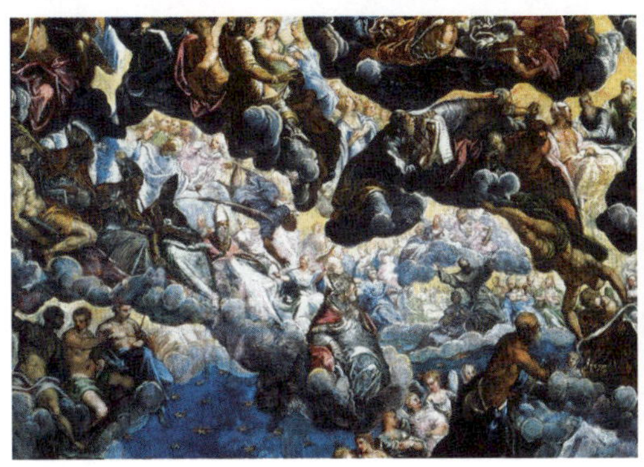
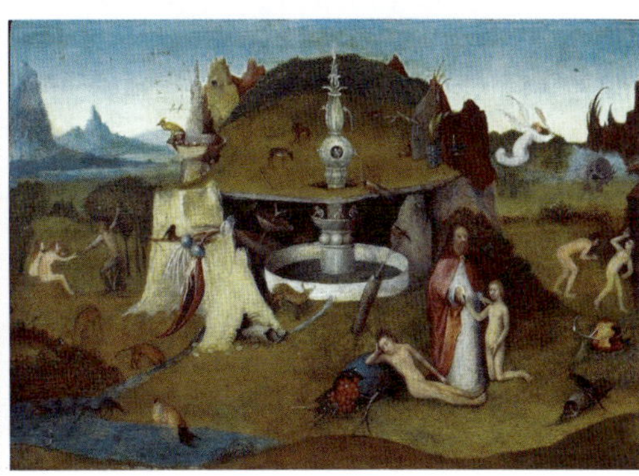

006
007

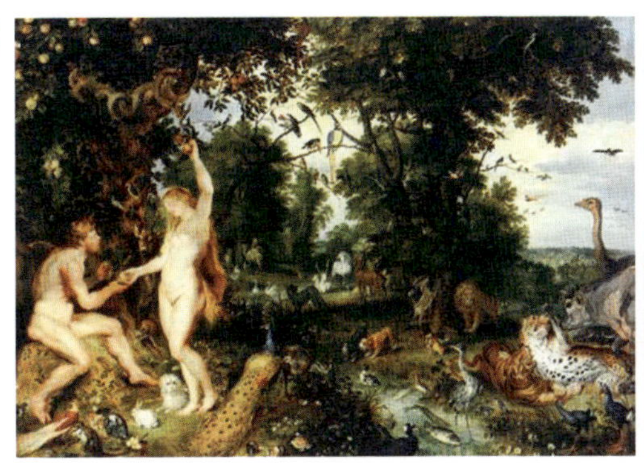
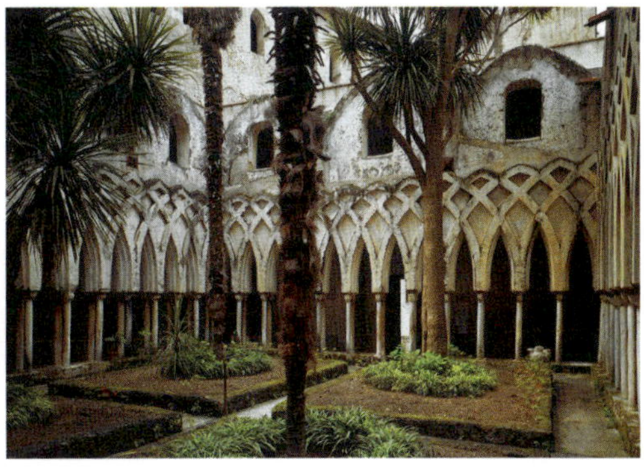

008
009

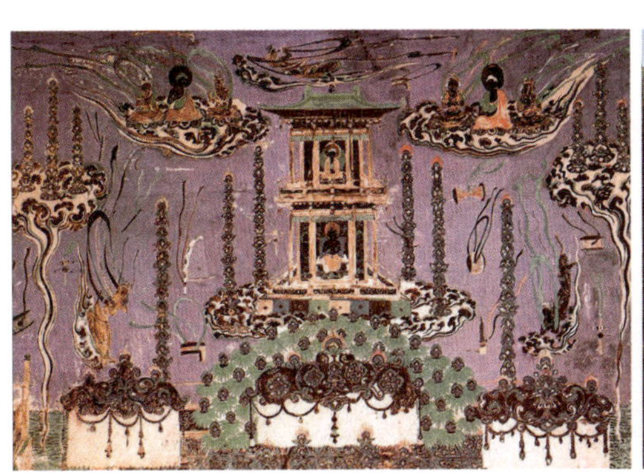
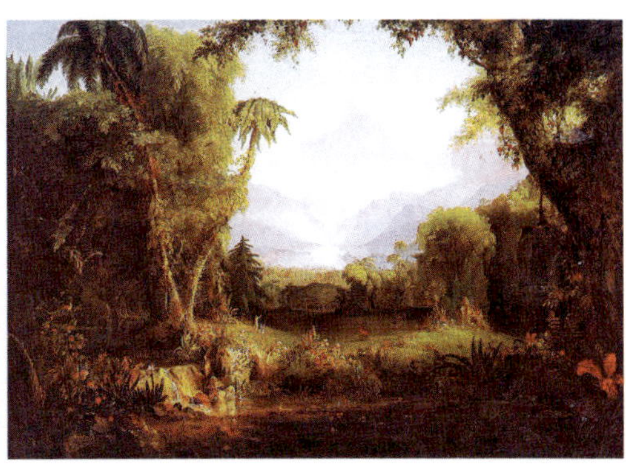

010
011

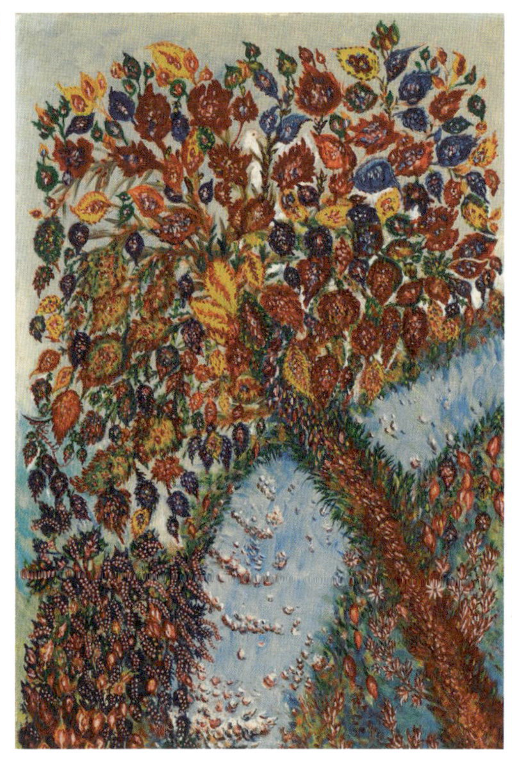
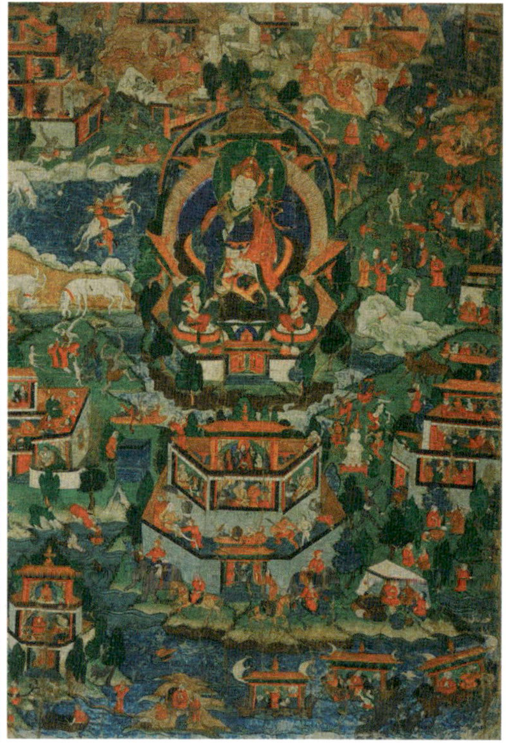

012
013

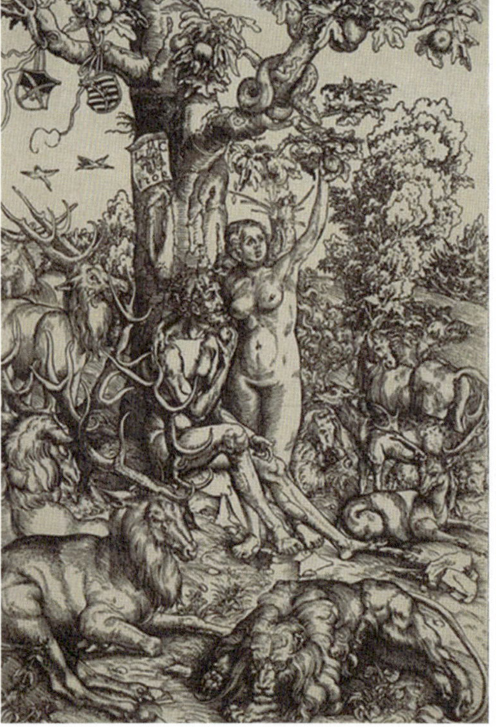
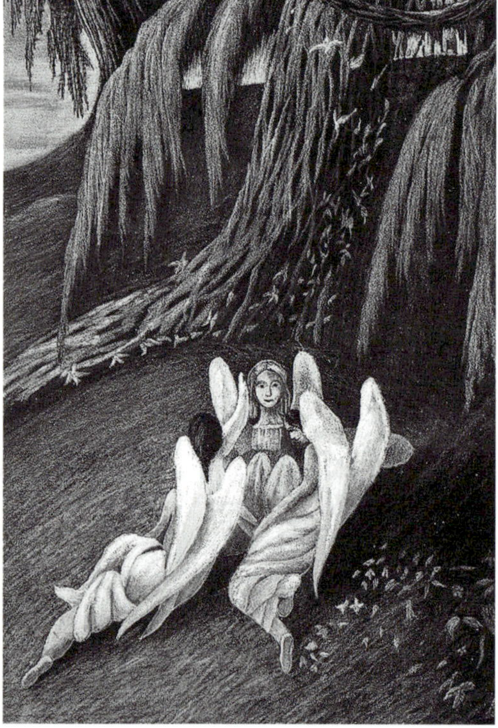

001 ADAM AND EVE IN THE GARDEN OF
EDEN [EARTHLY DELIGHTS]
CREATOR Hieronymus Bosch
SOURCE americanpicturelinks.com

002 GARDEN OF EDEN
CREATOR Unknown [German]
SOURCE www.wga.hu
DATE c. 1410

003 ADAM AND EVE IN THE GARDEN
OF EDEN
CREATOR Jan Brueghel the Elder
SOURCE americanpicturelinks.com
DATE 1615

004 PARADISE [DETAIL]
CREATOR Tintoretto
SOURCE Museo Thyssen-Bornemisza

005 GARDEN OF PARADISE
CREATOR Workshop of
Hieronymus Bosch
SOURCE The Art Institute
of Chicago

006 PARADISE
CREATOR Peter Paul Rubens
SOURCE www.kunstkopie.de

007 CLOISTER OF PARADISE
SOURCE library.artstor.org

008 SCENE FROM THE WESTERN PARADISE
OF SUKHAVATI BASED ON THE
AMITO JING
SOURCE The Huntington Archive,
Ohio State University

009 THE GARDEN OF EDEN
CREATOR Cole Thomas
SOURCE en.wikipedia.org

010 TREE OF PARADISE
CREATOR Séraphine Louis
SOURCE Museum of Modern Art,
New York

011 PADMASAMBHAVA'S PARADISE SURROUNDED
BY SCENES FROM THE LIFE OF PADMA
'OD 'BAR
CREATOR Unknown [Tibet]
SOURCE Philadelphia Museum of Art

012 ADAM AND EVE IN PARADISE
CREATOR Lucas Cranach the Elder
SOURCE de.academic.ru

013 GARDEN OF PARADISE
SOURCE library.artstor.org

001
002

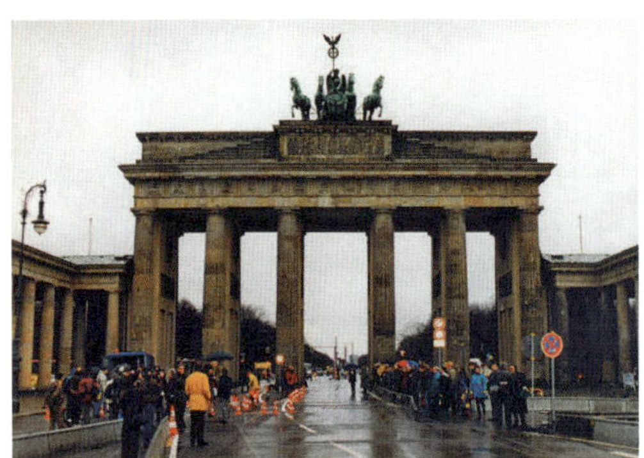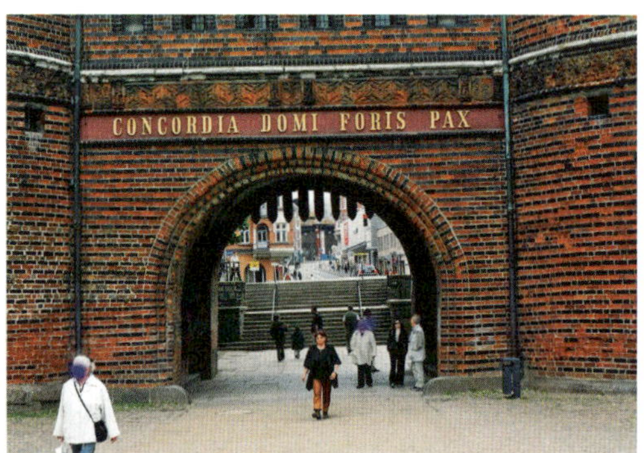

003
004

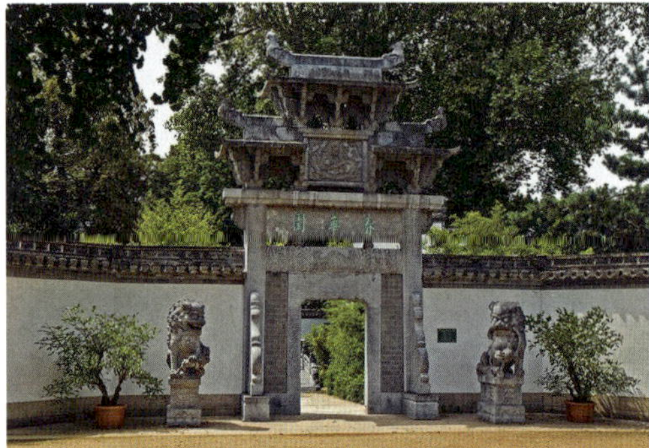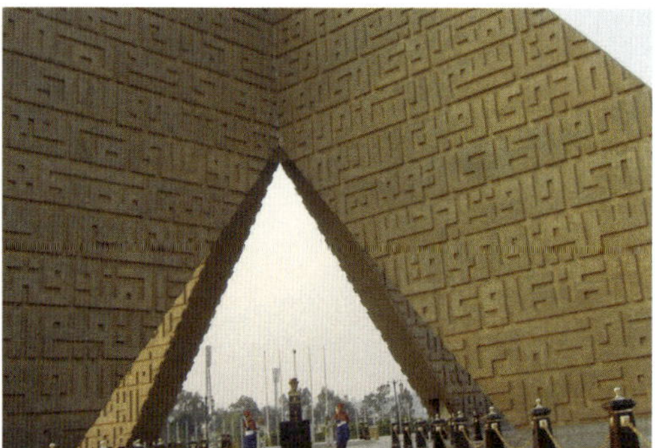

005
006

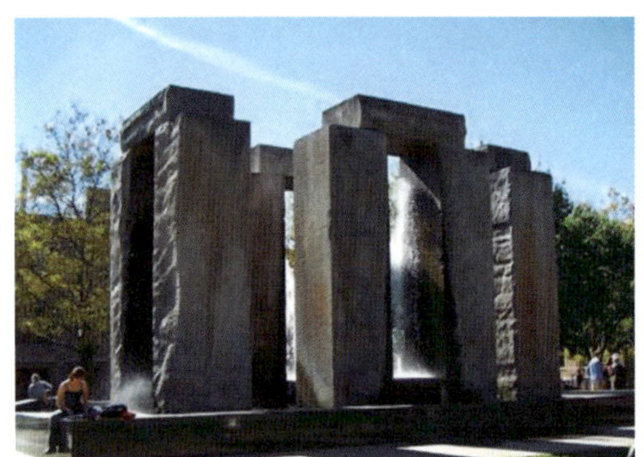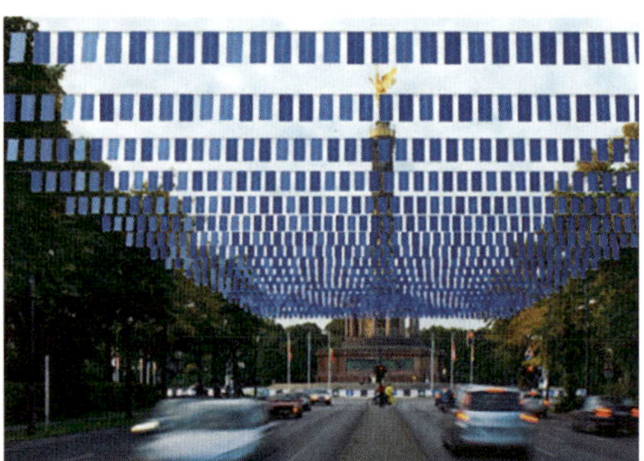

007
008

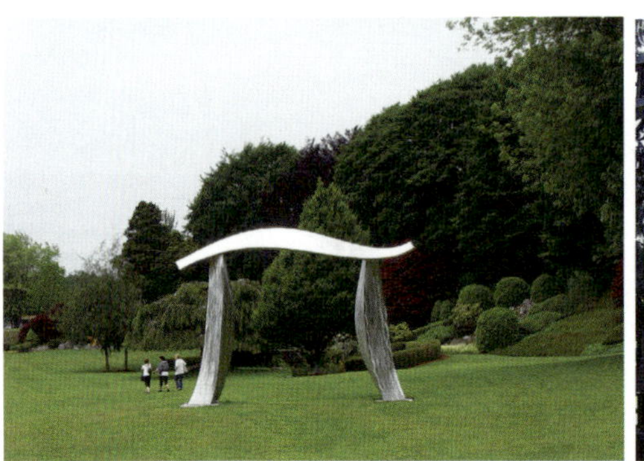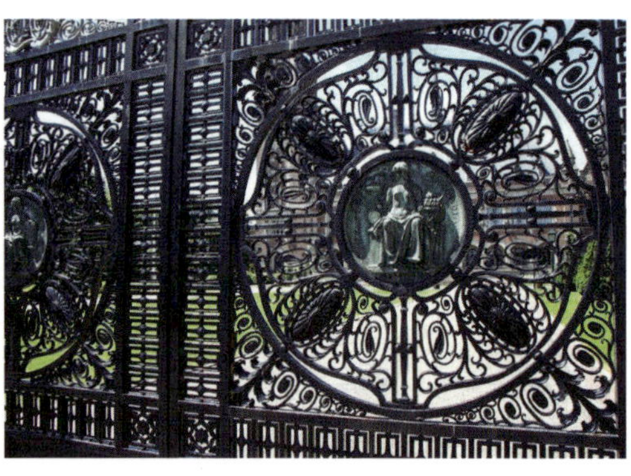

009
010

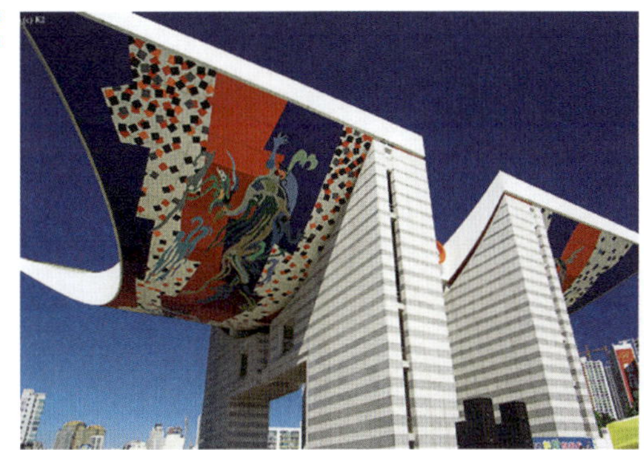
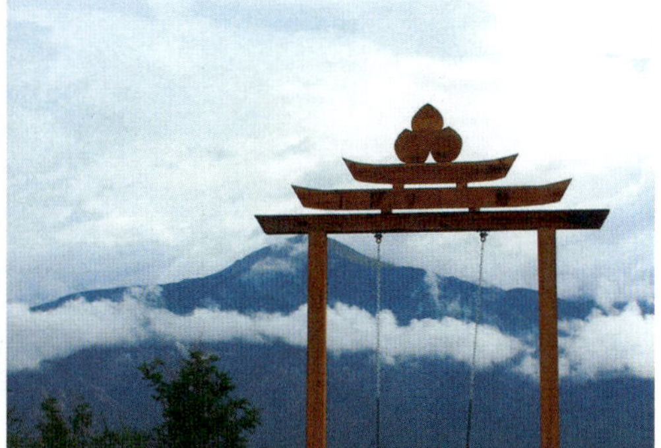

011
012

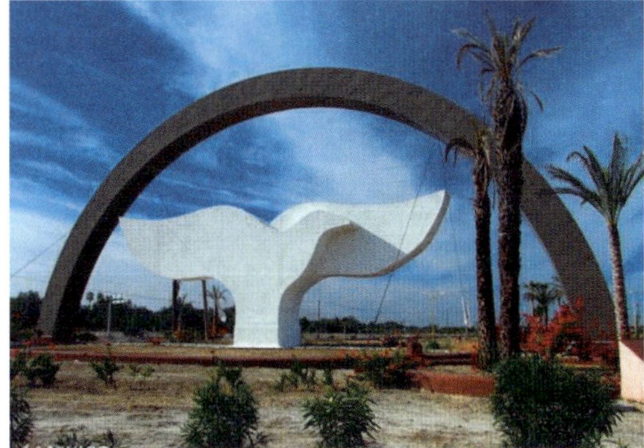
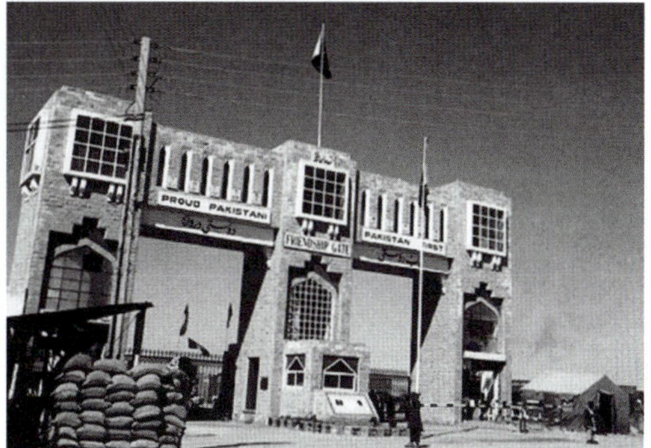

013
014

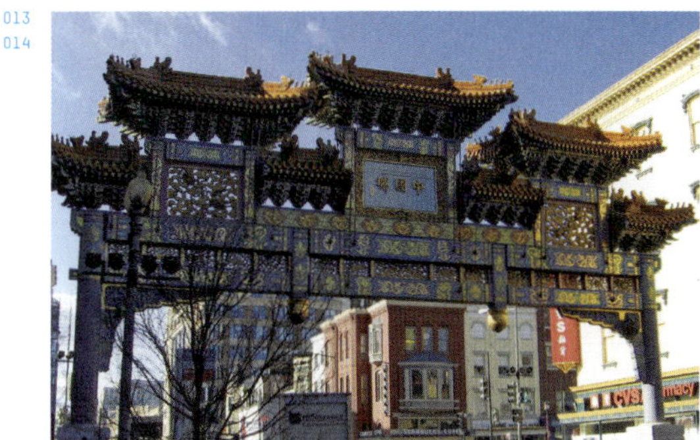
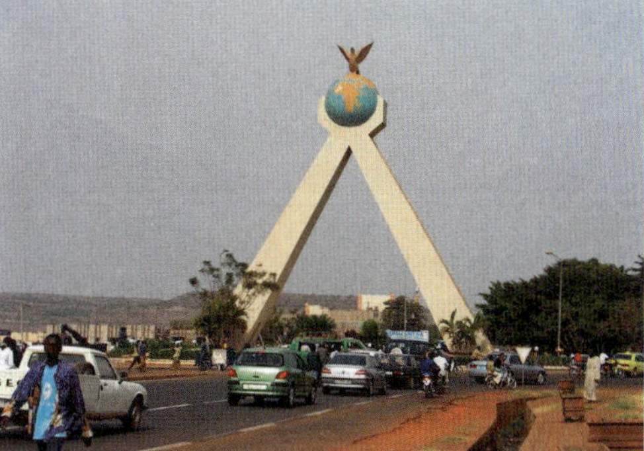

015
016

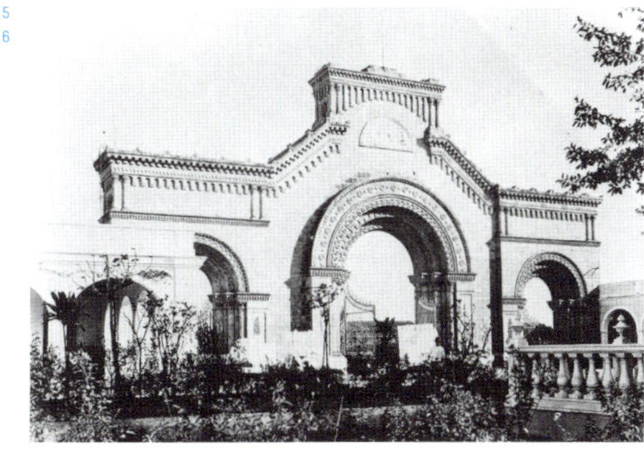
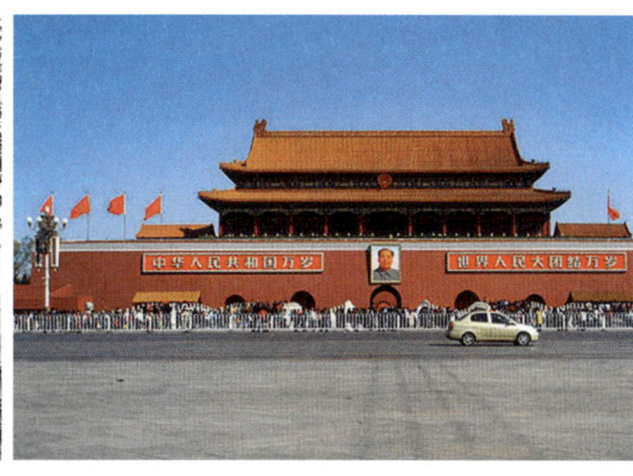

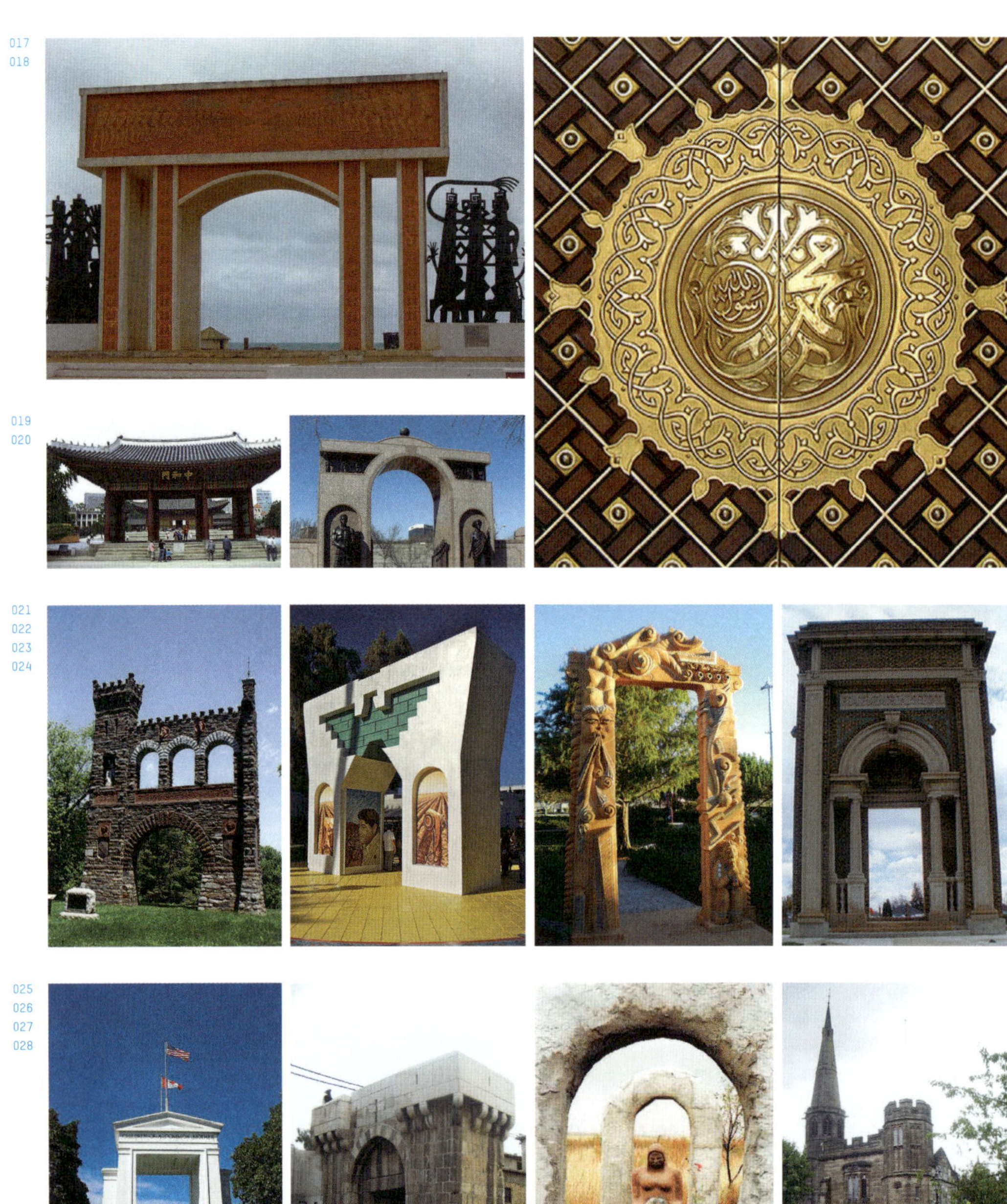

001 BRANDENBURG GATE
CREATOR Heiko Burkhardt
SOURCE ojersjo.wikispaces.com

002 CONCORDIA DOMI FORIS PAX
[UNITY INSIDE, PEACE OUTSIDE]
CREATOR Heiko Burkhardt
SOURCE www.roland-harder.de

003 MAIN GATE TO THE GARDEN OF
CELESTIAL PEACE
CREATOR KS aus F
SOURCE de.wikipedia.org

004 VICTORY MEMORIAL & TOMB OF
ANWAR SADAT
CREATOR Provided by Mark Harrison
SOURCE www.flickr.com/photos/
harrisme/2991935563/

005 CLARKE PEACE MEMORIAL FOUNTAIN
CREATOR Michael Bohn
SOURCE replicahenge.wordpress.com

006 WORLD DAY OF PEACE, PEACE
INSTALLATION
CREATOR kulturpate e.v.
SOURCE www.kulturpate-ev.de

007 PEACE ARCH, US / CANADIAN BORDER
CREATOR Provided by geovisual
SOURCE peace.maripo.com

008 WROUGHT IRON GATE OF THE
PEACE PALACE
CREATOR Provided by Marianne
SOURCE www.planeteye.com

009 WORLD PEACE GATE
World Peace Gate in Olympic Park,
Seoul, Korea. It was designed by
Joongup Kim to celebrate the
Seoul Olympic Games.
CREATOR Provied by Shisun
SOURCE www.flickr.com/photos/
k2p/2336646118
DATE 1998

010 GATE TO FIVE ELEMENTS PEACE PARK
CREATOR Five Elements Peace Park
SOURCE 5elementspeacepark.net

011 DOVE OF PEACE, BAJA CALIFORNIA
CREATOR Provided by geovisual
SOURCE peace.maripo.com

012 FRIENDSHIP GATE
Friendship Gate, between
Chaman [Pakistan] & Spin
Boldak [Afghanistan].
CREATOR Provided by Alex Majoli
SOURCE peace.maripo.com

013 FRIENDSHIP ARCH, WASHINGTON, DC
CREATOR Provided by Postdlf
SOURCE en.wikipedia.org

014 VICTORY MEMORIAL & TOMB OF ANWAR
SADAT, MEDINET NASR

Near Cairo, Egypt
CREATOR peace.maripo.com
SOURCE peace.maripo.com

015 GATE OF PEACE
SOURCE de.academic.ru

016 GATE OF CELESTIAL PEACE
SOURCE www.amazink.de

017 GATE OF NO RETURN IN OUIDAH
CREATOR Provided by eauaime
SOURCE image12.webshots.com

018 PEACE GATE
Gate of Al-Masjed Al-Nabawi in
Al Madinah Al Monawwara.
CREATOR Provided by ALQABBANI
SOURCE www.flickr.com/photos/
qap/3065001137

019 PEACE GATE, SEOUL
CREATOR Provided by Shaoming Zou
SOURCE business.missouri.edu

020 FREEDMAN MEMORIAL ARCH
CREATOR Designed by David Newton,
Provided by Donna
SOURCE www.flickr.com/photos/
txdiva/416966832/

021 CIVIL WAR CORRESPONDENTS
MEMORIAL ARCH
SOURCE peace.maripo.com

022 ARCH OF DIGNITY, EQUALITY
& JUSTICE
[CESAR CHAVEZ MONUMENT]
CREATOR Provided by geovisual
SOURCE peace.maripo.com

023 GATEWAY TO PEACE
CREATOR Provided by geovisual
SOURCE peace.maripo.com

024 PEACE MEMORIAL PARK ON EAST
36TH STREET
CREATOR Provided by Tom Flemming
SOURCE www.flickr.com/photos/
tomflem/3030513326/

025 UNITED STATES SIDE OF THE
PEACE ARCH MONUMENT
CREATOR Provided by Arnold C
SOURCE en.wikipedia.org

026 BAB AL SALAM PEACE
GATE DAMASCUS
CREATOR Provided by woutervv
SOURCE www.flickr.com/photos/
woutervv/3019578455

027 PEACE FARM
CREATOR Provided by geovisual
SOURCE peace.maripo.com

028 ST WILFRID'S PARISH CHURCH,
STANDISH, PEACE GATE
CREATOR Provided by

Alexander P Kapp
SOURCE www.geograph.org.uk
DATE 1926

001
002

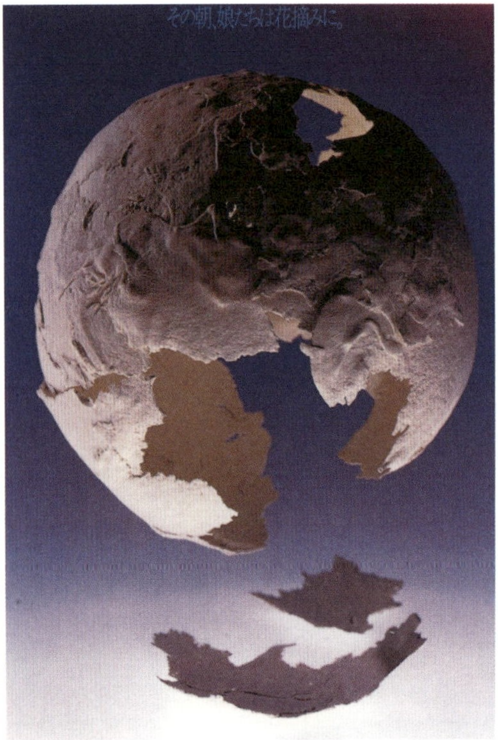

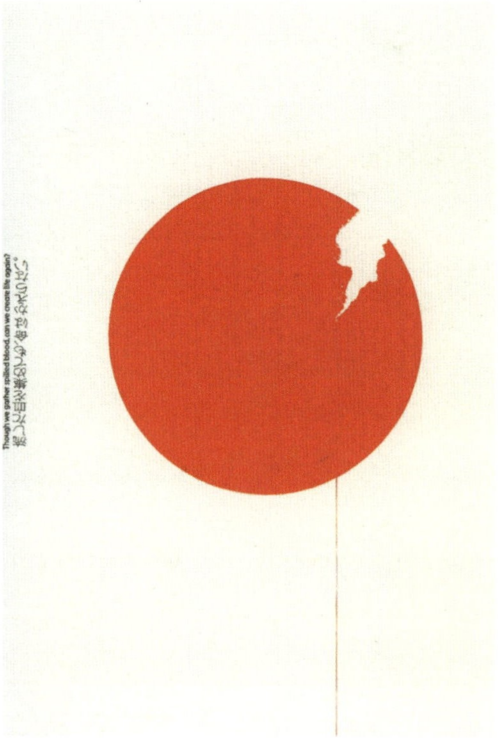

003
004

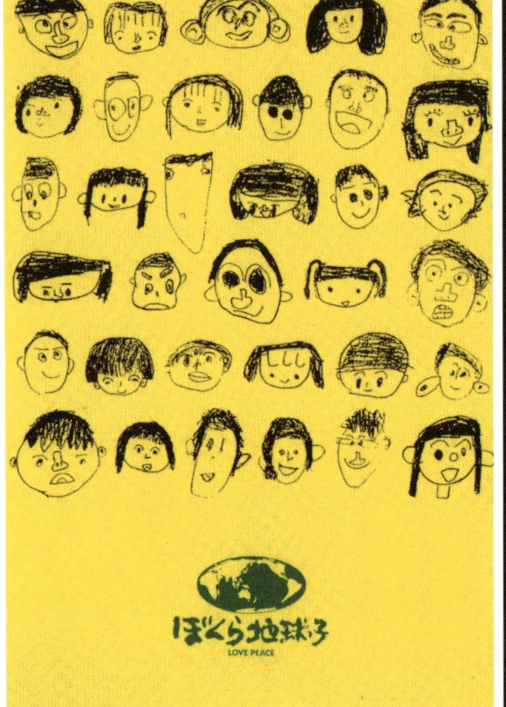

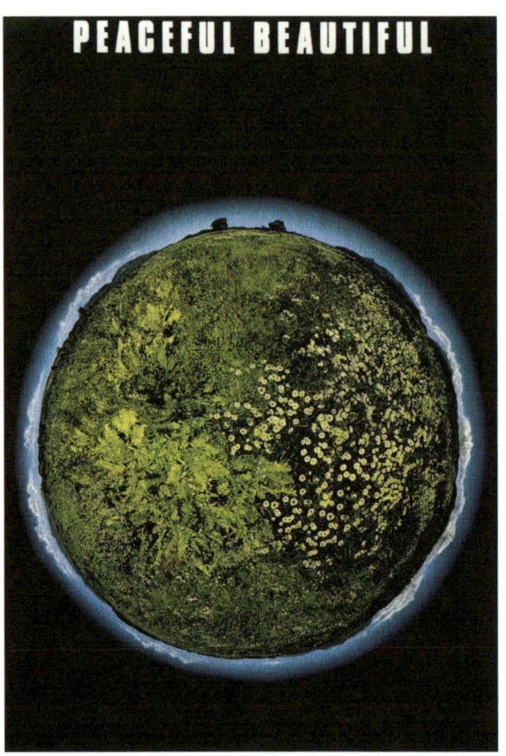

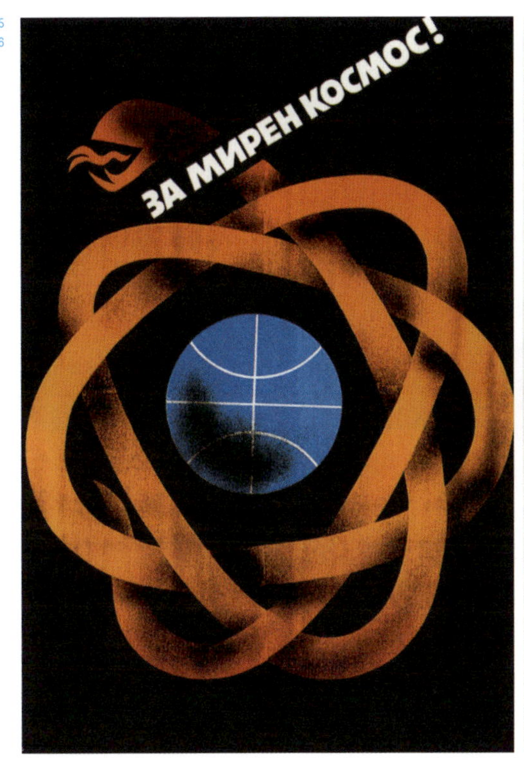
ЗА МИРЕН КОСМОС!

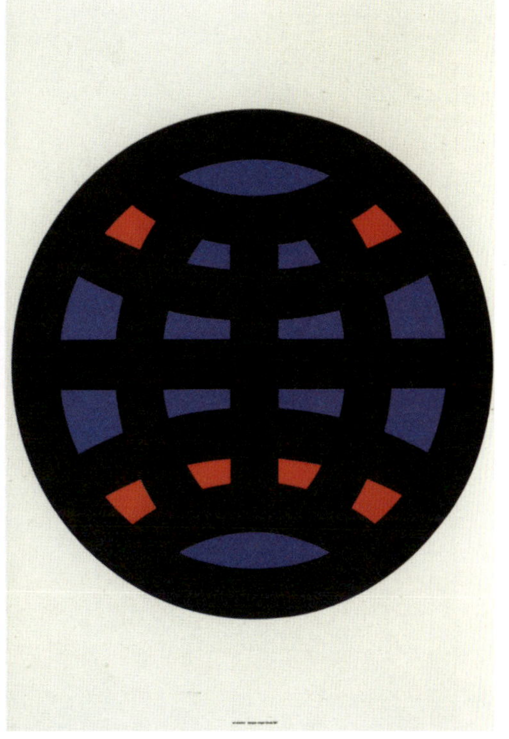

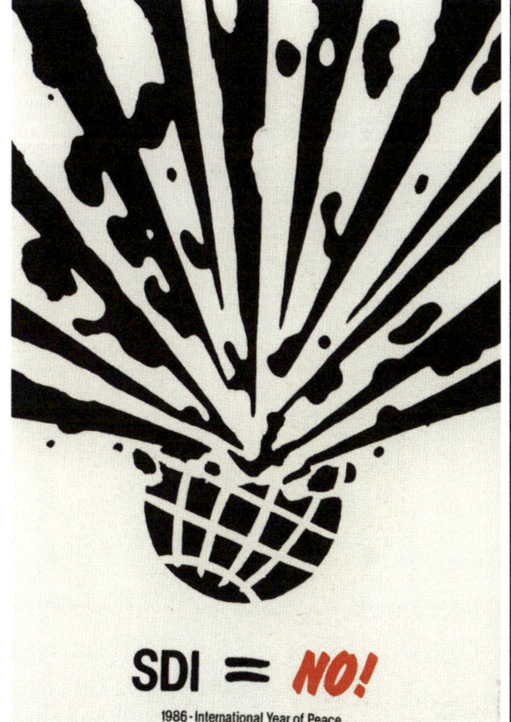
SDI = NO!
1986 · International Year of Peace

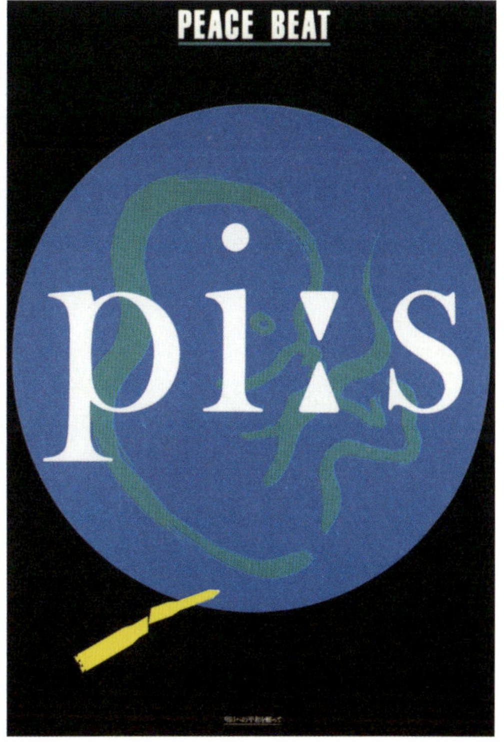
PEACE BEAT
pi s

009
010

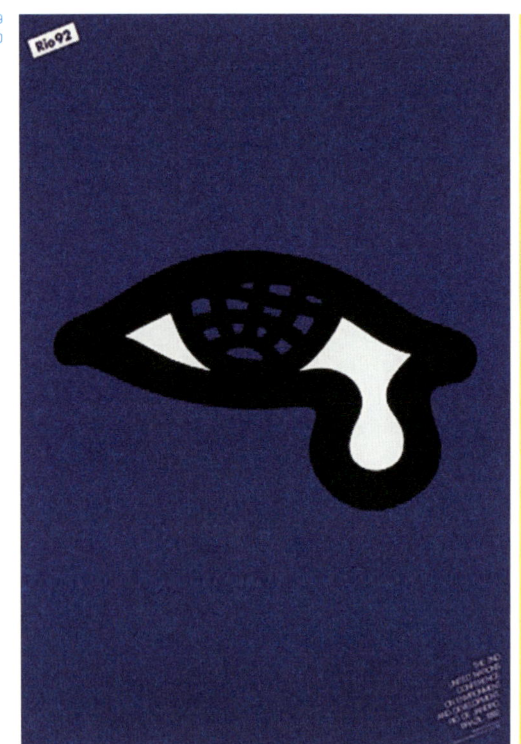

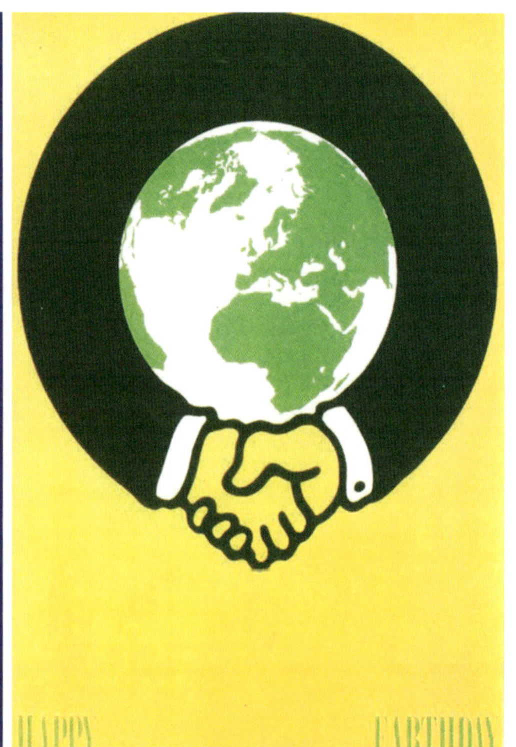

011
012

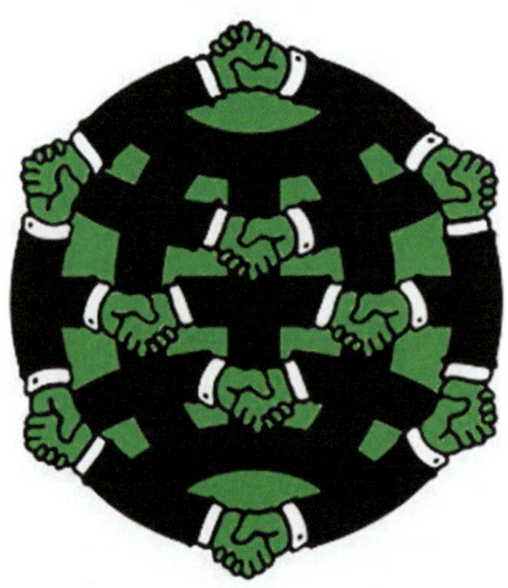

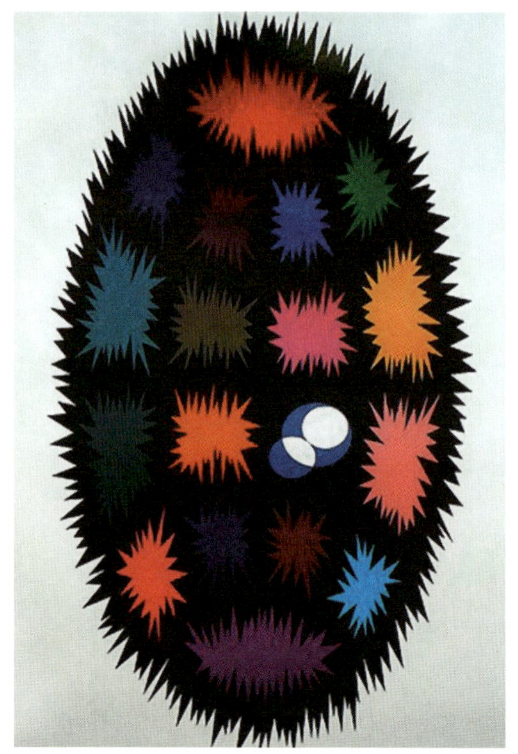

013

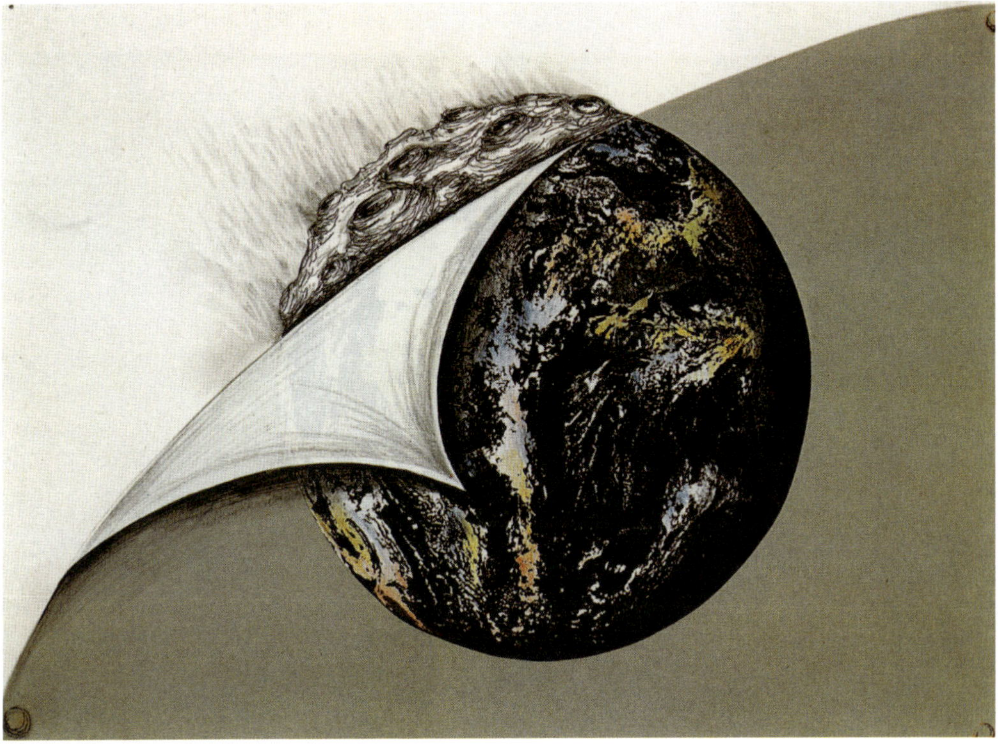

014

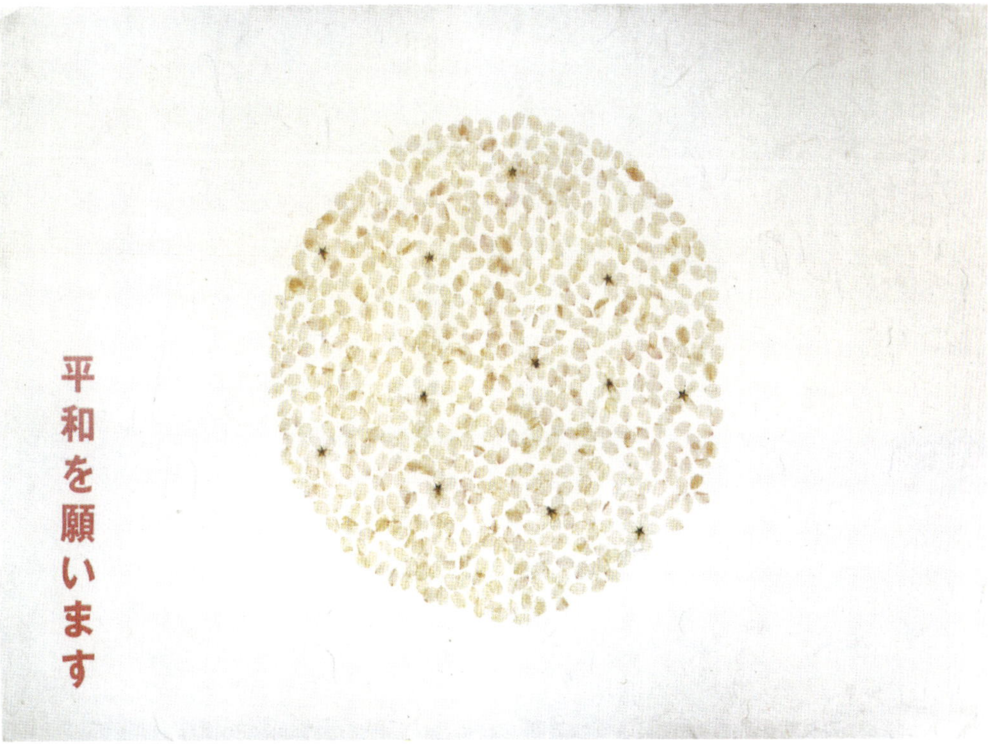

001 THE STAR OF NO RETURN
CREATOR Hitoshi Miura
SOURCE JAGDA Peace Posters
International Exhibition

002 IF WE SPILL OUR BLOOD,
WHAT REMAINS?...
CREATOR Tatsundo Hayashi
SOURCE JAGDA Peace Posters
International Exhibition

003 LOVE PEACE
CREATOR Yoichi Kotani
SOURCE JAGDA Peace Posters
International Exhibition

004 PEACEFUL BEAUTIFUL
CREATOR Yoshihiro Monjushiro
SOURCE JAGDA Peace Posters
International Exhibition

005 FOR PEACEFUL SPACE
CREATOR Dimitar Seresliev
SOURCE JAGDA Peace Posters
International Exhibition

006 HEY!
CREATOR Shigeo Fukuda
SOURCE JAGDA Peace Posters
International Exhibition

007 SID = NO / THE INTERNATIONAL
YEAR OF PEACE
CREATOR Shigeo Fukuda
SOURCE JAGDA Peace Posters
International Exhibition
DATE 1986

008 PEACE BEAT
CREATOR Toshio Katagiri
SOURCE JAGDA Peace Posters
International Exhibition

009 TOKYO
CREATOR Shigeo Fukuda
SOURCE www.robertlpeters.com

010 HAPPY EARTH DAY
CREATOR Shigeo Fukuda
SOURCE www.colectiva.tv

011 CREATOR Shigeo Fukuda
SOURCE temple-of-light.blogspot.ch

012 WORLD DESIGN EXPO, 1989
CREATOR Shigeo Fukuda
SOURCE vi.sualize.us

013 PEACE
CREATOR Tony Roberts
SOURCE JAGDA Peace Posters
International Exhibition

014 PEACE OF MIND
CREATOR Masayoshi Koide
SOURCE JAGDA Peace Posters
International Exhibition

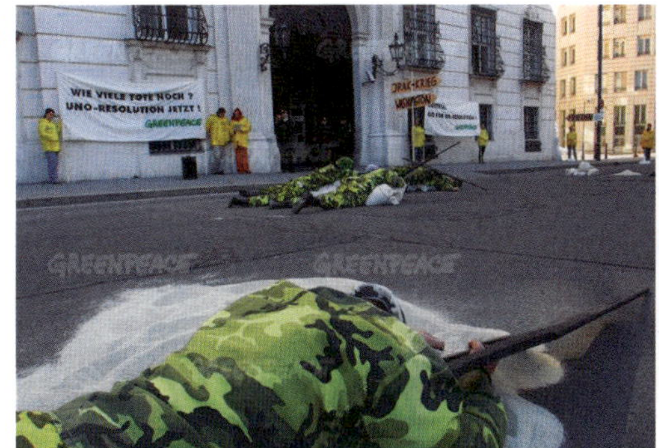

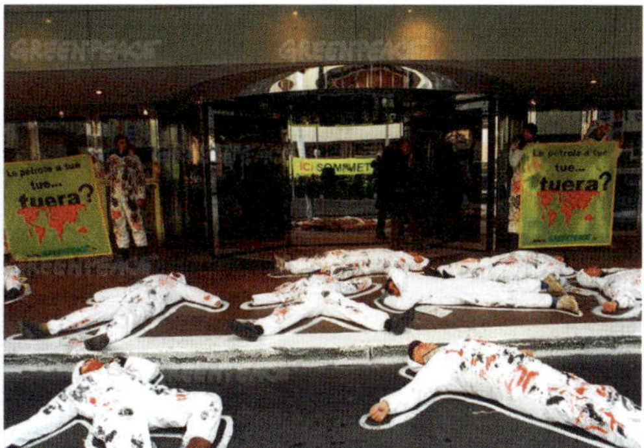

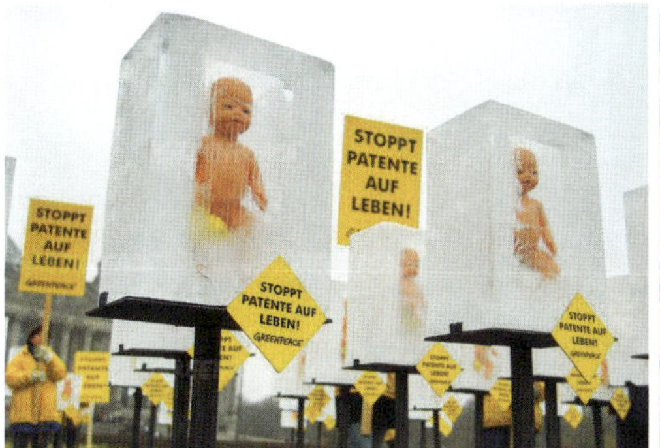
STOPPT
PATENTE
AUF
LEBEN!

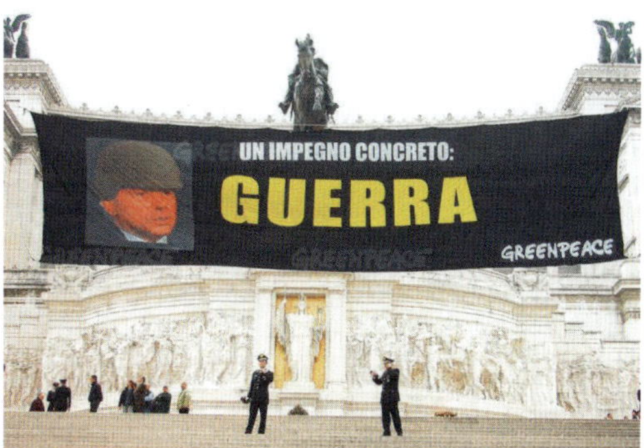
UN IMPEGNO CONCRETO:
GUERRA
GREENPEACE

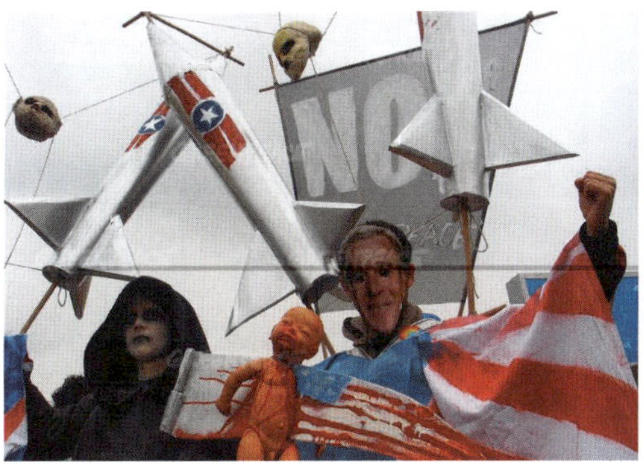

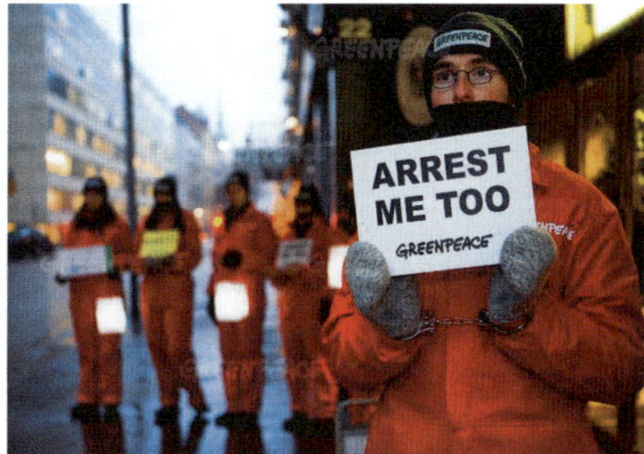
ARREST
ME TOO
GREENPEACE

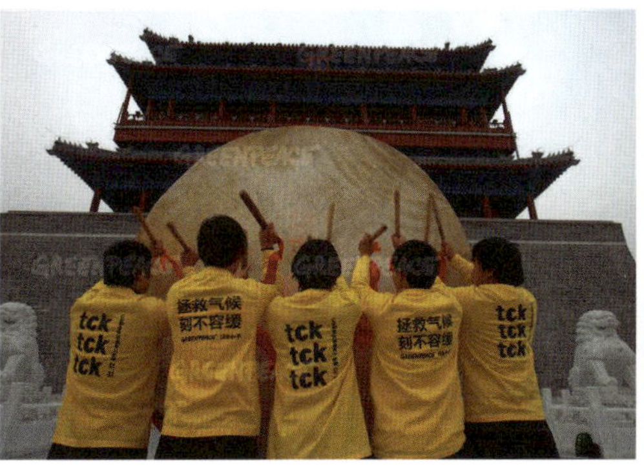
tck
tck
tck

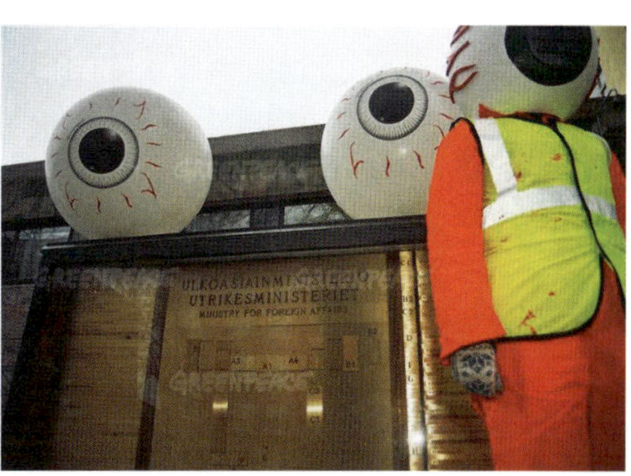

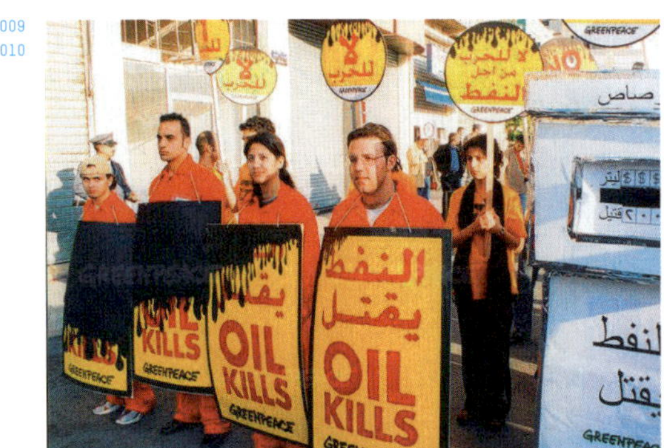
OIL KILLS
OIL KILLS
GREENPEACE

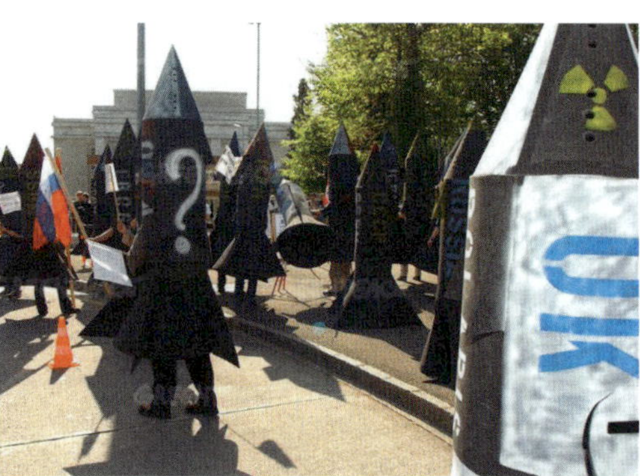
?
UK

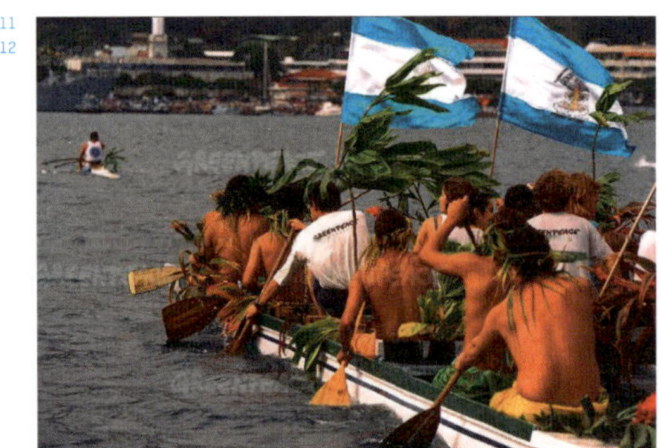

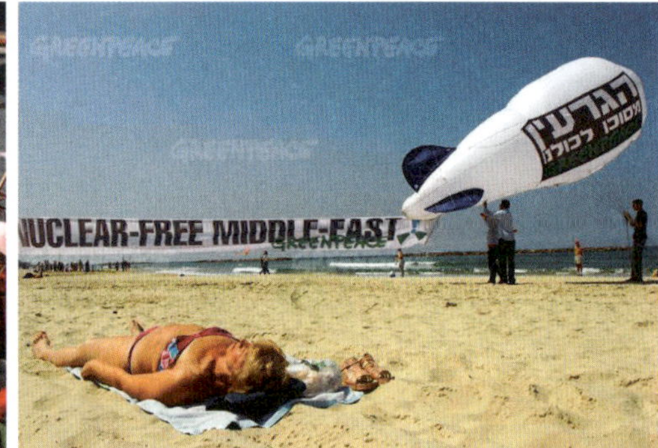
NUCLEAR-FREE MIDDLE-EAST

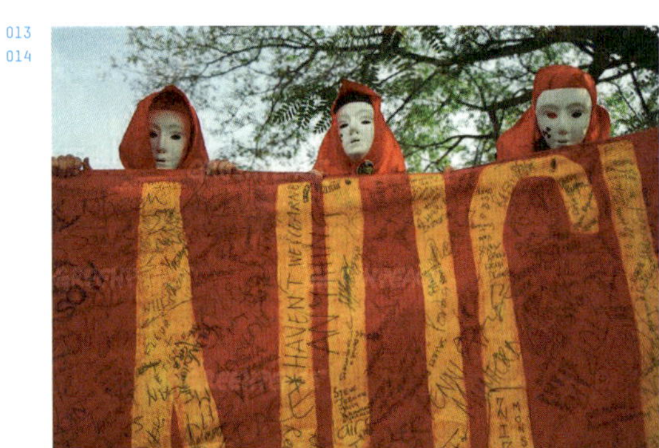

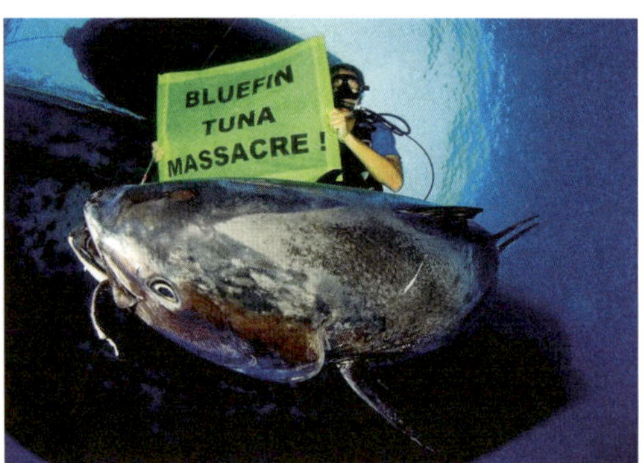
BLUEFIN TUNA MASSACRE !

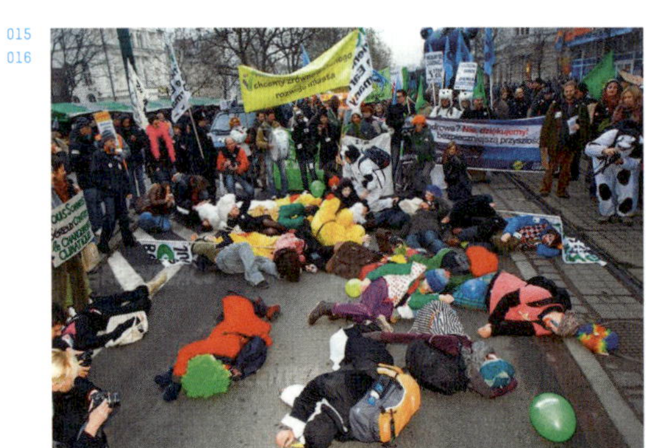

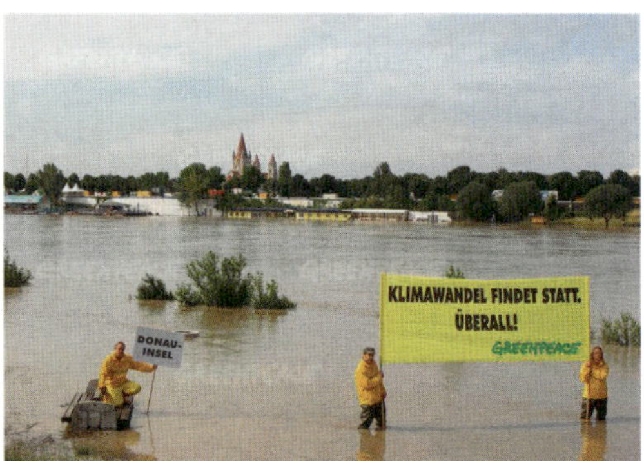
DONAU-INSEL
KLIMAWANDEL FINDET STATT. ÜBERALL!
GREENPEACE

017
018

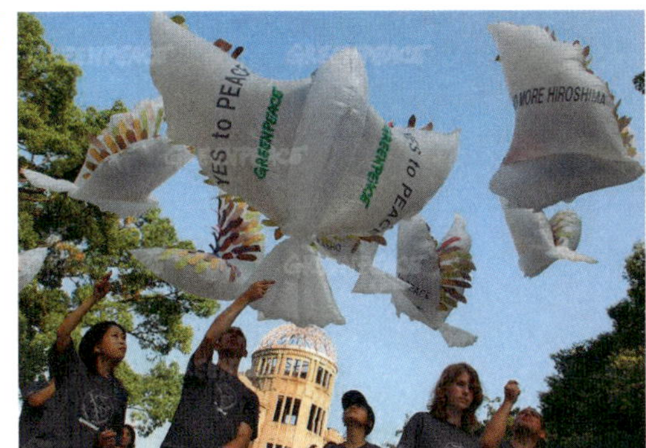

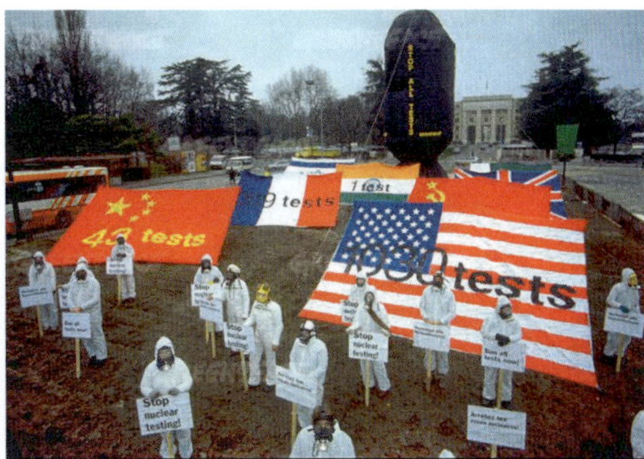

019
020

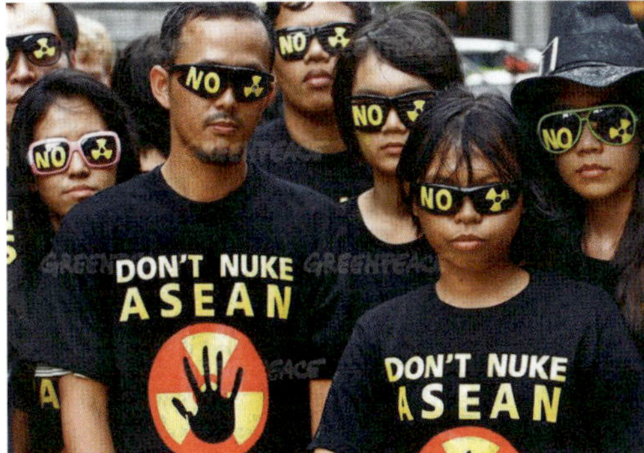

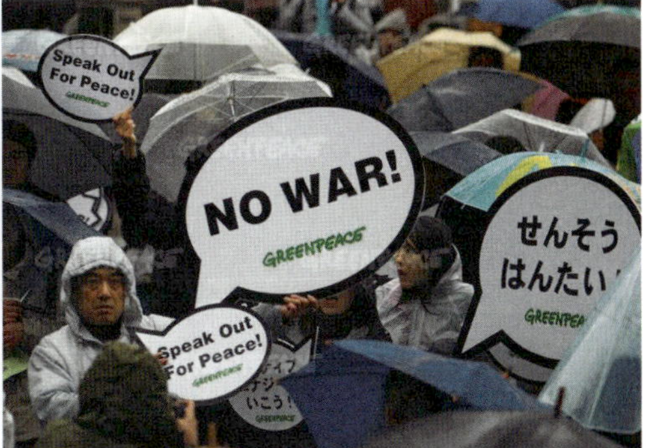

021
022

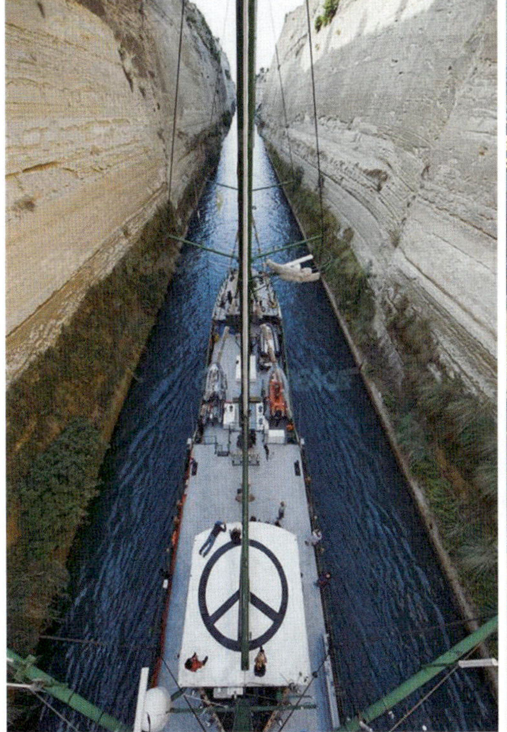

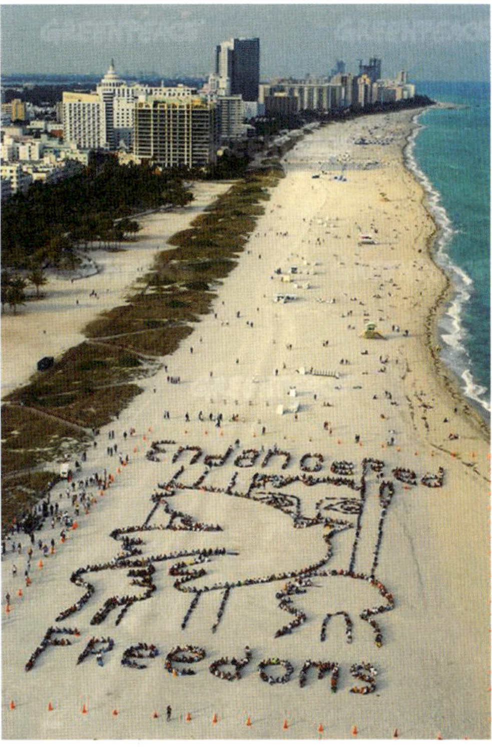

023
024

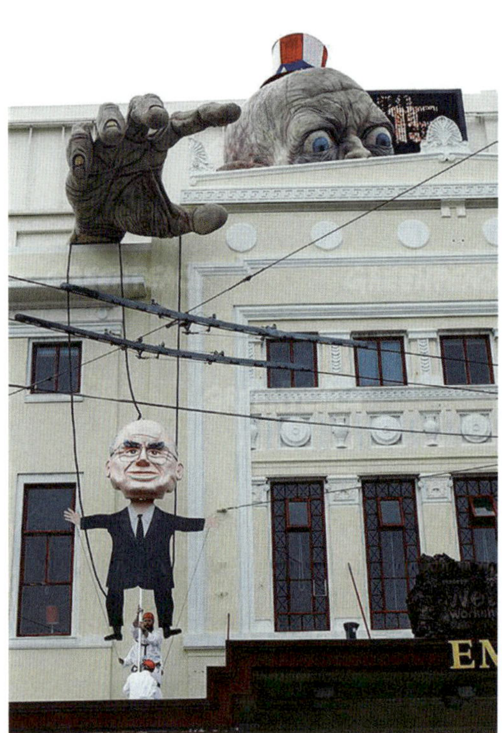

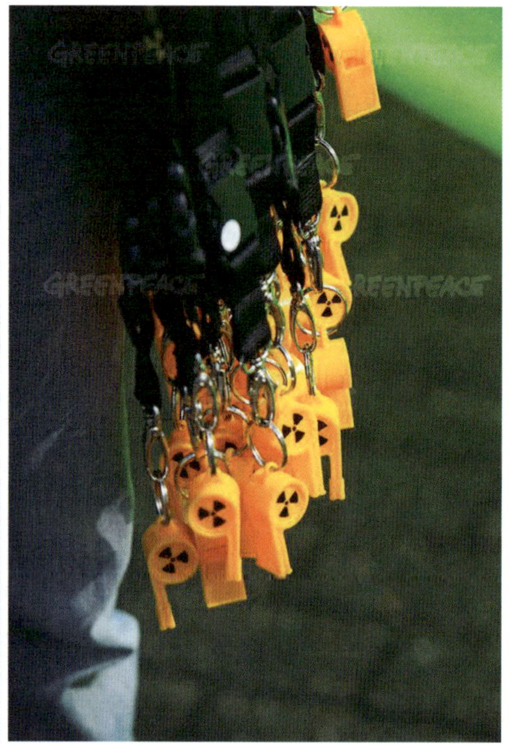

025
026

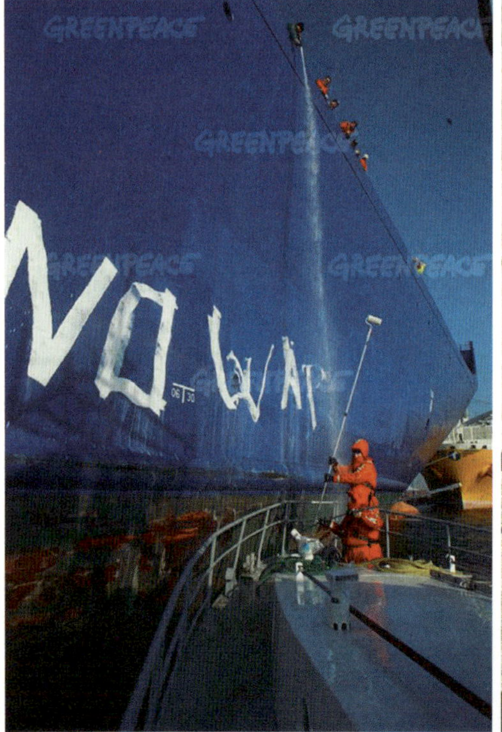

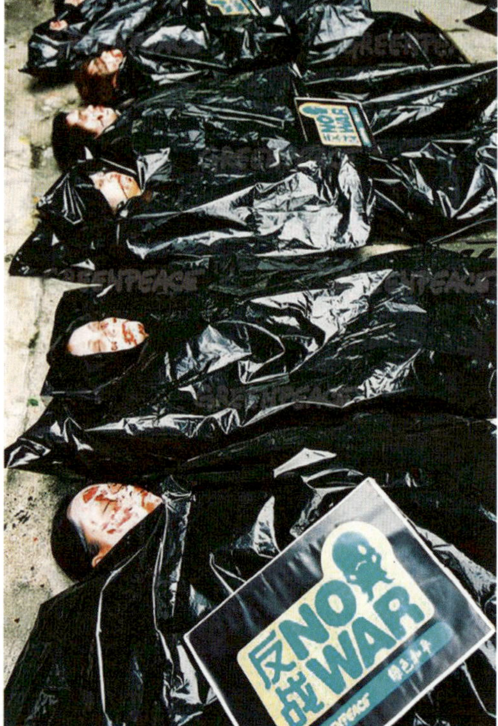

027
028

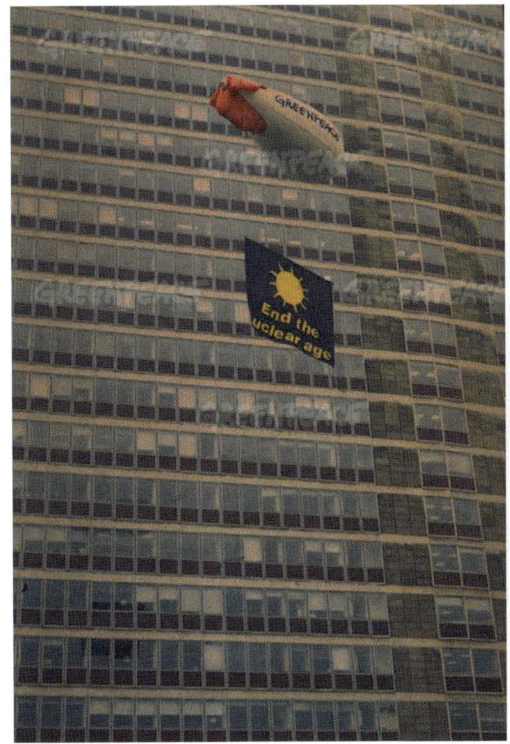
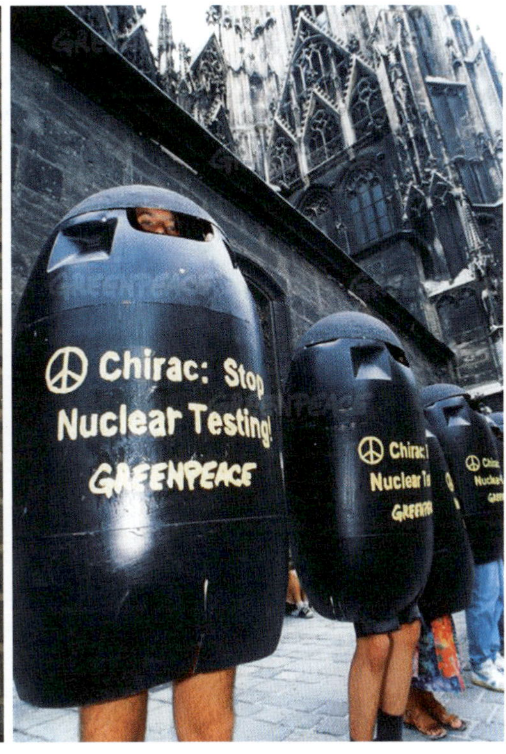

029
030

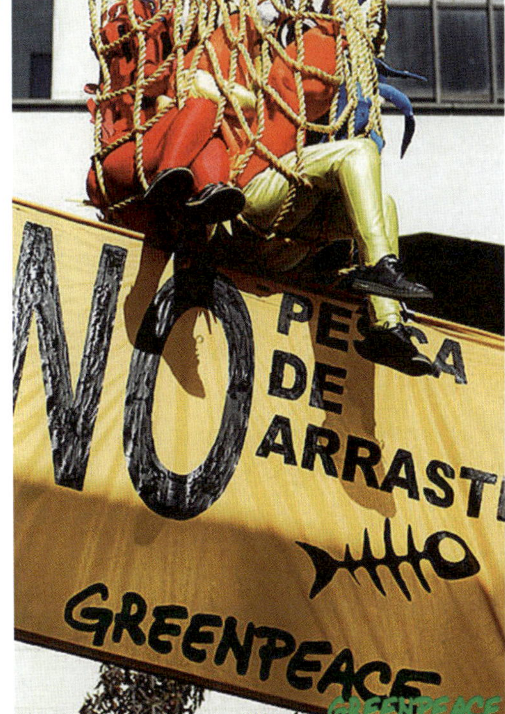

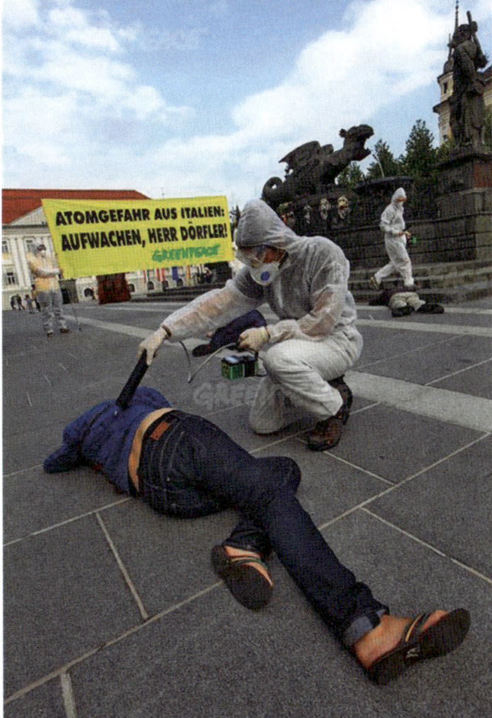

031

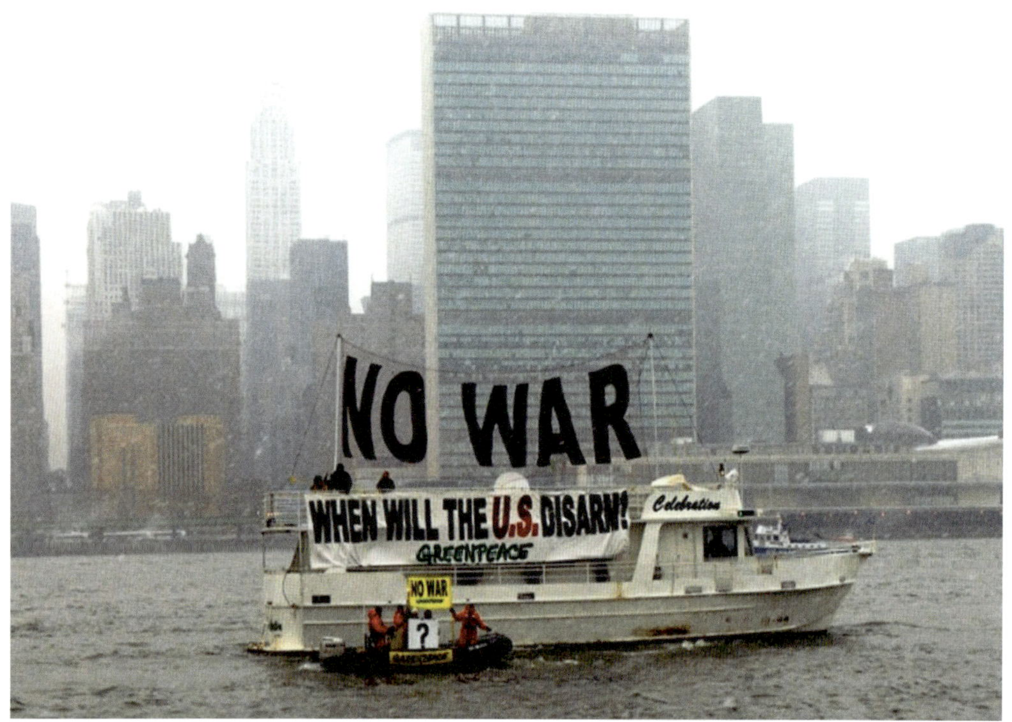

NO WAR
WHEN WILL THE U.S. DISARM?
GREENPEACE
Celebration
NO WAR
GREENPEACE
?

GREENPEACE

032

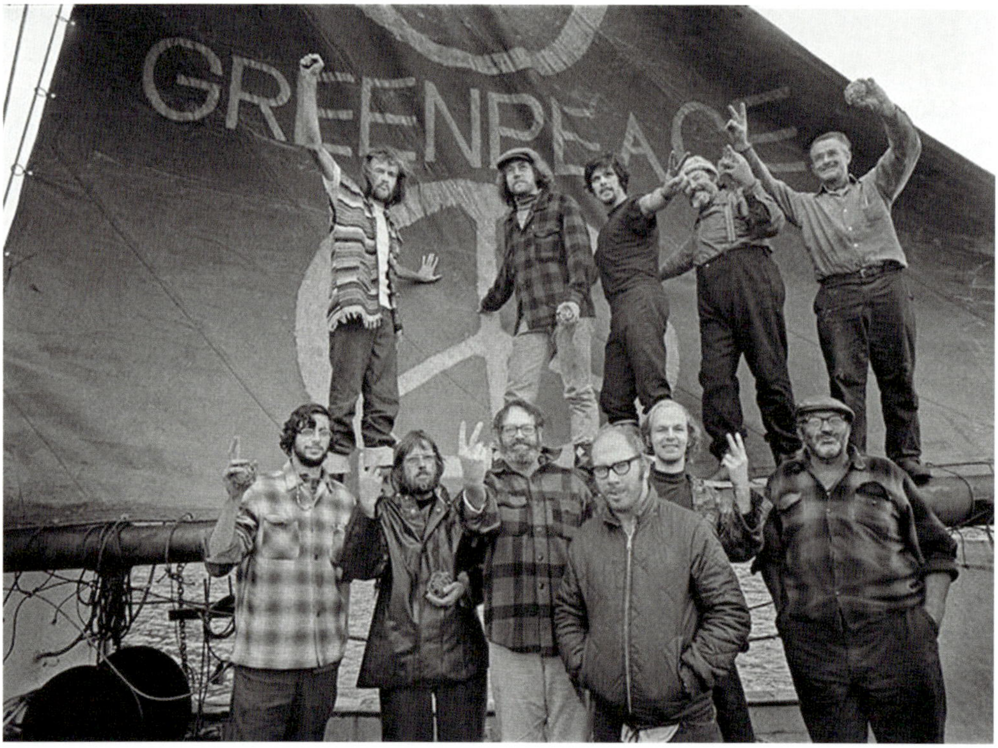

001 NO WAR ACTION AT AUSTRIAN
FOREIGN MINISTRY
CREATOR Ingrid Fankhauser
SOURCE Greenpeace
DATE 2003

002 NO WAR DEMONSTRATION IN FRANCE
CREATOR Matthieu Barret
SOURCE Greenpeace

003 GE ACTION AGAINST PATENTS ON
HUMAN DNA
CREATOR Paul Langrock
SOURCE Greenpeace

004 NO WAR DEMONSTRATION IN ITALY
CREATOR Massimo Vollaro
SOURCE Greenpeace

005 NO WAR DEMONSTRATION IN TURKEY
CREATOR G Yildirim
SOURCE Greenpeace

006 TOKYO 2 DEMONSTRATION FINLAND
CREATOR Matti Snellman
SOURCE Greenpeace
DATE 2008

007 COP15 GLOBAL DAY OF ACTION
IN BEIJING
CREATOR Lu Guang
SOURCE Greenpeace
DATE 2009

008 OCEANS ACTION AGAINST WHALING
IN FINLAND
CREATOR Hanna Weselius
SOURCE Greenpeace
DATE 2002

009 NO WAR DEMONSTRATION IN LEBANON
CREATOR Walid Abdelnour
SOURCE Greenpeace
DATE 2003

010 NUCLEAR ACTION UN HEADQUARTERS
CREATOR David Adair
SOURCE Greenpeace
DATE 2003

011 2000 TAHITIAN SUPPORTERS GREETED
THE RAINBOW WARRIOR AS IT
RETURNED TO TAHITI FROM MORUROA
CREATOR David Adair
SOURCE Greenpeace
DATE 1995

012 NUCLEAR-FREE MIDDLE EAST
BANNER ON BEACH
CREATOR Chen Leopold
SOURCE Greenpeace
DATE 2007

013 GREENPEACE DEMONSTRATION AGAINST
PLUTONIUM SHIPMENT OUTSIDE UK
CONSULATE. CAPE TOWN, SOUTH AFRICA
CREATOR Jason Mawdsley
SOURCE Greenpeace
DATE 1999

014 SAVING THE BLUEFIN TUNA
CREATOR Marco Care
SOURCE Greenpeace

015 GLOBAL DAY OF ACTION ON
CLIMATE CHANGE
CREATOR Konrad Konstantynowicz
SOURCE CEE, Poland
DATE 2008

016 CLIMATE BANNERS DURING
DANUBE FLOODING
CREATOR Barbara Tschann
SOURCE Greenpeace
DATE 2009

017 PEACE DOVES - HIROSHIMA ATOMIC
BOMBING 60TH ANNIVERSARY
CREATOR Jeremy Sutton-Hibbert
SOURCE Greenpeace
DATE 2005

018 NUCLEAR ACTION DURING CTBT
CONFERENCE IN GENEVA
CREATOR David Adair
SOURCE Greenpeace
DATE 1996

019 CLIMATE ACTION AGAINST NUCLEAR
ENERGY IN THAILAND
CREATOR Vinai Dithajohn
SOURCE Greenpeace
DATE 2008

020 WAR ANNIVERSARY DEMONSTRATION
IN TOKYO
CREATOR Jeremy Sutton-Hibbert
SOURCE Greenpeace
DATE 2004

021 RAINBOW WARRIOR IN CORINTH CANAL
CREATOR Pierre Gleizes
SOURCE Greenpeace
DATE 2008

022 GREENPEACE PROTEST MIAMI BEACH
CREATOR Robert Visser
SOURCE Greenpeace
DATE 2004

023 NO WAR DEMONSTRATION IN
NEW ZEALAND
CREATOR Anthony Phelps
SOURCE Greenpeace
DATE 2003

024 NUCLEAR ACTION SHAREHOLDERS'
MEETING ESSENT IN ARNHEM
CREATOR Sjoerd van Delden
SOURCE Greenpeace
DATE 2004

025 NO WAR ACTION
CREATOR Philip Reynaers
SOURCE Greenpeace
DATE 2003

026 NO WAR DEMONSTRATION
IN CHINA
CREATOR Sam Chan
SOURCE Greenpeace

027 END THE NUCLEAR AGE
CREATOR Unknown
SOURCE Greenpeace

028 PROTEST AT 50TH HIROSHIMA
ANNIVERSARY IN AUSTRIA
CREATOR W Watzl
SOURCE Greenpeace
DATE 1995

029 VALPARAISO, CHILE
CREATOR Lorenzo Moscia
SOURCE Greenpeace

030 AUSTRIAN ACTIVISTS PROTEST
ITALIAN NUCLEAR PROGRAM
CREATOR Juraj Rizman
SOURCE Greenpeace

031 WHEN WILL THE U.S. DISARM? NO WAR.
Sailing in front of the United
Nations headquarters in New York.
SOURCE Greenpeace
DATE 2006

032 AUSTRIAN ACTIVISTS PROTEST
ITALIAN NUCLEAR PROGRAM
In 1971, the first Greenpeace
crew unfurled their triangular
green sail, emblazoned with the
peace and ecology symbols, and
set out from Vancouver to change
the world.
SOURCE members.greenpeace.org/blog/
sebastianstelios/
DATE 1971

001
002

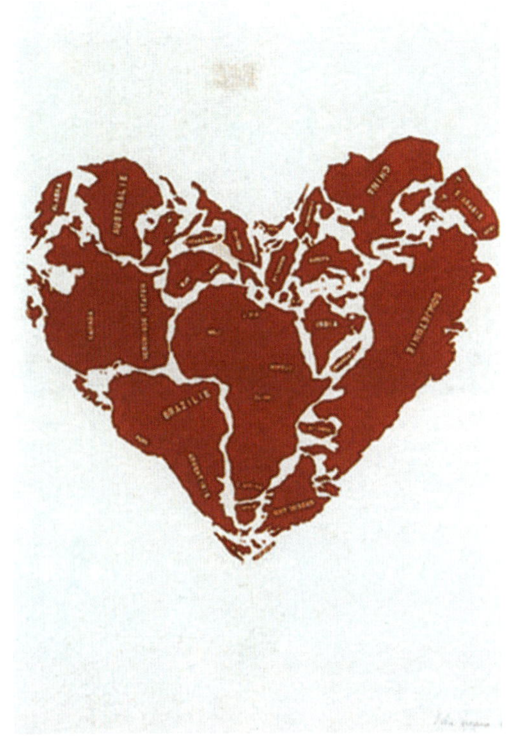

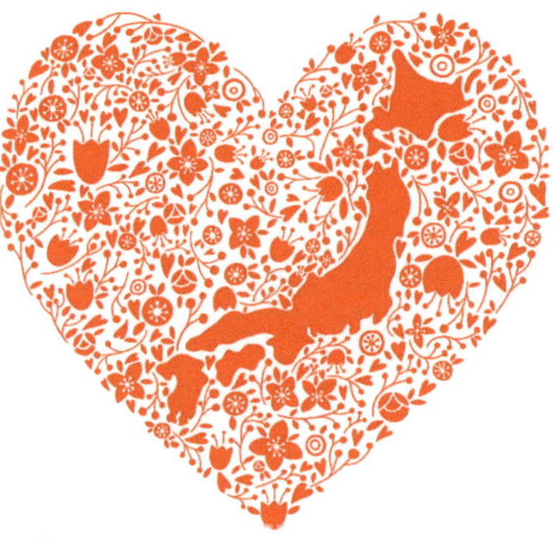

003
004

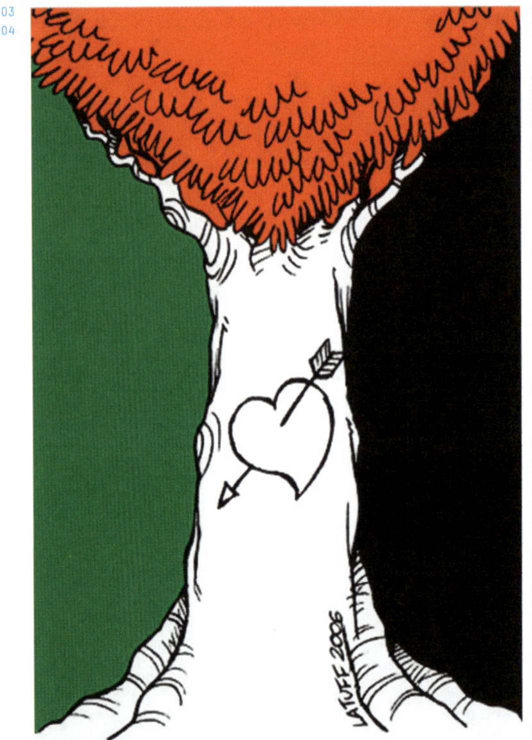

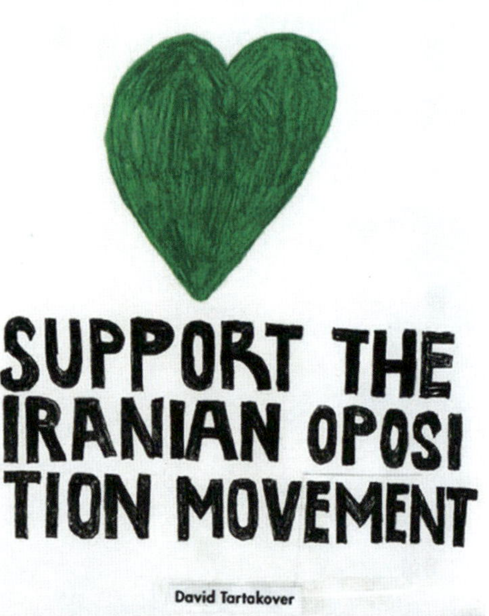

005

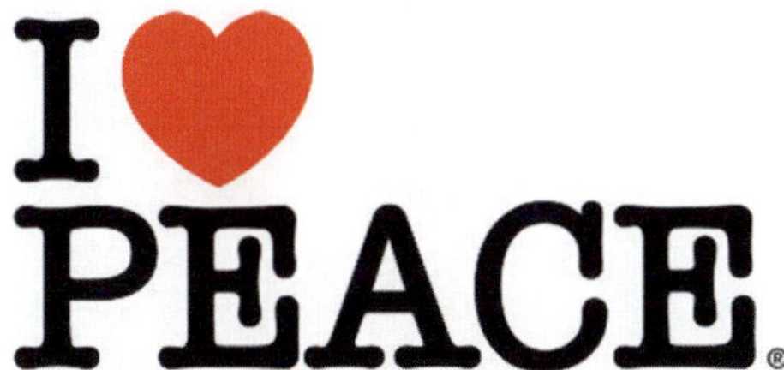

006

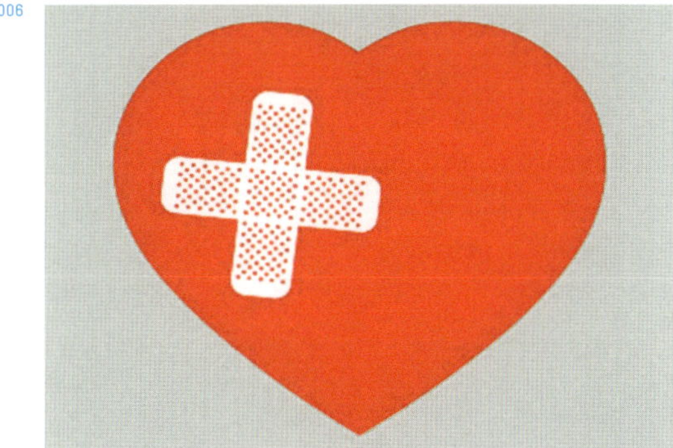

007

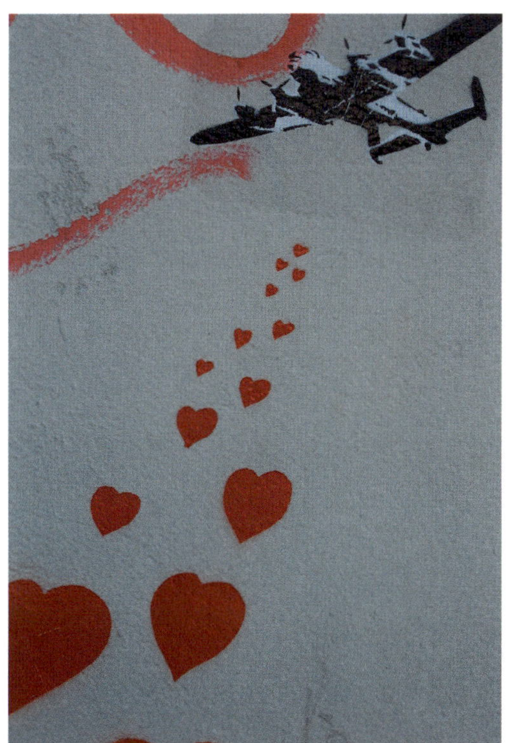

001 HET GEBROKEN HART
[THE BROKEN HEART]
SOURCE Milja Praagman

002 A THOUSAND PAPER CRANES FOR JAPAN
CREATOR This Paper Ship
SOURCE thispapership.com

003 IN LOVE WITH PALESTINE
CREATOR Latuff
SOURCE www.gazatimes.blogspot.ch/
DATE 2006

004 A POSTER FOR GREEN IRAN
CREATOR David Tartakover
SOURCE www.thelittlechimpsociety.
com

005 I HEART PEACE
CREATOR Gaertner Flo
SOURCE Beiträge macht Bilder

006 HAITI BENEFIT
CREATOR Shine MediaHouse
SOURCE shinemediahouse.com/

007 HEART BOMBER
CREATOR svennevenn
SOURCE www.flickr.com/photos/
makarellos/2358668253/sizes/o/in/
photostream/

001
002

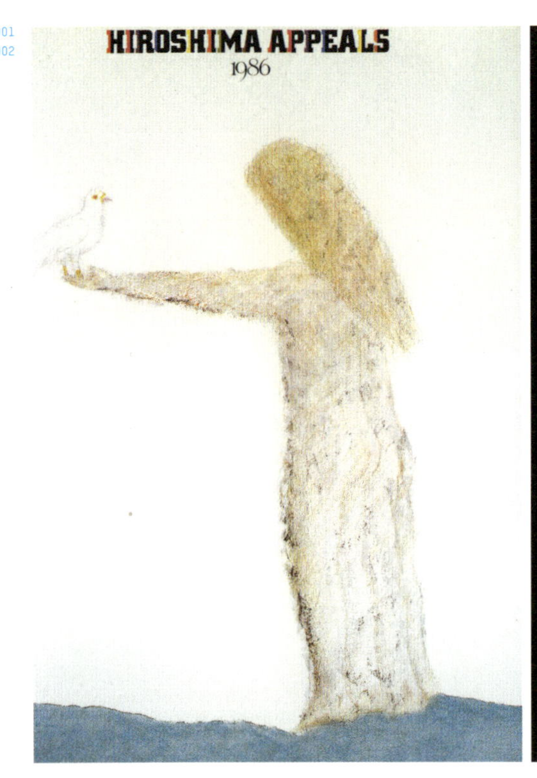
HIROSHIMA APPEALS
1986

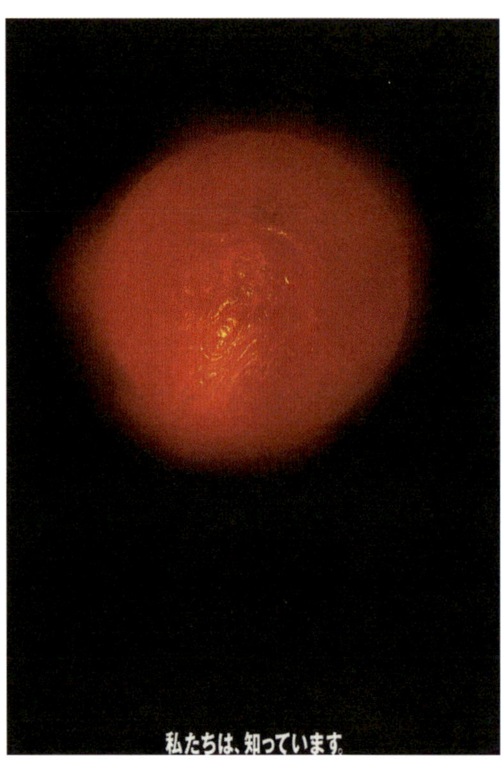
私たちは、知っています。

003
004

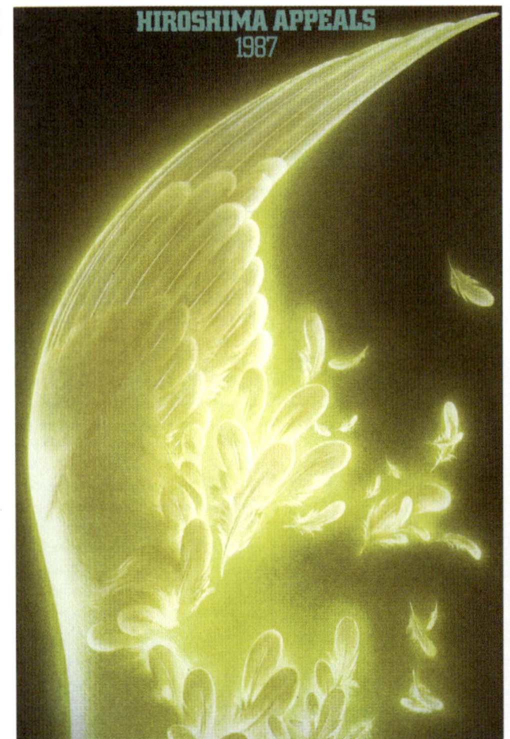
HIROSHIMA APPEALS
1987

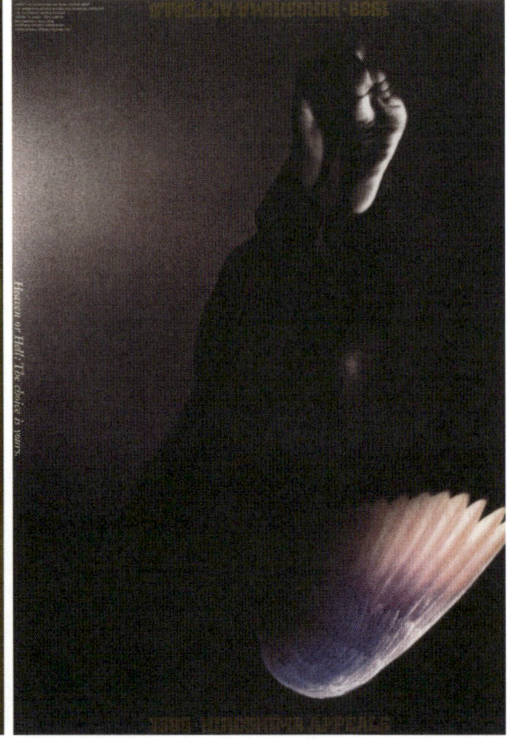
Heaven or Hell: The choice is yours.

005
006

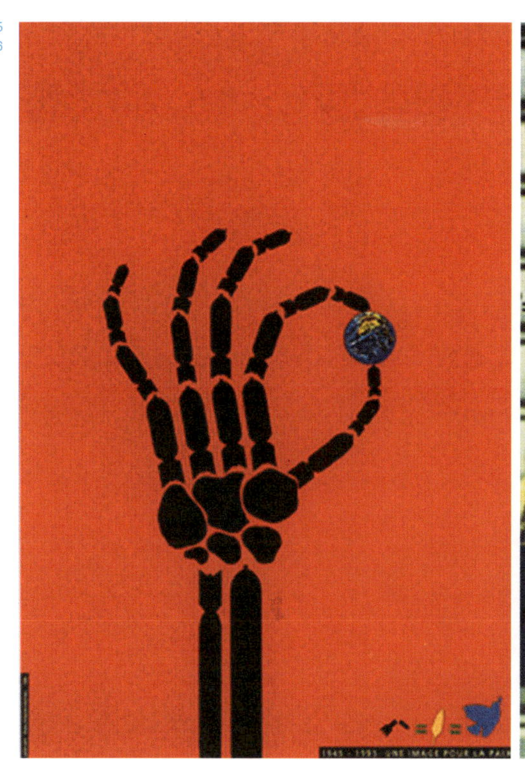

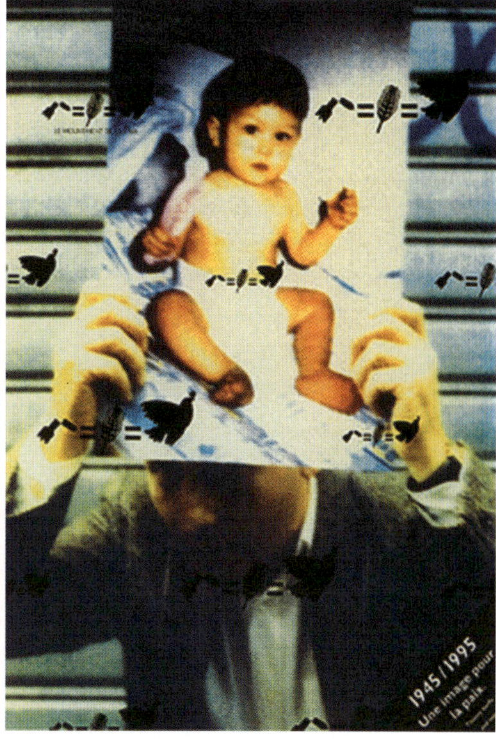

007
008

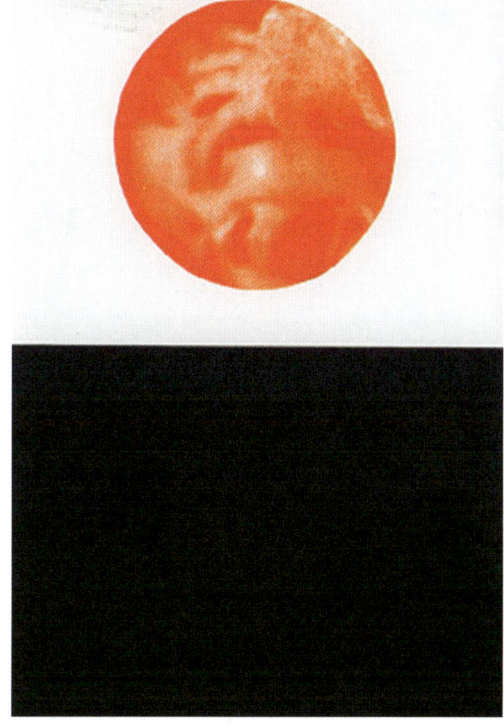

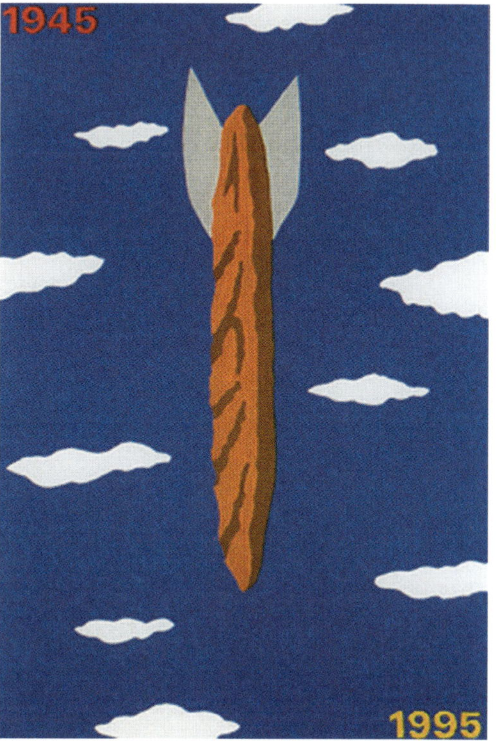

009
010

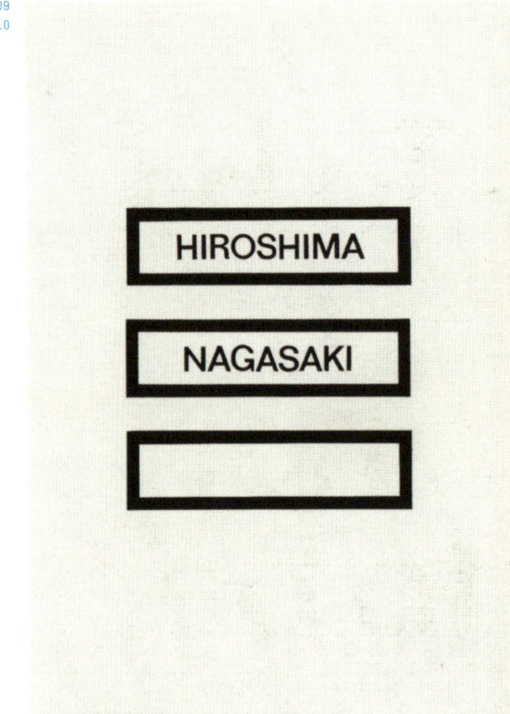

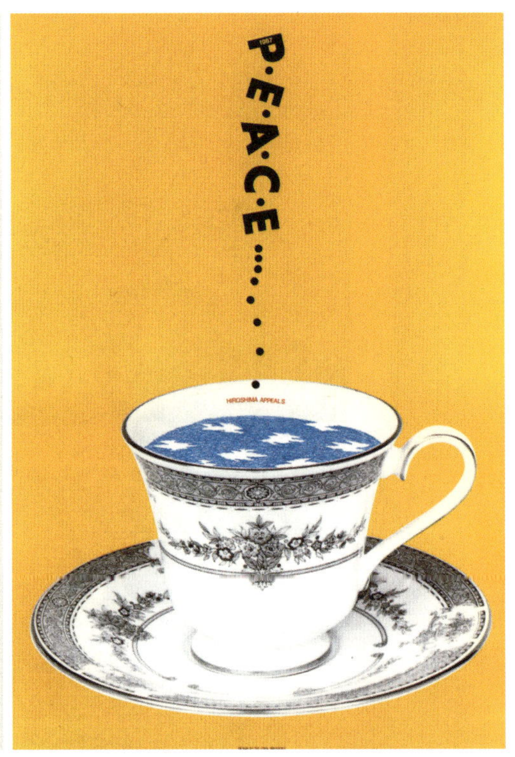

011
012

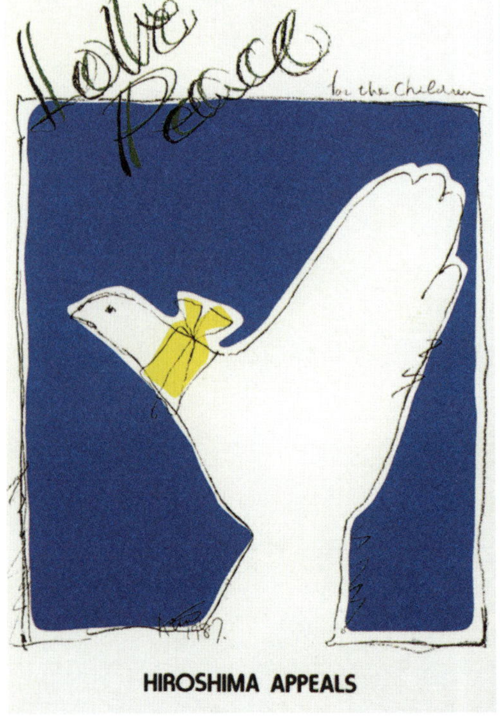

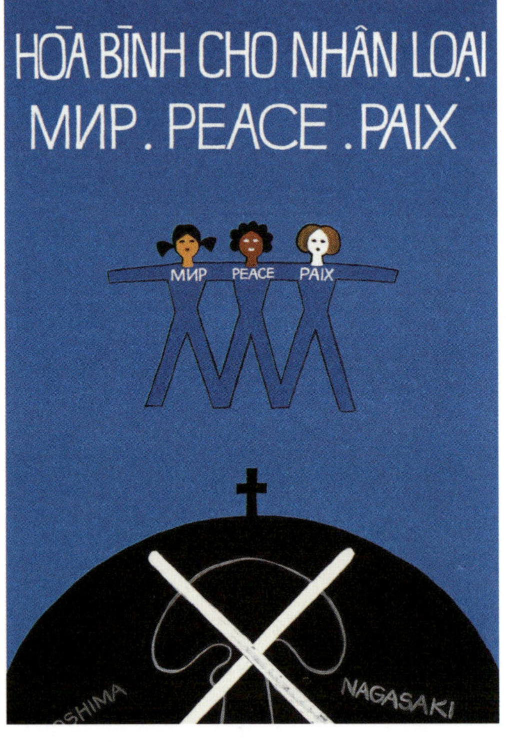

013
014

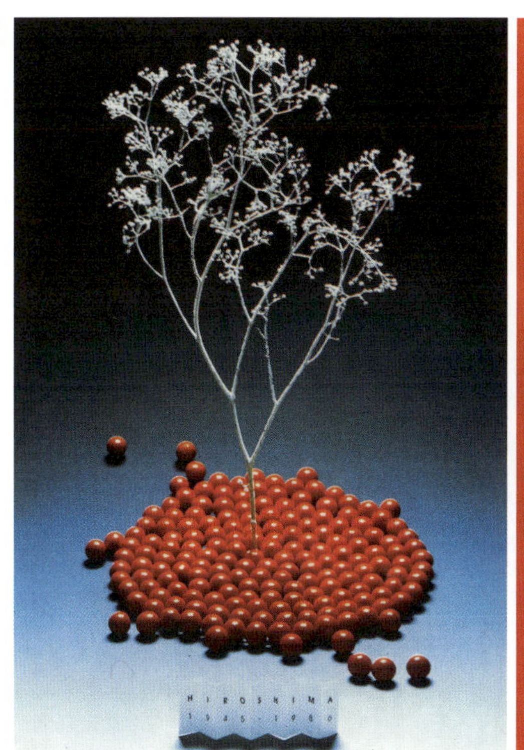

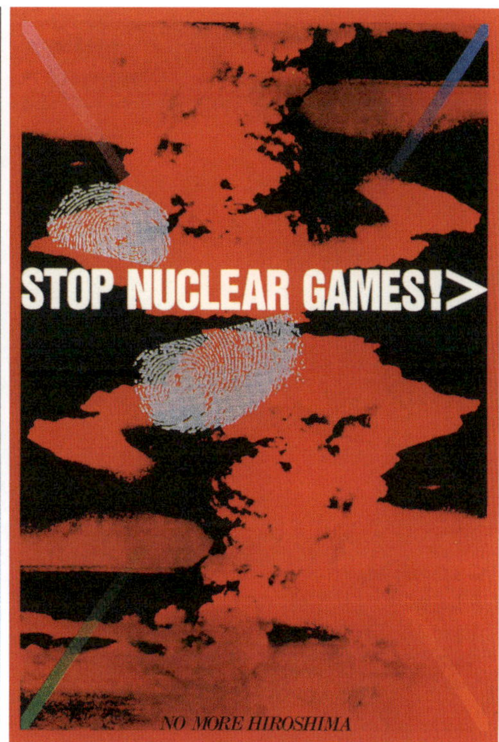

015
016

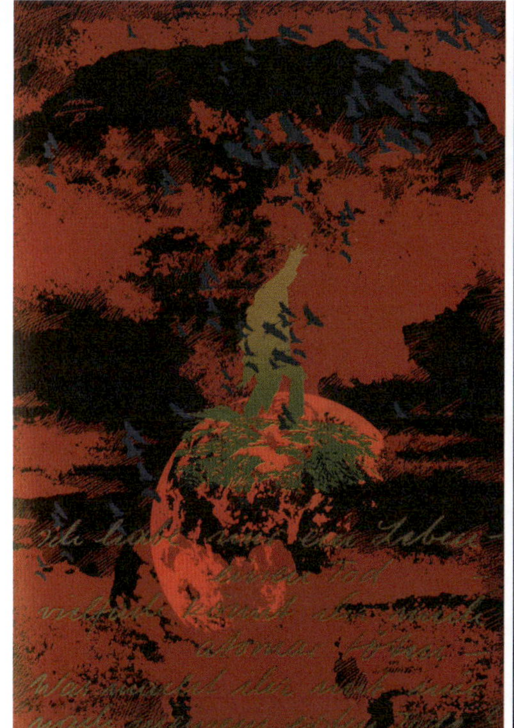

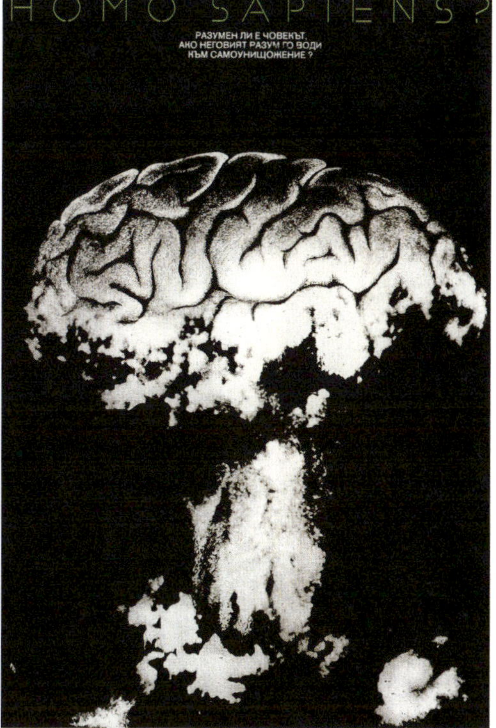

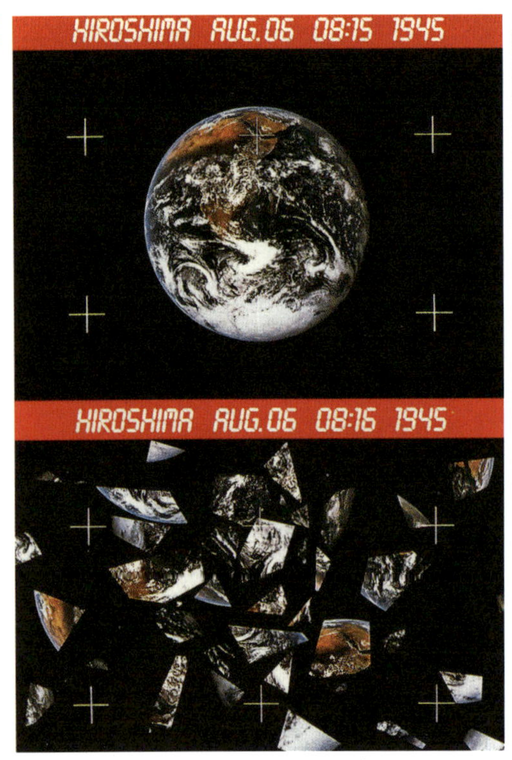

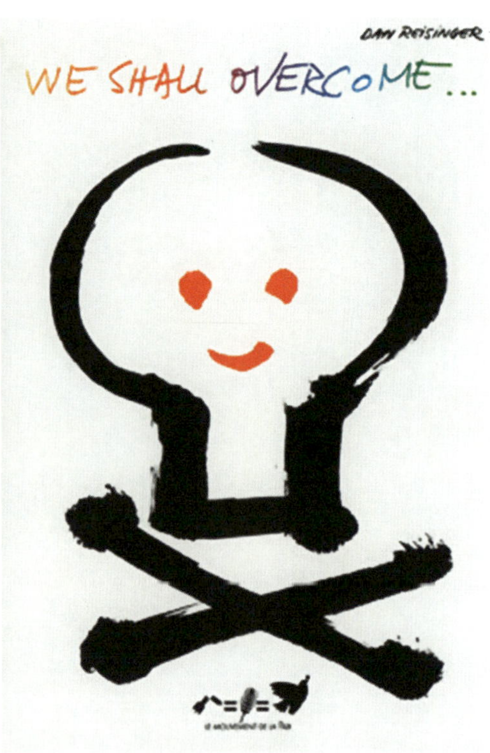

Ne pas oublier...

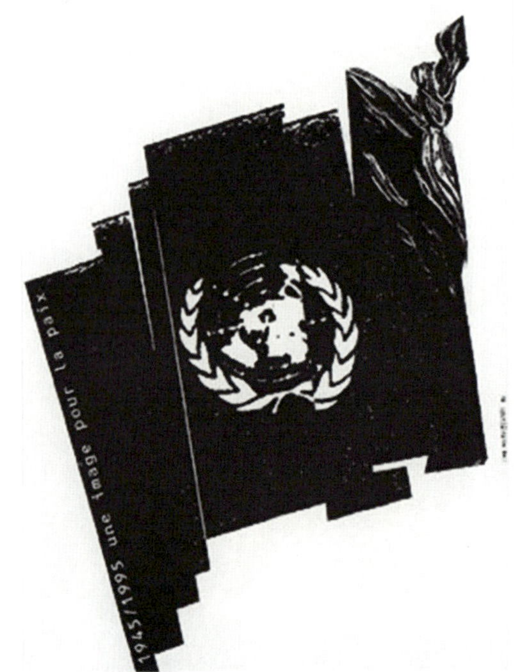

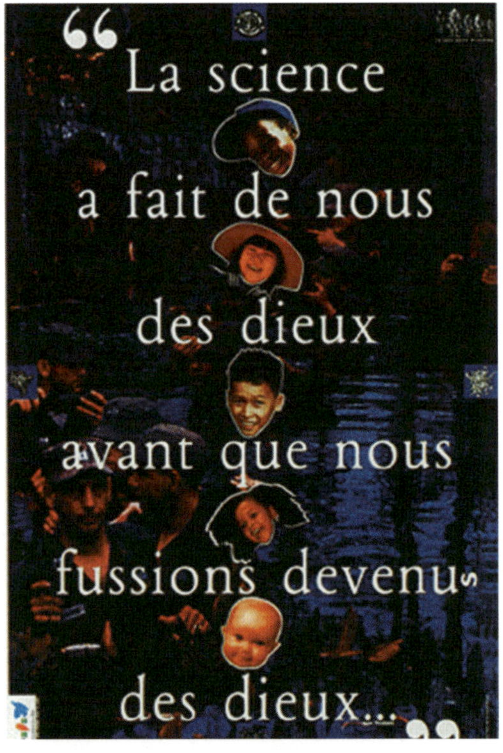

021
022

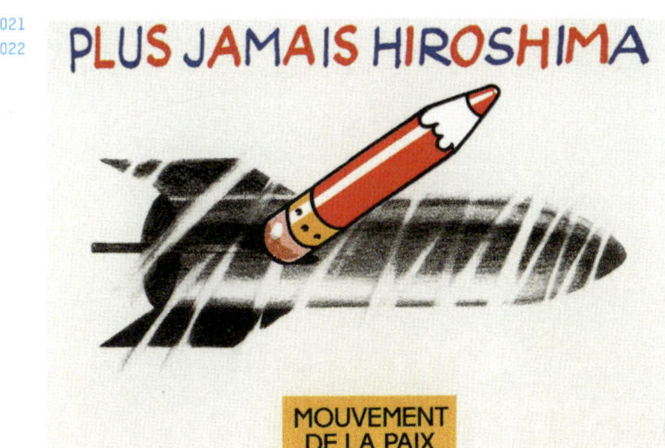

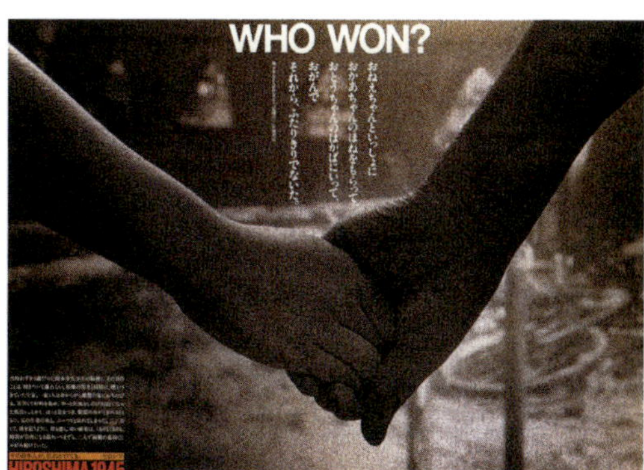

023
024

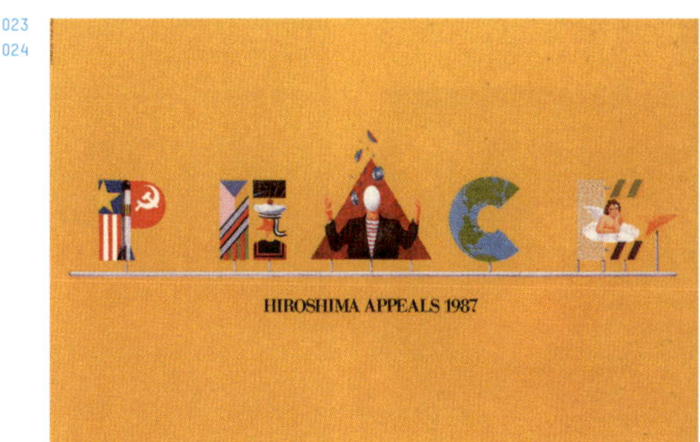

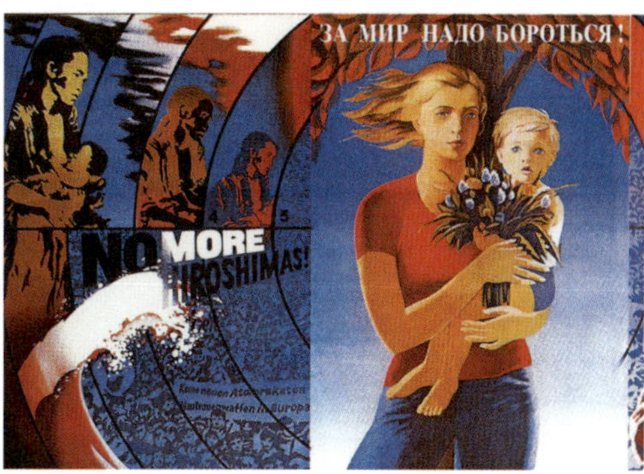

025
026

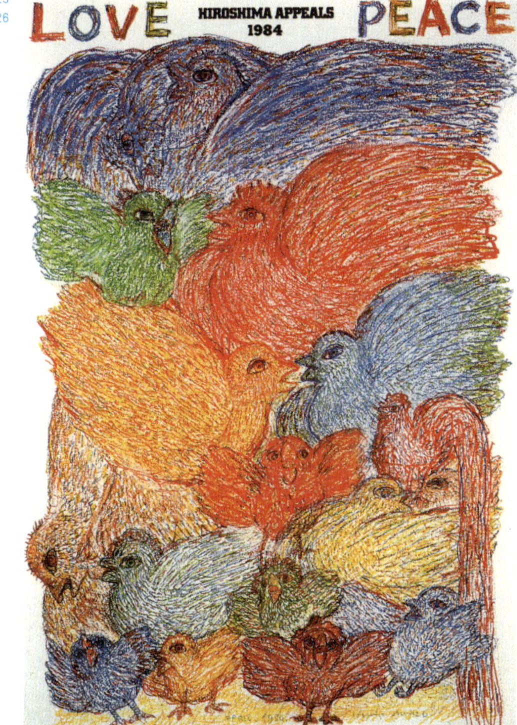

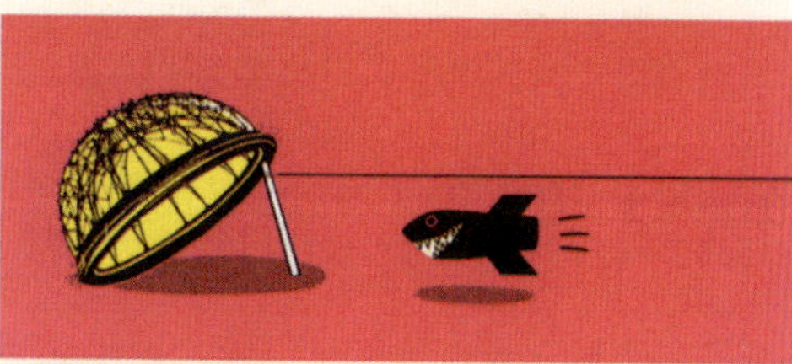

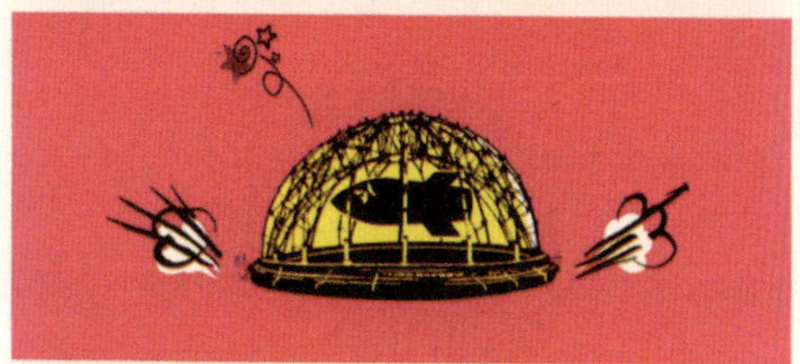

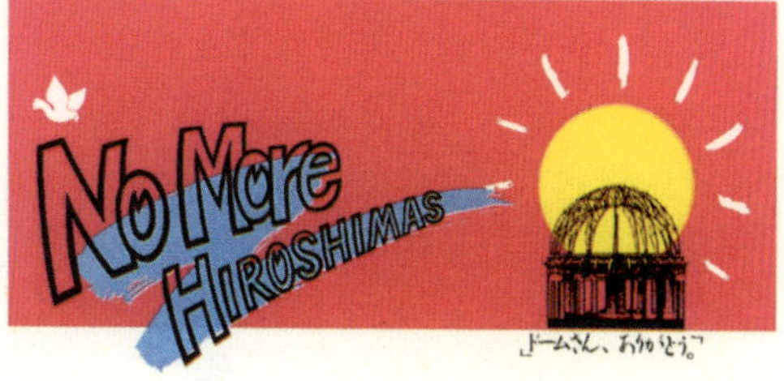

001 HIROSHIMA APPEALS
CREATOR Yoshio Hayakawa
SOURCE JAGDA Peace Posters
International Exhibition
DATE 1986

002 YES, WE KNOW
CREATOR Issei Ishisone
SOURCE JAGDA Peace Posters
International Exhibition

003 HIROSHIMA APPEALS
CREATOR Kazumasa Nagai
SOURCE JAGDA Peace Posters
International Exhibition
DATE 1987

004 HIROSHIMA APPEALS
CREATOR Mitsuo Katsui
SOURCE JAGDA Peace Posters
International Exhibition
DATE 1989

005 1945-1995 AN IMAGE FOR PEACE
CREATOR Marc-Antoine Mathieu
SOURCE Editions/Galerie l'Art
et la Paix
DATE 1995

006 1945-1995 AN IMAGE FOR PEACE
CREATOR Thierry Sarfis
SOURCE Editions/Galerie l'Art
et la Paix
DATE 1995

007 CREATOR Alex Jordan
SOURCE Editions/Galerie l'Art
et la Paix
DATE 1995

008 1945, 1995
CREATOR Nikolaus Troxler
SOURCE Editions/Galerie l'Art
et la Paix
DATE 1995

009 HIROSHIMA, NAGASAKI
CREATOR Witold Mysyrowicz
SOURCE JAGDA Peace Posters
International Exhibition

010 PEACE
CREATOR Tae-Chol Kim
SOURCE JAGDA Peace Posters
International Exhibition

011 LOVE PEACE
CREATOR Atsuko Matsumoto
SOURCE JAGDA Peace Posters
International Exhibition

012 PEACE FOR MANKIND
CREATOR Ngo Nhu Linh
SOURCE JAGDA Peace Posters
International Exhibition

013 HIROSHIMA
CREATOR David Murray
SOURCE JAGDA Peace Posters
International Exhibition
DATE 1986

014 STOP NUCLEAR GAMES!
CREATOR Masami Kawamura
SOURCE JAGDA Peace Posters
International Exhibition

015 I HAVE ONLY ONE LIFE ...
CREATOR Jochen Fiedler
SOURCE JAGDA Peace Posters
International Exhibition

016 HOMO SAPIENS?
CREATOR Nikola Nikolov
SOURCE JAGDA Peace Posters
International Exhibition

017 HIROSHIMA, 8:16 A.M. 1945
CREATOR Takaaki Matsumoto
SOURCE JAGDA Peace Posters
International Exhibition

018 WE SHALL OVERCOME...
CREATOR Dan Reisinger
SOURCE Editions/Galerie l'Art
et la Paix
DATE 1995

019 NE PAS OUBLIEZ
[DON'T FORGET]
CREATOR Ewa Maruszewska
SOURCE Editions/Galerie l'Art
et la Paix
DATE 1995

020 LA SCIENCE A FAIT DE NOUS DES
DIEUX AVANT QUE NOUS FUSSIONS
DEVENUS DES DIEUX
[SCIENCE MADE US GODS BEFORE
WE BECAME GODS...]
CREATOR Jèrôme Tham-Vo
SOURCE Editions/Galerie l'Art
et la Paix
DATE 1995

021 NO MORE HIROSHIMA
CREATOR Studio Tract
SOURCE JAGDA Peace Posters
International Exhibition

022 WHO ONE?
CREATOR Jutaro Itoh
SOURCE JAGDA Peace Posters
International Exhibition

023 PEACE
CREATOR Shuzo Kato
SOURCE JAGDA Peace Posters
International Exhibition

024 IT IS NECESSARY TO FIGHT
FOR PEACE
CREATOR V. Arlashhin, I. Chiveryova
SOURCE JAGDA Peace Posters
International Exhibition

025 HIROSHIMA APPEALS
CREATOR Kiyoshi Awazu
SOURCE JAGDA Peace Posters
International Exhibition
DATE 1984

026 NO MORE HIROSHIMA
SOURCE JAGDA Peace Posters
International Exhibition

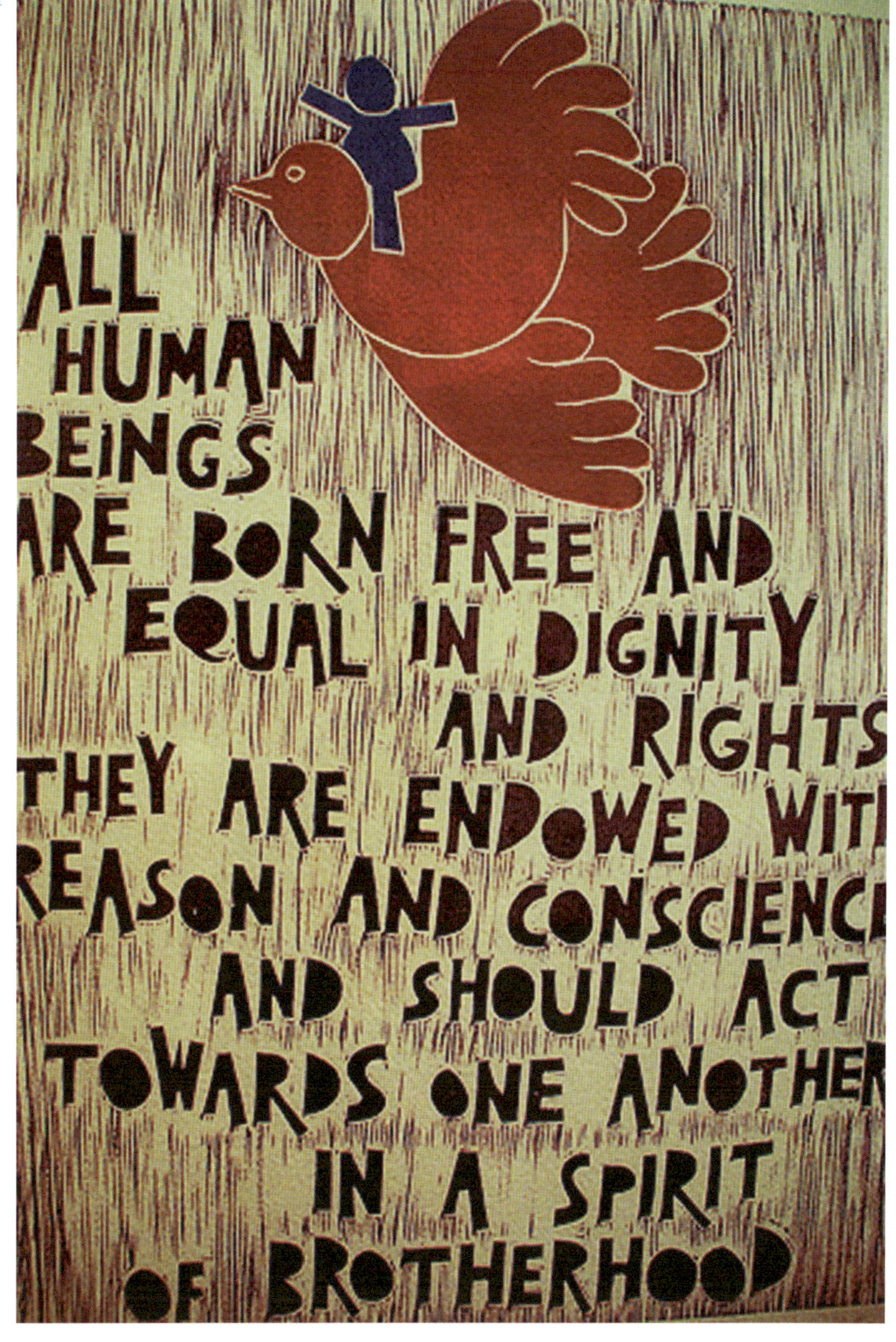
ALL HUMAN BEINGS ARE BORN FREE AND EQUAL IN DIGNITY AND RIGHTS THEY ARE ENDOWED WITH REASON AND CONSCIENCE AND SHOULD ACT TOWARDS ONE ANOTHER IN A SPIRIT OF BROTHERHOOD

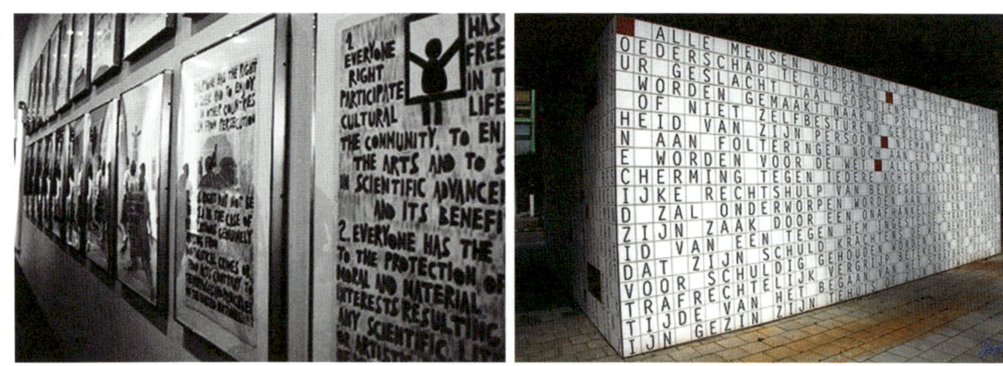

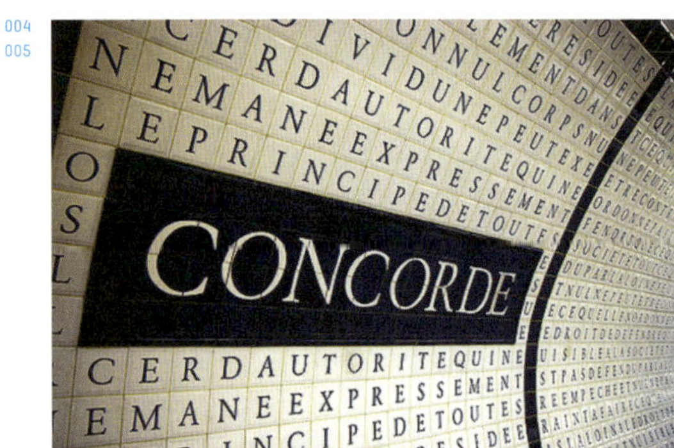
CONCORDE

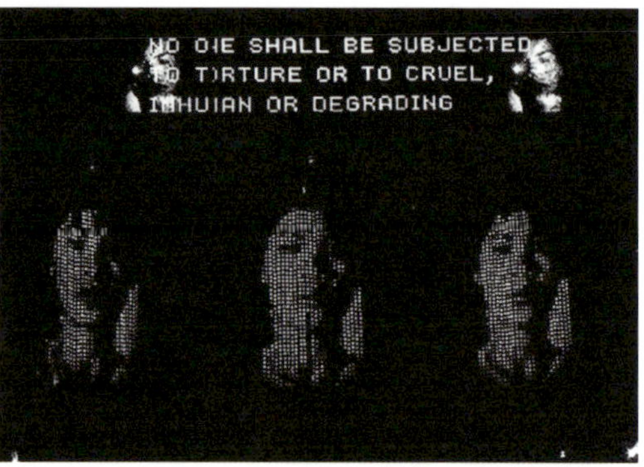
NO ONE SHALL BE SUBJECTED
TO TORTURE OR TO CRUEL,
INHUMAN OR DEGRADING

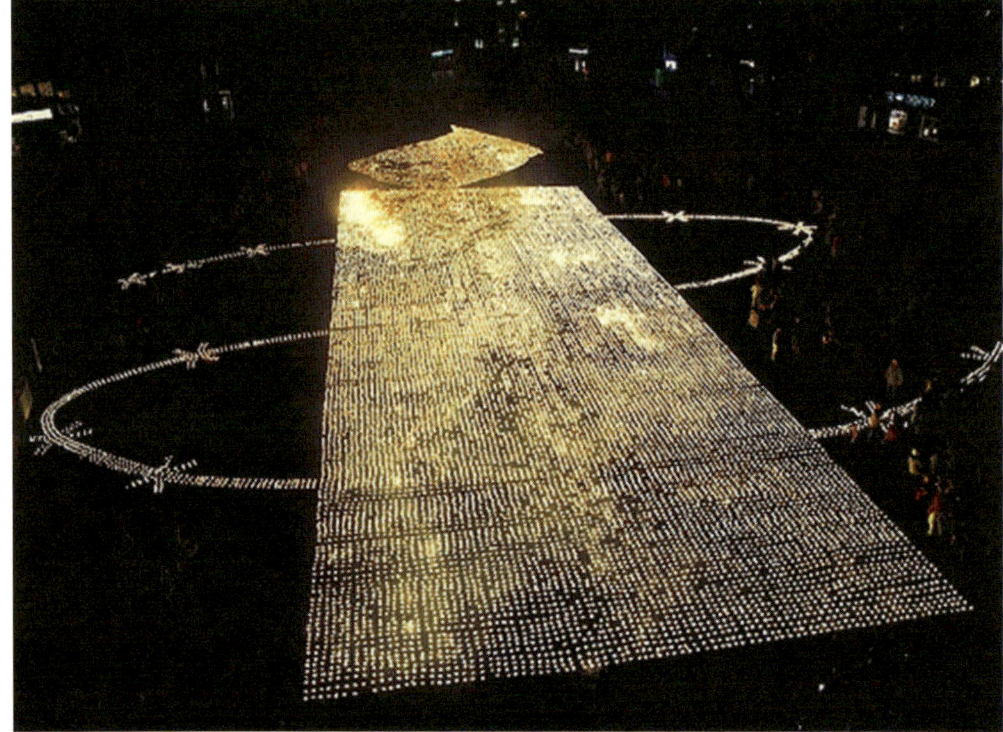

007
008

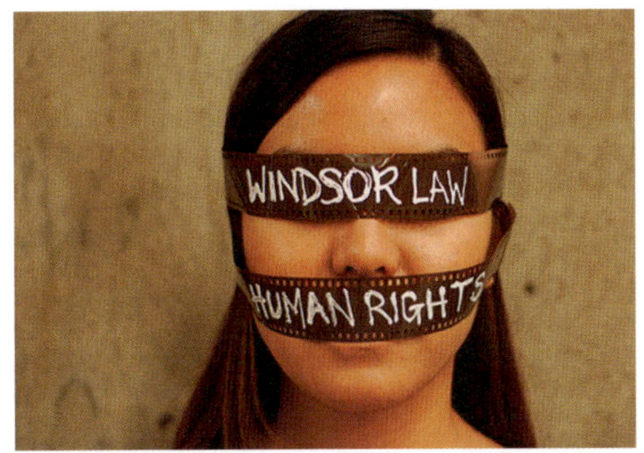

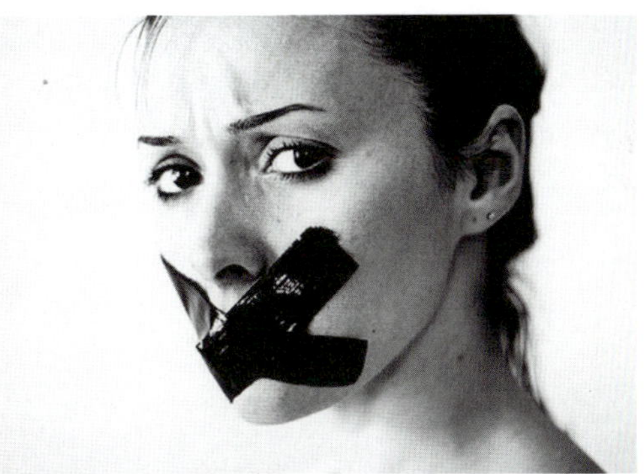

009
010

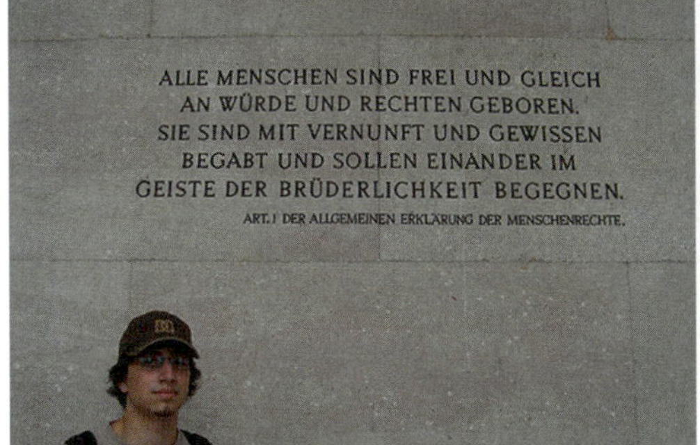

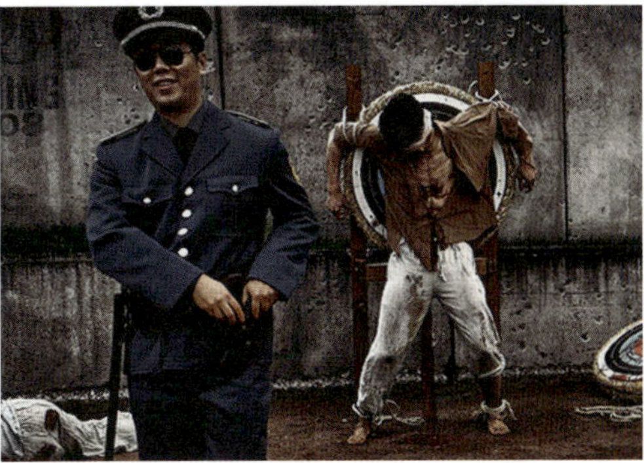

011
012

NEXT
013

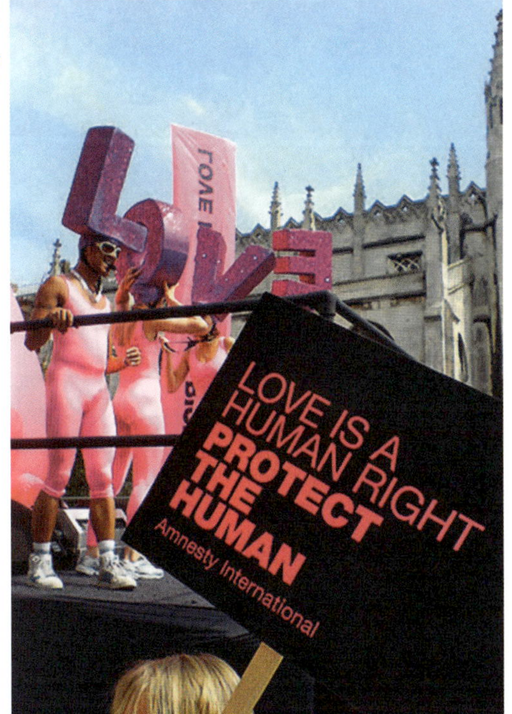

ICH SAGE, WAS ICH DENKE.
ICH SAGE, WAS ICH DENKE.
ICH SAGE,
ICH SAGE,
ICH SAGE,
ICH SAGE,
ICH SAGE,
ICH SAGE,
ICH SAGE,
ICH SAGE, WAS ICH DENKE.
ICH SAGE, WAS ICH DENKE.
ICH SAGE, WAS ICH DENKE.
ICH SAGE, WAS ICH DENKE.
ICH SAGE, WAS ICH DENKE.

ICH SAGE, WAS ICH DENKEN SOLL.

PEKING 2008 – WIR FORDERN

GOLD FÜR
MENSCHENRECHTE
WWW.GOLDFUERMENSCHENRECHTE.DE

AMNESTY
INTERNATIONAL

In China werden Andersdenkende zur
„Umerziehung" in Arbeitslagern inhaftiert.

Spendenkonto: 80 90 100. Bank für Sozialwirtschaft. BLZ 370 205 00.

Déclaration universelle des droits de l'homm

§ 1 Tous les êtres humains naissent libres et égaux en dignité et en droits. Ils sont doués de raison et de conscience et doivent agir les uns envers [les] autres dans un esprit de fraternité. **§ 2** 1. Chacun peut se prévaloir de tous les droits et de toutes les libertés proclamés dans la présente Déclarat[ion] sans distinction aucune, notamment de race, de couleur, de sexe, de langue, de religion, d'opinion politique ou de toute autre opinion, d'origine na[tio]nale ou sociale, de fortune, de naissance ou de toute autre situation. 2. De plus, il ne sera fait aucune distinction fondée sur le statut politique, jurid[ique] ou international du pays ou du territoire dont une personne est ressortissante, que ce pays ou territoire soit indépendant, sous tutelle, non auton[ome] ou soumis à une limitation quelconque de souveraineté. **§ 3** Tout individu a droit à la vie, à la liberté et à la sûreté de sa personne. **§ 4** Nul ne sera t[enu] en esclavage ni en servitude ; l'esclavage et la traite des esclaves sont interdits sous toutes leurs formes. **§ 5** Nul ne sera soumis à la torture, ni à [des] peines ou traitements cruels, inhumains ou dégradants. **§ 6** Chacun a le droit à la reconnaissance en tous lieux de sa personnalité juridique. **§ 7** T[ous] sont égaux devant la loi et ont droit sans distinction à une égale protection de la loi. Tous ont droit à une protection égale contre toute discrimina[tion] qui violerait la présente Déclaration et contre toute provocation à une telle discrimination. **§ 8** Toute personne a droit à un recours effectif devan[t les] juridictions nationales compétentes contre les actes violant les droits fondamentaux qui lui sont reconnus par la constitution ou par la loi. **§ 9** Nu[l ne] peut être arbitrairement arrêté, détenu ou exilé. **§ 10** Toute personne a droit, en pleine égalité, à ce que sa cause soit entendue équitablement et pu[bli]quement par un tribunal indépendant et impartial, qui décidera, soit de ses droits et obligations, soit du bien-fondé de toute accusation en matière p[éna]le dirigée contre elle. **§ 11** 1. Toute personne accusée d'un acte délictueux est présumée innocente jusqu'à ce que sa culpabilité ait été légalement é[ta]blie au cours d'un procès public où toutes les garanties nécessaires à sa défense lui auront été assurées. 2. Nul ne sera condamné pour des action[s ou] omissions qui, au moment où elles ont été commises, ne constituaient pas un acte délictueux d'après le droit national ou international. De même, [il ne] sera infligé aucune peine plus forte que celle qui était applicable au moment où l'acte délictueux a été commis. **§ 12** Nul ne sera l'objet d'immixt[ions] arbitraires dans sa vie privée, sa famille, son domicile ou sa correspondance, ni d'atteintes à son honneur et à sa réputation. Toute personne a dr[oit à] la protection de la loi contre de telles immixtions ou de telles atteintes. **§ 13** 1. Toute personne a le droit de circuler librement et de choisir sa rési[den]ce à l'intérieur d'un Etat. 2. Toute personne a le droit de quitter tout pays, y compris le sien, et de revenir dans son pays. **§ 14** 1. Devant la persécu[tion] toute personne a le droit de chercher asile et de bénéficier de l'asile en d'autres pays. 2. Ce droit ne peut être invoqué que dans le cas de poursuites [réel]lement fondées sur un crime de droit acommun ou sur des agissements contraires aux buts et aux principes des Nations Unies. **§ 15** 1. Tout individu [a droit] à une nationalité. 2. Nul ne peut être arbitrairement privé de sa nationalité, ni du droit de changer de nationalité. **§ 16** 1. A partir de l'âge nubile, l'hom[me] et la femme, sans aucune restriction quant à la race, la nationalité ou la religion, ont le droit de se marier et de fonder une famille. Ils ont des droits é[gaux] au regard du mariage, durant le mariage et lors de sa dissolution. 2. Le mariage ne peut être conclu qu'avec le libre et plein consentement des fu[turs] époux. 3. La famille est l'élément naturel et fondamental de la société et a droit à la protection de la société et de l'Etat. **§ 17** 1. Toute personne, [au]ssi bien seule qu'en collectivité, a droit à la propriété. 2. Nul ne peut être arbitrairement privé de sa propriété. **§ 18** Toute personne a droit à la liber[té de] pensée, de conscience et de religion ; ce droit implique la liberté de changer de religion ou de conviction ainsi que la liberté de manifester sa reli[gion] ou sa conviction seule ou en commun, tant en public qu'en privé, par l'enseignement, les pratiques, le culte et l'accomplissement des rites. **§ 19** Tout [indi]vidu a droit à la liberté d'opinion et d'expression, ce qui implique le droit de ne pas être inquiété pour ses opinions et celui de chercher, de recev[oir et] de répandre, sans considérations de frontières, les informations et les idées par quelque moyen d'expression que ce soit. **§ 20** 1. Toute personne a [droit] à la liberté de réunion et d'association pacifiques. 2. Nul ne peut être obligé de faire partie d'une association. **§ 21** 1. Toute personne a le droit de pren[dre] part à la direction des affaires publiques de son pays, soit directement, soit par l'intermédiaire de représentants librement choisis. 2. Toute pers[onne] a droit à accéder, dans des conditions d'égalité, aux fonctions publiques de son pays. 3. La volonté du peuple est le fondement de l'autorité des pou[voirs] publics ; cette volonté doit s'exprimer par des élections honnêtes qui doivent avoir lieu périodiquement, au suffrage universel égal et au vote secret ou [sui]vant une procédure équivalente assurant la liberté du vote. **§ 22** Toute personne, en tant que membre de la société, a droit à la sécurité sociale ; [elle] est fondée à obtenir la satisfaction des droits économiques, sociaux et culturels indispensables à sa dignité et au libre développement de sa person[nali]té, grâce à l'effort national et à la coopération internationale, compte tenu de l'organisation et des ressources de chaque pays. **§ 23** 1. Toute pers[onne] a droit au travail, au libre choix de son travail, à des conditions équitables et satisfaisantes de travail et à la protection contre le chômage. 2. Tou[s ont] droit, sans aucune discrimination, à un salaire égal pour un travail égal. 3. Quiconque travaille a droit à une rémunération équitable et satisfaisan[te] assurant ainsi qu'à sa famille une existence conforme à la dignité humaine et complétée, s'il y a lieu, par tous autres moyens de protection socia[le]. Toute personne a le droit de fonder avec d'autres des syndicats et de s'affilier à des syndicats pour la défense de ses intérêts. **§ 24** Toute person[ne a] droit au repos et aux loisirs et notamment à une limitation raisonnable de la durée du travail et à des congés payés périodiques. **§ 25** 1. Toute pe[rson]ne a droit à un niveau de vie suffisant pour assurer sa santé, son bien-être et ceux de sa famille, notamment pour l'alimentation, l'habillement, le [loge]ment, les soins médicaux ainsi que pour les services sociaux nécessaires ; elle a droit à la sécurité en cas de chômage, de maladie, d'invalidité, de [veu]vage, de vieillesse ou dans les autres cas de perte de ses moyens de subsistance par suite de circonstances indépendantes de sa volonté. 2. La mater[ni]té et l'enfance ont droit à une aide et à une assistance spéciales. Tous les enfants, qu'ils soient nés dans le mariage ou hors mariage, jouissent [de la] même protection sociale. **§ 26** 1. Toute personne a droit à l'éducation. L'éducation doit être gratuite, au moins en ce qui concerne l'enseignement élé[mentaire] et fondamental. L'enseignement élémentaire est obligatoire. L'enseignement technique et professionnel doit être généralisé ; l'accès aux ét[udes] supérieures doit être ouvert en pleine égalité à tous en fonction de leur mérite. 2. L'éducation doit viser au plein épanouissement de la personn[alité] humaine et au renforcement du respect des droits de l'homme et des libertés fondamentales. Elle doit favoriser la compréhension, la tolérance et [l'ami]tié entre toutes les nations et tous les groupes raciaux ou religieux, ainsi que le développement des activités des Nations Unies pour le maintien [de la] paix. 3. Les parents ont, par priorité, le droit de choisir le genre d'éducation à donner à leurs enfants. **§ 27** 1. Toute personne a le droit de prendre [part] librement à la vie culturelle de la communauté, de jouir des arts et de participer au progrès scientifique et aux bienfaits qui en résultent. 2. Chacun a [droit] à la protection des intérêts moraux et matériels découlant de toute production scientifique, littéraire ou artistique dont il est l'auteur. **§ 28** Toute pers[onne] a droit à ce que règne, sur le plan social et sur le plan international, un ordre tel que les droits et libertés énoncés dans la présente Déclaration [puis]sent y trouver plein effet. **§ 29** 1. L'individu a des devoirs envers la communauté dans laquelle seul le libre et plein développement de sa personn[alité] est possible. 2. Dans l'exercice de ses droits et dans la jouissance de ses libertés, chacun n'est soumis qu'aux limitations établies par la loi exclusive[ment] en vue d'assurer la reconnaissance et le respect des droits et libertés d'autrui et afin de satisfaire aux justes exigences de la morale, de l'ordre public [et du] bien-être général dans une société démocratique. 3. Ces droits et libertés ne pourront, en aucun cas, s'exercer contrairement aux buts et aux prin[cipes] des Nations Unies. **§ 30** Aucune disposition de la présente Déclaration ne peut être interprétée comme impliquant pour un Etat, un groupement [ou un] individu un droit quelconque de se livrer à une activité ou d'accomplir un acte visant à la destruction des droits et libertés qui y sont énoncés.

Ministère de l'Education nationale. Centre national de documentation pédagogique. Mission de l'éducation artistique et de l'action cult[urelle].
Ruedi Baur, 10 décembre 2001.

001 ALL HUMAN BEINGS ARE BORN FREE
The first article of the Universal Declaration of Human Rights,
linocut print by Otavio Roth.
CREATOR Provided by Zack Lee
SOURCE www.flickr.com/photos/
riacale/1347847390/

002 UNIVERSAL DECLARATION OF
HUMAN RIGHTS
Otavio Roth's linocut prints
of the thirty articles of the
Universal Declaration of Human
Rights, on display at the General
Assembly of the United Nations.
CREATOR Provided by Zack Lee
SOURCE www.flickr.com/photos/
riacale/1347846108/in/set-72157
601800761376/

003 UNIVERSAL DECLARATION OF HUMAN
RIGHTS, THE HAGUE
CREATOR Provided by Paul
SOURCE www.flickr.com/photos/
gravlax/849488349/

004 UNIVERSAL DECLARATION OF
HUMAN RIGHTS, CONCORDE
STATION, PARIS
CREATOR Françoise Schein;
provided by Hervé
SOURCE www.flickr.com/photos/
hervephotos/1157373739/

005 UNIVERSAL DECLARATION OF
HUMAN RIGHTS, ARTICLE 5
CREATOR Carrie Musgrave
SOURCE Livebabylive.com

006 HUMAN RIGHTS FOR CHINA - BELGIUM
Amesty International Belgium made
the AI logo from 26,105 candles
in a candlelit vigil in support
of Chinese human rights activists.
CREATOR Provided by The
China Debate
SOURCE www.flickr.com/photos/2755
4618@N07/2805269403/
DATE 4 June 2008

007 WINDSOR LAW: HUMAN RIGHTS
FILM FESTIVAL
CREATOR Provided by Anthony
Van Pham
SOURCE www.flickr.com/photos/avp17/
1905906741/
DATE 2007

008 NO VOICE = NO HUMAN RIGHTS
CREATOR _iamimp_
SOURCE www.flickr.com

009 UNIVERSAL DECLARATION OF
HUMAN RIGHTS, ARTICLE 1,
AUSTRIAN PARLIAMENT, VIENNA
CREATOR Provided by
Szilveszter Farkas
SOURCE www.flickr.com/photos/
szilveszter_farkas/251250342/

010 AMNESTY INTERNATIONAL
OLYMPIC GAMES HUMAN RIGHTS
TORTURE ARCHERY
CREATOR TBWA / PARIS for
Amnesty International
SOURCE www.flickr.com/photos/
8663589@N04/2616932102

011 LOVE IS A HUMAN RIGHT - PROTECT
THE HUMAN
CREATOR Provided by Matt Hamm
SOURCE www.flickr.com/photos/
matthamm/208123136/

012 GOLD FÜR MENSCHENRECHTE
[GOLD FOR HUMAN RIGHTS]
CREATOR Harald - HK, Amnesty
International
SOURCE Unknown

013 DÉCLARATION UNIVERSELLE
DES DROITS DE L'HOMME
[UNIVERSAL DECLARATION
OF HUMAN RIGHTS]
CREATOR Ruedi Baur

001
002

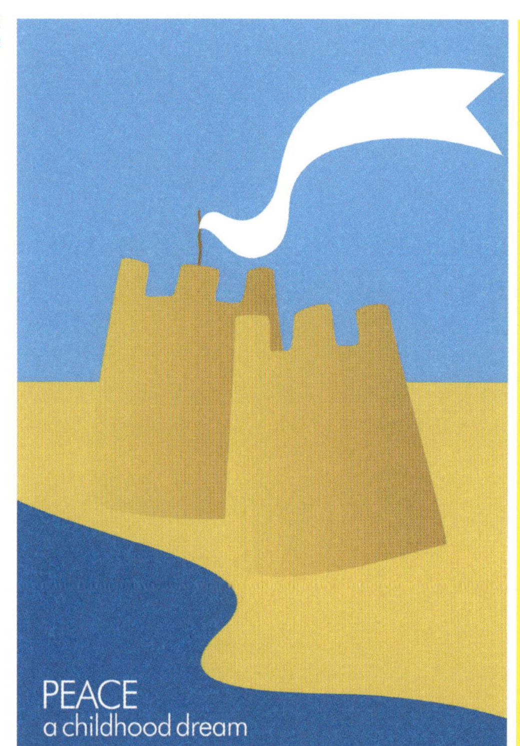

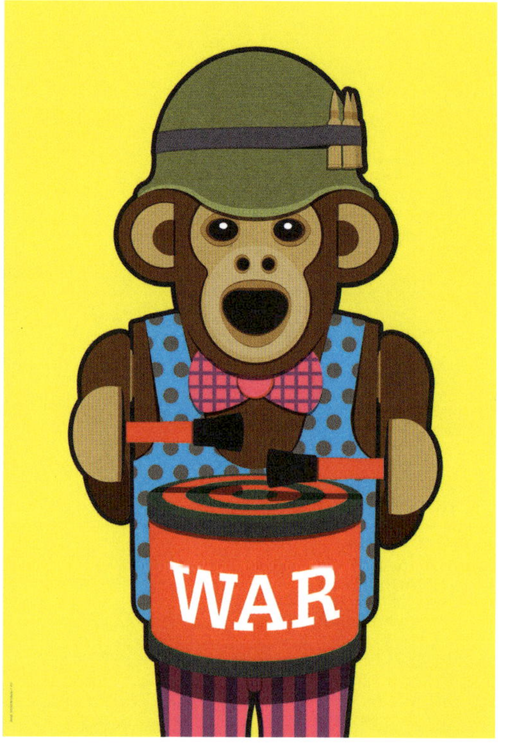

003
004

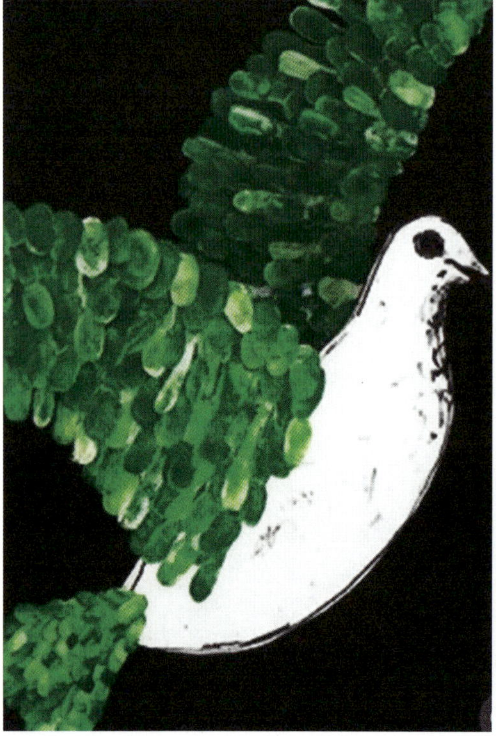

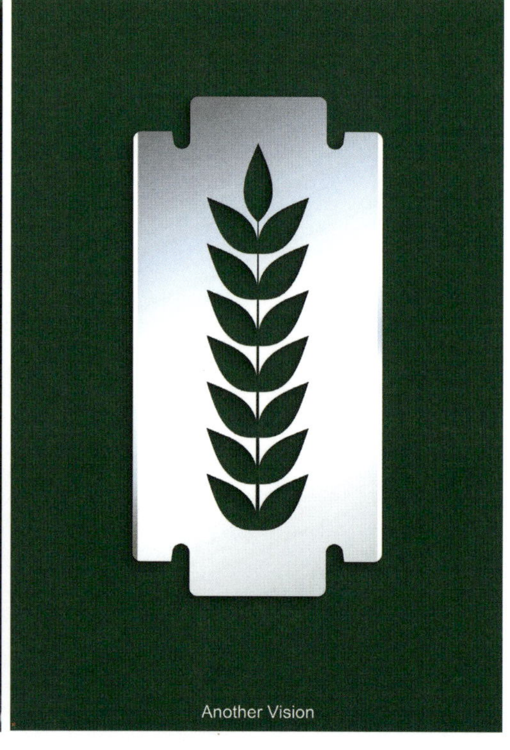

005
006

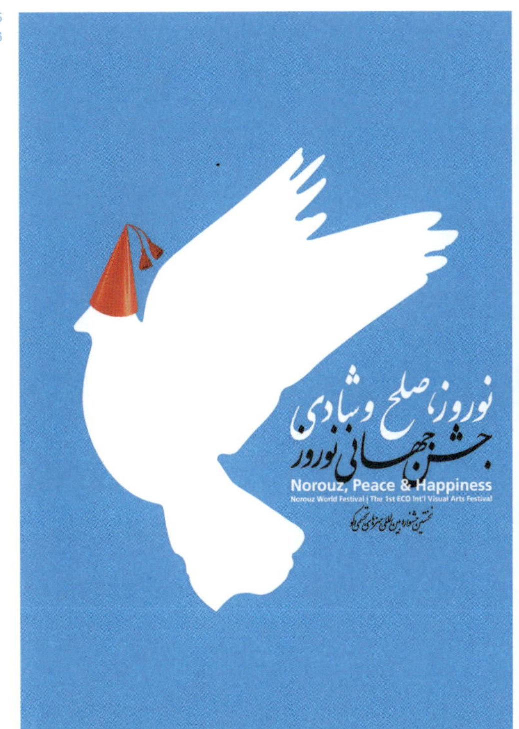

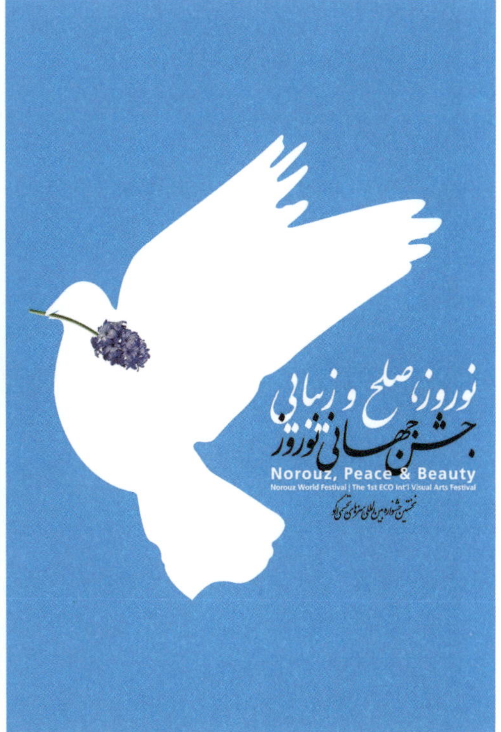

007
008

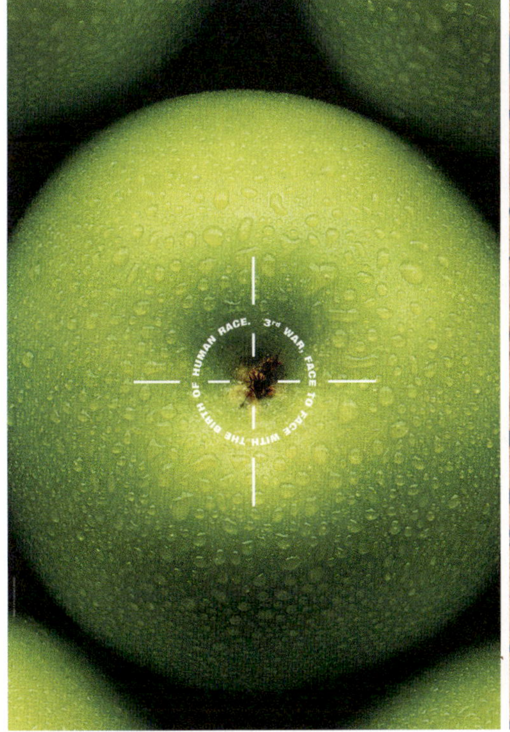

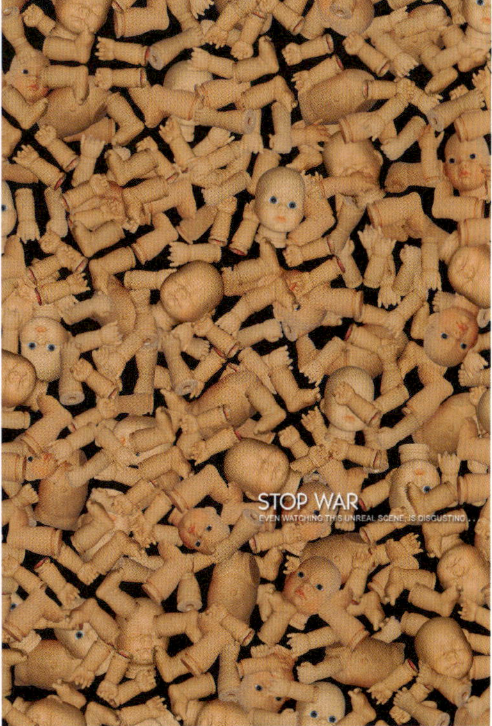

009
010

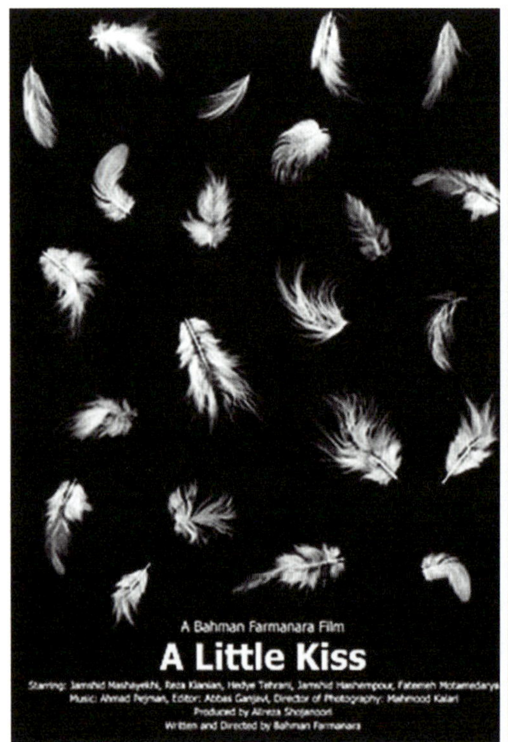
A Bahman Farmanara Film
A Little Kiss
Starring: Jamshid Mashayekhi, Reza Kianian, Hedye Tehrani, Jamshid Hashempour, Fatemeh Motamedarya
Music: Ahmad Pejman, Editor: Abbas Ganjavi, Director of Photography: Mahmood Kalari
Produced by Alireza Shojanoori
Written and Directed by Bahman Farmanara

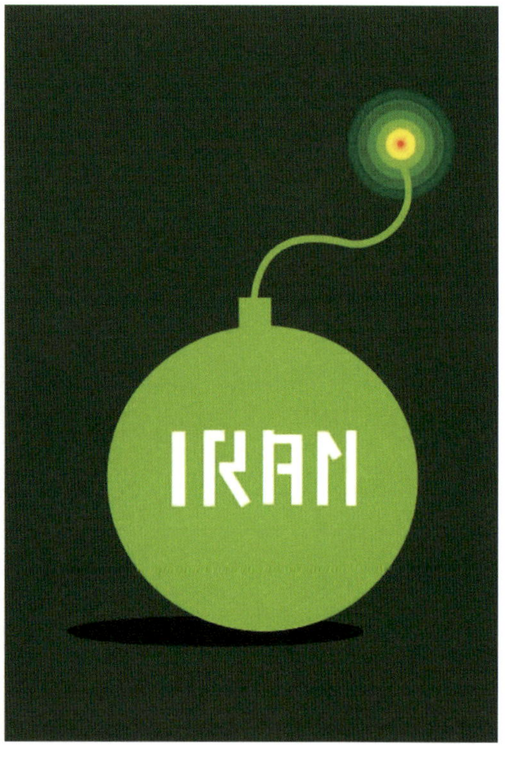
IRAN

011

PEACE

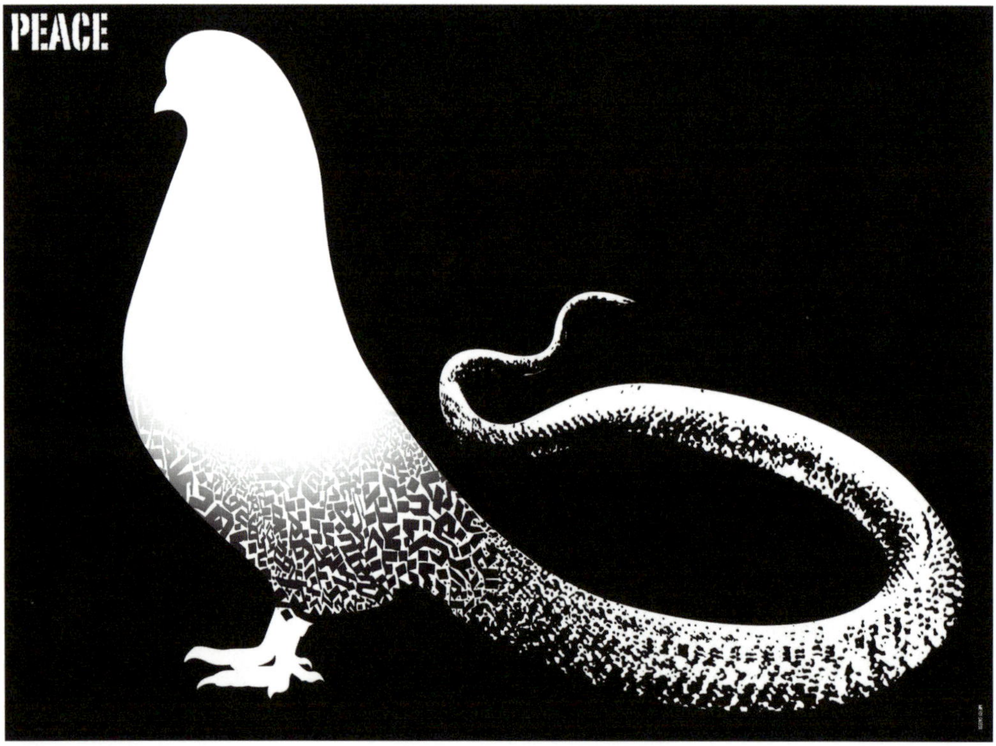

012
013

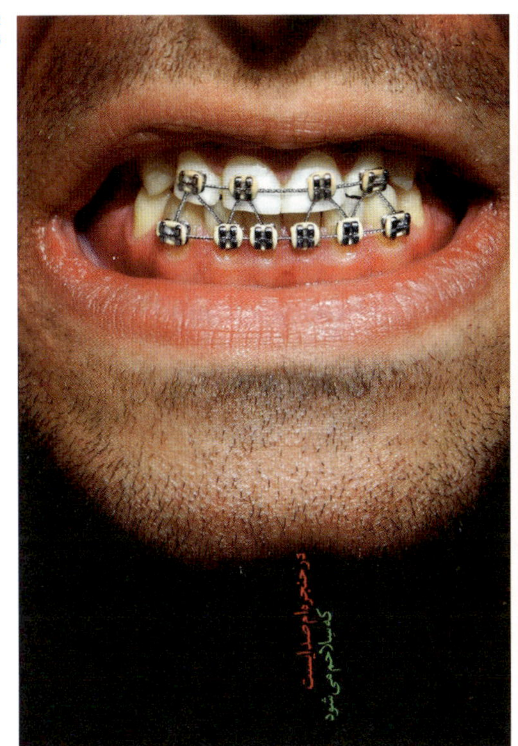

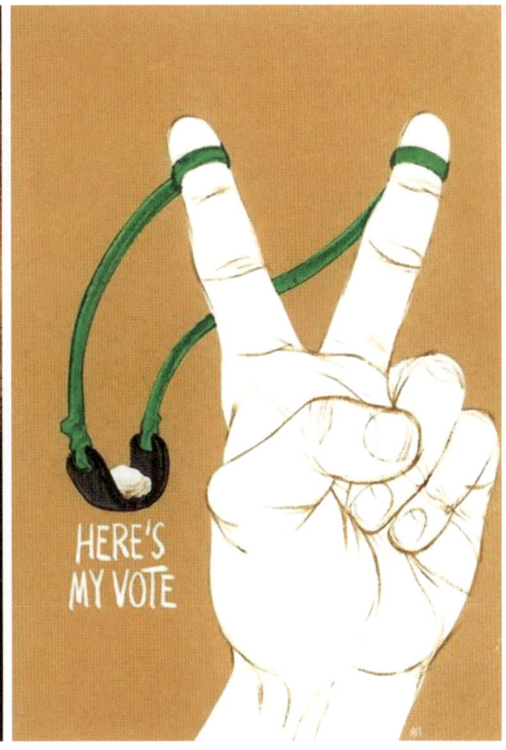

014
015

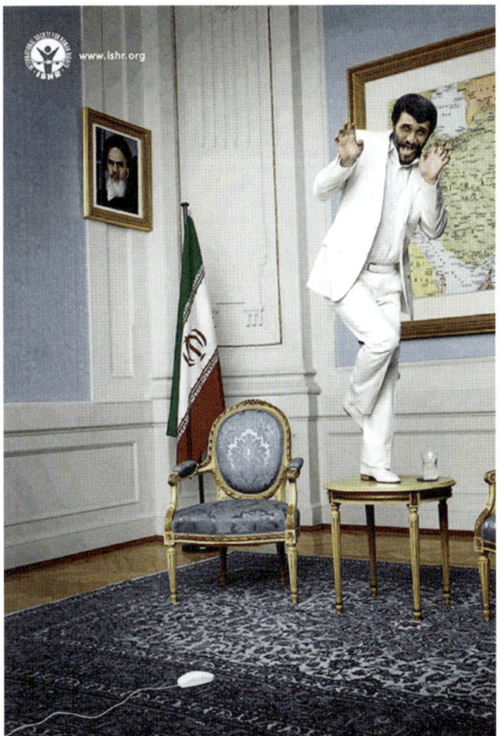

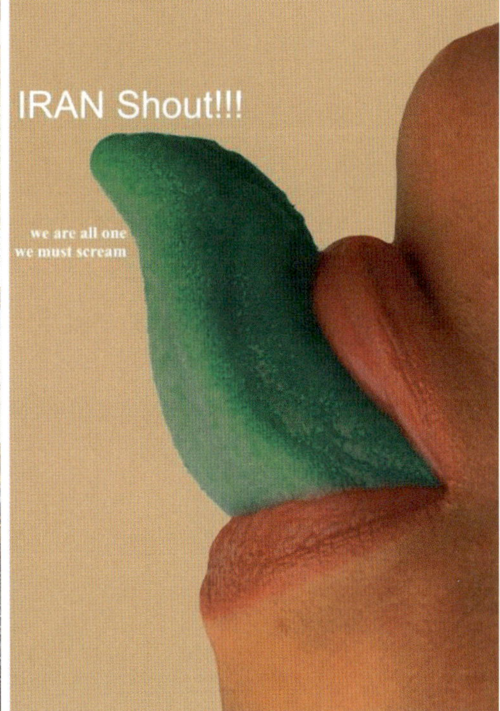

016
017

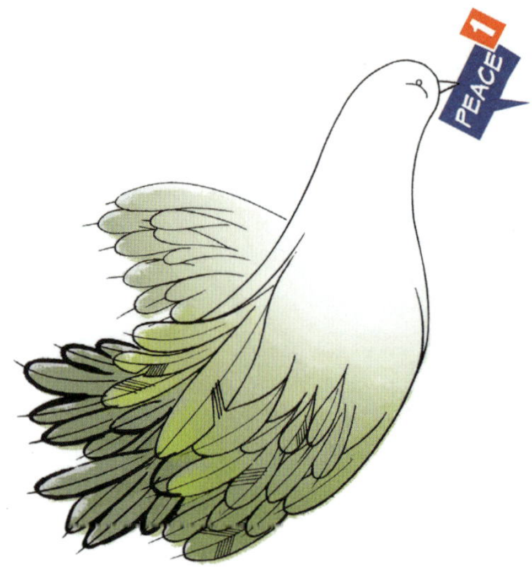

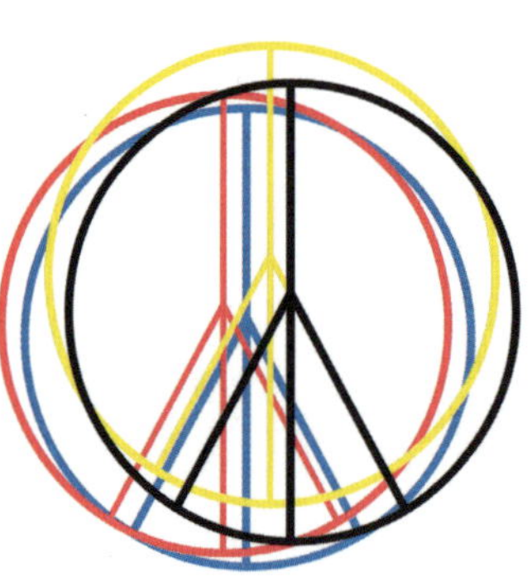
Let's register it!

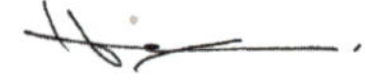

018
019

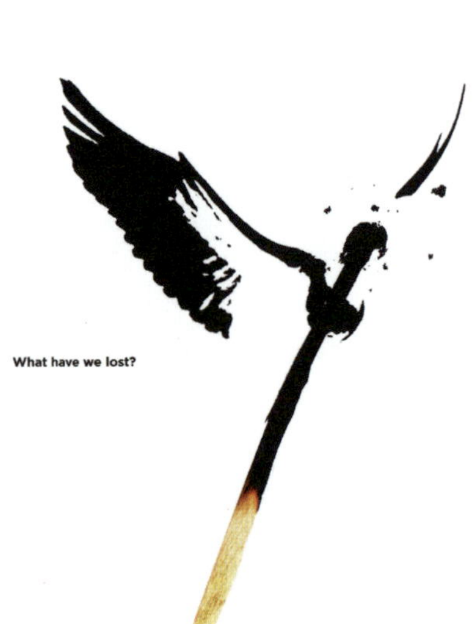

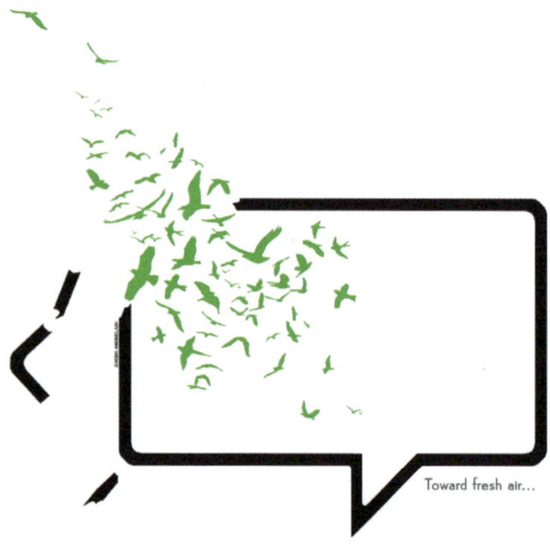

020
021

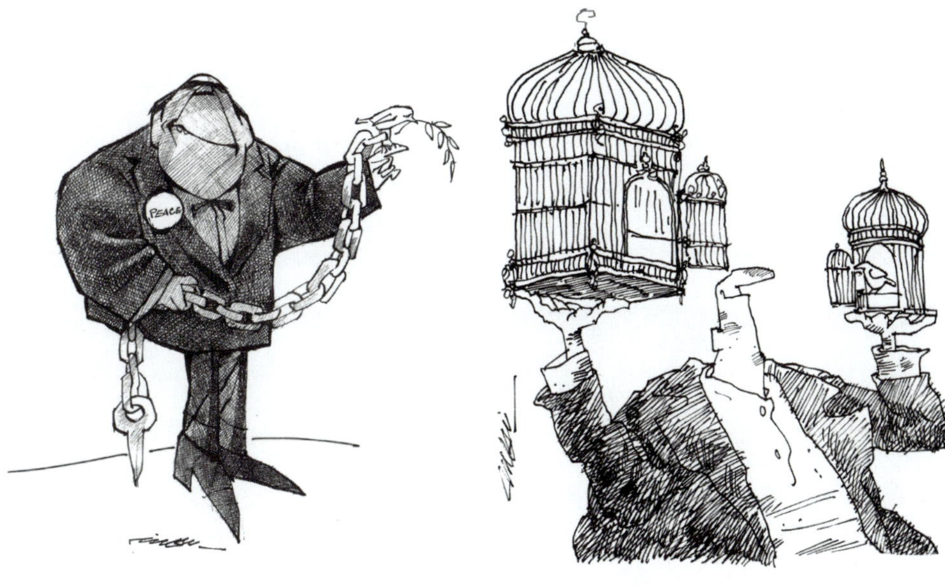

022
023

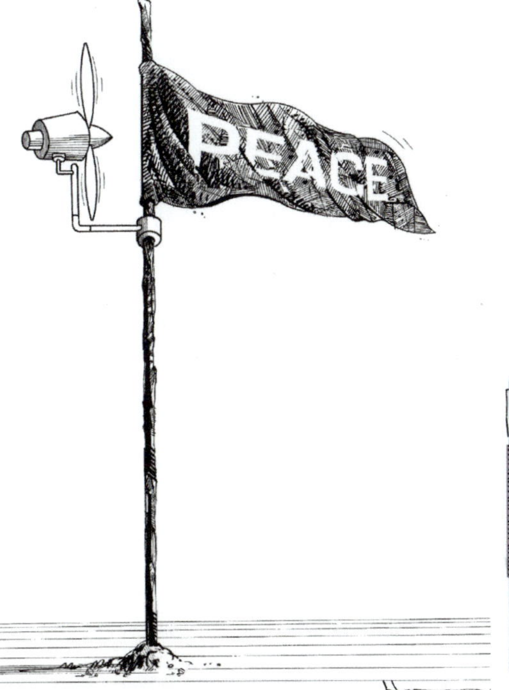

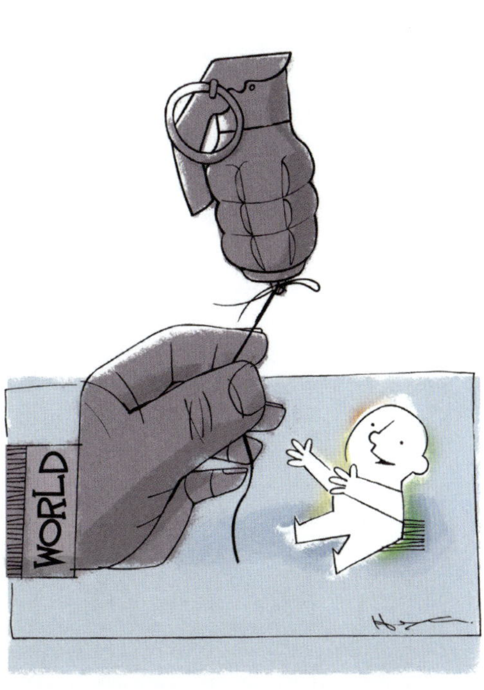

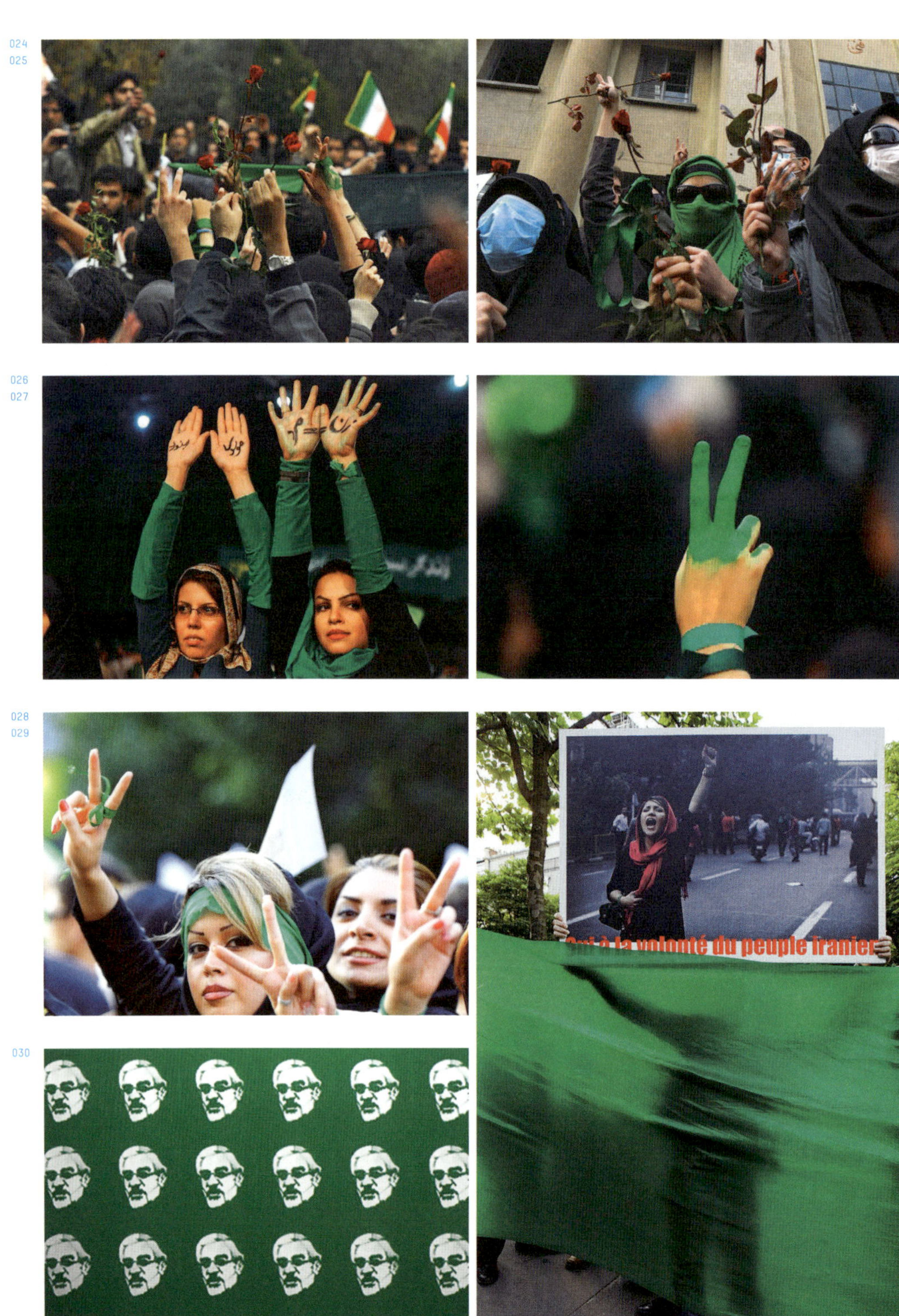
Oui à la volonté du peuple iranien

001 PEACE, A CHILDHOOD DREAM
     CREATOR Alireza Mostafazadeh
     DATE 2007

002 FUNNY GAMES
     CREATOR Behzad Motebaheri
     DATE 2010

003 SUPPORT IRAN
     CREATOR Lauren Rolwing
     SOURCE www.logorevue.sk

004 ANOTHER VERSION
     CREATOR Sohrab Marzban
     DATE 2009

005 NOROUZ, PEACE AND HAPPINESS
     CREATOR Ramina Naghioun
     DATE 2012

006 NOROUZ, PEACE AND BEAUTY
     CREATOR Ramina Naghioun
     DATE 2012

007 3RD WAR, FACE-TO-FACE WITH THE
     BIRTH OF THE HUMAN RACE
     CREATOR Tahamtan Aminian
     DATE 2005

008 STOP WAR
     CREATOR Onish Aminelahi
     DATE 2008

009 A LITTLE KISS
     CREATOR Saed Meshki
     SOURCE www.logorevue.sk

010 IRAN
     CREATOR Elzbieta Chojna
     SOURCE www.logorevue.sk

011 PEACE
     CREATOR Mehdi Saeedi
     DATE 2011

012 MY VOICE IS STUCK IN MY THROAT
     CREATOR Mohammad Hadi Jamali
     SOURCE www.logorevue.sk

013 HERE'S MY VOTE
     CREATOR Alex Nabaum
     SOURCE www.logorevue.sk

014 ISHR SCARED DICTATORS AND THE MOUSE
     International Society for Human
     Rights ran an award-winning
     advertising campaign, "Scared
     Dictators," which shows Hugo
     Chavez [Venezuela], Raul Castro
     [Cuba] and Mahmoud Ahmadinejad
     [Iran] attempting to escape
     a computer mouse.
     CREATOR International Society
     for Human Rights
     SOURCE theinspirationroom.com

015 IRAN SHOUT!!!
     CREATOR Osvaldo Gaona
     SOURCE www.logorevue.sk

016 YOU HAVE A MESSAGE
     CREATOR Hassan Karimzadeh
     DATE 2012

017 LET'S REGISTER IT
     CREATOR Fatemeh Karkehabadi
     DATE 2006

018 WHAT HAVE WE LOST?
     CREATOR Pedram Harby
     DATE 2006

019 TOWARD FRESH AIR
     CREATOR Onish Aminelahi
     DATE 2009

020 UNTITLED
     CREATOR Ahmad Sakhavarz
     DATE 1980

021 UNTITLED
     CREATOR Ahmad Sakhavarz
     DATE 2010

022 PEACE FLAG-WAVING
     CREATOR Hassan Karimzadeh
     DATE 2004

023 UNTITLED
     CREATOR Hassan Karimzadeh
     DATE 2010

024 MOUSAVI SUPPORTERS HOLD RED
     ROSES AND SHOW VICTORY SIGNS
     SOURCE www.guardian.co.uk
     DATE 7 December 2009

025 MOUSAVI SUPPORTERS HOLD
     RED ROSES
     SOURCE www.guardian.co.uk
     DATE 7 December 2009

026 IRAN'S ELECTION
     CREATOR Zohreh Soleimani
     SOURCE www.theatlantic.com
     DATE 8 June 2009

027 SOURCE andrewsullivan.thedaily
     beast.com

028 IRAN: 5TH GREEN DAY - 3V
     CREATOR Hamed Saber
     SOURCE www.flickr.com/photos/hamed

029 PROTEST AGAINST IRAN'S VIOLENT
     REPRESSION TOWARD ITS PEOPLE
     CREATOR Provided by
     looking4poetry
     SOURCE www.flickr.com/photos/
     looking4poetry/3654598591

030 BY THE HORSES WHO RUN PAINTING
     CREATOR Shahab Fotouhi
     SOURCE ingreen.tumblr.com

001
002

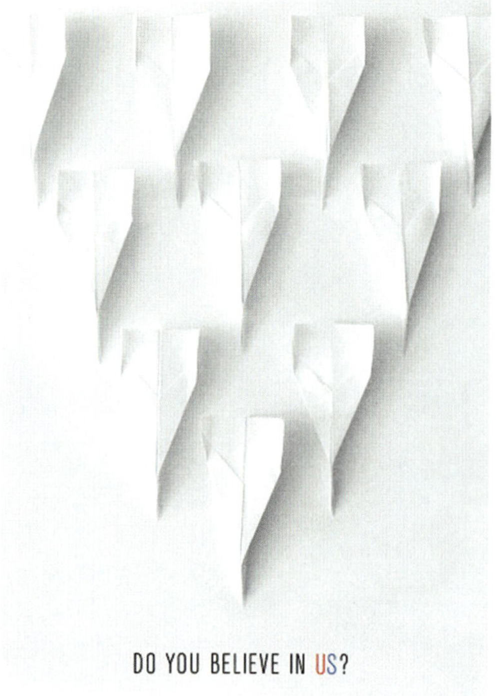

003
004

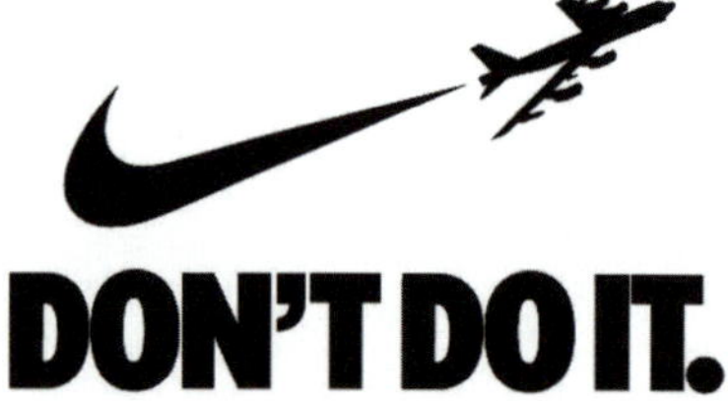

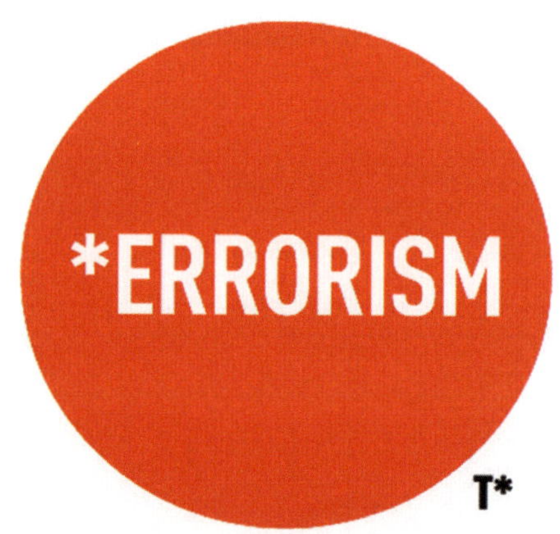

005
006

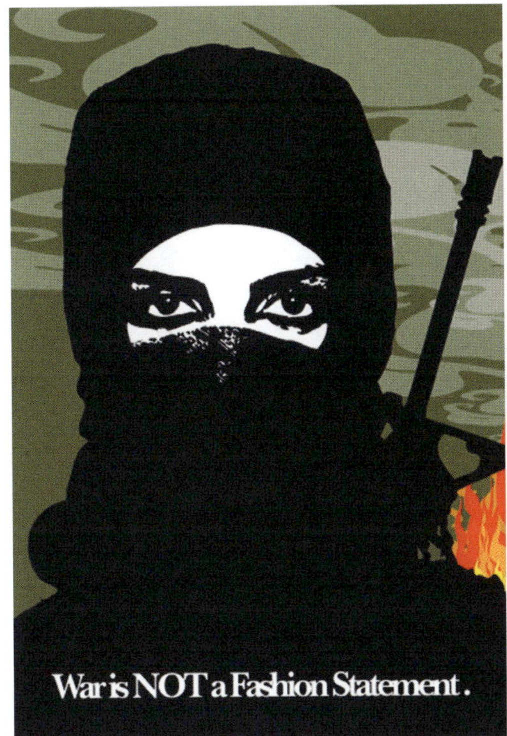

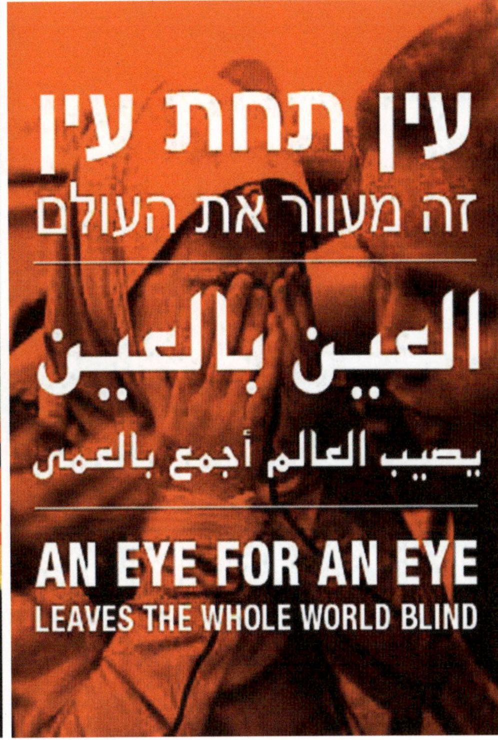

007
008

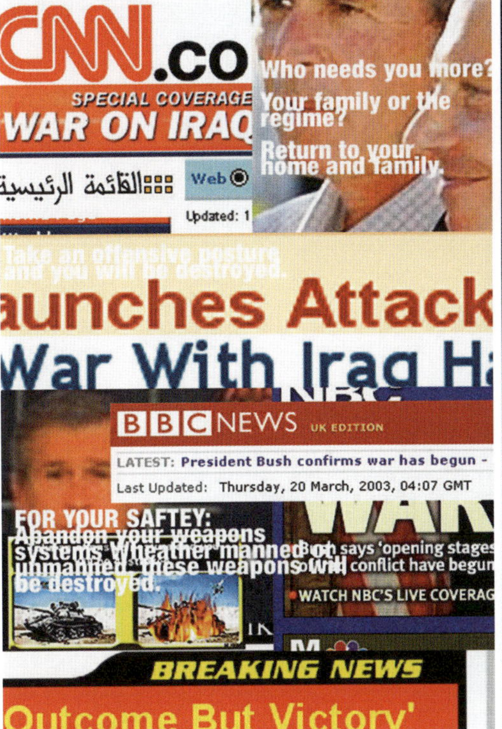

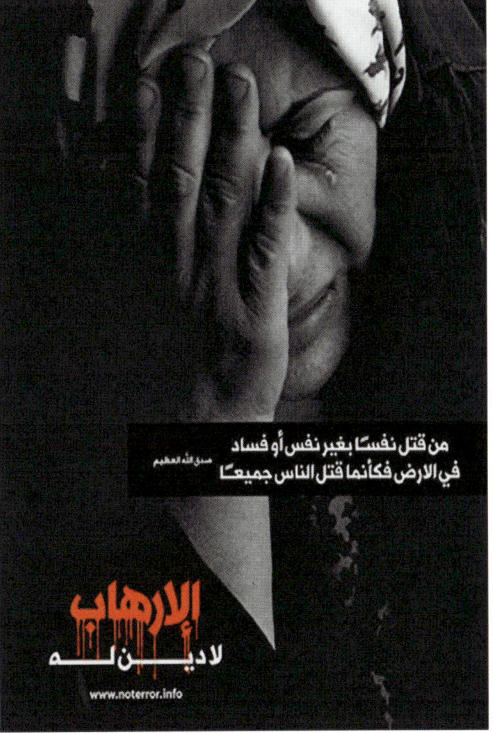

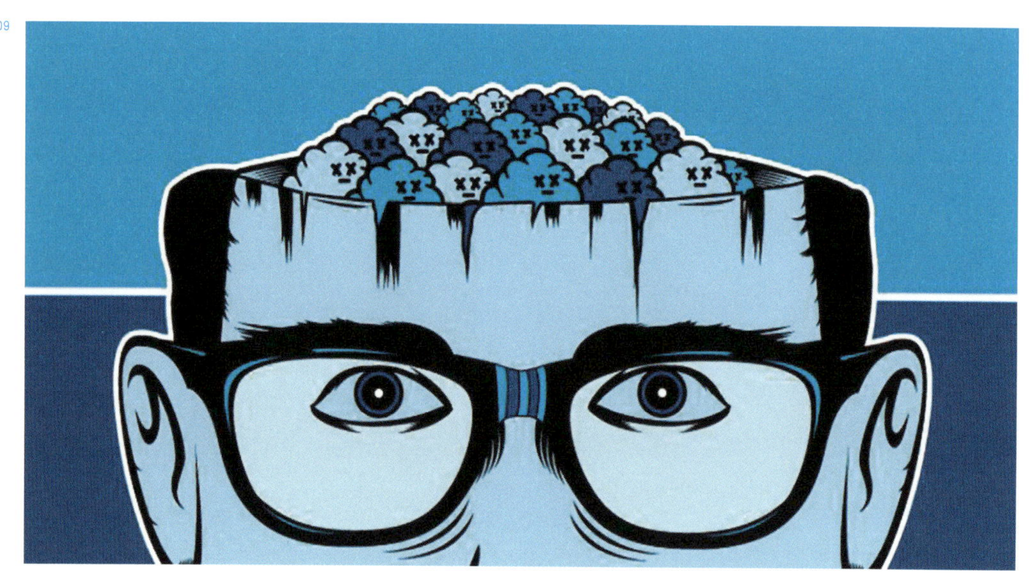

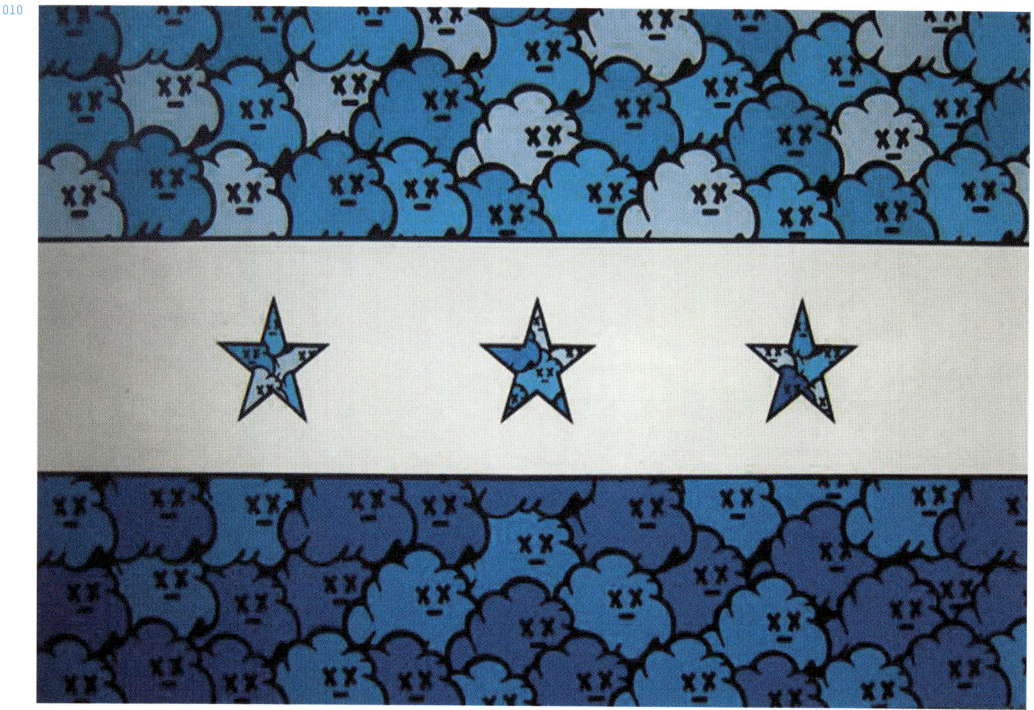

011
012

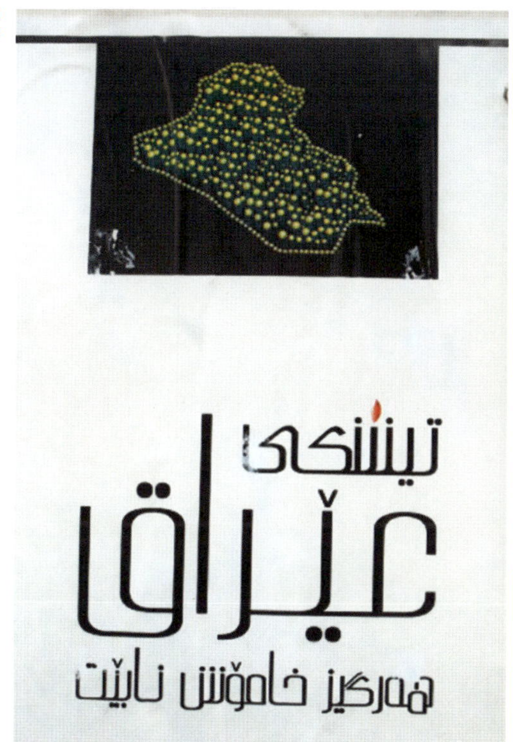

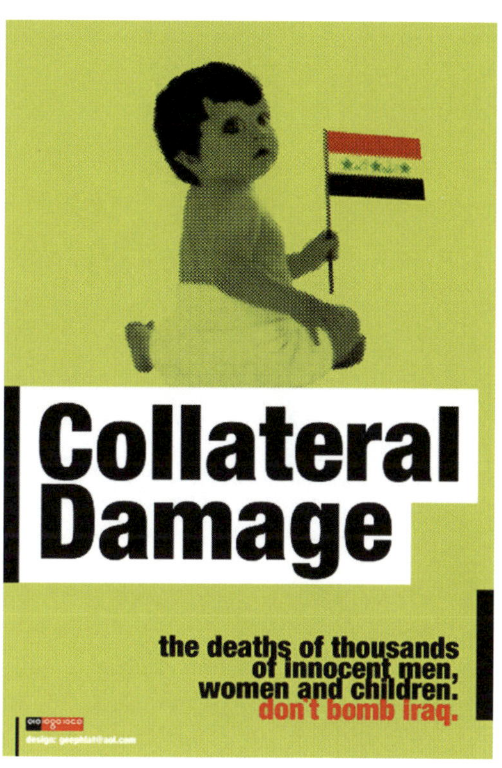

013

NEXT
014

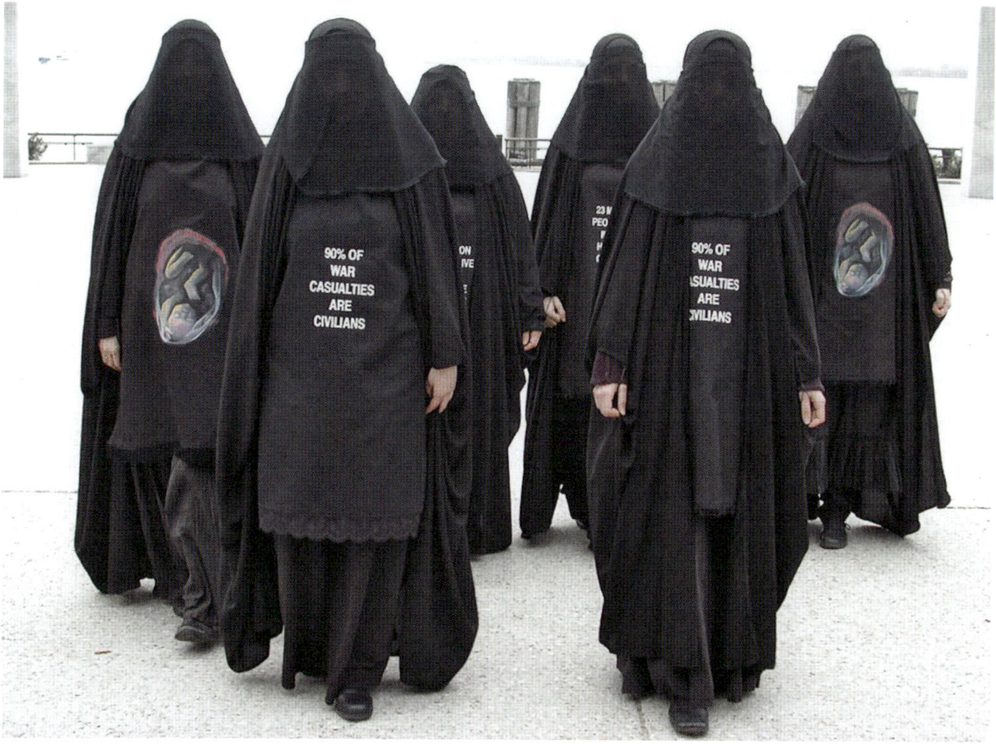

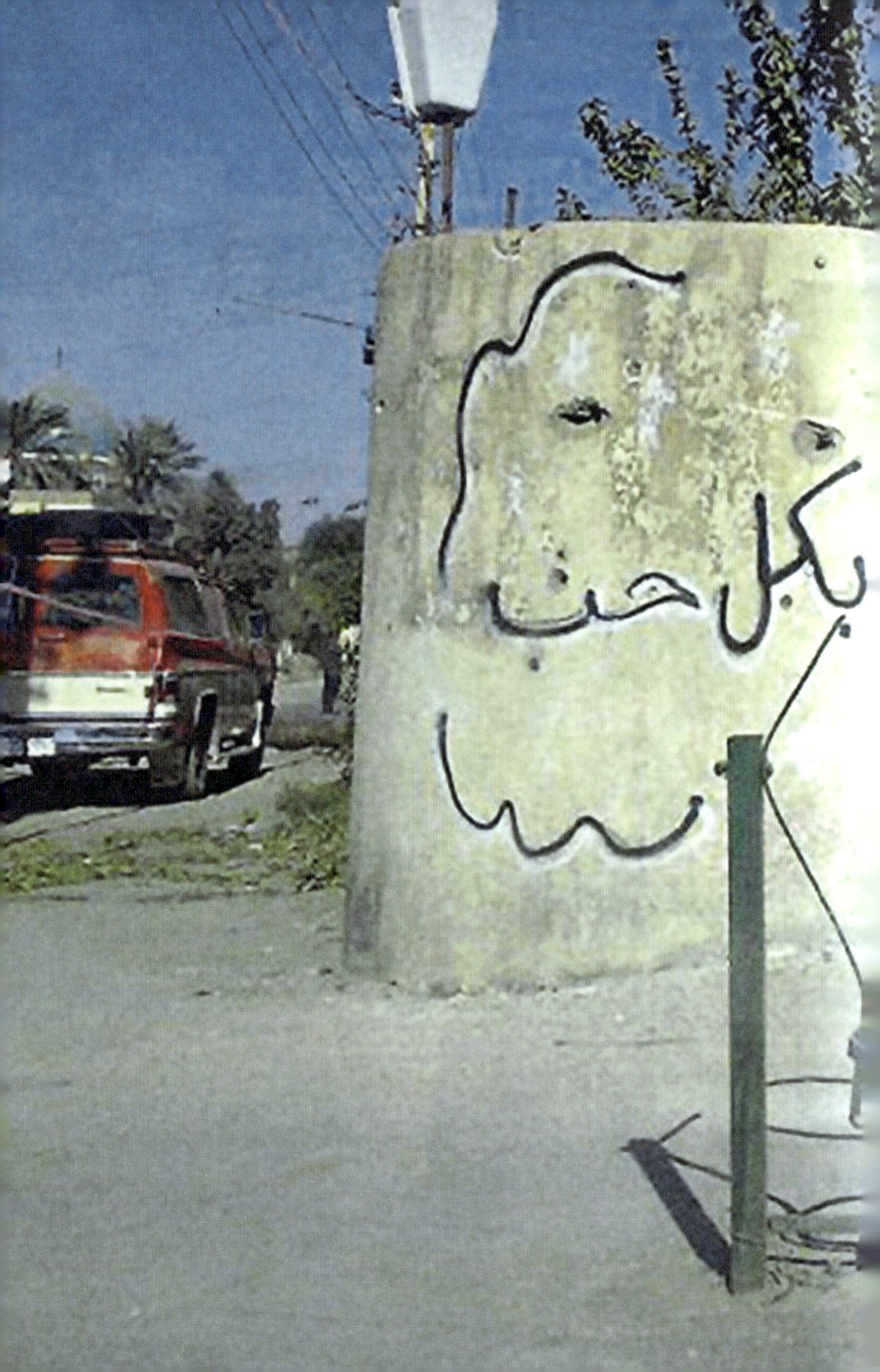

بكل حب
سلا

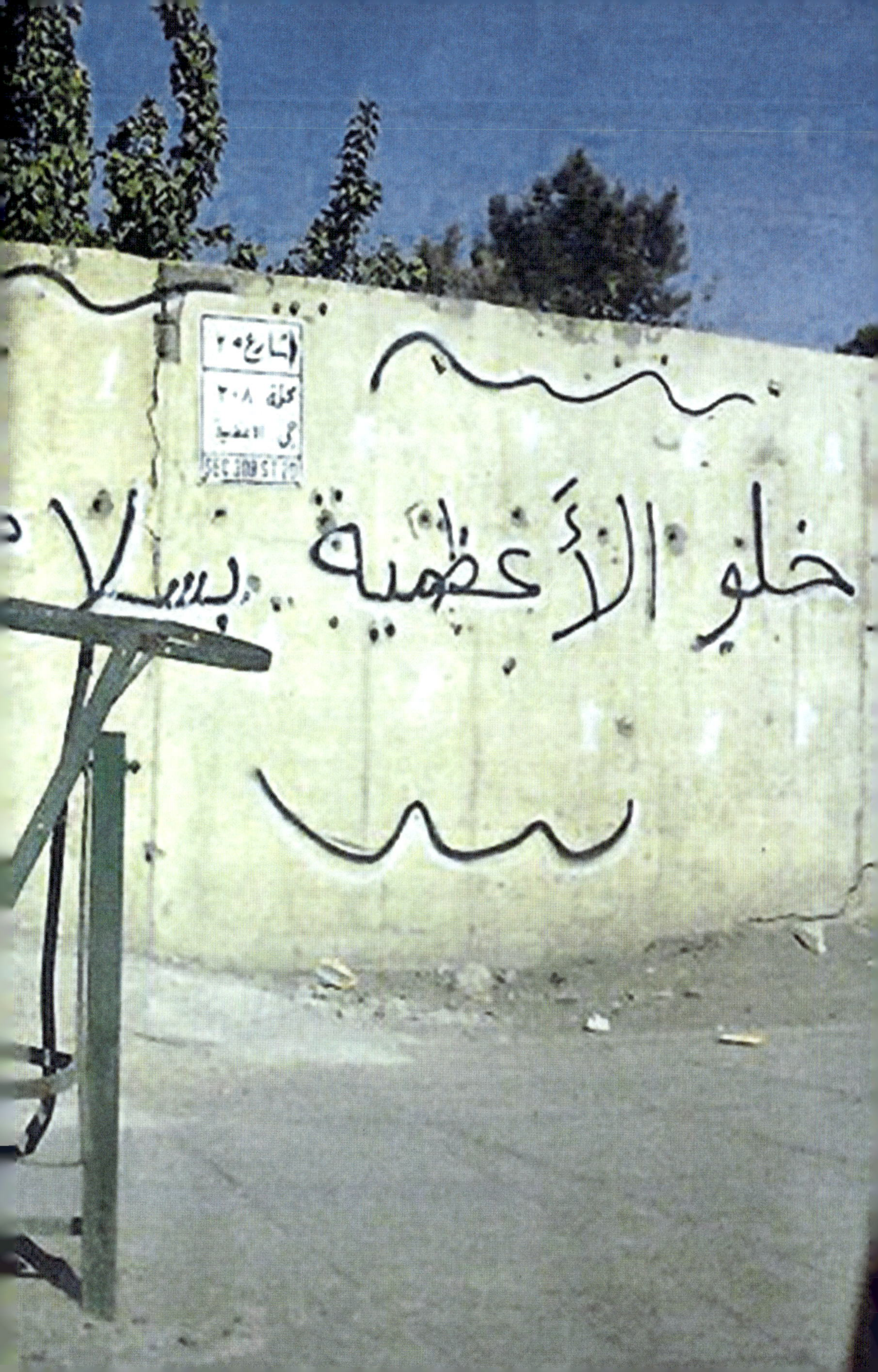
شارع ٢٠٤
محلة ٢٠٨
حي الأعظمية
خلو الأعظمية

015

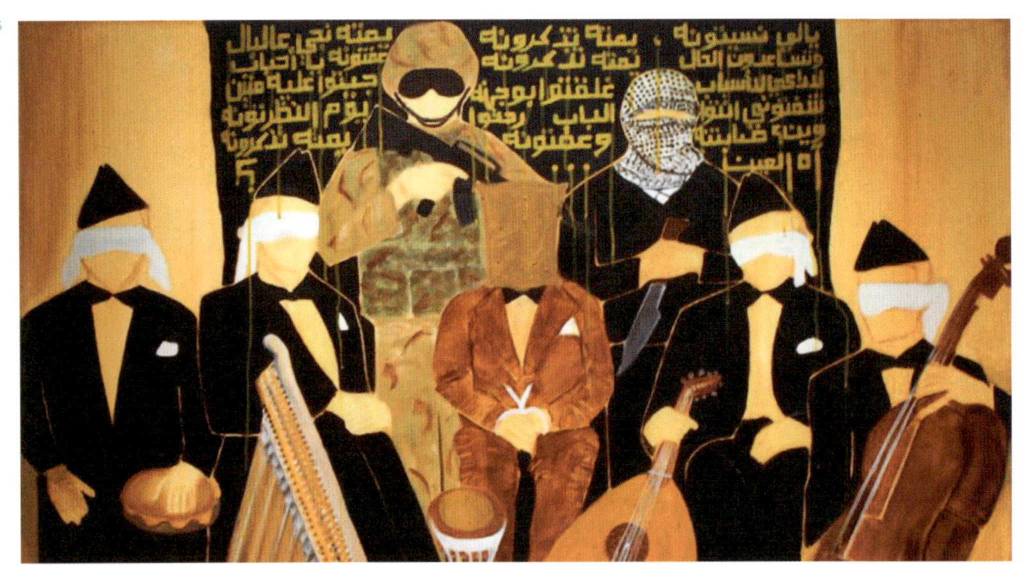

016

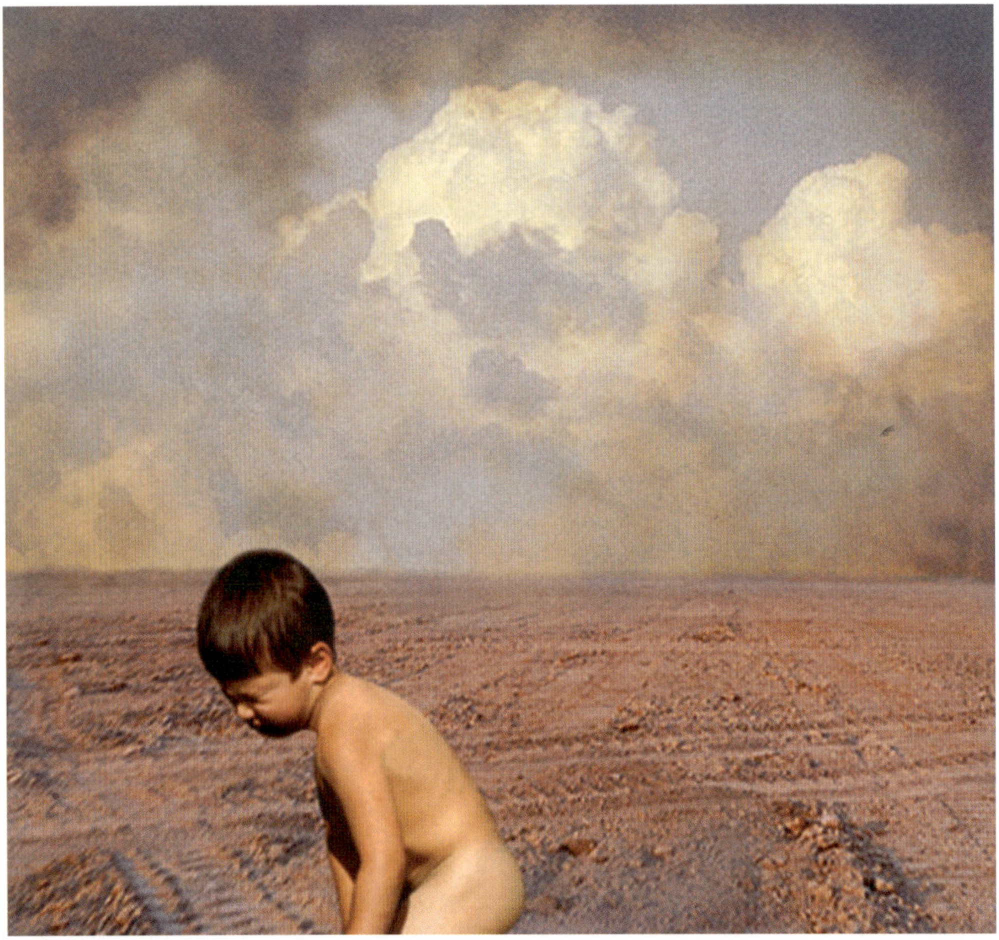

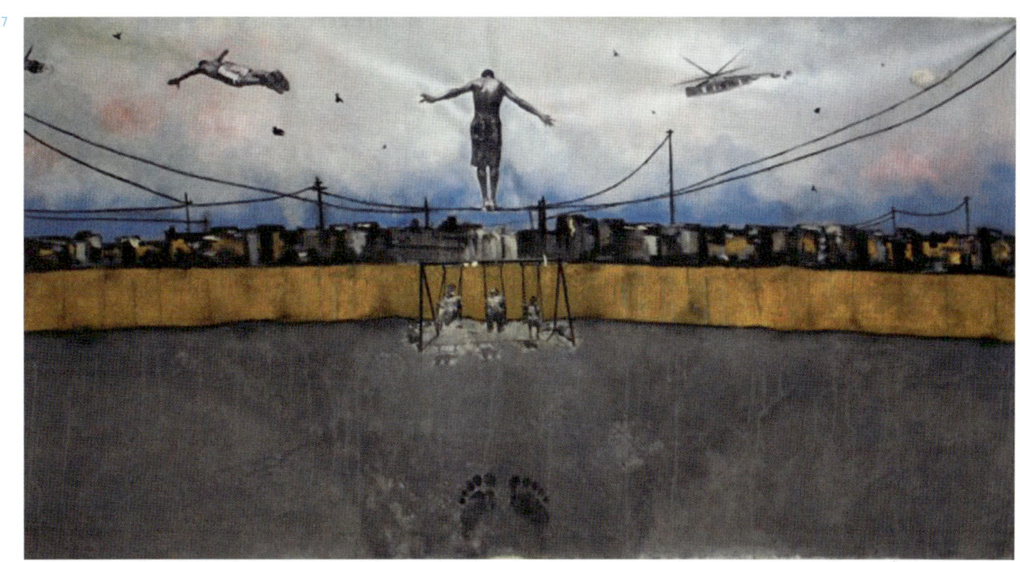

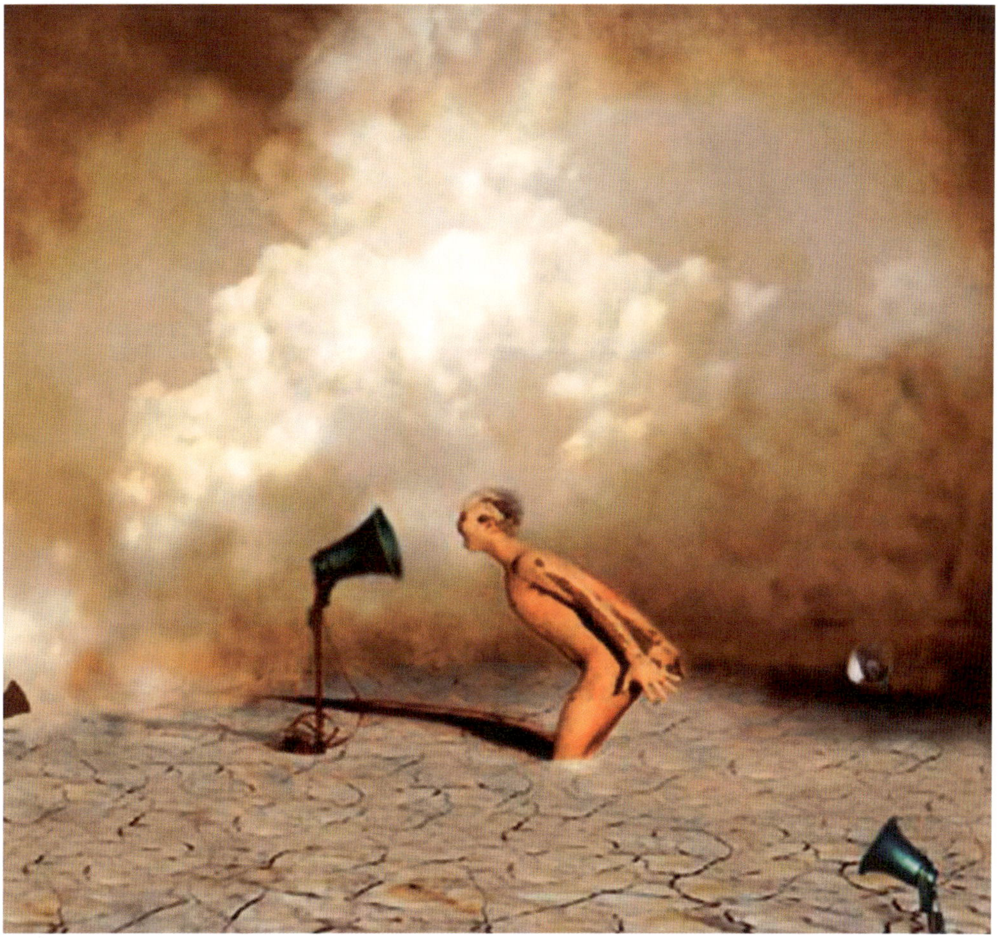

019

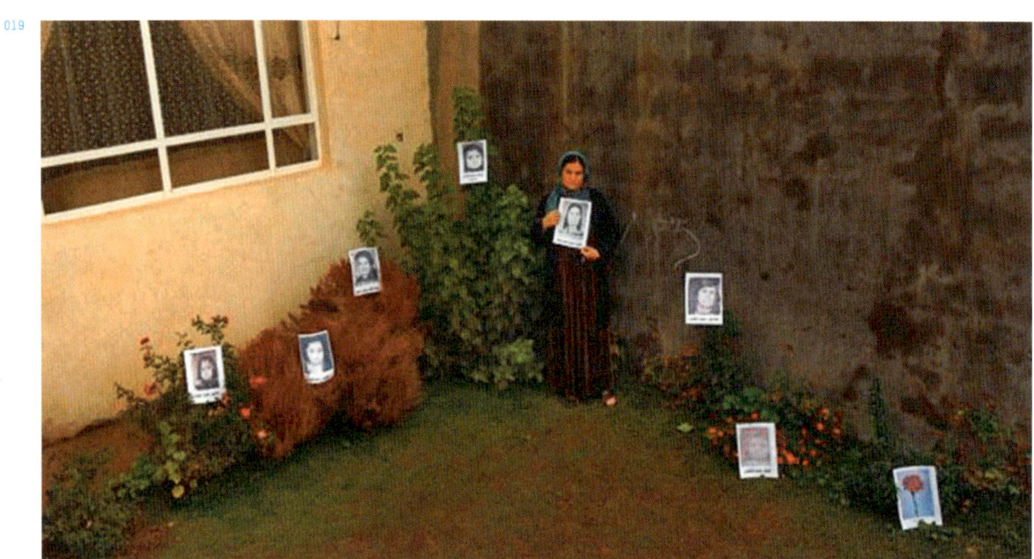

020

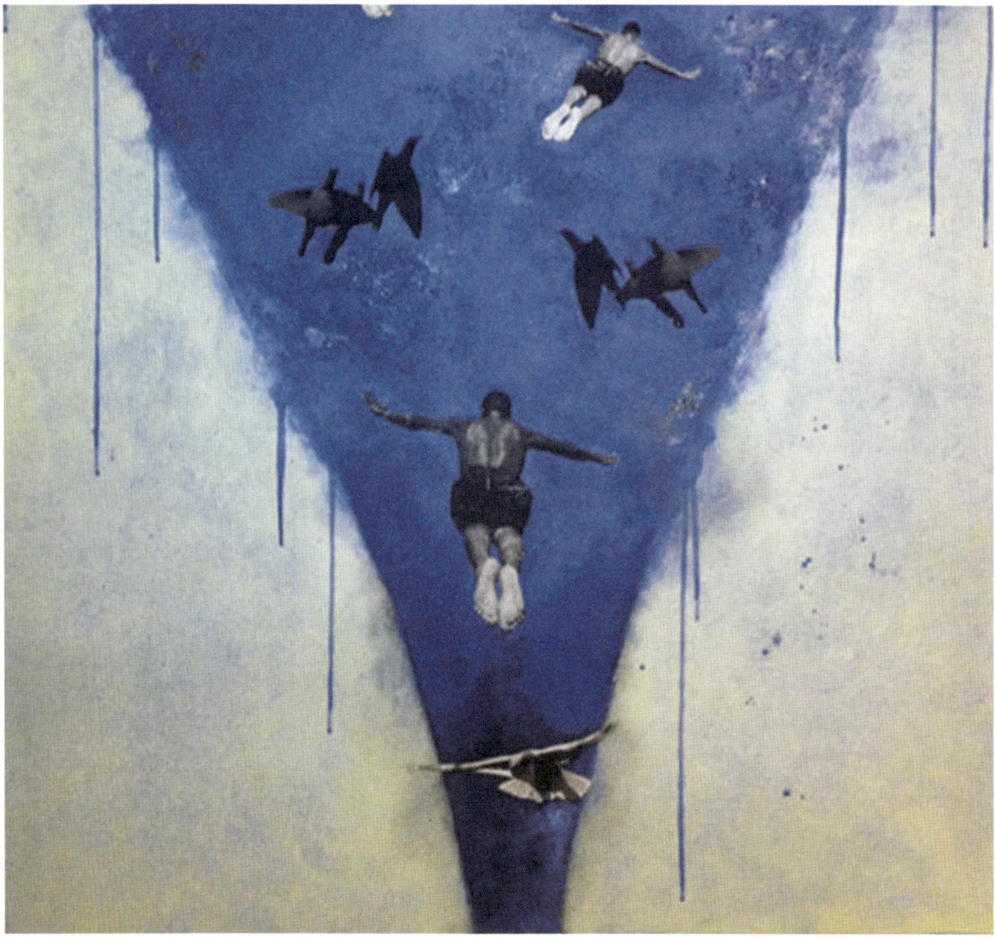

001 YOU BELIEVE IN US?
CREATOR Armin Vit
SOURCE www.miniaturegigantic.com

002 CONNECT
CREATOR DJK
SOURCE www.miniaturegigantic.com

003 DON'T DO IT
SOURCE www.miniaturegigantic.com

004 *ERRORISM
SOURCE www.miniaturegigantic.com

005 WAR IS NOT A FASHION STATEMENT
SOURCE www.miniaturegigantic.com

006 AN EYE FOR AN EYE LEAVES THE
WHOLE WORLD BLIND
CREATOR John, Social Design Notes
SOURCE blog.alrdesign.com

007 MEDIA OVERLOAD
CREATOR Luis Vazquez
SOURCE www.miniaturegigantic.com

008 SAY NO TO TERROR [TERROR HAS
NO RELIGION]
CREATOR Luis Vazquez
SOURCE blog.alrdesign.com

009 ALL IN MY HEAD
CREATOR Myne
SOURCE www.intheframe.org

010 CLOUD
CREATOR Myne
SOURCE www.intheframe.org

011 THE LIGHT OF IRAQ WILL NOT GO OUT
SOURCE www.michaeltotten.com

012 COLLATERAL DAMAGE
CREATOR geephlat
SOURCE www.miniaturegigantic.com

013 THE PEACE PIECE
CREATOR Adelle Lutz
SOURCE www.creativetime.org

014 UNTITLED
The writing on the wall reads:
"Enter Al-Adamiya with love and
peace." You can see all of the
bullets and shots after a fight
with an Al-Qaeda group.
SOURCE Geert von Kesteren,
*Baghdad Calling: Reports from
Turkey, Syria, Jordan and Iraq*
[Rotterdam: Episode Publishers,
2008], pp. 372-73.

015 THE FORGOTTEN
CREATOR Sundus Abdul-Hadi
SOURCE www.intheframe.org

016 INDIGENOUS
CREATOR Wafaa Bilal
SOURCE www.mocp.org

017 THE FLIGHT, BAGHDAD
CREATOR Sundus Abdul-Hadi
SOURCE www.intheframe.org

018 AJRASS
CREATOR Wafaa Bilal
SOURCE www.mocp.org
DATE 2002

019 THE FORGOTTEN
CREATOR Sundus Abdul-Hadi
SOURCE www.intheframe.org

020 THE FLIGHT, BAGHDAD
CREATOR Sundus Abdul-Hadi
SOURCE www.tamarabdulhadi.com/

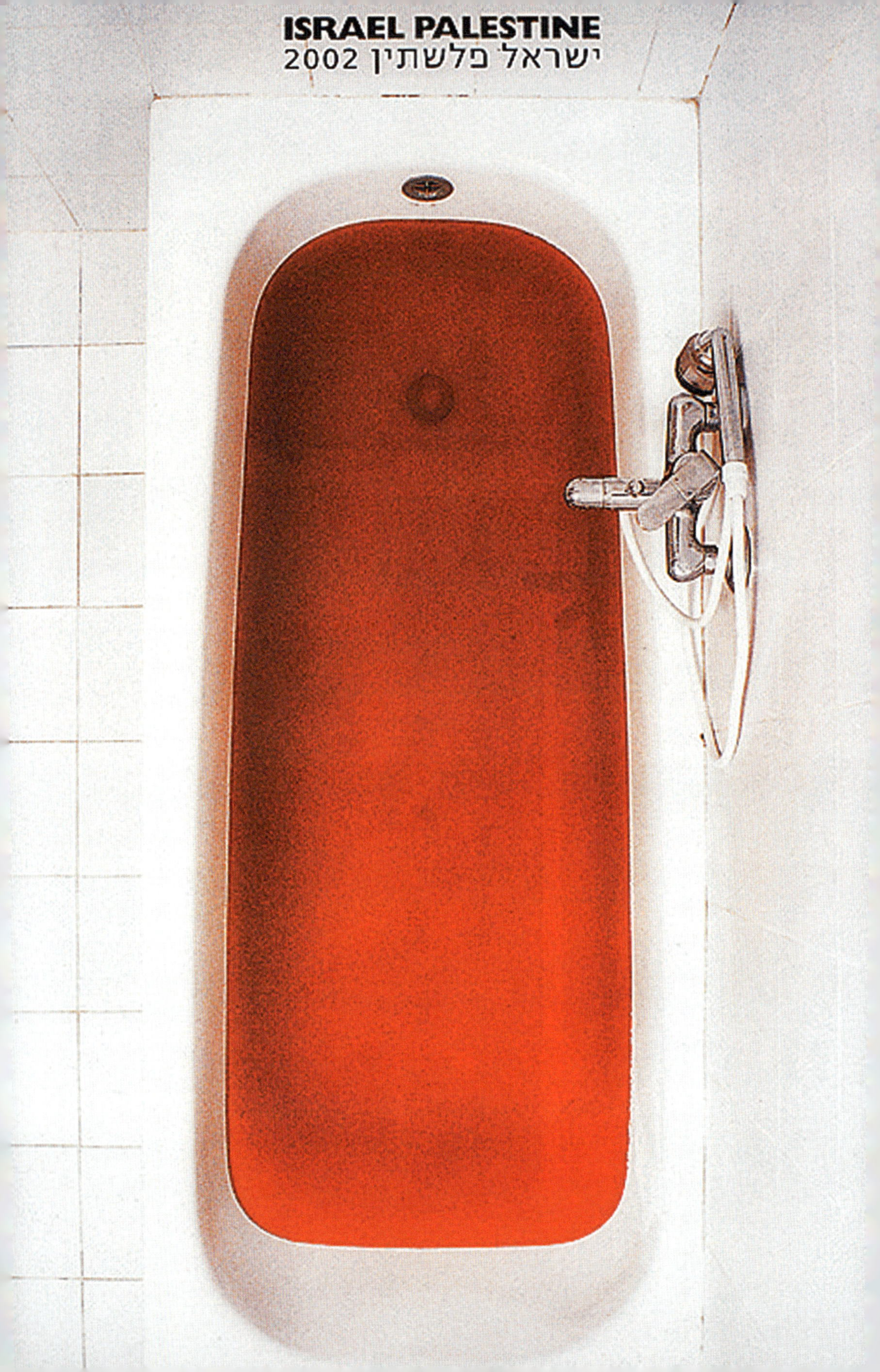
ISRAEL PALESTINE
ישראל פלשתין 2002

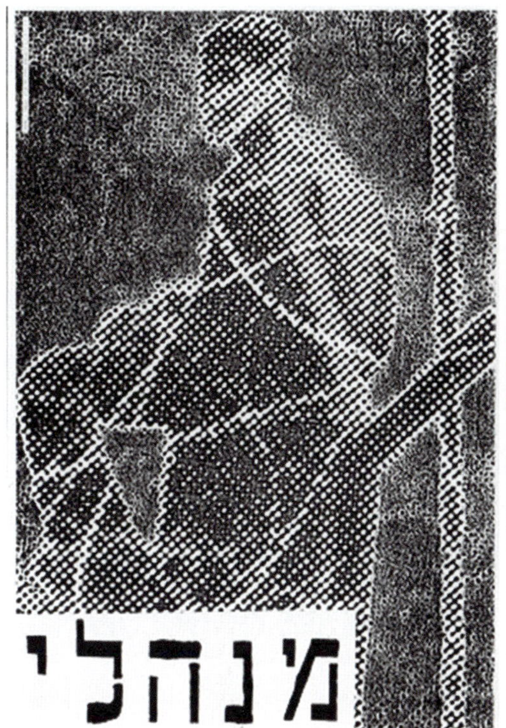
מנהלי

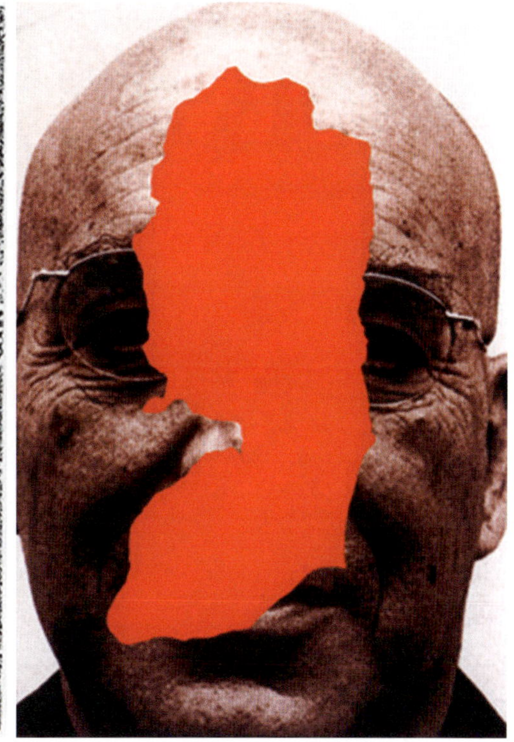

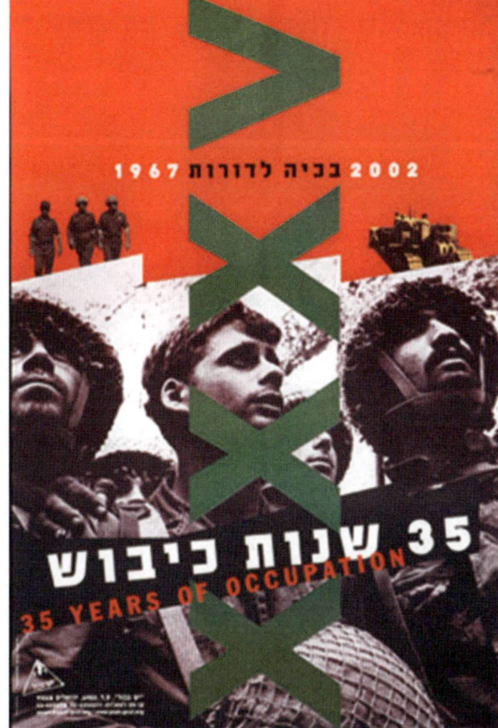
1967 בכיה לדורות 2002
XXXV
שנות כיבוש 35
35 YEARS OF OCCUPATION

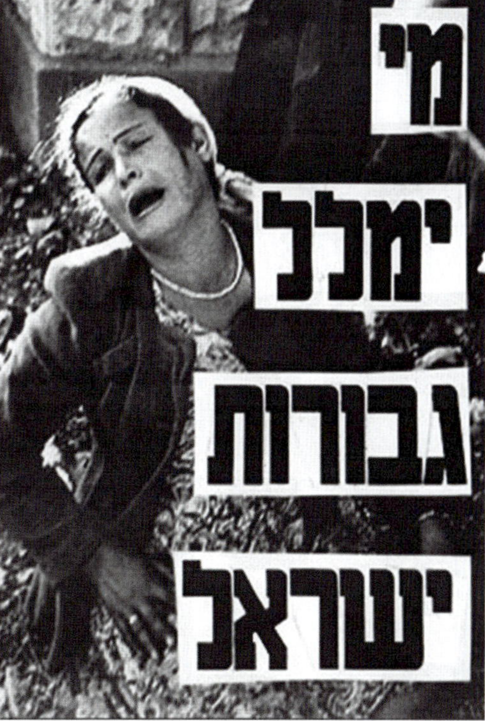
מי
ימלל
גבורות
ישראל

006
007

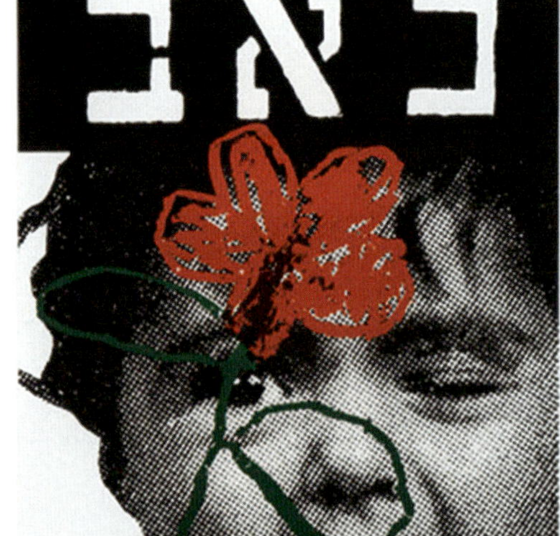

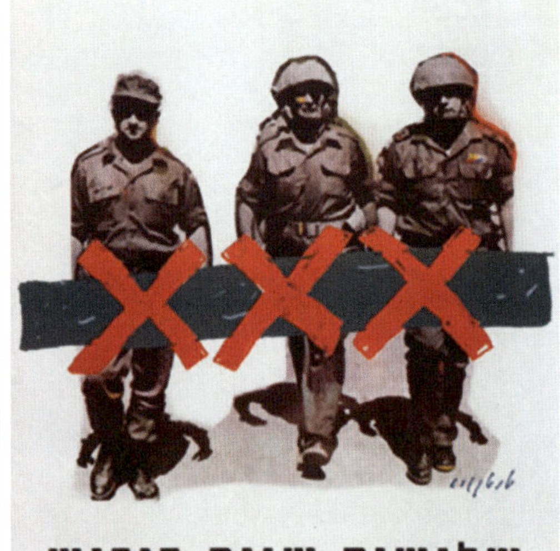

008
009

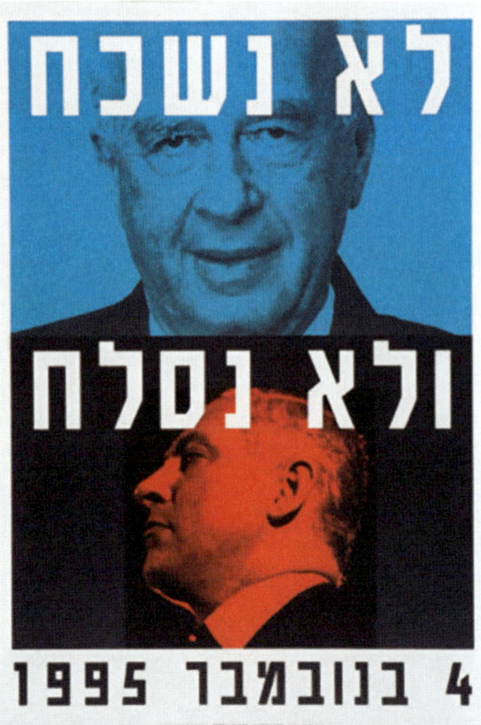

010
011

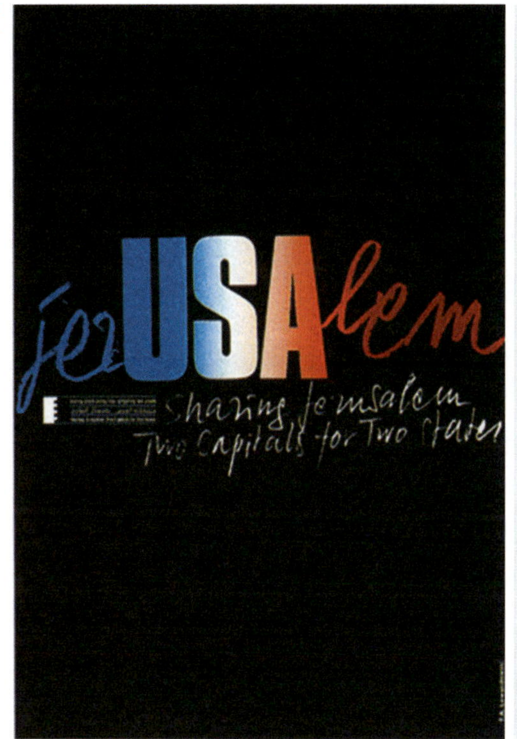

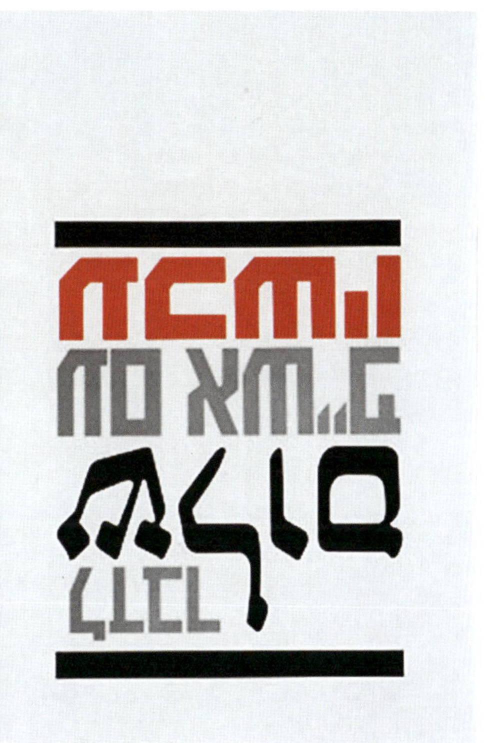

012
013

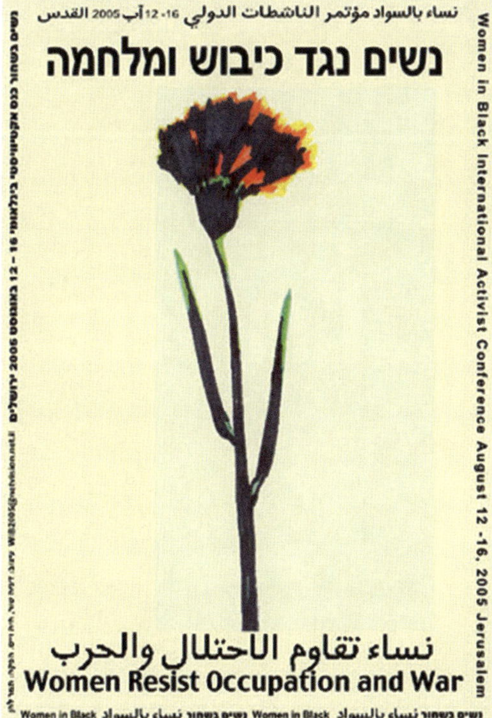

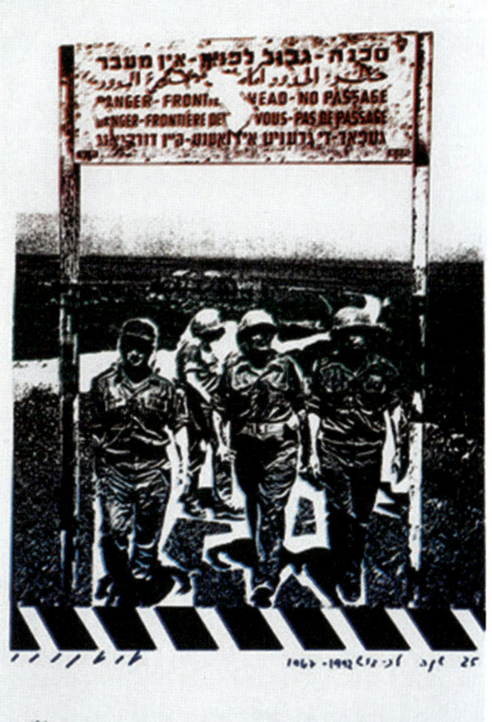

014
015

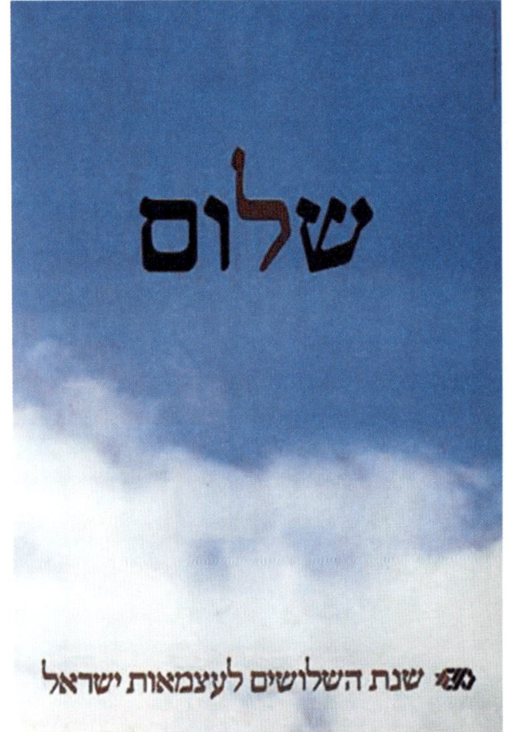

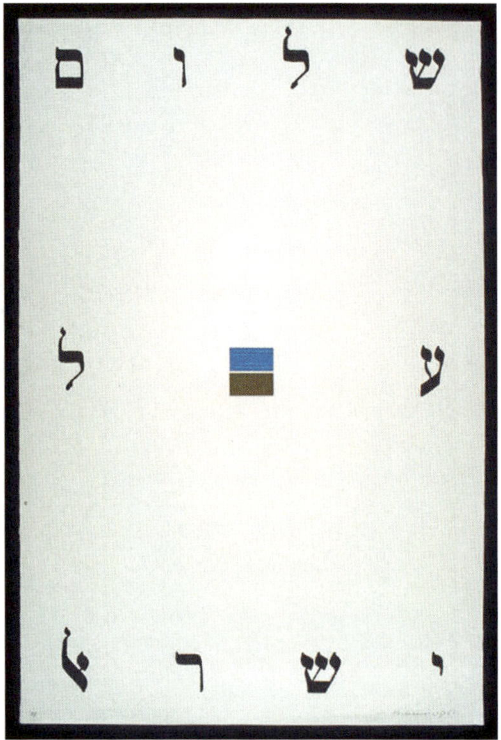

016
017
RIGHT
018

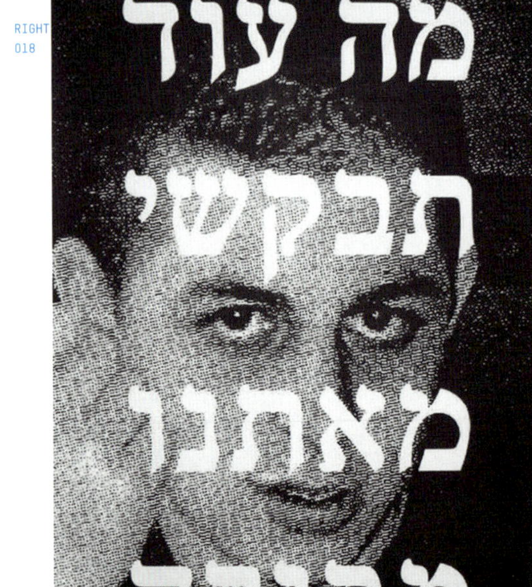

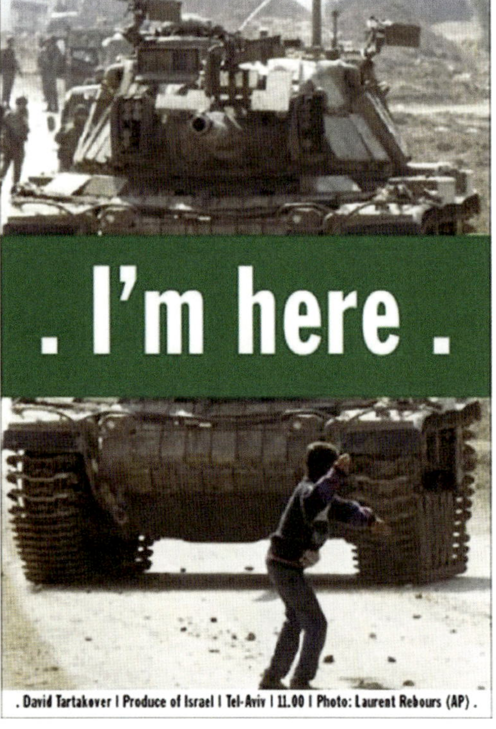

DOWN WITH THE OCCUPATION

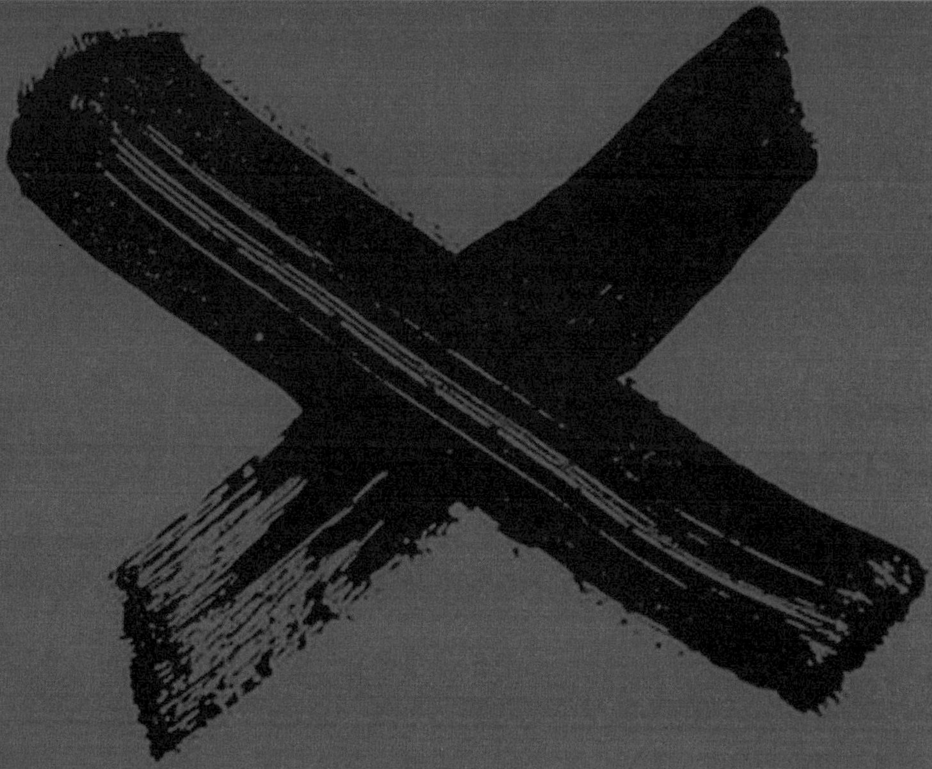

019
020

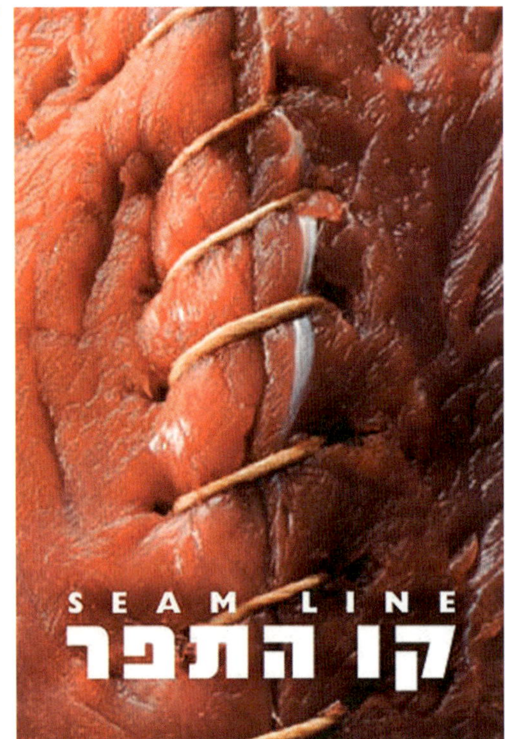

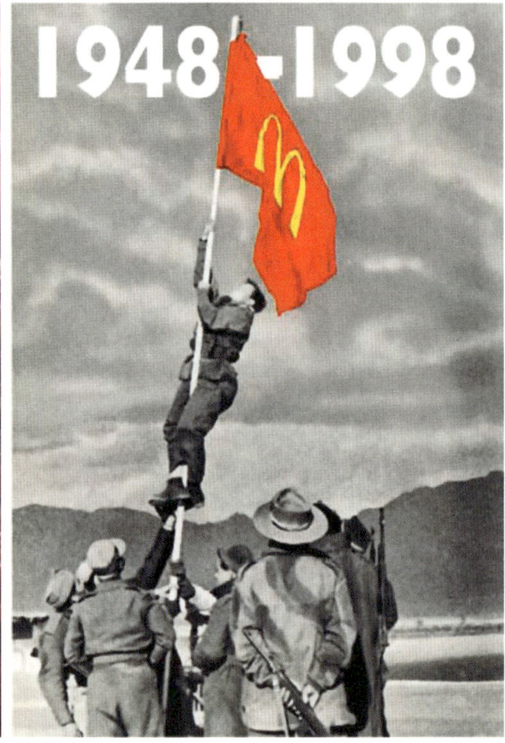

021
022

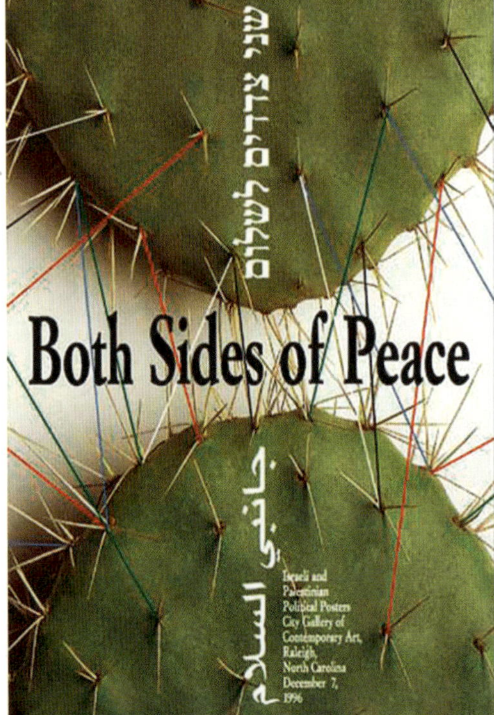

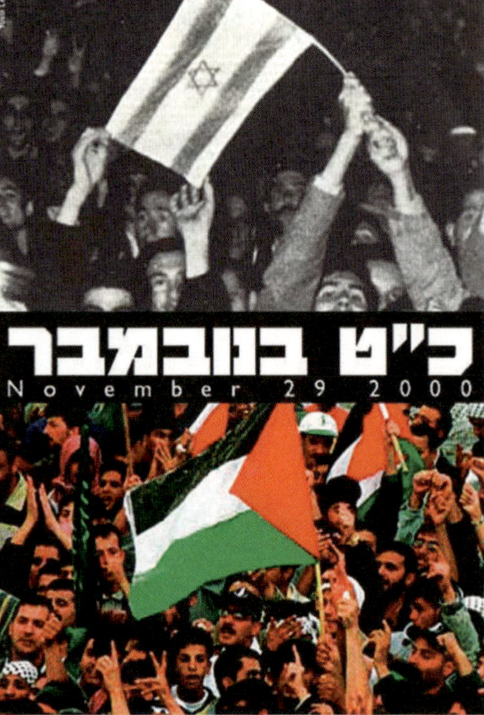

023
024

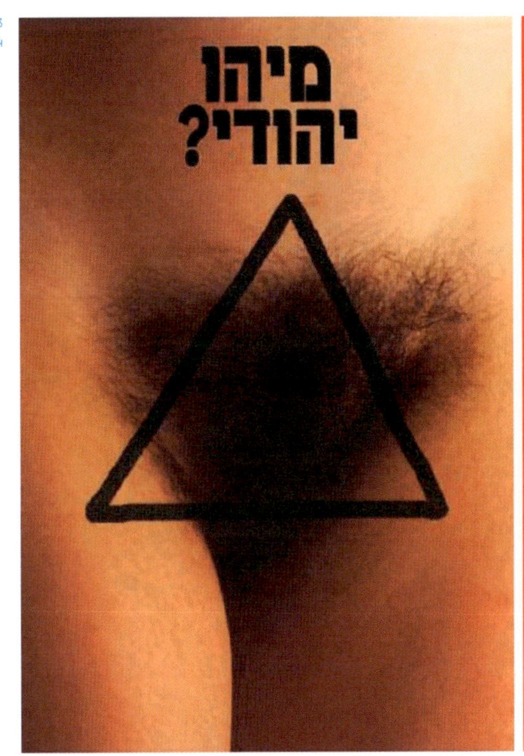

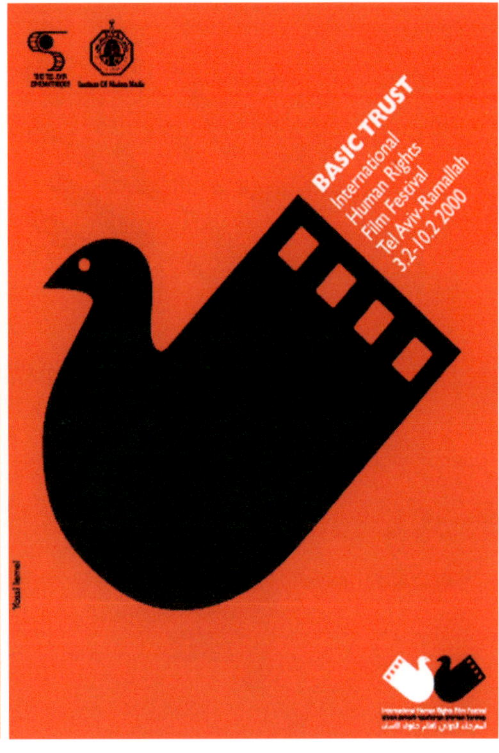

025
026

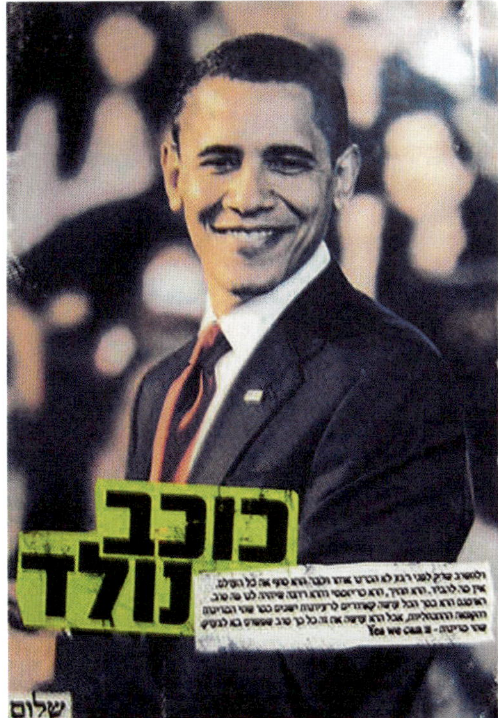

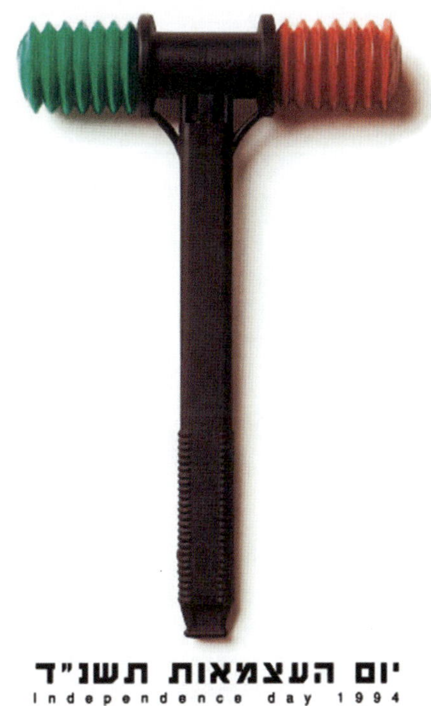

027
028

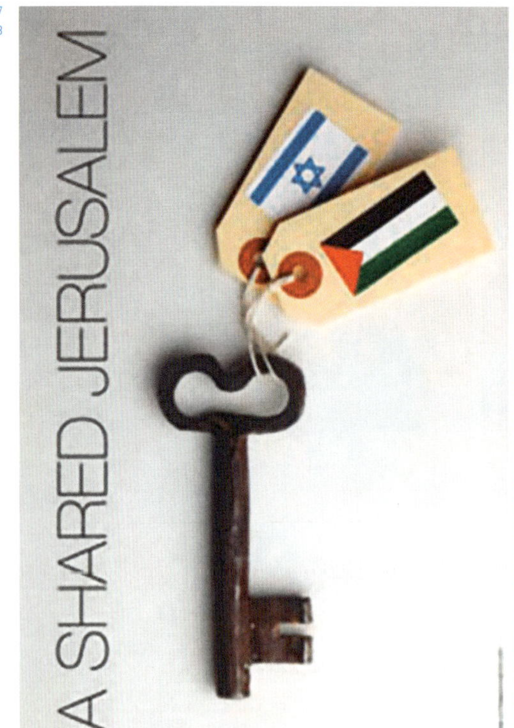

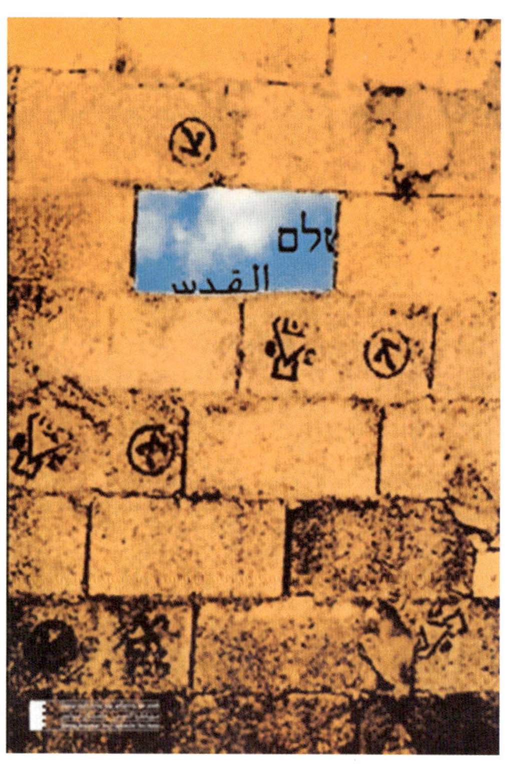

029
030

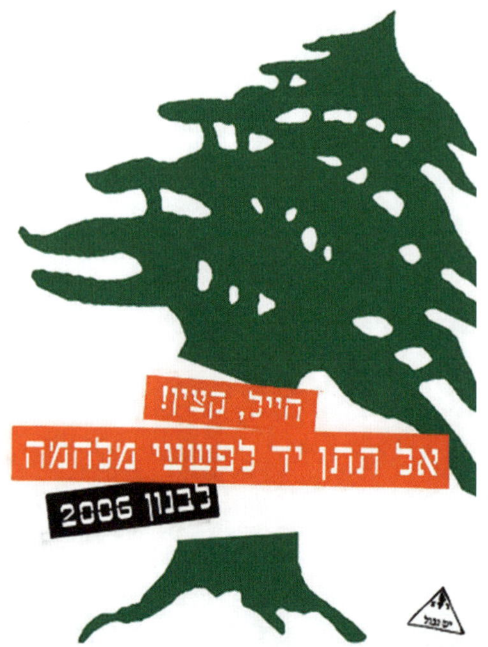

031

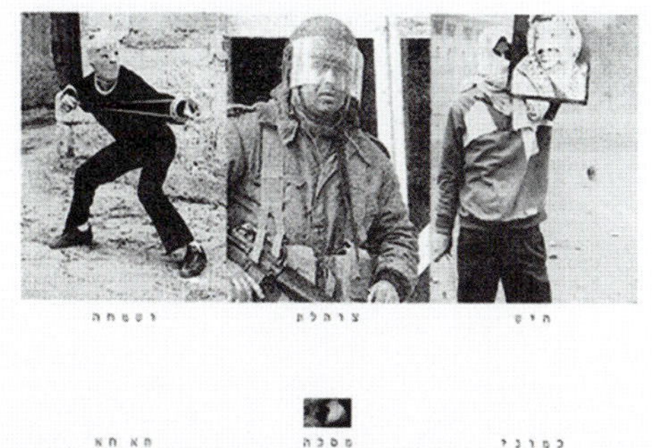
ושתה
צולבת
חיים
מא כא
מכבה
כולל

032

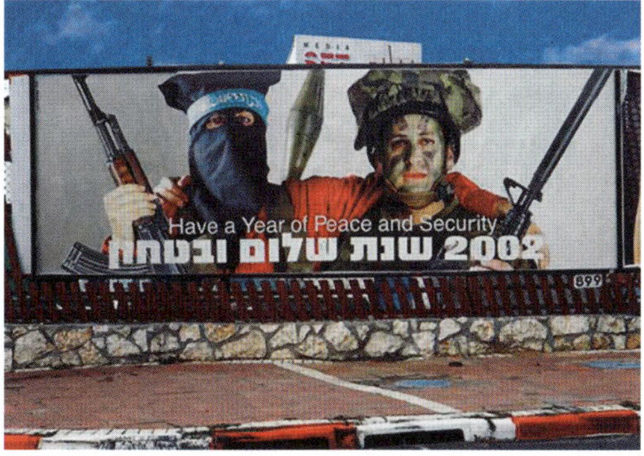
MEDIA
Have a Year of Peace and Security
שנת שלום ובטחה 2002
B99

033

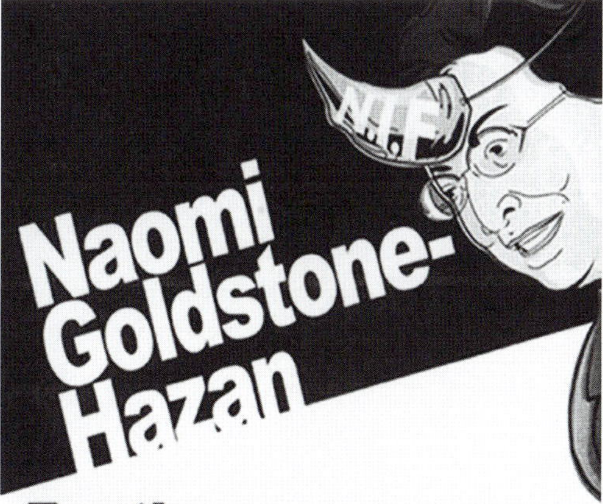
NIF

Naomi
Goldstone-
Hazan

Fact! Without the New Israel Fund,
there could be no Goldstone Report,
and Israel would not be facing
international accusations of war crimes

● Naomi Hazan's fund is behind 90% of the Goldstone war crimes allegations from non-official Israeli sources.

● In the past three years Naomi's fund has given $8 million to 16 anti-Zionist Israeli organizations
that volunteered to provide Goldstone incriminating "information" on the IDF's "war crimes"
during Operation Cast Lead.

● Nearly one in four allegations in the Goldstone Report that IDF soldiers murdered civilians
come from New Israel Fund organizations.

● Major NIF organizations signed a letter calling on Britain
to prosecute senior IDF officers for war crimes.

All the truth about the N.I.F: www.imb.org.il

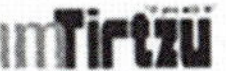
imTirtzu

001 ISRAEL PALESTINE 2002 BLOODBATH
CREATOR Yossi Lemel
SOURCE www.flickr.com/photos/
oregonstateuniversity/4518383706/
DATE 2002

002 ADMINISTRATIVE
CREATOR David Tartakover
SOURCE Plakatsammlung Museum
für Gestaltung Zürich

003 CREATOR David Tartakover
SOURCE Plakatsammlung Museum
für Gestaltung Zürich

004 35 YEARS OF OCCUPATION
CREATOR David Tartakover
SOURCE Plakatsammlung Museum
für Gestaltung Zürich

005 WHO WILL SPEAK ABOUT THE
MONSTROUS DEEDS OF ISRAEL?
CREATOR David Tartakover
SOURCE Plakatsammlung Museum
für Gestaltung Zürich

006 PAIN
CREATOR David Tartakover
SOURCE Plakatsammlung Museum
für Gestaltung Zürich

007 1967-1997, 30 YEARS OF OCCUPATION
CREATOR David Tartakover
SOURCE Plakatsammlung Museum
für Gestaltung Zürich

008 AND IT WILL COME TO PASS WHEN
YOU COME...
CREATOR David Tartakover
SOURCE Plakatsammlung Museum
für Gestaltung Zürich

009 WE WILL NEVER FORGET, AND WE WILL
NEVER FORGIVE
CREATOR David Tartakover
SOURCE Plakatsammlung Museum
für Gestaltung Zürich

010 JERUSALEM
CREATOR Tadeusz Lewandowski
SOURCE "L'engagement politique
et social," Le festival d'affiches,
Chaumont, 19 May - 16 July 2000

011 TALK WITH THE PLO ABOUT PEACE NOW
CREATOR David Tartakover
SOURCE Plakatsammlung Museum
für Gestaltung Zürich

012 INTERNATIONAL WOMEN IN BLACK
CONFERENCE, JERUSALEM
CREATOR Zhenia Schorr, Tamar Lehan
SOURCE www.gilasvirsky.com
DATE 2005

013 25 YEARS OF OCCUPATION
CREATOR David Tartakover
SOURCE Plakatsammlung Museum
für Gestaltung Zürich

014 PEACE-SHALOM
CREATOR David Tartakover
SOURCE www.peaceart.us
DATE 1977

015 PEACE-SHALOM
CREATOR David Tartakover
SOURCE www.palestineposter
project.org
DATE 1979

016 WHAT MORE WILL YOU ASK OF US,
MOTHERLAND?
CREATOR David Tartakover
SOURCE www.palestineposter
project.org
DATE 2009

017 I'M HERE
CREATOR David Tartakover
SOURCE www.palestineposter
project.org
DATE 2000

018 DOWN WITH THE OCCUPATION
CREATOR David Tartakover
SOURCE www.palestineposter
project.org

019 SEAM LINE
CREATOR Yossi Lemel
SOURCE www.lemel.co.il

020 ISRAEL, 50TH ANNIVERSARY
CREATOR Yossi Lemel
SOURCE www.lemel.co.il
DATE 1998

021 BOTH SIDES OF PEACE
CREATOR Yossi Lemel
SOURCE www.palestineposter
project.org
DATE 1995

022 NOVEMBER 29TH
CREATOR Yossi Lemel
SOURCE www.lemel.co.il
DATE 2000

023 WHO'S A JEW?
CREATOR Yossi Lemel
SOURCE www.lemel.co.il
DATE 1996

024 INTERNATIONAL HUMAN
RIGHTS FESTIVAL
CREATOR Yossi Lemel
SOURCE www.lemel.co.il

025 A STAR IS BORN
CREATOR Ido [Sany] Araz
SOURCE www.peacenow.org.il

026 INDEPENDENCE DAY, AN ISRAELI
SYMBOL [PLASTIC HAMMER] IN
PALESTINIAN COLORS
CREATOR Yossi Lemel
SOURCE www.lemel.co.il
DATE 1994

027 A SHARED JERUSALEM
SOURCE wws.princeton.edu

028 SHARING JERUSALEM: TWO CAPITALS
FOR TWO STATES
CREATOR David Tartakover
SOURCE Plakatsammlung Museum
für Gestaltung Zürich

029 SOLDIER, OFFICER! DON'T TAKE PART
IN WAR CRIMES
CREATOR Poster by the
Organization Yesh Gvul, Provided
by Lahav Halevy
SOURCE www.flickr.com/photos/
maarav/210931570/5/

030 YOU KNOW WHEN YOU HAVE TO GO
SOURCE www.peacenow.org.il

031 MASKS
CREATOR David Tartakover
SOURCE Plakatsammlung Museum
für Gestaltung Zürich

032 POSTER FOR NEW YEAR, HAVE A
YEAR OF PEACE AND SECURITY
CREATOR Yossi Lemel
SOURCE www.lemel.co.il
DATE 2002

033 THE SECOND ZIONIST REVOLUTION
The Hebrew phrase, "im tirtzu," is
the conditional opening premise
of Theodor Herzl's famous slogan
which became the foundational
rallying cry of political Zionism,
"if you will it [a Jewish state]
it is no dream." It is used today
by neo-Zionist organizations such
as Im Tirtzu in an effort to
re-invigorate Zionist ideals
within Israel.
SOURCE www.palestineposter
project.org

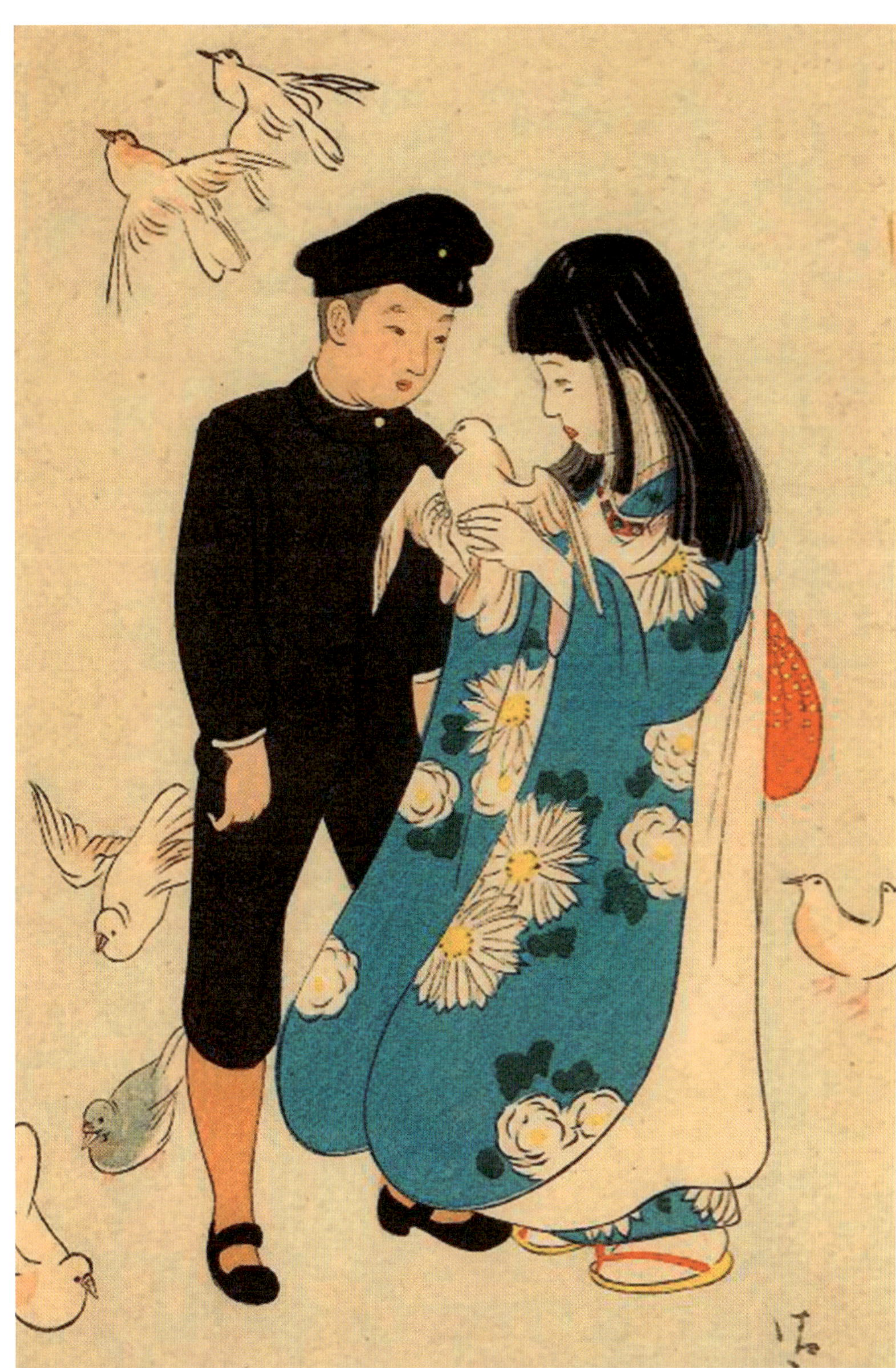

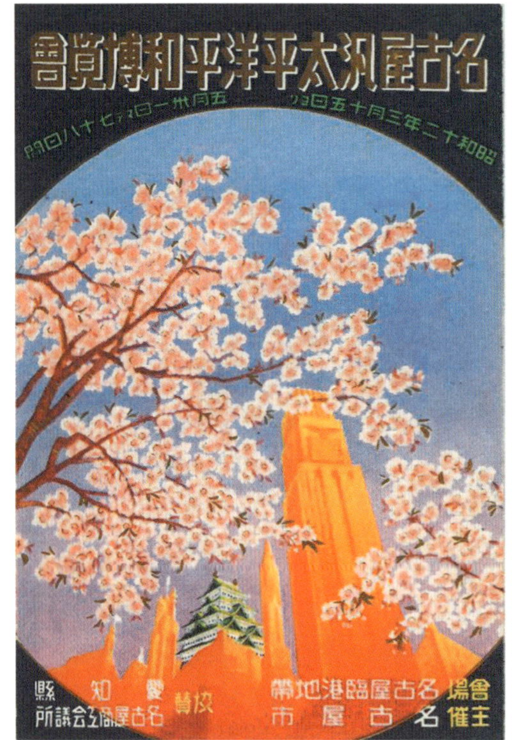

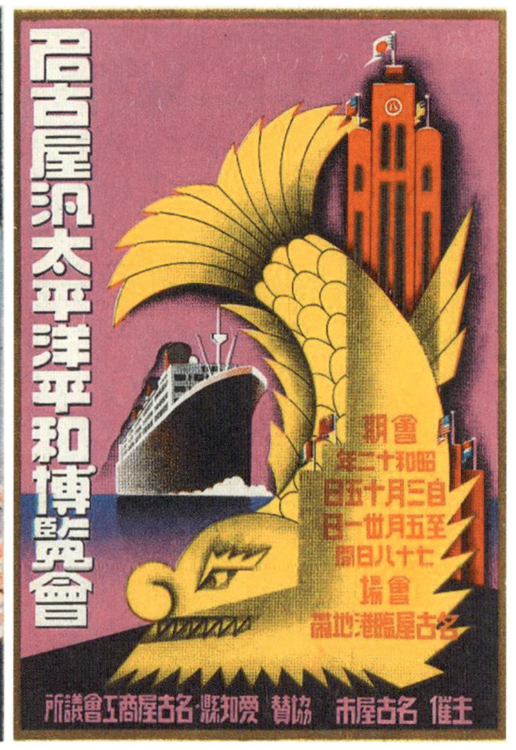

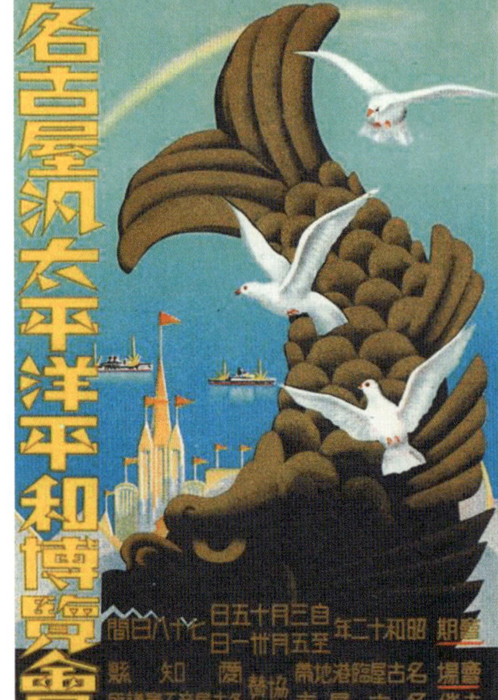

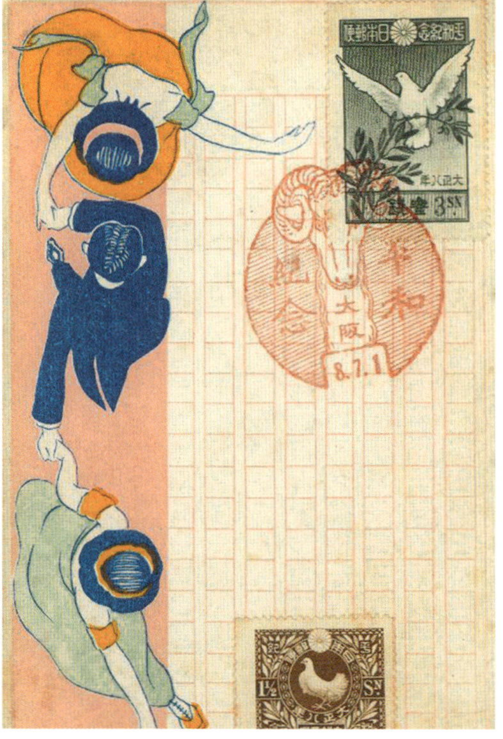

006
007
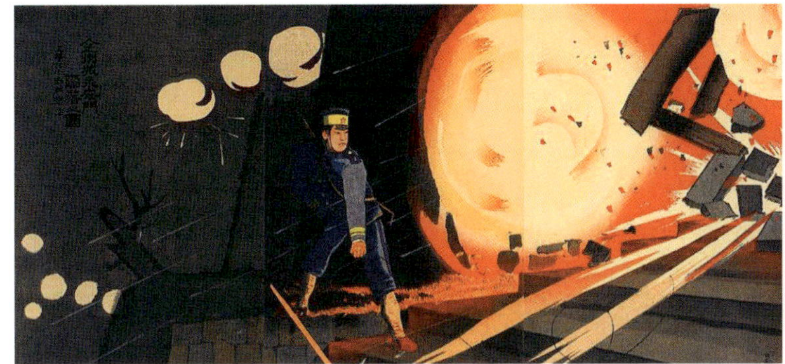
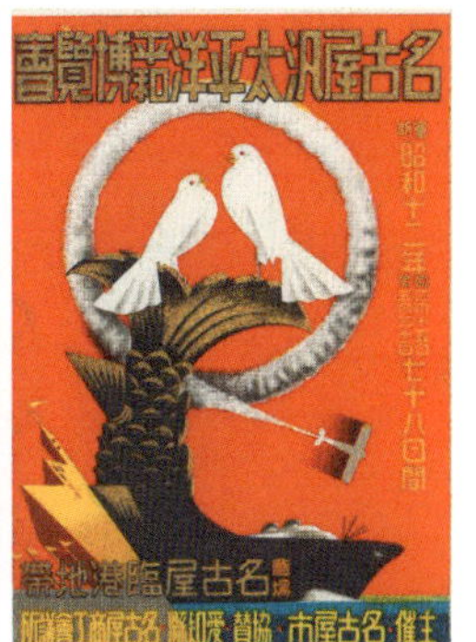

008
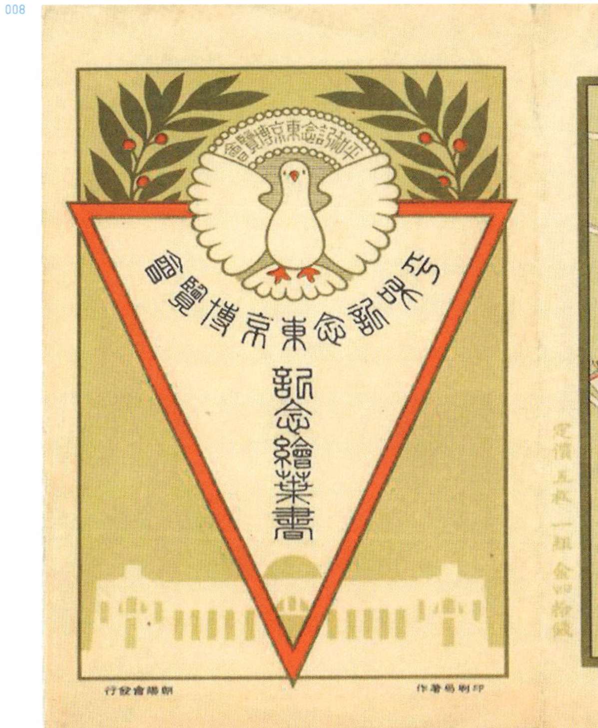
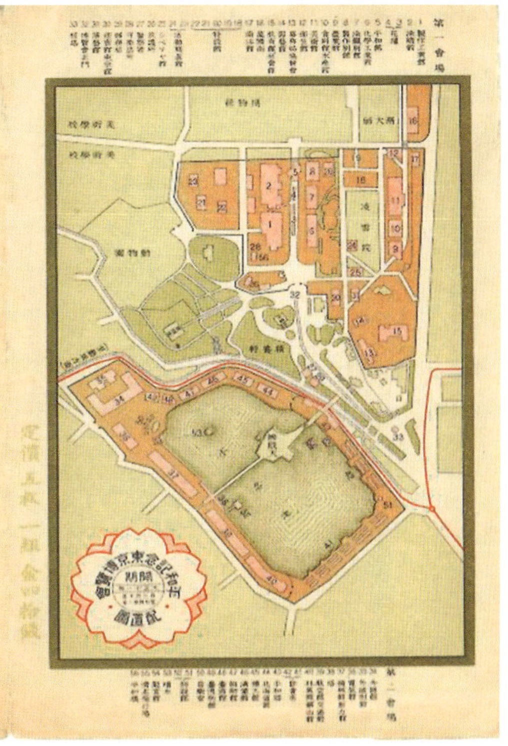

009
010
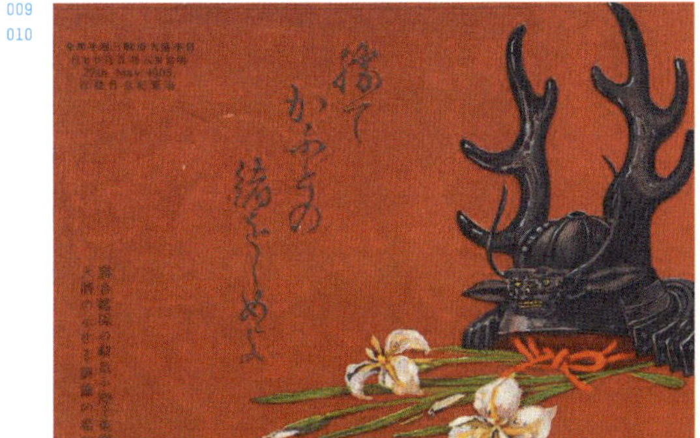
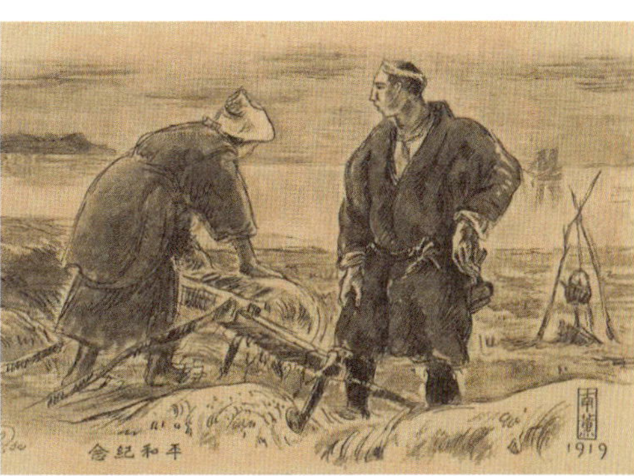

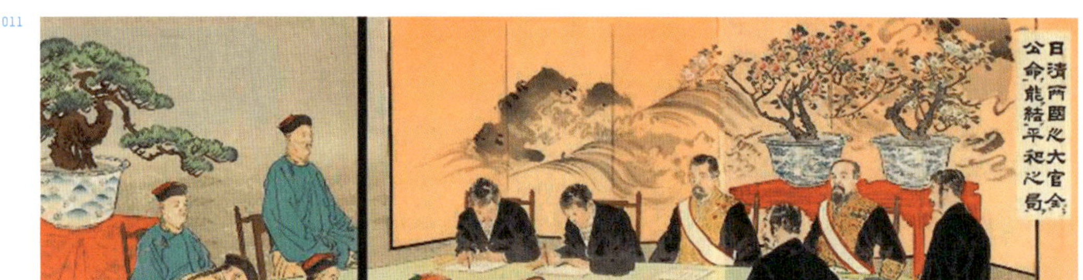

日清両國之大官金
公命能結平和之局

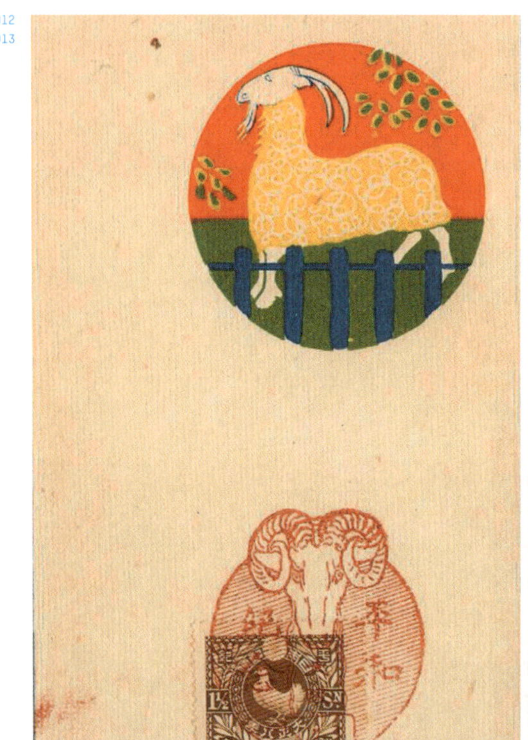

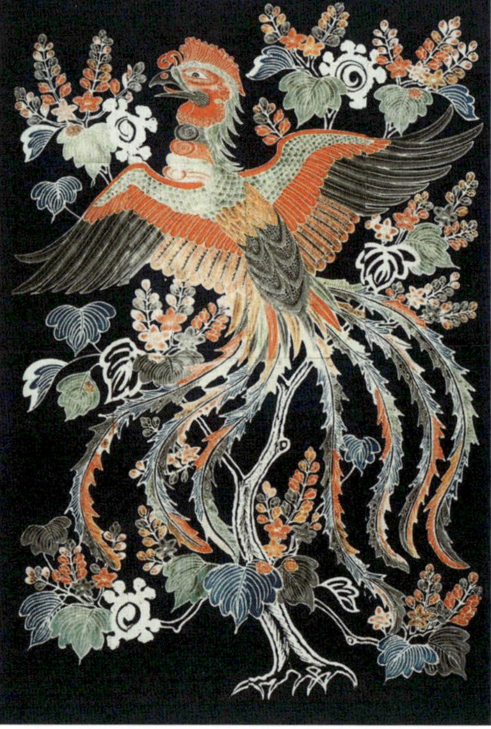

001 YOUNG BOY AND GIRL WITH DOVES
FROM THE SERIES COMMEMORATION OF
PEACE [HEIWA KINEN]
CREATOR Kaburaki Kiyokata
SOURCE www.mfa.org
DATE 1919

002 EXPOSITION OF THE PEACE OF THE
PAN PACIFIC, NAGOYA
CREATOR Unknown [Japanese]
SOURCE www.mfa.org
DATE 1937

003 EXPOSITION OF THE PEACE OF THE
PAN PACIFIC, NAGOYA
CREATOR Unknown [Japanese]
SOURCE www.mfa.org
DATE 1937

004 EXPOSITION OF THE PEACE OF THE
PAN PACIFIC, NAGOYA
CREATOR Unknown [Japanese]
SOURCE www.mfa.org
DATE 1937

005 VIEW OF DANCERS FROM ABOVE
CREATOR Unknown [Japanese]
SOURCE www.mfa.org

006 THE FALL OF THE YONGANMEN [GATE
OF ETERNAL PEACE] AT JINZHOUCHENG
CREATOR Kobayashi Kiyochika
SOURCE www.mfa.org

007 EXPOSITION OF THE PEACE OF THE
PAN PACIFIC, NAGOYA
CREATOR Unknown [Japanese]
SOURCE www.mfa.org
DATE 1937

008 POSTCARD ENVELOPE FOR THE SERIES
THE COMMEMORATION OF THE PEACE
EXHIBITION IN TOKYO
CREATOR Unknown [Japanese]
SOURCE www.mfa.org
DATE 1922

009 JAPANESE HELMET WITH ADMIRAL
TOGO'S VERSE
CREATOR Unknown [Japanese]
SOURCE www.mfa.org
DATE 1908

010 WORKERS FROM THE SERIES
COMMEMORATION OF THE PEACE
CREATOR Unknown [Japanese]
SOURCE www.mfa.org
DATE 1919

011 JAPANESE AND CHINESE DIGNITARIES
ACCOMPLISH THEIR MISSIONS
IN SUCCESSFULLY CONCLUDING
A PEACE TREATY
CREATOR Ogata Gekkô
SOURCE www.mfa.org
DATE 19th century

012 NEW YEAR'S CARD: GOAT
CREATOR Unknown [Japanese]
SOURCE www.mfa.org
DATE 19th century

013 FUTON COVER
CREATOR Unknown [Japanese]
SOURCE www.mfa.org
DATE 19th century

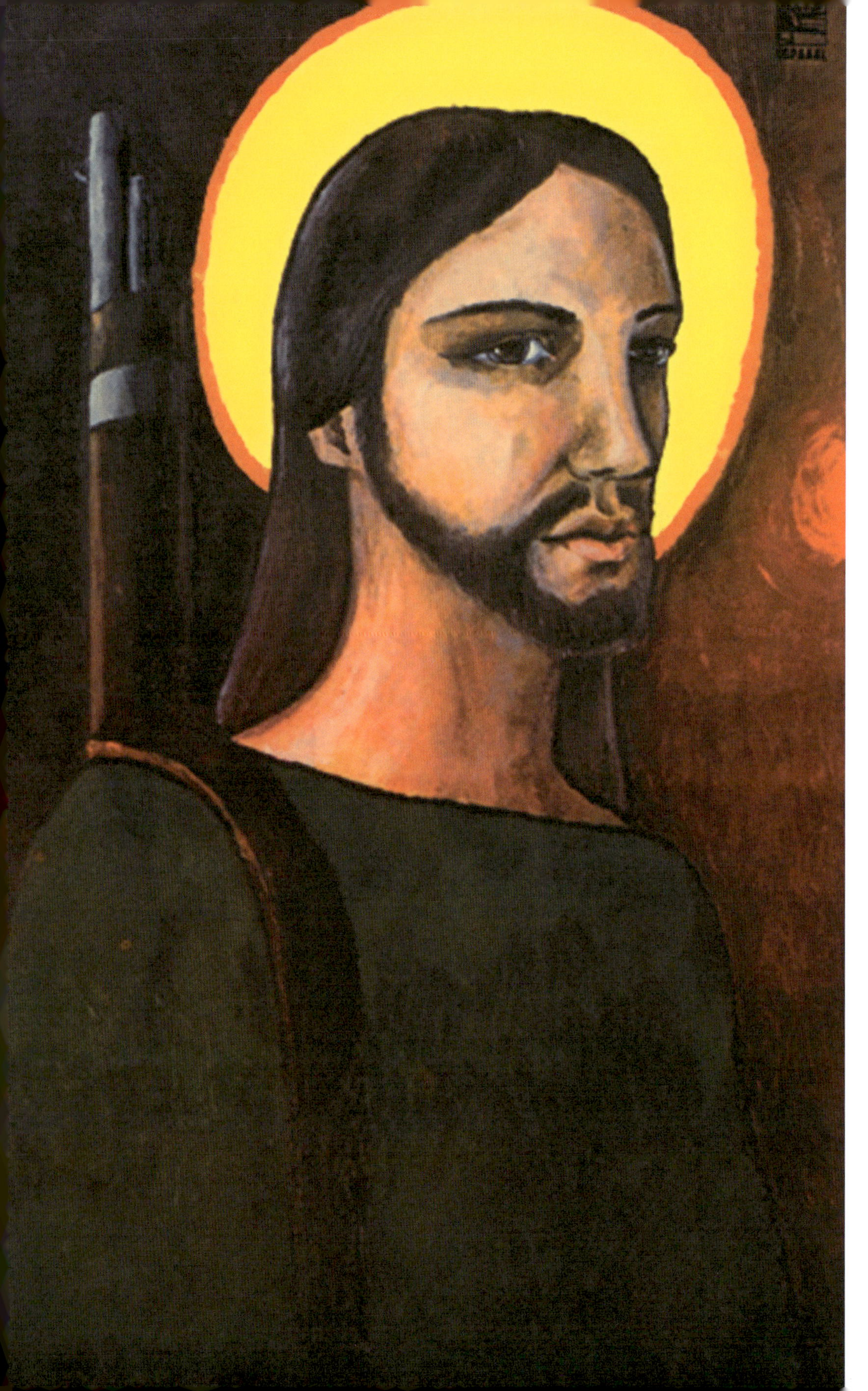

LEFT
001

002

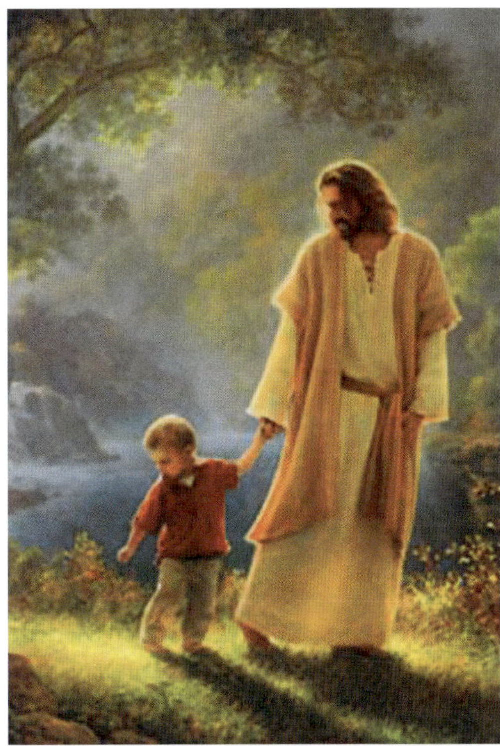

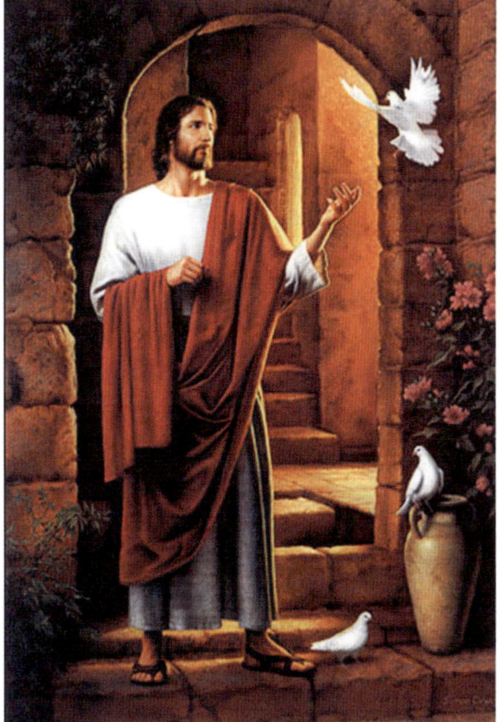

001 UNTITLED
CREATOR Alfredo G. Rostgaard
SOURCE Frick, ed., *The Triconti-
nental Solidarity Poster* [Bern:
Comedia, 2003].
DATE 1969

002 FIND PEACE IN JESUS CHRIST
SOURCE fr.christ.org

003 JESUS
SOURCE www.practicalspiritualwar
fare.com

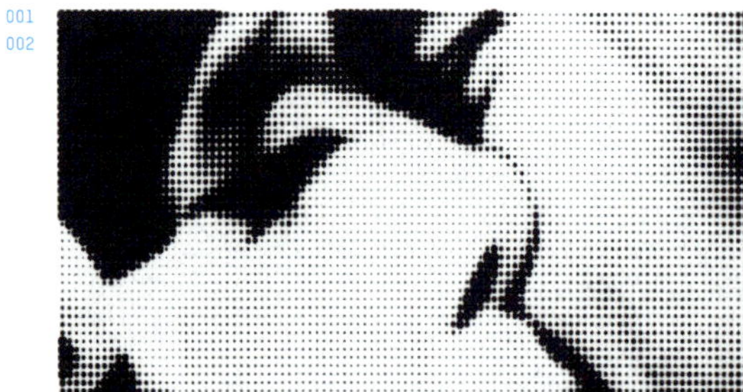

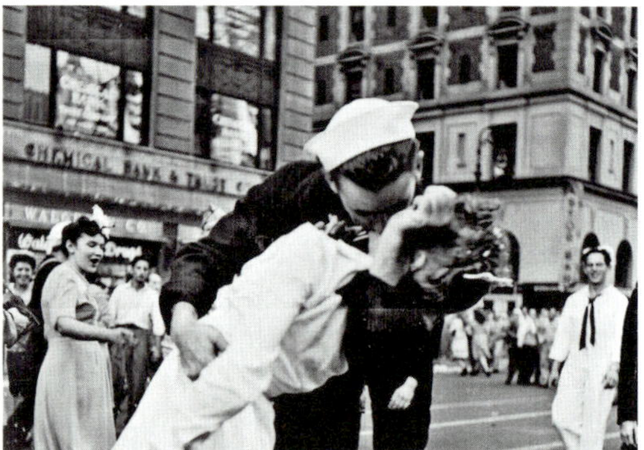

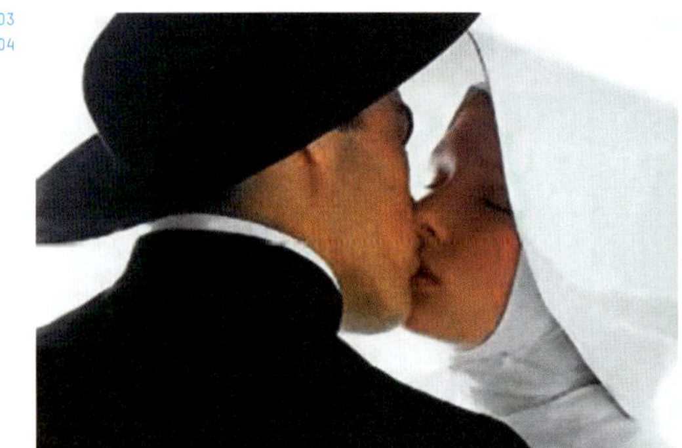

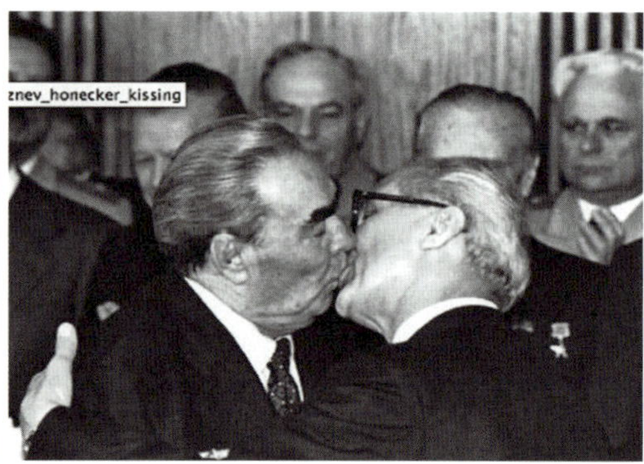
znev_honecker_kissing

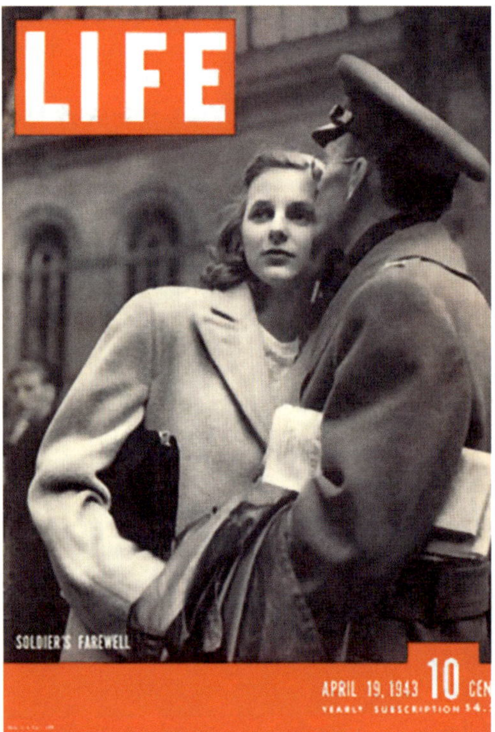
LIFE
SOLDIER'S FAREWELL
APRIL 19, 1943 10 CEN
YEARLY SUBSCRIPTION $4.

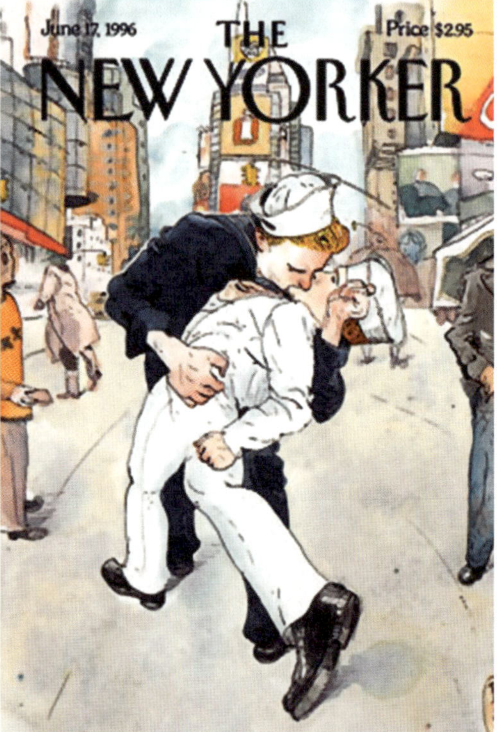
June 17, 1996
THE NEW YORKER
Price $2.95

007
008

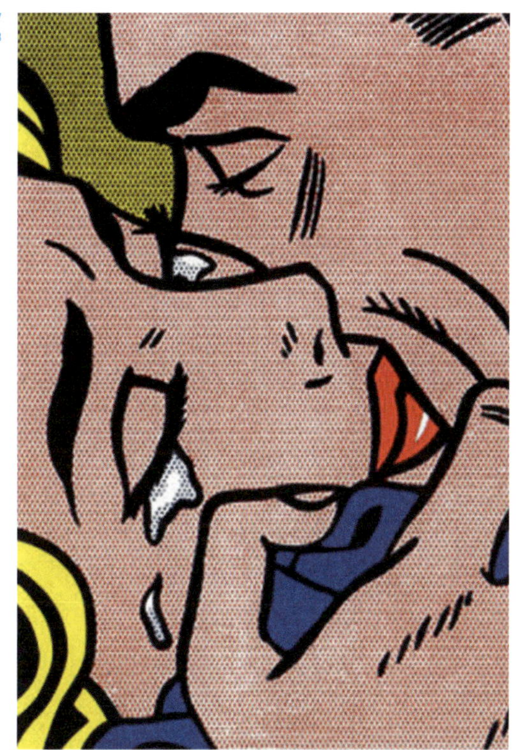

009
010

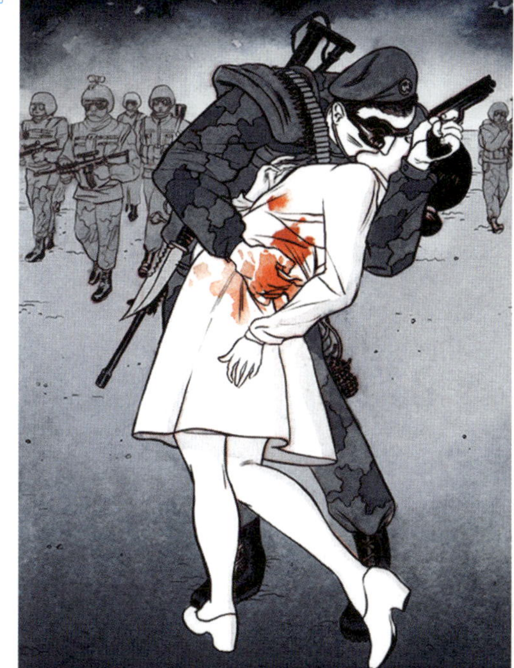

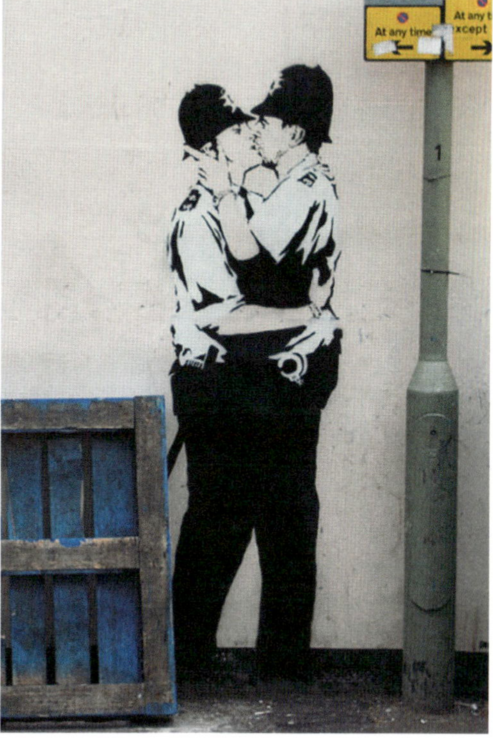

011

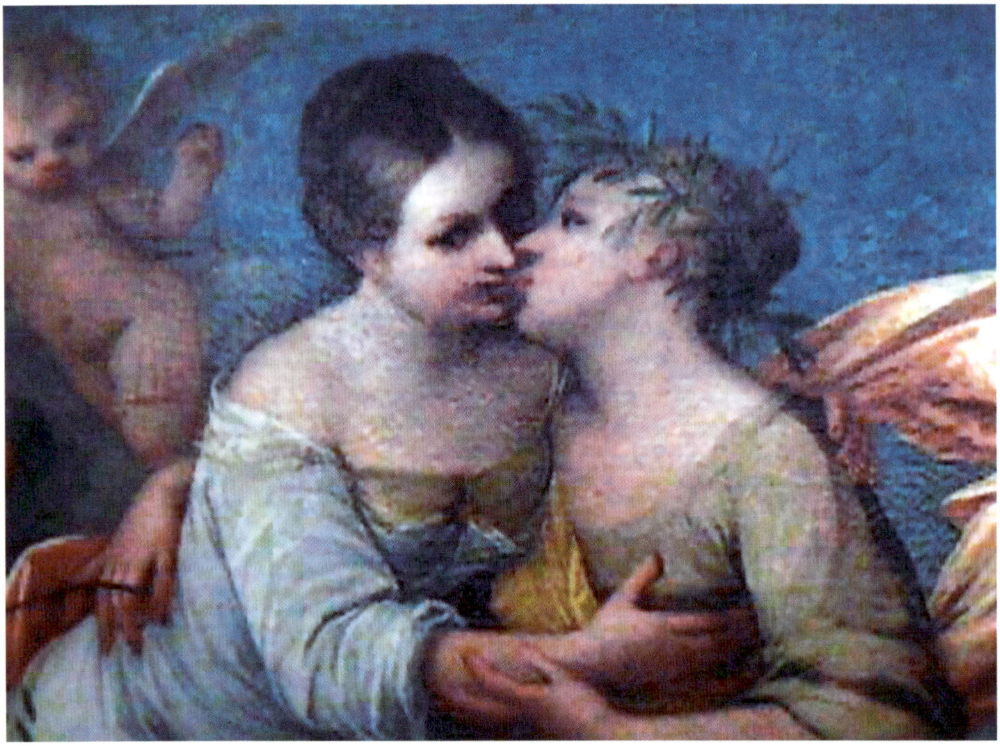

012

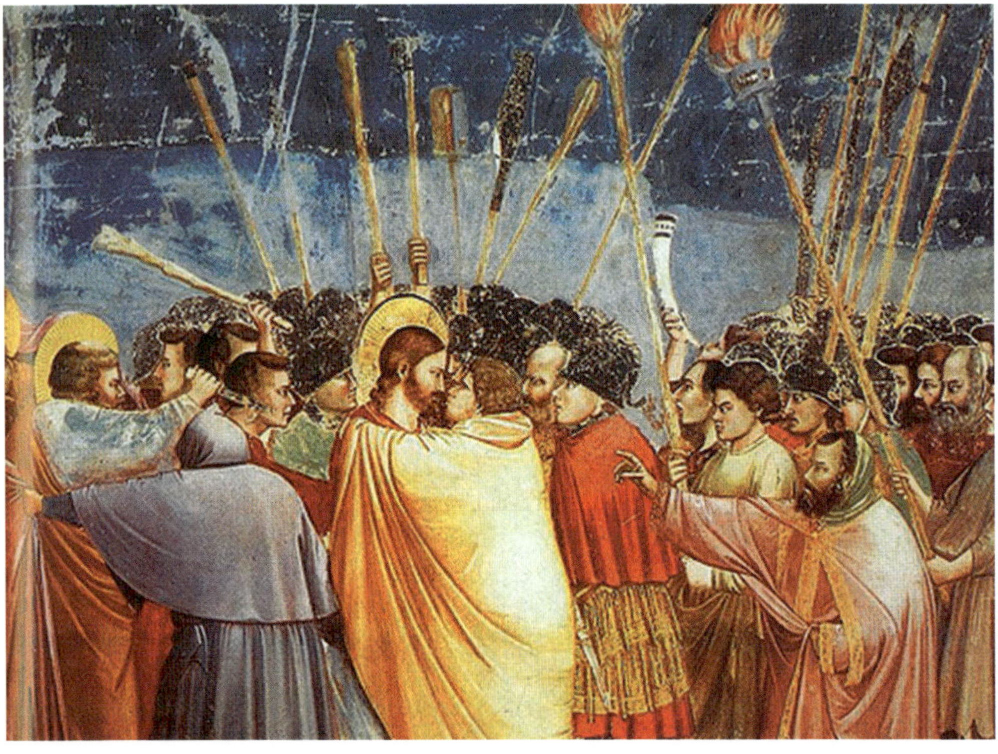

013

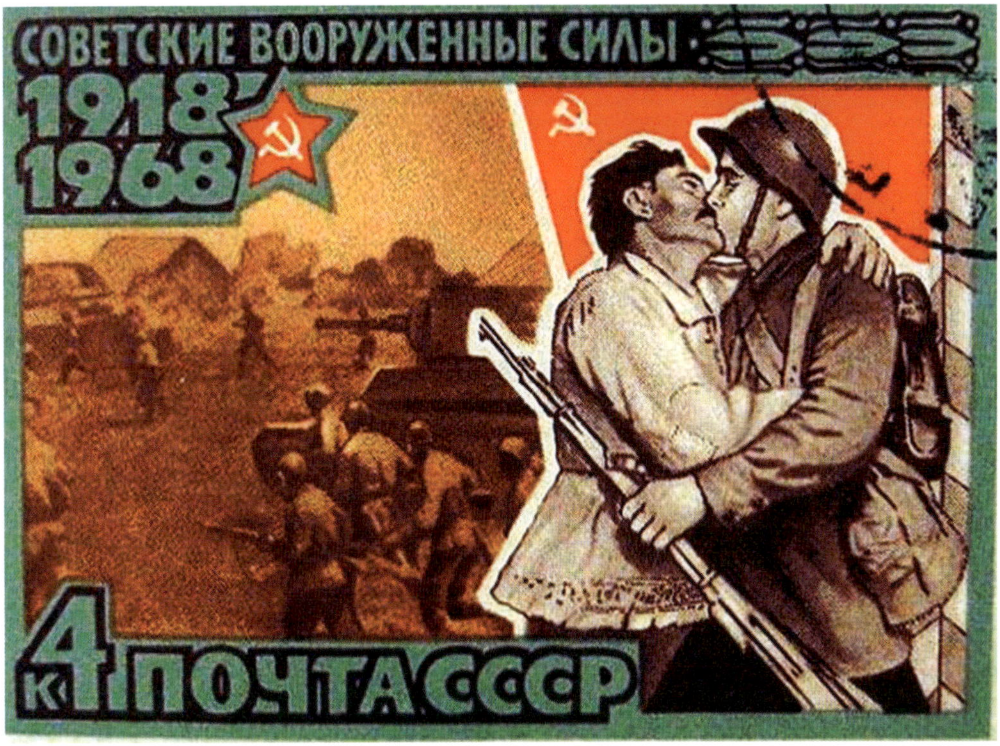

СОВЕТСКИЕ ВООРУЖЕННЫЕ СИЛЫ
1918
1968
4 к ПОЧТА СССР

KISSING
THE
BLARNEY
STONE

014

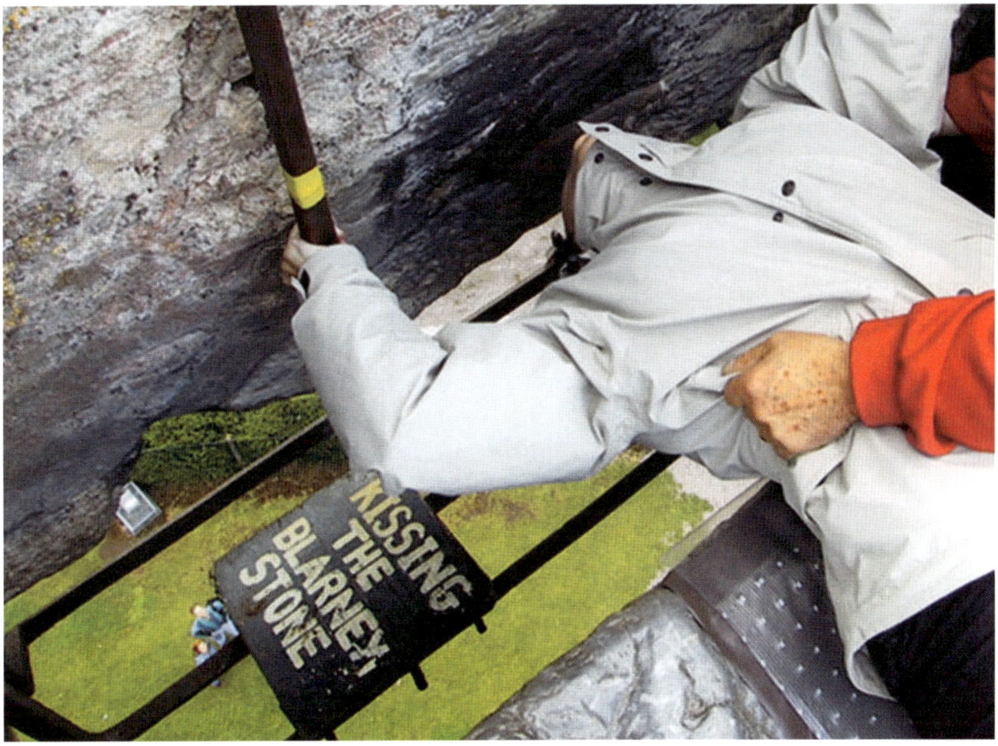

001 MÄRZ [MARCH]
     CREATOR Markus Weisbeck
     SOURCE Beiträge macht Bilder

002 KISSING THE WAR GOOD-BYE
     Sailor kissing a nurse in Times
     Square, during the celebration
     to mark V-J Day, the end of World
     War II.
     CREATOR Lt. Victor Jorgensen
     SOURCE en.wikipedia.org
     DATE 14 August 1945

003 KISSING NUN
     CREATOR Oliviero Toscani
     SOURCE iconicphotos.wordpress.com
     DATE 1992

004 THE FRATERNAL KISS
     Aging Soviet leader Leonid
     Brezhnev was the guest of
     honor at the DDR's thirtieth
     anniversary celebrations. When
     Brezhnev finished his speech,
     East German President Erich
     Honecker gave him a kiss.
     CREATOR Régis Bossu
     SOURCE iconicphotos.wordpress.com
     DATE 1979

005 SOLDIER'S FAREWELL
     CREATOR Alfred Eisenstaedt
     SOURCE cbi-theater-1.home.
     comcast.net
     DATE 19 April 1943

006 DON'T ASK
     CREATOR Bill Blitt
     SOURCE www.journalofamerican-
     history.org
     DATE 17 June 1996

007 KISS V
     CREATOR Roy Lichtenstein
     SOURCE artblogbybob.blogspot.ch
     DATE 1964

008 BESOS ROBADOS POSTER
     CREATOR René Azcuy Cardenas
     SOURCE Revolucion! Cuban Poster Art
     DATE 1970

009 KISSING THE WAR GOODBYE
     CREATOR Koren Shadmi
     SOURCE www.nocaptionneeded.com/
     2008/01/kissing-war-and-tasting-
     victory/

010 SOLDIERS KISS
     CREATOR Bansky
     SOURCE vostokzapad.wordpress.com

011 JUSTICE AND PEACE KISS EACH OTHER,
     PINACOTECA TOSIO MARTINENGO,
     BRESCIA [ITALY]
     CREATOR Giovanni Dall'Orto
     SOURCE commons.wikimedia.org

012 KISS OF JUDAS
     CREATOR Giotto
     SOURCE commons.wikimedia.org
     DATE 1304-06

013 PEASANT KISSING A RED
     ARMY SOLDIER
     SOURCE www.mentalfloss.com
     DATE 1968

014 BLARNEY STONE, BLARNEY
     CASTLE, IRELAND
     SOURCE en.wikipedia.org
     DATE 2002

001

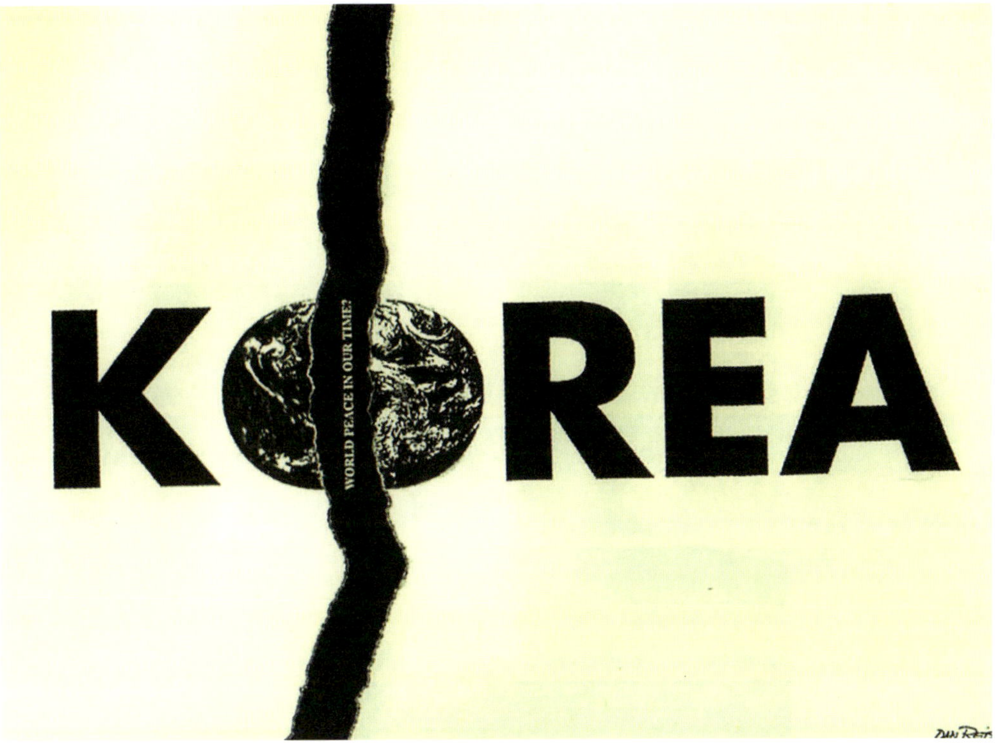

002

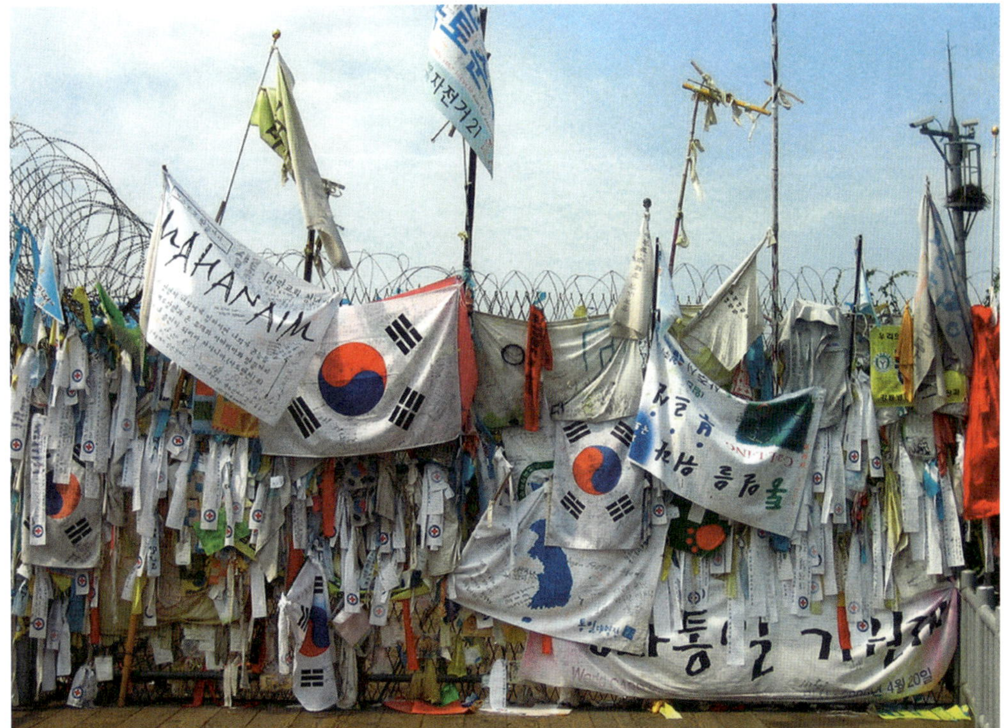

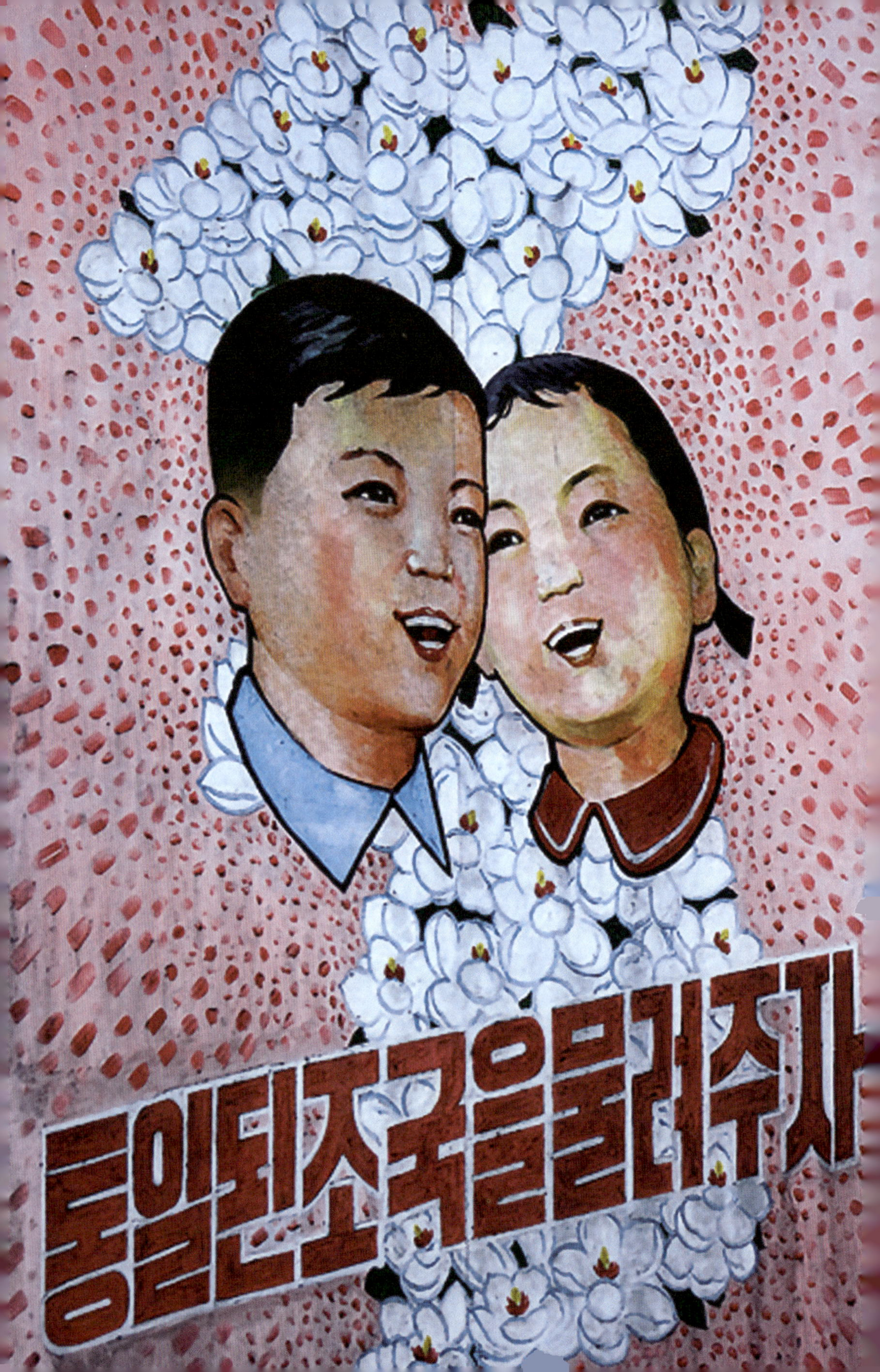

통일이 된 조국을 물려주자

LEFT
003
004
005

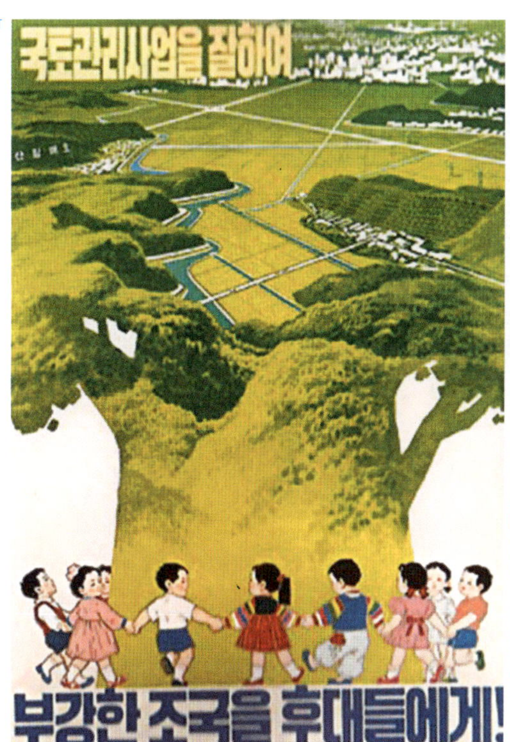
국토관리사업을 잘하여
부강한 조국을 후대들에게!

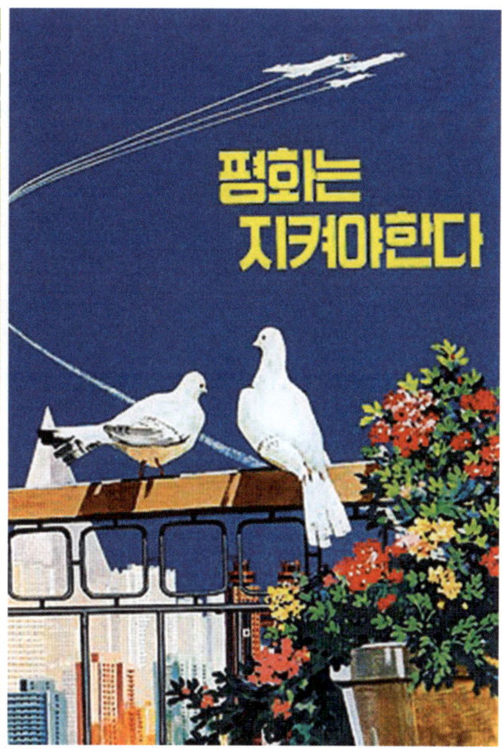
평화는
지켜야한다

006

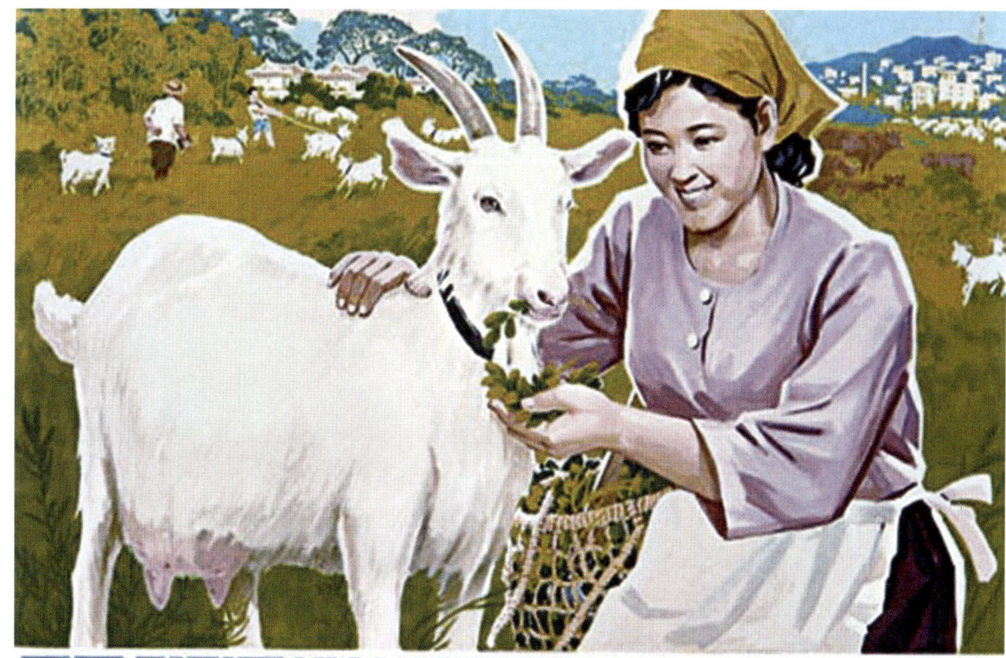
모든 가정들에서 염소를 대대적으로 기르자!

007

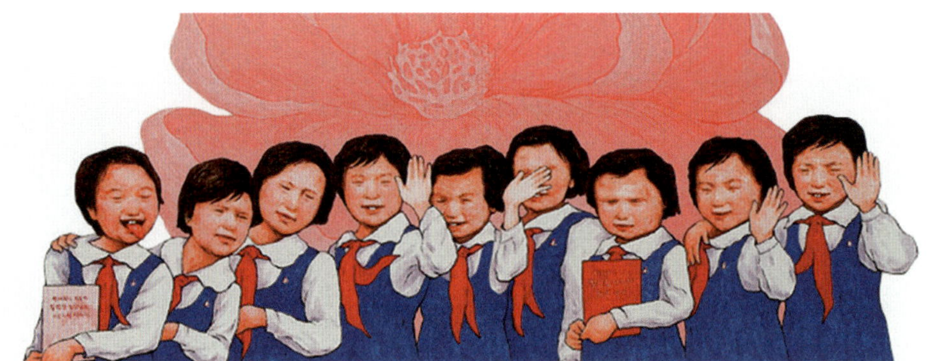

008

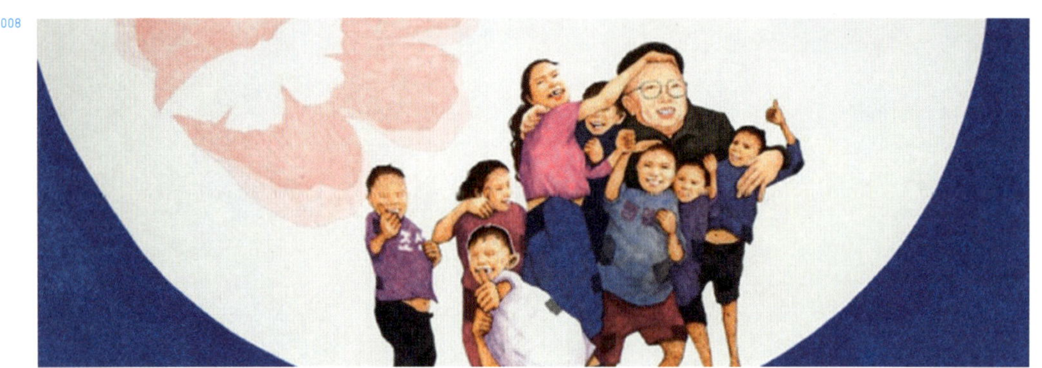

009
RIGHT
010

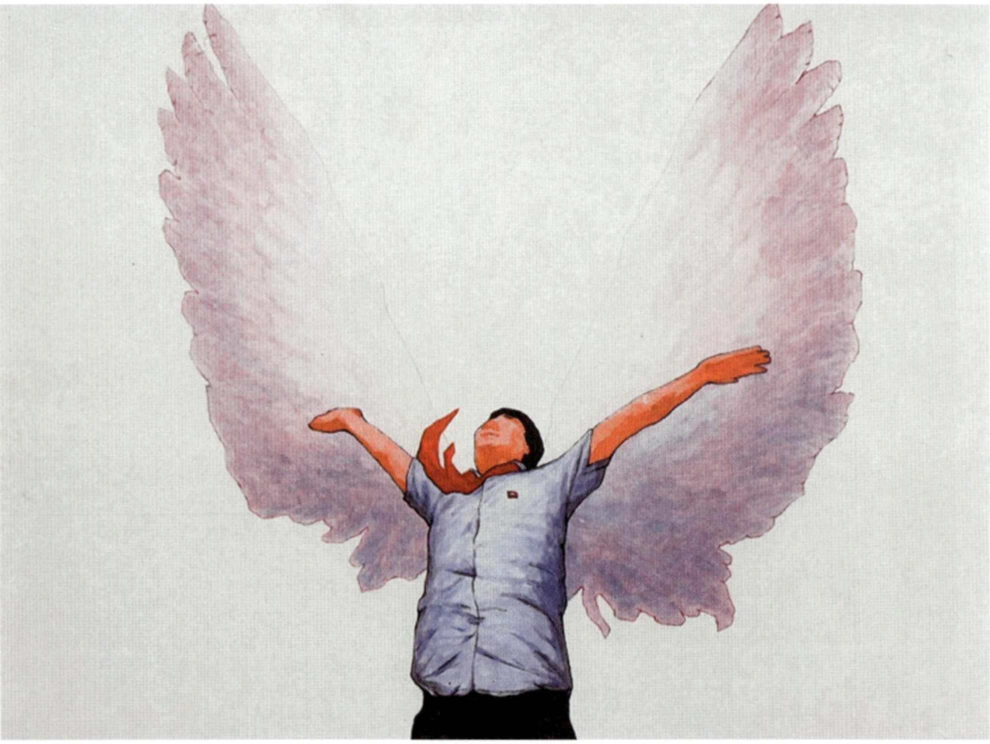

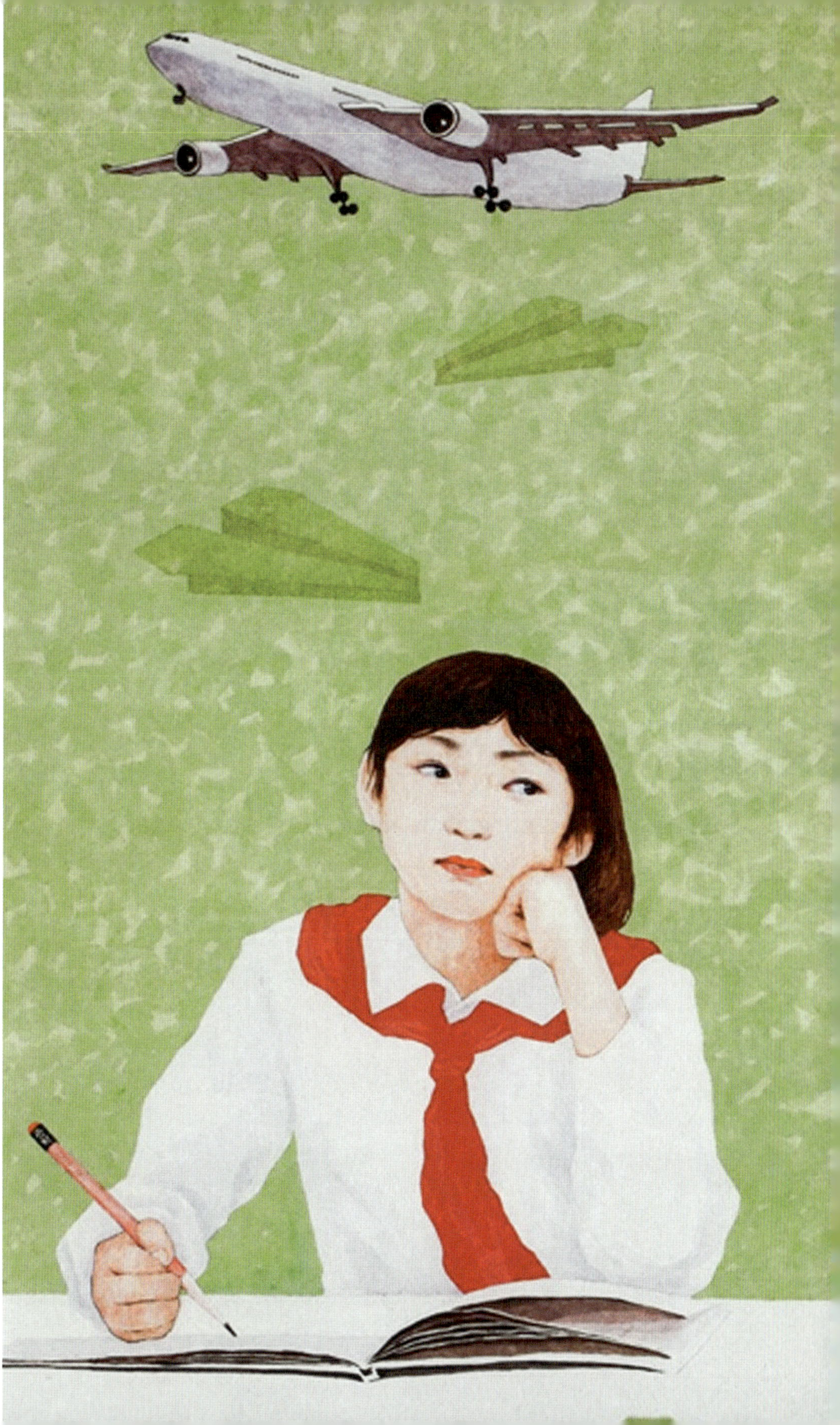

011

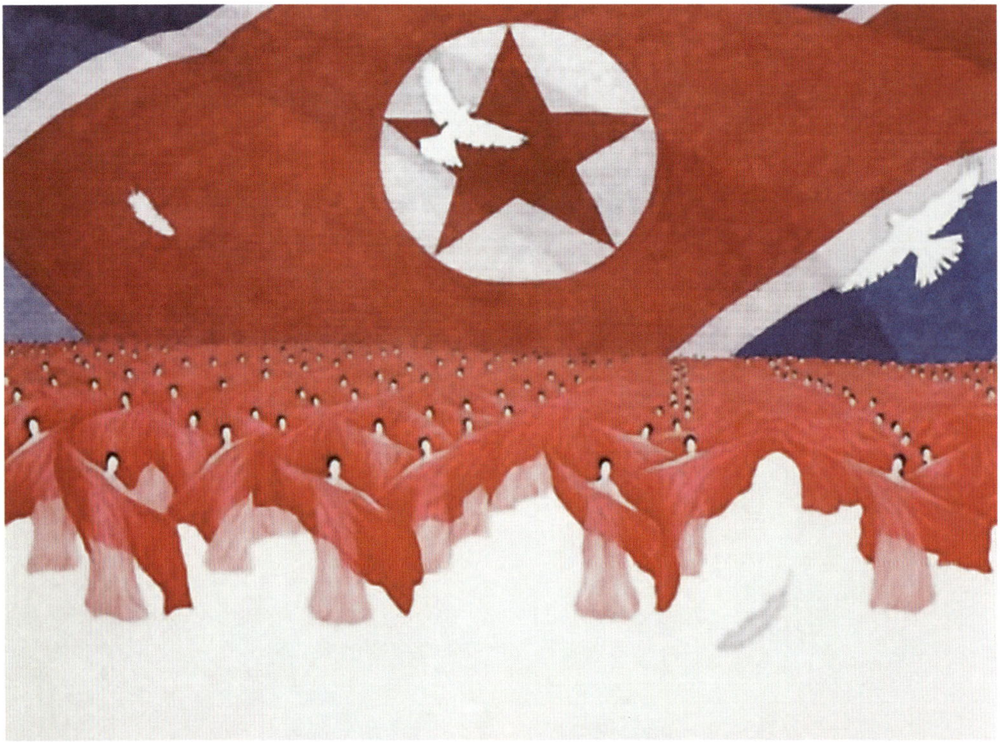

012

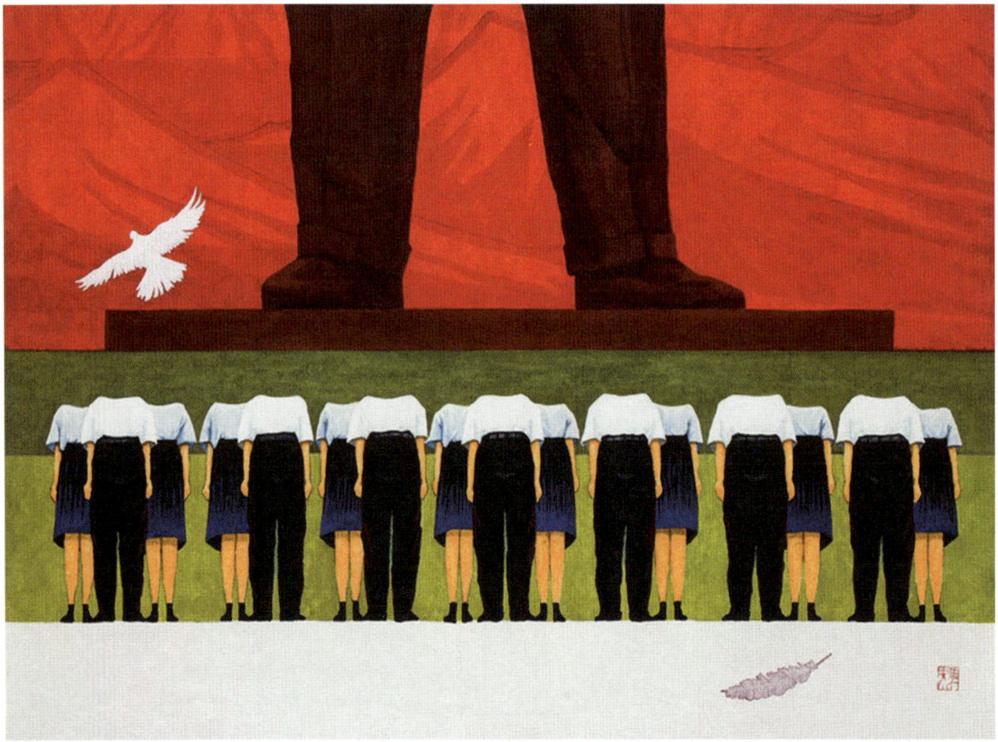

013
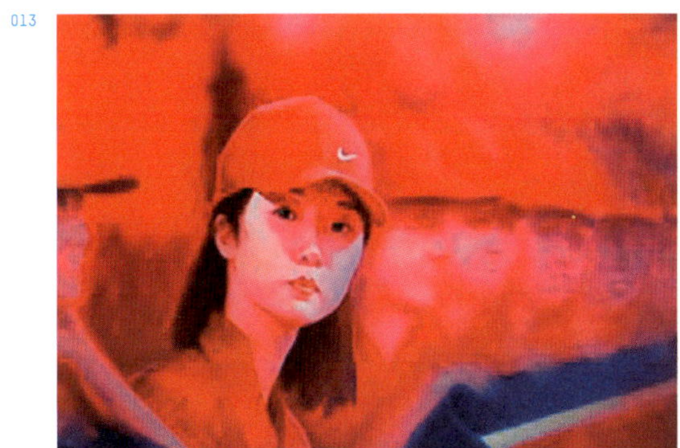

014
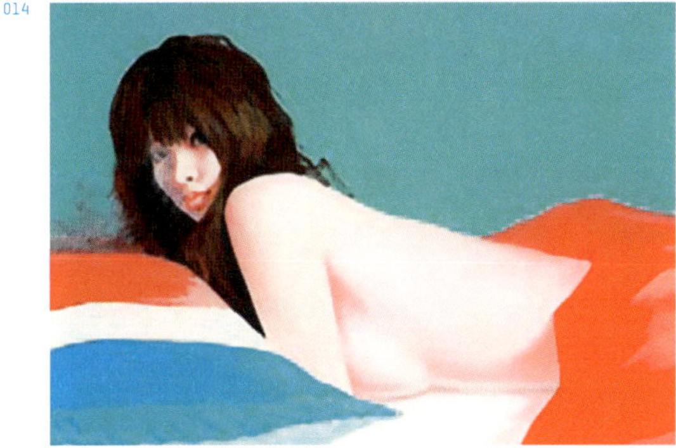

015
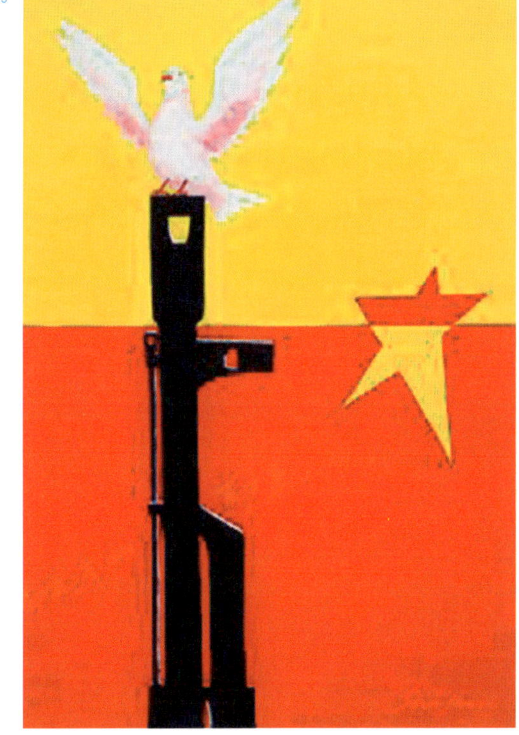

001 KOREA, WORLD PEACE IN OUR TIME?
     CREATOR Dan Reisinger
     SOURCE mfarrelltypoblog.blogspot.ch

002 FREEDOM BRIDGE, SOUTH KOREA / NORTH
     KOREA BORDER
     12,733 POWs returned to South
     Korea across this bridge. However,
     there are still families that are
     divided by the DMZ.
     CREATOR Provided by FoodieJP / Julie
     SOURCE www.flickr.com/photos/
     foodiejp/402228751/

003 PEACEFUL UNIFICATION KAESONG
     PROPAGANDA
     Unified Korea at the DMZ.
     CREATOR Provided by Joseph
     A Ferris III
     SOURCE www.flickr.com/photos/
     josephferris76/6116744034/

004 WITH LAND MANAGEMENT WORK
     PROPERLY DONE, A STRONG AND
     PROSPEROUS FATHERLAND FOR
     FUTURE GENERATIONS!
     SOURCE David Heather and Koen
     de Ceuster, *North Korean Posters:
     The David Heather Collection*
     [Munich. Prestel, 2008].

005 PEACE HAS TO BE DEFENDED
     SOURCE David Heather and Koen
     de Ceuster, *North Korean Posters:
     The David Heather Collection*
     [Munich: Prestel, 2008].

006 UNTITLED
     SOURCE David Heather and Koen
     de Ceuster, *North Korean Posters:
     The David Heather Collection*
     [Munich: Prestel, 2008].

007 FLOWER CHILDREN
     CREATOR Song Byeok
     SOURCE songbyeok.com
     DATE 2010

008 A LOVING FATHER AND HIS CHILDREN
     CREATOR Song Byeok
     SOURCE songbyeok.com
     DATE 2011

009 HOPE
     CREATOR Song Byeok
     SOURCE songbyeok.com
     DATE 2010

010 DREAMING OF SOMETHING ELSE
     CREATOR Song Byeok
     SOURCE songbyeok.com
     DATE 2010

011 MASS GAMES
     CREATOR Song Byeok
     SOURCE songbyeok.com
     DATE 2010

012 BELOVED LEADER
     CREATOR Song Byeok
     SOURCE songbyeok.com
     DATE 2010

013 I REALLY WANT TO BE HAPPY
     CREATOR Sun Mu
     SOURCE www.crestock.com
     DATE 2006

014 In propaganda posters of the
     People's Republic, displays of
     women as anything but burly,
     manlike workers were practically
     unheard of until well into
     the 1980s.
     CREATOR Sun Mu
     SOURCE www.crestock.com

015 GUNS AND PEACE
     CREATOR Sun Mu
     SOURCE www.crestock.com

001

NEXT
002
003

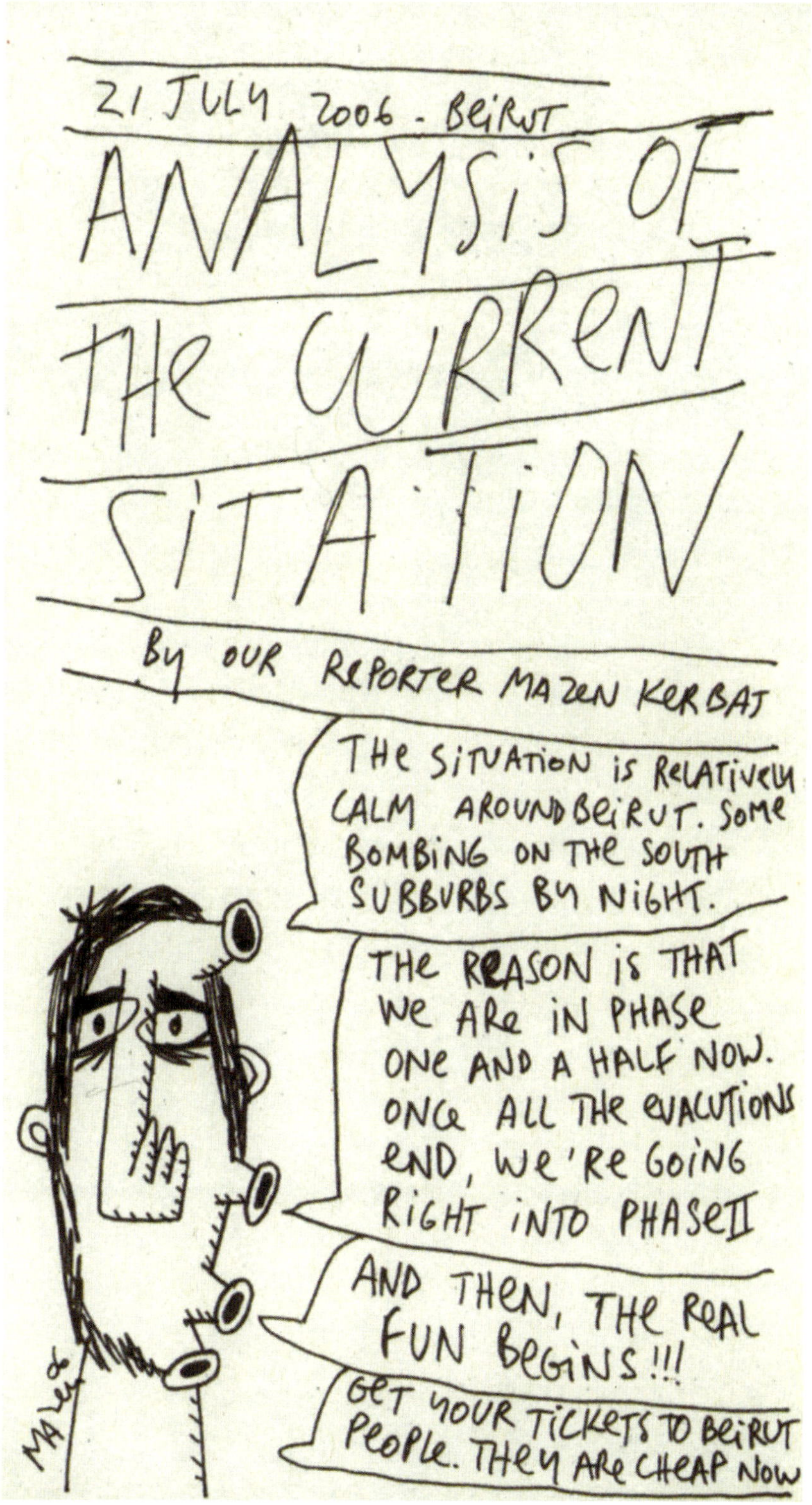

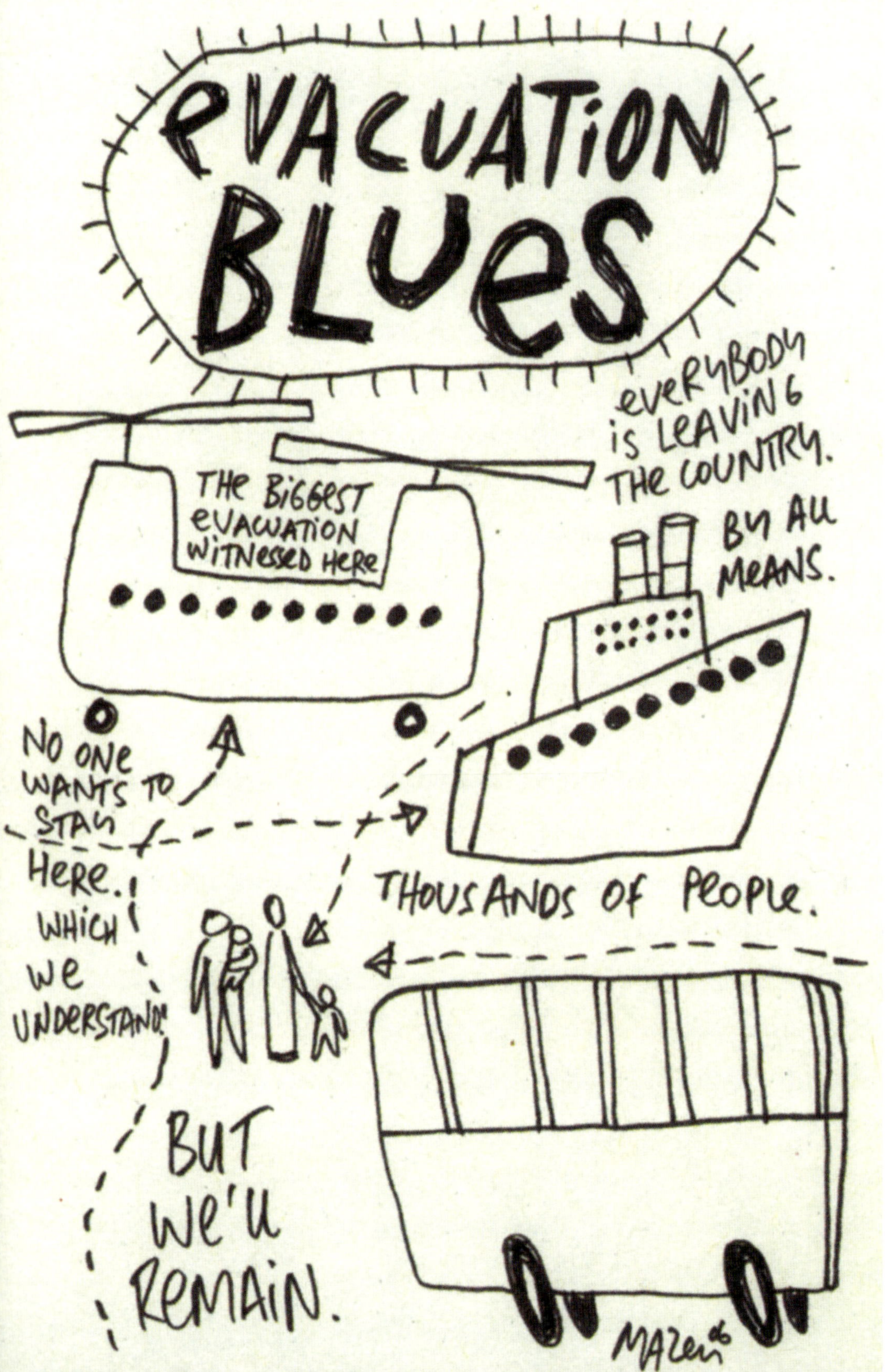

EVACUATION BLUES

THE BIGGEST EVACUATION WITNESSED HERE

EVERYBODY IS LEAVING THE COUNTRY.

BY ALL MEANS.

NO ONE WANTS TO STAY HERE. WHICH WE UNDERSTAND.

THOUSANDS OF PEOPLE.

BUT WE'LL REMAIN.

MAZEN

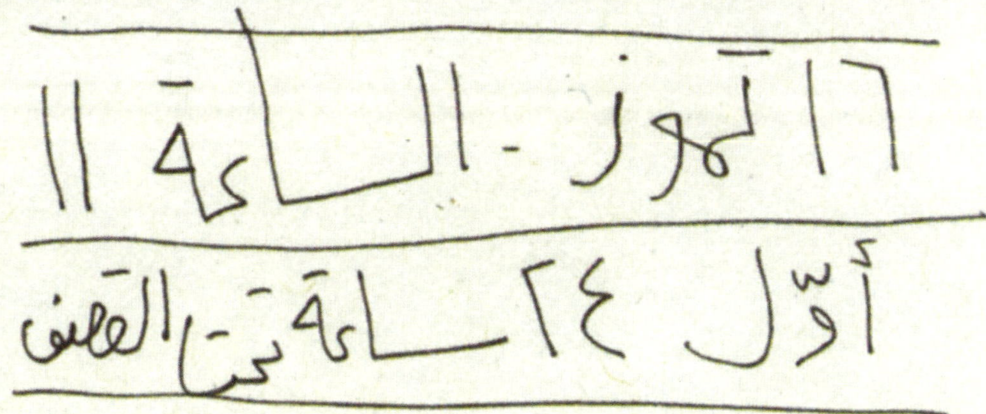

٦ ا لموز - ا لـا ٩ة ١١
أول ٢٤ سا٩ة تحت القصف

ما بعرف
كيفا نمت
ساعتين
...

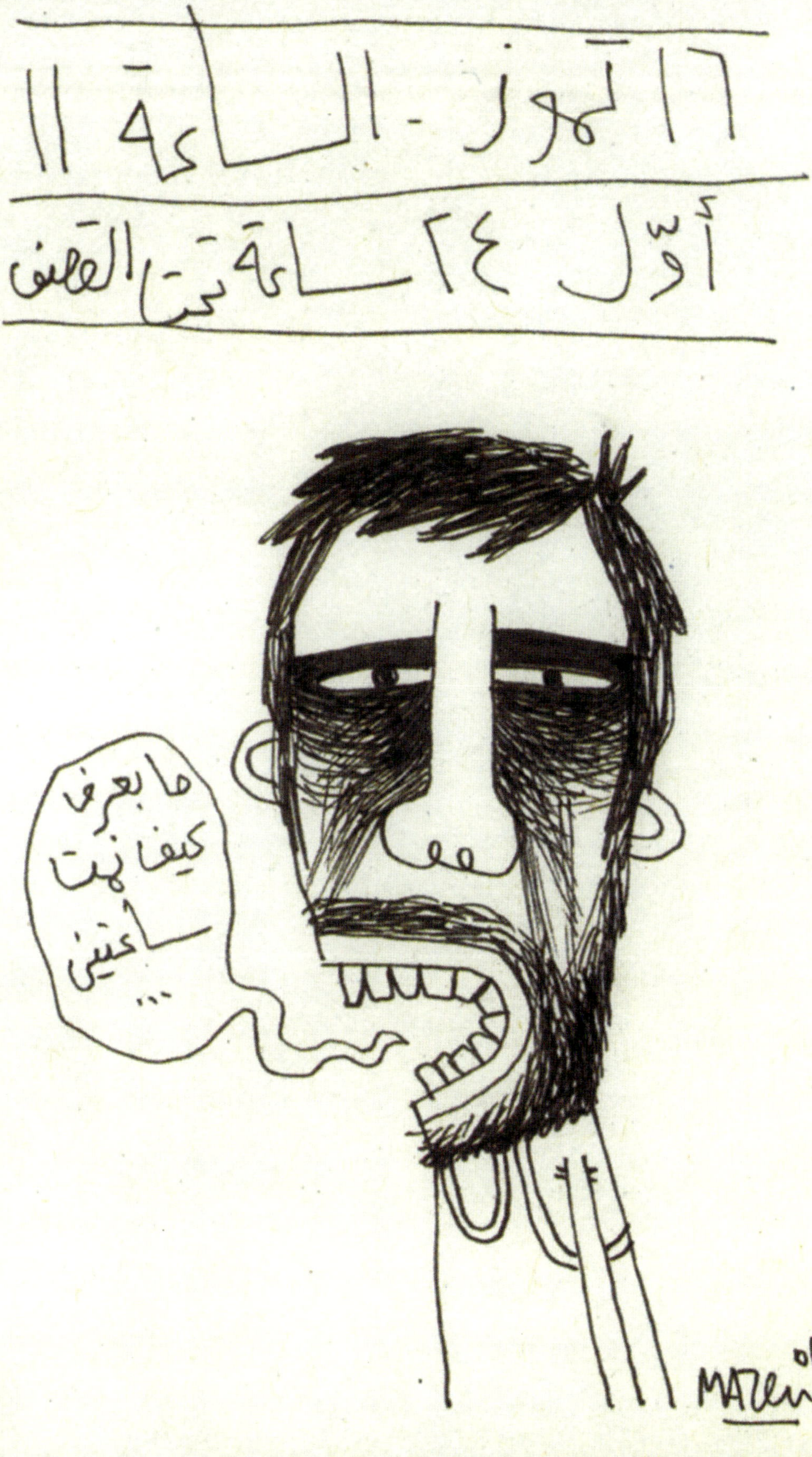

Mazen 06

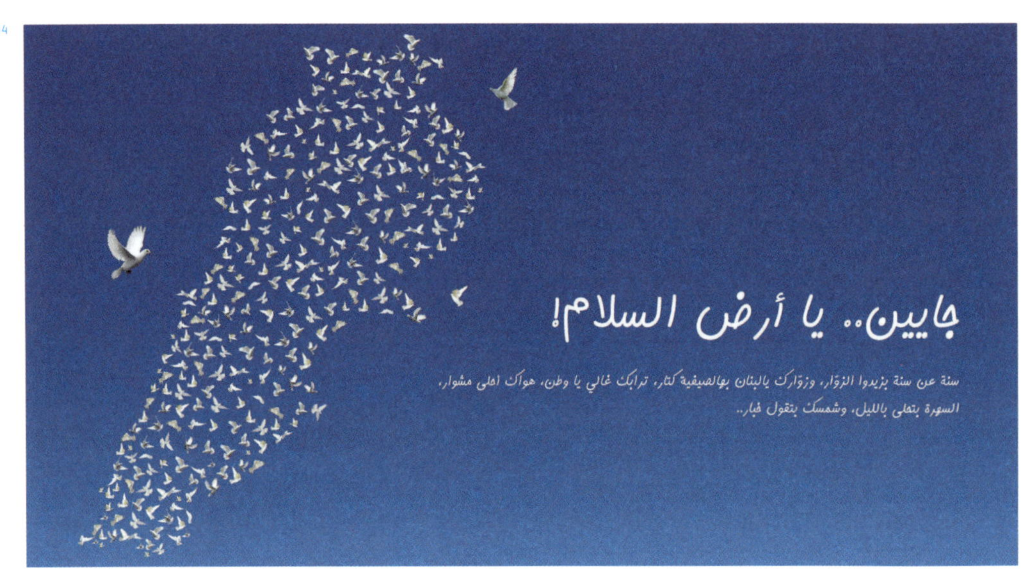

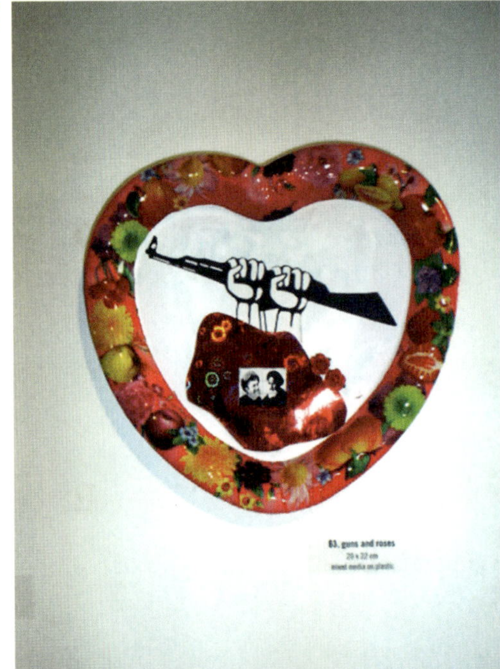

83. guns and roses
28 x 32 cm
mixed media on plastic.

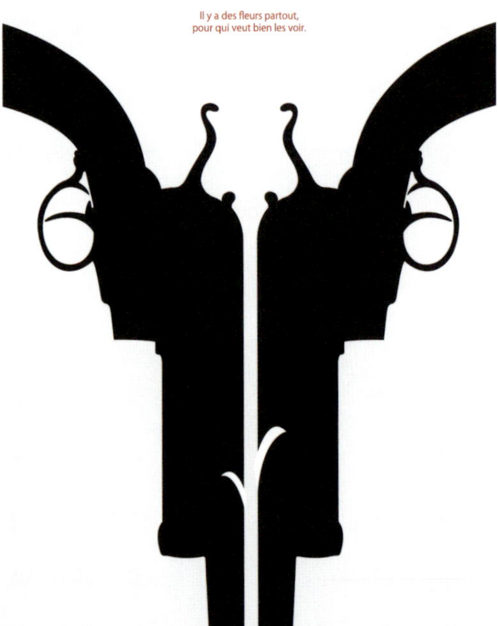

007

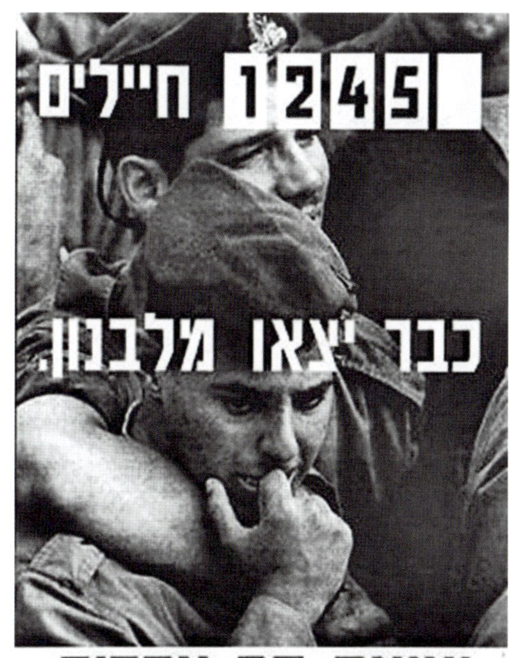

008

001 STARRY NIGHT
As bombs were dropped on Beirut
on the night of 15 July 2006,
Mazen Kerbaj played the trumpet
on his balcony and later uploaded
the recording of music and back-
ground explosions to the Internet
under the title "Starry Night."
CREATOR Mazen Kerbaj
SOURCE theaterofpeace.org
DATE July 2006

002 STARRY NIGHT
CREATOR Mazen Kerbaj
SOURCE theaterofpeace.org
DATE July 2006

003 STARRY NIGHT
CREATOR Mazen Kerbaj
SOURCE theaterofpeace.org
DATE July 2006

004 HEADING OFF TO THE LAND OF PEACE
CREATOR Lebanese Embassy, Kuwait
SOURCE www.ads2blog.com
DATE 2008

005 63. GUNS AND ROSES
CREATOR Zena el Khalil
SOURCE iconicphotos.wordpress.com
DATE 1979

006 IL Y A DES FLEURS PARTOUT, POUR
QUI VEUT BIEN LES VOIR.
[THERE ARE FLOWERS EVERYWHERE,
FOR ANYONE WHO WANTS TO SEE THEM]
CREATOR Mira Abou Malhab

007 LA PAIX ... AVEC MOI-MÊME
[PEACE ... WITH MYSELF]
CREATOR Alexandre Maalouf
SOURCE Unknown

008 1245 ISRAELI SOLDIERS HAVE
ALREADY LEFT LEBANON IN
A UNILATERAL WITHDRAWAL
CREATOR David Tartakover
SOURCE Plakatsammlung Museum
für Gestaltung Zürich
DATE 1998

001
002

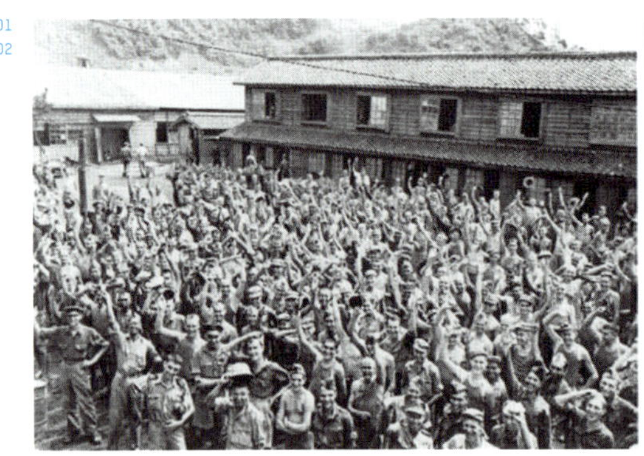
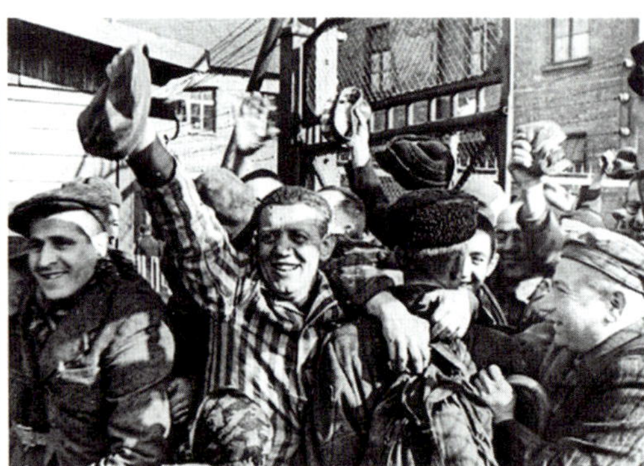

003
004

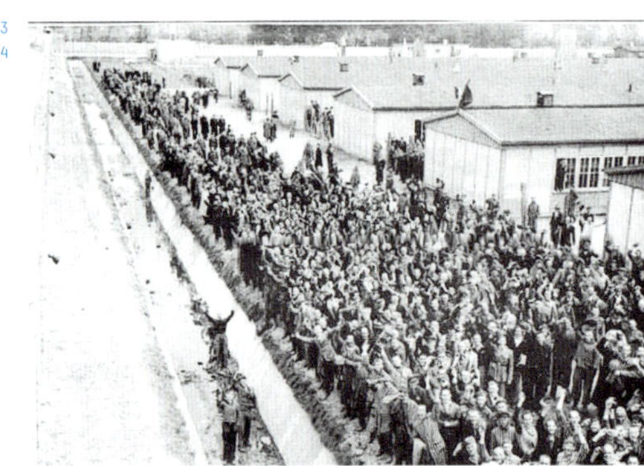
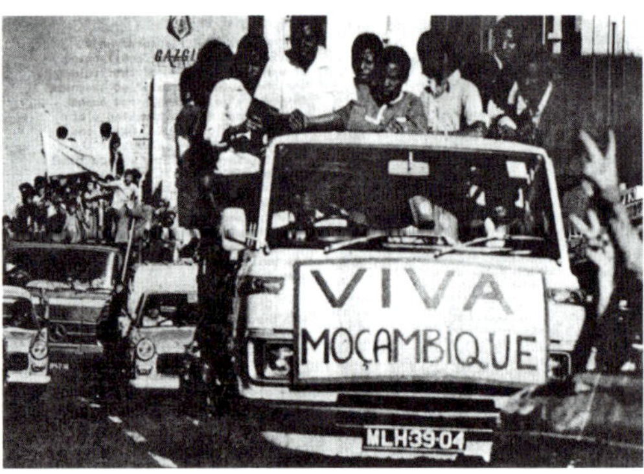

005
006

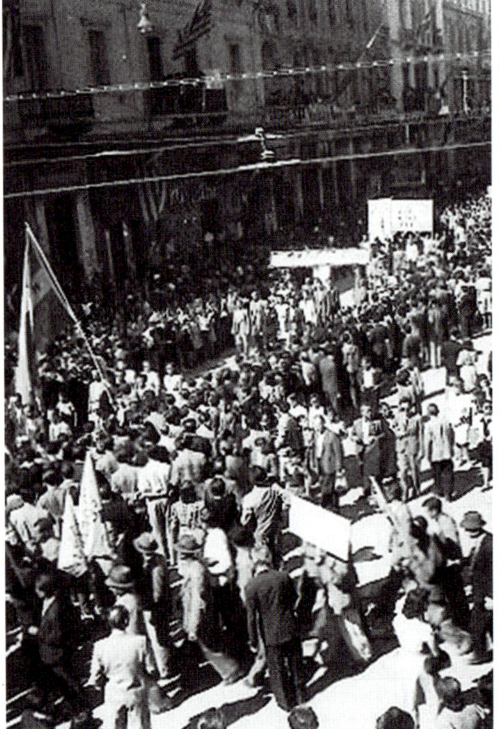
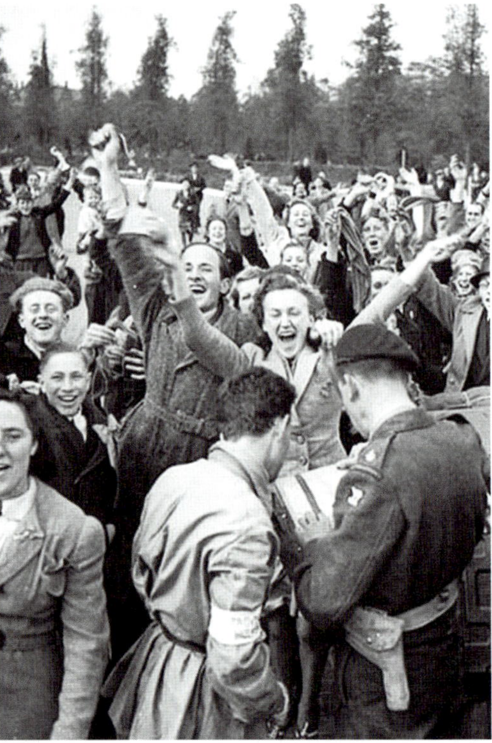

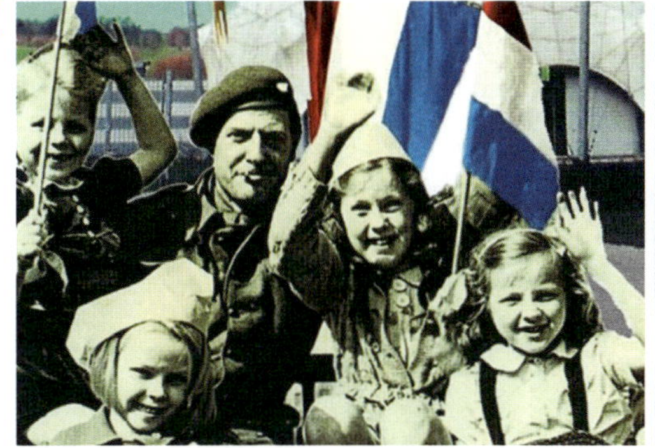
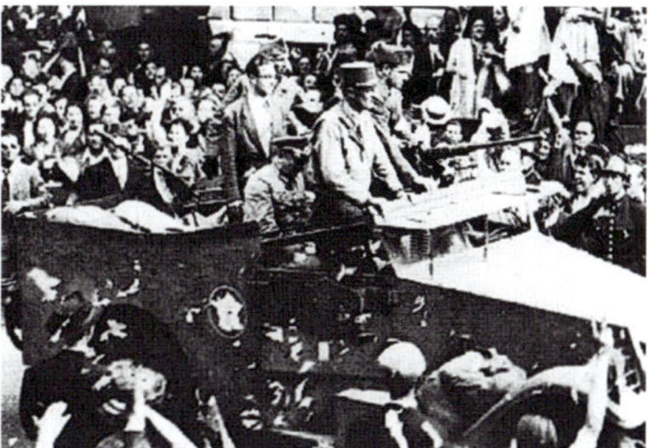
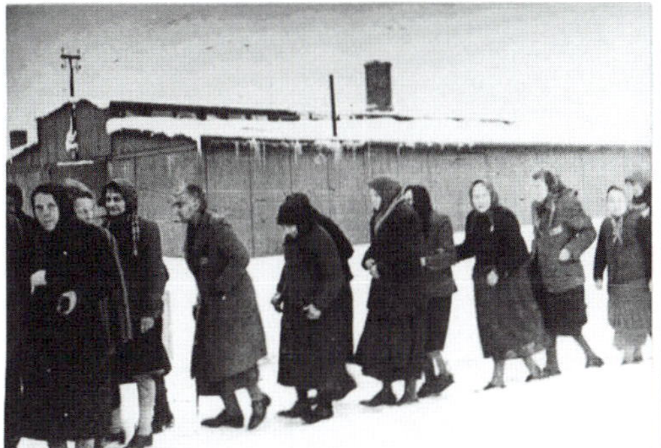
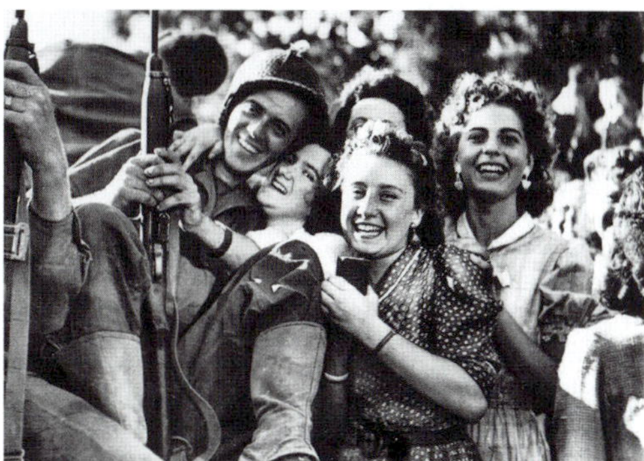
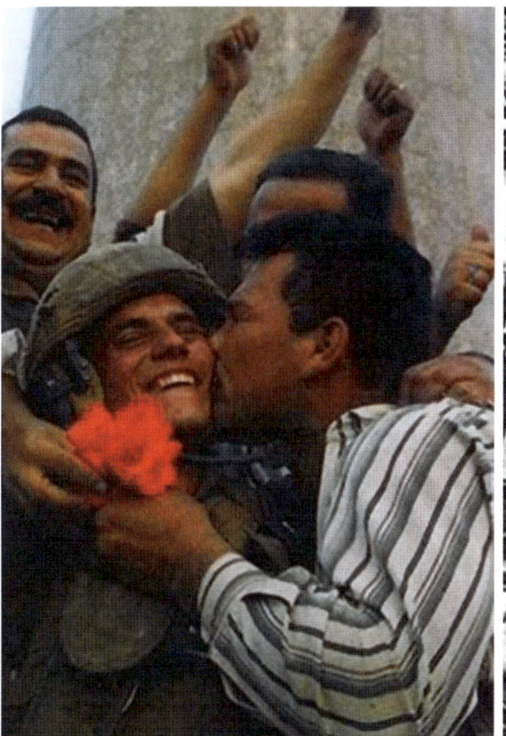
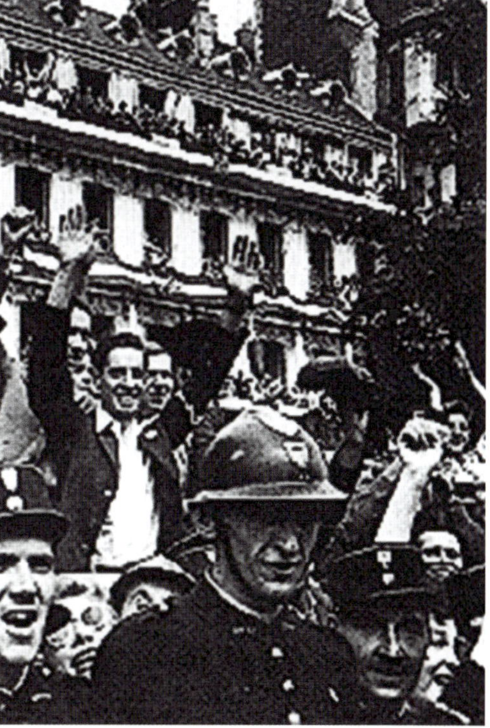

001 PRISONERS CELEBRATE END OF WAR,
     CAMP FUKUOKA #6, JAPAN
     SOURCE Unknown
     DATE 15 September 1945

002 PRISONERS OF AUSCHWITZ
     GREET THEIR LIBERATORS
     SOURCE Belarusian State Archive
     of Documentary Film and Photography
     DATE 27 January 1945

003 PRISONERS SOON AFTER
     THE LIBERATION OF DACHAU
     CONCENTRATION CAMP
     SOURCE US Holocaust Museum
     DATE 29 April 1945

004 CELEBRATIONS AT INDEPENDENCE
     OF MOZAMBIQUE
     SOURCE Unknown
     DATE 25 June 1975

005 LIBERATION OF ATHENS
     SOURCE AKG Images
     DATE 12 October 1944

006 DUTCH CELEBRATING THE LIBERATION
     OF UTRECHT, NETHERLANDS
     CREATOR Alexander Stirton
     SOURCE Unknown
     DATE 7 May 1945

007 CHILDREN RIDE ON A JEEP
     DURING THE LIBERATION OF
     VELP, NETHERLANDS
     CREATOR Sgt Hewitt, No 5 Army
     Film & Photographic Unit
     SOURCE Unknown
     DATE 16 April 1945

008 LIBERATION OF PARIS
     General Dietrich von Choltitz,
     commander of German forces in
     Paris, surrenders to Colonel
     Henri Rol-Tanguy and Maurice
     Kriegel-Valrimont [on left].
     CREATOR Roger-Viollet
     SOURCE rebellyon.info

009 FEMALE SURVIVORS TRUDGE THROUGH
     THE SNOW IMMEDIATELY AFTER THE
     LIBERATION OF AUSCHWITZ-BIRKENAU
     SOURCE www.eastrenfrewshire.gov.uk

010 LIBERATION OF PARIS, WOMEN
     AND SOLDIERS
     SOURCE AKG Images
     DATE 1944

011 VICTORY DAY IN IRAQ? NOT SO FAST!
     SOURCE cyberray-rays.blogspot.com

012 LIBERATION PARIS
     SOURCE mapage.noos.fr

001
002

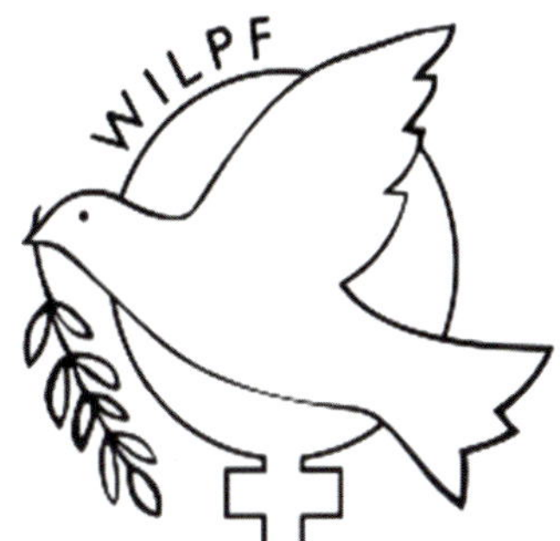

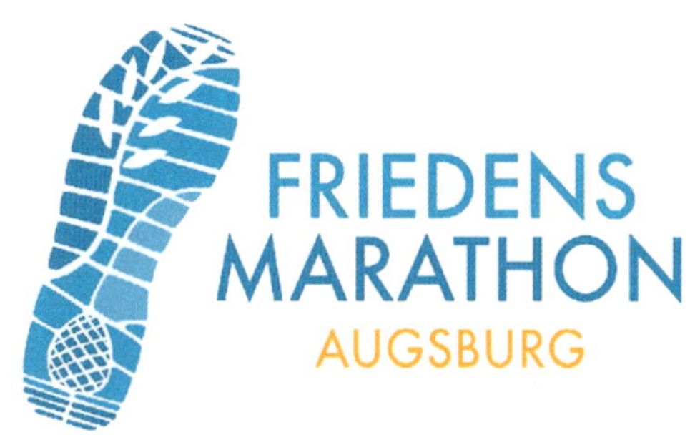

003
004

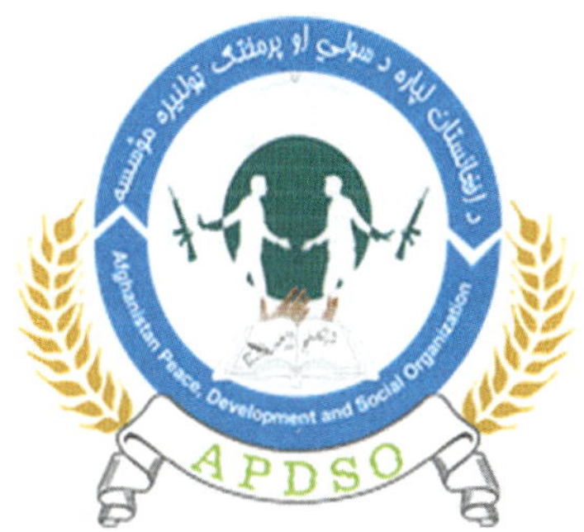

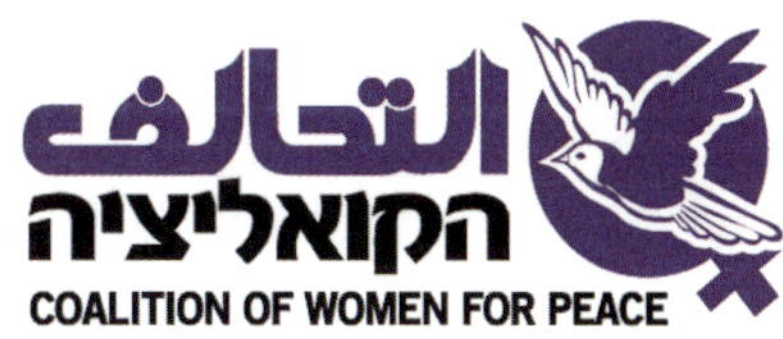

005
006

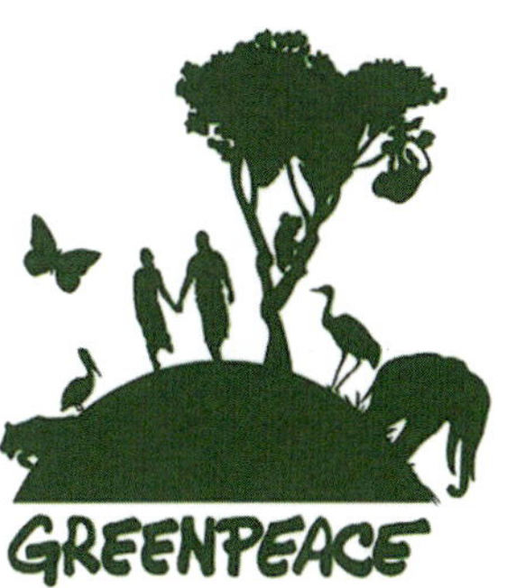

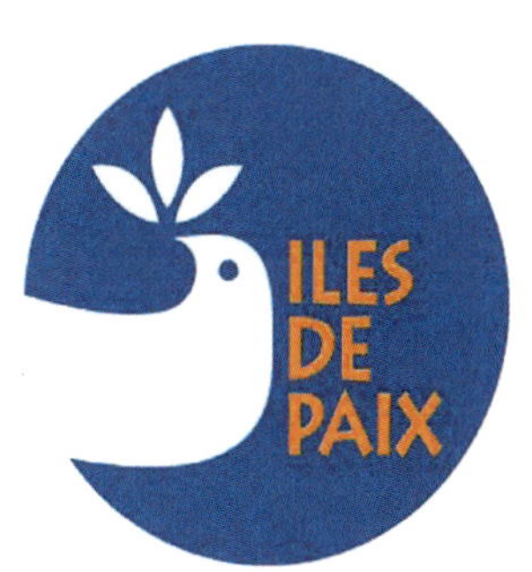

007
008

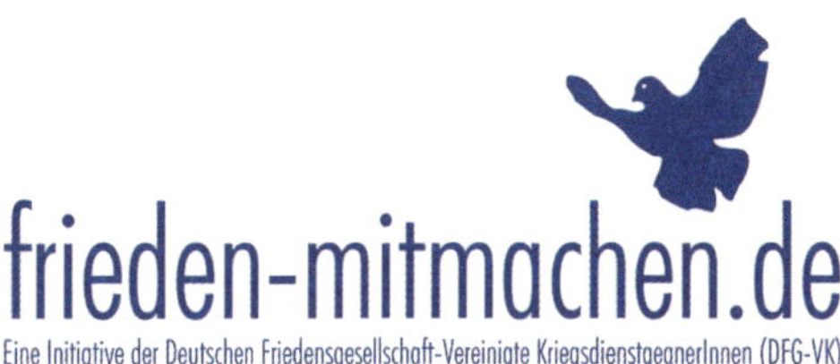

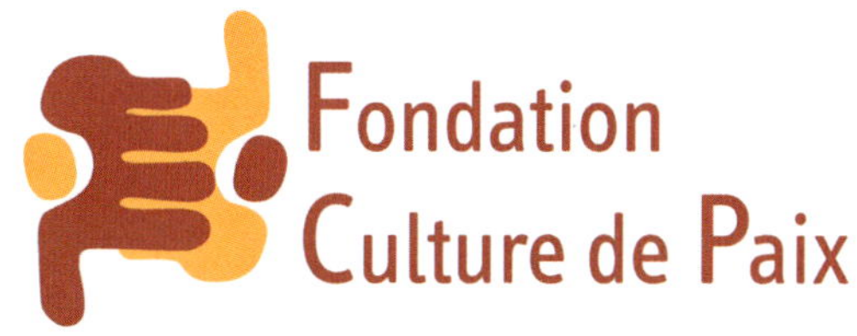

009

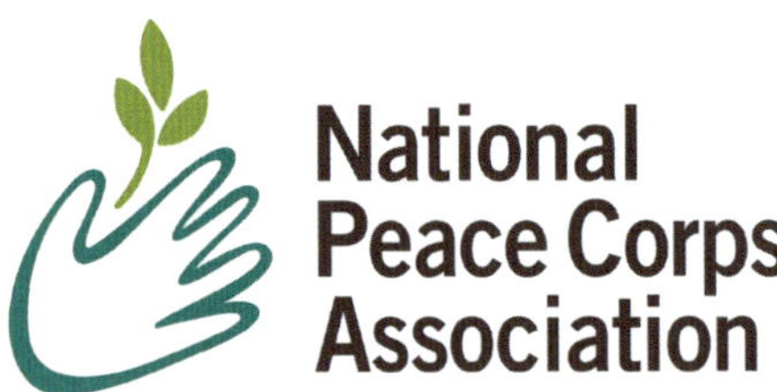

010

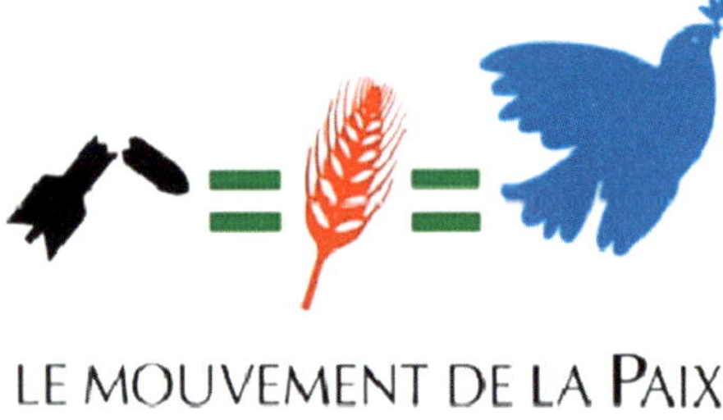

011

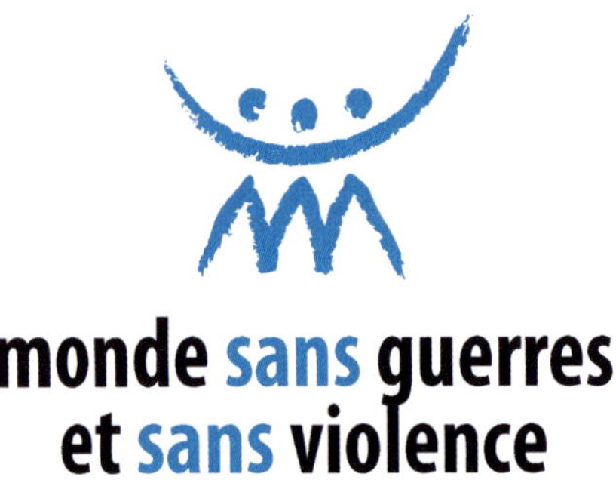

012

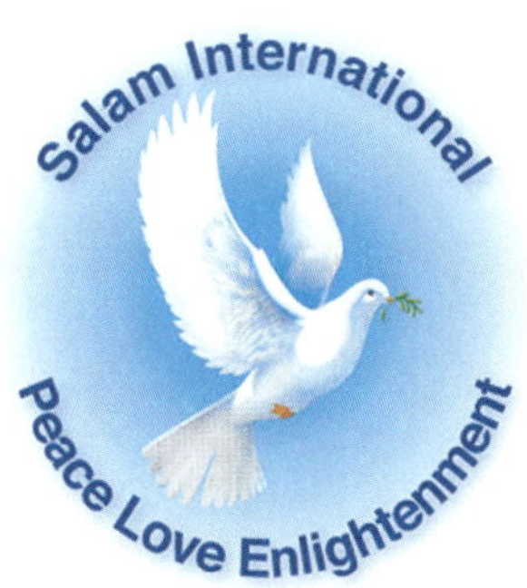

001
002

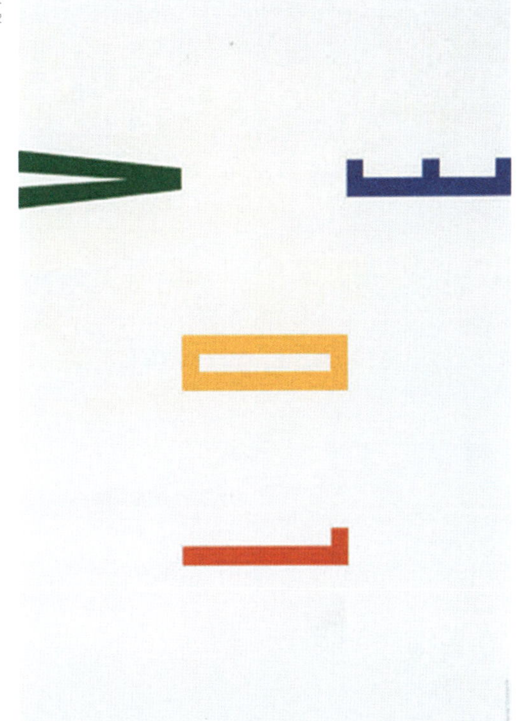

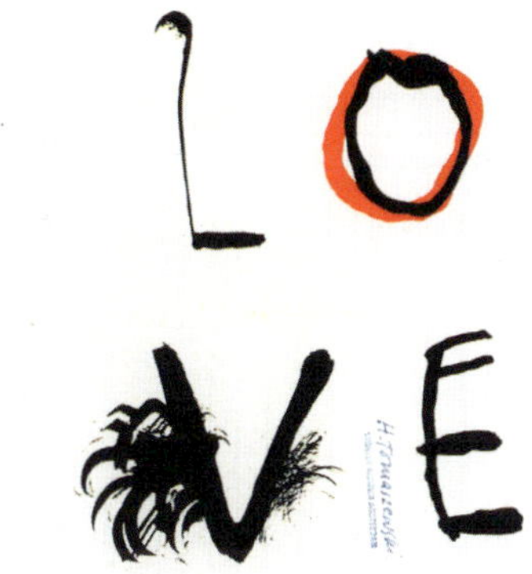

003
004

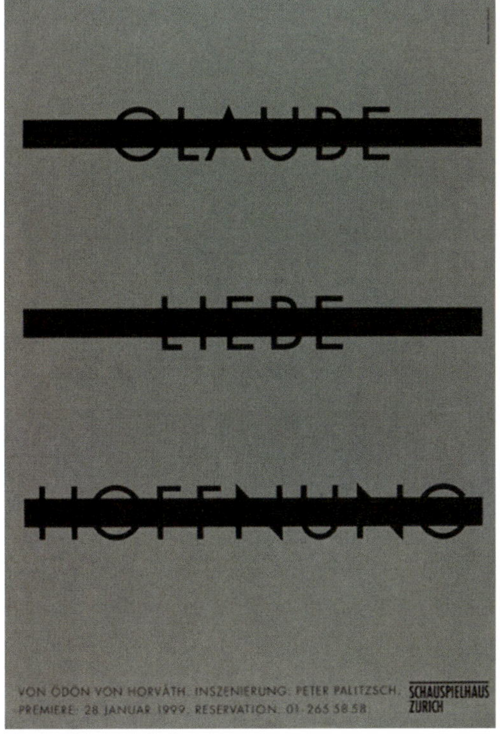

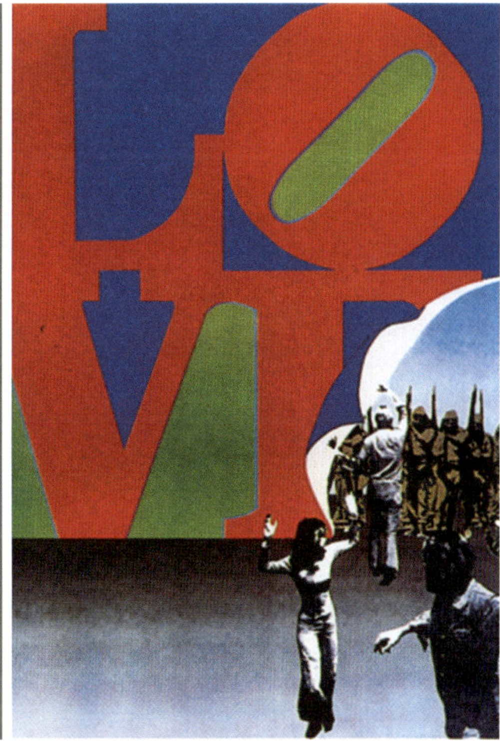

001 LOVE
     CREATOR Vladimir Caika
     SOURCE Plakatsammlung Museum
     für Gestaltung Zürich

002 LOVE
     CREATOR Henryk Tomaszewski
     SOURCE Pierre Peronnet and
     Wijntje van Rooijen, *Chaumont
     2006* (Paris: Pyramyd, 2006).
     DATE 2006

003 GLAUBE - LIEBE - HOFFNUNG
     [FAITH - LOVE - HOPE]
     SOURCE Plakatsammlung Museum
     für Gestaltung Zürich
     DATE 1999

004 LOVE
     CREATOR Bruce Kaiper
     SOURCE Bruno Margadant and
     Hans-Rudolf Lutz, *Hoffnung und
     Widerstand: das 20 Jahrhundert
     im Plakat der internationalen
     Arbeiter- und Friedensbewegung*
     [Zurich: Lutz, 1998].

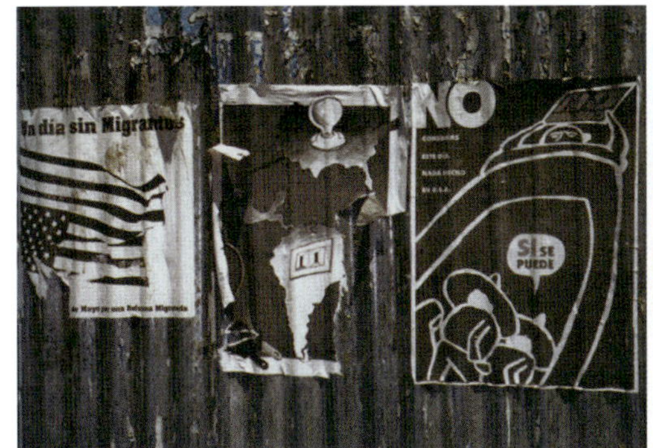
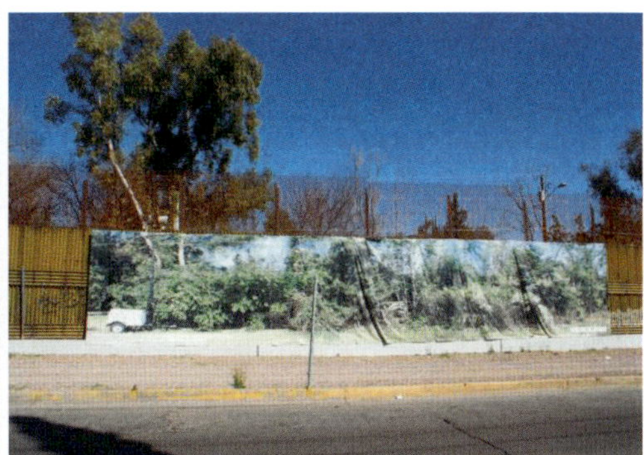

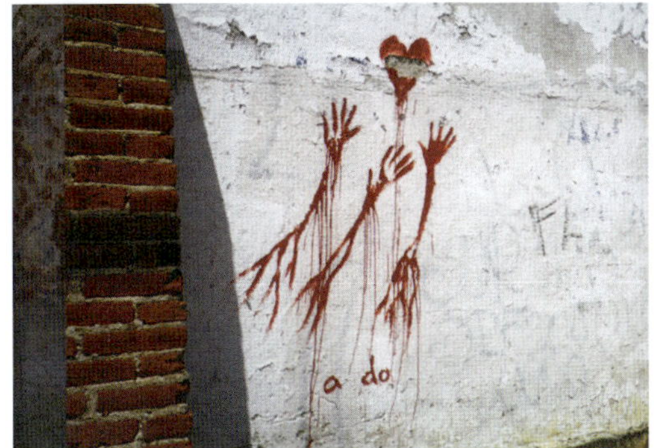
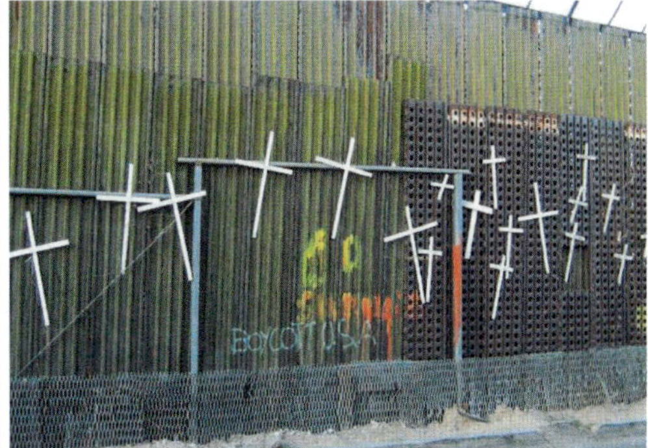

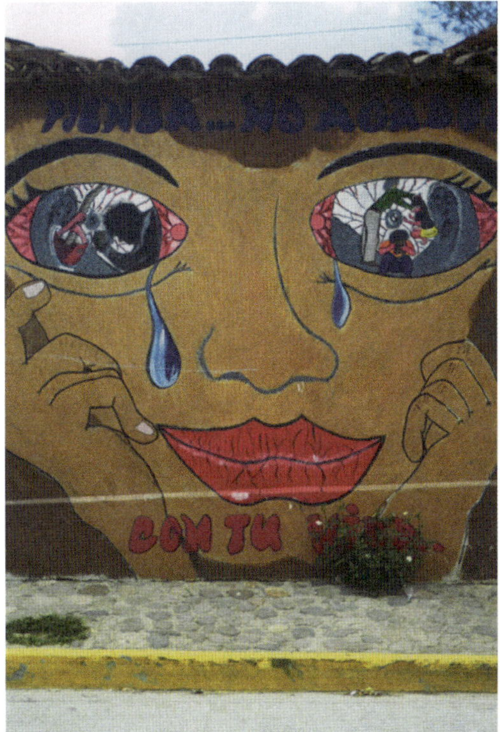
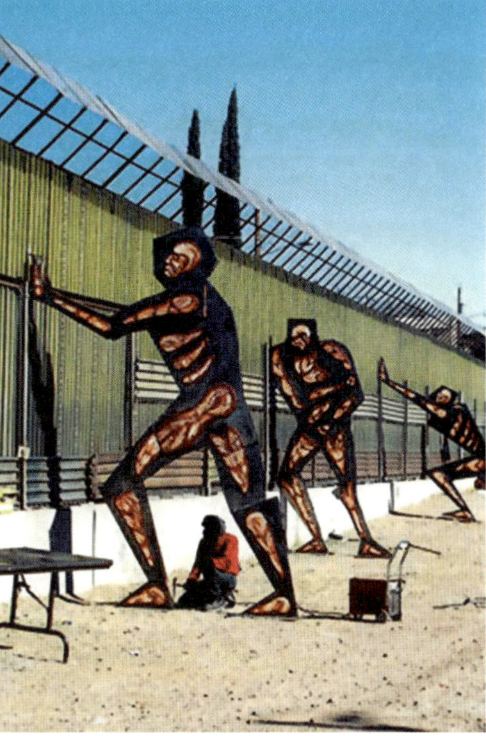

007
008

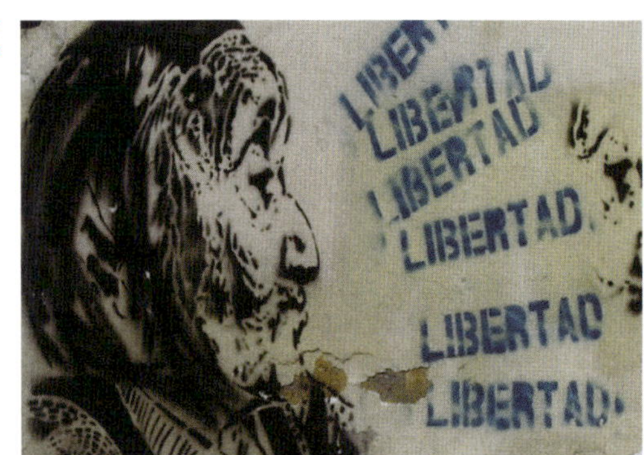

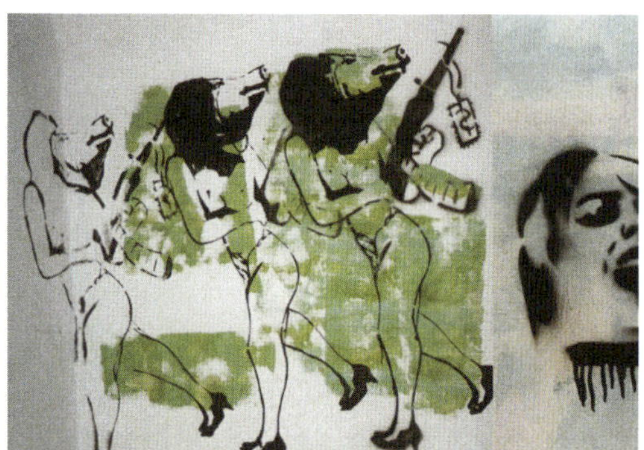

009
010

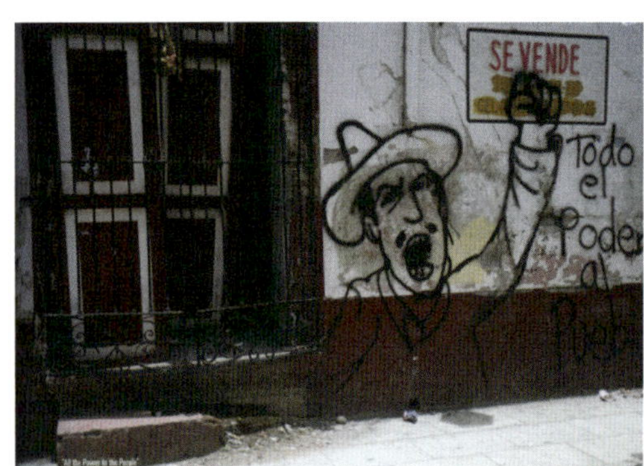

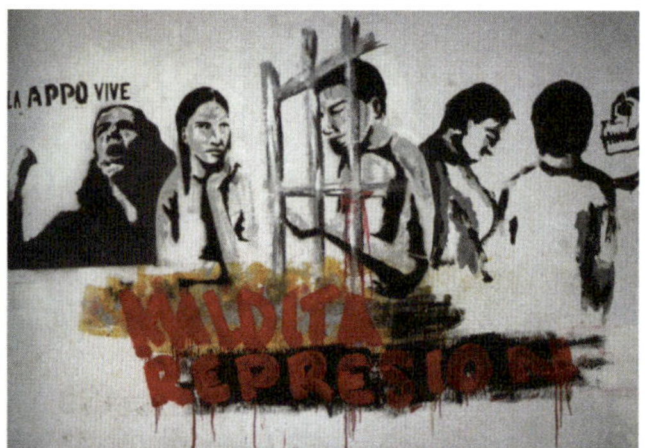

011
012

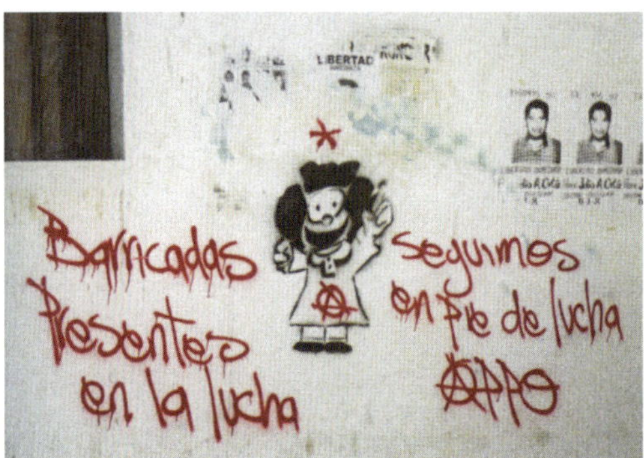

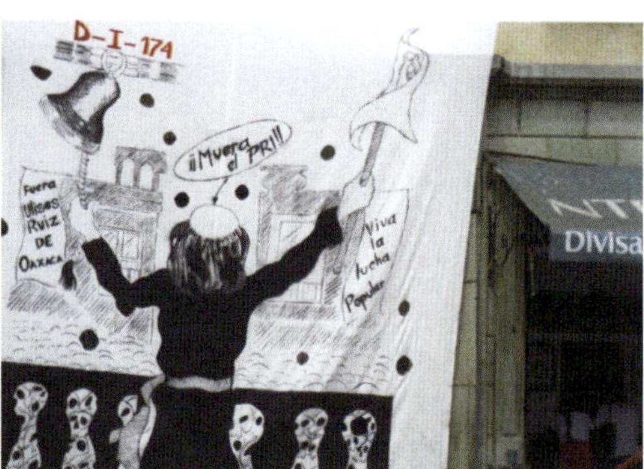

013
014

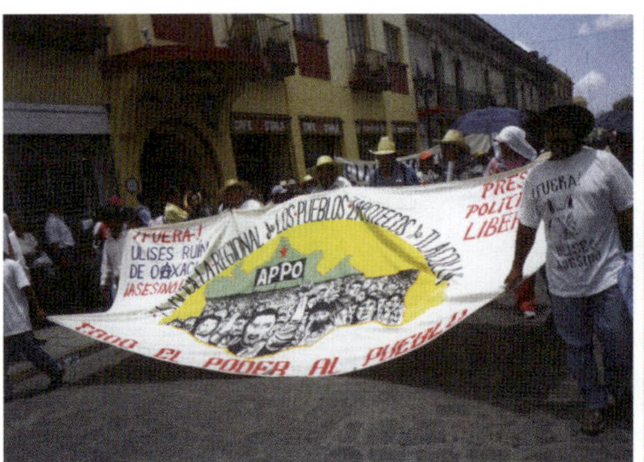

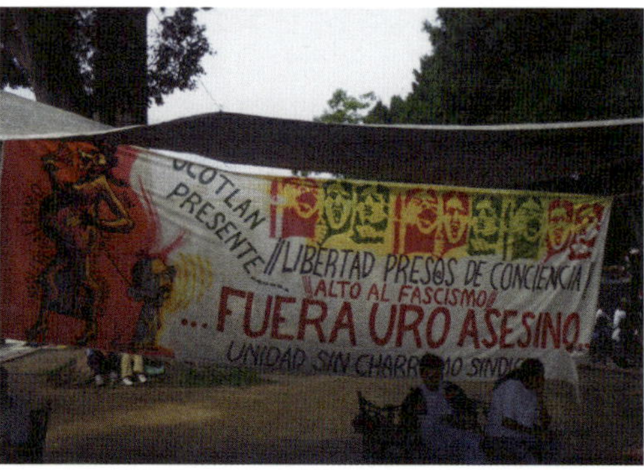

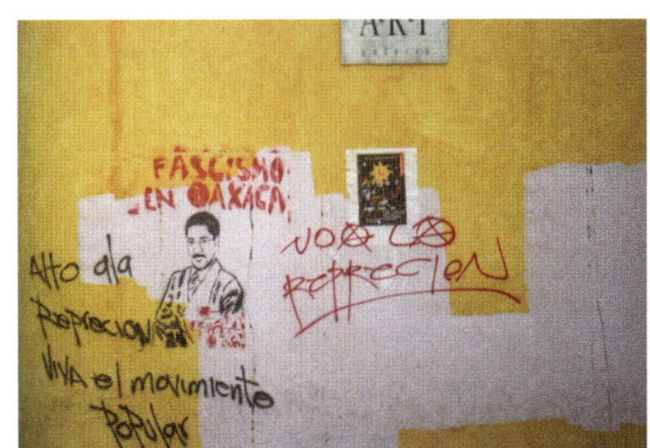
FASCISMO
EN OAXACA
NO A LA
REPRECION
Alto a la
Represion
Viva el movimiento
Popular

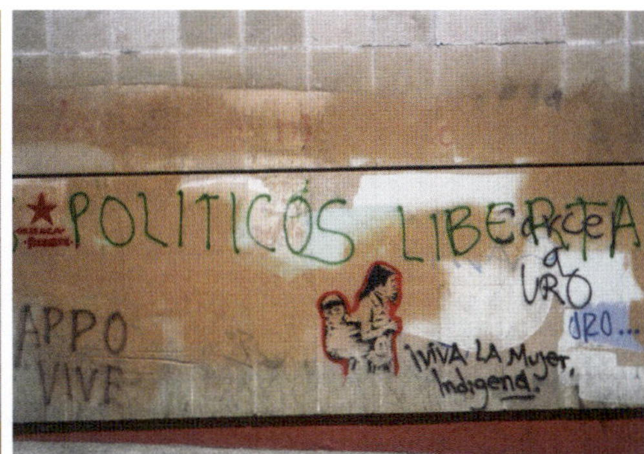
POLITICOS LIBER
URO
URO...
APPO
VIVE
VIVA LA Mujer
Indigena

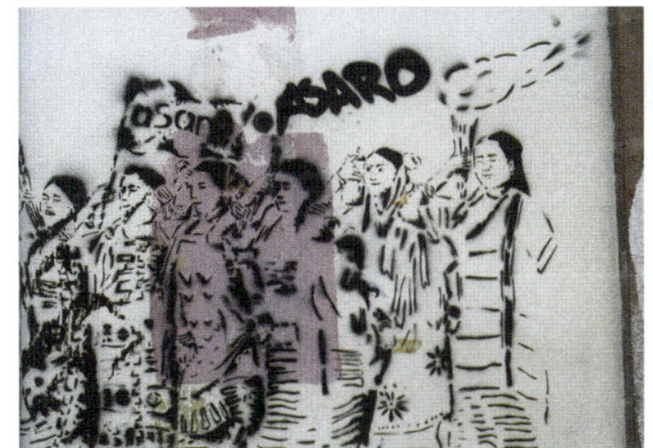
ASARO

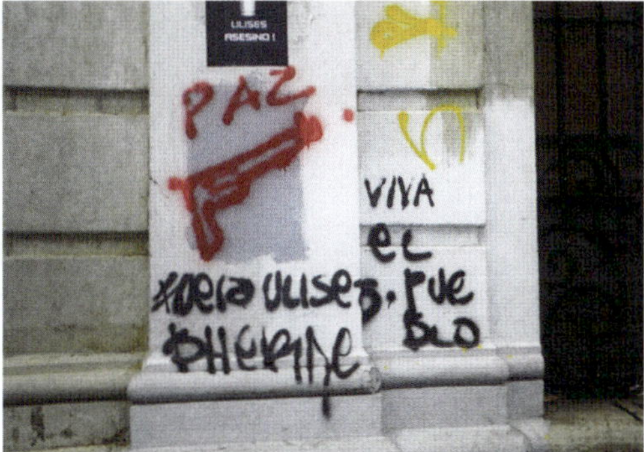
ULISES
ASESINO !
PAZ
VIVA
el
ULISES pue
DHERDE blo

MARISCOS LA RED
LA PAZ KE NOS
OFRECEN ES LA
PAZ DE OPRESOR

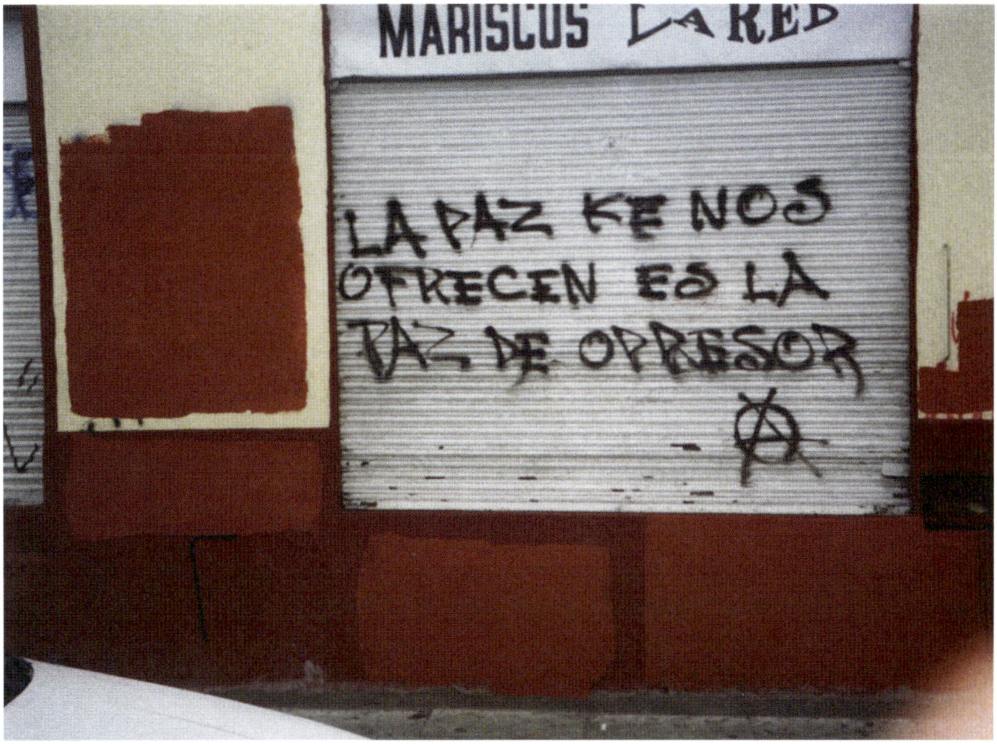

020
021
022

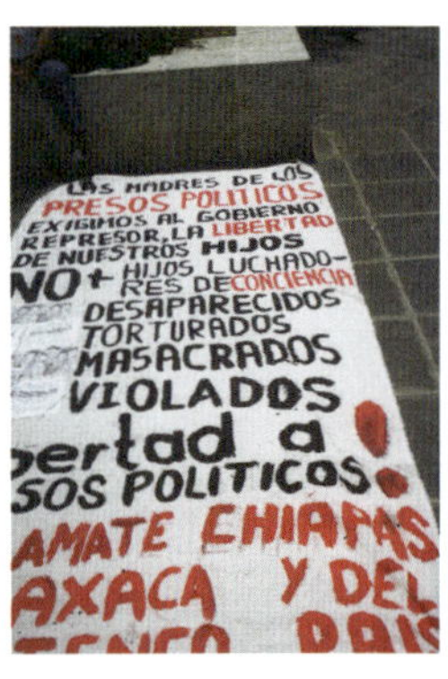
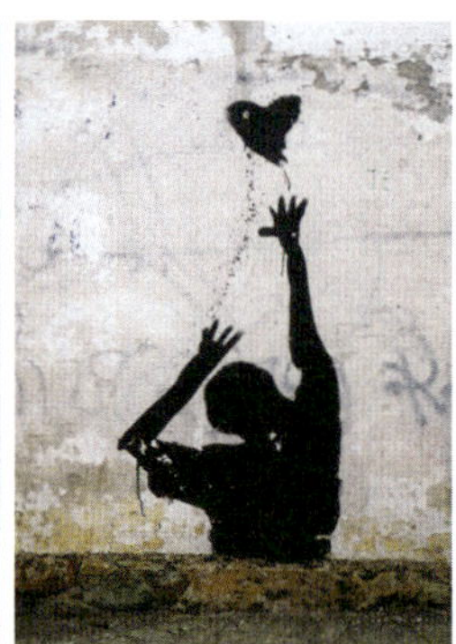
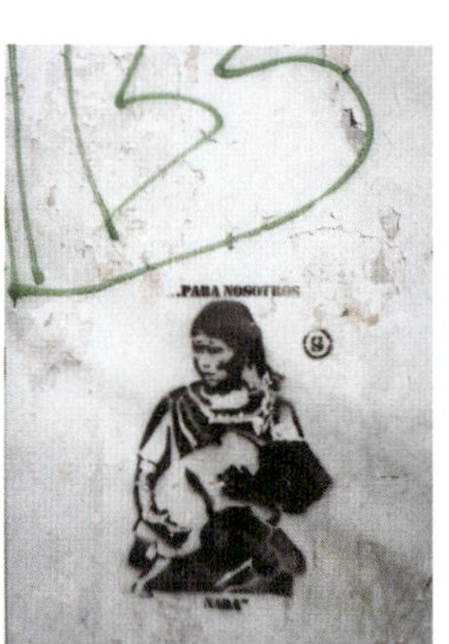

023
024
025

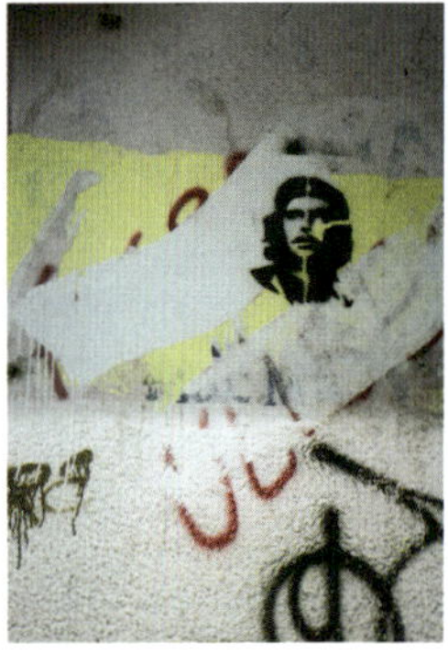
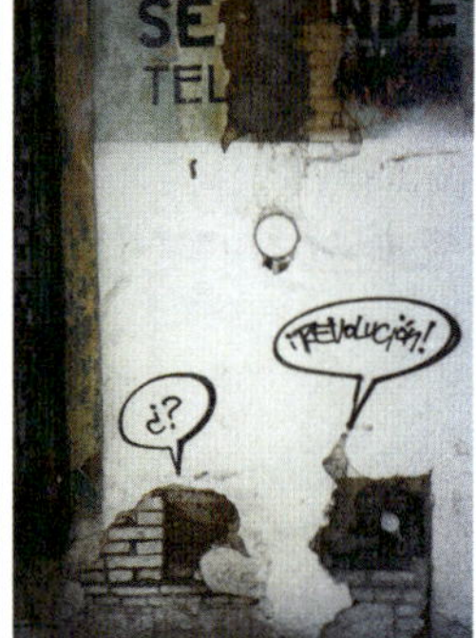
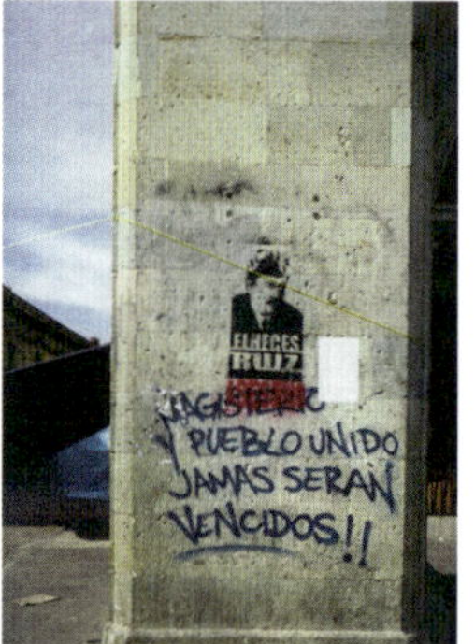

026
027
028

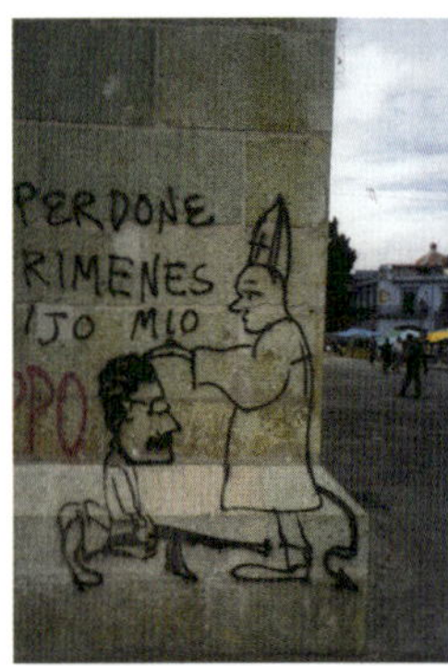
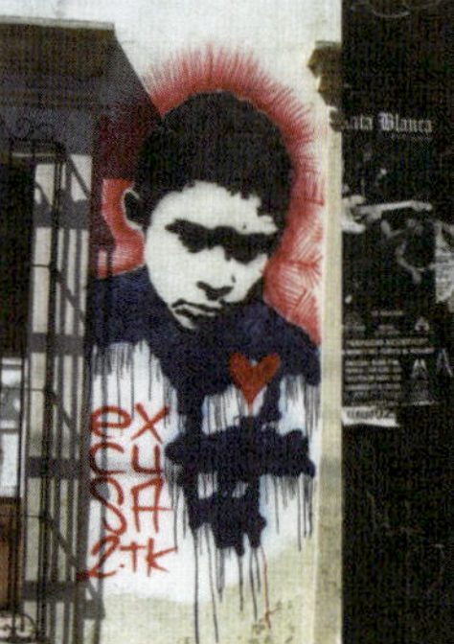
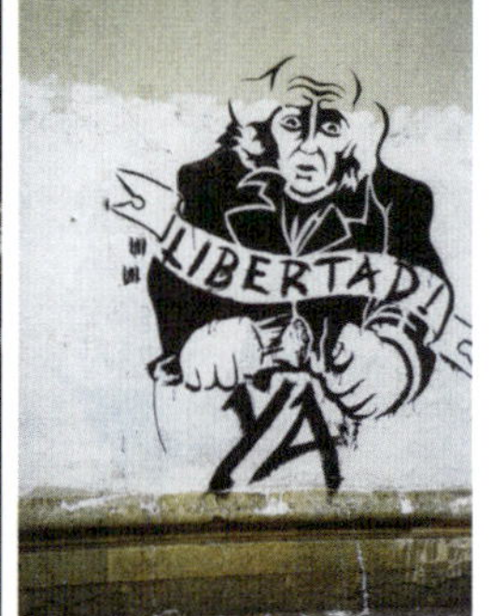

029
030

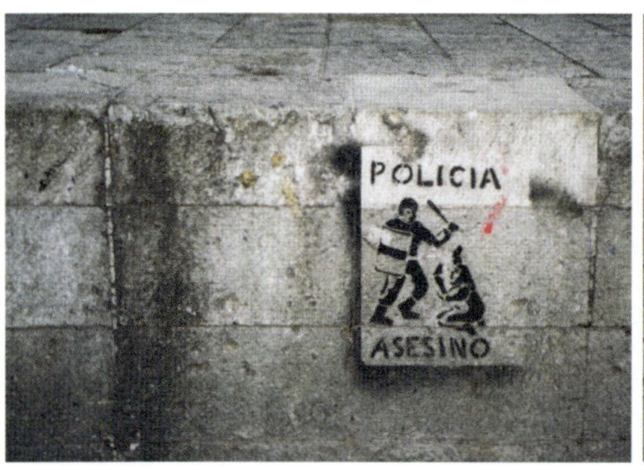
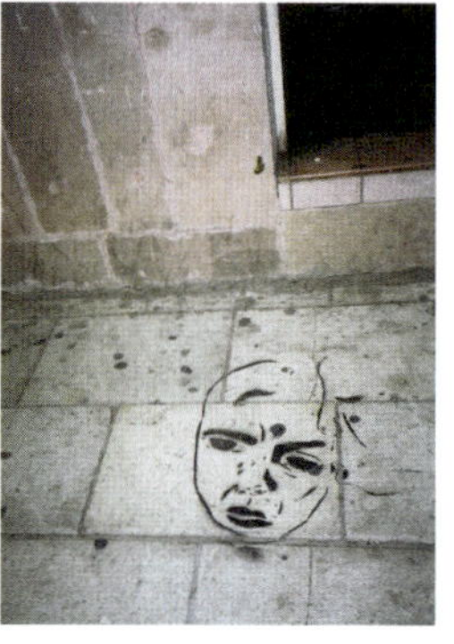

001 UNTITLED
CREATOR Photograph by Elaine Sendyk
SOURCE Louis E. V. Nevaer and
Elaine Sendyk, *Protest Graffiti
Mexico: Oaxaca* [New York: Mark
Batty Publisher, 2009].

002 VIRTUAL DISAPPEARANCE OF
A SECTION OF THE BORDER
FENCE BETWEEN NOGALES, SONORA
[MEXICO] FROM NOGALES, ARIZONA
[UNITED STATES]
SOURCE www.muralesfrontera.org

003 UNTITLED
CREATOR Photograph by Elaine Sendyk
SOURCE Louis E. V. Nevaer and
Elaine Sendyk, *Protest Graffiti
Mexico: Oaxaca* [New York: Mark
Batty Publisher, 2009].

004 BORDER WALL IN NOGALES, MEXICO
WITH BORDER DEATH MEMORIAL
SOURCE www.800milewall.org

005 UNTITLED
CREATOR Photograph by Elaine Sendyk
SOURCE Louis E. V. Nevaer and
Elaine Sendyk, *Protest Graffiti
Mexico: Oaxaca* [New York: Mark
Batty Publisher, 2009].

006 BORDER DYNAMICS, WINTER 2003
SOURCE www.muralesfrontera.org

007 UNTITLED
CREATOR Photograph by Elaine Sendyk
SOURCE Louis E. V. Nevaer and
Elaine Sendyk, *Protest Graffiti
Mexico: Oaxaca* [New York: Mark
Batty Publisher, 2009].

008 UNTITLED
CREATOR Photograph by Elaine Sendyk
SOURCE Louis E. V. Nevaer and
Elaine Sendyk, *Protest Graffiti
Mexico: Oaxaca* [New York: Mark
Batty Publisher, 2009].

009 UNTITLED
CREATOR Photograph by Elaine Sendyk
SOURCE Louis E. V. Nevaer and
Elaine Sendyk, *Protest Graffiti
Mexico: Oaxaca* [New York: Mark
Batty Publisher, 2009].

010 UNTITLED
CREATOR Photograph by Elaine Sendyk
SOURCE Louis E. V. Nevaer and
Elaine Sendyk, *Protest Graffiti
Mexico: Oaxaca* [New York: Mark
Batty Publisher, 2009].

011 UNTITLED
CREATOR Photograph by Elaine Sendyk
SOURCE Louis E. V. Nevaer and
Elaine Sendyk, *Protest Graffiti
Mexico: Oaxaca* [New York: Mark
Batty Publisher, 2009].

012 UNTITLED
CREATOR Photograph by Elaine Sendyk
SOURCE Louis E. V. Nevaer and
Elaine Sendyk, *Protest Graffiti
Mexico: Oaxaca* [New York: Mark
Batty Publisher, 2009].

013 UNTITLED
CREATOR Photograph by Elaine Sendyk
SOURCE Louis E. V. Nevaer and
Elaine Sendyk, *Protest Graffiti
Mexico: Oaxaca* [New York: Mark
Batty Publisher, 2009].

014 UNTITLED
CREATOR Photograph by Elaine Sendyk
SOURCE Louis E. V. Nevaer and
Elaine Sendyk, *Protest Graffiti
Mexico: Oaxaca* [New York: Mark
Batty Publisher, 2009].

015 UNTITLED
CREATOR Photograph by Elaine Sendyk
SOURCE Louis E. V. Nevaer and
Elaine Sendyk, *Protest Graffiti
Mexico: Oaxaca* [New York: Mark
Batty Publisher, 2009].

016 UNTITLED
CREATOR Photograph by Elaine Sendyk
SOURCE Louis E. V. Nevaer and
Elaine Sendyk, *Protest Graffiti
Mexico: Oaxaca* [New York: Mark
Batty Publisher, 2009].

017 UNTITLED
CREATOR Photograph by Elaine Sendyk
SOURCE Louis E. V. Nevaer and
Elaine Sendyk, *Protest Graffiti
Mexico: Oaxaca* [New York: Mark
Batty Publisher, 2009].

018 UNTITLED
CREATOR Photograph by Elaine Sendyk
SOURCE Louis E. V. Nevaer and
Elaine Sendyk, *Protest Graffiti
Mexico: Oaxaca* [New York: Mark
Batty Publisher, 2009].

019 UNTITLED
CREATOR Photograph by Elaine Sendyk
SOURCE Louis E. V. Nevaer and
Elaine Sendyk, *Protest Graffiti
Mexico: Oaxaca* [New York: Mark
Batty Publisher, 2009].

020 UNTITLED
CREATOR Photograph by Elaine Sendyk
SOURCE Louis E. V. Nevaer and
Elaine Sendyk, *Protest Graffiti
Mexico: Oaxaca* [New York: Mark
Batty Publisher, 2009].

021 UNTITLED
CREATOR Photograph by Elaine Sendyk
SOURCE Louis E. V. Nevaer and
Elaine Sendyk, *Protest Graffiti
Mexico: Oaxaca* [New York: Mark
Batty Publisher, 2009].

022 UNTITLED
CREATOR Photograph by Elaine Sendyk
SOURCE Louis E. V. Nevaer and
Elaine Sendyk, *Protest Graffiti
Mexico: Oaxaca* [New York: Mark
Batty Publisher, 2009].

023 UNTITLED
CREATOR Photograph by Elaine Sendyk
SOURCE Louis E. V. Nevaer and
Elaine Sendyk, *Protest Graffiti
Mexico: Oaxaca* [New York: Mark
Batty Publisher, 2009].

024 UNTITLED
CREATOR Photograph by Elaine Sendyk
SOURCE Louis E. V. Nevaer and
Elaine Sendyk, *Protest Graffiti
Mexico: Oaxaca* [New York: Mark
Batty Publisher, 2009].

025 UNTITLED
CREATOR Photograph by Elaine Sendyk
SOURCE Louis E. V. Nevaer and
Elaine Sendyk, *Protest Graffiti
Mexico: Oaxaca* [New York: Mark
Batty Publisher, 2009].

026 UNTITLED
CREATOR Photograph by Elaine Sendyk
SOURCE Louis E. V. Nevaer and
Elaine Sendyk, *Protest Graffiti
Mexico: Oaxaca* [New York: Mark
Batty Publisher, 2009].

027 UNTITLED
CREATOR Photograph by Elaine Sendyk
SOURCE Louis E. V. Nevaer and
Elaine Sendyk, *Protest Graffiti
Mexico: Oaxaca* [New York: Mark
Batty Publisher, 2009].

028 UNTITLED
CREATOR Photograph by Elaine Sendyk
SOURCE Louis E. V. Nevaer and
Elaine Sendyk, *Protest Graffiti
Mexico: Oaxaca* [New York: Mark
Batty Publisher, 2009].

029 UNTITLED
CREATOR Photograph by Elaine Sendyk
SOURCE Louis E. V. Nevaer and
Elaine Sendyk, *Protest Graffiti
Mexico: Oaxaca* [New York: Mark
Batty Publisher, 2009].

030 UNTITLED
CREATOR Photograph by Elaine Sendyk
SOURCE Louis E. V. Nevaer and
Elaine Sendyk, *Protest Graffiti
Mexico: Oaxaca* [New York: Mark
Batty Publisher, 2009].

001
002

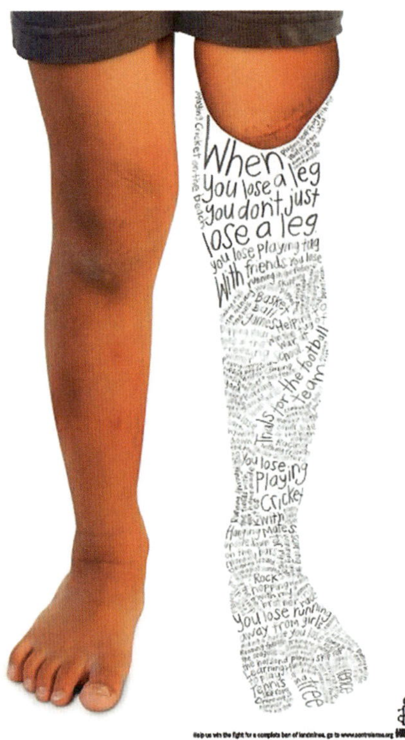

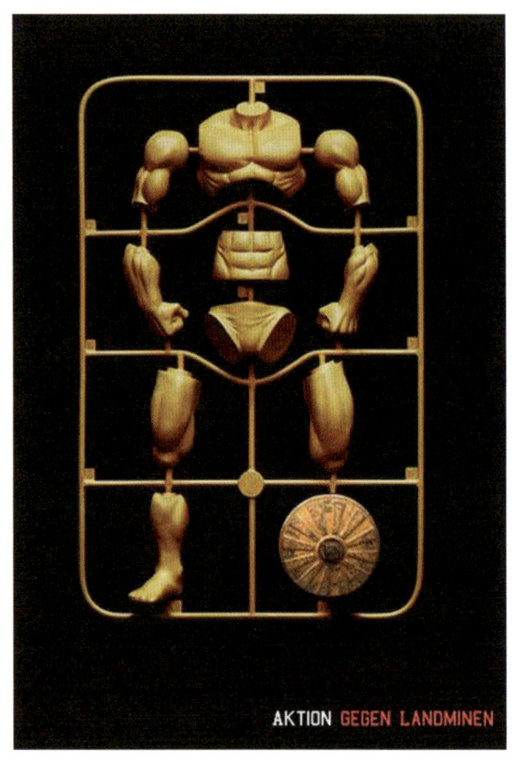

003
004

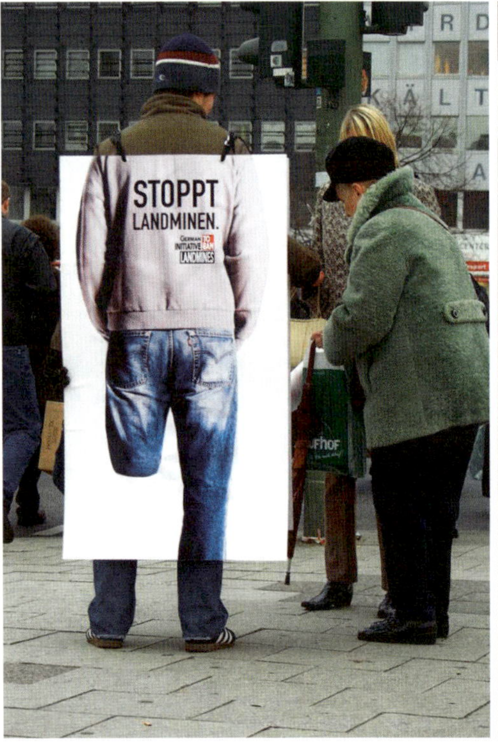

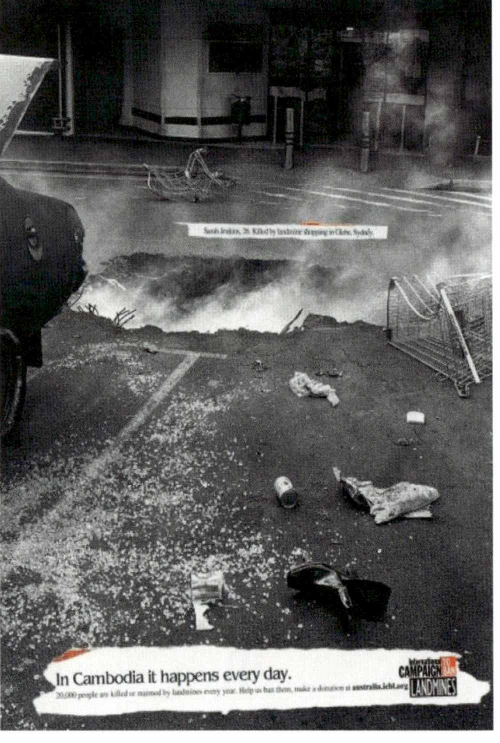

005
006

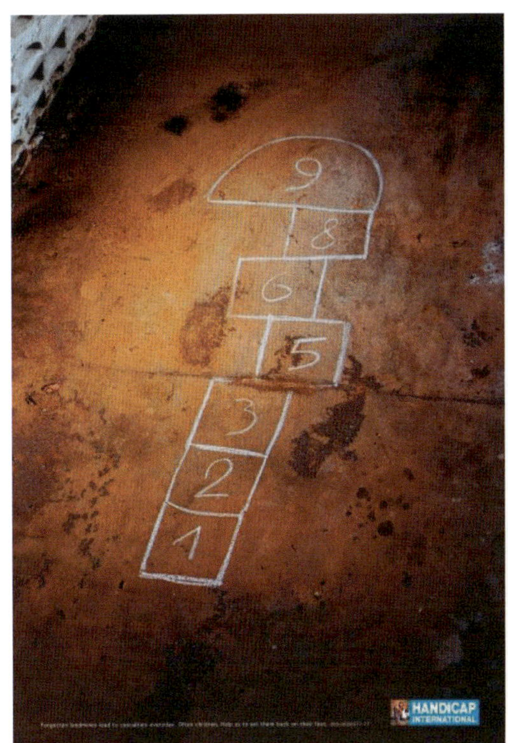
HANDICAP
INTERNATIONAL

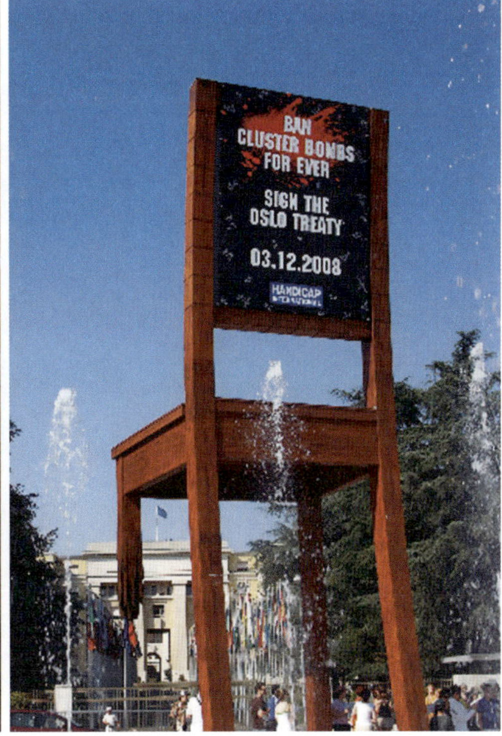
BAN
CLUSTER BOMBS
FOR EVER

SIGN THE
OSLO TREATY

03.12.2008

HANDICAP
INTERNATIONAL

007

Aujourd'hui, 37 pays continuent de produire
des mines antipersonnel et des bombes à sous-munitions.
Pour arrêter le massacre, signez la pétition sur www.sousmunitions.org

HANDICAP
INTERNATIONAL

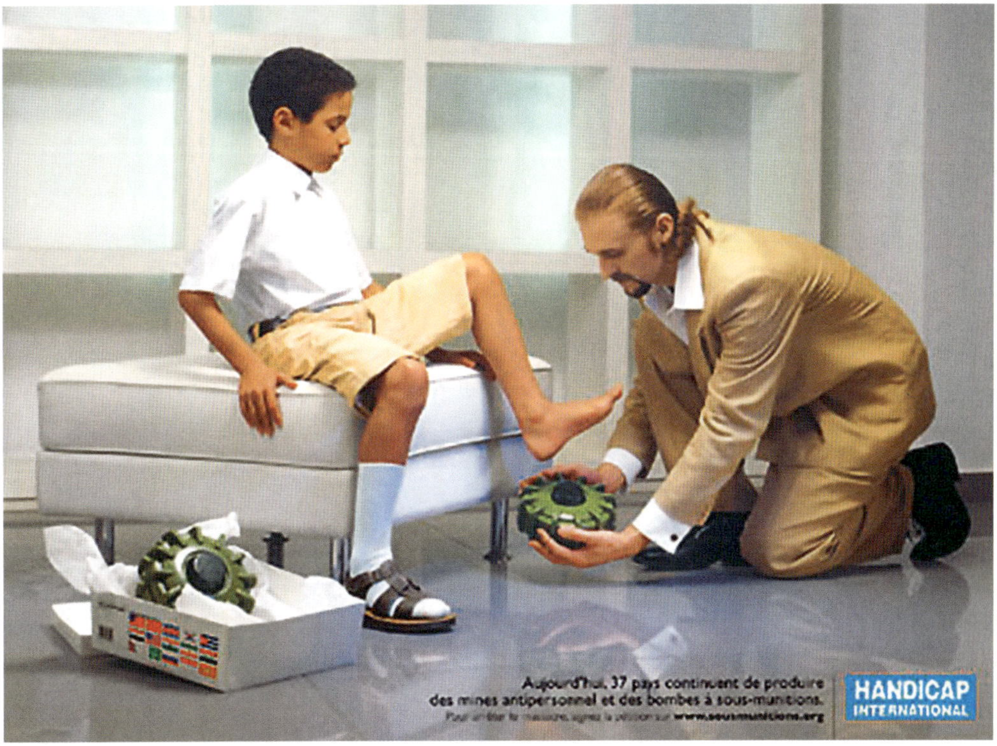

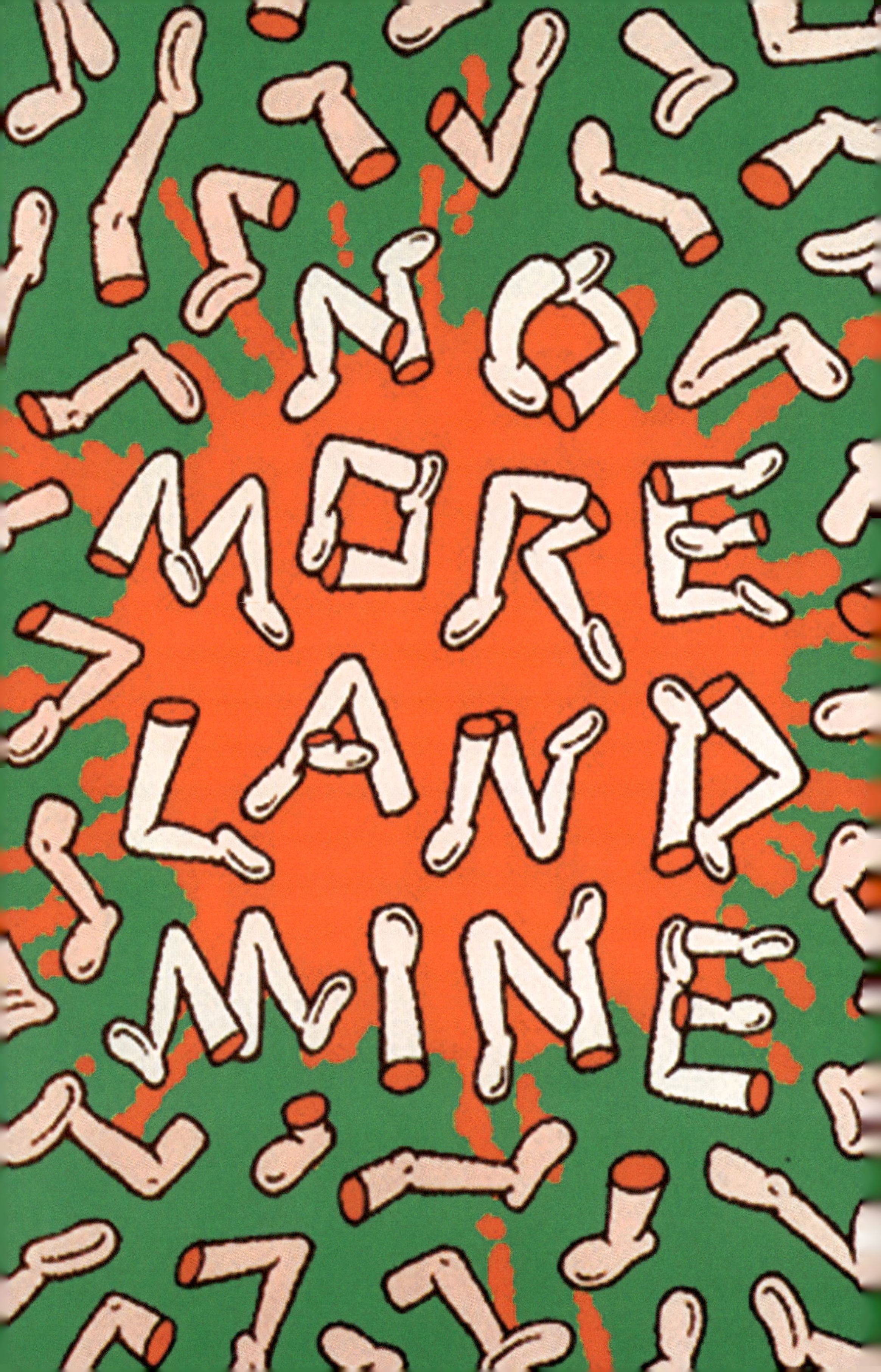
NO MORE LAND MINE

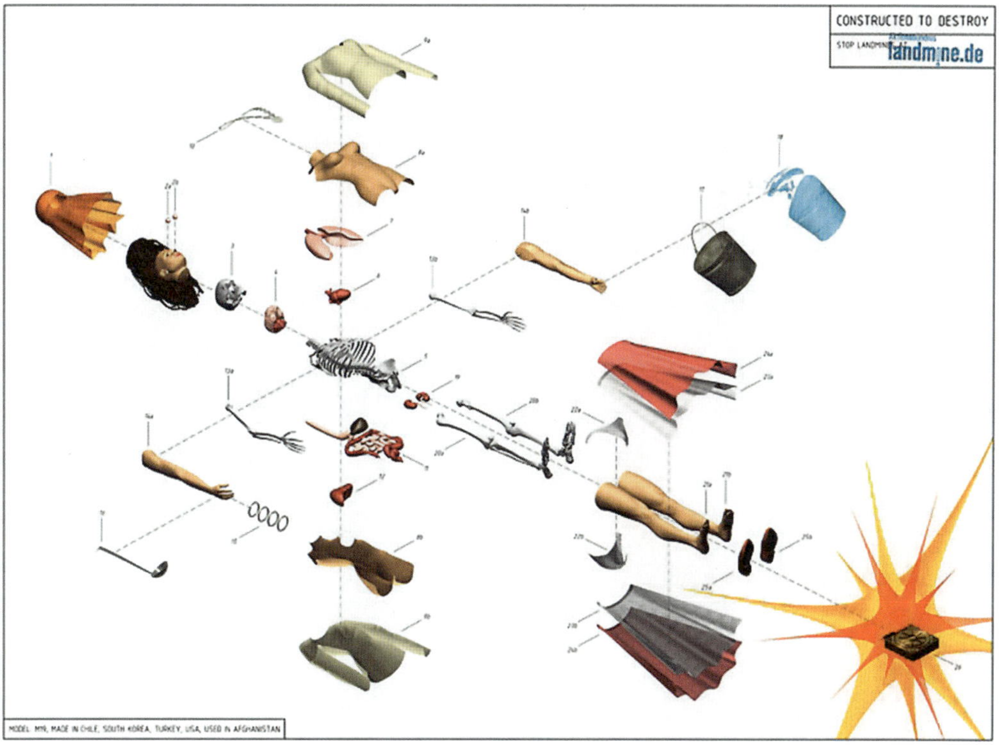

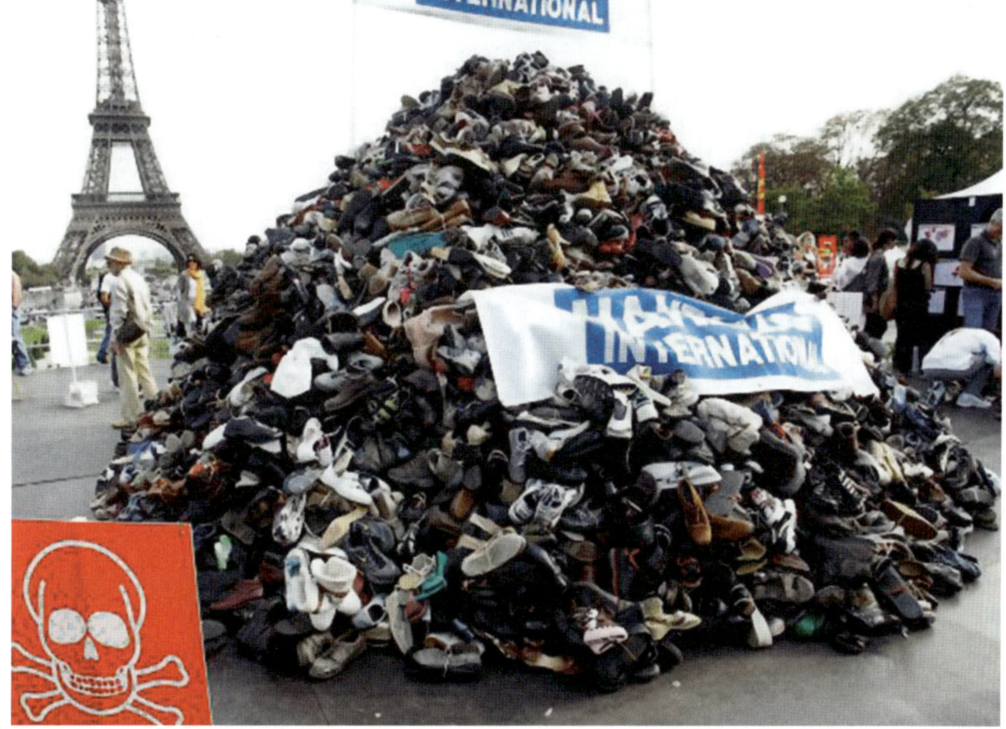
CONSTRUCTED TO DESTROY
STOP LANDMINES AT landmine.de
MODEL M14, MADE IN CHILE, SOUTH KOREA, TURKEY, USA, USED IN AFGHANISTAN

INTERNATIONAL
HANDICAP INTERNATIONAL

011
012

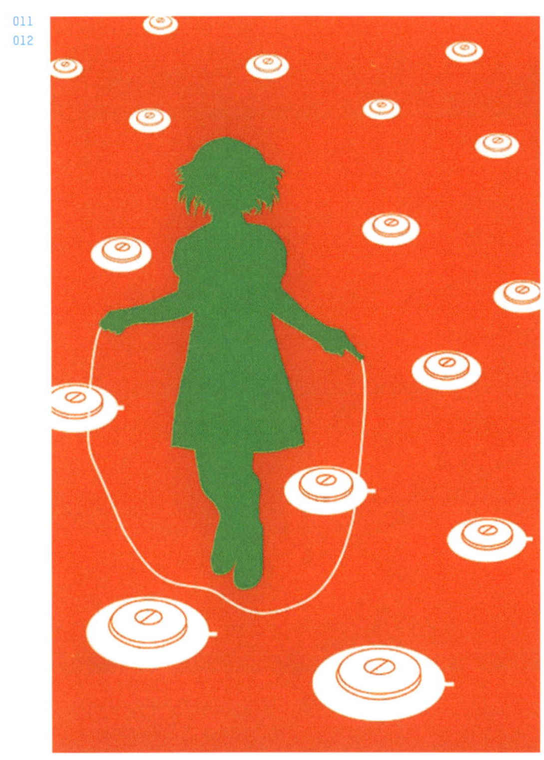

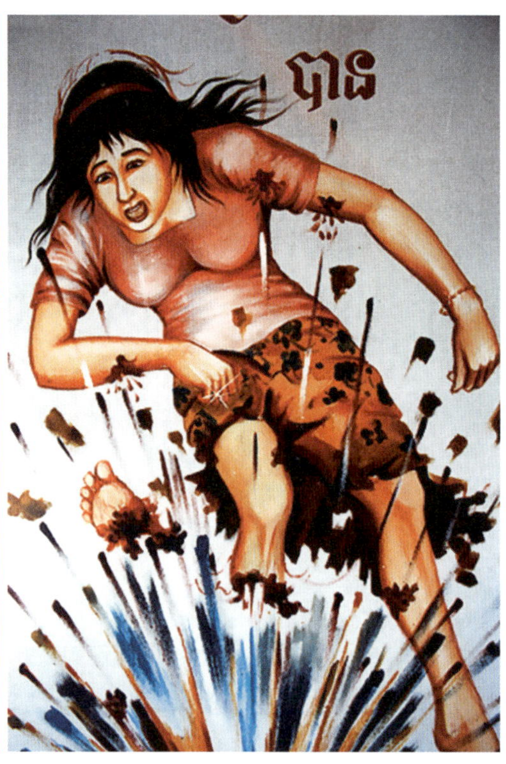

013
014

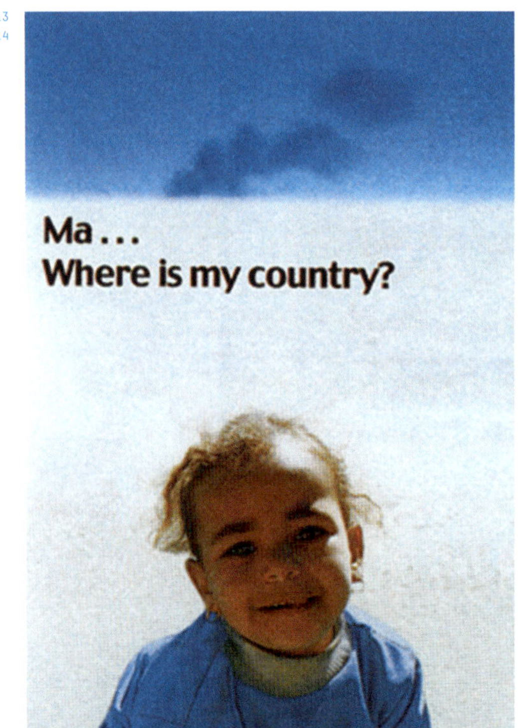

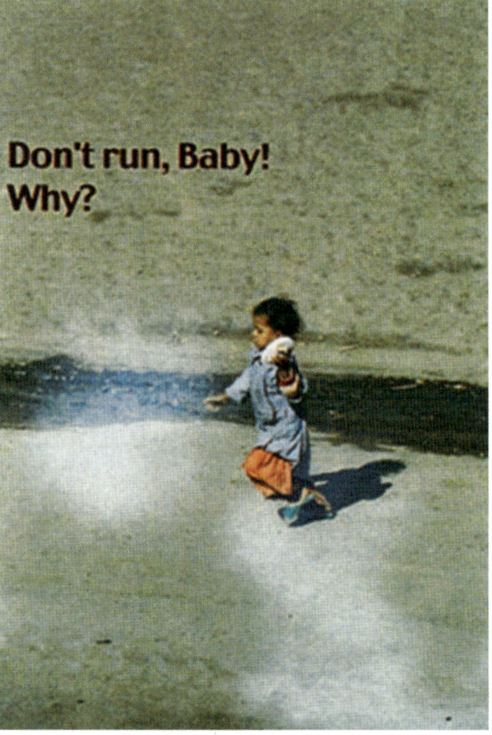

001 LEG
CREATOR Amnesty International
SOURCE theinspirationroom.com

002 AKTION GEGEN LANDMINEN
[ACTION AGAINST LANDMINES]
SOURCE print.sanjeev.net

003 STOPPT LANDMINEN
[INITIATIVE AGAINST LANDMINES]
SOURCE ingohoentschke.de

004 CAMBODIAN AD AGAINST LANDMINES
CREATOR DDB
SOURCE coloribus.com
DATE 2004

005 HOPSCOTCH
CREATOR TBWA / Belgium
SOURCE www.coloribus.com
DATE 2006

006 BROKEN CHAIR
CREATOR Handicap International
SOURCE www.stopclustermunitions.org

007 TODAY, 37 COUNTRIES STILL
PRODUCE ANTIPERSONNEL MINES
AND CLUSTER BOMBS
CREATOR Handicap International
SOURCE osocio.org

008 NO MORE LANDMINE
CREATOR Takashi Sekiguchi
SOURCE Pierre Peronnet and Wijntje
van Rooijen, *Chaumont 2006* [Paris:
Pyramyd, 2006].

009 CONSTRUCTED TO DESTROY
CREATOR Aktionsbüendnis Landmine
SOURCE www.osocio.org

010 PYRAMID OF SHOES, PARIS
SOURCE www.20min.ch
DATE 24 September 2011

011 CREATOR Demian Conrad
SOURCE Beiträge macht Bilder

012 WOMAN LANDMINE VICTIM POSTER
CREATOR Keo Sara
SOURCE www.flickr.com/photos/
pictim/2636425698/

013 MA... WHRE IS MY COUNTRY?
CREATOR Yoshito Nakano
SOURCE "L'engagement politique
et social," Le festival d'affiches,
Chaumont, 19 May - 16 July 2000

014 DON'T RUN, BABY! WHY?
CREATOR Yoshito Nakano
SOURCE "L'engagement politique
et social," Le festival d'affiches,
Chaumont, 19 May - 16 July 2000

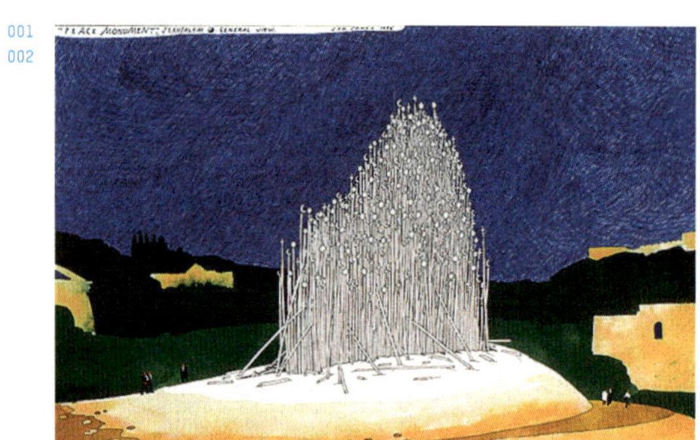
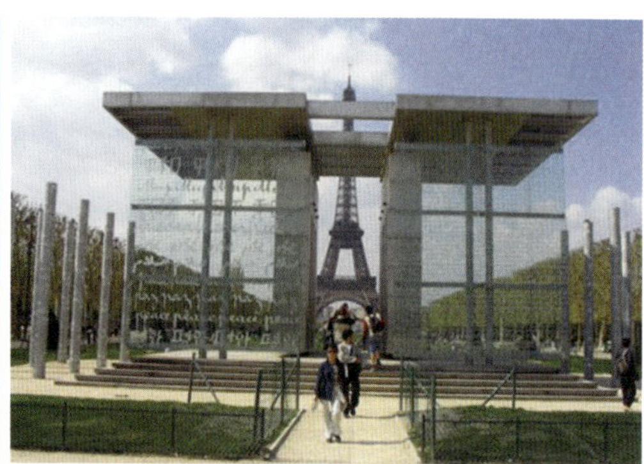
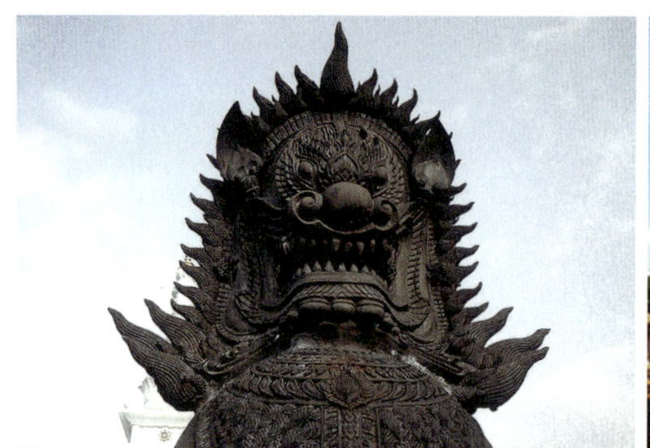
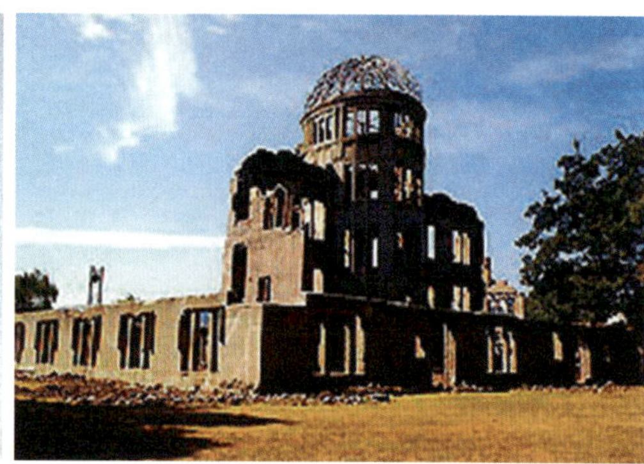
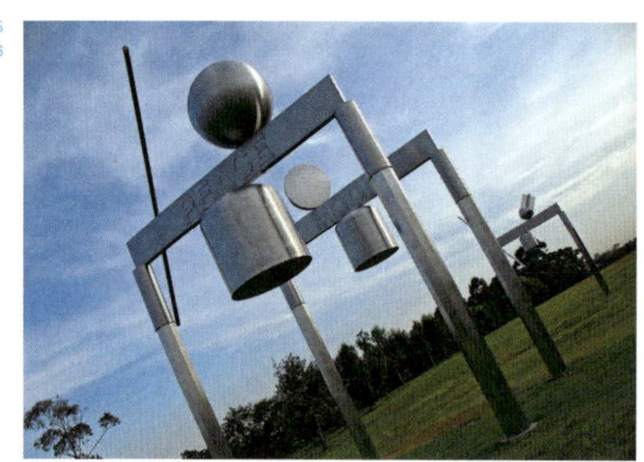
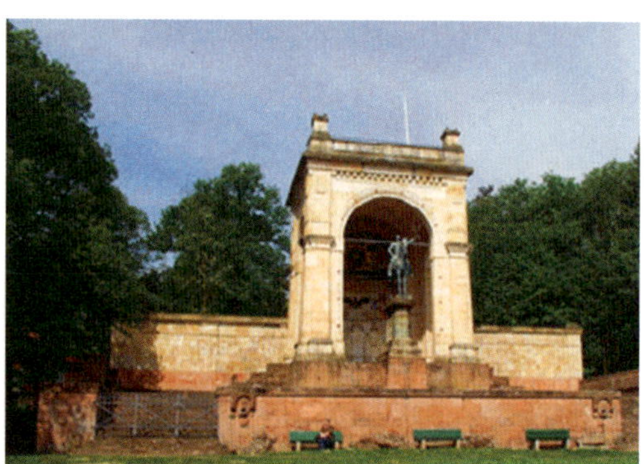
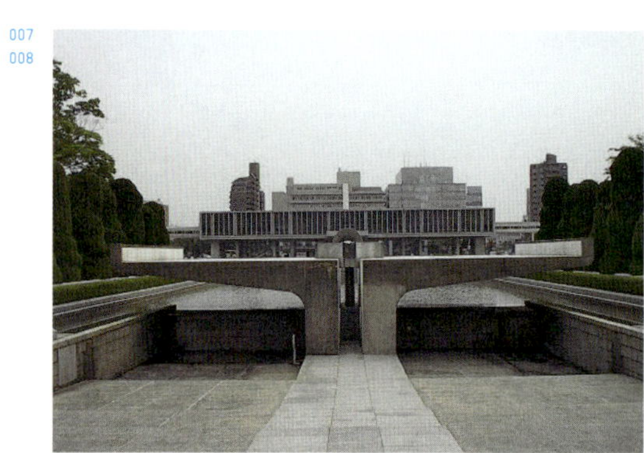
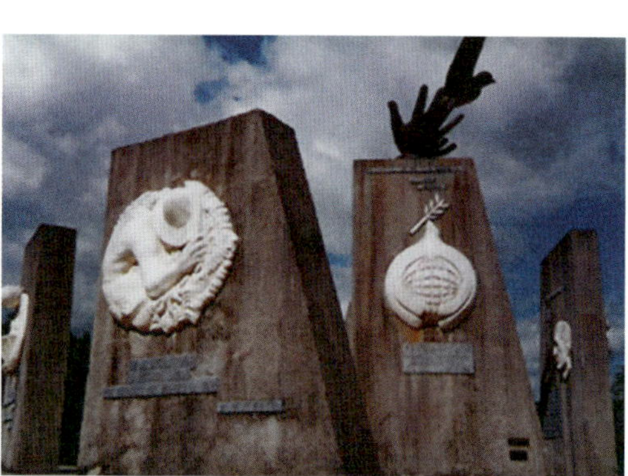

009
010

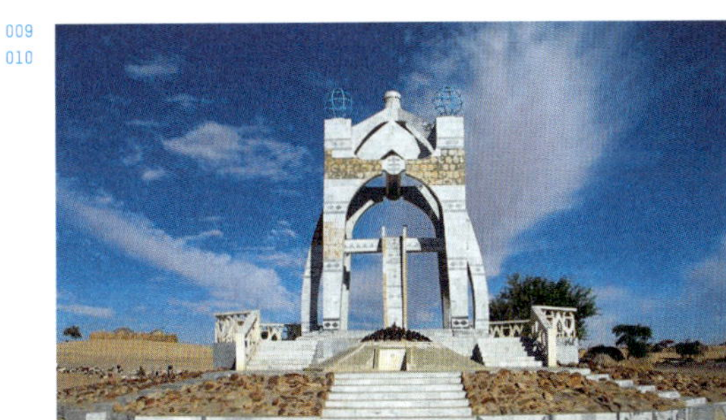

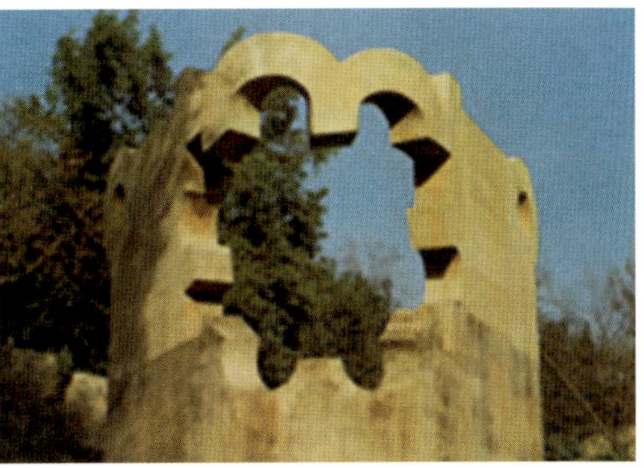

011
012

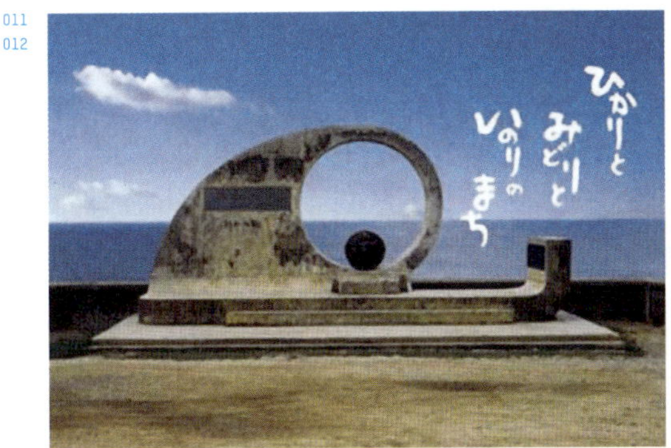

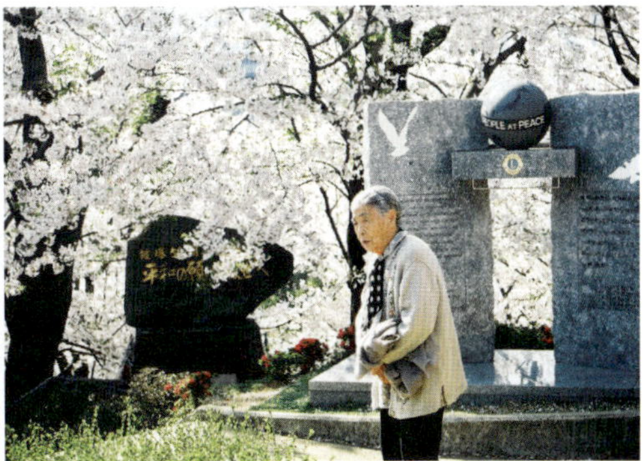

013
014

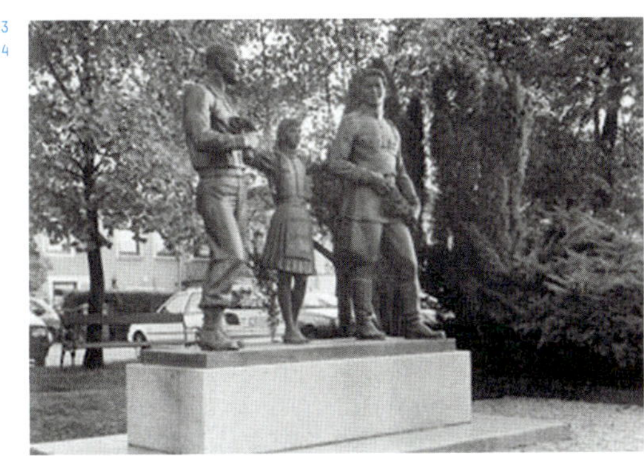

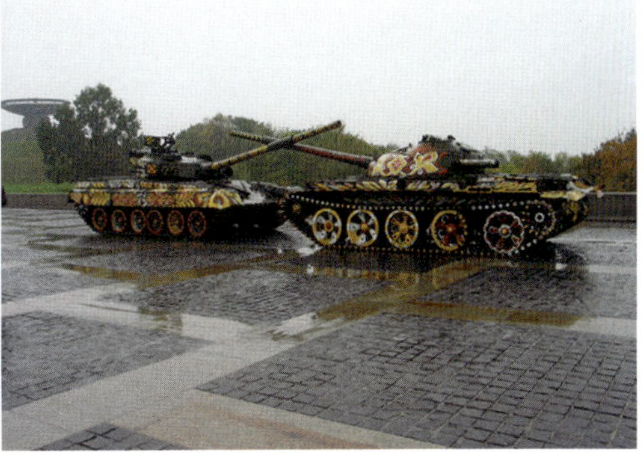

015
016

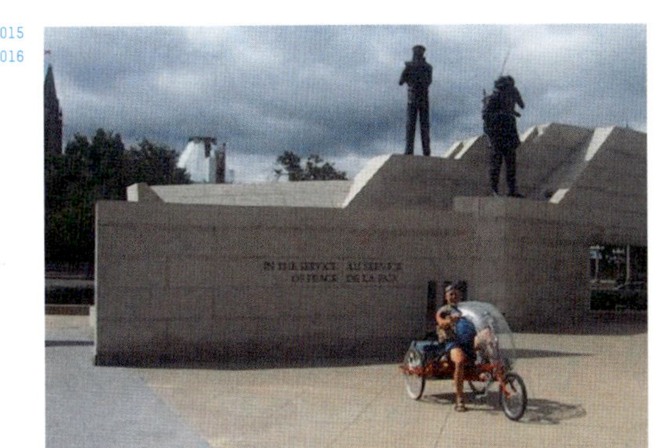

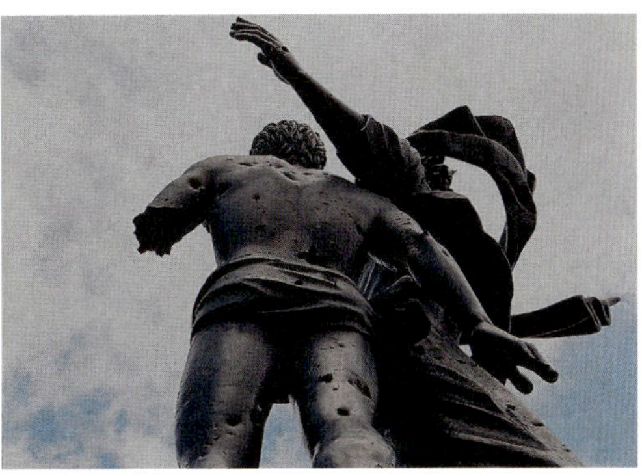

017
018

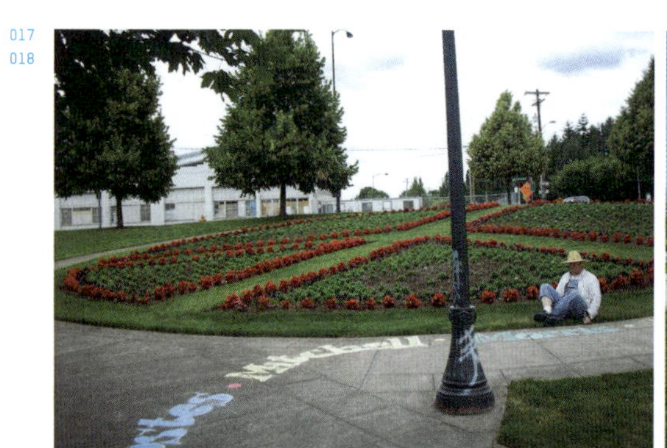
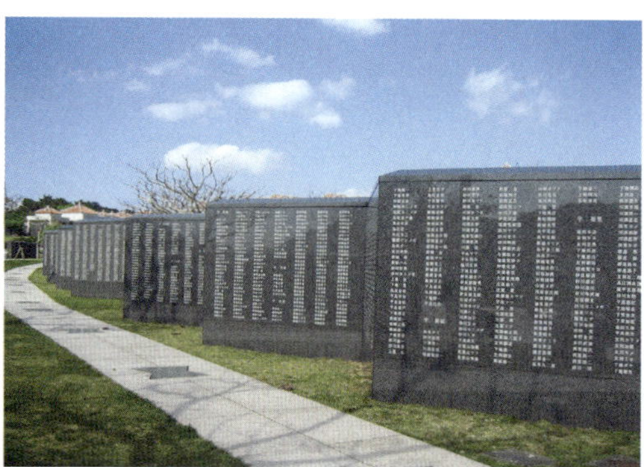

019
020

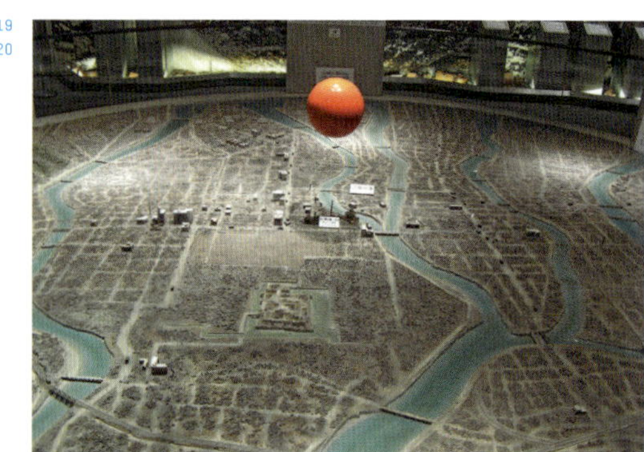
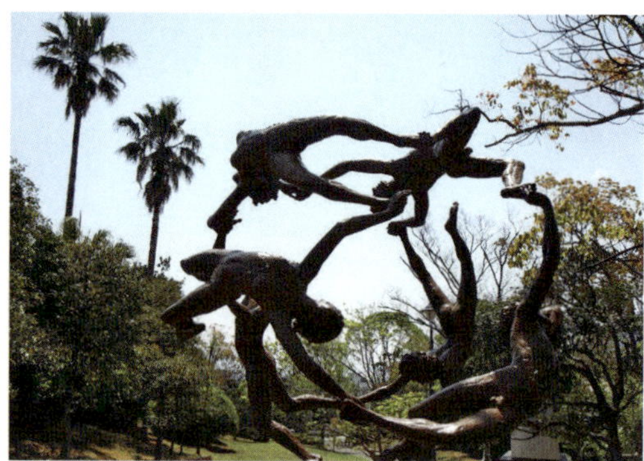

021
022

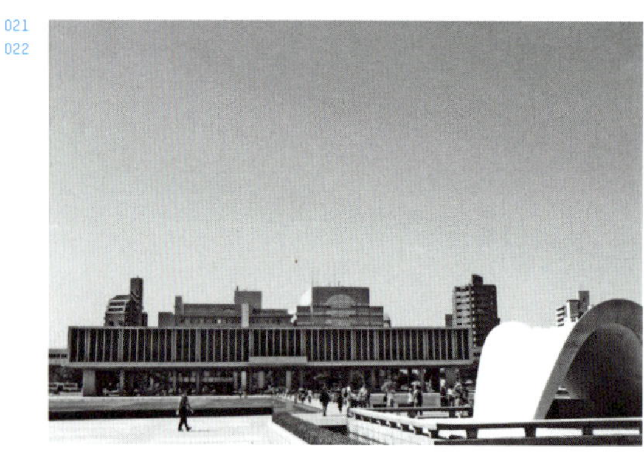
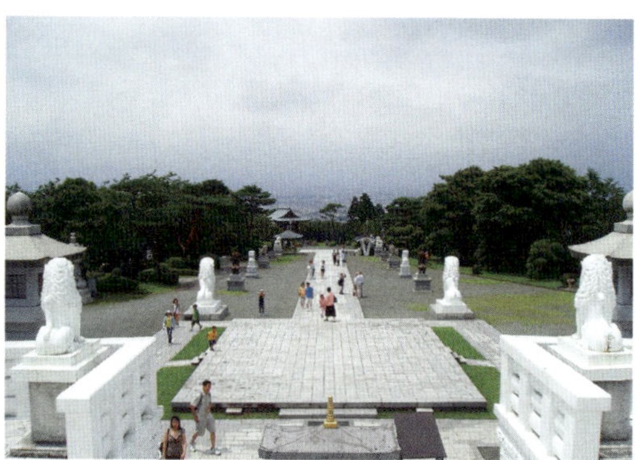

023
024

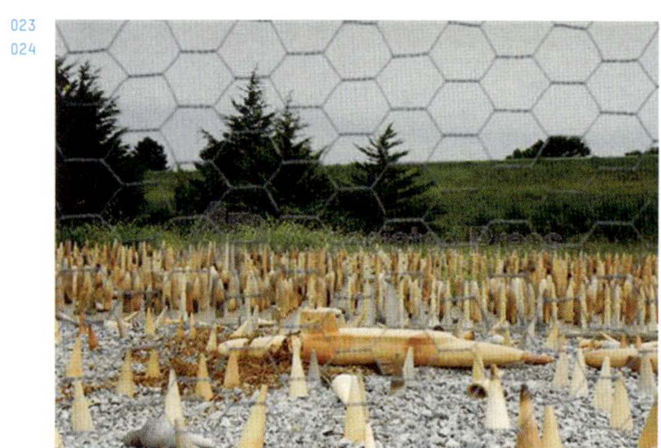
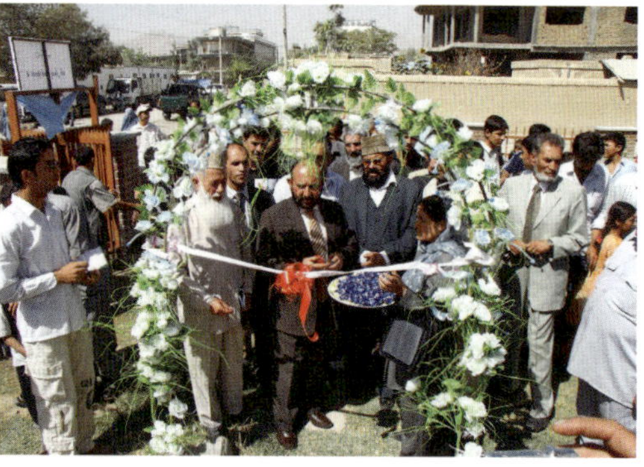

025
026
027
028

029
030
031
032

033
034
035
036

037
038
039

040
041

NEXT
042

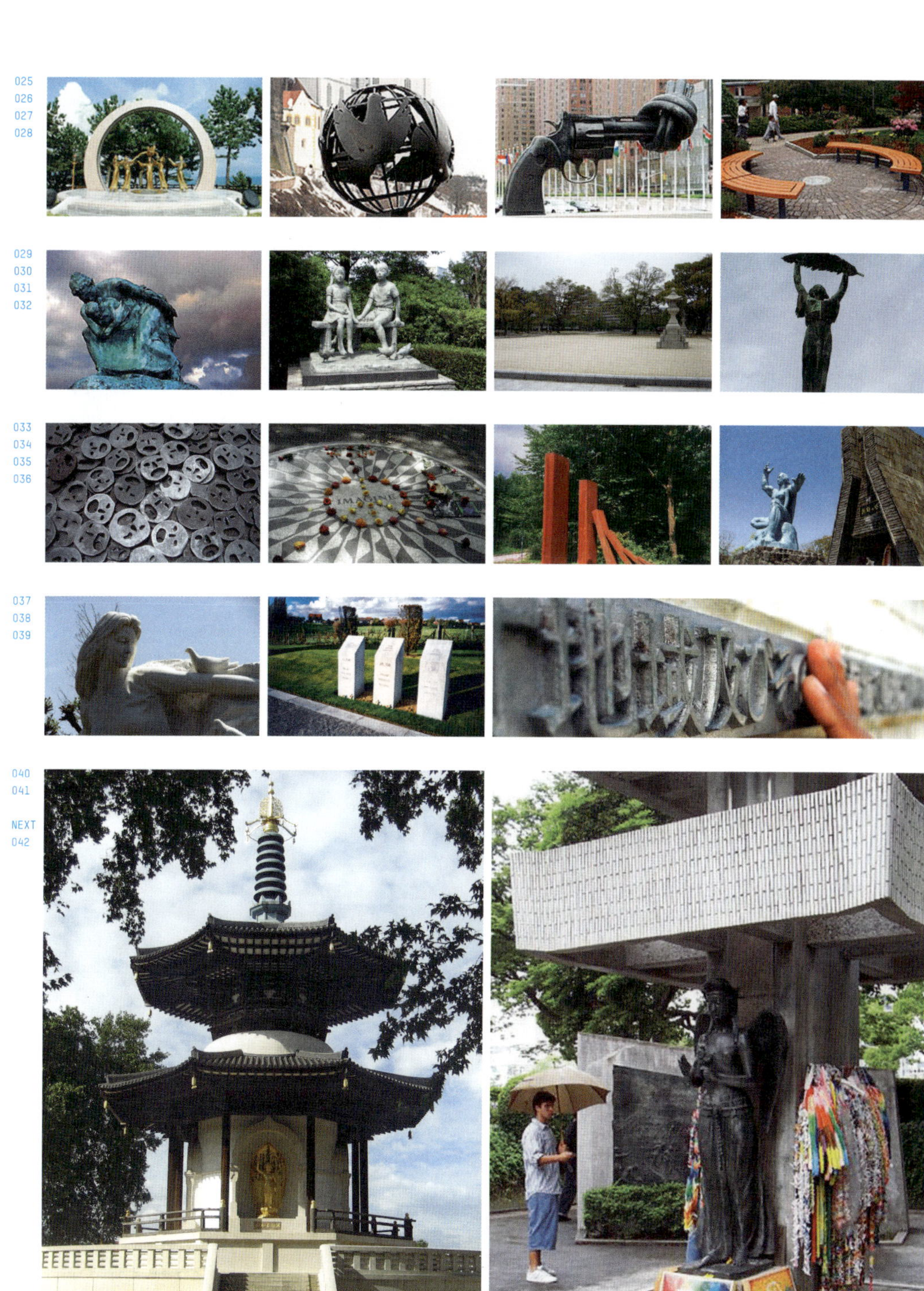

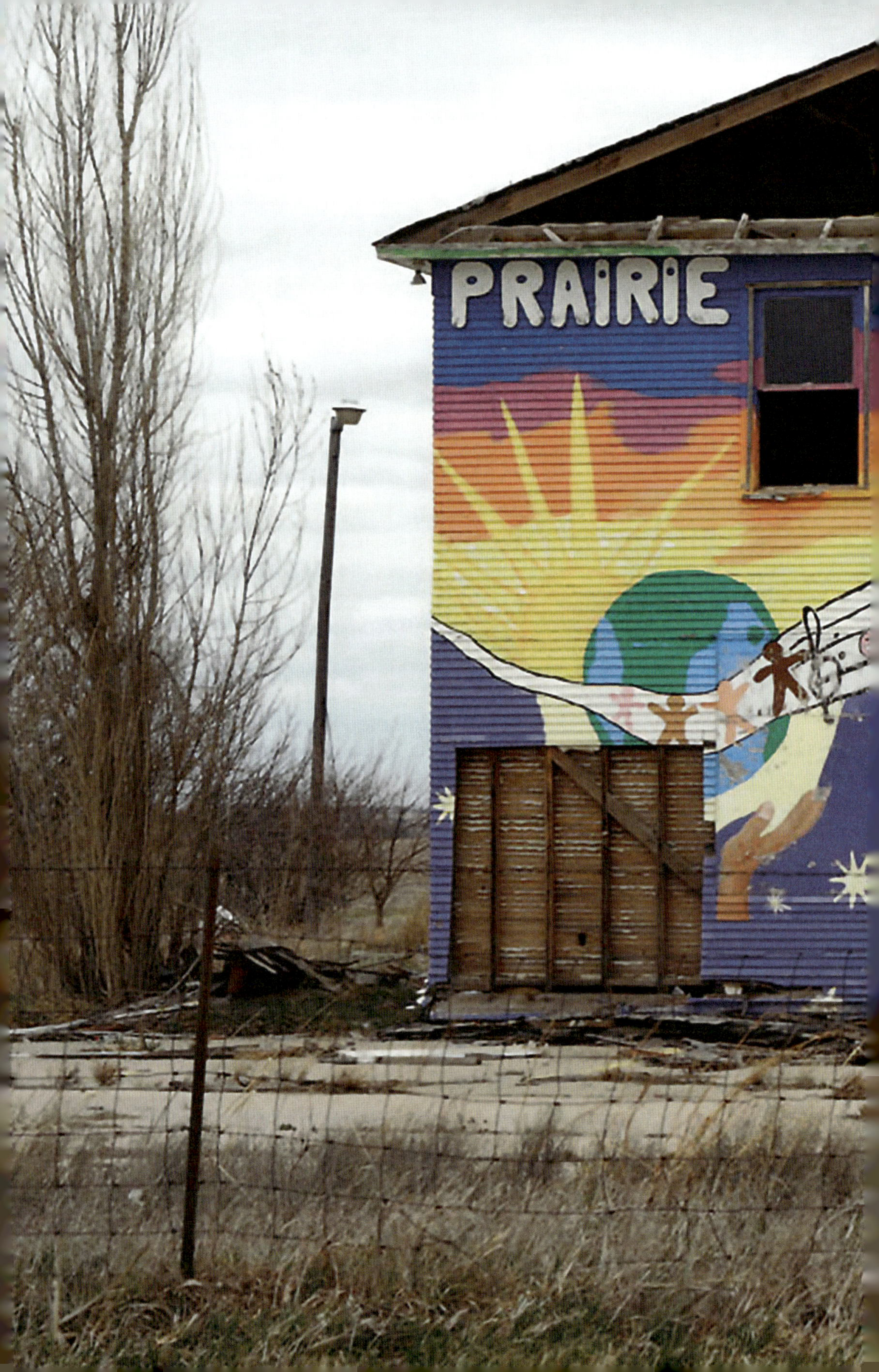
PRAIRIE

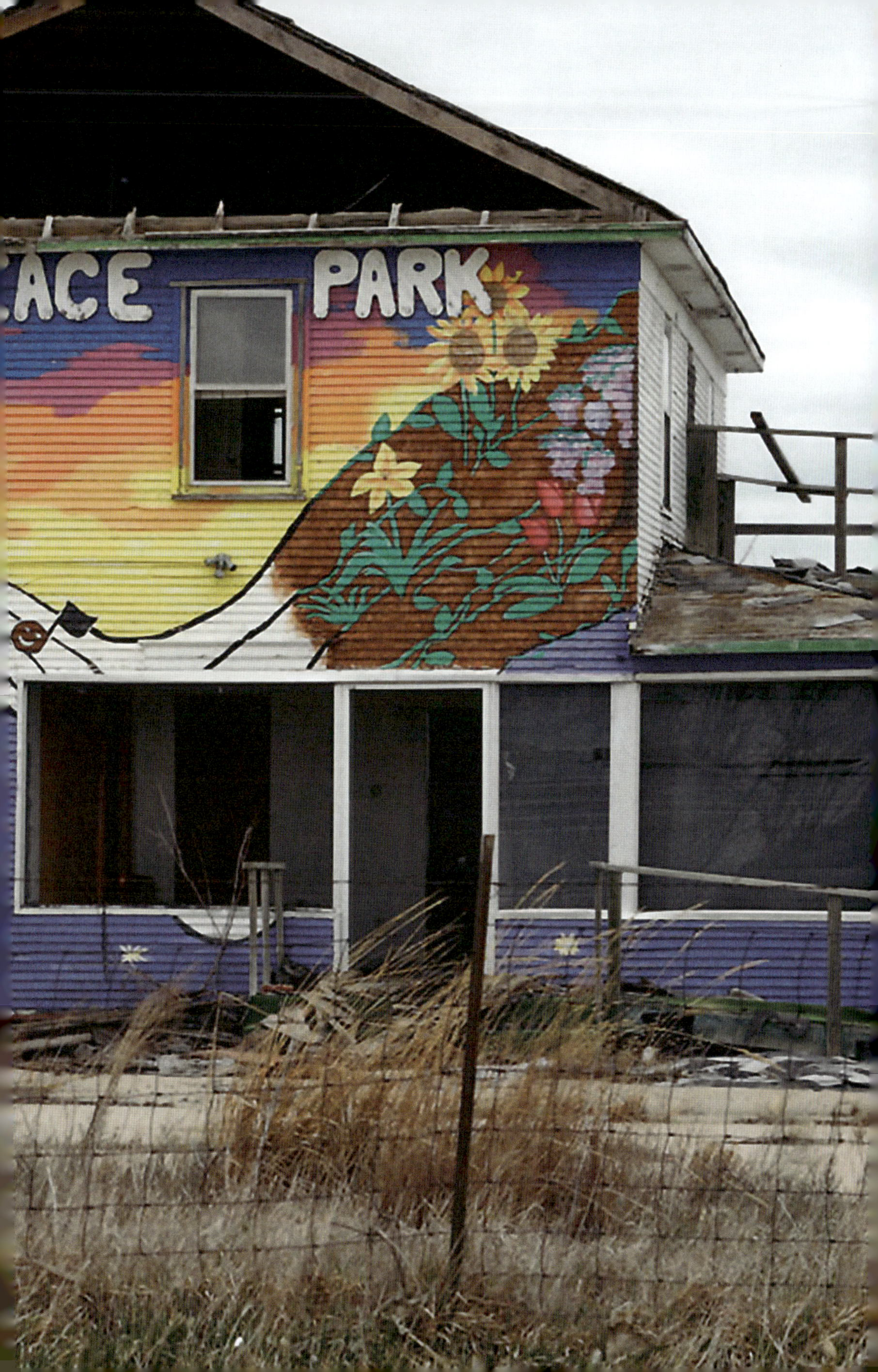
ACE
PARK

001 THE JERUSALEM PEACE MONUMENT
CREATOR Jan Sawka
SOURCE www.jansawka.com
DATE 2010

002 PEACE MONUMENT [WORLD PEACE
GATE], PARIS
CREATOR Provided by daywalker
SOURCE www.wicked86.de

003 TIGER SCULPTURE FROM HAKONE
PEACE PARK, JAPAN
CREATOR Provided by booogiemonster
SOURCE www.flickr.com/photos/
theunseen/366982882/

004 A-BOMB DOME, HIROSHIMA, JAPAN
SOURCE www.japan-photo.de

005 PEACE MOON BETWEEN
CREATOR Sculpture by
Michael Kitching, Provided
by funfunautobahn
SOURCE www.flickr.com/photos/
12147086@N00/338342760/

006 PEACE MONUMENT, EDENKOBEN, GERMANY
Originally built to celebrate
German unification at the end of
the Franco-Prussian war, it was
rededicated as a peace monument
in 1945.
SOURCE fotos-aktuell.de/

007 PEACE PARK ETERNAL FLAME
CREATOR Provided by expressoky
SOURCE www.flickr.com/photos/
expresso/166955765/

008 MONUMENT TO DISARMAMENT, WORK
AND PEACE, UNIVERSITY FOR PEACE,
COSTA RICA
CREATOR Thelvia Marín
SOURCE www.iexplore.com

009 PEACE MONUMENT, TIMBUKTU, MALI
SOURCE www.iexplore.com

010 PEACE MONUMENT, GUERNICA, SPAIN
CREATOR Eduardo Chillida
SOURCE www.stadt-pforzheim.de

011 PEACE MONUMENT AT CAPE KYAN
IN SOUTHERN OKINAWA, JAPAN
SOURCE www.city.itoman.okinawa.jp

012 PEACE PARK NAGASAKI, JAPAN
CREATOR Provided by bovinemagnet
SOURCE www.flickr.com/photos/
bovinemagnet/97733336/

013 PEACE MEMORIAL, ERLAUF, AUSTRIA
This statue of Russian and American
officers who met in Erlauf on 8
May 1945, together with a work by
Jenny Holzer, is conceptualized
as a peace memorial.
CREATOR Oleg Komov
SOURCE www.publicart.at

014 CREATOR Ex Oriente Lux Reisen
SOURCE www.eol-reisen.de

015 PEACEKEEPING MONUMENT,
OTTAWA, CANADA
CREATOR Provided by lightfoot-
cycles.com
SOURCE lightfootcycles.com

016 MARTYRS' SQUARE STATUE IN DOWNTOWN
BEIRUT, LEBANON
CREATOR Provided by teomaxxx
SOURCE www.gfy.com

017 PEACE MEMORIAL PARK, PORTLAND,
OREGON, USA
CREATOR Provided by Names Project
SOURCE www.flickr.com/photos/
iraqnamesproject/616574255/

018 CORNERSTONE OF PEACE, OKINAWA
PREFECTURAL PEACE MEMORIAL MUSEUM
The slabs are inscribed with
more than 240,000 names of
civilians and military personnel
who died in the 1945 Battle
of Okinawa, Japan.
CREATOR Provided by mdid
SOURCE www.flickr.com/photos/
mdid/930751183/

019 BLAST LOCATION, HIROSHIMA, JAPAN
CREATOR Provided by Micha L. Rieser
SOURCE commons.wikimedia.org

020 CONSTELLATION EARTH, NAGASAKI
PEACE PARK, JAPAN
CREATOR Paul Granlund, provided
by kamoda
SOURCE www.flickr.com/photos/
kamoda/466867170/

021 HIROSHIMA PEACE MEMORIAL PARK
CREATOR Provided by motocchio
SOURCE www.flickr.com/photos/
motofoto/1291318664/

022 HAKONE PEACE PARK, JAPAN
This park was created to inspire
world peace. It has contributions
from various countries and is
aimed at promoting the idea of
brotherhood and peace.
CREATOR Provided by Ehegi
SOURCE www.flickr.com/photos/
10064484@N05/847807100/

023 AMBER WAVES OF GRAIN
The 32,000-piece sculpture
representing the nuclear rockets,
missiles, planes, and submarines
of the Cold War, sits in the
Prairie Peace Park, 10 miles
west of Lincoln, Nebraska.
CREATOR J. Pat Carter
SOURCE www.apimages.com

024 PEACE PARK OPENING, KABUL
CREATOR Provided by Jon Bormet

SOURCE www.flickr.com/photos/
jonbormet/1423053965/
DATE 19 September 2007

025 WORLD PEACE MONUMENT, KOREA
The six bronze statues represent
the continents.
SOURCE www.sgi.org

026 PEACE MONUMENT
SOURCE www.allsoulsnyc.org

027 KNOTTED GUN, UNITED NATIONS
BUILDING, NYC
CREATOR Carl Fredrik Reutersward
SOURCE www.bmz.de

028 PEACE MONUMENT, BRANDEIS CAMPUS,
WALTHAM, MA, USA
CREATOR Dennis Nealon
SOURCE my.brandeis.edu

029 MOTHER AND CHILD, HIROSHIMA, JAPAN
SOURCE www.japan-photo.de

030 PEACE PARK MEMORIAL
CREATOR Provided by MShades
SOURCE www.flickr.com/photos/
mshades/238962992/

031 PEACE PARK MEMORIAL IN
HIROSHIMA, JAPAN
CREATOR Provided by marreka
SOURCE www.flickr.com/photos/
matthewk/138679969/

032 STATUE OF LIBERTY MEMORIAL
ON TOP OF GELLERT HILL TO
COMEMORATE PEACE AFTER THE
WORLD WAR II, BUDAPEST, HUNGARY
SOURCE www.euxus.de

033 FALLEN LEAVES
CREATOR Artwork by Menashe
Kadishman, provided by Gakas
SOURCE www.flickr.com/photos/
gakas/64837007/

034 NYC, CENTRAL PARK: STRAWBERRY
FIELDS, IMAGINE MOSAIC
CREATOR Artwork by Yoko Ono,
provided by wallyg
SOURCE www.flickr.com/photos/
wallyg/24686555

035 PEACE MEMORIAL, ULM, GERMANY
This monument commemorates
soldiers who deserted the
Wehrmacht during World War II.
CREATOR R. Thie
SOURCE www.ippnw-ulm.de

036 NAGASAKI PEACE PARK, JAPAN
CREATOR Provided by kamoda
SOURCE www.flickr.com/photos/
kamoda/466867278/

037 NAGASAKI PEACE PARK, JAPAN
CREATOR Provided by kamoda

<u>SOURCE</u> http://www.flickr.com/photos/
kamoda/466867296

038 ISLAND OF IRELAND PEACE
PARK, FLANDERS, BELGIUM
The memorial is in Messines,
location of a battle that marks
one of the few times when
Irishmen, regardless of religion,
united against a common enemy.
The pillars list the number
of killed, wounded, and missing
for each of the three divisions
of Irish soldiers who fought
in World War I.
<u>CREATOR</u> Provided by Redvers
<u>SOURCE</u> www.flickr.com/photos/
redvers/502502120/

039 LABUAN PEACE PARK, MALAYSIA
The Peace Park was built by the
Japanese government as tribute
to all those who lost their lives
in Borneo during World War II.
<u>CREATOR</u> Provided by Travel Sick
<u>SOURCE</u> www.flickr.com/photos/
travelsick/179787981/

040 PEACE PAGODA, BATTERSEA
PARK, LONDON
<u>CREATOR</u> Provided by adrian.b
<u>SOURCE</u> www.flickr.com/photos/
burky/235360570/

041 HIROSHIMA PEACE PARK, JAPAN
<u>CREATOR</u> Provided by
Purple-Passionl
<u>SOURCE</u> www.flickr.com/photos/
11288669@N00/172497197/

042 PRAIRIE PEACE PARK, NEBRASKA, USA
<u>CREATOR</u> Provided by andyofne
<u>SOURCE</u> www.flickr.com/photos/
andyofne/2415593020/

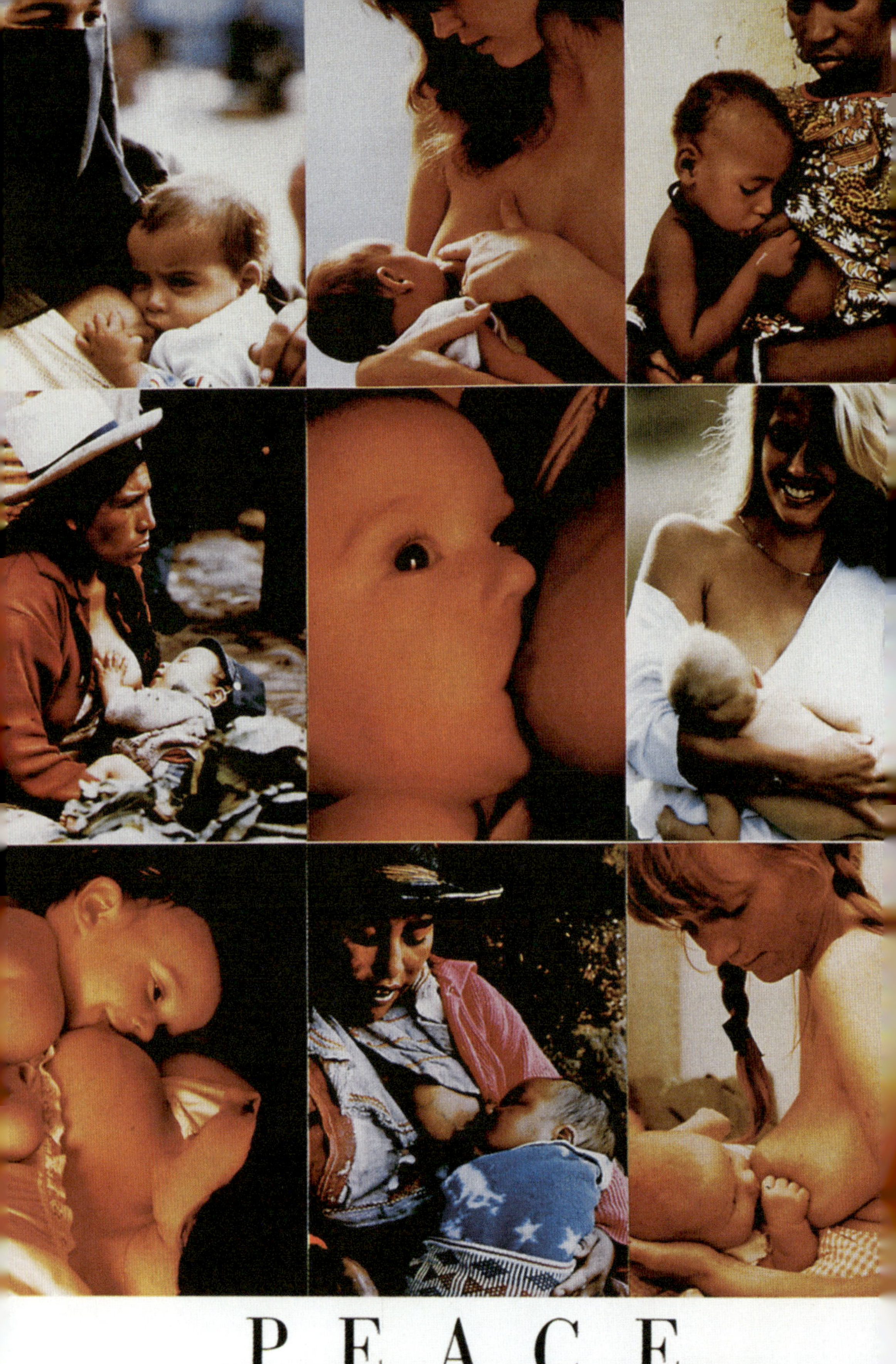

P E A C E

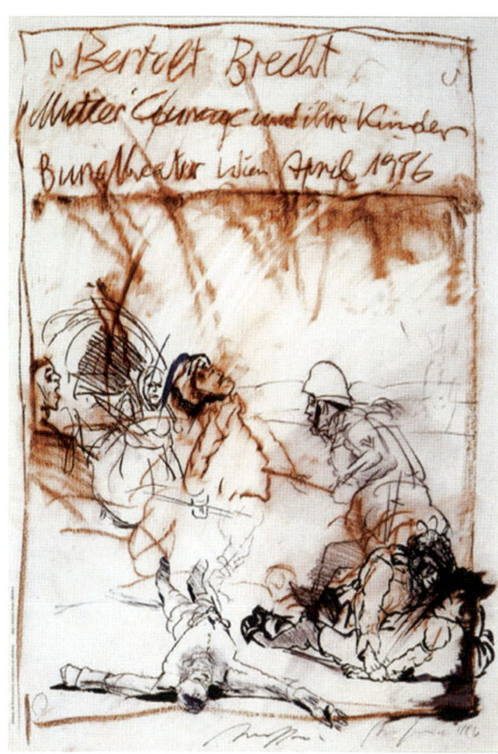

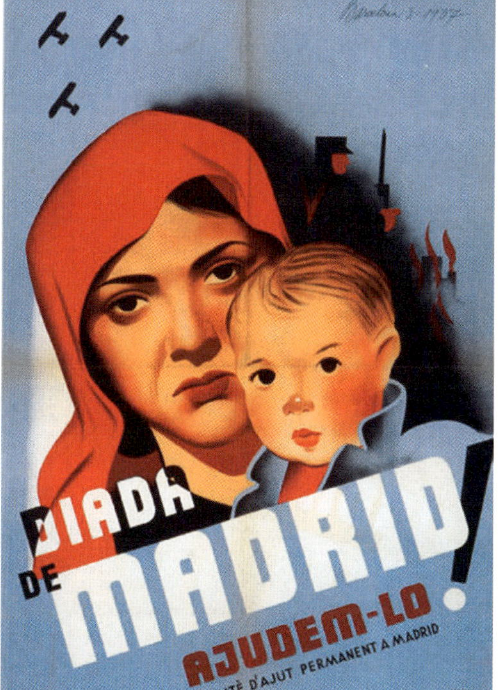

LEFT
001
002

001 PEACE – MOTHERS
<u>CREATOR</u> Varis Kyöst
<u>SOURCE</u> JAGDA Peace Posters
International Exhibition

002 BERTOLT BRECHT, MUTTER COURAGE
UND IHRE KINDER
[MOTHER COURAGE AND HER CHILDREN]
<u>CREATOR</u> Alfred Hrdlicka
<u>SOURCE</u> Plakatsammlung Museum
für Gestaltung Zürich

003 DIADA DE MADRID – AJUDEM-LO
COMITÉ D'AUJUT PERMANENT A MADRID
[MADRID DAY – LET US HELP YOU]
<u>SOURCE</u> Plakatsammlung Museum
für Gestaltung Zürich

003

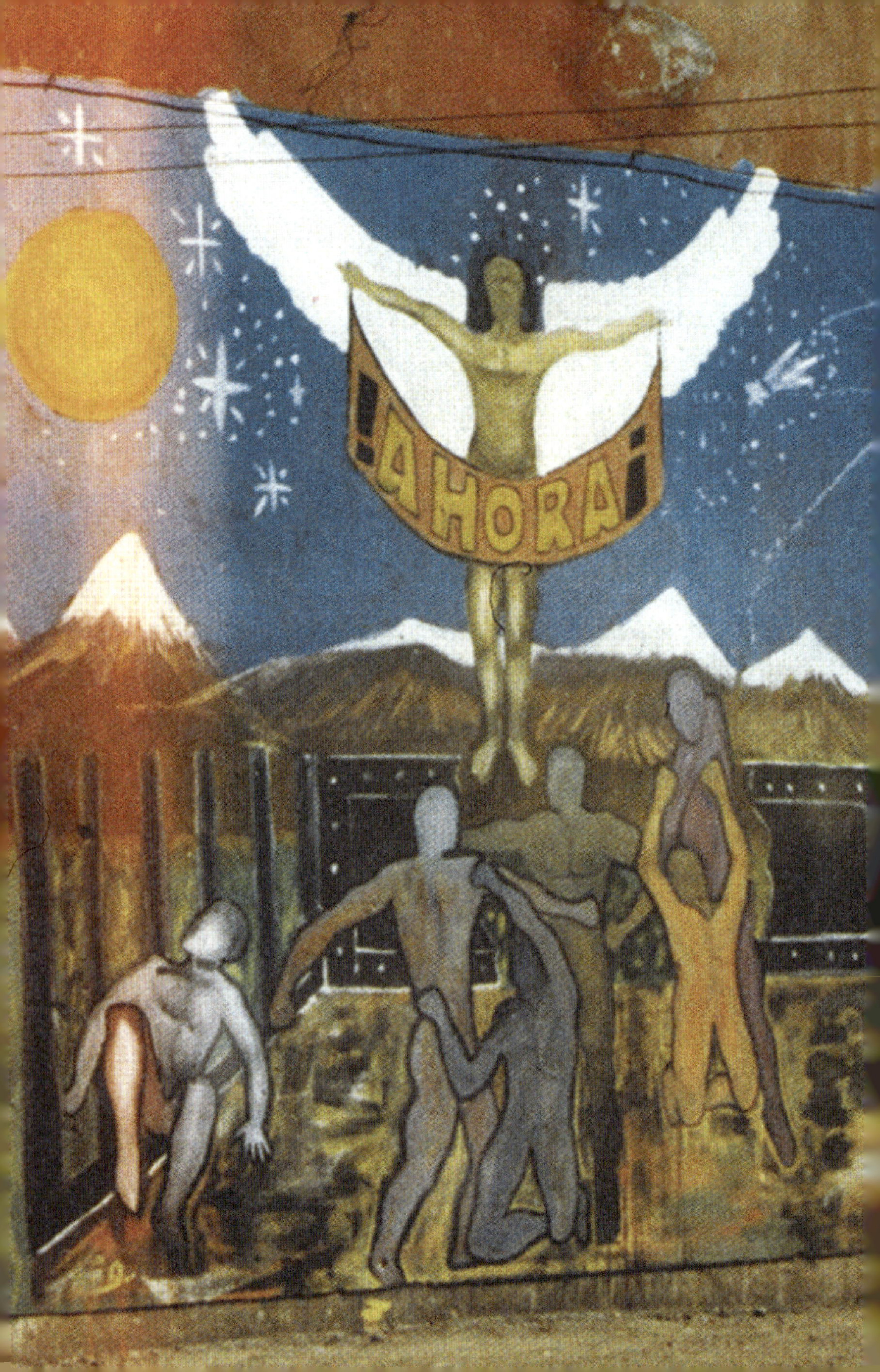

¡AHORA¡

LEFT
001
002

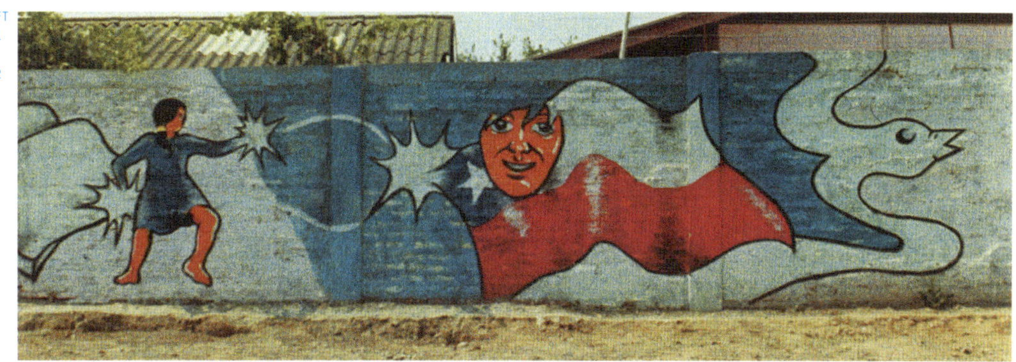

003
004

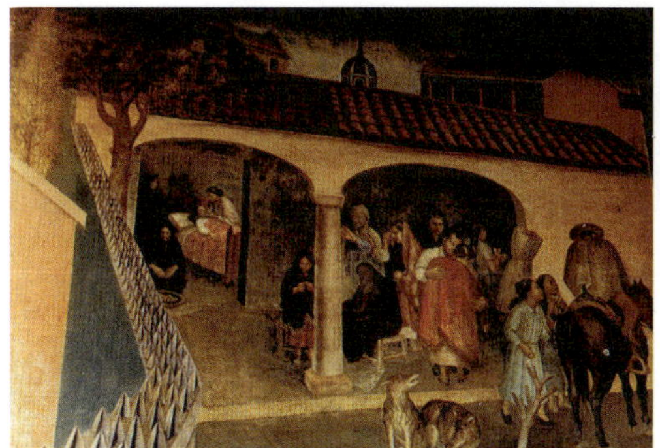
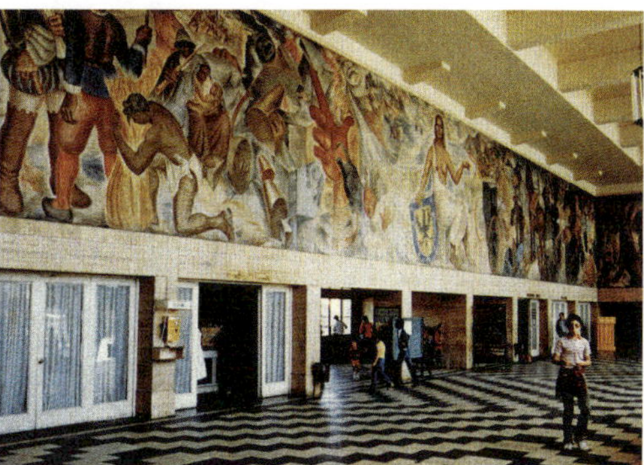

005

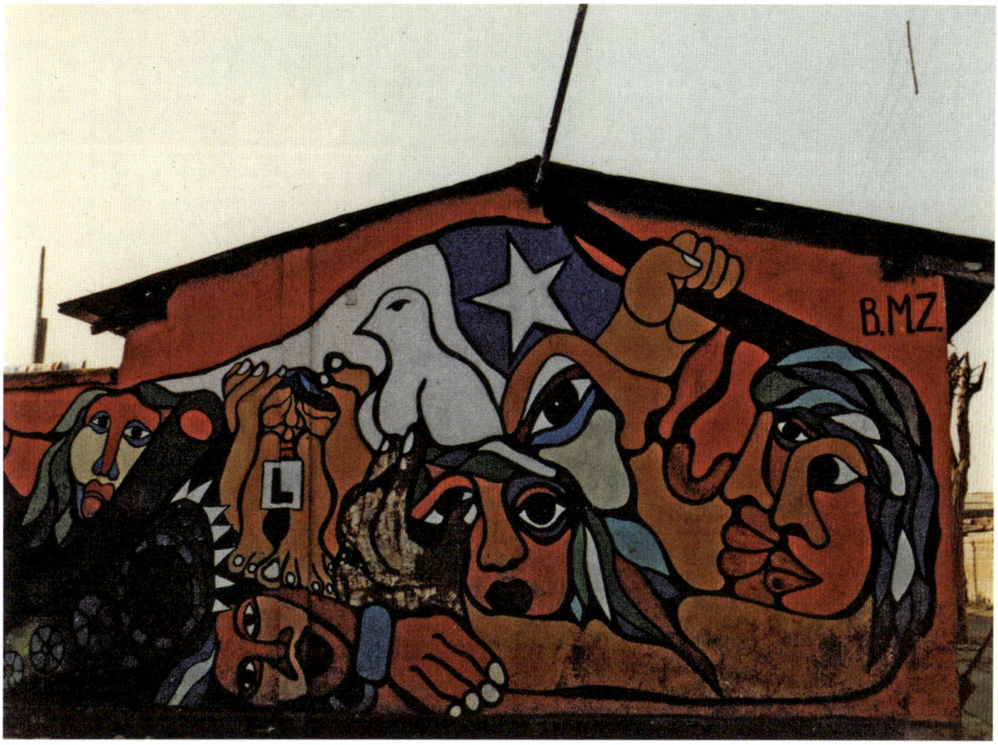

B.MZ.
L

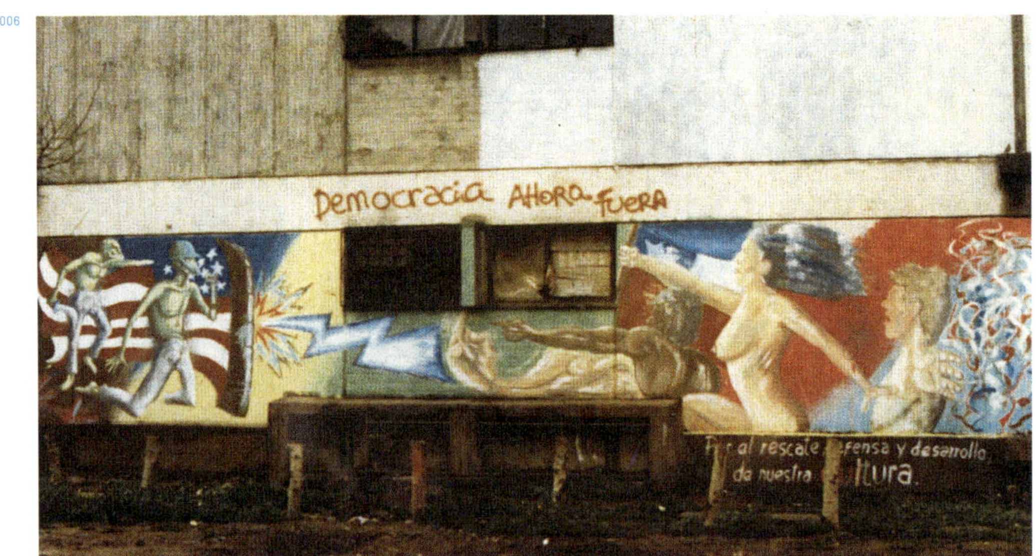

Democracia Ahora. Fuera
ar al rescate defensa y desarrollo
da nuestra ...ltura.

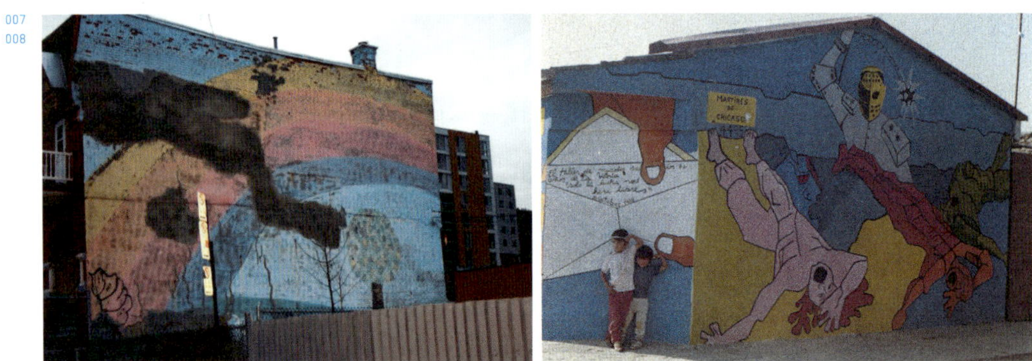

MARTIRES DE CHICAGO

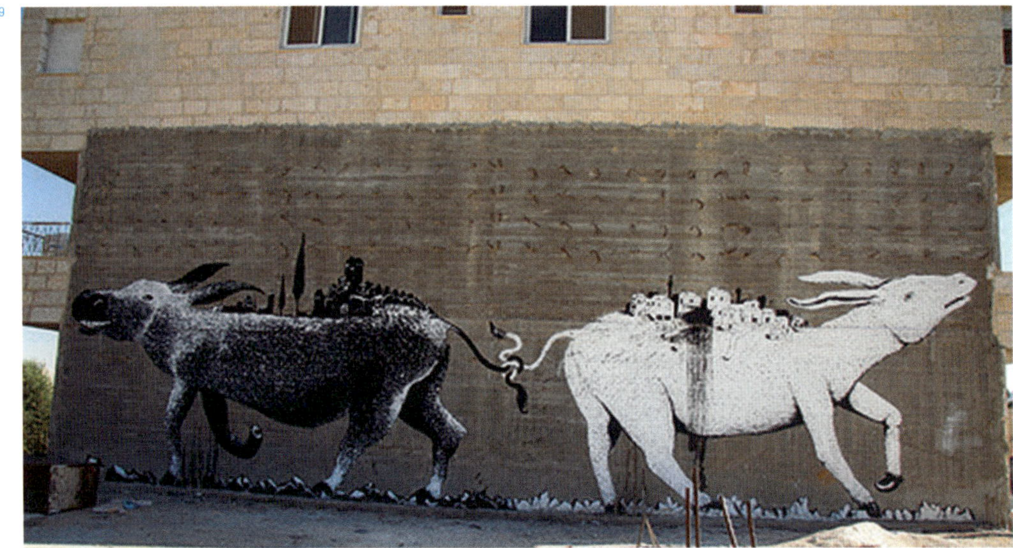

010

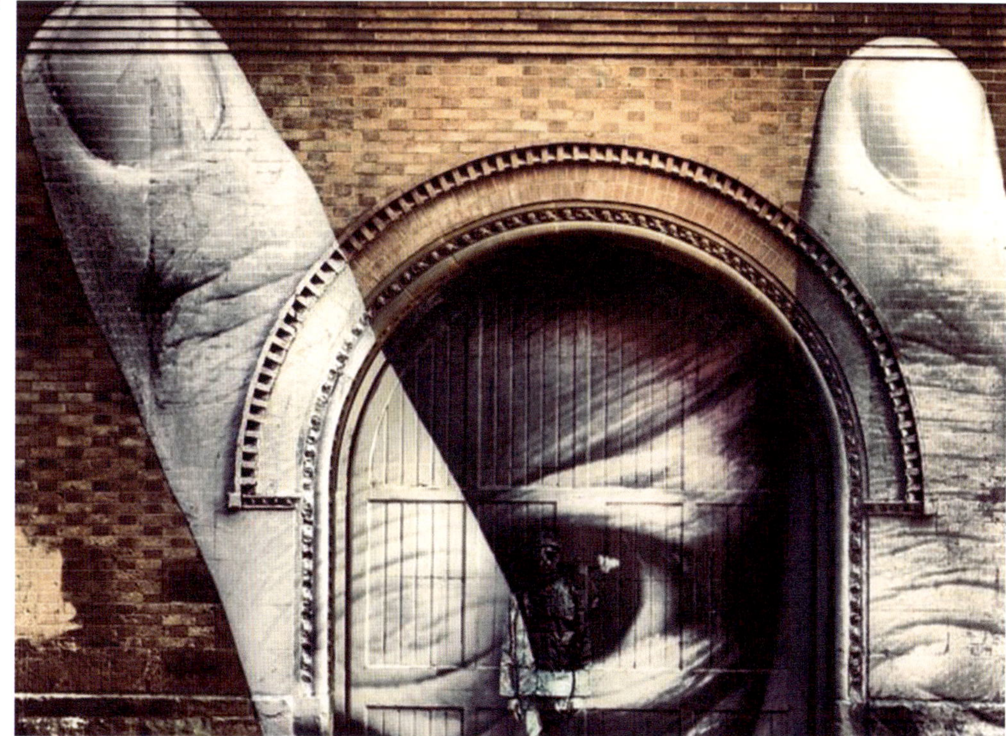

011

012
013

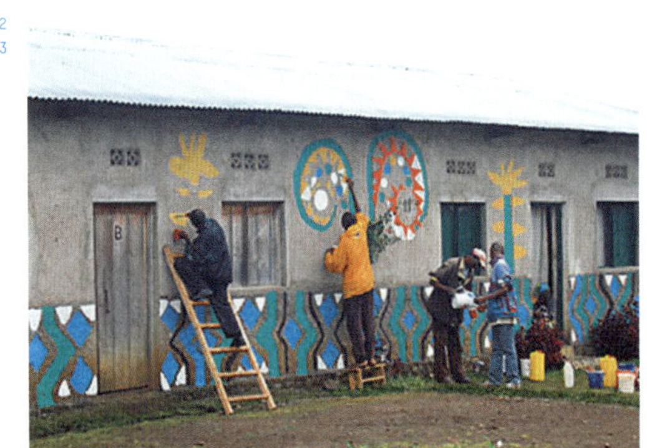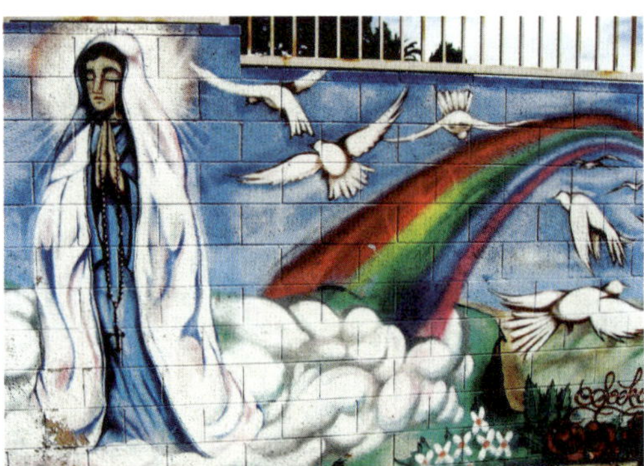

014
015

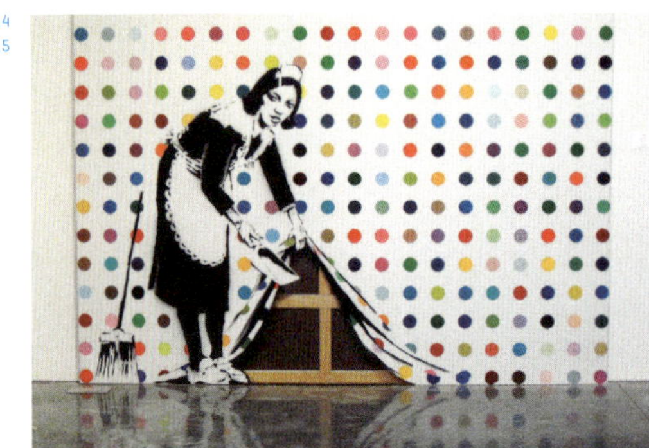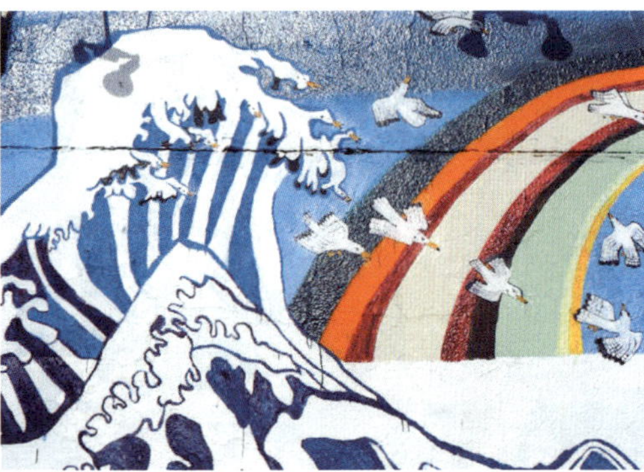

016

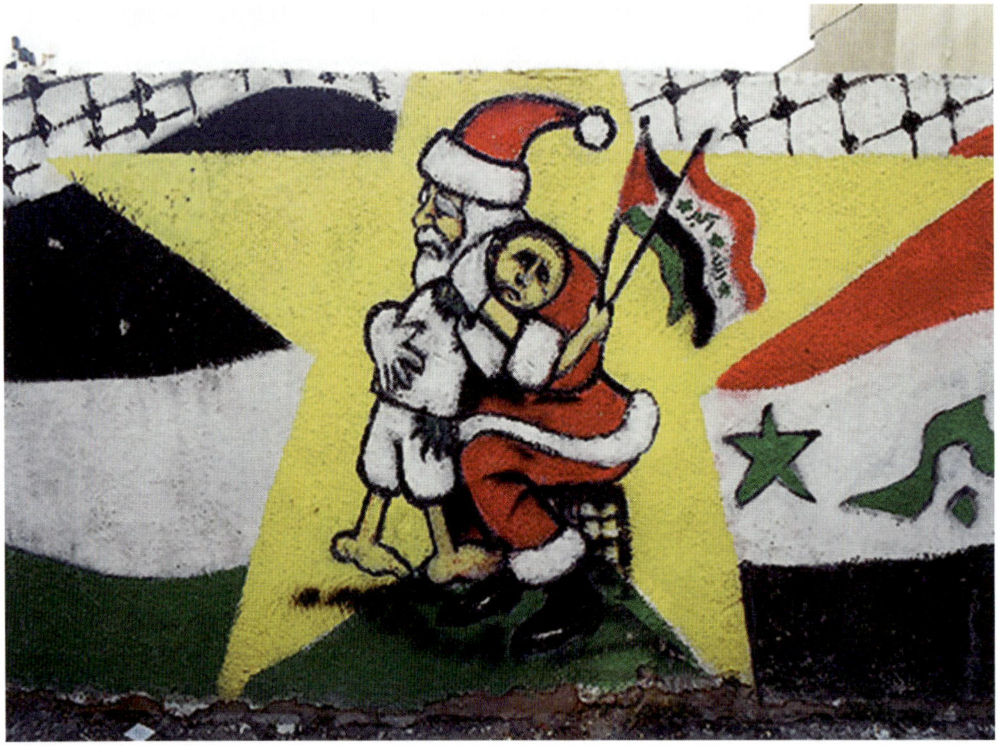

001 UNTITLED
SOURCE Comité de Defensa de
la Cultura Chilena, *Muralismo:
arte en la cultura popular chilena*
[St. Gallen: Edition Diá, 1990].

002 UNTITLED
SOURCE Comité de Defensa de
la Cultura Chilena, *Muralismo:
arte en la cultura popular chilena*
[St. Gallen: Edition Diá, 1990].

003 UNTITLED
SOURCE Comité de Defensa de
la Cultura Chilena, *Muralismo:
arte en la cultura popular chilena*
[St. Gallen: Edition Diá, 1990].

004 UNTITLED
SOURCE Comité de Defensa de
la Cultura Chilena, *Muralismo:
arte en la cultura popular chilena*
[St. Gallen: Edition Diá, 1990].

005 UNTITLED
SOURCE Comité de Defensa de
la Cultura Chilena, *Muralismo:
arte en la cultura popular chilena*
[St. Gallen: Edition Diá, 1990].

006 UNTITLED
SOURCE Comité de Defensa de
la Cultura Chilena, *Muralismo:
arte en la cultura popular chilena*
[St. Gallen: Edition Diá, 1990].

007 GRAY RAINBOW, MONTREAL
CREATOR Provided by flintsparc
SOURCE www.flickr.com/photos/
flintsparc/459542794/

008 UNTITLED
SOURCE Comité de Defensa de
la Cultura Chilena, *Muralismo:
arte en la cultura popular chilena*
[St. Gallen: Edition Diá, 1990].

009 ISRAEL AND PALESTINE, WEST BANK
CREATOR Provided by hazy jenius
SOURCE www.flickr.com/photos/
hazy_jenius/2548452477/

010 FACE 2 FACE, ISRAEL & PALESTINE
CREATOR JR
SOURCE www.jr-art.net
DATE 2007

011 JR X LIU BOLIN
CREATOR JR
SOURCE www.jr-art.net

012 THE RWANDA HEALING PROJECT
CREATOR Barefoot Artists
SOURCE www.jr-art.net

013 SOMEWHERE OVER THE RAINBOW
CREATOR Provided by NoAverageJoe
SOURCE www.flickr.com/photos/
74761448@N00/1449915875/

014 KEEP IT SPOTLESS
CREATOR Banksy and Damien Hirst
SOURCE www.flickr.com/photos/
nicolettesara/2263430933/
DATE 2008

015 ON HOKUSAI, WITH GULLS INSTEAD
OF BUNNIES
CREATOR Provided by gwen
SOURCE www.flickr.com/photos/
gwen/2198679118/

016 IRAQI-PALESTINIAN SOLIDARITY
CREATOR Provided by Shabtai Gold
SOURCE www.flickr.com/photos/
velvetart/94110447/

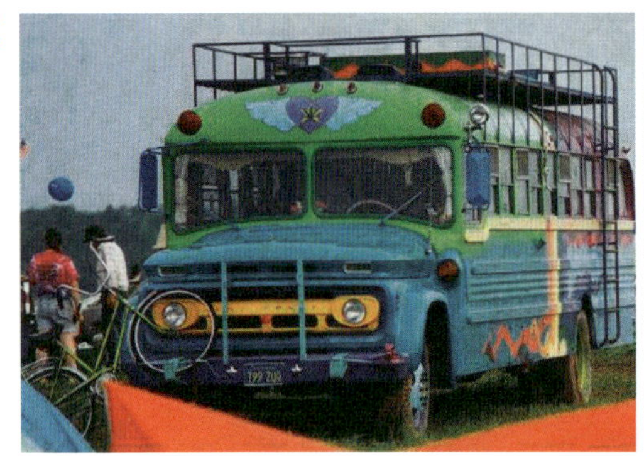

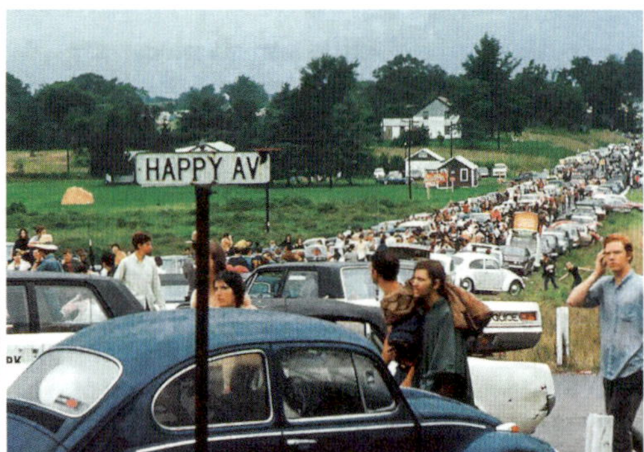
HAPPY AV"

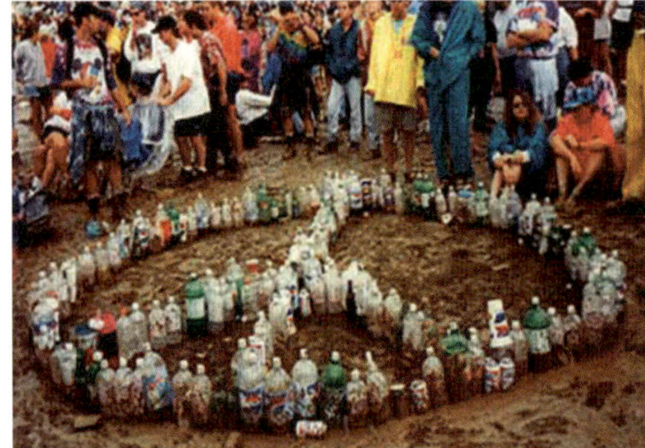

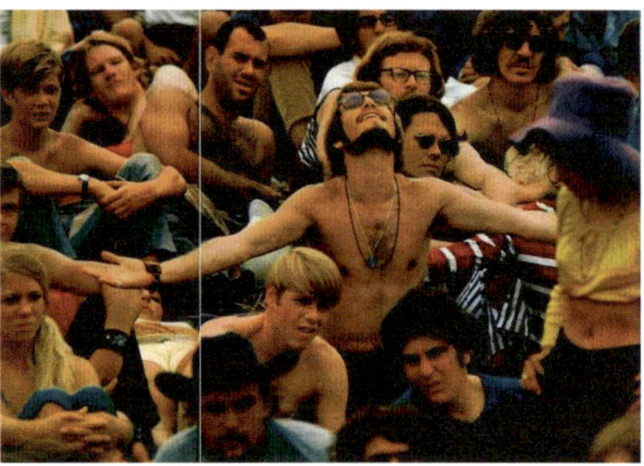

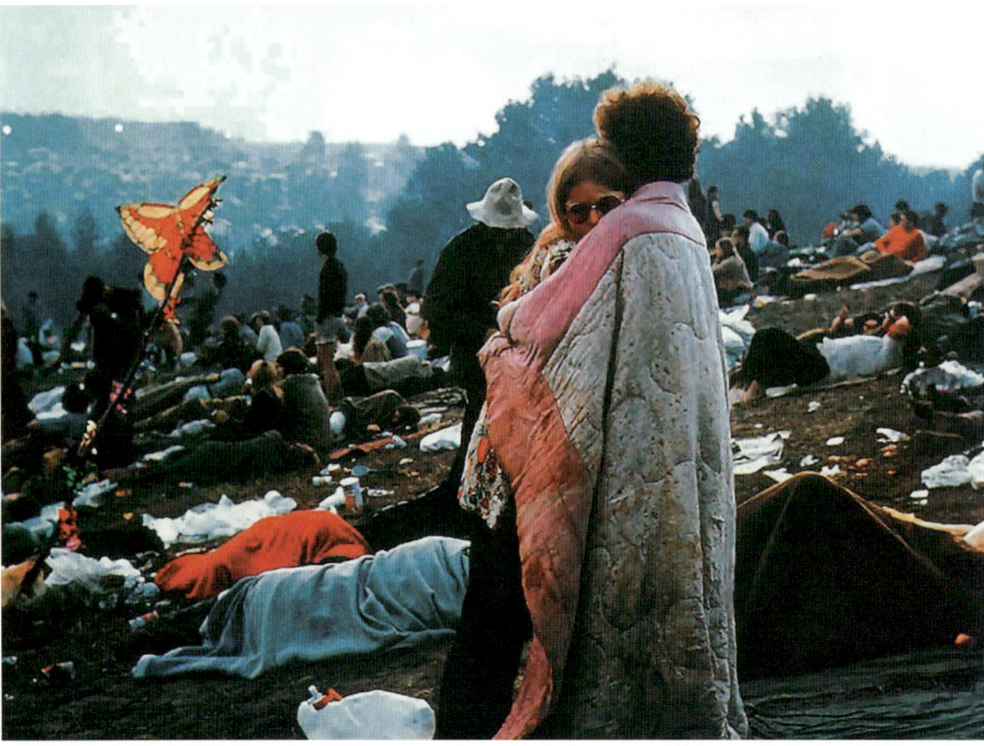

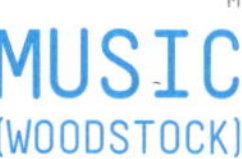

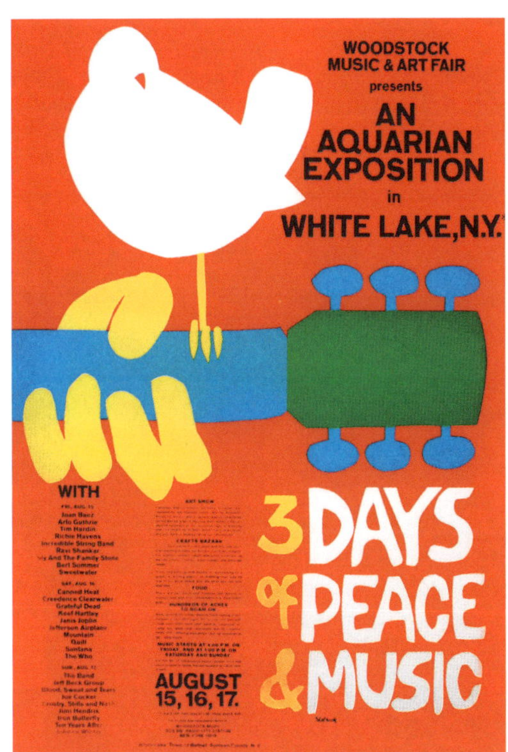

006

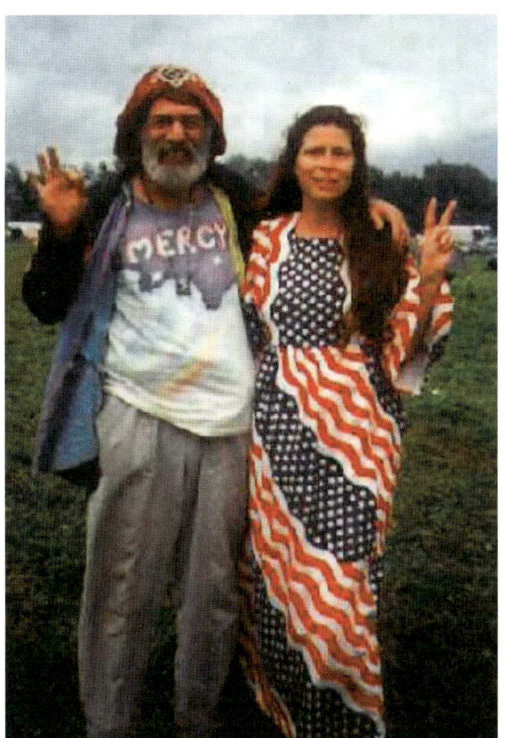

007

001 WOODSTOCK 1969
SOURCE donaldschwab.com

002 HAPPY AVENUE
SOURCE donaldschwab.com

003 WOODSTOCK 1994
CREATOR Michael Taylor
SOURCE www.the40yearplan.com/
article_081309_woodstock_94.php
DATE 1994

004 WOODSTOCK 1969
SOURCE donaldschwab.com

005 LOVE IN 1969
Nick and Bobbi Ercoline were
immortalized on the cover of the
original *Woodstock* album in 1970,
as well as on the movie poster.
CREATOR Burk Uzzle
SOURCE www.examiner.com/

006 3 DAYS OF PEACE & MUSIC
CREATOR Arnold Kolnick
SOURCE Plakatsammlung Museum
für Gestaltung Zürich

007 WOODSTOCK
SOURCE absolventi.gymcheb.cz

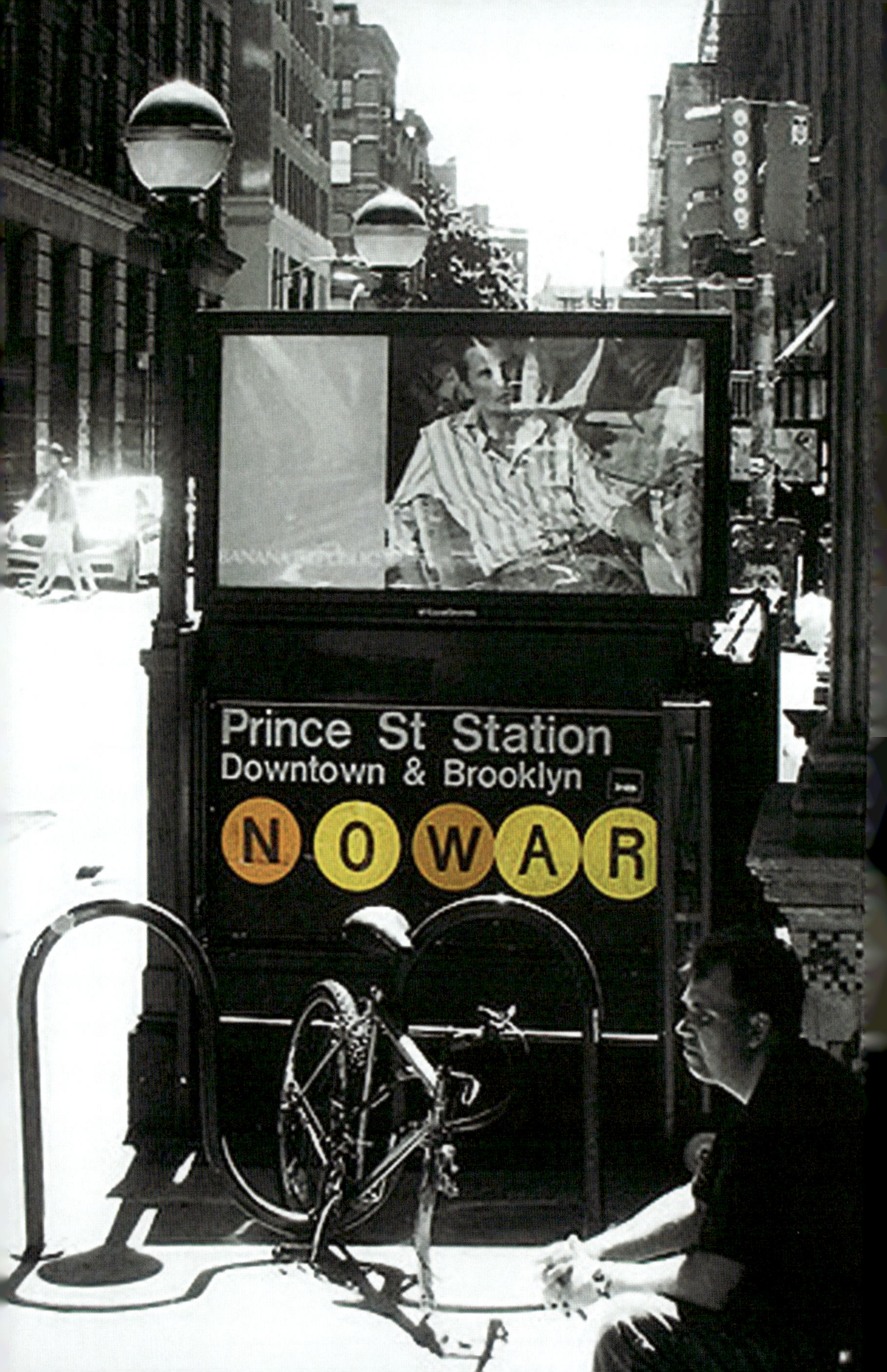

Prince St Station
Downtown & Brooklyn
N O W A R

LEFT
001
002
003

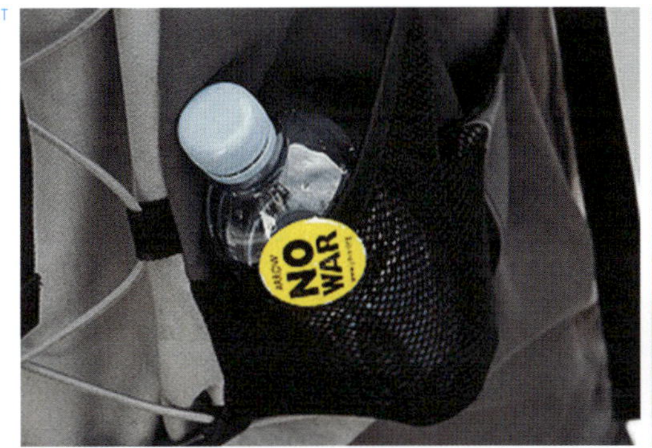

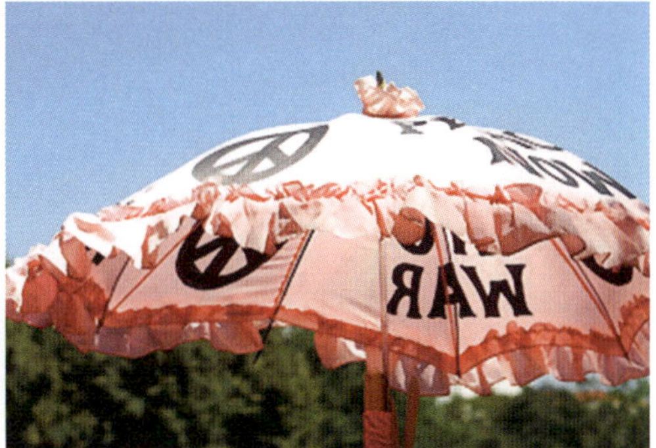

004
005

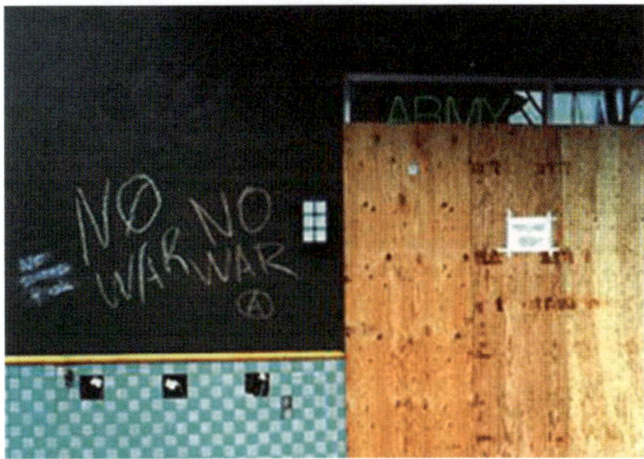

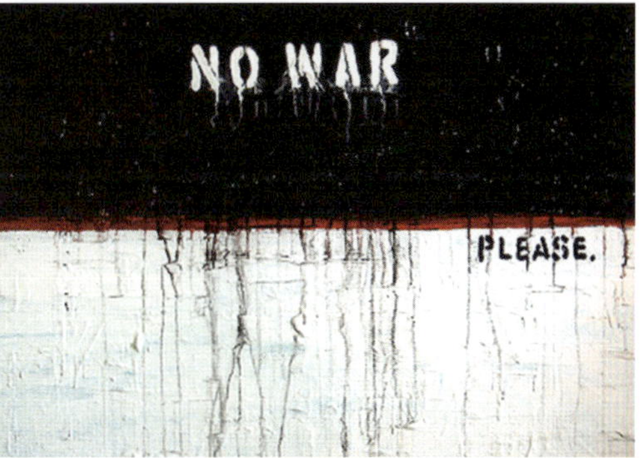

006
007

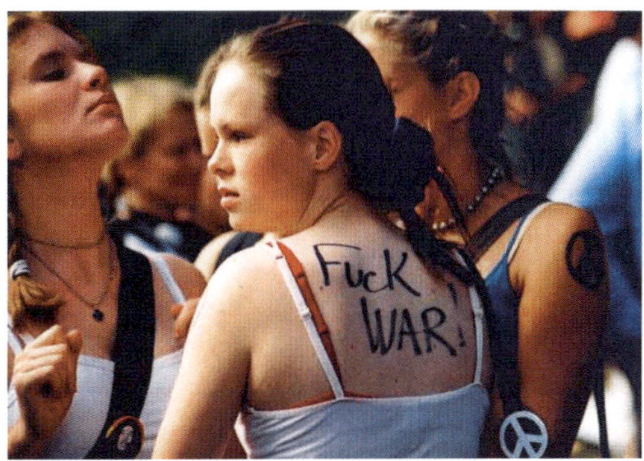

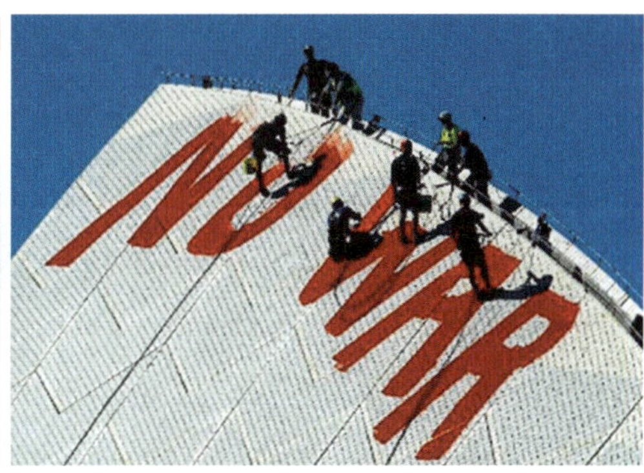

008
009

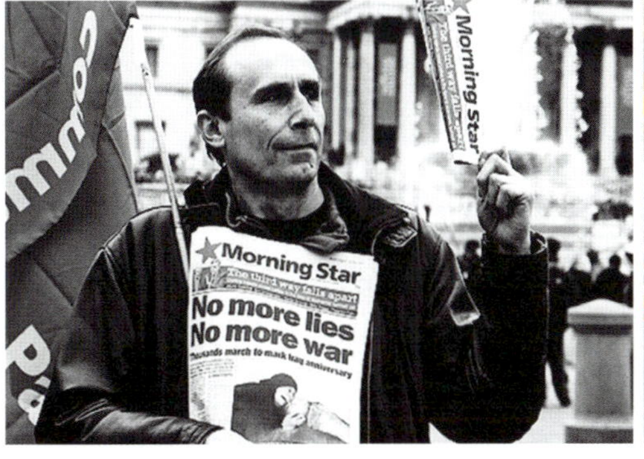

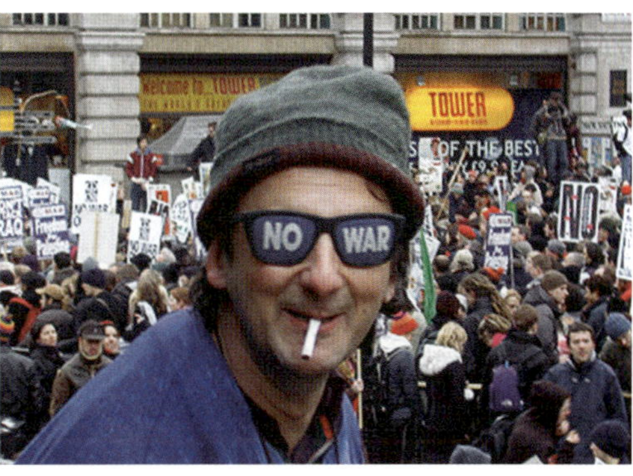

010 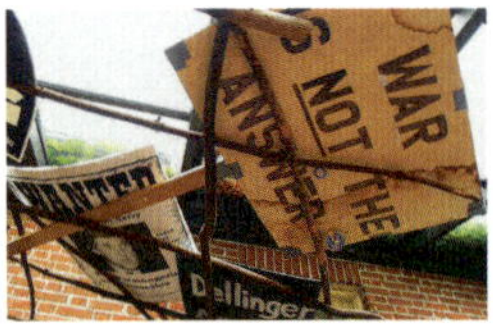
011 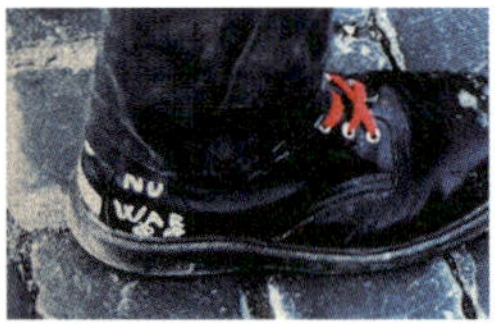
012 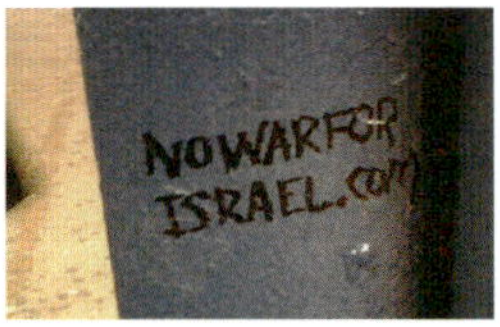
013

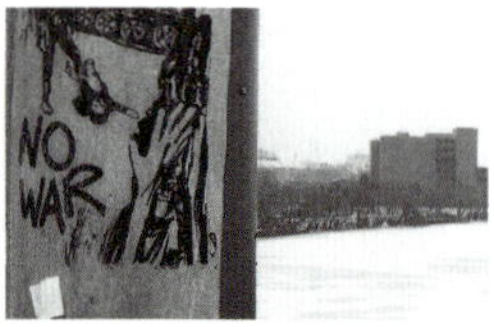

014 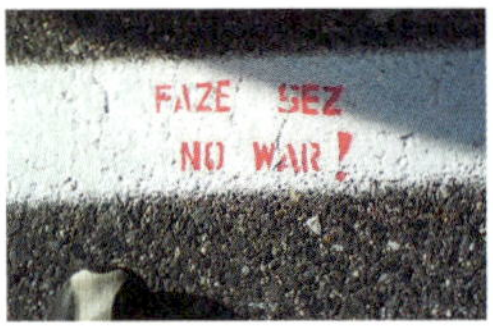
015 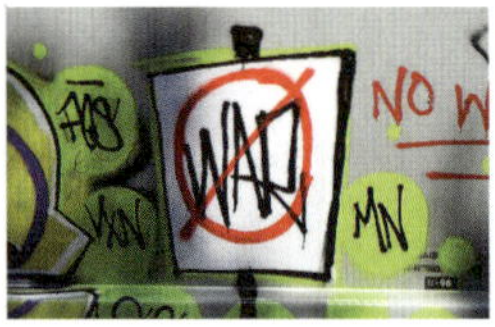
016 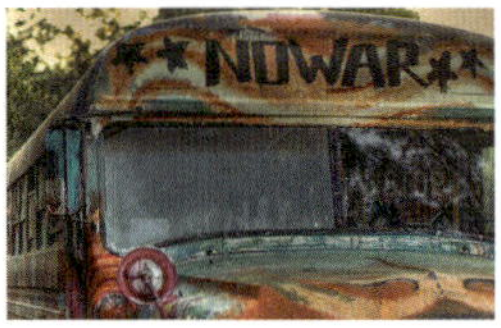
017

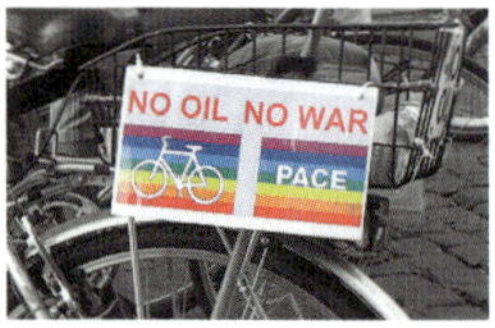

018 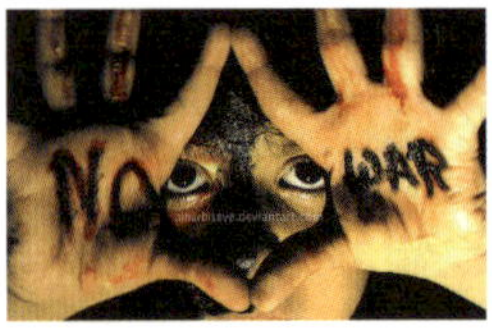
019 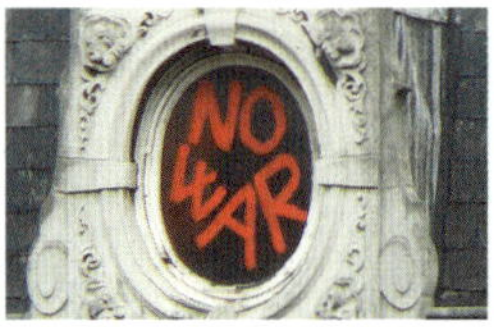
020 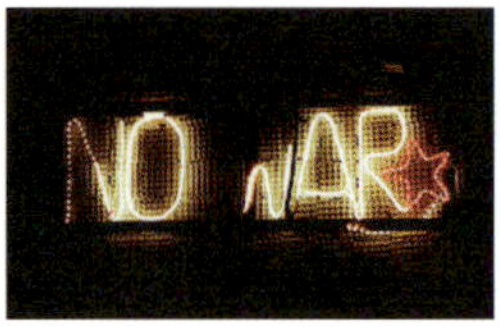
021

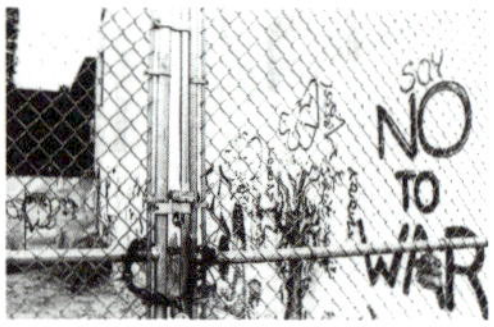

022 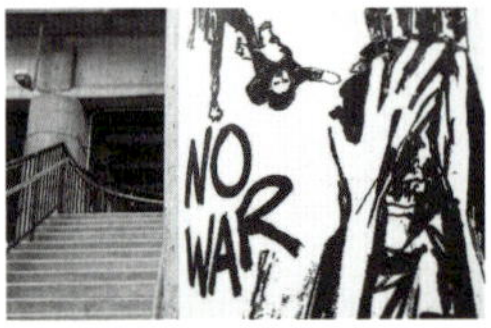
023 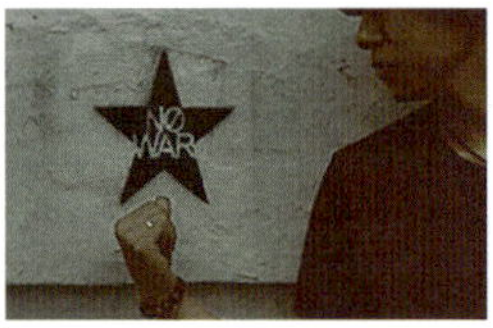
024 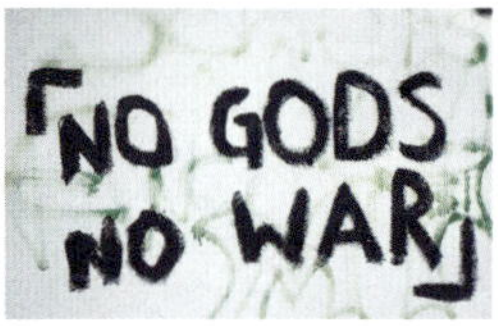
025

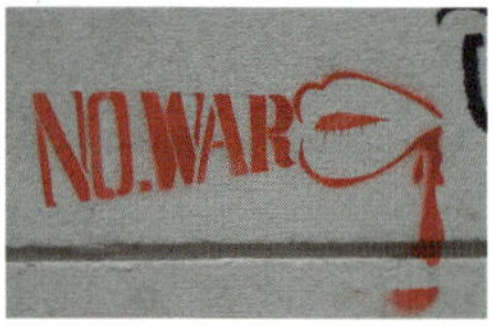

026

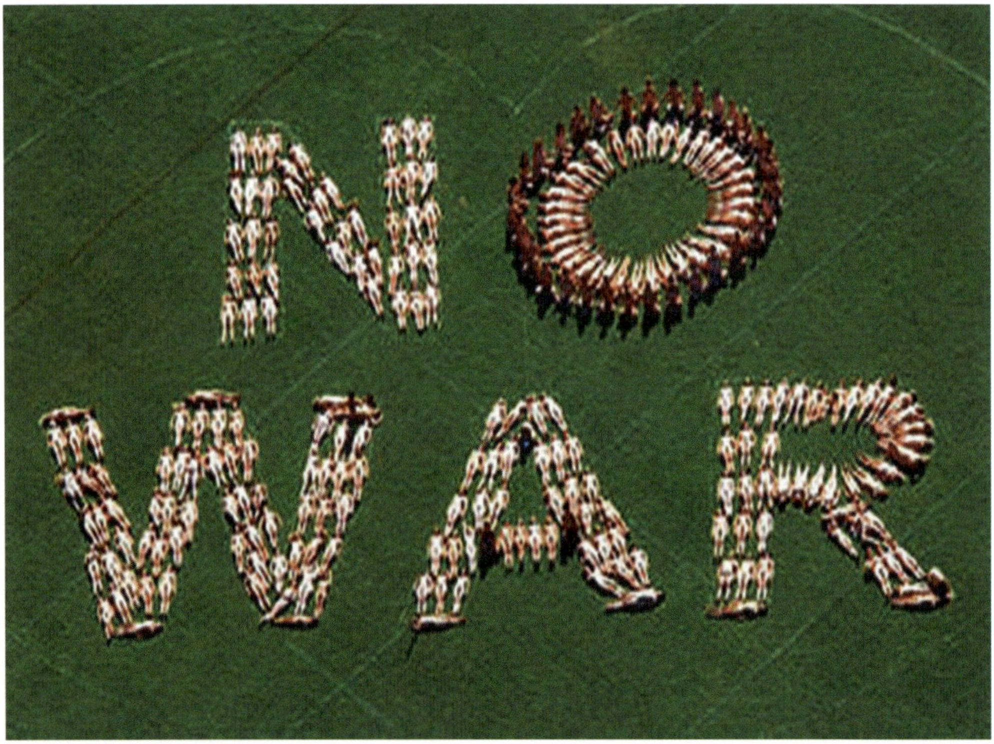

027
028
029
030

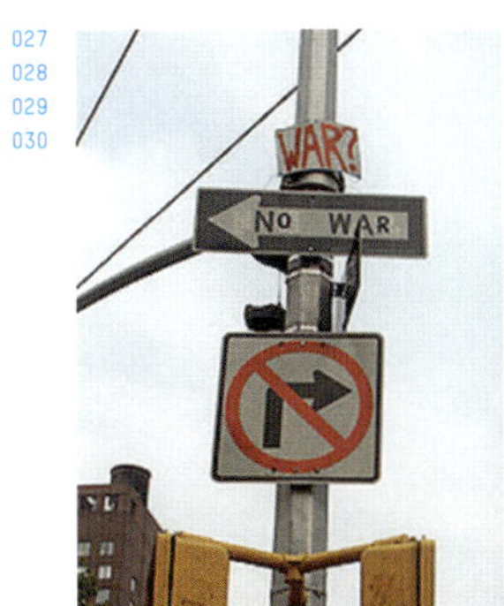

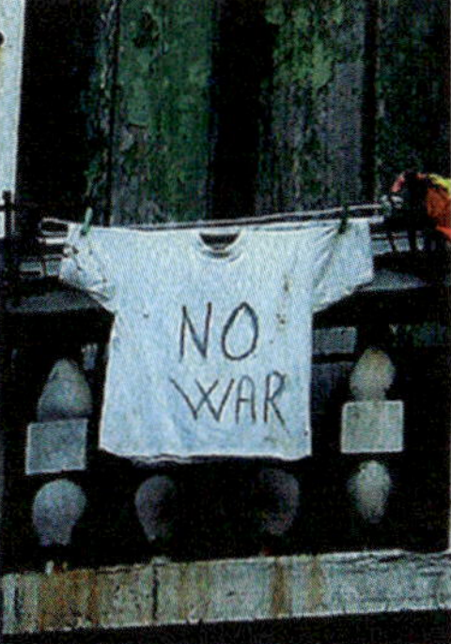

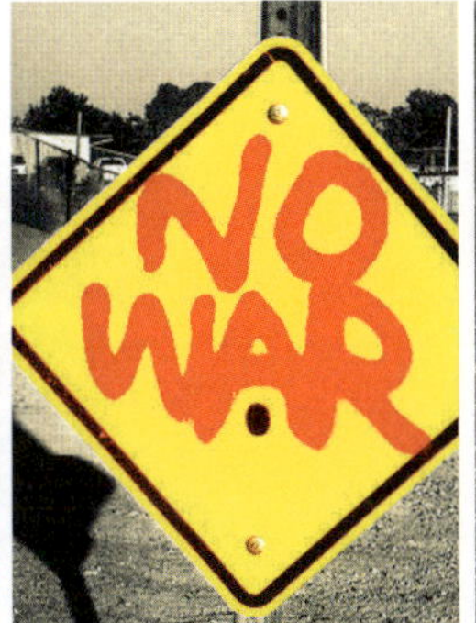

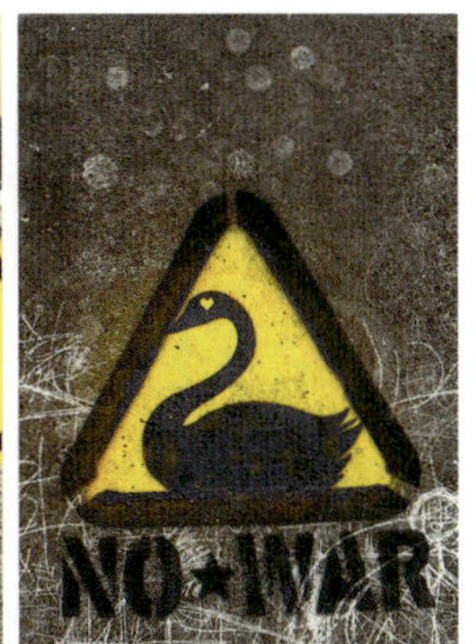

031
032
033

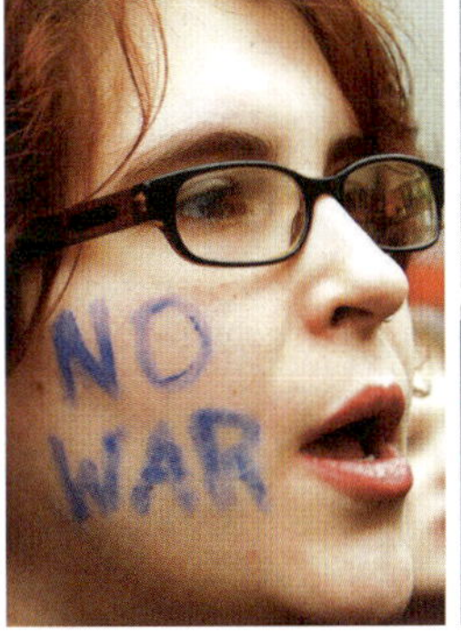

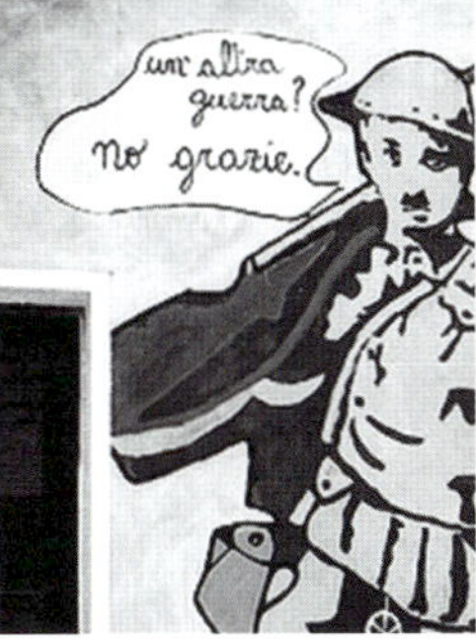

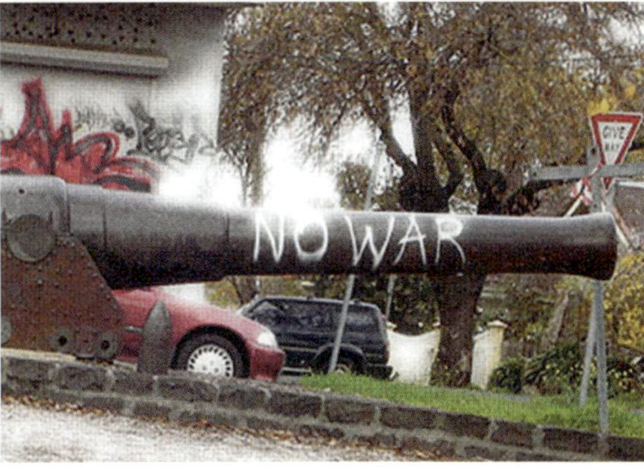

034

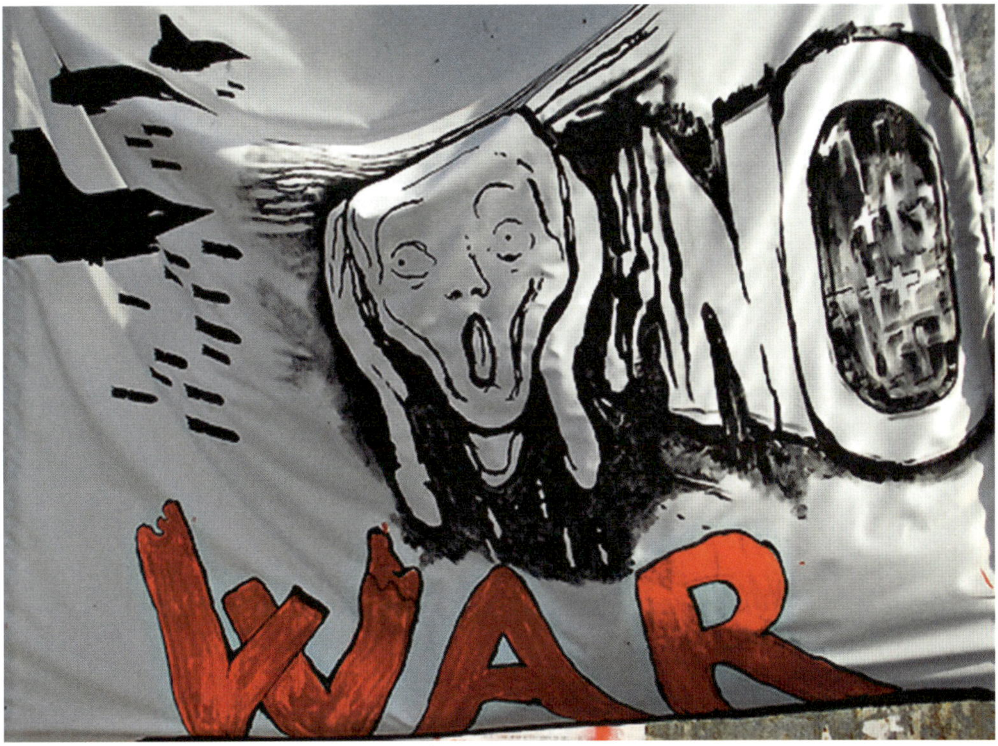

035

1986·Année Internationale de la Paix
NO STAR WAR

036

No Star Wars

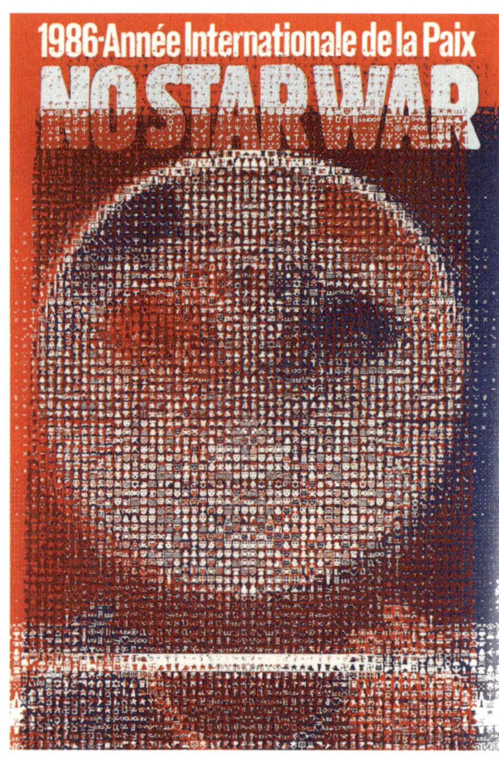

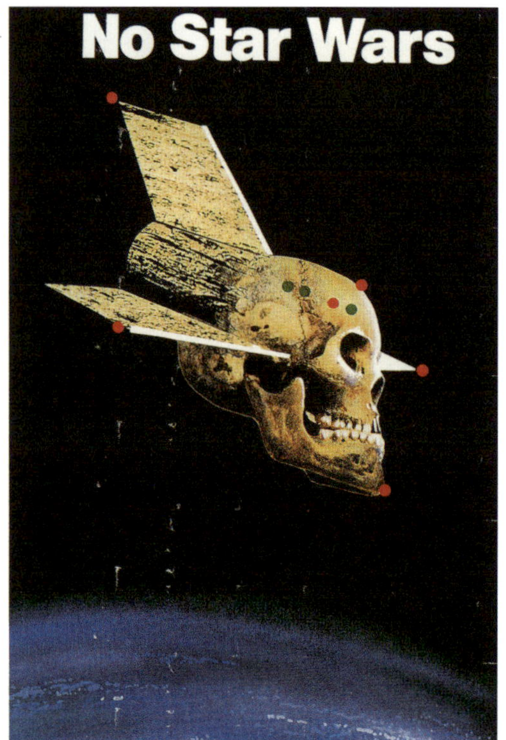

001 NO WAR
CREATOR Provided by asbestos
SOURCE www.flickr.com/photos/
asbestos/534666247/
DATE 2007

002 LIVE 8 - NO WAR
CREATOR Provided by madewithpixels
SOURCE www.flickr.com/photos/made-
withpixels/62946441/
DATE 2005

003 NO WAR
CREATOR Provided by Jadydangel
SOURCE www.flickr.com/
search/?q=Jadydangel
DATE 2008

004 NO WAR
CREATOR Christopher Rainone
SOURCE www.anti-war.us

005 NO WAR, PLEASE
CREATOR Provided by Kami Lerner
SOURCE www.flickr.com/photos/
45496170@N00/231492692/
DATE 2005

006 FUCK WAR
SOURCE www.thedigitalmuseum.org

007 NO WAR, SYDNEY OPERA HOUSE
CREATOR Provided by Jo
SOURCE joanne-horniman.blogspot.ch
DATE 2012

008 NO MORE LIES, NO MORE WAR
CREATOR Provided by lutonian
SOURCE www.flickr.com/
search/?q=lutonian&f=hp

009 NO WAR, LONDON ANTIWAR RALLY
CREATOR Provided by Ayman Haykal
SOURCE www.flickr.com/photos/
damascene/140556977/
DATE 2003

010 NO WAR
CREATOR Provided by neonlike
SOURCE www.flickr.com/photos/
neonlike59

011 NO WAR
CREATOR Provided by ZampArt
SOURCE www.flickr.com

012 NO WAR FOR ISRAEL - JAY ST, NYC
CREATOR Provided by intifada
SOURCE www.flickr.com/photos/
intifadah/436127655/

013 NO WAR
CREATOR Provided by caramaralyn
SOURCE www.flickr.com/photos/
caramaralyn/390830843/

014 FAZE SEZ NO WAR!
CREATOR Provided by Matt Oliphant
SOURCE www.flickr.com/photos/fajalar

015 NO WAR
CREATOR Provided by p...kin...e
SOURCE www.flickr.com/photos/
kinne/234230936/

016 NO WAR
CREATOR Provided by huntjump
SOURCE www.flickr.com/photos/
huntjump/2337826021/

017 NO OIL NO WAR
CREATOR Provided by Calicanthus
SOURCE www.flickr.com/photos/
calicanthus/1888674258/

018 NO WAR
CREATOR Provided by Alharbiseye
SOURCE www.flickr.com/photos/
alharbiseye/1241700895/

019 NO WAR
CREATOR Provided by noj.johnson
SOURCE www.flickr.com/photos/
noj-johnson/354291894/

020 NO WAR
CREATOR Provided by febbrile
SOURCE www.flickr.com/photos
/liberodicrederci/491605735/

021 SAY NO TO WAR
CREATOR Provided by
common people
SOURCE www.flickr.com/photos/
78196733@N00/119429338/

022 NO WAR
CREATOR Provided by Fen Branklin
SOURCE www.flickr.com

023 NO WAR
CREATOR Provided by grafix9
SOURCE www.flickr.com/photos/
afixlim/2802646058/

024 NO GODS - NO WAR
CREATOR Provided by Andreas B.
SOURCE www.flickr.com/photos/
andreasbehr/2729177468/

025 NO WAR
CREATOR Provided by Dr Case
SOURCE www.flickr.com/photos/
justin_case/54062138/

026 NO WAR
CREATOR Provided mrami
SOURCE www.flickr.com/photos/
meenoorami/9017483/

027 NO WAR
CREATOR Provided by DawnOne
SOURCE www.flickr.com/photos/dawnone

028 NO WAR
CREATOR Provided by
peaceloveandola
SOURCE www.flickr.com/photos/
peaceloveandola/370649017/

029 NO WAR
CREATOR Provided by Jessica Hellman
SOURCE www.flickr.com/photos/
heyheyitsjessica

030 NO WAR
CREATOR Provided by KonradS
SOURCE www.flickr.com

031 NO WAR
CREATOR Gregory by Varano
SOURCE www.flickr.com

032 NO WAR IN ORGOSOLO
CREATOR Provided by iperio
SOURCE www.flickr.com

033 NO WAR
CREATOR Provided by suerâ
SOURCE www.flickr.com

034 NO WAR, MILITARY BASE, ITALY
CREATOR Provided by indrasensi
SOURCE www.flickr.com/photos/
indrasensi

035 NO STAR WORLD
CREATOR Carlos Rolando Dotto
SOURCE JAGDA Peace Posters
International Exhibition

036 NO STAR WARS
CREATOR Karol Åśliwka
SOURCE JAGDA Peace Posters
International Exhibition

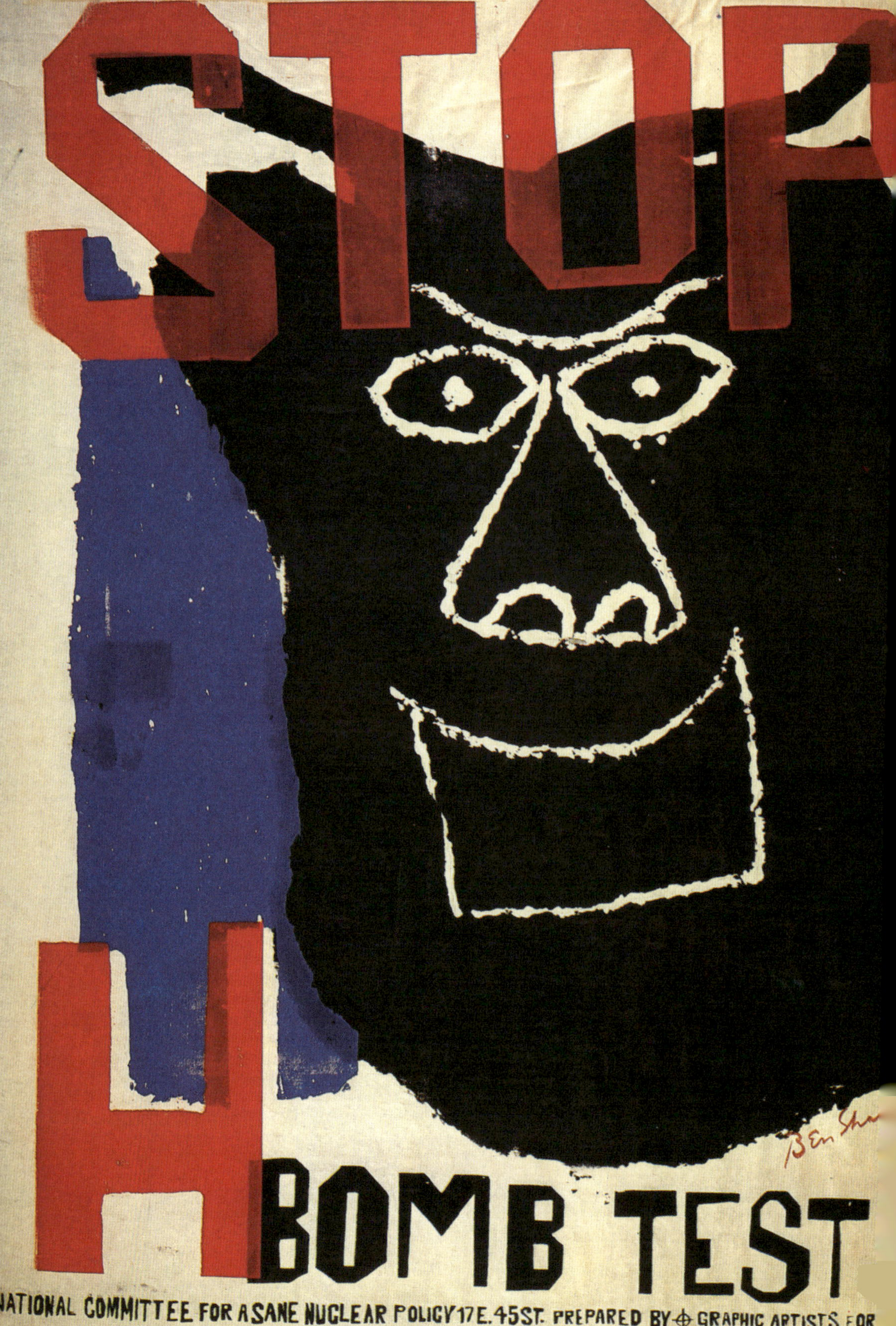

STOP
H
BOMB TEST
Ben Shn
NATIONAL COMMITTEE FOR A SANE NUCLEAR POLICY 17 E. 45 ST. PREPARED BY GRAPHIC ARTISTS FOR

LEFT
001
002
003

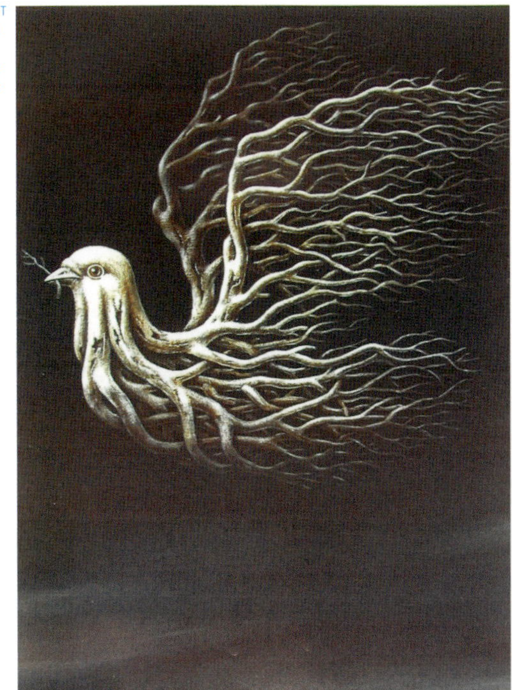

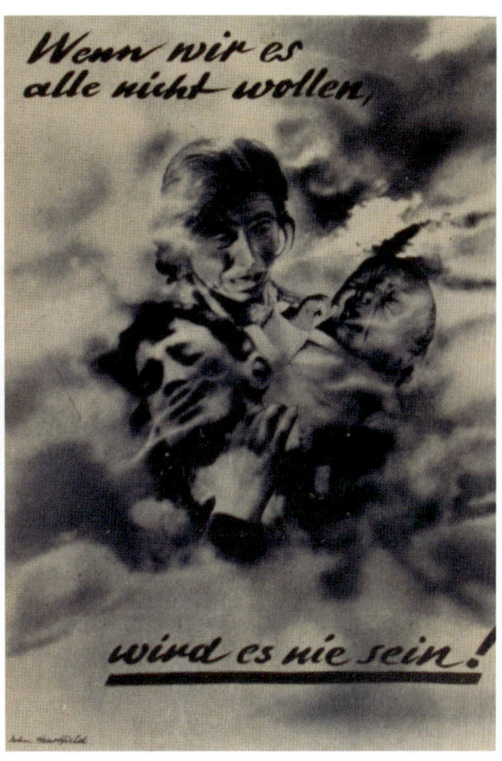

004
005

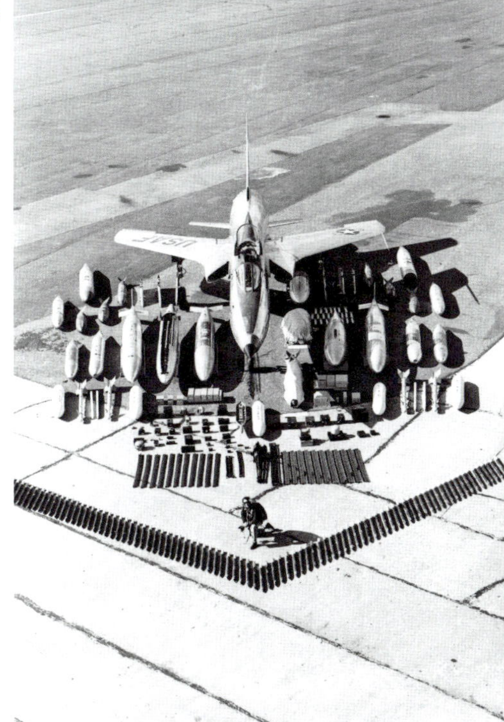

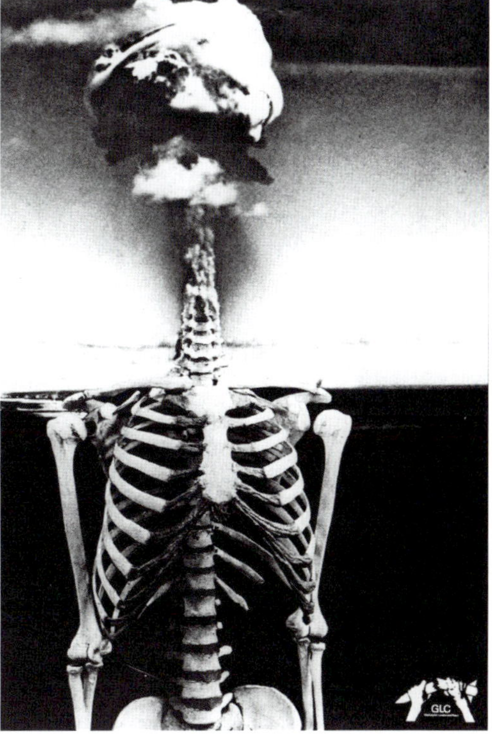

006
007

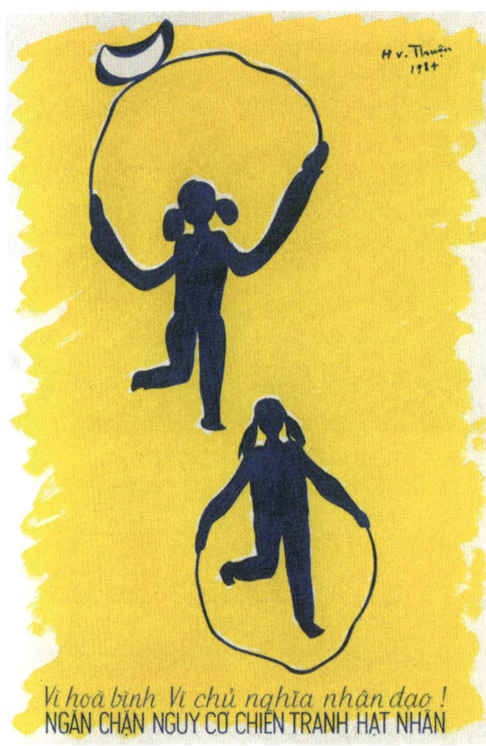

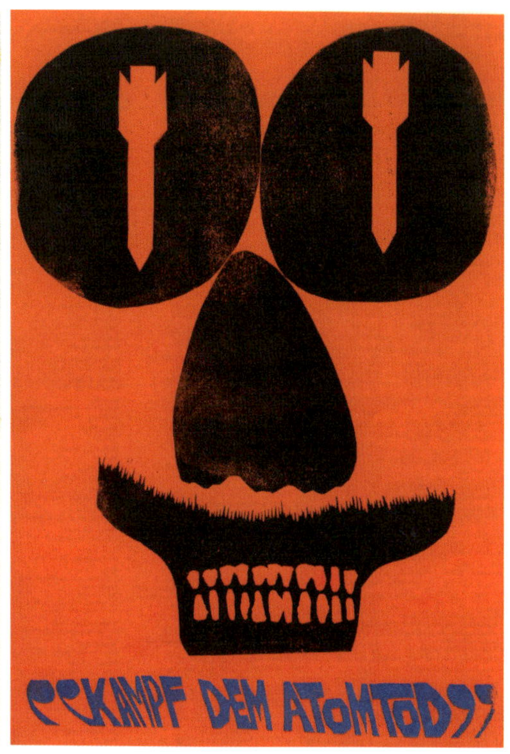

008
009

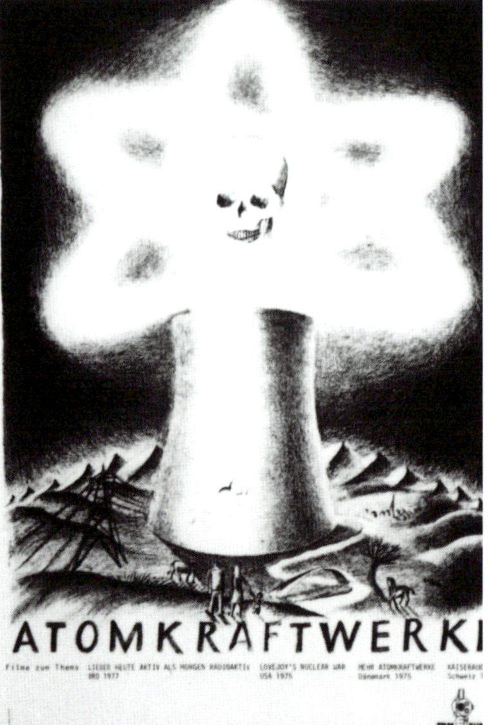

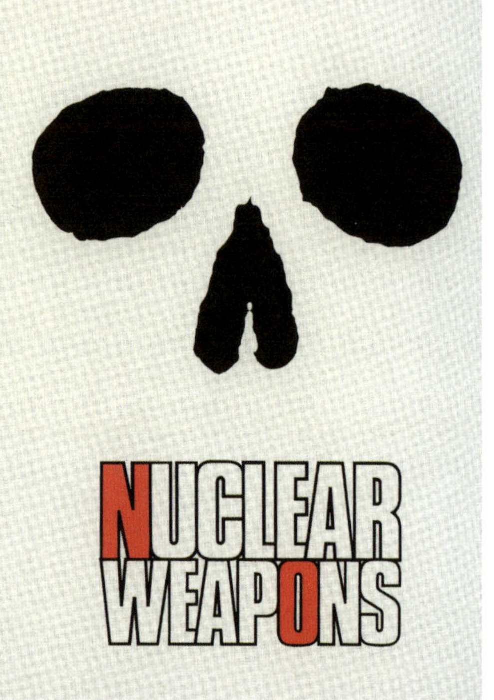

010
011

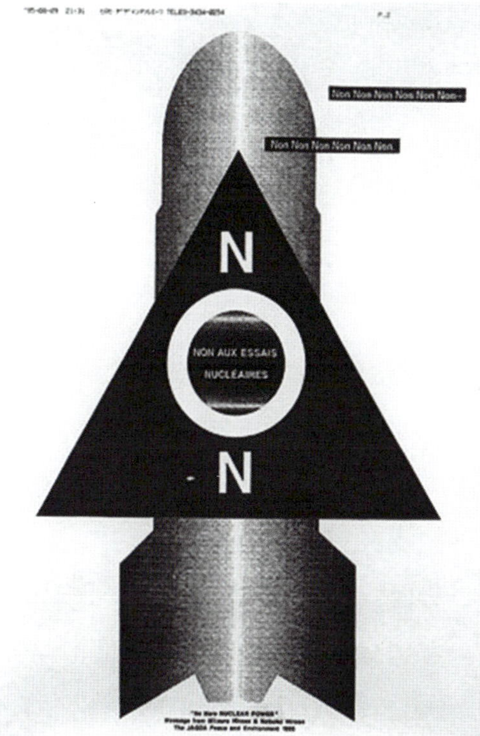

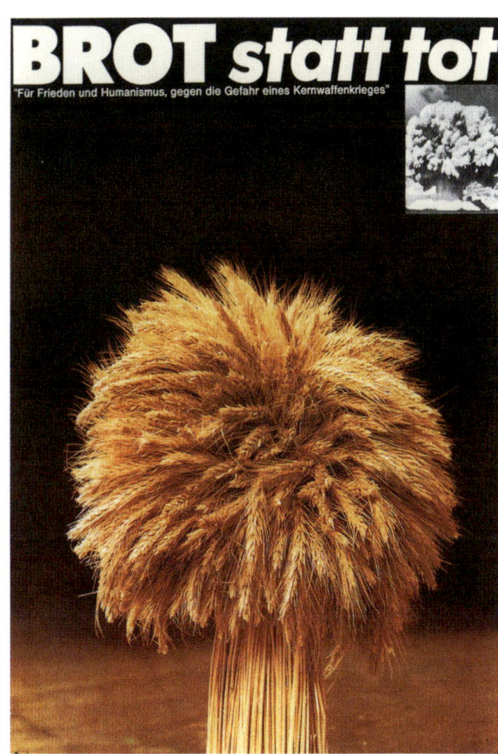

012
013

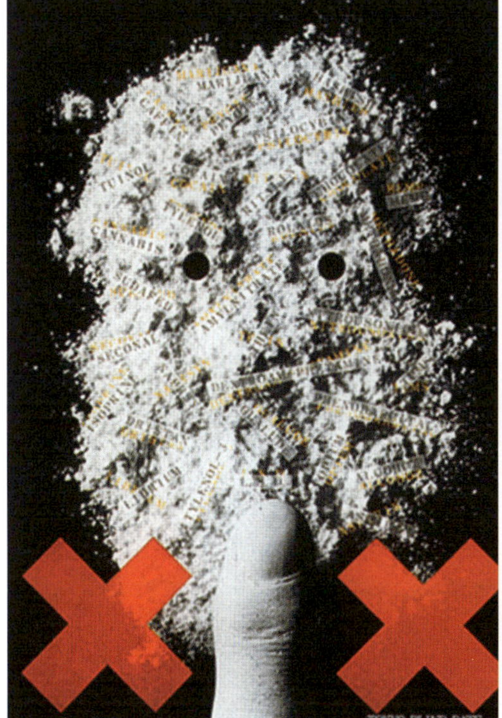

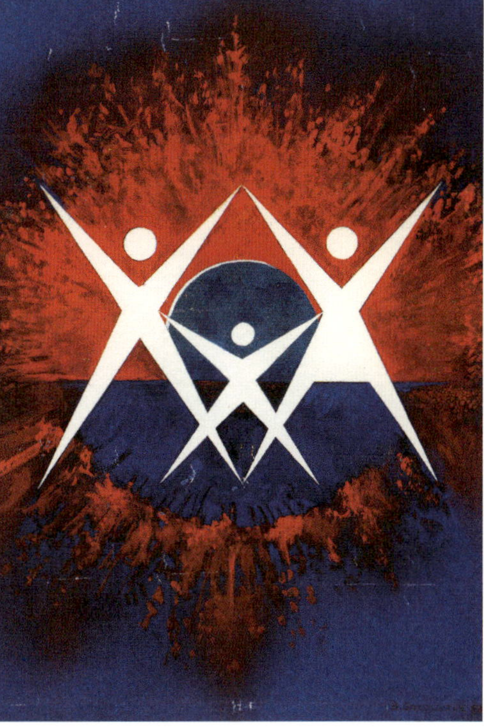

014
015

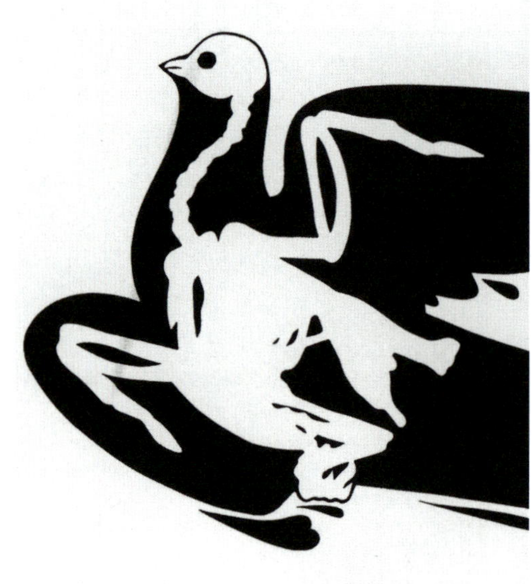

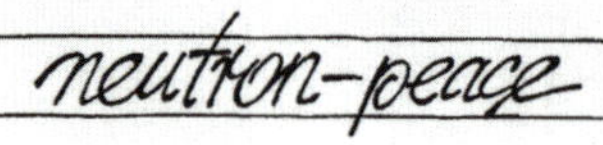

016
017

RIGHT
018

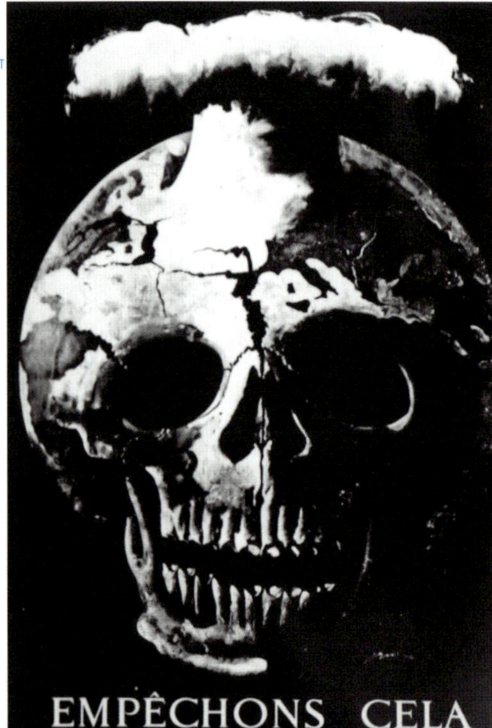

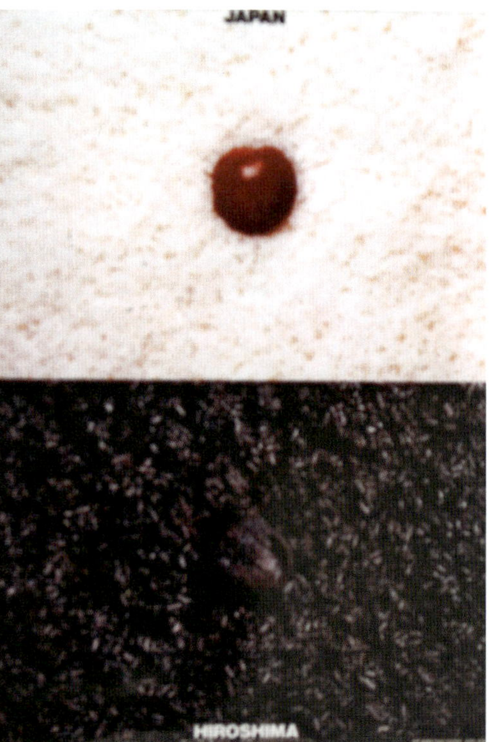

We want "PEACE".

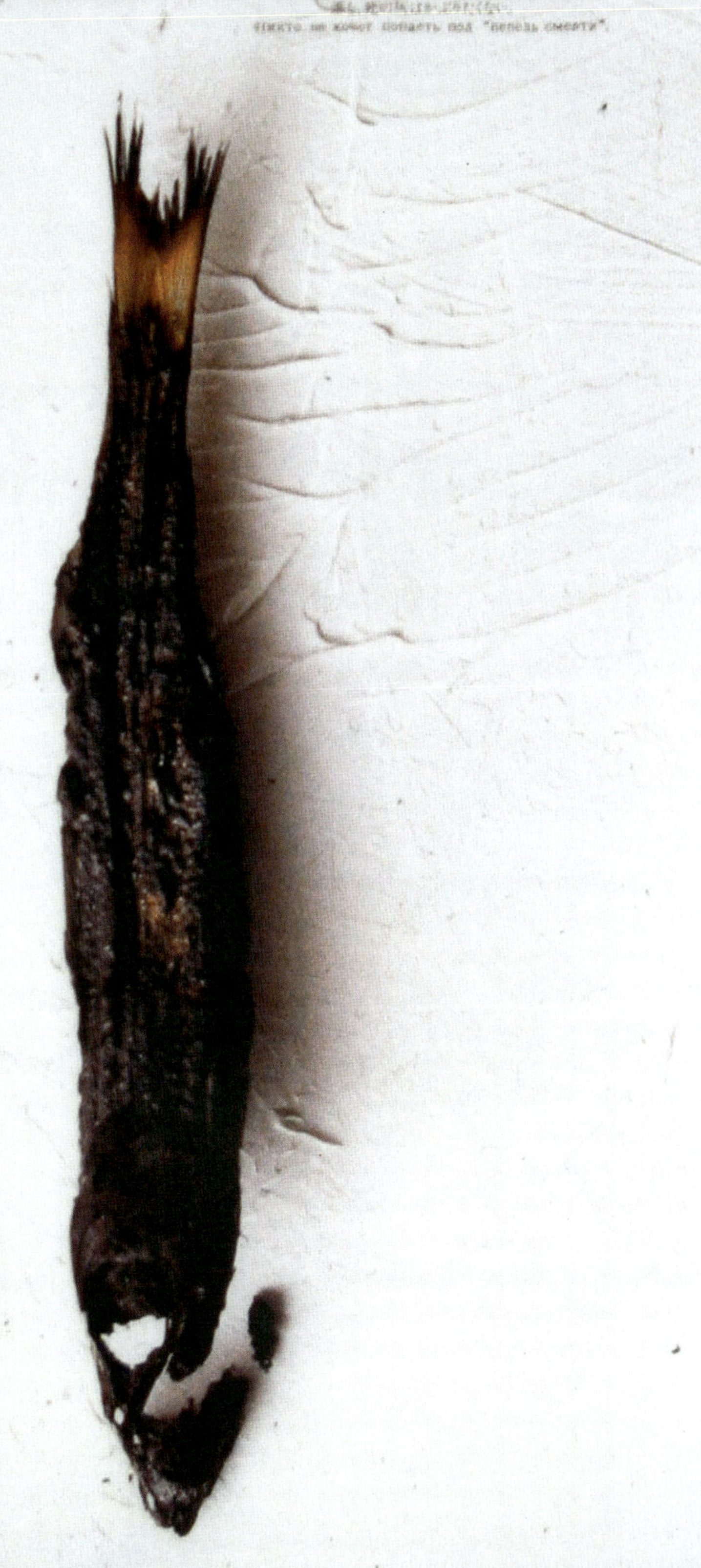

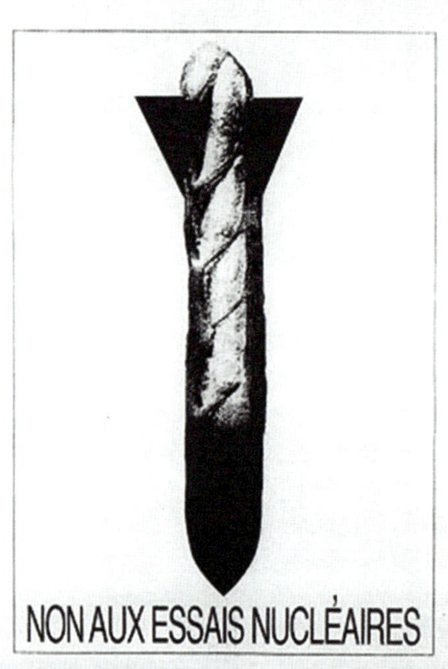
NON AUX ESSAIS NUCLÉAIRES
Toshio Imata

NON
AUX
ESSAIS
KEIZO MATSUI
Yuko Araki
NOMI. T

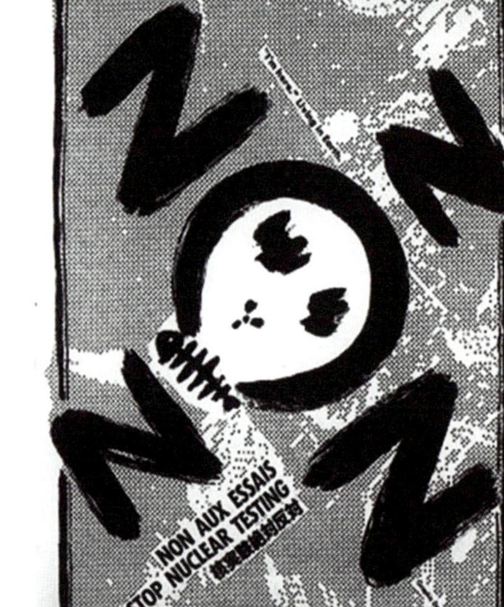
NON
NON AUX ESSAIS
STOP NUCLEAR TESTING

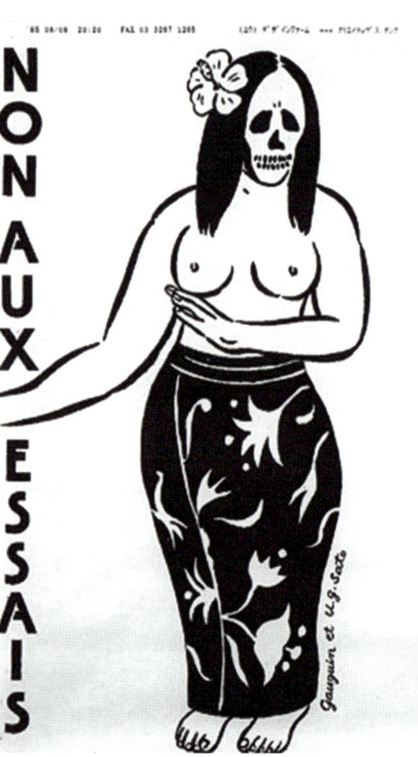
NON AUX ESSAIS
NUCLÉAIRES
Gauguin et U.S. Soto

023
024

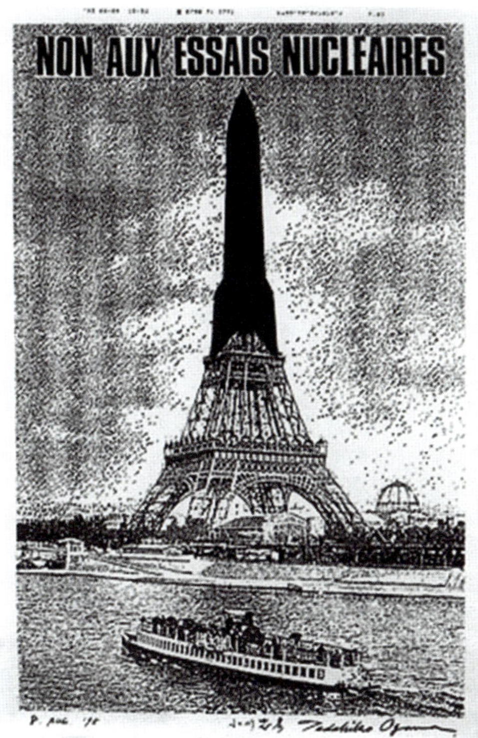

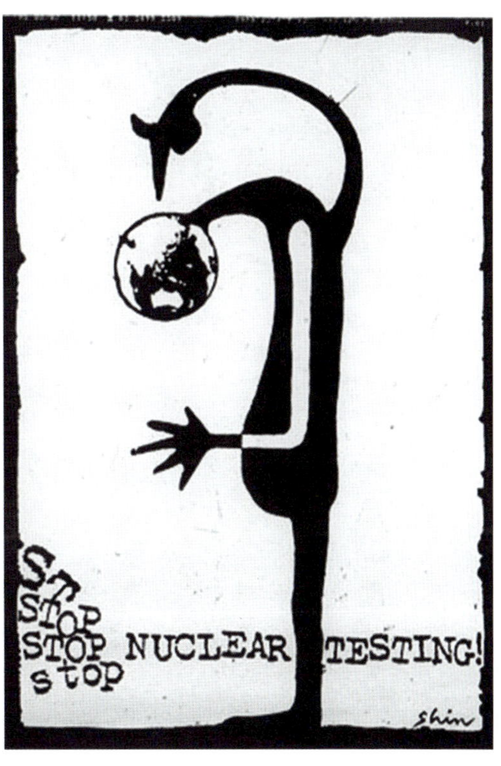

025
026

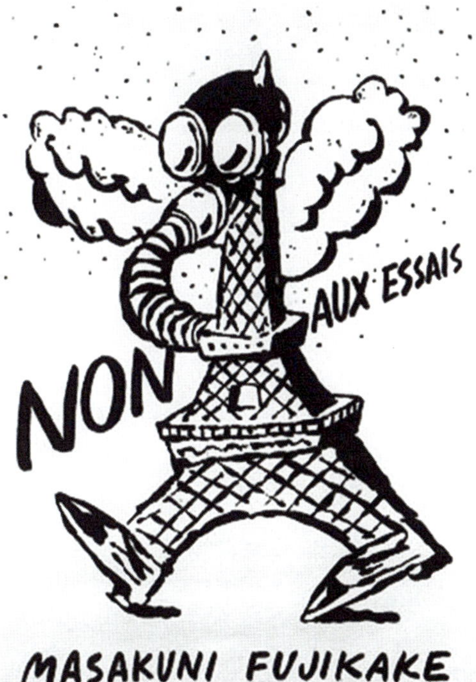

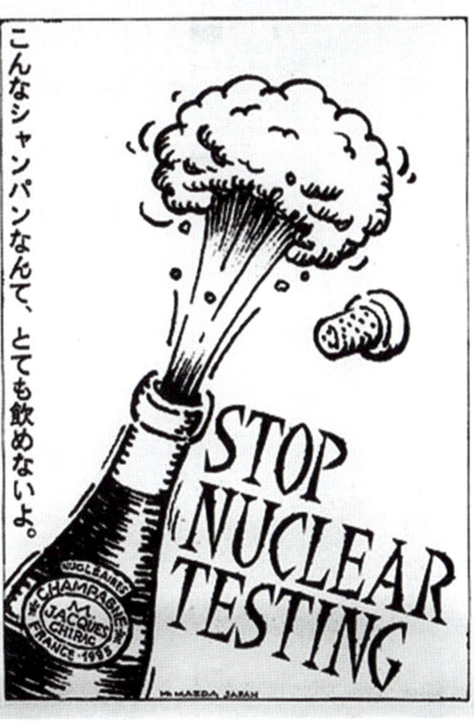

027

HIROSHIMA
never again
FEDERATION HABU HIROSHIMA

028

Protecting ourselves against pollution from nuclear power
also protects the persons we love.
自分を守ることは、
愛する人たちを守ることです。
原子力の平和利用を考える会
P.A.E.A.

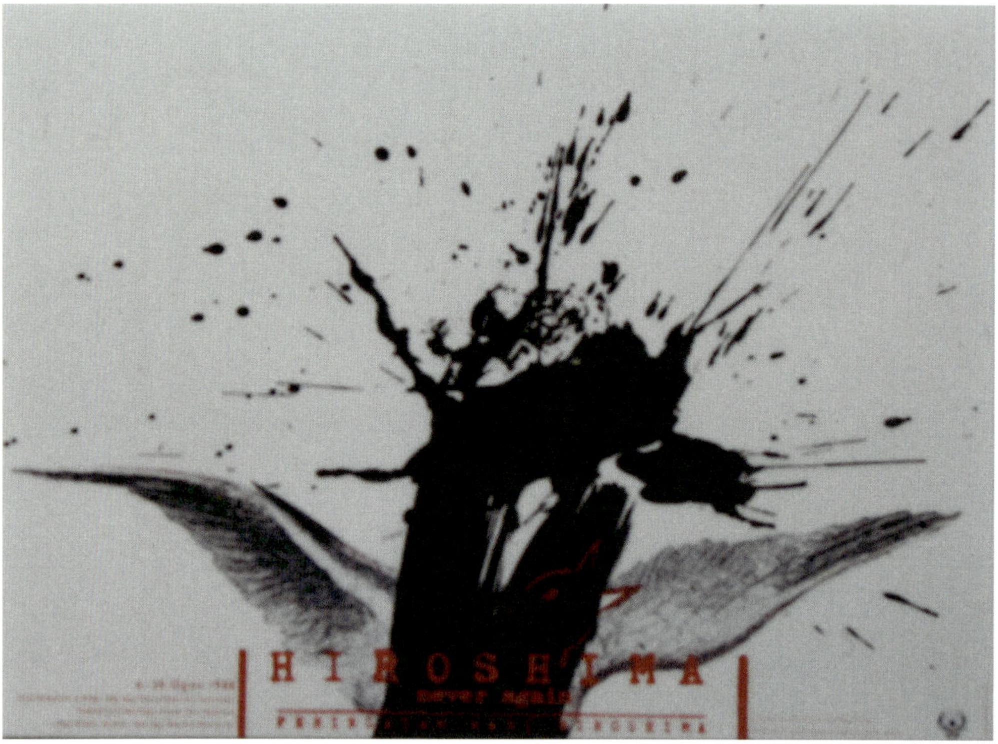

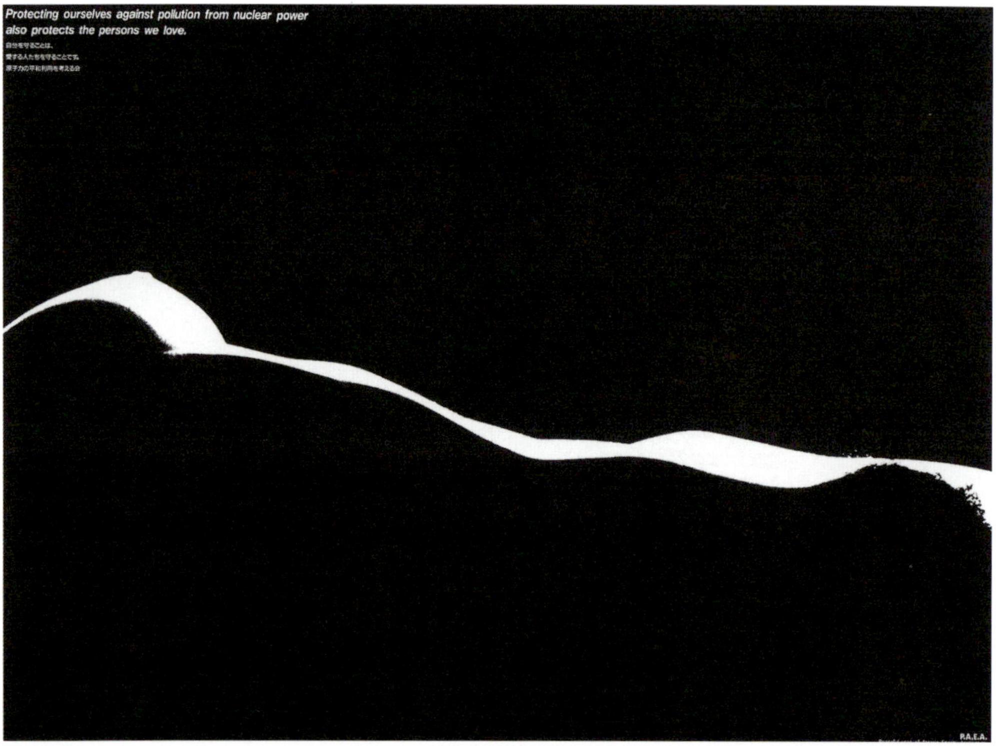

001 STOP H-BOMB TESTS
CREATOR Ben Shahn
SOURCE D. J. R. Bruckner, Seymour
Chwast, and Steven Heller, eds.,
Kunst Gegen den Krieg [Basel:
Birkhäuser, 1984], p. 103.

002 THERE IS NO PEACE AFTER
NUCLEAR WAR!
CREATOR Rafal Olbinski
SOURCE www.polishhomefoundation.org

003 WENN WIR ES ALLE NICHT WOLLEN,
WIRD ES NIE SEIN
[UNLESS NONE OF US WANT IT, IT
WILL NOT HAPPEN]
CREATOR John Heartfield
SOURCE Plakatsammlung Museum
für Gestaltung Zürich
DATE 1957

004 ONE-MAN AIR FORCE
SOURCE U.S. Air Force
DATE 1950s

005 SOURCE D. J. R. Bruckner, Seymour
Chwast, and Steven Heller, eds.,
Kunst Gegen den Krieg [Basel:
Birkhäuser, 1984], p. 125.

006 FOR PEACE, FOR HUMANISM – PREVENT
THE RISK OF NUCLEAR WAR
CREATOR Van Thuan Huynh
SOURCE JAGDA Peace Posters
International Exhibition

007 KAMPF DEM ATOMTOD
[FIGHT AGAINST ATOMIC DEATH]
SOURCE D. J. R. Bruckner, Seymour
Chwast, and Steven Heller, eds.,
Kunst Gegen den Krieg [Basel:
Birkhäuser, 1984], p. 124.

008 ATOMKRAFTWERKE
[ATOMIC POWER PLANTS]
CREATOR Helen Rymann
SOURCE Plakatsammlung Museum
für Gestaltung Zürich

009 NUCLEAR WEAPONS
CREATOR Dragutin Dado
SOURCE JAGDA Peace Posters
International Exhibition

010 NON [NO]
CREATOR Mitsuru Hirose,
Nobuku Hirose
SOURCE "L'engagement politique et
social," Le festival d'affiches,
Chaumont, 19 May – 16 July 2000

011 BREAD NOT DEATH
CREATOR Lutz Grumbach
SOURCE JAGDA Peace Posters
International Exhibition

012 TOKYO BLIND DATE
CREATOR Sigel Shimo'Oka

SOURCE "L'engagement politique et
social," Le festival d'affiches,
Chaumont, 19 May – 16 July 2000

013 NEVER
CREATOR Benon Grzeszczuk
SOURCE JAGDA Peace Posters
International Exhibition

014 NEUTRON – PEACE
CREATOR Gyorgy Olah
SOURCE JAGDA Peace Posters
International Exhibition

015 NON AUX ESSAIS NUCLÉAIRES
[NO TO NUCLEAR TESTING]
CREATOR Tokashi Othaka
SOURCE "L'engagement politique et
social," Le festival d'affiches,
Chaumont, 19 May – 16 July 2000

016 EMPÉCHONS CELA
[LET'S PREVENT THIS]
CREATOR Hans Erni
SOURCE Plakatsammlung Museum
für Gestaltung Zürich
DATE 1954

017 JAPAN, HIROSHIMA – GOT NO
FORGOTTEN, GOT TO RELATE
EXPERIENCE
CREATOR Sigel Shimo'Oka
SOURCE Plakatsammlung Museum
für Gestaltung Zürich
DATE 1989

018 WE WANT PEACE – NO ONE WANTS TO
WEAR THE RADIOACTIVE ASH
CREATOR Sigel Shimo'Oka
SOURCE Plakatsammlung Museum
für Gestaltung Zürich
DATE 1987

019 NON AUX ESSAIS NUCLÉAIRES
[NO TO NUCLEAR TESTING]
CREATOR Toshio Iwata
SOURCE "L'engagement politique et
social," Le festival d'affiches,
Chaumont, 19 May – 16 July 2000

020 NON AUX ESSAIS
[NO TO TESTING]
CREATOR Keizo Matsui, Yuko Araki,
Nomi. T
SOURCE "L'engagement politique et
social," Le festival d'affiches,
Chaumont, 19 May – 16 July 2000

021 NON AUX ESSAIS
[STOP NUCLEAR TESTING]
CREATOR Hideo Yamashita
SOURCE "L'engagement politique et
social," Le festival d'affiches,
Chaumont, 19 May – 16 July 2000

022 NON AUX ESSAIS NUCLÉAIRES
[NO TO NUCLEAR TESTING]
CREATOR U.G. Sato

SOURCE "L'engagement politique et
social," Le festival d'affiches,
Chaumont, 19 May – 16 July 2000

023 NON AUX ESSAIS NUCLÉAIRES
[NO TO NUCLEAR TESTING]
CREATOR Tadahiko Ogawa
SOURCE "L'engagement politique et
social," Le festival d'affiches,
Chaumont, 19 May – 16 July 2000

024 STOP NUCLEAR TESTING
CREATOR Shin Matsunaga
SOURCE "L'engagement politique et
social," Le festival d'affiches,
Chaumont, 19 May – 16 July 2000

025 NON AUX ESSAIS
[NO TO TESTING]
CREATOR Masakuni Fujikake
SOURCE "L'engagement politique et
social," Le festival d'affiches,
Chaumont, 19 May – 16 July 2000

026 STOP NUCLEAR TESTING
CREATOR Mineo Maeda
SOURCE "L'engagement politique et
social," Le festival d'affiches,
Chaumont, 19 May – 16 July 2000

027 HIROSHIMA NEVER AGAIN
CREATOR Tung Ming
SOURCE Plakatsammlung Museum
für Gestaltung Zürich
DATE 1988

028 PEACEFUL USES OF ATOMIC ENERGY
CREATOR Yoshiteru Asai
SOURCE JAGDA Peace Posters
International Exhibition

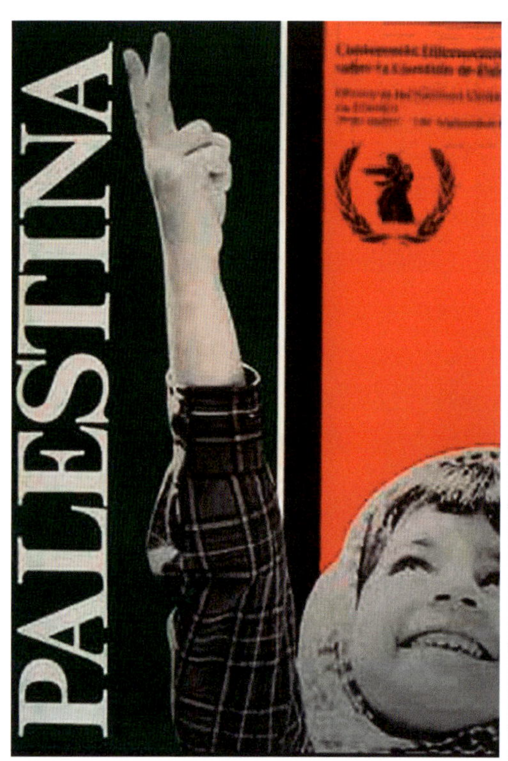
PALESTINA

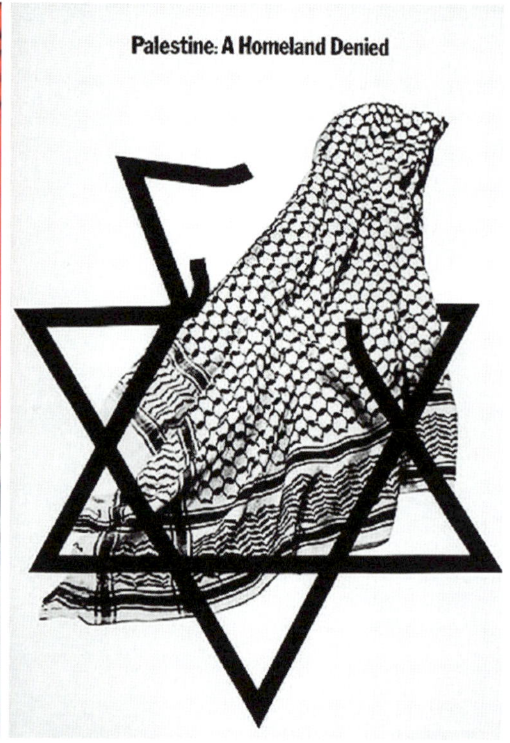
Palestine: A Homeland Denied

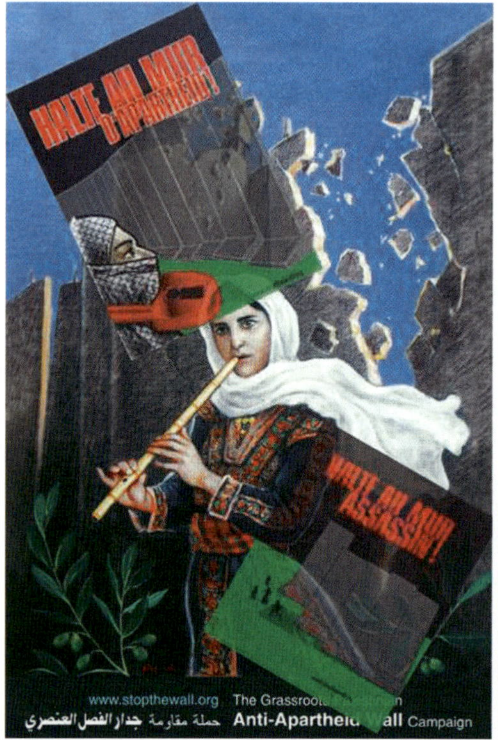
HALTE AU MUR
D'APARTHEID!
HALTE AU MUR
ASSASSIN!
www.stopthewall.org   The Grassroots
Anti-Apartheid Wall Campaign
حملة مقاومة جدار الفصل العنصري

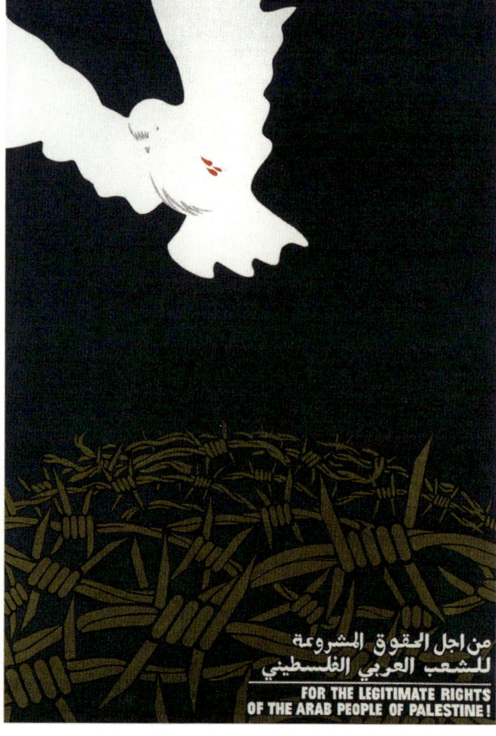
من اجل الحقوق المشروعة
للشعب العربي الفلسطيني
FOR THE LEGITIMATE RIGHTS
OF THE ARAB PEOPLE OF PALESTINE !

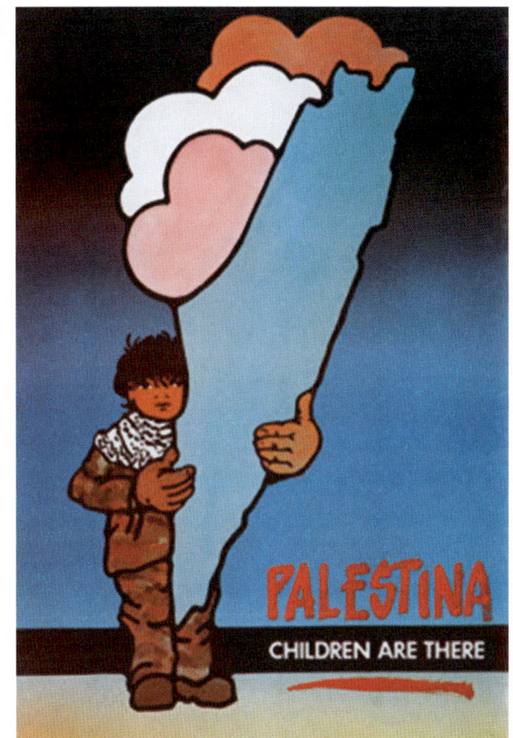
PALESTINA
CHILDREN ARE THERE

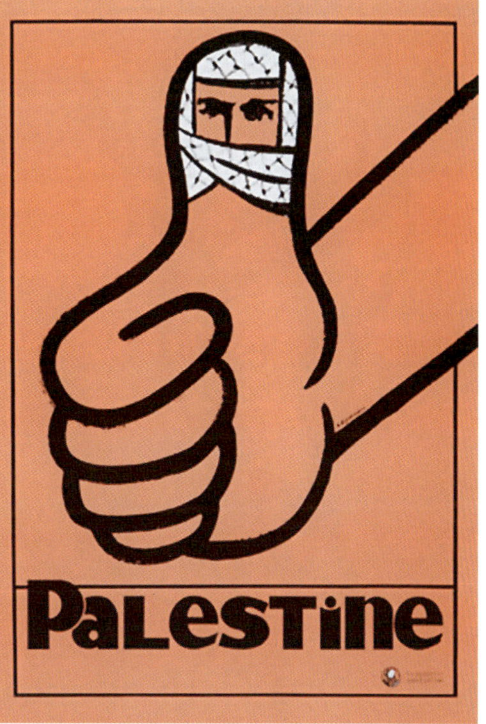
Palestine

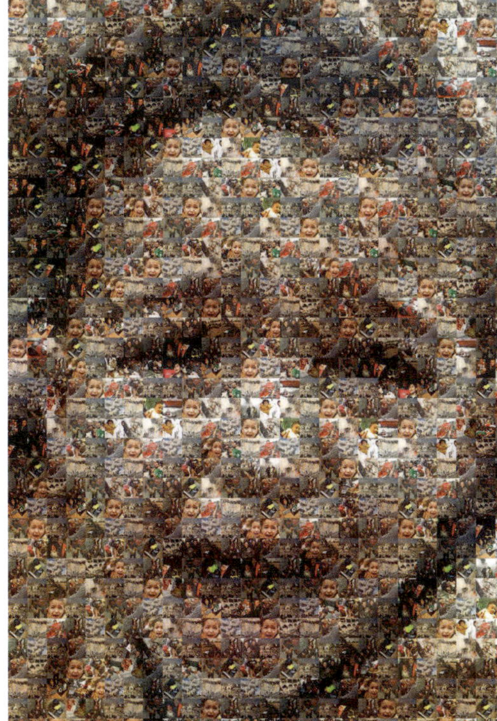

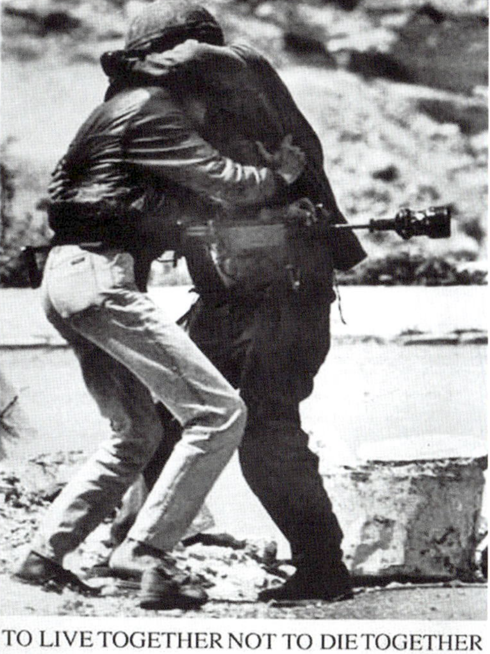
TO LIVE TOGETHER NOT TO DIE TOGETHER
I·T·S
P·O·S·S
I·B·L·E
الحياة معًا لا الموت معًا

009
010

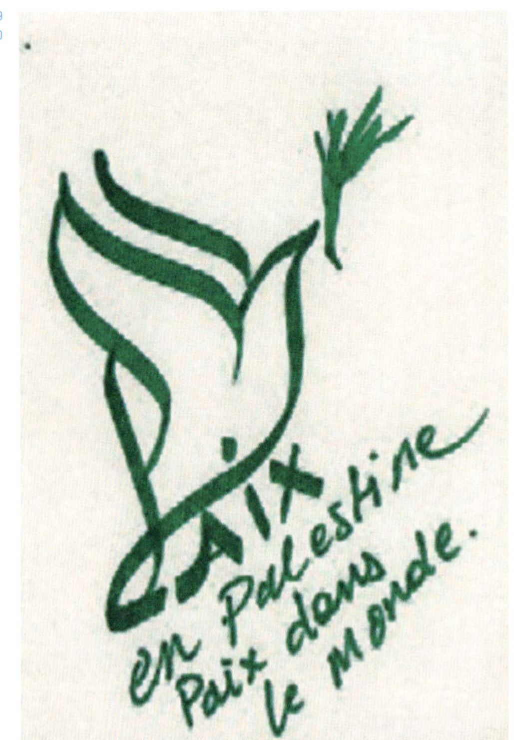

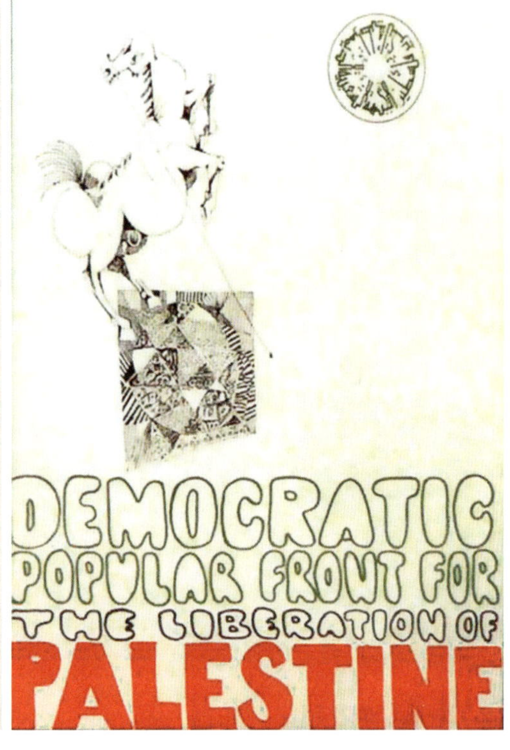

011
012

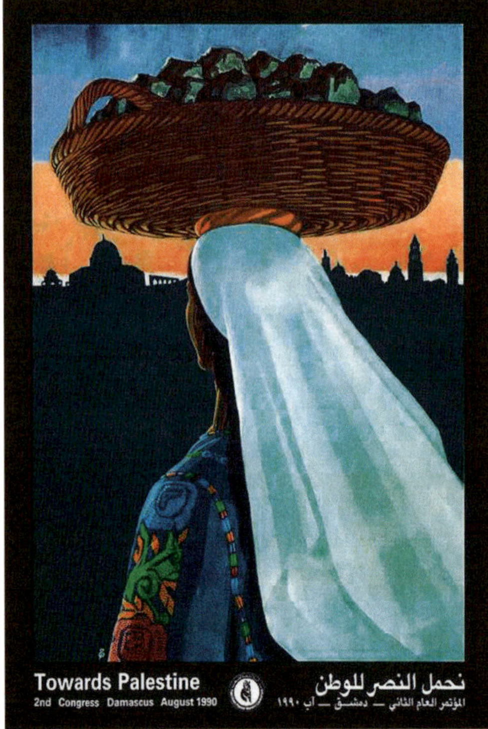

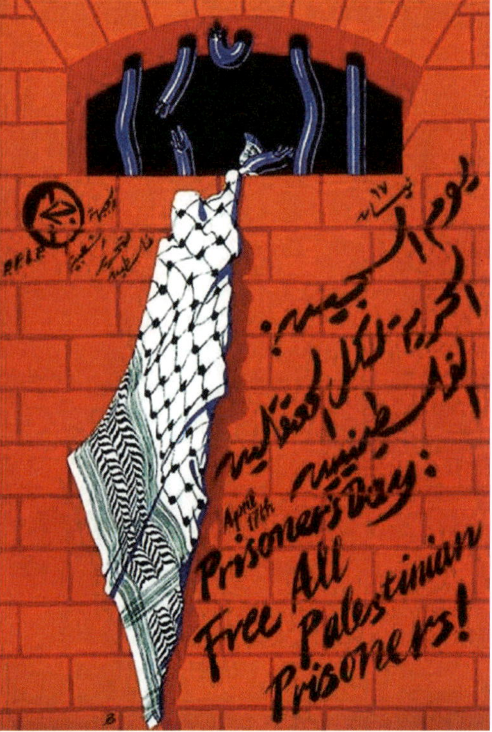

013
014

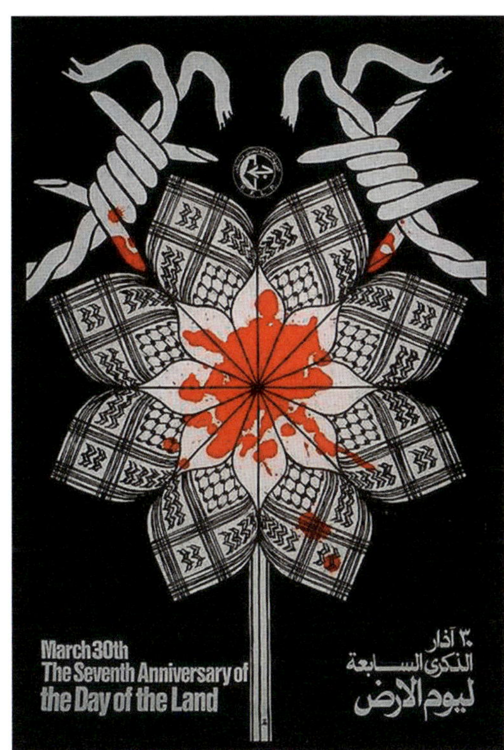

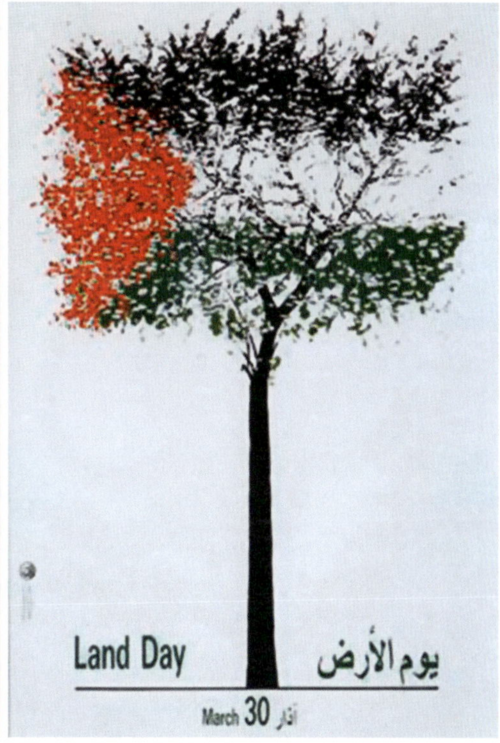

015
016

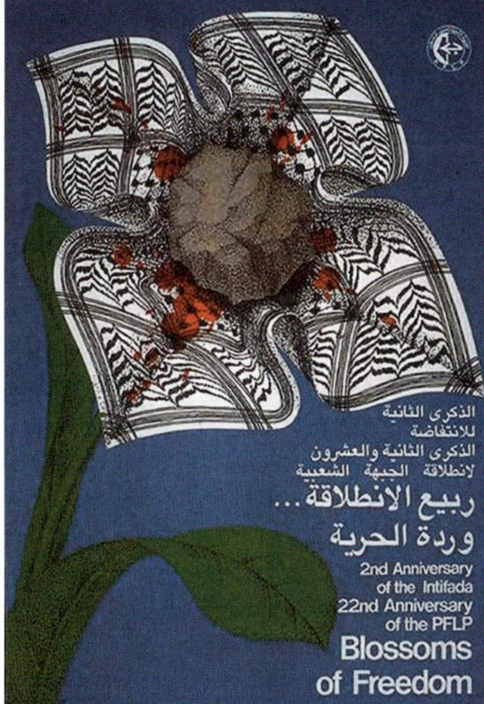

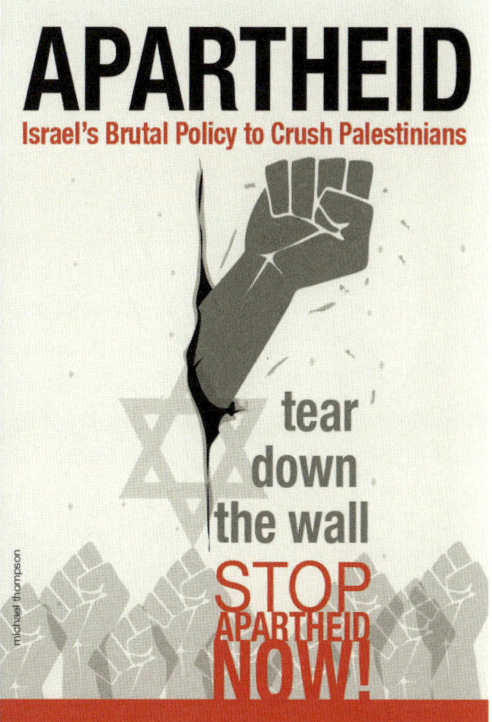

017

Moscow
Москва
Да здравствует мир, и антиимпериалистическая солидари
For Peace and Anti-Imperialist Solidarit
OOII-PLO
Youth of the Palestine National Salvation F
12.студенчичиский фестиваль
12th World Festival of Youth and Students

018

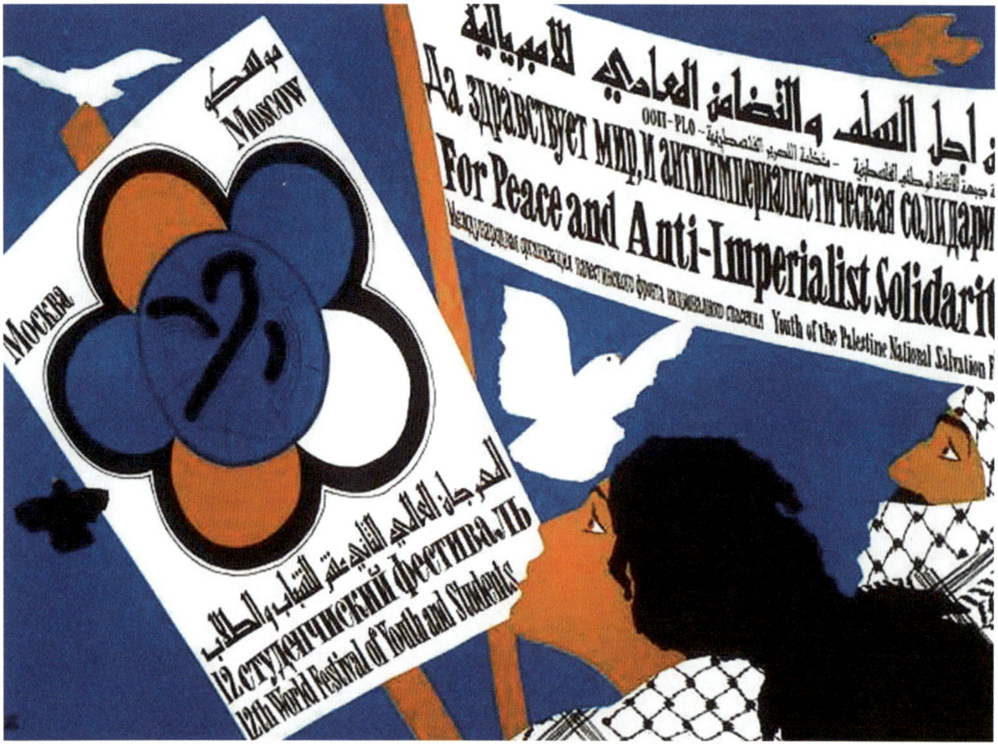

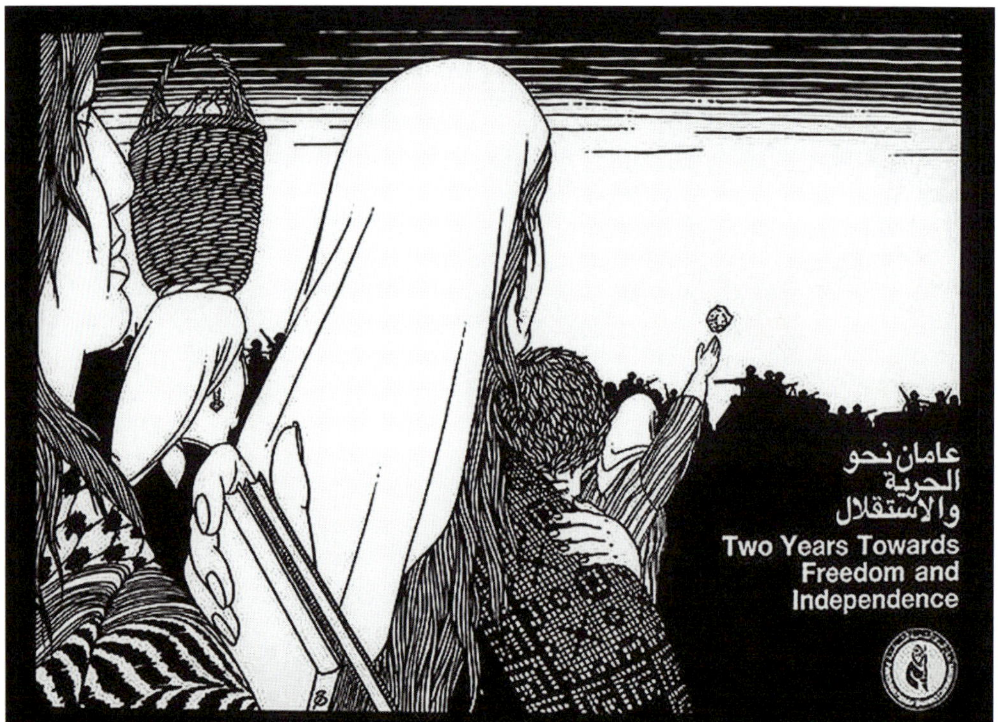

عامان نحو
الحرية
والاستقلال
Two Years Towards
Freedom and
Independence

019
020
021

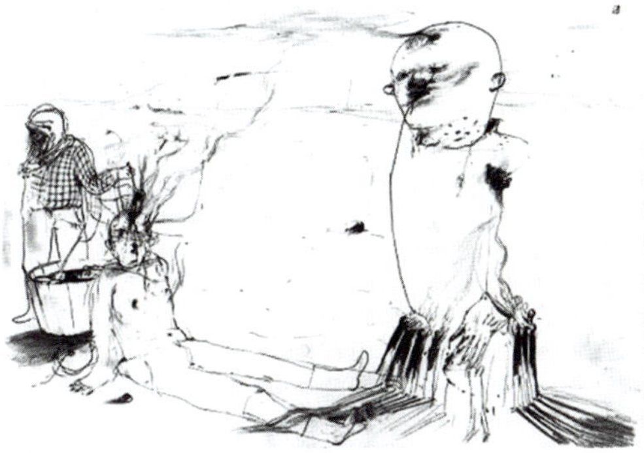

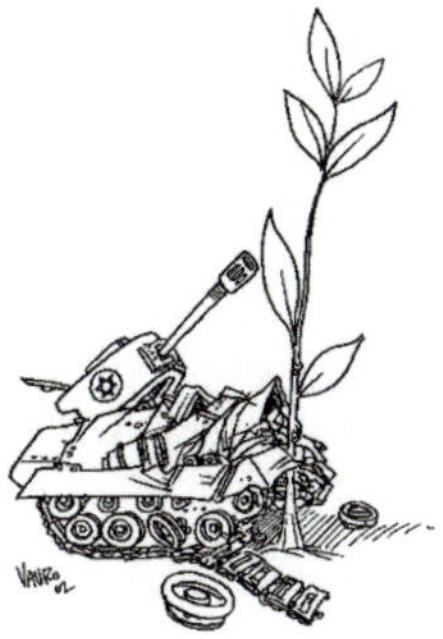

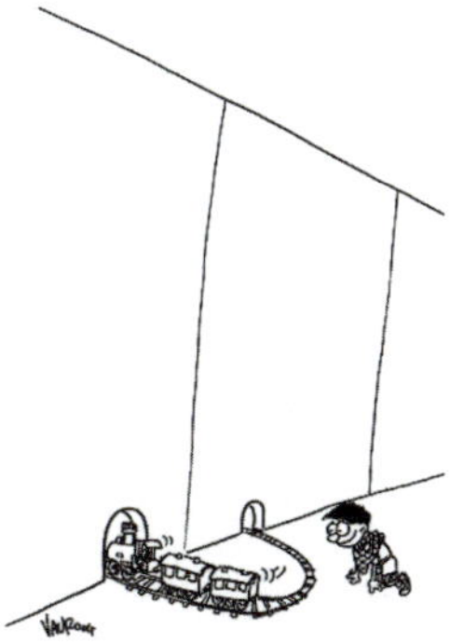

022
023

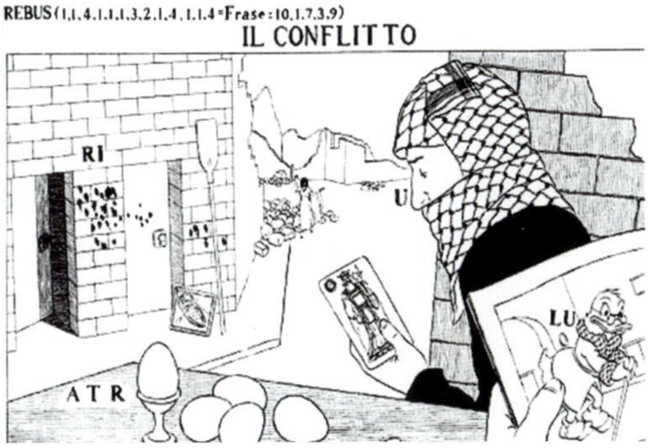

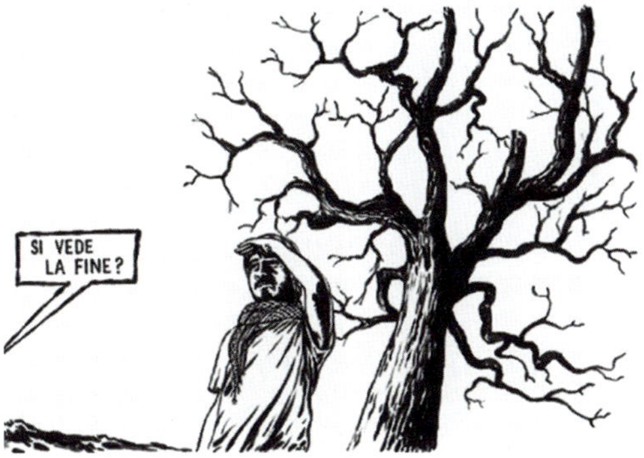

REBUS (1,1,4.1.1.1.3,2.1.4,1.1.4=Frase:10,1.7.3.9)
IL CONFLITTO
RI
U
LU
ATR
SI VEDE LA FINE?

024

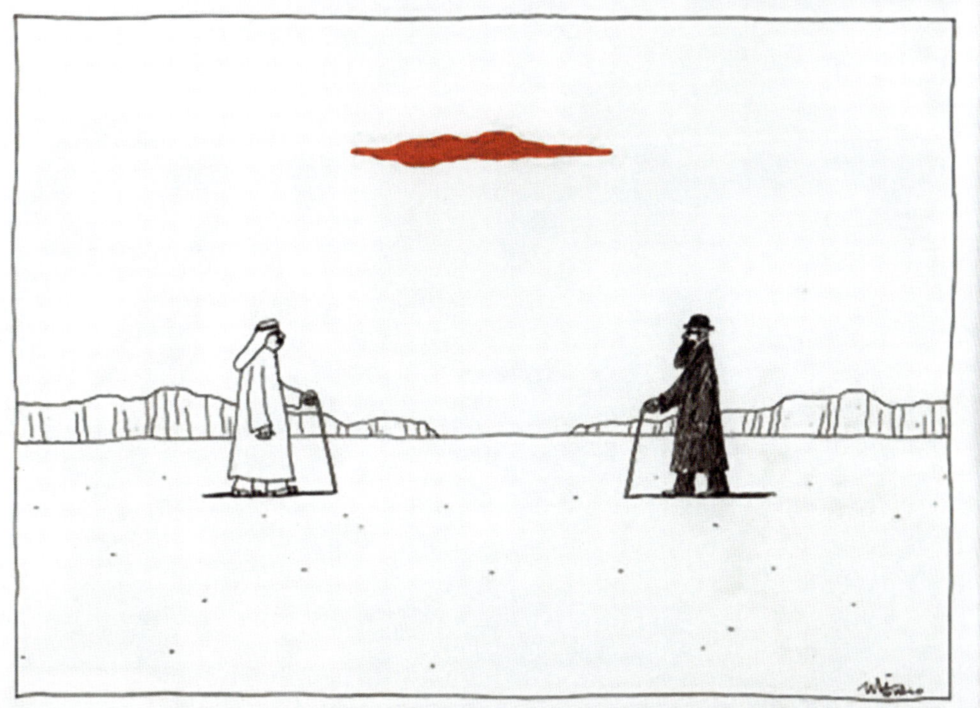

025

I AM A PALESTINIAN ARAB
I WAS BORN IN JERUSALEM
PALESTINE IS MY HOMELAND
BUT I CANNOT RETURN THERE
I AM AN AMERICAN JEW
I WAS BORN IN U.S.A.
ISRAEL IS NOT MY HOMELAND
BUT I CAN "RETURN" THERE

026

نعم لتطبيق قرار الأمم المتحدة 3236
حقوق الشعب الفلسطيني غير القابلة للتصرف
الحق في الحرية وتقرير المصير وإقامة الدولة والسيادة
وعودة اللاجئين إلى ديارهم وممتلكاتهم
اللجنة الوطنية العليا لإحياء ذكرى النكبة ـ فلسطين

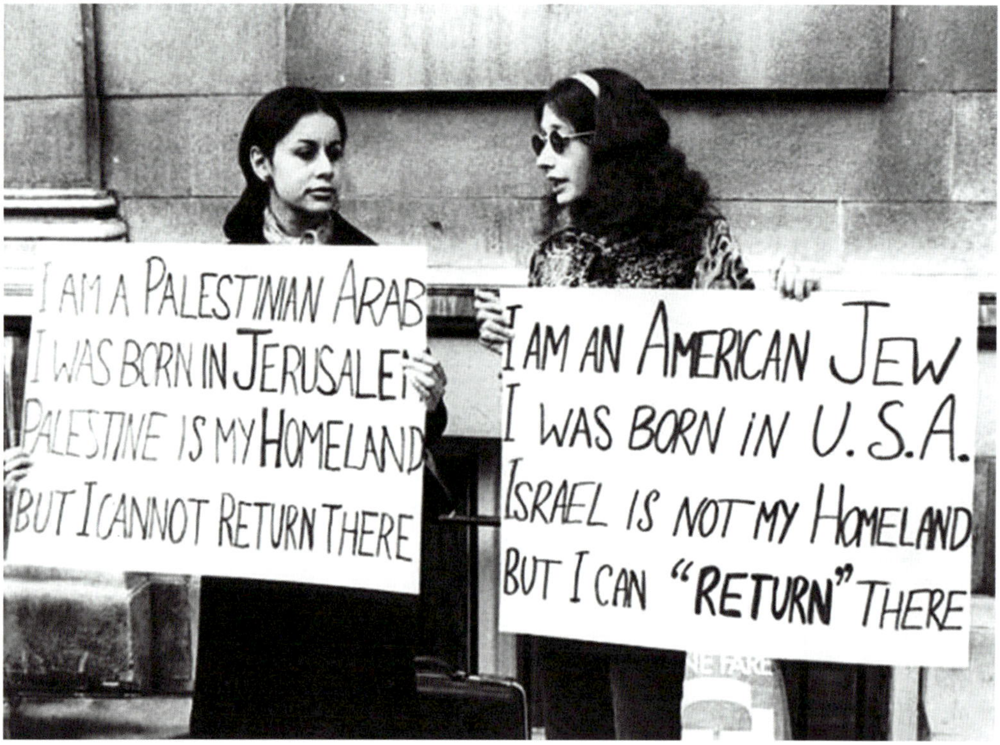

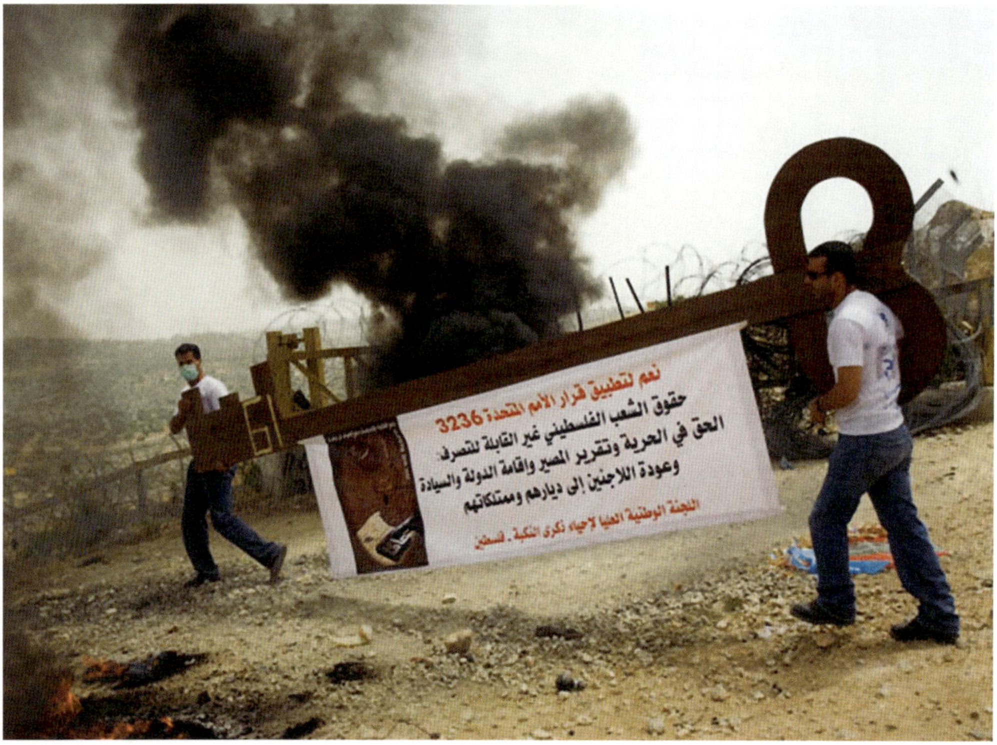

001 UNITED NATIONS CONFERENCE ON THE
QUESTION OF PALESTINE
CREATOR United Nations Public
Information Office
SOURCE Palestinian Poster Project,
www.palestineposterproject.org

002 HOMELAND DENIED
CREATOR Marian Nowinski
SOURCE Palestinian Poster Project,
www.palestineposterproject.org

003 ANTI-APARTHEID WALL CAMPAIGN
SOURCE D. J. R. Bruckner, Seymour
Chwast, and Steven Heller, eds.,
Kunst Gegen den Krieg [Basel:
Birkhäuser, 1984], p. 103.

004 FOR THE LEGITIMATE RIGHTS OF THE
ARAB PEOPLE OF PALESTINE!
CREATOR Vitalij M. Levtsenko
SOURCE JAGDA Peace Posters
International Exhibition

005 PALESTINA - CHILDREN ARE THERE
SOURCE Plakatsammlung Museum
für Gestaltung Zürich

006 PALESTINE
CREATOR A. Lyszkiewicz
SOURCE Plakatsammlung Museum
für Gestaltung Zürich

007 GAZA CHILDREN ARE STILL CRYING
CREATOR Provided by Mo7amaD
SOURCE www.flickr.com/photos/
mOh/3190921689/

008 TO LIVE TOGETHER NOT TO
DIE TOGETHER
CREATOR The Cooper Union for the
Advancement of Science and Art
SOURCE Palestinian Poster Project,
www.palestineposterproject.org
DATE 1988

009 PAIX EN PALESTINE PAIX
DANS LE MONDE
[PEACE IN PALESTINE, PEACE
ON EARTH]
SOURCE www.stopusa.be/

010 THE WHITE STALLION
CREATOR Progressive List for Peace
SOURCE Palestinian Poster Project,
www.palestineposterproject.org
DATE 1969

011 TOWARDS PALESTINE
We carry victory to the homeland.
Poster for Palestinian Women's
Organization [PWO]
CREATOR Marc Rudin
SOURCE Palestinian Poster Project,
www.palestineposterproject.org

012 PRISONER'S DAY - FREE ALL
PALESTINIAN PRISONERS
Poster for Palestinian Women's
Organization [PWO]
CREATOR Marc Rudin
SOURCE Palestinian Poster Project,
www.palestineposterproject.org
DATE 1990

013 SEVENTH ANNIVERSARY THE DAY
OF THE LAND
Poster for Palestinian Women's
Organization [PWO]
CREATOR Marc Rudin
SOURCE Palestinian Poster Project,
www.palestineposterproject.org

014 LAND DAY
SOURCE Plakatsammlung Museum
für Gestaltung Zürich
DATE 30 March 1990

015 BLOSSOMS OF FREEDOM
Poster for Popular Front
for the Liberation of
Palestine [PFLP]
CREATOR Marc Rudin
SOURCE Palestinian Poster Project,
www.palestineposterproject.org

016 APARTHEID - ISRAEL'S BRUTAL POLICY
TO CRUSH PALESTINIANS
SOURCE www.flickr.com/
photos/31466986@N08/3246929893

017 FOR PEACE AND ANTI-IMPERIALIST
SOLIDARITY
Poster for Popular Front for the
Liberation of Palestine [PFLP]
CREATOR Marc Rudin
SOURCE Palestinian Poster Project,
www.palestineposterproject.org
DATE 1985

018 TWO YEARS TOWARDS FREEDOM
AND INDEPENDENCE
Poster for Palestinian Popular
Women's Committees.
CREATOR Marc Rudin
SOURCE Palestinian Poster Project,
www.palestineposterproject.org

019 UNTITLED
CREATOR Michelangelo Setola
SOURCE www.inguine.net
DATE 2002

020 CREATOR Vauro
SOURCE www.inguine.net
DATE 2002

021 CREATOR Vauro
SOURCE www.inguine.net
DATE 2004

022 CREATOR Giacomo Nanni
SOURCE www.inguine.net
DATE 2002

023 CREATOR Matteo Bergamelli
SOURCE www.inguine.net
DATE 2002

024 CREATOR Franco Matticchio
SOURCE www.inguine.net
DATE 2002

025 GHADA KARMI AND ELLEN SIEGEL
PROTESTING OUTSIDE THE ISRAELI
EMBASSY IN LONDON
SOURCE prrprotest.tumblr.com/
DATE 1973

026 PROTEST AGAINST THE APARTHEID
WALL, BILIN, PALESTINE
CREATOR Oren Ziv [activestills.org]
SOURCE www.flickr.com/photos/
activestills/3536266981/

001
002

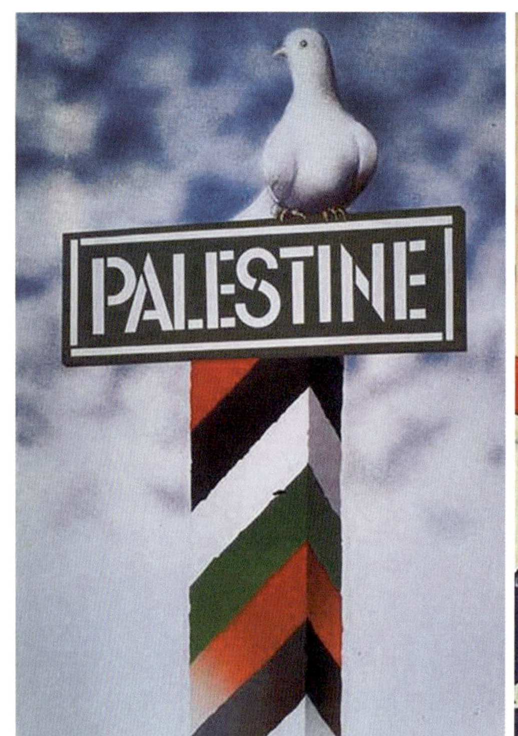

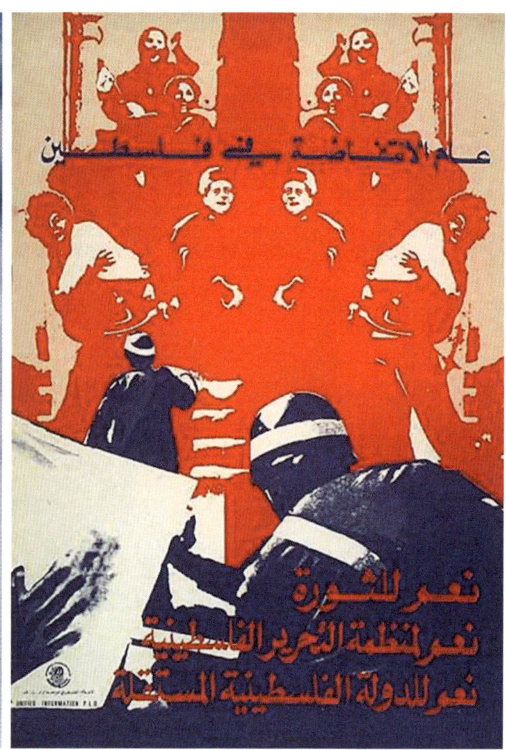

003
004

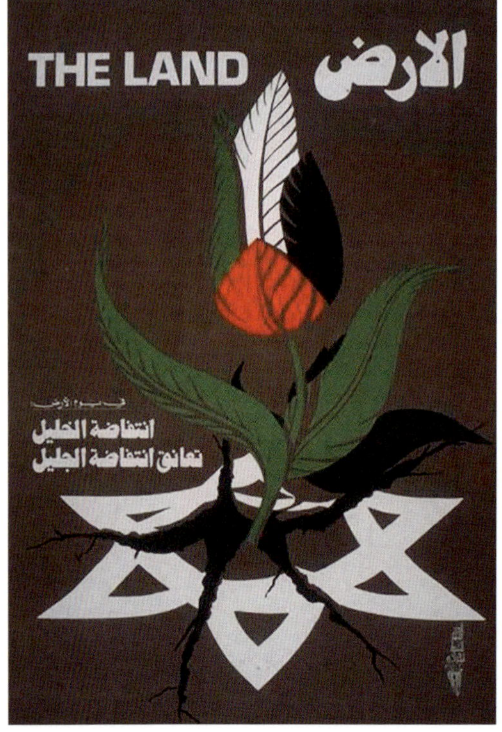

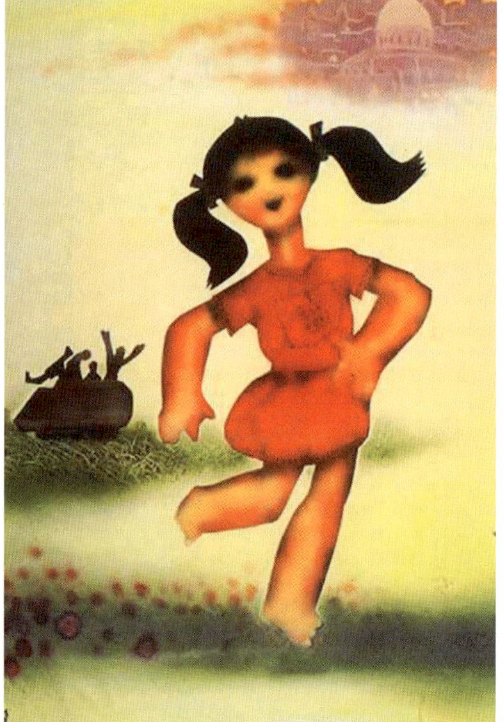

005
006

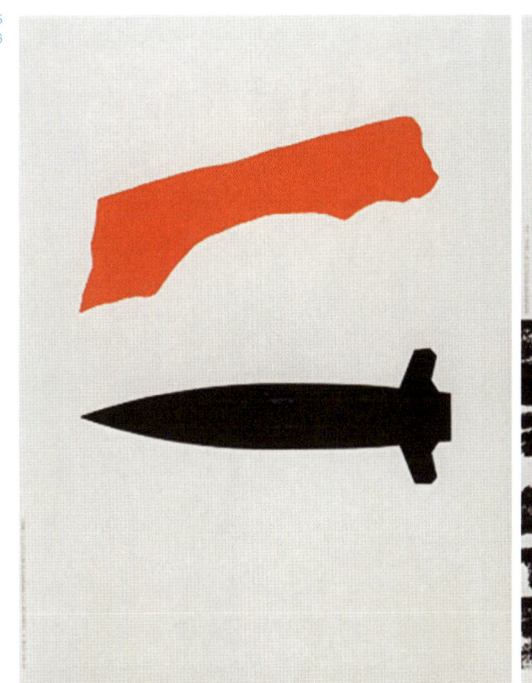

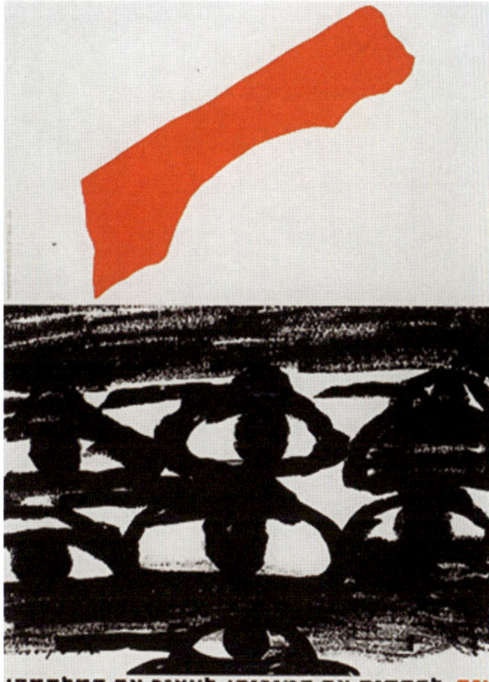

007
008

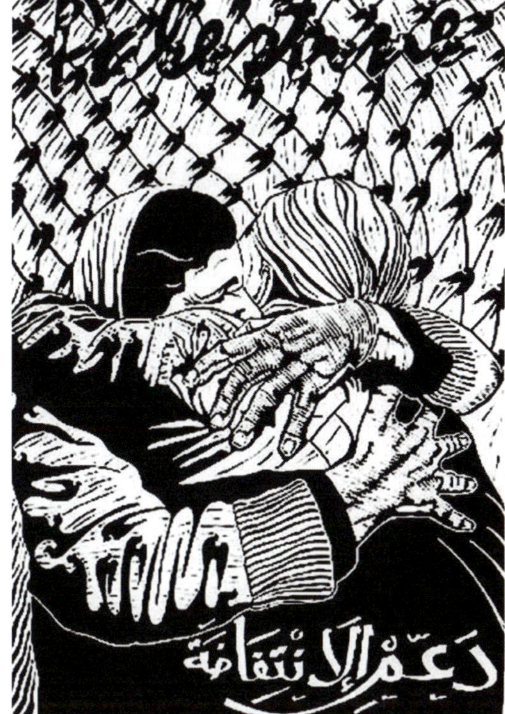

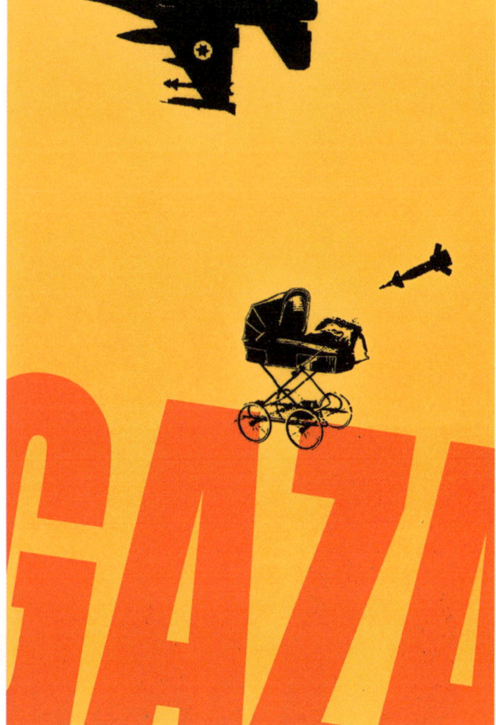

009
010

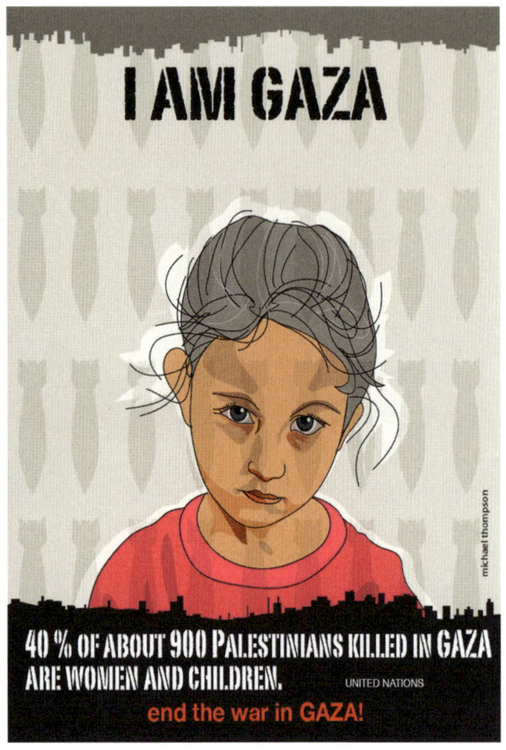

011
012

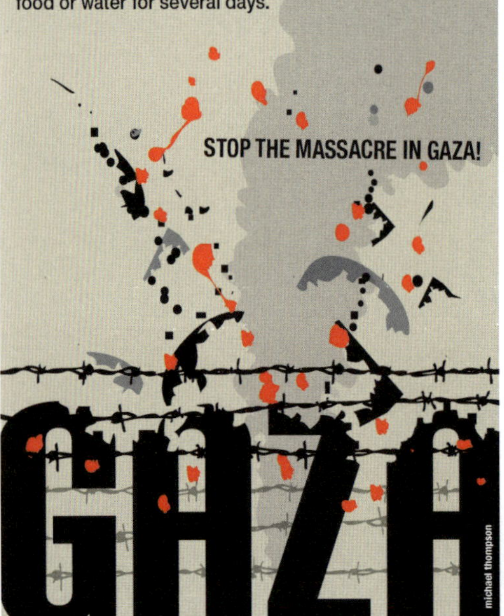

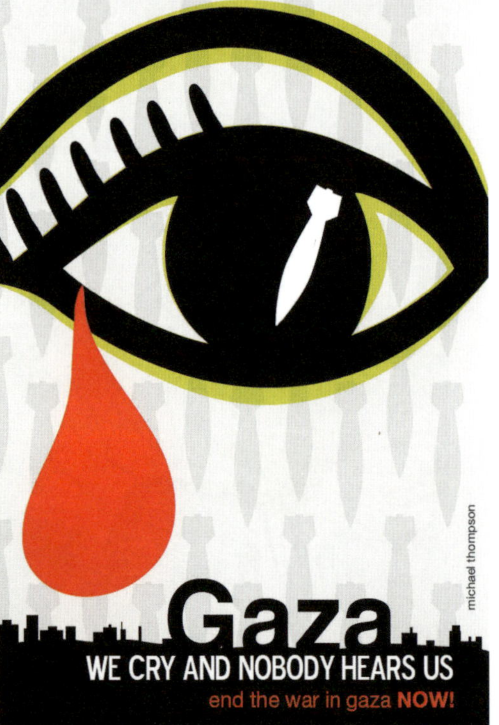

013
014

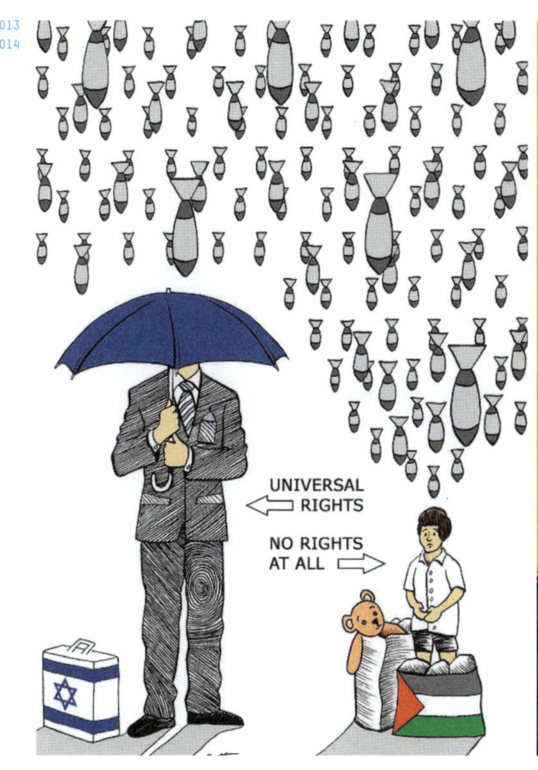

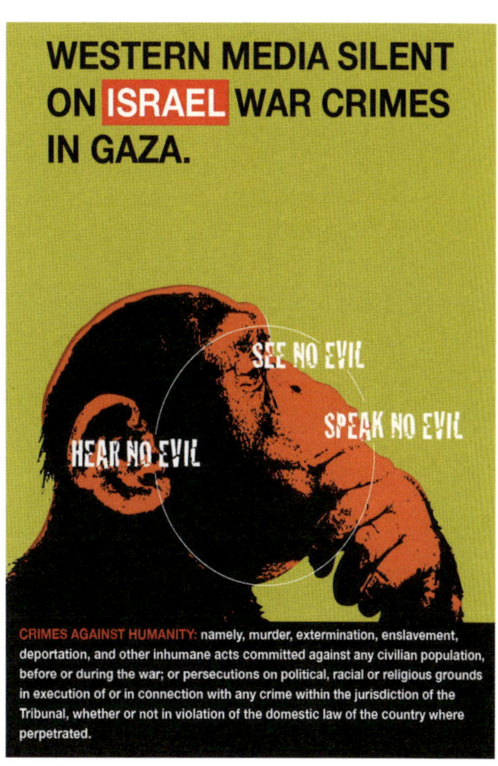

015
016

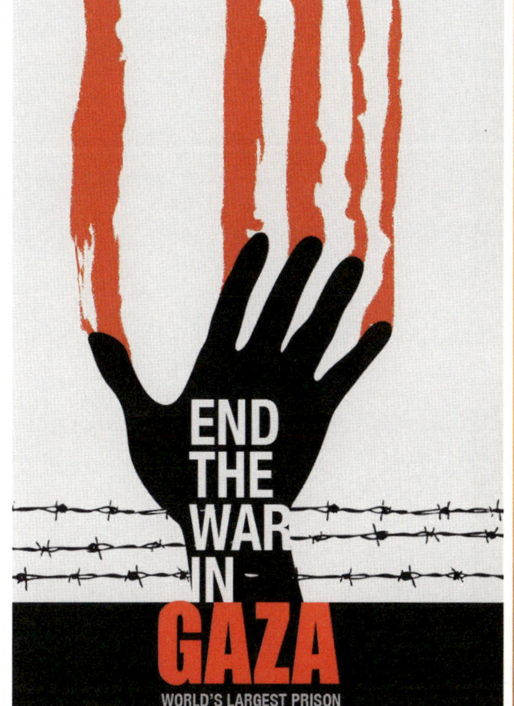

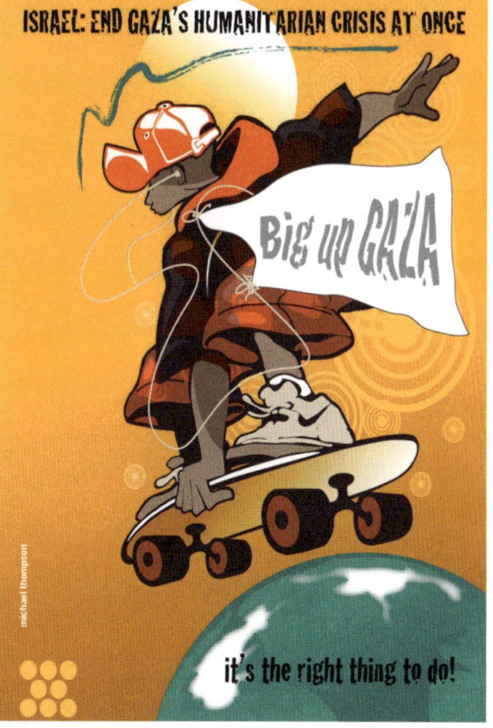

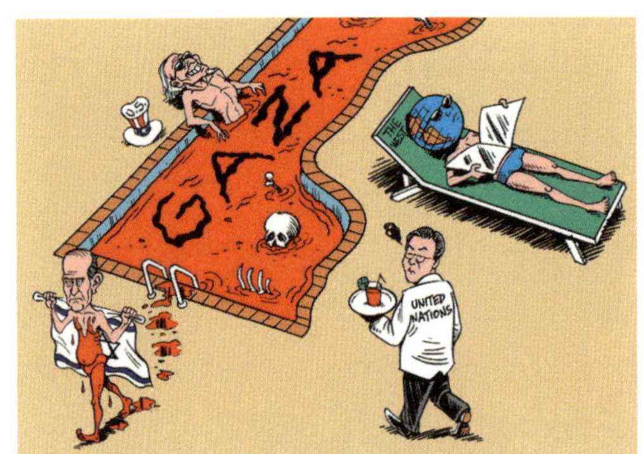
GAZA
UNITED
NATIONS

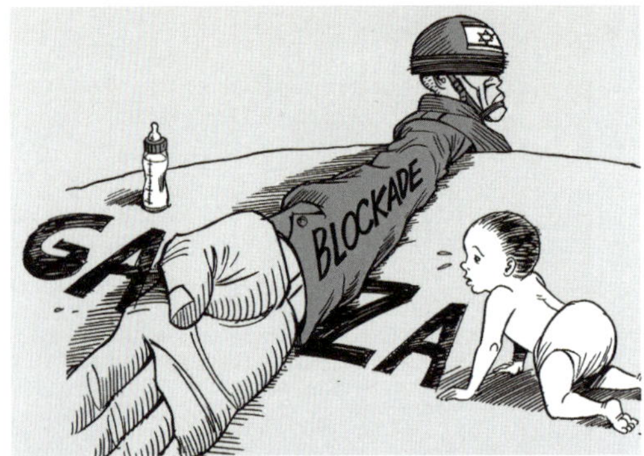
GAZA
BLOCKADE

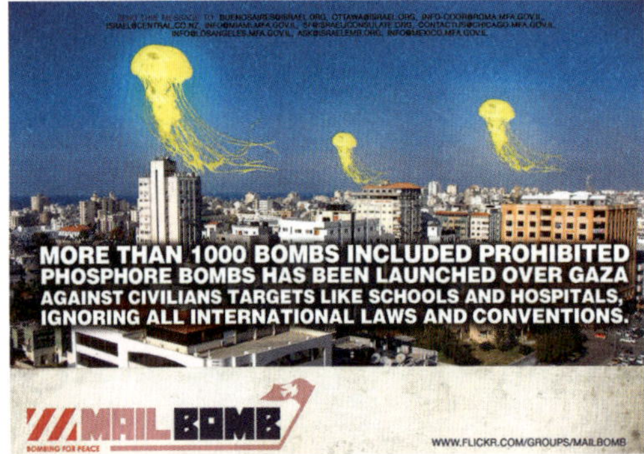
MORE THAN 1000 BOMBS INCLUDED PROHIBITED
PHOSPHORE BOMBS HAS BEEN LAUNCHED OVER GAZA
AGAINST CIVILIANS TARGETS LIKE SCHOOLS AND HOSPITALS,
IGNORING ALL INTERNATIONAL LAWS AND CONVENTIONS.
MAILBOMB
BOMBING FOR PEACE
WWW.FLICKR.COM/GROUPS/MAILBOMB

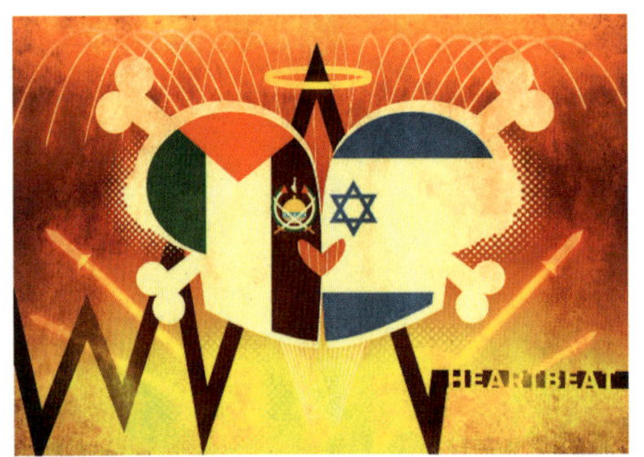
HEARTBEAT

001 INTIFADA 89
     CREATOR PLO Office [Tunis]
     SOURCE Palestinian Poster Project,
     www.palestineposterproject.org
     DATE 1989

002 YES – YES – YES
     SOURCE Palestinian Poster Project,
     www.palestineposterproject.org
     DATE 1988

003 INTIFADA KHALIL, INTIFADA JALEEL
     CREATOR Marc Rudin
     SOURCE Palestinian Poster Project,
     www.palestineposterproject.org
     DATE 1980

004 FROM PALESTINE, WITH LOVE
     CREATOR Jamal al Afghani
     SOURCE Palestinian Poster Project,
     www.palestineposterproject.org
     DATE 1990

005 GAZA: STOP THE MADNESS!
     STOP THE WAR!
     CREATOR David Tartakover
     SOURCE www.flickr.com/photos/
     realcreation3

006 GAZA: STOP THE MADNESS!
     STOP THE WAR!
     CREATOR David Tartakover
     SOURCE www.flickr.com/photos/
     realcreation3

007 SUPPORT THE INTIFADA
     CREATOR Juan Fuentes
     SOURCE Palestinian Poster Project,
     www.palestineposterproject.org

008 GAZA
     CREATOR Carlos Latuff
     SOURCE israels60thbirthday.com

009 FREE GAZA
     CREATOR Rory Madigan
     SOURCE www.flickr.com/photos/
     omigadesign/3175897605/

010 I AM GAZA
     CREATOR freestylee
     SOURCE www.flickr.com/photos/
     freestylee/3194579911/

011 STOP THE MASSACRE IN GAZA
     CREATOR freestylee
     SOURCE www.flickr.com/photos/
     freestylee/3189219058/

012 WE CRY AND NOBODY HEARS US
     CREATOR freestylee
     SOURCE www.flickr.com/photos/
     freestylee/3187629871/

013 SOMETHING WRONG
     CREATOR Ben Heine
     SOURCE benheine.deviantart.com

014 WESTERN MEDIA SILENT ON ISRAEL
     WAR CRIMES IN GAZA
     CREATOR freestylee
     SOURCE www.flickr.com/photos/
     freestylee/3201200829/

015 END THE WAR IN GAZA
     CREATOR freestylee
     SOURCE www.flickr.com/photos/
     freestylee/3187204544/

016 FREE GAZA!
     CREATOR freestylee
     SOURCE www.flickr.com/photos/
     freestylee/3203941801

017 SAVE GAZA NOW
     CREATOR Carlos Latuff
     SOURCE latuff2.deviantart.com/
     gallery/?q=Gaza#/dpnrpy
     DATE 15 November 2006

018 GAZA BLOCKADE
     CREATOR freestylee
     SOURCE israelsbirthday.files.
     wordpress.com

019 MAILBOMB: JELLYFISHES IN THE
     SKY OF GAZA
     CREATOR Jenkah DSR
     SOURCE www.flickr.com/photos/
     jenkah/3208084159/

020 HEARTBEAT
     CREATOR Mau Russo Design
     SOURCE www.flickr.com/photos/
     maustuff/3182770024/

001

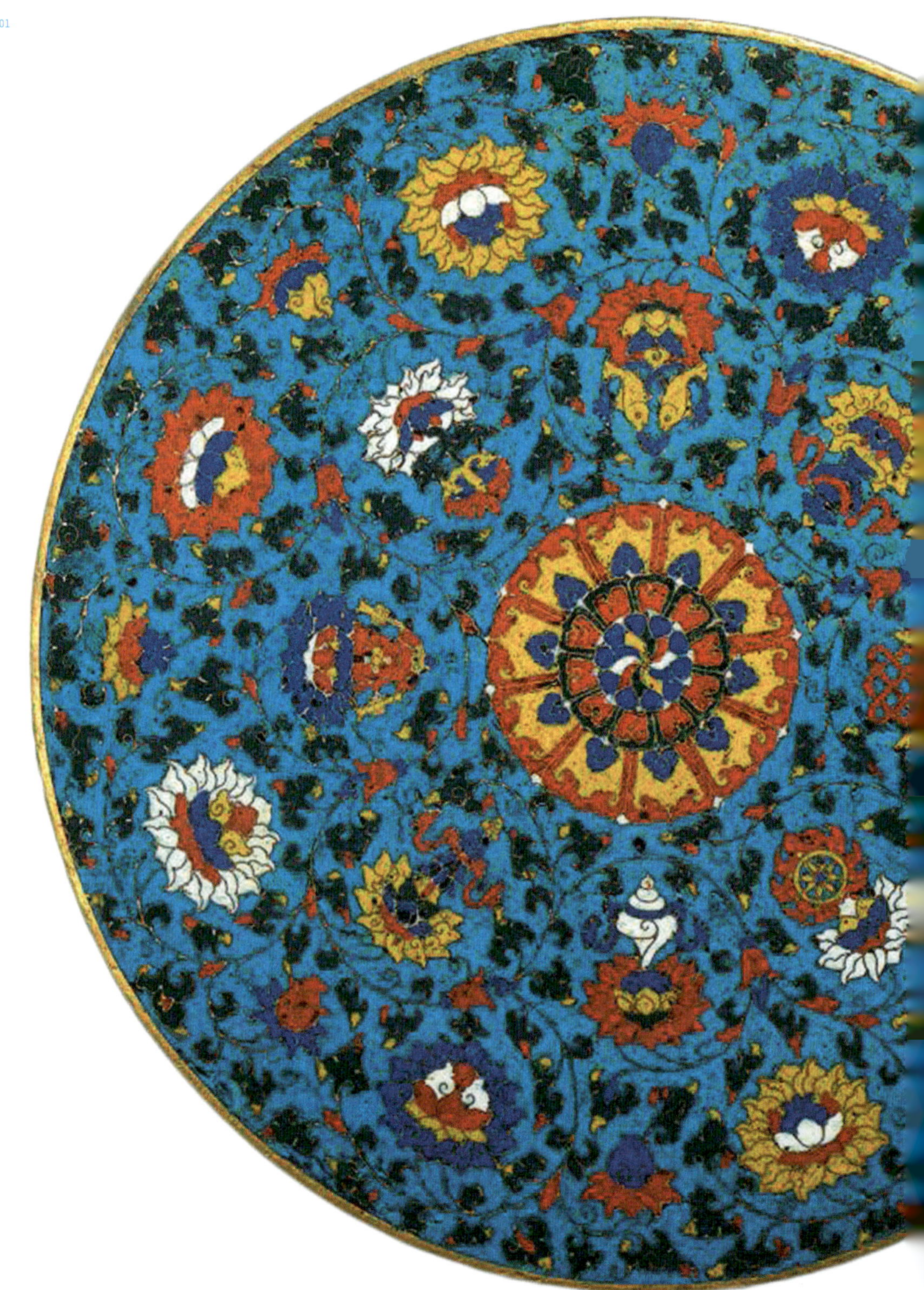

PAX MONGOLICA ^P

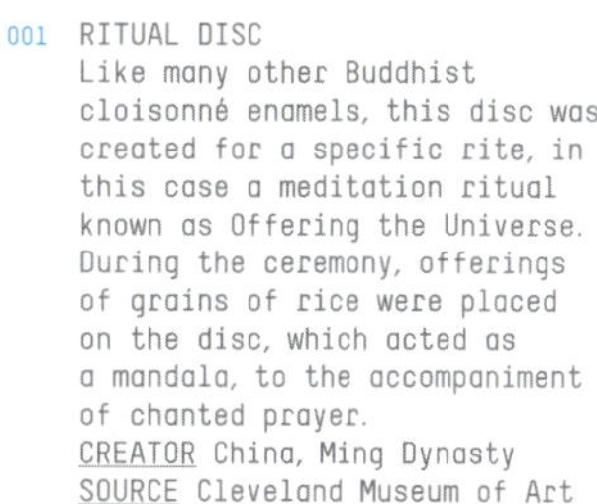

001 RITUAL DISC
Like many other Buddhist
cloisonné enamels, this disc was
created for a specific rite, in
this case a meditation ritual
known as Offering the Universe.
During the ceremony, offerings
of grains of rice were placed
on the disc, which acted as
a mandala, to the accompaniment
of chanted prayer.
CREATOR China, Ming Dynasty
SOURCE Cleveland Museum of Art

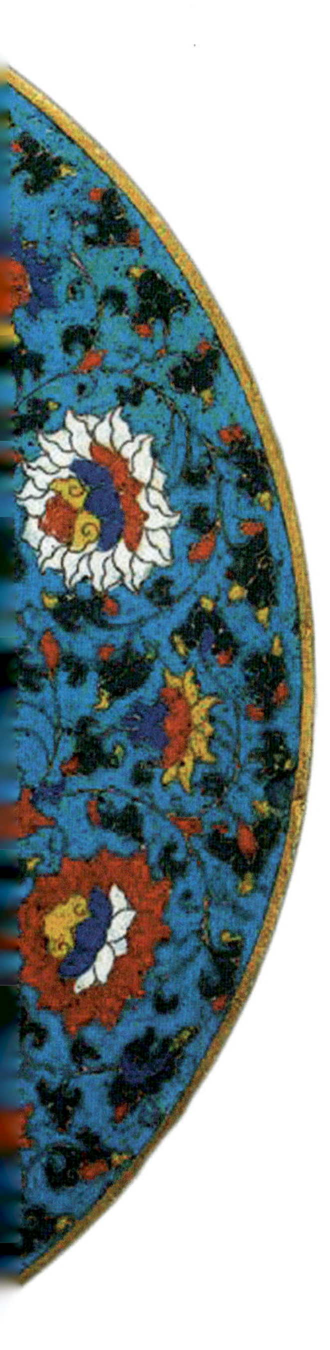

001

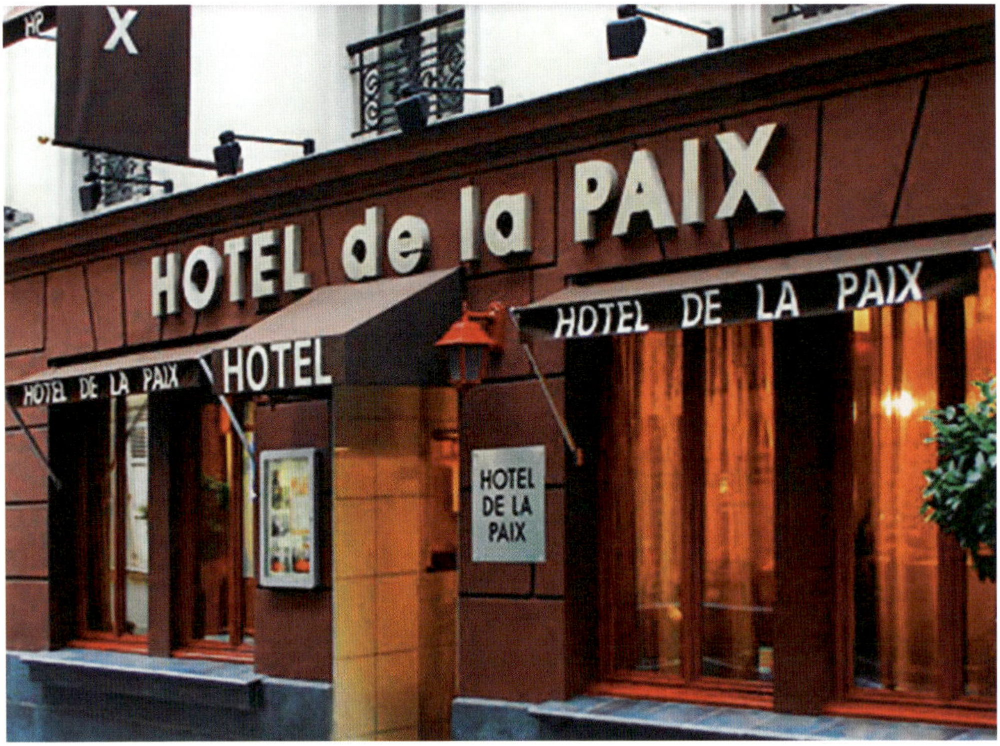

HOTEL de la PAIX
HOTEL DE LA PAIX
HOTEL DE LA PAIX
HOTEL
HOTEL
DE LA
PAIX

PEACE HOTEL

002

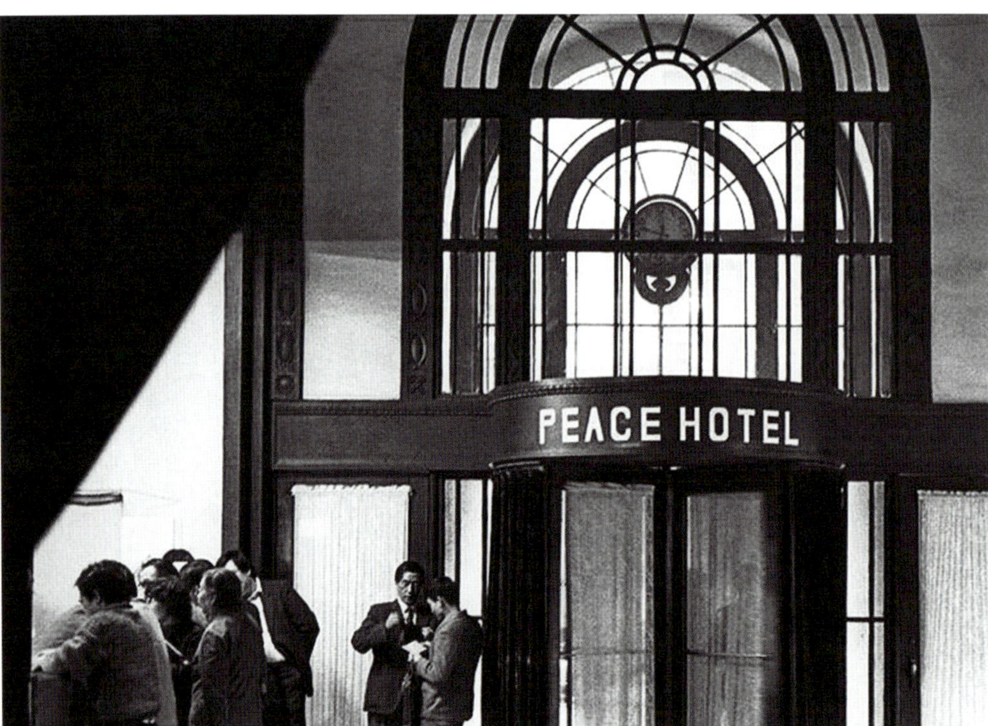

PEACE HOTEL

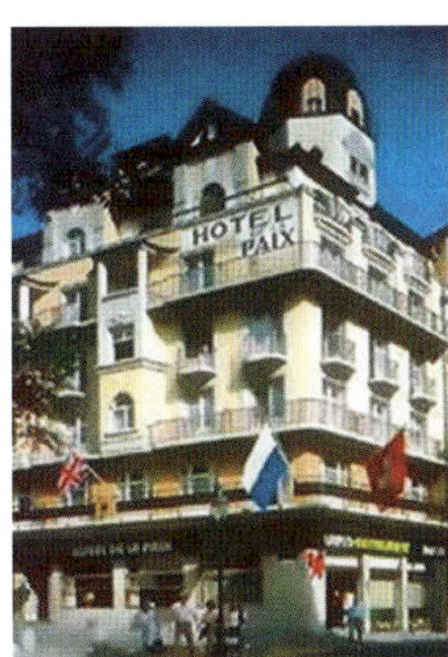
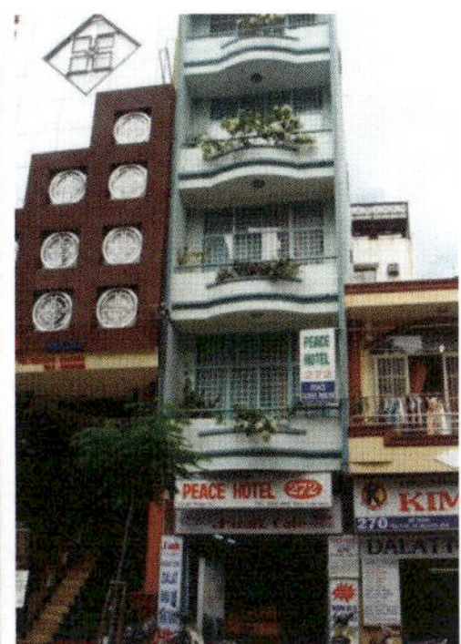
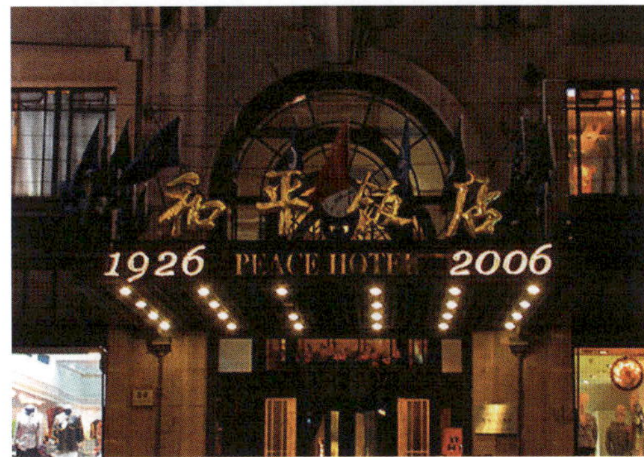
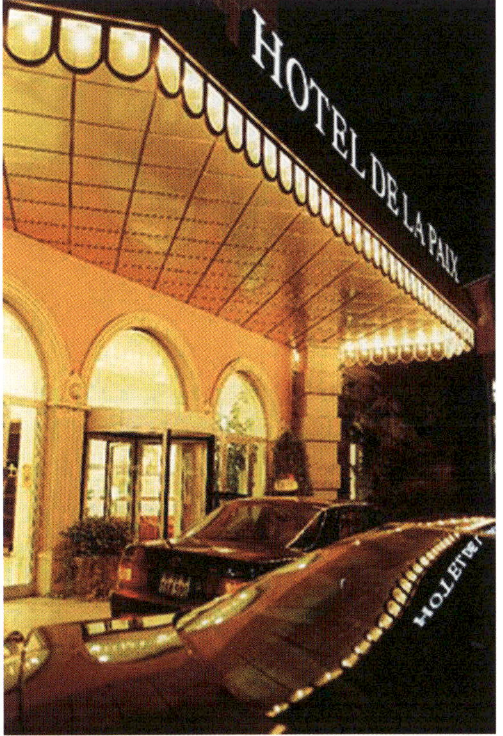

001 HOTEL DE LA PAIX, PARIS, FRANCE
[PEACE HOTEL]
SOURCE www.hotelparispaix.com/

002 PEACE HOTEL, SHANGHAI, CHINA
CREATOR Raymond Depardon
SOURCE Magnum Photos
DATE 1985

003 HOTEL DE LA PAIX,
LUGANO, SWITZERLAND
[PEACE HOTEL]
SOURCE www.fr.asiarooms.com

004 PEACE HOTEL
SOURCE www.hostels.com

005 PEACE HOTEL
SOURCE www.mir.com.my

006 HOTEL DE LA PAIX, LUGANO,
SWITZERLAND
[PEACE HOTEL]
SOURCE www.delapaix.ch/

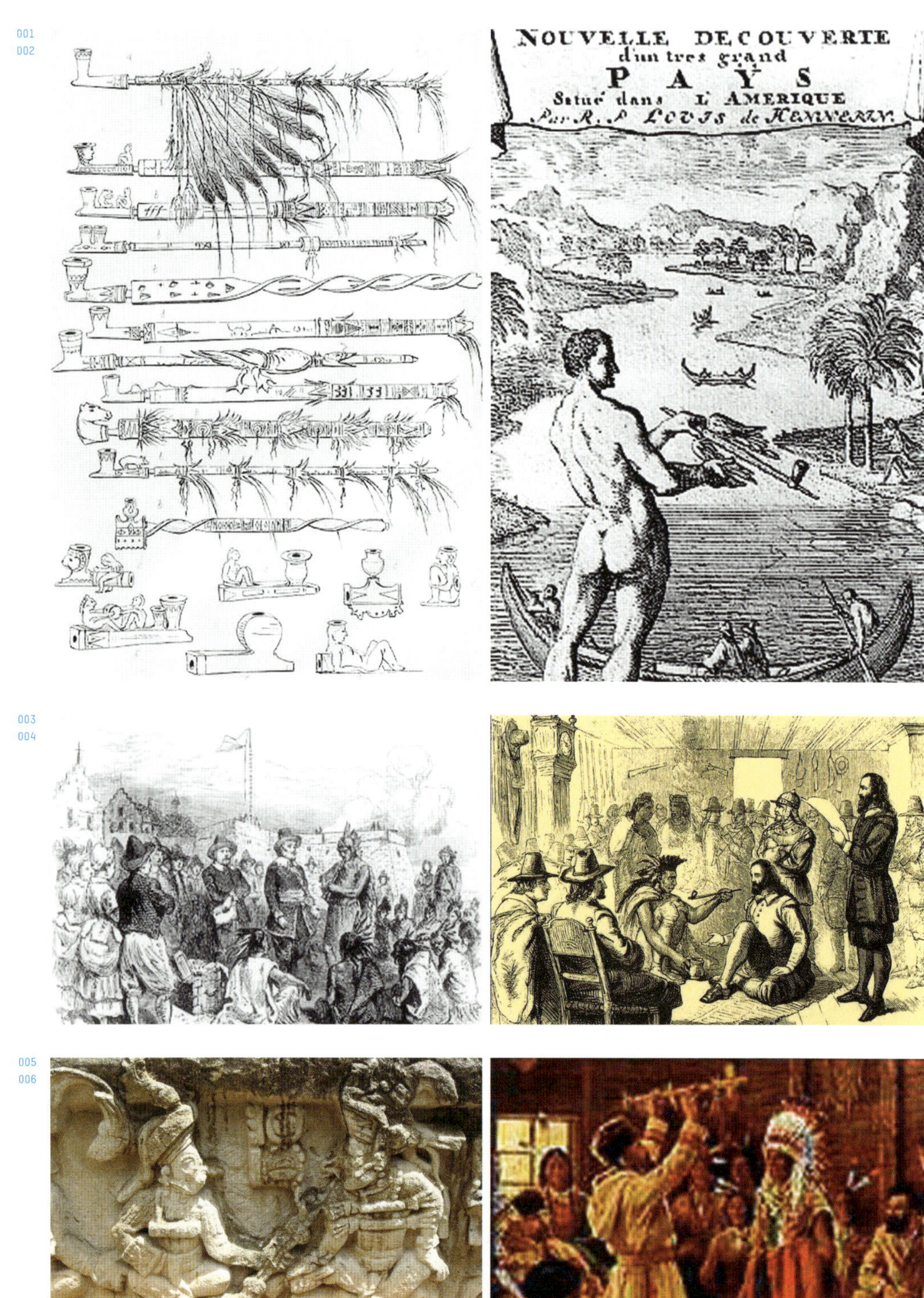
NOUVELLE DECOUVERTE
d'un tres grand
PAYS
Situé dans L'AMERIQUE
Par R. P. LOUIS de HENNEPIN

007

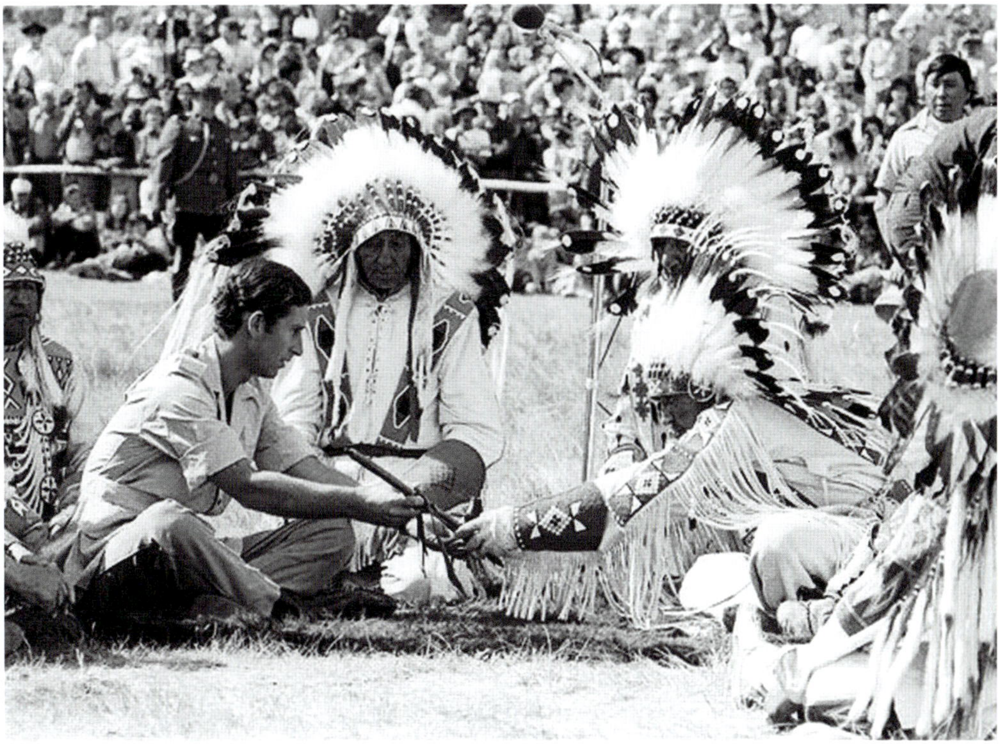

008

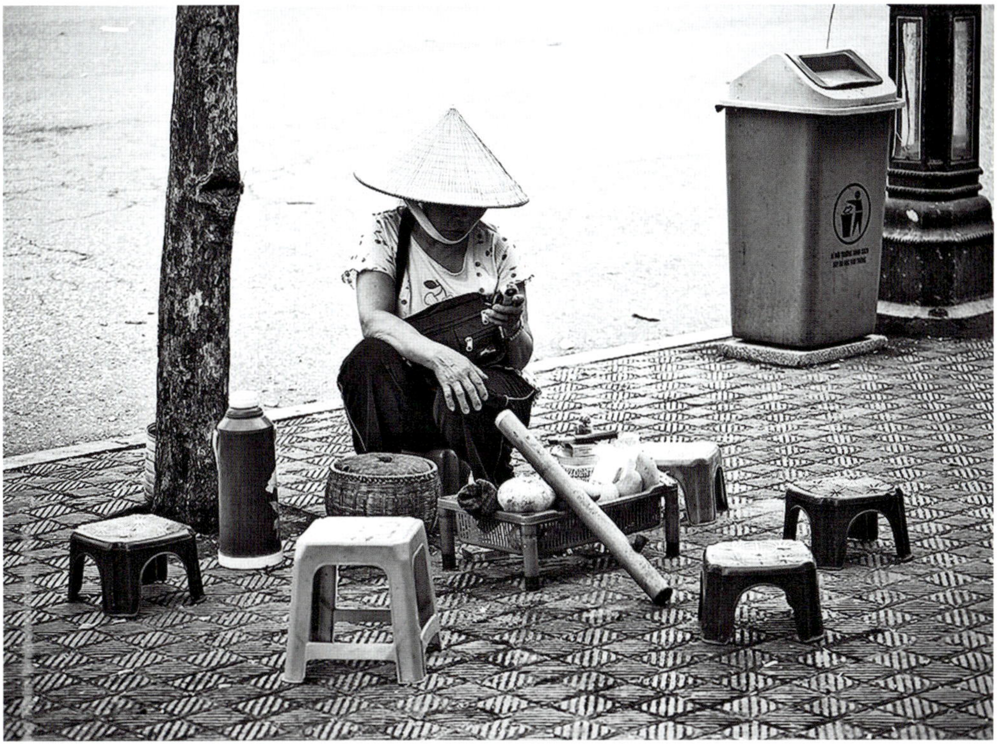

001 NATIVE AMERICAN SIOUX PEACE PIPES
     <u>SOURCE</u> memory.loc.gov

002 NOUVELLE DECOUVERTE D'UN
     TRES GRAND PAYS
     [NEW DISCOVERY OF A VERY
     LARGE COUNTRY]
     <u>SOURCE</u> Corbis

003 NEW NETHERLAND, PEACE PIPE
     <u>SOURCE</u> commons.wikimedia.org

004 MASSASOIT AND GOVERNOR JOHN
     CARVER MAKING A PEACE PIPE
     <u>SOURCE</u> Sutro Library, San
     Francisco, USA

005 THE PEACE PIPE
     <u>CREATOR</u> Provided by Tracy M
     <u>SOURCE</u> www.canadiana.ca

006 UNTITLED
     <u>SOURCE</u> www.canadiana.ca

007 PRINCE CHARLES SMOKING
     A PEACE PIPE
     In Alberta, Canada, Prince
     Charles smoked a peace pipe
     with medicine man Ben Calfrope
     during a re-enactment ceremony
     of a treaty signed between the
     Blackfoot Confederacy and the
     British government in 1877.
     <u>SOURCE</u> Corbis
     <u>DATE</u> 15 July 1977

008 PEACE PIPE
     <u>CREATOR</u> Ming Thein
     <u>SOURCE</u> www.flickr.com/photos/
     mingthein/2376131131/
     <u>DATE</u> 2008

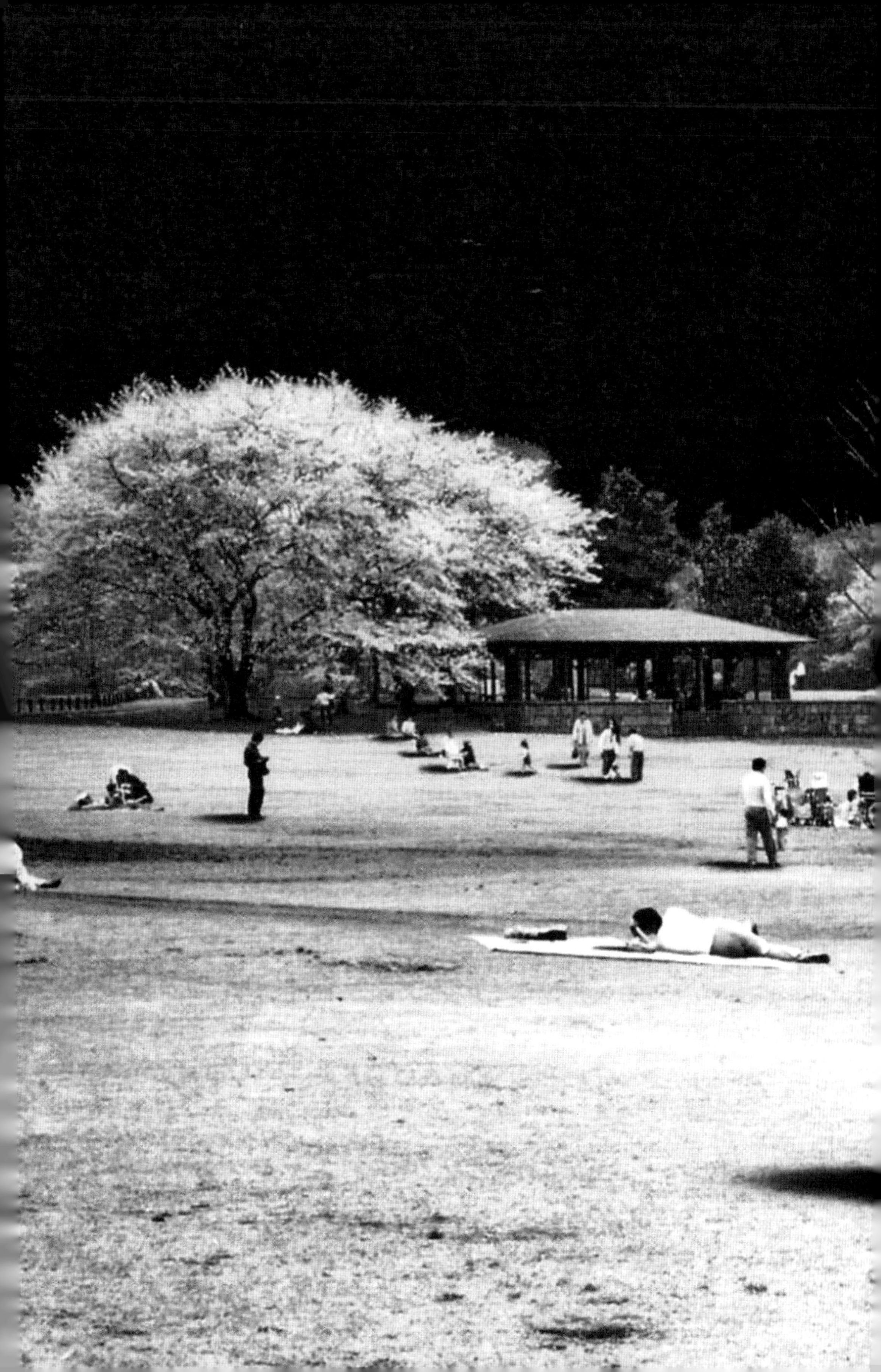

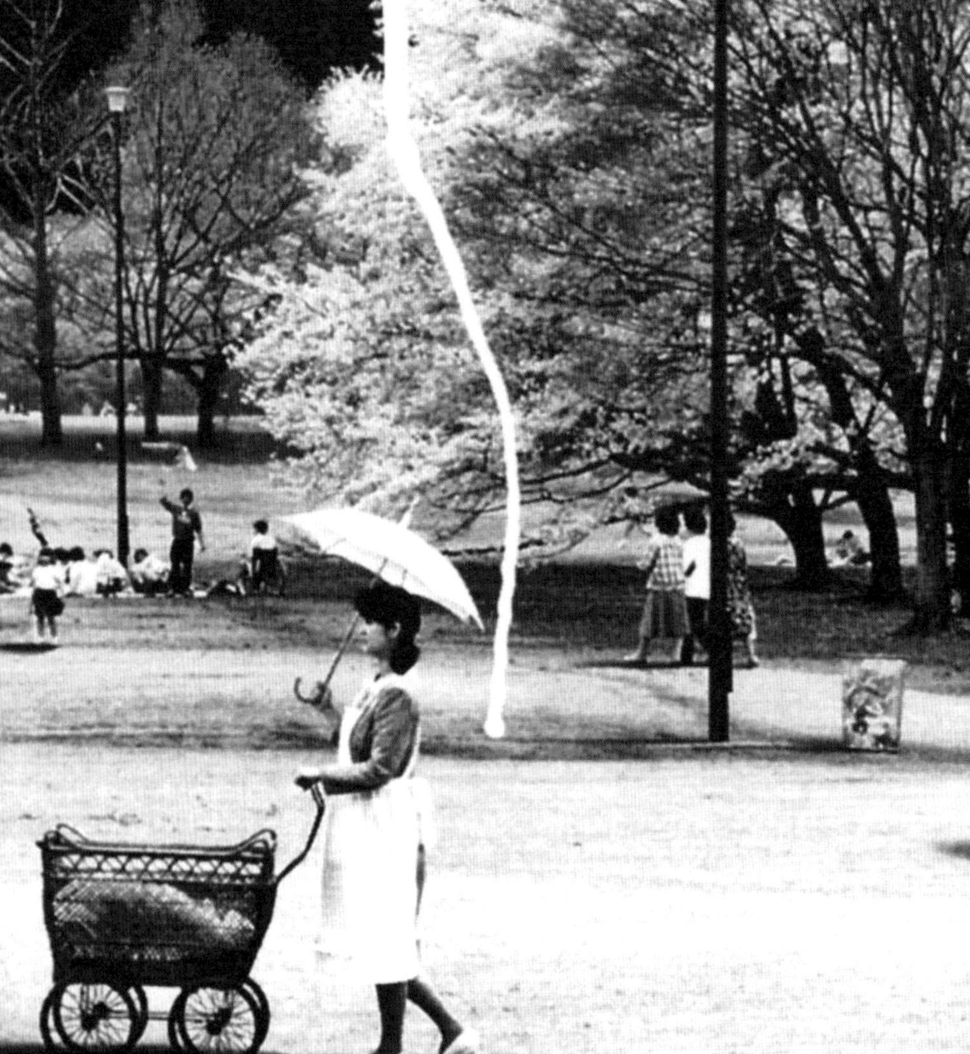

ASK NOT WHAT SOMEONE ELSE CAN DO FOR PEACE-MAKING;
ASK WHAT YOU CAN DO FOR IT.
誰かが守ってくれる、ではいけないのかもしれない。
PEACE

LEFT
001
002

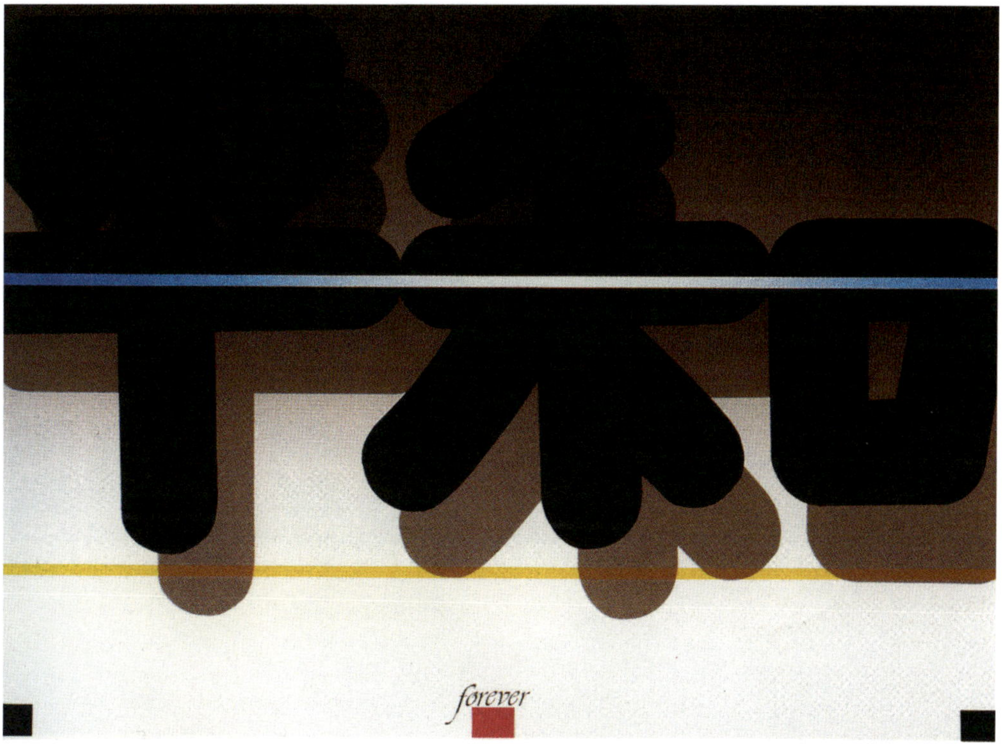

forever

003

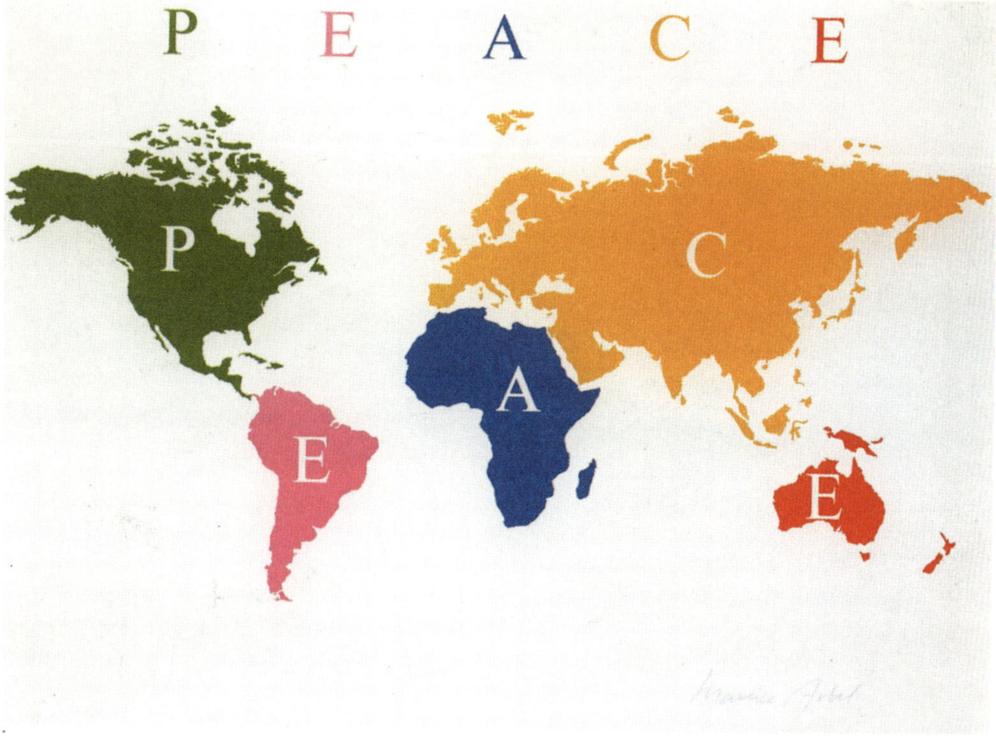

P E A C E
P
E
A
C
E

004

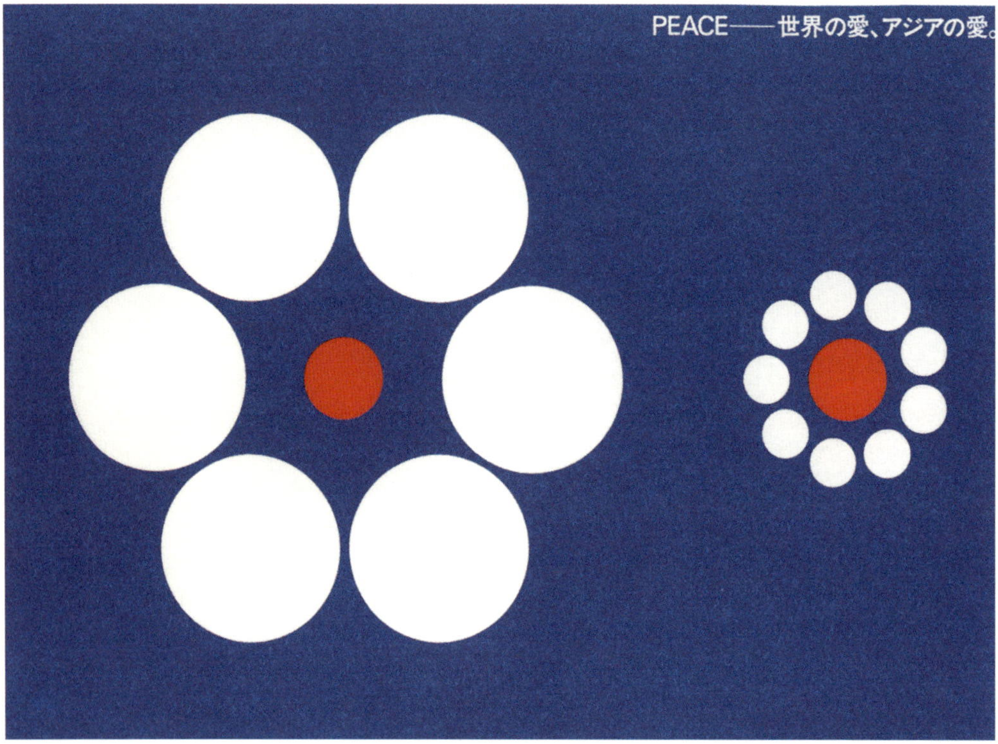

005

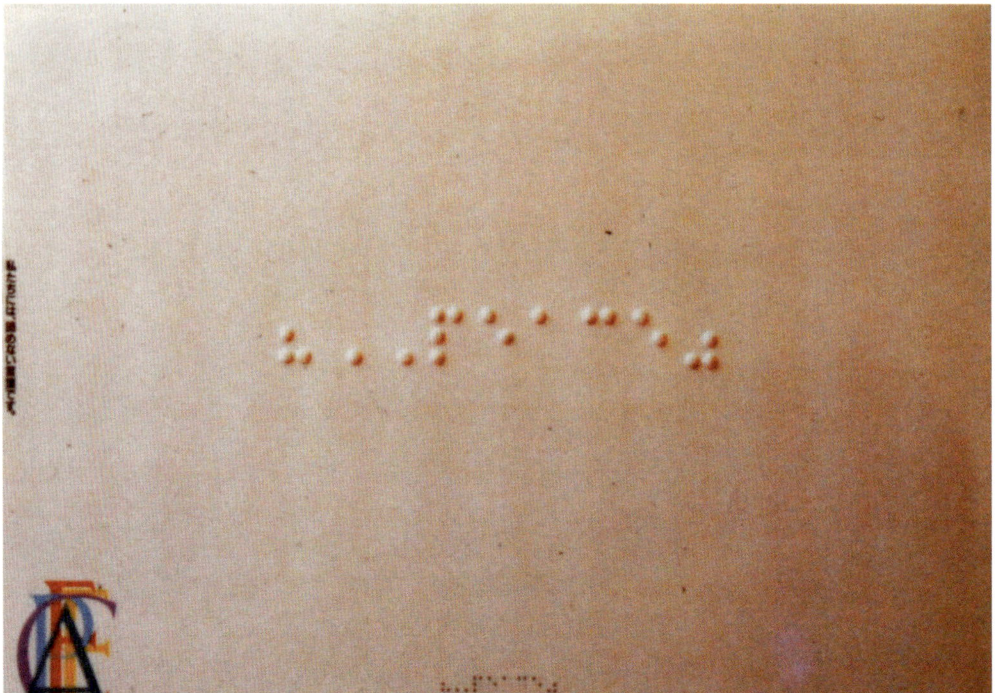

006

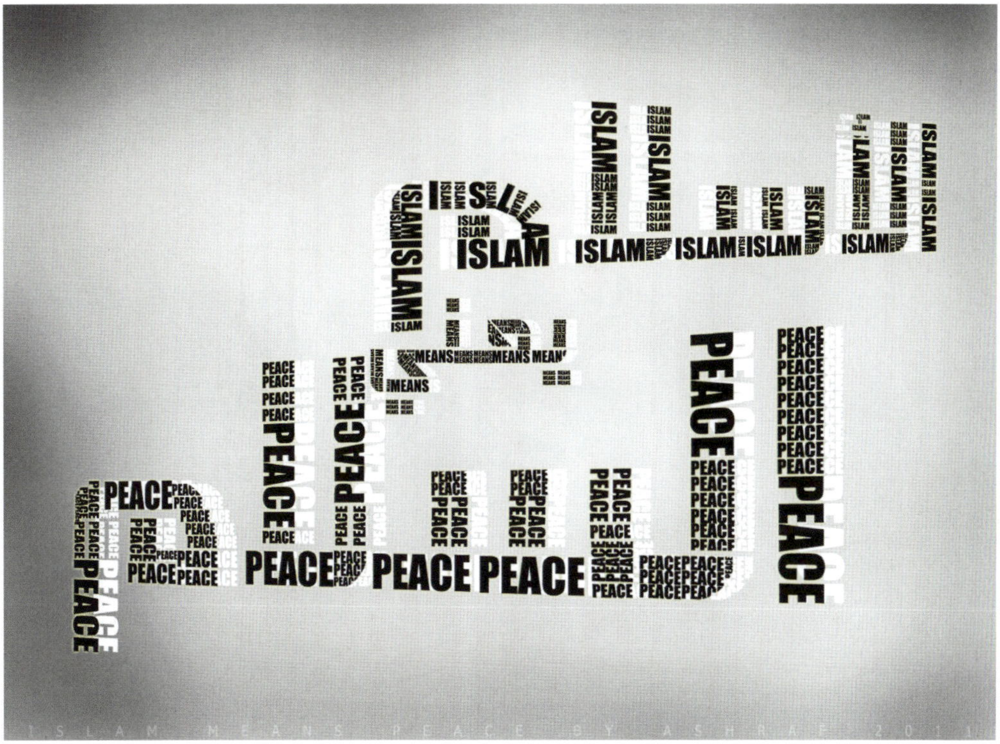

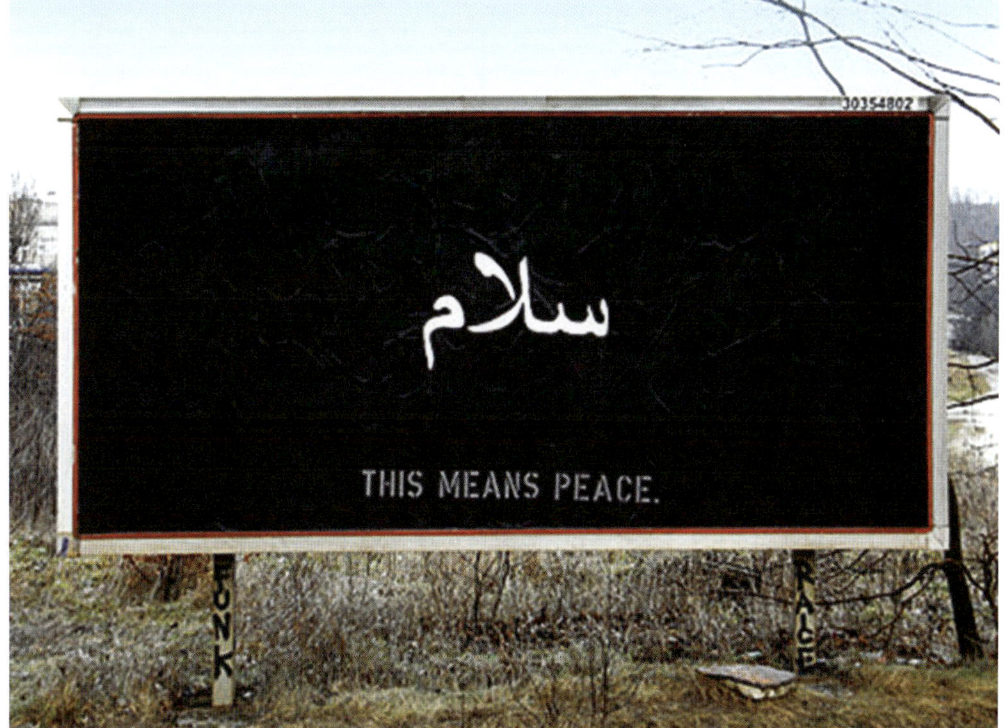

007

008
009

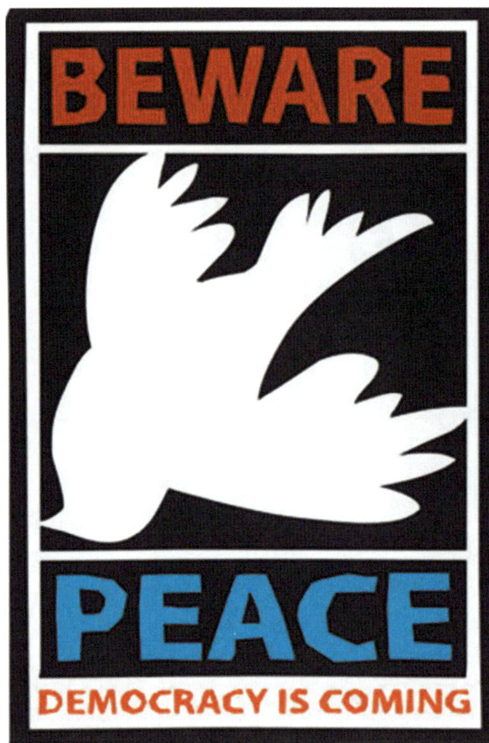

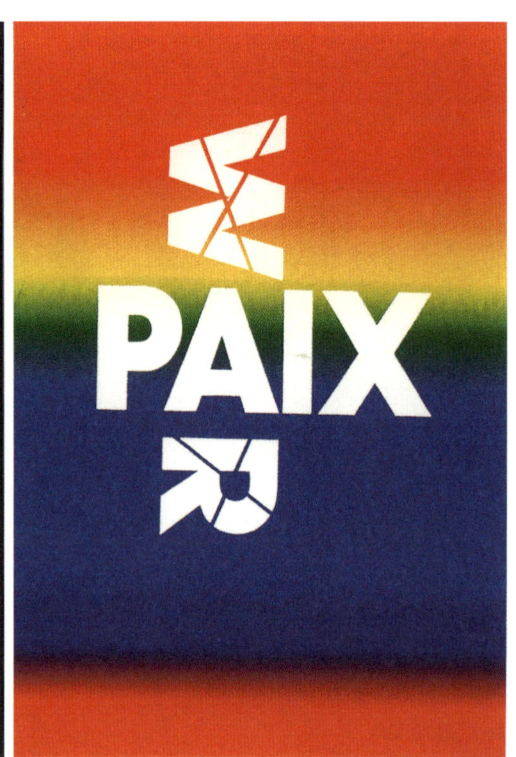

010
011

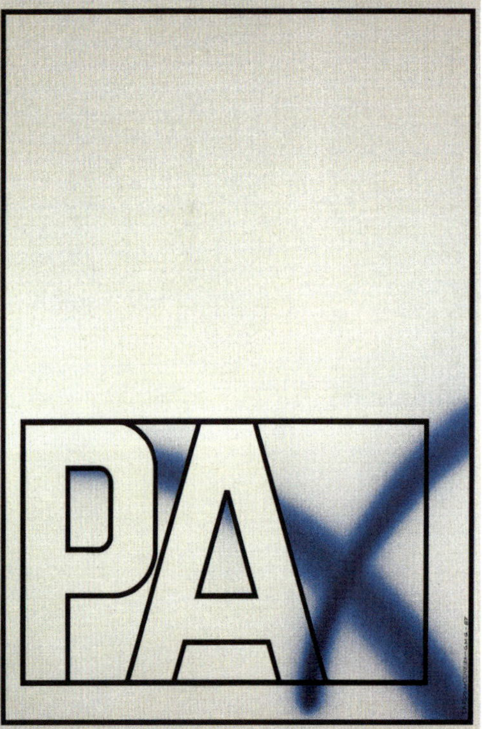

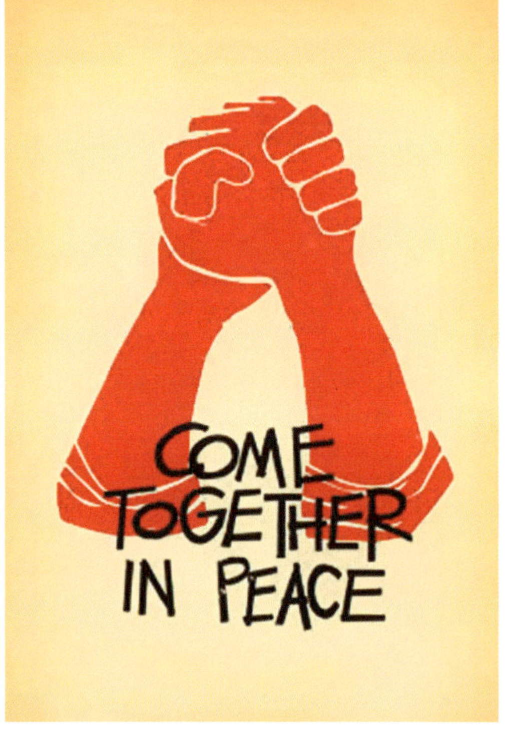

001 HEIWA
     CREATOR Katsu Asano
     SOURCE JAGDA Peace Posters
     International Exhibition

002 PEACE
     CREATOR Marco Sauro
     SOURCE JAGDA Peace Posters
     International Exhibition

003 PEACE
     CREATOR Maurice Arbel
     SOURCE JAGDA Peace Posters
     International Exhibition
     DATE c. 1969

004 LOVE OF THE WORLD, LOVE OF ASIA
     CREATOR Takeharu Igo
     SOURCE JAGDA Peace Posters
     International Exhibition

005 PEACE, THESE WORDS ARE
     STRANGE TO US
     CREATOR Sigel Shimo'Oka
     SOURCE JAGDA Peace Posters
     International Exhibition
     DATE 1990

006 PEACE
     CREATOR ASHRAF-GFX
     SOURCE ashraf-gfx.deviantart.com

007 THIS MEANS PEACE
     CREATOR Visual Poetry
     SOURCE hackschnitzelblog.blogspot.ch

008 BEWARE PEACE, DEMOCRACY IS COMING
     SOURCE www.popsiclesandgrenades.com

009 WAR / PEACE
     CREATOR Max Huber
     SOURCE JAGDA Peace Posters
     International Exhibition

010 PEACE
     CREATOR Carlos Oliveira
     SOURCE JAGDA Peace Posters
     International Exhibition

011 COME TOGETHER IN PEACE
     SOURCE www.internationalposter.com
     DATE c. 1969

001
002

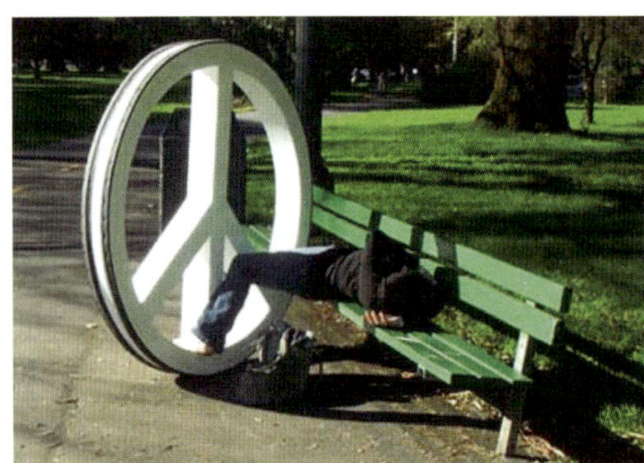
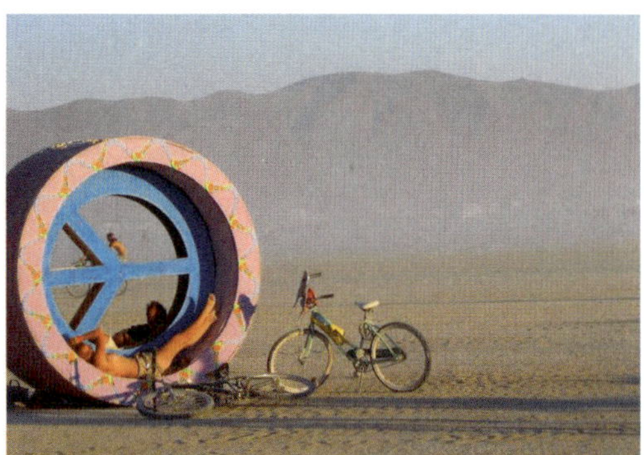

003
004

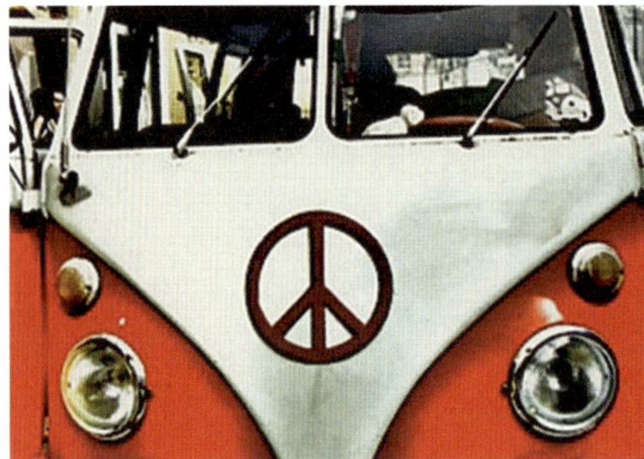
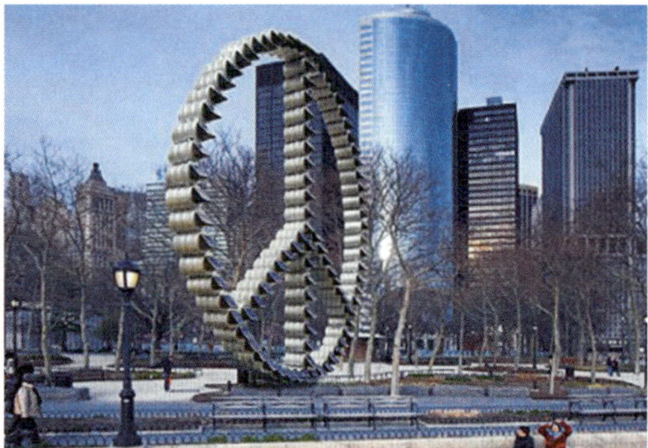

005
006

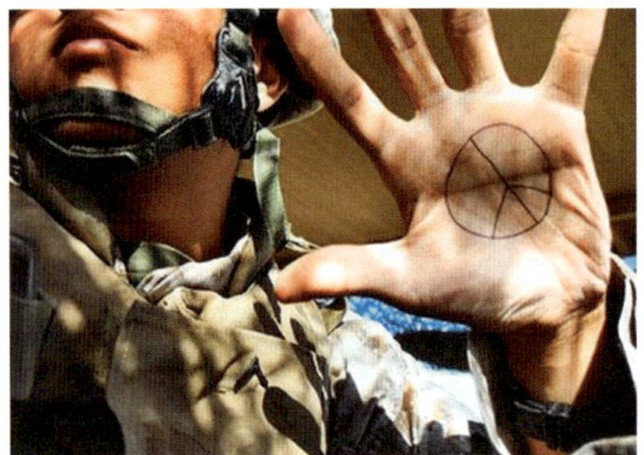
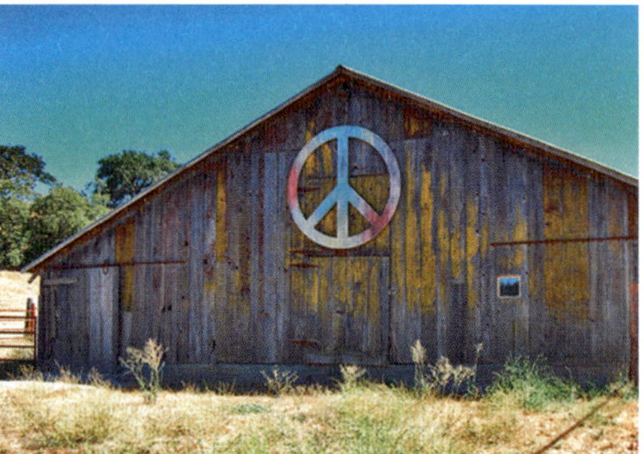

007
008

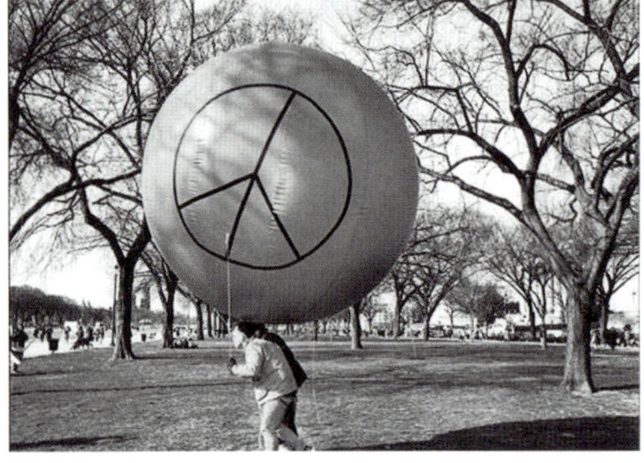
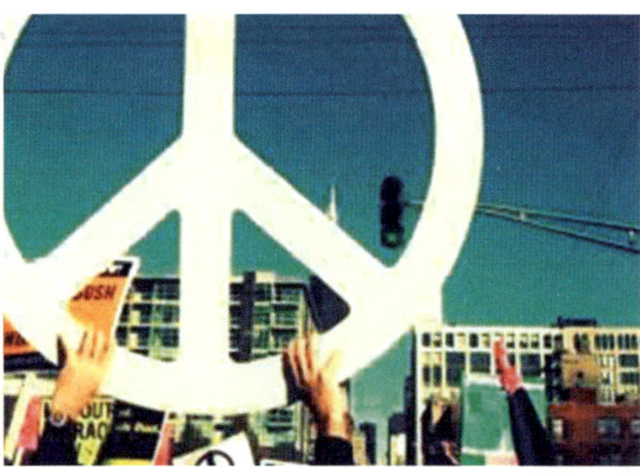

PEACE SIGN

009
010
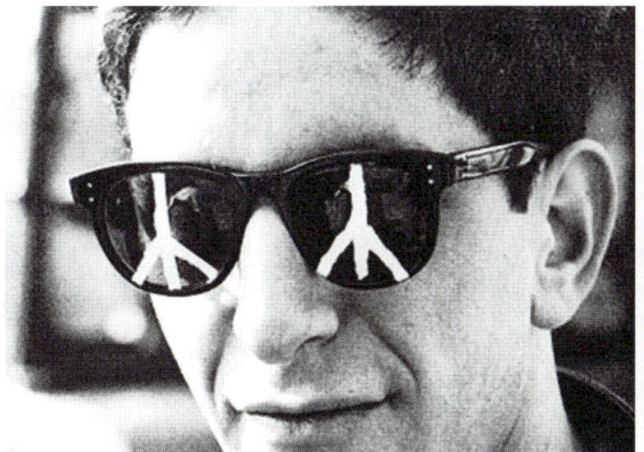
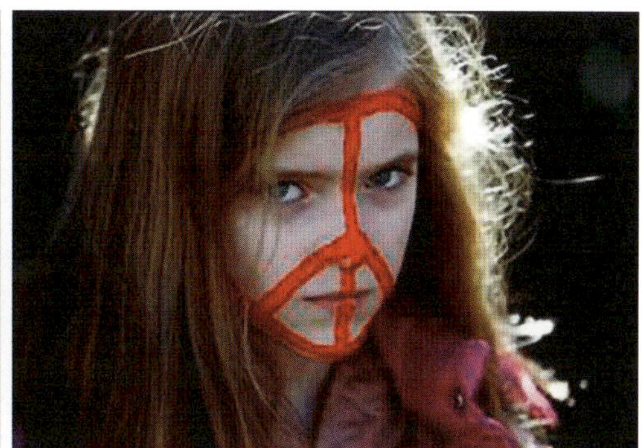

011
012
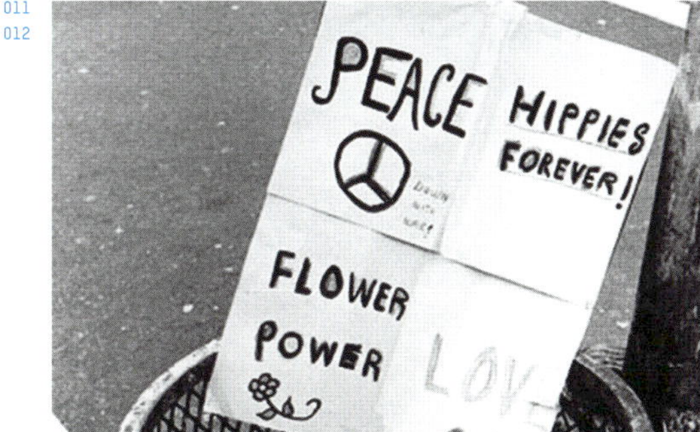

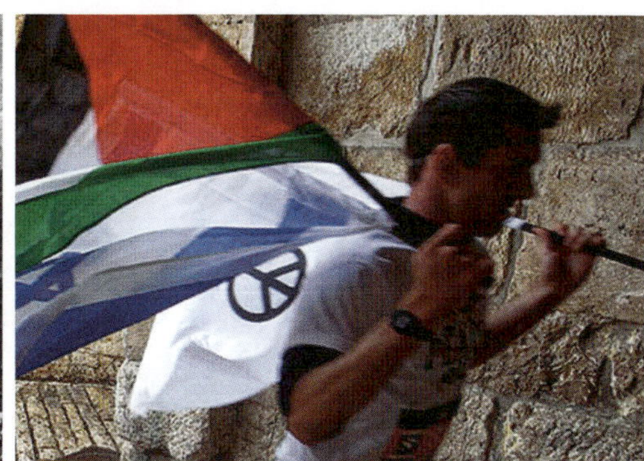

013
014
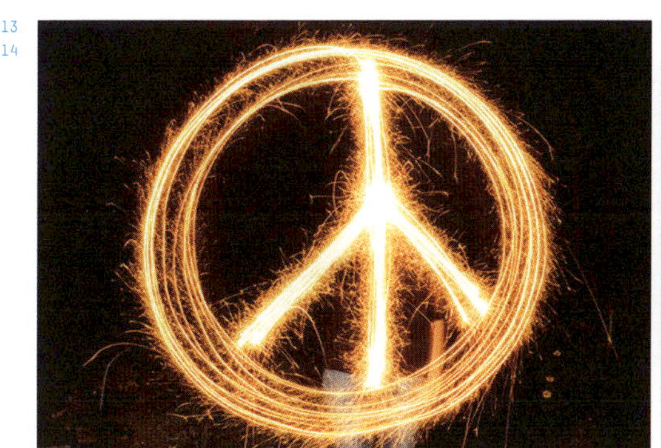
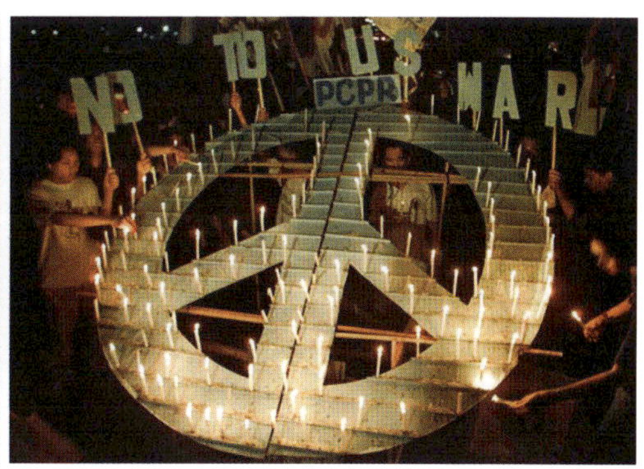

015
016
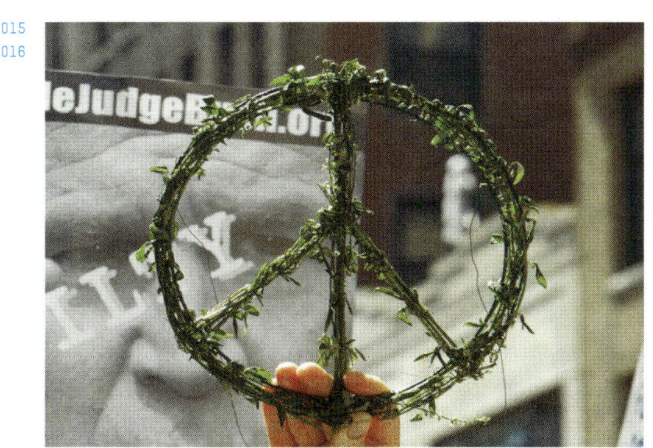

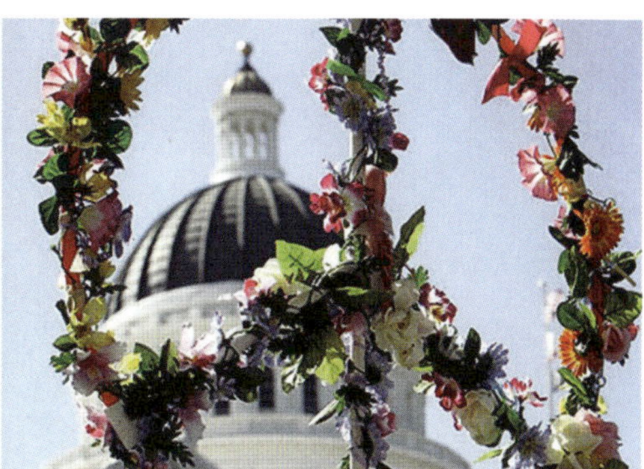

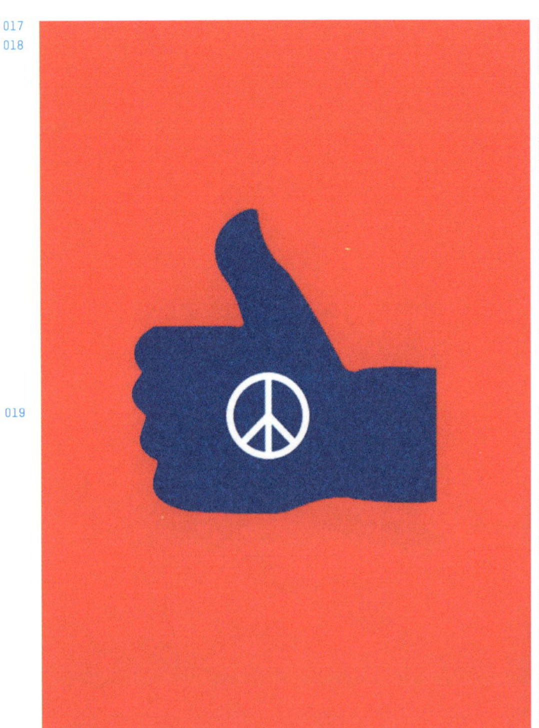

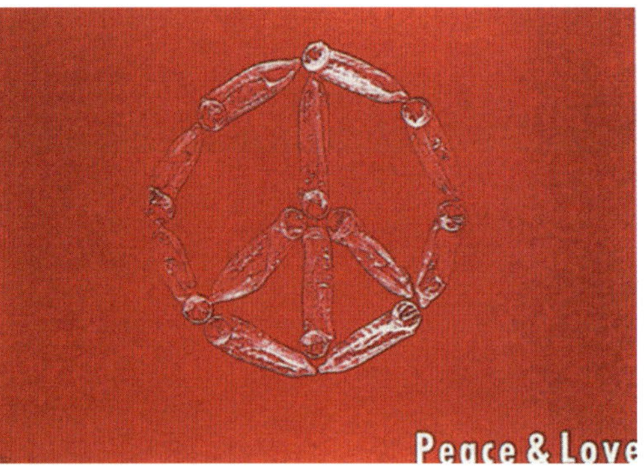
Schaffhausen-
Zürich
Peace & Love

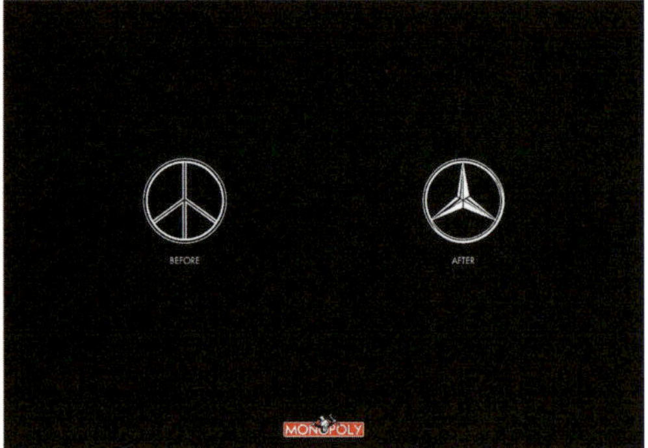
BEFORE
AFTER
MONOPOLY

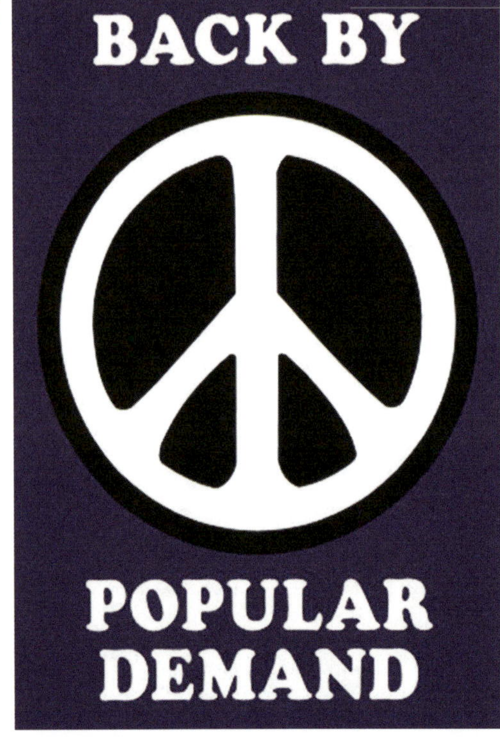
BACK BY
POPULAR
DEMAND

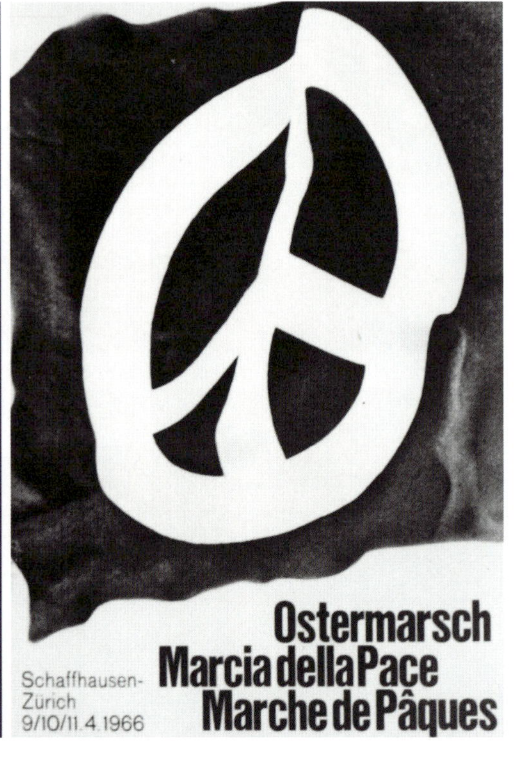
Ostermarsch
Marcia della Pace
Marche de Pâques
Schaffhausen-
Zürich
9/10/11.4.1966

001 UNTITLED
SOURCE ilovethisworld.com

002 PEACE SYMBOL AT SUNSET,
BURNING MAN
SOURCE pic.templetons.com
DATE 2003

003 PEACE SYMBOL TURNS 50, LONDON, UK
SOURCE www.robertlpeters.com

004 PROPOSED SOLAR PEACE SIGN
SCULPTURE MADE FROM 80 METAL
OIL BARRELS
CREATOR Artwork by Fred George
SOURCE inhabitat.com

005 SOLDIER WITH PEACE SYMBOL
ON HIS HAND
CREATOR Provided by Jayel Aheram
SOURCE visualinsights.blogspot.ch

006 PEACE SYMBOL BARN, SANTA BARBARA
SOURCE shereshevsky.wordpress.com
DATE 2009

007 PEACE PROTEST, DEMONSTRATION
AGAINST THE IRAQ WAR
CREATOR Carl De Kreyzer
SOURCE maryt.wordpress.com

008 PEACE
CREATOR Lukschi
SOURCE s260.photobucket.com

009 A PROTESTOR WEARS THE CAMPAIGN
FOR NUCLEAR DISARMAMENT [PEACE]
SYMBOL ON HIS SUNGLASSES DURING
A BAN-THE-BOMB MARCH
CREATOR John Franks
SOURCE www.guardian.co.uk
DATE 1960

010 UNTITLED
SOURCE www.commondreams.org

011 A SIGN FOR HIPPIES, PEACE, LOVE,
AND FLOWERS RESTS IN A GARBAGE
CAN OF A NEW YORK CITY PARK
CREATOR Owen Franken
SOURCE www.guardian.co.uk
DATE c. 1970

012 A MARATHON RUNNER CARRIES
PALESTINIAN AND ISRAELI FLAGS AS
WELL AS A WHITE FLAG WITH A PEACE
SYMBOL AS HE ENTERS THE ZION GATE
CREATOR Jim Hollander
SOURCE framework.latimes.com
DATE 2012

013 PEACE SIGN WITH SPARKLERS
CREATOR Jeff Wignall
SOURCE jeffwignall.com

014 PEACE MOVEMENT, PHILIPPINES
SOURCE www.britannica.com

015 GIVE PEACE A CHANCE
CREATOR Provided by Erica
SOURCE ericaakers.blogspot.ch

016 PEACE SYMBOL MADE OF FLOWERS,
DEMONSTRATION AGAINST THE WAR
IN IRAQ
CREATOR Rich Pedroncelli
SOURCE blog.syracuse.com

017 PEACE
SOURCE www.republicofpeace.com

018 PEACE AND LOVE
CREATOR Polymago, Juliette
Weisbuch
SOURCE "L'engagement politique et
social," Le festival d'affiches,
Chaumont, 19 May – 16 July 2000

019 BEFORE / AFTER
SOURCE www3.spotanatomy.info/

020 PEACE, BACK BY POPULAR DEMAND
SOURCE www.allposters.com

021 OSTERMARSCH
[EASTER MARCH]
CREATOR Roland Gretler, Peter Brun
SOURCE Plakatsammlung Museum
für Gestaltung Zürich

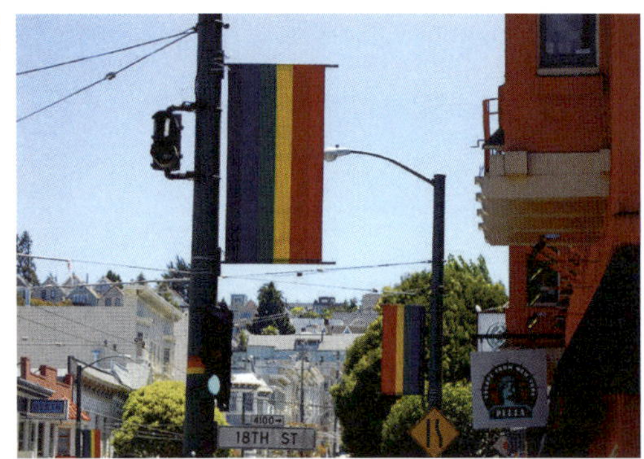
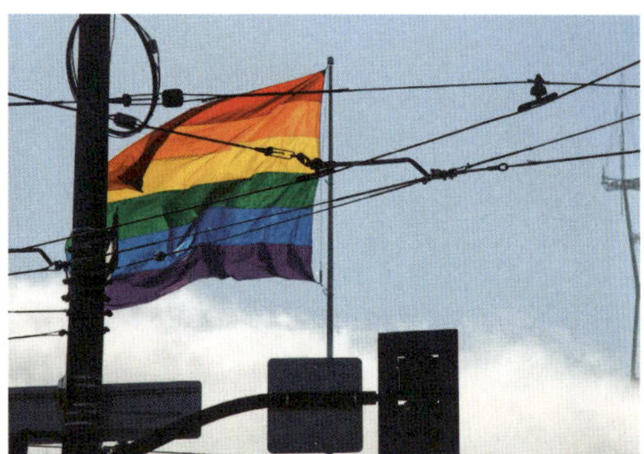
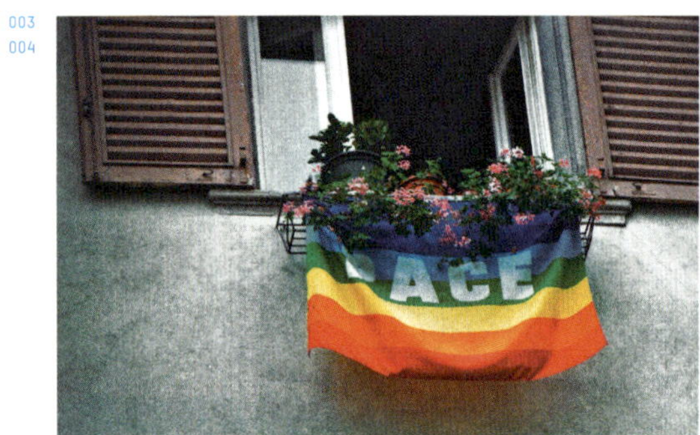
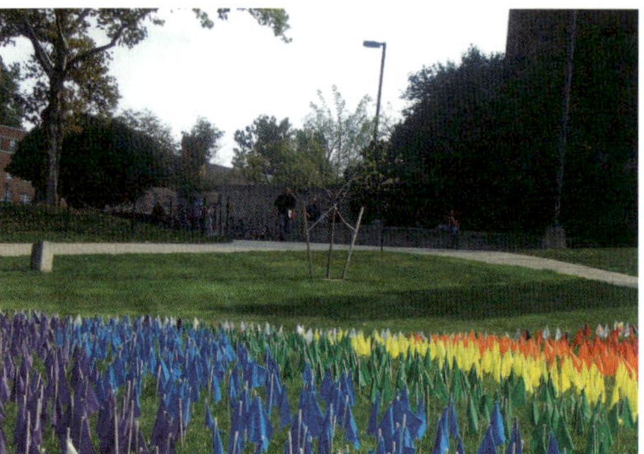
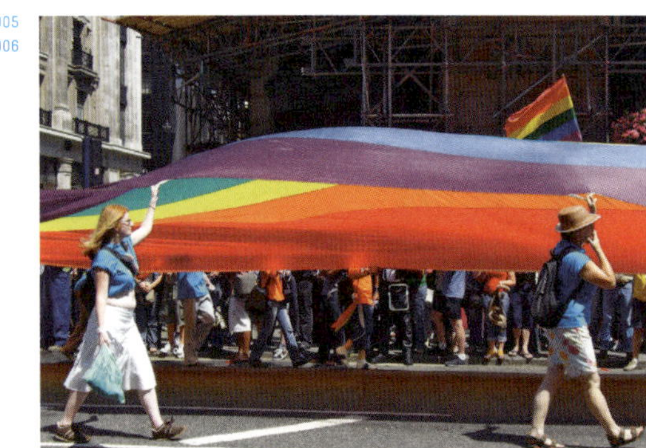
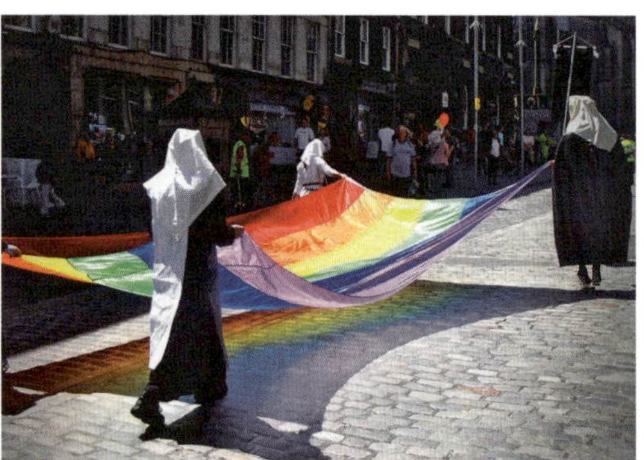
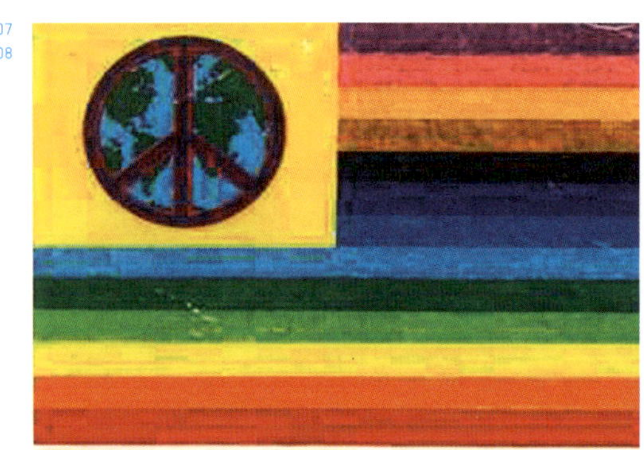
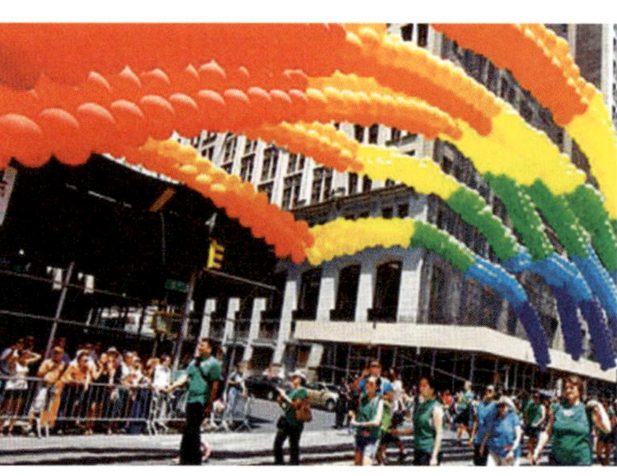

009
010
011
012

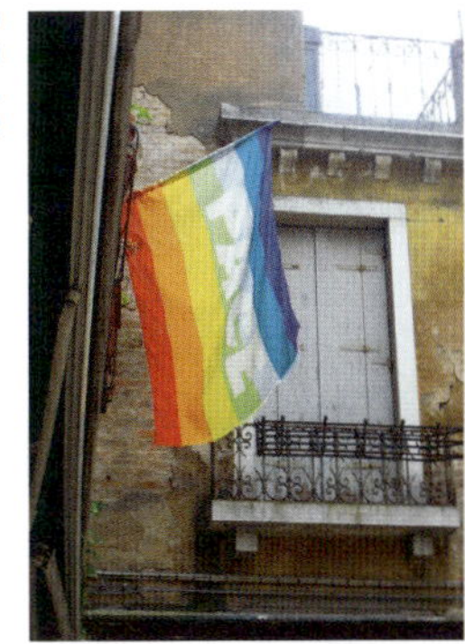
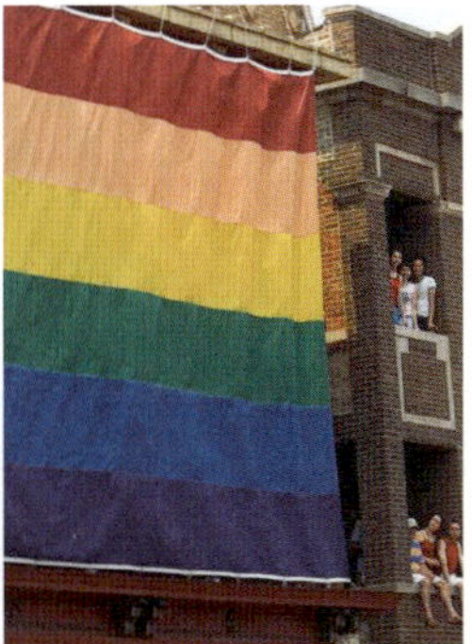
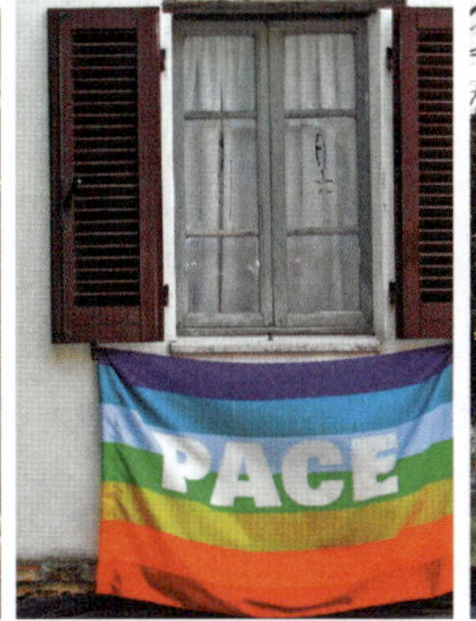
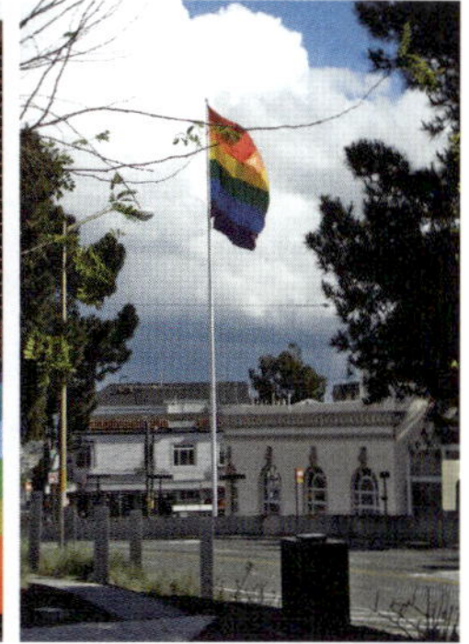

013
014
015
016

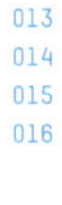
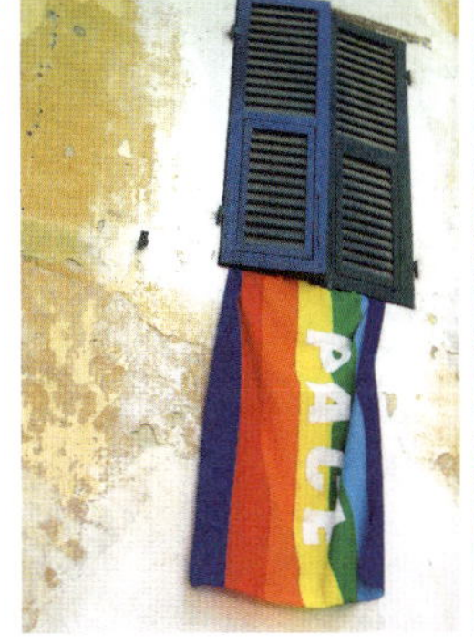
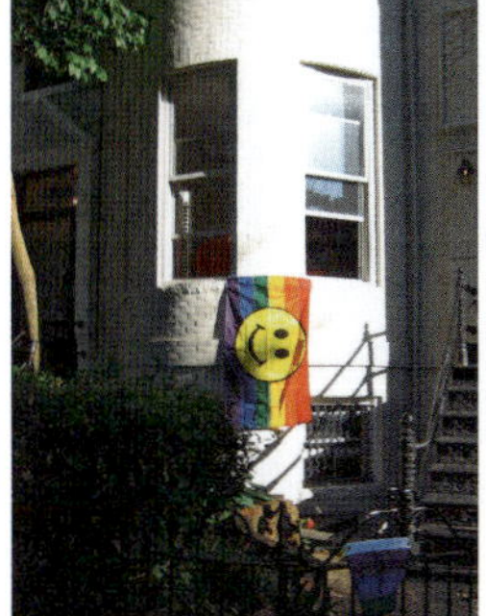
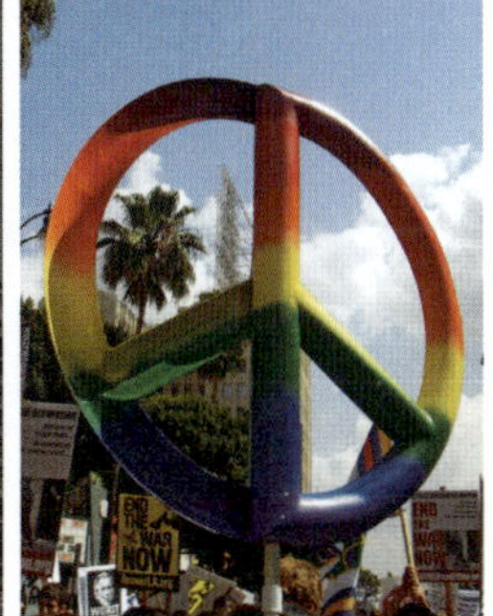
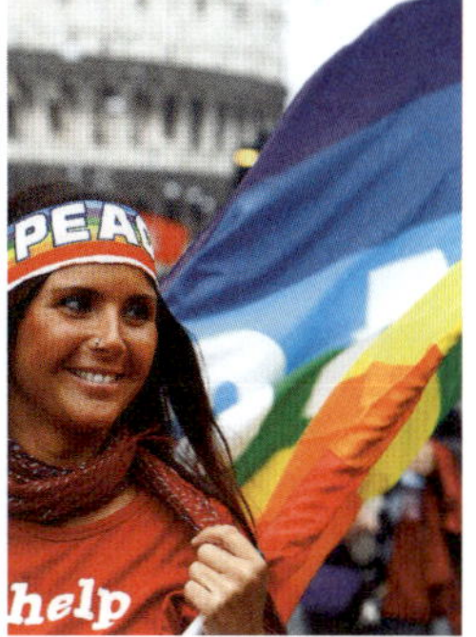

017
018
019
020

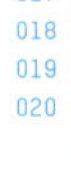
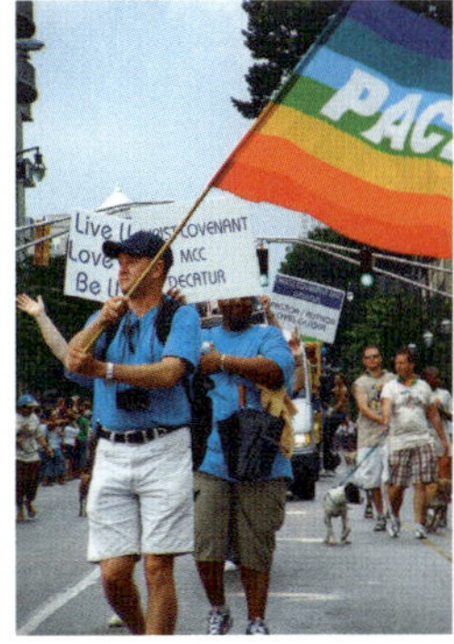
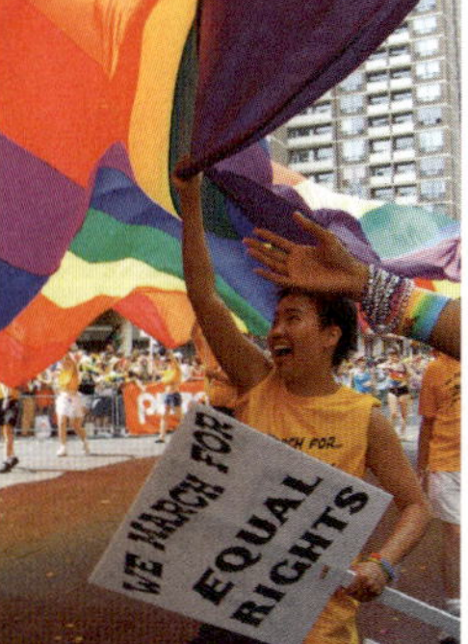
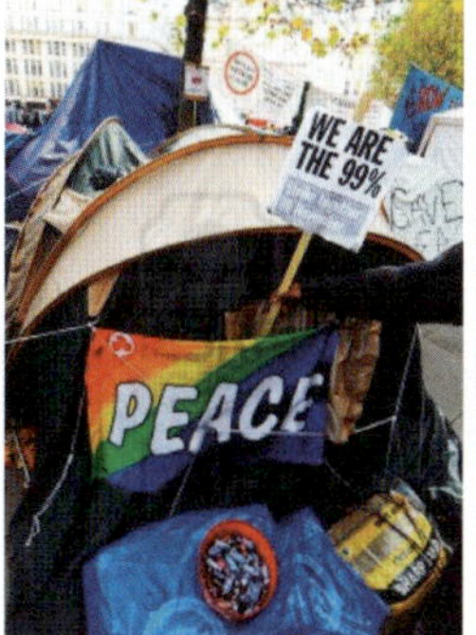
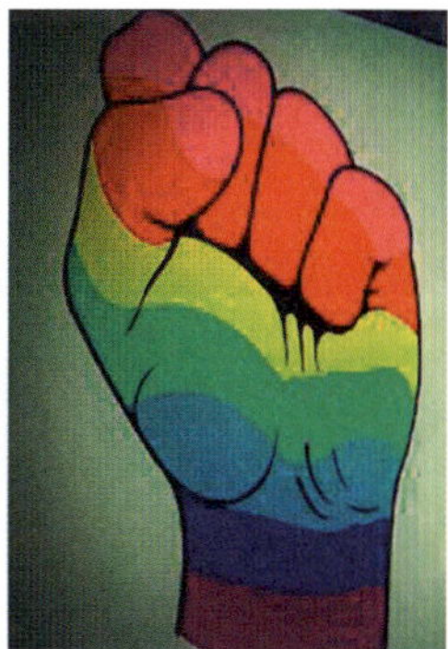

021
022
023
024

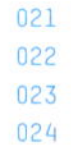
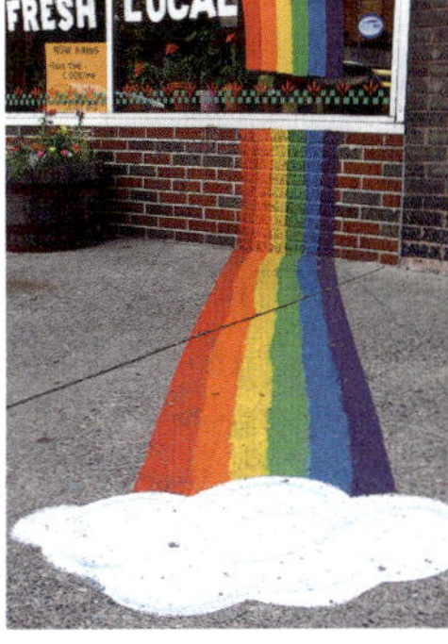
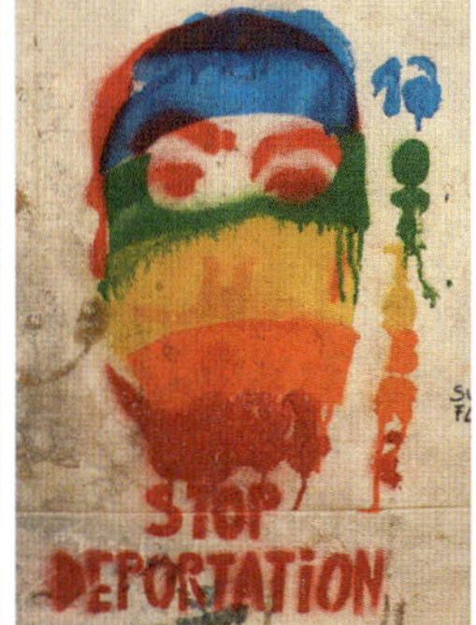
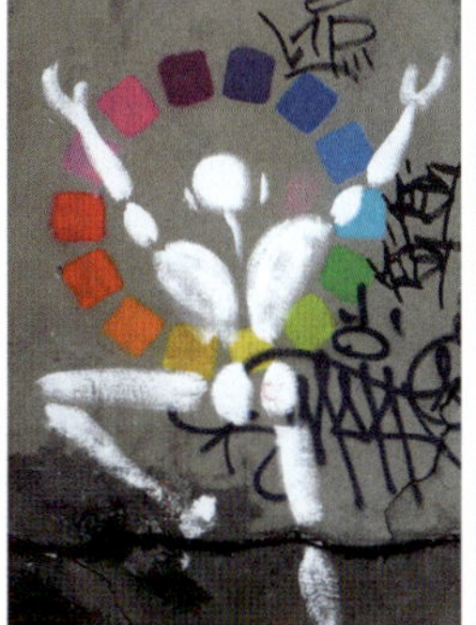
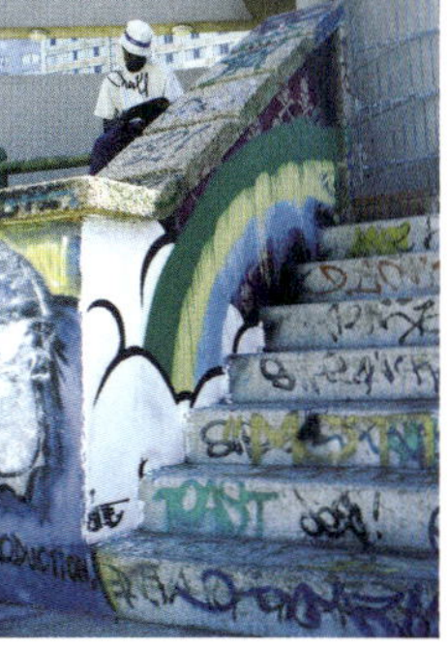

001 SAN FRANCISCO RAINBOW FLAG,
CASTRO DISTRICT
CREATOR Provided by svonkastell
SOURCE www.flickr.com/photos/
vonkastell/1028611220/

002 RAINBOW FLAG
CREATOR Provided by eisenzahn
SOURCE www.flickr.com/photos/
eisenzahn/2011565351/

003 PEACE FLAG, VERONA, ITALY
CREATOR Provided by Fugue
SOURCE www.flickr.com/photos/
fugue/12899977/

004 RAINBOW FLAGS
CREATOR Provided by
mybeautifulromance1
SOURCE www.flickr.com/photos/
mybeautifulromance1/1518288400/

005 PRIDE RAINBOW FLAG, LONDON
CREATOR Provided by Loodle
SOURCE www.flickr.com/photos/
loodle/179588931/
DATE 2006

006 RAINBOW FLAG, LONDON
CREATOR Provided by alephnaught
SOURCE www.flickr.com/photos/
alephnaught/21806346/

007 PEACE FLAG
CREATOR Provided by misa penguin
SOURCE www.flickr.com/photos/
25124962@N06/2516451586/sizes/m/
DATE 2006

008 RAINBOW BALOONS, PRIDE
MARCH, NYC
SOURCE www.mid-day.com
DATE 24 June 2012

009 PEACE FLAG
CREATOR Provided by DerekL
SOURCE www.flickr.com/photos/
derekl/15750558/

010 SUPPORT
CREATOR Provided by uBookworm
SOURCE www.flickr.com/photos/
ubookworm/21946949/

011 PEACE, SAN CASCIANO DEI BAGNI
CREATOR Provided by ingirogiro
SOURCE www.flickr.com/photos/
ingirogiro/79301027/
DATE 2003

012 RAINBOW FLAG
CREATOR Provided by SFAntti
SOURCE www.flickr.com/photos/
sfantti/5281655/

013 PEACE
CREATOR Provided by fulmini
SOURCE www.flickr.com/photos/
fulminiesaette/21733869/

014 SMILEY RAINBOW FLAG
CREATOR Provided by jtowns
SOURCE www.flickr.com/photos/
jtowns/165425869/

015 NOT GIVEN
CREATOR Provided by elleinad
SOURCE www.flickr.com/photos/
-elleinad-/2340966781/
DATE 2008

016 PROTEST FOR LABOR, PROTEST
FOR PEACE, ROME
CREATOR Pier Paolo Cito
SOURCE www.jezebel.com
DATE 16 October 2010

017 PROTEST FOR LABOR, PROTEST
FOR PEACE, ROME
CREATOR Provided by kuzquiano
SOURCE www.flickr.com/photos/
kuzquiano/175562625/

018 TORONTO GAY PRIDE PARADE
CREATOR Provided by Nenners
SOURCE www.flickr.com/photos/
nenners/301222054/
DATE 2006

019 OCCUPY LONDON PROTEST
SOURCE www.123rf.com
DATE 19 November 2011

020 RAINBOW HAND, PARIS
CREATOR Marie C. Cudraz

021 UNTITLED
CREATOR Minn
SOURCE www.flickr.com

022 VENICE
CREATOR Provided by TorCad
SOURCE www.flickr.com/photos/
96805000@N00/976116059/

023 PARIS
CREATOR Provided by melina1965
SOURCE www.flickr.com/photos/
8989278@N03/2225898288/
DATE 27 January 2008

024 SOMEWHERE OVER THE RAINBOW
CREATOR Provided by skullboy
SOURCE www.flickr.com/photos/
skullboy/1477567529/

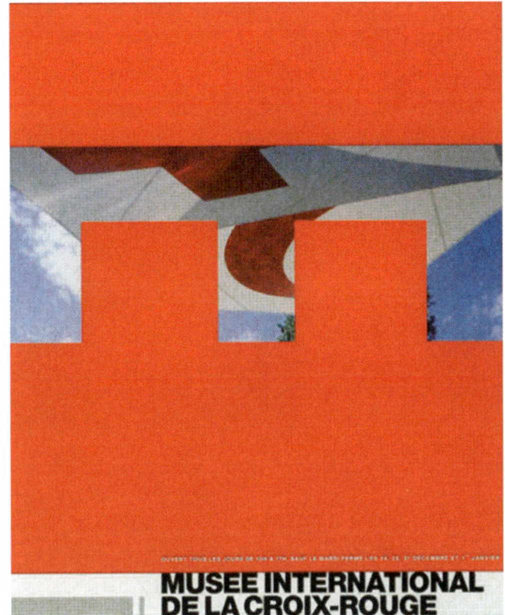
MUSEE INTERNATIONAL
DE LA CROIX-ROUGE
ET DU CROISSANT-ROUGE
17, AVENUE DE LA PAIX
CH-1202 GENEVE
WWW.MICR.ORG
TEL +41 22 748 95 25

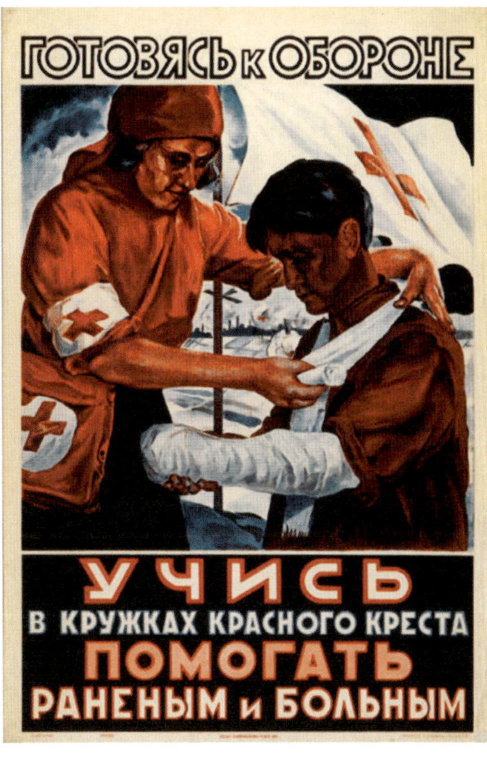
ГОТОВЯСЬ к ОБОРОНЕ
УЧИСЬ
В КРУЖКАХ КРАСНОГО КРЕСТА
ПОМОГАТЬ
РАНЕНЫМ и БОЛЬНЫМ

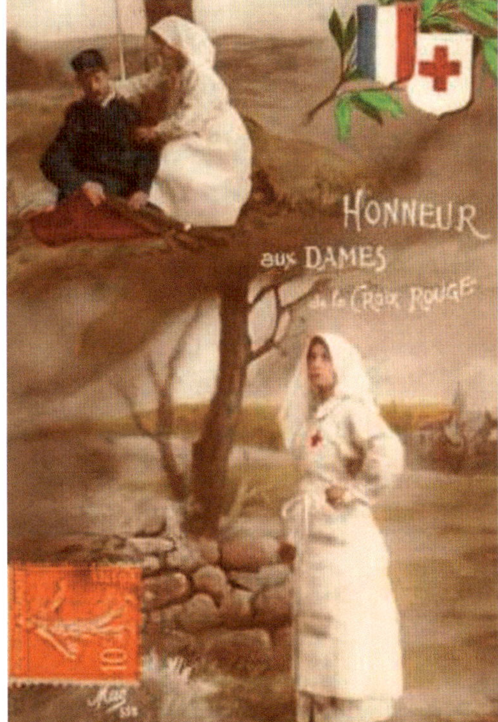
HONNEUR
aux DAMES
de la CROIX ROUGE

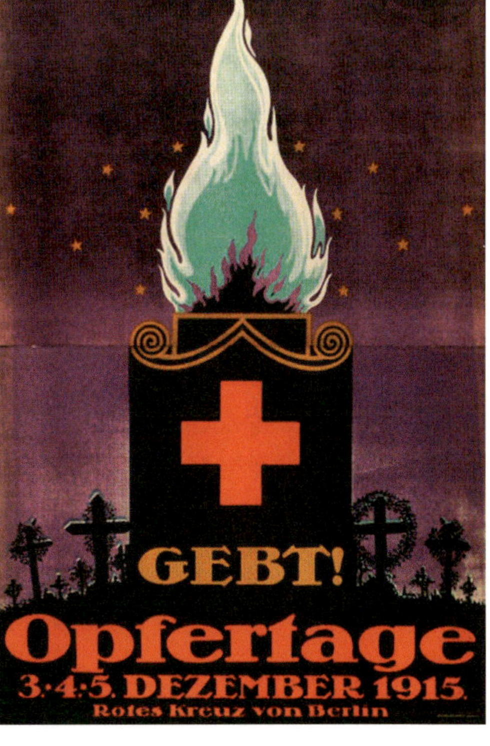
GEBT!
Opfertage
3·4·5. DEZEMBER 1915.
Rotes Kreuz von Berlin

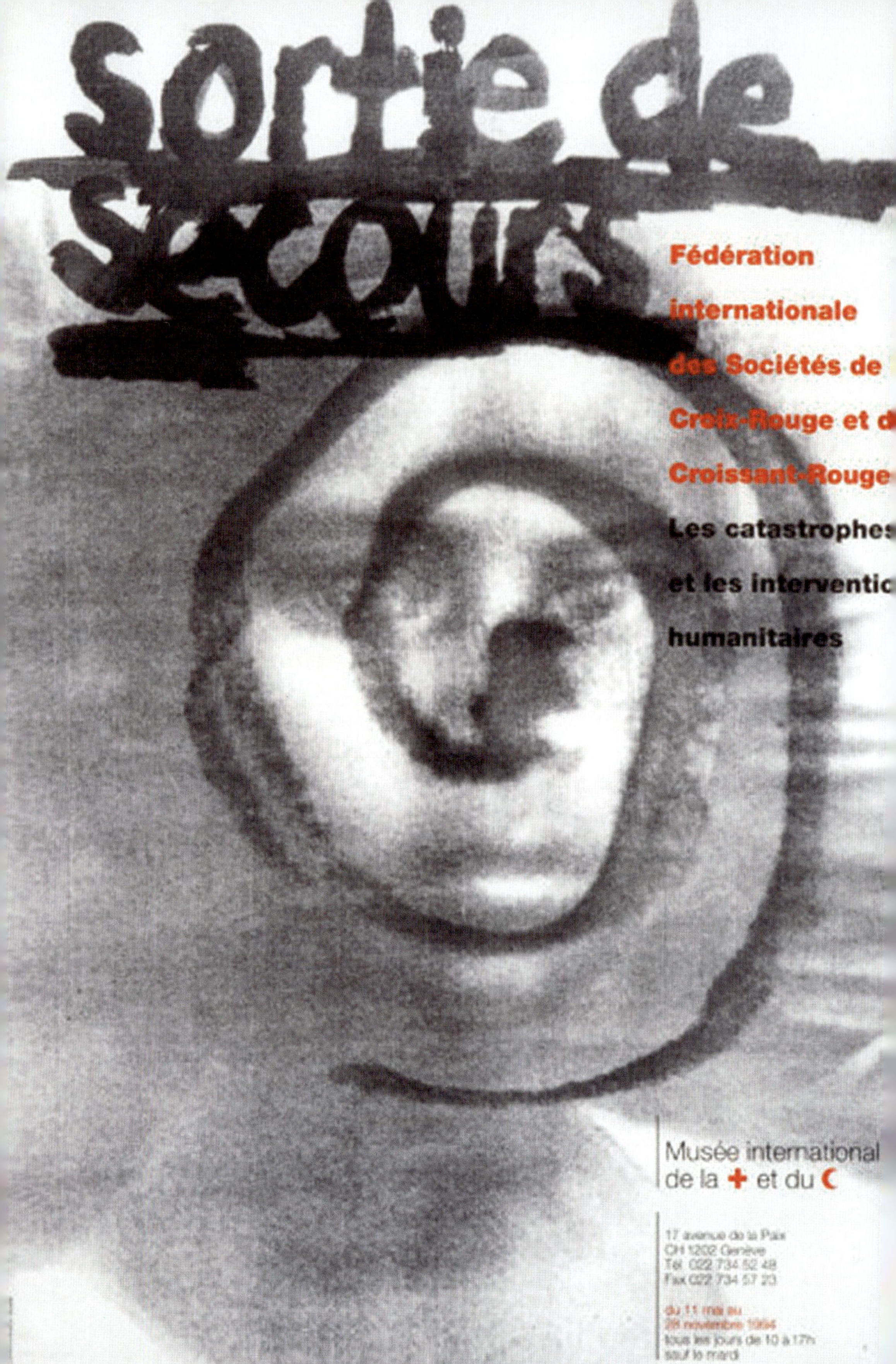
sortie de secours

Fédération
internationale
des Sociétés de
Croix-Rouge et de
Croissant-Rouge

Les catastrophes
et les interventions
humanitaires

Musée international
de la + et du (

17 avenue de la Paix
CH 1202 Genève
Tél 022 734 52 48
Fax 022 734 57 23

du 11 mai au
26 novembre 1994
tous les jours de 10 à 17h
sauf le mardi

001 MUSÉE INTERNATIONAL DE LA
CROIX-ROUGE ET DU CROISSANT-ROUGE
[THE INTERNATIONAL RED CROSS AND
RED CRESCENT MUSEUM]
CREATOR Izet Shesivari
SOURCE Plakatsammlung Museum
für Gestaltung Zürich
DATE 2001

002 HELP DEFEND YOUR COUNTRY: LEARN
HOW TO CARE FOR THE WOUNDED AND
SICK IN THE LOCAL BRANCH OF THE
RED CROSS. USSR, 1927
SOURCE Plakatsammlung Museum
für Gestaltung Zürich

003 HONNEUR À LA CROIX-ROUGE
[PRAISE FOR THE RED CROSS]
SOURCE commons.wikimedia.org
DATE 1915

004 GEBT!
[GIVE!]
CREATOR Martin Jacoby-Boy
SOURCE Plakatsammlung Museum
für Gestaltung Zürich
DATE 1915

005 SORTIE DE SECOURS
[EMERGENCY EXIT]
CREATOR Roger Pfund, Sophie Pfund,
Ateilier Pfund
SOURCE Plakatsammlung Museum
für Gestaltung Zürich

WAR
PEACE

FRIEDEN
bonjour

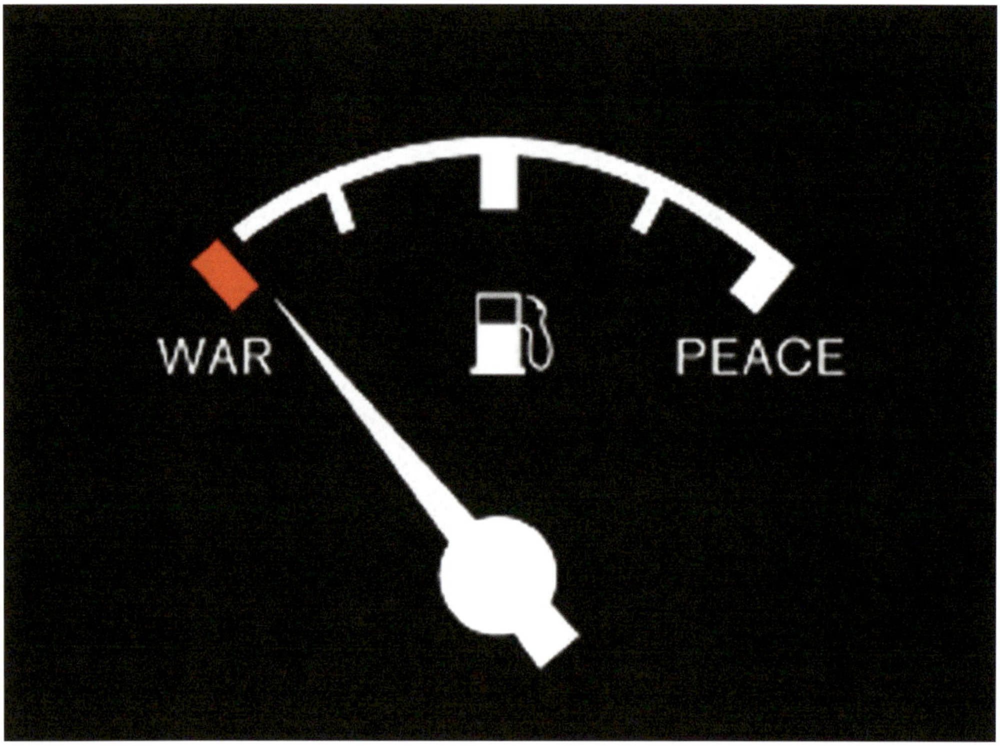

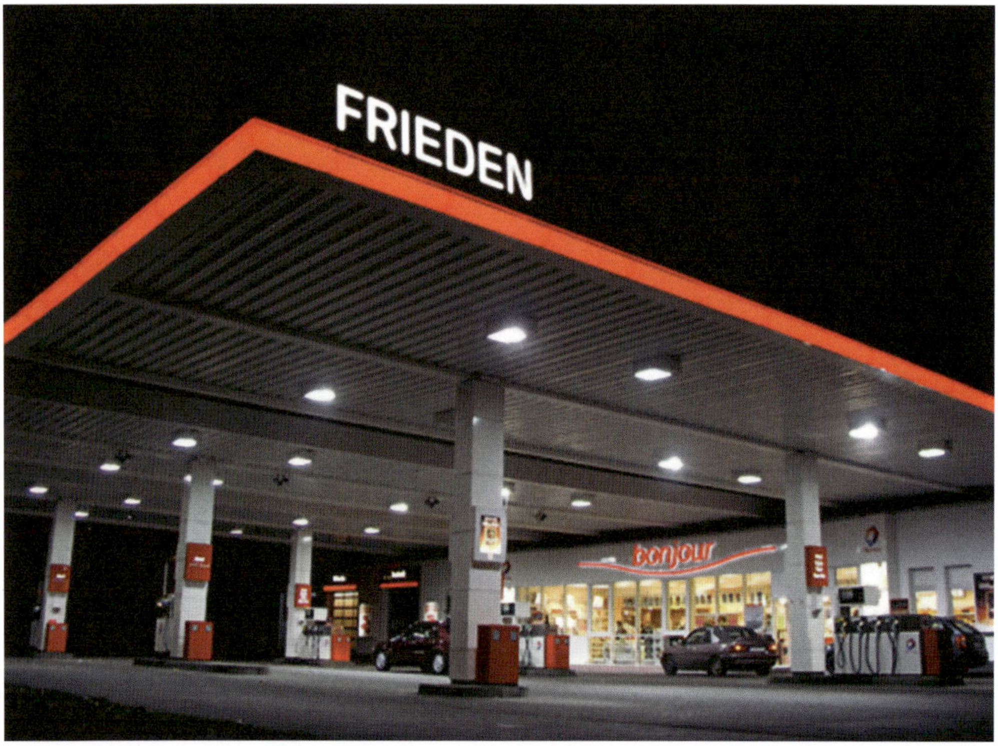

001 PEACE POSTERS PROJECT
     CREATOR Marten Lindquist
     SOURCE www.brushstroke.tv
     DATE 2003

002 PEACE POSTERS PROJECT
     CREATOR Marten Lindquist
     SOURCE www.brushstroke.tv
     DATE 2003

001
002

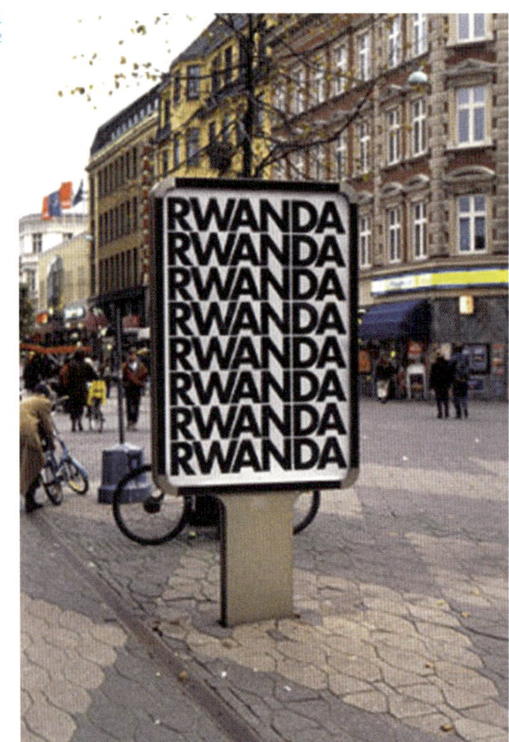

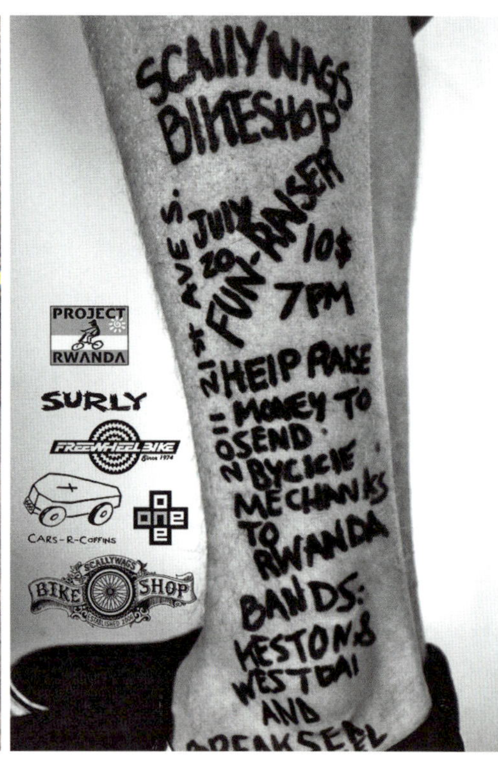

003
004

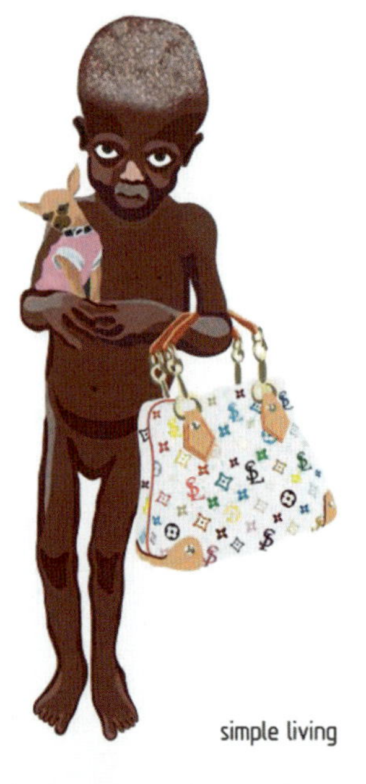

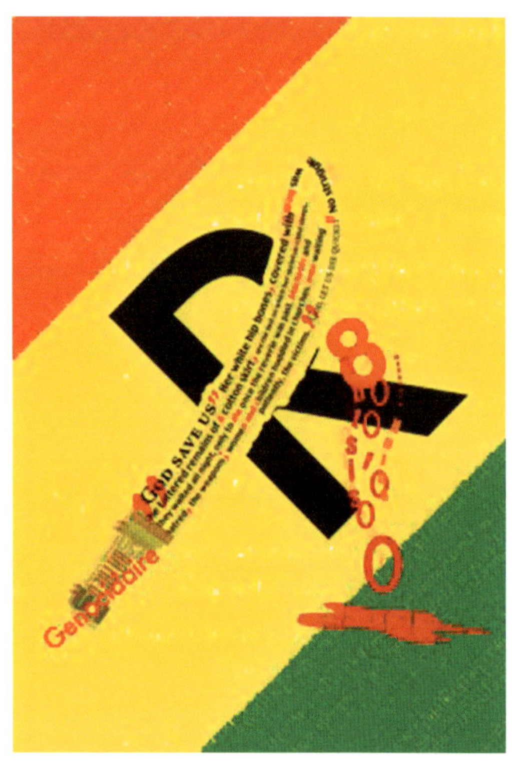

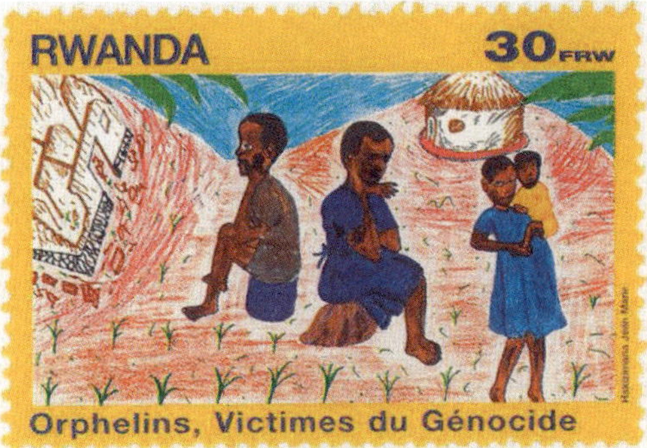

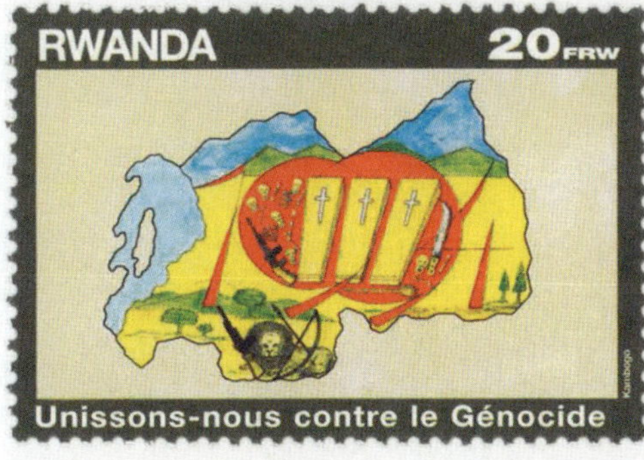

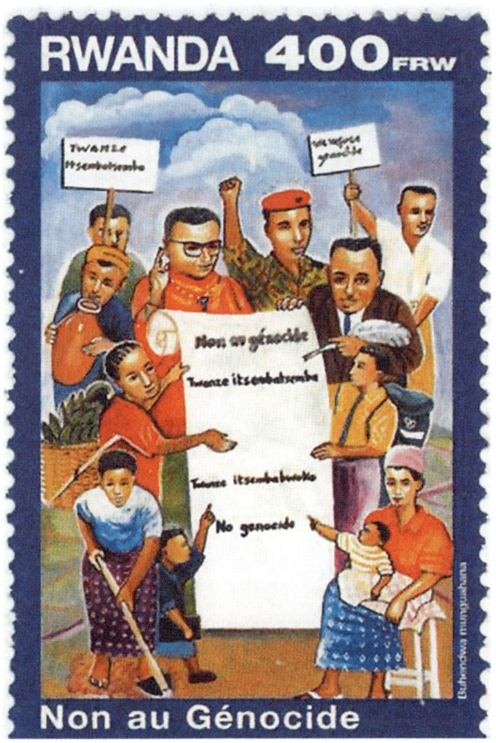

001 RWANDA, RWANDA
These posters, scattered around the streets and squares of Malmo were a raw gesture, produced out of frustration and anger. If all of the images of slaughter and piled corpses, and all of the reportage did so little, perhaps a simple sign, in the form of an insistent cry, would get their attention.
CREATOR Alfredo Jaar
SOURCE memory.loc.gov
DATE 1994

002 FUND-RAISER TO SEND MECHANICS TO RWANDA
CREATOR The Scallywags Bike Shop
SOURCE www.surlybikes.com

003 SIMPLE LIVING
CREATOR Nadia Plesner
SOURCE osocio.org

004 GENOCIDAIRE
SOURCE mrbruns.21publish.com

005 ORPHANS, VICTIMS OF GENOCIDE
SOURCE www.chgs.umn.edu

006 LET US UNITE AGAINST GENOCIDE
SOURCE www.chgs.umn.edu

007 NO TO GENOCIDE
SOURCE www.chgs.umn.edu

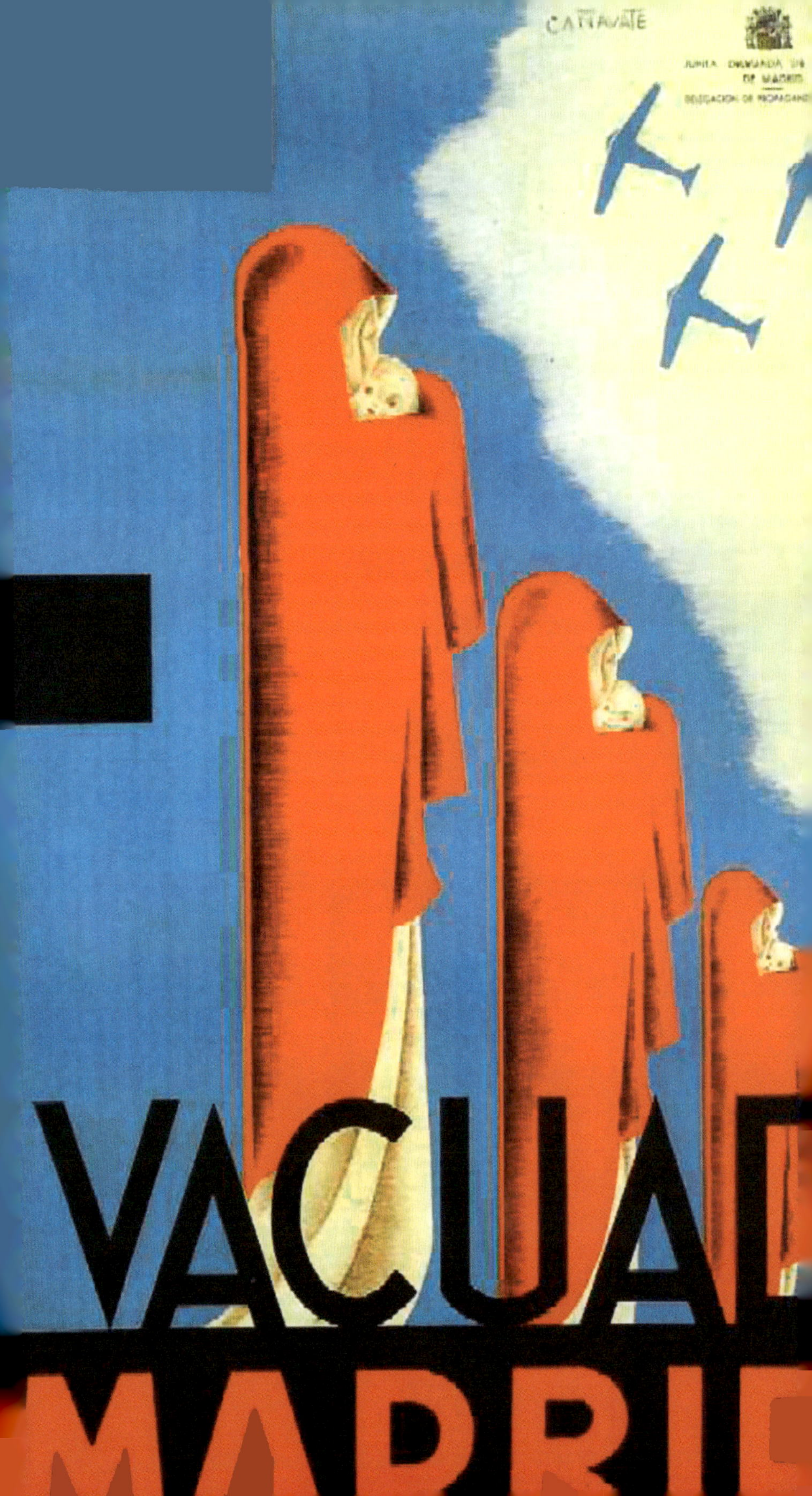

CAÑAVATE
JUNTA DELEGADA DE MADRID
DELEGACIÓN DE PROPAGANDA
VACUAD
MADRID

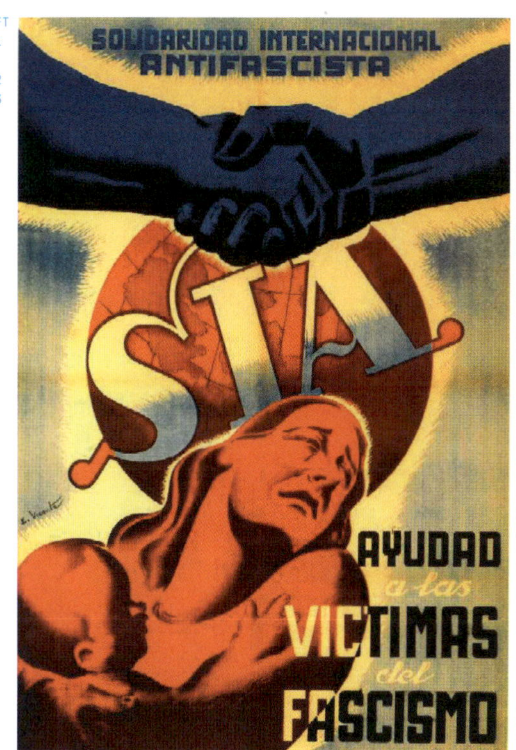
SOLIDARIDAD INTERNACIONAL
ANTIFASCISTA
S.I.A.
AYUDAD
a las
VICTIMAS
del
FASCISMO

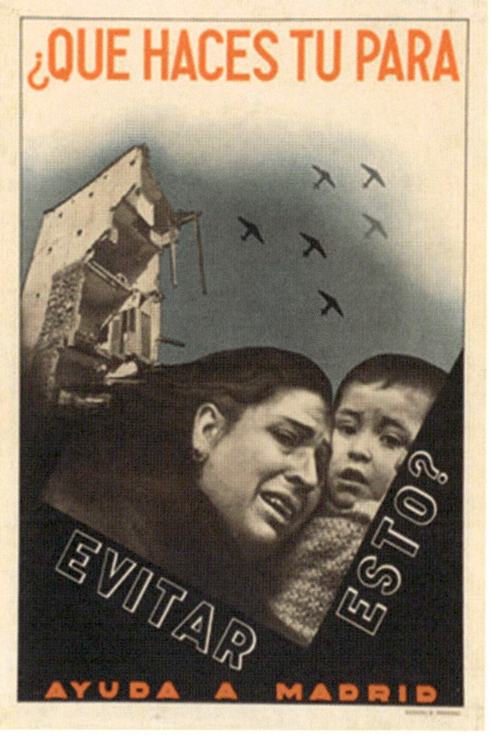
¿QUE HACES TU PARA
EVITAR
ESTO?
AYUDA A MADRID

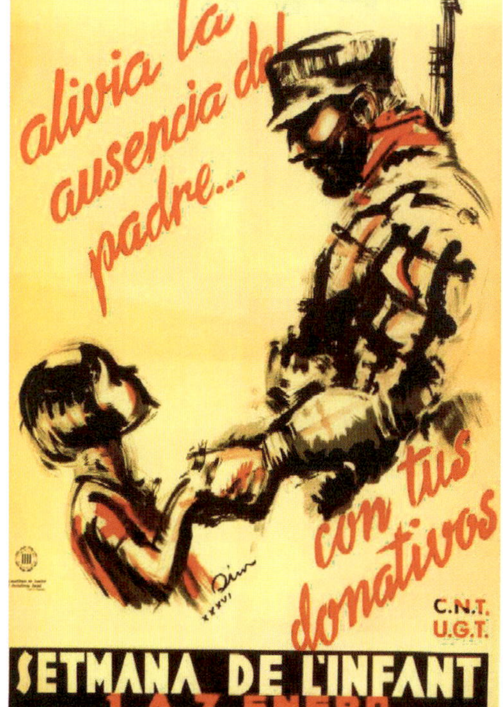
alivia la
ausencia del
padre...
con tus
donativos
C.N.T.
U.G.T.
SETMANA DE L'INFANT
1 A 7 ENERO

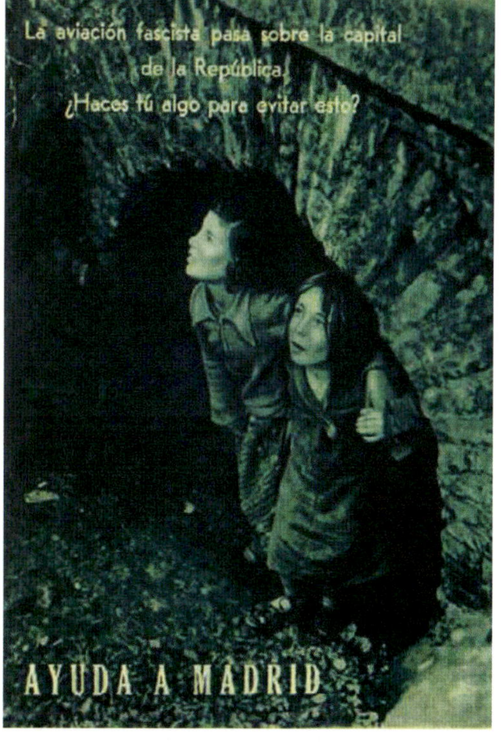
La aviación fascista pasa sobre la capital
de la República.
¿Haces tú algo para evitar esto?
AYUDA A MADRID

006
007

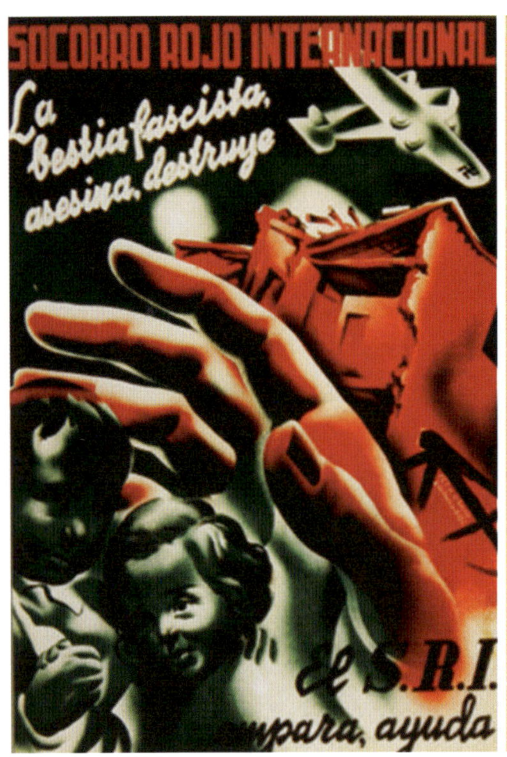

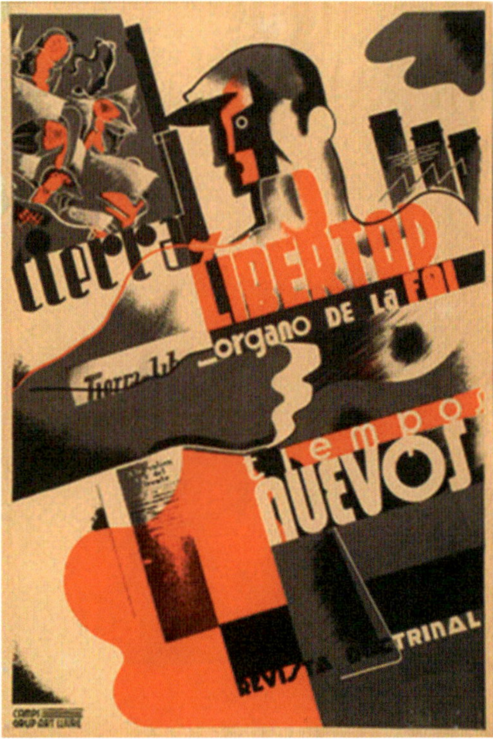

008
009

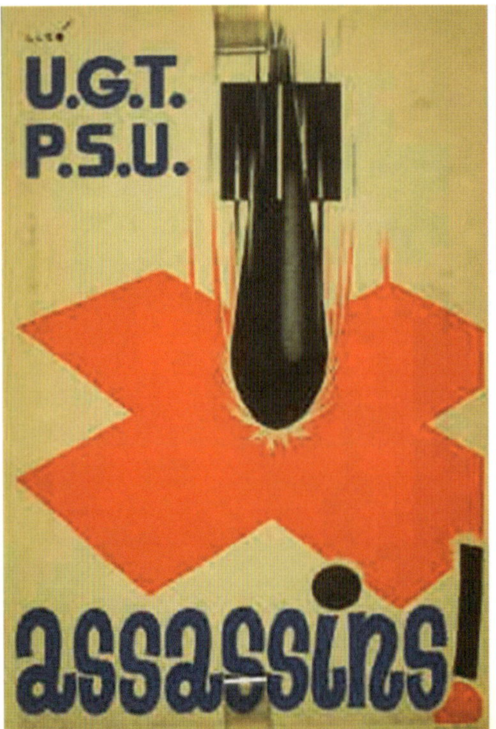

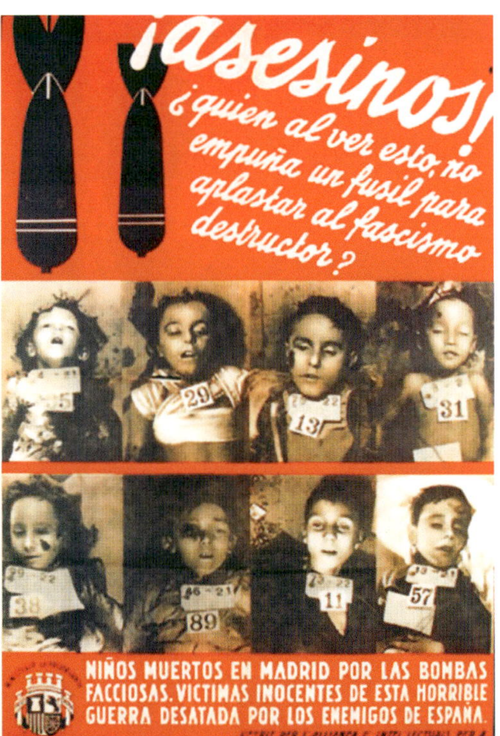

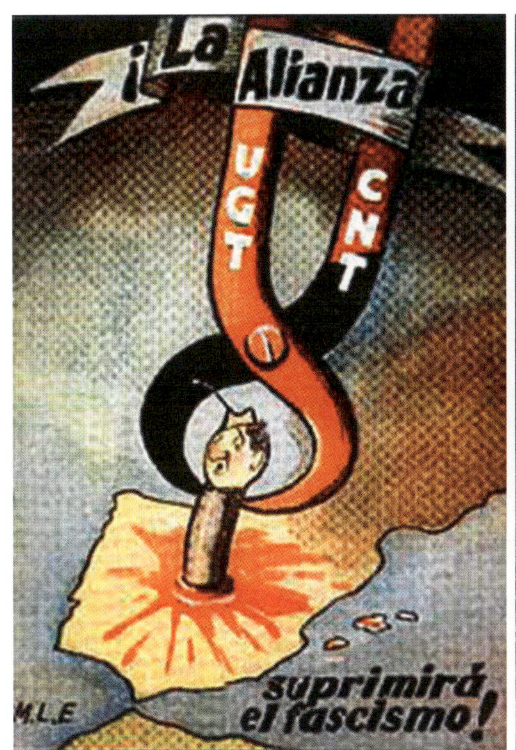
¡La Alianza
UGT
CNT
M.L.E
suprimirá
el fascismo!

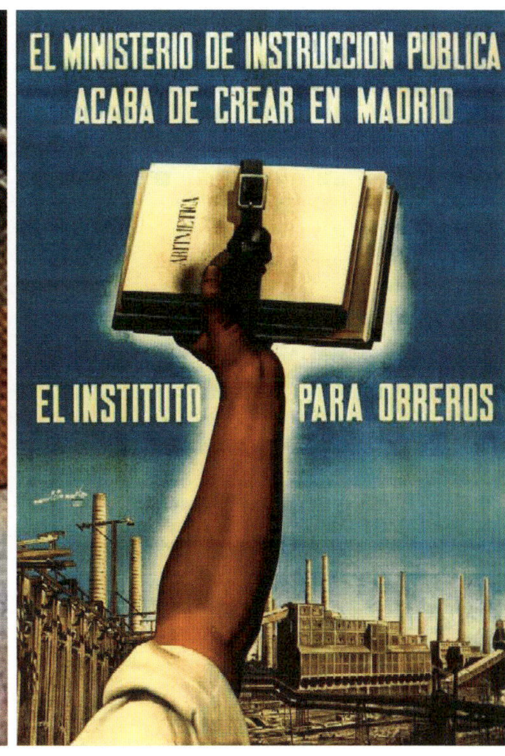
EL MINISTERIO DE INSTRUCCION PUBLICA
ACABA DE CREAR EN MADRID
ARITMETICA
EL INSTITUTO PARA OBREROS

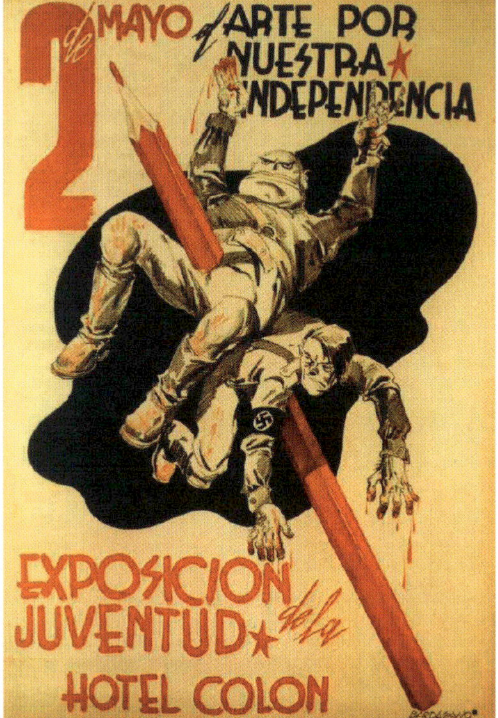
2 de MAYO el ARTE POR
NUESTRA
INDEPENDENCIA
EXPOSICION
JUVENTUD de la
HOTEL COLON

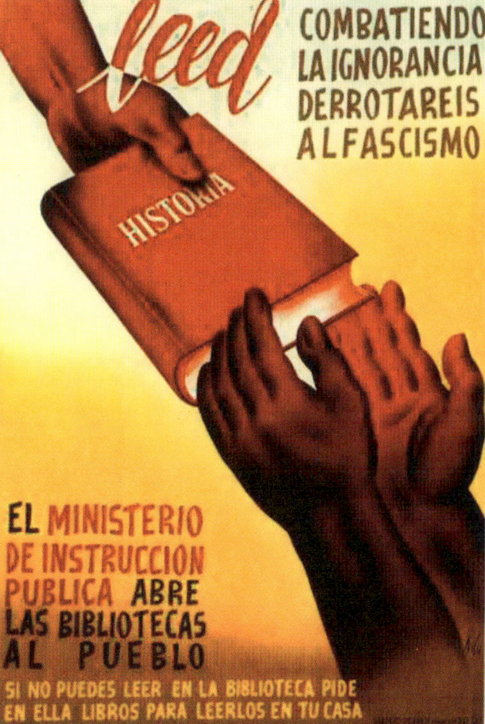
leed COMBATIENDO
LA IGNORANCIA
DERROTAREIS
AL FASCISMO
HISTORIA
EL MINISTERIO
DE INSTRUCCION
PUBLICA ABRE
LAS BIBLIOTECAS
AL PUEBLO
SI NO PUEDES LEER EN LA BIBLIOTECA PIDE
EN ELLA LIBROS PARA LEERLOS EN TU CASA

014
015

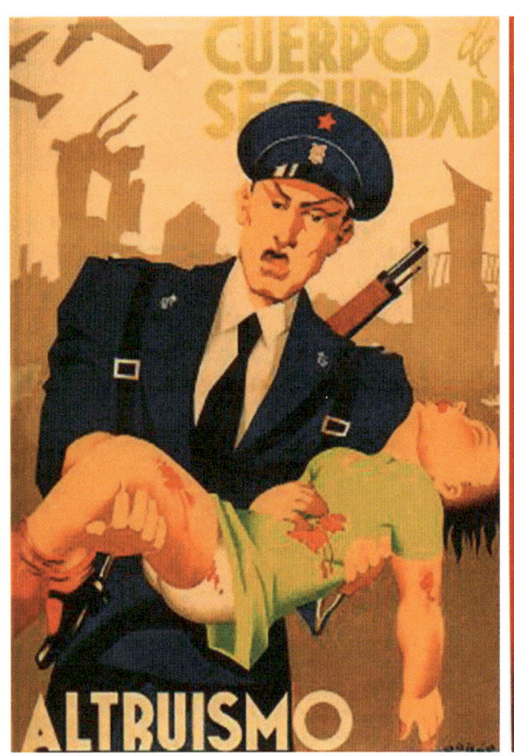

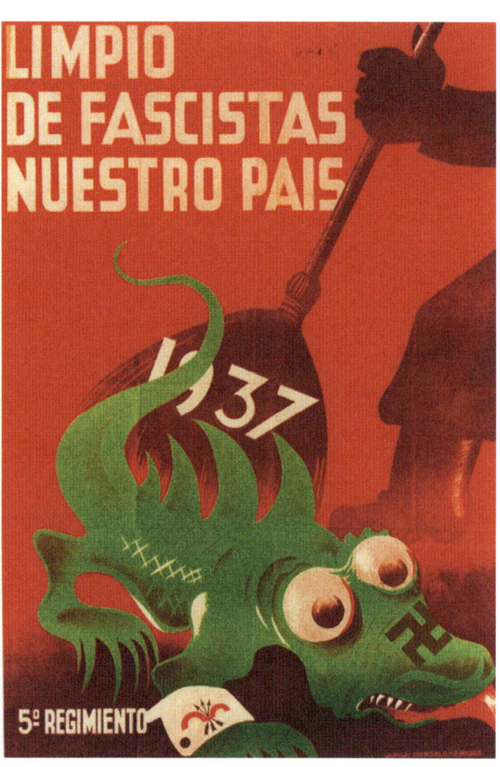

016
017

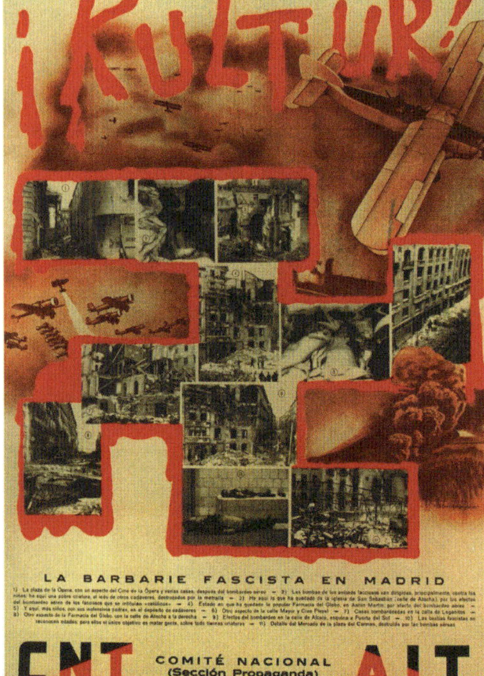

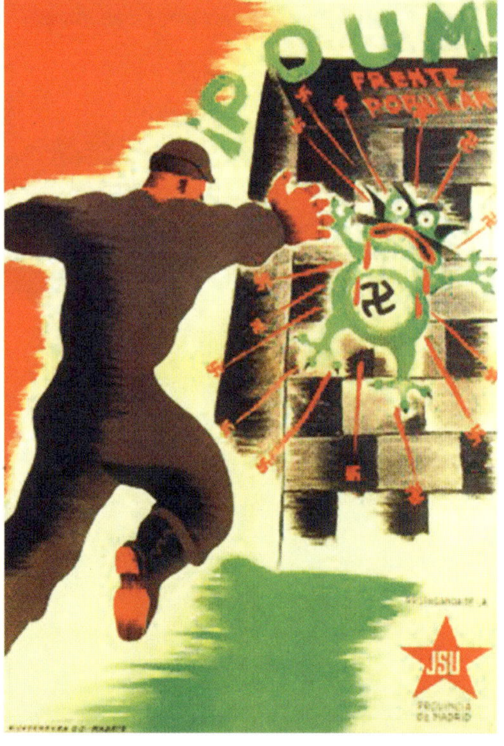

018
019

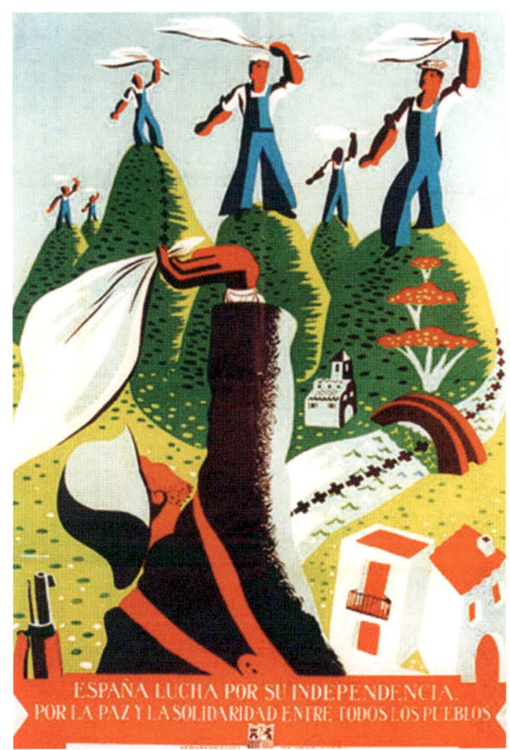

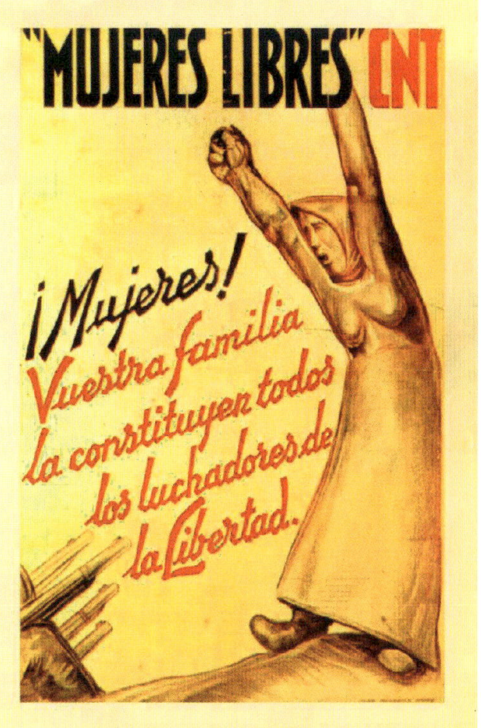

020
021

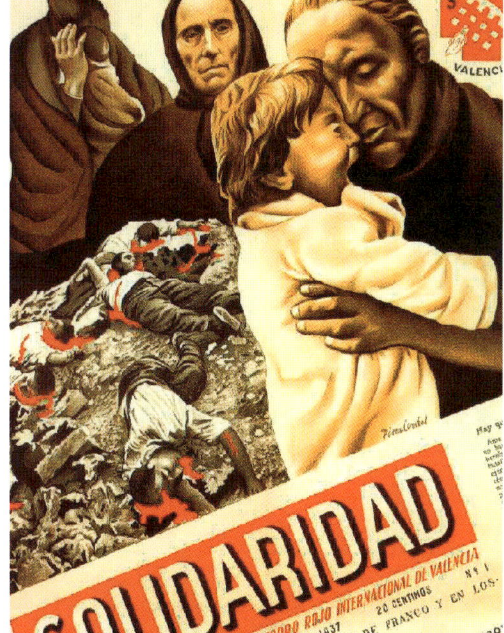

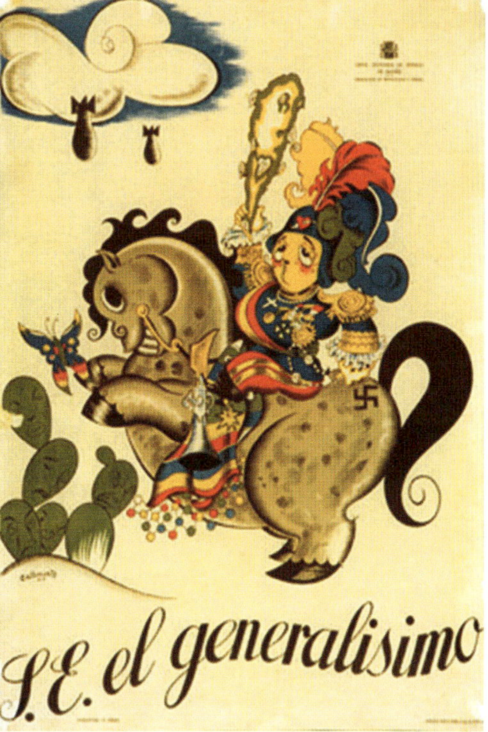

022

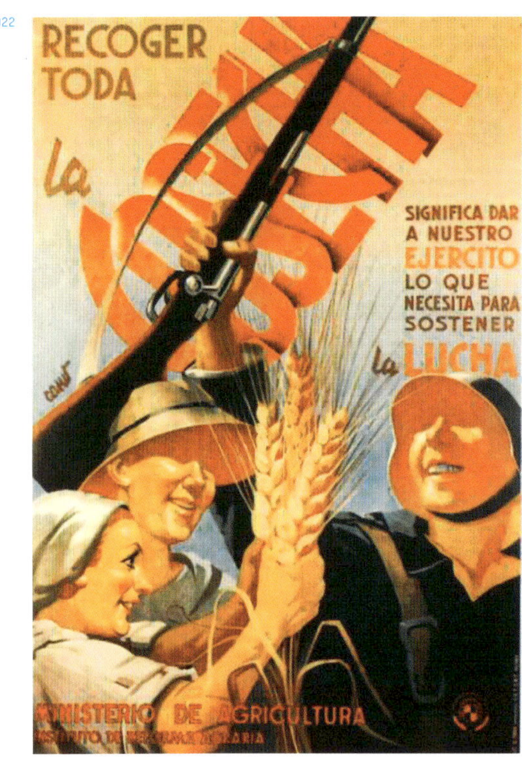
RECOGER TODA
la COSECHA
SIGNIFICA DAR A NUESTRO EJERCITO LO QUE NECESITA PARA SOSTENER la LUCHA
MINISTERIO DE AGRICULTURA

023

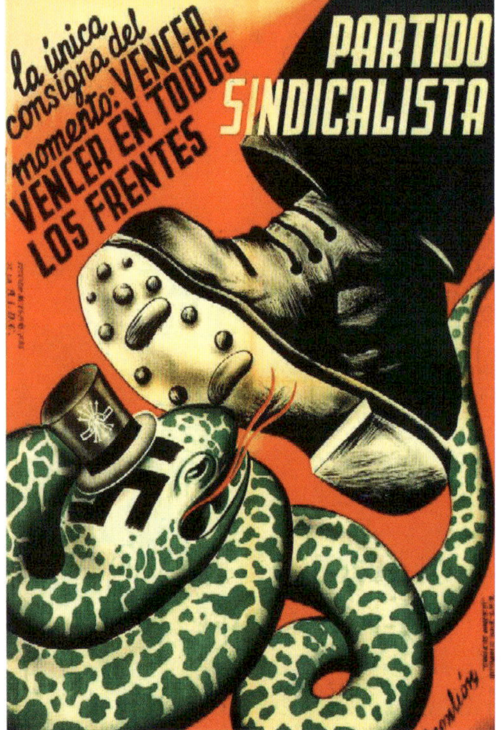
la única consigna del momento: VENCER, VENCER EN TODOS LOS FRENTES
PARTIDO SINDICALISTA

001 EVACUAD MADRID
[EVACUATE MADRID]
CREATOR CAÑ'AVATE
SOURCE www.guerracivil.org

002 AYUDAD A LAS VICTIMAS DEL FASCISMO
[HELP THE VICTIMS OF FASCISM]
SOURCE www.ugt.es

003 QUE HACES TU PARA
EVITAR ESTO?
[WHAT ARE YOU DOING TO
AVOID THIS?]
CREATOR Augusto
SOURCE Plakatsammlung Museum
für Gestaltung Zürich
DATE 1937

004 SETMANA DE L'ENFANT
[CHILDREN'S WEEK]
CREATOR José Luis Rey Vila
SOURCE www.guerracivil.org

005 AYUDA A MADRID
[HELP MADRID]
SOURCE www.ugt.es

006 SOCORRO ROJO INTERNACIONAL
[INTERNATIONAL RED AID]
CREATOR Seccion Artes
Plasticas A.I.D.C.
SOURCE Plakatsammlung Museum
für Gestaltung Zürich
DATE 1937

007 TIERRA Y LIBERTAD
[LAND AND LIBERTY]
CREATOR Champs, Barcelona
SOURCE Plakatsammlung Museum
für Gestaltung Zürich
DATE 1937

008 ASSASSINS!
[MURDERERS!]
SOURCE www.ugt.es

009 ASESINOS! QUIEN AL VER ESTO,
NO EMPUNA UN FUSIL PARA APLASTAR
AL FASCISMO DESTRUCTOR?
[MURDERERS! WHO, SEEING THIS,
WOULDN'T TAKE UP WEAPONS TO
DESTROY FASCISM?]
SOURCE www.ugt.es

010 LA ALIANZA SUPRIMIRÁ EL FASCISMO!
[THE ALLIANCE WILL DEFEAT FASCISM!]
SOURCE www.ugt.es

011 EL MINISTERIO DE INSTRUCCION
PUBLICA ACABA DE CREAR EN MADRID
EL INSTITUTO PARA OBREROS
[THE MINISTRY OF MUNICIPAL
SERVICES IN MADRID HAS JUST
CREATED THE INSTITUTE FOR WORKERS]
SOURCE www.guerracivil.org

012 ARTE POR NUESTRA INDEPENDENCIA
[ART FOR OUR INDEPENDENCE]
SOURCE www.ugt.es

013 LEED HISTORIA - COMBATIENDO
LA IGNORANCIA DERROTAREIS
AL FASCISMO
[READ HISTORY - BATTLE IGNORANCE
TO DEFEAT FASCISM]
CREATOR Wila
SOURCE www.guerracivil.org

014 ALTRUISMO
[ALTRUISM]
SOURCE www.ugt.es

015 LIMPIO DE FASCISTAS NUESTRO PAIS
[RID OUR LAND OF FASCISTS!]
CREATOR Garay
SOURCE Alfonso Guerra, ed., *Carteles
de la guerra, 1936-1939* [Barcelona:
Lunwerg Editores, 2004], p. 155.
DATE 1937

016 KULTUR! LA BARBARIE FASCISTA
EN MADRID
[CULTURE! FASCIST BARBARISM
IN MADRID]
CREATOR Muro
SOURCE Alfonso Guerra, ed., *Carteles
de la guerra, 1936-1939* [Barcelona:
Lunwerg Editores, 2004], p. 112.

017 POUM!
SOURCE www.ugt.es

018 ESPAÑA LUCHA POR SU INDEPENDENCIA
POR LA PAZ Y LA SOLIDARIDAD ENTRE
TODOS PUEBLOS
[SPAIN FIGHTING FOR INDEPENDENCE
FOR PEACE AND SOLIDARITY AMONG
ALL PEOPLES]
SOURCE www.elcantodelbuho.org

019 "MUJERES LIBRES" - ¡MUJERES!
VUESTRA FAMILIA LA CONSTITUYEN
TODOS LOS LUCHADORES DE
LA LIBERTAD
[FREE WOMEN - WOMEN! YOUR FAMILY
ARE ALL FREEDOM FIGHTERS]
SOURCE www.elcantodelbuho.org

020 SOLIDARIDAD
[SOLIDARITY]
SOURCE www.guerracivil.org

021 S.E. EL GENERALISIMO
[HIS EXCELLENCY THE GENERALISSIMO]
CREATOR Canavate
SOURCE Plakatsammlung Museum
für Gestaltung Zürich
DATE 1937

022 RECOGER TODA LA COSECHA
[HARVEST THE CROPS]
CREATOR Vicente Canet
SOURCE www.guerracivil.org

023 PARTIDO SINDICALISTA
[SYNDICALIST PARTY]
CREATOR Manuel Monleón
SOURCE www.guerracivil.org

001

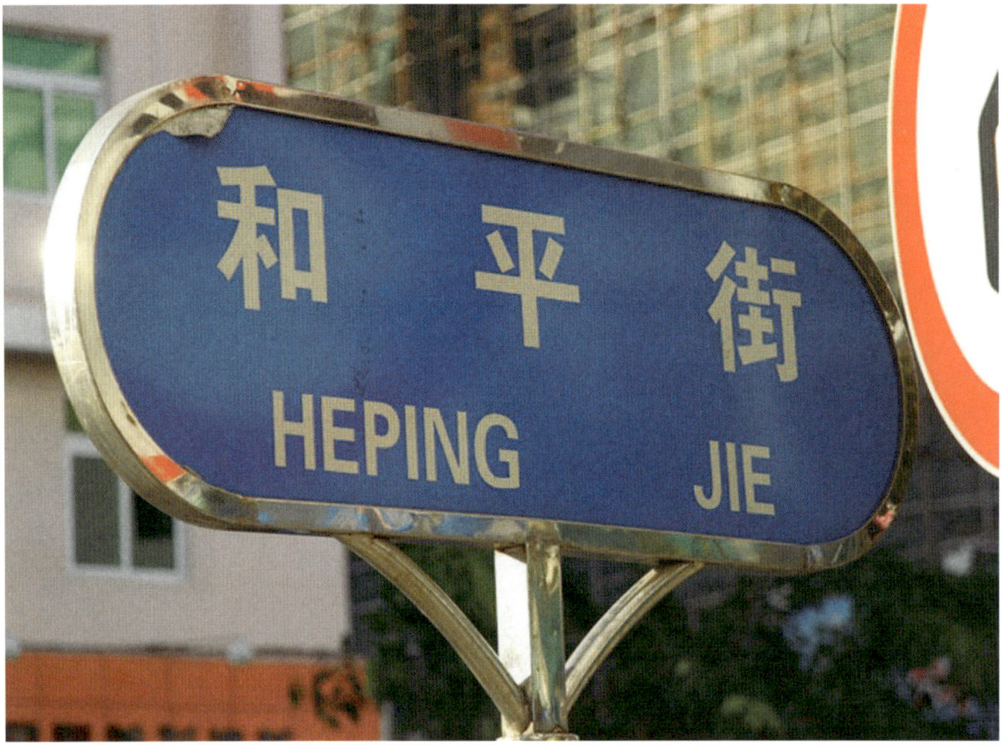

002

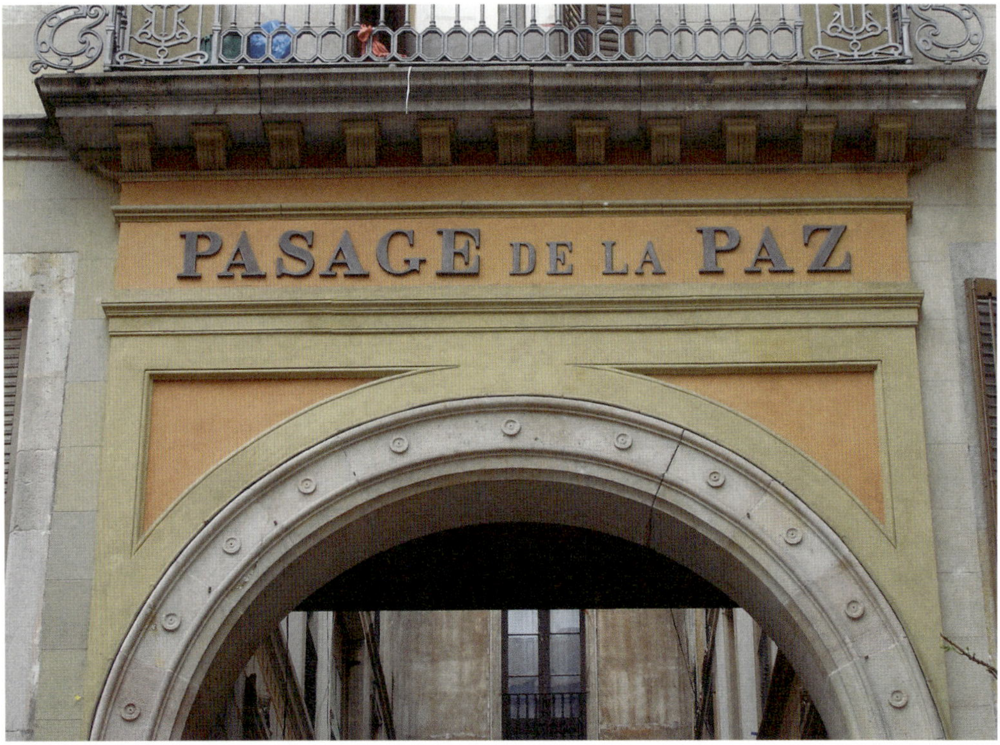

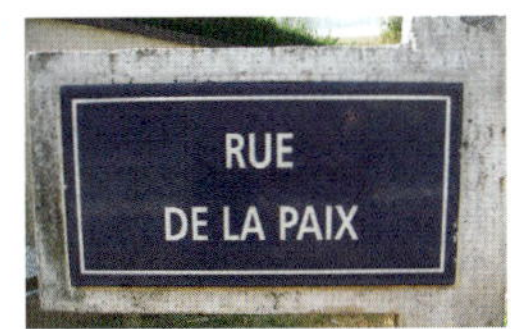

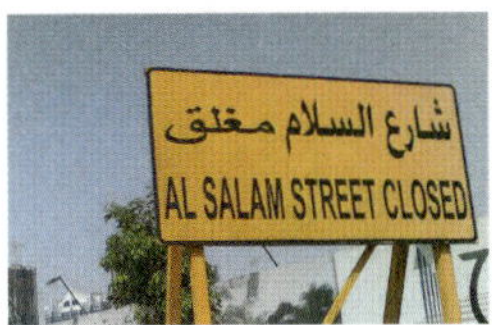

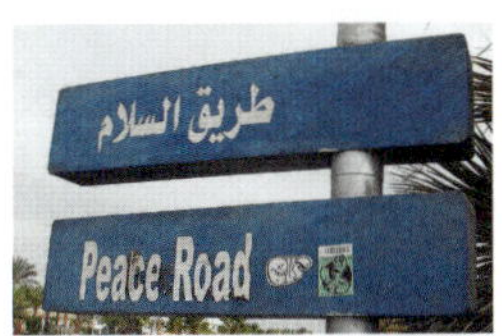

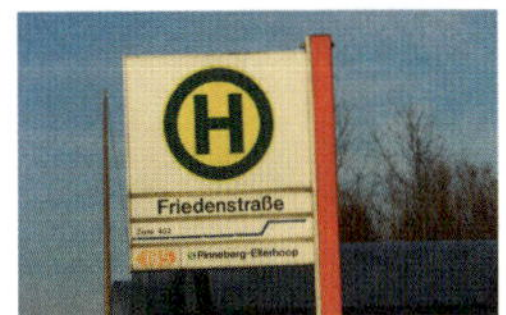

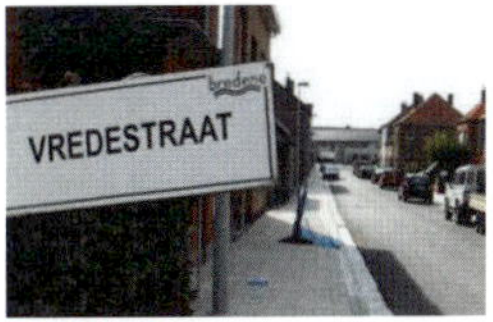

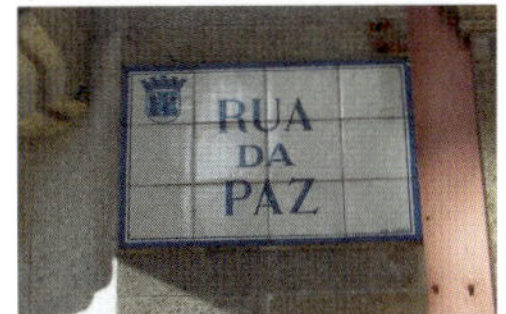

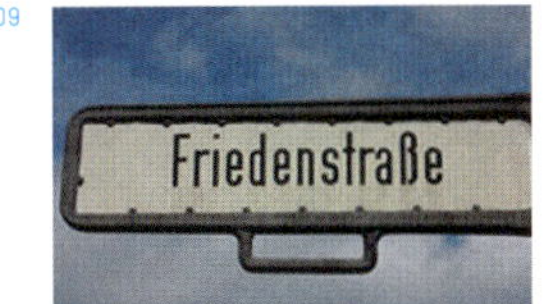

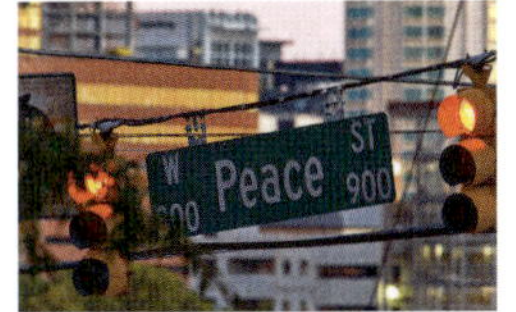

001 PEACE STREET, HAINAN, CHINA
CREATOR Provided by angelinaf
SOURCE www.flickr.com/photos/
angelspin/350862071/

002 PASAGE DE LA PAZ [PEACE PASSAGE],
BARCELONA, SPAIN
CREATOR Ruedi Baur

003 RUE DE LA PAIX [PEACE STREET], PARIS
SOURCE fr.wikipedia.org

004 AL SALAAM STREET [PEACE STREET],
CLOSED, ABU DHABI
SOURCE shalabieh.wordpress.com

005 PEACE ROAD, EGYPT
CREATOR Provided by Josh
SOURCE www.flickr.com/photos/
question-josh/3178088428/

006 HVV BUSHALTESTELLE FRIEDENSTRASSE
[HVV BUS STOP PEACE STREET]
SOURCE www.nachbarschaft.
immobilienscout24.de

007 VREDESTRAAT [PEACE STREET],
BREDENE, BELGIUM
SOURCE www.bredene-breed.be

008 RUA DA PAZ [PEACE STREET],
VISEU, PORTUGAL
SOURCE www.calcadaportuguesa-
roc2c.blogspot.ch

009 FRIEDENSTRASSE [PEACE STREET], BERLIN
SOURCE www.xhain.info

010 PEACE STREET, RALEIGH,
NORTH CAROLINA, USA
CREATOR Matt Robinson
SOURCE www.raleighskyline.com

001

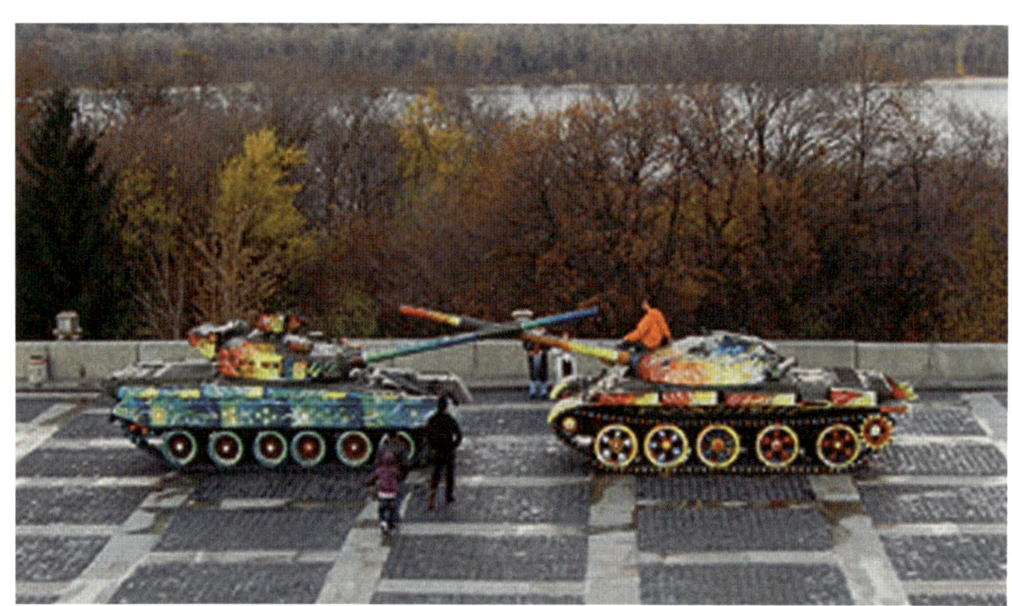

002
STINKFIST
COMES AROUND.
STOP THE IRAQ WAR.
Global Coalition For Peace.org

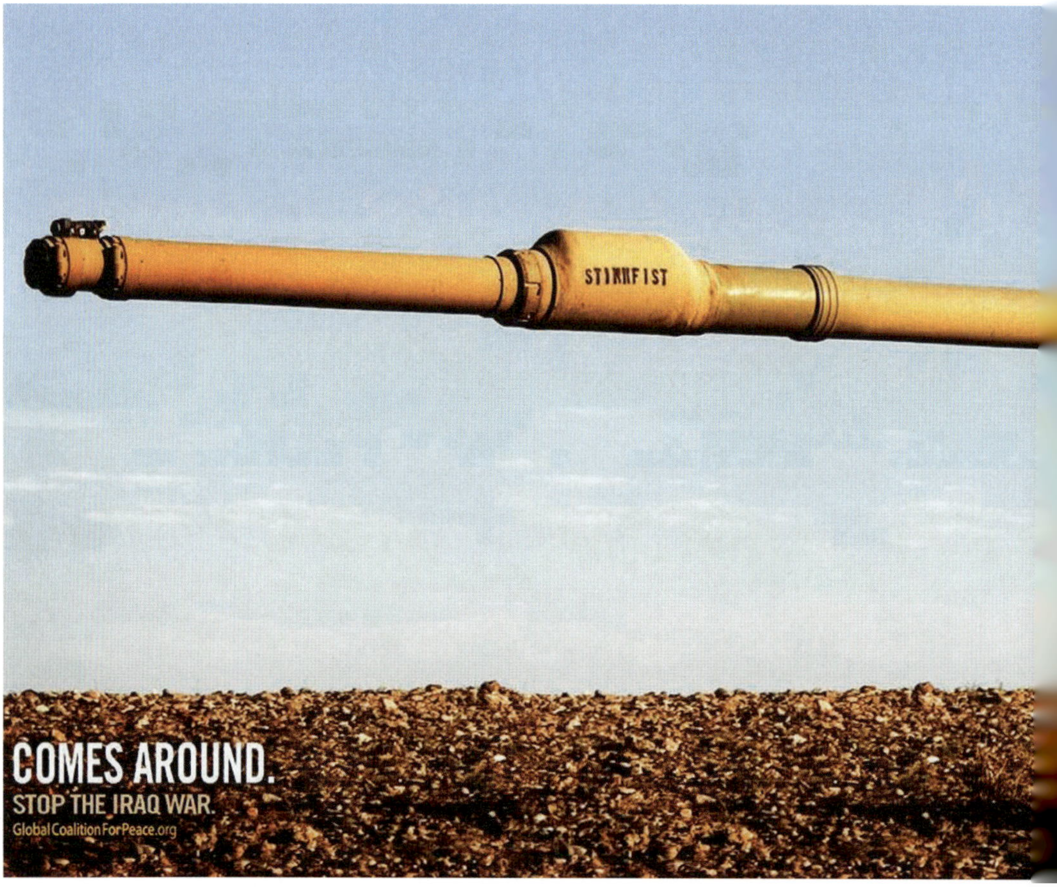

003

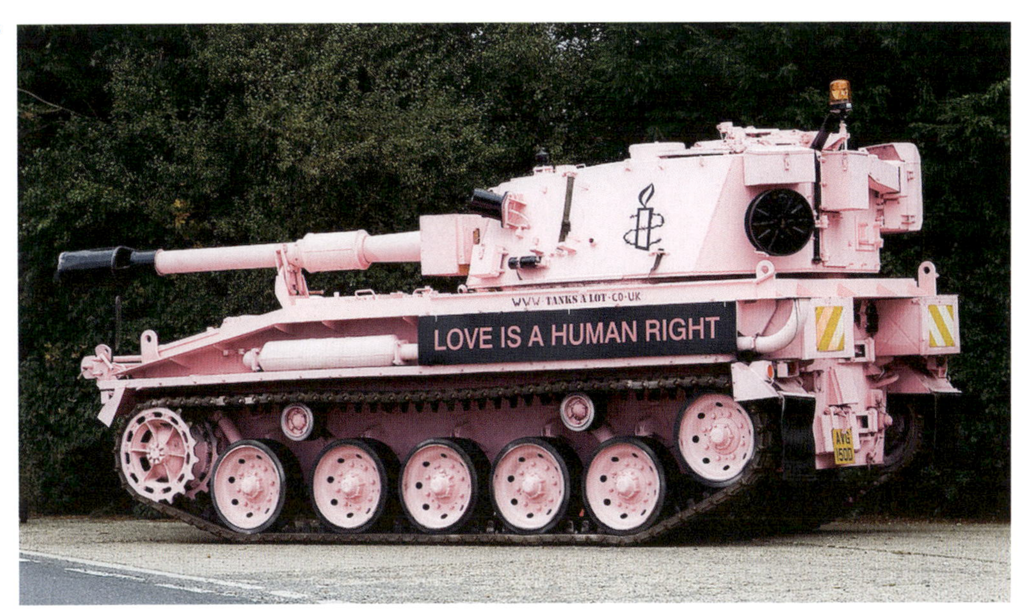

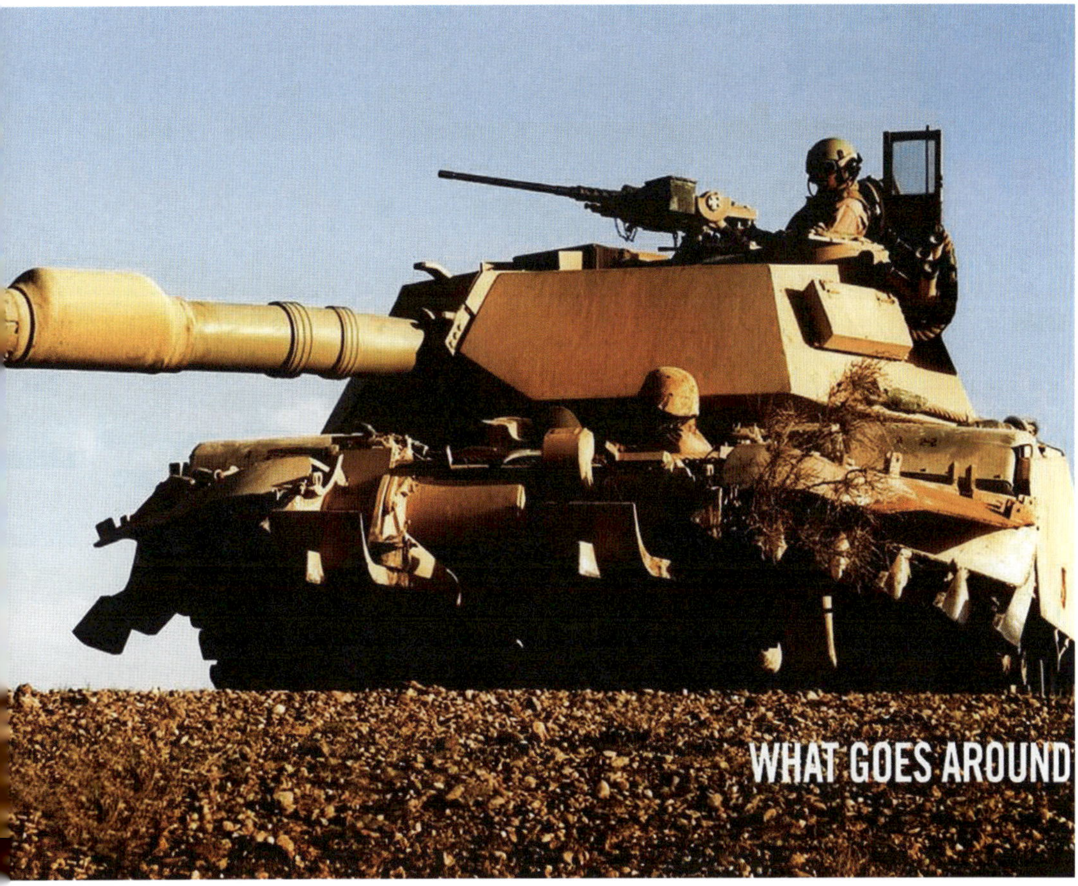

001 PEACE TANKS, KIEV
     CREATOR Provided by cooldogphotos
     SOURCE www.flickr.com/photos/
     cooldogphotos/2049621103/
     DATE 2007

002 WHAT GOES AROUND COMES AROUND
     CREATOR Big Ant
     SOURCE www.ibelieveinadv.com

003 PINK TANK, NORTHAMPTONSHIRE, UK
     CREATOR Provided by d.anny
     SOURCE www.flickr.com/photos/
     dannytucker/994025567/

TIANANMEN

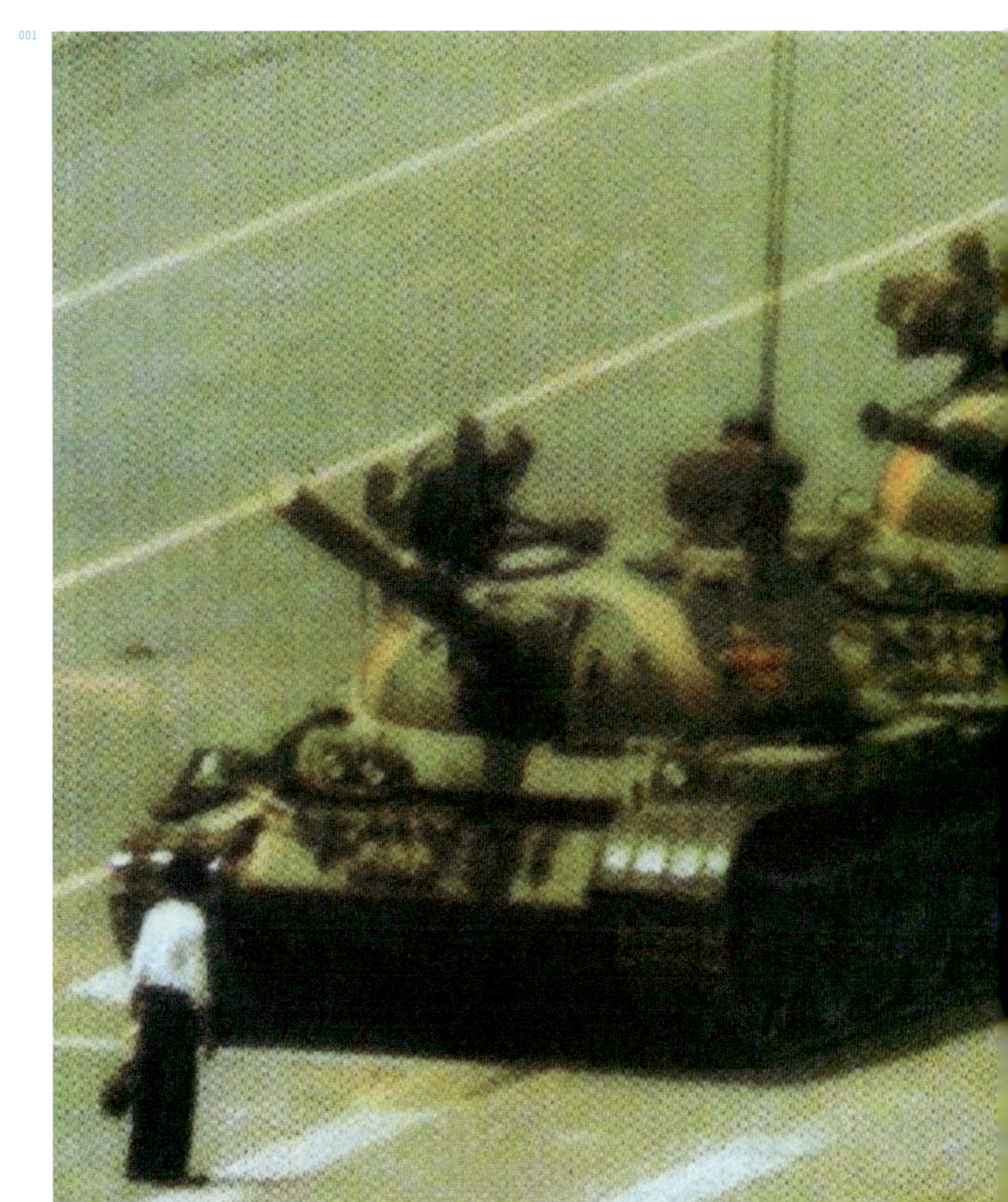

001 TANK MAN, CHANG'AN AVENUE
CREATOR Jeff Widener
SOURCE en.wikipedia.org
DATE 1989

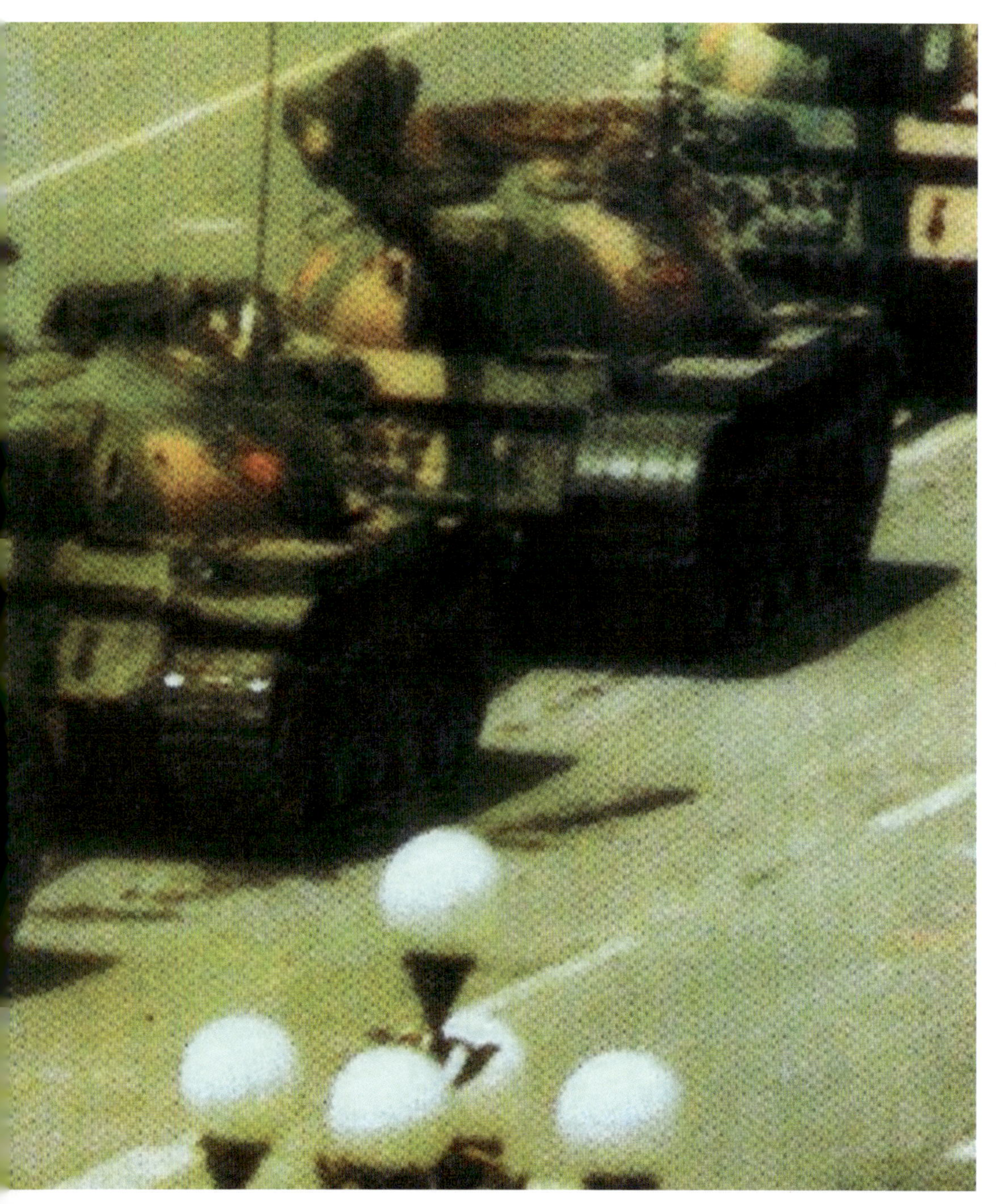

001

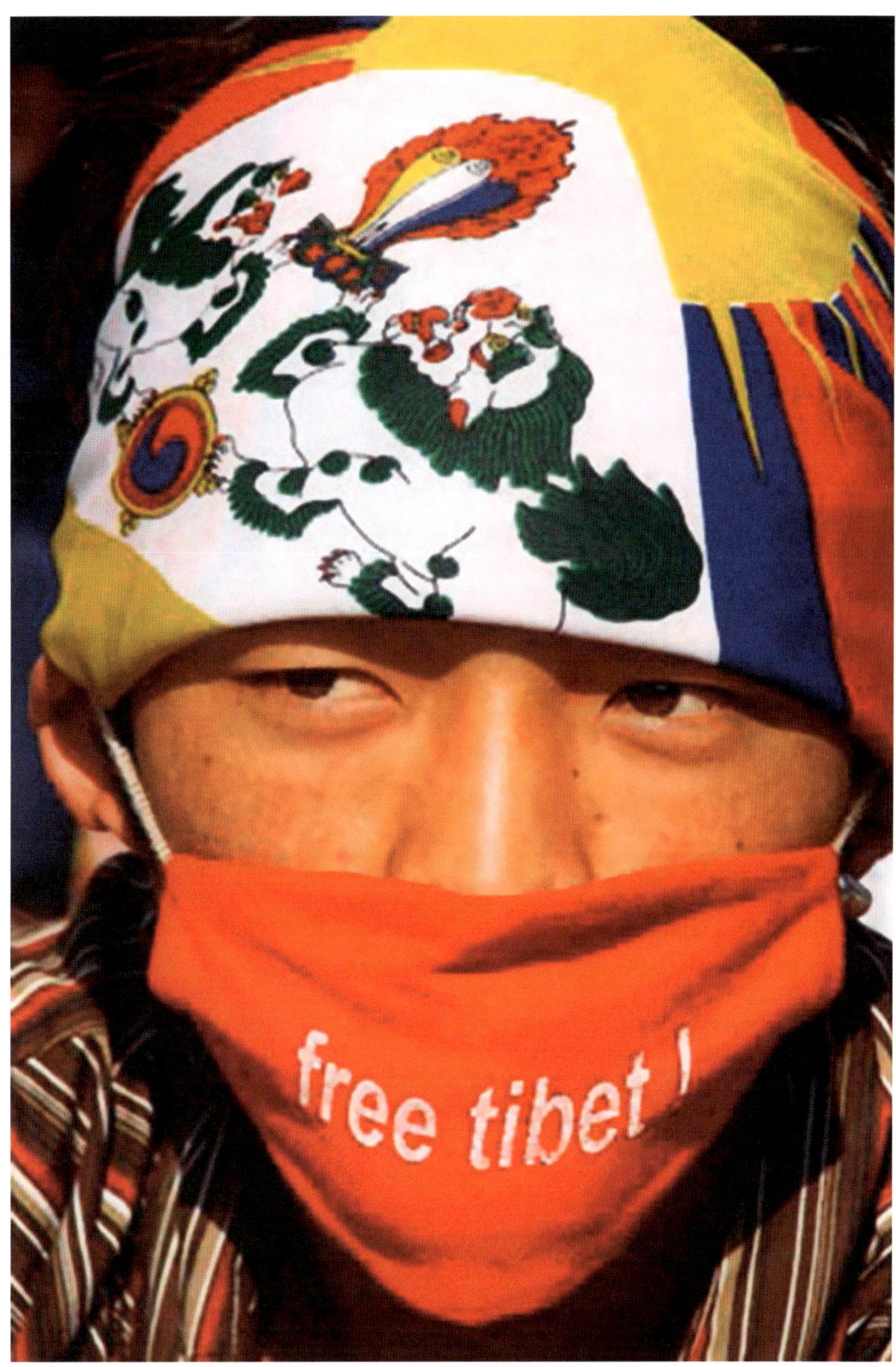

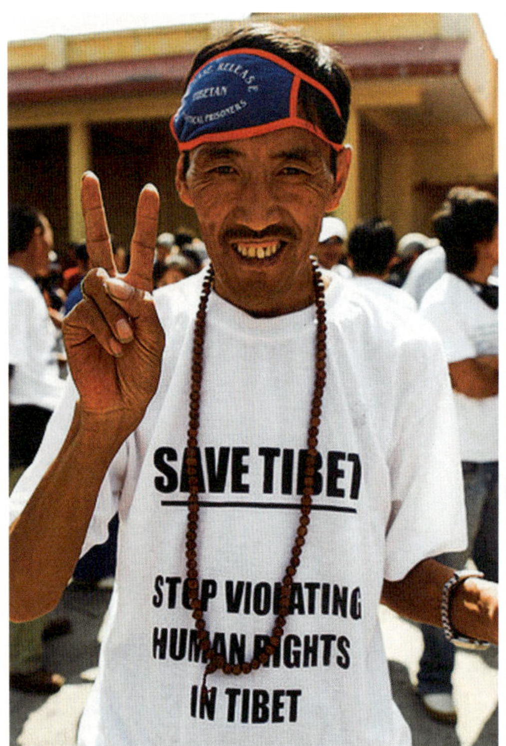
SAVE TIBET
STOP VIOLATING
HUMAN RIGHTS
IN TIBET

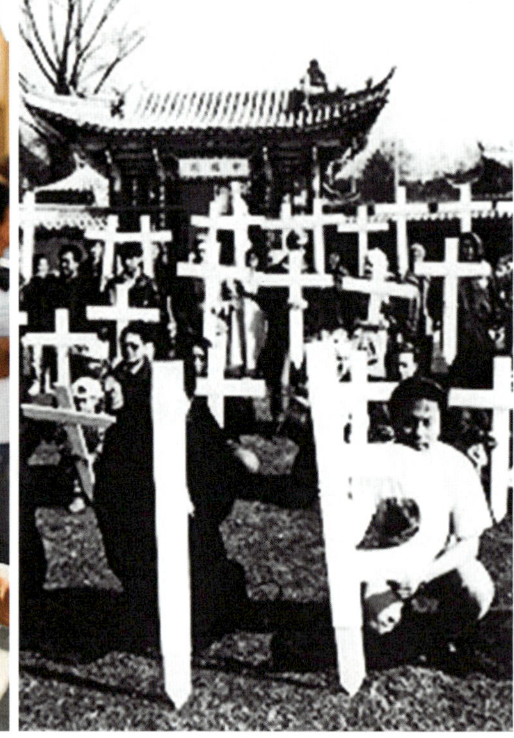

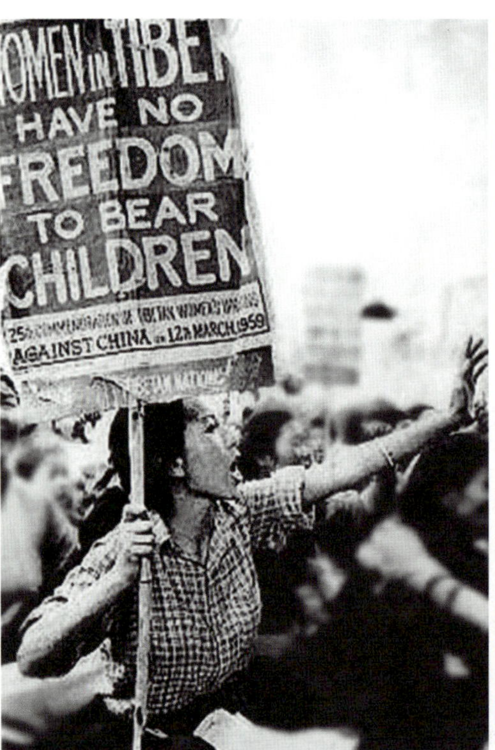
OMEN in TIBET
HAVE NO
FREEDOM
TO BEAR
CHILDREN
25th ANNIVERSARY OF TIBETAN WOMEN UPRISING
AGAINST CHINA on 12th MARCH 1959

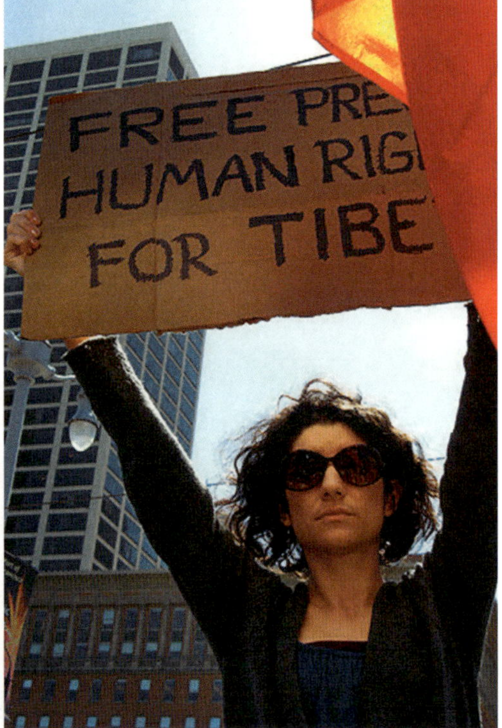
FREE PRE
HUMAN RIG
FOR TIBE

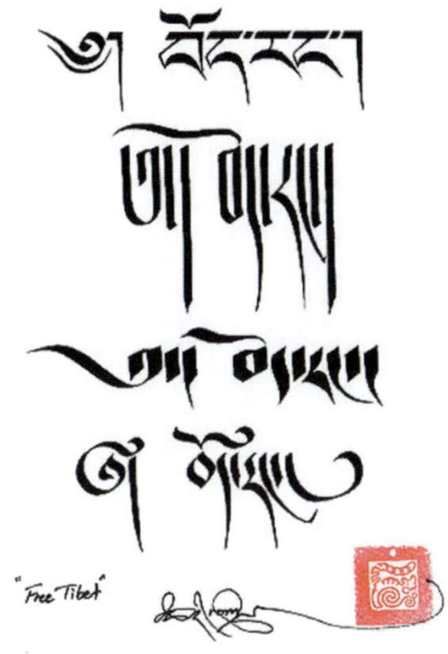
"Free Tibet"

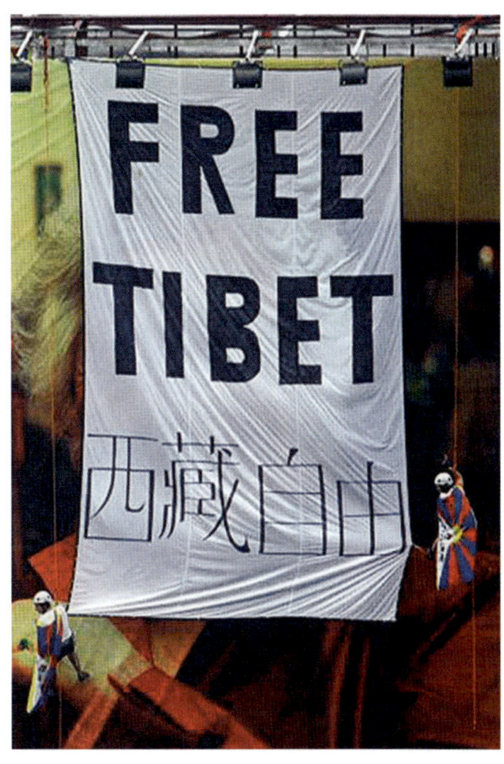
FREE
TIBET
西藏自由

The games of Beijing. With Tibet.
Free Tibet

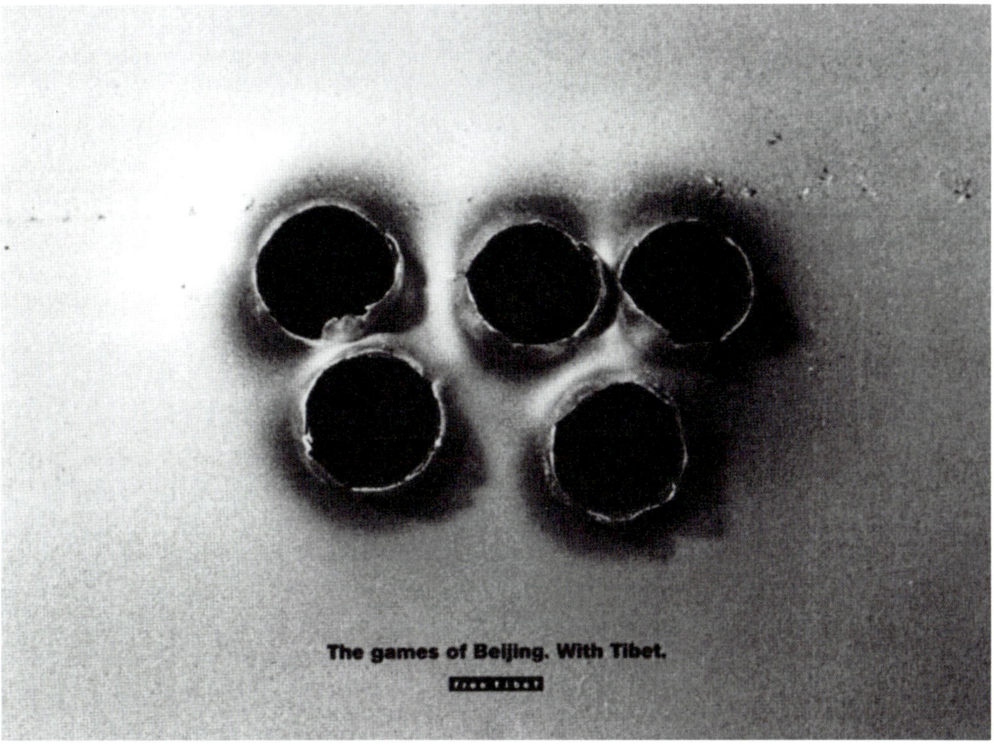

001 FREE TIBET
     SOURCE images.photomania.com

002 STOP VIOLATING HUMAN RIGHTS
     IN TIBET, KATHMANDU
     Buddhist monks and nuns led
     a silent protest of about 5,000
     people who held candles and
     covered their mouths with masks.
     Starting from a hilltop stupa the
     march proceeded to the office of
     the United Nations' rights group,
     where the demonstrators requested
     that UN observers be dispatched
     to monitor the situation in Tibet.
     CREATOR Provided by zorro
     SOURCE www.flickr.com/photos/
     cactus23/2449225260/

003 TIBET
     CREATOR McCann-Erickson S.A.
     SOURCE Plakatsammlung Museum
     für Gestaltung Zürich

004 WOMEN IN TIBET HAVE NO FREEDOM
     TO BEAR CHILDREN
     CREATOR Provided by Ark-Angel
     SOURCE www.flickr.com/photos/
     7692825@N03/2475750966/

005 FREE PRESS, HUMAN RIGHTS FOR TIBET
     CREATOR Provided by tingley
     SOURCE www.flickr.com/photos/
     tingley/2401377711/

006 FREE TIBET [4 TIBETAN SCRIPT STYLES]
     CREATOR Tashi Mannox
     SOURCE nn.wikipedia.org

007 FREE TIBET [IN ENGLISH + CHINESE]
     Two pro-Tibet activists rappeled
     from the top of a large
     Olympic billboard and unfurled a
     375-square-foot/115-square-meter
     banner in front of Chinese state
     television's new headquarters
     in Beijing.
     SOURCE latimesblogs.latimes.com
     DATE 16 August 2008

008 THE GAMES OF BEIJING WITH TIBET
     CREATOR Euro RSCG Switzerland
     SOURCE Steven Heller and Carol
     Wells, eds., *The Graphic
     Imperative: International Posters
     for Peace, Social Justice, and the
     Environment, 1965-2005* [Boston:
     Massachusetts College of Arts,
     2005], p. 32.

001

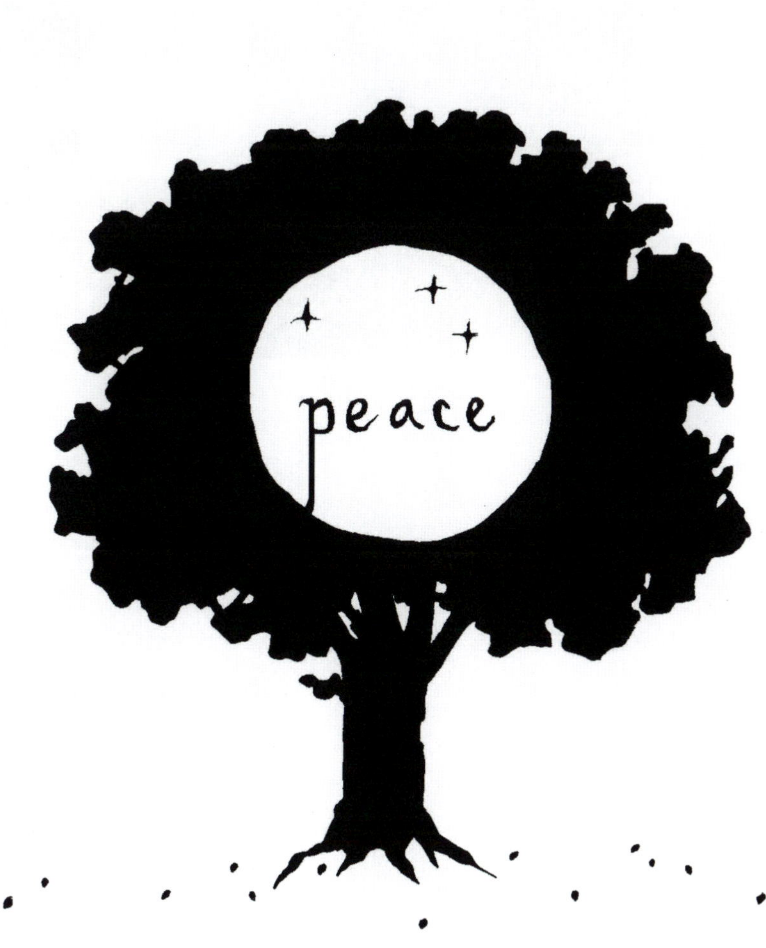

002
003

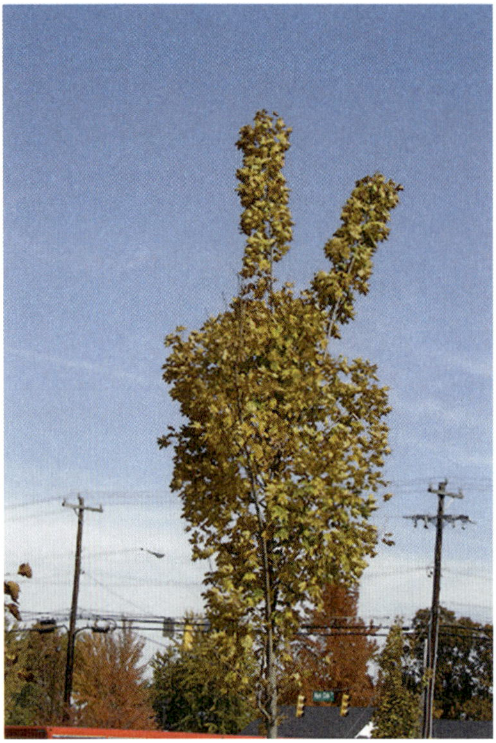

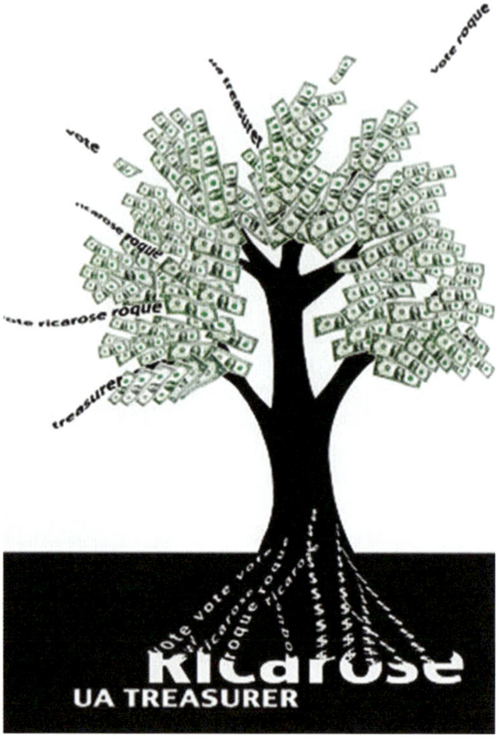

004
005

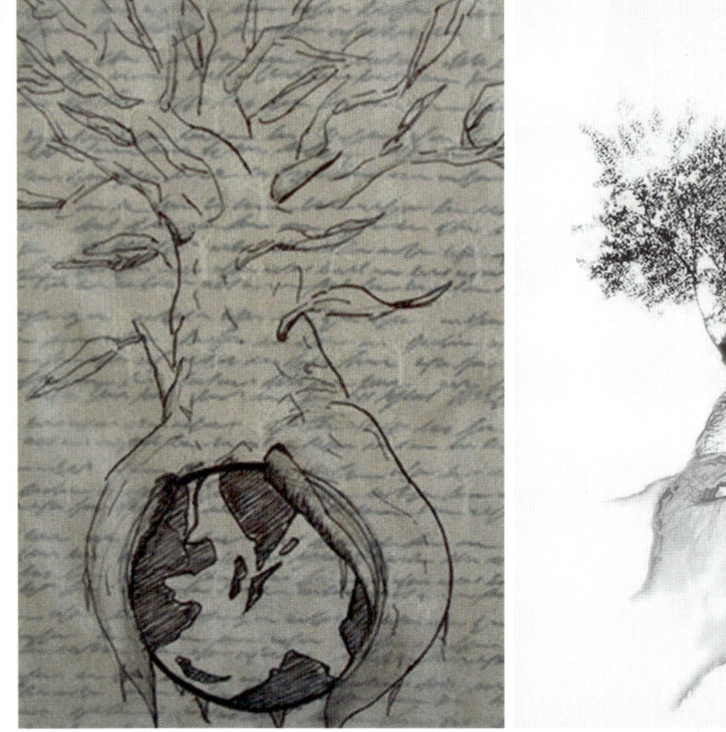
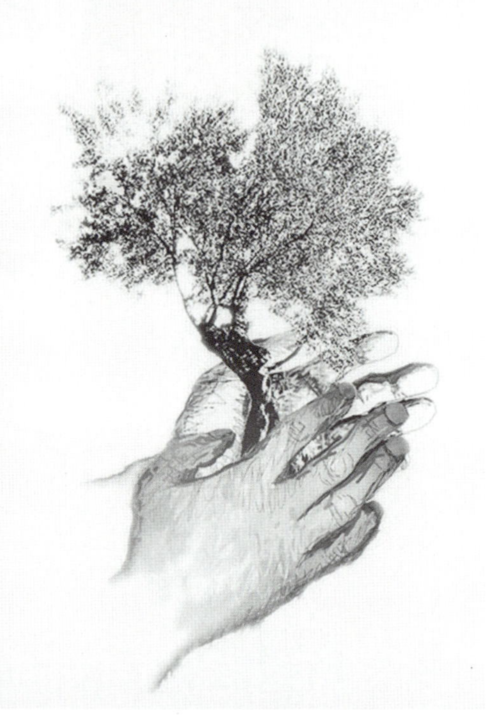

006
007

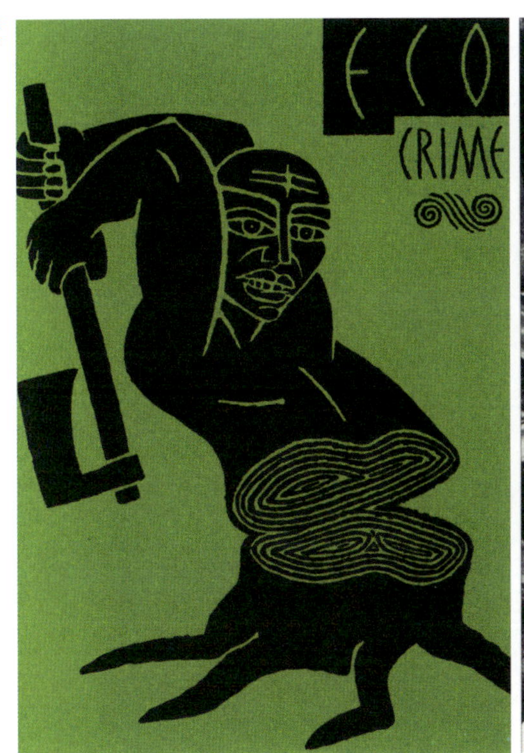

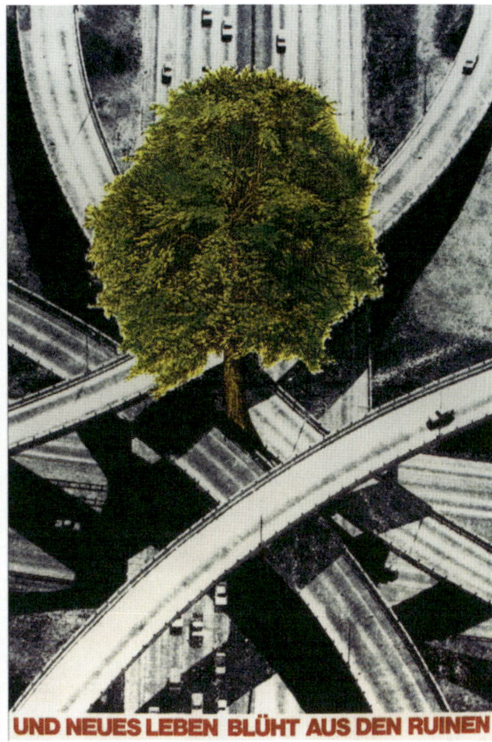

008
009

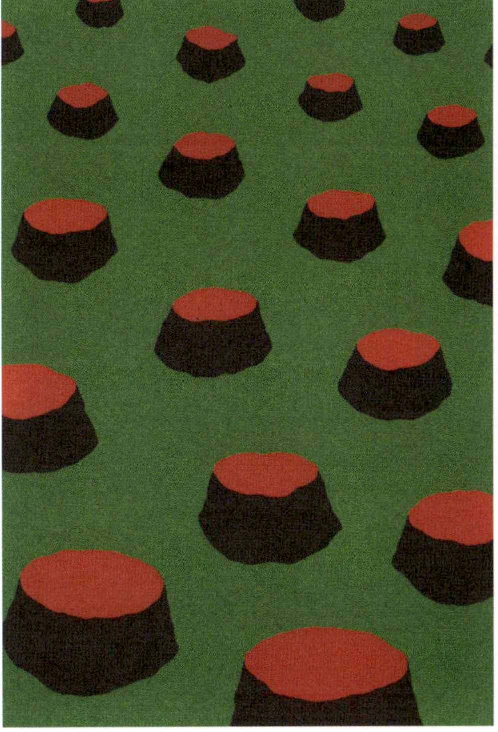

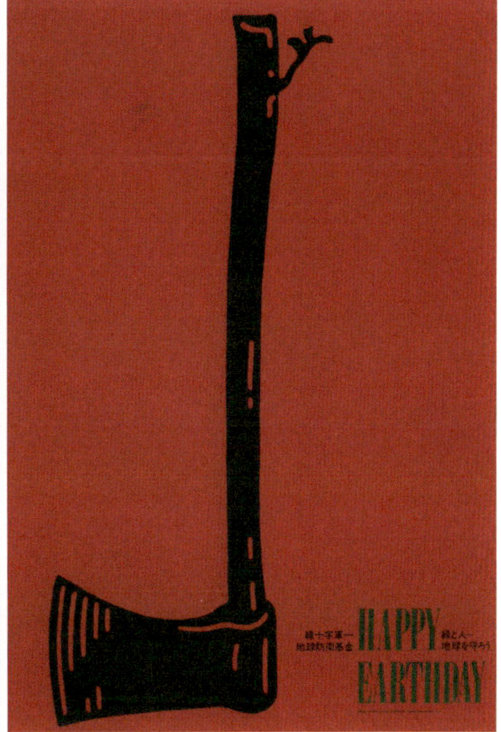

010
011

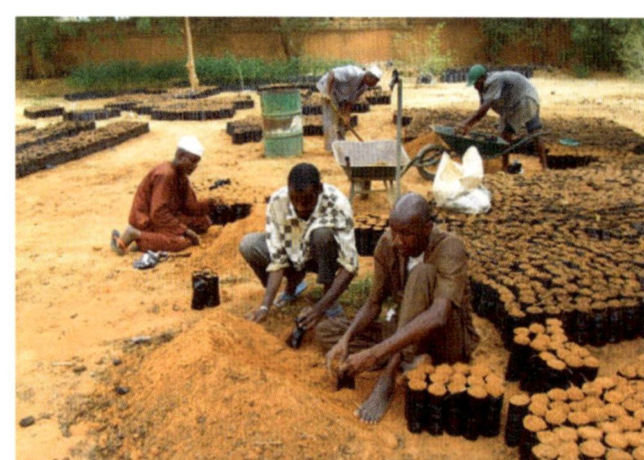

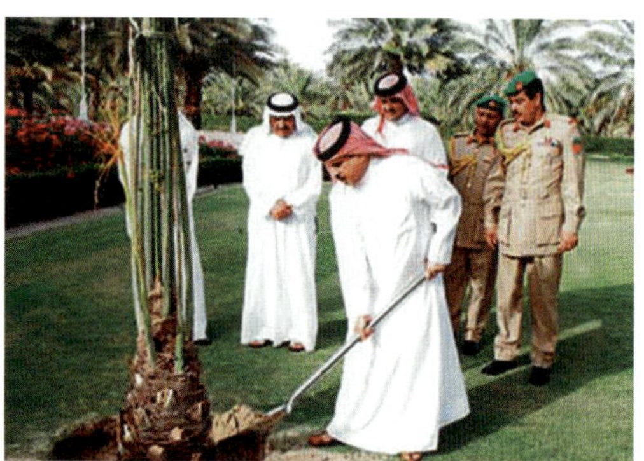

012
013

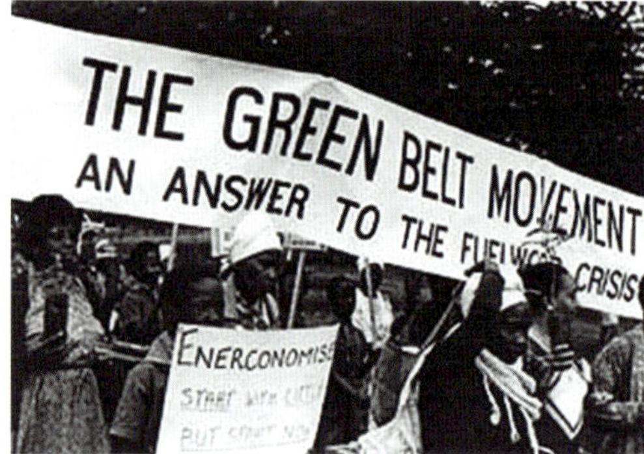

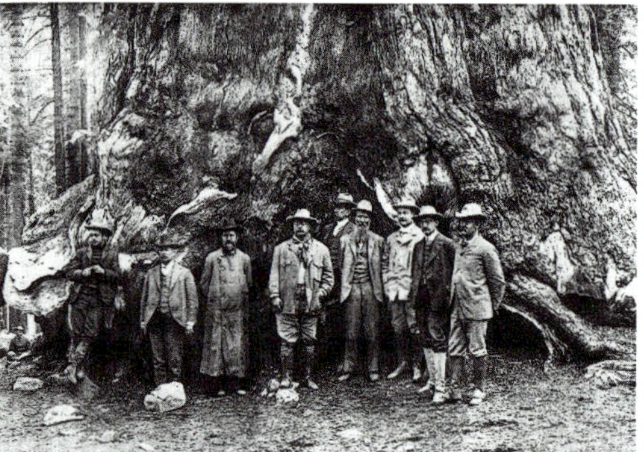

014
015

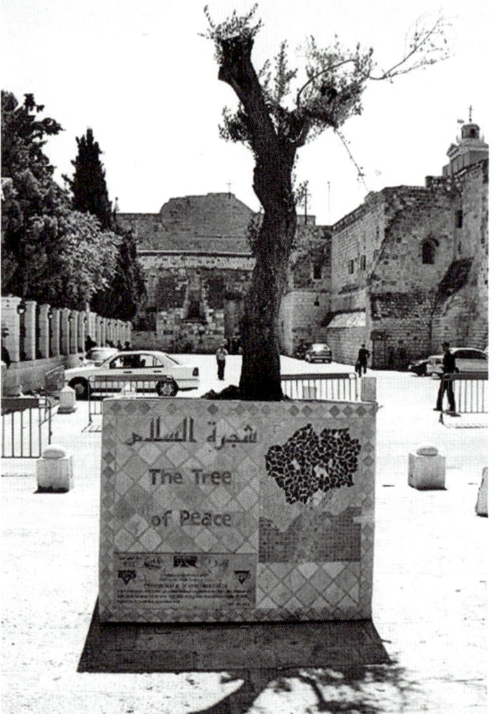

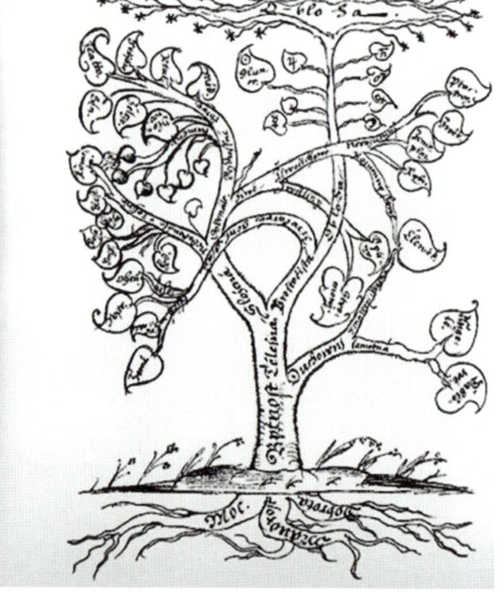

001 PEACE TREE
CREATOR Provided by alphanunu
SOURCE www.flickr.com/photos/
alphanunu/980382146/

002 PEACE TREE
CREATOR Provided by semicursedlife
SOURCE www.flickr.com/photos/
semicursedlife/286538856/

003 RICAROSE, UA TREASURER
CREATOR Ricarose Roque
SOURCE acg.media.mit.edu/

004 UNTITLED
SOURCE Beiträge macht Bilder

005 1000 OLIVE TREES FOR PEACE
CREATOR l'association Palestine
Amitie [Besançon]
SOURCE reseaudolepaixjusteau
procheorient.blogspot.ch/

006 ECO CRIME
CREATOR Luba Lukova
SOURCE Steven Heller and
Carol Wells, eds., *The Graphic
Imperative: International Posters
for Peace, Social Justice, and
the Environment, 1965-2005*
[Boston: Massachusetts College
of Arts, 2005], p. 47.

007 UND NEUES LEBEN BLÜHT AUS
DEN RUINEN
[AND NEW LIFE RISES FROM
THE RUINS]
CREATOR Klaus Staeck
SOURCE Steven Heller and
Carol Wells, eds., *The Graphic
Imperative: International Posters
for Peace, Social Justice, and
the Environment, 1965-2005*
[Boston: Massachusetts College
of Arts, 2005], p. 47.

008 DEAD TREES
CREATOR Nikolaus Troxler
SOURCE Steven Heller and
Carol Wells, eds., *The Graphic
Imperative: International Posters
for Peace, Social Justice, and
the Environment, 1965-2005*
[Boston: Massachusetts College
of Arts, 2005], p. 48.

009 HAPPY BIRTHDAY
CREATOR Shigeo Fukuda
SOURCE Steven Heller and
Carol Wells, eds., *The Graphic
Imperative: International Posters
for Peace, Social Justice, and
the Environment, 1965-2005*
[Boston: Massachusetts College
of Arts, 2005], p. 48.

010 FILLING UP PROCESS OF THE POTS
SOURCE www.tree-nation.com

011 UNITED NATIONS ENVIRONMENT
PROGRAMME
Bahrain: His Majesty Hamad Bin
Isa Al-Khalifa, King of Bahrain
planting a tree.
SOURCE www.unep.org

012 THE GREEN BELT MOVEMENT
SOURCE www.womenaid.org

013 PRESIDENT ROOSEVELT WITH
NATURALIST AND CONSERVATIONIST
JOHN MUIR
SOURCE portal.picture-alliance.com
DATE 1903

014 TREE OF PEACE, ISRAEL
CREATOR Provided by jacqueline_r
SOURCE www.flickr.com/photos/
jacqueline_r/379535578/

015 TREE OF LIFE
CREATOR Komensky
SOURCE commons.wikimedia.org

001

NOBEL PEACE PRIZE 1988
UNITED NATIONS PEACE-KEEPING

002
003

UNITED NATIONS
We, 1,750,000,000 People
for understanding—for peace

United Nations Day
OCTOBER 24TH
Peace Works

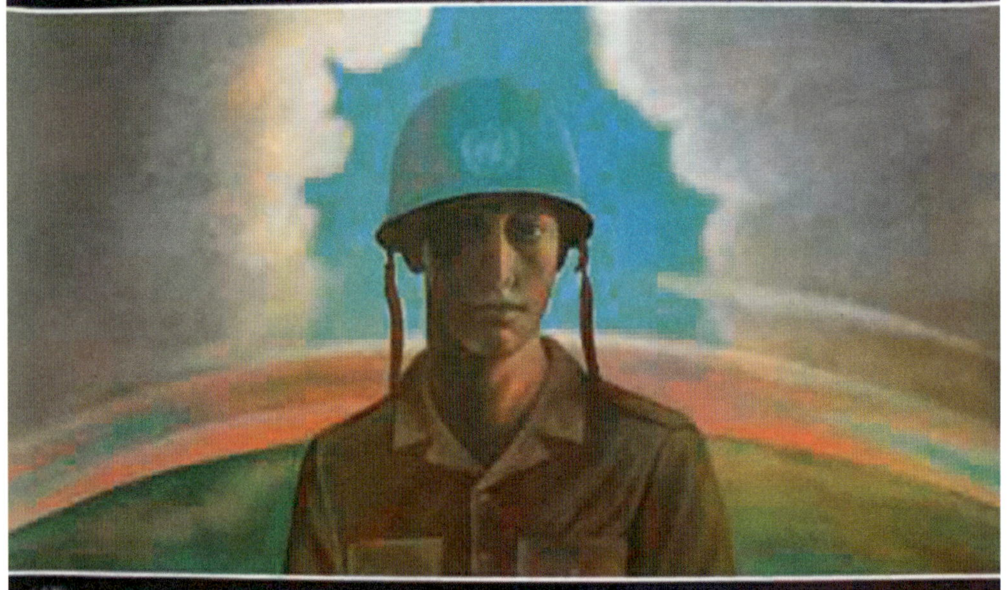

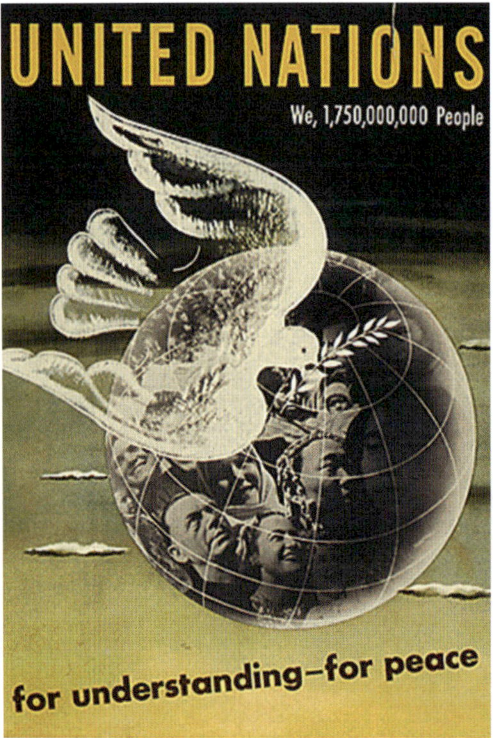

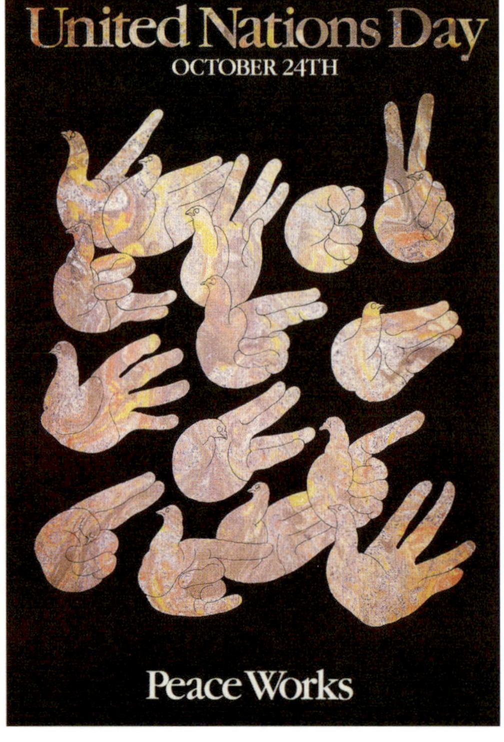

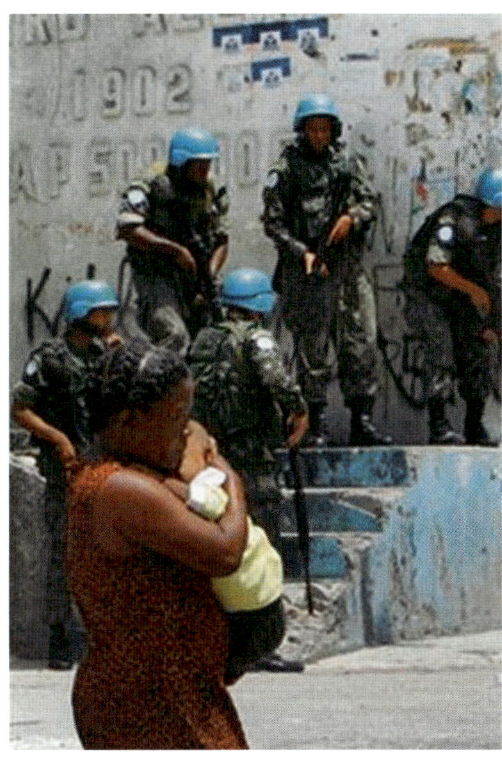

004

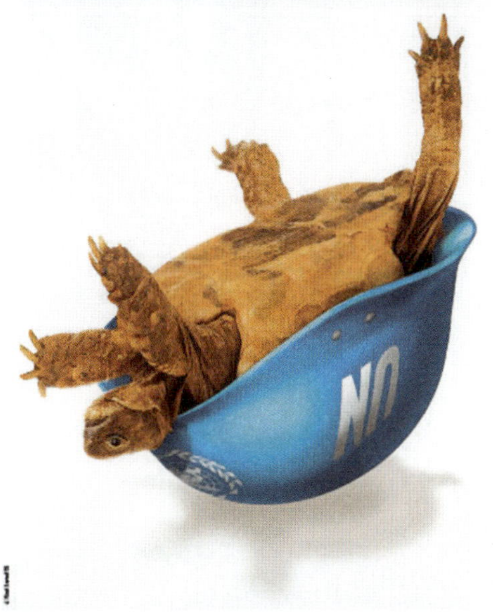

005

001 NOBEL PEACE PRIZE 1988, UNITED
NATIONS PEACE-KEEPING
SOURCE webapp1.dlib.indiana.edu

002 UNITED NATIONS POSTER
SOURCE Unknown
DATE 1945

003 PEACE WORKS
CREATOR Milton Glaser
SOURCE JAGDA Peace Posters
International Exhibition

004 HAITI
SOURCE www.haitiechange.org

005 50TH ANNIVERSARY
Criticism of the UN and its role
in the Bosnian war.
CREATOR Yossi Lemel
SOURCE www.lemel.co.il
DATE 1995

001
002

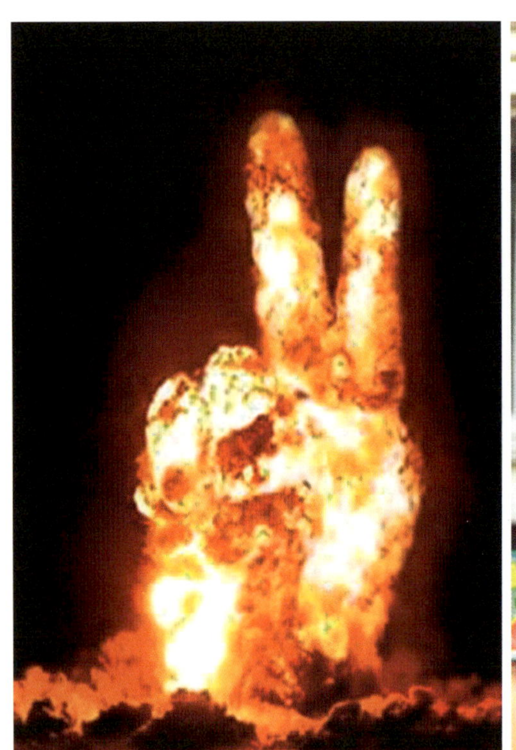

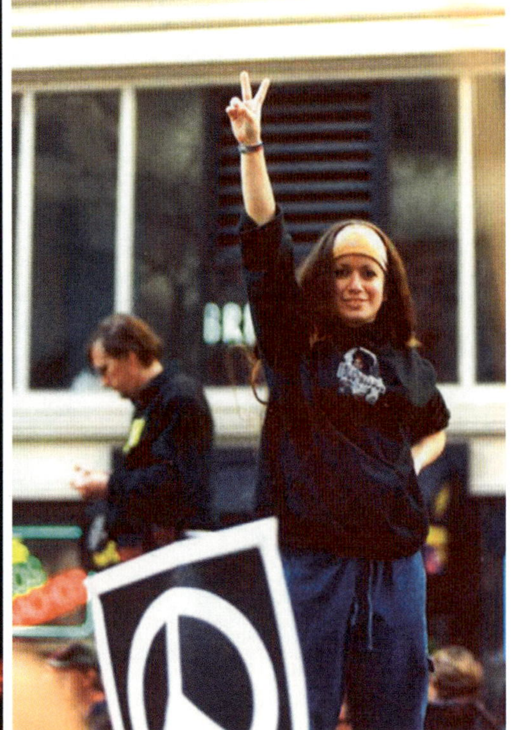

003
004

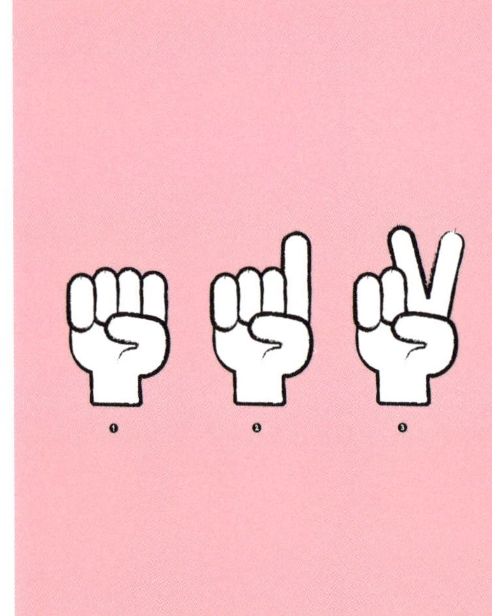

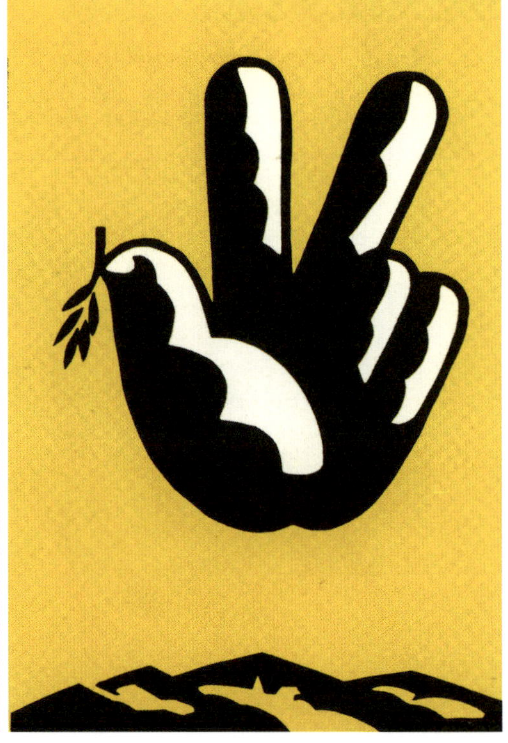

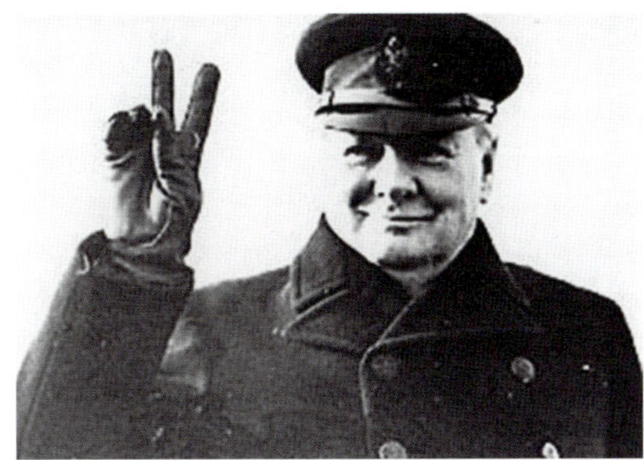

005

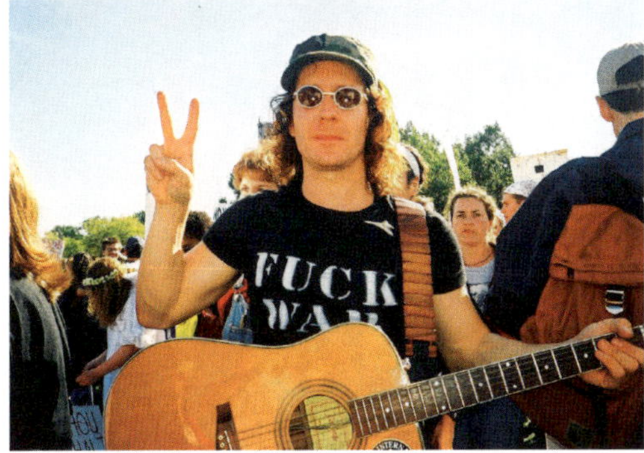

006

007

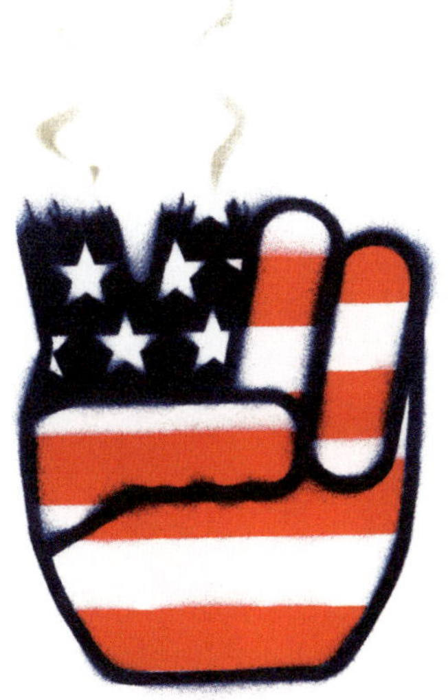

001 UNTITLED
SOURCE favoritechoses.typepad.com

002 SAN FRANCISCO
SOURCE www.sierrafoot.org

003 UNTITLED
CREATOR Frei Christoph
SOURCE Unknown

004 UNTITLED
CREATOR Gerd Kehrer
SOURCE JAGDA Peace Posters
International Exhibition

005 WINSTON CHURCHILL
SOURCE www.wwwarketing.coma

006 FUCK WAR
CREATOR Danny Hammontree / Ed Hale
SOURCE Unknown

007 UNTITLED
SOURCE John Carr, ed., *Yo! What
Happened to Peace?* [Rome: Federico
Zesi, 2007].

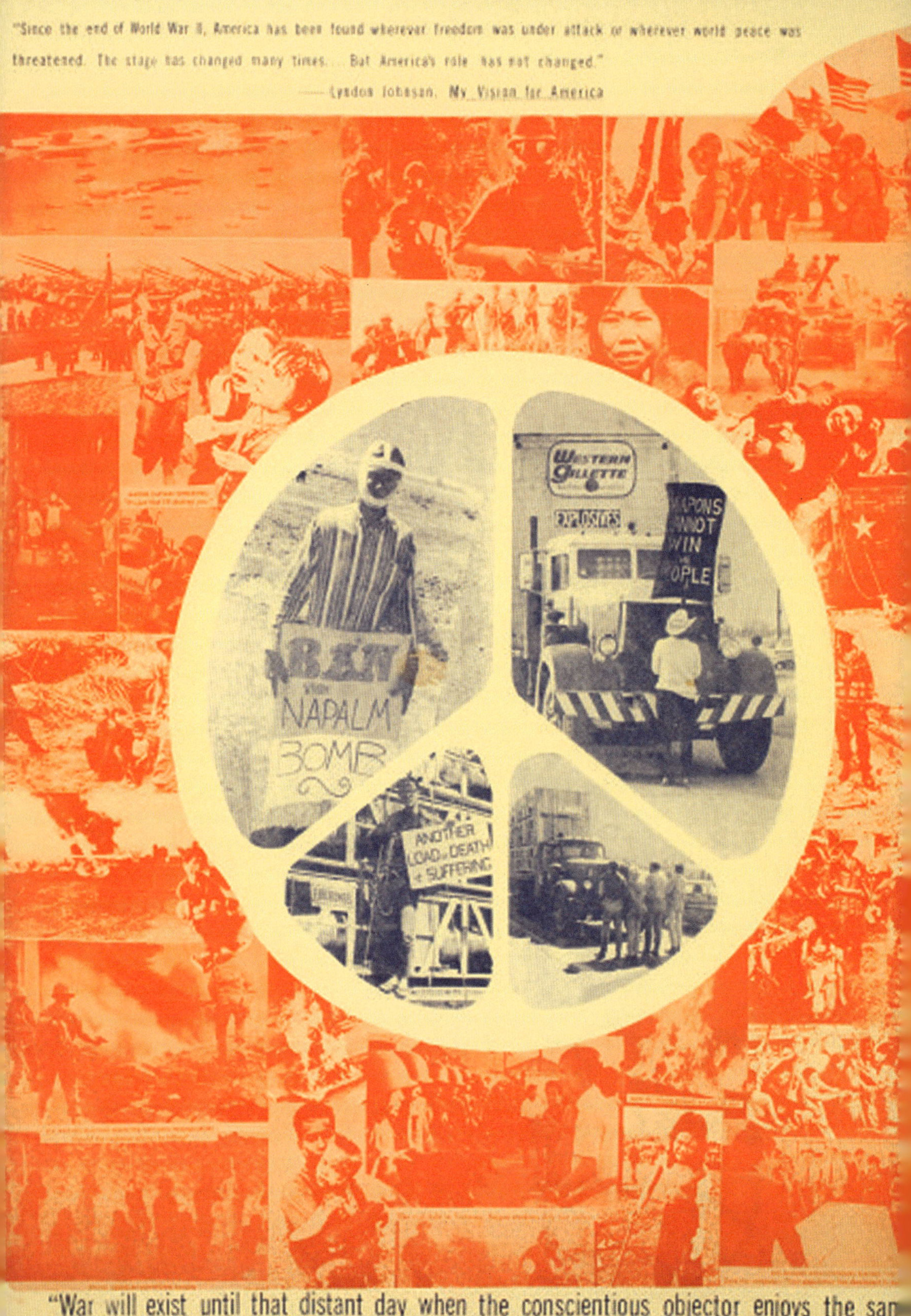

"Since the end of World War II, America has been found wherever freedom was under attack or wherever world peace was threatened. The stage has changed many times... But America's role has not changed."
— Lyndon Johnson, My Vision for America
BAN NAPALM BOMB
Western Gillette
EXPLOSIVES
WEAPONS CANNOT WIN THE PEOPLE
ANOTHER LOAD OF DEATH & SUFFERING
"War will exist until that distant day when the conscientious objector enjoys the same reputation and prestige that the warrior does today." —— John Fitzgerald Kennedy
PORT CHICAGO VIGIL - CONTINUOUS WITNESS AGAINST WAR SINCE HIROCHIMA DAY, 6 AUGUST 1965. FIFTY-EIGHT CITIZENS HAVE BEEN ARRESTED FOR CONFRONTING THE WAR MACHINE AT AMERICA'S MAJOR MUNITIONS PORT (THE CONCORD NAVAL WEAPONS STATION AT SAN FRANCISCO'S SUISUN BAY WHICH SHIPS 96% OF ALL MILITARY EXPLOSIVES INCLUDING NAPALM. THE DEFENDANTS ARE NOW PUTTING THE GOVERNMENT ON TRIAL FOR VIOLATIONS OF THE 1954 GENEVA ACCORDS, THE UNITED NATIONS CHARTER, THE NUREMBERG PRECEDENTS, AND THE UNITED STATES CONSTITUTION.
PORT CHICAGO DEFENDANTS COMM.
P.O. BOX 897, BERKELEY, CALIF.
DESIGN © 1967 PerCv-IntCv.

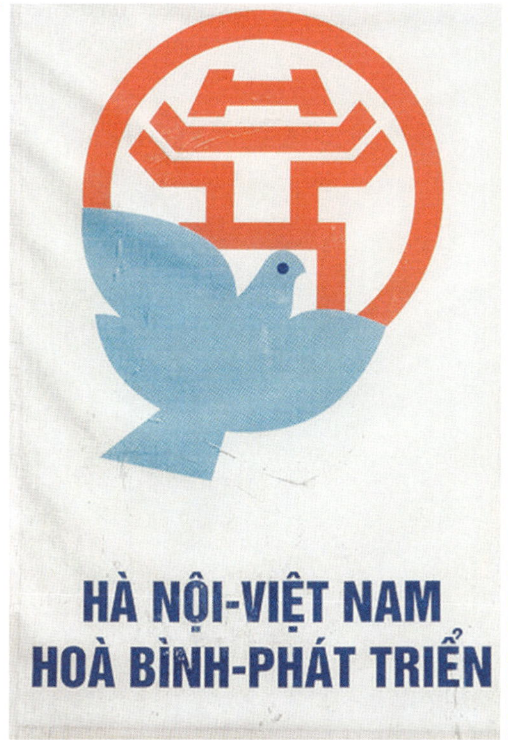
HÀ NỘI-VIỆT NAM
HOÀ BÌNH-PHÁT TRIỂN

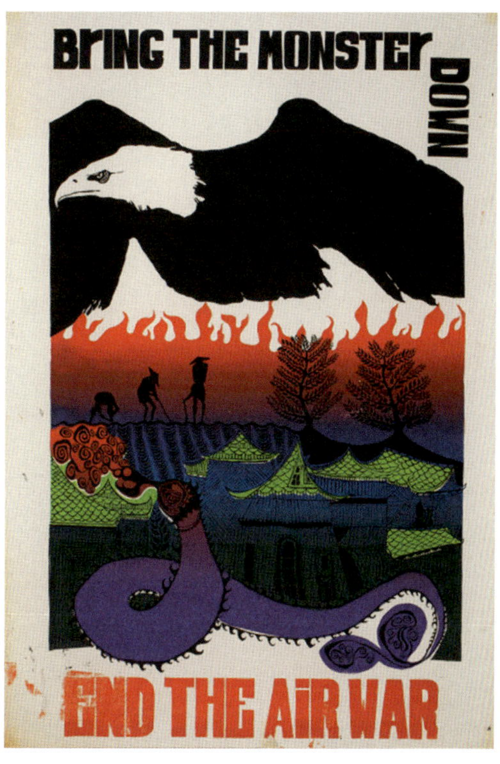
BRING THE MONSTER DOWN
END THE AIR WAR

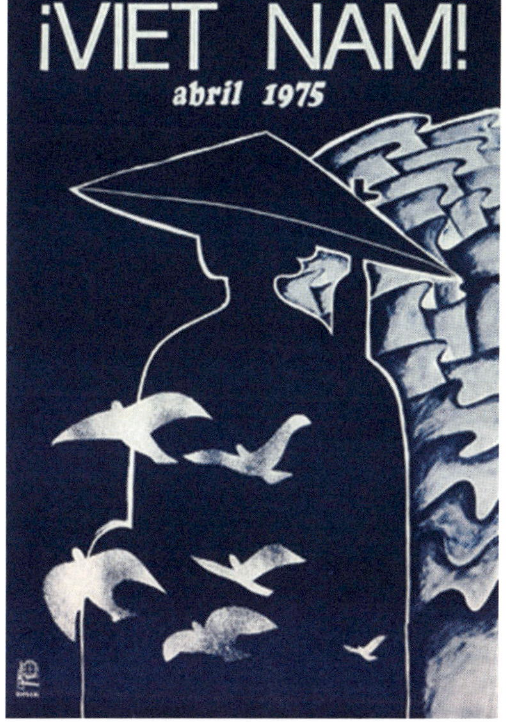
¡VIET NAM!
abril 1975

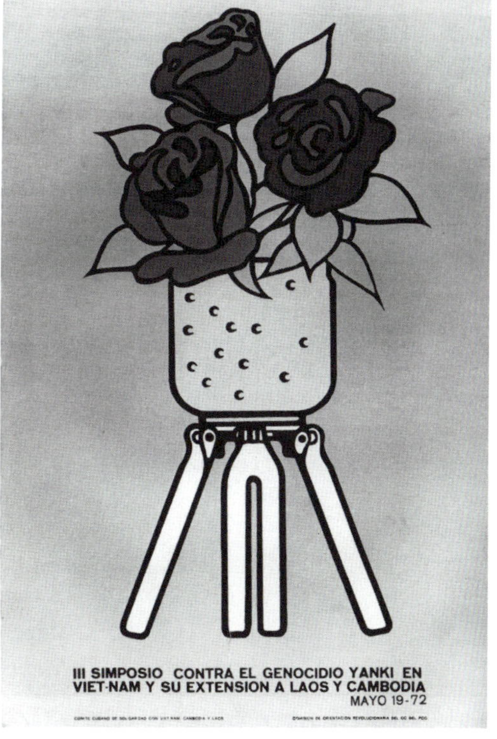
III SIMPOSIO CONTRA EL GENOCIDIO YANKI EN
VIET-NAM Y SU EXTENSION A LAOS Y CAMBODIA
MAYO 19-72

006
007

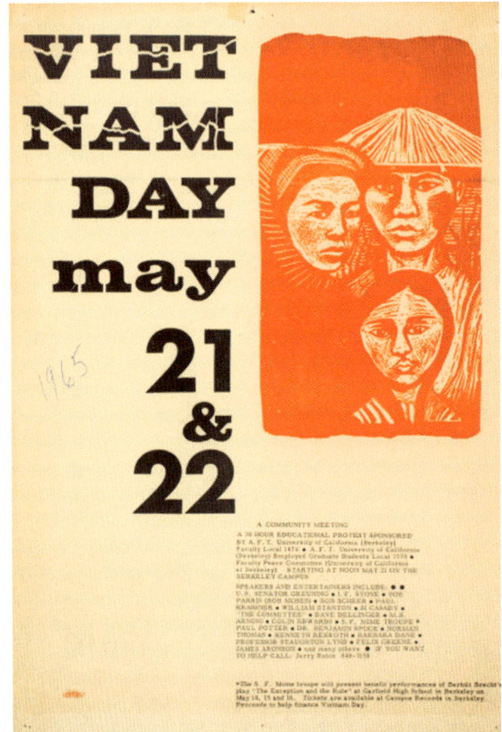

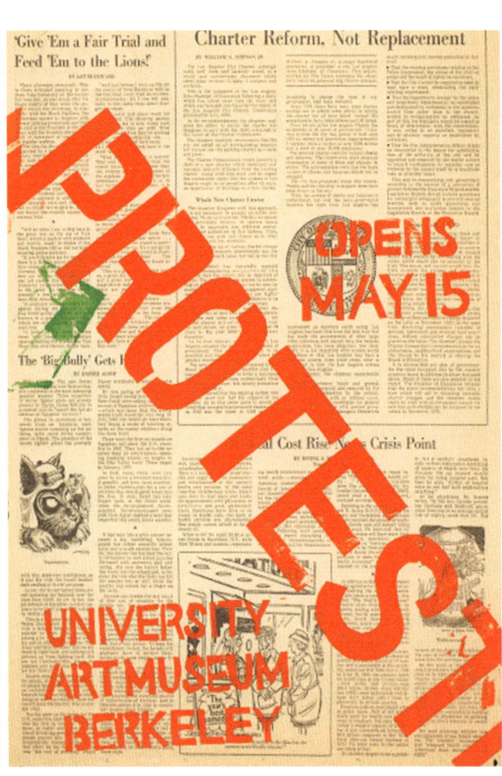

008
009

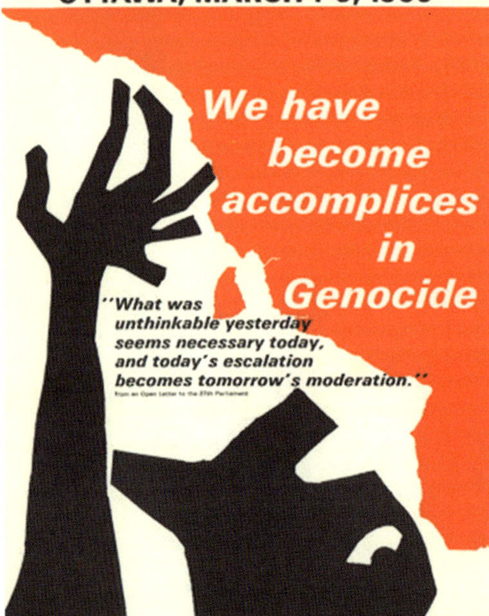

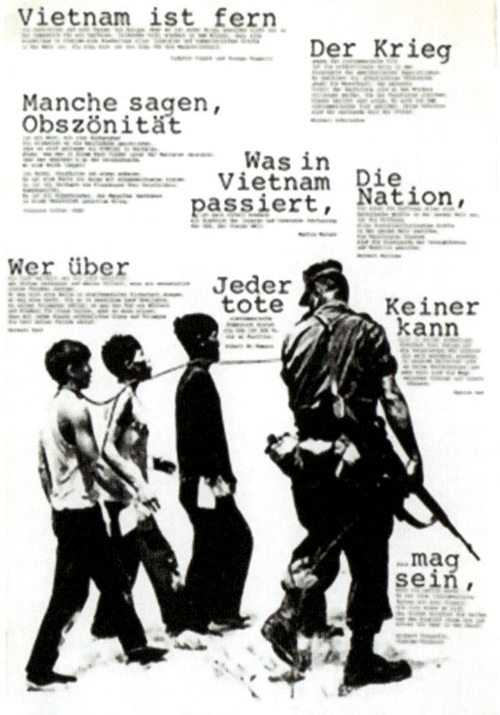

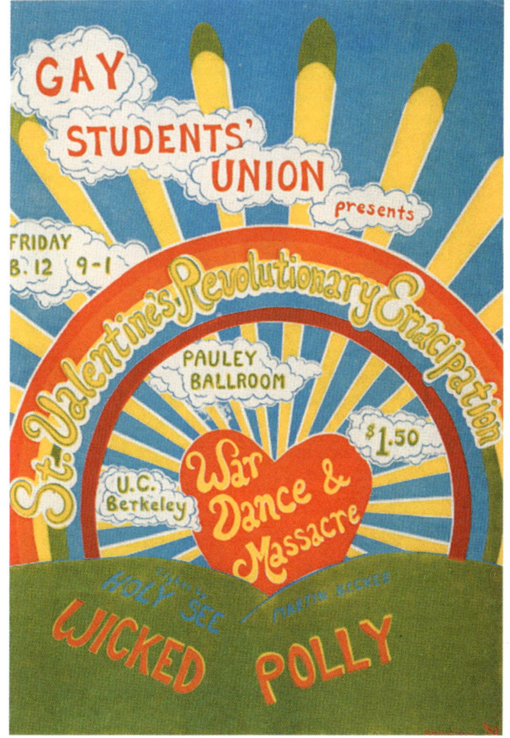
GAY
STUDENTS'
UNION
presents
FRIDAY
B. 12 9-1
St. Valentine's Revolutionary Emancipation
PAULEY
BALLROOM
U.C.
Berkeley
$1.50
War
Dance &
Massacre
HOLY SEE
MARTIN BECKER
WICKED
POLLY

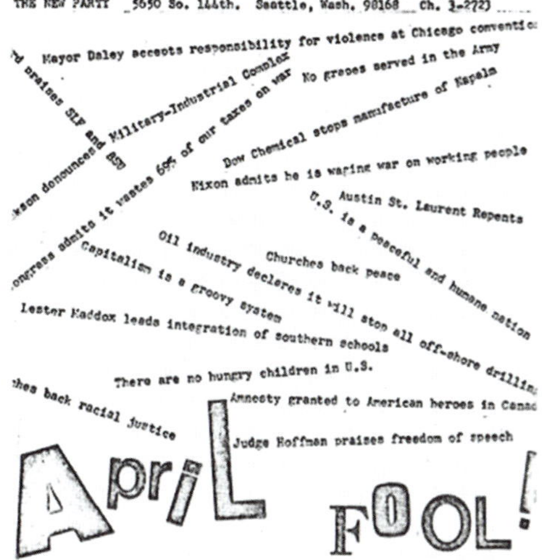
U. S. DECLARES
PEACE ON WORLD &
WINS !
THE NEW PARTY _5650 So. 144th. Seattle, Wash. 98168_ Ch. 1-2721 ____
Mayor Daley accepts responsibility for violence at Chicago convention
Johnson denounces Military-Industrial Complex
praises SIF
Reagan denounces war
No graves served in the Army
No taxes on war
Dow Chemical stops manufacture of Napalm
Nixon admits he is waging war on working people
U.S. is a peaceful and humane nation
Austin St. Laurent Repents
Congress admits it wastes 60% of our taxes on war
Oil industry declares it will stop all off-shore drilling
Capitalism is a groovy system
Churches back peace
Lester Maddox leads integration of southern schools
There are no hungry children in U.S.
wishes back racial justice
Amnesty granted to American heroes in Canada
Judge Hoffman praises freedom of speech
APRIL   FOOL!
Join our "victory" celebration 10-2 Wed., April 1 in the Westlake
Mall. Bring signs, noisemakers, confetti, flags and friends. 20
moderate to radical peace and civil-rights speakers will present
their views of how to bring justice and humanity to the   United
States.

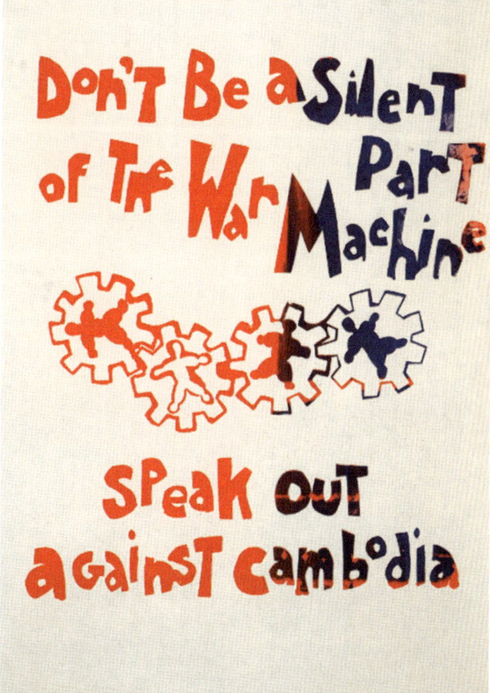
BERKELEY LIBERATION
PROGRAM
THE PEOPLE OF BERKELEY PASSIONATELY DESIRE HUMAN SOLIDARITY,
CULTURAL FREEDOM AND PEACE.
1 WE WILL MAKE TELEGRAPH AVENUE AND THE SOUTH
CAMPUS A STRATEGIC FREE TERRITORY
FOR REVOLUTION.
2 WE WILL CREATE OUR REVOLUTIONARY CULTURE EVERYWHERE.
3 WE WILL TURN THE SCHOOLS
INTO TRAINING GROUNDS FOR LIBERATION.
4 WE WILL DESTROY THE UNIVERSITY UNLESS IT SERVES THE PEOPLE.
5 WE WILL STRUGGLE FOR
THE FULL LIBERATION
OF WOMEN
AS A NECESSARY PART
OF THE REVOLUTIONARY PROCESS.
6 WE WILL TAKE COMMUNAL RESPONSIBILITY FOR BASIC
HUMAN NEEDS.
7 WE WILL PROTECT AND EXPAND OUR
DRUG CULTURE.
8 WE WILL BREAK THE POWER OF THE LANDLORDS
AND PROVIDE BEAUTIFUL
HOUSING FOR EVERYONE.
9 WE WILL TAX THE CORPORATIONS,
NOT THE WORKING PEOPLE.
10 WE WILL DEFEND OURSELVES AGAINST
LAW AND ORDER.
11 WE WILL CREATE A SOULFUL
SOCIALISM IN BERKELEY.
12 WE WILL CREATE A PEOPLE'S GOVERNMENT.
13 WE WILL UNITE WITH OTHER MOVEMENTS THROUGHOUT THE WORLD
TO DESTROY THIS MOTHERFUCKING RACISTCAPITALISTIMPERIALIST SYSTEM.
WE CALL FOR SISTERS AND BROTHERS TO FORM LIBERATION COMMITTEES
TO CARRY OUT THE BERKELEY STRUGGLE.
Sisters and Brothers,
Unite for Survival,
Resist and Create,
Fight for a Revolutionary Berkeley,
With your Friends, your Dope, your Guns,
Form Liberation Committees,
Carry Out the Program,
Choose the Action and Do It,
Set Examples and Spread the Word:
POWER TO THE
IMAGINATION
ALL POWER
TO THE PEOPLE

DON'T BE A SILENT
PART
OF THE War
Machine
SPEAK OUT
AGAINST cambodia

014
015

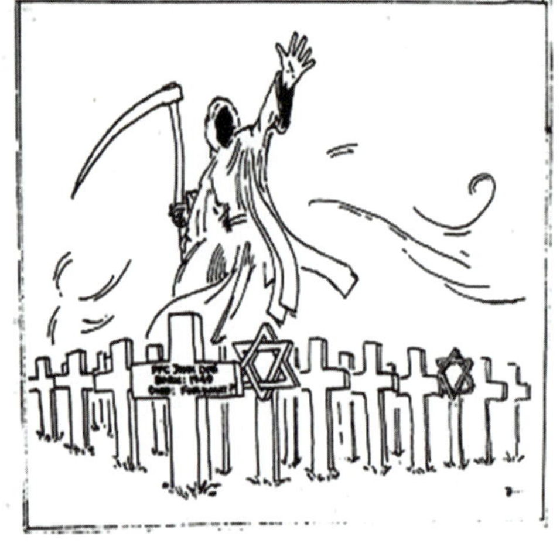

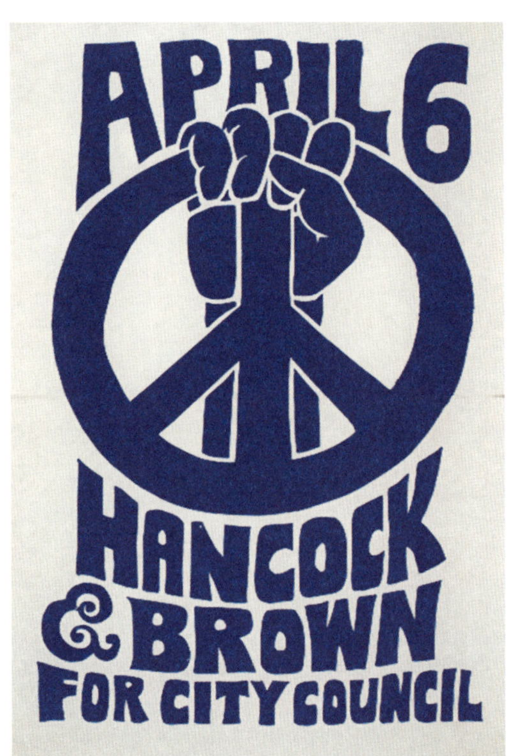

016
017

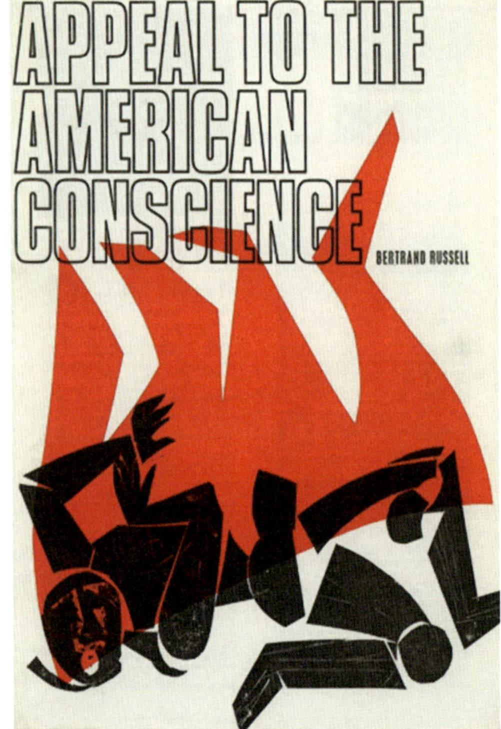

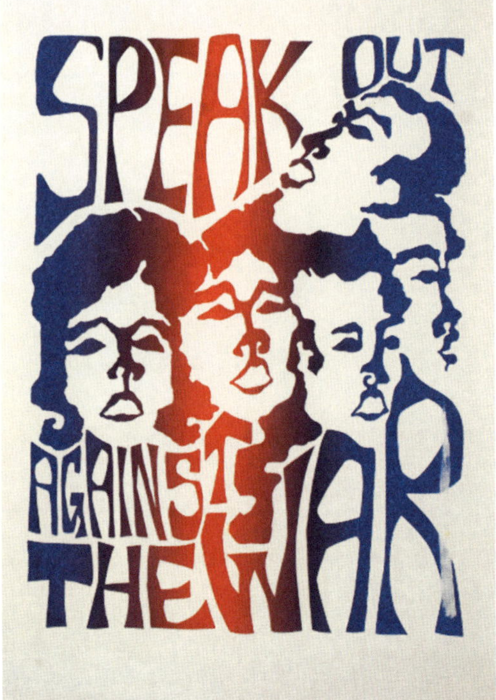

018
019

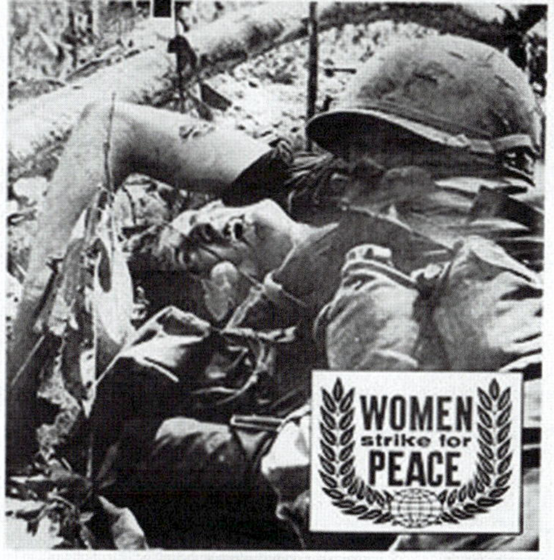

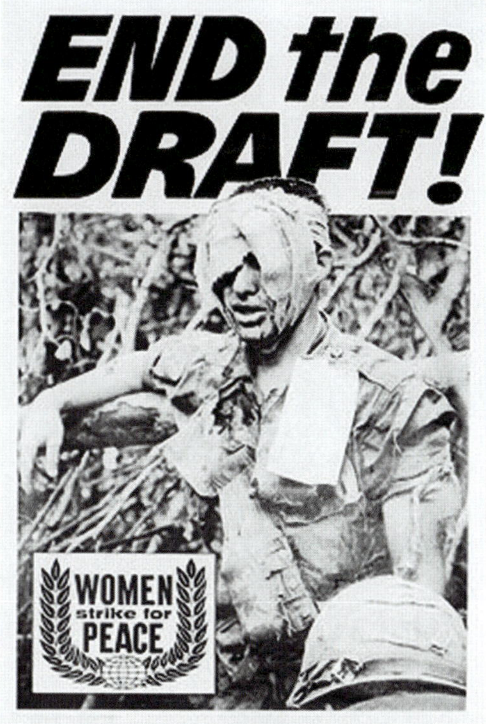

020
021

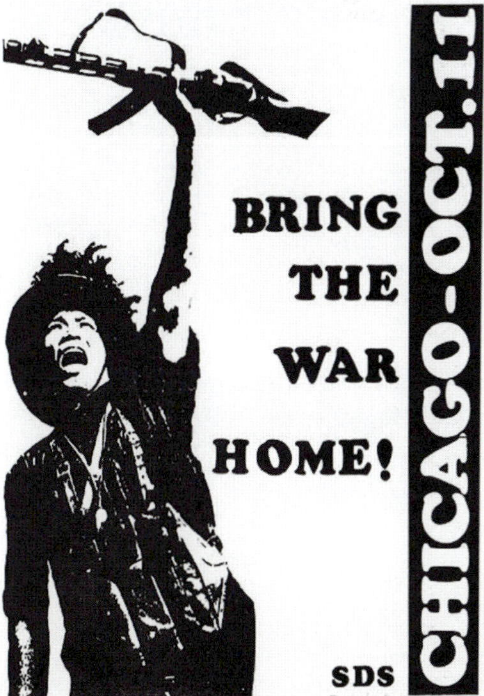

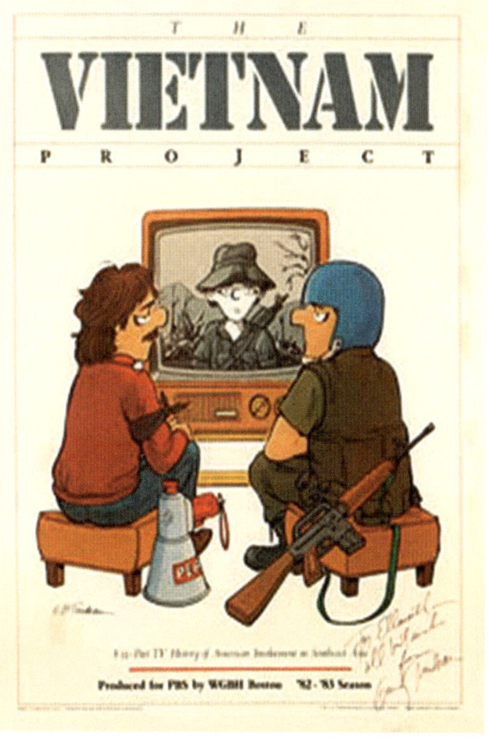

022
023

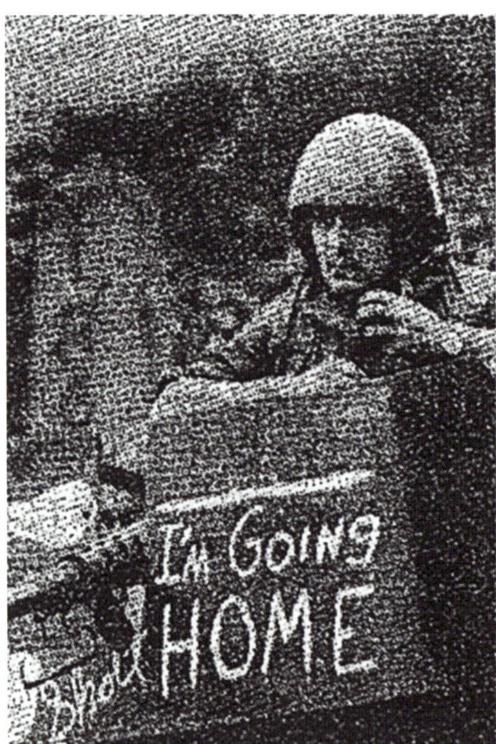

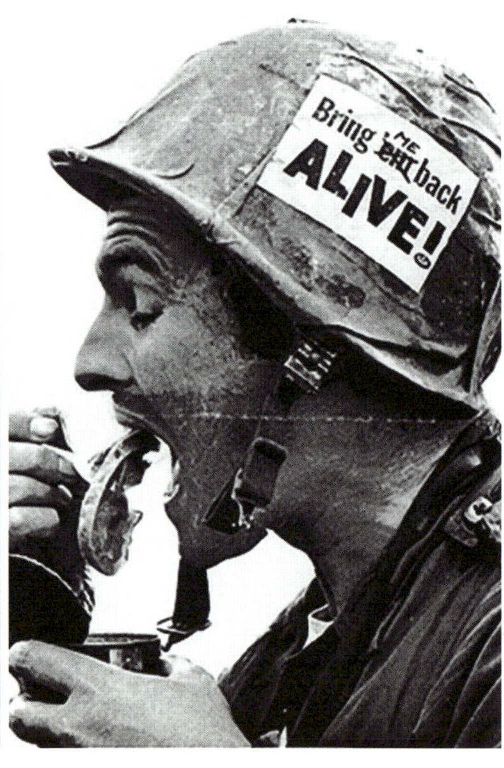

024
025

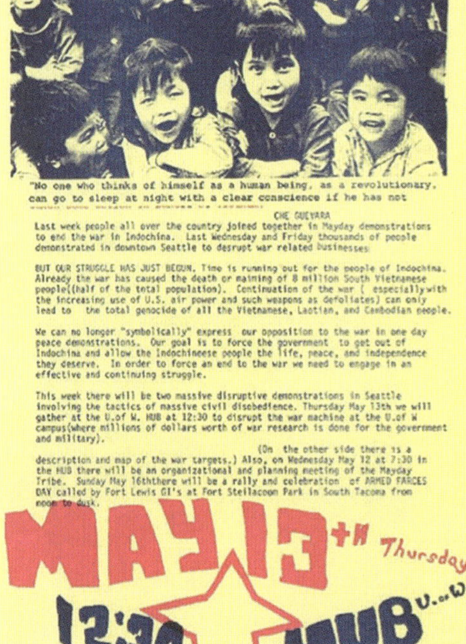

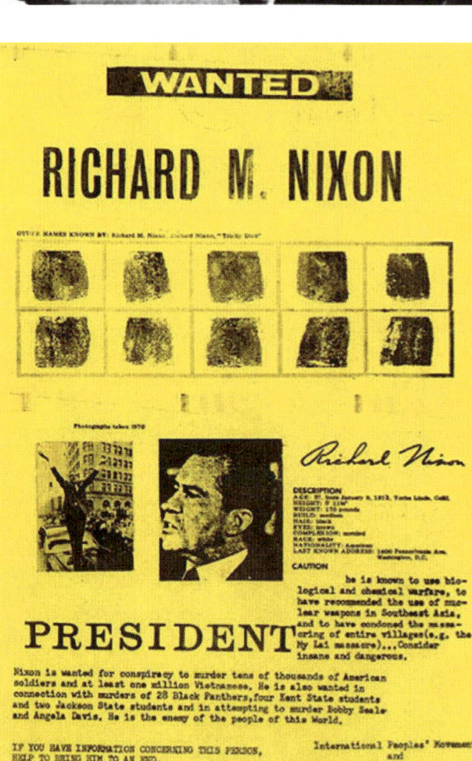

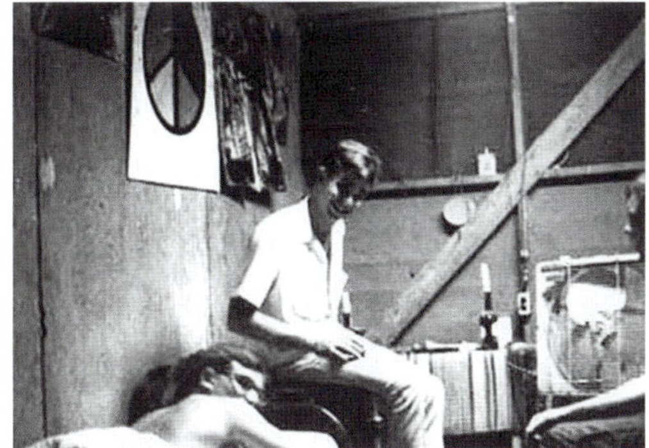

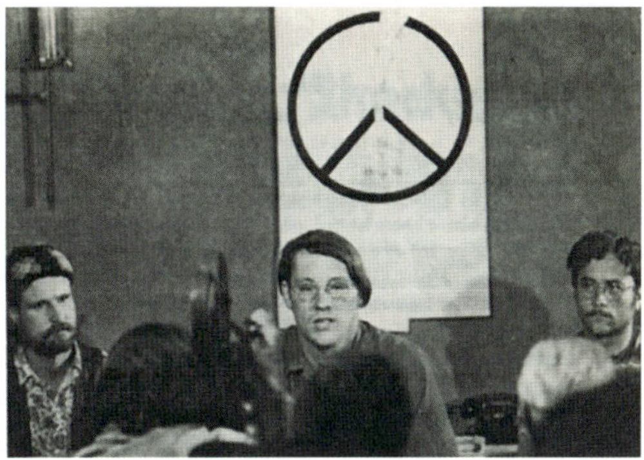

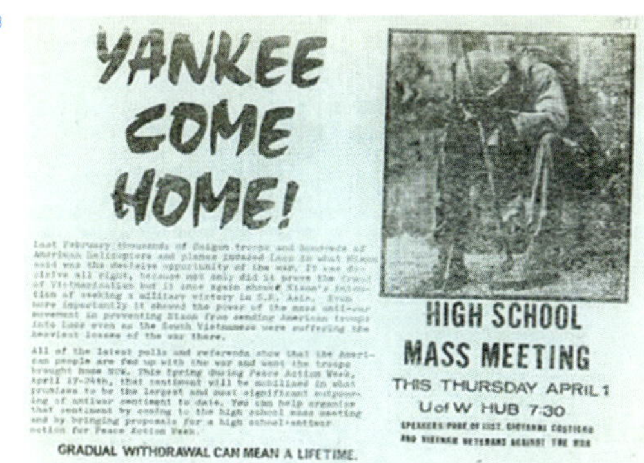
YANKEE COME HOME!
HIGH SCHOOL MASS MEETING
THIS THURSDAY APRIL 1
U of W HUB 7:30
SPEAKERS: PROF. OF HIST. GIOVANNI COSTIGAN
AND VIETNAM VETERANS AGAINST THE WAR
GRADUAL WITHDRAWAL CAN MEAN A LIFETIME.

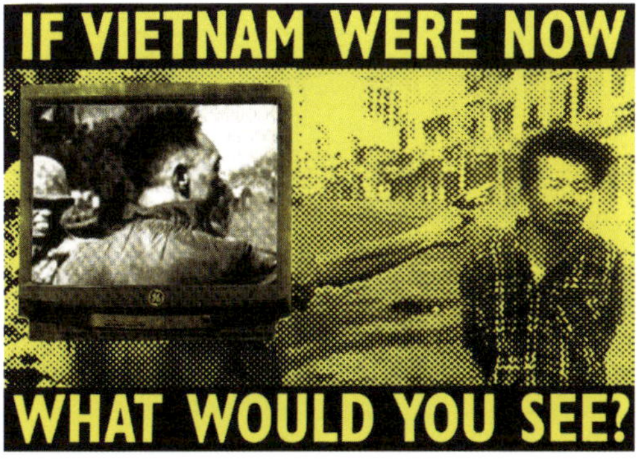
IF VIETNAM WERE NOW
WHAT WOULD YOU SEE?

001
002

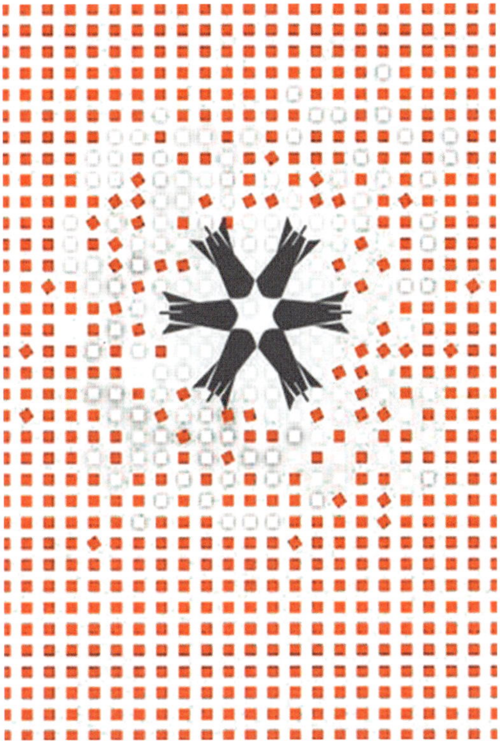

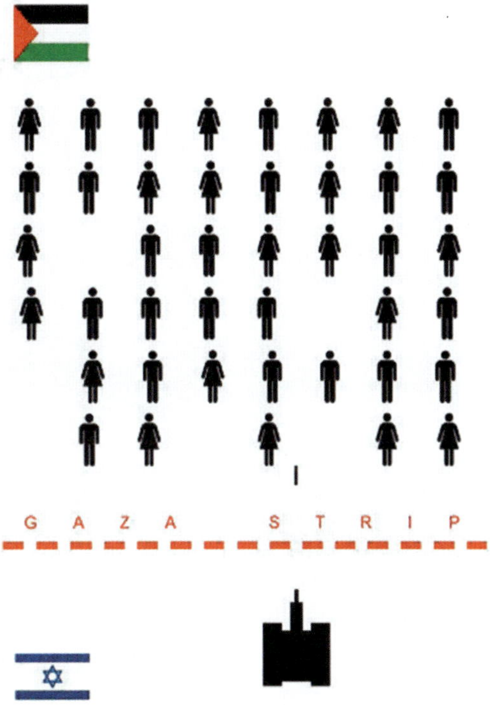

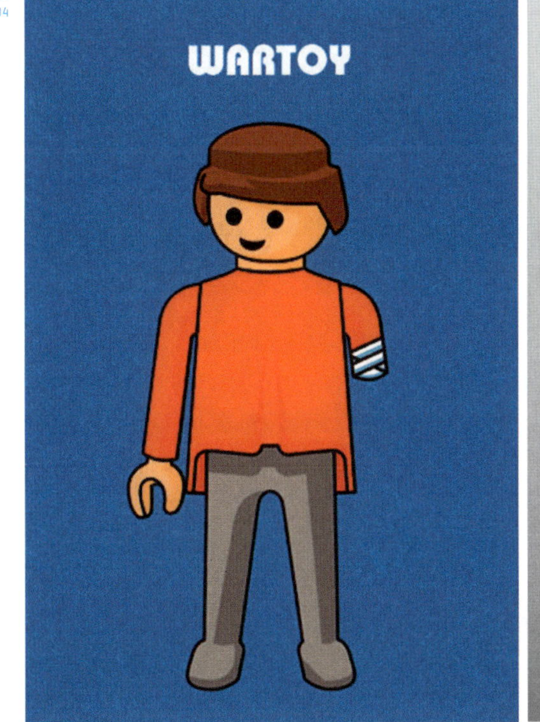

003
004

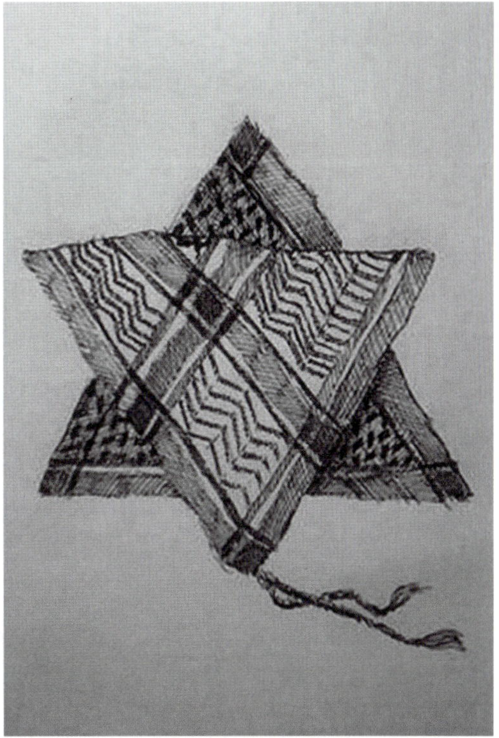

005
006

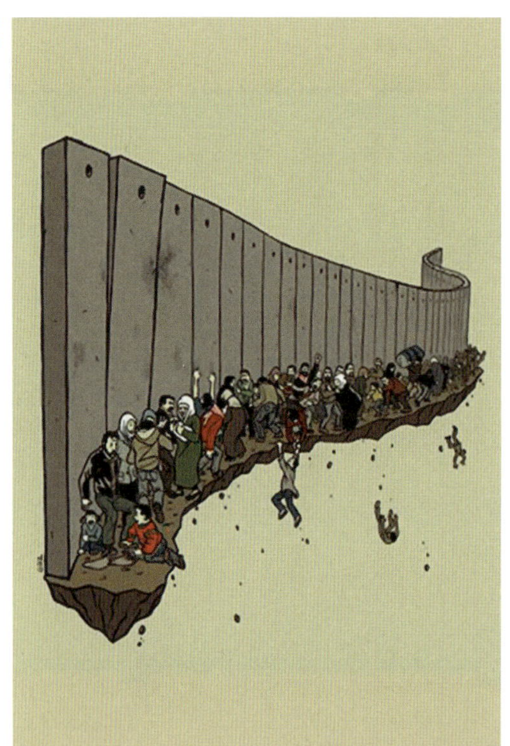

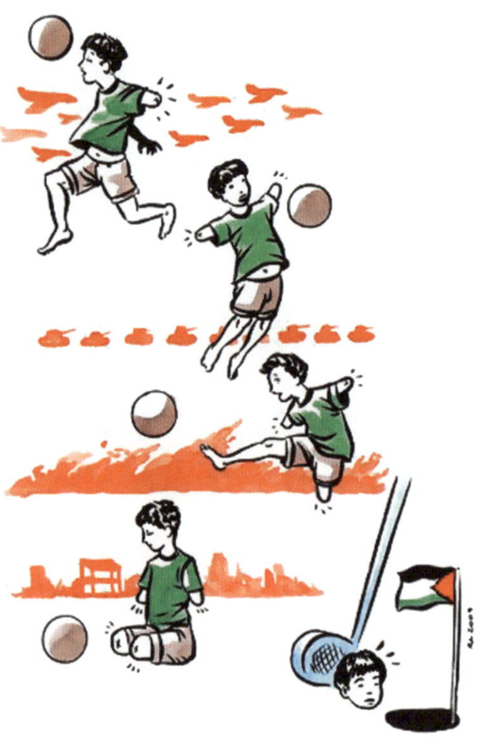

007
008

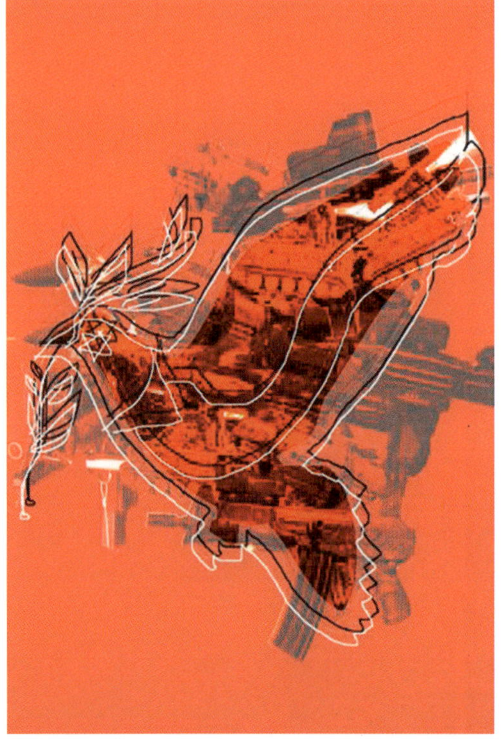

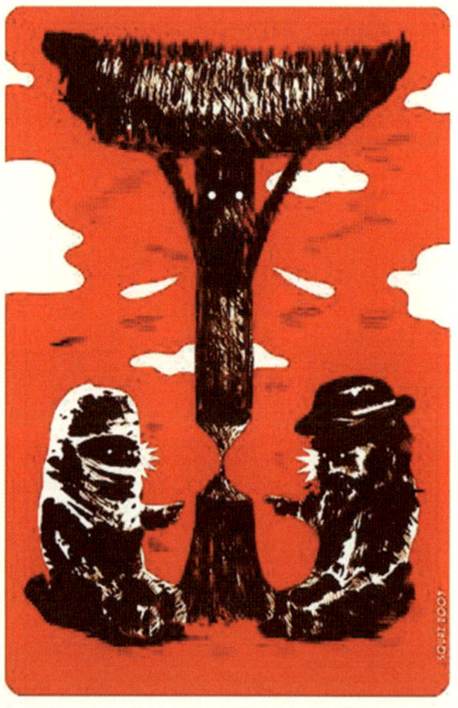

009
010
011
012

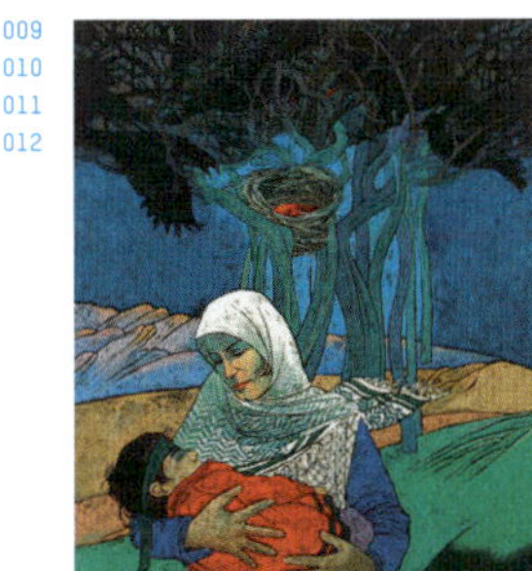
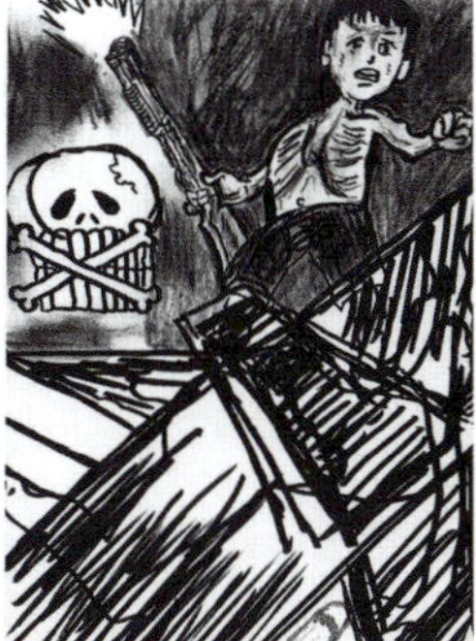
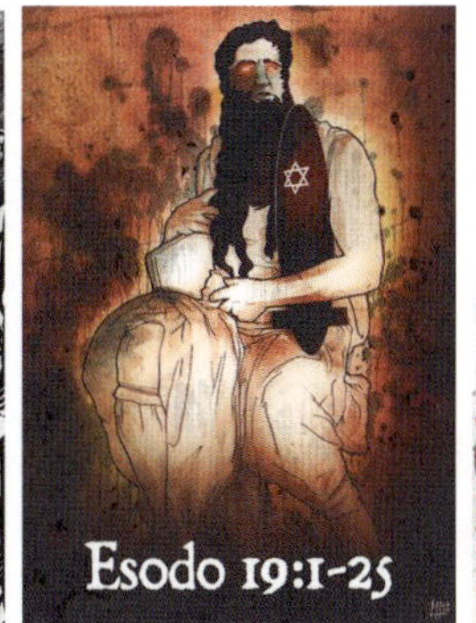

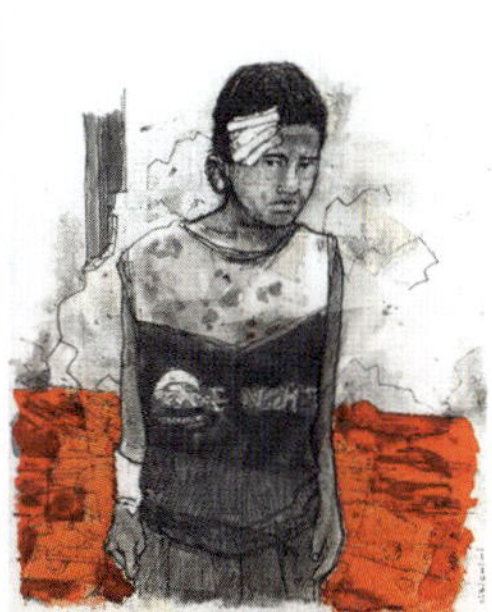

013
014

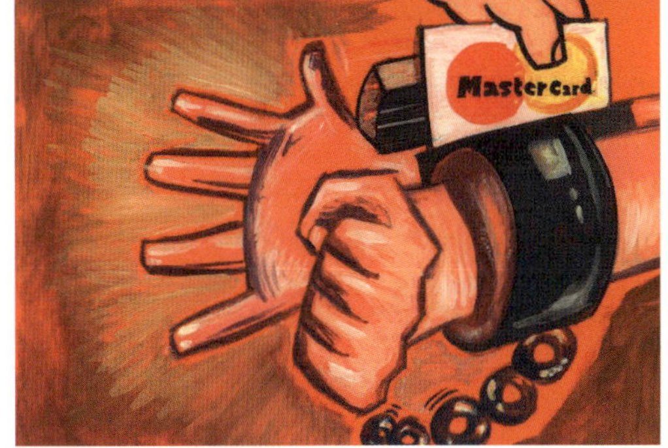

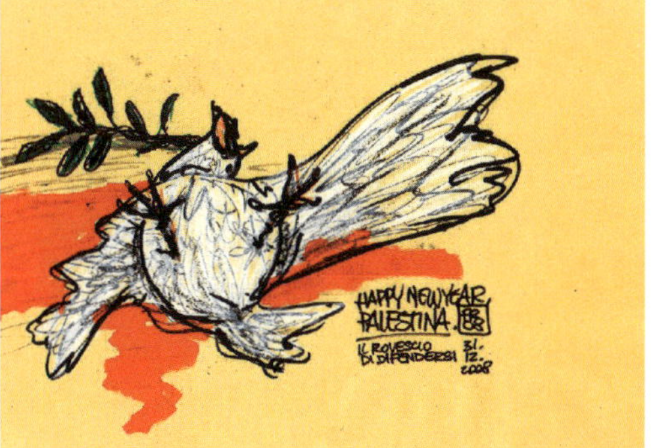

015
016

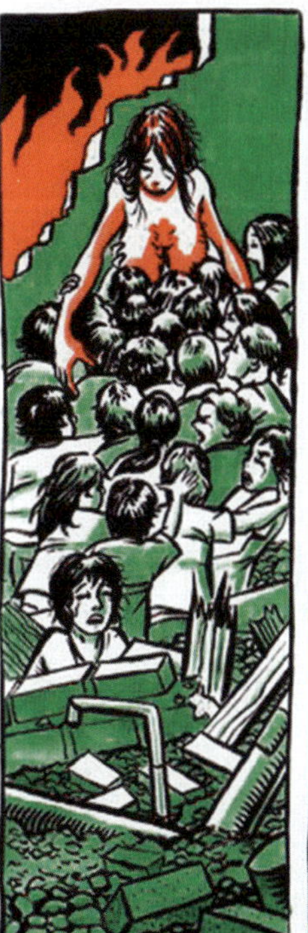
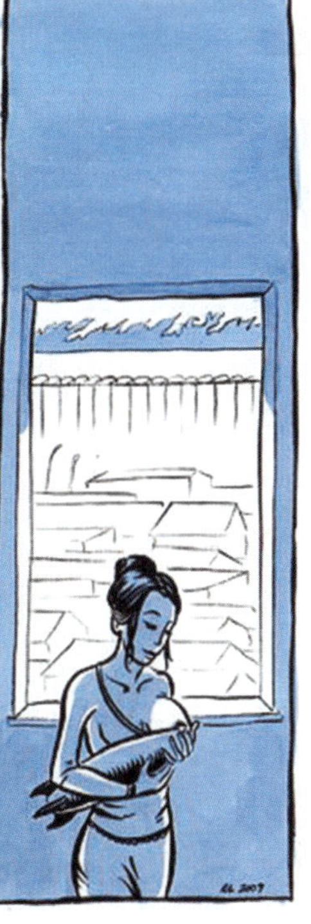
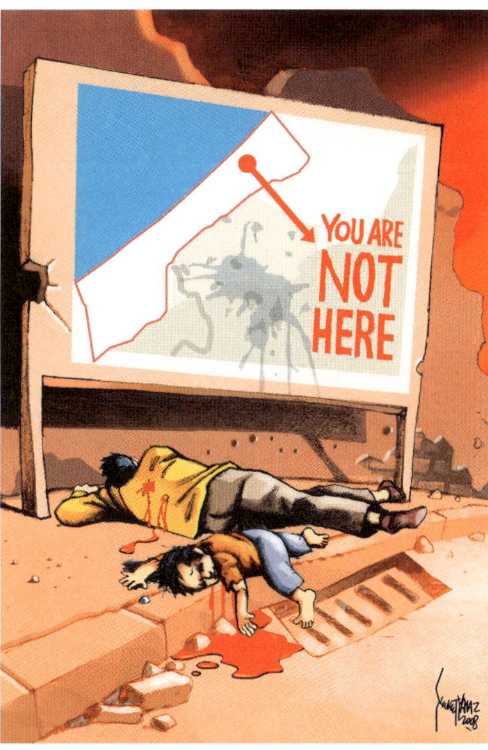

017
018

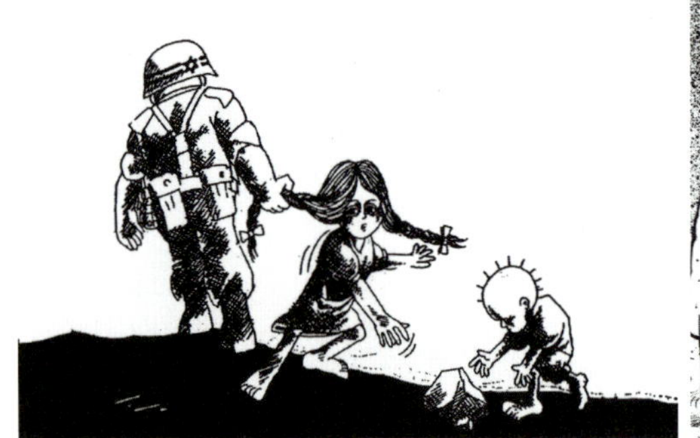

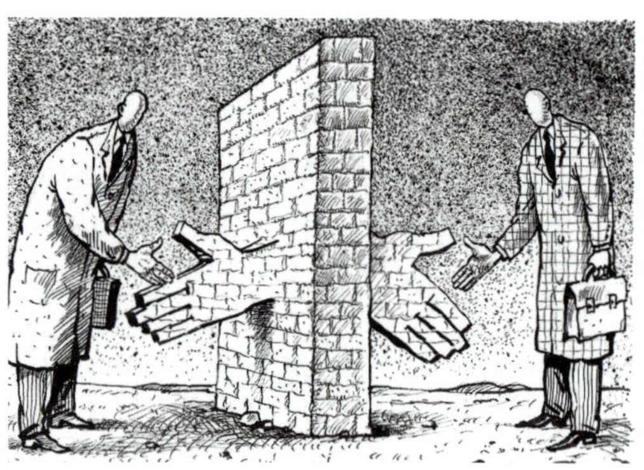

019
020

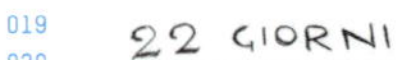

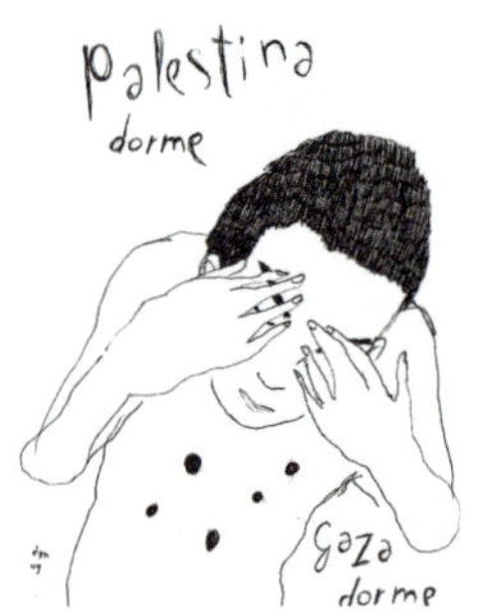

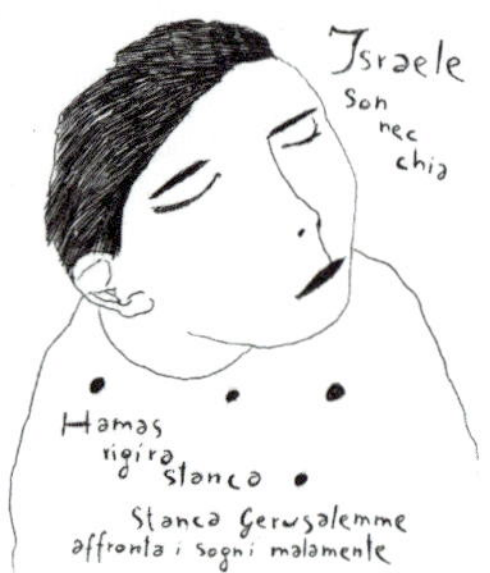

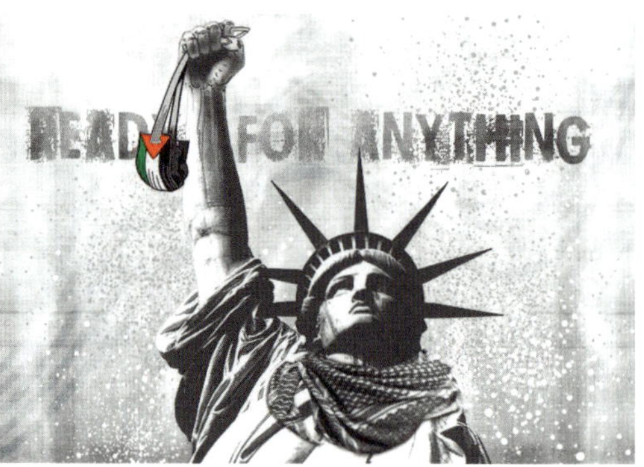

021
022

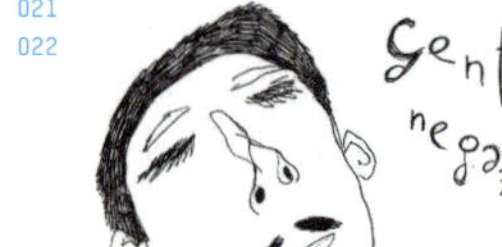

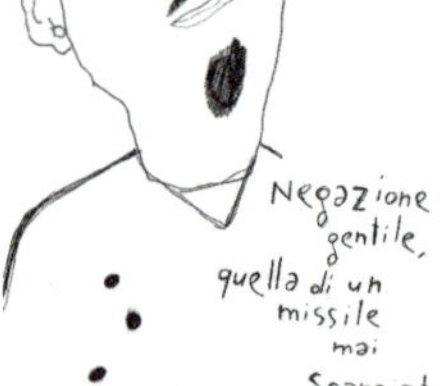

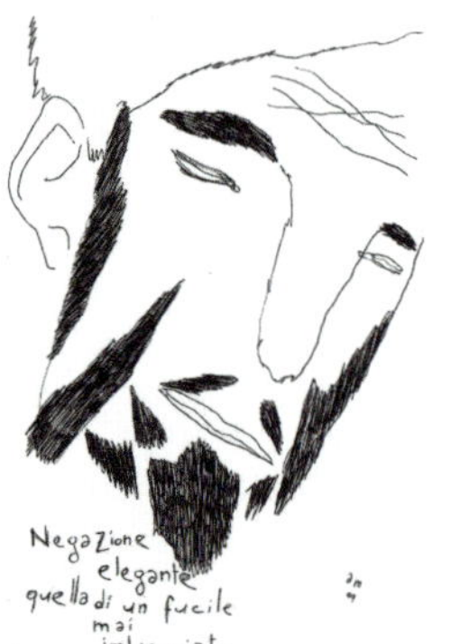

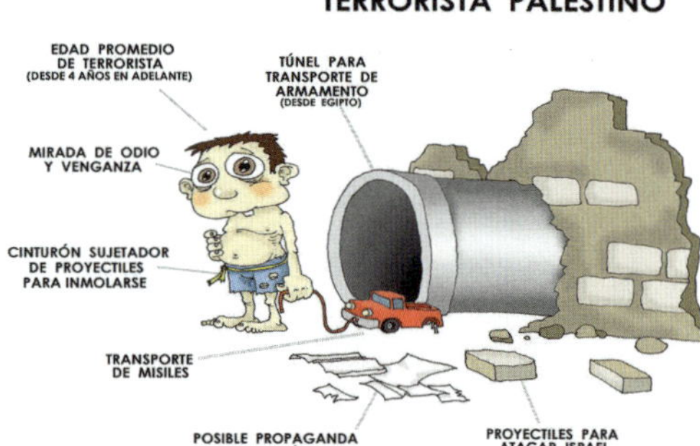

023

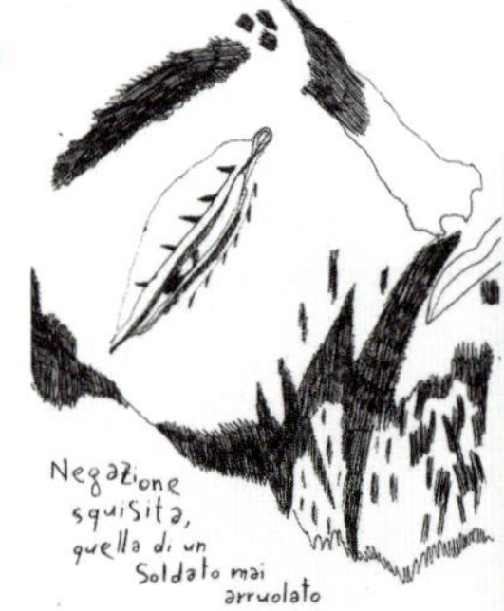

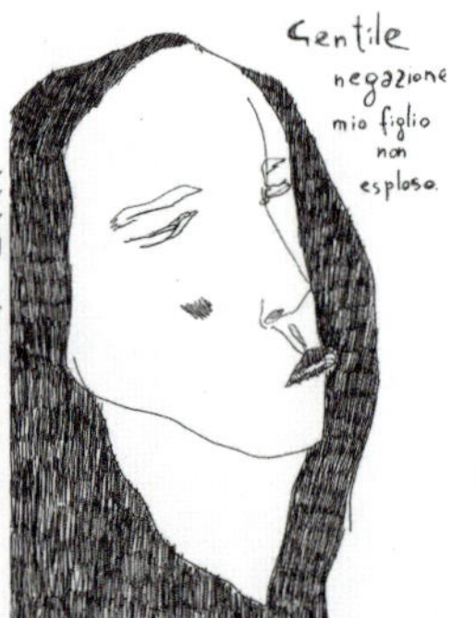

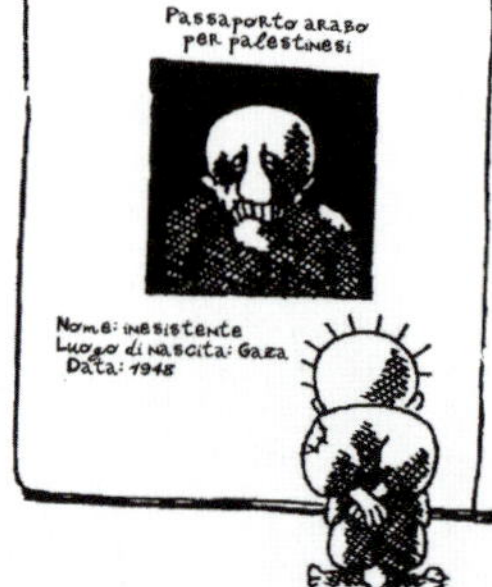

001 UNTITLED
<u>CREATOR</u> Delikatessen
<u>SOURCE</u> visualintifada.blogspot.com

002 GAZA STRIP
<u>CREATOR</u> Jose Sala
<u>SOURCE</u> visualintifada.blogspot.com

003 WAR TOY
<u>CREATOR</u> Giovanni Di Modica
<u>SOURCE</u> visualintifada.blogspot.com

004 UNTITLED
<u>CREATOR</u> Alessio Marazzi
<u>SOURCE</u> visualintifada.blogspot.com

005 UNTITLED
<u>CREATOR</u> Roberto Grossi
<u>SOURCE</u> visualintifada.blogspot.com

006 UNTITLED
<u>CREATOR</u> Rocco Lombardi
<u>SOURCE</u> visualintifada.blogspot.com

007 UNTITLED
<u>CREATOR</u> Âclaricedesign
<u>SOURCE</u> visualintifada.blogspot.com

008 UNTITLED
<u>CREATOR</u> Squaz
<u>SOURCE</u> visualintifada.blogspot.com

009 UNTITLED
<u>SOURCE</u> visualintifada.blogspot.com

010 UNTITLED
<u>CREATOR</u> Tetsuro Susumu
<u>SOURCE</u> visualintifada.blogspot.com

011 EXODUS 19:1-25
<u>CREATOR</u> Matteo Cuccato
<u>SOURCE</u> visualintifada.blogspot.com

012 UNTITLED
<u>CREATOR</u> Maurizio Ribichini
<u>SOURCE</u> visualintifada.blogspot.com

013 MASTERCARD
<u>CREATOR</u> Sales of the Freedom
<u>SOURCE</u> visualintifada.blogspot.com

014 HAPPY NEW YEAR, PALESTINE
<u>CREATOR</u> Filippo Ricca
<u>SOURCE</u> visualintifada.blogspot.com

015 UNTITLED
<u>CREATOR</u> Rocco Lombardi
<u>SOURCE</u> visualintifada.blogspot.com

016 YOU ARE NOT HERE
<u>CREATOR</u> Sevket Yalaz
<u>SOURCE</u> visualintifada.blogspot.com

017 UNTITLED
<u>CREATOR</u> Mostra di Naji Al Ali
<u>SOURCE</u> visualintifada.blogspot.com

018 UNTITLED
<u>CREATOR</u> Igor Smirnov
<u>SOURCE</u> visualintifada.blogspot.com

019 22 GIORNI
[22 DAYS]
<u>CREATOR</u> Angelo Mennillo
<u>SOURCE</u> visualintifada.blogspot.com

020 READY FOR ANYTHING
<u>CREATOR</u> Vinicio Trugli
<u>SOURCE</u> visualintifada.blogspot.com

021 GENTILE NEGAZIONE
[GENTLE DENIAL]
<u>CREATOR</u> Angelo Mennillo
<u>SOURCE</u> visualintifada.blogspot.com

022 TERRORISTA PALESTINO
[PALESTINIAN TERRORIST]
<u>CREATOR</u> Luis Ligarribay
<u>SOURCE</u> visualintifada.blogspot.com

023 ARABIC PASSPORT FOR PALESTINIANS
<u>CREATOR</u> NAJI AL ALI
<u>SOURCE</u> visualintifada.blogspot.com

001

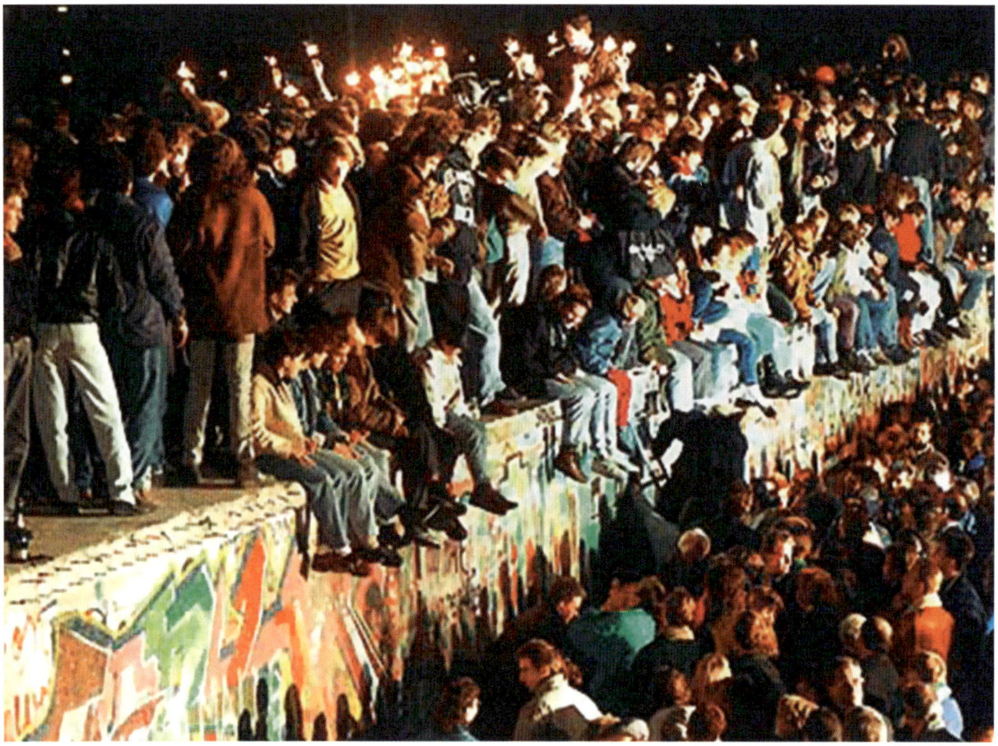

002

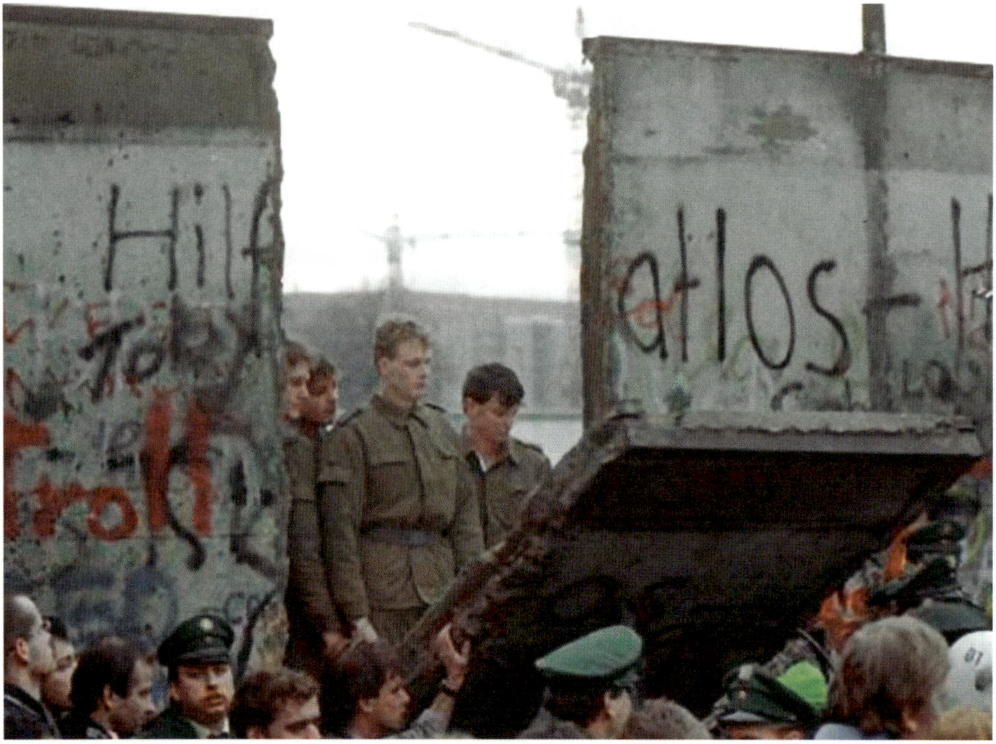

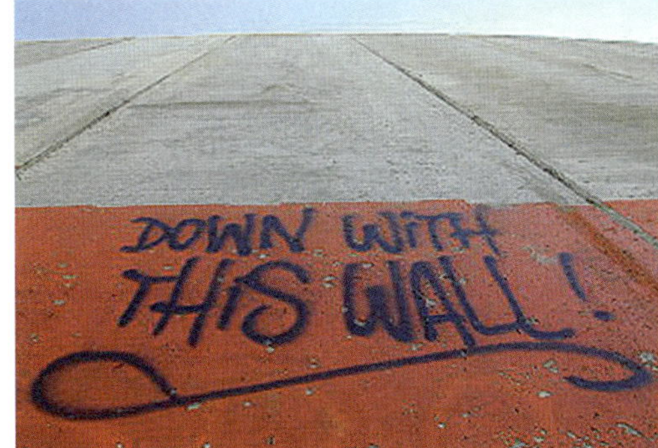
DOWN WITH
THIS WALL!

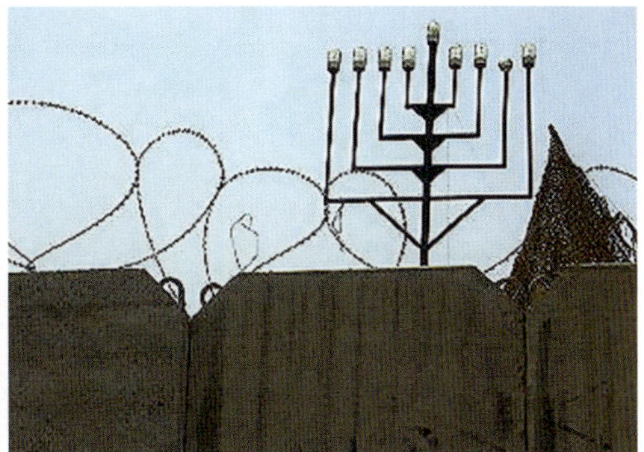

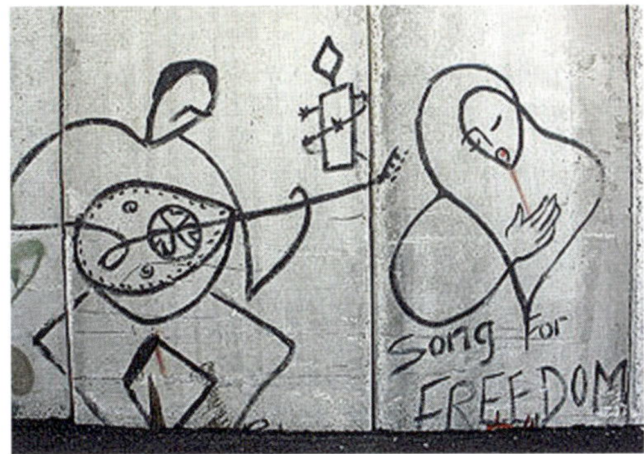
Song for
FREEDOM

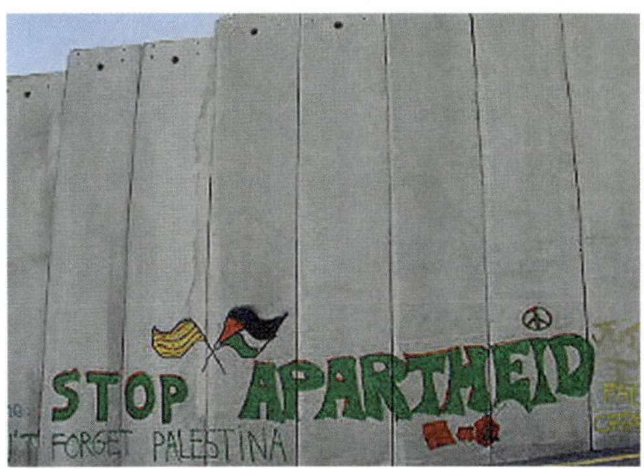
STOP APARTHEID
'T FORGET PALESTINA

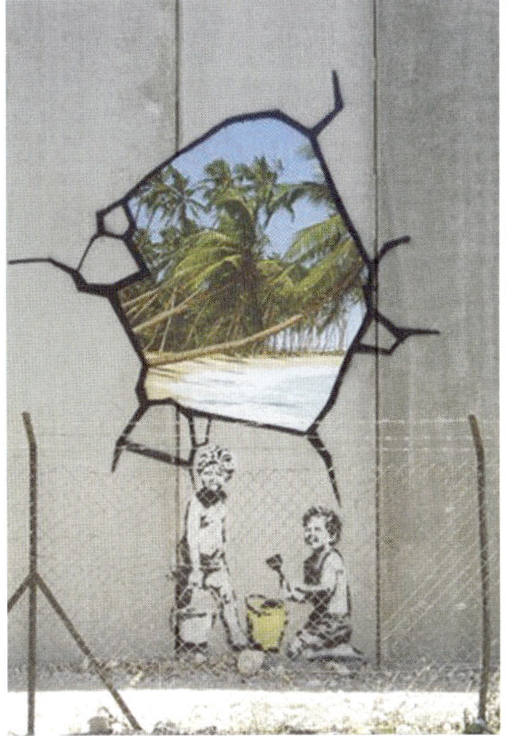

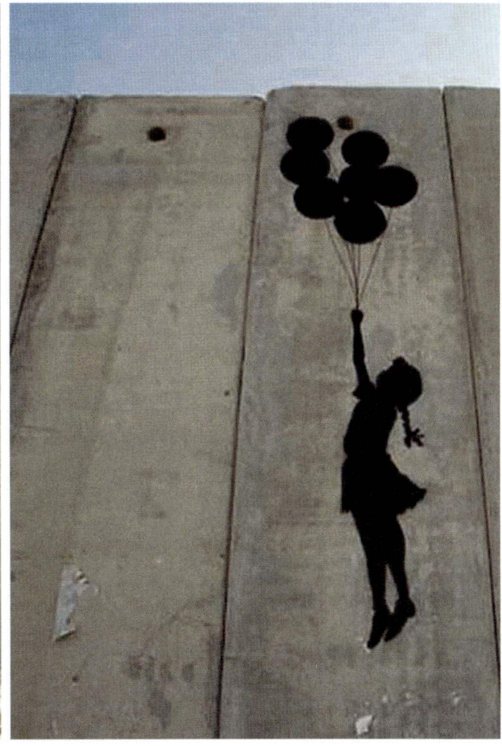

009 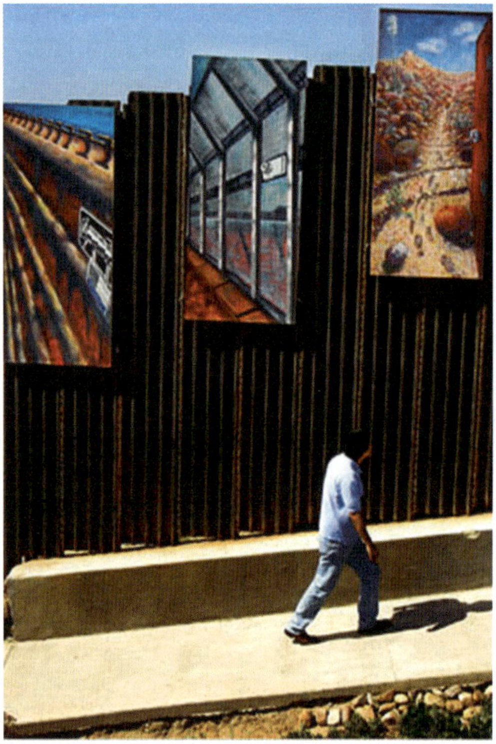
010

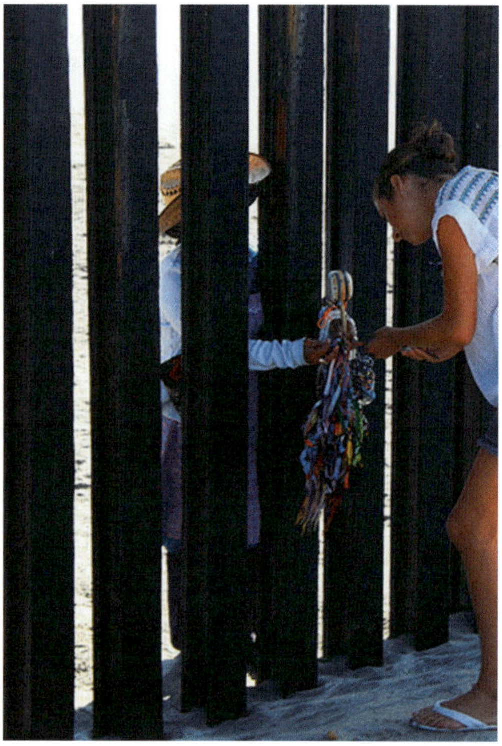

011

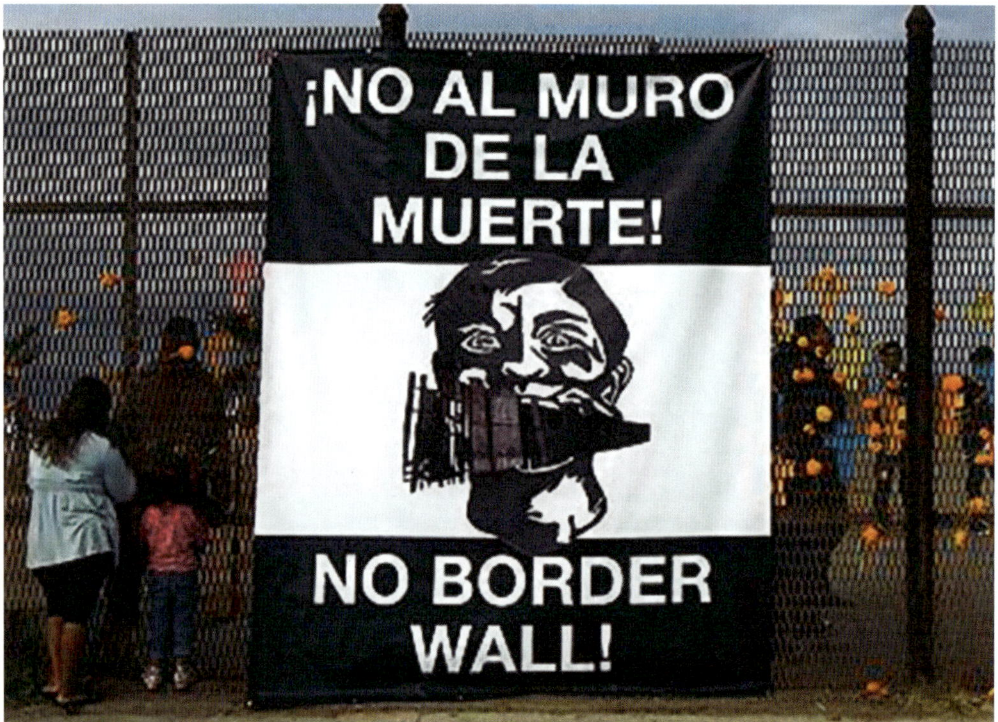

001 THE BERLIN WALL COMES DOWN
SOURCE www.americanproject.tv
DATE 9 November 1989

002 AND THEN THE WALL CAME
TUMBLING DOWN, BERLIN
SOURCE www.bbc.co.uk
DATE 9 November 1989

003 ISRAEL-PALESTINE WALL
SOURCE www.arbeiterfotografie.com

004 ISRAELI MILITARY POST AT THE
ENTRANCE TO BETHLEHEM - WITH
NATO BARBED WIRE AND LIGHTS FOR
THE HANUKKAH FESTIVAL
CREATOR Gilad Ronnen / Mitsuru
Nakamura
SOURCE www.arbeiterfotografie.com

005 ISRAEL-PALESTINE WALL
SOURCE www.arbeiterfotografie.com

006 ISRAEL-PALESTINE WALL
SOURCE www.arbeiterfotografie.com

007 ISRAEL-PALESTINE WALL
CREATOR Bansky
SOURCE l.salsa.net
DATE 14 February 2009

008 ISRAEL-PALESTINE WALL
CREATOR Bansky
SOURCE arabisraelibookreview.com

009 THE OTHER SIDE OF TIJUANA
SOURCE foreignpolicyblogs.com

010 TRADE ALONG THE US-MEXICO BORDER
SOURCE www.flickriver.com

011 NO BORDER WALL
A sign hung by the Raza
Rights Coalition hangs on
the Mexican side of the border
fence in Friendship Park.
SOURCE www.telegraph.co.uk

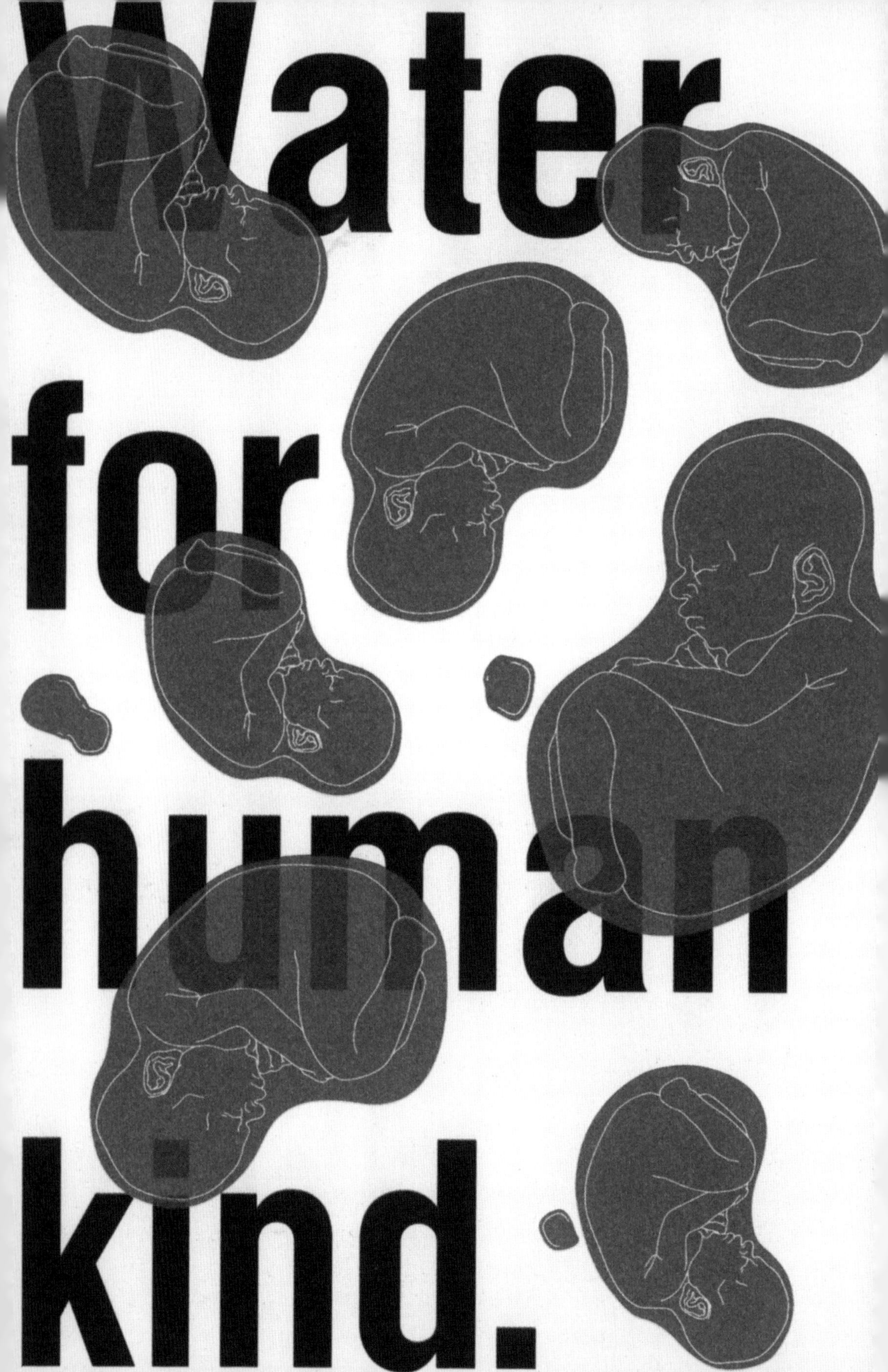
Water
for
human
kind.

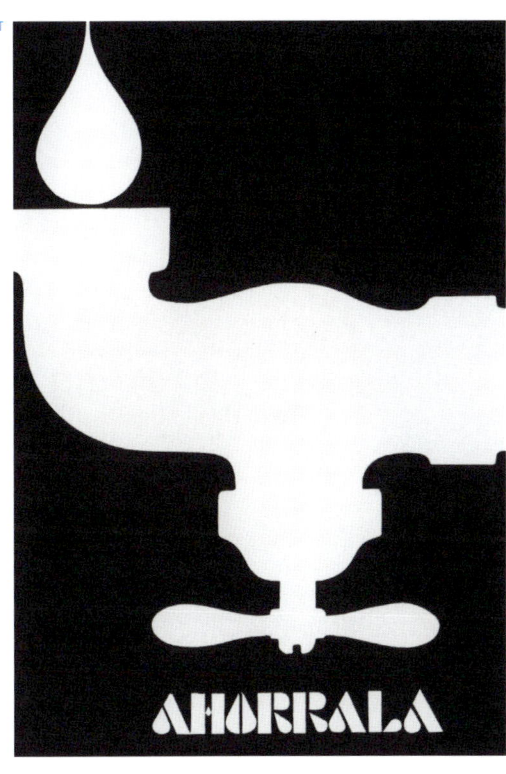

LEFT
001
002

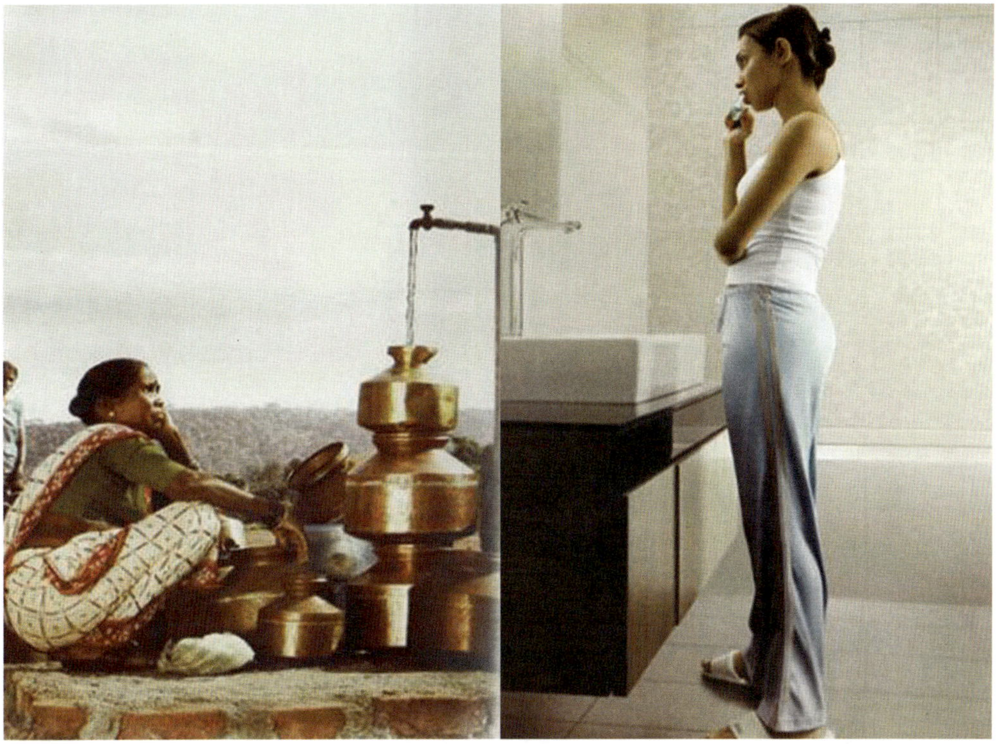

001   WATER FOR HUMAN KIND
CREATOR Yuri Surkov
SOURCE Steven Heller and
Carol Wells, eds., *The Graphic
Imperative: International
Posters for Peace, Social Justice,
and the Environment, 1965-2005*
[Boston: Massachusetts College
of Arts, 2005], p. 52.

002   SAVE IT! [WATER]
CREATOR Faustion Pèrez Organero
SOURCE Steven Heller and
Carol Wells, eds., *The Graphic
Imperative: International
Posters for Peace, Social Justice,
and the Environment, 1965-2005*
[Boston: Massachusetts College
of Arts, 2005], p. 52.

003   VANARAI FOUNDATION: WATER WASTE
CREATOR McCann Worldgroup, Mumbai
SOURCE www.ibelieveinadv.com

003

001
002

The Coalition of the Killing

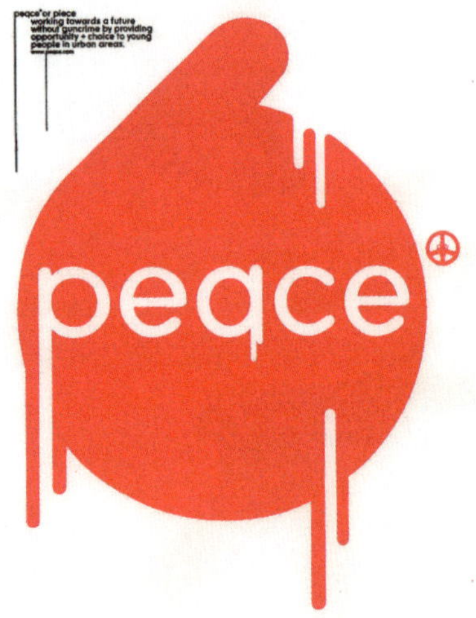

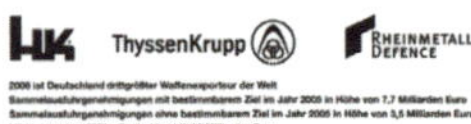

2006 ist Deutschland drittgrößter Waffenexporteur der Welt
Sammelausfuhrgenehmigungen mit bestimmbarem Ziel im Jahr 2006 in Höhe von 7,7 Milliarden Euro
Sammelausfuhrgenehmigungen ohne bestimmbarem Ziel im Jahr 2006 in Höhe von 5,5 Milliarden Euro
Militärausgaben 2006 in Deutschland 27,97 Milliarden Euro

003

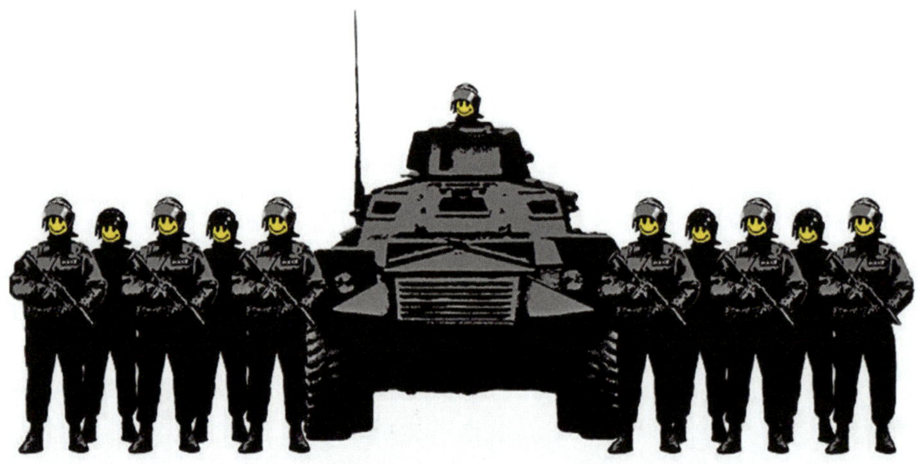

004

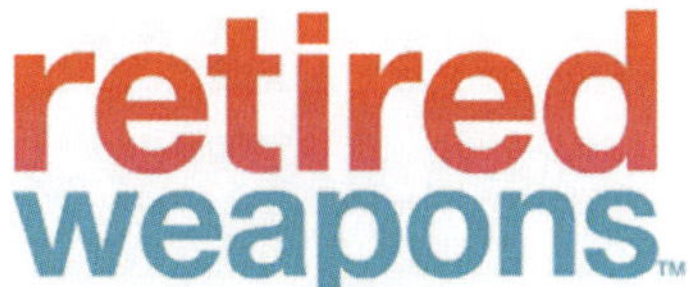

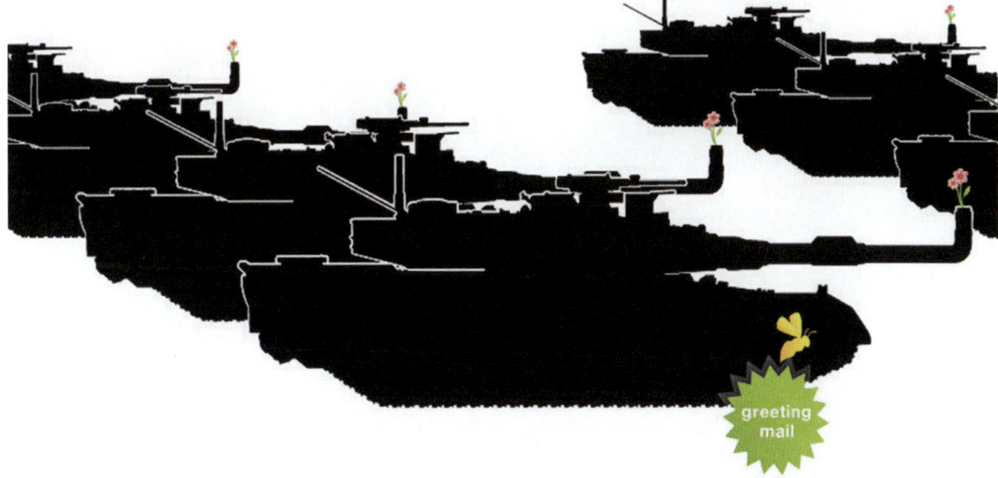

005

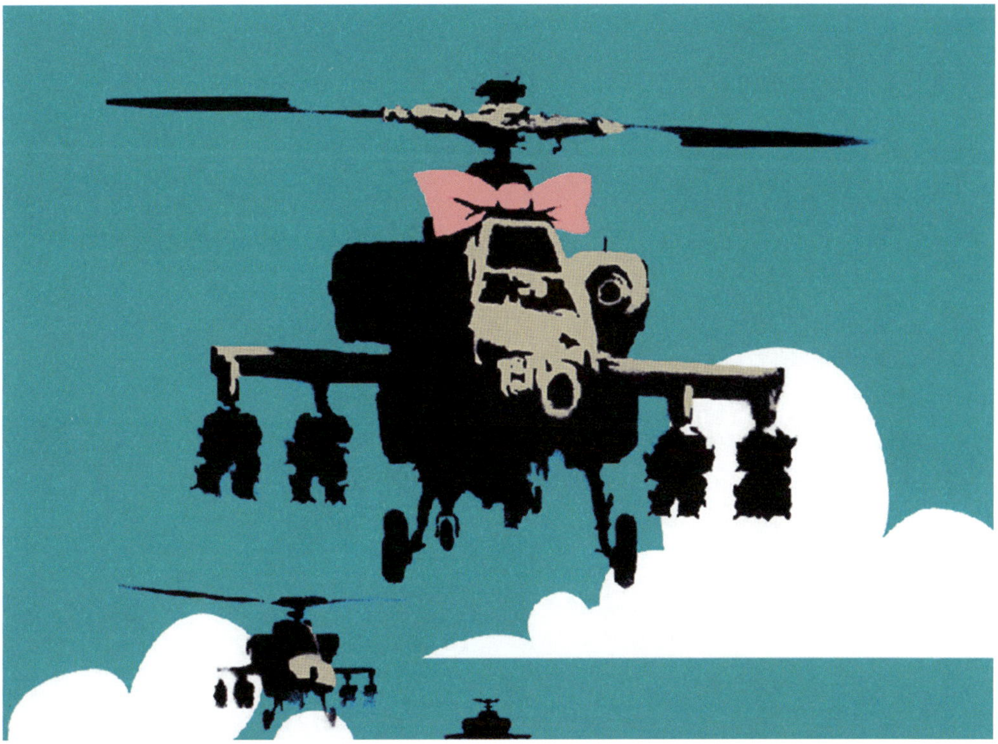

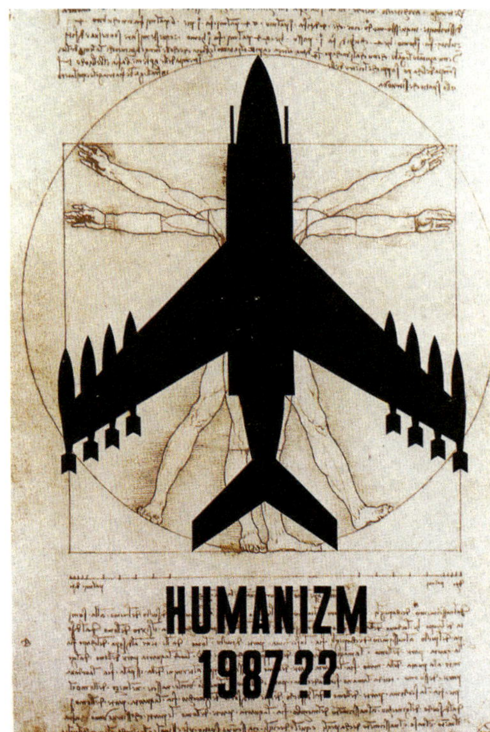
Come Here
PEACE

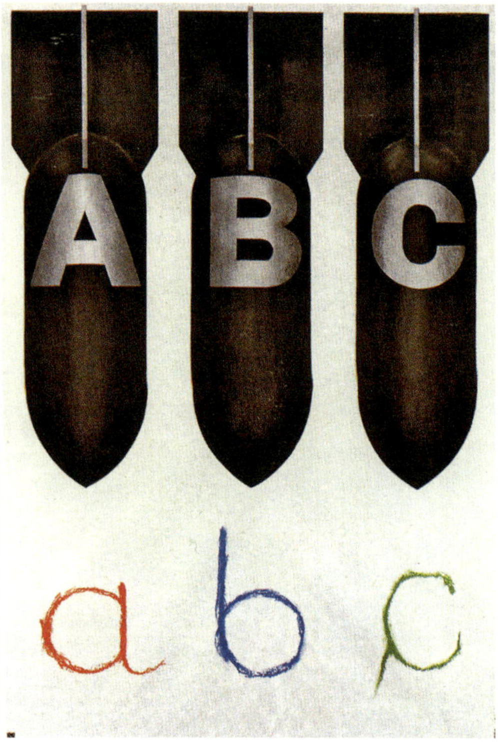

A B C
a b c

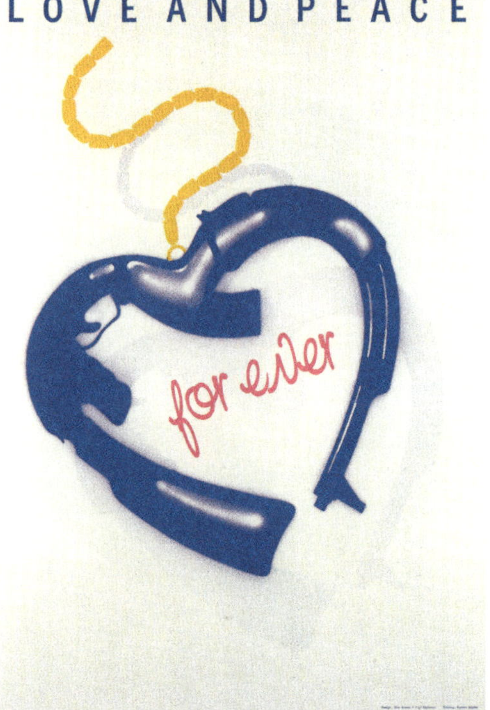
HUMANIZM
1987 ??

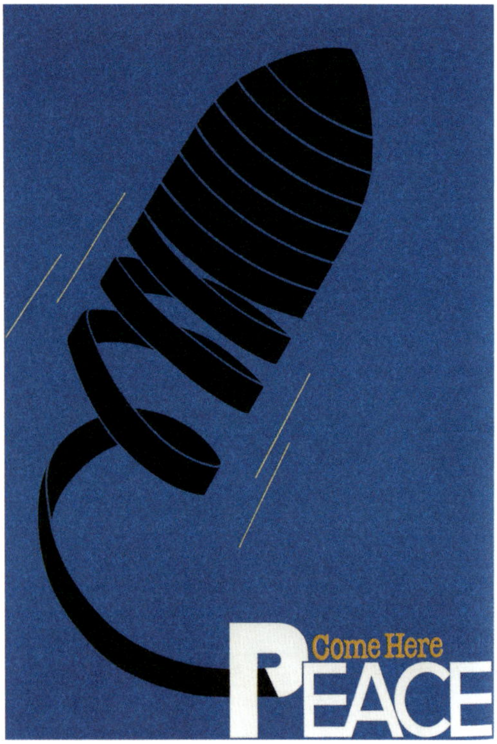

LOVE AND PEACE
for ever

010
011

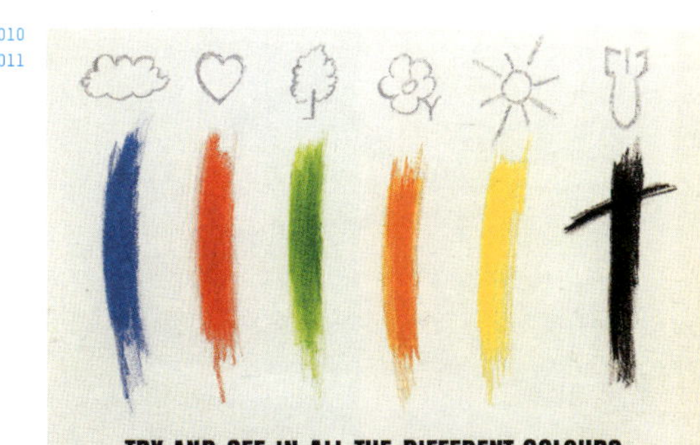

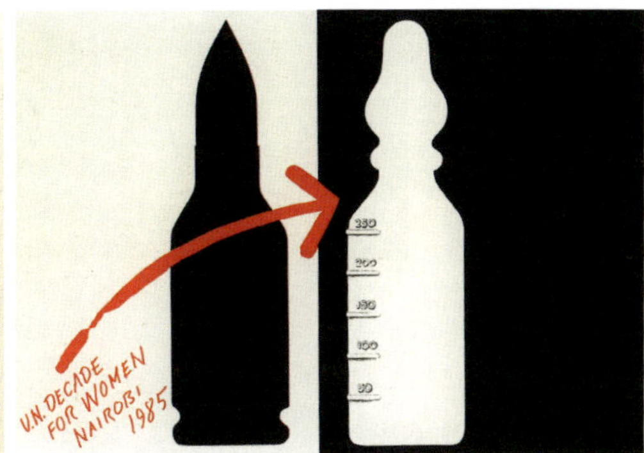

012
013

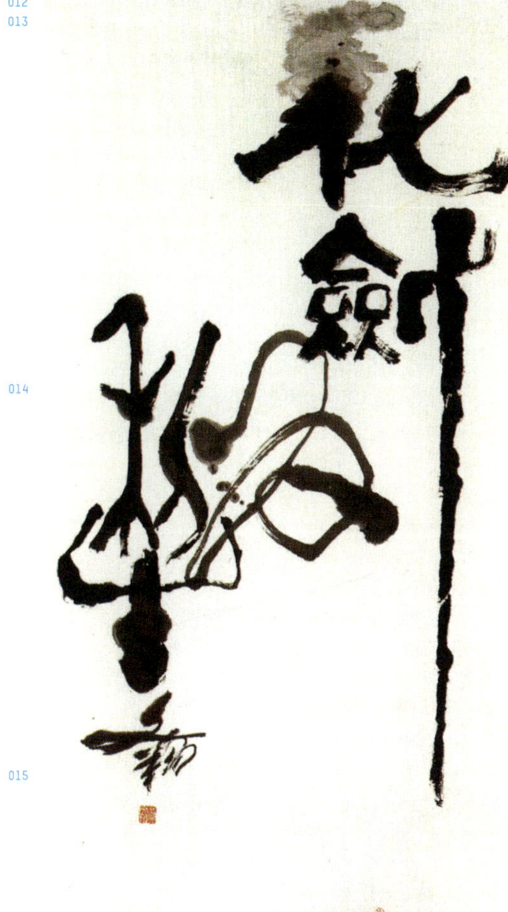

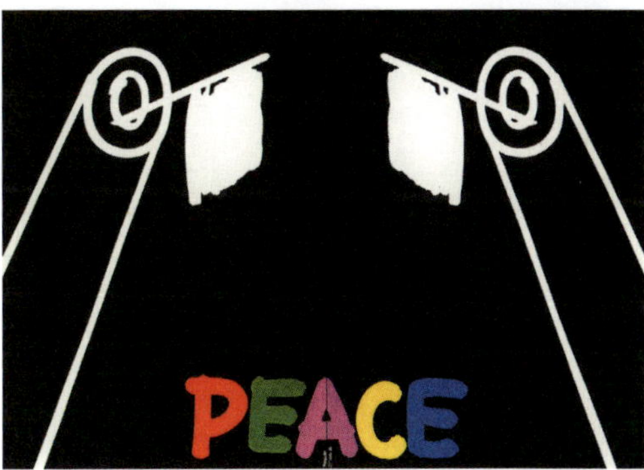

014

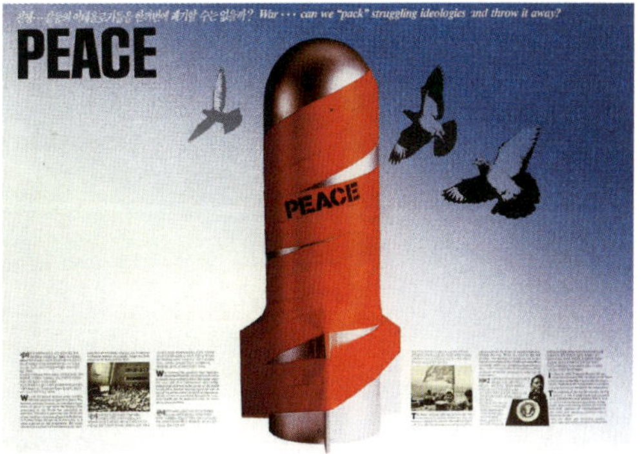

015

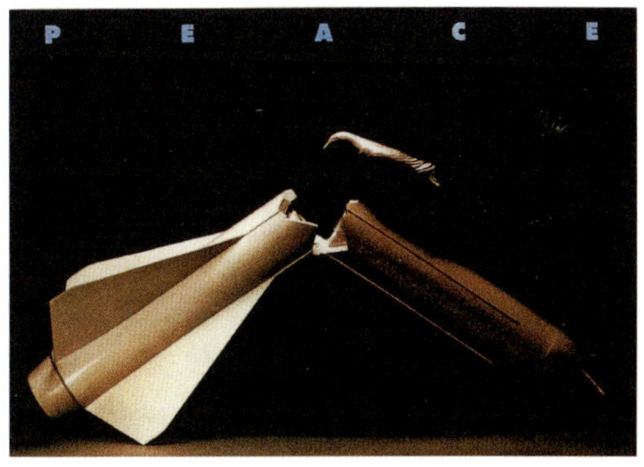

016
017

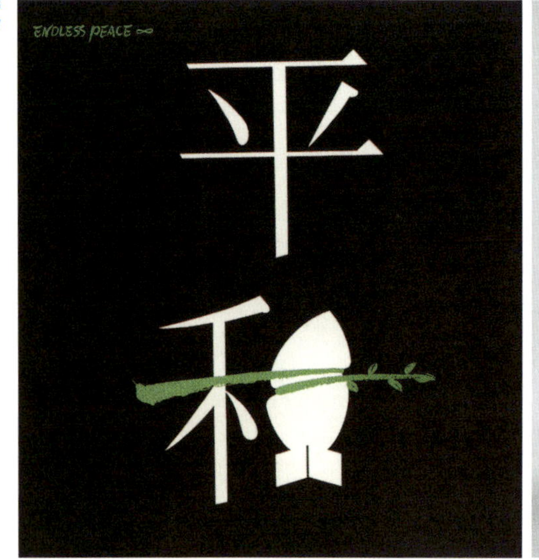

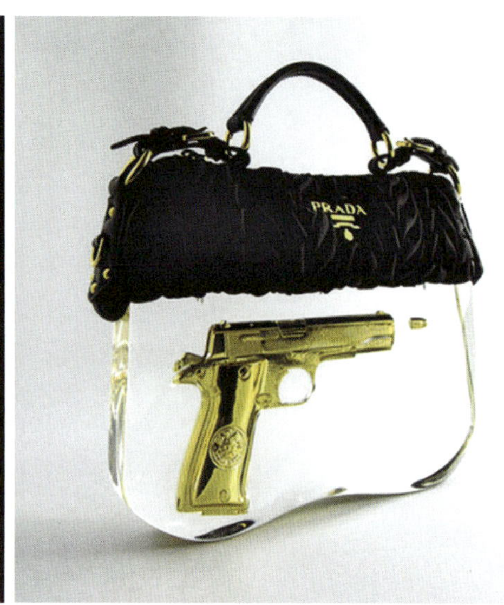

018
019

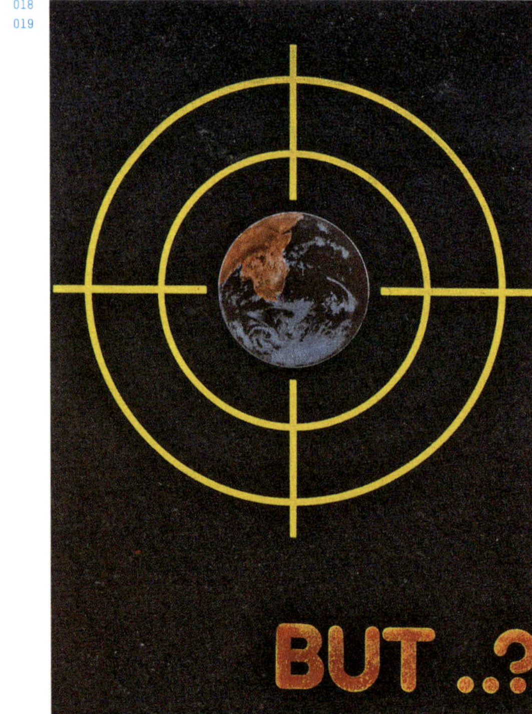

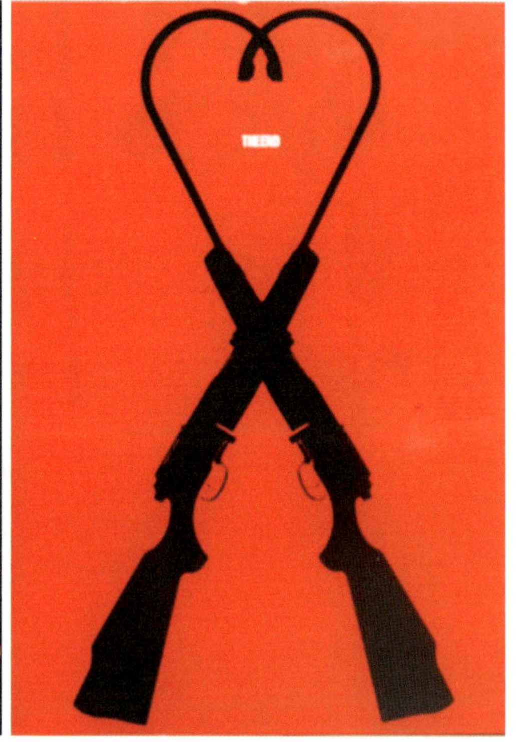

001 COALITION OF THE KILLING
CREATOR Tobias Honert

002 PEACE ANTIGUN CRIME
CREATOR Ben Edwards
SOURCE www.flickr.com/photos/
27530296@N03/2569535719/

003 HAVE A NICE DAY
CREATOR Banksy
SOURCE www.banksy.co.uk

004 RETIRED WEAPONS
SOURCE www.retired.jp

005 HAPPY CHOPPER
CREATOR Banksy
SOURCE www.banksy.co.uk

006 COME HERE PEACE
CREATOR Hun-Hyouk Im
SOURCE JAGDA Peace Posters
International Exhibition

007 ABC
CREATOR Maciej Urbaniec
SOURCE JAGDA Peace Posters
International Exhibition

008 HUMANIZM 1987??
CREATOR Jerzy Burski
SOURCE JAGDA Peace Posters
International Exhibition

009 FOREVER
CREATOR Shin Enami
SOURCE JAGDA Peace Posters
International Exhibition

010 TRY AND SEE IN ALL THE
DIFFERENT COLOURS
CREATOR Andrzej Lipiea
SOURCE JAGDA Peace Posters
International Exhibition

011 UN DECADE FOR WOMEN NAIROBI
CREATOR Jarosaaw Jasiaski
SOURCE JAGDA Peace Posters
International Exhibition
DATE 1985

012 CHANGE SWORD FOR PLOUGH
CREATOR Wen-Xiang Huang
SOURCE JAGDA Peace Posters
International Exhibition
DATE 1987

013 PEACE
CREATOR Alexandr Petrovitsh Segal,
Alexandr Vladimirovitsh Faldin
SOURCE JAGDA Peace Posters
International Exhibition

014 PEACE
CREATOR Soo Geoun Moon, Il Jae Park
SOURCE JAGDA Peace Posters
International Exhibition

015 PEACE
CREATOR Bu-Yong Hwag
SOURCE JAGDA Peace Posters
International Exhibition

016 ENDLESS PEACE
CREATOR Jai-Myung Jeon
SOURCE JAGDA Peace Posters
International Exhibition

017 LADY K BAG NR.4
CREATOR Atelier Ted Noten

018 BUT... ?
CREATOR Wladyslaw Targosz
SOURCE JAGDA Peace Posters
International Exhibition

019 THE END
CREATOR Masuteru Aoba
SOURCE Plakatsammlung Museum
für Gestaltung Zürich

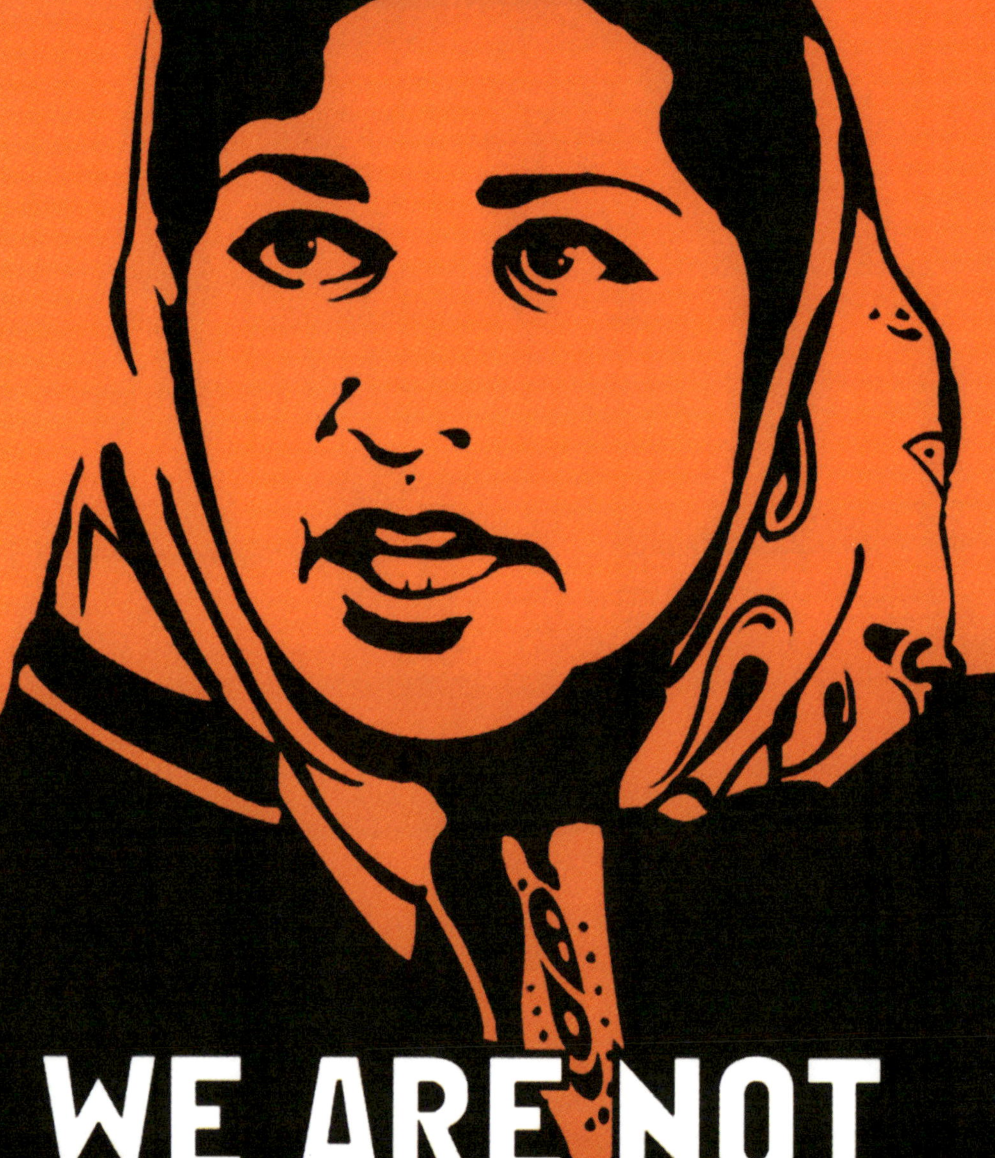

GENOCIDE ≠ JUSTICE
WE ARE NOT THE ENEMY
INCITE! Women of Color Against Violence
www.incite-national.org
P.O. Box 6861 Minneapolis MN 55406

LEFT
001

002

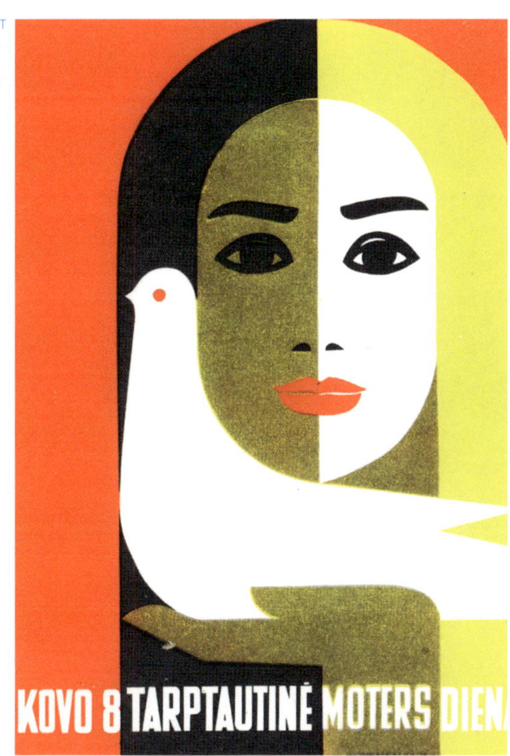

003

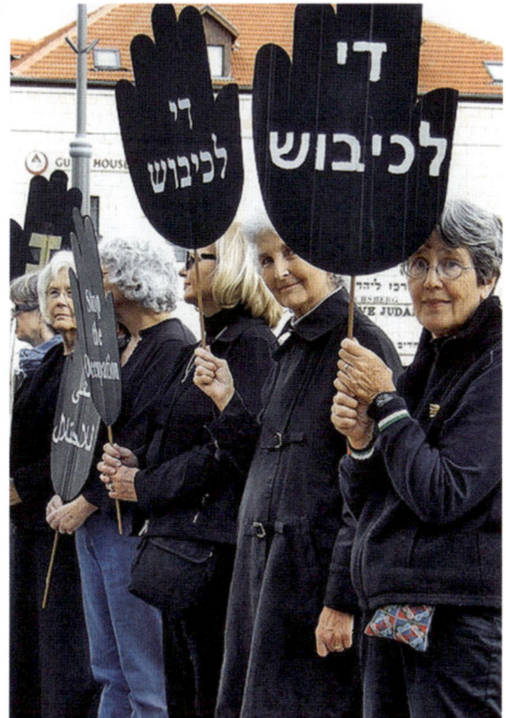

001 WE ARE NOT THE ENEMY
     CREATOR Yuri Surkov
     SOURCE John Carr, ed., *Yo!*
     What Happened to Peace?
     (Rome: Federico Zesi, 2007).

002 KOVO 8 TARPTAUTINE MOTERS DIENA
     [INTERNATIONAL WOMEN'S DAY
     IN LITHUANIA]
     CREATOR Yuri Surkov
     SOURCE www.sovietposters.com

003 WOMEN IN BLACK, AGAINST
     MILITARY ENGAGEMENTS
     SOURCE www.worldette.com

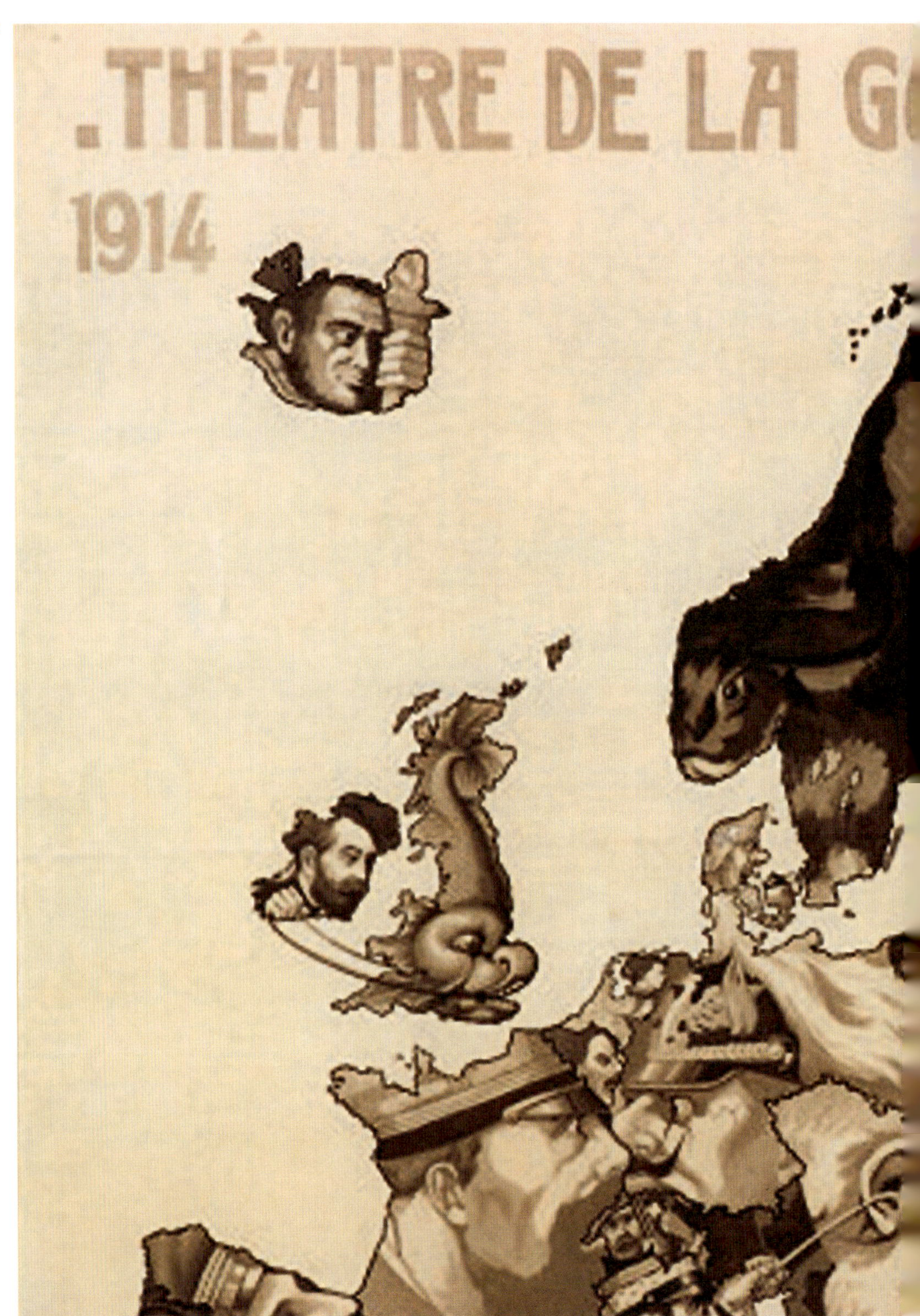
.THÉÂTRE DE LA G
1914

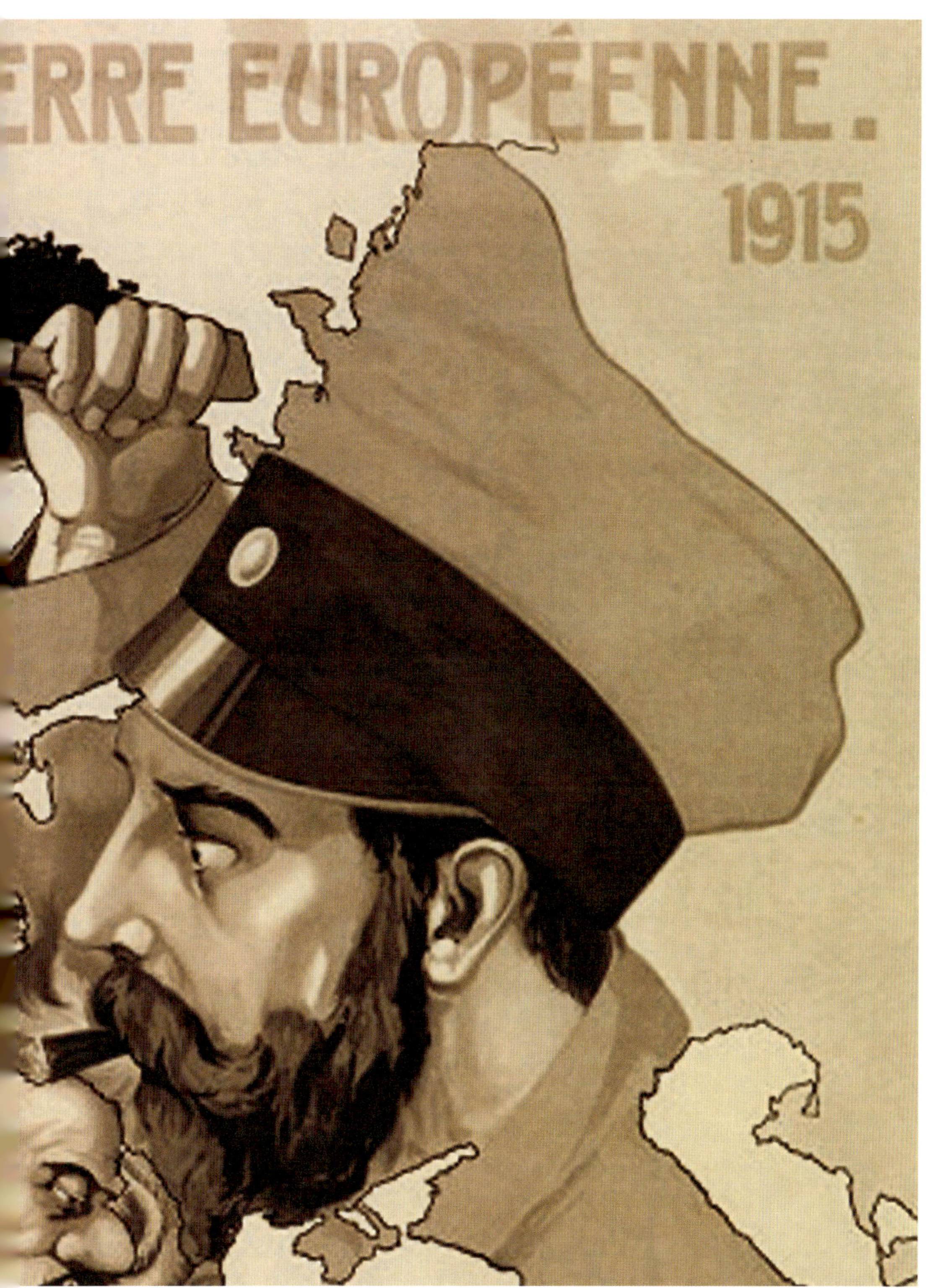
ERRE EUROPÉENNE.
1915

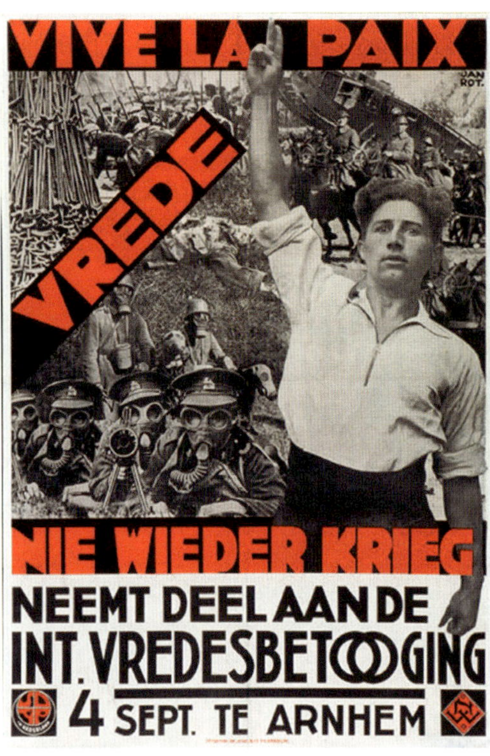

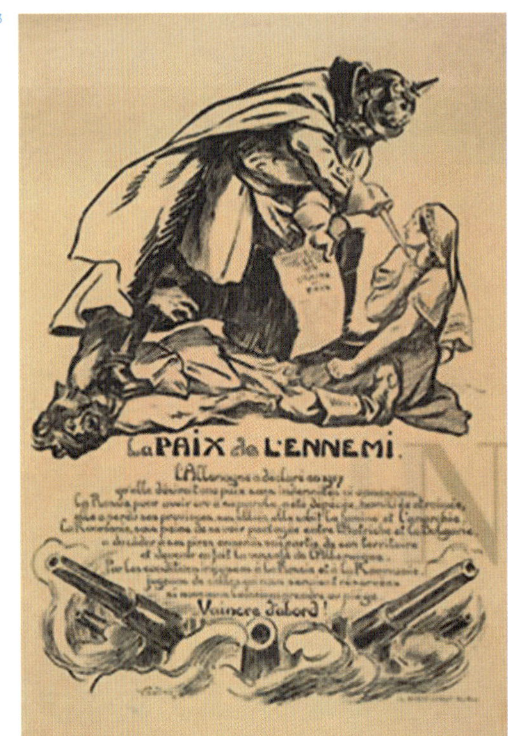

001 THÉÂTRE DE LA GUERRE EUROPÉENNE
     [EUROPEAN THEATER OF WAR]
     CREATOR André Huguenin-Dumittan
     SOURCE Plakatsammlung Museum
     für Gestaltung Zürich
     DATE 1914-1915

002 VIVE LA PAIX
     [LONG LIVE PEACE]
     CREATOR Jan Rot
     SOURCE Plakatsammlung Museum
     für Gestaltung Zürich

003 LA PAIX DE L'ENNEMI
     [THE ENEMY'S PEACE]
     SOURCE purl.pt

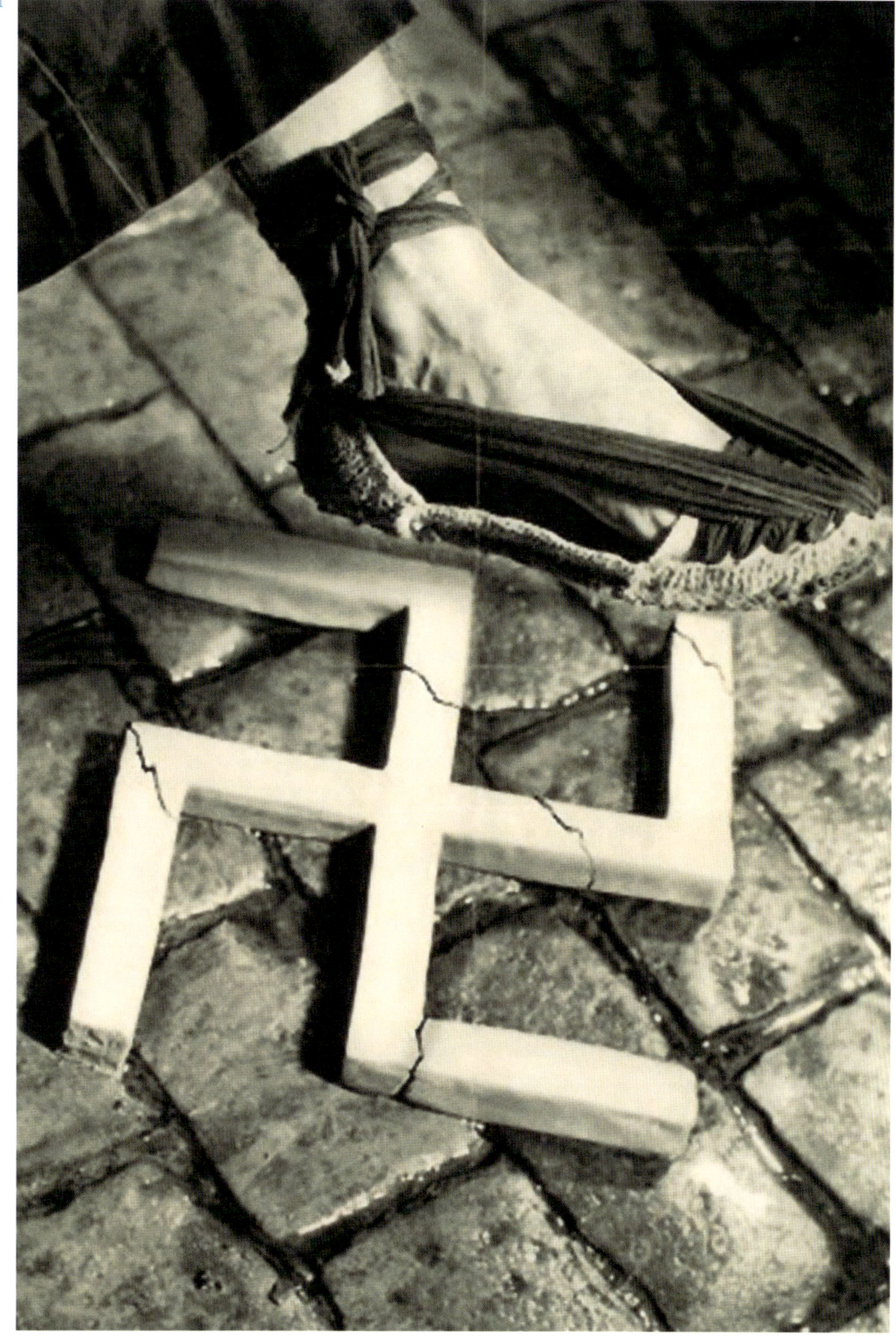

002
003

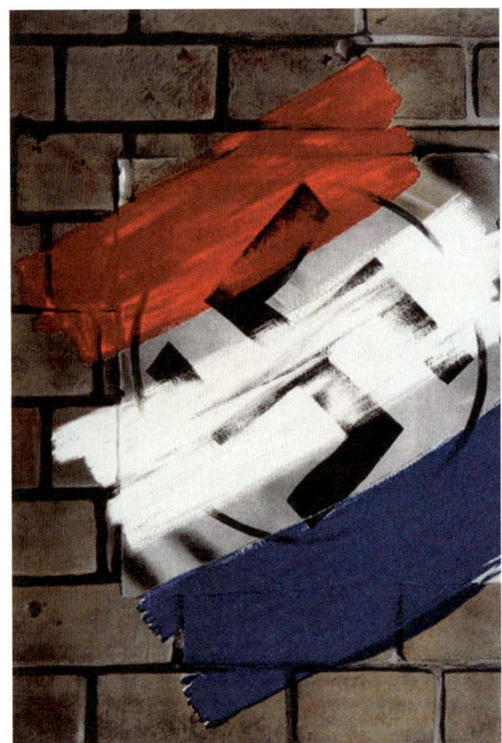

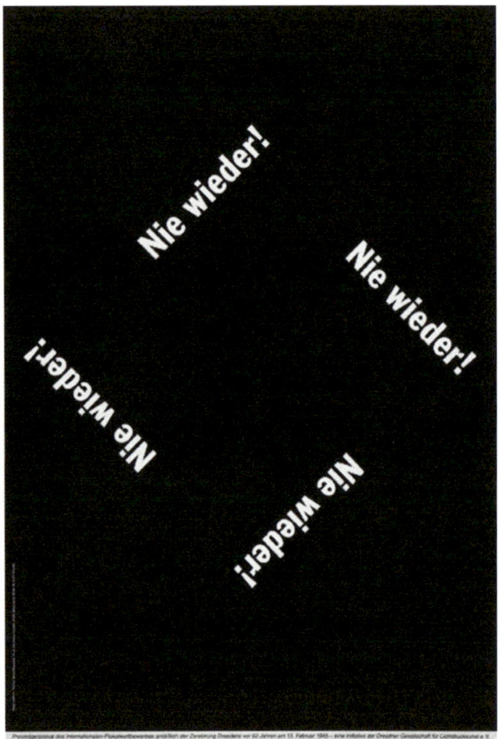

004
005

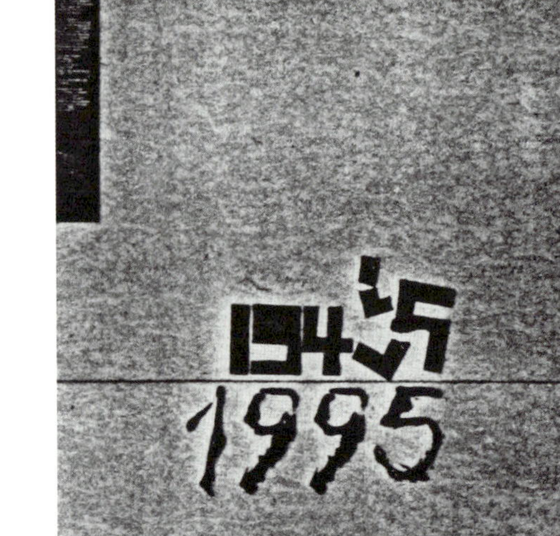

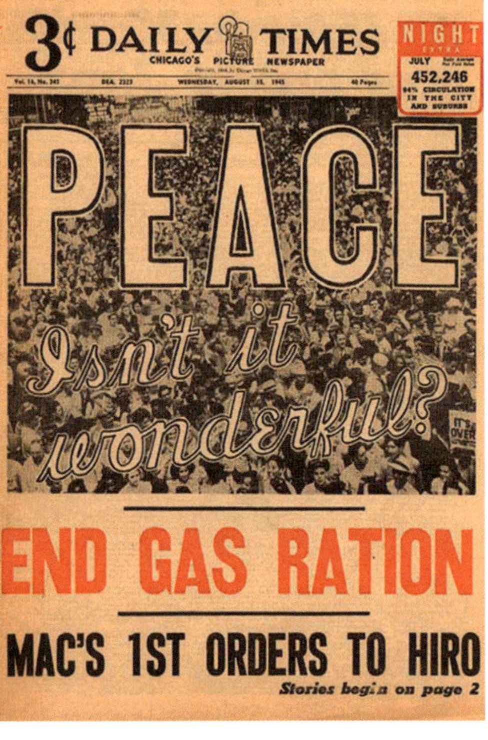

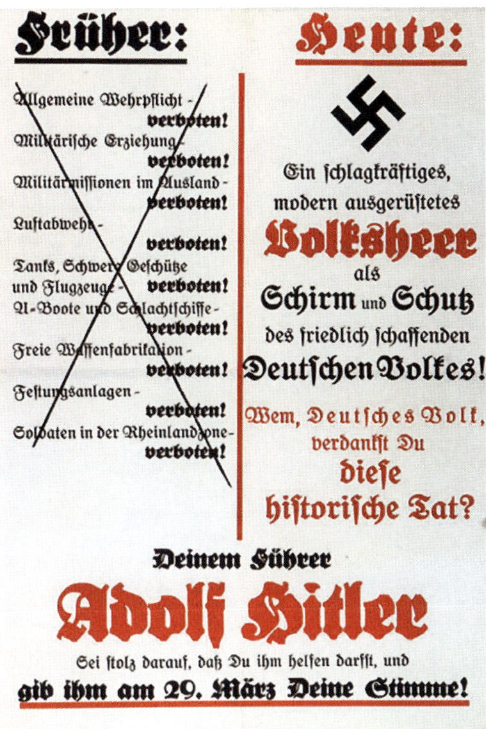
Früher:
Heute:
Allgemeine Wehrpflicht -
verboten!
Militärische Erziehung -
verboten!
Militärmissionen im Ausland -
verboten!
Luftabwehr -
verboten!
Tanks, Schwere Geschütze
und Flugzeuge - verboten!
U-Boote und Schlachtschiffe -
verboten!
Freie Waffenfabrikation -
verboten!
Festungsanlagen -
verboten!
Soldaten in der Rheinlandzone -
verboten!
Ein schlagkräftiges,
modern ausgerüstetes
Volksheer
als
Schirm und Schutz
des friedlich schaffenden
Deutschen Volkes!
Wem, Deutsches Volk,
verdankst Du
diese
historische Tat?
Deinem Führer
Adolf Hitler
Sei stolz darauf, daß Du ihm helfen darfst, und
gib ihm am 29. März Deine Stimme!

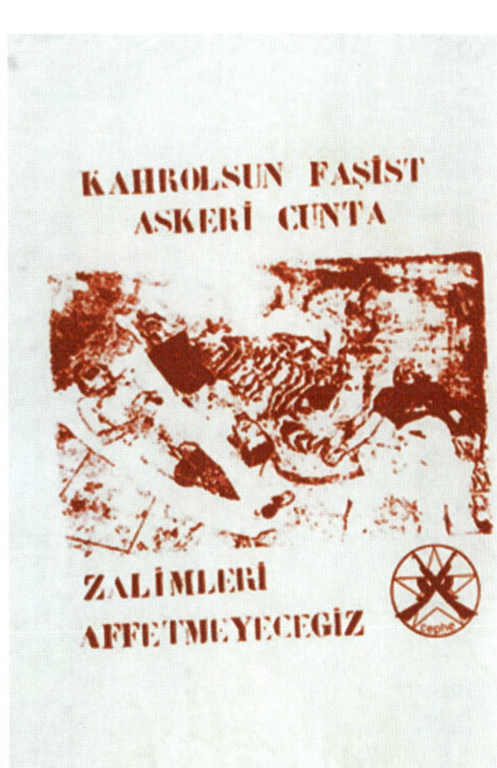
KAHROLSUN FAŞİST
ASKERİ CUNTA
ZALİMLERİ
AFFETMEYECEGİZ

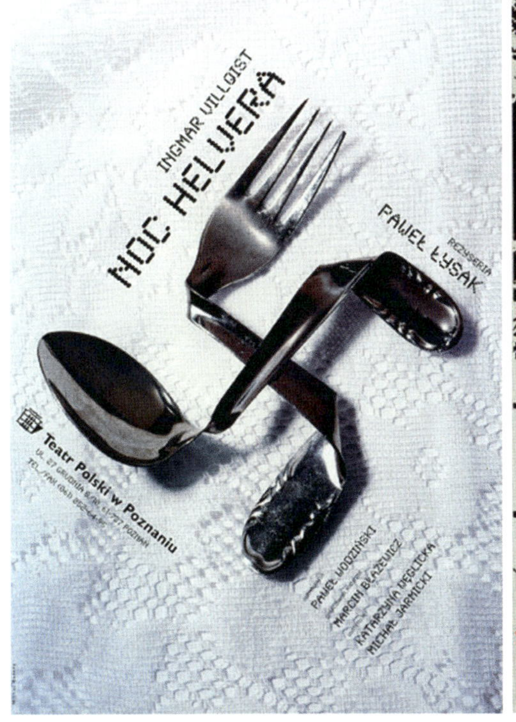
INGMAR VILLQIST
NOC HELVERA
PAWEŁ ŁYSAK
Teatr Polski w Poznaniu

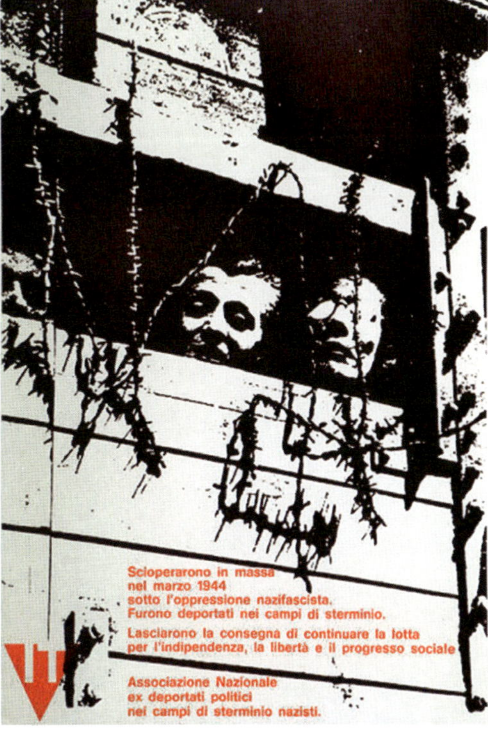
Scioperarono in massa
nel marzo 1944
sotto l'oppressione nazifascista.
Furono deportati nei campi di sterminio.
Lasciarono la consegna di continuare la lotta
per l'indipendenza, la libertà e il progresso sociale
Associazione Nazionale
ex deportati politici
nei campi di sterminio nazisti.

001 AIXAFEM EL FEIXISME
[SMASH FASCISM]
SOURCE Plakatsammlung Museum
für Gestaltung Zürich
DATE 1937

002 UNTITLED
SOURCE Plakatsammlung Museum
für Gestaltung Zürich
DATE 1944

003 NIE WIEDER
[NEVER AGAIN]
CREATOR Holger Giffhorn
SOURCE Plakatsammlung Museum
für Gestaltung Zürich

004 50 LET POBEDY
[50 YEARS OF VICTORY]
CREATOR Dan Reisinger
SOURCE Plakatsammlung Museum
für Gestaltung Zürich
DATE 1995

005 PEACE – ISN'T IT WONDERFUL
CREATOR *Chicago Daily Times*
SOURCE www.loc.gov

006 FRÜHER – HEUTE
[EARLIER – TODAY]
SOURCE Plakatsammlung Museum
für Gestaltung Zürich
DATE 1936

007 KAHROLSUN FASIST ASKERI CUNTA
[DOWN WITH THE FASCIST
MILITARY JUNTA]
SOURCE Plakatsammlung Museum
für Gestaltung Zürich

008 NOC HELVERA
CREATOR Michal Batory
SOURCE Plakatsammlung Museum
für Gestaltung Zürich
DATE 2001

009 FURONO DEPORTATI NEI CAMPI
DI STERMINIO
[THEY WERE DEPORTED TO
EXTERMINATION CAMPS]
CREATOR Albe Steiner
SOURCE Plakatsammlung Museum
für Gestaltung Zürich
DATE 2001

001
002
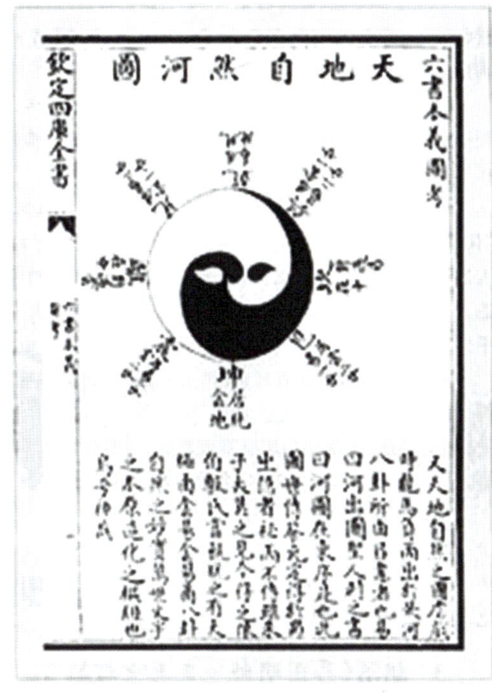

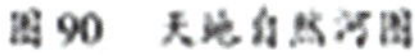
圖90　天地自然河圖

003
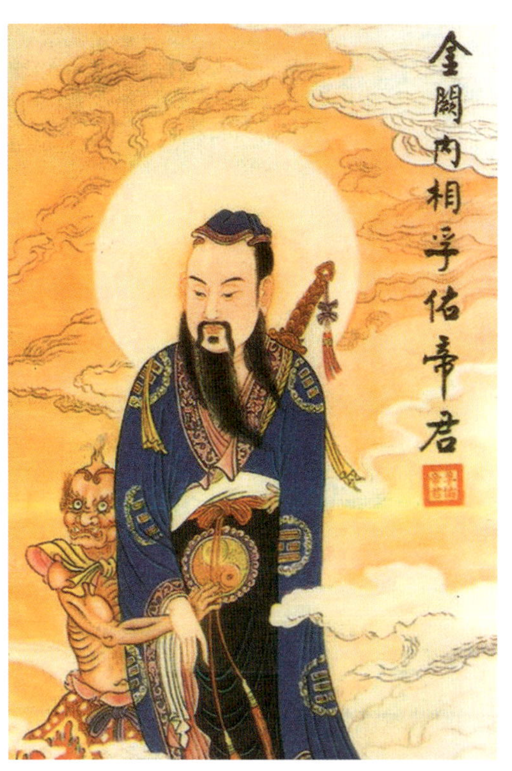

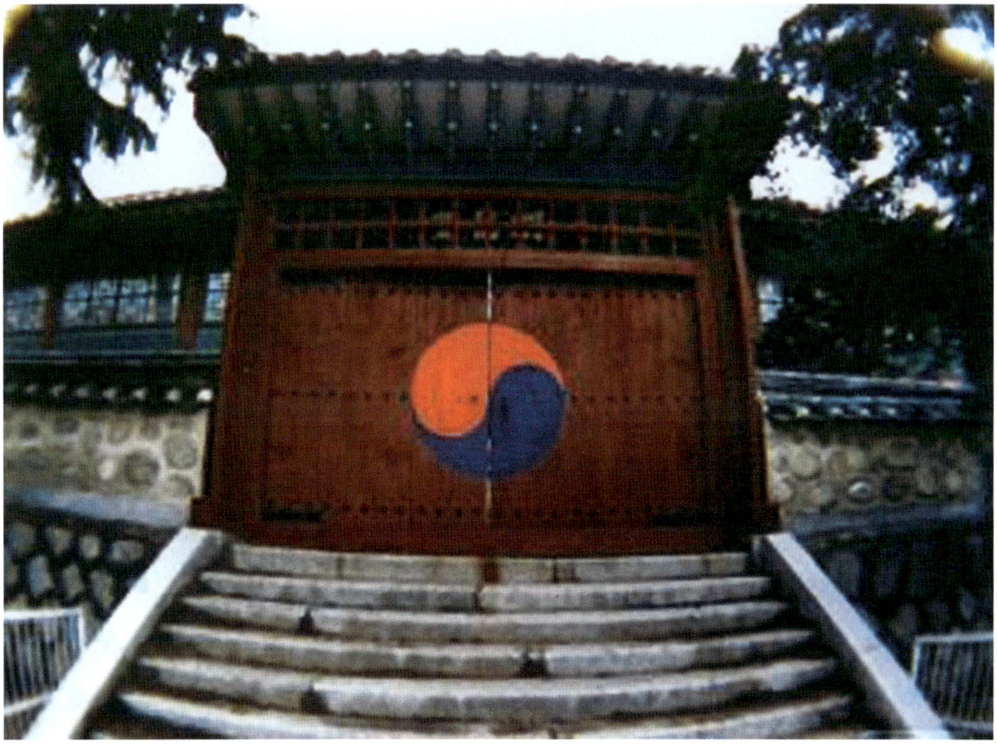

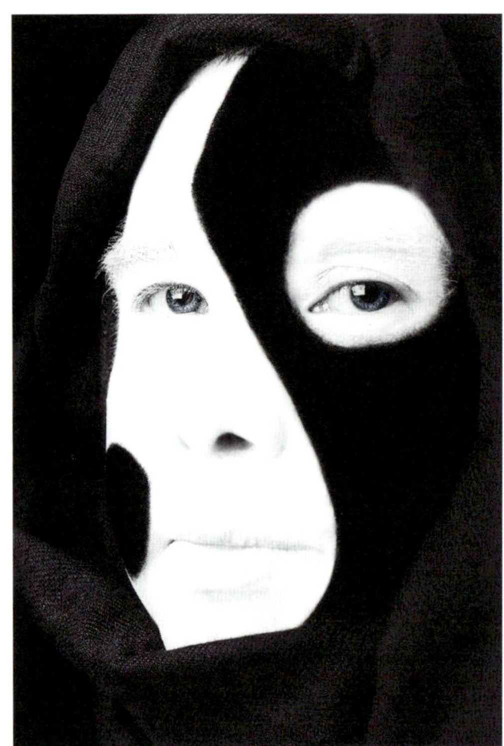

004

005

001 YIN YANG
SOURCE www.iep.utm.edu

002 UNTITLED
SOURCE kaleidoscope.cultural
china.com/

003 THE DOORWAY TO A CONFUCIAN
SCHOOL OF THOUGHT
SOURCE morethanjustkpop.
wordpress.com

004 YIN YANG
CREATOR Martina Karlsso
SOURCE www.flickr.com/photos/
martinakarlsso

005 ZHUGE BAGUA VILLLAGE
Zhuge is the surname of most
of the villagers and Bagua
describes the layout of the
village in the shape of the
Bagua or Eight Diagrams from
the classic Chinese work, the
I Ching or the Book of Changes.
CREATOR Vilma Salazar
SOURCE www.flickr.com/photos/
vilmasalazar/3057382282/

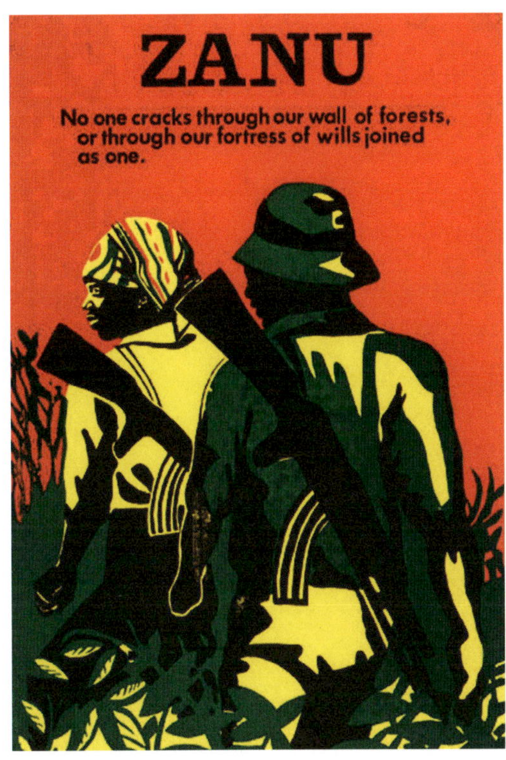

001 ZANU
SOURCE Plakatsammlung Museum
für Gestaltung Zürich
DATE 1975

002 ZIMBABWE FREEDOM RALLY!
CREATOR David King
SOURCE Plakatsammlung Museum
für Gestaltung Zürich
DATE 1975

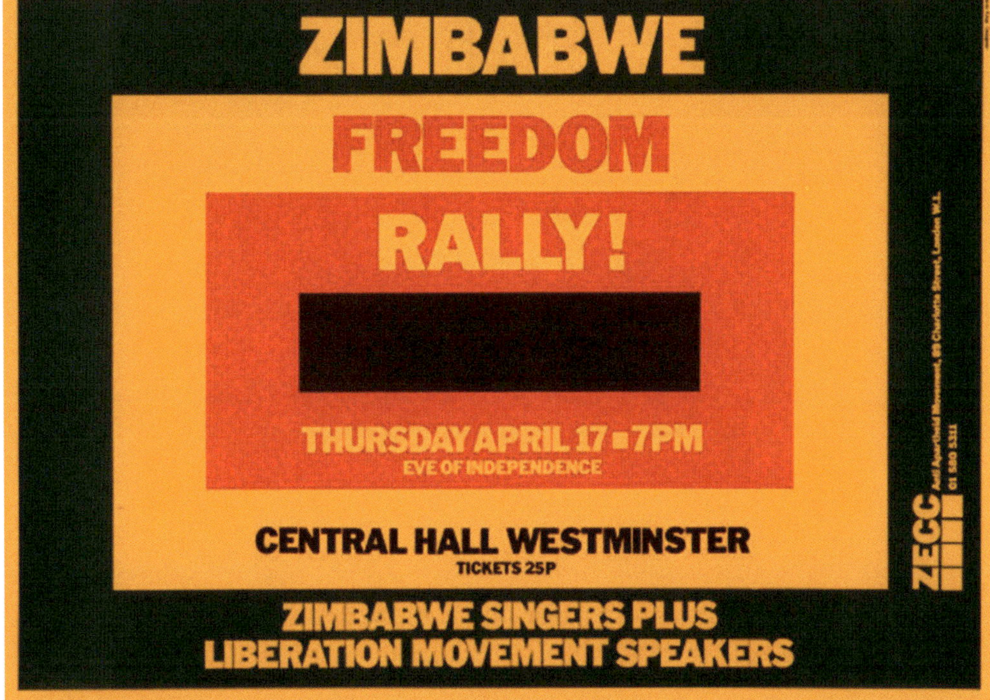

VERA BAUR KOCKOT IS A SOCIOLOGIST AND CULTURE AND
ICONOGRAPHY THEORIST. COFOUNDER AND CODIRECTOR OF THE
POSTGRADUATE PROGRAM CIVIC CITY AT HEAD IN GENEVA,
AND OF THE INSTITUTE FOR CRITICAL RESEARCH AND SCIENCES
IN DESIGN, PARIS, SHE IS ALSO A MEMBER OF THE BOARD OF
DIRECTORS FOR THE SOCIETY FOR INTERDISCIPLINARY IMAGE
STUDIES (GIB). SHE WAS FORMERLY WITH THE DIRECTORSHIP
AT THE INSTITUTE FOR ART, DESIGN, AND MEDIA TECHNOLOGY
IN NUREMBERG, AND AT THE INSTITUTE DESIGN2CONTEXT AT
THE ZURICH UNIVERSITY OF THE ARTS. IN 1989 SHE FOUNDED
INTERDIS, THE INSTITUTE FOR INTERDISCIPLINARITY, BERLIN.

RUEDI BAUR, BORN IN PARIS IN 1956, IS A GRAPHIC DESIGNER.
HE IS THE FOUNDER AND HEAD OF INTÉGRAL RUEDI BAUR
ET ASSOCIÉS, ZURICH, AND PARIS, AND DIRECTOR OF THE
INSTITUTE FOR DESIGN RESEARCH DESIGN2CONTEXT AT THE
ZURICH UNIVERSITY OF THE ARTS. HE IS A PROFESSOR AT
ENSAD, PARIS, AND HEADS THE INTERNATIONAL SNF-SPONSORED
RESEARCH PROGRAM COHABITATION OF SIGNS. HE IS THE
COFOUNDER AND CODIRECTOR OF THE POSTGRADUATE PROGRAM
CIVIC CITY AT HEAD IN GENEVA, AND OF THE INSTITUTE
FOR CRITICAL RESEARCH AND SCIENCES IN DESIGN, PARIS.

SIGNS FOR PEACE
AN IMPOSSIBLE VISUAL ENCYCLOPEDIA

EDITED BY RUEDI BAUR AND VERA BAUR KOCKOT AND
THE INSTITUTE DESIGN2CONTEXT ZHDK ZURICH

IN COLLABORATION WITH CLEMENS BELLUT, MERIEM BOUHARA,
MARIA FAHRINGER, MEGAN HALL, MARU MARTINEZ, MONYA PLETSCH,
KARIN PRÄTORIUS, CHRIS STEURER, AND SÉBASTIEN THIERRY.

TRANSLATIONS JOHN O'TOOLE (FR.-ENGL.), IAN PEPPER (GER.-ENGL.)

COPYEDITING JONATHAN FOX (INTRODUCTION), KEONAONA PETERSON

DESIGN RUEDI BAUR AND MEGAN HALL

LITHOGRAPHY AST & FISCHER, WABERN, SWITZERLAND

PRINTING AND BINDING KÖSEL, ALTUSRIED-KRUGZELL, GERMANY

THIS BOOK WAS PRINTED ON ECO-FRIENDLY PAPER: LESSEBO
DESIGN SMOOTH WHITE, 130 G/M^2, SUPPLIED BY GEESE PAPIER,
HENSTEDT-ULZBURG/GERMANY. WWW.GEESE.DE

LARS MÜLLER PUBLISHERS
ZÜRICH, SWITZERLAND
WWW.LARS-MUELLER-PUBLISHERS.COM

ISBN 978-3-03778-243-9

PRINTED IN GERMANY

PUBLISHED WITH THE GENEROUS SUPPORT OF HAMASIL FOUNDATION,
ZURICH